Lethbridge—Alberta

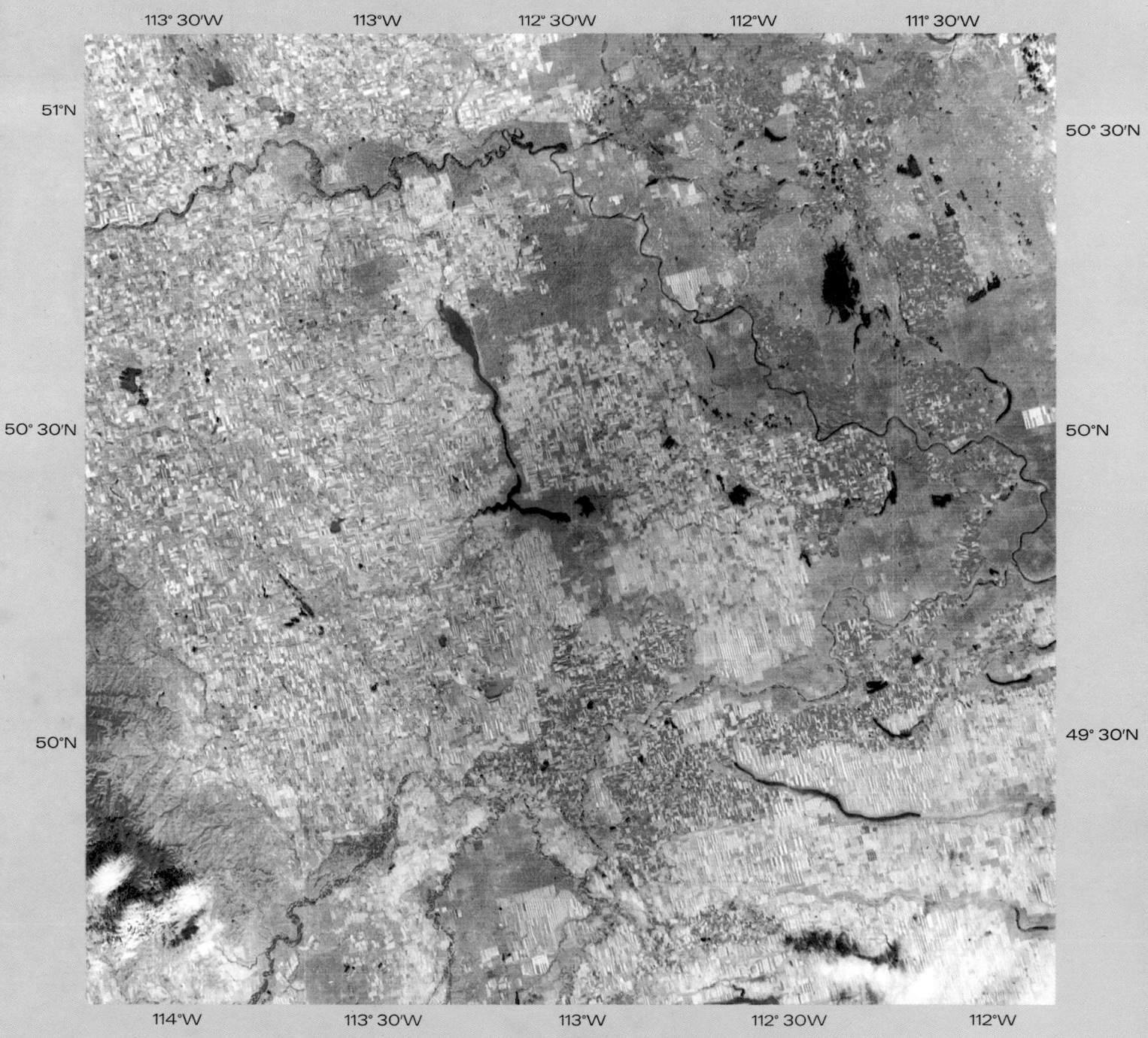

This area of southwestern Alberta is dominated by agriculture with several patterns of land-use. In the northeast, pasture and rangeland with the relative absence of field divisions is brown. The dry high plains of Alberta makes irrigation advisable where possible, and irrigation areas stand out as bright red, growing corn, sugar beet, potatoes and other green crops. Several reservoirs can be seen where rivers have been dammed for irrigation purposes. Wheat and other cereals are grown on the fields with a light tan colour, while mixed farming occupies the remainder of the agricultural area in the smaller, darker, more rectangular fields (especially in the west of the area). In the southwest are the Porcupine Hills – foothills of the Rocky Mountains – covered with forest which gives them a red colour. Lethbridge itself, not clearly visible, lies in the lower centre.

(23 August 1973)

The images shown on the endpapers were produced by the Landsat spacecraft which orbits the earth at an altitude of 900 km. (Images from NASA).

George Philip Raintree Inc.
205 West Highland Avenue
MILWAUKEE, WISCONSIN 53203, USA

© **1979 George Philip and Son Ltd.**

ISBN 0 89810 001 1 (Standard Edition)
ISBN 0 89810 002 X (Deluxe Edition)
ISBN 0 89810 004 6 (Library Edition)

Printed in Great Britain by George Philip Printers Ltd., London

Preface

The easier and more rapid means of communication, the increase in global trade and exchanges, the growth of world organizations of all kinds and the pace of international events all demand of anyone who is careful to co-ordinate his information a convenient reference source and there is nothing better for this than an atlas. To be of the greatest use, it is essential that the maps should be detailed, accurate, legible and up-to-date; in addition, the index must enable the reader to find any place quickly. Also it is considered helpful that the detailed maps should be complemented by thematic maps, tables and illustrations to analyse and portray on the one hand the physical environment (such as geology, climate and vegetation) and on the other man and his activities, production and trade.

The ATLAS OF CANADA AND THE WORLD, it is hoped, meets these needs. The Atlas is of an easily portable size, convenient for frequent use, and able to stand on a bookshelf. At the same time, the content has been arranged to give regional maps on a large scale because it is only at such scales that a precision and wealth of detail can be satisfactorily presented.

The Atlas gives firstly an overall view of the earth in space, the composition of the earth and its surrounding atmosphere, then physical, demographic, economic and political maps followed by studies in depth of the continents by means of specialized maps and the more detailed regional maps. As befits the requirements of Canadian readers, a considerable section of the Atlas is given to special maps dealing with the country as a whole, as well as with each of the provinces. Thematic maps of Canada portray in the first place the physical conditions – geology, soils, vegetation – followed by specific maps on population and economic activities in agriculture, forestry, fishing, mining, energy production and industry. Regional maps on scales of 1:7M and 1:10M are amplified by larger scale maps, 1:2.5M, of the important more densely settled parts of the provinces, with yet more detailed maps of the Metropolitan regions, whilst the larger cities and capitals are shown on maps of 1:250,000 complemented by photographs. Neighbouring countries in the North and Latin America are given special treatment e.g. Northeastern United States, the Chicago-St. Louis region, California and Washington, Mexico and the Caribbean.

The design of the maps takes advantage of new developments in map reproduction. Lighter yet clearer layer colours have made possible the inclusion of a hill-shading to bring out clearly the character of the land and relief features without impairing the legibility of names, settlements and communications.

The opportunity of new reproduction has been taken to incorporate latest changes up to the date of printing and is shown in the most recent state of boundaries, political and administrative divisions and communications. International boundaries are drawn to show the *de facto* situation where there are rival claims to territory.

Spellings of Canadian names are the forms given in the Gazetteer of Canada by the Canadian Permanent Committee on Geographic Names and in the Répertoire Géographique du Québec by the Commission de Géographie. Spellings of names in other parts of the world are in the forms given in the latest official list and generally agree with the rules of the Permanent Committee on Geographical Names and the United States Board on Geographic Names. The comprehensive index locates over 35,000 places and geographical features by coordinates of latitude and longitude.

H. FULLARD

Contents

The Universe, Earth and Man

Maps 1–136

The World

North America

Contents-II

Canada

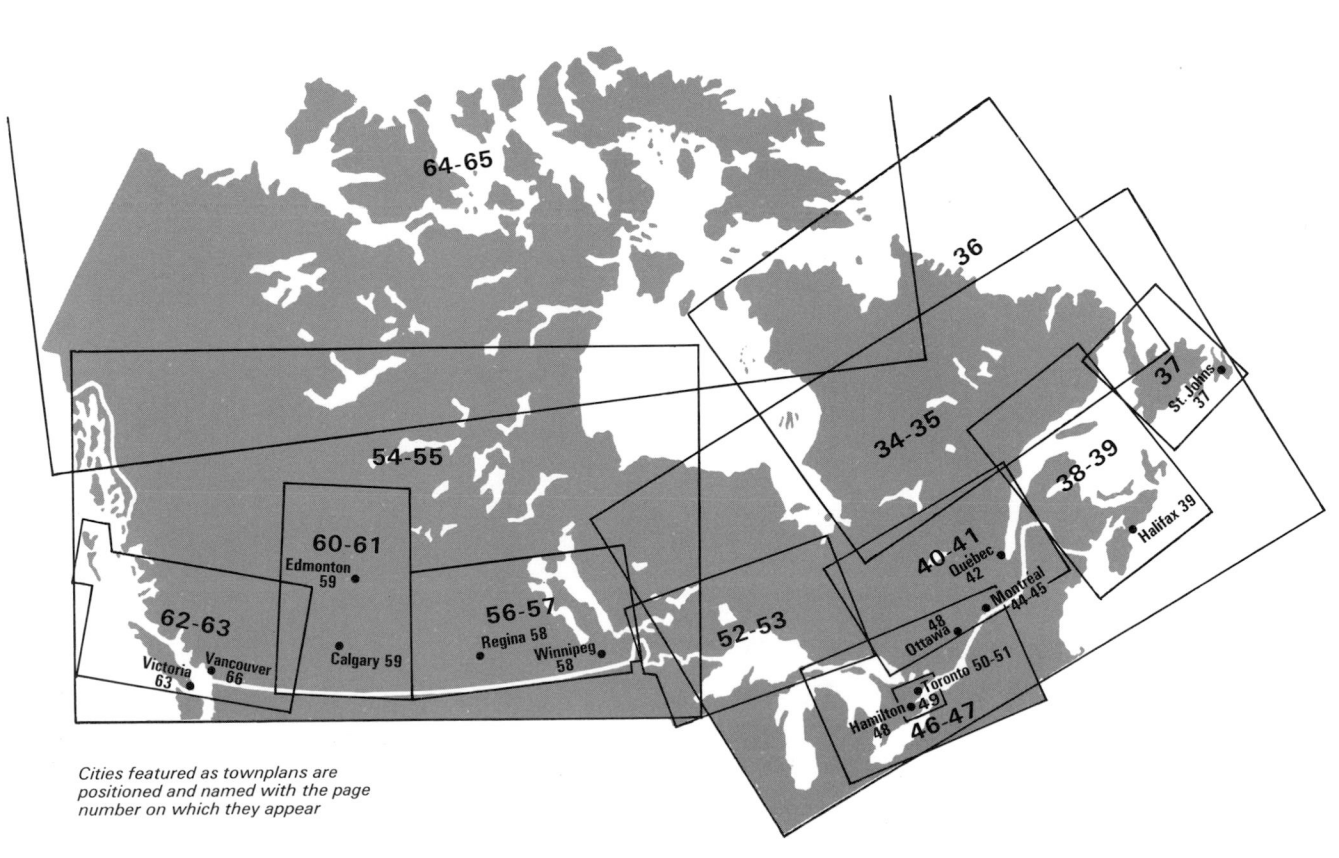

Cities featured as townplans are positioned and named with the page number on which they appear

Contents–III

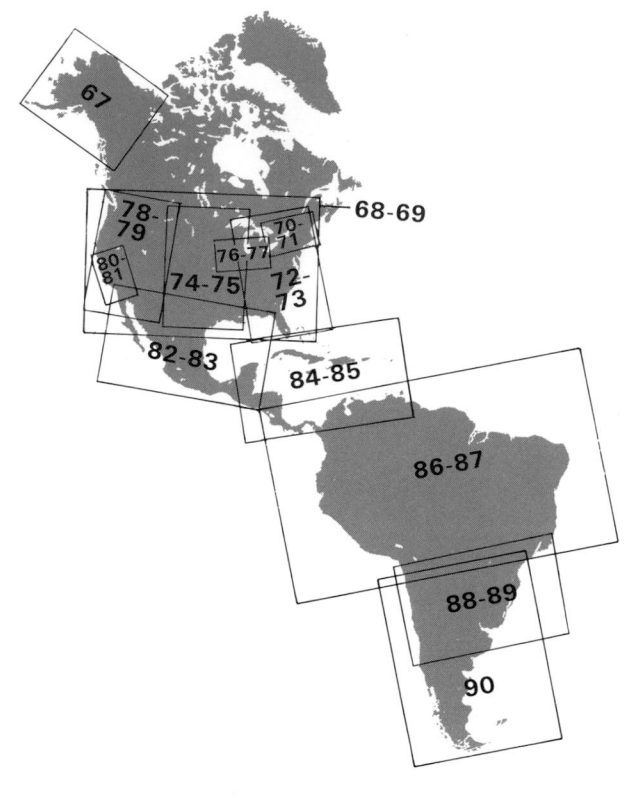

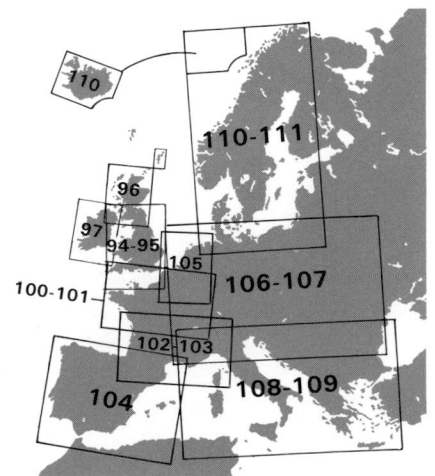

Contents-IV

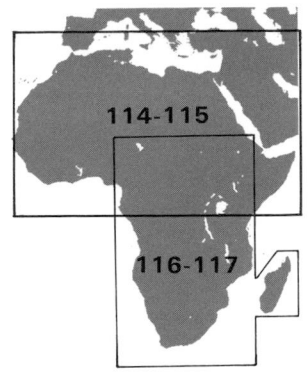

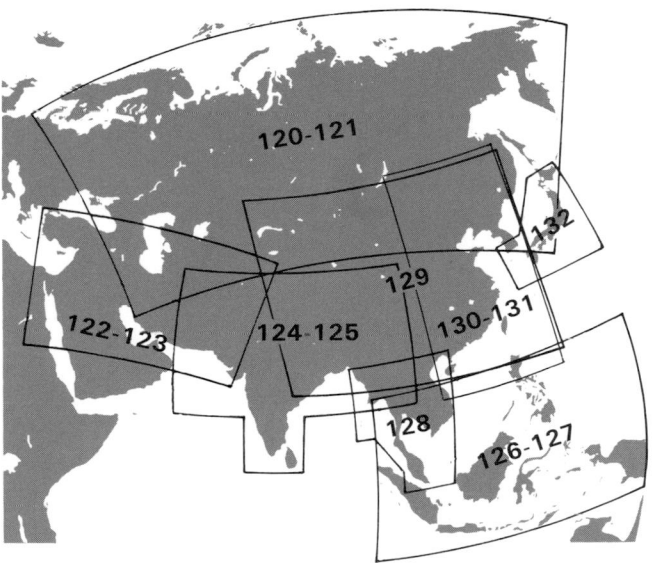

Index

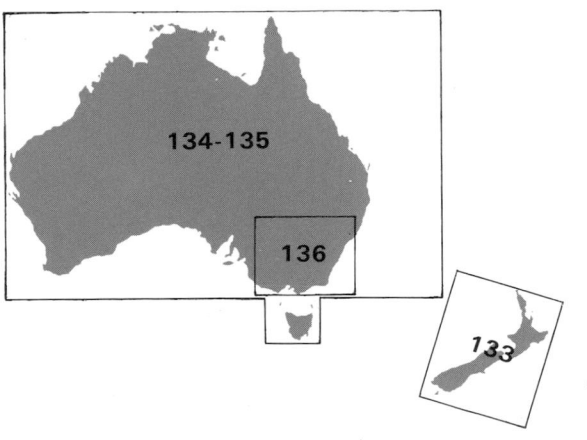

Chart of the Stars

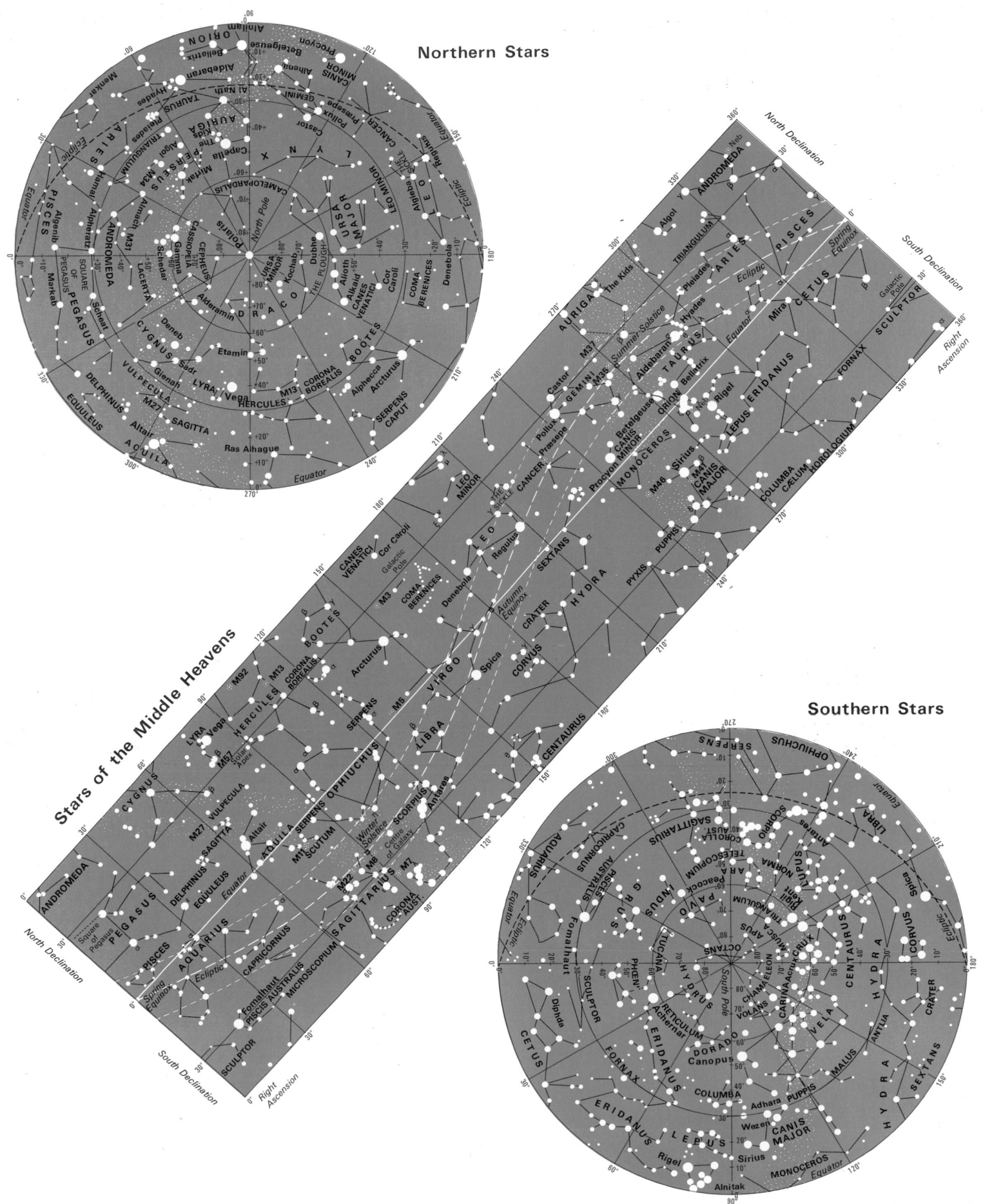

Northern Stars

Southern Stars

Stars of the Middle Heavens

The Solar System

The Solar System is a minute part of one of the innumerable galaxies that make up the universe. Our Galaxy is represented in the drawing to the right and The Solar System (S) lies near the plane of spiral-shaped galaxy, but 27 000 light-years from the centre. The System consists of the Sun at the centre with planets, moons, asteroids, comets, meteors, meteorites, dust and gases revolving around it. It is calculated to be at least 4 700 million years old.

The Solar System can be considered in two parts: the Inner Region planets- Mercury, Venus, Earth and Mars - all small and solid; the Outer Region planets - Jupiter, Saturn, Uranus and Neptune - all gigantic in size, and on the edge of the system the smaller Pluto.

Our galaxy

Inner region planets

Outer region planets

Mars
Venus
Earth
Mercury

Pluto
Neptune
Uranus
Saturn
Jupiter
Mars

The planets

All planets revolve round the Sun in the same direction, and mostly in the same plane. Their orbits are shown (left) - they are not perfectly circular paths.

The table below summarizes the dimensions and movements of the Sun and planets.

The Sun

The Sun has an interior with temperatures believed to be of several million °C brought about by continuous thermo-nuclear fusions of hydrogen into helium. This immense energy is transferred by radiation into surrounding layers of gas the outer surface of which is called the chromosphere. From this "surface" with a temperature of many thousands °C "flames" (solar prominences) leap out into the diffuse corona which can best be seen at times of total eclipse (see photo right). The bright surface of the Sun, the photosphere, is calculated to have a temperature of about 6 000 °C. and when viewed through a telescope has a mottled appearance, the darker patches being called sunspots - the sites of large disturbances of the surface.

Total eclipse of the sun

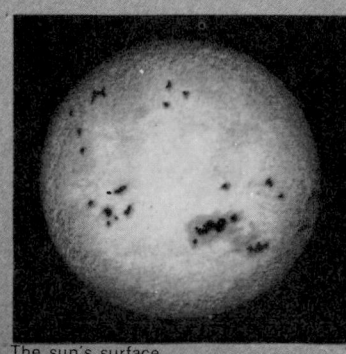
The sun's surface

	Equatorial diameter in km	Mass (earth=1)	Mean distance from sun in millions km	Radii of orbit (earth=1)	Orbital inclination	Sidereal period	Period of rotation on axis	Number of satellites
Sun	1 392 000	333 434	—	—	—	—	25 days 9hrs	—
Mercury	4 840	0·04	58	0·39	7°	88d	59 days	0
Venus	12 300	0·83	108	0·72	3°24'	225d	244 days	0
Earth	12 756	1·00	150	1·00	—	1 year	23hrs 56m	1
Mars	6 790	0·11	228	1·52	1°51'	1y 322d	24hrs 37m	2
Jupiter	143 200	318	778	5·20	1°18'	11y 315d	9hrs 50m	12
Saturn	119 300	95	1 427	9·54	2°29'	29y 167d	10hrs 14m	10
Uranus	47 100	15	2 870	19·19	0°46'	84y 6d	10hrs 49m	5
Neptune	51 000	17	4 497	30·07	1°46'	164y 288d	15hrs 48m	2
Pluto	5 900	0·06	5 950	39·46	17°06'	247y 255d	6d 9hrs 17m	

The Sun's diameter is 109 times greater than that of the Earth.

Distances from sun in millions km

58	Mercury
108	Venus
150	Earth
228	Mars
778	Jupiter
1427	Saturn
2870	Uranus
4497	Neptune
5950	Pluto

Mercury is the smallest planet and nearest to the Sun. It is composed mostly of metals and probably has an atmosphere of heavy inert gases.

Venus is similar in size to the Earth, and probably in composition. It is, however, much hotter and has a dense atmosphere of carbon dioxide which obscures our view of its surface.

Earth is the largest of the inner planets. It has a dense iron-nickel core surrounded by layers of silicate rock. The surface is approximately $\frac{3}{8}$ land and $\frac{5}{8}$ water, and the lower atmosphere consists of a mixture of nitrogen, oxygen and other gases supplemented by water vapour. With this atmosphere and surface temperatures usually between −50°C and +40°C, life is possible.

Mars, smaller than the Earth, has a noticeably red appearance. Recent photographs sent back by satellite show clearly the cratered surface and the ice areas at the poles made from condensed carbon dioxide.

The Asteroids orbit the Sun mainly between Mars and Jupiter. They consist of thousands of bodies of varying sizes with diameters ranging from yards to hundreds of miles.

Jupiter is the largest planet of the Solar System. It shines brightly in the sky (magnitude −2·5), and is notable for its cloud belts and the Great Red Spot.

Saturn, the second largest planet consists of hydrogen, helium and other gases. Its density is less than that of water. It is unique in appearance because of its equatorial rings believed to be made of ice-covered particles.

Uranus was discovered in 1781 by Herschel. It is extremely remote yet faintly visible to the naked eye. Methane in its atmosphere gives it a slightly green appearance.

Neptune, yet more remote than Uranus and larger. It is composed of gases and has a bluish green appearance when seen in a telescope. As with Uranus, little detail can be observed on its surface.

Pluto No details are known of its composition or surface. The existence of this planet was firstly surmised in a computed hypothesis, which was tested by repeated searches by large telescopes until in 1930 the planet was found.

The Earth

Seasons, Equinoxes and Solstices

The Earth revolves around the Sun once a year and rotates daily on its axis, which is inclined at $66\frac{1}{2}°$ to the orbital plane and always points into space in the same direction. At midsummer (N.) the North Pole tilts towards the Sun, six months later it points away and half way between the axis is at right angles to the direction of the Sun (right).

Earth data

Maximum distance from the Sun (Aphelion) 152 007 016 km
Minimum distance from the Sun (Perihelion) 147 000 830 km
Obliquity of the ecliptic 23° 27′ 08″
Length of year - tropical (equinox to equinox) 365.24 days
Length of year - sidereal (fixed star to fixed star) 365.26 days
Length of day - mean solar day 24h 03m 56s
Length of day - mean sidereal day 23h 56m 04s

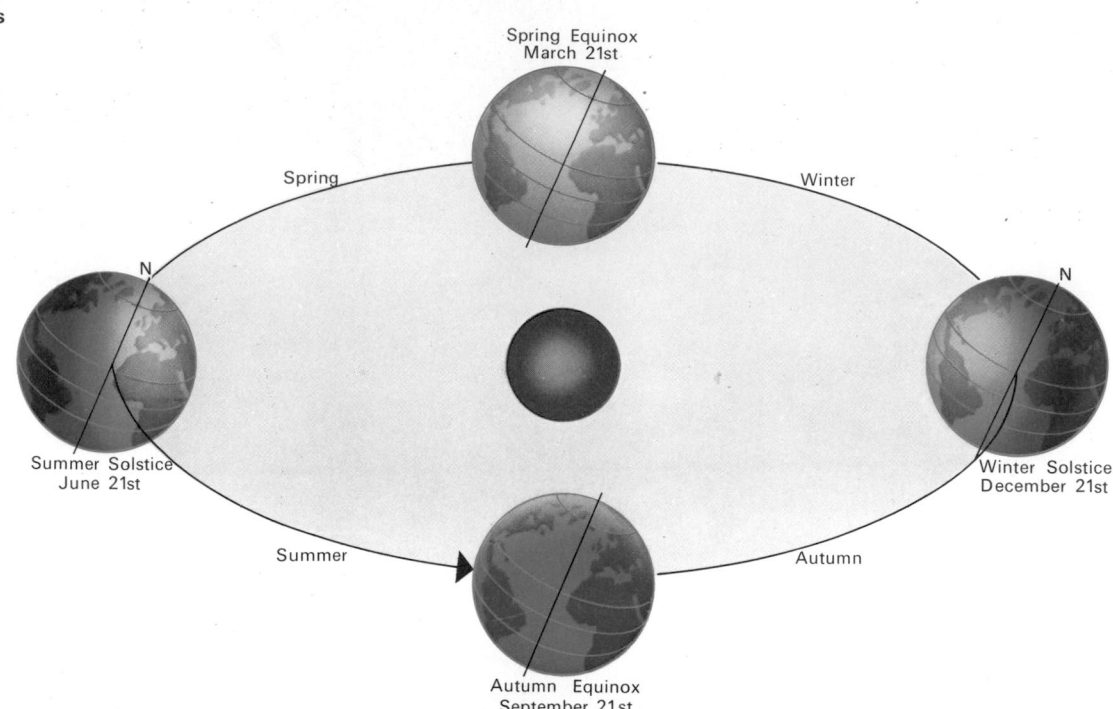

Length of day and night

At the summer solstice in the northern hemisphere, the Arctic has total daylight and the Antarctic total darkness. The opposite occurs at the winter solstice. At the equator, the length of day and night are almost equal all the year, at 30° the length of day varies from about 14 hours to 10 hours and at 50° from about 16 hours to 8 hours.

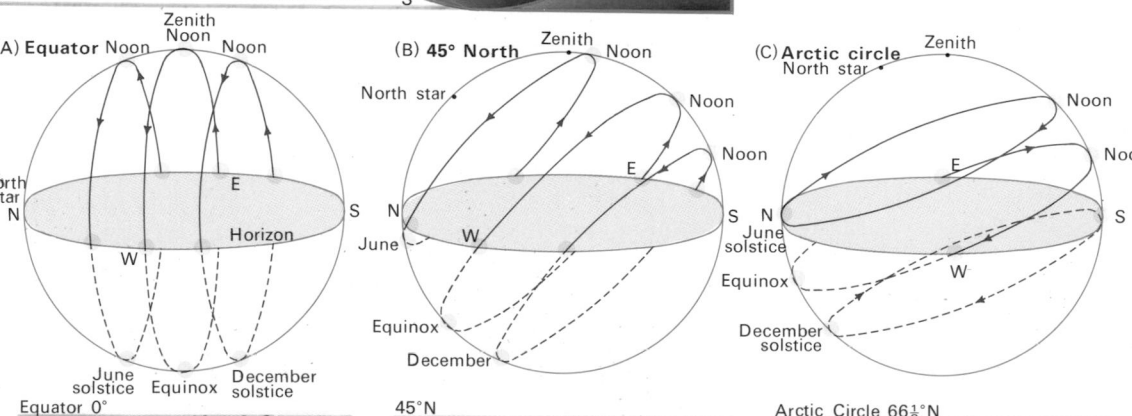

Apparent path of the Sun

The diagrams (right) illustrate the apparent path of the Sun at A the equator, B in mid latitudes say 45°N, C at the Arctic Circle $66\frac{1}{2}°$ and D at the North Pole where there is six months continuous daylight and six months continuous night

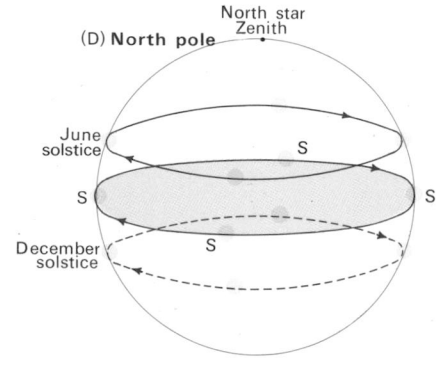

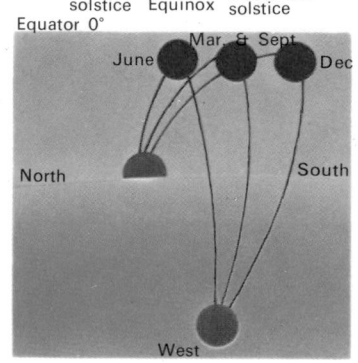

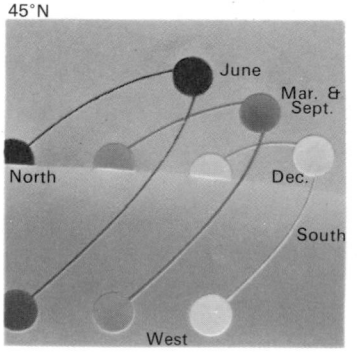

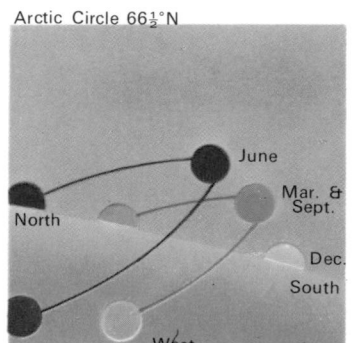

4

The Moon

The Moon rotates slowly making one complete turn on its axis in just over 27 days. This is the same as its period of revolution around the Earth and thus it always presents the same hemisphere ('face') to us. Surveys and photographs from space-craft have now added greatly to our knowledge of the Moon, and, for the first time, views of the hidden hemisphere.

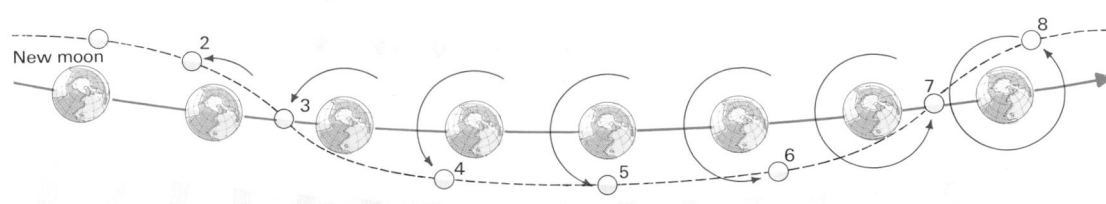

Phases of the Moon
The interval between one full Moon and the next is approximately 29½ days - thus there is one new Moon and one full Moon every month. The diagrams and photographs (right) show how the apparent changes in shape of the Moon from new to full arise from its changing position in relation to the Earth and both to the fixed direction of the Sun's rays.

| Crescent moon(2) | Half moon, first quarter(3) | Gibbous moon (4) | Full moon (5) | The waning moon (6) | Half moon, last quarter(7) | The old moon (8) |

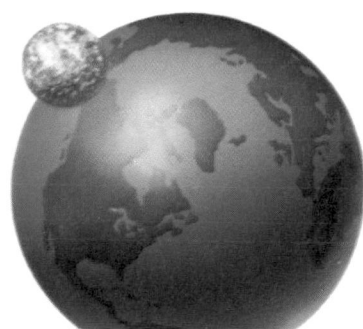

Moon data
Distance from Earth 356 410 km
    to 406 685 km
Mean diameter 3 473 km
Mass approx. $\frac{1}{81}$ of that of Earth
Surface gravity $\frac{1}{6}$ of that of Earth
Atmosphere - none, hence no clouds,
    no weather, no sound.
Diurnal range of temperature at the Equator +200°C

Landings on the Moon
Left are shown the landing sites of the U.S. Apollo programme.
Apollo 11 Sea of Tranquility (1°N 23°E) 1969
Apollo 12 Ocean of Storms (3°S 24°W) 1969
Apollo 14 Fra Mauro (4°S 17°W) 1971
Apollo 15 Hadley Rill (25°N 4°E) 1971
Apollo 16 Descartes (9°S 15°E) 1972
Apollo 17 Sea of Serenity (20°N 31°E) 1972

Eclipses of Sun and Moon
When the Moon passes between Sun and Earth it causes a partial eclipse of the Sun (right 1) if the Earth passes through the Moon's outer shadow (P), or a total eclipse (right 2), if the inner cone shadow crosses the Earth's surface.
    In a lunar eclipse, the Earth's shadow crosses the Moon and gives either total or partial eclipses.

Partial eclipse (1)

Total eclipse (2)

Lunar eclipse

Tides
Ocean water moves around the Earth under the gravitational pull of the Moon, and, less strongly, that of the Sun. When solar and lunar forces pull together - near new and full Moon - high spring tides result. When solar and lunar forces are not combined - near Moon's first and third quarters - low neap tides occur.

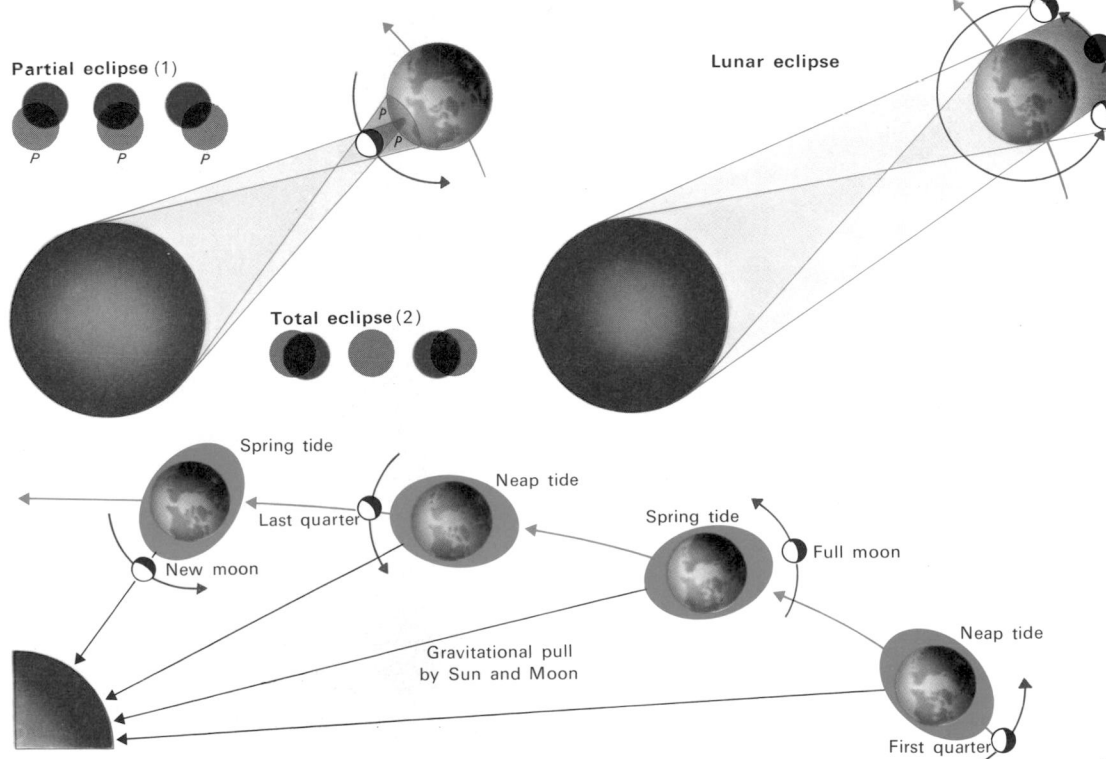

Spring tide

Neap tide

Last quarter

Spring tide

Full moon

New moon

Neap tide

Gravitational pull by Sun and Moon

First quarter

Time

Time measurement
The basic unit of time measurement is the day, one rotation of the earth on its axis. The subdivision of the day into hours and minutes is arbitrary and simply for our convenience. Our present calendar is based on the solar year of $365\frac{1}{4}$ days, the time taken for the earth to orbit the sun. A month was anciently based on the interval from new moon to new moon, approximately $29\frac{1}{2}$ days - and early calendars were entirely lunar.

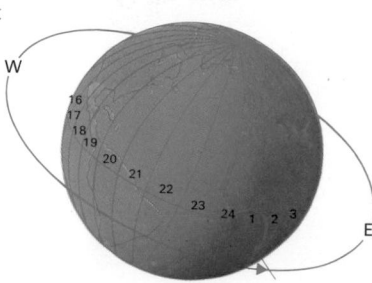
Rotation of the Earth

Greenwich Observatory

Prime Meridian

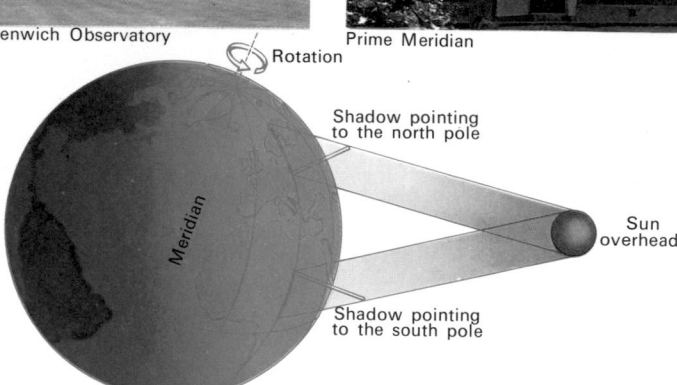

Solar time
The time taken for the earth to complete one rotation about its own axis is constant and defines a day but the speed of the earth along its orbit around the sun is inconstant. The length of day, or 'apparent solar day', as defined by the apparent successive transits of the sun is irregular because the earth must complete more than one rotation before the sun returns to the same meridian.

Sidereal time
The constant sidereal day is defined as the interval between two successive apparent transits of a star, or the first point of Aries, across the same meridian. If the sun is at the equinox and overhead at a meridian on one day, then the next day the sun will be to the east by approximately 1°; thus the sun will not cross the meridian until about 4 minutes after the sidereal noon.

The International Date Line
When it is 12 noon at the Greenwich meridian, 180° east it is midnight of the same day while 180° west the day is only just beginning. To overcome this the International Date Line was established, approximately following the 180° meridian. Thus, for example, if one travelled eastwards from Japan (140° East) to Samoa (170° West) one would pass from Sunday night into Sunday morning.

Time zones
The world is divided into 24 time zones, each centred on meridians at 15° intervals which is the longitudinal distance the sun appears to travel every hour. The meridian running through Greenwich passes through the middle of the first zone. Successive zones to the east of Greenwich zone are ahead of Greenwich time by one hour for every 15° of longitude, while zones to the west are behind by one hour.

Night and day
As the earth rotates from west to east the sun appears to rise in the east and set in the west: when the sun is setting in Shanghai on the directly opposite side of the earth New York is just emerging into sunlight. Noon, when the sun is directly overhead, is coincident at all places on the same meridian with shadows pointing directly towards the poles.

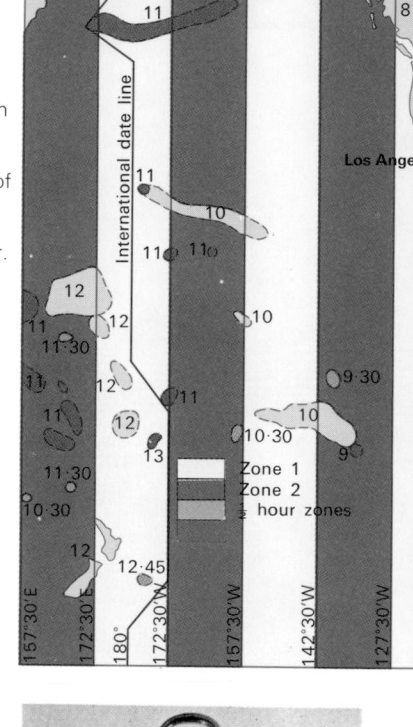

Astronomical clock, Delhi

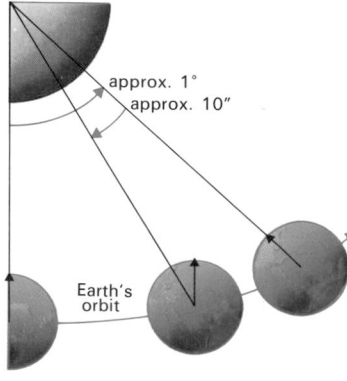

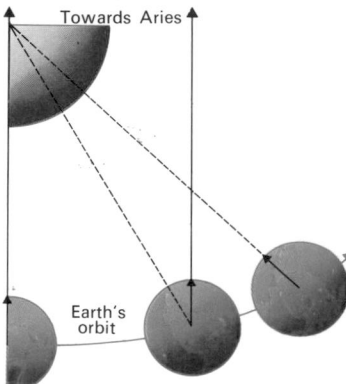

Sundials
The earliest record of sundials dates back to 741 BC but they undoubtedly existed as early as 2000 BC although probably only as an upright stick or obelisk. A sundial marks the progress of the sun across the sky by casting the shadow of a central style or gnomon on the base. The base, generally made of stone, is delineated to represent the hours between sunrise and sunset.

Kendall's chronometer

Chronometers
With the increase of sea traffic in the 18th century and the need for accurate navigation clockmakers were faced with an intriguing problem. Harrison, an English carpenter, won a British award for designing a clock which was accurate at sea to one tenth of a second per day. He compensated for the effect of temperature changes by incorporating bi-metallic strips connected to thin wires and circular balance wheels.

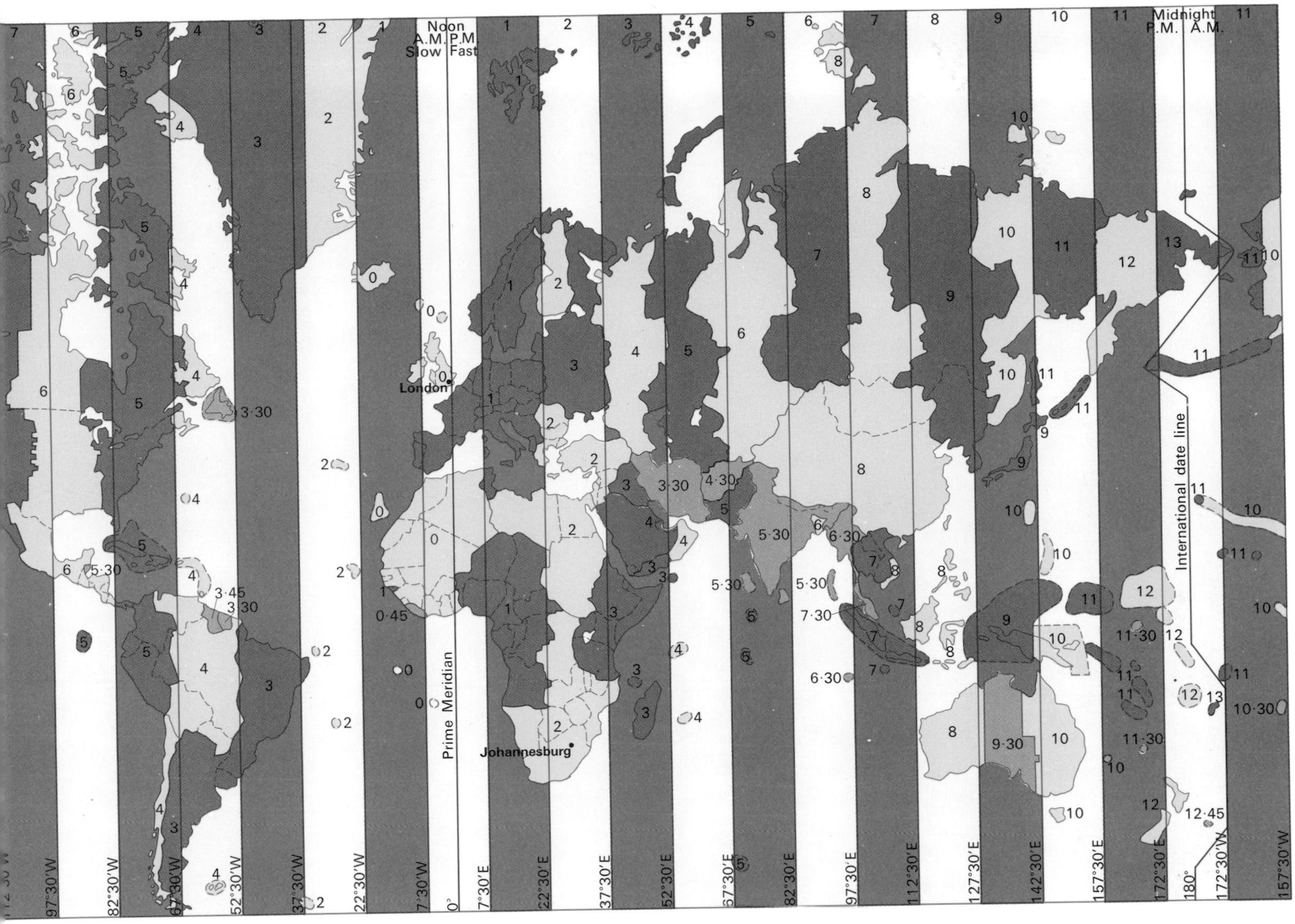

Noon
A.M. P.M.
Slow Fast
Midnight
P.M. A.M.
London
Johannesburg
Prime Meridian
International date line
97°30'W
82°30'W
67°30'W
52°30'W
37°30'W
22°30'W
7°30'W
0°
7°30'E
22°30'E
37°30'E
52°30'E
67°30'E
82°30'E
97°30'E
112°30'E
127°30'E
142°30'E
157°30'E
172°30'E
180°
172°30'W
157°30'W

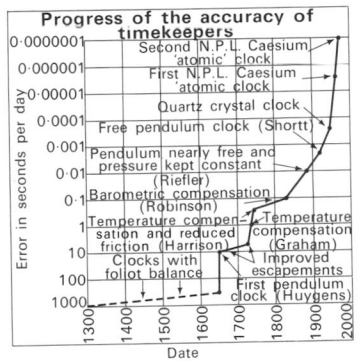

Progress of the accuracy of timekeepers
Second N.P.L. Caesium 'atomic' clock
First N.P.L. Caesium 'atomic' clock
Quartz crystal clock
Free pendulum clock (Shortt)
Pendulum nearly free and pressure kept constant (Riefler)
Barometric compensation (Robinson)
Temperature compensation and reduced friction (Harrison)
Temperature compensation (Graham)
Clocks with foliot balance
Improved escapements
First pendulum clock (Huygens)
0·0000001
0·000001
0·00001
0·0001
0·001
0·01
0·1
1
10
100
1000
Error in seconds per day
1300
1400
1500
1600
1700
1800
1900
2000
Date

Vibration of quartz ring

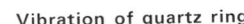

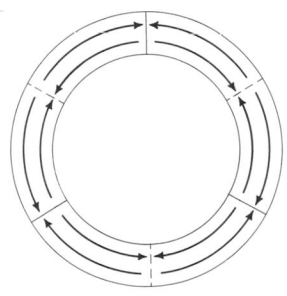

Time difference when travelling by air

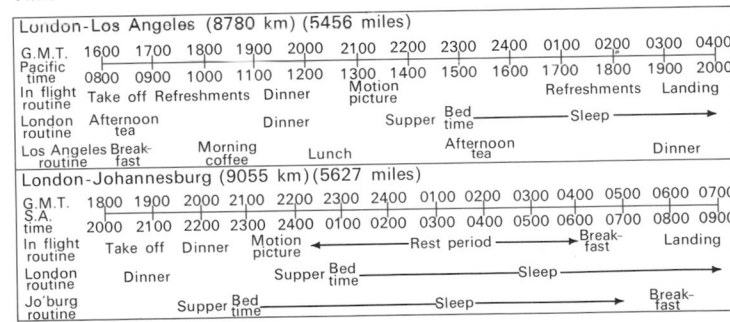

London-Los Angeles (8780 km) (5456 miles)													
G.M.T.	1600	1700	1800	1900	2000	2100	2200	2300	2400	0100	0200	0300	0400
Pacific time	0800	0900	1000	1100	1200	1300	1400	1500	1600	1700	1800	1900	2000
In flight routine	Take off	Refreshments			Dinner	Motion picture					Refreshments		Landing
London routine	Afternoon tea				Dinner		Supper	Bed time	———	Sleep ——→			
Los Angeles routine	Breakfast		Morning coffee			Lunch		Afternoon tea				Dinner	

London-Johannesburg (9055 km) (5627 miles)														
G.M.T.	1800	1900	2000	2100	2200	2300	2400	0100	0200	0300	0400	0500	0600	0700
S.A. time	2000	2100	2200	2300	2400	0100	0200	0300	0400	0500	0600	0700	0800	0900
In flight routine		Take off	Dinner	Motion picture		←———		Rest period	———→		Breakfast		Landing	
London routine		Dinner			Supper	Bed time	———		Sleep	———	——→			
Jo'burg routine			Supper	Bed time	———		Sleep	———	——→			Breakfast		

Chronographs

The invention of the chronograph by Charles Wheatstone in 1842 made it possible to record intervals of time to an accuracy of one sixtieth of a second. The simplest form of chronograph is the stop-watch. This was developed to a revolving drum and stylus and later electrical signals. A recent development is the cathode ray tube capable of recording to less than one ten-thousanth of a second.

Quartz crystal clocks

The quartz crystal clock, designed originally in America in 1929, can measure small units of time and radio frequencies. The connection between quartz clocks and the natural vibrations of atoms and molecules mean that the unchanging frequencies emitted by atoms can be used to control the oscillator which controls the quartz clock. A more recent version of the atomic clock is accurate to one second in 300 years.

International date line

Date line
Gain a day
Date line
Lose a day

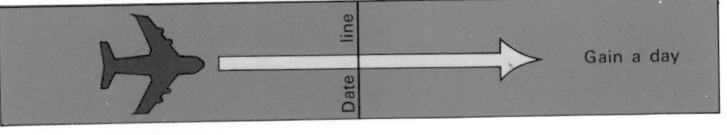

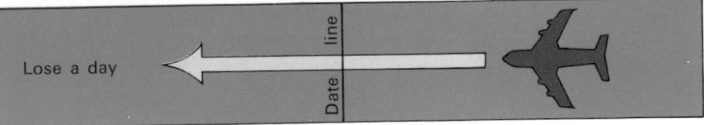

The Atmosphere and Clouds

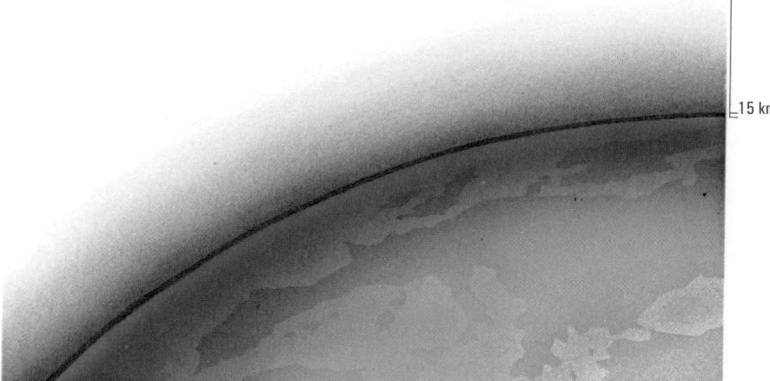

Earth's thin coating *(right)*
The atmosphere is a blanket of protective gases around the earth providing insulation against otherwise extreme alternations in temperature. The gravitational pull increases the density nearer the earth's surface so that 5/6ths of the atmospheric mass is in the first 15 kms. It is a very thin layer in comparison with the earth's diameter of 12 680 kms., like the cellulose coating on a globe.

Exosphere *(1)*
The exosphere merges with the interplanetary medium and although there is no definite boundary with the ionosphere it starts at a height of about 600 kms. The rarified air mainly consists of a small amount of atomic oxygen up to 600 kms. and equal proportions of hydrogen and helium with hydrogen predominating above 2 400 kms.

Ionosphere *(2)*
Air particles of the ionosphere are electrically charged by the sun's radiation and congregate in four main layers, D, E, F1 and F2, which can reflect radio waves. Aurorae, caused by charged particles deflected by the earth's magnetic field towards the poles, occur between 65 and 965 kms. above the earth. It is mainly in the lower ionosphere that meteors from outer space burn up as they meet increased air resistance.

Stratosphere *(3)*
A thin layer of ozone contained within the stratosphere absorbs ultra-violet light and in the process gives off heat. The temperature ranges from about -55°C at the tropopause to about -60°C in the upper part, known as the mesosphere, with a rise to about 2°C just above the ozone layer. This portion of the atmosphere is separated from the lower layer by the tropopause.

Troposphere *(4)*
The earth's weather conditions are limited to this layer which is relatively thin, extending upwards to about 8 kms. at the poles and 15 kms. at the equator. It contains about 85% of the total atmospheric mass and almost all the water vapour. Air temperature falls steadily with increased height at about 1°C for every 100 metres above sea level.

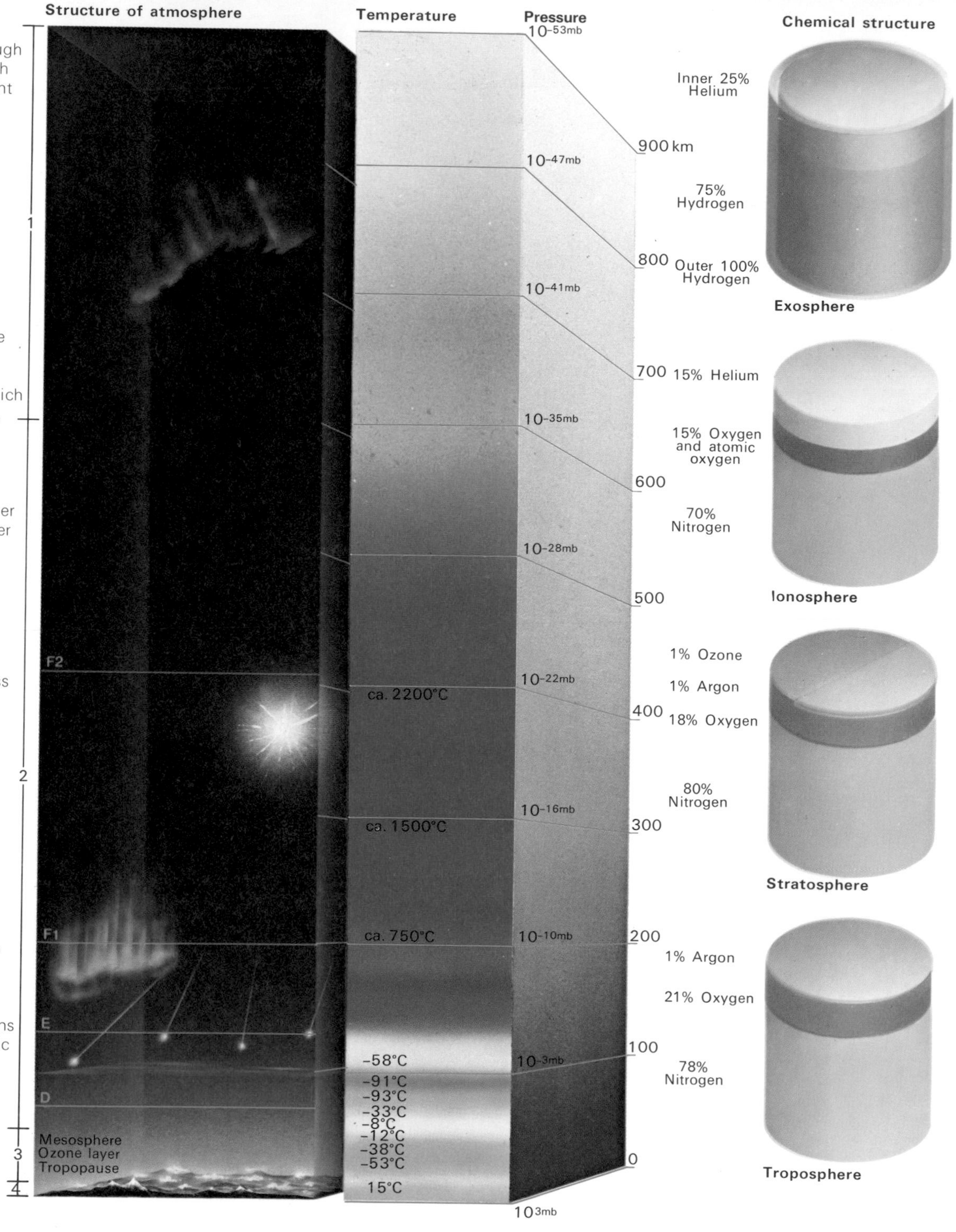

600 km
15 km

Structure of atmosphere

Temperature

Pressure

Chemical structure

10^{-53}mb

10^{-47}mb — 900 km

10^{-41}mb — 800

10^{-35}mb — 700

600

10^{-28}mb — 500

ca. 2200°C — 10^{-22}mb — 400

ca. 1500°C — 10^{-16}mb — 300

ca. 750°C — 10^{-10}mb — 200

F2
F1
E
D

-58°C — 10^{-3}mb — 100
-91°C
-93°C
-33°C
-8°C
-12°C
-38°C — 0
-53°C

Mesosphere
Ozone layer
Tropopause
15°C

1
2
3
4

10^{3}mb

Inner 25% Helium
75% Hydrogen
Outer 100% Hydrogen
Exosphere

15% Helium
15% Oxygen and atomic oxygen
70% Nitrogen
Ionosphere

1% Ozone
1% Argon
18% Oxygen
80% Nitrogen
Stratosphere

1% Argon
21% Oxygen
78% Nitrogen
Troposphere

Pacific Ocean
Cloud patterns over the Pacific show the paths of prevailing winds.

Circulation of the air

30° N

Equator

30° S

Circulation of the air
Owing to high temperatures in equatorial regions the air near the ground is heated, expands and rises producing a low pressure belt. It cools, causing rain, spreads out then sinks again about latitudes 30° north and south forming high pressure belts.

High and low pressure belts are areas of comparative calm but between them, blowing from high to low pressure, are the prevailing winds. These are deflected to the right in the northern hemisphere and to the left in the southern hemisphere (Corolis effect). The circulations appear in three distinct belts with a seasonal movement north and south following the overhead sun.

Cloud types
Clouds form when damp air is cooled, usually by rising. This may happen in three ways: when a wind rises to cross hills or mountains; when a mass of air rises over, or is pushed up by another mass of denser air; when local heating of the ground causes convection currents.

Cirrus *(1)* are detached clouds composed of microscopic ice crystals which gleam white in the sun resembling hair or feathers. They are found at heights of 6 000 to 12 000 metres.

Cirrostratus *(2)* are a whitish veil of cloud made up of ice crystals through which the sun can be seen often producing a halo of bright light.

Cirrocumulus *(3)* is another high altitude cloud formed by turbulence between layers moving in different directions.

Altostratus *(4)* is a grey or bluish striated, fibrous or uniform sheet of cloud producing light drizzle.

Altocumulus *(5)* is a thicker and fluffier version of cirro cumulus, it is a white and grey patchy sheet of cloud.

Nimbostratus *(6)* is a dark grey layer of cloud obscuring the sun and causing almost continuous rain or snow.

Cumulus *(7)* are detached heaped up, dense low clouds. The sunlit parts are brilliant white while the base is relatively dark and flat.

Stratus *(8)* forms dull overcast skies associated with depressions and occurs at low altitudes up to 1500 metres.

Cumulonimbus *(9)* are heavy and dense clouds associated with storms and rain. They have flat bases and a fluffy outline extending up to great altitudes.

High clouds

Middle clouds

Low clouds

Thousands of metres

1 Cirrus

2 Cirrostratus

3 Cirrocumulus

4 Altostratus

5 Altocumulus

6 Nimbostratus

7 Cumulus

9 Cumulonimbus

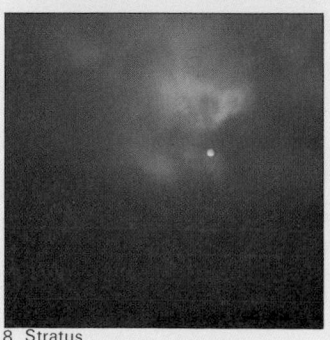

8 Stratus

Climate and Weather

All weather occurs over the earth's surface in the lowest level of the atmosphere, the troposphere. Weather has been defined as the condition of the atmosphere at any place at a specific time with respect to the various elements: temperature, sunshine, pressure, winds, clouds, fog, precipitation. Climate, on the other hand, is the average of weather elements over previous months and years.

Climate graphs *right*
Each graph typifies the kind of climatic conditions one would experience in the region to which it is related by colour to the map. The scale refers to degrees Celsius for temperature and millimetres for rainfall, shown by bars. The graphs show average observations based over long periods of time, the study of which also compares the prime factors for vegetation differences.

Development of a depression *below*
In an equilibrium front between cold and warm air masses (i) a wave disturbance develops as cold air undercuts the warm air (ii). This deflects the air flow and as the disturbance progresses a definite cyclonic circulation with warm and cold fronts is created (iii). The cold front moves more rapidly than the warm front eventually overtaking it, and occlusion occurs as the warm air is pinched out (iv).

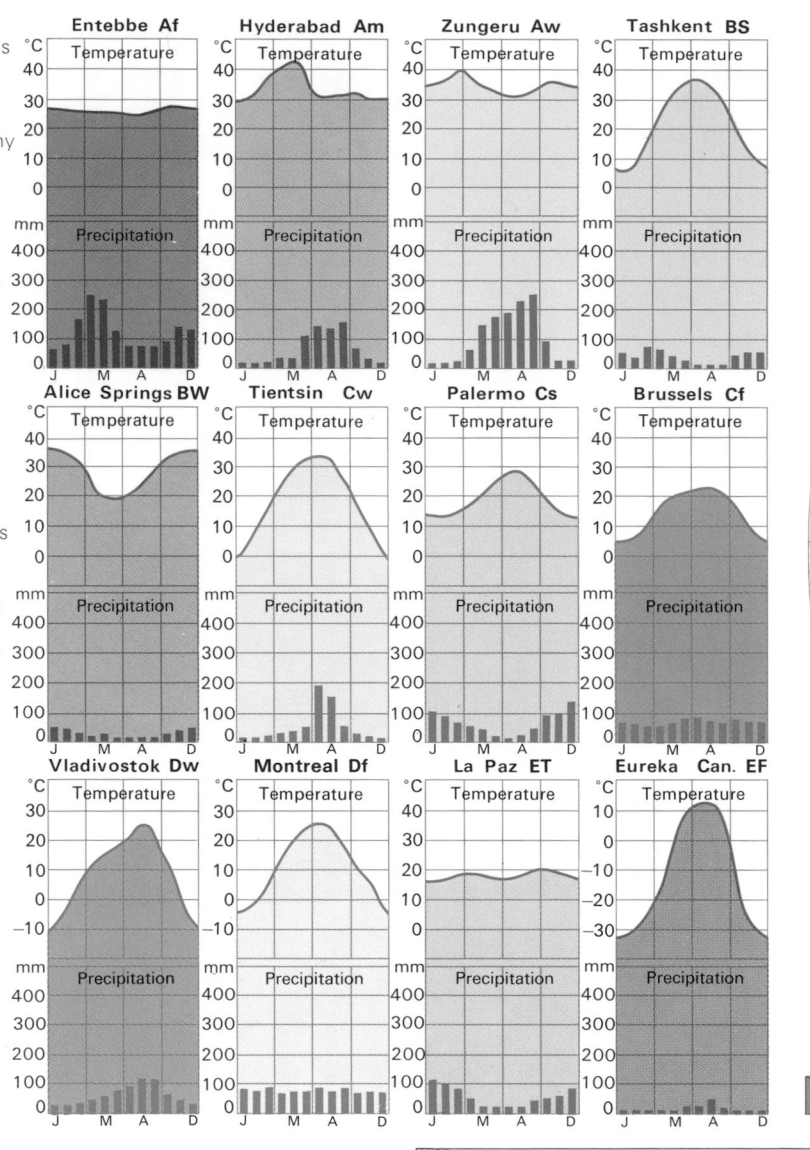

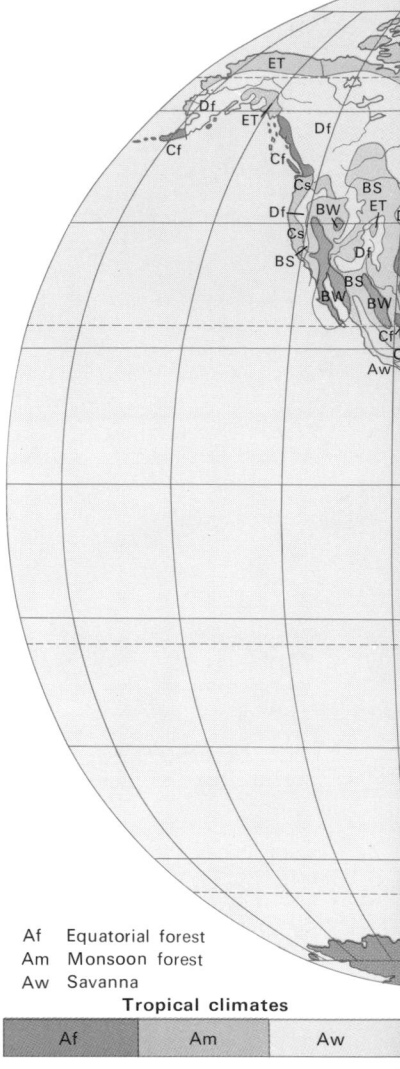

Af Equatorial forest
Am Monsoon forest
Aw Savanna

Tropical climates

Af	Am	Aw

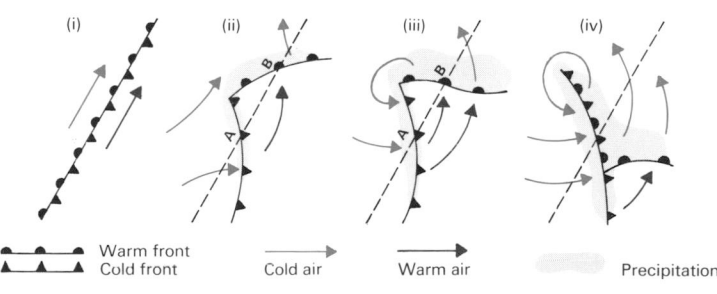

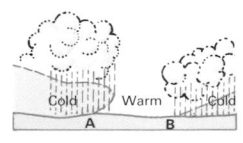 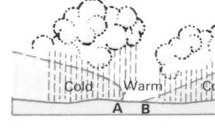 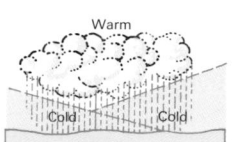

Warm front
Cold front
Cold air
Warm air
Precipitation

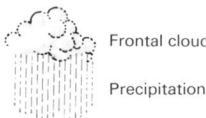

Frontal cloud

Precipitation

The upper diagrams show in plan view stages in the development of a depression.
The cross sections below correspond to stages (ii) to (iv).

Kinds of precipitation
Rain The condensation of water vapour on microscopic particles of dust, sulphur, soot or ice in the atmosphere forms water particles. These combine until they are heavy enough to fall as rain.

Hail Water particles, carried to a great height, freeze into ice particles which fall and become coated with fresh moisture. They are swept up again and refrozen. This may happen several times before falling as hail-stones.

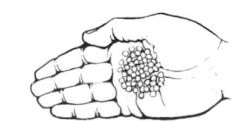

Frost Hoar, the most common type of frost, is precipitated instead of dew when water vapour changes directly into ice crystals on the surface of ground objects which have cooled below freezing point.

Snow is the precipitation of ice in the form of flakes, or clusters, of basically hexagonal ice crystals. They are formed by the condensation of water vapour directly into ice.

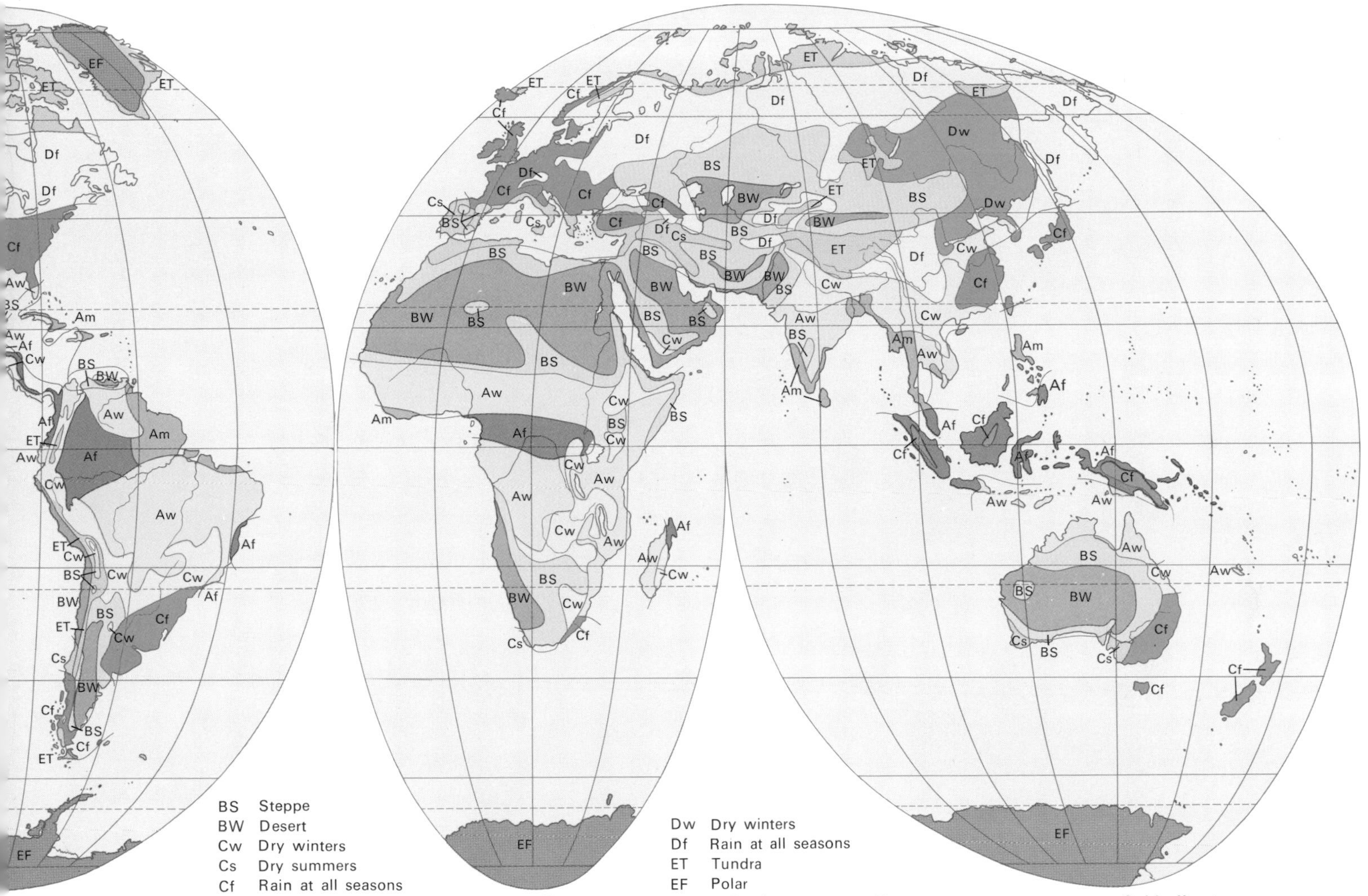

BS Steppe
BW Desert
Cw Dry winters
Cs Dry summers
Cf Rain at all seasons

Dw Dry winters
Df Rain at all seasons
ET Tundra
EF Polar

Dry climates **Warm temperate climates** **Cool temperate climates** **Cold climates**

| BS | BW | Cw | Cs | Cf | Dw | Df | ET | EF |

Tropical storm tracks *below*

A tropical cyclone, or storm, is designated as having winds of gale force (60 kph) but less than hurricane force (120 kph). It is a homogenous air mass with upward spiralling air currents around a windless centre, or eye. An average of 65 tropical storms occur each year, over 50% of which reach hurricane force. They originate mainly during the summer over tropical oceans.

Extremes of climate & weather *right*

Tropical high temperatures and polar low temperatures combined with wind systems, altitude and unequal rainfall distribution result in the extremes of tropical rain forests, inland deserts and frozen polar wastes. Fluctuations in the limits of these extreme zones and extremes of weather result in occasional catastrophic heat-waves and drought, floods and storms, frost and snow.

Hurricane devastation

Hot desert

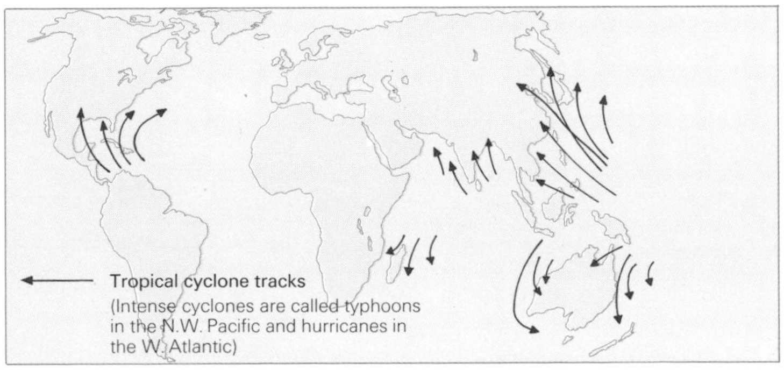

← Tropical cyclone tracks
(Intense cyclones are called typhoons in the N.W. Pacific and hurricanes in the W. Atlantic)

Tornado

Arctic dwellings

The Earth from Space

Mount Etna, Sicily *left*
Etna is at the top of the photograph, the Plain of Catania in the centre and the Mediterranean to the right. This is an infra-red photograph; vegetation shows as red, water as blue/black and urban areas as grey. The recent lava flows, as yet with no vegetation, show up as blue/black unlike the cultivated slopes which are red and red/pink.

Hawaii, Pacific Ocean *above*
This is a photograph of Hawaii, the largest of the Hawaiian Islands in the Central Pacific. North is at the top of the photograph. The snowcapped craters of the volcanoes Mauna Kea (dormant) in the north centre and Mauna Loa (active) in the south centre of the photograph can be seen. The chief town, Hilo, is on the north east coast.

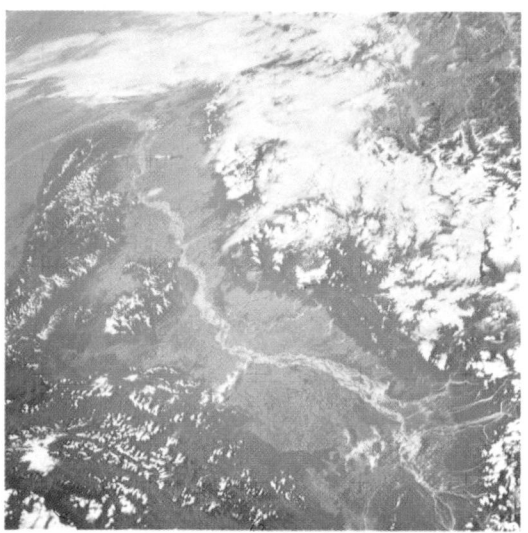

River Brahmaputra, India *left*
A view looking westwards down the Brahmaputra with the Himalayas on the right and the Khasi Hills of Assam to the left.

Szechwan, China *right*
The River Tachin in the mountainous region of Szechwan, Central China. The lightish blue area in the river valley in the north east of the photograph is a village and its related cultivation.

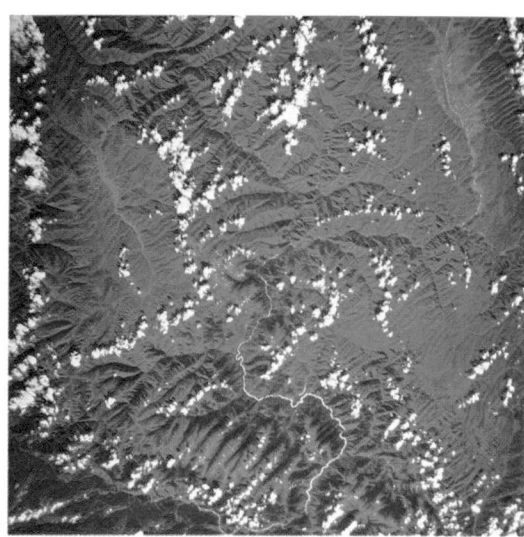

New York, U.S.A. *left*
This infra-red photograph shows the western end of Long Island and the entrance to the Hudson River. Vegetation appears as red, water as blue/black and the metropolitan areas of New York, through the cloud cover, as grey.

The Great Barrier Reef, Australia *right*
The Great Barrier Reef and the Queensland coast from Cape Melville to Cape Flattery. The smoke from a number of forest fires can be seen in the centre of the photograph.

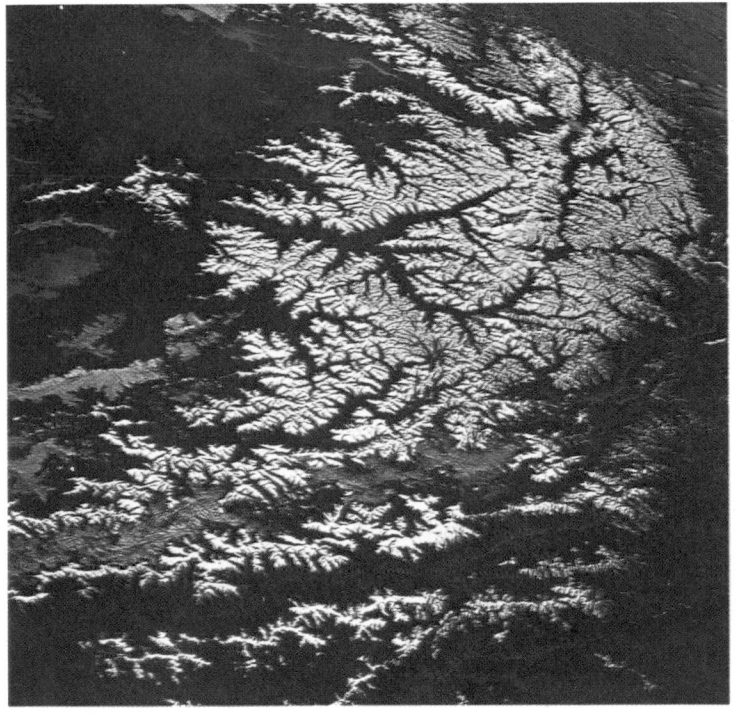

Eastern Himalayas, Asia
above left
A view from Apollo IX looking
north-westwards over the
snowcapped, sunlit mountain
peaks and the head waters of
the Mekong, Salween,
Irrawaddy and, in the distance,
with its distinctive loop, the
Brahmaputra.

Atacama Desert, Chile
above right
This view looking eastwards
from the Pacific over the
Mejillones peninsula with the
city of Antofagasta in the
southern bay of that peninsula.
Inland the desert and salt-pans
of Atacama, and beyond, the
Andes.

The Alps, Europe *right*
This vertical photograph shows
the snow-covered mountains
and glaciers of the Alps along
the Swiss-Italian-French
border. Mont Blanc and the
Matterhorn are shown and, in
the north, the Valley of the
Rhône is seen making its sharp
right-hand bend near Martigny.
In the south the head waters
of the Dora Baltea flow
towards the Po and, in the
north-west, the Lac d'Annecy
can be seen.

The Evolution of the Continents

The origin of the earth is still open to much conjecture although the most widely accepted theory is that it was formed from a solar cloud consisting mainly of hydrogen. Under gravitation the cloud condensed and shrank to form our planets orbiting around the sun. Gravitation forced the lighter elements to the surface of the earth where they cooled to form a crust while the inner material remained hot and molten. Earth's first rocks formed over 3500 million years ago but since then the surface has been constantly altered.

Until comparatively recently the view that the primary units of the earth had remained essentially fixed throughout geological time was regarded as common sense, although the concept of moving continents has been traced back to references in the Bible of a break up of the land after Noah's floods. The continental drift theory was first developed by Antonio Snider in 1858 but probably the most important single advocate was Alfred Wegener who, in 1915, published evidence from geology, climatology and biology. His conclusions are very similar to those reached by current research although he was wrong about the speed of break-up.

The measurement of fossil magnetism found in rocks has probably proved the most influential evidence. While originally these drift theories were openly mocked, now they are considered standard doctrine.

The jigsaw
As knowledge of the shape and structure of the earth's surface grew, several of the early geographers noticed the great similarity in shape of the coasts bordering the Atlantic. It was this remarkable similarity which led to the first detailed geological and structural comparisons. Even more accurate fits can be made by placing the edges of the continental shelves in juxtaposition.

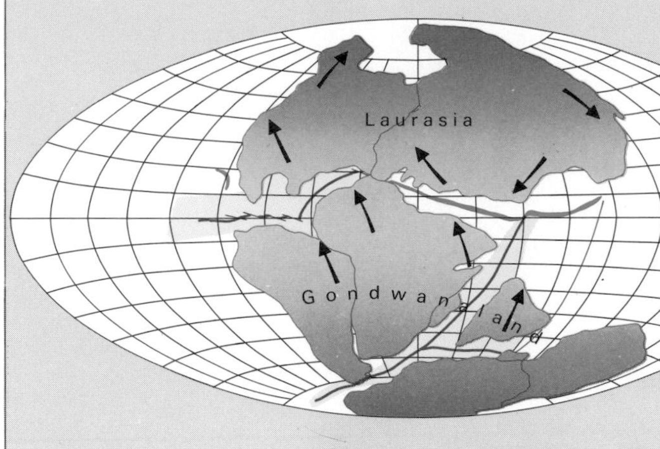

180 million years ago.
The original Pangaea land mass had split into two major continental groups. The southern group, Gondwanaland, had itself started to break up, India and Antarctica-Australia becoming isolated. A rift had begun to appear between South America and Africa and, in the East, Africa was closing up the Tethys Sea.

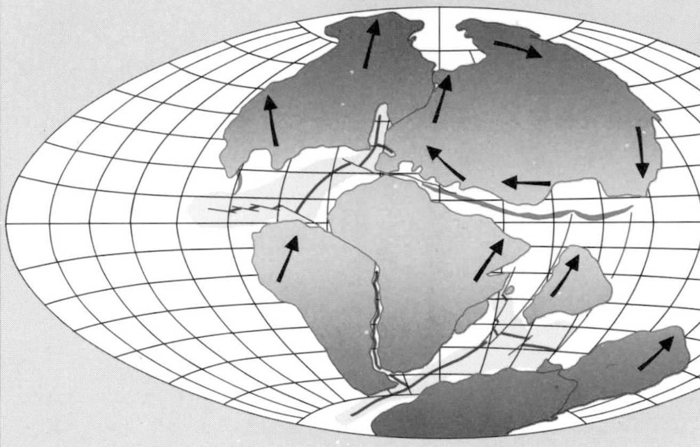

135 million years ago.
Both Gondwanaland and Laurasia continued to drift northwards but the widening of the splits in the North Atlantic and Indian Oceans persisted. The South Atlantic rift continued to lengthen and a further perpendicular rift appeared which will eventually separate Greenland from North America. India continues heading northward towards Asia.

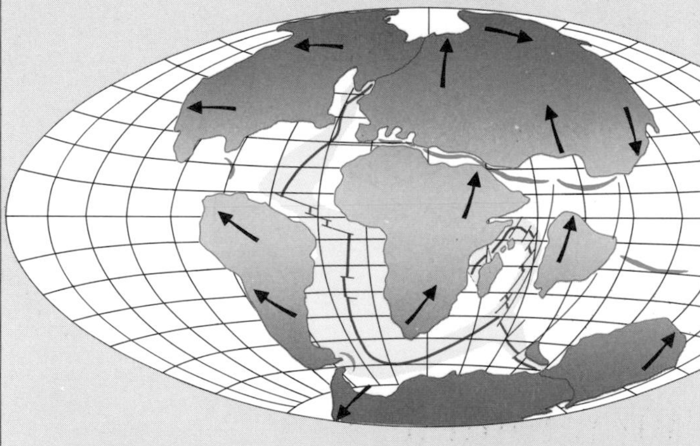

65 million years ago.
South America, completely separated from Africa, moved quickly north and westwards. Madagascar broke free from Africa but, as yet, there is no sign of the Red Sea Rift which will split Africa from the Arabian Peninsula. The Mediterranean sea is recognizable. In the south, Australia is still connected to Antarctica.

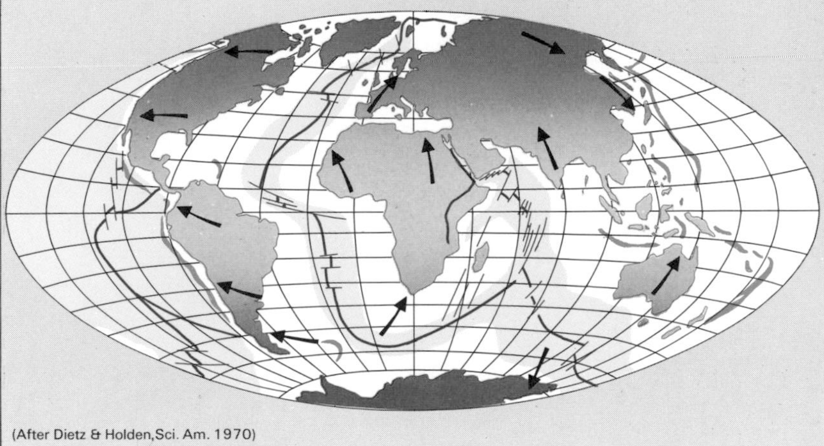

Today.
India has moved northwards and is colliding with Asia, crumpling up the sediments to form the folded mountain range of the Himalayas. South America has rotated and moved west to connect with North America. Australia has separated from Antarctica.

Laurasia

Gondwanaland

(After Dietz & Holden, Sci. Am. 1970)

	Trench
	Rift
	New Ocean Floor
	Zones of slippage

Plate tectonics

The original debate about continental drift was only a prelude to a more radical idea; plate tectonics. The basic theory is that the earth's crust is made up of a series of rigid plates which float on a soft layer of the mantle and are moved about by convection currents in the earth's interior. These plates converge and diverge along margins marked by earthquakes, volcanoes and other seismic activity. Plates diverge from mid-ocean ridges where molten lava pushes upwards and forces the plates apart at a rate of up to 30mm. a year. Converging plates form either a trench, where the oceanic plate sinks below the lighter continental rock, or mountain ranges where two continents collide. This explains the paradox that while there have always been oceans none of the present oceans contain sediments more than 150 million years old.

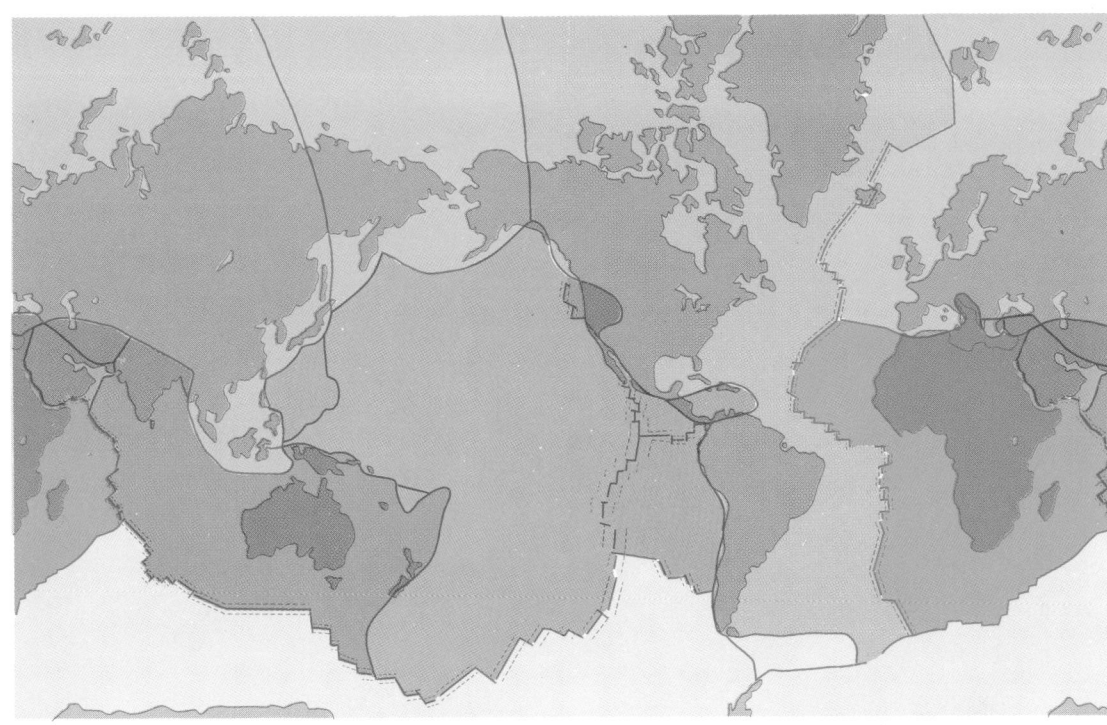

Trench boundary

The present explanation for the comparative youth of the ocean floors is that where an ocean and a continent meet the ocean plate dips under the less dense continental plate at an angle of approximately 45°. All previous crust is then ingested by downward convection currents. In the Japanese trench this occurs at a rate of about 120mm. a year.

Transform fault

The recent identification of the transform, or transverse, fault proved to be one of the crucial preliminaries to the investigation of plate tectonics. They occur when two plates slip alongside each other without parting or approaching to any great extent. They complete the outline of the plates delineated by the ridges and trenches and demonstrate large scale movements of parts of the earth's surface

Ridge boundary

Ocean rises or crests are basically made up from basaltic lavas for although no gap can exist between plates, one plate can ease itself away from another. In that case hot, molten rock instantly rises from below to fill in the incipient rift and forms a ridge. These ridges trace a line almost exactly through the centre of the major oceans.

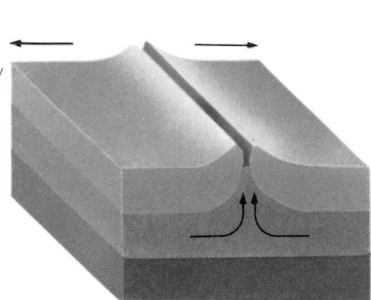

Destruction of ocean plates.

As the ocean plate sinks below the continental plate some of the sediment on its surface is scraped off and piled up on the landward side. This sediment is later incorporated in a folded mountain range which usually appears on the edge of the continent, such as the Andes. Similarly if two continents collide the sediments are squeezed up into new mountains.

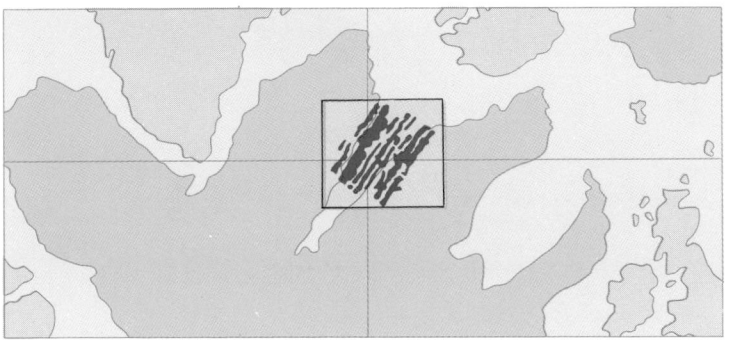

Sea floor spreading

Reversals in the earth's magnetic field have occured throughout history. As new rock emerges at the ocean ridges it cools and is magnetised in the direction of the prevailing magnetic field. By mapping the magnetic patterns either side of the ridge a symmetrical stripey pattern of alternating fields can be observed (see inset area in diagram). As the dates of the last few reversals are known the rate of spreading can be calculated.

The Unstable Earth

The earth's surface is slowly but continually being rearranged. Some changes such as erosion and deposition are extremely slow but they upset the balance which causes other more abrupt changes often originating deep within the earth's interior. The constant movements vary in intensity, often with stresses building up to a climax such as a particularly violent volcanic eruption or earthquake.

The crust *(below and right)*
The outer layer or crust of the earth consists of a comparatively low density, brittle material varying from 5 to 50 kilometres deep beneath the continents. Under this is a layer of rock consisting predominately of silica and aluminium; hence it is called 'sial'. Extending under the ocean floors and below the sial is a basaltic layer known as 'sima', consisting mainly of silica and magnesium.

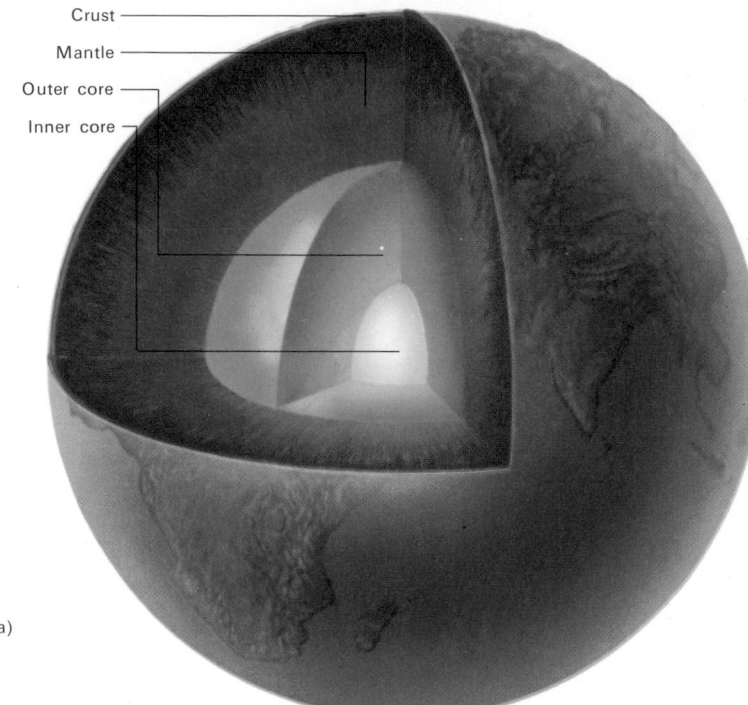

Crust
Mantle
Outer core
Inner core

Continental crust   Ocean crust

Sediment
Granite rock (sial)
Basaltic layer (sima)
Mantle

Volcanoes *(right, below and far right)*
Volcanoes occur when hot liquefied rock beneath the crust reaches the surface as lava. An accumulation of ash and cinders around a vent forms a cone. Successive layers of thin lava flows form an acid lava volcano while thick lava flows form a basic lava volcano. A caldera forms when a particularly violent eruption blows off the top of an already existing cone.

The mantle *(above)*
Immediately below the crust, at the mohorovicic discontinuity line, there is a distinct change in density and chemical properties. This is the mantle - made up of iron and magnesium silicates - with temperatures reaching 1 600°C. The rigid upper mantle extends down to a depth of about 1 000 km., below which is the more viscous lower mantle which is about 1 900 km. thick.

The core *(above)*
The outer core, approximately 2 100 km. thick, consists of molten iron and nickel at 2 000°C to 5 000°C possibly separated from the less dense mantle by an oxidised shell. About 5 000 km. below the surface is the liquid transition zone, below which is the solid inner core, a sphere of 2 740 km. diameter where rock is three times as dense as in the crust.

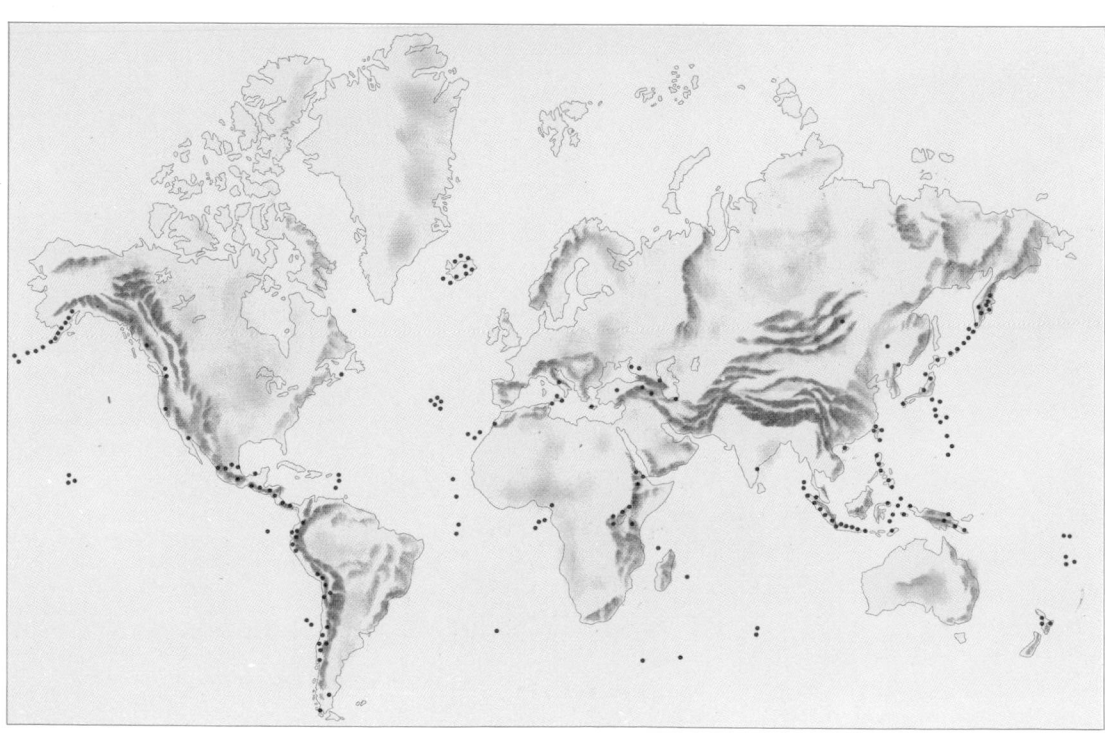

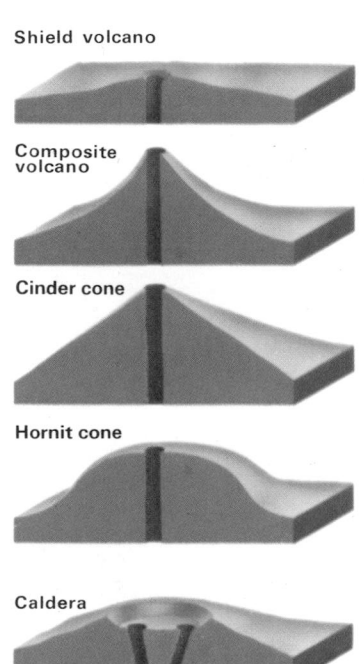

Shield volcano

Composite volcano

Cinder cone

Hornit cone

Caldera

Major earthquakes in the last 100 years	numbers killed
1896 Japan (tsunami)	22 000
1906 San Francisco	destroyed
1906 Chile, Valparaiso	22 000
1908 Italy, Messina	77 000
1920 China, Kansu	180 000
1923 Japan, Tokyo	143 000
1930 Italy, Naples	2 100
1931 Napier	destroyed
1931 Nicaragua, Managua	destroyed
1932 China, Kansu	70 000
1935 India, Quetta	60 000
1939 Chile, Chillan	20 000
1939/40 Turkey, Erzincan	30 000
1948 Japan, Fukui	5 100
1956 N. Afghanistan	2 000
1957 W. Iran	2 500
1960 Morocco, Agadir	12 000
1962 N.W. Iran	10 000
1963 Yugoslavia, Skopje	1 000
1966 U.S.S.R., Tashkent	destroyed
1970 N. Peru	66 800
1972 Nicaragua, Managua	7 000
1974 N. Pakistan	10 000
1975 Turkey, Lice	2 300
1976 China, Tangshan	650 000
1976 Turkey, Van	3 800

Sea Land + Earthquake foci
Regions with frequent earthquake disturbances
Regions with occasional earthquake disturbances

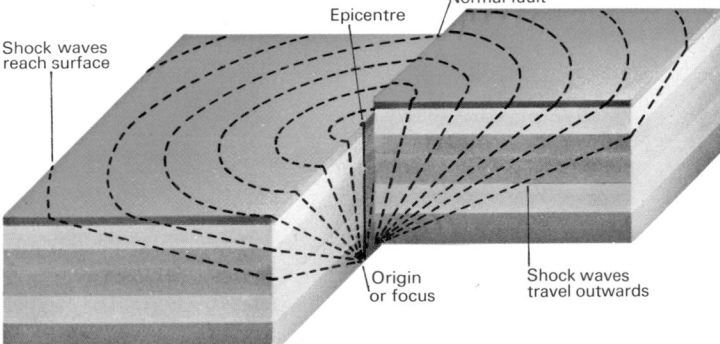

Epicentre
Normal fault
Shock waves reach surface
Origin or focus
Shock waves travel outwards

Earthquakes *(right and above)*

Earthquakes are a series of rapid vibrations originating from the slipping or faulting of parts of the earth's crust when stresses within build up to breaking point. They usually happen at depths varying from 8-30 km. Severe earthquakes cause extensive damage when they take place in populated areas destroying structures and severing communications. Most loss of life occurs due to secondary causes i.e. falling masonry, fires or tsunami waves.

Alaskan earthquake, 1964

Tsunami waves *(left)*

A sudden slump in the ocean bed during an earthquake forms a trough in the water surface subsequently followed by a crest and smaller waves. A more marked change of level in the sea bed can form a crest, the start of a Tsunami which travels up to 60 kph with waves up to 60 metres high. Seismographic detectors continuously record earthquake shocks and warn of the Tsunami which may follow it.

Seismic Waves *(right)*

The shock waves sent out from the epicentre of an earthquake are of three main kinds each with distinct properties. Primary (P) waves are compressional waves which can be transmitted through both solids and liquids and therefore pass through the earth's liquid core. Secondary (S) waves are shear waves and can only pass through solids. They cannot pass through the core and are reflected at the core-mantle boundary taking a concave course back to the surface. The core also refracts the P waves causing them to alter course, and the net effect of this reflection and refraction is the production of a shadow zone at a certain distance from the epicentre, free from P and S waves. Due to their different properties P waves travel about 1·7 times faster than S waves. The third main kind of wave is a long (L) wave, a slow wave which travels along the earth's surface, its motion being either horizontal or vertical.

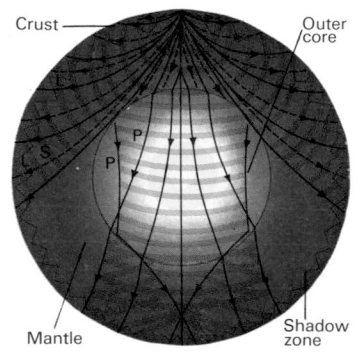

Crust
Outer core
Mantle
Shadow zone

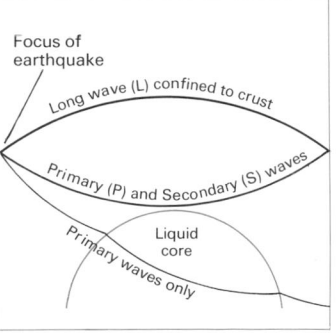

Focus of earthquake
Long wave (L) confined to crust
Primary (P) and Secondary (S) waves
Primary waves only
Liquid core

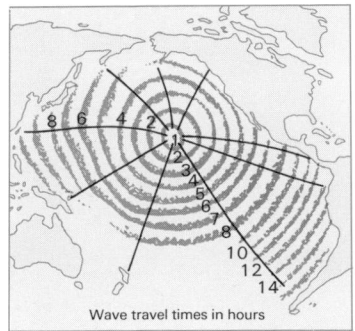

Wave travel times in hours

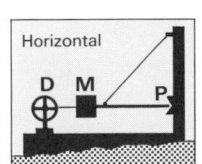

Horizontal
D M P

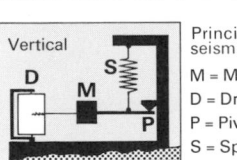

Vertical
D M P
S

Principles of seismographs (left)
M = Mass
D = Drum
P = Pivot
S = Spring

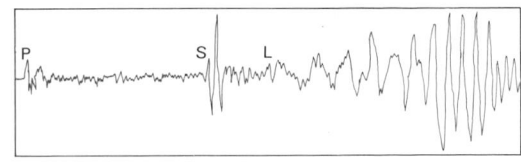

P   S   L

Seismographs

Seismographs are delicate instruments capable of detecting and recording vibrations due to earthquakes thousands of miles away. P waves cause the first tremors. S the second, and L the main shock.

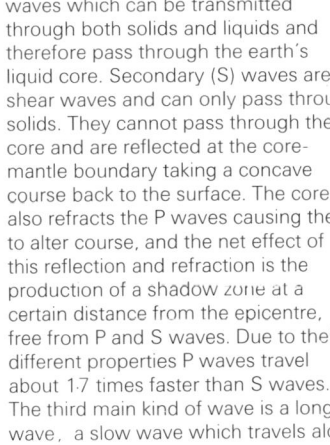

17

The Making of Landscape

The making of landscape

The major forces which shape our land would seem to act very slowly in comparison with man's average life span but in geological terms the erosion of rock is in fact very fast. Land goes through a cycle of transformation. It is broken up by earthquakes and other earth movements, temperature changes, water, wind and ice. Rock debris is then transported by water, wind and glaciers and deposited on lowlands and on the sea floor. Here it builds up and by the pressure of its own weight is converted into new rock strata. These in turn can be uplifted either gently as plains or plateaux or more irregularly to form mountains. In either case the new higher land is eroded and the cycle recommences.

A Peneplain

Uplifted peneplain

Rivers

Rivers shape the land by three basic processes: erosion, transportation and deposition. A youthful river flows fast eroding downwards quickly to form a narrow valley (1) As it matures it deposits some debris and erodes laterally to widen the valley (2). In its last stage it meanders across a wide flat flood plain depositing fine particles of alluvium (3).

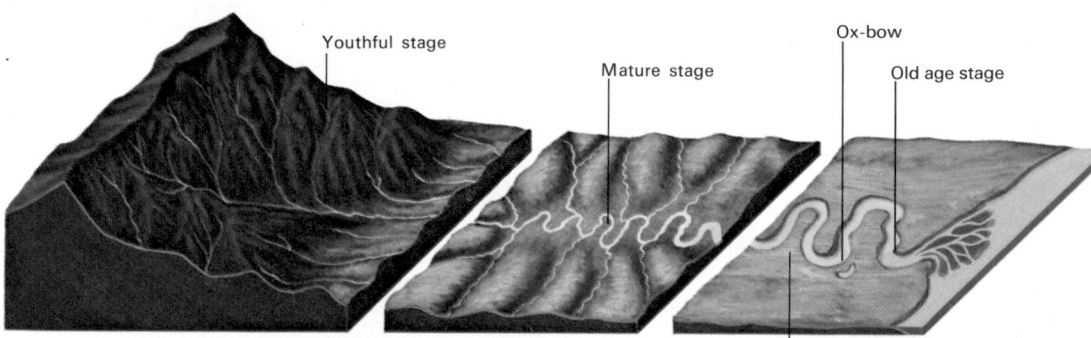

Youthful stage   Mature stage   Ox-bow   Old age stage   Meanders

Underground water

Water enters porous and permeable rocks from the surface moving downward until it reaches a layer of impermeable rock. Joints in underground rock, such as limestone, are eroded to form underground caves and caverns. When the roof of a cave collapses a gorge is formed. Surface entrances to joints are often widened to form vertical openings called swallow holes.

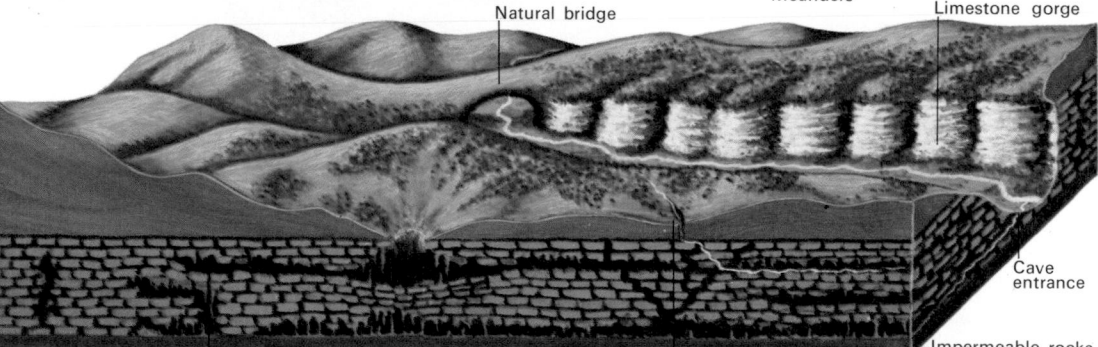

Natural bridge   Limestone gorge   Cave entrance   Impermeable rocks

Cave with stalactites and stalagmites   River disappears down swallow hole

Wind

Wind action is particularly powerful in arid and semi-arid regions where rock waste produced by weathering is used as an abrasive tool by the wind. The rate of erosion varies with the characteristics of the rock which can cause weird shapes and effects (right). Desert sand can also be accumulated by the wind to form barchan dunes (far right) which slowly travel forward, horns first.

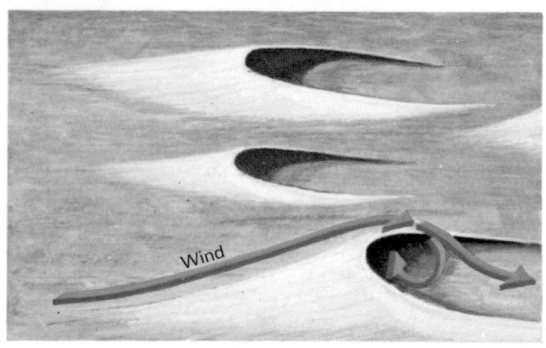

Wind

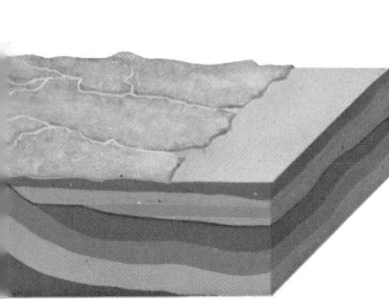

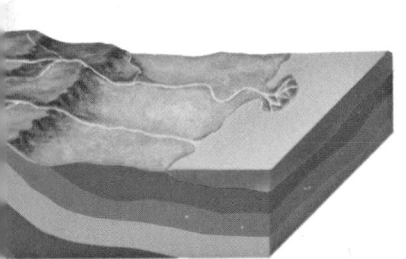

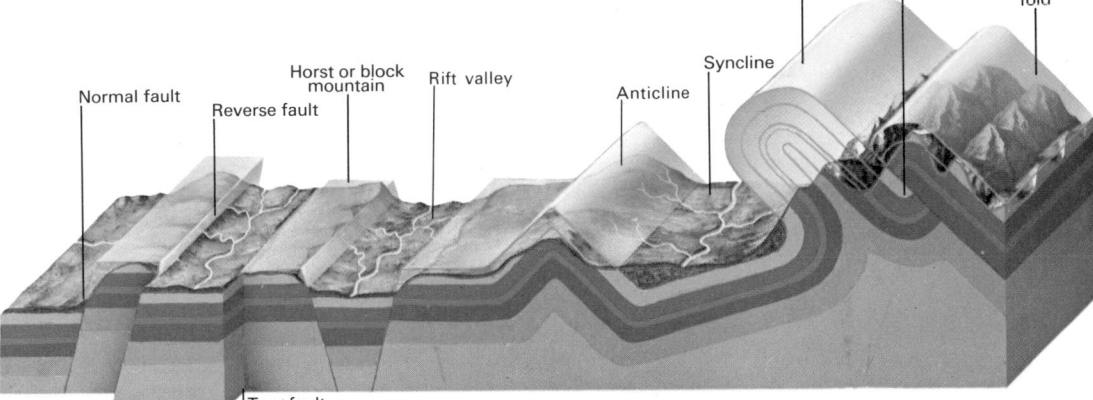

Folding and faulting

A vertical displacement in the earth's crust is called a fault or reverse fault; lateral displacement is a tear fault. An uplifted block is called a horst, the reverse of which is a rift valley. Compressed horizontal layers of sedimentary rock fold to form mountains. Those layers which bend up form an anticline, those bending down form a syncline : continued pressure forms an overfold.

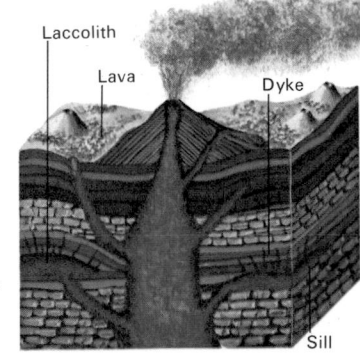

Volcanic activity

When pressure on rocks below the earth's crust is released the normally semi-solid hot rock becomes liquid magma. The magma forces its way into cracks of the crust and may either reach the surface where it forms volcanoes or it may collect in the crust as sills dykes or lacoliths. When magma reaches the surface it cools to form lava.

Waves

Coasts are continually changing, some retreat under wave erosion while others advance with wave deposition. These actions combined form steep cliffs and wave cut platforms. Eroded debris is in turn deposited as a terrace. As the water becomes shallower the erosive power of the waves decreases and gradually the cliff disappears. Wave action can also create other features (far right).

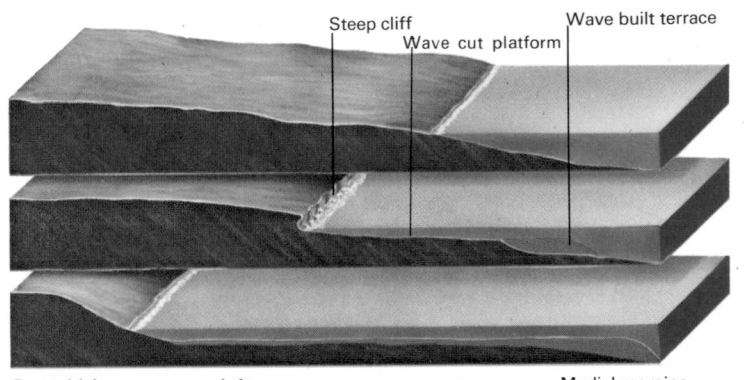

Ice

These diagrams (right) show how a glaciated valley may have formed. The glacier deepens, straightens and widens the river valley whose interlocking spurs become truncated or cut off. Intervalley divides are frost shattered to form sharp aretes and pyramidal peaks. Hanging valleys mark the entry of tributary rivers and eroded rocks form medial moraine. Terminal moraine is deposited as the glacier retreats.

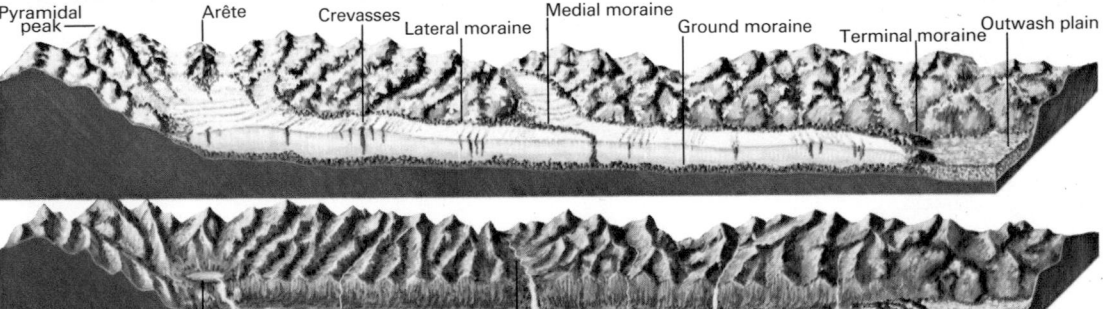

Subsidence and uplift

As the land surface is eroded it may eventually become a level plain - a peneplain, broken only by low hills, remnants of previous mountains. In turn this peneplain may be uplifted to form a plateau with steep edges. At the coast the uplifted wave platform becomes a coastal plain and in the rejuvenated rivers downward erosion once more predominates.

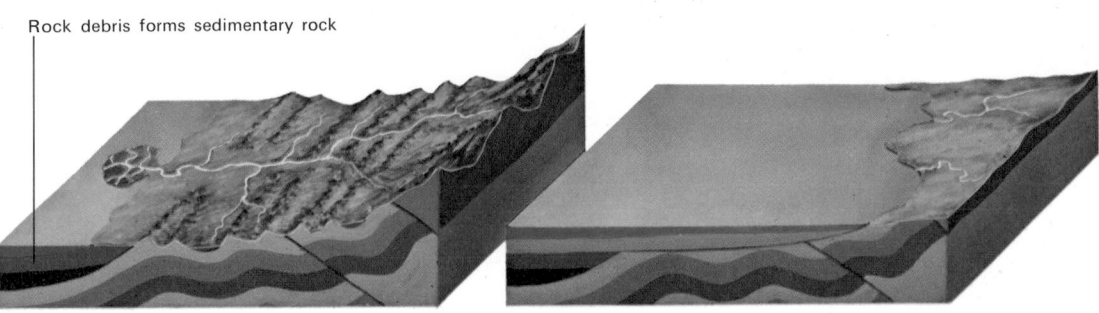

The Earth: Physical Dimensions

Its surface

Highest point on the earth's surface: Mt. Everest, Tibet - Nepal boundary   8 848 m
Lowest point on the earth's surface: The Dead Sea, Jordan   below sea level 395 m
Greatest ocean depth.: Challenger Deep, Mariana Trench   11 022 m
Average height of land   840 m
Average depth of seas and oceans   3 808 m

Dimensions

Superficial area	510 000 000 km²
Land surface	149 000 000 km²
Land surface as % of total area	29·2 %
Water surface	361 000 000 km²
Water surface as % of total area	70·8 %
Equatorial circumference	40 077 km
Meridional circumference	40 009 km
Equatorial diameter	12 756·8 km
Polar diameter	12 713·8 km
Equatorial radius	6 378·4 km
Polar radius	6 356·9 km
Volume of the Earth	1 083 230 x 10⁶ km³
Mass of the Earth	5·9 x 10²¹ tonnes

The Figure of Earth

An imaginary sea-level surface is considered and called a geoid. By measuring at different places the angles from plumb lines to a fixed star there have been many determinations of the shape of parts of the geoid which is found to be an oblate spheriod with its axis along the axis of rotation of the earth. Observations from satellites have now given a new method of more accurate determinations of the figure of the earth and its local irregularities.

Land and Sea Hemispheres.

About 85% of the total land area is contained in the hemisphere centred on a point between Paris and Brussels.

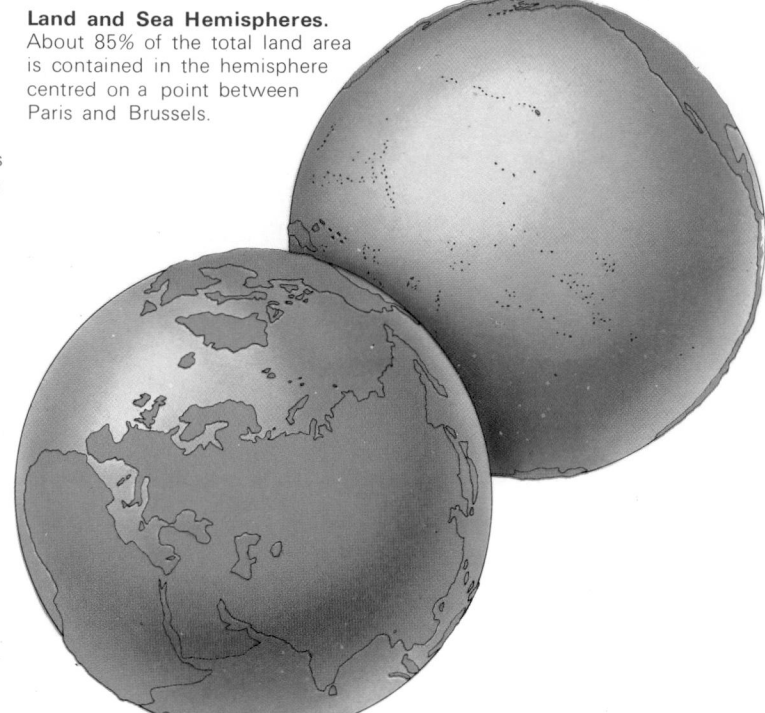

Oceans and Seas
Area in 1000 km²

Pacific Ocean	165 721	North Sea	575
Atlantic Ocean	81 660	Black Sea	448
Indian Ocean	73 442	Red Sea	440
Arctic Ocean	14 351	Baltic Sea	422
Mediterranean Sea	2 966	Persian Gulf	238
Bering Sea	2 274	St. Lawrence, Gulf of	236
Caribbean Sea	1 942	English Channel & Irish Sea	179
Mexico, Gulf of	1 813	California, Gulf of	161
Okhotsk, Sea of	1 528		
East China Sea	1 248		
Hudson Bay	1 230		
Japan, Sea of	1 049		

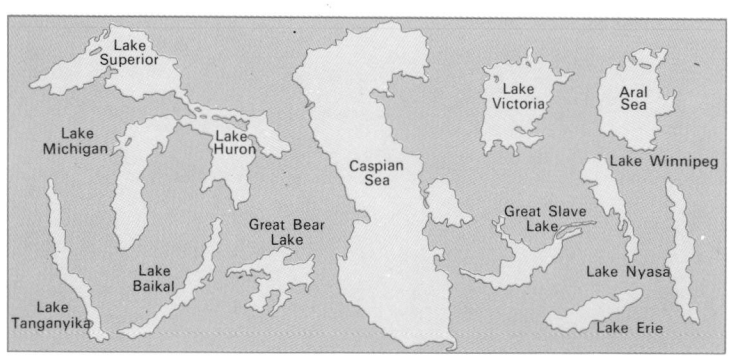

Lakes and Inland Seas
Areas in 1000 km²

Caspian Sea, Asia	424·2	Lake Ontario, N.America	19·5
Lake Superior, N.America	82·4	Lake Ladoga, Europe	18·4
Lake Victoria, Africa	69·5	Lake Balkhash, Asia	17·3
Aral Sea (Salt), Asia	63·8	Lake Maracaibo, S.America	16·3
Lake Huron, N.America	59·6	Lake Onega, Europe	9·8
Lake Michigan, N.America	58·0	Lake Eyre (Salt), Australia	9·6
Lake Tanganyika, Africa	32·9	Lake Turkana (Salt), Africa	9·1
Lake Baikal, Asia	31·5	Lake Titicaca, S.America	8·3
Great Bear Lake, N.America	31·1	Lake Nicaragua, C.America	8·0
Great Slave Lake, N.America	28·9	Lake Athabasca, N.America	7·9
Lake Nyasa, Africa	28·5	Reindeer Lake, N.America	6·3
Lake Erie, N.America	25·7	Issyk-Kul, Asia	6·2
Lake Winnipeg, N.America	24·3	Lake Torrens (Salt), Australia	6·1
Lake Chad, Africa	20·7	Koko Nor (Salt), Asia	6·0
		Lake Urmia, Asia	6·0
		Vänern, Europe	5·6

Longest rivers

	km.
Nile, Africa	6 690
Amazon, S.America	6 280
Mississipi - Missouri, N.America	6 270
Yangtze, Asia	4 990
Zaire, Africa	4 670
Amur, Asia	4 410
Hwang Ho (Yellow), Asia	4 350
Lena, Asia	4 260
Mekong, Asia	4 180
Niger, Africa	4 180
Mackenzie, N.America	4 040
Ob, Asia	4 000
Yenisei, Asia	3 800

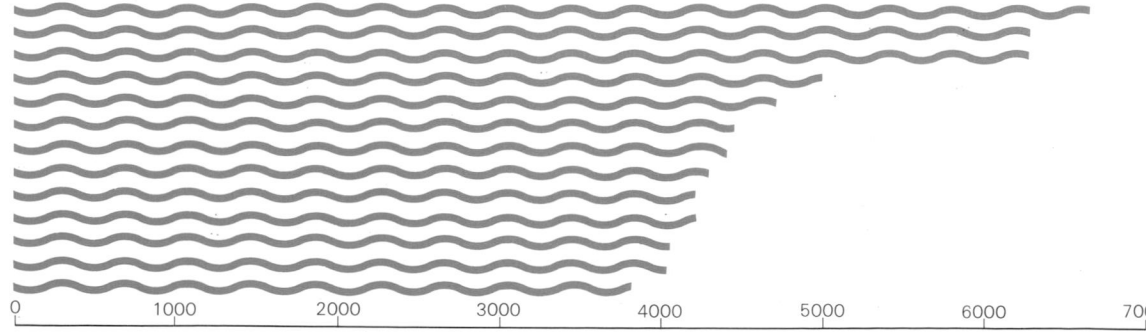

The Highest Mountains and the Greatest Depths.

Mount Everest defied the world's greatest mountaineers for 32 years and claimed the lives of many men. Not until 1920 was permission granted by the Dalai Lama to attempt the mountain, and the first successful ascent came in 1953. Since then the summit has been reached several times. The world's highest peaks have now been climbed but there are many as yet unexplored peaks in the Himalayas some of which may be over 7 600 m.

The greatest trenches are the Puerto Rico deep (9 200m.). The Tonga (10 822 m) and Mindanao (10 497 m) trenches and the Mariana Trench (11 022 m) in the Pacific. The trenches represent less than 2% of the total area of the sea-bed but are of great interest as lines of structural weakness in the Earth's crust and as areas of frequent earthquakes.

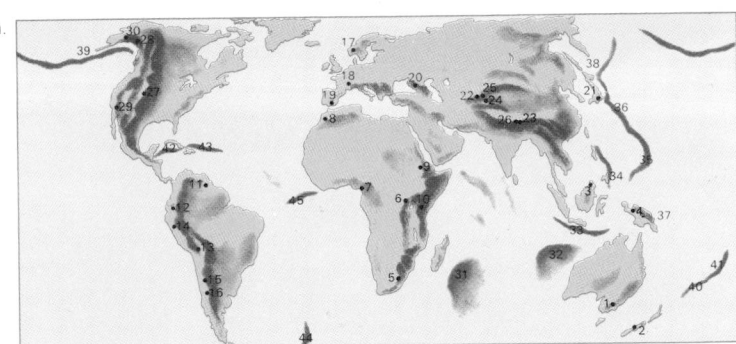

Mountain heights in metres

Ocean depths in metres

High mountains

Bathyscaphe

Waterfall

Dam

Notable Waterfalls
heights in metres

Angel, Venezuela	980
Tugela, S. Africa	853
Mongefossen, Norway	774
Yosemite, California	738
Mardalsfossen, Norway	655
Cuquenan, Venezuela	610
Sutherland, N.Z.	579
Reichenbach, Switzerland	548
Wollomombi, Australia	518
Ribbon, California	491
Gavarnie, France	422
Tyssefallene, Norway	414

Krimml, Austria	370
King George VI, Guyana	366
Silver Strand, California	356
Geissbach, Switzerland	350
Staubbach, Switzerland	299
Trümmelbach, Switzerland	290
Chirombo, Zambia	268
Livingstone, Zaïre	259
King Edward VIII, Guyana	256
Gersoppa, India	253
Vettifossen Norway	250
Kalambo, Zambia	240
Kaieteur, Guyana	226
Maletsunyane, Lesotho	192

Terui, Italy	180
Murchison, Uganda	122
Victoria, Rhodesia - Zambia	107
Cauvery, India	97
Stanley, Zaïre	61
Niagara, N.America	51
Schaffhausen, Switzerland	30

Notable Dams
heights in metres

Africa

Cabora Bassa, Zambezi R.	168
Akosombo Main Dam, Volta R.	141
Kariba, Zambezi R.	128
Aswan High Dam, Nile R.	110

Asia

Nurek, Vakhsh R., U.S.S.R.	317
Bhakra, Sutlej R., India	226
Kurobegawa, Kurobe R., Jap.	186
Charvak, Chirchik R., U.S.S.R.	168
Okutadami, Tadami R., Jap.	157
Bhumiphol, Ping R., Thai.	154

Australasia

Warragamba, N.S.W., Australia	137
Eucumbene, N.S.W., Australia	116

Europe

Grande Dixence, Switz.	284
Vajont, Vajont, R., Italy	261
Mauvoisin, Drance R., Switz.	237
Contra , Verzasca R., Switz.	230
Luzzone, Brenno R., Switz.	208
Tignes, Isère R., France	180
Amir Kabir, Karadj R., U.S.S.R.	180
Vidraru, Arges R., Rum.	165
Kremasta, Acheloos R., Greece	165

North America

Oroville, Feather R.,	235
Hoover, Colorado R.,	221
Glen Canyon, Colorado R.,	216
Daniel Johnson, Can.	214
New Bullards Bar, N. Yuba R.	194
Mossyrock, Cowlitz R.,	184
Shasta, Sacramento R.,	183
W.A.C. Bennett, Canada.	183
Don Pedro, Tuolumne R.,	178
Hungry Horse, Flathead R.,	172
Grand Coulee, Columbia R.,	168

Central and South America

Guri, Caroni R., Venezuela.	106

Distances

Kms

	Berlin	Bombay	Buenos Aires	Cairo	Calcutta	Caracas	Chicago	Copenhagen	Darwin	Hong Kong	Honolulu	Johannesburg	Lagos	Lisbon	(London →)
		3907	7400	1795	4370	5241	4402	222	8044	5440	7310	5511	3230	1436	5…
			9275	2706	1034	9024	8048	3990	4510	2683	8024	4334	4730	4982	44…
				7341	10268	3167	5599	7498	9130	11481	7558	5025	4919	5964	69…
					3541	6340	6127	1992	7216	5064	8838	3894	2432	2358	21…
Berlin						9609	7978	4395	3758	1653	7048	5256	5727	5639	49…
Bombay	6288						2502	5215	11221	10166	6009	6847	4810	4044	46…
Buenos Aires	11909	14925						4250	9361	7783	4247	8689	5973	3992	39…
Cairo	2890	4355	11814						8017	5388	7088	5732	3436	1540	5…
Calcutta	7033	1664	16524	5699						2654	5369	6611	8837	9391	86…
Caracas	8435	14522	5096	10203	15464						5543	6669	7360	6853	59…
Chicago	7084	12953	9011	3206	12839	4027						11934	10133	7821	72…
Copenhagen	357	6422	12067	9860	7072	8392	6840						2799	5089	56…
Darwin	12946	7257	14693	11612	6047	18059	15065	12903						2360	31…
Hong Kong	8754	4317	18478	8150	2659	16360	12526	8671	4271						9…
Honolulu	11764	12914	12164	14223	11343	9670	6836	11407	8640	8921					
Johannesburg	8870	6974	8088	6267	8459	11019	13984	9225	10639	10732	19206				
Lagos	5198	7612	7916	3915	9216	7741	9612	5530	14222	11845	16308	4505			
Lisbon	2311	8018	9600	3794	9075	6501	6424	2478	15114	11028	12587	8191	3799		
London	928	7190	11131	3508	7961	7507	6356	952	13848	9623	11632	9071	5017	1588	
Los Angeles	9311	14000	9852	12200	13120	5812	2804	9003	12695	11639	4117	16676	12414	9122	87…
Mexico City	9732	15656	7389	12372	15280	3586	2726	9514	14631	14122	6085	14585	11071	8676	89…
Moscow	1610	5031	13477	2902	5534	9938	8000	1561	11350	7144	11323	9161	6254	3906	24…
Nairobi	6370	4532	10402	3536	6179	11544	12883	6706	10415	8776	17282	2927	3807	6461	68…
New York	6385	12541	8526	9020	12747	3430	1145	6188	16047	12950	7980	12841	8477	5422	55…
Paris	876	7010	11051	3210	7858	7625	6650	1026	13812	9630	11968	8732	4714	1454	3…
Peking	7822	4757	19268	7544	3269	14399	10603	7202	6011	1963	8160	11710	11457	9668	81…
Reykjavik	2385	8335	11437	5266	8687	6915	4757	2103	13892	9681	9787	10938	6718	2948	18…
Rio de Janeiro	10025	13409	1953	9896	15073	4546	8547	10211	16011	17704	13342	7113	6035	7734	92…
Rome	1180	6175	11151	2133	7219	8363	7739	1531	13265	9284	12916	7743	4039	1861	14…
Singapore	9944	3914	15879	8267	2897	18359	15078	9969	3349	2599	10816	8660	11145	11886	108…
Sydney	16096	10160	11800	14418	9138	15343	14875	16042	3150	7374	8168	11040	15519	18178	169…
Tokyo	8924	6742	18362	9571	5141	14164	10137	8696	5431	2874	6202	13547	13480	11149	95…
Toronto	6497	12488	9093	9233	12561	3873	700	6265	15498	12569	7465	13374	8948	5737	57…
Wellington	18140	12370	9981	16524	11354	13122	13451	17961	5325	9427	7513	11761	16050	19575	188…

Mileage distance chart.

Distances to Los Angeles, Mexico City, Moscow, Nairobi, New York, Paris, Peking, Reykjavik, Rio de Janeiro, Rome, Singapore, Sydney, Tokyo, Toronto, Wellington

Los Angeles	Mexico City	Moscow	Nairobi	New York	Paris	Peking	Reykjavik	Rio de Janeiro	Rome	Singapore	Sydney	Tokyo	Toronto	Wellington	
785	6047	1000	3958	3967	545	4860	1482	6230	734	6179	10002	5545	4037	11272	Berlin
700	9728	3126	2816	7793	4356	2956	5179	8332	3837	2432	6313	4189	7760	7686	Bombay
122	4591	8374	6463	5298	6867	11972	7106	1214	6929	9867	7332	11410	5650	6202	Buenos Aires
580	7687	1803	2197	5605	1994	4688	3272	6149	1325	5137	8959	5947	5737	10268	Cairo
152	9494	3438	3839	7921	4883	2031	5398	9366	4486	1800	5678	3195	7805	7055	Calcutta
612	2228	6175	7173	2131	4738	8947	4297	2825	5196	11407	9534	8801	2406	8154	Caracas
742	1694	4971	8005	711	4132	6588	2956	5311	4809	9369	9243	6299	435	8358	Chicago
594	5912	970	4167	3845	638	4475	1306	6345	951	6195	9968	5403	3892	11160	Copenhagen
888	9091	7053	6472	9971	8582	3735	8632	9948	8243	2081	1957	3375	9630	3309	Darwin
232	8775	4439	5453	8047	5984	1220	6015	11001	5769	1615	4582	1786	7810	5857	Hong Kong
558	3781	7036	10739	4958	7437	5070	6081	8290	8026	6721	5075	3854	4638	4669	Honolulu
362	9063	5692	1818	7979	5426	7276	6797	4420	4811	5381	6860	8418	8310	7308	Johannesburg
713	6879	3886	2366	5268	2929	7119	4175	3750	2510	6925	9643	8376	5560	9973	Lagos
668	5391	2427	4015	3369	903	6007	1832	4805	1157	7385	11295	6928	3565	12163	Lisbon
442	5552	1552	4237	3463	212	5057	1172	5778	889	6743	10558	5942	3545	11691	London
	1549	6070	9659	2446	5645	6251	4310	6310	6331	8776	7502	5475	2170	6719	Los Angeles
		6664	9207	2090	5717	7742	4635	4780	6365	10321	8058	7024	2018	6897	Mexico City
			3942	4666	1545	3600	2053	7184	1477	5237	9008	4651	4637	10283	Moscow
				7358	4029	5727	5395	5548	3350	4635	7552	6996	7570	8490	Nairobi
					3626	6828	2613	4832	4280	9531	9935	6741	356	8951	New York
						5106	1384	5708	687	6671	10539	6038	3738	11798	Paris
							4897	10773	5049	2783	5561	1304	6557	6700	Peking
								6135	2048	7155	10325	5469	2600	10725	Reykjavik
									5725	9763	8389	11551	5180	7367	Rio de Janeiro
										6229	10143	6127	4399	11523	Rome
											3915	3306	9350	5298	Singapore
												4861	9800	1383	Sydney
													6410	5762	Tokyo
														8820	Toronto
															Wellington

Miles (lower-left triangle — columns: Los Angeles, Mexico City, Moscow, Nairobi, New York, Paris, Peking, Reykjavik, Rio de Janeiro, Rome, Singapore, Sydney, Tokyo, Toronto)

Los Angeles	Mexico City	Moscow	Nairobi	New York	Paris	Peking	Reykjavik	Rio de Janeiro	Rome	Singapore	Sydney	Tokyo	Toronto	
2493														Mexico City
9769	10724													Moscow
5544	14818	6344												Nairobi
3936	3364	7510	11842											New York
0085	9200	2486	6485	5836										Paris
0060	12460	5794	9216	10988	8217									Peking
6936	7460	3304	8683	4206	2228	7882								Reykjavik
0155	7693	11562	8928	7777	9187	17338	9874							Rio de Janeiro
0188	10243	2376	5391	6888	1105	8126	3297	9214						Rome
4123	16610	8428	7460	15339	10737	4478	11514	15712	10025					Singapore
2073	12969	14497	12153	15989	16962	8949	16617	13501	16324	6300				Sydney
3811	11304	7485	11260	10849	9718	2099	8802	18589	9861	5321	7823			Tokyo
3492	3247	7462	12183	574	6015	10552	4184	8336	7080	15047	15772	10316		Toronto
0814	11100	16549	13664	14405	18987	10782	17260	11855	18545	8526	2226	9273	14194	Wellington

Water Resources and Vegetation

Water resources and vegetation
Fresh water is essential for life on earth and in some parts of the world it is a most precious commodity. On the other hand it is very easy for industrialised temperate states to take its existence for granted, and man's increasing demand may only be met finally by the desalination of earth's 1250 million cubic kilometres of salt water. 70% of the earth's fresh water exists as ice.

The hydrological cycle
Water is continually being absorbed into the atmosphere as vapour from oceans, lakes, rivers and vegetation transpiration. On cooling the vapour either condenses or freezes and falls as rain, hail or snow. Most precipitation falls over the sea but one quarter falls over the land of which half evaporates again soon after falling while the rest flows back into the oceans.

Distribution of water

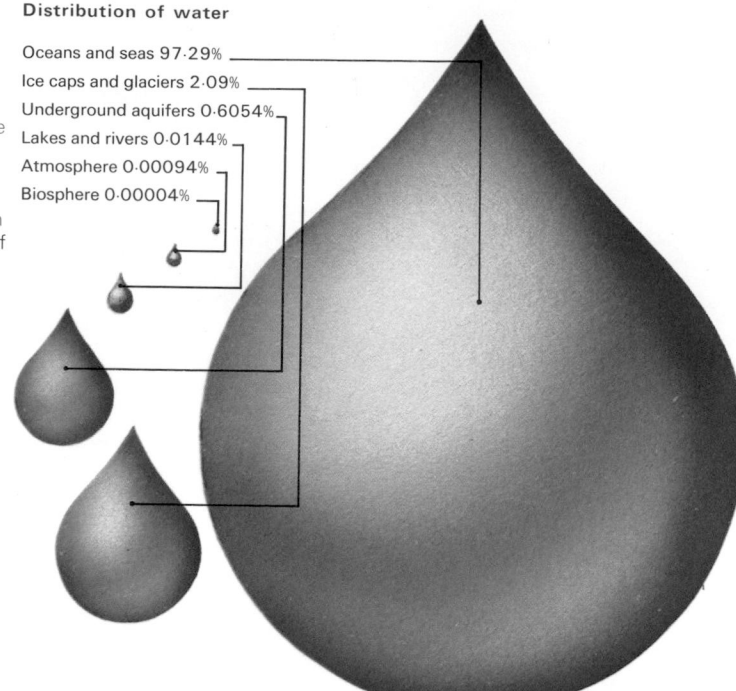

Oceans and seas 97·29%
Ice caps and glaciers 2·09%
Underground aquifers 0·6054%
Lakes and rivers 0·0144%
Atmosphere 0·00094%
Biosphere 0·00004%

Tundra

Mediterranean scrub

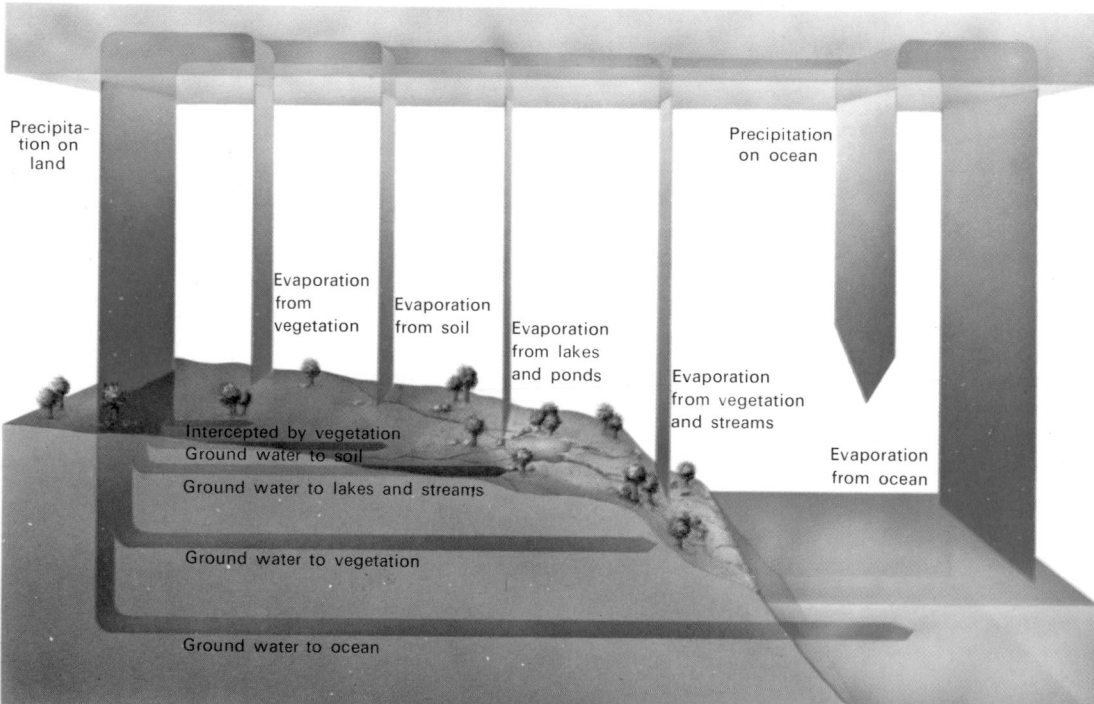

Precipitation on land

Precipitation on ocean

Evaporation from vegetation

Evaporation from soil

Evaporation from lakes and ponds

Evaporation from vegetation and streams

Evaporation from ocean

Intercepted by vegetation
Ground water to soil
Ground water to lakes and streams
Ground water to vegetation
Ground water to ocean

Domestic consumption of water
An area's level of industrialisation, climate and standard of living are all major influences in the consumption of water. On average Europe consumes 636 litres per head each day of which 180 litres is used domestically. In the U.S.A. domestic consumption is slightly higher at 270 litres per day. The graph (right) represents domestic consumption in the U.K. in 1970.

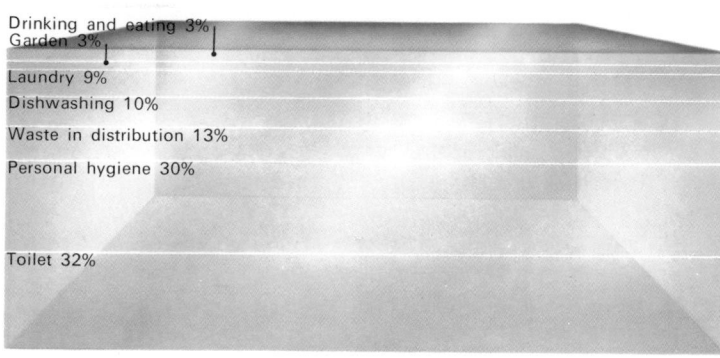

Drinking and eating 3%
Garden 3%
Laundry 9%
Dishwashing 10%
Waste in distribution 13%
Personal hygiene 30%
Toilet 32%

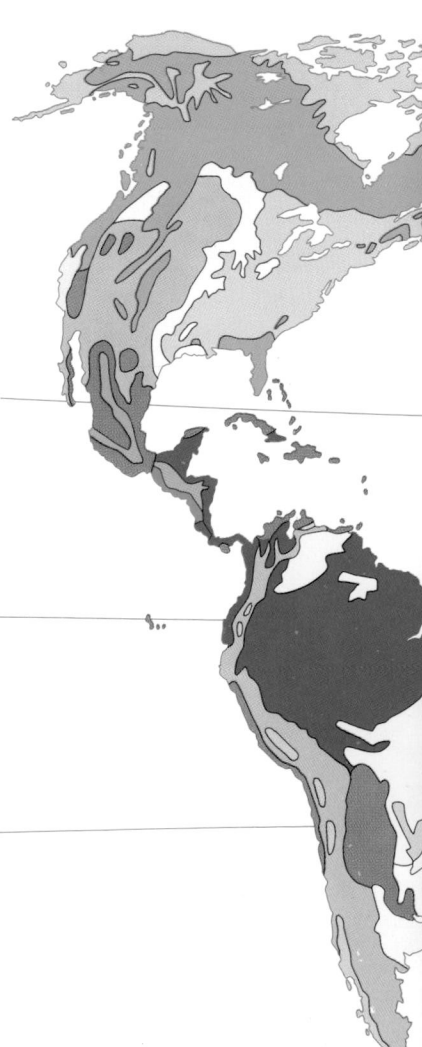

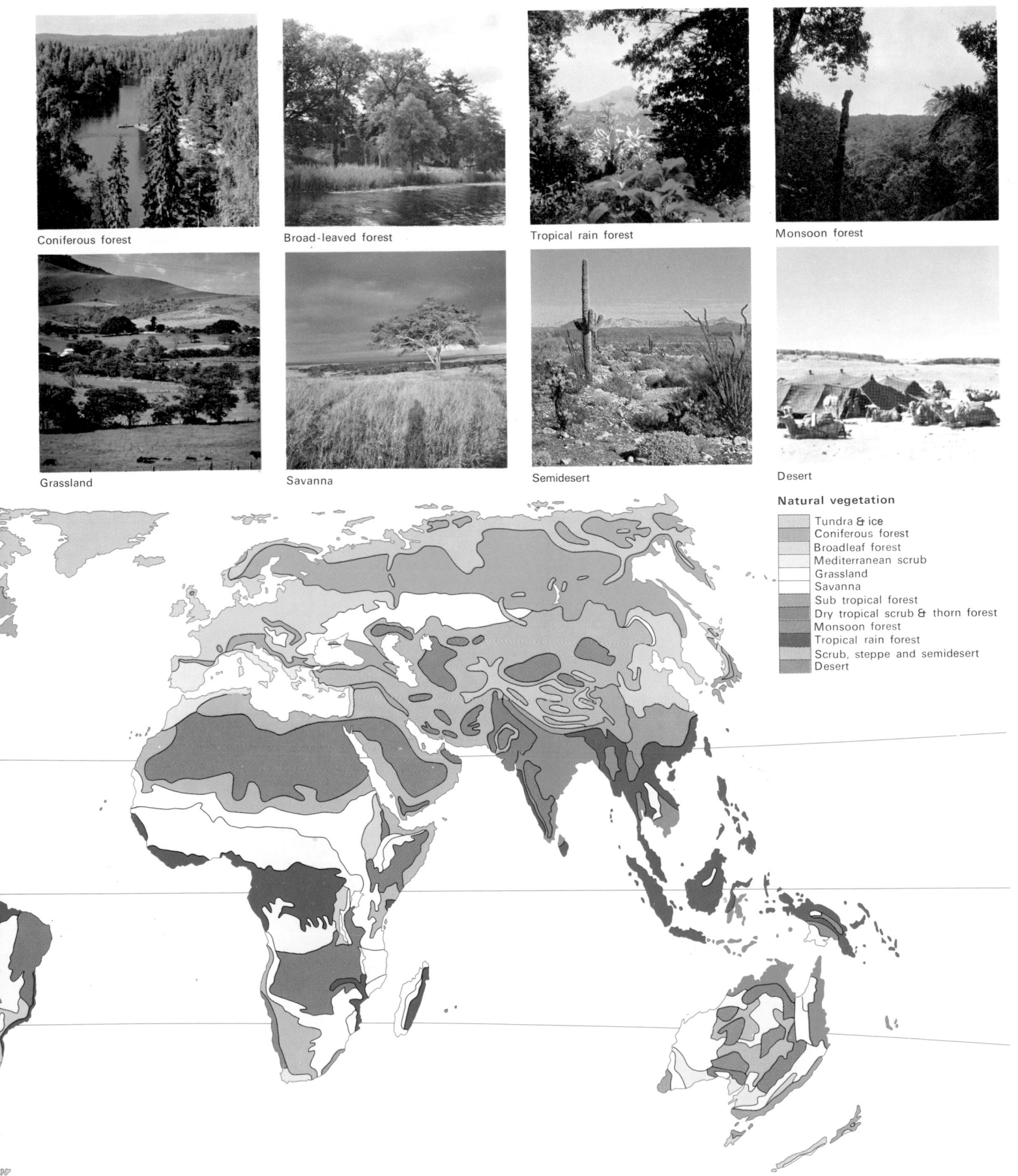

Coniferous forest

Broad-leaved forest

Tropical rain forest

Monsoon forest

Grassland

Savanna

Semidesert

Desert

Natural vegetation

Tundra & ice
Coniferous forest
Broadleaf forest
Mediterranean scrub
Grassland
Savanna
Sub tropical forest
Dry tropical scrub & thorn forest
Monsoon forest
Tropical rain forest
Scrub, steppe and semidesert
Desert

Population

Population distribution
(right and lower right)
People have always been unevenly distributed in the world. Europe has for centuries contained nearly 20% of the world's population but after the 16-19th century explorations and consequent migrations this proportion has rapidly reduced. In 1750 the Americas had 2% of the world's total: in 2000 AD they are expected to contain 16%.

The most densely populated regions are in India, China and Europe where the average density is between 100 and 200 per square km. although there are pockets of extremely high density elsewhere. In contrast Australia has only 1·5 people per square km. The countries in the lower map have been redrawn to make their areas proportional to their populations.

U.S.A. (1972)
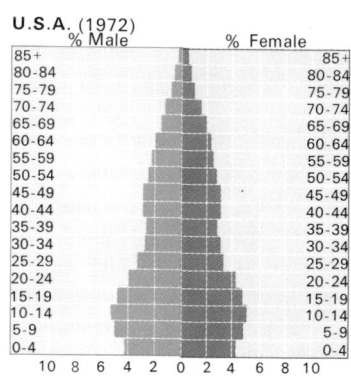

France (1972)
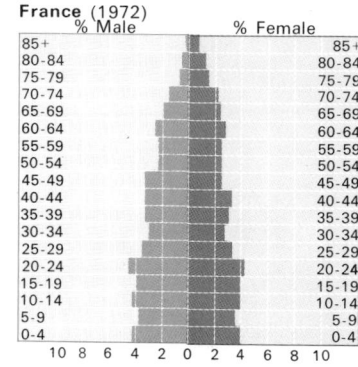

Brazil (1971)
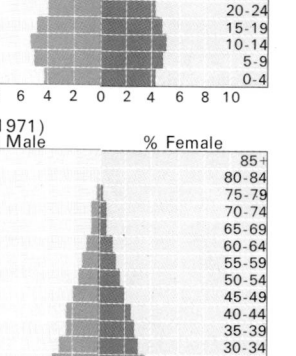

U.S.S.R. (1970)
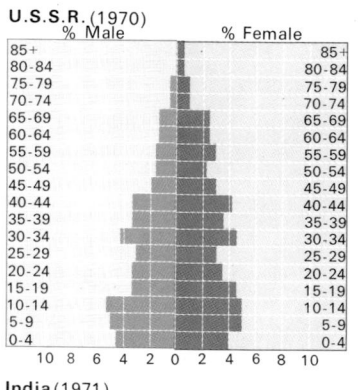

Ghana (1970)
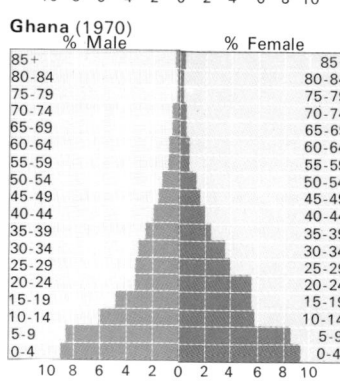

India (1971)
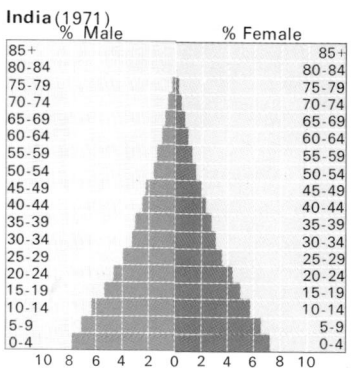

Age distribution
France shows many demographic features characteristic of European countries. Birth and death rates have declined with a moderate population growth - there are nearly as many old as young. In contrast, India and several other countries have few old and many young because of the high death rates and even higher birth rates. It is this excess that is responsible for the world's population explosion.

World population increase
Until comparatively recently there was little increase in the population of the world. About 6000 BC it is thought that there were about 200 million people and in the following 7000 years an increase of just over 100 million. In the 1800's there were about 1000 million; at present there are over 3500 million and by the year 2000 if present trends continue there would be at least 7000 million.

1650 1700 1750 1800

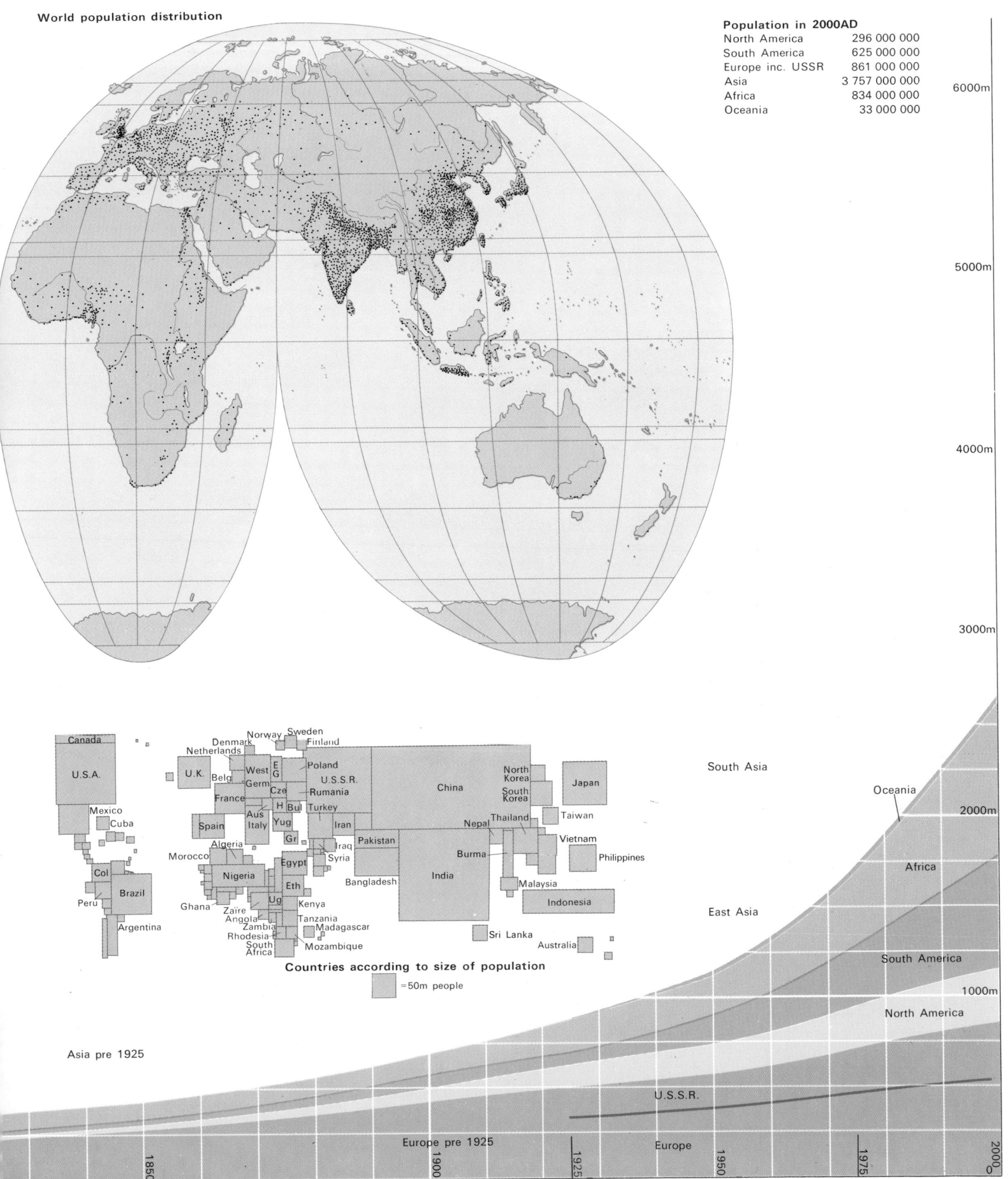

World population distribution

Population in 2000AD

North America	296 000 000
South America	625 000 000
Europe inc. USSR	861 000 000
Asia	3 757 000 000
Africa	834 000 000
Oceania	33 000 000

Countries according to size of population

=50m people

Language

Languages may be blamed partly for the division and lack of understanding between nations. While a common language binds countries together it in turn isolates them from other countries and groups. Thus beliefs, ideas and inventions remain exclusive to these groups and different cultures develop.

There are thousands of different languages and dialects spoken today. This can cause strife even within the one country, such as India, where different dialects are enough to break down the country into distinct groups.

As a result of colonization and the spread of internationally accepted languages, many countries have superimposed a completely unrelated language in order to combine isolated national groups and to facilitate international understanding, for example Spanish in South America, English in India.

Related languages

Certain languages showing marked similarities are thought to have developed from common parent languages for example Latin. After the retreat of the Roman Empire wherever Latin had been firmly established it remained as the new nation's language. With no unifying centre divergent development took place and Latin evolved into new languages.

Calligraphy

Writing was originally by a series of pictures, and these gradually developed in styles which were influenced by the tools generally used. Carved alphabets, such as that used by the Sumerians, tended to be angular, while those painted or written tended to be curved, as in Egyptian hieroglyphics development of which can be followed through the West Semitic, Greek and Latin alphabets to our own.

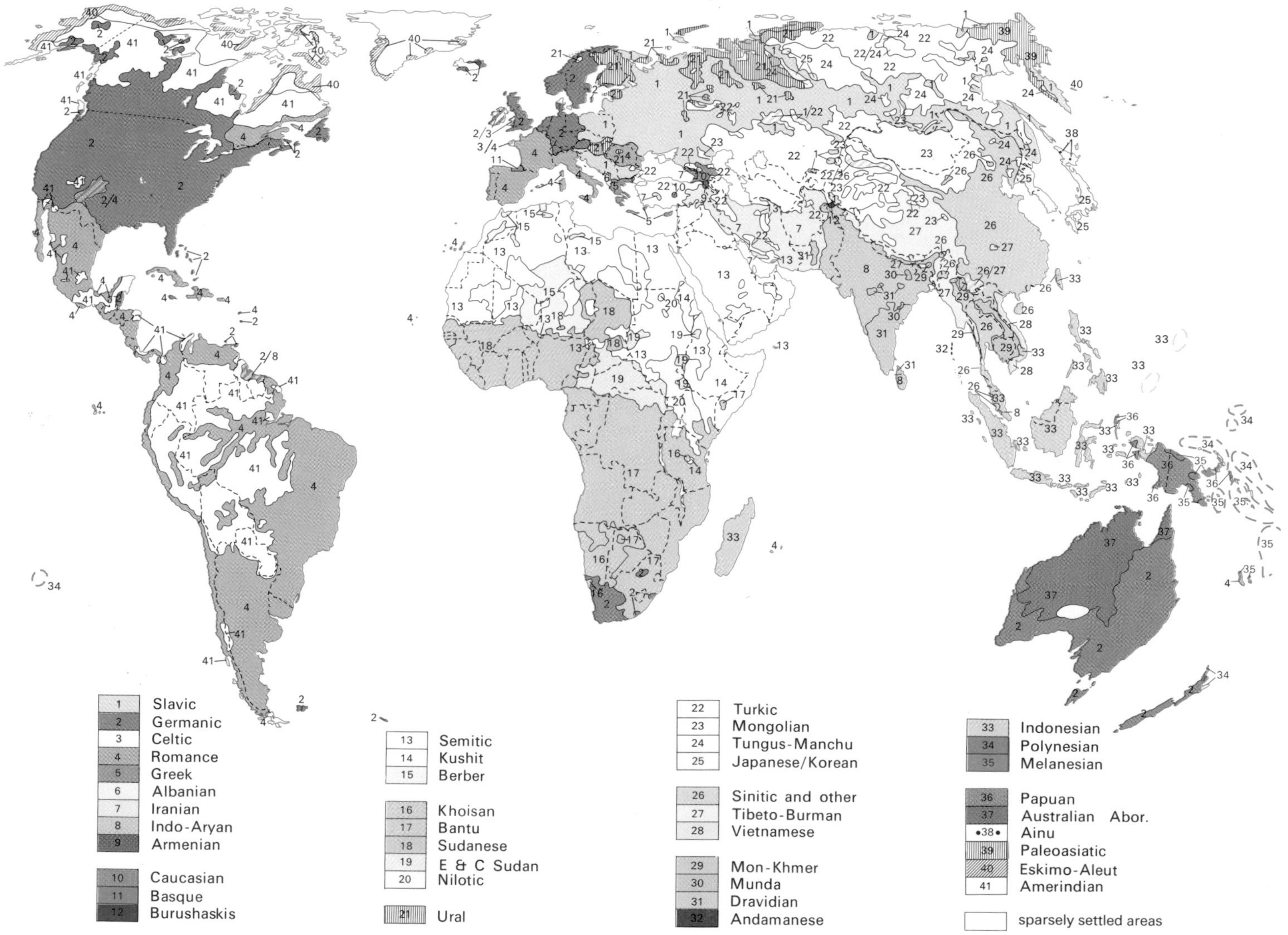

Assyrian (carved)

Ancient Hebrew (painted)

Egyptian hieroglyphic (painted)

Some modern non-latin type faces

Greek
ΑΒΓΔΕΖΗΘΙΚΛΜΝΞΟΠΡΣΤΥΦΧΨΩς

Cyrillic
АБВГДЕЖЗИЙІКЛМНОПРСТУФХЦЏЧШ

Arabic
فى عام ١٨٩٧ وصل إلى إنجلترا أ نموذج

Bengali
১৮৯৭ খ্রীস্টাব্দে আধুনিক মডেলের একটি

Telugu
నిన్న న్యూయింటికి వచ్చిన యతిథ యేమియు

Japanese
国土の位置と地形

Chinese
父獨子出有之限地位司，
司在提印芬刷奧業司上有

1	Slavic
2	Germanic
3	Celtic
4	Romance
5	Greek
6	Albanian
7	Iranian
8	Indo-Aryan
9	Armenian
10	Caucasian
11	Basque
12	Burushaskis

13	Semitic
14	Kushit
15	Berber
16	Khoisan
17	Bantu
18	Sudanese
19	E & C Sudan
20	Nilotic
21	Ural

22	Turkic
23	Mongolian
24	Tungus-Manchu
25	Japanese/Korean
26	Sinitic and other
27	Tibeto-Burman
28	Vietnamese
29	Mon-Khmer
30	Munda
31	Dravidian
32	Andamanese

33	Indonesian
34	Polynesian
35	Melanesian
36	Papuan
37	Australian Abor.
38	Ainu
39	Paleoasiatic
40	Eskimo-Aleut
41	Amerindian
	sparsely settled areas

Religion

Throughout history man has had beliefs in supernatural powers based on the forces of nature which have developed into worship of a god and some cases gods.

Hinduism honours many gods and goddesses which are all manifestations of the one divine spirit, Brahma, and incorporates beliefs such as reincarnation, worship of cattle and the caste system.

Buddhism, an offshoot of Hinduism, was founded in north east India by Gautama Buddha (563-483 BC) who taught that spiritual and moral discipline were essential to achieve supreme peace.

Confucianism is a mixture of Buddhism and Confucius' teachings which were elaborated to provide a moral basis for the political structure of Imperial China and to cover the already existing forms of ancestor worship.

Judaism dates back to c. 13th century B.C. The Jews were expelled from the Holy Land in AD70 and only reinstated in Palestine in 1948.

Christian monastery

Jewish holy place

Hindu temple

Islam, founded in Mecca by Muhammad (570-632 AD) spread across Asia and Africa and in its retreat left isolated pockets of adherent communities.

Christianity was founded by Jesus of Nazareth in the 1st century AD The Papal authority, established in the 4th century, was rejected by Eastern churches in the 11th century. Later several other divisions developed eg. Roman Catholicism, Protestantism.

Mohammedan mosque

Buddhist temple

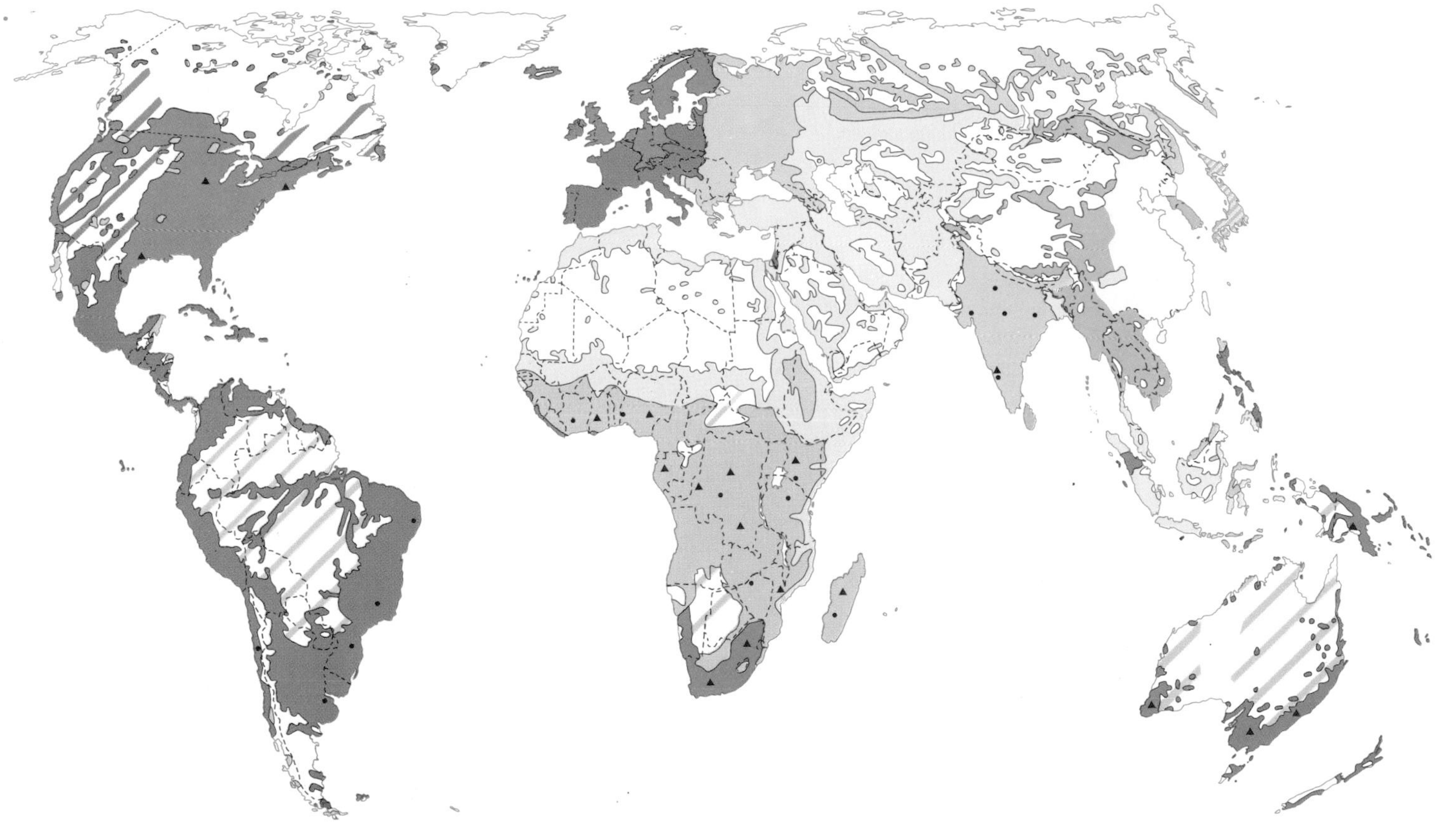

Roman Catholicism	Shiah Islam	Judaism
Orthodox and other Eastern Churches	Buddhism	Shintoism
Protestantism	Hinduism	Primitive religions
Sunni Islam	Confucianism	Uninhabited

The Growth of Cities

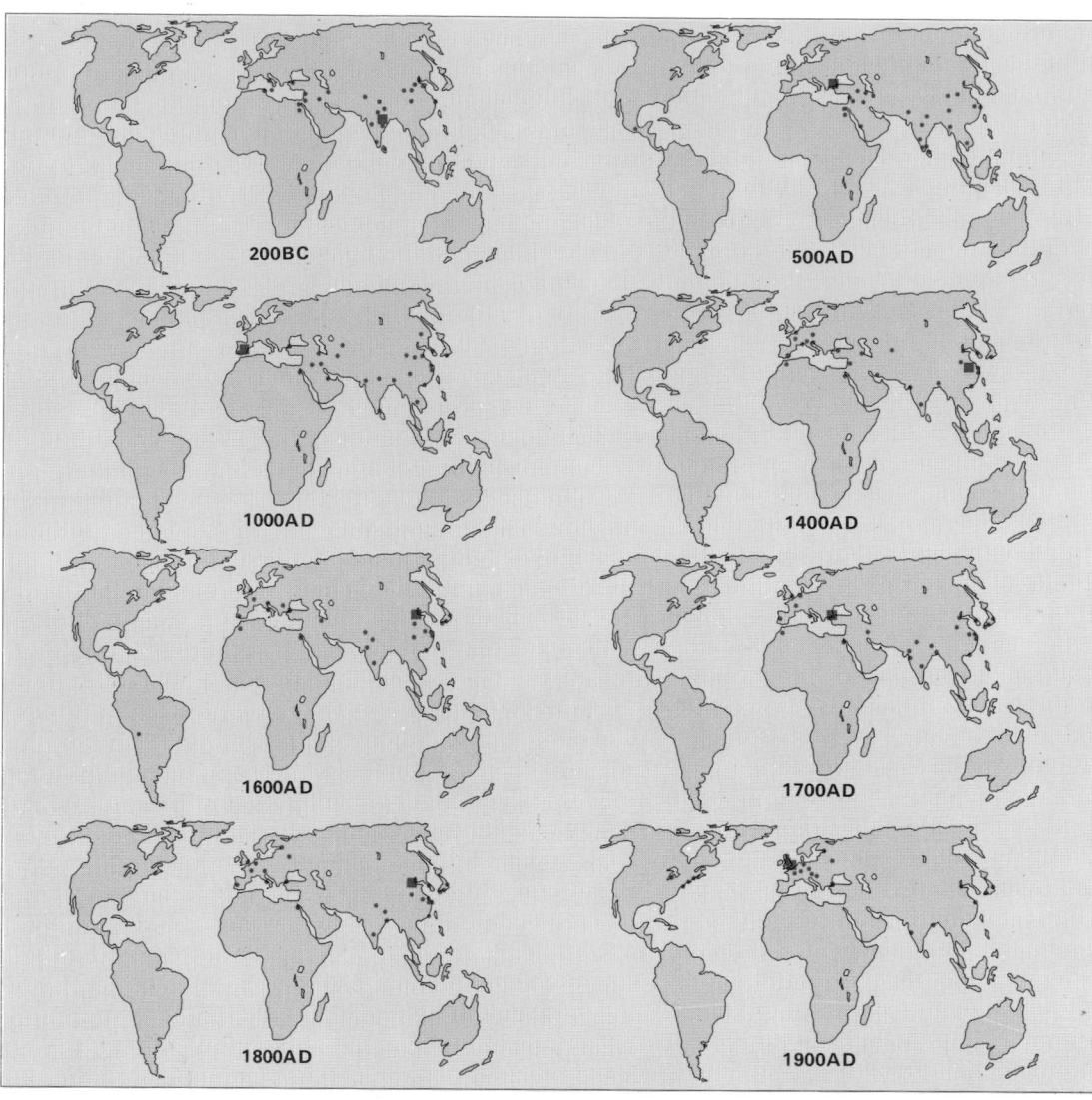

200BC
500AD
1000AD
1400AD
1600AD
1700AD
1800AD
1900AD

Cities through history

The evolution of the semi-permanent Neolithic settlements into a city took from 5000 until 3500 BC. Efficient communications and exchange systems were developed as population densities increased as high as 30 000 to 50 000 per square kilometre in 2000BC in Egypt and Babylonia, compared with New York City today at 10 000.

■ The largest city in the world

· The twenty five largest cities in the world

Sao Paulo

Increase in urbanisation

The increase in urbanisation is a result primarily of better sanitation and health resulting in the growth of population and secondarily to the movement of man off the land into industry and service occupations in the cities. Generally the most highly developed industrial nations are the most intensely urbanised although exceptions such as Norway and Switzerland show that rural industrialisation can exist.

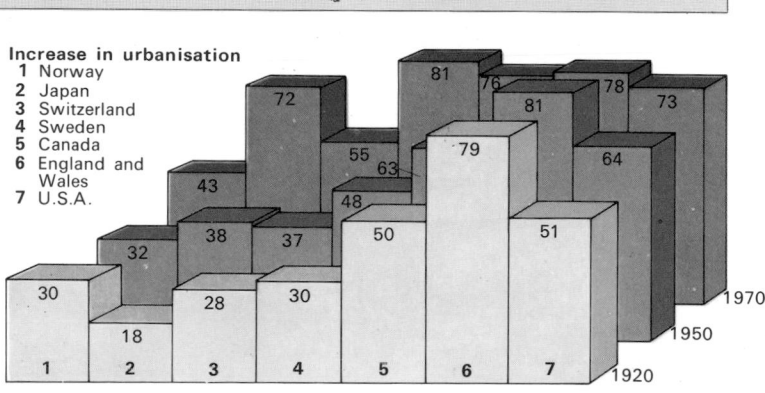

Increase in urbanisation
1 Norway
2 Japan
3 Switzerland
4 Sweden
5 Canada
6 England and Wales
7 U.S.A.

1970
1950
1920

Metropolitan areas

A metropolitan area can be defined as a central city linked with surrounding communities by continuous built-up areas controlled by one municipal government. With improved communications the neighbouring communities generally continue to provide the city's work-force. The graph (right) compares the total populations of the world's ten largest cities.

City populations

1	Tokyo	11 623 000
2	New York	11 571 000
3	Mexico	11 340 000
4	Shanghai	10 820 000
5	Paris	9 863 000
6	Moscow	7 632 000
7	Peking	7 570 000
8	London	7 168 000
9	Los Angeles	7 032 000
10	Calcutta	7 005 000

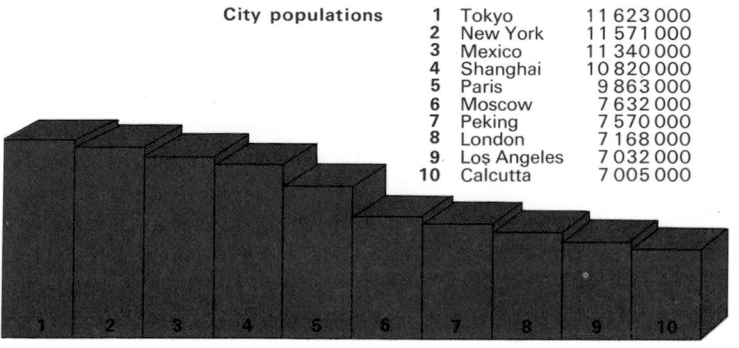

Major cities

Normally these are not only major centres of population and wealth but also of political power and trade. They are the sites of international airports and characteristically are great ports from which imported goods are distributed using the roads and railways which focus on the city. Their staple trades and industries are varied and flexible and depend on design and fashion rather than raw material production.

New York

Sydney

Moscow

Tokyo

Hong Kong

Bombay

London

Cairo

Rio de Janeiro

Rome

◆ Cities over 5 000 000 inhabitants

■ 2 000 000 - 5 000 000 inhabitants

■ 1 000 000 - 2 000 000 inhabitants

■ 250 000 - 1 000 000 inhabitants

31

Food Resources: Vegetable

Cocoa, tea , coffee
These tropical or sub-tropical crops are grown mainly for export to the economically advanced countries. Tea and coffee are the world's principal beverages. Cocoa is used more in the manufacture of chocolate.

Sugar beet, sugar cane
Cane Sugar - a tropical crop - accounts for the bulk of the sugar entering into international trade. Beet Sugar, on the other hand, demands a temperate climate and is produced primarily for domestic consumption.

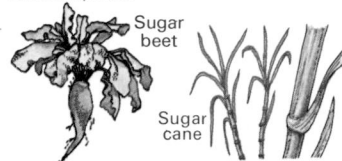

Fruit million tonnes

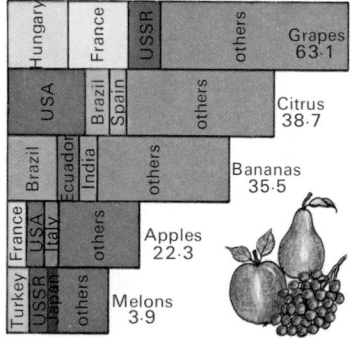

Vegetable oilseeds and oils
Despite the increasing use of synthetic chemical products and animal and marine fats, vegetable oils extracted from these crops grow in quantity, value and importance. Food is the major use- in margarine and cooking fats.

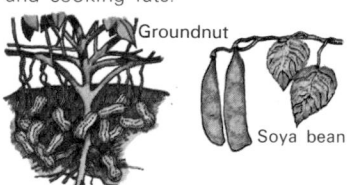

Groundnuts are also a valuable subsistence crop and the meal is used as animal feed. Soya-bean meal is a growing source of protein for humans and animals. The Mediterranean lands are the prime source of olive oil.

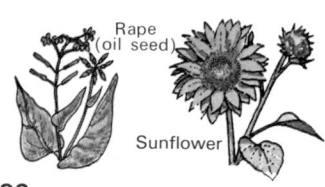

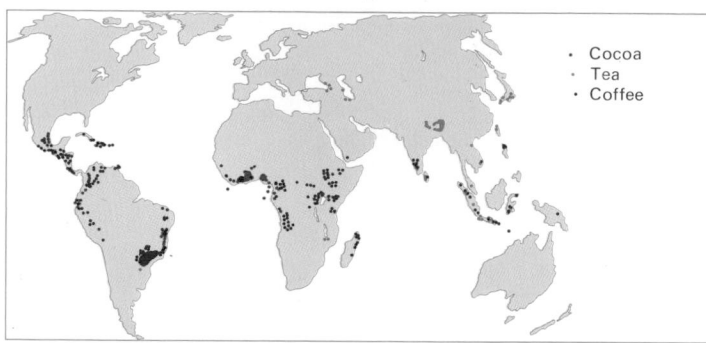

- Cocoa
- Tea
- Coffee

- Sugar beet
- Sugar cane

Wine

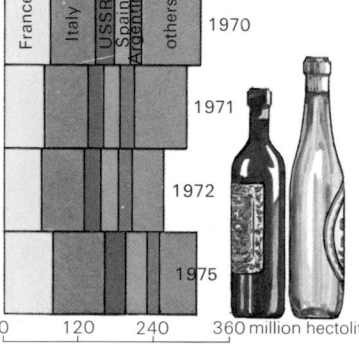

0   120   240   360 million hectolitres

Fruit, wine
With the improvements in canning, drying and freezing, and in transport and marketing, the international trade and consumption of deciduous and soft fruits, citrus fruits and tropical fruits has greatly increased. Recent developments in the use of the peel will give added value to some of the fruit crops.

Over 80% of grapes are grown for wine and over a half in countries bordering the Mediterranean.

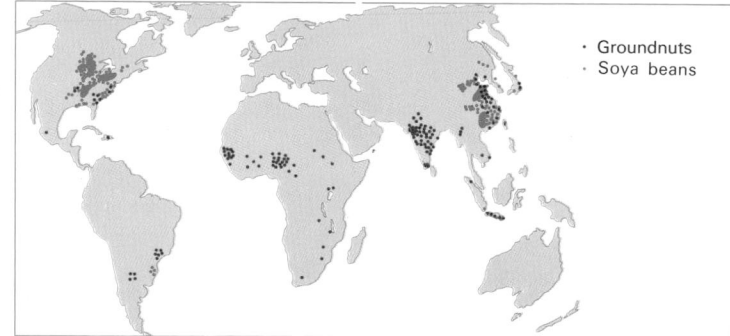

- Groundnuts
- Soya beans

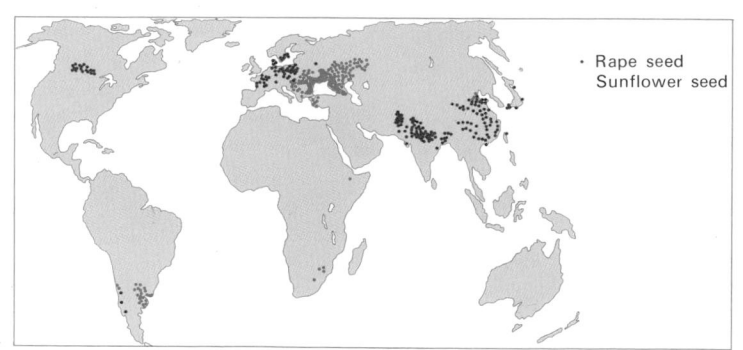

- Rape seed
  Sunflower seed

Cereals
Cereals include those members of the grain family with starchy edible seeds - wheat, maize, barley, oats, rye, rice, millets and sorghums.

Cereals and potatoes (not a cereal but starch-producing) are the principal source of food for our modern civilisations because of their high yield in bulk and food value per unit of land and labour required. They are also easy to store and transport, and provide food also for animals producing meat, fat, milk and eggs. Wheat is the principal bread grain of the temperate regions in which potatoes are the next most important food source. Rice is the principal cereal in the hotter. humid regions. especially in Asia. Oats, barley and maize are grown mainly for animal feed; millets and sorghums as main subsistence crops in Africa and India.

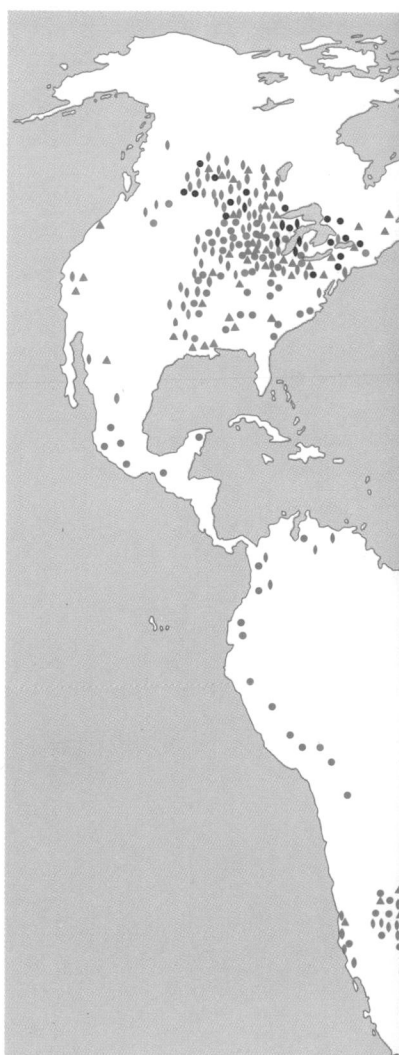

Maize (or Corn)   Needs plenty of sunshine, summer rain or irrigation and frost free for 6 months. Important as animal feed and for human food in Africa, Latin America and as a vegetable and breakfast cereal.

U.S.A.   China   Brazil

World production 320·6 million tonnes

Barley   Has the widest range of cultivation requiring only 8 weeks between seed time and harvest. Used mainly as animal-feed and by the malting industry.

U.S.S.R.   China   France   Canada

World production 157·1 million tonnes

Oats   Widely grown in temperate regions with the limit fixed by early autumn frosts. Mainly fed to cattle. The best quality oats are used for oatmeal, porridge and breakfast foods.

U.S.S.R.   U.S.A.   Canada   W.Germany   Poland

World production 50·5 million tonnes

Rice   Needs plains or terraces which can be flooded and abundant water in the growing season. The staple food of half the human race. In the husk, it is known as paddy.

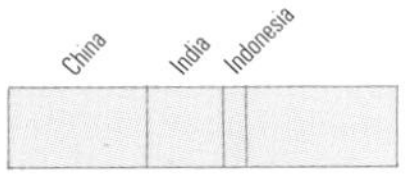

China   India   Indonesia

World production 342·9 million tonnes

Wheat   The most important grain crop in the temperate regions though it is also grown in a variety of climates e.g. in Monsoon lands as a winter crop.

U.S.S.R.   U.S.A.   China   India

World production 362·6 million tonnes

Rye   The hardiest of cereals and more resistant to cold, pests and disease than wheat. An important foodstuff in Central and E. Europe and the U.S.S.R.

U.S.S.R.   Poland   W.Germany

World production 26·0 million tonnes

Millets   The name given to a number of related members of the grass family, of which sorghum is one of the most important. They provide nutritious grain.

India   China   U.S.A.

World production 52·3 million tonnes

Potato   An important food crop though less nutritious weight for weight than grain crops. World production is over 300 million tonnes.

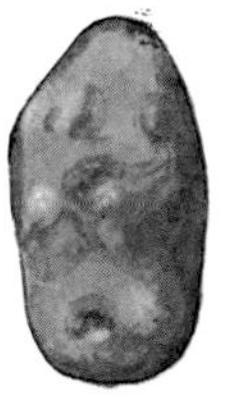

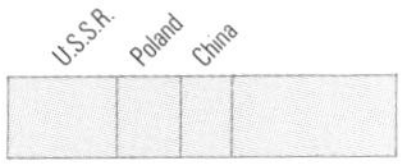

U.S.S.R.   Poland   China

World production 301·6 million tonnes

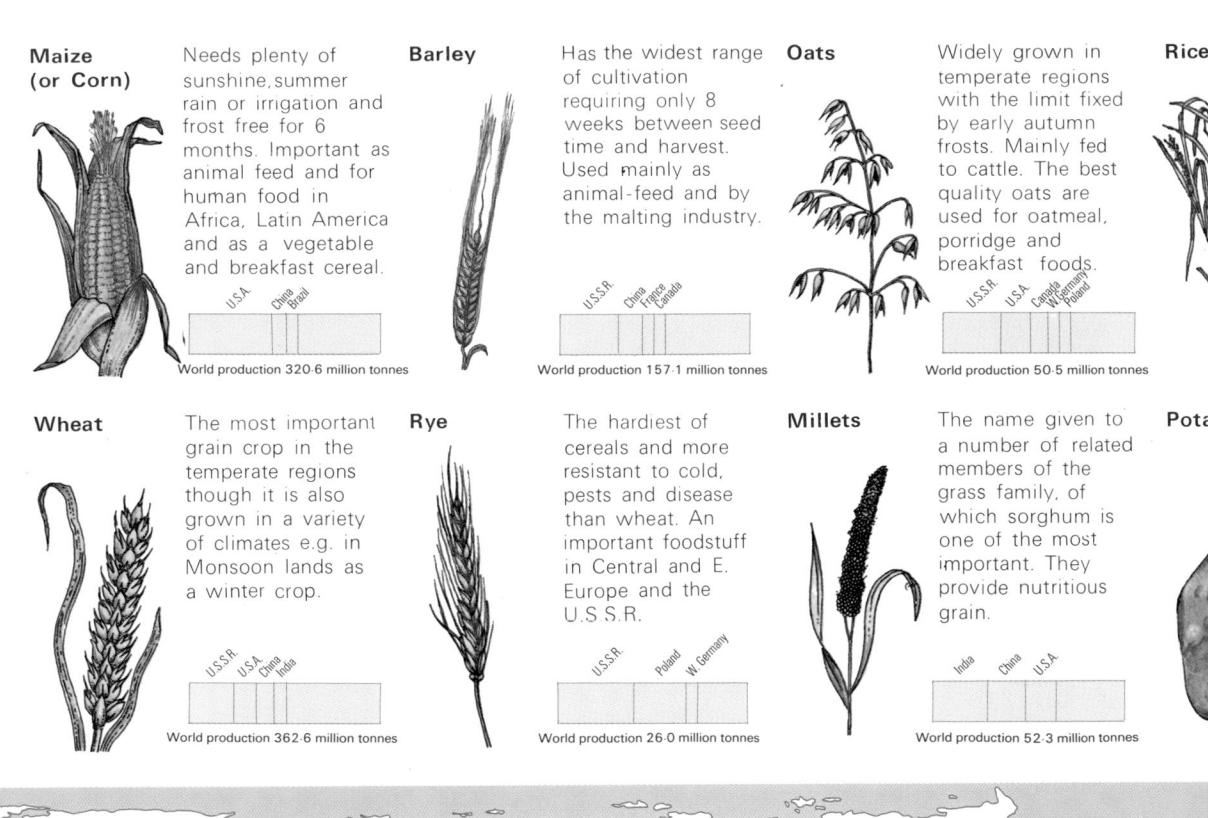

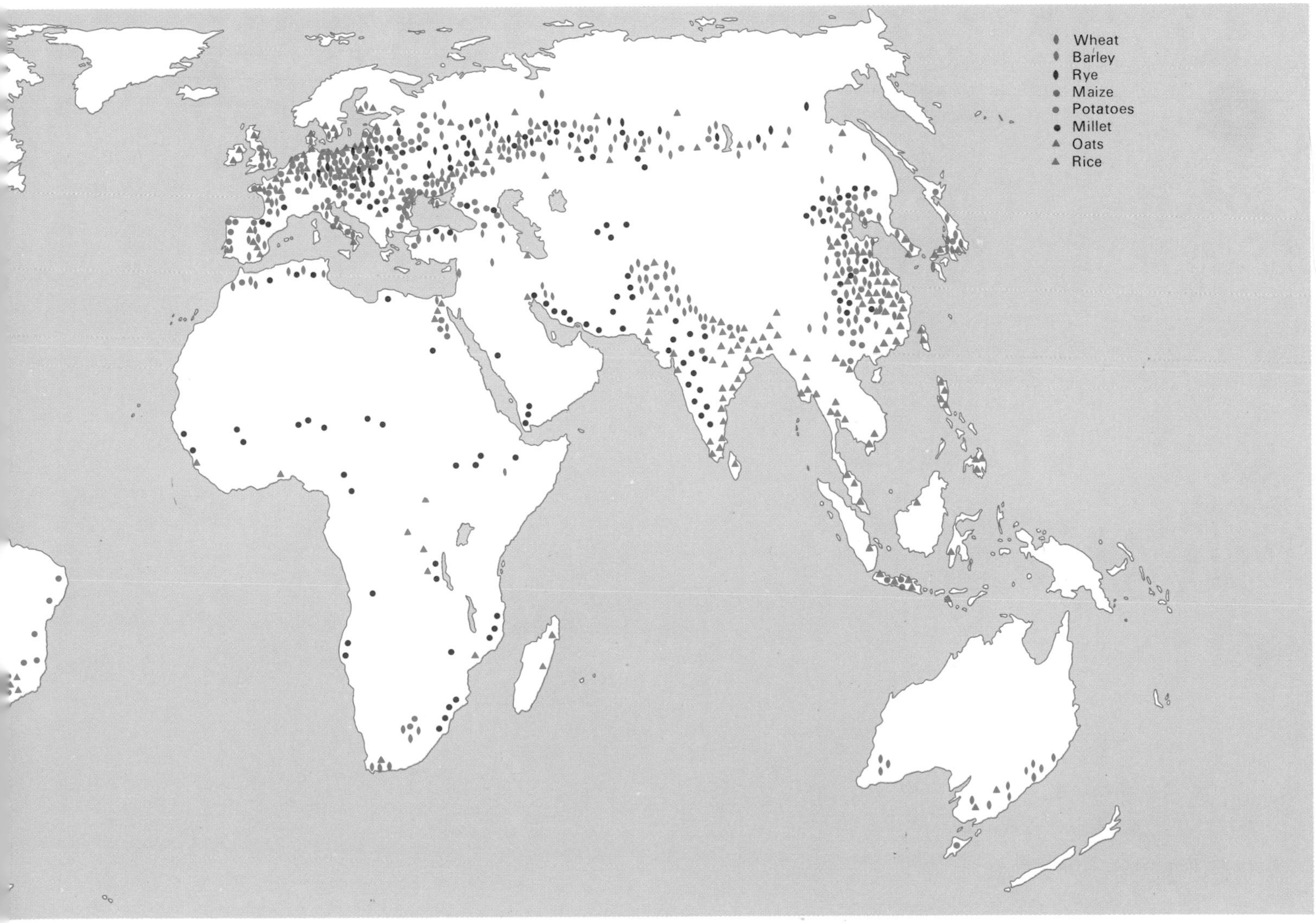

- Wheat
- Barley
- Rye
- Maize
- Potatoes
- Millet
- Oats
- Rice

Food Resources: Animal

Food resources: Animal
Meat, milk and allied foods are prime protein-providers and are also sources of essential vitamins. Meat is mainly a product of continental and savannah grasslands and the cool west coasts, particularly in Europe. Milk and cheese, eggs and fish - though found in some quantity throughout the world - are primarily a product of the temperate zones.

Beef cattle Australia, New Zealand and Argentina provide the major part of international beef exports. Western U.S.A. and Europe have considerable production of beef for their local high demand.

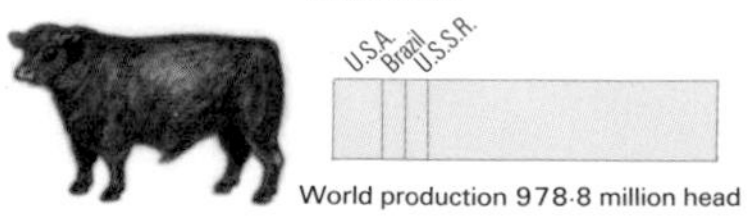

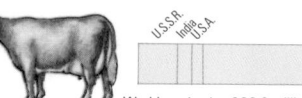
World production 978·8 million head

Dairy Cattle The need of herds for a rich diet and for nearby markets result in dairying being characteristic of densely-populated areas of the temperate zones - U.S.A., N.W. Europe, N. Zealand and S.E. Australia.

World production 200·0 million head

Cheese The principal producers are the U.S.A., India, W. Europe, U.S.S.R., and New Zealand and principal exporters Netherlands, New Zealand, Denmark and France.

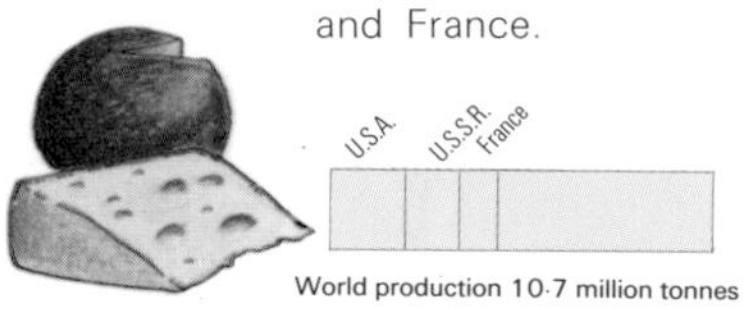

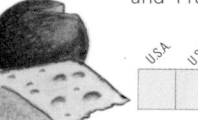
World production 10·7 million tonnes

Sheep Raised mostly for wool and meat, the skins and cheese from their milk are important products in some countries. The merino yields a fine wool and crossbreds are best for meat.

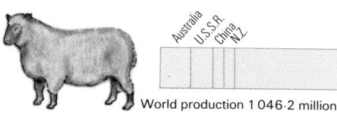
World production 1 046·2 million head

Pigs Can be reared in most climates from monsoon to cool temperate. They are abundant in China, the corn belt of the U.S.A. N.W. and C. Europe, Brazil and U.S.S.R.

 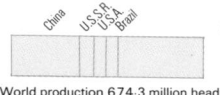
World production 674·3 million head

Fish Commercial fishing requires large shoals of fish of one species within reach of markets. Freshwater fishing is also important. A rich source of protein, fish will become an increasingly valuable food source.

 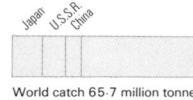
World catch 65·7 million tonnes

Butter The biggest producers are U.S.S.R., W. Europe, U.S.A., New Zealand and Australia.

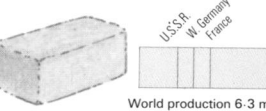
World production 6·3 million tonnes

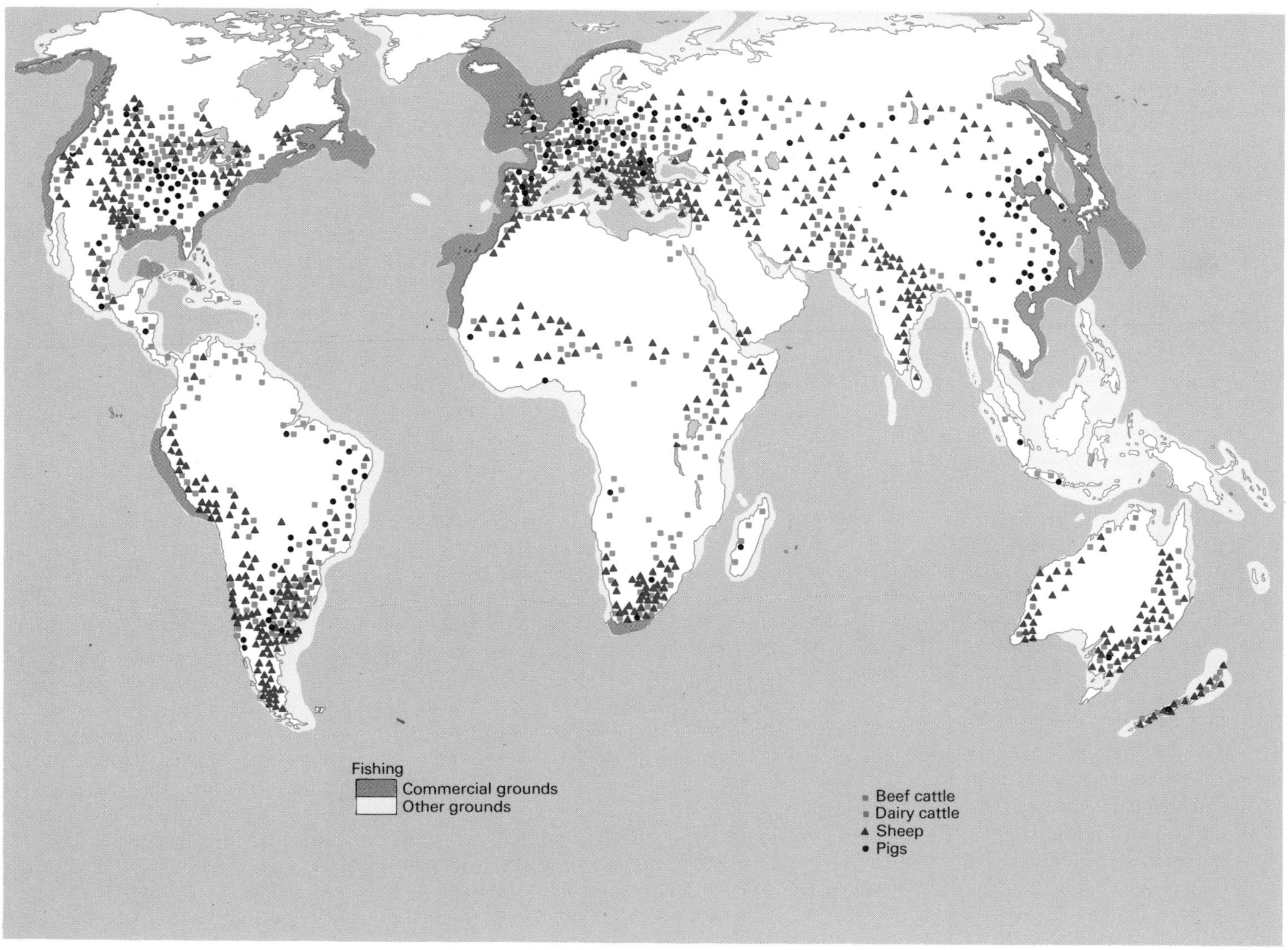

Fishing
Commercial grounds
Other grounds

■ Beef cattle
■ Dairy cattle
▲ Sheep
● Pigs

Nutrition

Foodstuffs fall, nutritionally, into three groups - providers of energy, protein and vitamins. Cereals and oil-seeds provide energy and second-class protein'; milk, meat and allied foods provide protein and vitamins, fruit and vegetables provide vitamins, especially Vitamin C, and some energy. To avoid malnutrition, a minimum level of these three groups of foodstuffs is required: the maps and diagrams show how unfortunately widespread are low standards of nutrition and even malnutrition.

Comparison of daily diets

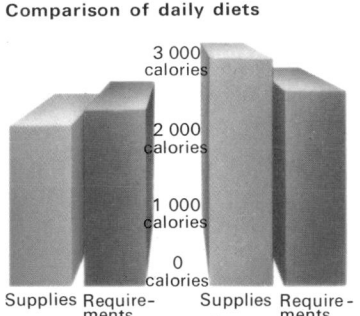

Supplies | Require-ments
Far East, Near East, Africa & Latin America

Supplies | Require-ments
Europe, Oceania & North America

Malnutrition

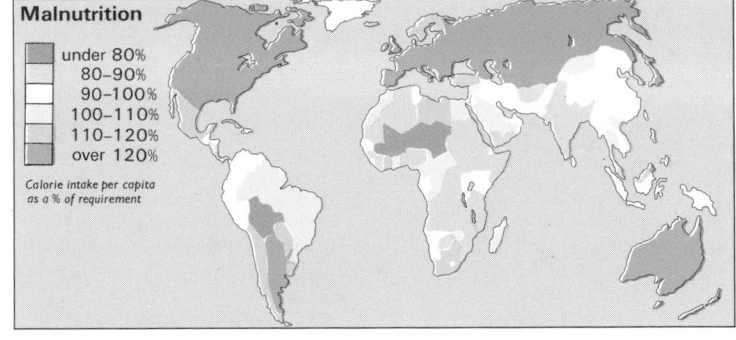

- under 80%
- 80–90%
- 90–100%
- 100–110%
- 110–120%
- over 120%

Calorie intake per capita as a % of requirement

Proportions of calories

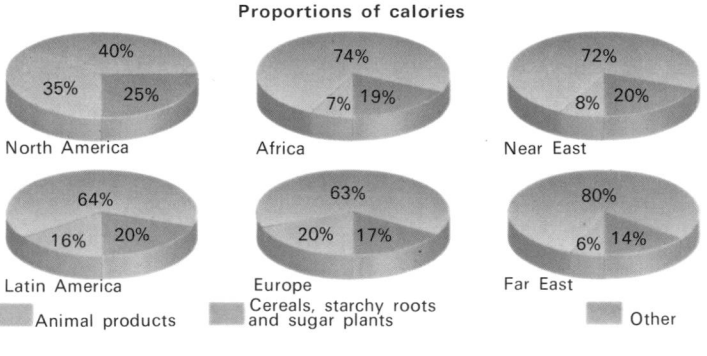

North America 40% 35% 25%

Africa 74% 7% 19%

Near East 72% 8% 20%

Latin America 64% 16% 20%

Europe 63% 20% 17%

Far East 80% 6% 14%

- Animal products
- Cereals, starchy roots and sugar plants
- Other

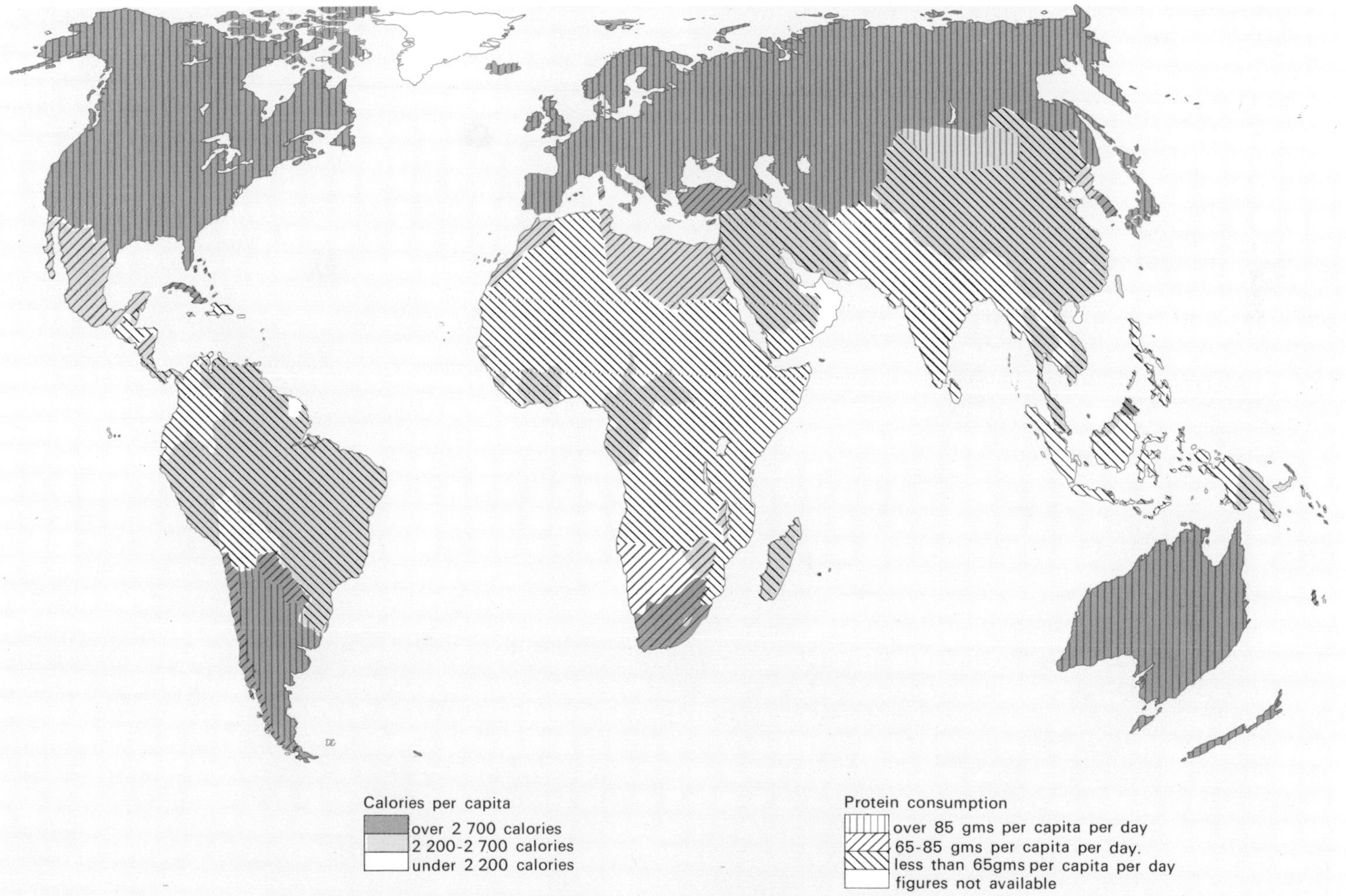

People and tractors engaged in agriculture

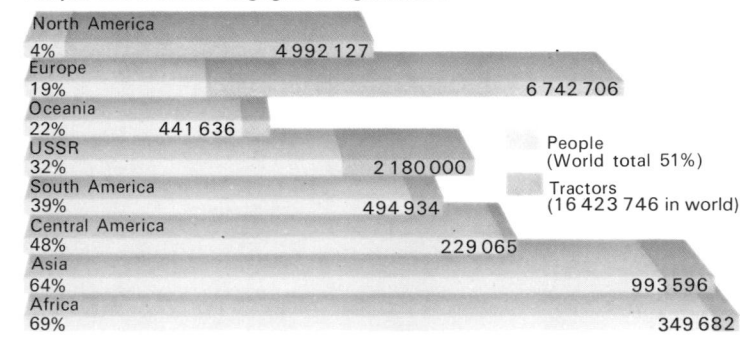

North America 4% — 4 992 127
Europe 19% — 6 742 706
Oceania 22% — 441 636
USSR 32% — 2 180 000
South America 39% — 494 934
Central America 48% — 229 065
Asia 64% — 993 596
Africa 69% — 349 682

People (World total 51%)
Tractors (16 423 746 in world)

Calories per capita
- over 2 700 calories
- 2 200-2 700 calories
- under 2 200 calories

Protein consumption
- over 85 gms per capita per day
- 65-85 gms per capita per day.
- less than 65gms per capita per day
- figures not available

Mineral Resources I

Primitive man used iron for tools and vessels and its use extended gradually until iron, and later steel, became the backbone of the Modern World with the Industrial Revolution in the late 18th Century. At first, local ores were used, whereas today richer iron ores in huge deposits have been discovered and are mined on a large scale, often far away from the areas where they are used; for example, in Western Australia, Northern Sweden, Venezuela and Liberia. Iron smelting plants are today increasingly located at coastal sites, where the large ore carriers can easily discharge their cargo.

Steel is refined iron with the addition of other minerals, ferro-alloys, giving to the steel their own special properties; for example, resistance to corrosion (chromium, nickel, cobalt), hardness (tungsten, vanadium), elasticity (molybdenum), magnetic properties (cobalt), high tensile strength (manganese) and high ductility (molybdenum).

Production of Ferro-alloy metals

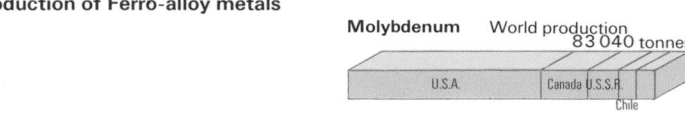

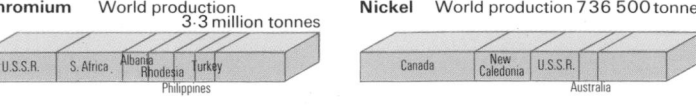

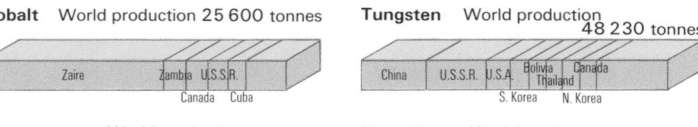

Iron and Steel Industry of Western Europe

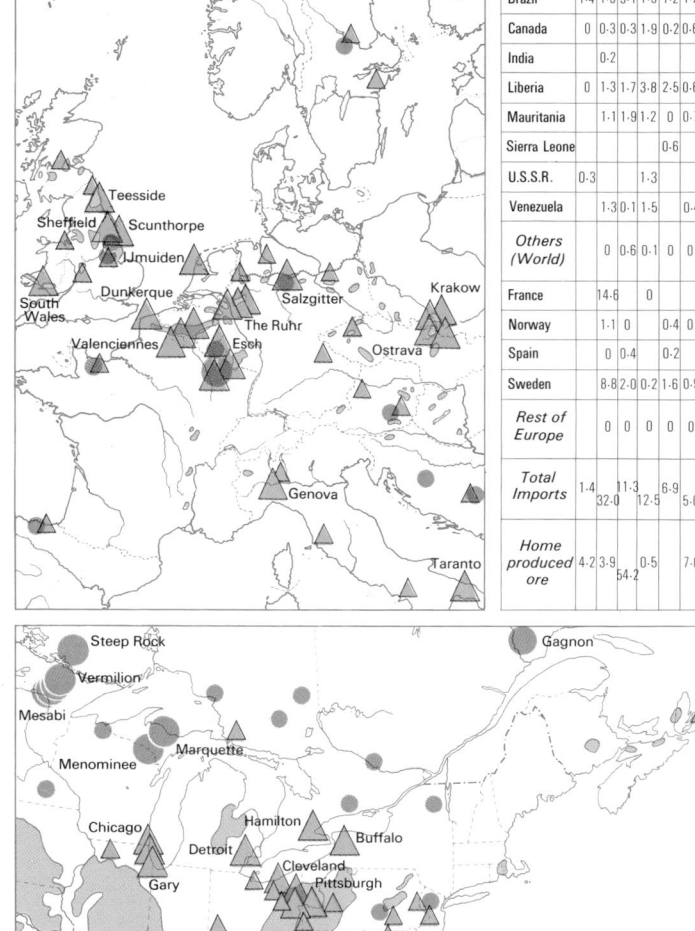

Major Centre / Other Important Centre
- ● / ● Iron ore
- ▲ / ▲ Iron and steel plant
- Coalfields

Kiruna, Gällivare, Teesside, Sheffield, Scunthorpe, IJmuiden, South Wales, Dunkerque, Salzgitter, Krakow, Valenciennes, The Ruhr, Esch, Ostrava, Genova, Taranto

Sources of Iron ore imported into Western Europe
million tonnes

Imports from ▼	Austria	Belgium-Lux.	France	Italy	Netherlands	Spain	U.K.	W.Germany
Angola		0·2	0·4	0·1			0·8	1·4
Australia	0	1·8	0·8	1·8	0·2	0·6	1·2	27·8
Brazil	1·4	1·3	3·1	1·9	1·2	1·2	2·4	11·0
Canada	0	0·3	0·3	1·9	0·2	0·6	5·5	3·9
India	0·2						0	0
Liberia	0	1·3	1·7	3·8	2·5	0·6	0·9	8·5
Mauritania		1·1	1·9	1·2	0	0·7	2·2	1·0
Sierra Leone					0·6		0	0·7
U.S.S.R.	0·3			1·3			0·1	0·1
Venezuela		1·3	0·1	1·5		0·4	1·7	2·6
Others (World)	0	0·6	0·1	0	0	0	0·4	0·7
France	14·6		0					3·5
Norway	1·1	0			0·4	0	1·1	1·9
Spain	0	0·4		0·2			0·3	1·0
Sweden	8·8	2·0	0·2	1·6	0·9		4·9	10·9
Rest of Europe	0	0	0	0	0	0	0	0
Total Imports	1·4 32·0	11·3	54·2 12·5	6·9	5·0	21·4	74·9
Home produced ore	4·2	3·9	54·2	0·5		7·0	7·1	88·7

Iron and Steel Industry of Eastern North America

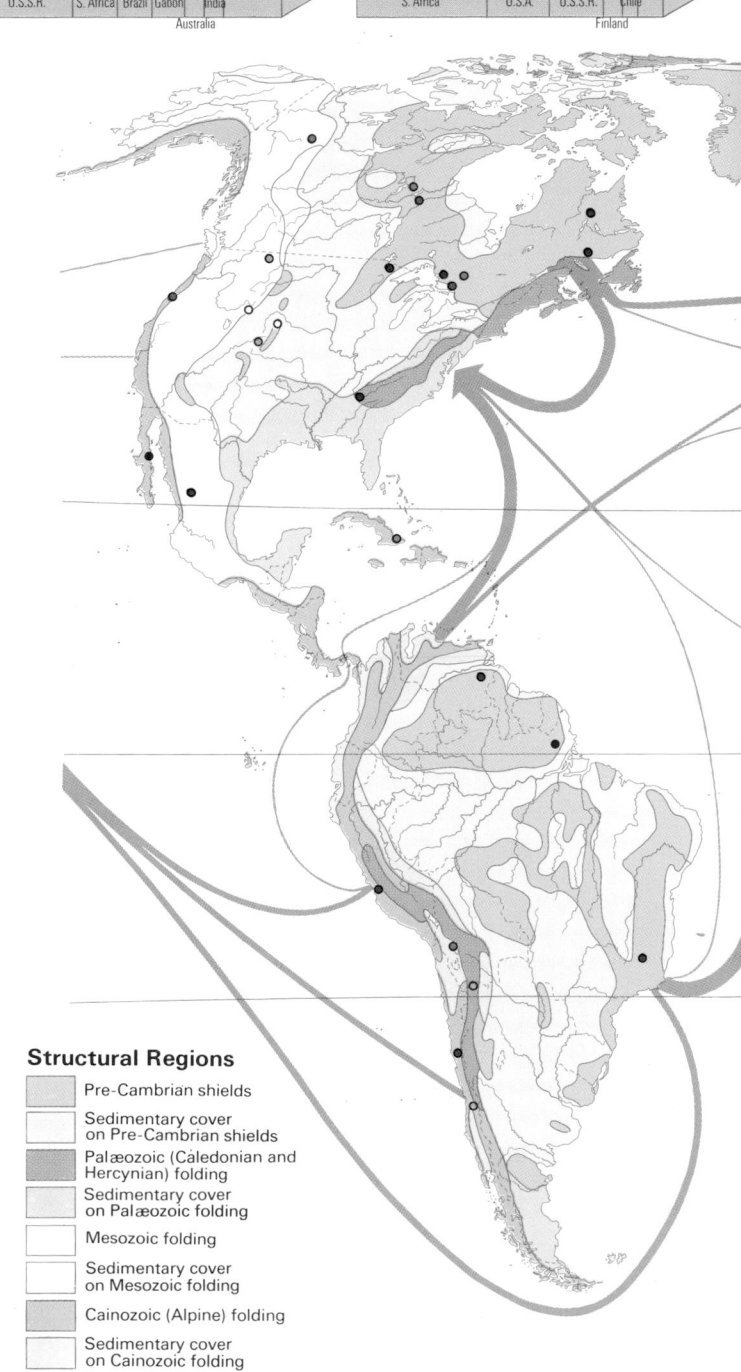

Steep Rock, Gagnon, Vermilion, Mesabi, Marquette, Menominee, Chicago, Hamilton, Buffalo, Detroit, Cleveland, Gary, Pittsburgh, Sparrows Point, Birmingham

Major Centre / Other Important Centre
- ● / ● Iron ore
- ▲ / ▲ Iron and steel plant
- Coalfields

Structural Regions

- Pre-Cambrian shields
- Sedimentary cover on Pre-Cambrian shields
- Palæozoic (Caledonian and Hercynian) folding
- Sedimentary cover on Palæozoic folding
- Mesozoic folding
- Sedimentary cover on Mesozoic folding
- Cainozoic (Alpine) folding
- Sedimentary cover on Cainozoic folding

World production of Pig iron and Ferro-alloys

Total World production 530 million tonnes

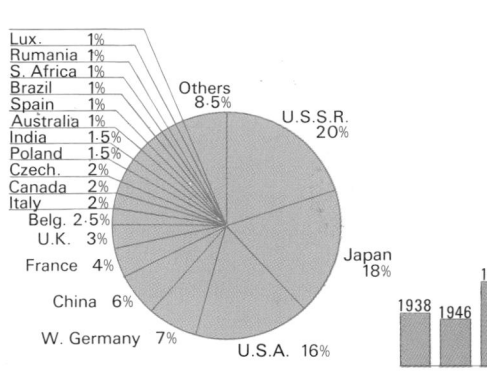

Lux. 1%
Rumania 1%
S. Africa 1%
Brazil 1%
Spain 1%
Australia 1%
India 1·5%
Poland 1·5%
Czech. 2%
Canada 2%
Italy 2%
Belg. 2·5%
U.K. 3%
France 4%
China 6%
W. Germany 7%
Others 8·5%
U.S.S.R. 20%
Japan 18%
U.S.A. 16%

Growth of World production of Pig iron and Ferro-alloys

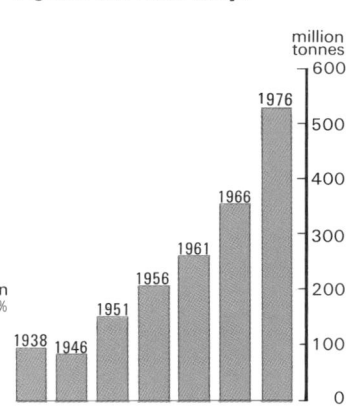

million tonnes
600
500
400
300
200
100
0
1938
1946
1951
1956
1961
1966
1976

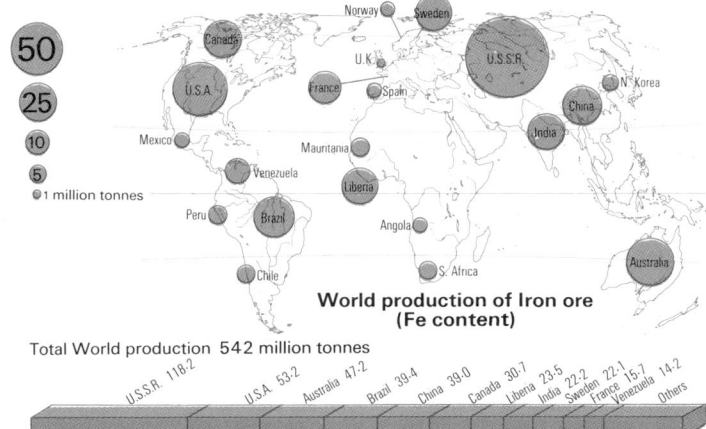

50
25
10
5
1 million tonnes
Norway
Sweden
Canada
U.K.
U.S.S.R.
U.S.A.
France
Spain
N. Korea
China
India
Mexico
Mauritania
Venezuela
Liberia
Peru
Brazil
Angola
Chile
S. Africa
Australia

World production of Iron ore (Fe content)

Total World production 542 million tonnes

U.S.S.R. 118·2
U.S.A. 53·2
Australia 47·2
Brazil 39·4
China 39·0
Canada 30·7
Liberia 23·5
India 22·2
Sweden 22·1
France 15·7
Venezuela 14·2
Others

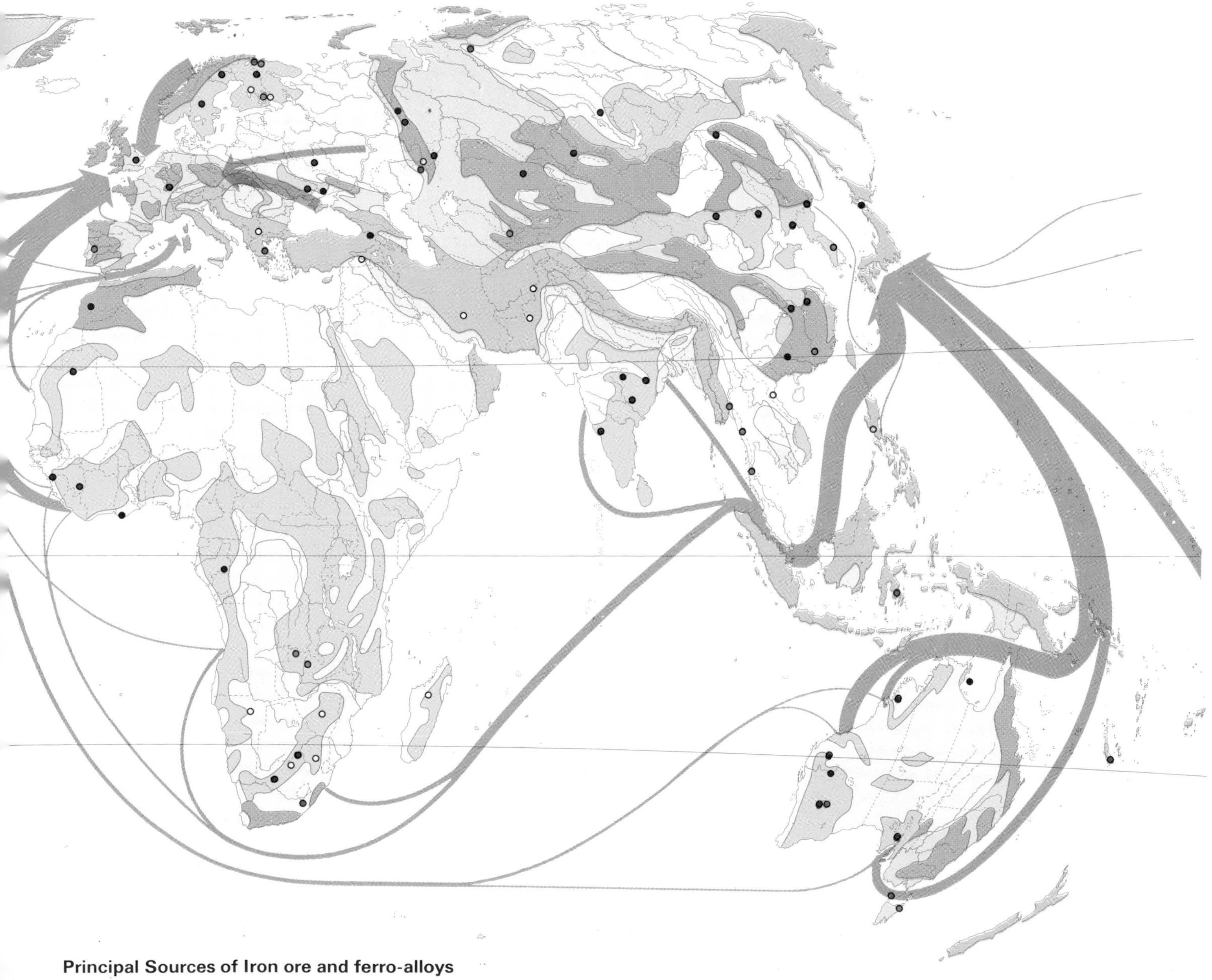

Principal Sources of Iron ore and ferro-alloys

- ● Iron
- ○ Chrome
- ● Cobalt
- ● Manganese
- ● Molybdenum
- ● Nickel
- ● Tungsten
- ○ Vanadium
- Iron ore trade flow

Mineral Resources II

Antimony – imparts hardness when alloyed to other metals, especially lead.
Uses: type metal, pigments to paints, glass and enamels, fireproofing of textiles.

World production 78 478 tonnes

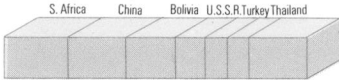

S. Africa China Bolivia U.S.S.R. Turkey Thailand

Lead – heavy, soft, malleable, acid resistant.
Uses: storage batteries, sheeting and piping, cable covering, ammunition, type metal, weights, additive to petrol.

World production 3·57 million tonnes

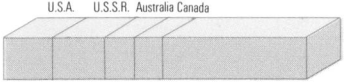

U.S.A. U.S.S.R. Australia Canada

Tin – resistant to attacks by organic acids, malleable.
Uses: canning, foils, as an alloy to other metals (brass and bronze).

World production 217 200 tonnes

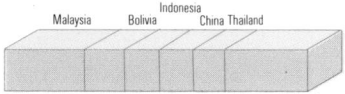

Malaysia Bolivia Indonesia China Thailand

Aluminium – light, resists corrosion, good conductor.
Uses: aircraft, road and rail vehicles, domestic utensils, cables, makes highly tensile and light alloys.

World production 81·22 million tonnes (of Bauxite)

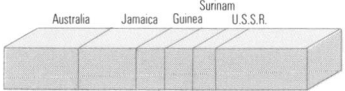

Australia Jamaica Guinea Surinam U.S.S.R.

Gold – untarnishable and resistant to corrosion, highly ductile and malleable, good conductor. The pure metal is soft and it is alloyed to give it hardness.
Uses: bullion, coins, jewellery, gold-leaf, electronics.

World production 1 135 tonnes

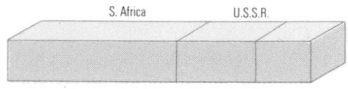

S. Africa U.S.S.R.

Copper – excellent conductor of electricity and heat, durable, resistant to corrosion, strong and ductile.
Uses: wire, tubing, brass (with zinc and tin), bronze (with tin), (compounds) – dyeing.

World production 7·89 million tonnes

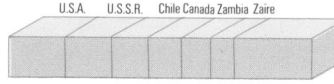

U.S.A. U.S.S.R. Chile Canada Zambia Zaire

Mercury – the only liquid metal, excellent conductor of electricity.
Uses: thermometers, electrical industry, gold and silver ore extraction, (compounds) – drugs, pigments, chemicals, dentistry.

World production 8932 tonnes

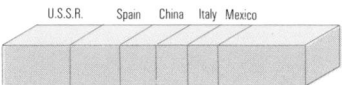

U.S.S.R. Spain China Italy Mexico

Zinc – hard metal, low corrosion factor.
Uses: brass (with copper and tin), galvanising, diecasting, medicines, paints and dyes.

World production 5·89 million tonnes

Canada U.S.S.R. Australia U.S.A. Peru

Diamonds – very hard and resistant to chemical attack, high lustre, very rare.
Uses: jewellery, cutting and abrading other materials.

World production 44·63 million carats

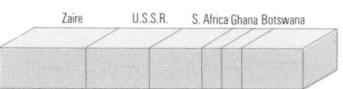

Zaire U.S.S.R. S. Africa Ghana Botswana

Silver – ductile and malleable, a soft metal and must be alloyed for use in coinage.
Uses: coins, jewellery, photography, electronics, medicines.

World production 9306 tonnes

U.S.S.R. Canada Peru Mexico U.S.A Australia

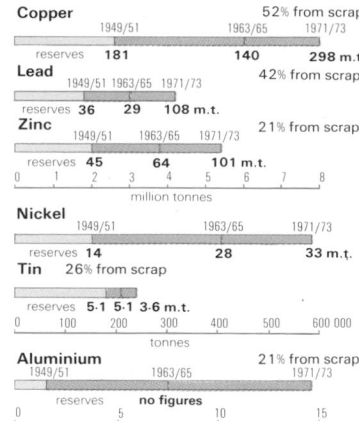

World consumption of non-ferrous metals

These diagrams show the average yearly world consumption of certain refined metals for 1949/51, 1963/65 and 1971/73 and also the percentage of the latter produced from scrap. The figures beneath each diagram show estimates made in 1950, 1964 and 1973 of reserves in the Western World.

While indicating that the reserves are by no means infinite the figures show how widely these estimates have differed over 10 years and take no account of unknown reserves, particularly in the sea-bed, or advances in mining technology which will make it economic to mine low-content ores.

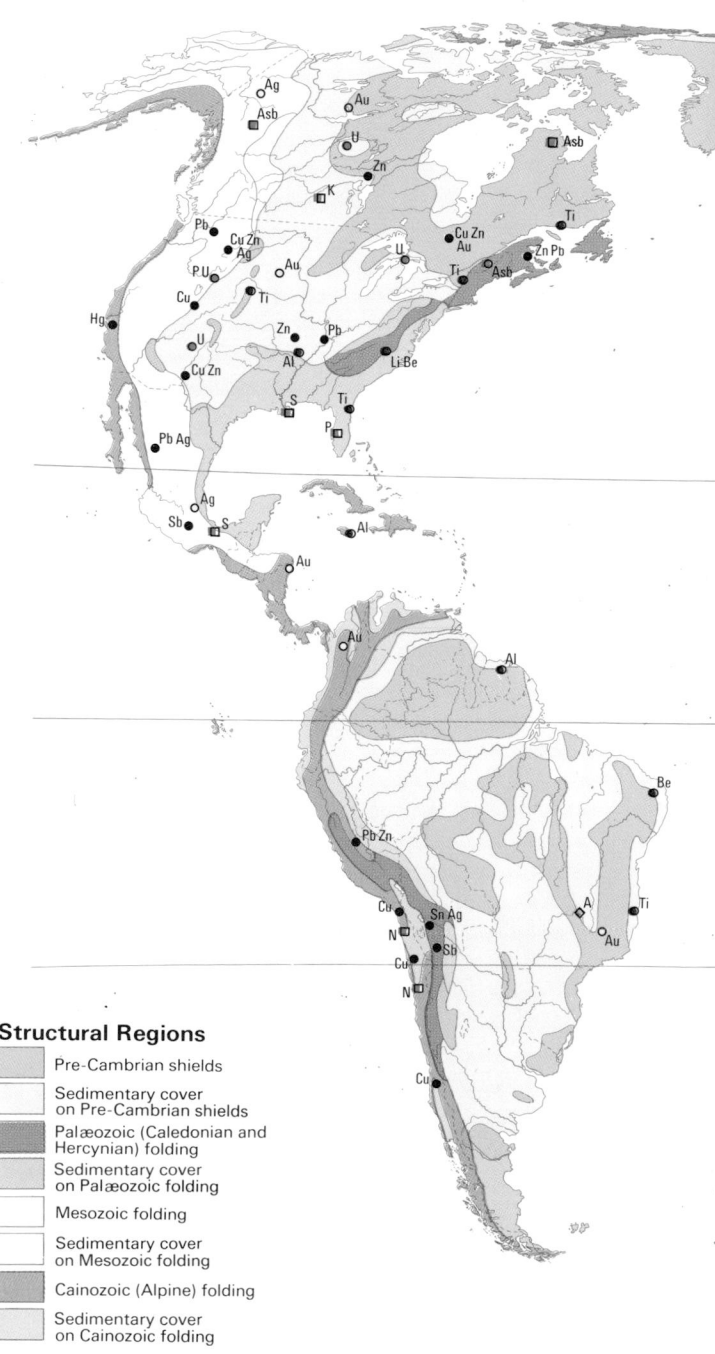

Structural Regions

- Pre-Cambrian shields
- Sedimentary cover on Pre-Cambrian shields
- Palæozoic (Caledonian and Hercynian) folding
- Sedimentary cover on Palæozoic folding
- Mesozoic folding
- Sedimentary cover on Mesozoic folding
- Cainozoic (Alpine) folding
- Sedimentary cover on Cainozoic folding

million tonnes

15   10   5   1

Artificial Fertilizers are produced from the minerals sodium nitrate, potassium, salt, phosphate and potash, and as by-products of other industries.

Tonnes of fertilizer per 1000 hectares of arable land

0   20   50   100   200   300+

Fertilizers— principal producers

Fertilizers— principal consumers

Developing world — Developed world

◄3.9% 1961-65 average
Total world production 40 million tonnes

◄7.3% 1976
Total world production 92 million tonnes

Developing world — Developed world

◄9% 1961-65 average
Total world consumption 38 million tonnes

15% 1976
Total world consumption 89 million tonnes

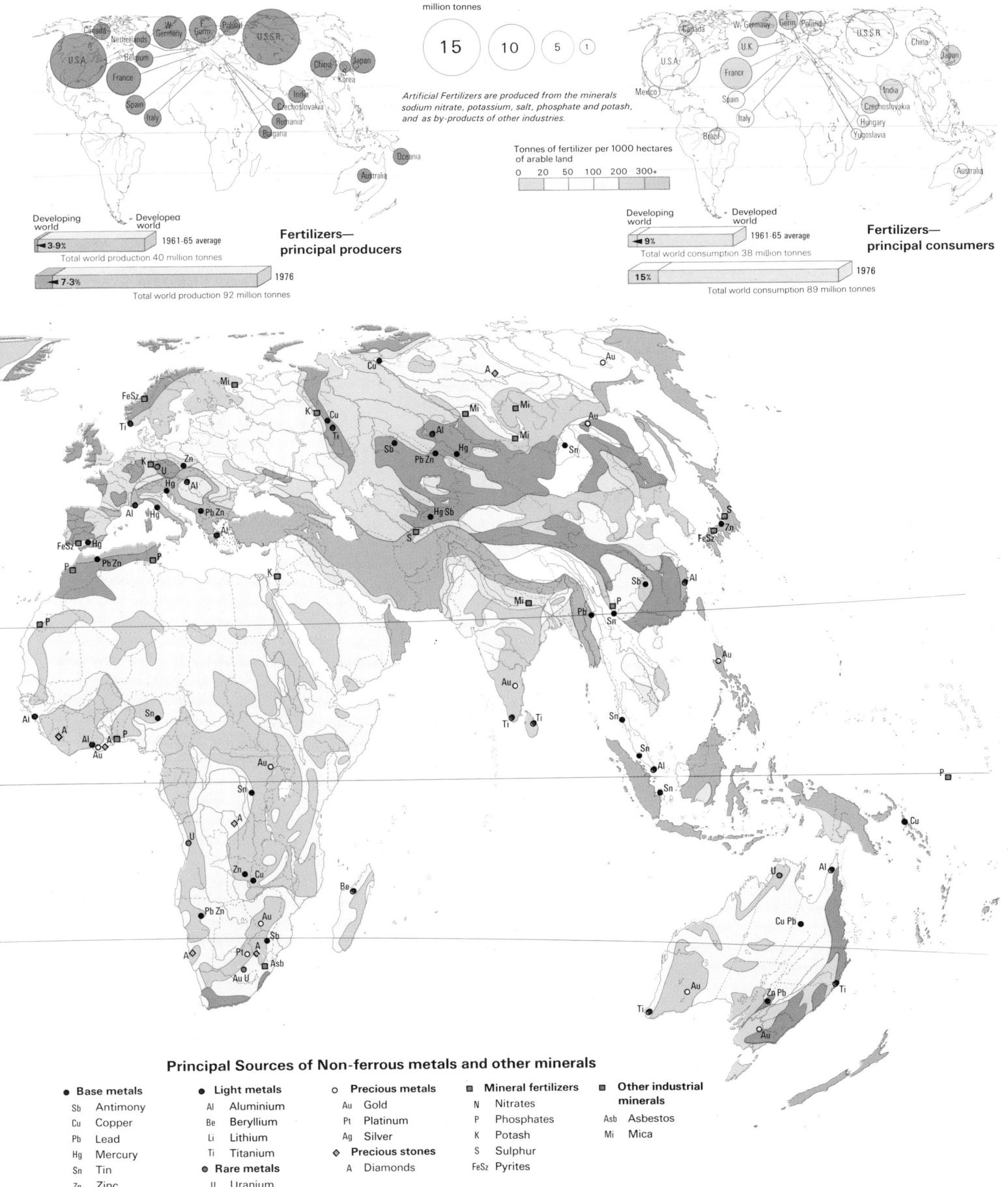

Principal Sources of Non-ferrous metals and other minerals

● **Base metals**

Sb Antimony
Cu Copper
Pb Lead
Hg Mercury
Sn Tin
Zn Zinc

● **Light metals**

Al Aluminium
Be Beryllium
Li Lithium
Ti Titanium

● **Rare metals**

U Uranium

○ **Precious metals**

Au Gold
Pt Platinum
Ag Silver

◇ **Precious stones**

A Diamonds

■ **Mineral fertilizers**

N Nitrates
P Phosphates
K Potash
S Sulphur
FeSz Pyrites

■ **Other industrial minerals**

Asb Asbestos
Mi Mica

Fuel and Energy

Coal

Coal is the result of the accumulation of vegetation over millions of years. Later under pressure from overlying sediments, it is hardened through four stages: peat, lignite, bituminous coal, and finally anthracite. Once the most important source of power, coal's importance now lies in the production of electricity and as a raw material in the production of plastics, heavy chemicals and disinfectants.

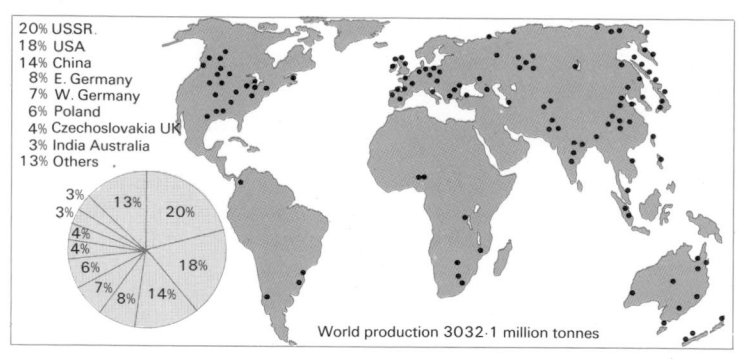

20% USSR.
18% USA
14% China
8% E. Germany
7% W. Germany
6% Poland
4% Czechoslovakia UK
3% India Australia
13% Others

World production 3032·1 million tonnes

Coal mine

Oil

Oil is derived from the remains of marine animals and plants, probably as a result of pressure, heat and chemical action. It is a complex mixture of hydrocarbons which are refined to extract the various constituents. These include products such as gasolene, kerosene and heavy fuel oils. Oil is rapidly replacing coal because of easier handling and reduced pollution.

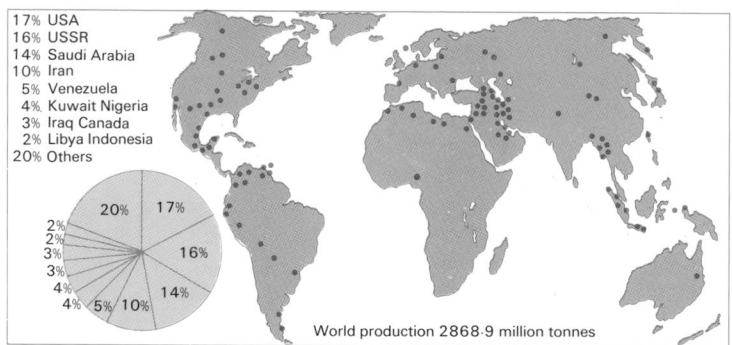
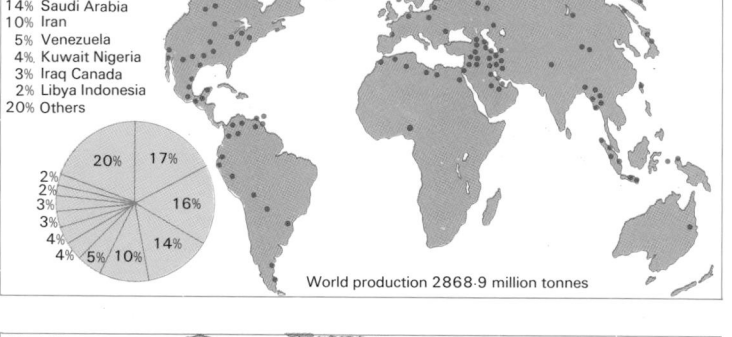

17% USA
16% USSR
14% Saudi Arabia
10% Iran
5% Venezuela
4% Kuwait Nigeria
3% Iraq Canada
2% Libya Indonesia
20% Others

World production 2868·9 million tonnes

Oil derrick

Natural gas

Since the early 1960's natural gas (methane) has become one of the largest single sources of energy. By liquefaction its volume can be reduced to 1/600 of that of gas and hence is easily transported. It is often found directly above oil reserves and because it is both cheaper than coal gas and less polluting it has great potential.

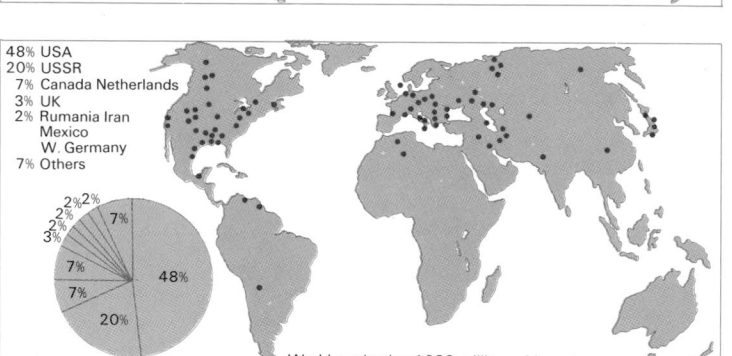

48% USA
20% USSR
7% Canada Netherlands
3% UK
2% Rumania Iran
Mexico
W. Germany
7% Others

World production 1280 million cubic metres

North sea gas rig

Water

Hydro-electric power stations use water to drive turbines which in turn generate electricity. The ideal site is one in which a consistently large volume of water falls a considerable height, hence sources of H.E.P. are found mainly in mountainous areas. Potential sources of hydro-electricity using waves or tides are yet to be exploited widely.

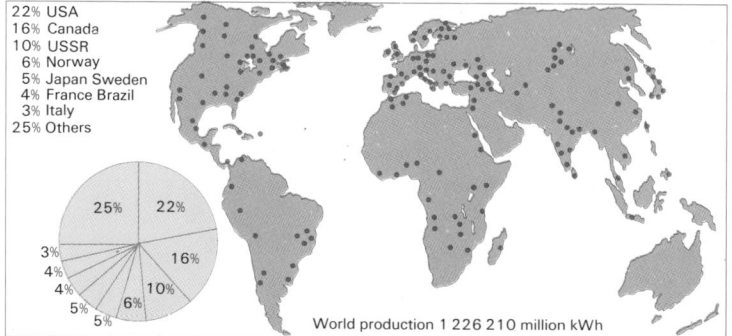

22% USA
16% Canada
10% USSR
6% Norway
5% Japan Sweden
4% France Brazil
3% Italy
25% Others

World production 1 226 210 million kWh

Water power

Nuclear energy

The first source of nuclear power was developed in Britain in 1956. Energy is obtained from heat generated by the reaction from splitting atoms of certain elements, of which uranium and plutonium are the most important. Although the initial installation costs are very high the actual running costs are low because of the slow consumption of fuel.

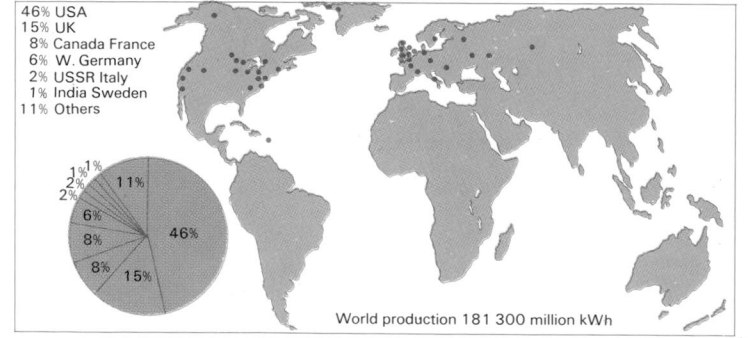

46% USA
15% UK
8% Canada France
6% W. Germany
2% USSR Italy
1% India Sweden
11% Others

World production 181 300 million kWh

Nuclear power station

40

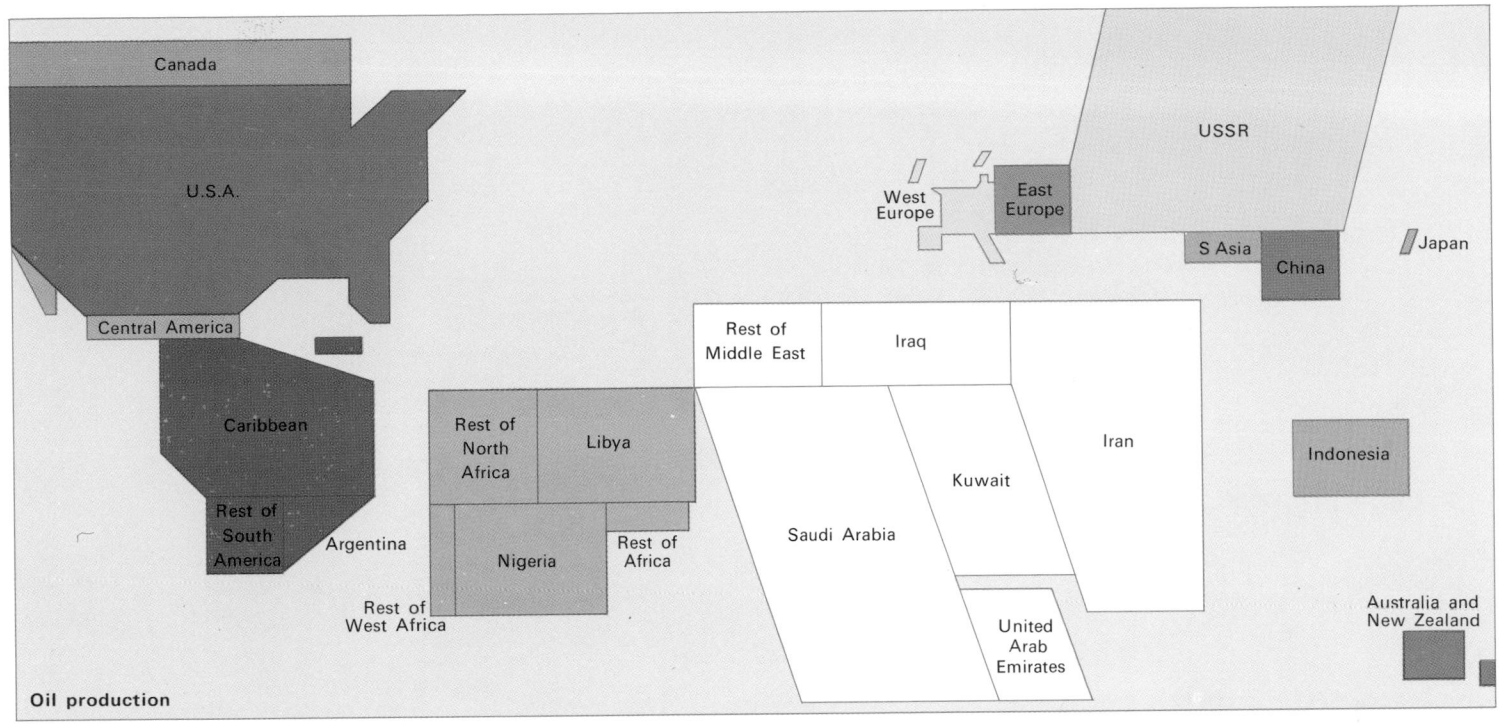

Oil production

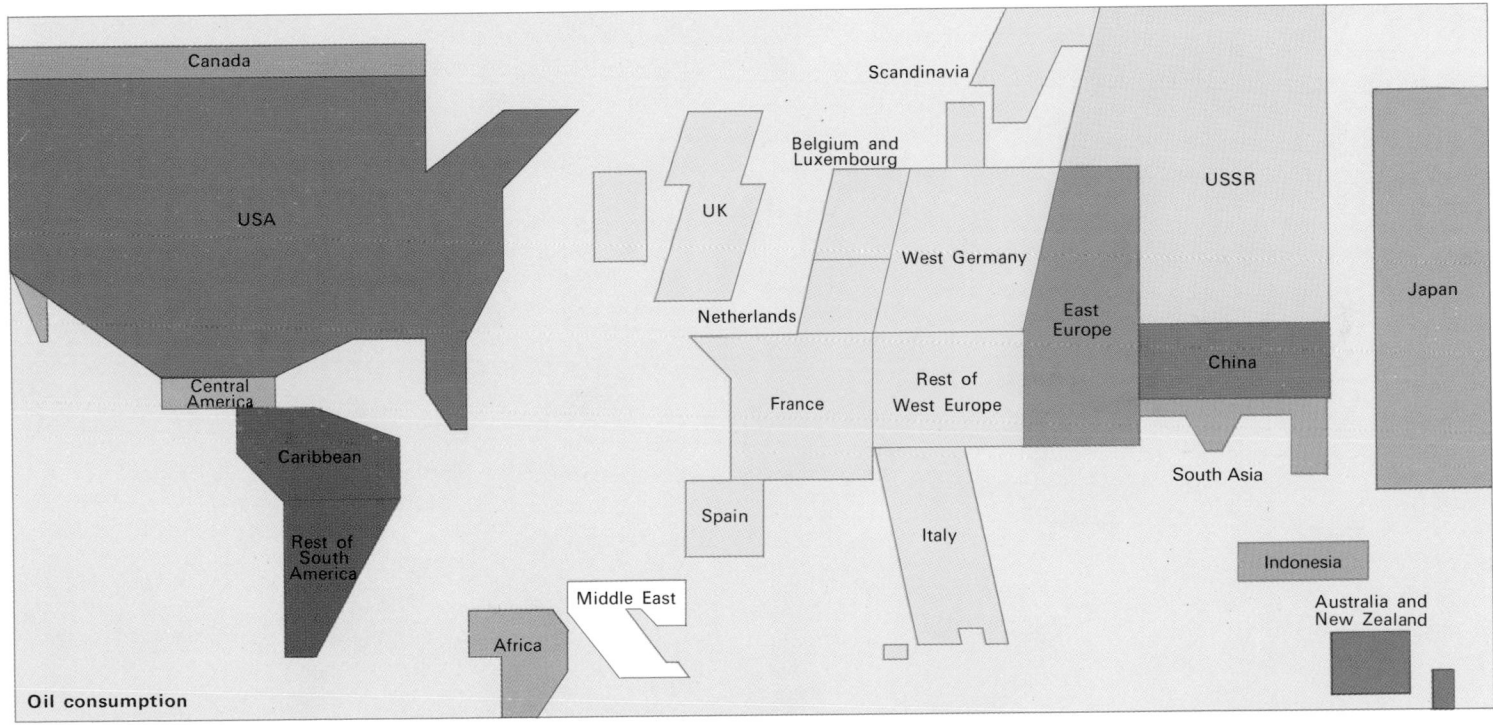

Oil consumption

Oil's new super-powers *above*
When countries are scaled
according to their production and
consumption of oil they take on
new dimensions. At present, large
supplies of oil are concentrated in
a few countries of the Caribbean,
the Middle East and North Africa,
except for the vast indigenous
supplies of the U.S.A. and U.S.S.R.
The Middle East, with 55% of the
world's reserves, produces 37% of
the world's supply and yet
consumes less than 3%. The U.S.A.,

despite its great production, has
a deficiency of nearly 300 million
tons a year, consuming 30% of the
world's total. Estimates show that
Western Europe, at present
consuming 747 million tons or 27%
of the total each year, may by
1980 surpass the U.S. consumption.
Japan is the largest importer of
crude oil with an increase in
consumption of 440% during the
period 1963-73.

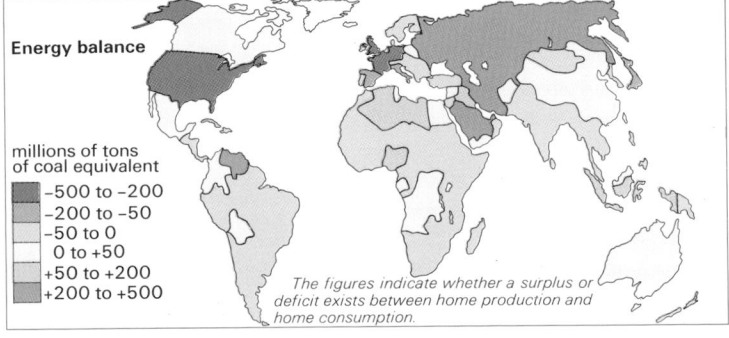

Energy balance

millions of tons
of coal equivalent

- −500 to −200
- −200 to −50
- −50 to 0
- 0 to +50
- +50 to +200
- +200 to +500

*The figures indicate whether a surplus or
deficit exists between home production and
home consumption.*

Occupations

Proportion employed in

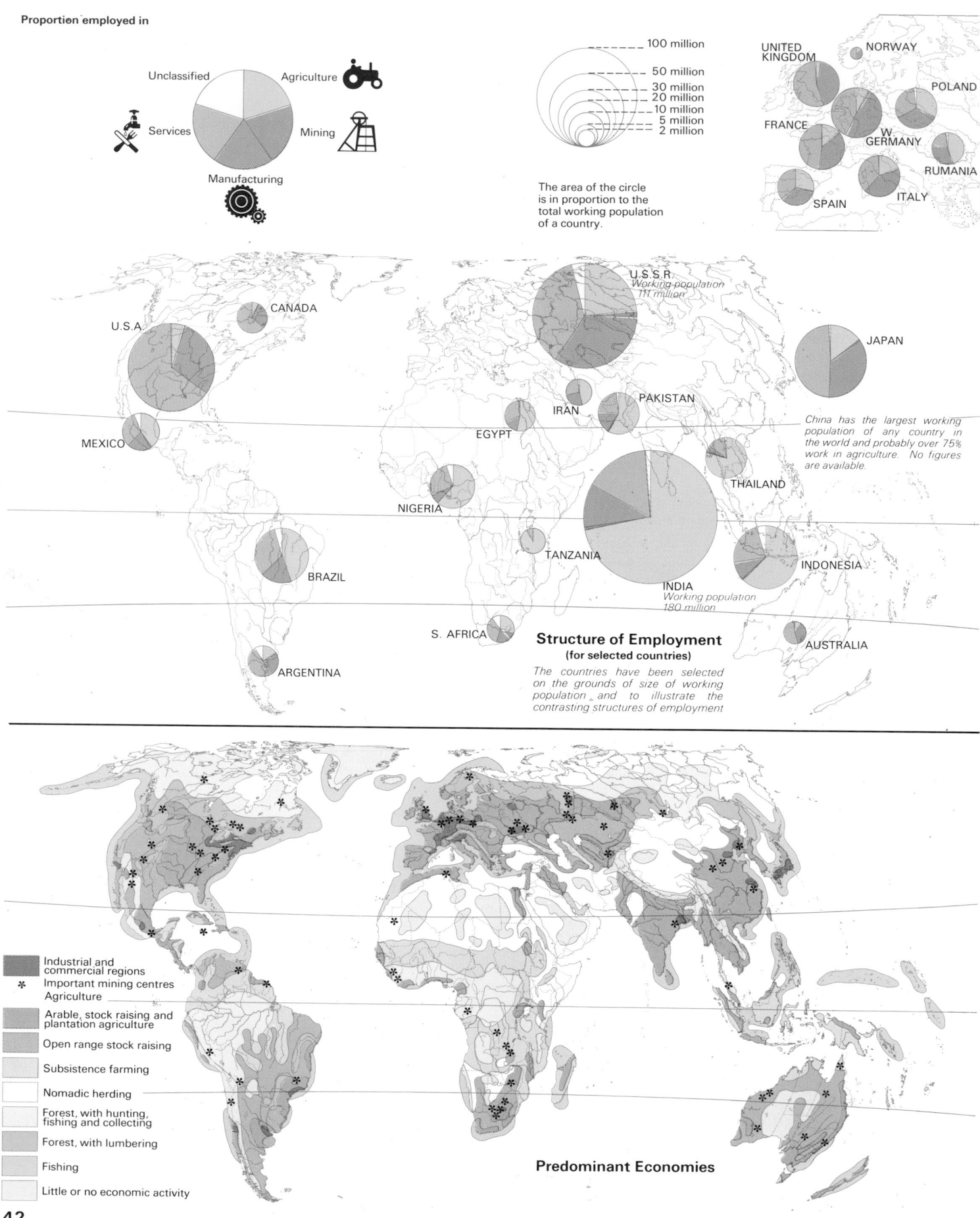

Unclassified

Agriculture

Services

Mining

Manufacturing

100 million
50 million
30 million
20 million
10 million
5 million
2 million

The area of the circle
is in proportion to the
total working population
of a country.

UNITED
KINGDOM

NORWAY

POLAND

FRANCE

W.
GERMANY

RUMANIA

SPAIN

ITALY

CANADA

U.S.A.

U.S.S.R.
*Working population
111 million*

JAPAN

MEXICO

IRAN

PAKISTAN

EGYPT

*China has the largest working
population of any country in
the world and probably over 75%
work in agriculture. No figures
are available.*

THAILAND

NIGERIA

TANZANIA

INDIA
*Working population
180 million*

INDONESIA

S. AFRICA

Structure of Employment
(for selected countries)

*The countries have been selected
on the grounds of size of working
population and to illustrate the
contrasting structures of employment*

AUSTRALIA

ARGENTINA

Industrial and
commercial regions
* Important mining centres
Agriculture

Arable, stock raising and
plantation agriculture

Open range stock raising

Subsistence farming

Nomadic herding

Forest, with hunting,
fishing and collecting

Forest, with lumbering

Fishing

Little or no economic activity

Predominant Economies

42

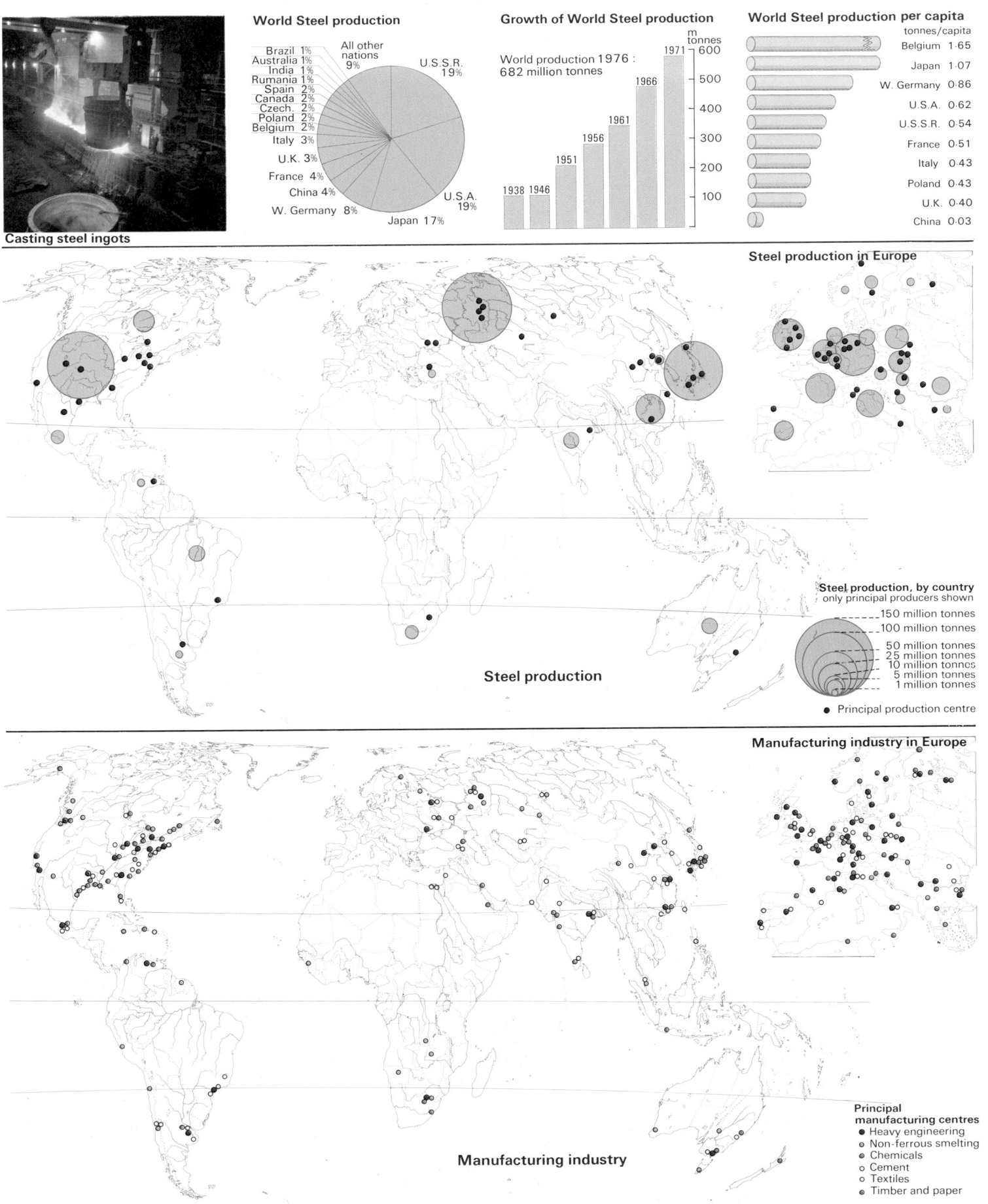

Casting steel ingots

World Steel production

Brazil 1%
Australia 1%
India 1%
Rumania 1%
Spain 2%
Canada 2%
Czech. 2%
Poland 2%
Belgium 2%
Italy 3%
U.K. 3%
France 4%
China 4%
W. Germany 8%
Japan 17%
All other nations 9%
U.S.S.R. 19%
U.S.A. 19%

Growth of World Steel production

World production 1976 : 682 million tonnes

m tonnes
600 — 1971
500 — 1966
400 — 1961
300 — 1956
200 — 1951
100 — 1938 1946

World Steel production per capita

tonnes/capita

Belgium	1·65
Japan	1·07
W. Germany	0·86
U.S.A.	0·62
U.S.S.R.	0·54
France	0·51
Italy	0·43
Poland	0·43
U.K.	0·40
China	0·03

Steel production in Europe

Steel production

Steel production, by country
only principal producers shown

150 million tonnes
100 million tonnes
50 million tonnes
25 million tonnes
10 million tonnes
5 million tonnes
1 million tonnes

● Principal production centre

Manufacturing industry in Europe

Manufacturing industry

Principal manufacturing centres
● Heavy engineering
◐ Non-ferrous smelting
◑ Chemicals
○ Cement
○ Textiles
◒ Timber and paper

43

Transport

Shipyards

Japan 17 609	
Sweden 2206	
West Germany 2151	
Spain 1428	
France 1349	
U.K. 1281	
Denmark 1125	
Italy 1028	
Norway 1012	
U.S.A. 801	
Yug. 774	
Neth. 723	

Shipbuilding
tonnage launched
in thousand gross
registered tons

● Principal shipbuilding centres

Europe

Japan

Concorde and Boeing 747

Aircraft Industry

In 1975 there were approximately
10 000 civil passenger airliners in
service. This diagram shows where they
were built.

U.S.A. 53%	U.S.S.R. 33%	U.K. 6% Netherlands 3% France 2%

Trade in Aircraft and Aircraft Engines

	Exports	*million U.S. $*		Imports	
	Aircraft.	Engines		Aircraft.	Engines
U.S.A.	4143	714	U.S.A.	563	218
U.K.	605	591	Canada	438	108
France	360	150	France	400	250
Canada	325	132	U.K.	389	393
W. Germ.	200		Australia	342	20
Neth.	192	89	W. Germ.	279	
Italy	137		Japan	236	107

● Principal aircraft manufacturing centres

Motor vehicles

Production *thousand units*		Exports *million U.S. $*	Imports *million U.S. $*
U.S.A. 12 638		6076	1005
Japan 7088		4899	193
W. Germany 3949		9107	996
France 3596		3779	1903
U.K. 2164		2701	1599
Italy 1960		1963	1263
Canada 1604		4814	5349
U.S.S.R. 1604		611	240
Belgium 938		2215	1457

Locomotive works

Railway vehicles

Exports *million U.S. $*		Imports *million U.S. $.*	
U.S.A.	219·2	Yugoslavia	109·2
France	210·2	Brazil	65·8
Japan	186·3	S. Africa	48·4
W. Germany	157·7	W. Germany	47·4
Canada	76·1	U.S.A.	39·0
Yugoslavia	59·6	Belg.-Lux.	34·9
Italy	42·2	Netherlands	34·4
Spain	42·2	France	31·3
U.K.	38·6	Canada	30·0
Sweden	24·2	Argentina	25·7
Belg.-Lux.	22·0	Italy	22·9
Portugal	14·4	Sweden	19·4
Austria	11·8	S. Korea	18·8

Car assembly line

Europe

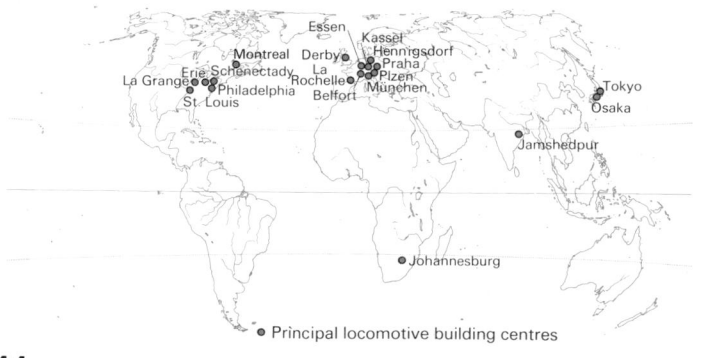

● Principal locomotive building centres

● Principal motor vehicle plants

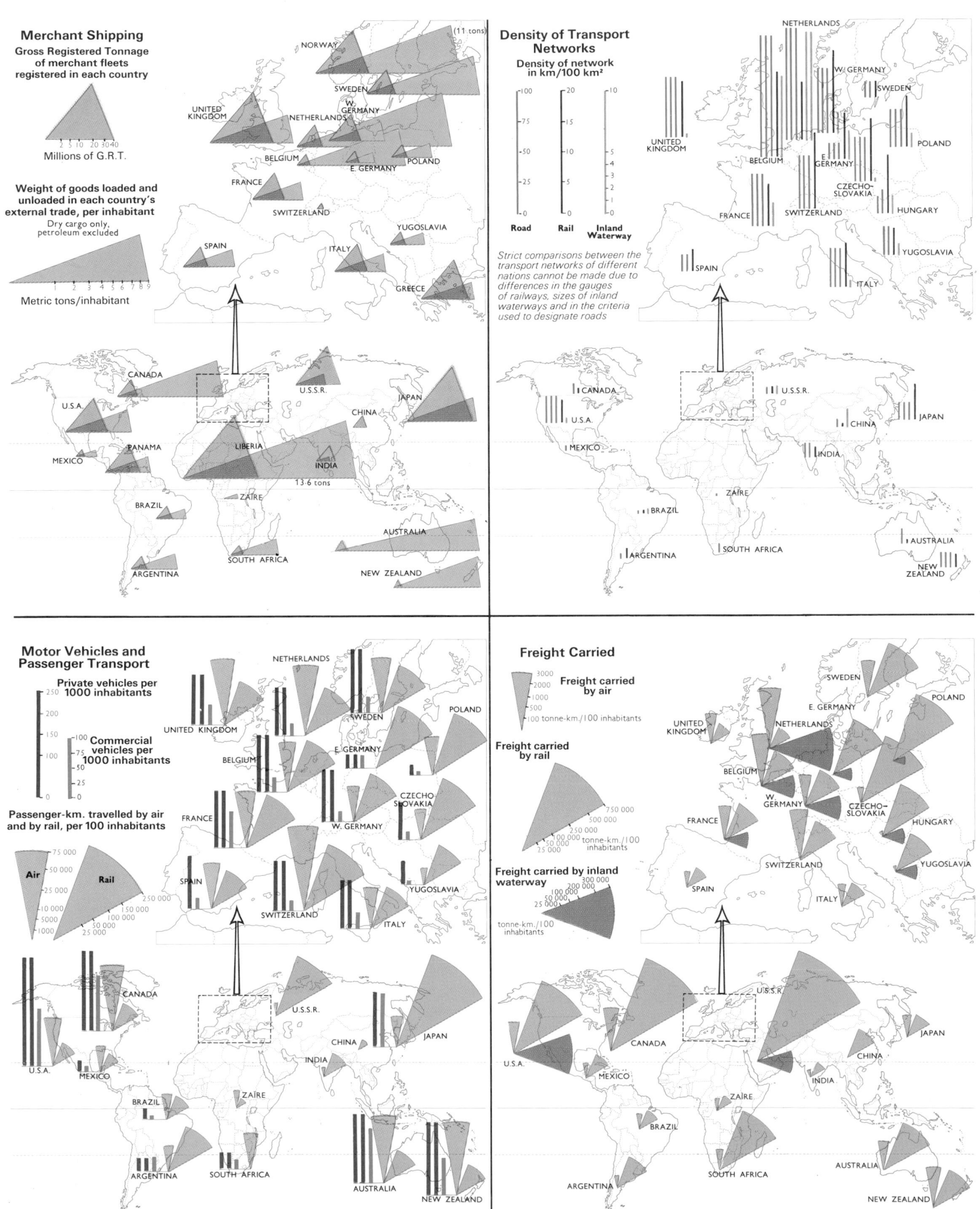

Merchant Shipping

Gross Registered Tonnage of merchant fleets registered in each country

2 5 10 20 30 40
Millions of G.R.T.

Weight of goods loaded and unloaded in each country's external trade, per inhabitant

Dry cargo only, petroleum excluded

1 2 3 4 5 6 7 8 9
Metric tons/inhabitant

Density of Transport Networks

Density of network in km/100 km²

Road	Rail	Inland Waterway

Strict comparisons between the transport networks of different nations cannot be made due to differences in the gauges of railways, sizes of inland waterways and in the criteria used to designate roads

Motor Vehicles and Passenger Transport

Private vehicles per 1000 inhabitants

Commercial vehicles per 1000 inhabitants

Passenger-km. travelled by air and by rail, per 100 inhabitants

Air   Rail

Freight Carried

Freight carried by air

100 tonne-km./100 inhabitants

Freight carried by rail

tonne-km./100 inhabitants

Freight carried by inland waterway

tonne-km./100 inhabitants

Trade

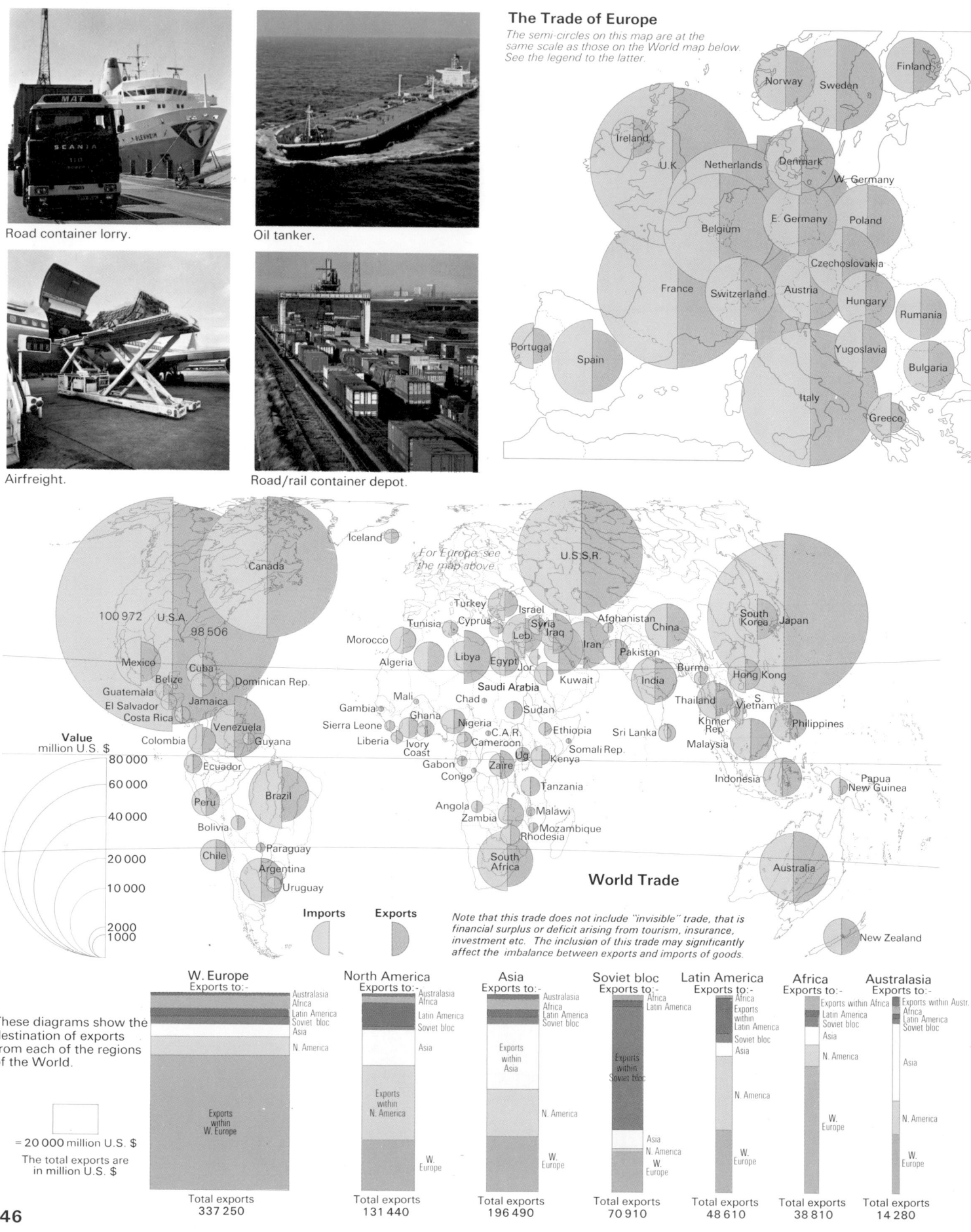

Road container lorry.

Oil tanker.

Airfreight.

Road/rail container depot.

The Trade of Europe

The semi-circles on this map are at the same scale as those on the World map below. See the legend to the latter.

Norway · Sweden · Finland
Ireland · U.K. · Netherlands · Denmark · W. Germany
Belgium · E. Germany · Poland
France · Switzerland · Austria · Czechoslovakia · Hungary · Rumania
Portugal · Spain · Yugoslavia · Bulgaria
Italy · Greece

World Trade

Iceland · Canada · U.S.S.R.
For Europe see the map above.
100 972 · U.S.A. · 98 506
Mexico · Cuba · Dominican Rep. · Turkey · Israel · Afghanistan · China · South Korea · Japan
Belize · Morocco · Tunisia · Cyprus · Syria · Iraq · Iran · Pakistan
Guatemala · Jamaica · Algeria · Libya · Egypt · Jor. · Kuwait · India · Burma · Hong Kong
El Salvador · Costa Rica · Leb. · Saudi Arabia · Thailand · S. Vietnam · Philippines
Colombia · Venezuela · Guyana · Gambia · Mali · Chad · Sudan · Khmer Rep. · Malaysia
Ecuador · Sierra Leone · Ghana · Nigeria · C.A.R. · Ethiopia · Sri Lanka
Peru · Liberia · Ivory Coast · Cameroon · Somali Rep. · Indonesia · Papua New Guinea
Brazil · Gabon · Congo · Zaire · Ug. · Kenya
Bolivia · Angola · Tanzania
Chile · Paraguay · Zambia · Malawi · Mozambique · Rhodesia · Australia
Argentina · Uruguay · South Africa
New Zealand

Value million U.S. $
80 000
60 000
40 000
20 000
10 000
2000
1000

Imports · Exports

Note that this trade does not include "invisible" trade, that is financial surplus or deficit arising from tourism, insurance, investment etc. The inclusion of this trade may significantly affect the imbalance between exports and imports of goods.

These diagrams show the destination of exports from each of the regions of the World.

☐ = 20 000 million U.S. $
The total exports are in million U.S. $

W. Europe
Exports to:-
Australasia
Africa
Latin America
Soviet bloc
Asia
N. America
Exports within W. Europe
Total exports
337 250

North America
Exports to:-
Australasia
Africa
Latin America
Soviet bloc
Asia
Exports within N. America
W. Europe
Total exports
131 440

Asia
Exports to:-
Australasia
Africa
Latin America
Soviet bloc
Exports within Asia
N. America
W. Europe
Total exports
196 490

Soviet bloc
Exports to:-
Africa
Latin America
Exports within
Latin America
Exports within Soviet bloc
Asia
N. America
W. Europe
Total exports
70 910

Latin America
Exports to:-
Africa
Exports within Latin America
Soviet bloc
Asia
N. America
W. Europe
Total exports
48 610

Africa
Exports to:-
Exports within Africa
Africa
Soviet bloc
Asia
N. America
W. Europe
Total exports
38 810

Australasia
Exports to:-
Exports within Austr.
Africa
Latin America
Soviet bloc
Asia
N. America
W. Europe
Total exports
14 280

46

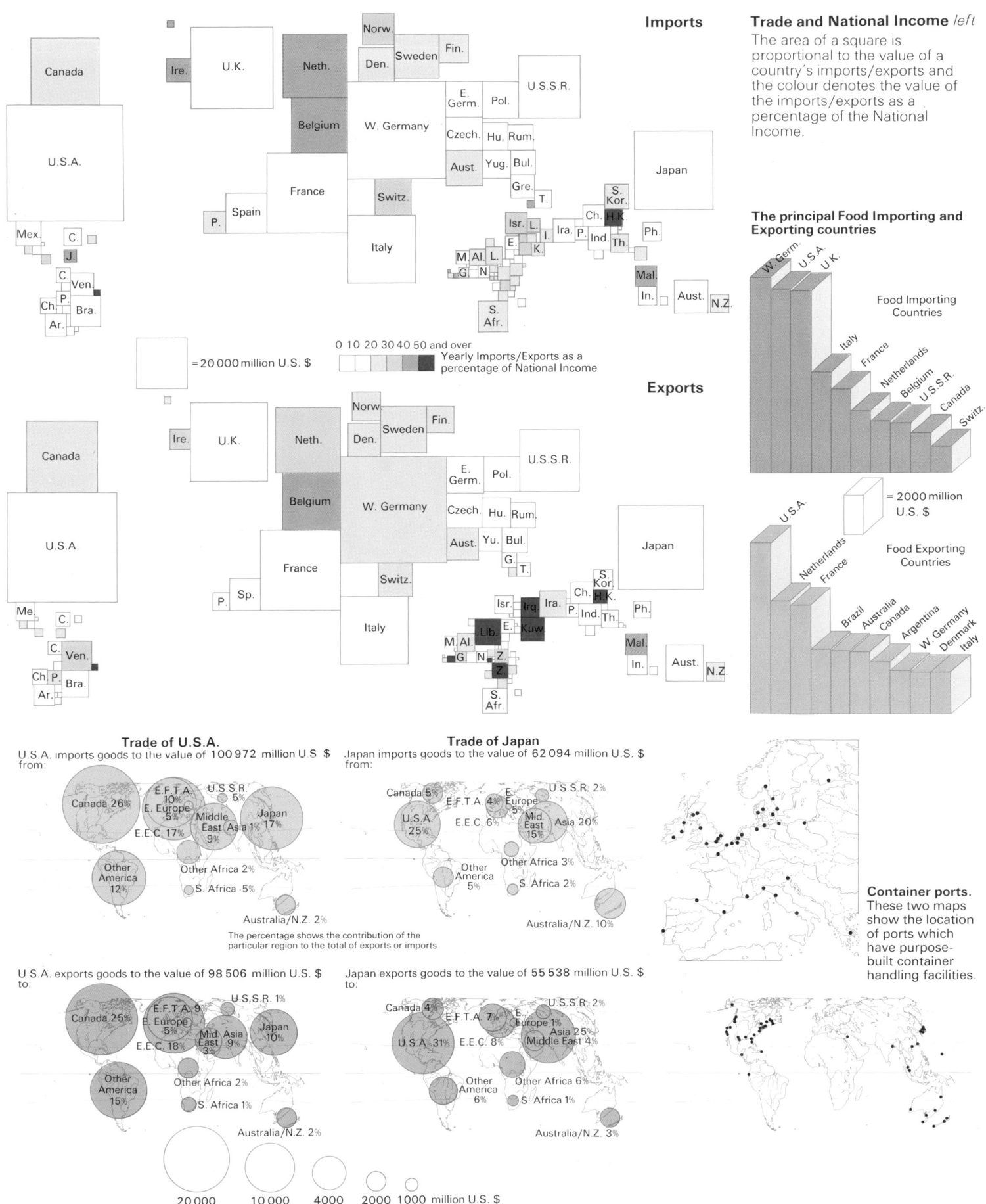

Imports

Trade and National Income *left*
The area of a square is proportional to the value of a country's imports/exports and the colour denotes the value of the imports/exports as a percentage of the National Income.

The principal Food Importing and Exporting countries

Food Importing Countries

W. Germ. U.S.A. U.K. Italy France Netherlands Belgium U.S.S.R. Canada Switz.

= 2000 million U.S. $

Food Exporting Countries

U.S.A. Netherlands France Brazil Australia Canada Argentina W. Germany Denmark Italy

= 20 000 million U.S. $

0 10 20 30 40 50 and over
Yearly Imports/Exports as a percentage of National Income

Exports

Trade of U.S.A.
U.S.A. imports goods to the value of 100 972 million U.S. $ from:

Canada 26%
E.F.T.A. 10%
E. Europe 5%
U.S.S.R. 5%
E.E.C. 17%
Middle East 9%
Asia 1%
Japan 17%
Other America 12%
Other Africa 2%
S. Africa 5%
Australia/N.Z. 2%

The percentage shows the contribution of the particular region to the total of exports or imports

Trade of Japan
Japan imports goods to the value of 62 094 million U.S. $ from:

Canada 5%
E.F.T.A. 4%
E. Europe 5%
U.S.S.R. 2%
U.S.A. 25%
E.E.C. 6%
Mid. East 15%
Asia 20%
Other America 5%
Other Africa 3%
S. Africa 2%
Australia/N.Z. 10%

U.S.A. exports goods to the value of 98 506 million U.S. $ to:

Canada 25%
E.F.T.A. 9%
E. Europe 5%
U.S.S.R. 1%
E.E.C. 18%
Mid East 3%
Asia 9%
Japan 10%
Other America 15%
Other Africa 2%
S. Africa 1%
Australia/N.Z. 2%

Japan exports goods to the value of 55 538 million U.S. $ to:

Canada 4%
E.F.T.A. 7%
E. Europe 1%
U.S.S.R. 2%
U.S.A. 31%
E.E.C. 8%
Middle East 4%
Asia 25%
Other America 6%
Other Africa 6%
S. Africa 1%
Australia/N.Z. 3%

20 000   10 000   4000   2000 1000 million U.S. $

Container ports.
These two maps show the location of ports which have purpose-built container handling facilities.

Wealth

The living standard of a few highly developed, urbanised, industrialised countries is a complete contrast to the conditions of the vast majority of economically undeveloped, agrarian states. It is this contrast which divides mankind into rich and poor, well fed and hungry. The developing world is still an overwhelmingly agricultural world: over 70% of all its people live off the land and yet the output from that land remains pitifully low. Many Africans, South Americans and Asians struggle with the soil but the bad years occur only too frequently and they seldom have anything left over to save. The need for foreign capital then arises.

National Income *see right*

The gap between developing and developed worlds is in fact widening eg. in 1938 the incomes for the United States and India were in the proportions of 1:15; now they are 1:35.

Islands *see map right*

a Antilles
b Martinique
c Barbados
d Cape Verde
e Bahrein
f Comoro
g Reunion
h Mauritius
j Solomon
k New Hebrides
l Fiji
m New Caledonia
n Tonga

Incomes per capita in U.S. dollars

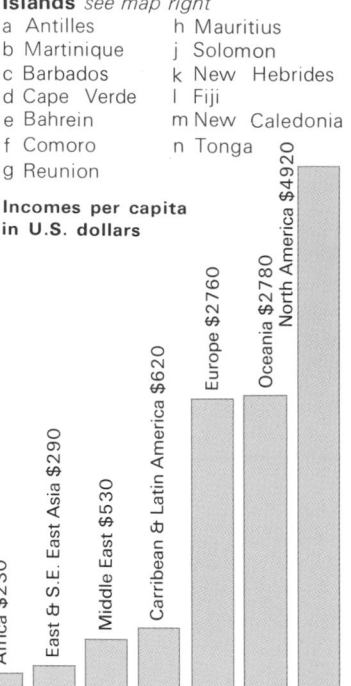

- Africa $230
- East & S.E. East Asia $290
- Middle East $530
- Carribean & Latin America $620
- Europe $2760
- Oceania $2780
- North America $4920

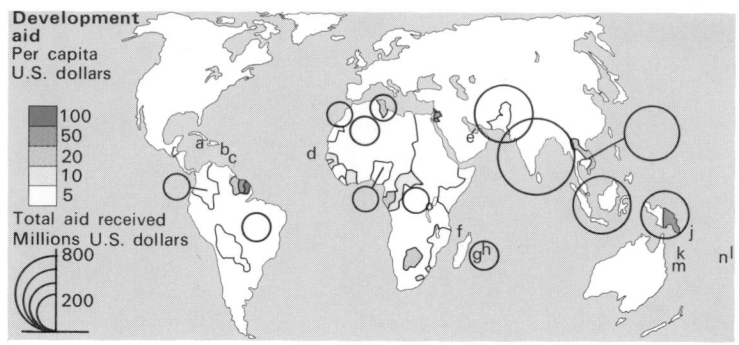

Development aid
Per capita
U.S. dollars

- 100
- 50
- 20
- 10
- 5

Total aid received
Millions U.S. dollars

- 800
- 200

Development aid

The provision of foreign aid, defined as assistance on concessional terms for promoting development, is today an accepted, though controversial aspect of the economic policies of most advanced countries towards less developed countries. Aid for development is based not merely on economic considerations but also on social, political and historical factors. The most important international committee set up after the war was that of the U.N.; practically all aid however has been given bi-laterally direct from an industrialised country to an under-developed country. Although aid increased during the 1950's the donated proportion of industrialised countries GNP has diminished from 0·5 to 0·4%. Less developed countries share of world trade also decreased and increased population invalidated any progress made:

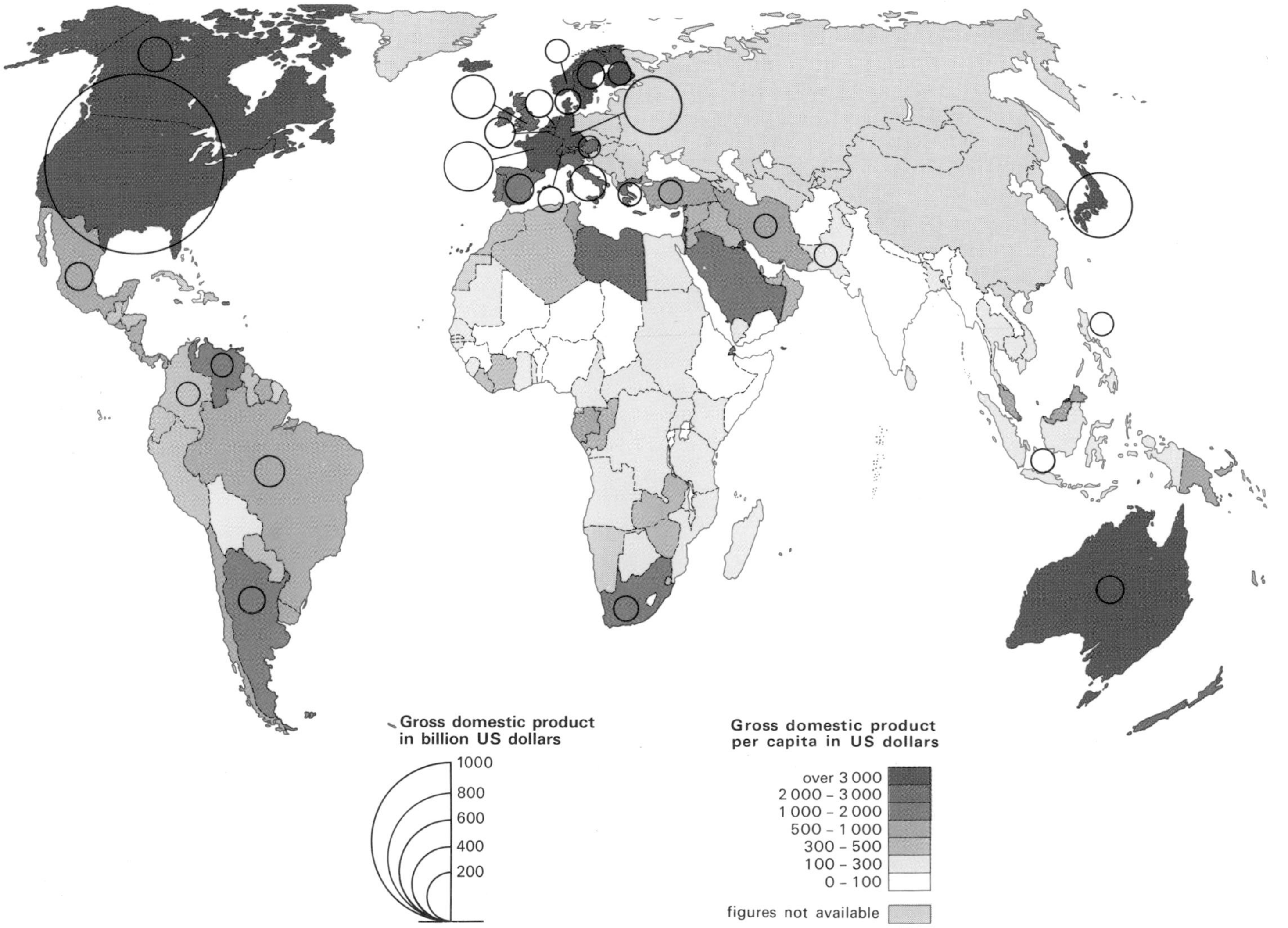

Gross domestic product in billion US dollars

- 1000
- 800
- 600
- 400
- 200

Gross domestic product per capita in US dollars

- over 3 000
- 2 000 – 3 000
- 1 000 – 2 000
- 500 – 1 000
- 300 – 500
- 100 – 300
- 0 – 100

figures not available

SETTLEMENTS

Settlement symbols in order of size

LONDON
MONTRÉAL
Stuttgart
Hamilton
Sevilla
Moose Jaw
Bergen
Prince Rupert
Bath
Gaspé
Biarritz
Banff
Srikolayatji
Miquelon

Settlement symbols and type styles vary according to
the scale of each map and indicate the importance of
towns on the map rather than specific population figures

∴ Sites of Archæological or
Historical importance

BOUNDARIES

—————— International Boundaries

— — — International Boundaries
(Undemarcated or Undefined)

·········· Internal Boundaries

International boundaries show the *de facto* situation
where there are rival claims to territory

National and
Provincial Parks

COMMUNICATIONS

===== Freeways

========= Freeways under construction

—o— Trans-Canada Highway

—————— Principal Roads

⌒ Other Roads

‒‒‒‒‒ Tracks and Seasonal Roads

⌒ Principal Railways

⌒ Other Railways

‒‒·‒‒· Railways under construction

⊐‒‒⊏ Railway Tunnels

⊐‒‒⊏ Road Tunnels

‿ Passes

············· Principal Canals

—·—·— Principal Oil Pipelines

_3386_ Principal Shipping Routes
(Distances in Nautical Miles)

—————— Principal Air Routes

✈ + ✿ Airports

PHYSICAL FEATURES

⌒ Perennial Streams

‒‒‒‒‒ Seasonal Streams

▲ 8848 Spot Height
in metres

⊂⊃ Seasonal Lakes, Salt Flats

Swamps, Marshes

▾ 8050 Sea Depths.
in metres

Permanent Ice

⌣ Wells in Desert

1134 Height of Lake Surface
Above Sea Level, in metres

Height of Land
Above Sea Level
in metres

Land Below
Sea Level

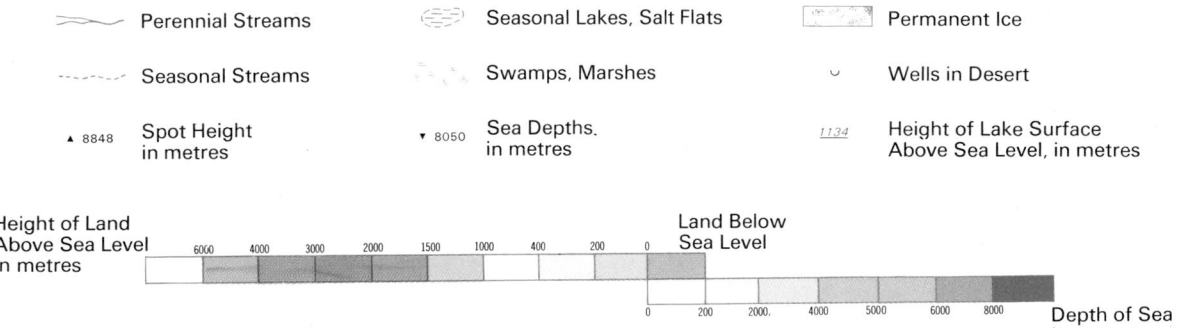

6000 4000 3000 2000 1500 1000 400 200 0

0 200 2000. 4000 5000 6000 8000

Depth of Sea
in metres

Some of the maps have different contours to
highlight and clarify the principal relief features

Abbreviations of measures used   mm Millimetres   m Metres   km Kilometres   °C Degrees Celsius   mb Millibars

GEOLOGY
after
Beyschlag, Nalivkin and others

1:90 000 000

Ⓐ

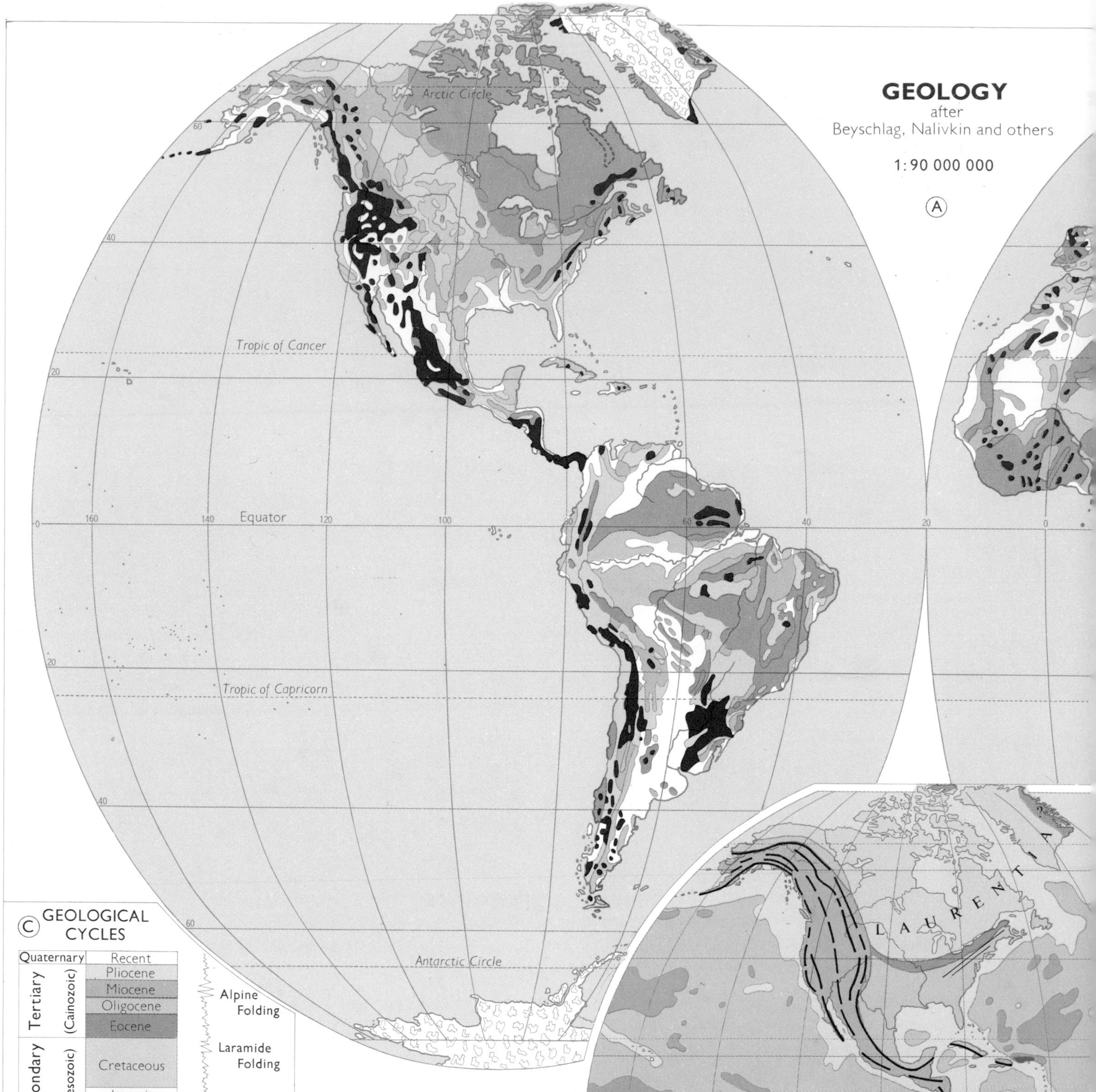

Arctic Circle

60

40

Tropic of Cancer

20

160   140   Equator   120   100   60   40   20   0

20

Tropic of Capricorn

40

60

Antarctic Circle

Ⓒ GEOLOGICAL CYCLES

Quaternary		Recent	
Tertiary (Cainozoic)		Pliocene	Alpine Folding
		Miocene	
		Oligocene	
		Eocene	
Secondary (Mesozoic)		Cretaceous	Laramide Folding
		Jurassic	
		Triassic	
		Permian	
Primary (Palæozoic)	Upper	Carboniferous	Hercynian Folding
		Devonian	
	Lower	Silurian	Caledonian Folding
		Ordovician	
		Cambrian	
Archæan		Pre-Cambrian	

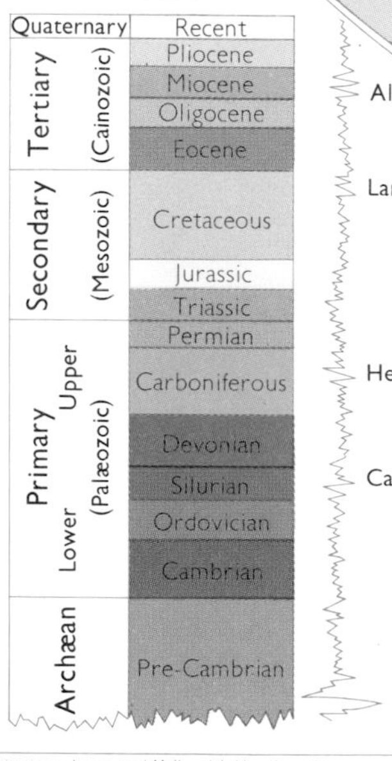

Ⓑ   An Interpretation of
STRUCTURE
showing
the distribution of rigid masses and folded regions
after L. Kober and others

Pre-Cambrian tables composite in structure, rigid since the Cambrian period and forming stable elements separating the geo-synclines of later times.

Regions of Caledonian folding; Siluro-Devonian earth movements.

Regions of Hercynian folding; Carbo-Permian earth movements.

Regions of Tertiary folding; Cretaceo-Tertiary earth movements.

The Great Rift Valley

Main Trend lines

LAURENTIA

G

Projections: Interrupted Mollweide's Homolographic

3

Sedimentary Rocks
Quaternary
Cainozoic
Mesozoic
Upper Palæozoic
Lower Palæozoic
Pre-Cambrian and Metamorphic

Igneous Rocks
Volcanic
Intrusive

Ice caps
Unexplored regions

Arctic Circle

Tropic of Cancer

Equator

Tropic of Capricorn

60

20

40

60

80

140

160

180

0

20

40

60

Sea Depths
m
4000
6000
8000

1:126 000 000

BALTICA

SIBERIAN TABLE
(ANGARALAND)

CHINESE
TABLE

G O N D W A N A L A N D

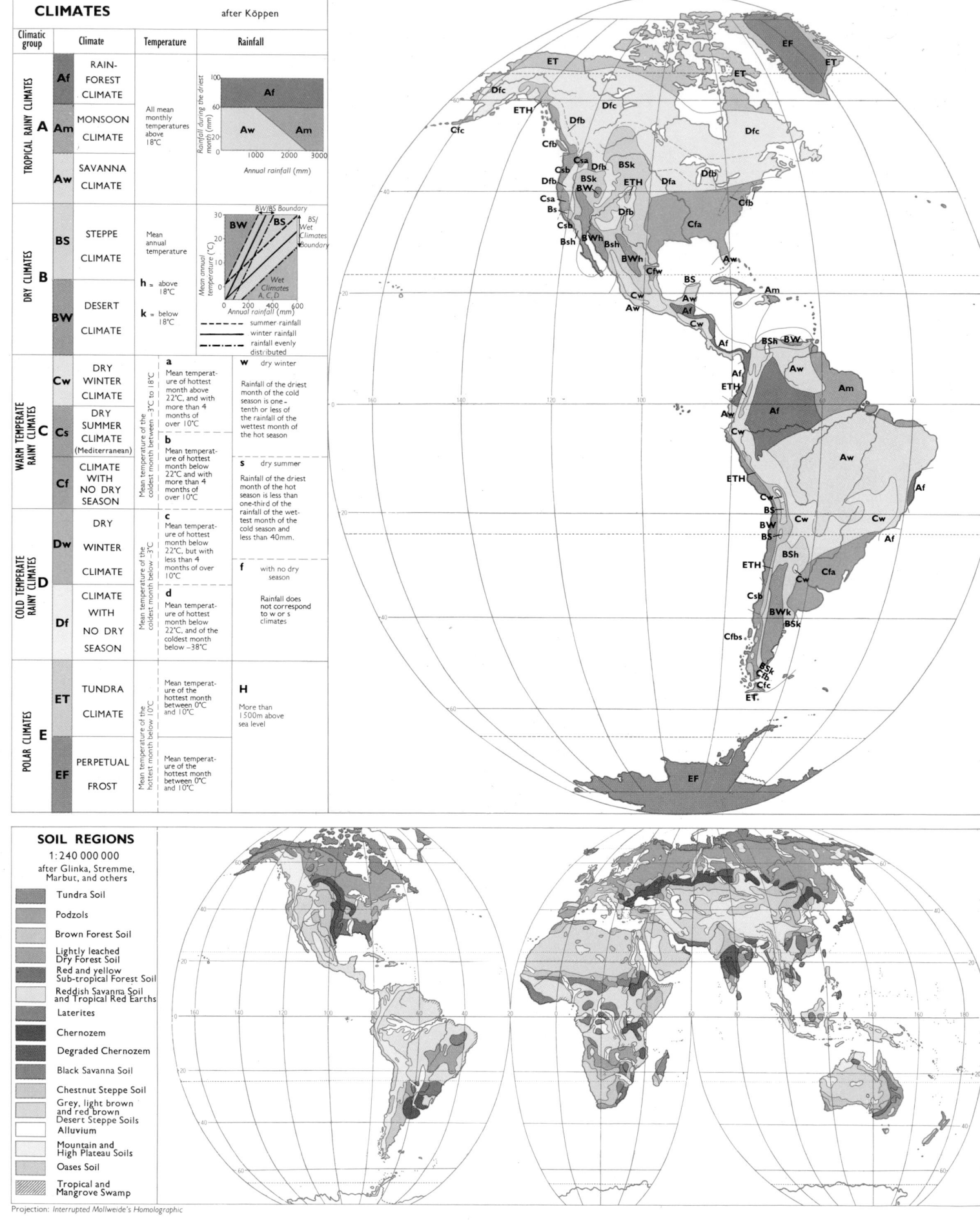

CLIMATES

after Köppen

Climatic group		Climate	Temperature	Rainfall
TROPICAL RAINY CLIMATES **A**	Af	RAIN-FOREST CLIMATE	All mean monthly temperatures above 18°C	
	Am	MONSOON CLIMATE		
	Aw	SAVANNA CLIMATE		
DRY CLIMATES **B**	BS	STEPPE CLIMATE	Mean annual temperature	
	BW	DESERT CLIMATE	h = above 18°C k = below 18°C	
WARM TEMPERATE RAINY CLIMATES **C**	Cw	DRY WINTER CLIMATE		
	Cs	DRY SUMMER CLIMATE (Mediterranean)		
	Cf	CLIMATE WITH NO DRY SEASON		
COLD TEMPERATE RAINY CLIMATES **D**	Dw	DRY WINTER CLIMATE		
	Df	CLIMATE WITH NO DRY SEASON		
POLAR CLIMATES **E**	ET	TUNDRA CLIMATE	Mean temperature of the hottest month between 0°C and 10°C	H More than 1500m above sea level
	EF	PERPETUAL FROST	Mean temperature of the hottest month between 0°C and 10°C	

Temperature details for C and D groups:

Mean temperature of the coldest month between −3°C to 18°C:
- **a** Mean temperature of hottest month above 22°C, and with more than 4 months of over 10°C
- **b** Mean temperature of hottest month below 22°C and with more than 4 months of over 10°C

Mean temperature of the coldest month below −3°C:
- **c** Mean temperature of hottest month below 22°C, but with less than 4 months of over 10°C
- **d** Mean temperature of hottest month below 22°C, and of the coldest month below −38°C

Rainfall details:
- **w** dry winter — Rainfall of the driest month of the cold season is one-tenth or less of the rainfall of the wettest month of the hot season
- **s** dry summer — Rainfall of the driest month of the hot season is less than one-third of the rainfall of the wettest month of the cold season and less than 40mm.
- **f** with no dry season — Rainfall does not correspond to w or s climates

Rainfall graph (Af): Rainfall during the driest month (mm) vs Annual rainfall (mm) — Af, Aw, Am zones, 1000/2000/3000 mm

Temperature graph: Mean annual temperature (°C) vs Annual rainfall (mm) — BW, BS, Wet Climates A,C,D zones; BW/BS Boundary, BS/Wet Climates Boundary; summer rainfall, winter rainfall, rainfall evenly distributed

SOIL REGIONS

1:240 000 000

after Glinka, Stremme, Marbut, and others

- Tundra Soil
- Podzols
- Brown Forest Soil
- Lightly leached Dry Forest Soil
- Red and yellow Sub-tropical Forest Soil
- Reddish Savanna Soil and Tropical Red Earths
- Laterites
- Chernozem
- Degraded Chernozem
- Black Savanna Soil
- Chestnut Steppe Soil
- Grey, light brown and red brown Desert Steppe Soils
- Alluvium
- Mountain and High Plateau Soils
- Oases Soil
- Tropical and Mangrove Swamp

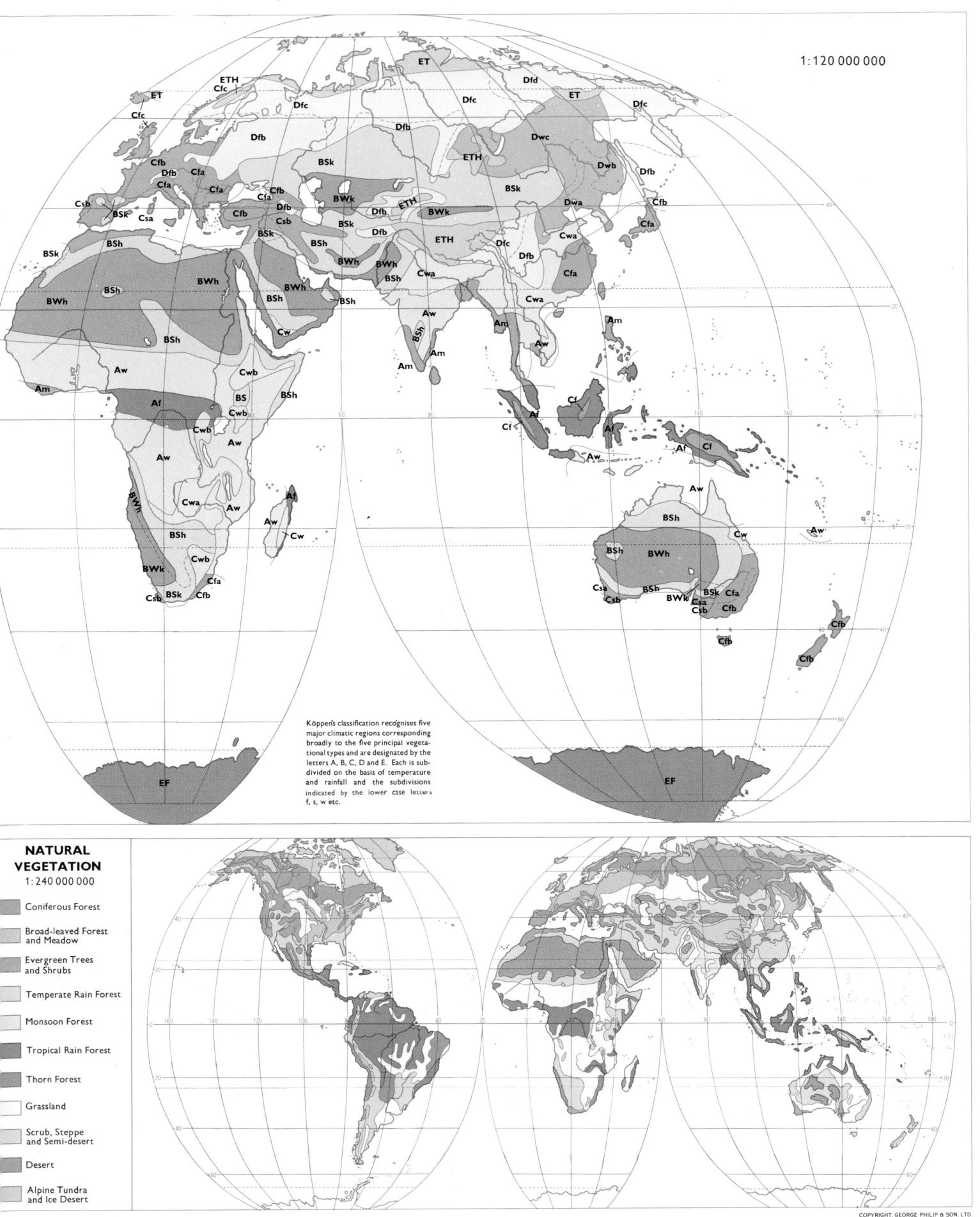

1:120 000 000

Köppen's classification recognises five major climatic regions corresponding broadly to the five principal vegetational types and are designated by the letters A, B, C, D and E. Each is subdivided on the basis of temperature and rainfall and the subdivisions indicated by the lower case letters f, s, w etc.

NATURAL VEGETATION

1:240 000 000

- Coniferous Forest
- Broad-leaved Forest and Meadow
- Evergreen Trees and Shrubs
- Temperate Rain Forest
- Monsoon Forest
- Tropical Rain Forest
- Thorn Forest
- Grassland
- Scrub, Steppe and Semi-desert
- Desert
- Alpine Tundra and Ice Desert

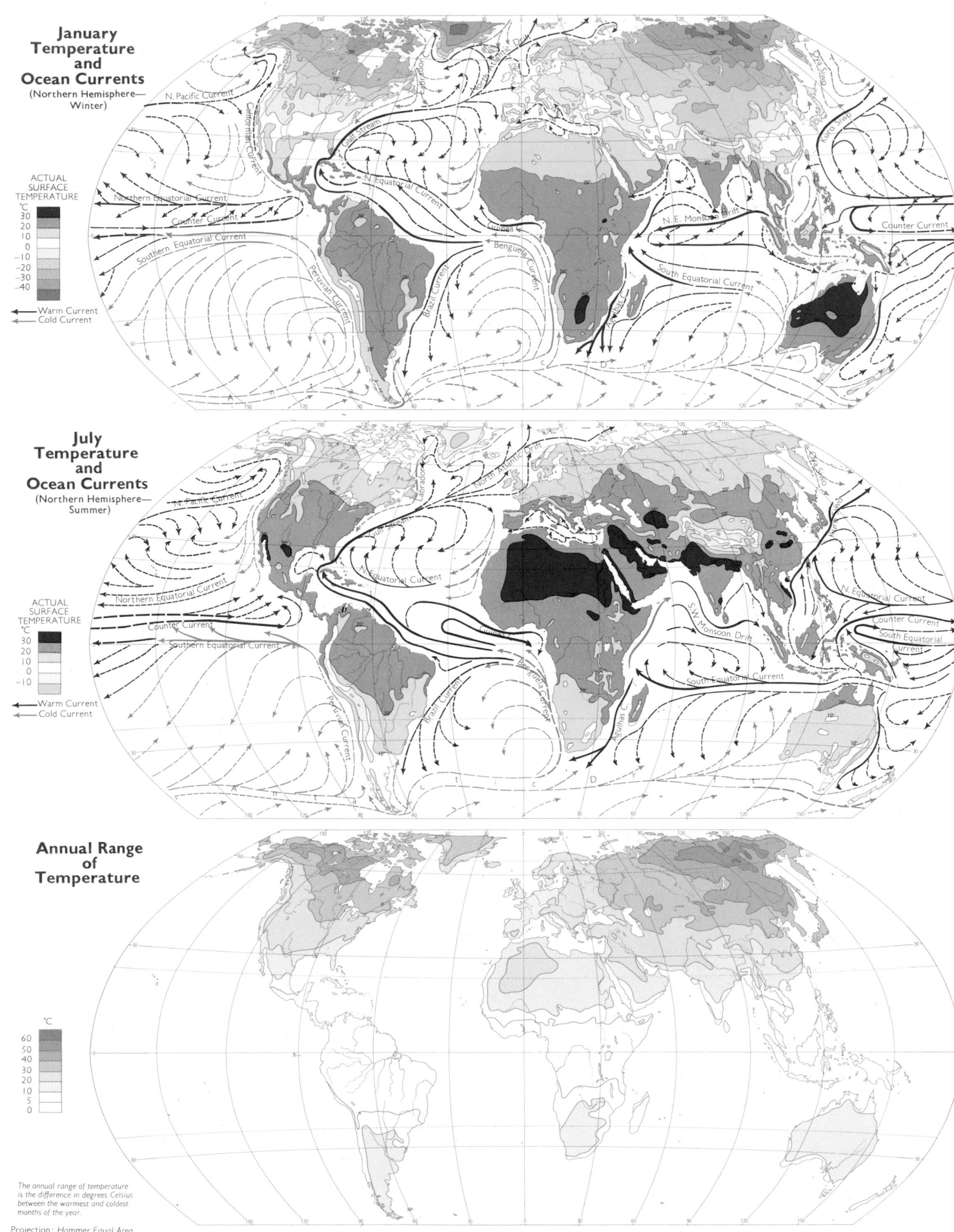

**January
Temperature
and
Ocean Currents**
(Northern Hemisphere—
Winter)

ACTUAL
SURFACE
TEMPERATURE
°C
30
20
10
0
-10
-20
-30
-40

⟶ Warm Current
⟶ Cold Current

**July
Temperature
and
Ocean Currents**
(Northern Hemisphere—
Summer)

ACTUAL
SURFACE
TEMPERATURE
°C
30
20
10
0
-10

⟶ Warm Current
⟶ Cold Current

**Annual Range
of
Temperature**

°C
60
50
40
30
20
10
5
0

The annual range of temperature
is the difference in degrees Celsius
between the warmest and coldest
months of the year.

Projection: Hammer Equal Area

1:190 000 000

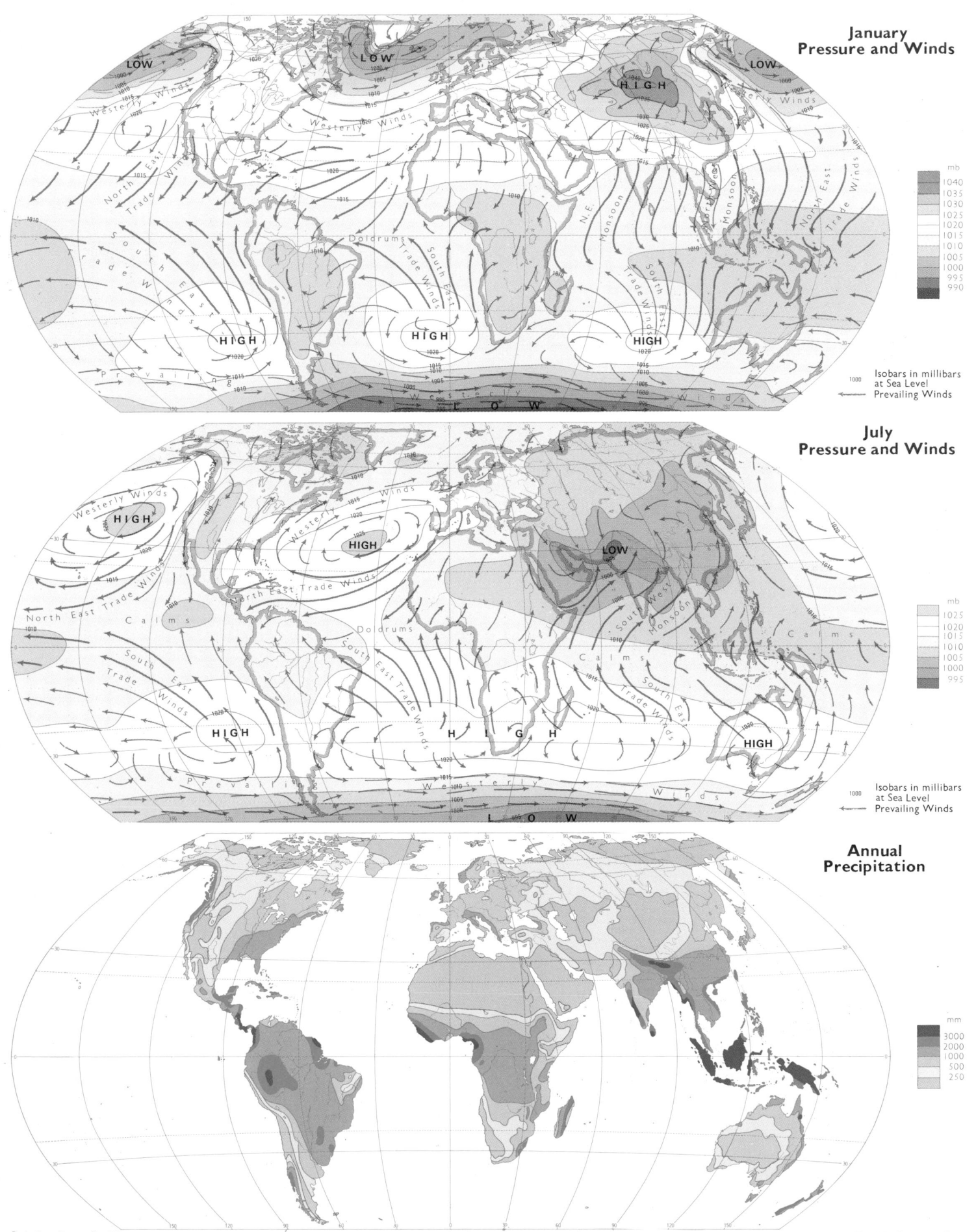

January
Pressure and Winds

mb
1040
1035
1030
1025
1020
1015
1010
1005
1000
995
990

1000 Isobars in millibars
at Sea Level
← Prevailing Winds

July
Pressure and Winds

mb
1025
1020
1015
1010
1005
1000
995

1000 Isobars in millibars
at Sea Level
← Prevailing Winds

Annual
Precipitation

mm
3000
2000
1000
500
250

Projection: Hammer Equal Area

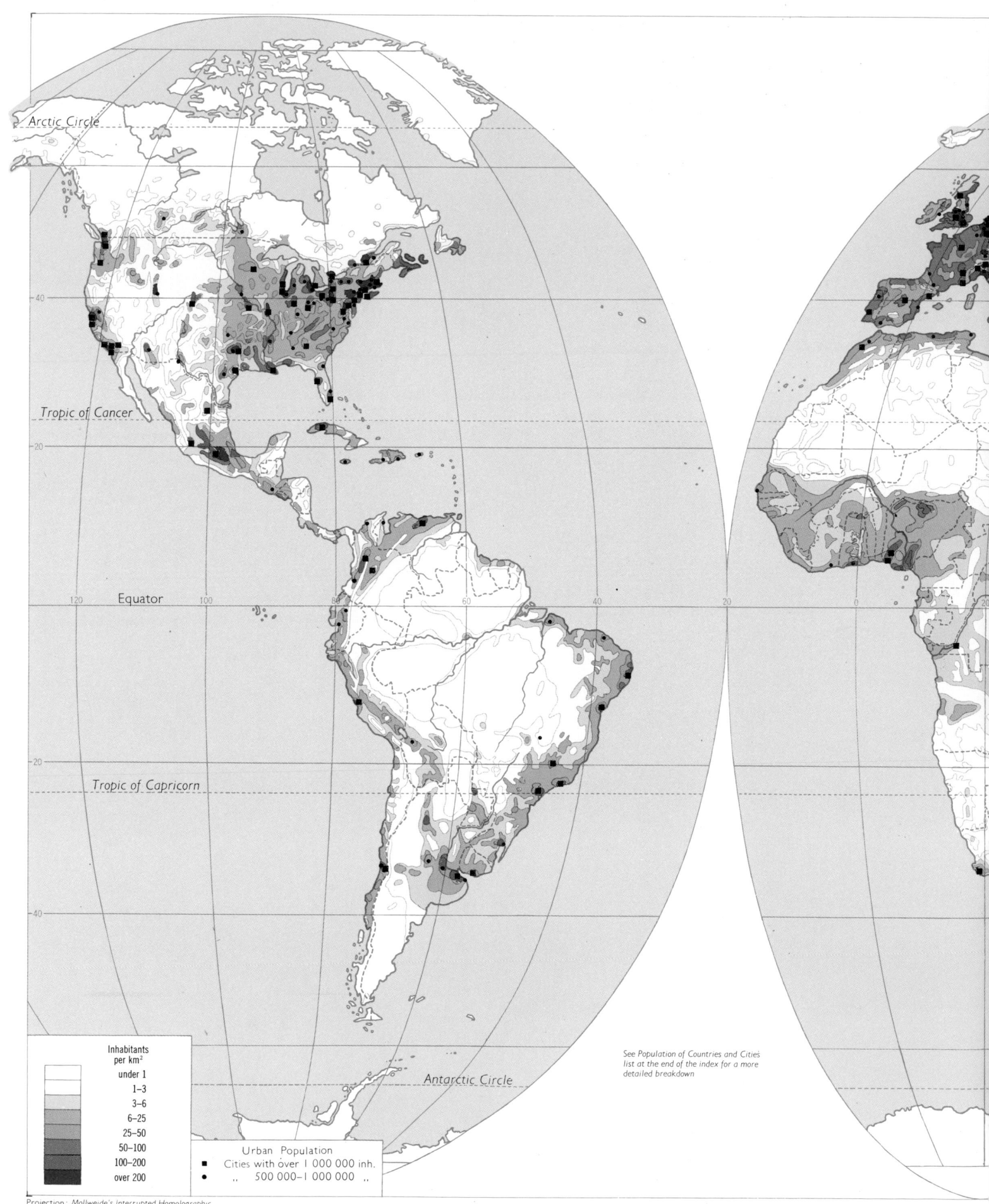

Arctic Circle

Tropic of Cancer

Equator

Tropic of Capricorn

Antarctic Circle

See Population of Countries and Cities
list at the end of the index for a more
detailed breakdown

Inhabitants
per km²

	under 1
	1–3
	3–6
	6–25
	25–50
	50–100
	100–200
	over 200

Urban Population
■ Cities with over 1 000 000 inh.
•   　,,   500 000–1 000 000   ,,

Projection: Mollweide's interrupted Homolographic

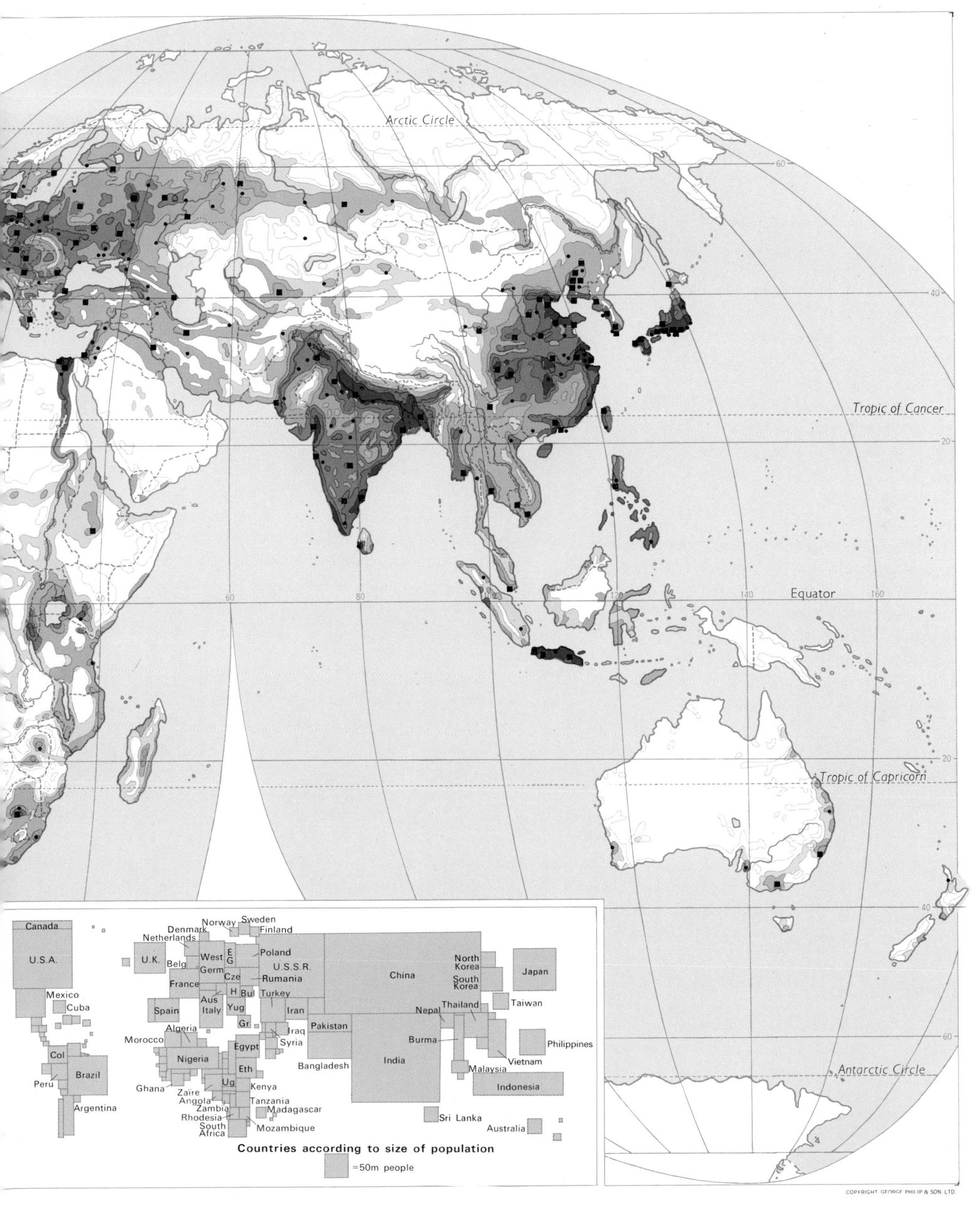

Arctic Circle

Tropic of Cancer

Equator

Tropic of Capricorn

Antarctic Circle

Canada

U.S.A.

Mexico

Cuba

Col

Peru

Brazil

Argentina

Norway Sweden

Denmark Finland

Netherlands

U.K. Poland

Belg West E U.S.S.R.

France Germ G Rumania

Cze H Bul

Spain Aus Yug Turkey

Italy Gr

Morocco Iran

Algeria Iraq

Egypt Syria

Nigeria

Eth

Ghana Ug Kenya

Zaïre

Angola Zambia Tanzania Madagascar

Rhodesia

South Mozambique

Africa

China North Korea Japan

South Korea Taiwan

Nepal Thailand

Pakistan Burma Philippines

India Vietnam

Bangladesh Malaysia

Indonesia

Sri Lanka

Australia

Countries according to size of population

=50m people

Projection: Hammer Equal Area

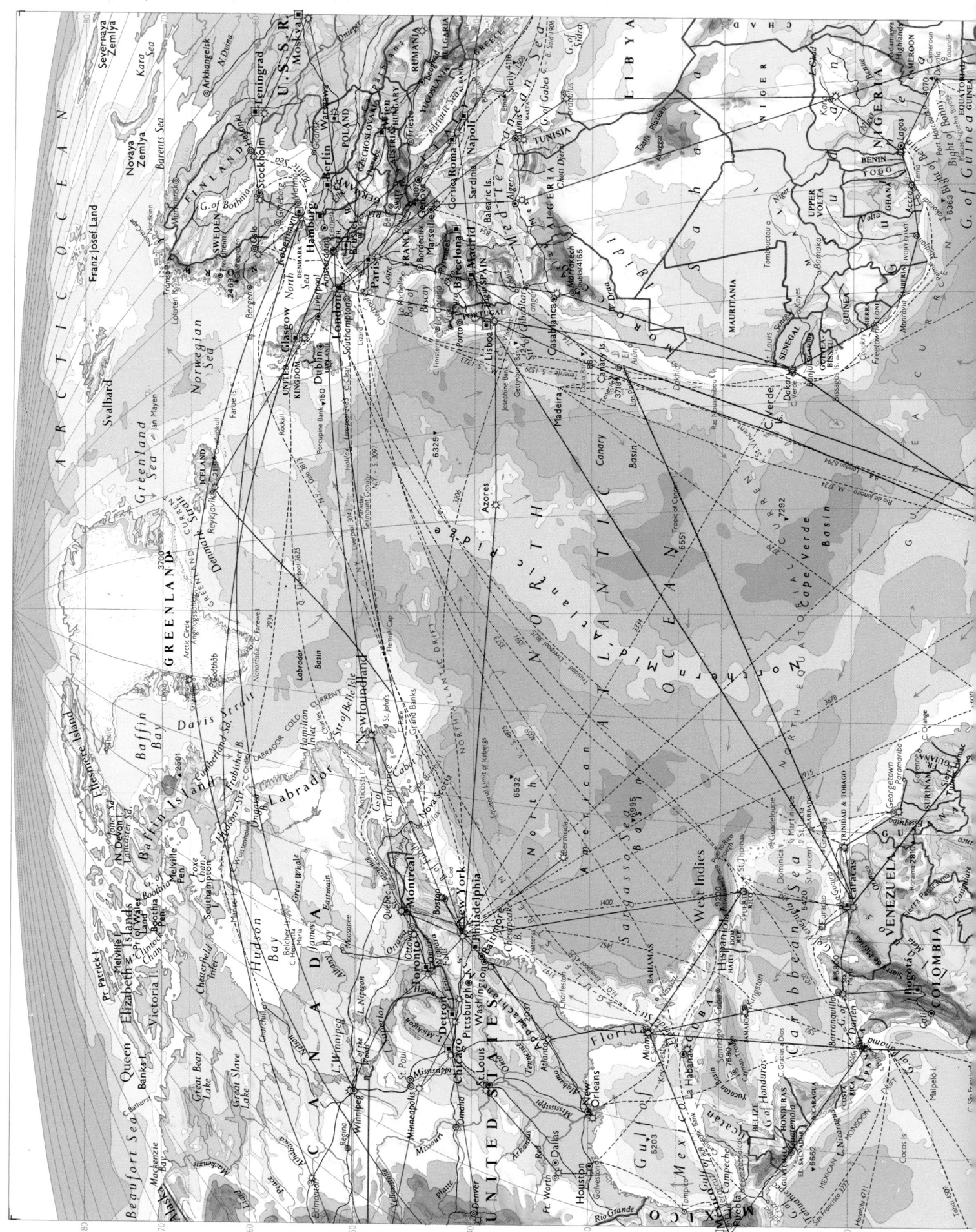

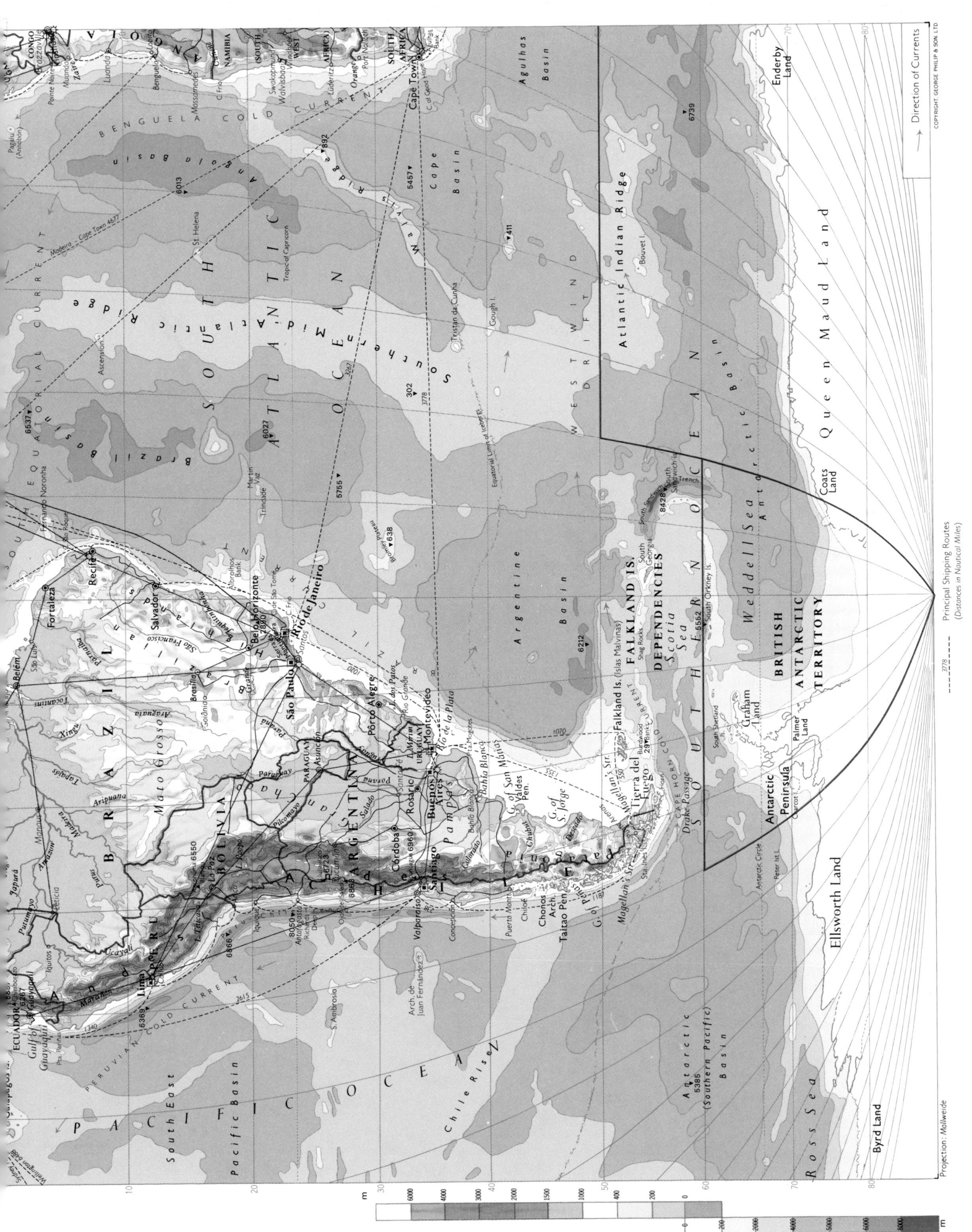

13

1:45 000 000

Projection: Mollweide

Principal Shipping Routes
(Distances in Nautical Miles)

Direction of Currents

COPYRIGHT GEORGE PHILIP & SON LTD

m
6000
4000
3000
2000
1500
1000
400
200
0

0
200
2000
4000
5000
6000
8000
m

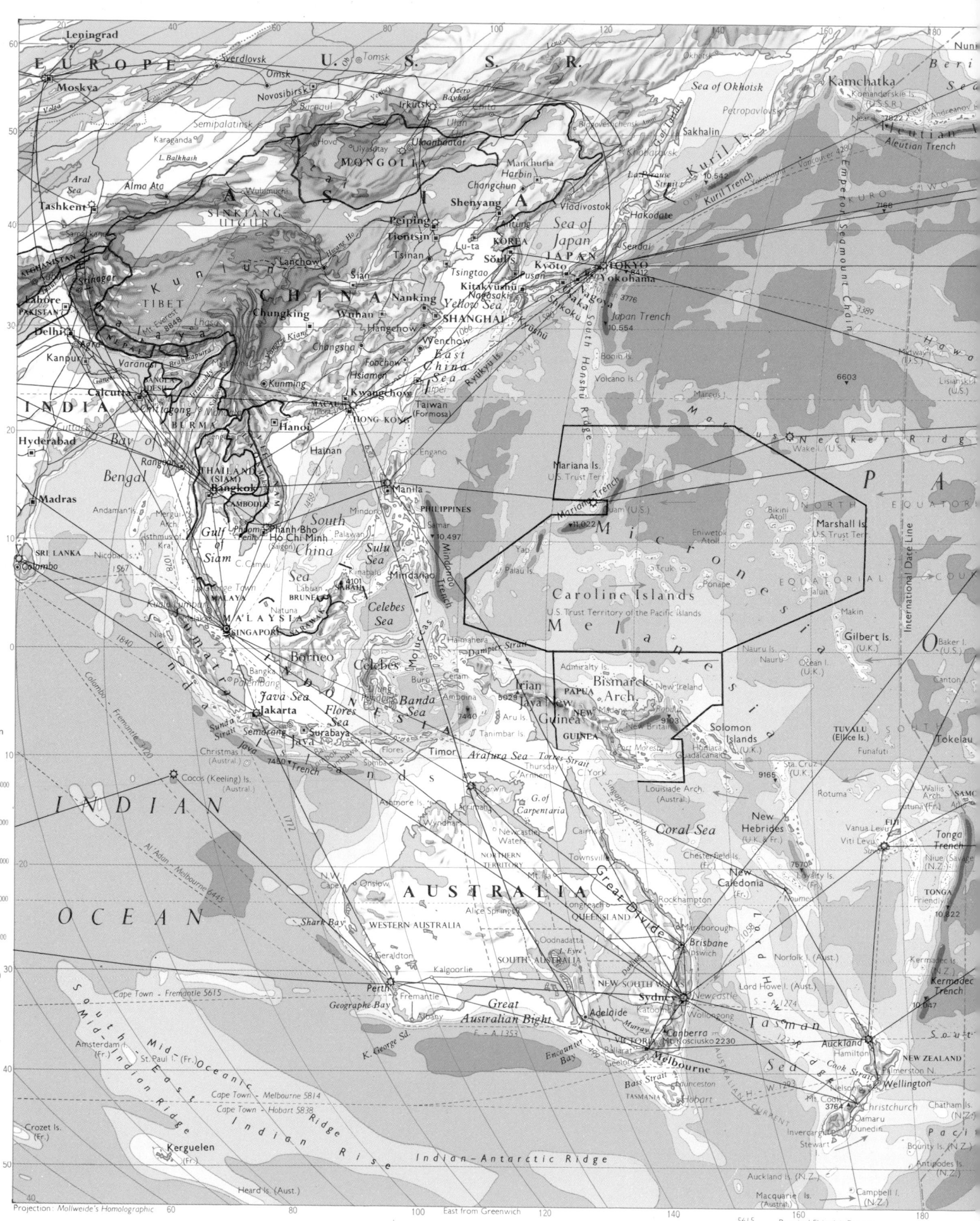

East from Greenwich

- - - - 5615 - - - - Principal Shipping Routes
(Distances in Nautical Miles)

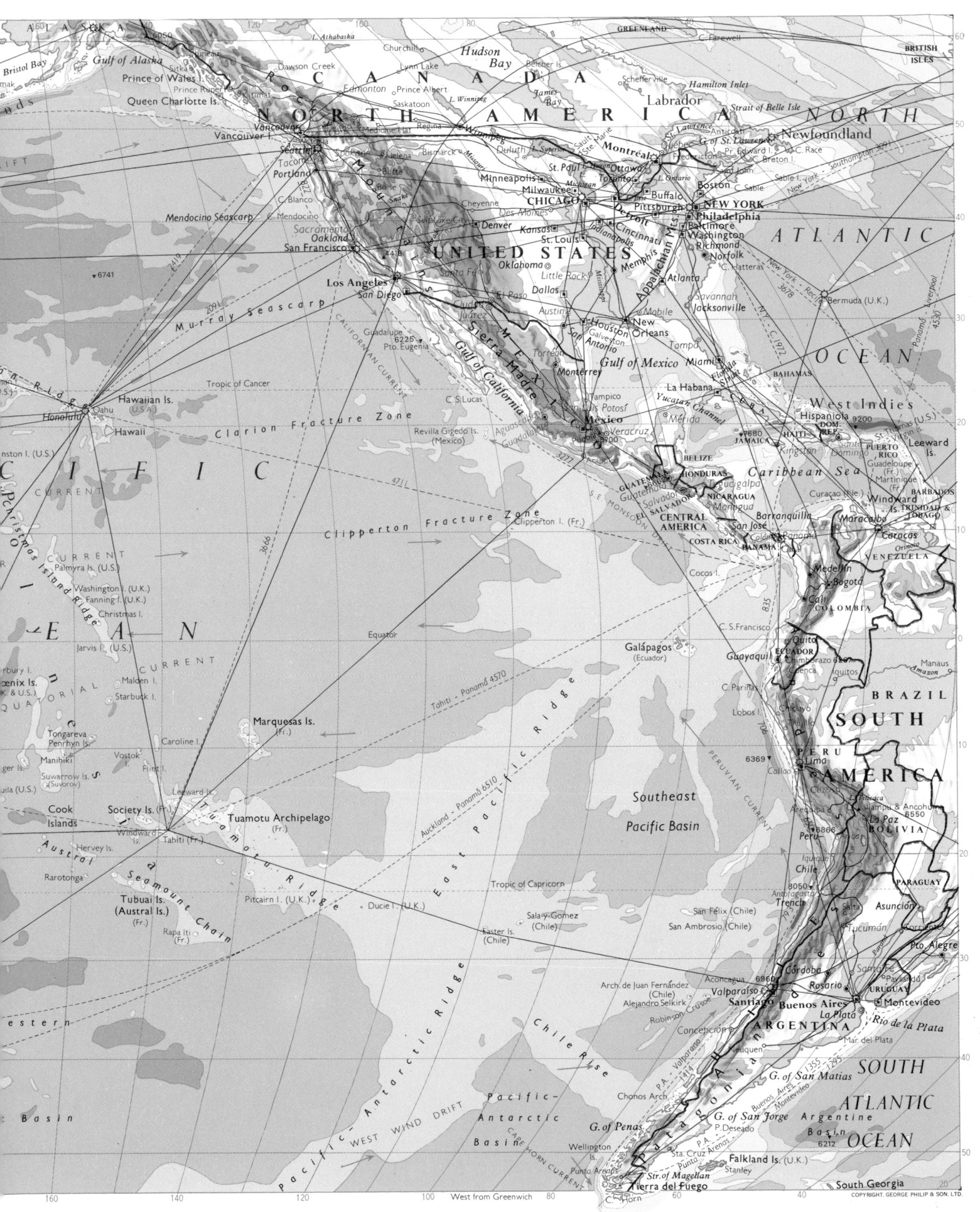

Equatorial Scale 1:50 000 000

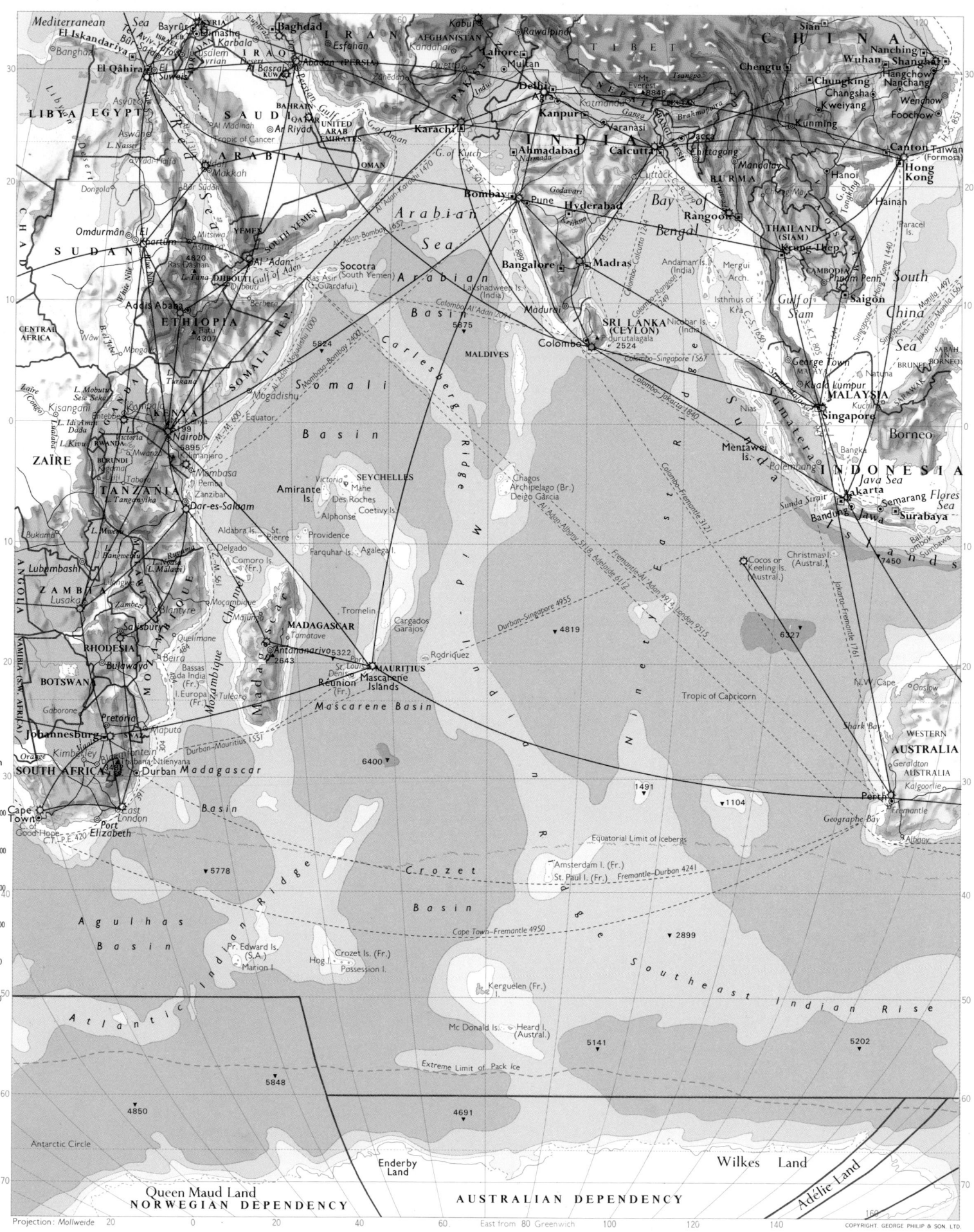

Projection: Mollweide

East from 80 Greenwich

COPYRIGHT GEORGE PHILIP & SON, LTD.

1:35 000 000

400   400   800   1200 km

ARCTIC REGIONS

EUREKA

TEMPERATURE
Range 51.7°C

Eureka
80°00N
85°56W

PRESSURE
M.S.L.

ANNUAL
PRECIPITATION
Total 58.2mm.

J F M A M J J A S O N D

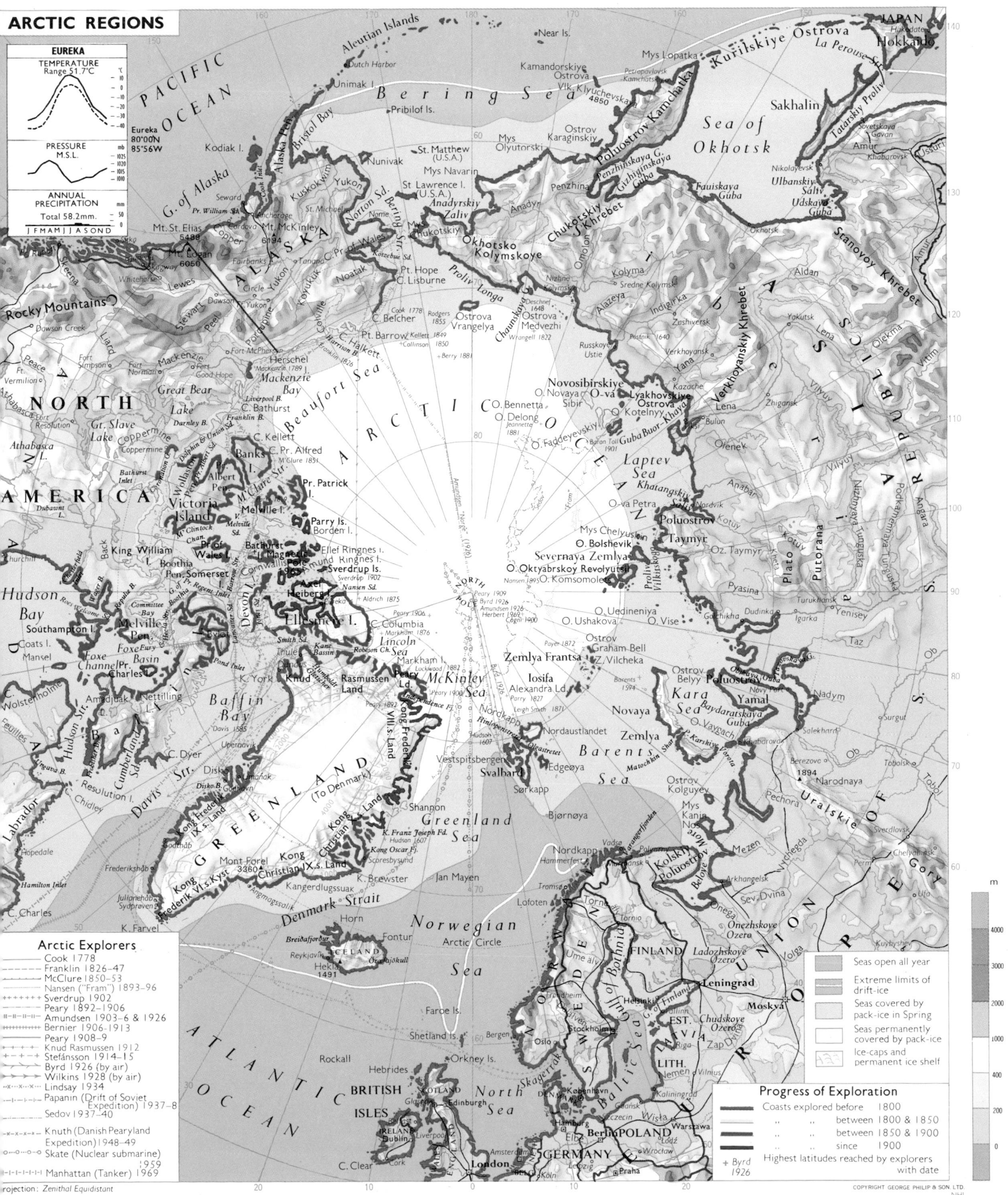

Arctic Explorers

———————— Cook 1778
– – – – – – Franklin 1826–47
················ McClure 1850–53
—·—·—·— Nansen ("Fram") 1893–96
+++++++ Sverdrup 1902
·········· Peary 1892–1906
■–■–■–■ Amundsen 1903–6 & 1926
++++++++ Bernier 1906–1913
———————— Peary 1908–9
+–+–+– Knud Rasmussen 1912
+·+·+·+ Stefánsson 1914–15
——————— Byrd 1926 (by air)
——————— Wilkins 1928 (by air)
—·—·—·— Lindsay 1934
—··—··— Papanin (Drift of Soviet
              Expedition) 1937–8
              Sedov 1937–40

—×—×—×— Knuth (Danish Pearyland
              Expedition) 1948–49
–○–○–○– Skate (Nuclear submarine)
              1959
–│–│–│– Manhattan (Tanker) 1969

Projection: Zenithal Equidistant

m
4000
3000
2000
1000
400
200
0

Seas open all year

Extreme limits of
drift-ice

Seas covered by
pack-ice in Spring

Seas permanently
covered by pack-ice

Ice-caps and
permanent ice shelf

Progress of Exploration

———————— Coasts explored before   1800
————————   „   „   between 1800 & 1850
————————   „   „   between 1850 & 1900
————————   „   „   since   1900
+ Byrd   Highest latitudes reached by explorers
1926   with date

COPYRIGHT GEORGE PHILIP & SON LTD.
NHI

1 : 30 000 000

200 0 200 400 600 800 1000 km

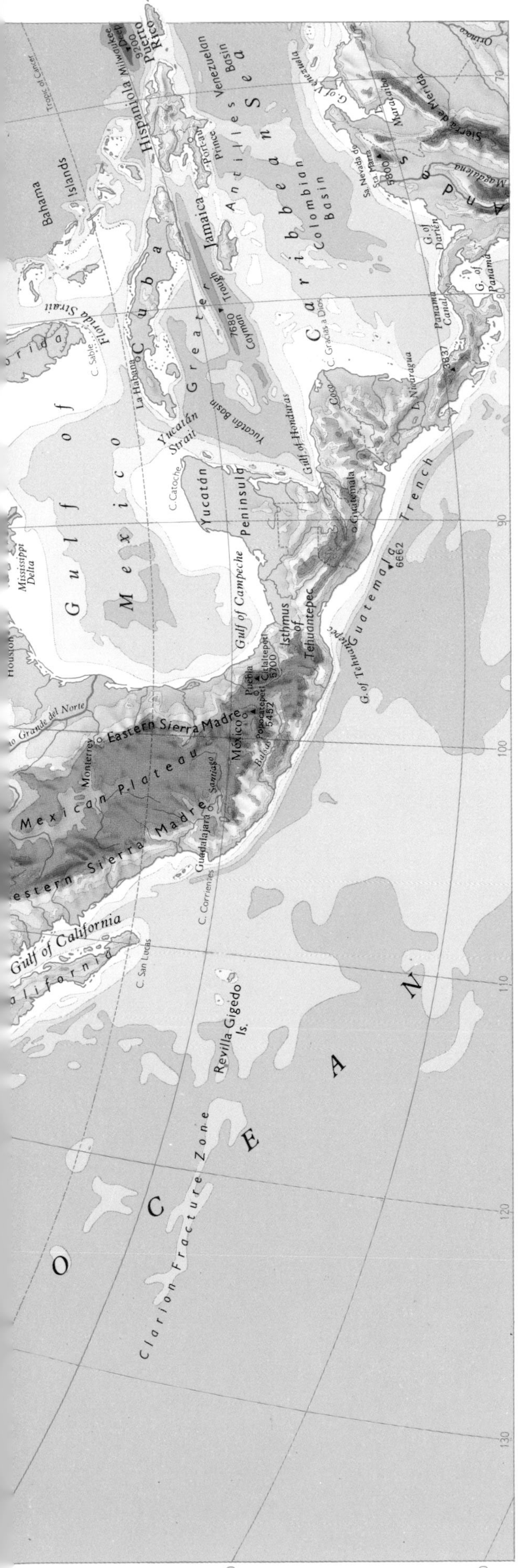

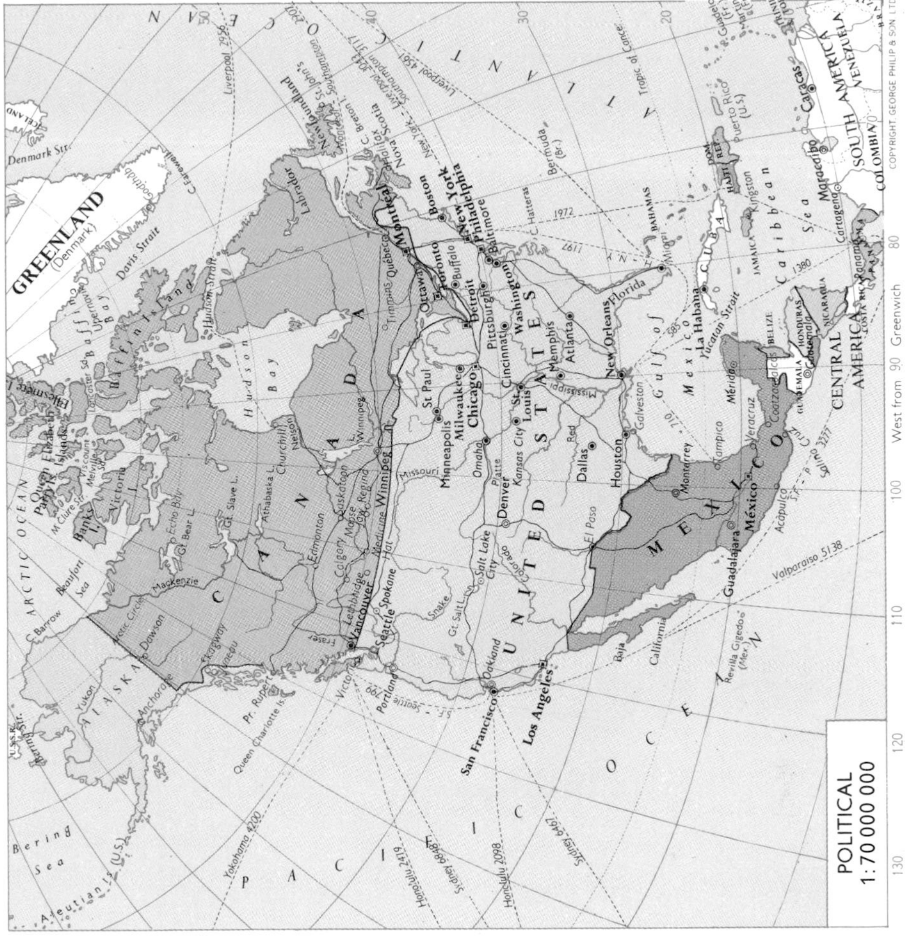

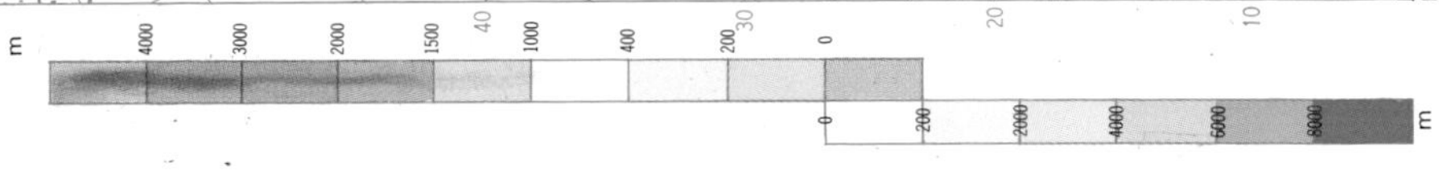

GREENLAND
(Denmark)

Bahama Islands

Puerto Rico

Milwaukee Deep

Hispaniola

Cuba

La Habana

Jamaica

Greater Antilles

Caribbean Sea

Prince Venezuelan Basin

Sierra de Perija

Colombian Basin

Yucatán Strait

Yucatán Basin

Yucatán Peninsula

C. Catoche

Gulf of Honduras

Gulf of Campeche

Guatemala

Gulf of **Mexico**

Mississippi Delta

Houston

Isthmus of Tehuantepec

G. of Tehuantepec

Eastern Sierra Madre

Monterrey

México

Mexican Plateau

Western Sierra Madre

Guadalajara

Gulf of California

Baja California

C. San Lucas

C. Corrientes

Revilla Gigedo Is.

Clarion Fracture Zone

P A C I F I C   O C E A N

CANADA

Labrador

Newfoundland

Hudson Bay

Quebec

Ottawa

Montreal

Toronto

Buffalo

Detroit

Boston

New York

Philadelphia

Baltimore

Washington

Pittsburgh

Cincinnati

Atlanta

Florida

Memphis

New Orleans

St Louis

Chicago

Milwaukee

St Paul

Minneapolis

Omaha

Kansas City

Denver

Salt Lake City

Winnipeg

Edmonton

Calgary

Vancouver

Seattle

Spokane

Portland

San Francisco

Los Angeles

El Paso

Dallas

Houston

Monterrey

Guadalajara

México

Veracruz

Mérida

MEXICO

UNITED STATES

Gulf of Mexico

La Habana

Yucatan Channel

Caribbean Sea

CENTRAL AMERICA

SOUTH AMERICA

Caracas

Maracaibo

VENEZUELA

COLOMBIA

ALASKA (U.S.)

Bering Sea

Aleutian Is.

ARCTIC OCEAN

Barrow

Beaufort Sea

Mackenzie

Victoria I.

Banks I.

Baffin Island

Davis Strait

Denmark Str.

COPYRIGHT GEORGE PHILIP & SON LTD

POLITICAL
1 : 70 000 000

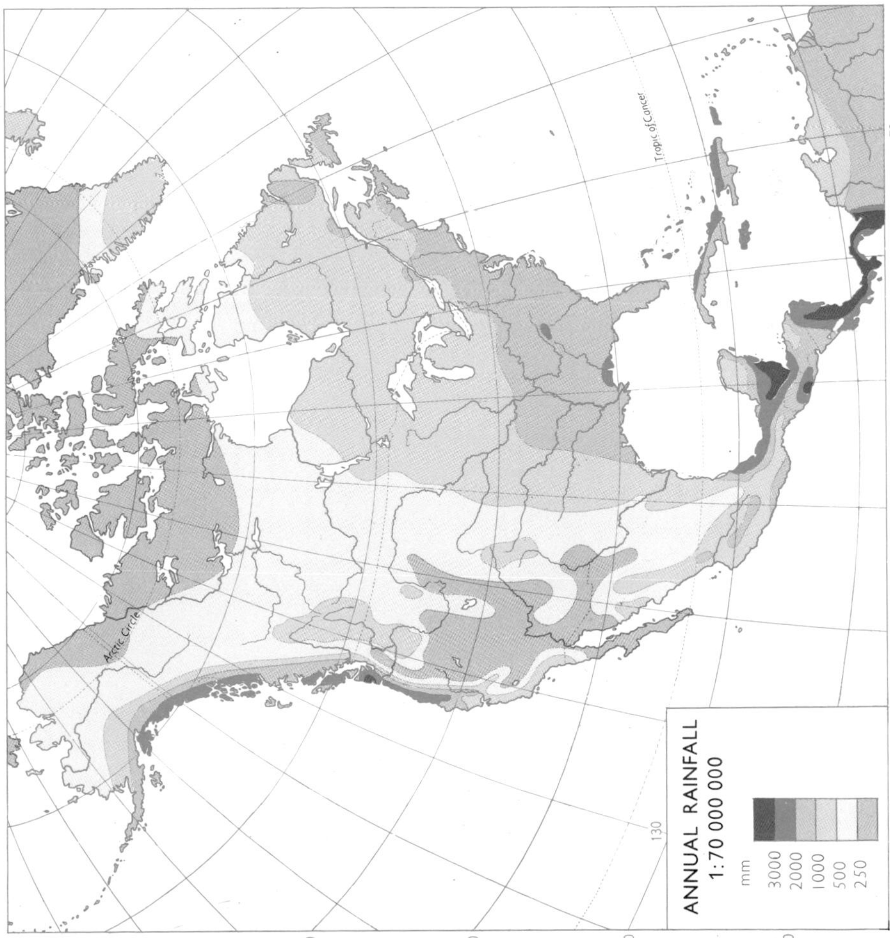

West from 90 Greenwich

ANNUAL RAINFALL
1 : 70 000 000

mm
3000
2000
1000
500
250

Projection: Bonne

West from 90 Greenwich

Tropic of Cancer

m
4000 3000 2000 1500 1000 400 200 0

0 200 4000 6000 m

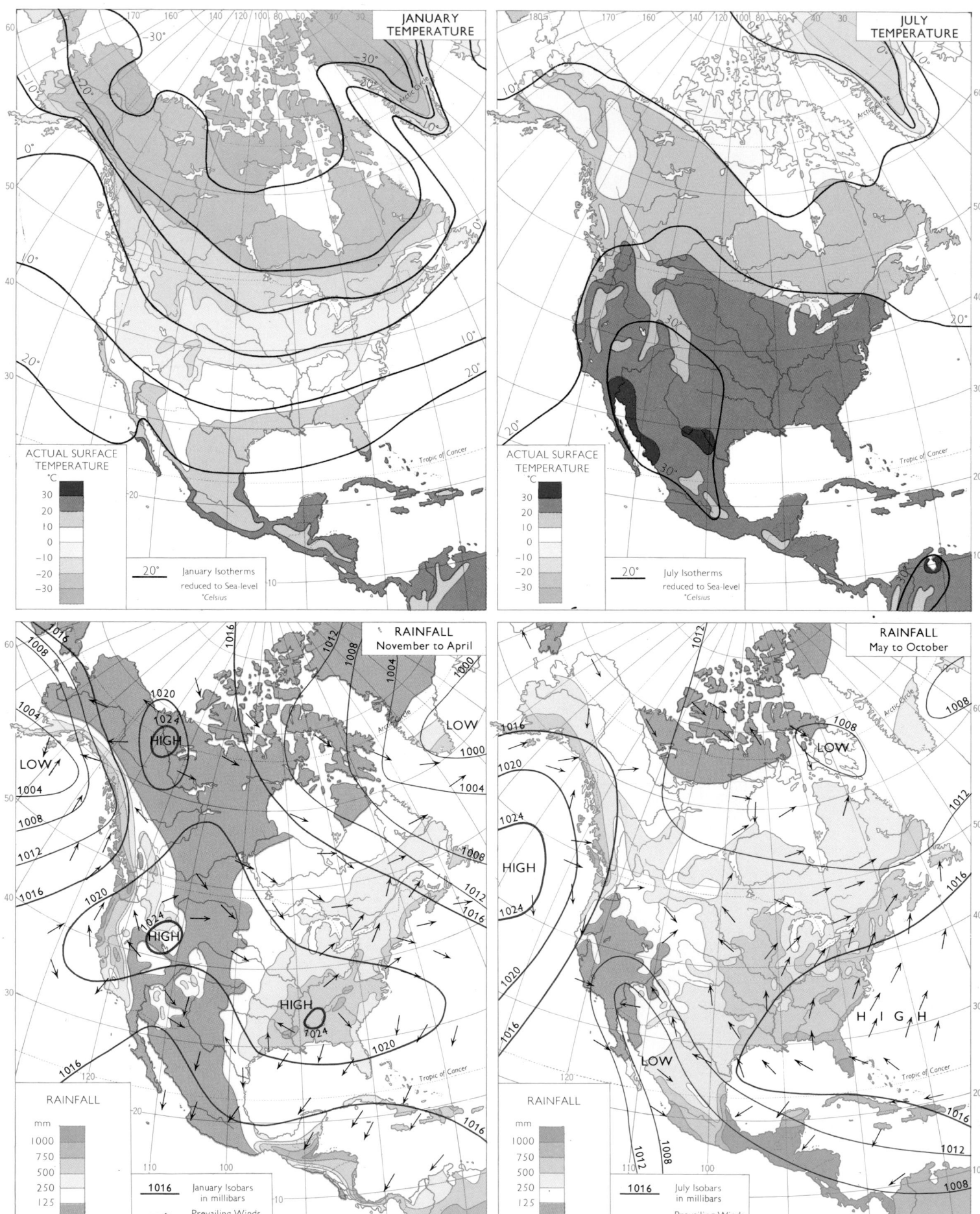

1 : 70 000 000

500   0   500   1000   1500   2000   2500 km

JANUARY TEMPERATURE

JULY TEMPERATURE

ACTUAL SURFACE TEMPERATURE
°C
30
20
10
0
-10
-20
-30

Tropic of Cancer

20°   January Isotherms
reduced to Sea-level
°Celsius

ACTUAL SURFACE TEMPERATURE
°C
30
20
10
0
-10
-20
-30

Tropic of Cancer

20°   July Isotherms
reduced to Sea-level
°Celsius

RAINFALL
November to April

LOW

HIGH

LOW

HIGH

HIGH

Tropic of Cancer

RAINFALL
mm
1000
750
500
250
125

1016   January Isobars
in millibars
⟶   Prevailing Winds

RAINFALL
May to October

LOW

HIGH

LOW

H I G H

Tropic of Cancer

RAINFALL
mm
1000
750
500
250
125

1016   July Isobars
in millibars
⟶   Prevailing Winds

Projection: Lambert's Equivalent Azimuthal   West from 70 Greenwich   COPYRIGHT. GEORGE PHILIP & SON. LTD

1 : 32 000 000

100 0 400 800 1200 km

Projection: Polyconic

West from Greenwich

Tropic of Cancer

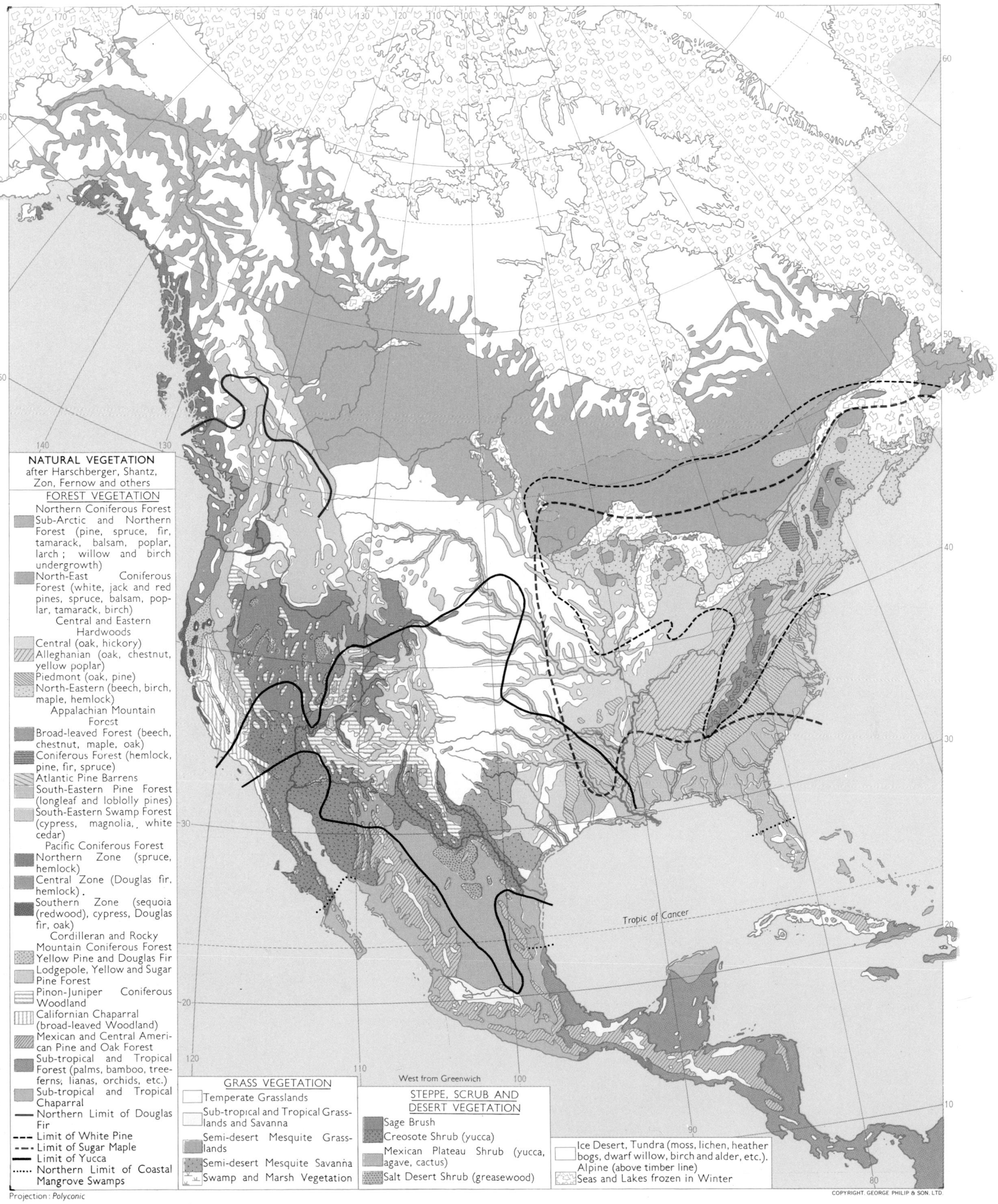

NATURAL VEGETATION
after Harschberger, Shantz,
Zon, Fernow and others

FOREST VEGETATION
Northern Coniferous Forest
Sub-Arctic and Northern
Forest (pine, spruce, fir,
tamarack, balsam, poplar,
larch ; willow and birch
undergrowth)
North-East   Coniferous
Forest (white, jack and red
pines, spruce, balsam, pop-
lar, tamarack, birch)
Central and Eastern
Hardwoods
Central (oak, hickory)
Alleghanian (oak, chestnut,
yellow poplar)
Piedmont (oak, pine)
North-Eastern (beech, birch,
maple, hemlock)
Appalachian Mountain
Forest
Broad-leaved Forest (beech,
chestnut, maple, oak)
Coniferous Forest (hemlock,
pine, fir, spruce)
Atlantic Pine Barrens
South-Eastern Pine Forest
(longleaf and loblolly pines)
South-Eastern Swamp Forest
(cypress, magnolia, white
cedar)
Pacific Coniferous Forest
Northern Zone (spruce,
hemlock)
Central Zone (Douglas fir,
hemlock)
Southern Zone (sequoia
(redwood), cypress, Douglas
fir, oak)
Cordilleran and Rocky
Mountain Coniferous Forest
Yellow Pine and Douglas Fir
Lodgepole, Yellow and Sugar
Pine Forest
Pinon-Juniper   Coniferous
Woodland
Californian Chaparral
(broad-leaved Woodland)
Mexican and Central Ameri-
can Pine and Oak Forest
Sub-tropical and Tropical
Forest (palms, bamboo, tree-
ferns, lianas, orchids, etc.)
Sub-tropical and Tropical
Chaparral
—— Northern Limit of Douglas
Fir
--- Limit of White Pine
—·— Limit of Sugar Maple
—— Limit of Yucca
······ Northern Limit of Coastal
Mangrove Swamps

GRASS VEGETATION
Temperate Grasslands
Sub-tropical and Tropical Grass-
lands and Savanna
Semi-desert Mesquite Grass-
lands
Semi-desert Mesquite Savanna
Swamp and Marsh Vegetation

STEPPE, SCRUB AND
DESERT VEGETATION
Sage Brush
Creosote Shrub (yucca)
Mexican Plateau Shrub (yucca,
agave, cactus)
Salt Desert Shrub (greasewood)

Ice Desert, Tundra (moss, lichen, heather
bogs, dwarf willow, birch and alder, etc.).
Alpine (above timber line)
Seas and Lakes frozen in Winter

West from Greenwich

1:17 500 000

200   0   200   400   600 km

GEOLOGY
1:35 000 000

IGNEOUS AND PLUTONIC ROCKS

Volcano
Carbonatite and syenite intrusion
Ultrabasic intrusion
Fault
Thrust

Acidic rocks
Basic rocks
Anorthosite
Granitic gneiss
Granulite
Gabbro dyke

SEDIMENTARY AND VOLCANIC ROCKS   Time Scale

Period	Era	(million years)
Cenozoic	Tertiary	2·5–65
Mesozoic	Secondary	65–225
Cretaceous		
Paleozoic	Primary	225–570
Late Paleozoic		
Devonian		
Early Paleozoic		
Proterozoic and Paleozoic		
Proterozoic	Precambrian	570–300
Hadrynian		
Helikian		
Neohelikian		
Paleohelikian		
Aphebian		
Archean		

Based on the Atlas of Canada

1 : 30 000 000

200   0   200   400   600   800   1000 km

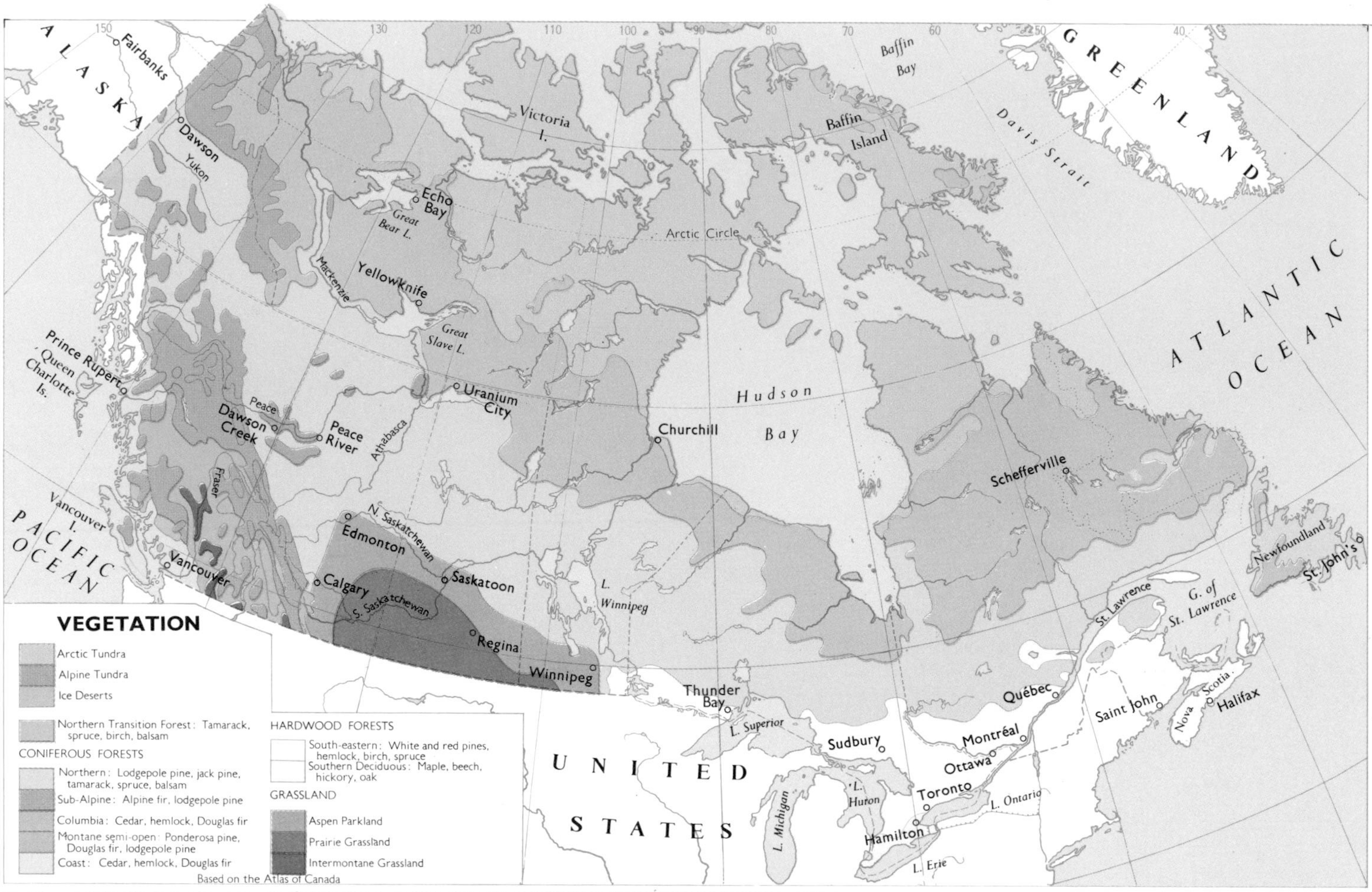

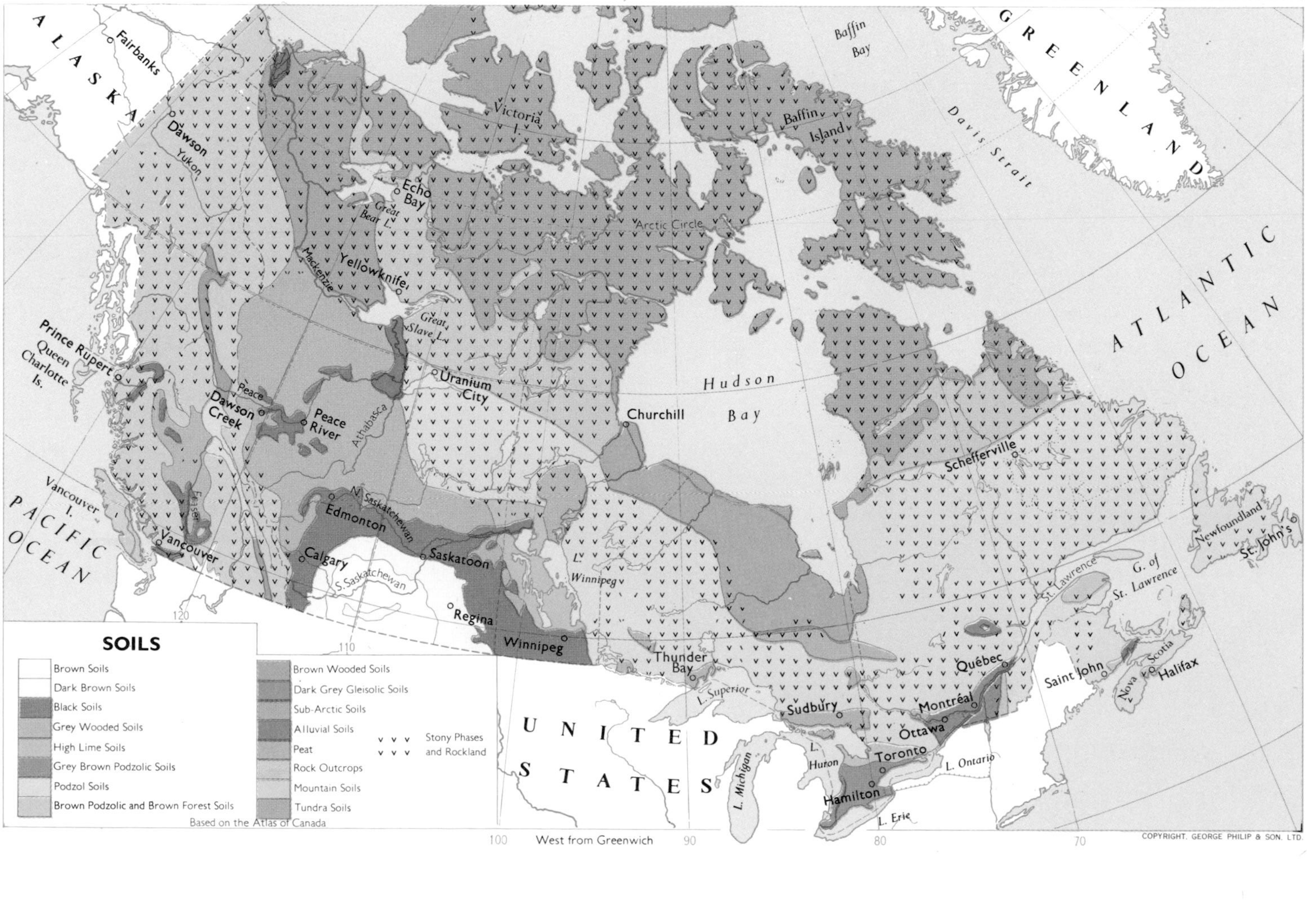

VEGETATION

Arctic Tundra

Alpine Tundra

Ice Deserts

Northern Transition Forest: Tamarack, spruce, birch, balsam

CONIFEROUS FORESTS

Northern: Lodgepole pine, jack pine, tamarack, spruce, balsam

Sub-Alpine: Alpine fir, lodgepole pine

Columbia: Cedar, hemlock, Douglas fir

Montane semi-open: Ponderosa pine, Douglas fir, lodgepole pine

Coast: Cedar, hemlock, Douglas fir

HARDWOOD FORESTS

South-eastern: White and red pines, hemlock, birch, spruce

Southern Deciduous: Maple, beech, hickory, oak

GRASSLAND

Aspen Parkland

Prairie Grassland

Intermontane Grassland

Based on the Atlas of Canada

SOILS

Brown Soils

Dark Brown Soils

Black Soils

Grey Wooded Soils

High Lime Soils

Grey Brown Podzolic Soils

Podzol Soils

Brown Podzolic and Brown Forest Soils

Brown Wooded Soils

Dark Grey Gleisolic Soils

Sub-Arctic Soils

Alluvial Soils

Peat

Rock Outcrops

Mountain Soils

Tundra Soils

v v v   Stony Phases
v v v   and Rockland

Based on the Atlas of Canada

West from Greenwich

COPYRIGHT. GEORGE PHILIP & SON, LTD.

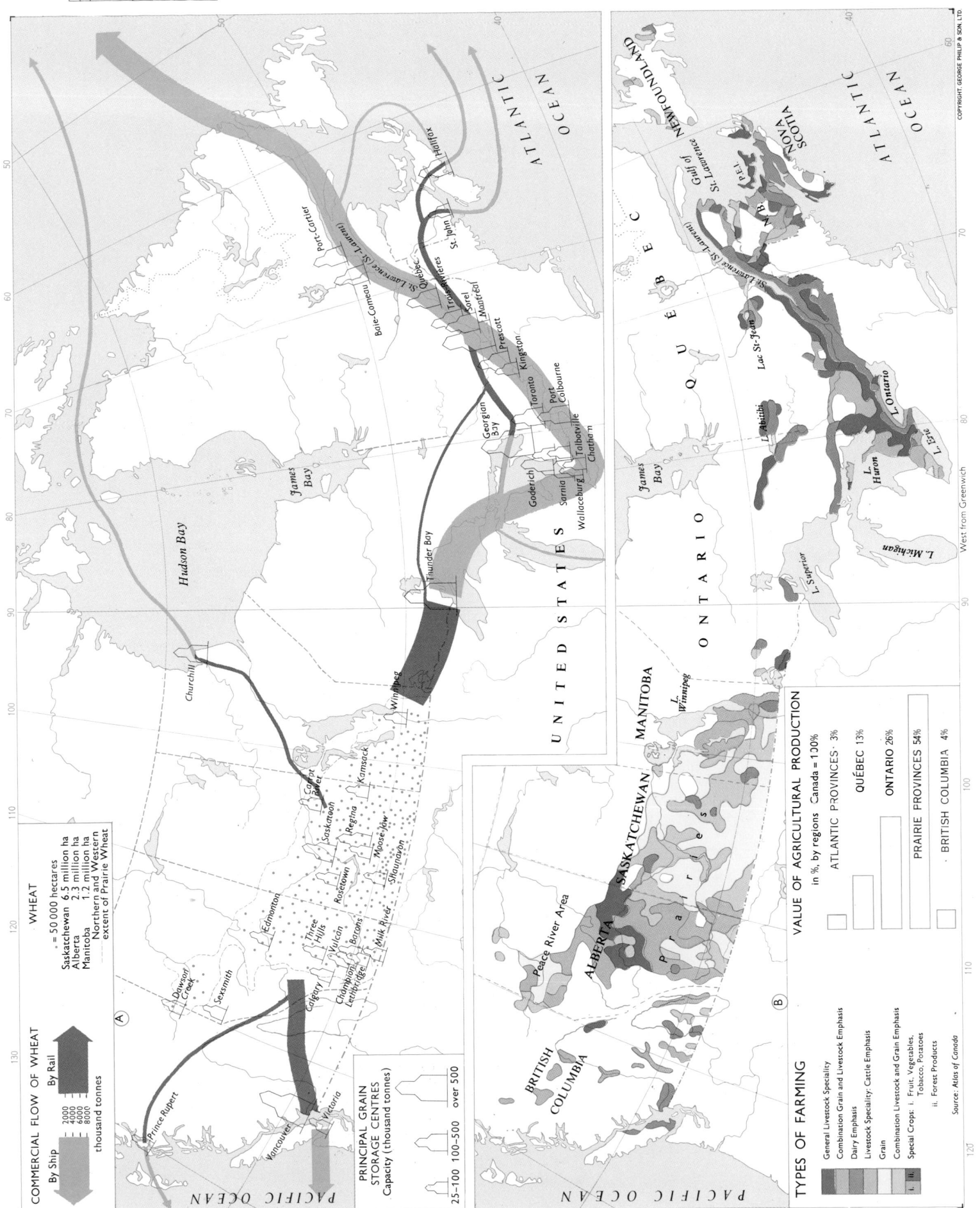

1 : 22 500 000

100 0   200   400   600 km

COMMERCIAL FLOW OF WHEAT

By Rail

By Ship

thousand tonnes

2000
4000
6000
8000

WHEAT

• = 50 000 hectares

Saskatchewan 6.5 million ha
Alberta   2.3 million ha
Manitoba   1.2 million ha
Northern and Western
extent of Prairie Wheat

PRINCIPAL GRAIN
STORAGE CENTRES
Capacity (thousand tonnes)

over 500

100–500

25–100

A

Hudson Bay

James Bay

Churchill

Port-Cartier

Baie-Comeau

St. Lawrence (S¹-Laurent)

Québec

Trois-Rivières

Sorel

Montréal

Prescott

Kingston

Toronto

Port Colbourne

Georgian Bay

Talbotville

Chatham

Goderich

Sarnia

Wallaceburg

Thunder Bay

Winnipeg

Carrot River

Kamsack

Saskatoon

Regina

Moose Jaw

Rosetown

Shaunavon

Edmonton

Three Hills

Vulcan

Botons

Milk River

Champion

Lethbridge

Calgary

Dawson Creek

Sexsmith

Prince Rupert

Vancouver

Victoria

PACIFIC OCEAN

ATLANTIC
OCEAN

Halifax

St. John

UNITED STATES

VALUE OF AGRICULTURAL PRODUCTION

in %, by regions   Canada = 100%

ATLANTIC PROVINCES· 3%

QUÉBEC 13%

ONTARIO 26%

PRAIRIE PROVINCES 54%

· BRITISH COLUMBIA 4%

TYPES OF FARMING

General Livestock Speciality

Combination Grain and Livestock Emphasis

Dairy Emphasis

Livestock Speciality: Cattle Emphasis

Grain

Combination Livestock and Grain Emphasis

Special Crops: i. Fruit, Vegetables,
               Tobacco, Potatoes
             ii. Forest Products

Source: Atlas of Canada

B

NEWFOUNDLAND

NOVA
SCOTIA

N.B.

P.E.I.

Gulf of
St. Lawrence

QUÉBEC

St. Lawrence (S¹-Laurent)

Lac St-Jean

L. Abitibi

ONTARIO

L. Ontario

L. Erie

L. Huron

L. Michigan

L. Superior

James
Bay

ATLANTIC

OCEAN

West from Greenwich

MANITOBA

L. Winnipeg

SASKATCHEWAN

ALBERTA

Peace River Area

Prairies

BRITISH
COLUMBIA

PACIFIC OCEAN

ATLANTIC

OCEAN

1:22 000 000

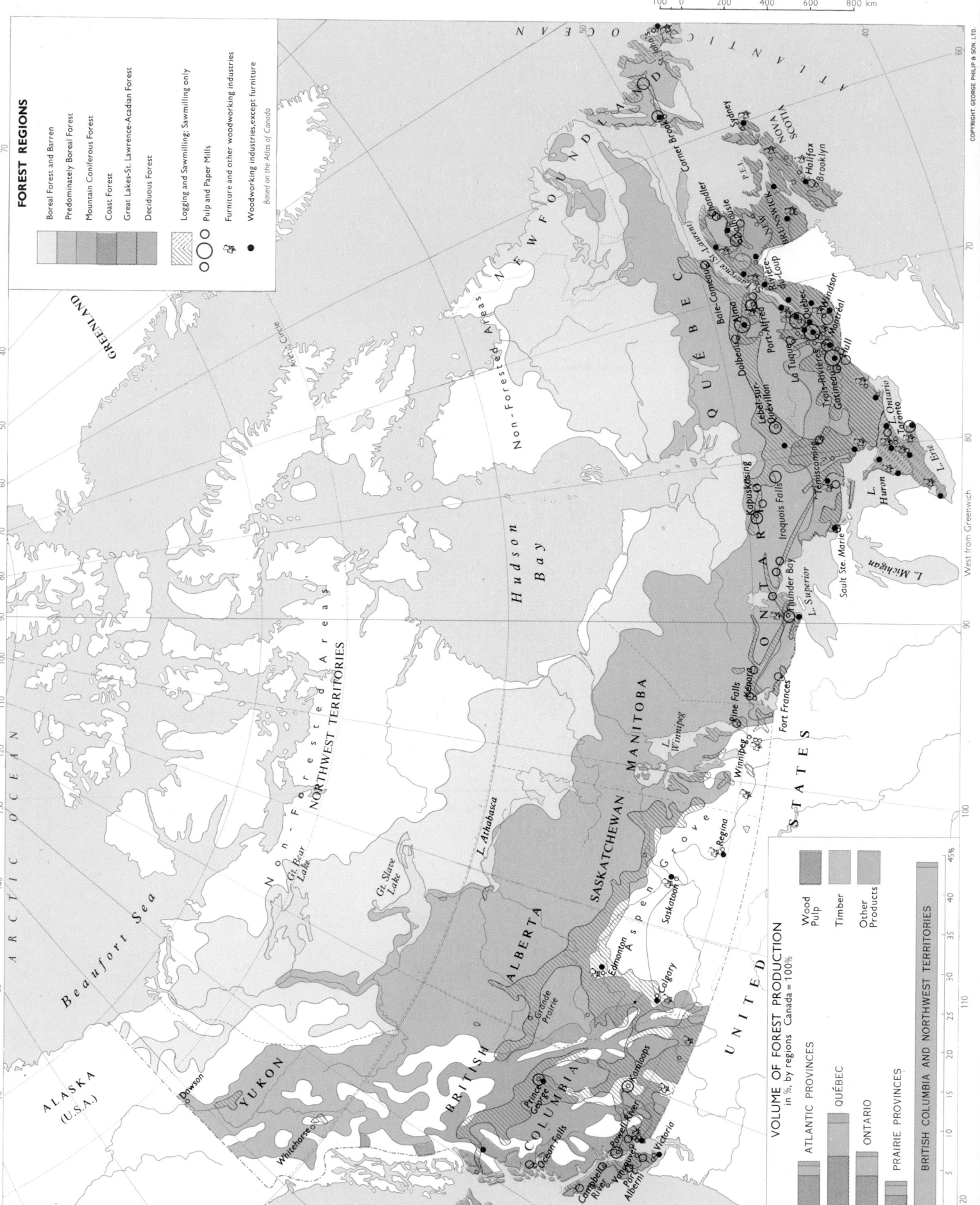

FOREST REGIONS

Boreal Forest and Barren
Predominately Boreal Forest
Mountain Coniferous Forest
Coast Forest
Great Lakes-St. Lawrence-Acadian Forest
Deciduous Forest

Logging and Sawmilling: Sawmilling only
Pulp and Paper Mills
Furniture and other woodworking industries
Woodworking industries, except furniture

Based on the Atlas of Canada

VOLUME OF FOREST PRODUCTION
in % by regions Canada = 100%

Wood Pulp
Timber
Other Products

ATLANTIC PROVINCES
QUÉBEC
ONTARIO
PRAIRIE PROVINCES
BRITISH COLUMBIA AND NORTHWEST TERRITORIES

COPYRIGHT GEORGE PHILIP & SON, LTD.

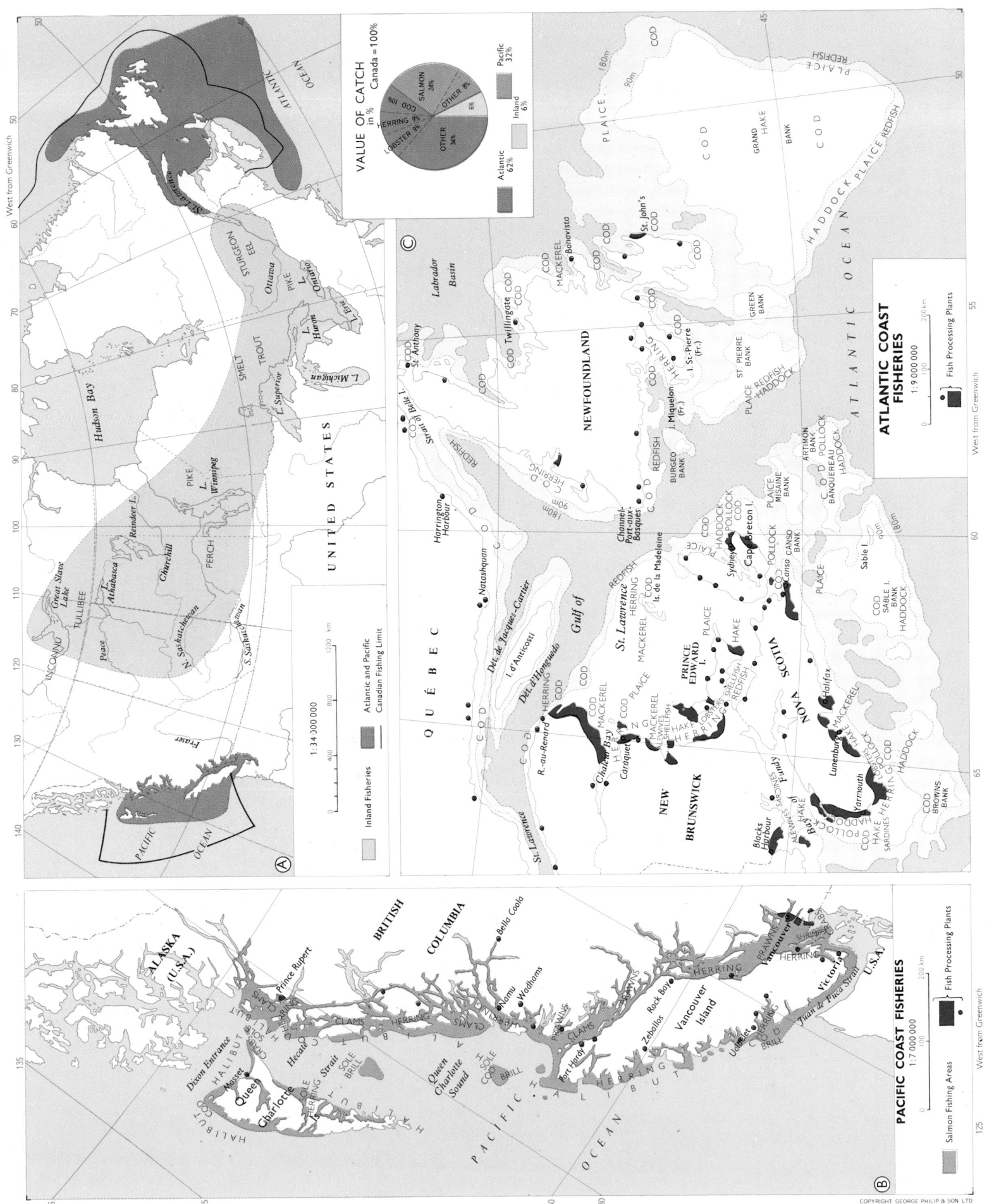

VALUE OF CATCH
in %
Canada = 100%

SALMON 24%
OTHER 6%
COD 10%
HERRING 9%
LOBSTER 9%
OTHER 34%

Pacific 32%
Inland 6%
Atlantic 62%

A
1:34 300 000

Inland Fisheries

Atlantic and Pacific
Canadian Fishing Limit

©
ATLANTIC COAST FISHERIES
1:9 000 000

Fish Processing Plants

B
PACIFIC COAST FISHERIES
1:7 000 000

Salmon Fishing Areas

Fish Processing Plants

COPYRIGHT GEORGE PHILIP & SON LTD

1:22 000 000

100 0 200 400 600 800 km

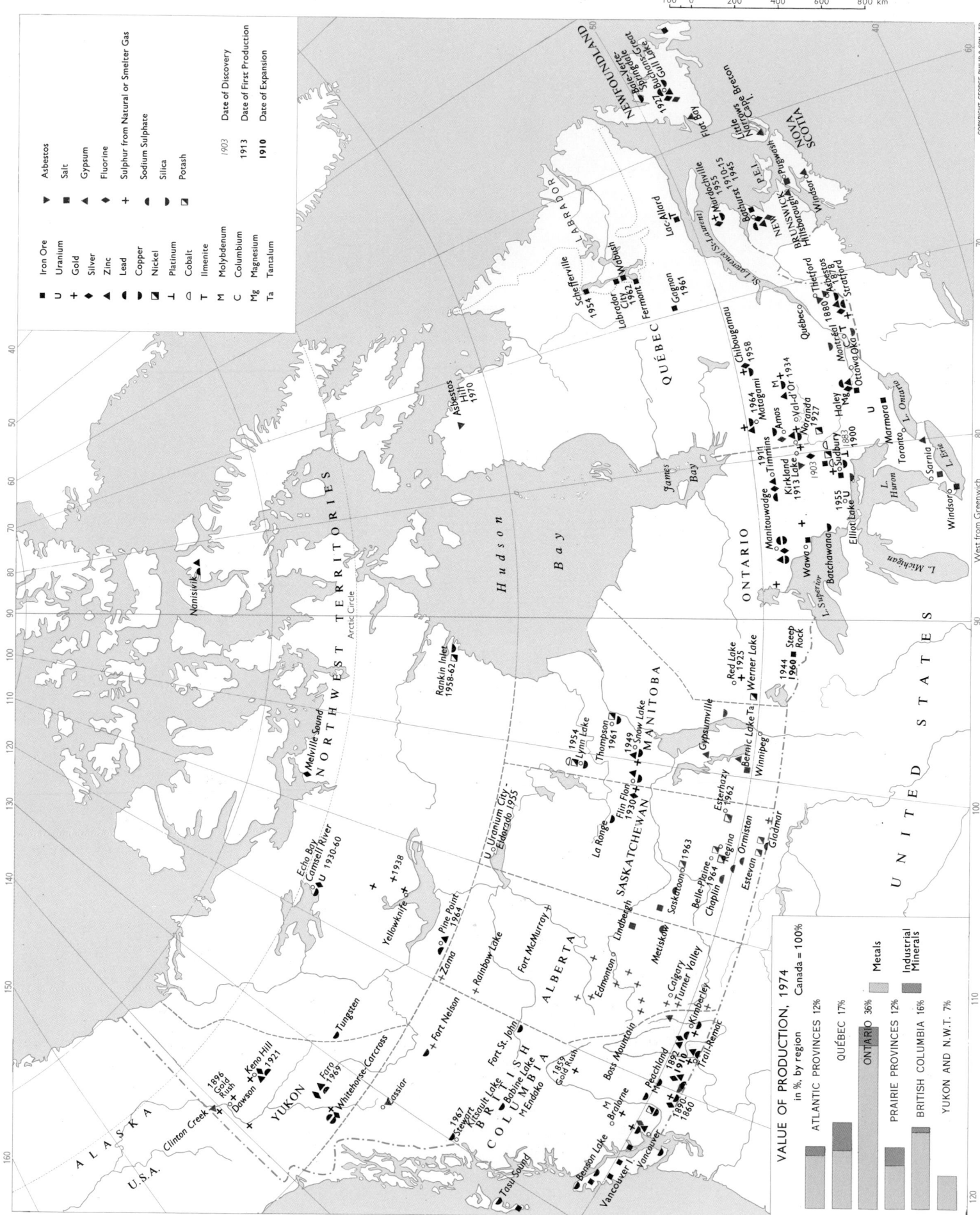

▶	Asbestos	
∪	Salt	
◀	Gypsum	
◆	Fluorine	
+	Sulphur from Natural or Smelter Gas	
◖	Sodium Sulphate	
◗	Silica	
◰	Potash	

1903 Date of Discovery
1913 Date of First Production
1910 Date of Expansion

■	Iron Ore	
∪	Uranium	
◆	Gold	
◀	Silver	
◖	Zinc	
◰	Lead	
⊥	Copper	
◗	Nickel	
◖	Platinum	
M	Cobalt	
C	Ilmenite	
T	Molybdenum	
	Columbium	
Mg	Magnesium	
Ta	Tantalum	

COPYRIGHT GEORGE PHILIP & SON LTD.

West from Greenwich

VALUE OF PRODUCTION, 1974
in %, by region Canada = 100%

Metals

Industrial
Minerals

ATLANTIC PROVINCES 12%
QUÉBEC 17%
ONTARIO 36%
PRAIRIE PROVINCES 12%
BRITISH COLUMBIA 16%
YUKON AND N.W.T. 7%

1:22 000 000

100 0 200 400 600 800 km

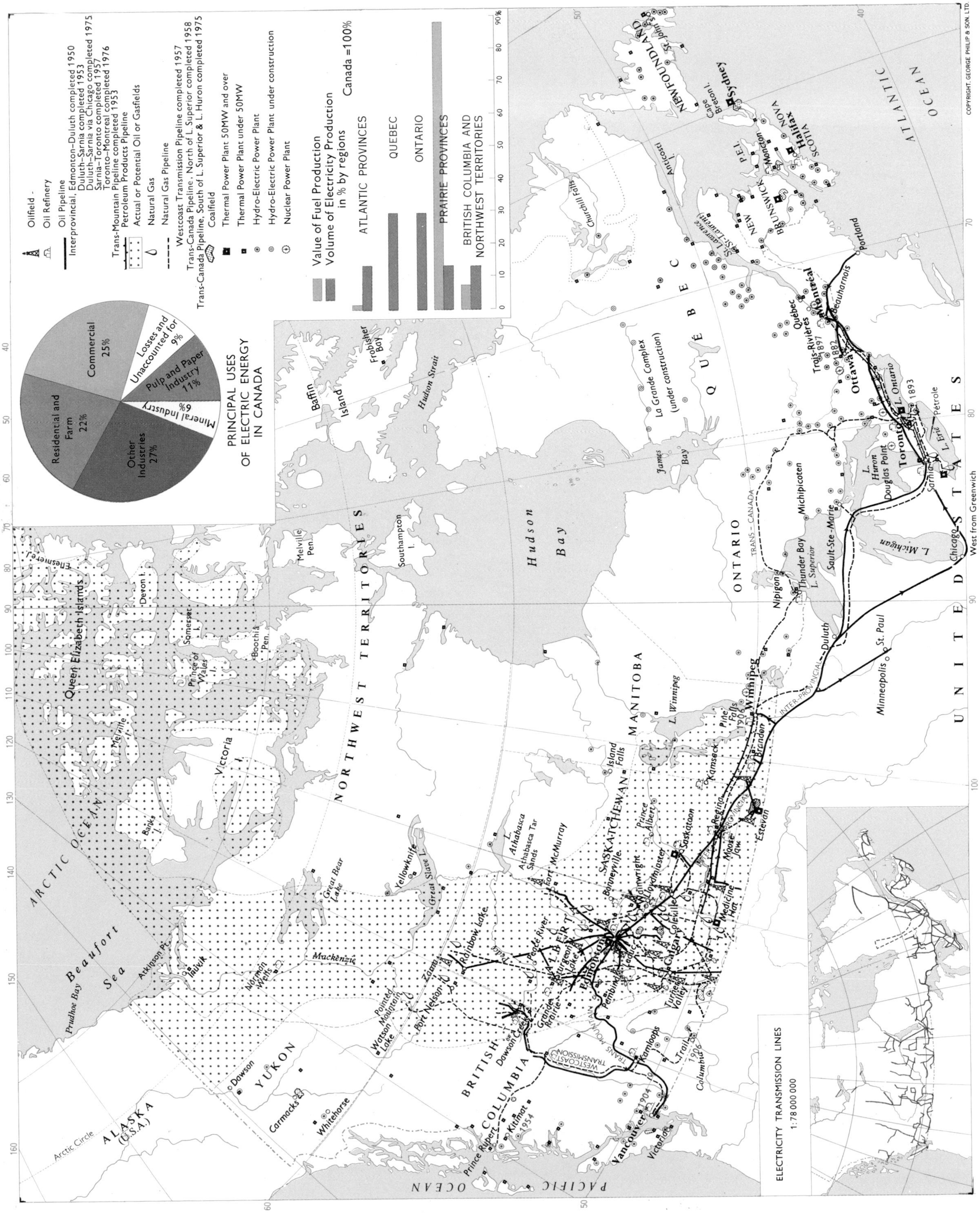

Legend:

- Oilfield
- Oil Refinery
- Oil Pipeline
- Interprovincial, Edmonton–Duluth completed 1950
  Duluth–Sarnia completed 1953
  Duluth–Sarnia via Chicago completed 1975
  Sarnia–Toronto completed 1957
  Toronto–Montreal completed 1976
- Petroleum Products Pipeline
- Trans-Mountain Pipeline completed 1953
- Actual or Potential Oil or Gasfields
- Natural Gas
- Natural Gas Pipeline
- Westcoast Transmission Pipeline completed 1957
- Trans-Canada Pipeline, North of L. Superior completed 1958
- Trans-Canada Pipeline, South of L. Superior & L. Huron completed 1975
- Coalfield
- Thermal Power Plant 50MW and over
- Thermal Power Plant under 50MW
- Hydro-Electric Power Plant
- Hydro-Electric Power Plant under construction
- Nuclear Power Plant

Value of Fuel Production
Volume of Electricity Production
in % by regions   Canada =100%

ATLANTIC PROVINCES
QUEBEC
ONTARIO
PRAIRIE PROVINCES
BRITISH COLUMBIA AND NORTHWEST TERRITORIES

PRINCIPAL USES OF ELECTRIC ENERGY IN CANADA

- Commercial 25%
- Losses and Unaccounted for 9%
- Pulp and Paper Industry 11%
- Mineral Industry 6%
- Other Industries 27%
- Residential and Farm 22%

COPYRIGHT GEORGE PHILIP & SON LTD.

Map labels:

ATLANTIC OCEAN
NEWFOUNDLAND
St. John's
Cape Breton I.
Sydney
NOVA SCOTIA
Halifax
P.E.I.
Moncton
NEW BRUNSWICK
Anticosti
Churchill Falls
Frobisher Bay
Baffin Island
Hudson Strait
Hudson Bay
James Bay
La Grande Complex (under construction)
QUEBEC
Québec
Trois-Rivières
Montréal
Beauharnois
Ottawa
Portland
Toronto
L. Ontario
Sarnia
Pte. au Petrole
L. Erie
Chicago
L. Michigan
Douglas Point
L. Huron
Sault-Ste-Marie
Michipicoten
Thunder Bay
L. Superior
Nipigon
ONTARIO
TRANS–CANADA
Duluth
St. Paul
Minneapolis
UNITED STATES
West from Greenwich

Melville Pen.
Southampton I.
Devon I.
Ellesmere I.
Queen Elizabeth Islands
Melville I.
Somerset I.
Prince of Wales I.
Boothia Pen.
Victoria I.
NORTHWEST TERRITORIES
ARCTIC OCEAN
Beaufort Sea
Prudhoe Bay
Atkinson Pt.
Tuktoyaktuk
Norman Wells
Mackenzie
Great Bear Lake
Yellowknife
Great Slave L.
Fort Nelson
Rainbow Lake
Zama
Pointed Mountain
Watson Lake
Fort McMurray
Athabasca Tar Sands
L. Athabasca
Peace River
MANITOBA
L. Winnipeg
Winnipeg
Brandon
Island Falls
Pine Falls
Kamsack
SASKATCHEWAN
Prince Albert
Saskatoon
Regina
Moose Jaw
Estevan
Medicine Hat
ALBERTA
Edmonton
Calgary
Lloydminster
Wainwright
Bonnyville
Grande Prairie
BRITISH COLUMBIA
Dawson Creek
WESTCOAST TRANS-MISSION
TRANS MOUNTAIN
Kamloops
Trail
Columbia
Kitimat
Prince Rupert
Kamloops
Vancouver
Victoria
PACIFIC OCEAN
YUKON
Dawson
Carmacks
Whitehorse
ALASKA (U.S.A.)
Arctic Circle

ELECTRICITY TRANSMISSION LINES
1:78 000 000

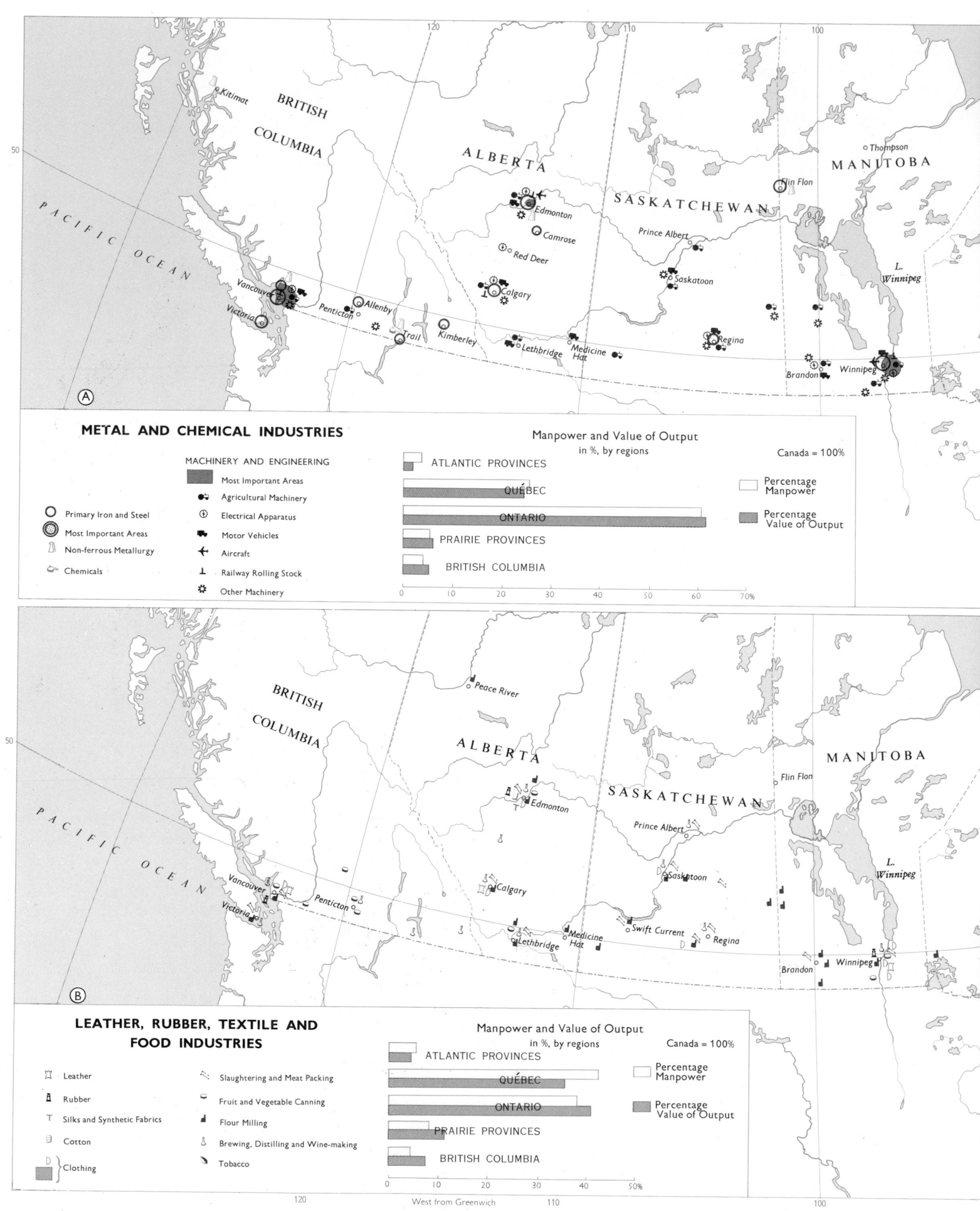

METAL AND CHEMICAL INDUSTRIES

MACHINERY AND ENGINEERING

Most Important Areas

○ Primary Iron and Steel

◎ Most Important Areas

⚗ Non-ferrous Metallurgy

☞ Chemicals

⚙ Agricultural Machinery

⊕ Electrical Apparatus

🚘 Motor Vehicles

✈ Aircraft

⊥ Railway Rolling Stock

✿ Other Machinery

Manpower and Value of Output
in %, by regions   Canada = 100%

ATLANTIC PROVINCES

QUÉBEC

ONTARIO

PRAIRIE PROVINCES

BRITISH COLUMBIA

☐ Percentage Manpower

▨ Percentage Value of Output

0   10   20   30   40   50   60   70%

LEATHER, RUBBER, TEXTILE AND FOOD INDUSTRIES

Leather

Rubber

Silks and Synthetic Fabrics

Cotton

Clothing

Slaughtering and Meat Packing

Fruit and Vegetable Canning

Flour Milling

Brewing, Distilling and Wine-making

Tobacco

Manpower and Value of Output
in %, by regions   Canada = 100%

ATLANTIC PROVINCES

QUÉBEC

ONTARIO

PRAIRIE PROVINCES

BRITISH COLUMBIA

☐ Percentage Manpower

▨ Percentage Value of Output

0   10   20   30   40   50%

West from Greenwich

1:15 000 000

100   0   100   200   300   400   500   600 km

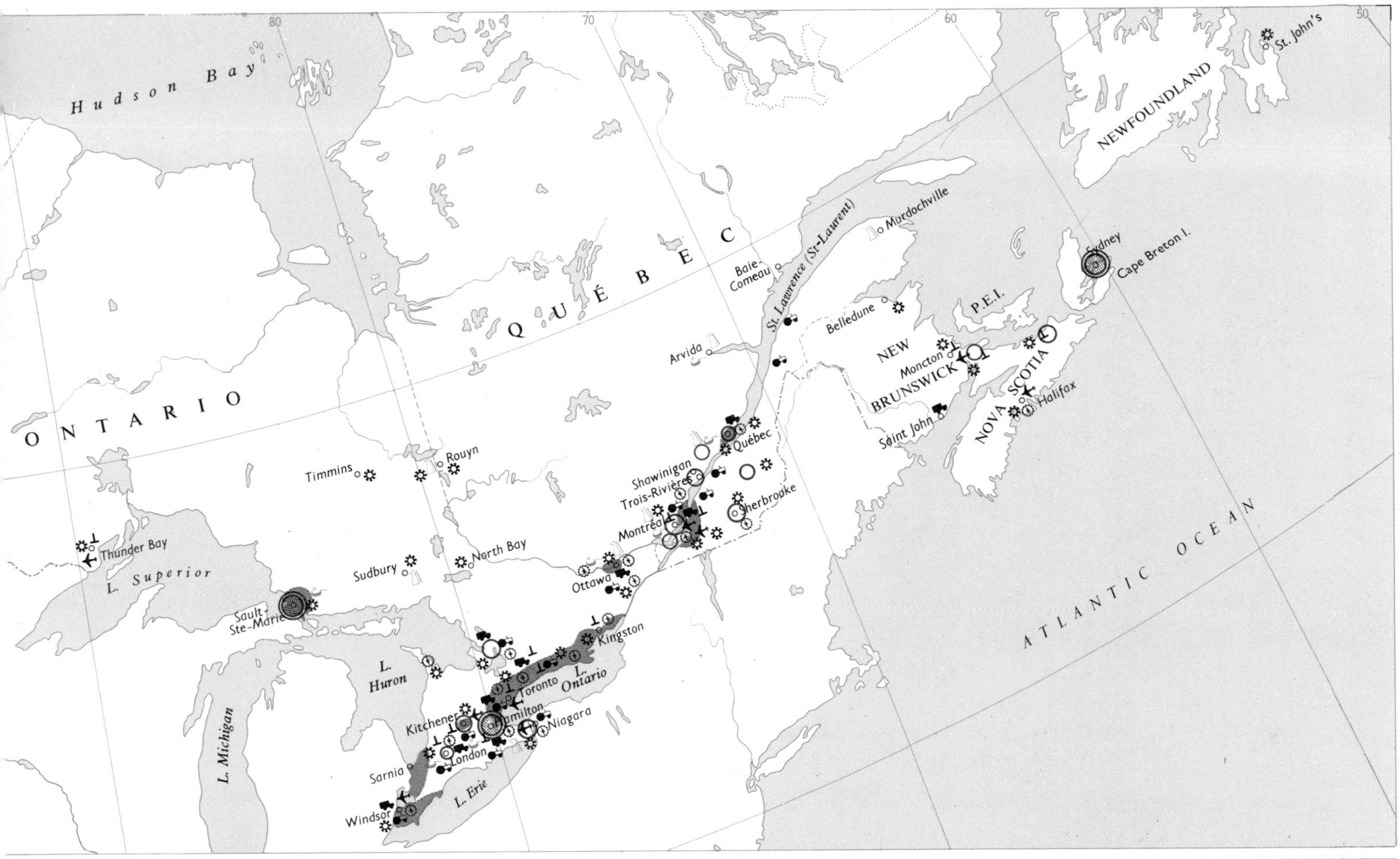

Top map:

Hudson Bay

QUÉBEC

ONTARIO

NEWFOUNDLAND

St. John's

Murdochville

Baie-Comeau

St. Lawrence (St-Laurent)

Belledune

NEW BRUNSWICK

P.E.I.

Moncton

Arvida

NOVA SCOTIA

Sydney   Cape Breton I.

Saint John

Halifax

Timmins   Rouyn

Shawinigan

Trois-Rivières   Québec

Sherbrooke

Thunder Bay

L. Superior

Sudbury   North Bay

Montréal

Ottawa

Sault-Ste-Marie

L. Huron

Kingston

L. Michigan

Toronto   L. Ontario

Kitchener   Hamilton   Niagara

Sarnia   London

L. Erie

Windsor

ATLANTIC OCEAN

Bottom map:

Hudson Bay

ONTARIO

QUÉBEC

NEWFOUNDLAND

St. John's

St. Lawrence (St-Laurent)

Chicoutimi

NEW BRUNSWICK

P.E.I.

Fredericton

Sydney   Cape Breton I.

NOVA SCOTIA

Halifax

Montmorency

Québec

Shawinigan   Drummondville

Sherbrooke

Thunder Bay

L. Superior

Montréal   Granby

Ottawa   Cornwall

Kingston

L. Huron

Toronto   L. Ontario

Kitchener   Hamilton   Welland

London   Brantford

Sarnia   Chatham

L. Erie

Windsor

L. Michigan

ATLANTIC OCEAN

90   80   West from Greenwich   70

COPYRIGHT. GEORGE PHILIP & SON. LTD.

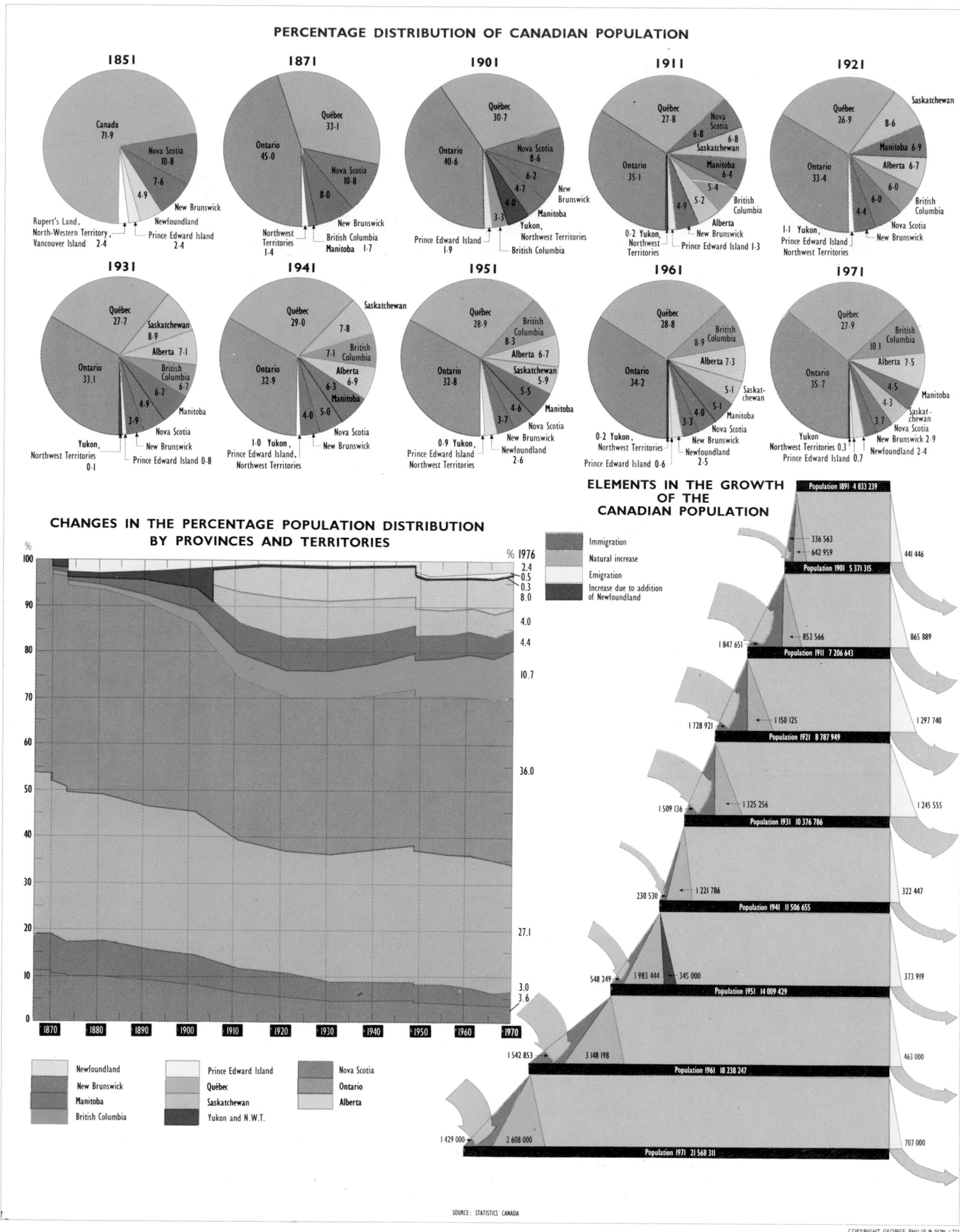

PERCENTAGE DISTRIBUTION OF CANADIAN POPULATION

1851
Canada 71·9
Nova Scotia 10·8
7·6
4·9
New Brunswick
Rupert's Land, North-Western Territory, Vancouver Island 2·4
Prince Edward Island 2·4
Newfoundland

1871
Québec 33·1
Ontario 45·0
Nova Scotia 10·8
8·0
New Brunswick
Northwest Territories 1·4
British Columbia
Manitoba 1·7

1901
Québec 30·7
Ontario 40·6
Nova Scotia 8·6
6·2
4·7
4·0
3·3
New Brunswick
Manitoba
Prince Edward Island 1·9
Yukon, Northwest Territories
British Columbia

1911
Québec 27·8
Nova Scotia 6·8
Saskatchewan 6·8
Ontario 35·1
Manitoba 6·4
5·4
5·2
4·9
British Columbia
Alberta
New Brunswick
0·2 Yukon, Northwest Territories
Prince Edward Island 1·3

1921
Québec 26·9
Saskatchewan 8·6
Manitoba 6·9
Alberta 6·7
6·0
6·0
4·4
Ontario 33·4
British Columbia
Nova Scotia
New Brunswick
1·1 Yukon, Prince Edward Island Northwest Territories

1931
Québec 27·7
Saskatchewan 8·9
Alberta 7·1
British Columbia 6·7
Ontario 33·1
6·7
4·9
3·9
Manitoba
Nova Scotia
New Brunswick
Yukon, Northwest Territories 0·1
Prince Edward Island 0·8

1941
Québec 29·0
Saskatchewan 7·8
British Columbia 7·1
Alberta 6·9
Ontario 32·9
6·3
5·0
4·0
Manitoba
Nova Scotia
New Brunswick
1·0 Yukon, Prince Edward Island, Northwest Territories

1951
Québec 28·9
British Columbia 8·3
Alberta 6·7
Saskatchewan 5·9
Ontario 32·8
5·5
4·6
3·7
Manitoba
Nova Scotia
New Brunswick
Newfoundland 2·6
0·9 Yukon, Prince Edward Island Northwest Territories

1961
Québec 28·8
British Columbia 8·9
Alberta 7·3
Saskat-chewan 5·1
Ontario 34·2
5·1
4·0
3·3
Manitoba
Nova Scotia
New Brunswick
Newfoundland 2·5
0·2 Yukon, Northwest Territories
Prince Edward Island 0·6

1971
Québec 27·9
British Columbia 10·1
Alberta 7·5
Ontario 35·7
4·5
4·3
3·7
Manitoba
Saskat-chewan
New Brunswick 2·9
Newfoundland 2·4
Yukon, Northwest Territories 0·3
Prince Edward Island 0·7

CHANGES IN THE PERCENTAGE POPULATION DISTRIBUTION BY PROVINCES AND TERRITORIES

%

%1976
2.4
0.5
0.3
8.0
4.0
4.4
10.7
36.0
27.1
3.0
3.6

1870 1880 1890 1900 1910 1920 1930 1940 1950 1960 1970

Newfoundland
New Brunswick
Manitoba
British Columbia
Prince Edward Island
Québec
Saskatchewan
Yukon and N.W.T.
Nova Scotia
Ontario
Alberta

ELEMENTS IN THE GROWTH OF THE CANADIAN POPULATION

Immigration
Natural increase
Emigration
Increase due to addition of Newfoundland

Population 1891 4 833 239
336 563
642 959
441 446
Population 1901 5 371 315
853 566
1 847 651
865 889
Population 1911 7 206 643
1 150 125
1 728 921
1 297 740
Population 1921 8 787 949
1 325 256
1 509 136
1 245 555
Population 1931 10 376 786
1 221 786
230 530
322 447
Population 1941 11 506 655
1 983 444 345 000
548 249
373 919
Population 1951 14 009 429
3 148 198
1 542 853
463 000
Population 1961 18 238 247
2 608 000
1 429 000
707 000
Population 1971 21 568 311

SOURCE: STATISTICS CANADA

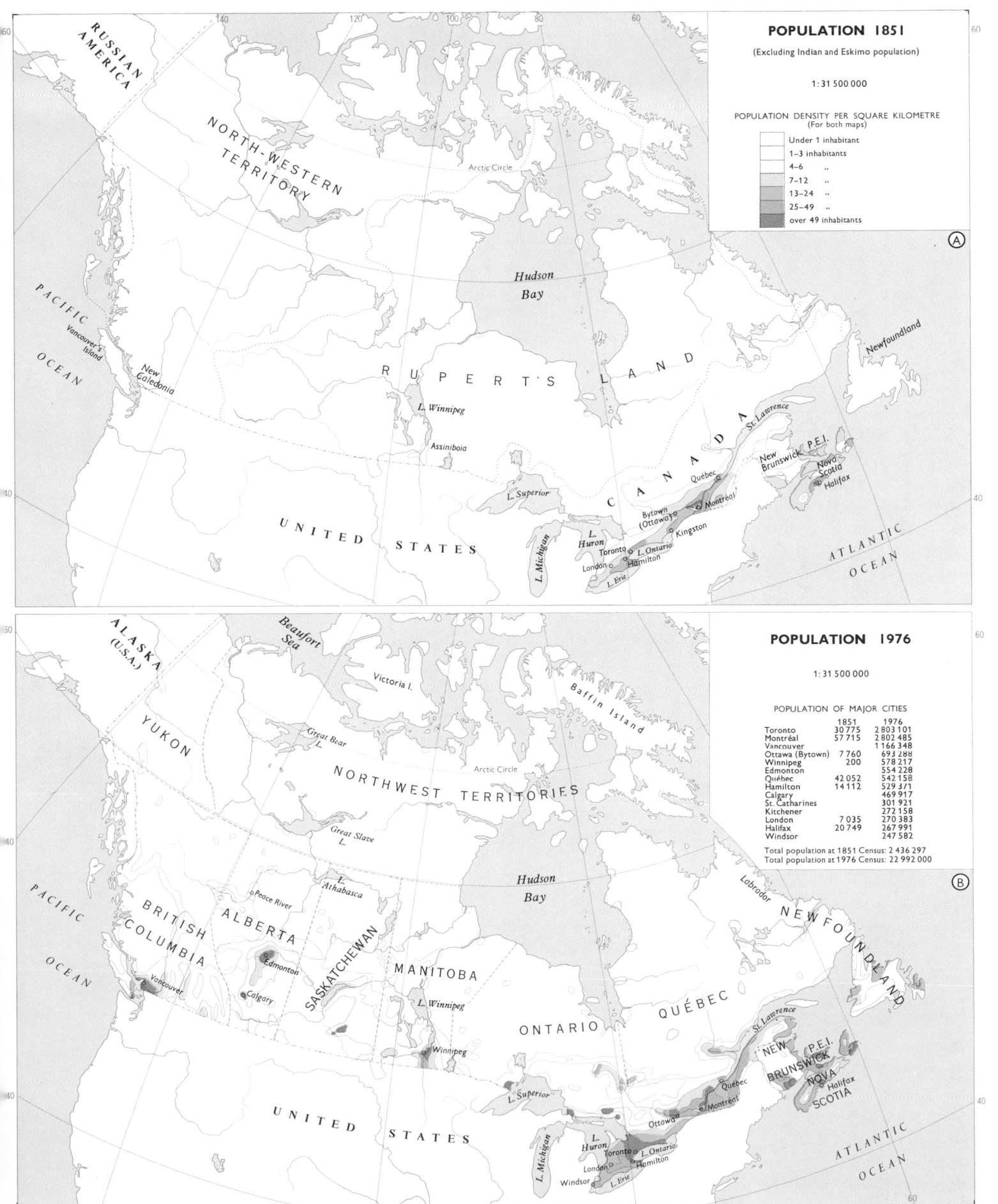

COPYRIGHT. GEORGE PHILIP & SON. LTD.
NHI

POPULATION 1851

(Excluding Indian and Eskimo population)

1 : 31 500 000

POPULATION DENSITY PER SQUARE KILOMETRE
(For both maps)

	Under 1 inhabitant
	1–3 inhabitants
	4–6 ,,
	7–12 ,,
	13–24 ,,
	25–49 ,,
	over 49 inhabitants

Ⓐ

POPULATION 1976

1 : 31 500 000

POPULATION OF MAJOR CITIES

	1851	1976
Toronto	30 775	2 803 101
Montréal	57 715	2 802 485
Vancouver		1 166 348
Ottawa (Bytown)	7 760	693 288
Winnipeg	200	578 217
Edmonton		554 228
Québec	42 052	542 158
Hamilton	14 112	529 371
Calgary		469 917
St. Catharines		301 921
Kitchener		272 158
London	7 035	270 383
Halifax	20 749	267 991
Windsor		247 582

Total population at 1851 Census: 2 436 297
Total population at 1976 Census: 22 992 000

Ⓑ

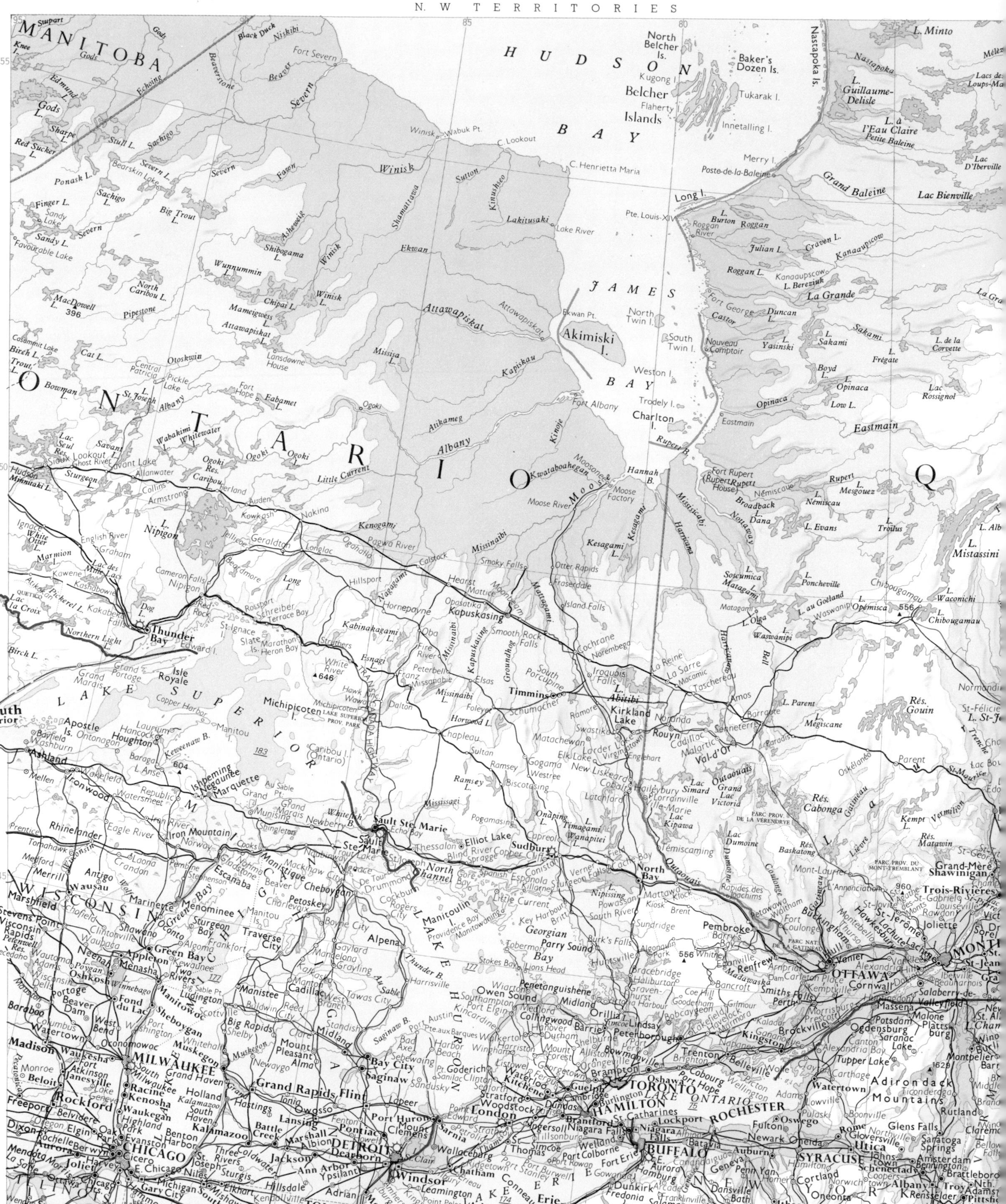

N.W TERRITORIES

MANITOBA

HUDSON

BAY

JAMES

BAY

North
Belcher
Is.

Baker's
Dozen Is.

Kugong I.

Belcher

Flaherty
Islands

Tukarak I.

Innetalling I.

Merry I.

Poste-de-la-Baleine

Long I.

Burton
Roggan

Roggan
River

Julian L.

Craven L.

Nouveau
Comptoir

Fort George

Duncan

La Grande

Sakami

Boyd

Opinaca

Low L.

Eastmain

Fort Rupert
(Rupert
House)

Rupert R.

Némiscau
Broadback

Dana

L. Evans

L. Olga

Matagami

Chibougamau

ONTARIO

QUÉBEC

LAKE SUPERIOR

Thunder
Bay

Duluth
Superior

WISCONSIN

MICHIGAN

Timmins

Kirkland
Lake

Rouyn

Val-d'Or

Sudbury

North
Bay

OTTAWA

MONTREAL

Trois-Rivières

LAKE HURON

Georgian
Bay

Parry Sound

TORONTO

HAMILTON

LAKE ONTARIO

ROCHESTER

BUFFALO

SYRACUSE

Milwaukee

Madison

Rockford

CHICAGO

Grand Rapids

DETROIT

TOLEDO

CLEVELAND

Windsor

London

LAKE ERIE

NEW YORK

MICHIGAN

INDIANA   OHIO   PENNSYLVANIA

Sault Ste Marie

Marquette

Lambert's Equivalent Azimuthal

1:7 000 000

50 0 50 100 150 200 250 300 km

COAST OF

LABRADOR

NEW FOUNDLAND

QUEBEC

NEWFOUNDLAND

GULF OF
ST. LAWRENCE

Î. d'Anticosti

PRINCE EDWARD
ISLAND

Charlottetown

Summerside

NEW
BRUNSWICK

Fredericton

Saint John

NOVA SCOTIA

Cape Breton
Island

Sydney

Halifax
Dartmouth

MAINE

Bangor

Augusta

Portland

BOSTON

ATLANTIC

OCEAN

Sable I.
(Nova Scotia)

SAINT-PIERRE
ET MIQUELON
(Fr.)

Avalon
Peninsula

St. John's

Cabot
Strait

1:7 000 000

50   0   50   100   150   200   250   300 km

Projection: Lambert's Equivalent Azimuthal

West from Greenwich

m   1500   1000   400   200   0

m   2000   4000

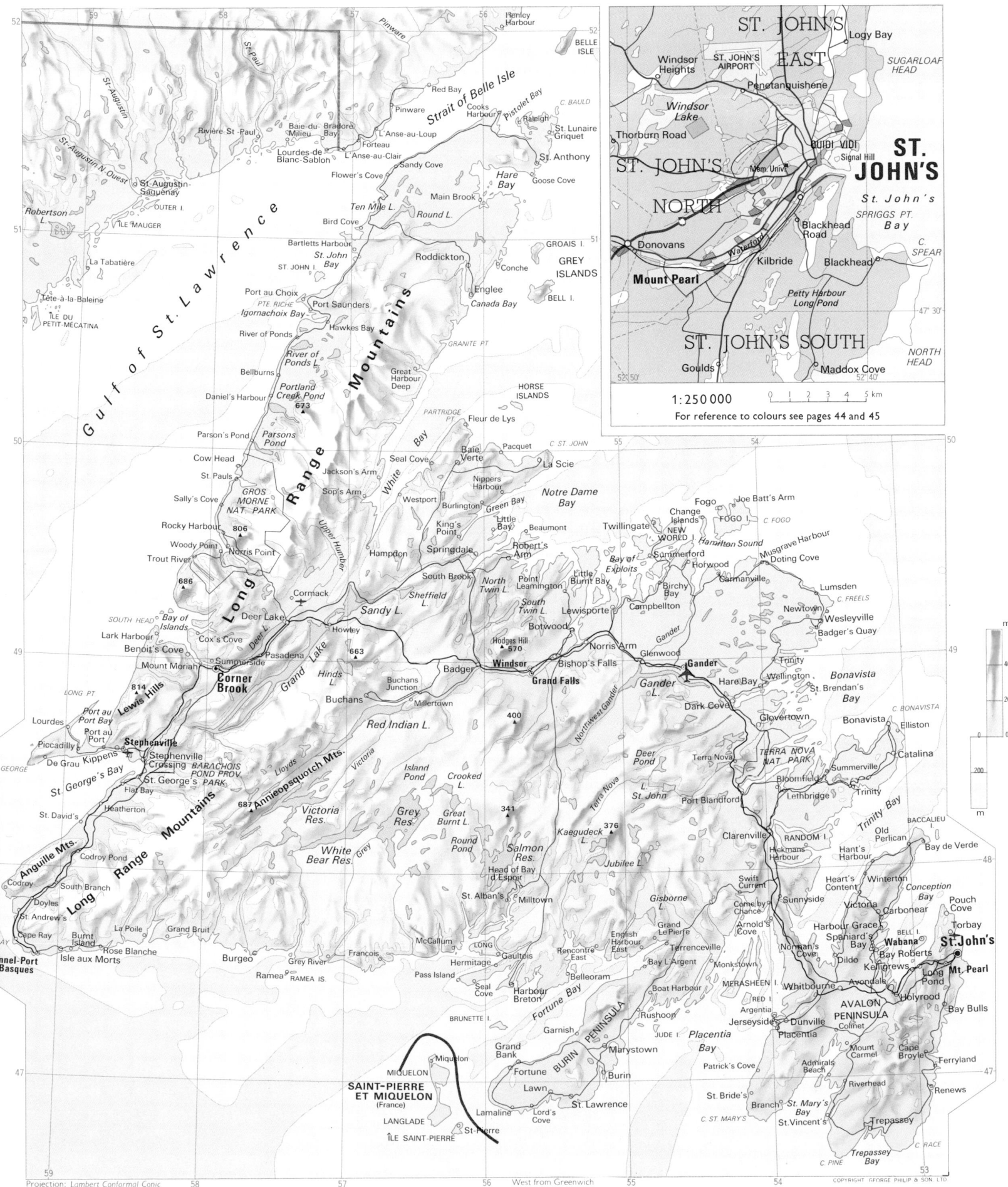

1:2 500 000

10 0 10 20 30 40 50 60 70 80 90 100 km

Gulf of St. Lawrence

Strait of Belle Isle

Long Range Mountains

GROS MORNE NAT. PARK

Notre Dame Bay

White Bay

Hare Bay

GREY ISLANDS

Corner Brook

Deer Lake

Grand Lake

Red Indian L.

Windsor

Grand Falls

Gander

Gander L.

Bonavista Bay

TERRA NOVA NAT. PARK

Trinity Bay

Conception Bay

St. John's

Mt. Pearl

AVALON PENINSULA

BURIN PENINSULA

Fortune Bay

Placentia Bay

St. Mary's Bay

SAINT-PIERRE ET MIQUELON (France)

MIQUELON

LANGLADE

ÎLE SAINT-PIERRE

ST. JOHN'S

1:250 000

0 1 2 3 4 5 km

For reference to colours see pages 44 and 45

ST. JOHN'S EAST

ST. JOHN'S NORTH

ST. JOHN'S SOUTH

Windsor Heights

Windsor Lake

St. John's Airport

Thorburn Road

Quidi Vidi

Mem. Univ.

Signal Hill

Mount Pearl

Donovans

Kilbride

Blackhead Road

Petty Harbour Long Pond

Goulds

Maddox Cove

SUGARLOAF HEAD

St. John's

SPRIGGS PT. Bay

C. SPEAR

NORTH HEAD

Projection: Lambert Conformal Conic   West from Greenwich   COPYRIGHT GEORGE PHILIP & SON, LTD.

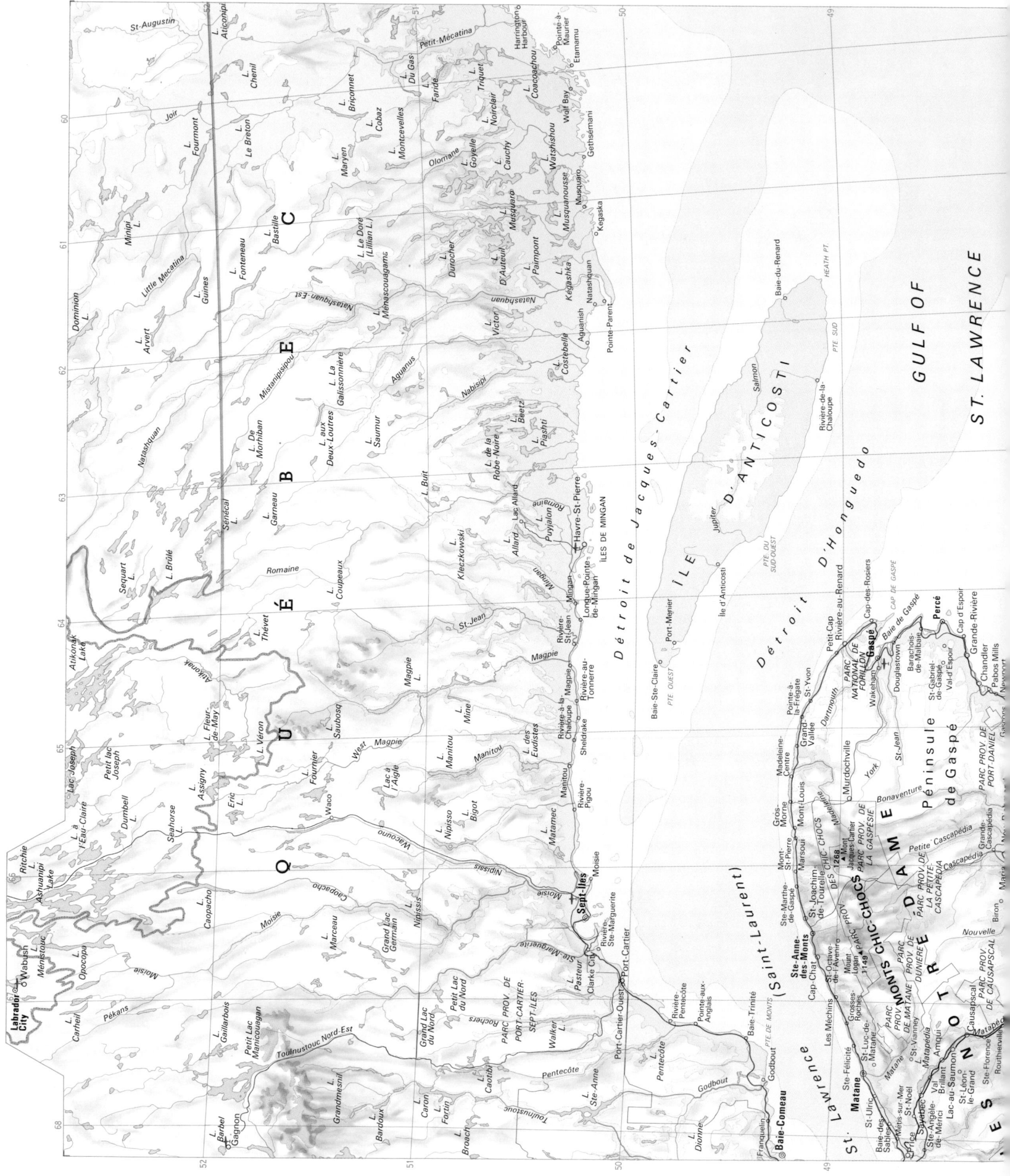

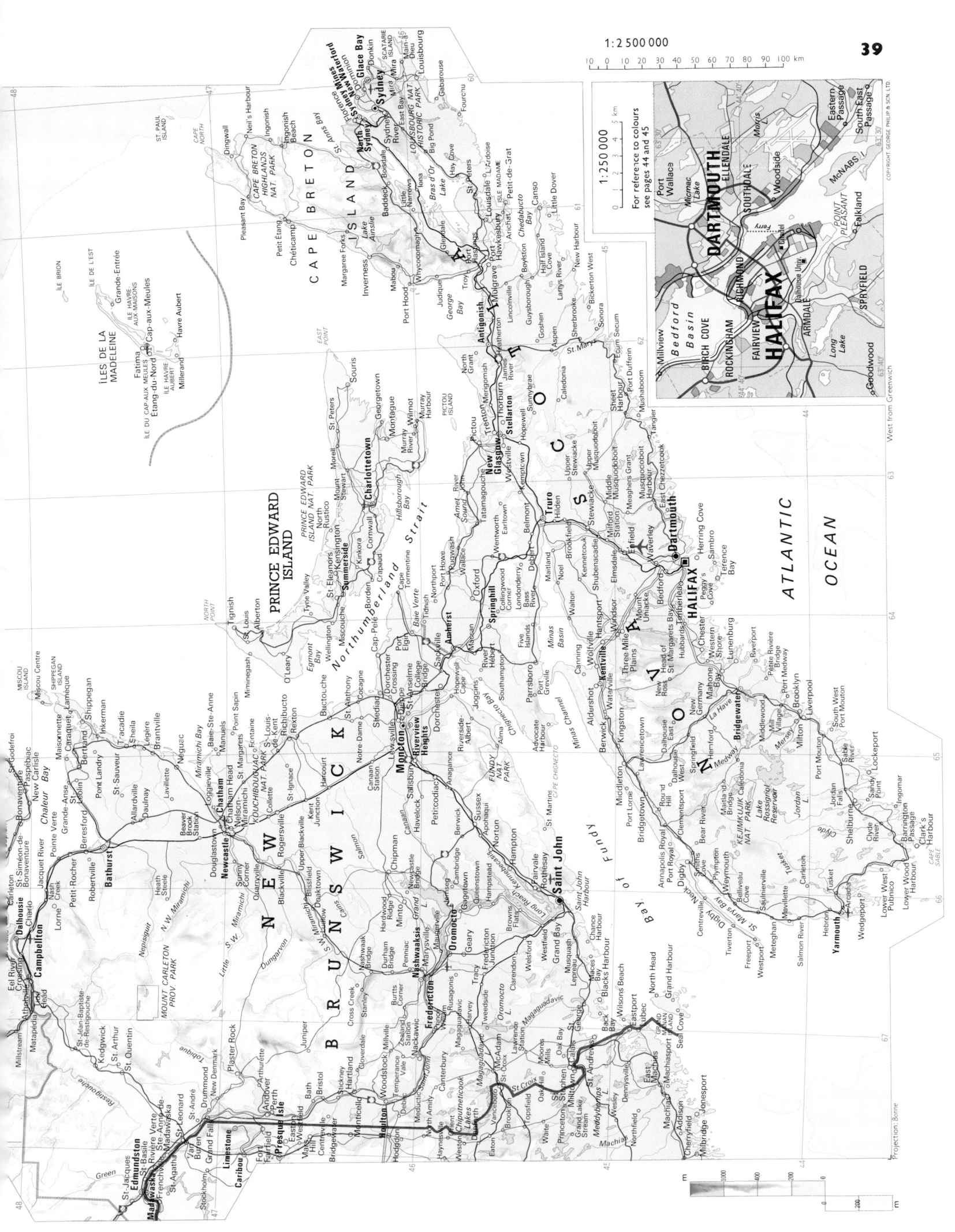

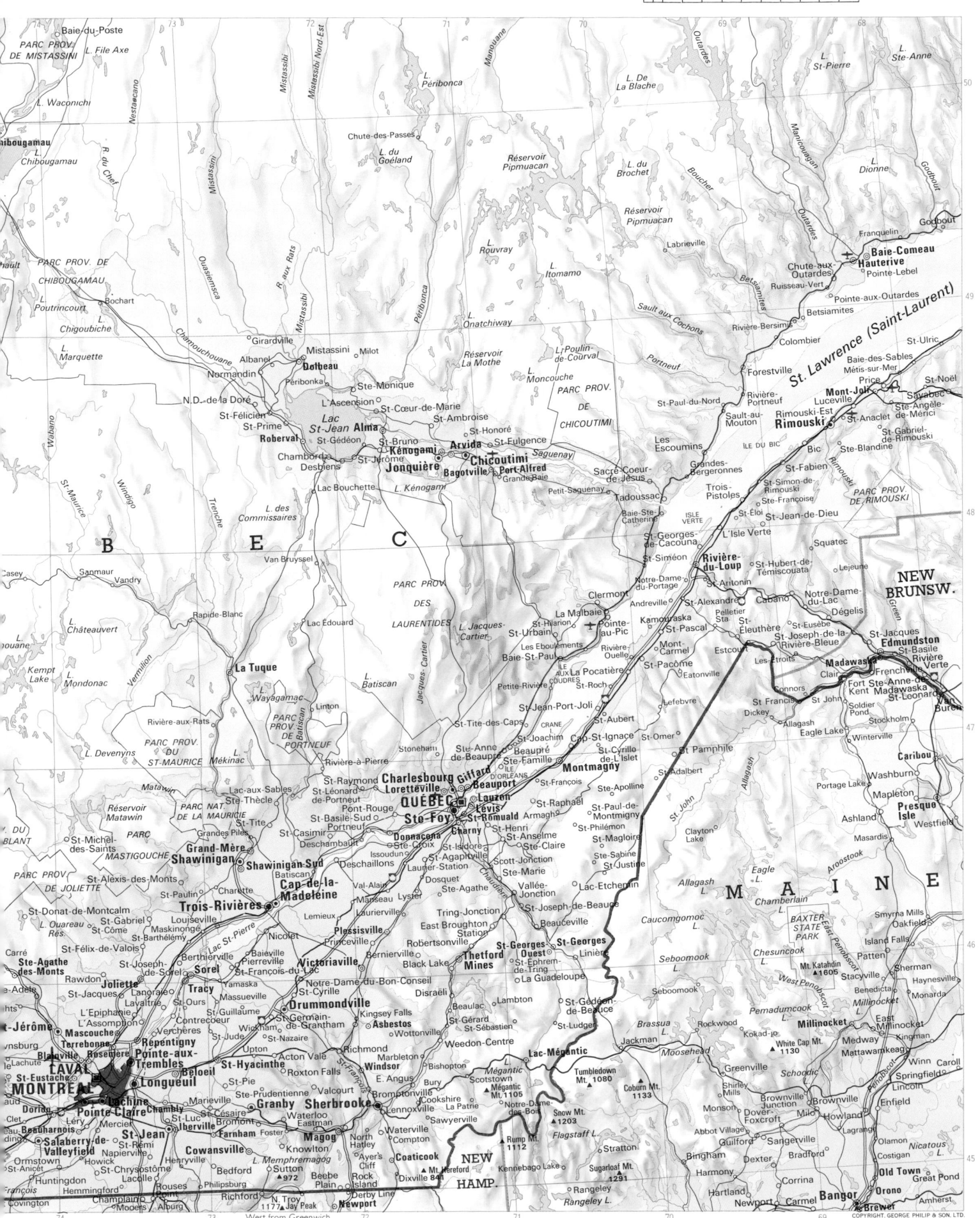

1 : 2 500 000

10 0 10 20 30 40 50 60 70 80 90 100 km

41

1:250 000

5 4 3 2 1 0   5   10 km

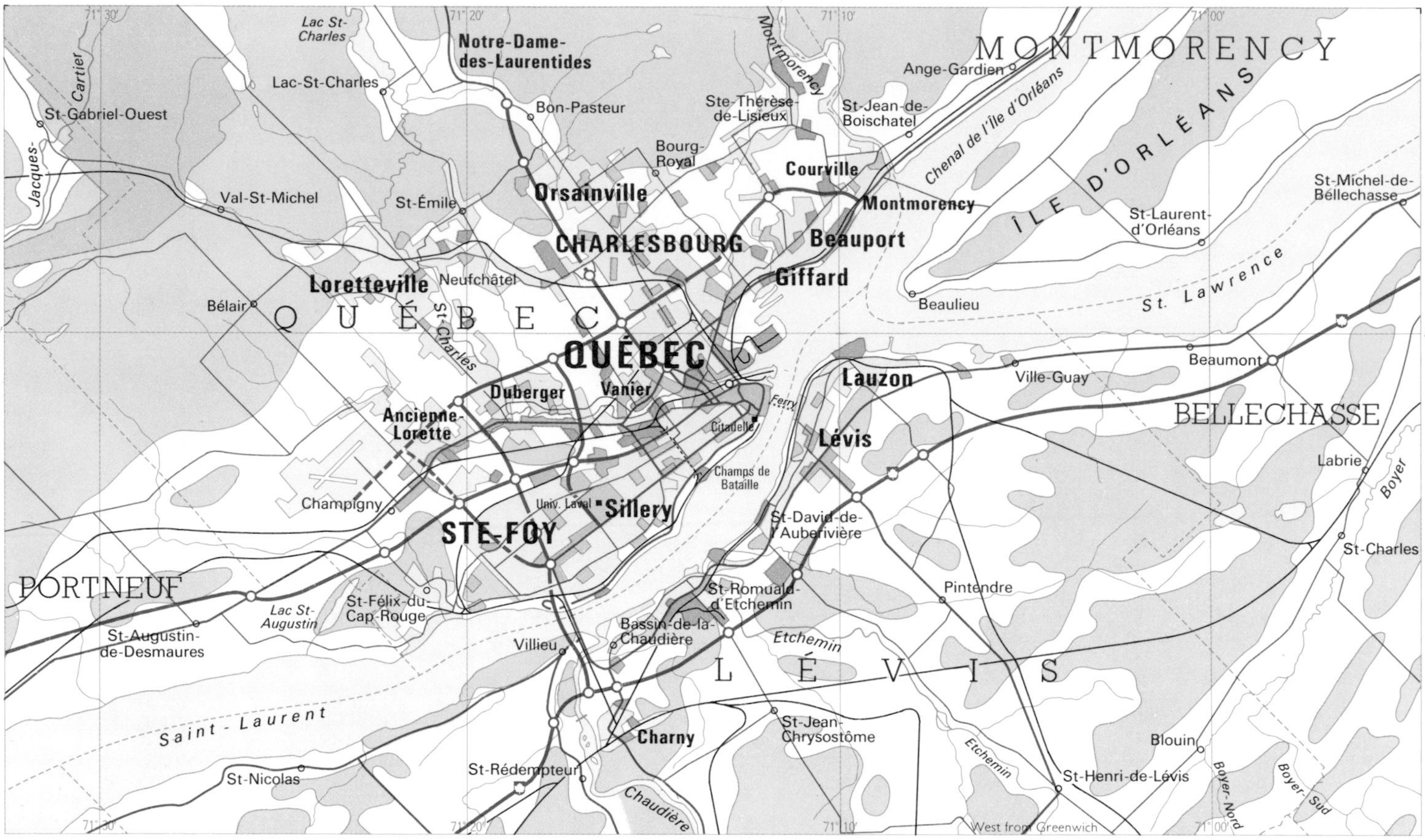

MONTMORENCY

Notre-Dame-des-Laurentides

Lac St-Charles

Lac-St-Charles

St-Gabriel-Ouest

Bon-Pasteur

Ste-Thérèse-de-Lisieux

Ange-Gardien

St-Jean-de-Boischatel

ÎLE D'ORLÉANS

Chenal de l'île d'Orléans

St-Michel-de-Béllechasse

Bourg-Royal

Courville

Montmorency

St-Laurent-d'Orléans

Val-St-Michel

St-Émile

Orsainville

St. Lawrence

Beauport

Beaulieu

CHARLESBOURG

Giffard

Loretteville

Neufchâtel

Bélair

QUÉBEC

Beaumont

QUÉBEC

Lauzon

Ville-Guay

BELLECHASSE

Duberger

Vanier

Lévis

Labrie

Ancienne-Lorette

Citadelle

Champs de Bataille

Champigny

Univ. Laval

Sillery

St-David-de-l'Auberivière

Boyer

STE-FOY

St-Charles

PORTNEUF

Lac St-Augustin

St-Félix-du-Cap-Rouge

St-Romuald-d'Etchemin

Pintendre

St-Augustin-de-Desmaures

Villieu

Bassin-de-la-Chaudière

Etchemin

LÉVIS

St-Nicolas

Charny

St-Jean-Chrysostôme

Etchemin

Blouin

Boyer-Nord

Boyer-Sud

St-Rédempteur

St-Henri-de-Lévis

Chaudière

West from Greenwich

Saint - Laurent

Jacques-

Cartier

St-Charles

Montmorency

	Residential		Industrial		Recreational		Transportation and utilities
	Commercial		Institutional		Woodland		Agricultural and other

─○─ Freeway with interchange
- - - Freeway under construction

─◇─ Trans-Canada Highway

─○─ Railway with station

- - - - - County Boundary

Québec looking north-east from Parliament Buildings across the St. Lawrence River.

Montréal looking east from Mont-Royal across the St. Lawrence River.

Projection: Transverse Mercator

1 : 600 000

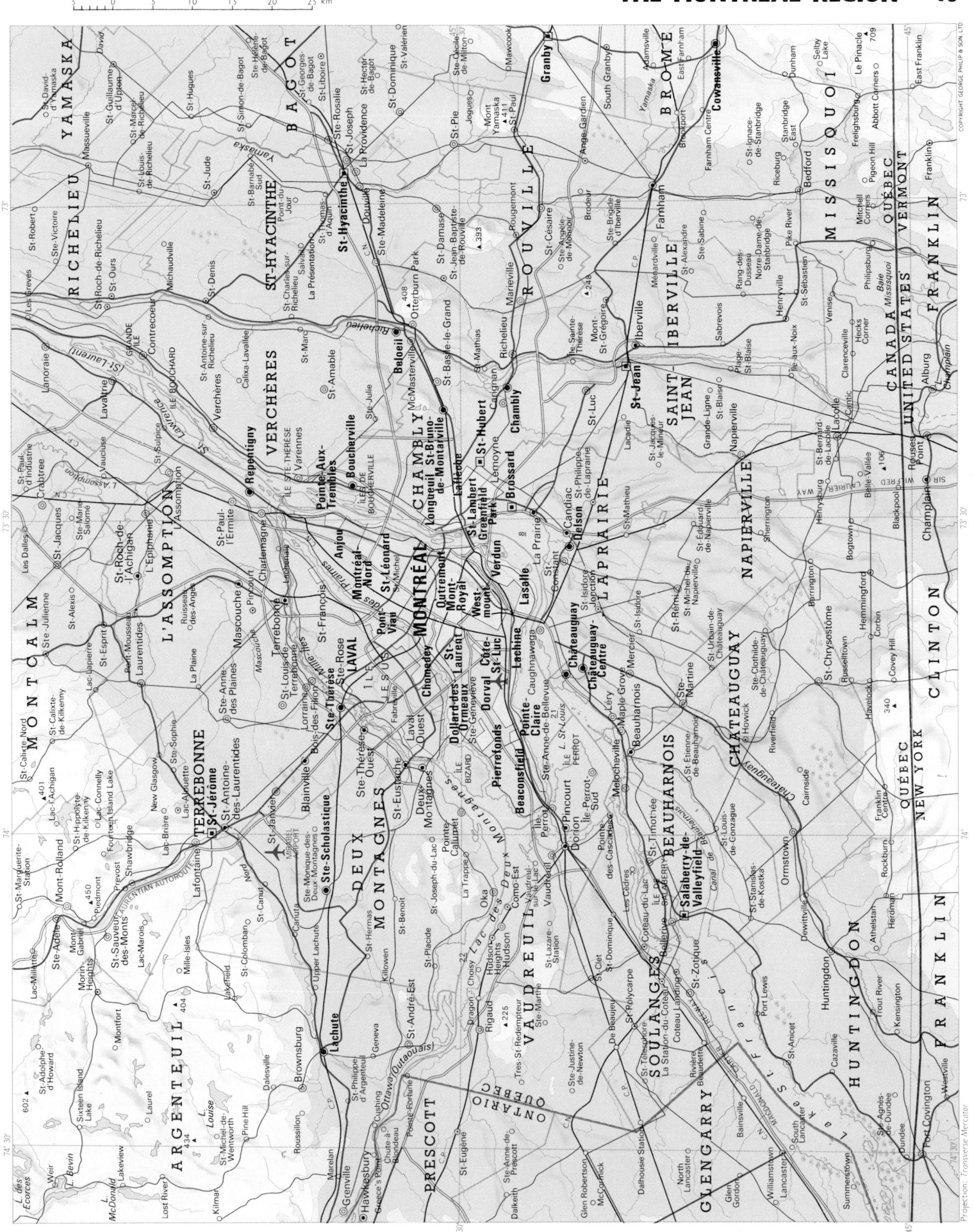

Projection: Transverse Mercator

COPYRIGHT GEORGE PHILIP & SON LTD

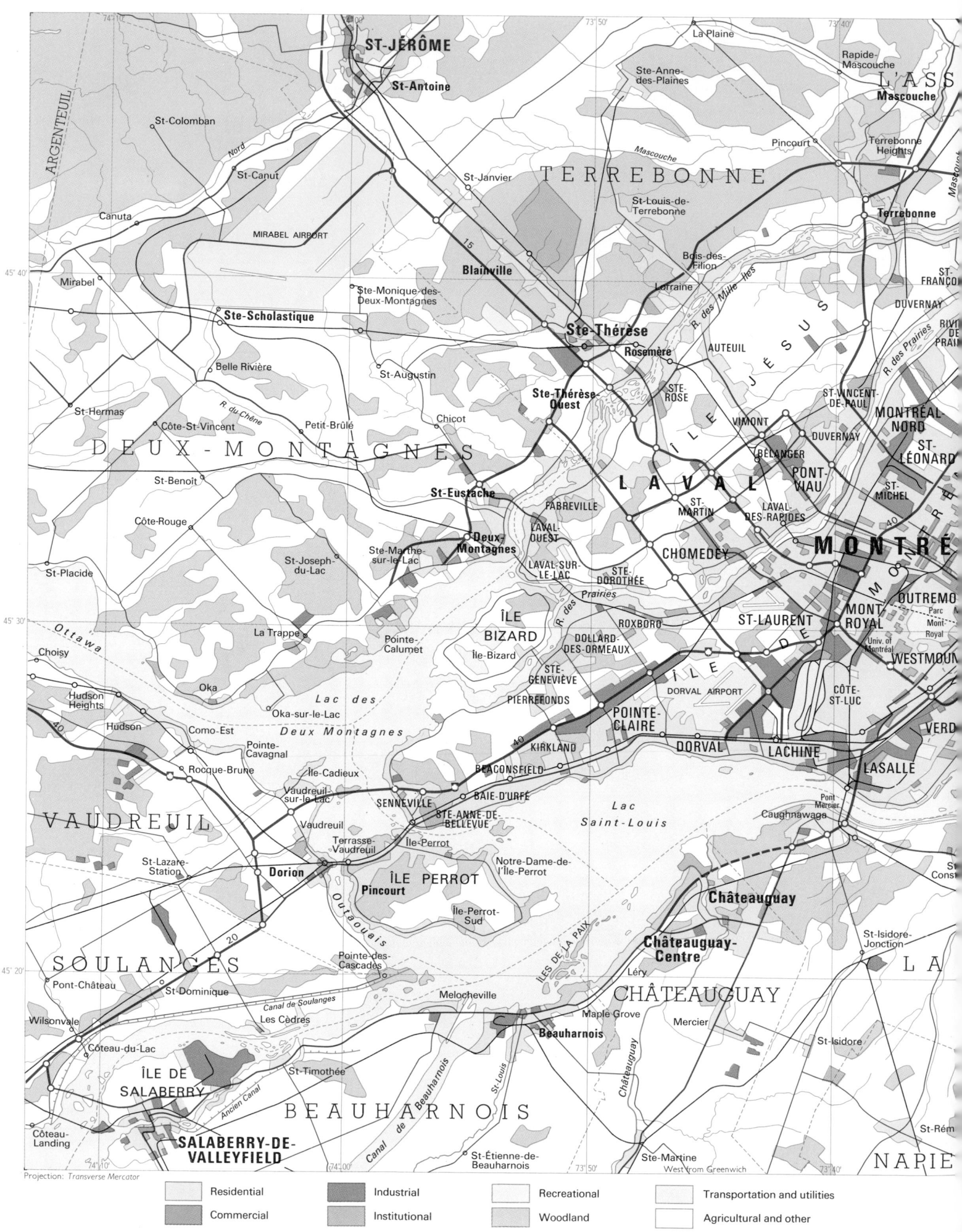

Residential	Industrial	Recreational	Transportation and utilities	
Commercial	Institutional	Woodland	Agricultural and other	

Projection: Transverse Mercator

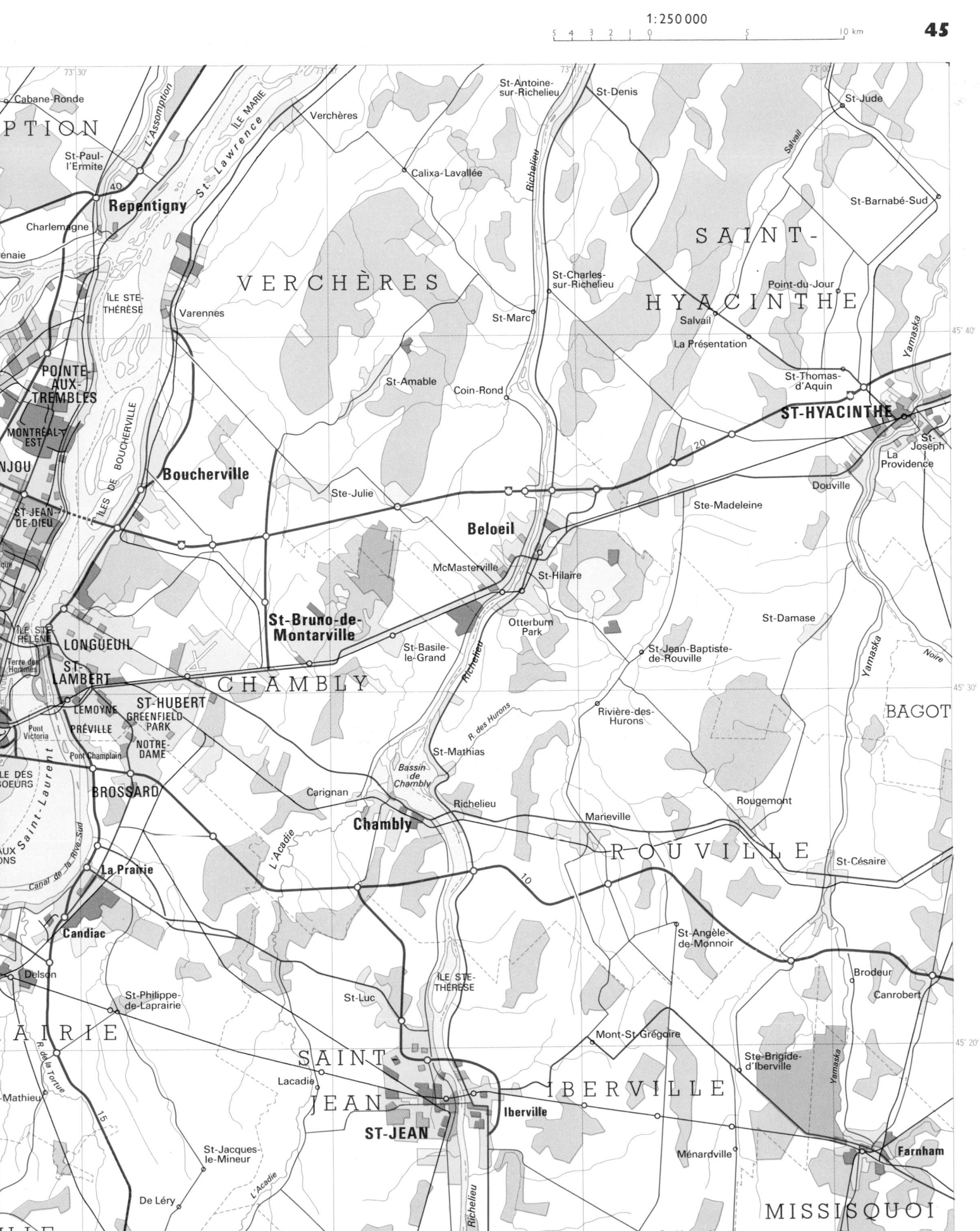

1:250 000

5 4 3 2 1 0   5   10 km

45

Cabane-Ronde

St-Paul-l'Ermite

Repentigny

Charlemagne

chénaie

ÎLE STE-THÉRÈSE

Varennes

POINTE-AUX-TREMBLES

MONTRÉAL-EST

ANJOU

ST-JEAN-DE-DIEU

Boucherville

Ste-Julie

ÎLES DE BOUCHERVILLE

ÎLE STE-HÉLÈNE

Terre des Hommes

LONGUEUIL

ST-LAMBERT

LEMOYNE

PRÉVILLE

ST-HUBERT

GREENFIELD PARK

NOTRE-DAME

Pont Victoria

Pont Champlain

ÎLE DES SOEURS

CHAMBLY

St-Bruno-de-Montarville

St-Basile-le-Grand

Beloeil

McMasterville

St-Hilaire

Otterburn Park

ÎLE MARIE

St-Lawrence

L'Assomption

40

Verchères

VERCHÈRES

Calixa-Lavallée

St-Amable

Coin-Rond

St-Antoine-sur-Richelieu

St-Denis

St-Charles-sur-Richelieu

St-Marc

La Présentation

Salvail

Point-du-Jour

SAINT-HYACINTHE

St-Barnabé-Sud

St-Jude

St-Thomas-d'Aquin

ST-HYACINTHE

St-Joseph

La Providence

Douville

Ste-Madeleine

St-Jean-Baptiste-de-Rouville

St-Damase

Noire

Yamaska

20

BROSSARD

La Prairie

Canal de la Rive-Sud

St-Laurent

AUX RONS

Carignan

Bassin de Chambly

Chambly

L'Acadie

Richelieu

R. des Hurons

St-Mathias

St-Basile-le-Grand

Rivière-des-Hurons

Richelieu

Marieville

Rougemont

ROUVILLE

BAGOT

St-Césaire

10

Candiac

Delson

St-Philippe-de-Laprairie

St-Luc

ÎLE STE-THÉRÈSE

St-Angèle-de-Monnoir

Brodeur

Canrobert

RAIRIE

R. de la Tortue

St-Mathieu

15

SAINT JEAN

Lacadie

De Léry

St-Jacques-le-Mineur

ST-JEAN

Iberville

Mont-St-Grégoire

Ste-Brigide-d'Iberville

IBERVILLE

Yamaska

Farnham

Ménardville

NAPIERVILLE

Richelieu

St-Alexandre

MISSISQUOI

ILLE

COPYRIGHT. GEORGE PHILIP & SON. LTD.

73° 30′   73° 20′   73° 10′   73° 00′

45° 40′

45° 30′

45° 20′

⊸○⊸ Freeway with interchange   ⊷┅┅⊷ Freeway with tunnel   ——— Subway   ⊸○⊸ Railway with station

- - - - Freeway under construction   ⊸○⊸ Trans-Canada Highway   - - - - - Subway under construction   - - - - - County Boundary

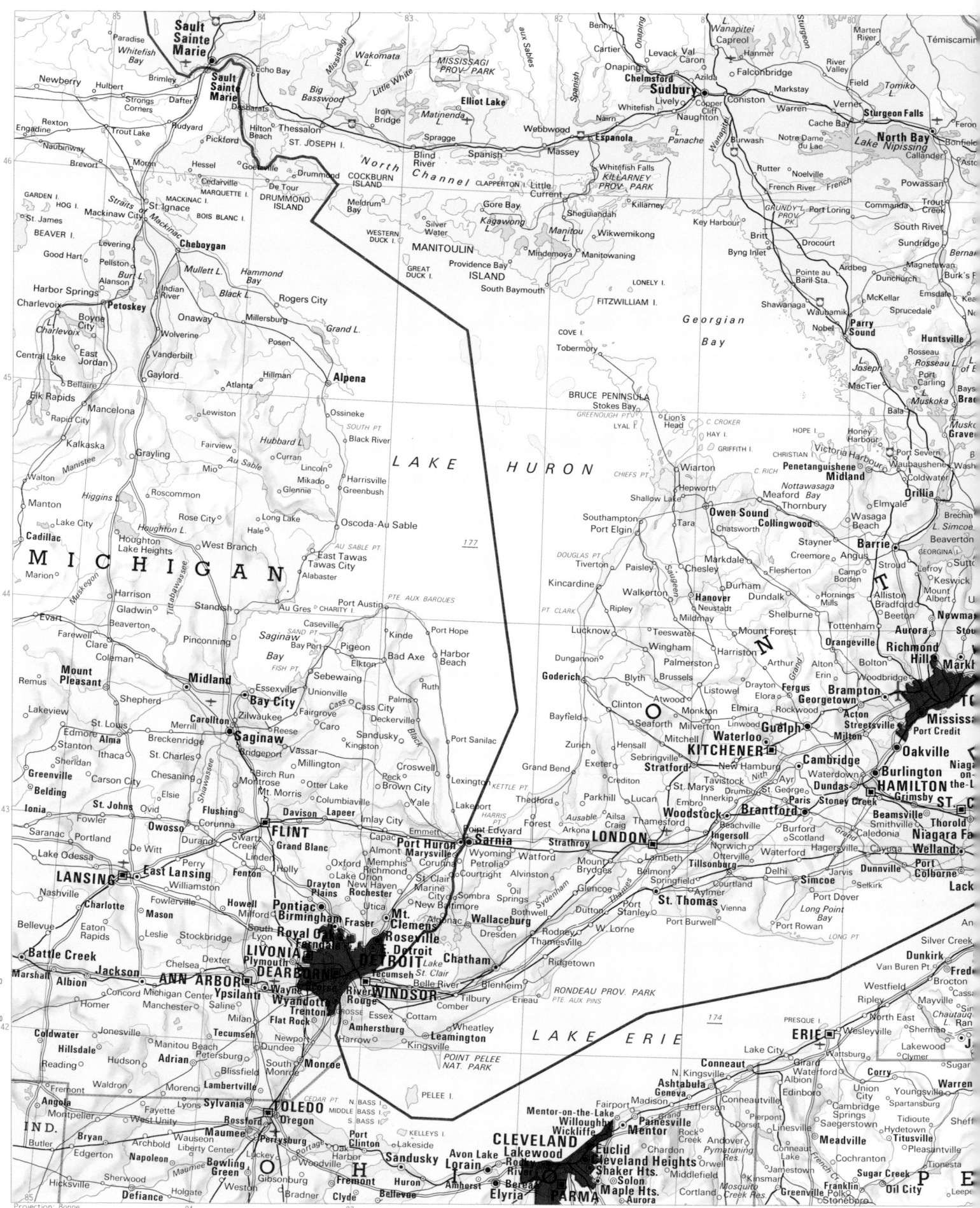

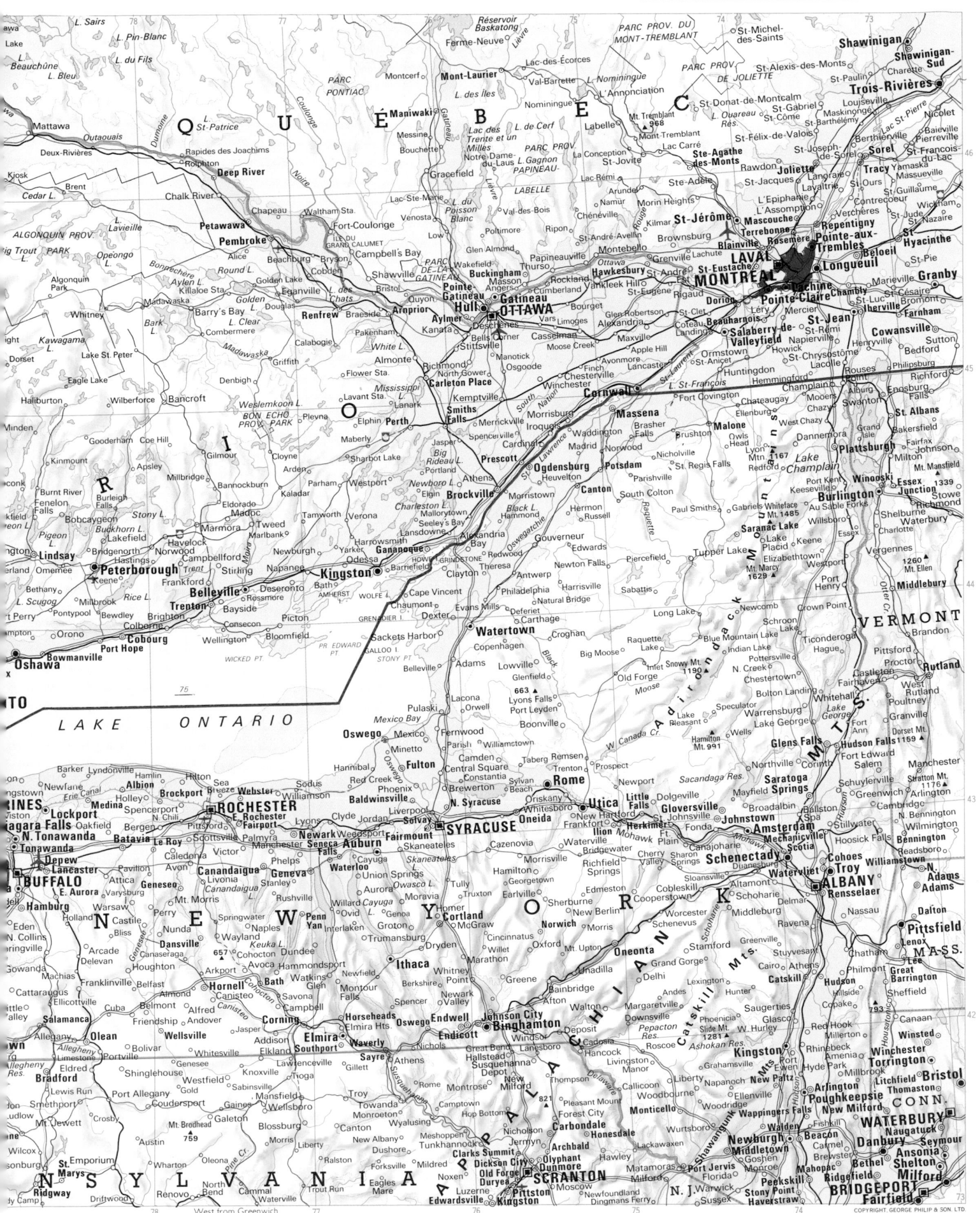

1:2 500 000

10 0 10 20 30 40 50 60 70 80 90 100 km

QUÉBEC

ONTARIO

NEW YORK

VERMONT

MASS.

CONN.

N.J.

PENNSYLVANIA

LAKE ONTARIO

Shawinigan
Shawinigan-Sud
Trois-Rivières
Sorel
MONTREAL
LAVAL
Longueuil
OTTAWA
Hull
Gatineau
Pembroke
Petawawa
Deep River
Kingston
Belleville
Peterborough
Cobourg
Oshawa
Bowmanville
ROCHESTER
SYRACUSE
BUFFALO
Niagara Falls
N. Tonawanda
Depew
Lancaster
Hamburg
Utica
Rome
ALBANY
Schenectady
Troy
Rensselaer
Cohoes
Watertown
Oswego
Fulton
Auburn
Ithaca
Elmira
Corning
Binghamton
SCRANTON
Pittsburgh
BRIDGEPORT
WATERBURY
Albany
Burlington
Plattsburgh
Saratoga Springs
Glens Falls
Rutland
Middlebury

West from Greenwich

COPYRIGHT. GEORGE PHILIP & SON. LTD.

1 : 250 000

Parliament Hill seen from the air, looking towards Hull.

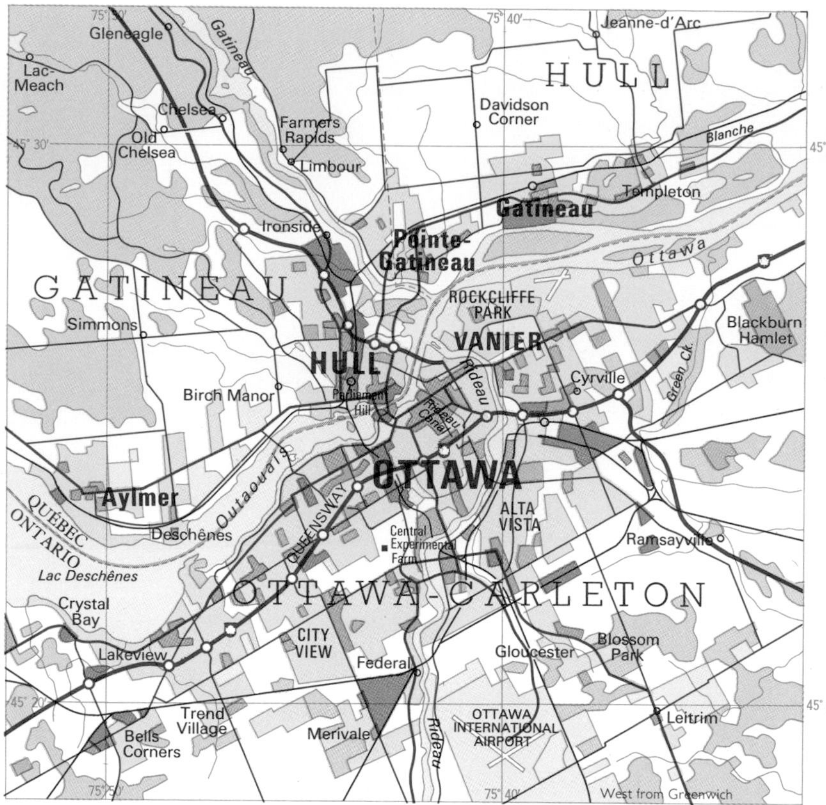

Residential	Institutional	Transportation and utilities
Commercial	Recreational	Agricultural and other
Industrial	Woodland	

Trans-Canada Highway

County or Regional Municipality Boundary

Freeway with interchange

Railway with station

Hamilton steelworks seen from Hamilton Harbour.

COPYRIGHT. GEORGE PHILIP & SON. LTD.

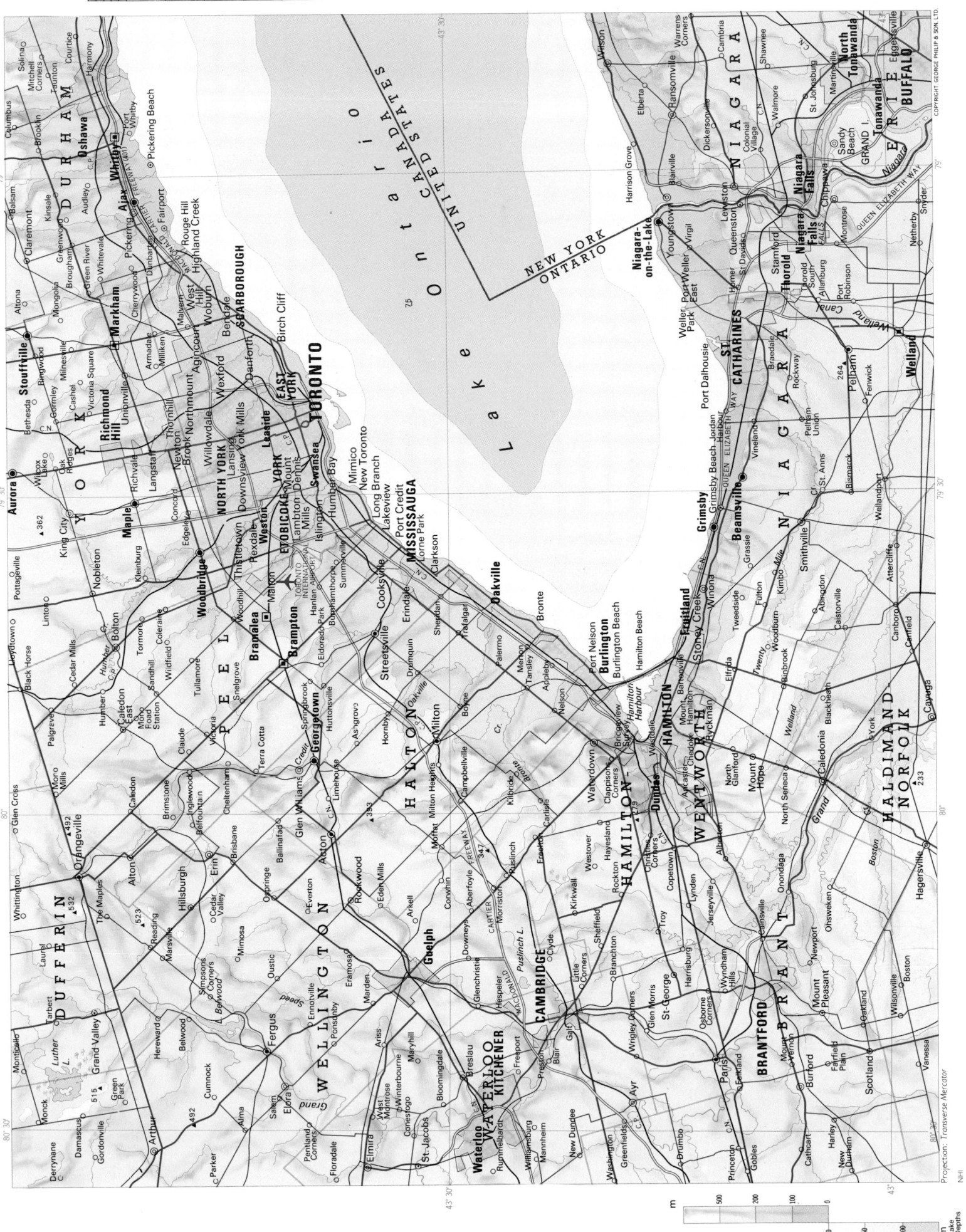

1 : 600 000

5 0 5 10 15 20 25 km

Projection: Transverse Mercator

Lake Ontario

UNITED STATES
CANADA

NEW YORK
ONTARIO

DURHAM
Oshawa
Whitby
Ajax
Pickering Beach
Port Whitby

YORK
Aurora
Markham
Richmond Hill
Stouffville
Maple

NORTH YORK
TORONTO
EAST YORK
SCARBOROUGH
Leaside
York
ETOBICOKE
MISSISSAUGA
Swansea
Mimico
New Toronto
Port Credit

PEEL
Brampton
Bramalea
Woodbridge

Oakville
Bronte

HALTON
Milton
Georgetown
Acton

WELLINGTON
Guelph
Fergus
Elora

WATERLOO
KITCHENER
Waterloo

CAMBRIDGE
Galt

BRANTFORD
BRANT
Paris

DUFFERIN
Orangeville

Port Nelson
Burlington
Burlington Beach
Hamilton Beach

HAMILTON
WENTWORTH
Dundas
Waterdown
Stoney Creek
Fruitland
Winona

NIAGARA
Grimsby
Beamsville
Vineland
ST. CATHARINES
Thorold
Niagara Falls
Niagara-on-the-Lake
Queenston
Lewiston
Welland
Pelham
Fenwick

NIAGARA
Ransomville
North Tonawanda
Tonawanda
BUFFALO
ERIE

HALDIMAND-NORFOLK
Caledonia
Cayuga

233

264

Projection: Transverse Mercator   West from Greenwich

1:250 000

5 4 3 2 1 0 5 10 km

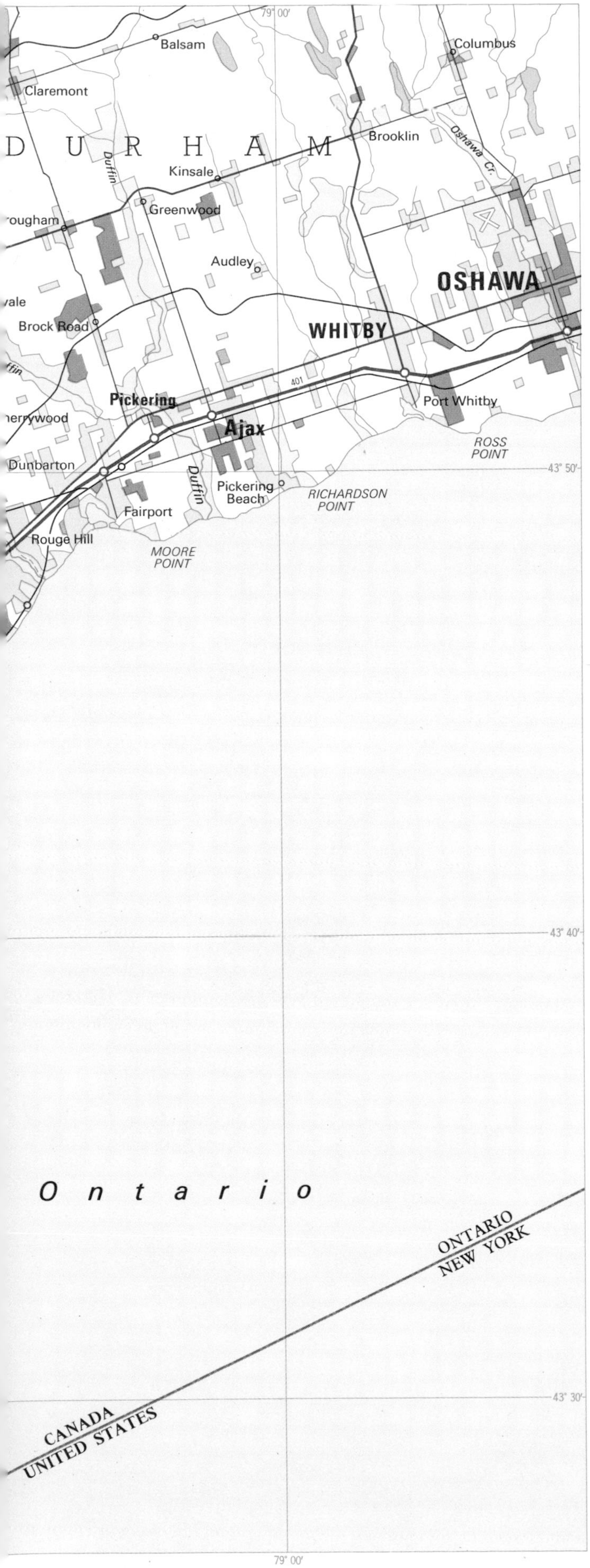

79° 00'
Balsam
Columbus
Claremont
D U R H A M
Brooklin
Oshawa Cr.
Duffin
Kinsale
Greenwood
rougham
Audley
OSHAWA
vale
Brock Road
WHITBY
401
Pickering
Port Whitby
nerrywood
Ajax
ROSS POINT
Dunbarton
Duffin
Pickering Beach
RICHARDSON POINT
43° 50'
Fairport
Rouge Hill
MOORE POINT
43° 40'
Ontario
ONTARIO
NEW YORK
CANADA
UNITED STATES
43° 30'
79° 00'

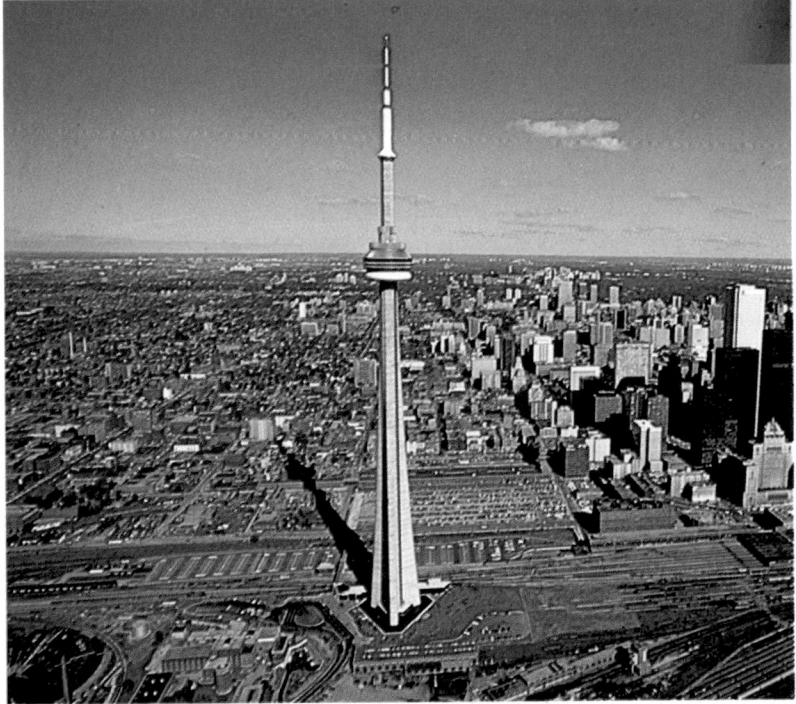

Toronto looking north with CN Tower (553 metres high) in foreground.

Residential
Commercial
Industrial
Institutional
Recreational
Woodland
Transportation and utilities
Agricultural and other

Freeway with interchange
Trans-Canada Highway
County or Regional Municipality Boundary
Subway
Subway under construction
Railway with station

Toronto's skyline seen from Toronto Harbour.

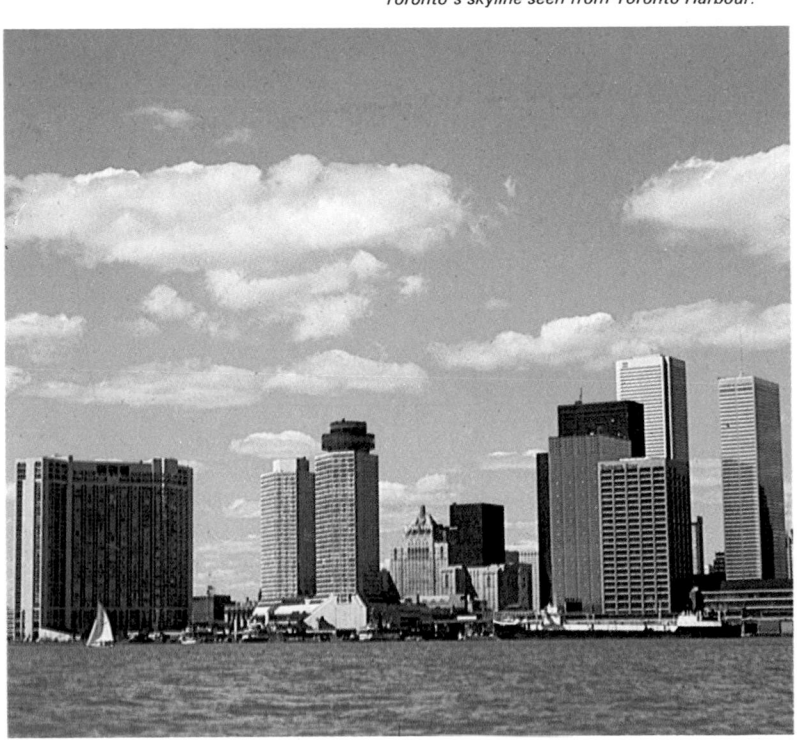

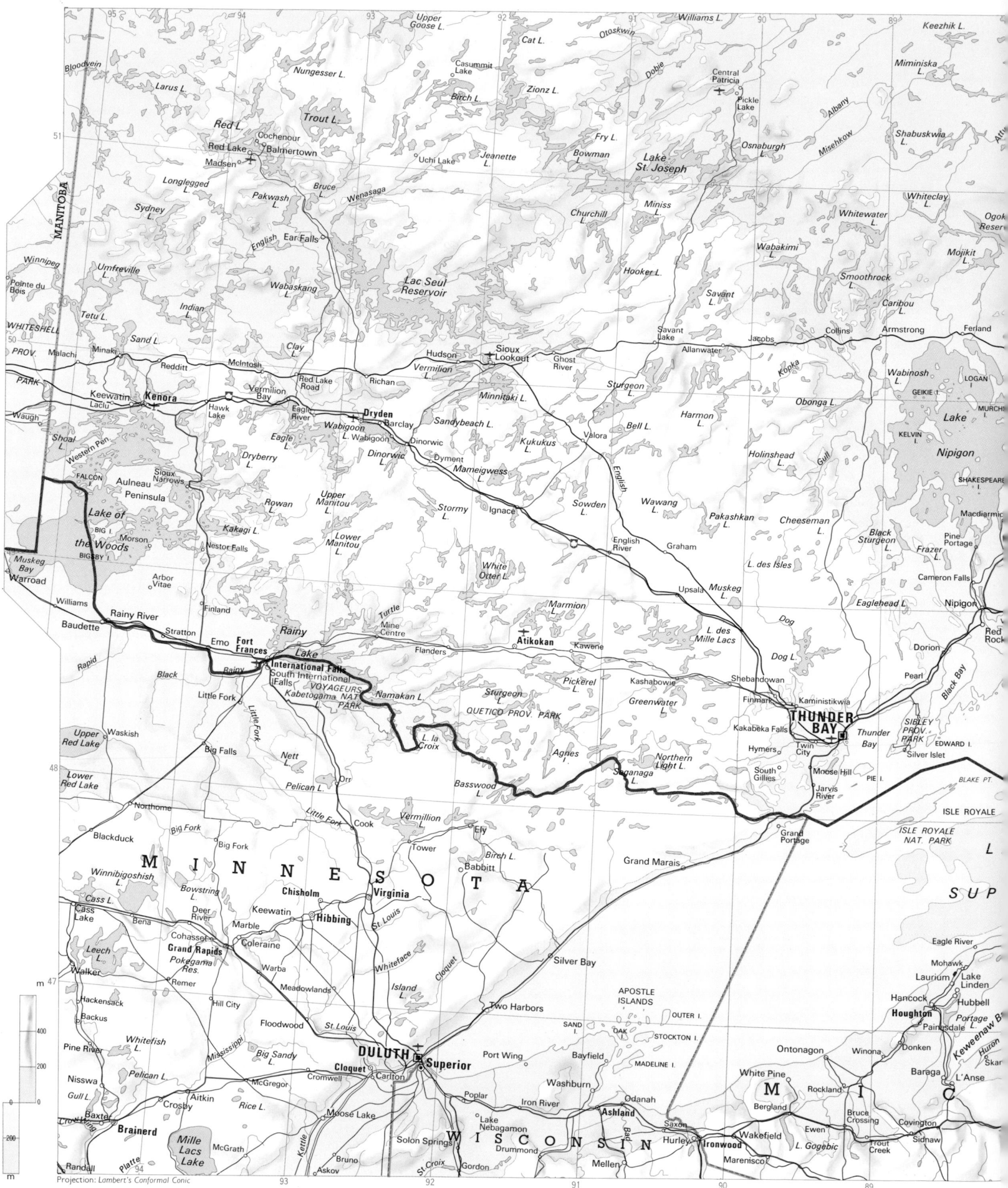

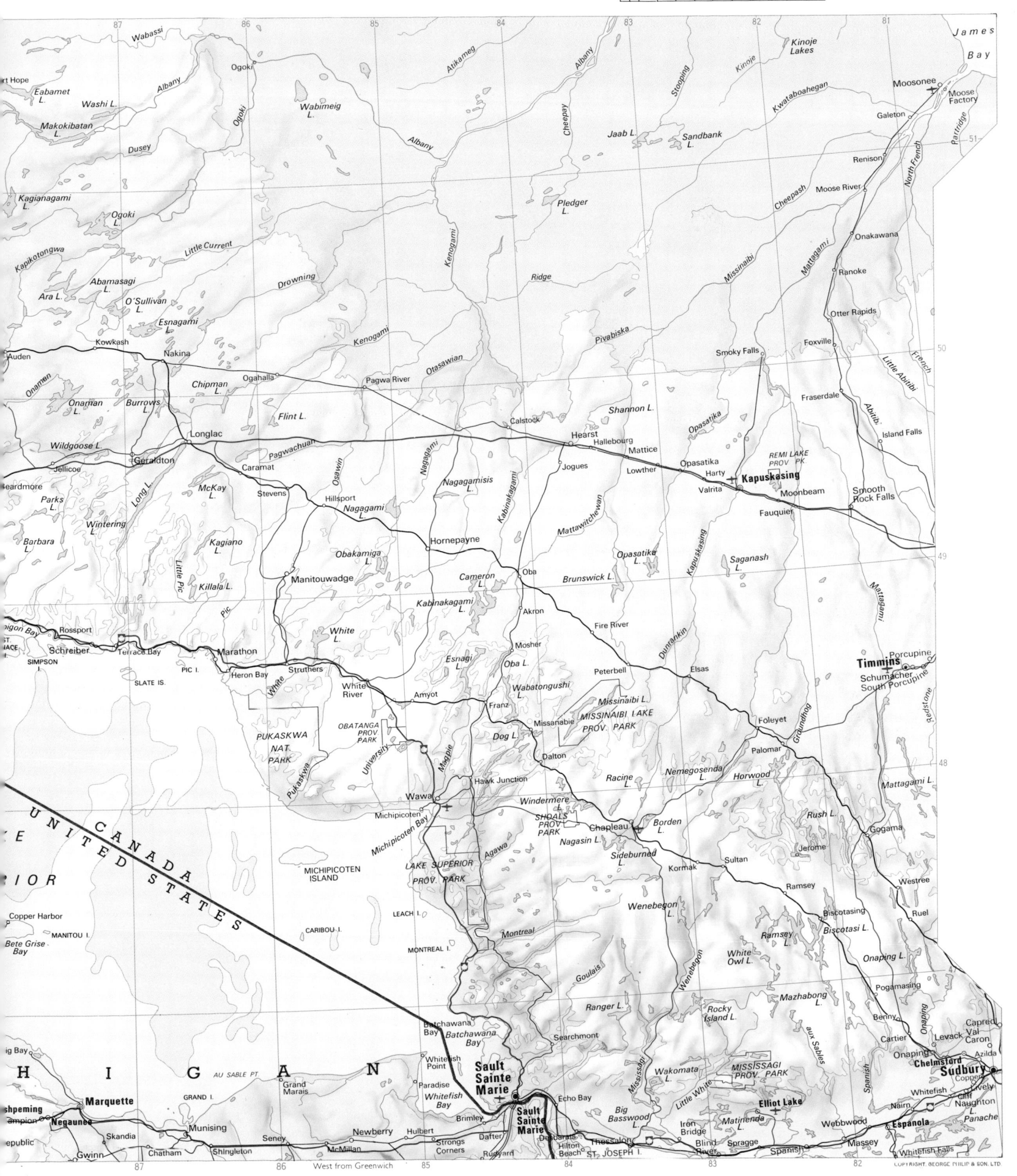

1 : 2 500 000

10 0 10 20 30 40 50 60 70 80 90 100 km

James Bay

Moosonee
Moose Factory
Galeton
Partridge

Kinoje Lakes
Stooping
Kinoje
Kwataboahegan

Cheepay
Albany
Jaab L.
Sandbank
Atikameg

Ogoki
Wabimeig L.

Wabassi
Albany
Washi L.
Makokibatan L.

rt Hope
Eabamet L.

Kagianagami L.
Ogoki L.

Little Current
Drowning
Kenogami

Pledger
Ridge

Cheepash
Moose River

Missinaibi
Pivabiska

Renison

51

Mattagami
Onakawana
Ranoke

Otter Rapids

Foxville
Smoky Falls
French
Little Abitibi

50

Ara L.
Abamasagi L.
O'Sullivan L.
Esnagami L.

Kowkash
Nakina
Chipman
Ogahalla
Pagwa River
Otasawian
Calstock
Hearst
Hallebourg
Mattice

Opasatika
Fraserdale
Abitibi
Island Falls

Burrows
Onaman
Onaman L.

Longlac
Flint L.
Pagwachuan
Nagagami

Jogues
Lowther
Opasatika
Harty
Valrita

Kapuskasing
Moonbeam
Fauquier
Smooth Rock Falls

REMI LAKE PROV. PK.

Geraldton
Caramat
Stevens
Oswin
Hillsport
Nagagamisis

Mattawitchewan

Saganash

49

Jellicoe
Wildgoose L.
Long L.

McKay L.
Nagagami

Hornepayne
Oba

Brunswick L.
Opasatika L.
Kapuskasing

Beardmore
Parks L.
Wintering L.
Barbara L.

Kagiano L.
Obakamiga L.
Cameron
Oba

Mattagami L.

Killala L.
Little Pic
Manitouwadge
Kabinakagami L.
Akron
Fire River

Rossport
Schreiber
Terrace Bay
Marathon
Pic I.
White
Esnagi
Oba L.
Mosher
Dunrankin
Elsas

Timmins
Porcupine
Schumacher
South Porcupine
Redstone

SIMPSON
SLATE IS.
Heron Bay
Struthers
White River
Amyot
Franz
Peterbell

Missinaibi L.
Foleyet
Groundhog

48

PUKASKWA NAT. PARK
OBATANGA PROV PARK
White
Missanabie
MISSINAIBI LAKE PROV. PARK
Palomar
Horwood
Mattagami L.

University
Pukaskwa
Magpie
Dog L.
Dalton
Racine
Nemegosenda
Rush L.
Gogama

Wawa
Hawk Junction
Windermere
SHOALS PROV PARK
Chapleau
Borden
Jerome

Michipicoten
Michipicoten Bay
Agawa
Nagasin L.
Sultan
Westree

MICHIPICOTEN ISLAND
LAKE SUPERIOR PROV. PARK
Kormak
Ramsey
Biscotasing
Biscotasi L.
Ruel

RIOR
Copper Harbor
MANITOU I.
Bete Grise Bay
CARIBOU I.
LEACH I.
Montreal
Wenebegon
Ramsey
White Owl L.
Onaping L.

MONTREAL I.
Goulais
Mazhabong
Pogamasing
Benny

Ranger L.
Rocky Island L.
aux Sables
Cartier
Onaping
Levack
Capreol
Val Caron

Batchawana Bay
Batchawana
Searchmont
MISSISSAGI PROV. PARK
Azilda
Chelmsford
Sudbury

CANADA
UNITED STATES

Whitefish Point
Sault Sainte Marie
Echo Bay
Wakomata L.
Elliot Lake
Whitefish
Nairn
Naughton
Panache

Paradise
Whitefish Bay
Sault Sainte Marie
Big Basswood
Iron Bridge
Matinenda
Webbwood
Espanola
Lively
Copper

H I G A N
Marquette
Negaunee
AU SABLE PT.
GRAND I.
Grand Marais
Brimley
Dafter
Desbarats
Hilton Beach
ST. JOSEPH I.
Thessalon
Blind River
Spragge
Massey
Whitefish Falls

shpeming
ampion
Republic
Gwinn
Skandia
Chatham
Munising
Shingleton
Seney
McMillan
Newberry
Hulbert
Strongs Corners
Rudyard
Spanish

West from Greenwich

COPYRIGHT GEORGE PHILIP & SON, LTD.

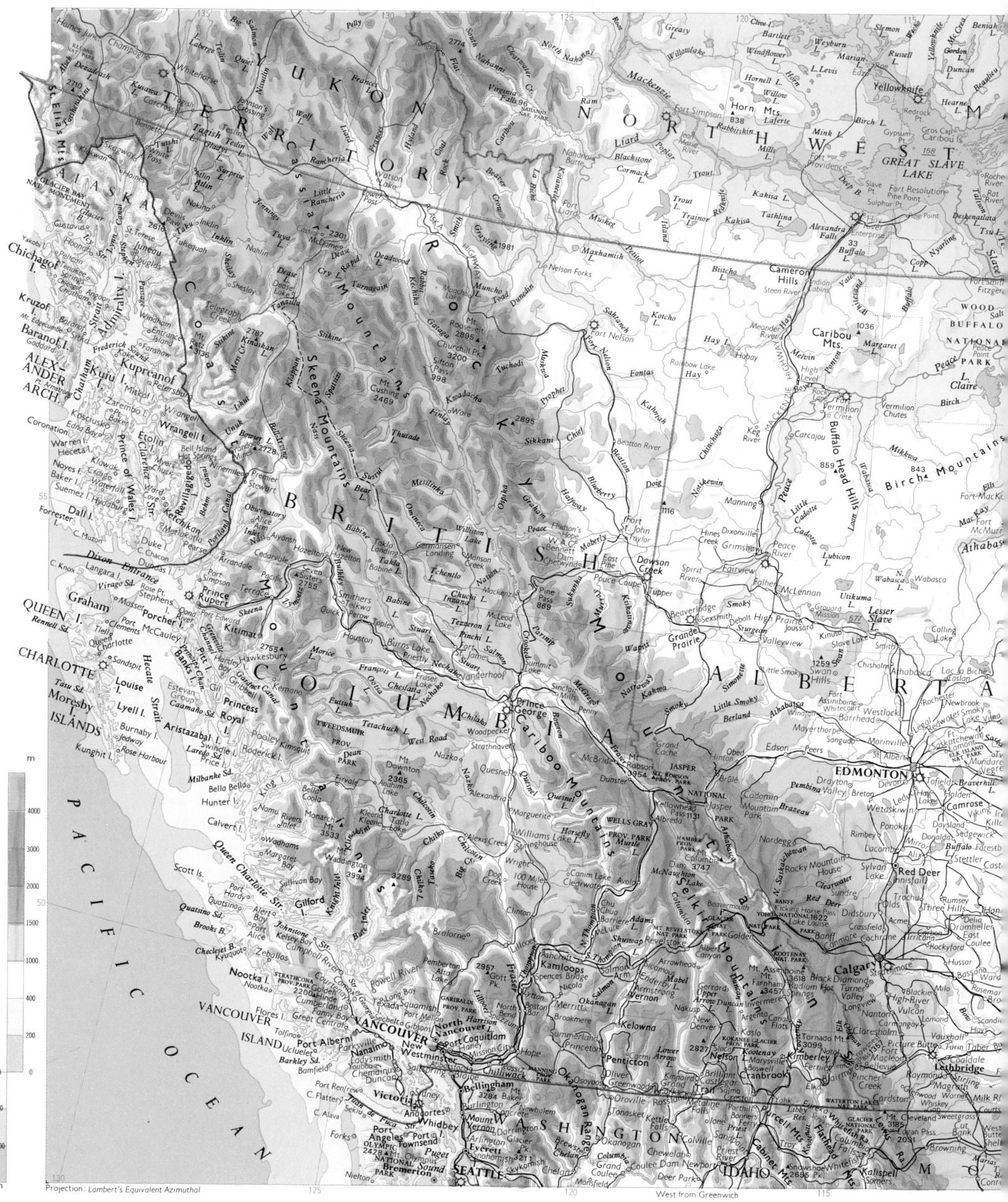

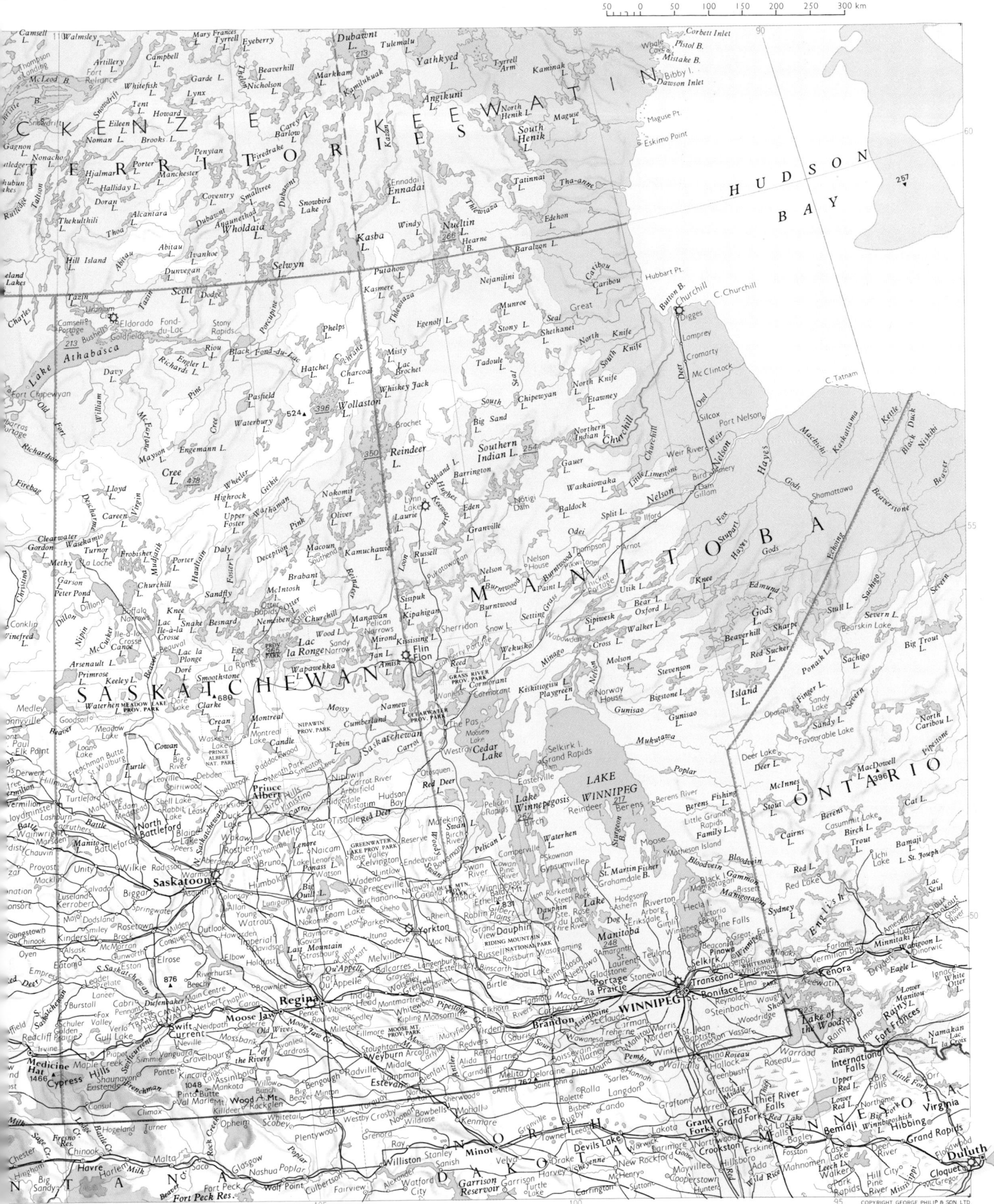

50 0   50   100   150   200   250   300 km

HUDSON

BAY

C K E N Z I E   T E R R I T O R I E S   K E E W A T I N

S A S K A T C H E W A N

M A N I T O B A

O N T A R I O

Lake Athabasca

LAKE WINNIPEG

Lake Winnipegosis

Prince Albert

North Battleford

Saskatoon

Yorkton

Regina

Moose Jaw

Swift Current

Medicine Hat

Brandon

WINNIPEG

Portage la Prairie

Selkirk

Lake of the Woods

N O R T H   D A K O T A

M I N N E S O T A

M O N T A N A

Duluth

Minot

Grand Forks

Bemidji

Fort Peck Res.

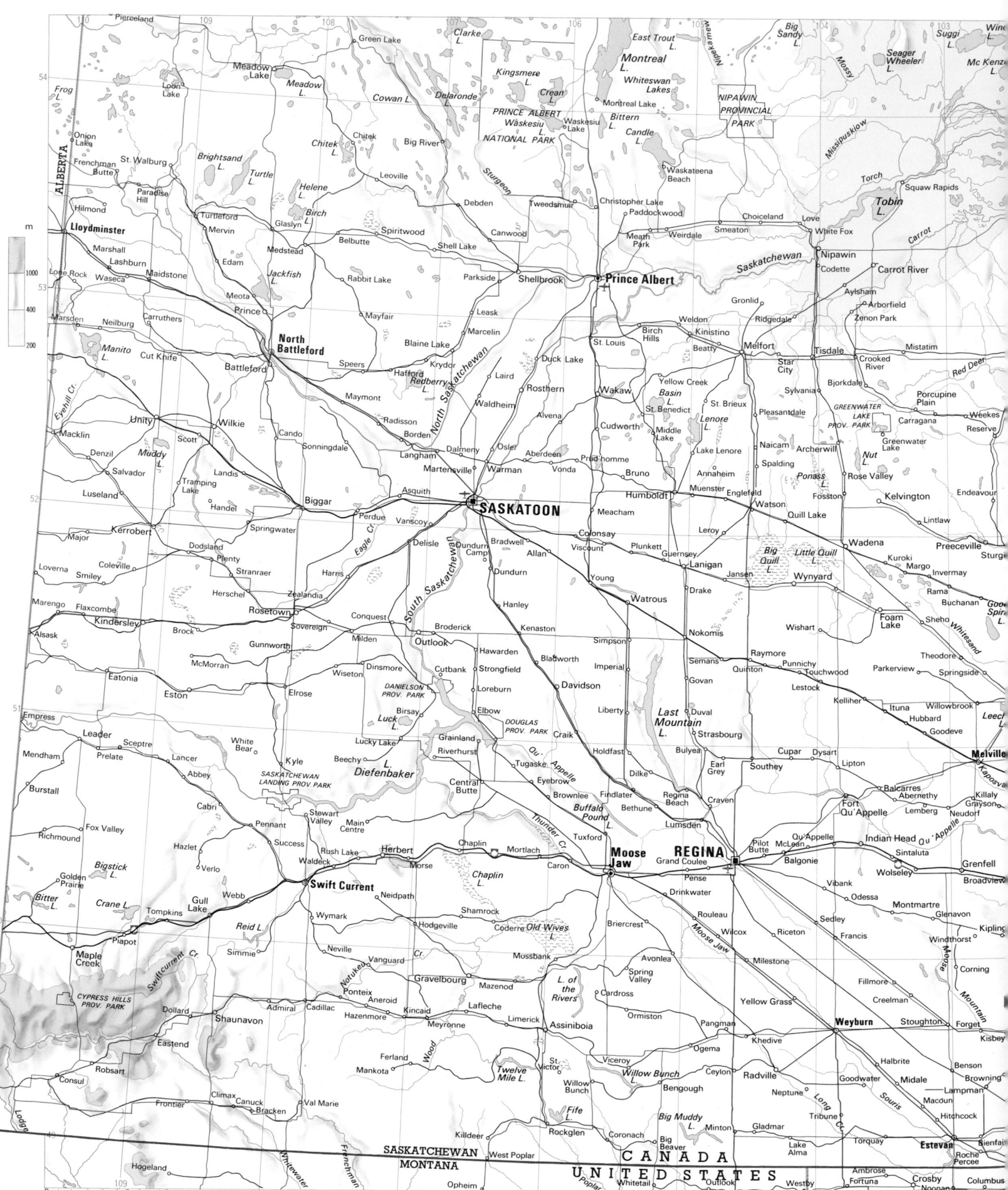

Projection: Lambert's Conformal Conic

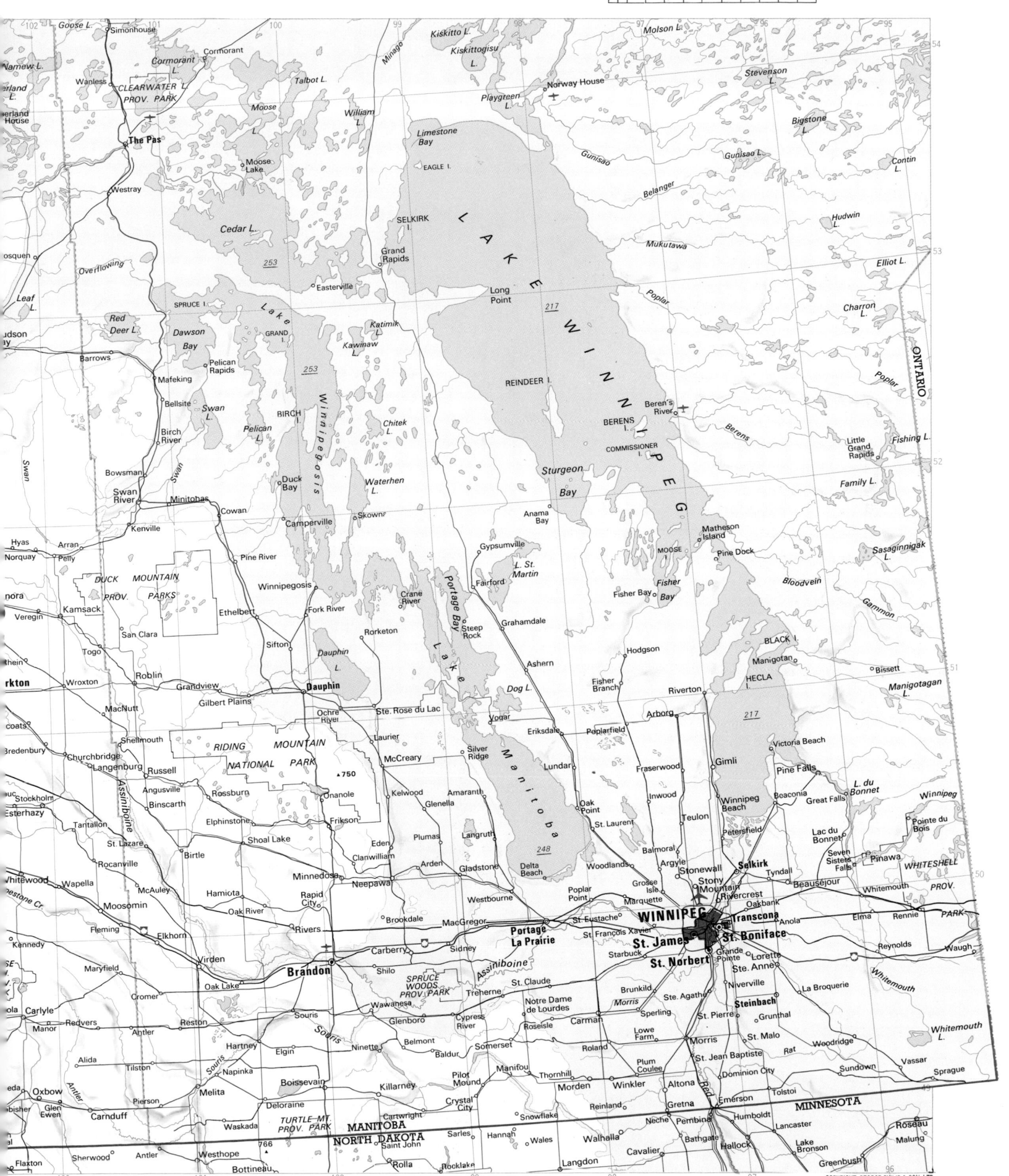

1:2 500 000

10 0 10 20 30 40 50 60 70 80 90 100 km

COPYRIGHT. GEORGE PHILIP & SON. LTD.

1:250 000

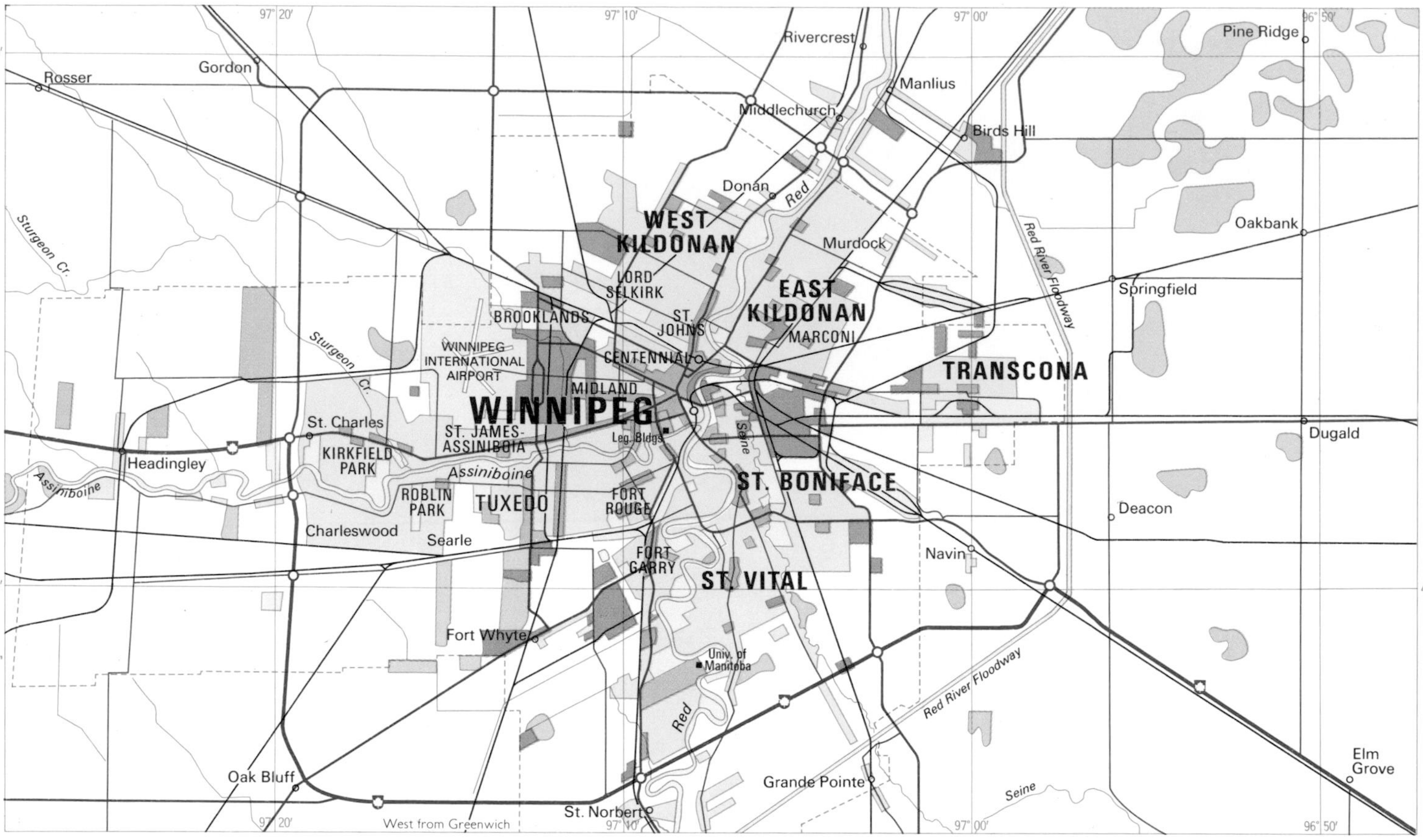

5 4 3 2 1 0 5 10 km

Winnipeg Map

50° 00'

97° 20' 97° 10' 97° 00' 96° 50'

Rivercrest
Pine Ridge
Rosser
Gordon
Manlius
Middlechurch
Birds Hill
Oakbank
Donan
Red
WEST KILDONAN
Murdock
Springfield
LORD SELKIRK
EAST KILDONAN
BROOKLANDS
ST. JOHNS
MARCONI
WINNIPEG INTERNATIONAL AIRPORT
CENTENNIAL
TRANSCONA
Sturgeon Cr.
Sturgeon
MIDLAND
WINNIPEG
St. Charles
ST. JAMES-ASSINIBOIA
Leg. Bldgs.
Dugald
KIRKFIELD PARK
Assiniboine
ST. BONIFACE
Headingley
Assiniboine
ROBLIN PARK
FORT ROUGE
Deacon
Charleswood
TUXEDO
Searle
FORT GARRY
Navin
49° 50'
ST. VITAL
Fort Whyte
Univ. of Manitoba
Red
Red River Floodway
Seine
Elm Grove
Oak Bluff
Grande Pointe
Seine
West from Greenwich
St. Norbert

Legend

| Residential | Industrial | Recreational | Transportation and utilities |
| Commercial | Institutional | Woodland | Agricultural and other |

—o— Freeway with interchange   —o— Trans-Canada Highway   —o— Railway with station   - - - - City Boundary

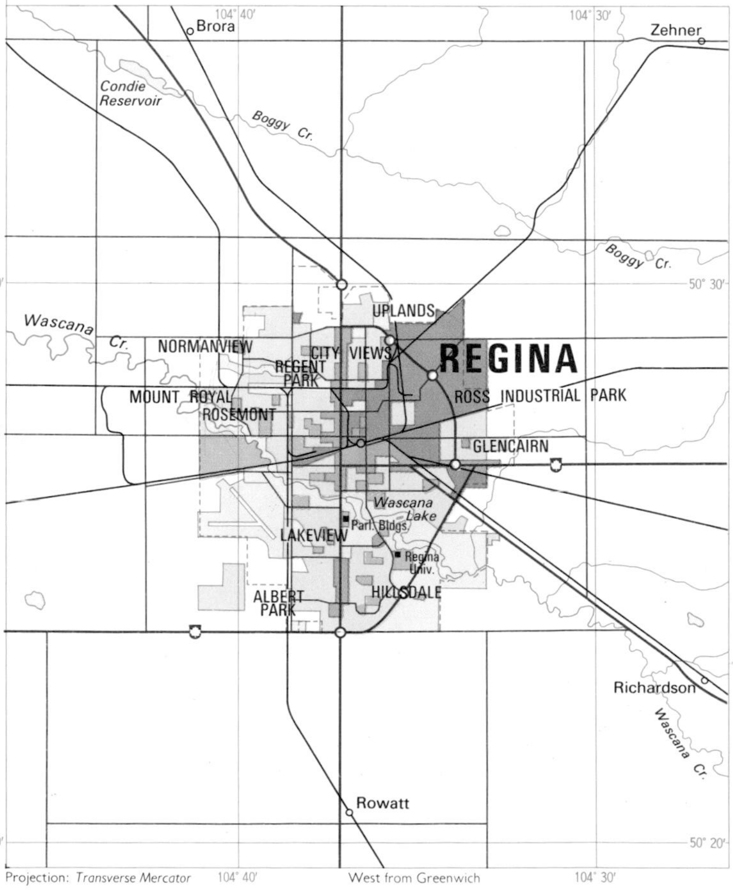

Regina Map

104° 40' 104° 30'

Brora
Zehner
Condie Reservoir
Boggy Cr.
50° 30'
Boggy Cr.
Wascana Cr.
UPLANDS
NORMANVIEW
CITY VIEWS
REGINA
REGENT PARK
MOUNT ROYAL
ROSS INDUSTRIAL PARK
ROSEMONT
GLENCAIRN
Wascana Lake
LAKEVIEW
Parl. Bldgs.
Regina Univ.
ALBERT PARK
HILLSDALE
Richardson
Wascana Cr.
Rowatt
50° 20'

Projection: Transverse Mercator   104° 40'   West from Greenwich   104° 30'

Winnipeg aerial view looking north.

Regina looking north across Wascana Lake.

1:250 000

5 4 3 2 1 0   5   10 km

Edmonton looking north with the Legislative Building in the centre and the city centre beyond.

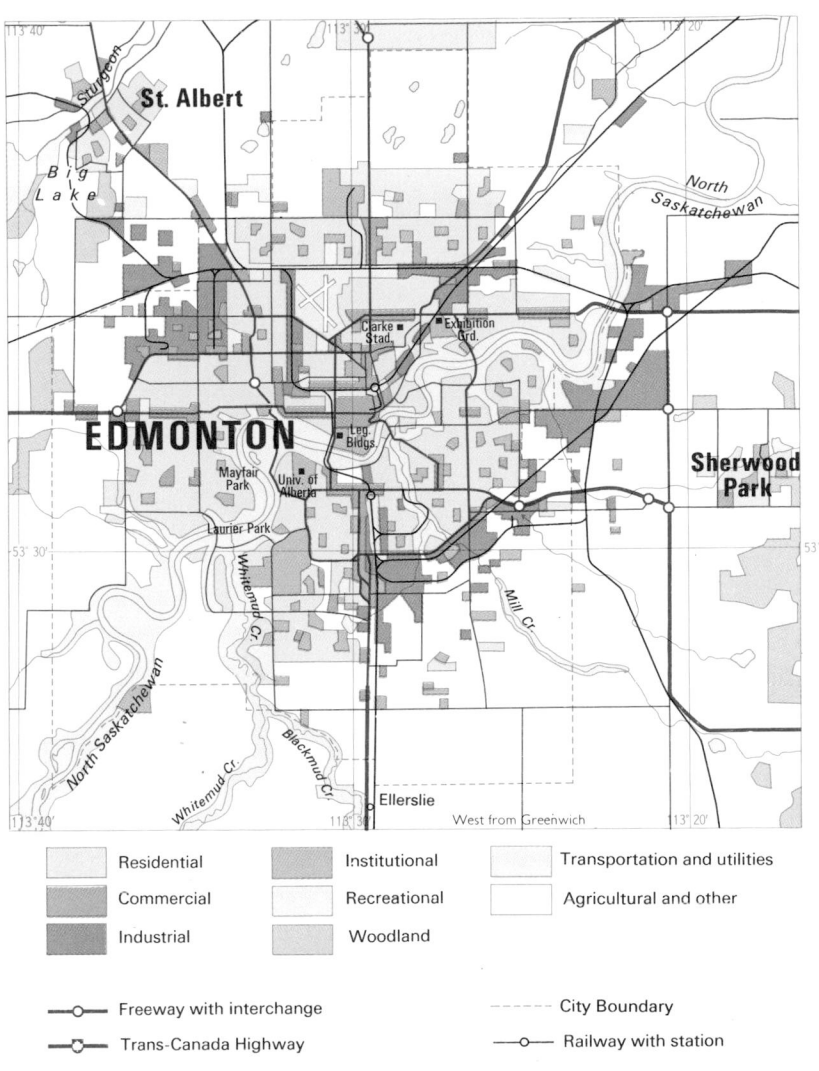

	Residential		Institutional		Transportation and utilities
	Commercial		Recreational		Agricultural and other
	Industrial		Woodland		

⊸○⊸ Freeway with interchange   - - - - City Boundary

⊸▭⊸ Trans-Canada Highway   —○— Railway with station

Calgary city centre looking south across Bow River, with Calgary Tower (188 metres high) at left.

Projection: Transverse Mercator

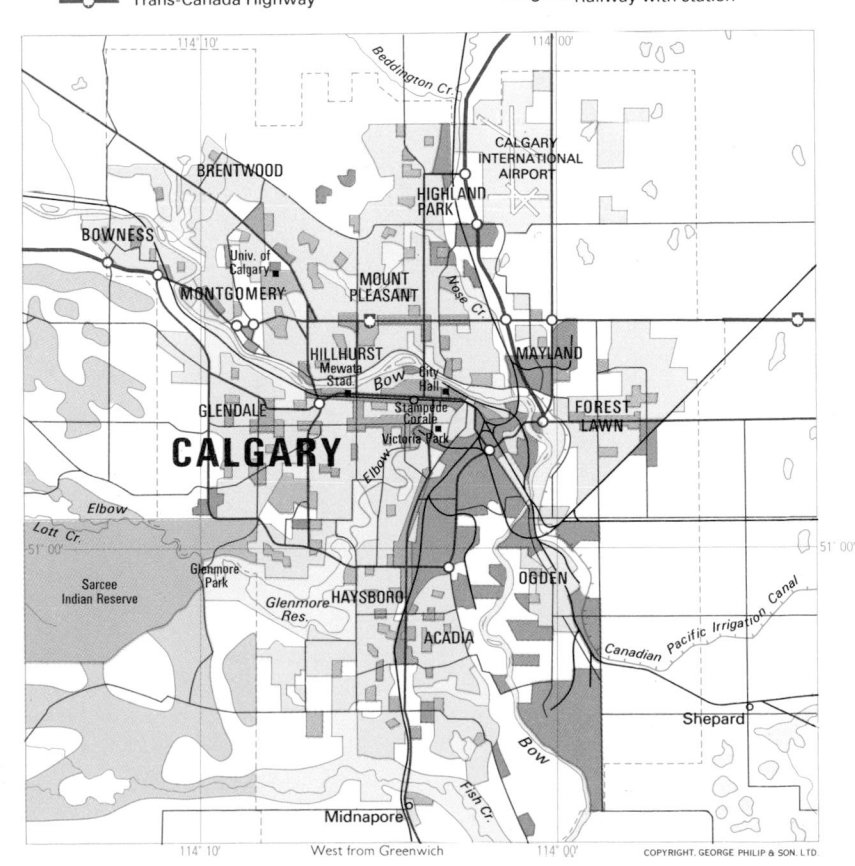

COPYRIGHT. GEORGE PHILIP & SON. LTD.

1:2 500 000

10　0　10　20　30　40　50　60　70　80　90　100 km

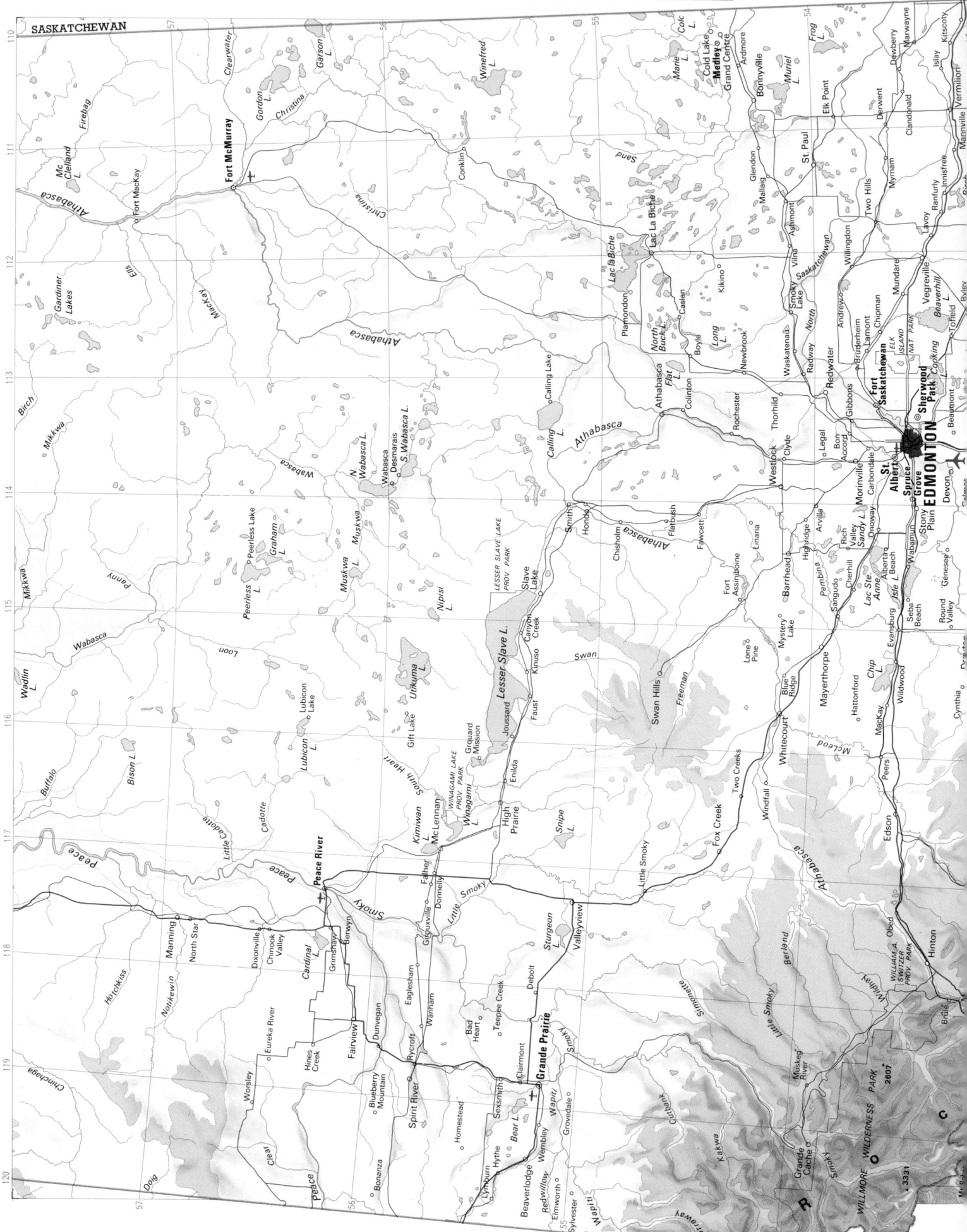

SASKATCHEWAN

Fort McMurray

EDMONTON

Peace River

Grande Prairie

Cold Lake
Medley
Grand Centre

Lac La Biche

Lesser Slave L.

Slave Lake

Fort Saskatchewan
Sherwood Park
St. Albert
Spruce Grove
Stony Plain

Hinton

WILLMORE WILDERNESS PARK

Projection: Lambert's Conformal Conic

West from Greenwich

COPYRIGHT GEORGE PHILIP & SON LTD.

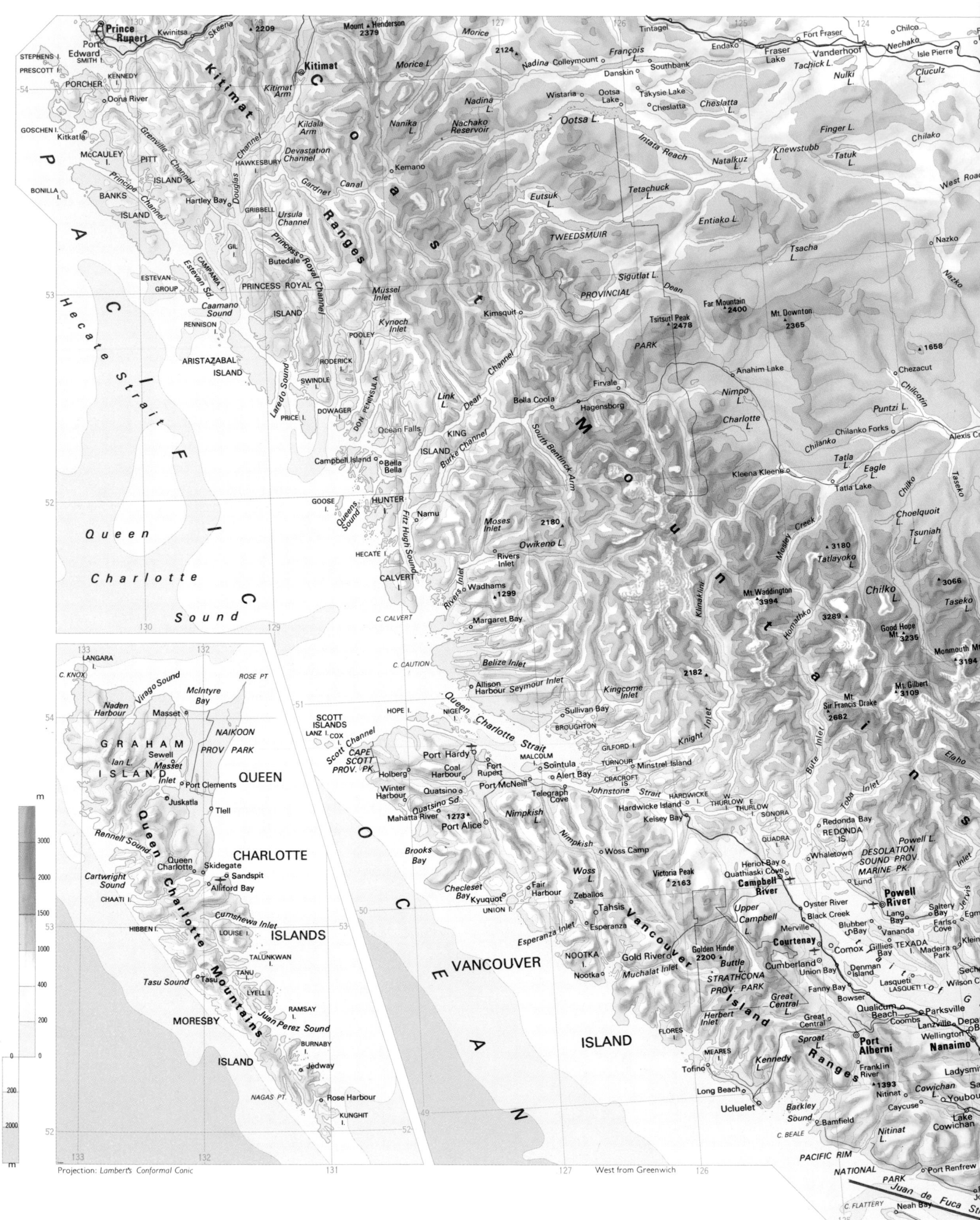

Projection: Lambert's Conformal Conic

West from Greenwich

1:2 500 000

10 0 10 20 30 40 50 60 70 80 90 100 km

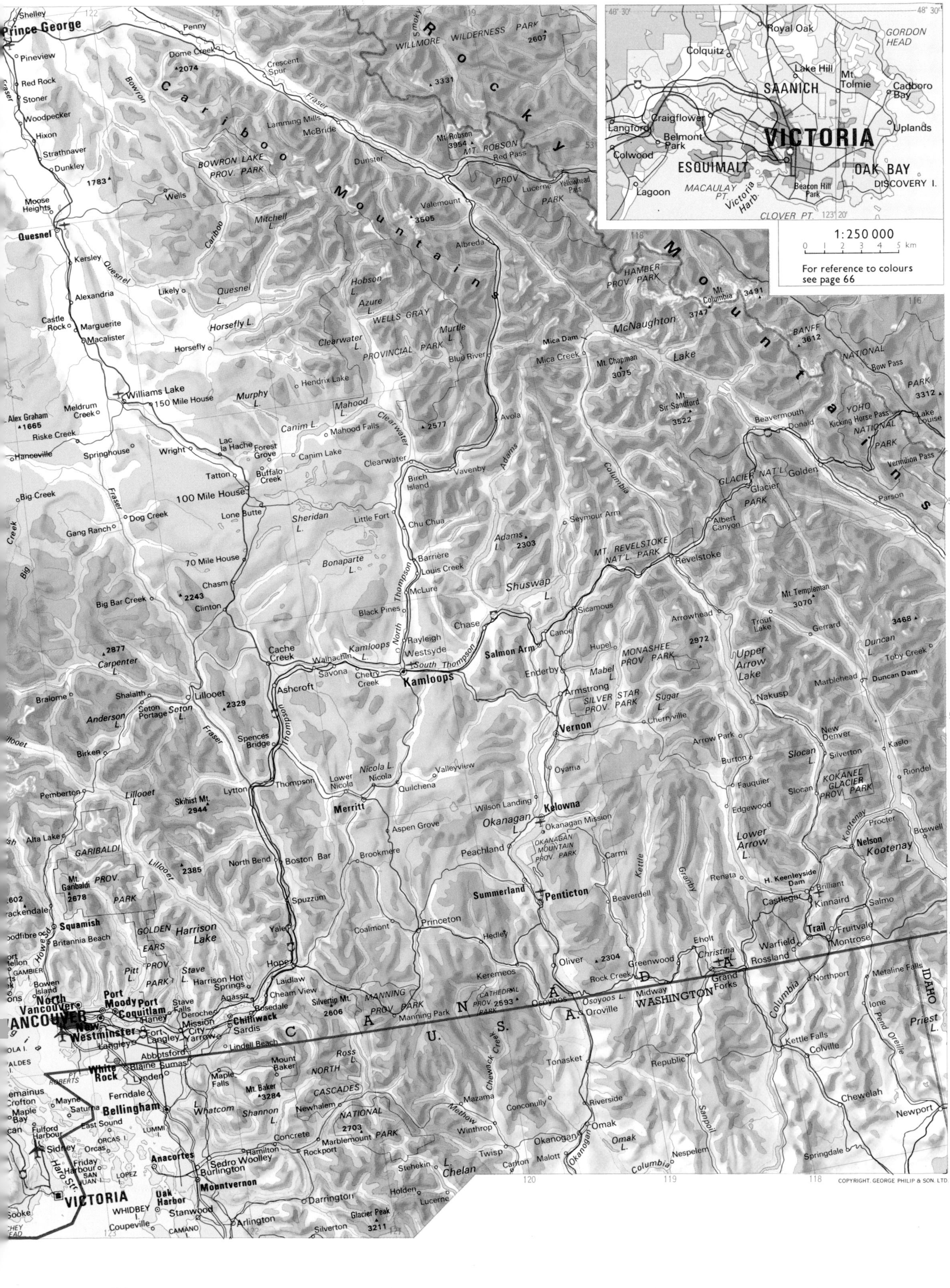

1:250 000

0 1 2 3 4 5 km

For reference to colours
see page 66

COPYRIGHT. GEORGE PHILIP & SON. LTD.

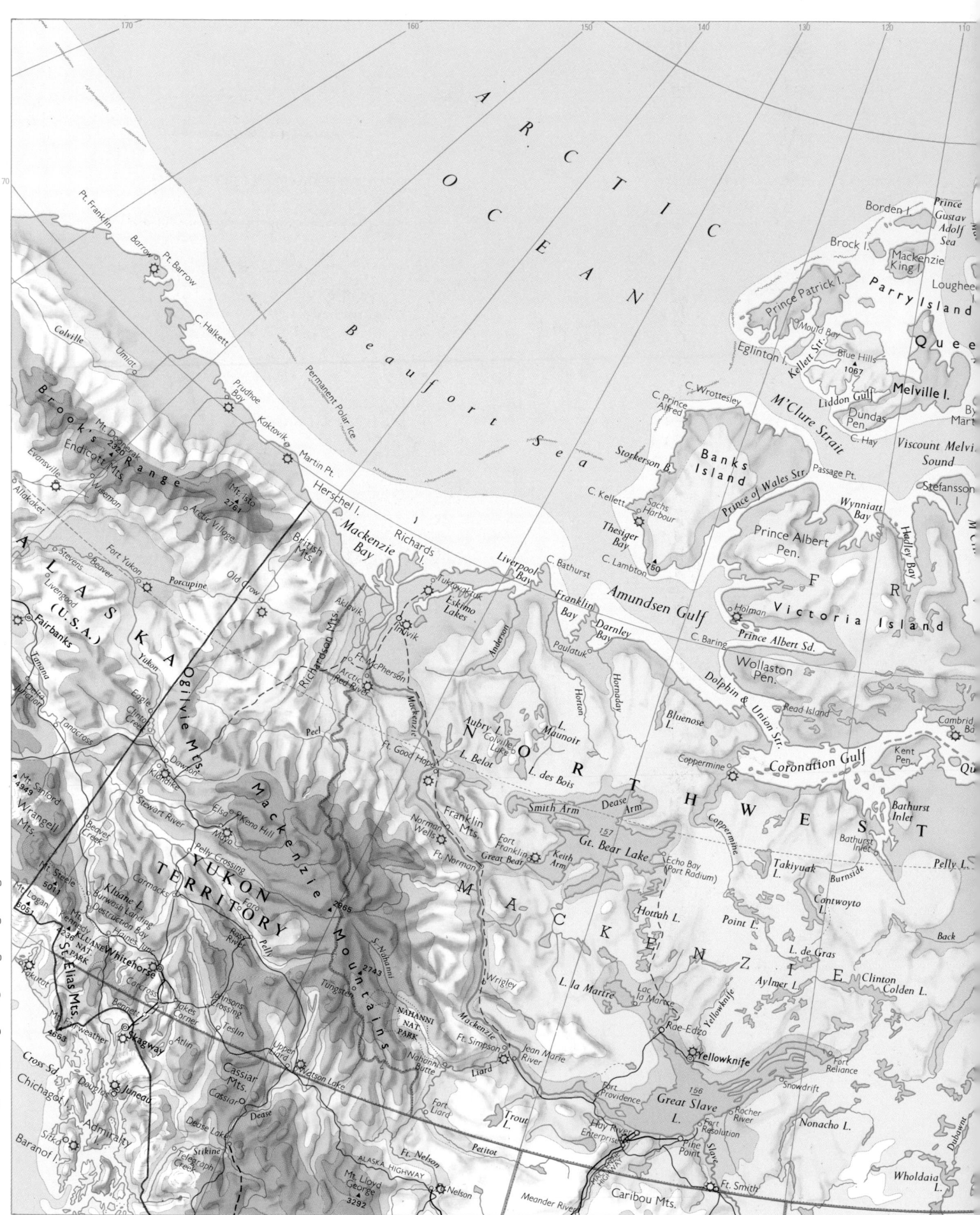

ARCTIC OCEAN

Beaufort Sea

Brook's Range

ALASKA (U.S.A.)

Banks Island

Victoria Island

Amundsen Gulf

NORTHWEST

MACKENZIE

YUKON TERRITORY

Mackenzie Mountains

Great Slave L.

Gt. Bear Lake

Yellowknife

Whitehorse

Juneau

Projection: Bonne

1:10 000 000

100   0   100   200   300   400 km

G R E E N L A N D

(DENMARK)

United States Range

Barbeau Pk.
2604

C. Thomas
Hubbard

Nansen Sd.

Greely Fd.

Kennedy Ch.

Kane
Basin

Humboldt
Glacier

Knud Rasmussen

Land

Princess
Margaret
Range

Eureka

Fosheim
Pen.

Victoria
and
Albert
Mts.

Axel
Heiberg
I.

2140

Ellesmere Island

Smith
B.

Kane
Basin

Inglefield Land

Inglefield
Gulf

Thule (Qanaq)

C. Parry

Kraulshavn

Sverdrup Chan.

Raanes
Pen.

Wolstenholme
Fjord

Dundas
(Thule)

Amund
Ringnes
I.

Norwegian
Bay

Graham
I.

Simmons
Pen.

Grise
Fiord

Coburg I.

C. York

Melville
Bay

Upernavik

Prøven

Cornwall I.

Belcher Channel

Lady Ann Str.

Glacier Str.

Svartenhuk
Peninsula

Umanak

Nugssuaq
Pen.

Penny Str.

Elizabeth

Is.

Jones Sound

Treuter Mts.

1887

Hyde Inlet

C. Cockburn

B a f f i n

Disko B.

Disko I.

Godthavn

Jakobshavn

North
Magnetic
Pole

Bathurst

Devon I.

C. Warrender

B a y

Cornwallis I.

Wellington
Chan.

Resolute

Barrow Str.

Lancaster Sound

C. Crawford

C. Liverpool

Nova
Zembla I.

C. Jameson

C. Hunter

Scott Inlet

C. Hewett

C. Raper

Holsteinsborg

Russell
I.

Somerset
I.

Prince Regent Inlet

Arctic
Bay

Numisivik

2134

Bylot I.

Pond Inlet

Pond Inlet

Bruce
Mts.

Clyde

C. Henry Kater

Home B.

D a v i s   S t r a i t

Prince
of
Wales I.

Boothia
Peninsula

Franklin Str.

C. Farrand

Brodeur

Peninsula

Borden
Peninsula

Eclipse Sd.

B a f f i n

Barnes
Icecap

Kivitoo

Broughton
Island

Podloping
Island

Cape Dyer

Gateshead
I.

573

Bernier B.

Admiralty Inlet

Steensby
Inlet

I s l a n d

Penny
Highland
2591

Cumberland Peninsula

Hoare B.

Hinson
Pen.

Gulf
of
Boothia

Thom Bay

Fury & Hecla Str.

C. Englefield

Igloolik

Rowley
I.

Foley I.

Baird
Pen.

Air
Force I.

Pangnirtung

C. Mercy

Admiralty

Spence Bay

Hall
Lake

Melville

Prince
Charles
I.

Cumberland Sound

Lemieux
Islands

King
William
I.

Simpson
Pen.

Pelly Bay

Wales

Peninsula

Committee B.

Nettilling
L.

Frobisher
Bay

Hall Pen.

Gjoa
Haven

T E R R I T O R I E S

Foxe Basin

C. Dominion

Amadjuak

Chantrey
Inlet

Rae
Isthmus

C. Dorchester

Amadjuak
L.

Everett Mts.

Resolution I.

Adelaide
Pen.

Repulse Bay

Arctic Circle

Vansittart

Cape Dorset

Lake
Harbour

Frobisher Bay

Macdougall
L.

Wager
Bay

Wager B.

Foxe Pen.

C. Chidley

Garry L.

Torsill
Mts.

Foxe

Channel

Salisbury

H u d s o n   S t r a i t

Port
Burwell

Chesterfield Inlet

Southampton I.

Coral
Harbour

Bell Pen.

Nottingham I.

Nottingham
Island

C. Hopes
Advance

Akpatok
I.

Baker
Lake

Baker L.

Chesterfield Inlet

Roes Welcome Sd.

C. Low

Fisher Strait

Coats
I.

Nottingham I.

Digges Is.

C. Wolstenholme

Wolstenholme

Ivugivik

Soglout

St. Louis Mts.

Koartac

Maricourt
(Wakeham)

Bellin
(Payne)

Ungava Bay

Port
Nouveau-Québec
(George R.)

K E E W A T I N

Dubawnt
L.

Rankin Inlet

Chesterfield
Inlet

Mansell I.

Arnaud
(Payne)

Port
Harrison

Yathkyed
L.

Kaminak
L.

Whale Cove

Cape Smith

Payne

Feuilles (Leaf)

Koksoak

Fort
Chimo

Padlei

Tavani

Povungnituk

Payne L.

Nueltin
L.

Eskimo Point

H u d s o n   B a y

Ottawa
Is.

Portland
Promontory

Inoucdjouac
Port Harrison

Mélèzes (Larch)

Caniapiscau

Thlewiaza

L. Minto

1 : 250 000

5 4 3 2 1 0   5   10 km

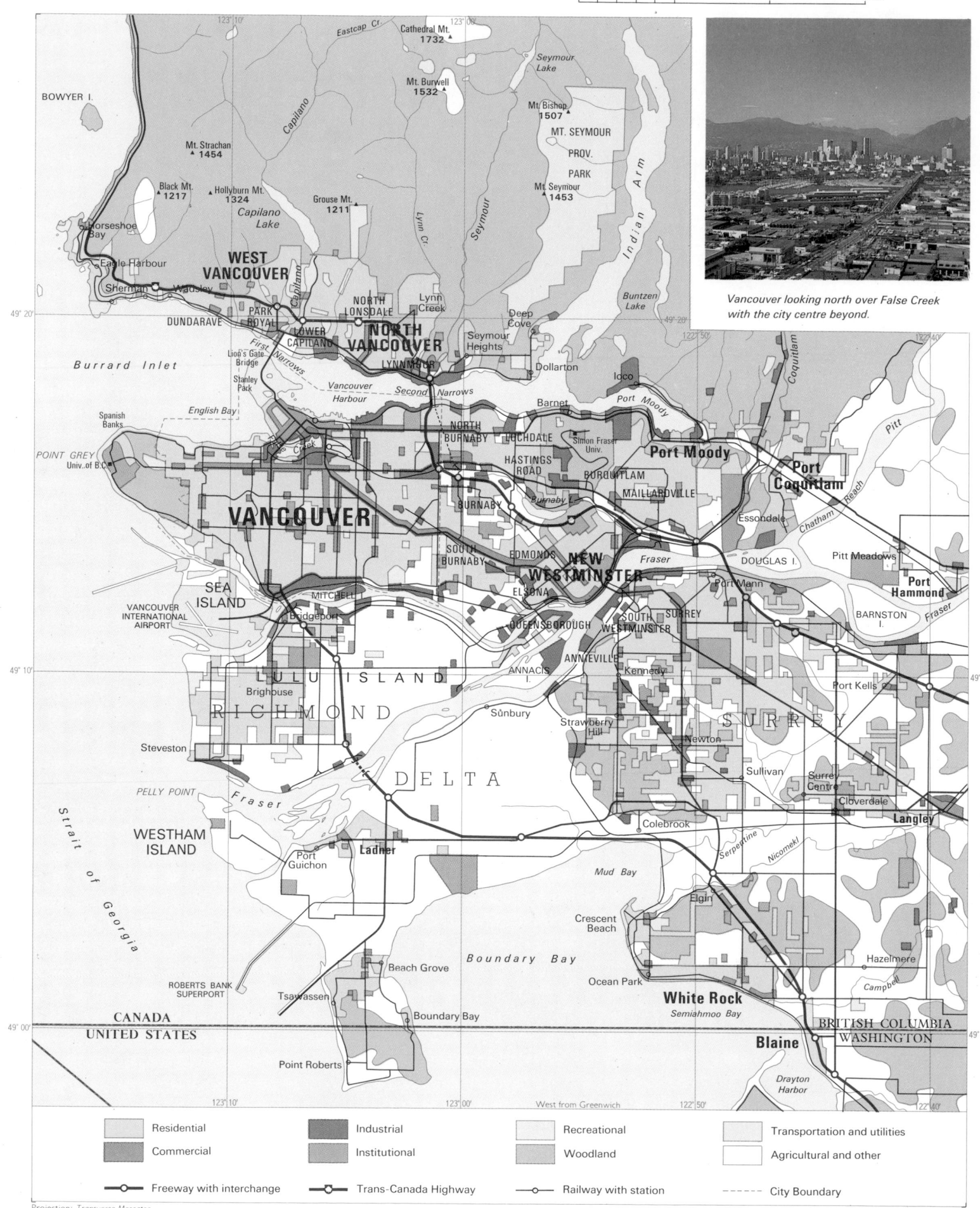

Vancouver looking north over False Creek with the city centre beyond.

BOWYER I.

Eastcap Cr.

Cathedral Mt.
▲ 1732

Seymour Lake

Mt. Burwell
▲ 1532

Mt Bishop
▲ 1507

MT. SEYMOUR

PROV.

Mt. Strachan
▲ 1454

PARK

Black Mt.
▲ 1217

Hollyburn Mt.
▲ 1324

Grouse Mt.
▲ 1211

Mt Seymour
▲ 1453

Capilano Lake

Horseshoe Bay

Eagle Harbour

WEST VANCOUVER

Sherman   Wadsley

DUNDARAVE

PARK ROYAL

NORTH LONSDALE

Lynn Creek

Buntzen Lake

Deep Cove

LOWER CAPILANO

NORTH VANCOUVER

LYNNMOUR

Seymour Heights

Dollarton

Lion's Gate Bridge

First Narrows

Burrard Inlet

Stanley Park

Vancouver Harbour

Second Narrows

Barnet

Ioco

Port Moody

English Bay

Spanish Banks

NORTH BURNABY

LOCHDALE

Simon Fraser Univ.

Port Moody

POINT GREY

Univ. of B.C.

False Creek

HASTINGS ROAD

BURQUITLAM

Port Coquitlam

VANCOUVER

BURNABY

MAILLARDVILLE

Burnaby L.

Coquitlam

Pitt

Essondale

SOUTH BURNABY

EDMONDS

NEW WESTMINSTER

Fraser

DOUGLAS I.

Pitt Meadows

Port Hammond

SEA ISLAND

MITCHELL

ELSONA

Port Mann

BARNSTON I.

VANCOUVER INTERNATIONAL AIRPORT

Bridgeport

QUEENSBOROUGH

SOUTH WESTMINSTER

SOUTH SURREY

Fraser

ANNACIS I.

ANNIEVILLE

Port Kells

LULU ISLAND

Brighouse

Kennedy

RICHMOND

Sunbury

Strawberry Hill

Newton

Sullivan

S U R R E Y

Surrey Centre

Steveston

Cloverdale

Langley

PELLY POINT

Fraser

D E L T A

Colebrook

Serpentine

Nicomekl

WESTHAM ISLAND

Port Guichon

Ladner

Strait of Georgia

Mud Bay

Elgin

Hazelmere

ROBERTS BANK SUPERPORT

Tsawwassen

Beach Grove

Boundary Bay

Crescent Beach

Ocean Park

Campbell

CANADA
UNITED STATES

Boundary Bay

White Rock

Semiahmoo Bay

BRITISH COLUMBIA
WASHINGTON

Blaine

Point Roberts

Drayton Harbor

West from Greenwich

Residential | Industrial | Recreational | Transportation and utilities
Commercial | Institutional | Woodland | Agricultural and other

⊶○⊶ Freeway with interchange   ━○━ Trans-Canada Highway   ─○─ Railway with station   ------ City Boundary

Projection: *Transverse Mercator*

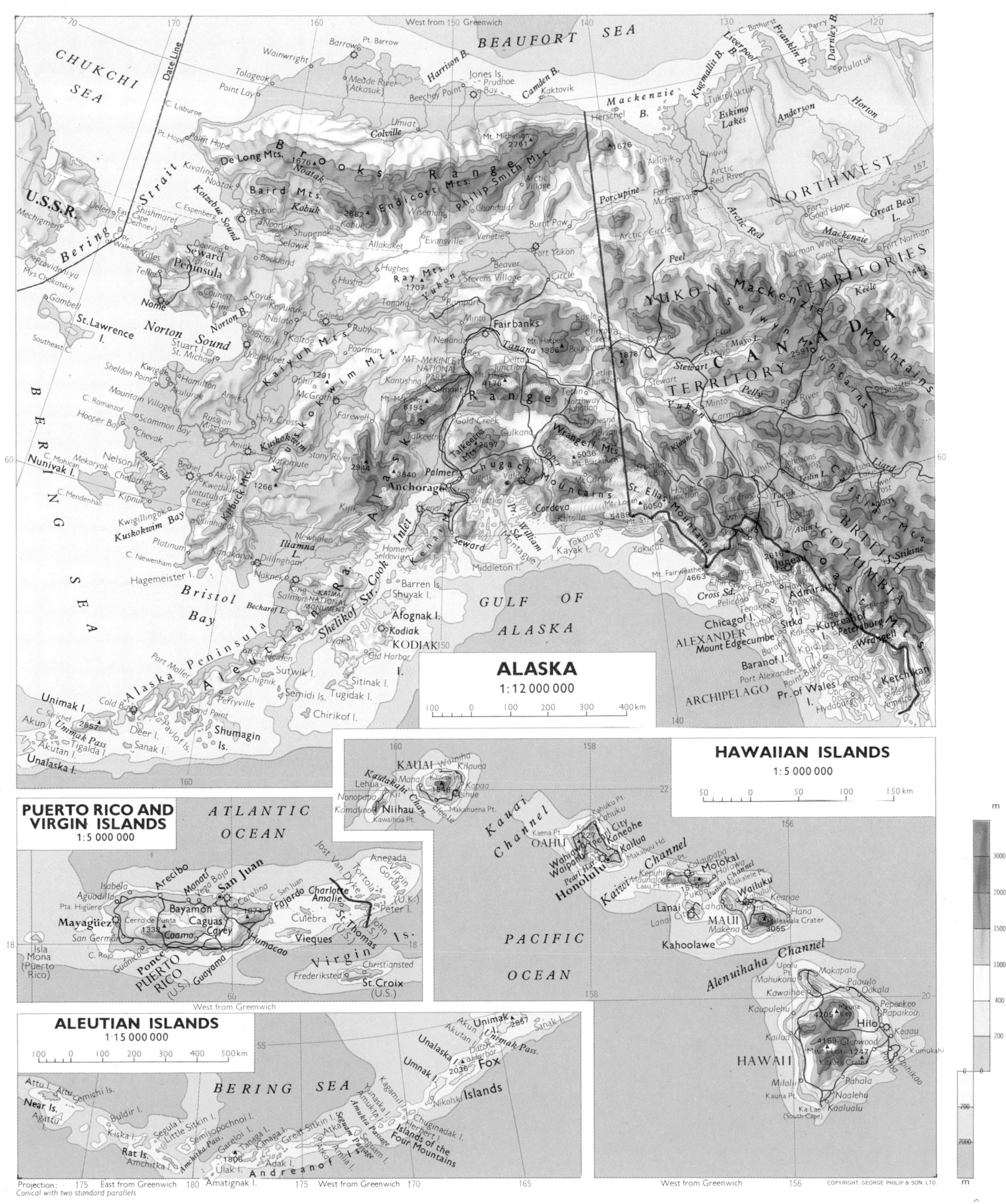

ALASKA
1:12 000 000

100 0 100 200 300 400 km

HAWAIIAN ISLANDS
1:5 000 000

50 0 50 100 150 km

PUERTO RICO AND VIRGIN ISLANDS
1:5 000 000

ALEUTIAN ISLANDS
1:15 000 000

100 0 100 200 300 400 500 km

Projection:
Conical with two standard parallels

COPYRIGHT. GEORGE PHILIP & SON. LTD

1:12 000 000

100   0   100   200   300   400   500 km

Projection: Bonne

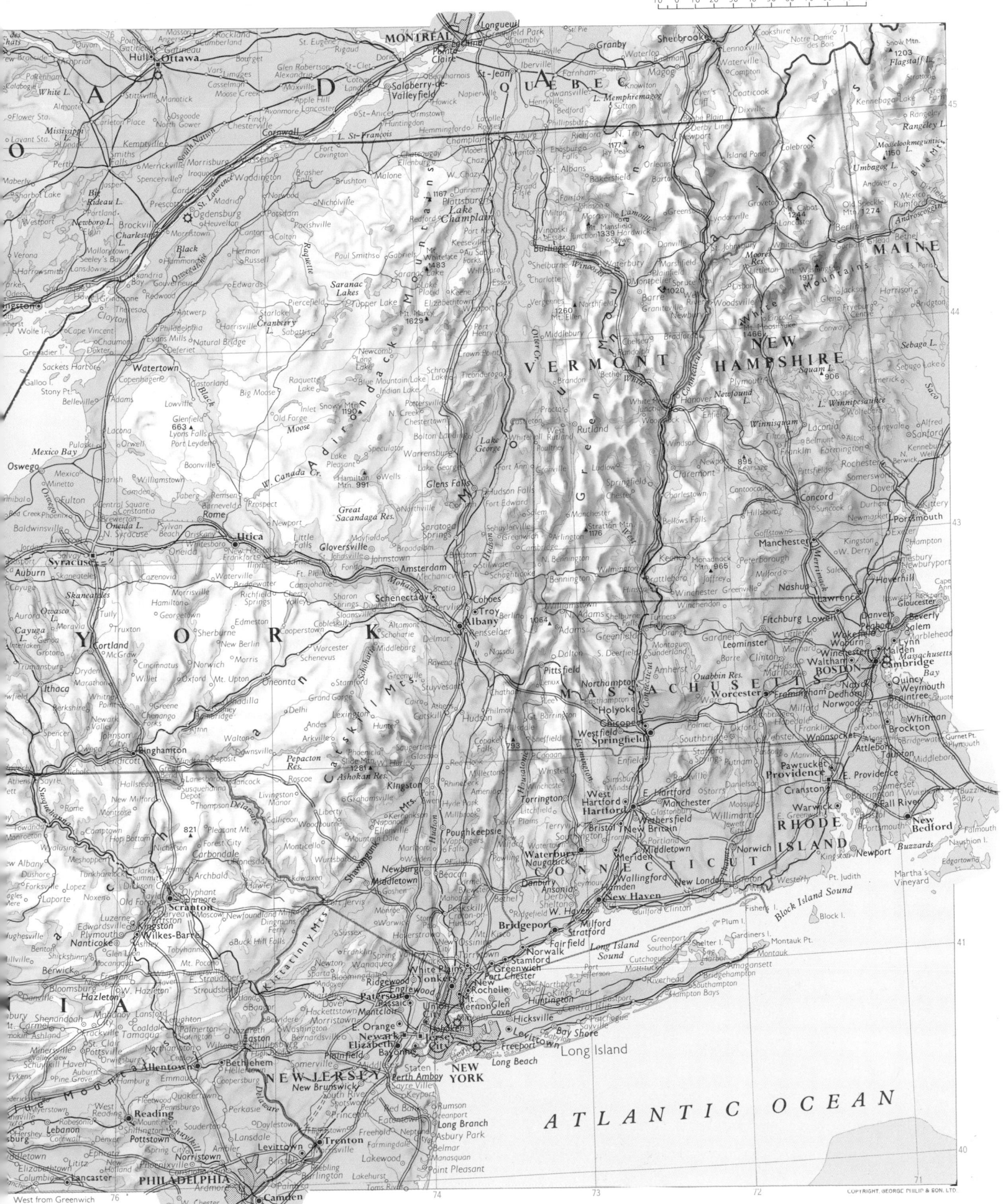

1 : 2 500 000

10 0 10 20 30 40 50 60 70 80 90 100 km

ATLANTIC OCEAN

West from Greenwich   COPYRIGHT, GEORGE PHILIP & SON, LTD.

QUEBEC

ONTARIO

NEW HAMPSHIRE

VERMONT

NEW YORK

NEW JERSEY

PENNSYLVANIA

MARYLAND

DELAWARE

VIRGINIA

WEST VIRGINIA

OHIO

KENTUCKY

INDIANA

MICHIGAN

WISCONSIN

LAKE SUPERIOR

LAKE HURON

LAKE ONTARIO

LAKE ERIE

Georgian Bay

Chesapeake Bay

MONTREAL

BOSTON

NEW YORK

PHILADELPHIA

BALTIMORE

WASHINGTON

PITTSBURGH

CLEVELAND

DETROIT

CHICAGO

MILWAUKEE

CINCINNATI

INDIANAPOLIS

BUFFALO

TORONTO

Ottawa

Quebec

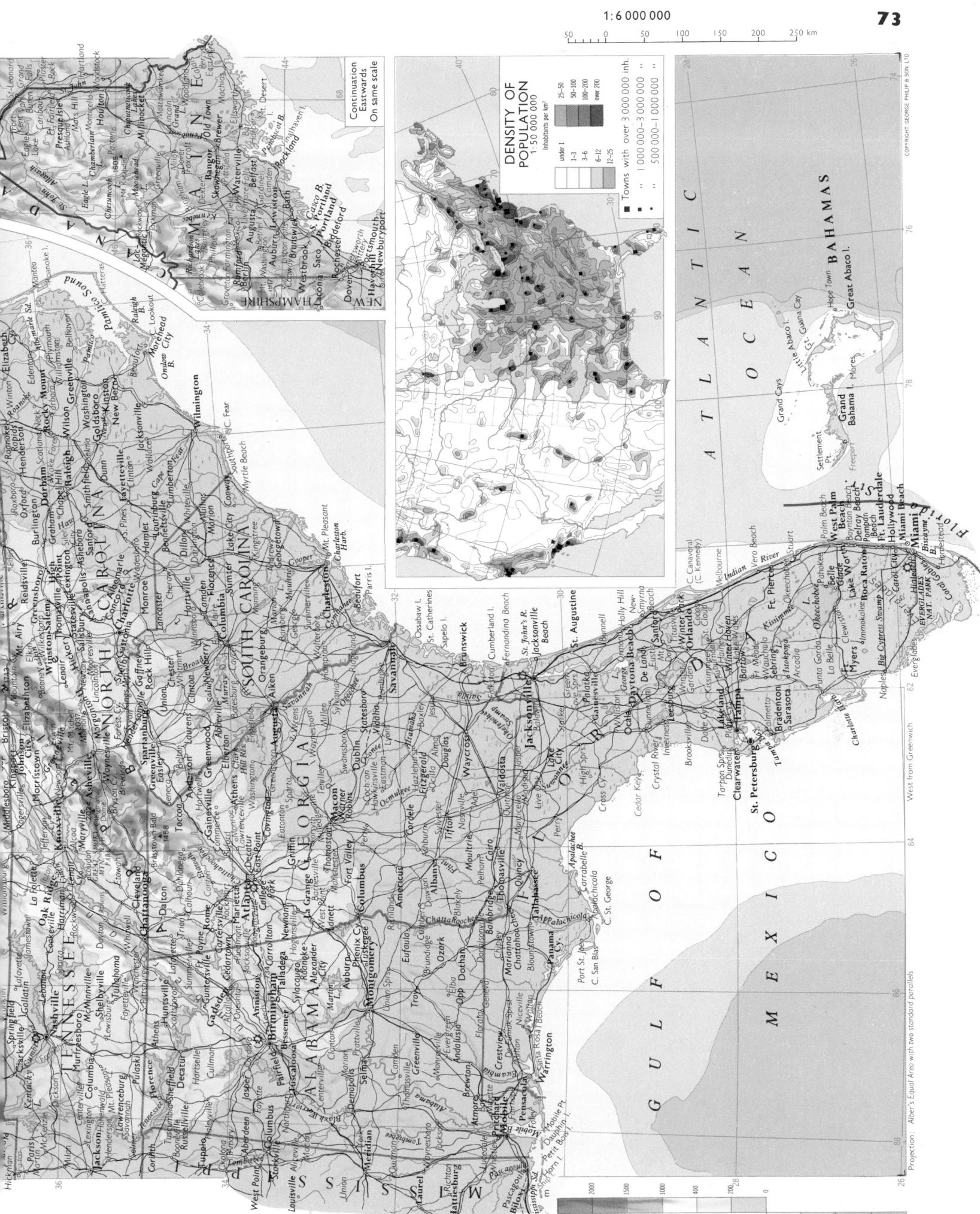

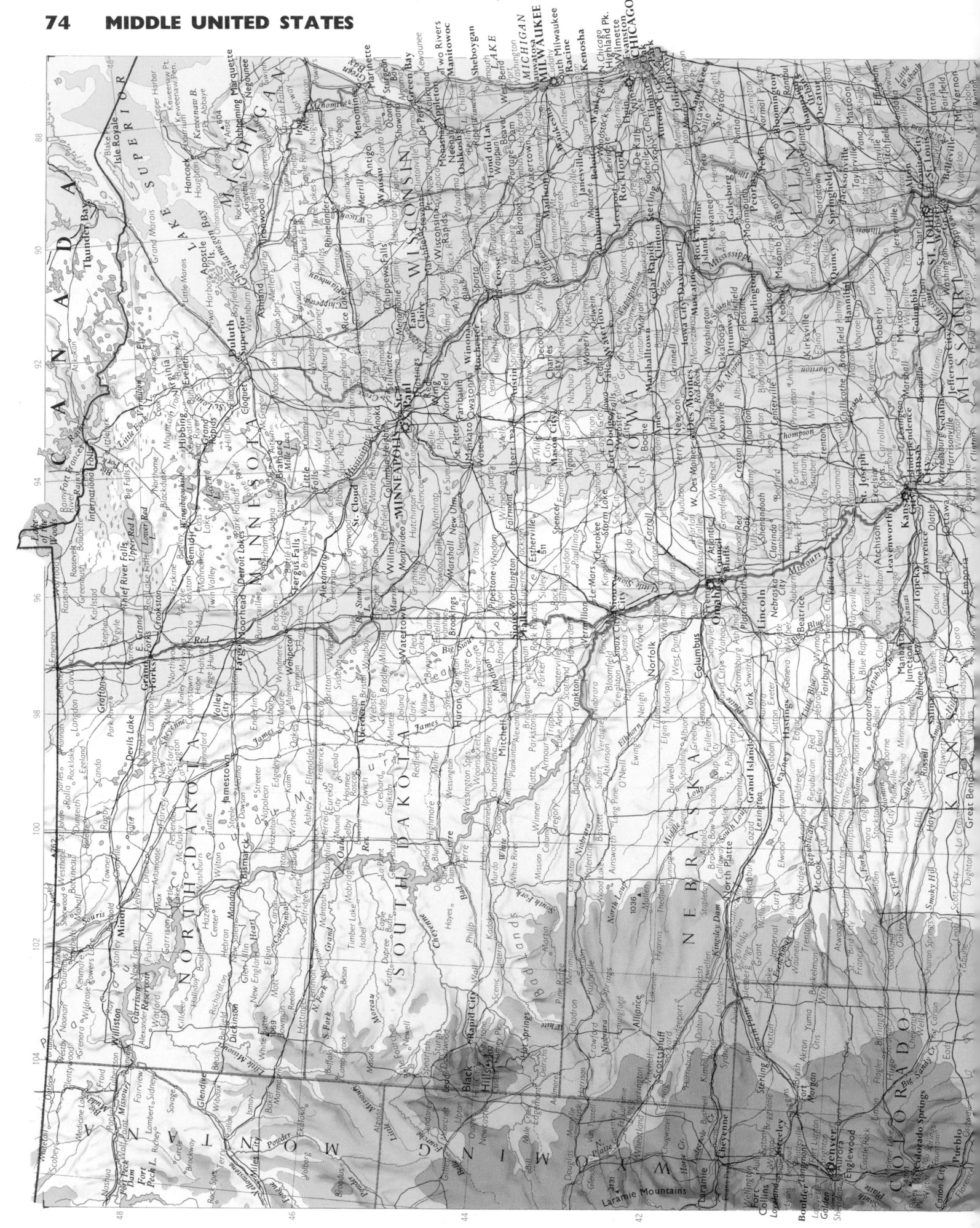

1:6 000 000

50   0   50   100   150   200   250 km

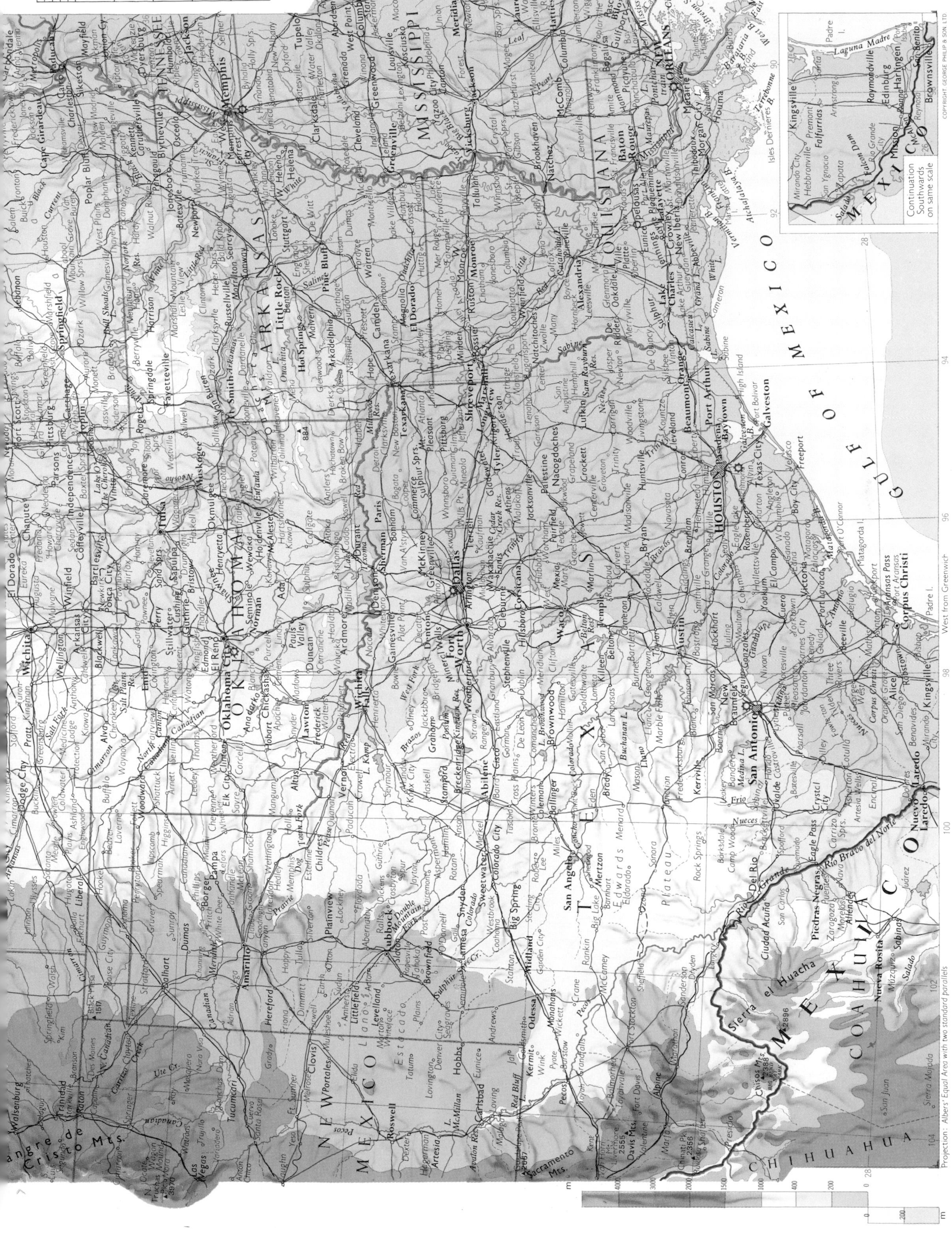

TENNESSEE

MISSISSIPPI

ARKANSAS

OKLAHOMA

LOUISIANA

T E X A S

NEW MEXICO

MEXICO

COAHUILA

CHIHUAHUA

GULF OF MEXICO

Memphis
Little Rock
Hot Springs
El Dorado
Shreveport
Texarkana
Baton Rouge
New ORLEANS
Jackson
Vicksburg
Natchez
Meridian
Tupelo
Oklahoma City
Tulsa
Wichita
Wichita Falls
Amarillo
Lubbock
Fort Worth
Dallas
Abilene
San Angelo
Austin
San Antonio
HOUSTON
Beaumont
Port Arthur
Galveston
Corpus Christi
Laredo
Nuevo Laredo
Piedras Negras
Ciudad Acuña
Del Rio
Midland
Odessa
Hobbs
Carlsbad
Roswell
Clovis
Tucumcari
Dodge City
Waco
Alexandria
Lake Charles
Monroe
Ruston
Baton Rouge
Laguna Madre
Brownsville
Harlingen
Kingsville

Sangre de Cristo Mts.

Sierra el Huacha

Edwards Plateau

Llano Estacado

Laguna Madre

Continuation Southwards on same scale

Projection: Albers' Equal Area with two standard parallels

West from Greenwich

COPYRIGHT GEORGE PHILIP & SON LTD

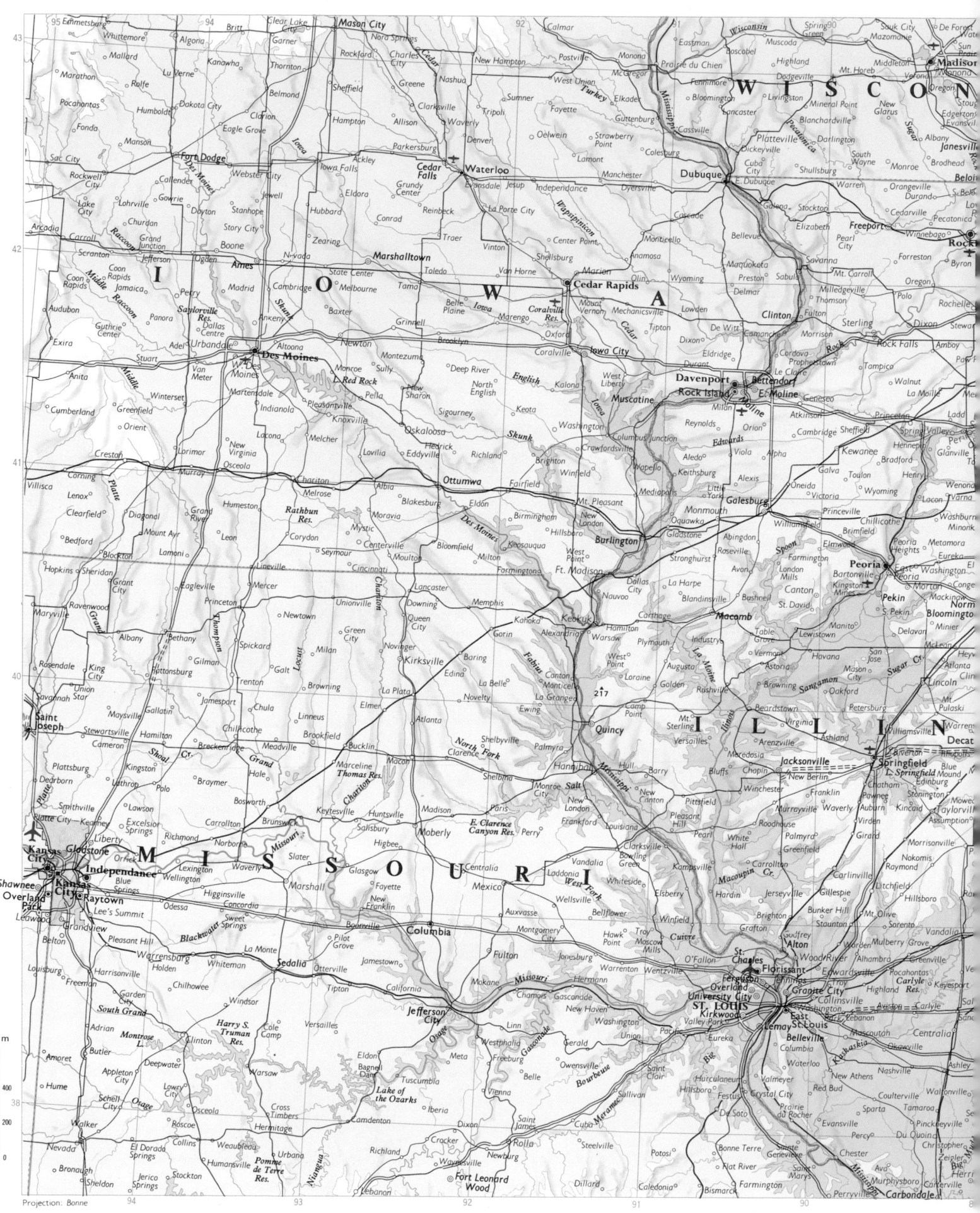

Projection: Bonne

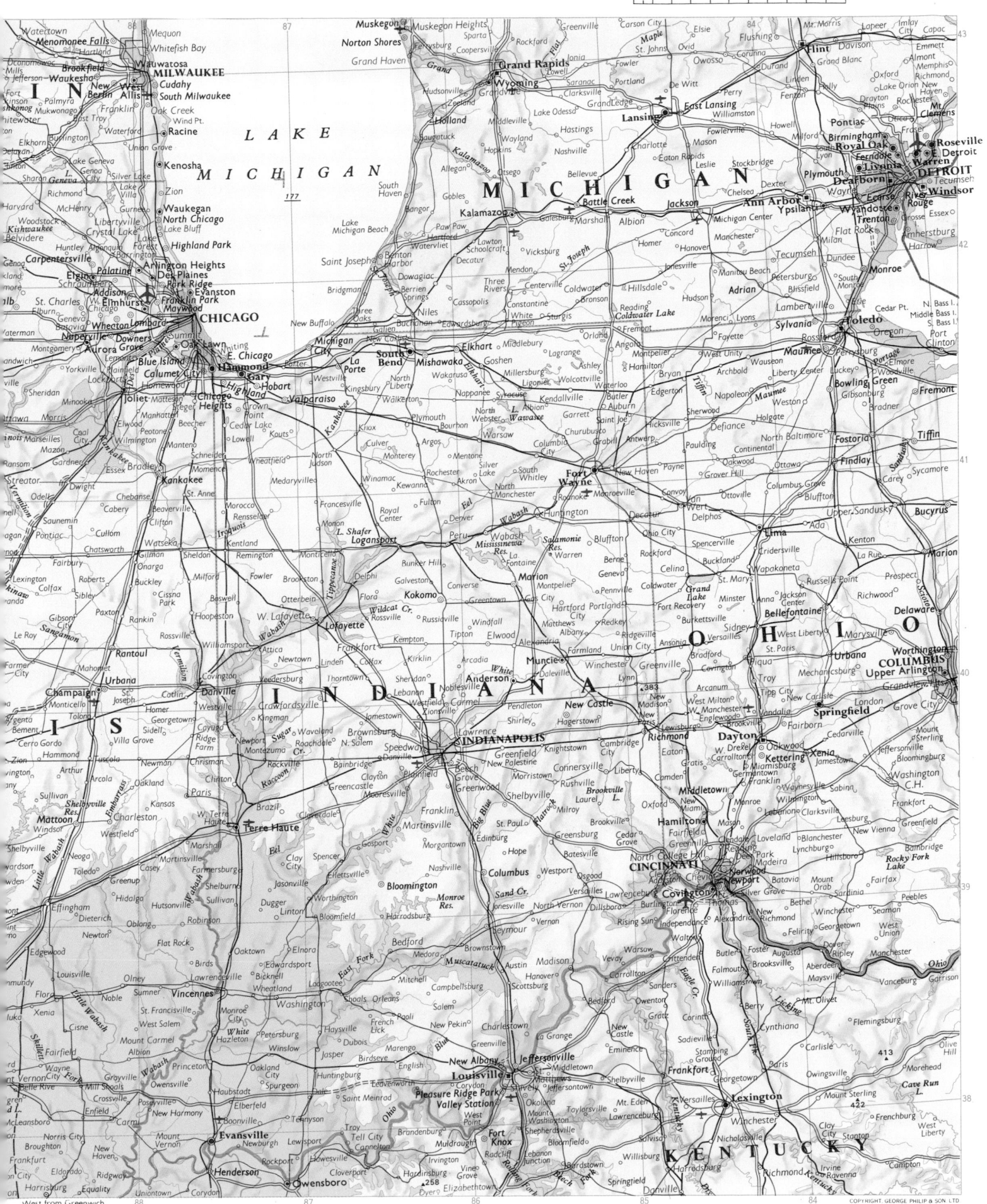

1 : 2 500 000

10 0 10 20 30 40 50 60 70 80 90 100 km

1:6 000 000

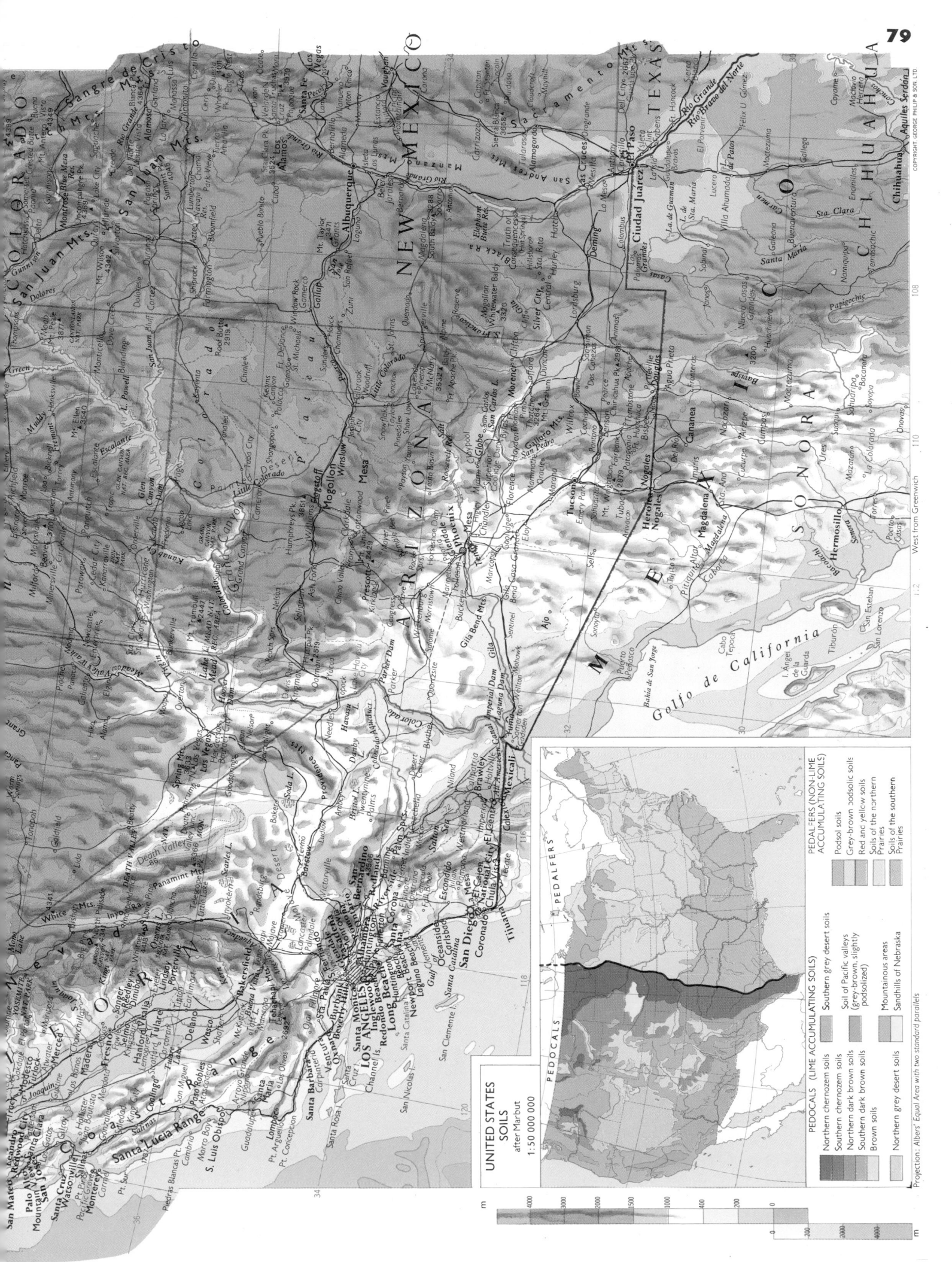

COLORADO

NEW MEXICO

ARIZONA

TEXAS

CHIHUAHUA

SONORA

MEXICO

Golfo de California

NEVADA

CALIFORNIA

Los Angeles
San Diego
Tijuana
Mexicali

Phoenix
Tucson

El Paso
Ciudad Juárez

Albuquerque
Santa Fe

Death Valley

**UNITED STATES
SOILS**
after Marbut
1:50 000 000

PEDOCALS (LIME ACCUMULATING SOILS)

Northern chernozem soils
Southern chernozem soils
Northern dark brown soils
Southern dark brown soils
Brown soils
Northern grey desert soils
Southern grey desert soils
Soil of Pacific valleys (grey-brown, slightly podsolized)

PEDALFERS (NON-LIME ACCUMULATING SOILS)

Podsol soils
Grey-brown podsolic soils
Red and yellow soils
Soils of the northern Prairies
Soils of the southern Prairies
Mountainous areas
Sandhills of Nebraska

PEDALFERS

PEDOCALS

Projection: Albers' Equal Area with two standard parallels

West from Greenwich

COPYRIGHT GEORGE PHILIP & SON, LTD.

m
4000
3000
2000
1500
1000
400
200
0

m
200
2000
4000

SEATTLE-PORTLAND REGION
On same scale

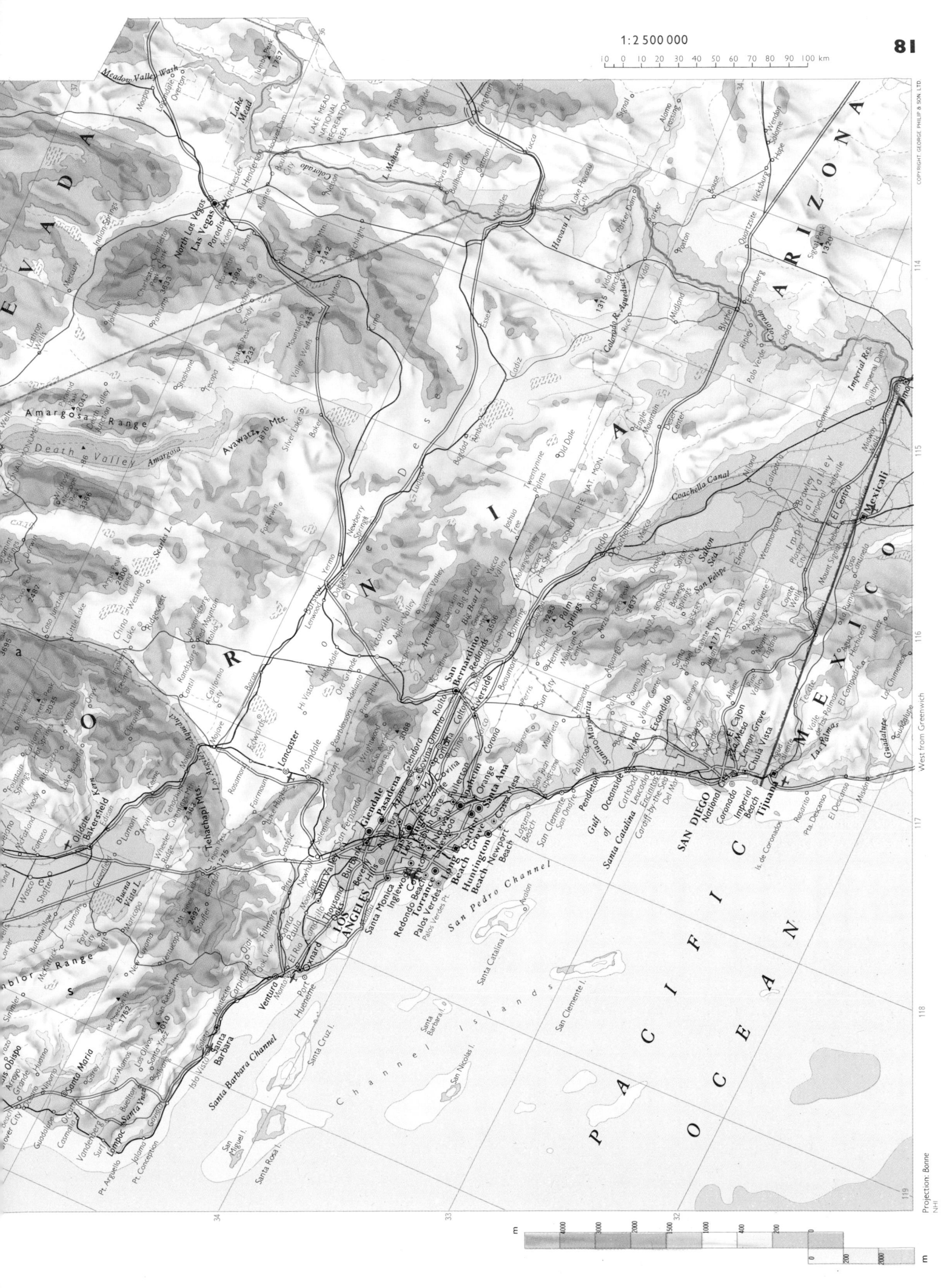

1:2 500 000

10 0 10 20 30 40 50 60 70 80 90 100 km

81

Projection: Bonne

NEVADA

ARIZONA

CALIFORNIA

M E X I C O

P A C I F I C   O C E A N

Meadow Valley Wash

Lake Mead

LAKE MEAD NATIONAL RECREATION AREA

Colorado

North Las Vegas
Las Vegas
Paradise

Death Valley

Amargosa Range

Avawatz Mts.

D e s e r t

M O J A V E   D E S E R T

Barstow

Colorado R. Aqueduct

Coachella Canal

Salton Sea

JOSHUA TREE NAT. MON.
Joshua Tree
Twentynine Palms

Palm Springs

Bakersfield

Lancaster
Palmdale

Mojave

Tehachapi Mts.

San Bernardino
Riverside
Redlands
Colton
Ontario
Pomona
Covina
Fullerton
Orange
Santa Ana

LOS ANGELES
Glendale
Pasadena
Burbank
Beverly Hills
Santa Monica
Inglewood
Torrance
Redondo Beach
Palos Verdes
Palos Verdes Pt.
Long Beach
Huntington Beach
Newport Beach
Laguna Beach
Costa Mesa
Garden Grove
Anaheim

Ventura
Port Hueneme
Oxnard

Santa Barbara

Santa Barbara Channel

C h a n n e l   I s l a n d s

San Miguel I.
Santa Rosa I.
Santa Cruz I.
Santa Barbara I.
San Nicolas I.

San Pedro Channel

Santa Catalina I.
Avalon

San Clemente I.

Oceanside
Carlsbad
Encinitas
Del Mar

SAN DIEGO
Coronado
Imperial Beach
Chula Vista
National City
La Mesa
El Cajon
Escondido
Vista

Tijuana

Mexicali
El Centro
Imperial
Brawley

Imperial Dam
Yuma

Signal Peak
1320

Santa Maria
Lompoc

West from Greenwich

COPYRIGHT GEORGE PHILIP & SON, LTD

34

33

32

114

115

116

117

118

119

m 4000 3000 2000 1500 1000 400 200 0 200 2000 m

REFERENCE TO NUMBERS

1 Federal District
2 Aguascalientes
3 Guanajuato
4 Hidalgo
5 México
6 Morelos
7 Querétaro
8 Tlaxcala

Projection: Bi-polar oblique Conical Orthomorphic

West from Greenwich

1 : 8 000 000

50 0 50 100 150 200 250 300 km

Wichita
Falls
Denison
Sherman
Paris Hope
Camden
Texarkana ARKANSAS
Texarkana El Dorado
Greenville
Greenwood
Tuscaloosa
Opelika
Columbus
McRae

FORT WORTH DALLAS
Denton Greenville
Marshall
Longview
Tyler
Corsicana
Monroe
Tallulah
Vicksburg
MISSISSIPPI
Meridian
Jackson
Montgomery
Selma
Phenix City
Americus
Albany
GEORGIA
Cordele
Tifton
Waycross

D
Cleburne
Ranger
Hillsboro
Palestine
Waco
Shreveport
Natchez
Laurel
Hattiesburg
Dothan
Chattahoochee
Valdosta

X Brownwood
Temple
Huntsville
Bryan
Lufkin
Nacogdoches
Alexandria
McComb
Bogalusa
Baton
Rouge
Hammond
FLORIDA
Lake
City

Austin
Navasota
Beaumont
Lake Charles
Lafayette
NEW
ORLEANS
Gulfport
Biloxi
MOBILE
Pensacola
Panama City
Apalchee
Bay
Suwannee
Clearwater

SAN
ANTONIO
HOUSTON
Port
Arthur
Rosenberg
Galveston
Breton Sound
Mississippi
Delta
C. San Blas

Dilley
Victoria
Atchafalaya
Bay
Terrebonne B.

Alice
Corpus Christi

Laredo
Kingsville
Nuevo Laredo
Zapata
GULF OF

Camargo
McAllen
Harlingen
Brownsville
Laguna Madre
MEXICO

Reynosa
Gomez
China
Matamoros
Santa Teresa

Montemorelos
Mendez
Laguna Madre

Linares
San Fernando

Villagran
Santander Jiménez
La Pesca
Soto la Marina

Ciudad
Victoria
Sierra de
Tamaulipas
CUBA
Guane
La Fe

Aldama
Pta. Jerez
Corrientes

Ciudad Mante
Isla
Desterrada
Isla Pérez
Canal de Yucatán
C. San Antonio

Ciudad Madero
Tampico
Pta.
Yalkubul
Rio Lagartos
C. Catoche
Pto. Juárez

Ciudad
Valles
Dzilam
de Bravo
El Cuyo
Pto. Morelos

Tempoal
C. Rojo
Progreso
Temax
Tizimín
El Díaz

Tantoyuca
Laguna de Tamiahua
Dzibilchaltun
Motul
Izamal
Espita
Valladolid
Isla
Cozumel

Poza Rica
Papantla
MÉRIDA
YUCATÁN
Chichén
Itzá
Cozumel

Huauchinango
Nautla
Maxcanú
Sotuta
Peto
Vigia Chico
B. de la Ascensión

Tulancingo
Teziutlán
Ticul
Tekax
Bolonchenticul
B. del Espíritu Santo

MEXICO
Jalapa
Zempoala
Tenabo
Peto

Coatepec
Veracruz
Campeche
Hopelchen
Felipe Carrillo
Puerto
QUINTANA

Orizaba
Córdoba
Alvarado
Golfo
de
Campeche
Champotón
San José Carpizo
ROO

Tehuacán
Cosamaloapan
San Andrés
Tuxtla
Chenkán
Juárez
Pedro Antonio Santos
Bacalar

Cárdenas
Villahermosa
Ciudad del
Carmen
Laguna de Términos
CAMPECHE
Chetumal
B. de
Chetumal

Minatitlán
Coatzacoalcos
Frontera
Paraíso
TABASCO
Concepción
Palizada
Orange Walk
Ambergris Cay

Acayucan
Istmo
de
Comalcalco
Belize
City
BELIZE

Oaxaca
OAXACA
Tehuantepec
CHIAPA
San Cristóbal de
las Casas
Maya Mts.
Golfo de Honduras
Islas de
la Bahía

Ixtepec
Juchitán
Tuxtla
Gutiérrez
Comitán
Puerto Barrios
San Pedro Sula

Tehuantepec
Salina Cruz
Arriaga
Tonalá
GUATEMALA
Cobán
HONDURAS
Tegucigalpa

Tapachula
Coatepec
GUATEMALA

GULF OF MEXICO

GREATER

CARI...

Isla Desterrada
Isla Pérez

Progreso
Mérida
YUCATÁN
Campeche
CAMPECHE
Ciudad del Carmen
Laguna de Términos

Tizimín
Valladolid
Isla Cozumel
Chichén Itzá
Ticul
Peto

QUINTANA ROO
Chetumal
Ambergris Cay

Canal de Yucatán

(Havana) LA HABANA
San Antonio de los Baños
MARIANAO
Pinar del Río
Guanajay
Guane
La Fé
San Luis
Los Palacios
Batabanó
Güines
Jagüey Grande
Matanzas
Colón
Cárdenas
Jovellanos
Santa Clara
Sagua la Grande
Caibarién
Placetas
Cienfuegos
Trinidad
Sancti Spíritus
Ciego de Ávila
Morón
Camagüey
Florida
Victoria de las Tunas
Manzanillo
Bayamo
Holguín
Sierra Maestra
SANTIAGO DE CUBA

Cayman Islands (Br.)
Georgetown
Grand Cayman
Little Cayman
Cayman Brac

Swan Islands (U.S.A. & Honduras)

Montego Bay
Lucea
Falmouth
St. Ann's Bay
Port Maria
JAMAICA
Savanna la Mar
Black River
Mandeville
May Pen
Spanish Town
KINGSTON

Pedro Cays (Jamaica)

GUATEMALA
Cobán
Huehuetenango
Quezaltenango
Antigua
GUATEMALA
Escuintla
San Marcos
Totonicapán

BELIZE
Belize City
Maya Mts.
Tikal
Flores

HONDURAS
San Pedro Sula
El Progreso
Santa Bárbara
Tegucigalpa
Comayagua
Juticalpa
Catacamas
La Ceiba
Tela
Puerto Cortés
Puerto Barrios
Trujillo
Islas de la Bahía
Roatán

Mosquitia
Laguna Caratasca
C. Gracias á Dios
Puerto Cabezas
Cayos Miskitos (Nicaragua)

EL SALVADOR
SAN SALVADOR
Santa Ana
Ahuachapán
Usulután
San Miguel
Golfo de Fonseca

NICARAGUA
MANAGUA
Masaya
Granada
León
Chinandega
Corinto
Matagalpa
Estelí
Boaco
Juigalpa
Bluefields
Lago de Managua
Lago de Nicaragua
Rivas
San Carlos
San Juan del Norte
Río Grande
Prinzapolca
El Bluff
Isla de Ometepe

I. de Providencia (Colombia)
I. de San Andrés (Colombia)
Cayos de Albuquerque (Colombia)
Cayos Roncador (U.S.A. & Colombia)
Islas del Maíz (Nicaragua, U.S.A.)
Bajo Nuevo (Colombia)

COSTA RICA
SAN JOSÉ
Cartago
Alajuela
Limón
Puntarenas
Liberia
Nicoya
Santa Cruz
Pen. de Nicoya
Pen. de Osa
Golfo Dulce
Puerto Armuelles

CANAL ZONE (U.S.A.)
PANAMÁ
David
Santiago
Chitré
Las Tablas
Colón
Portobelo
La Chorrera
Golfo de Panamá
Archipiélago de las Perlas
Golfo de Chiriquí
Serranía del Darién
Golfo del Darién

CARTA...

MIAMI
Fort Myers
Naples
Key West
Everglades
West Palm Beach
Boca Raton
Fort Lauderdale
Hialeah
Florida Keys
Florida Bay
Dry Tortugas

GREAT BAHAMA BANK
Grand Bahama I.
Little Abaco I.
Great Abaco I.
Berry Is.
Bimini Is.
Nassau
New Providence
Andros Town
Eleuthera
Great Exuma I.

Projection: Bi-polar oblique Conical Orthomorphic

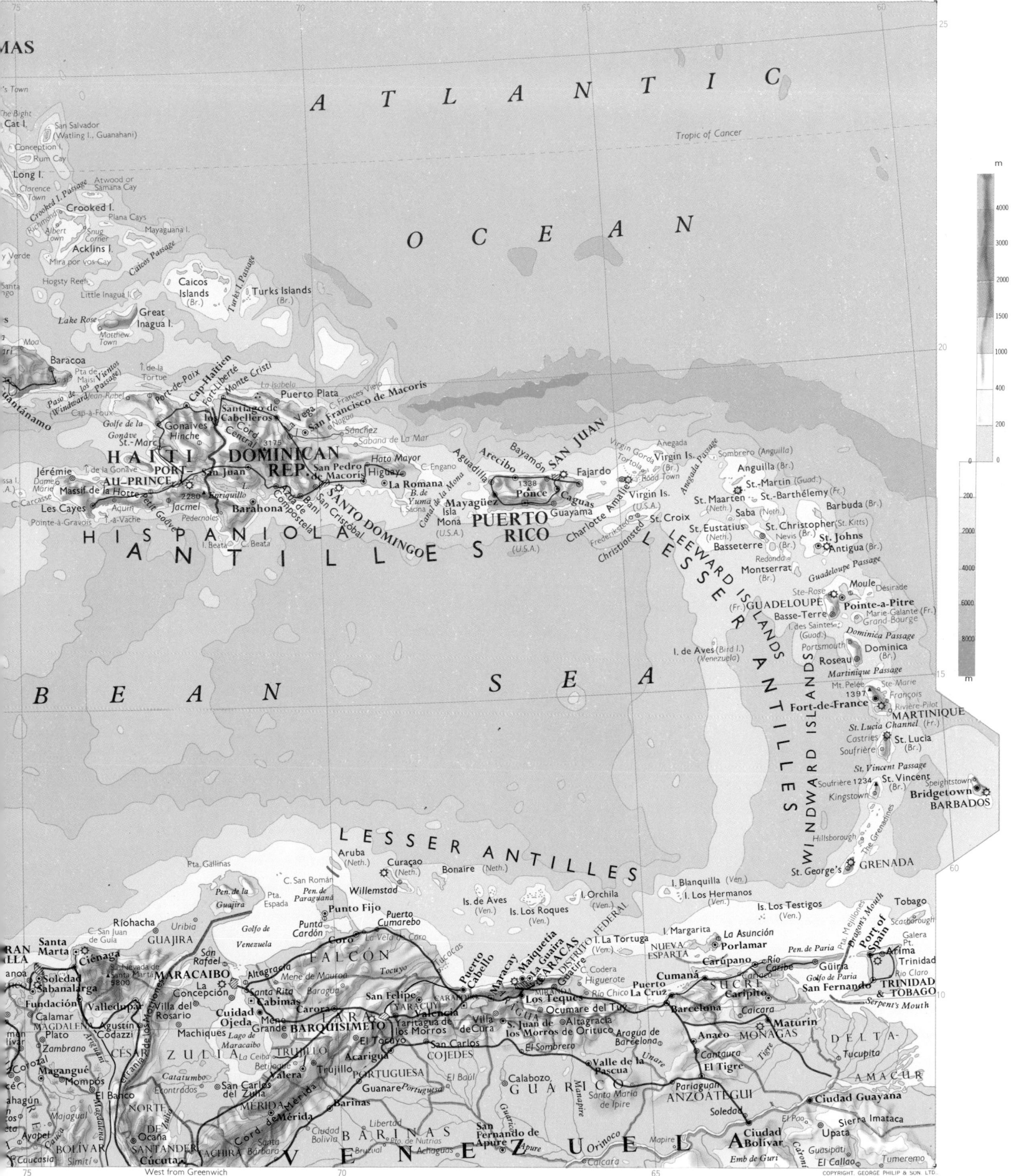

Projection: Sanson-Flamsteed's Sinusoidal

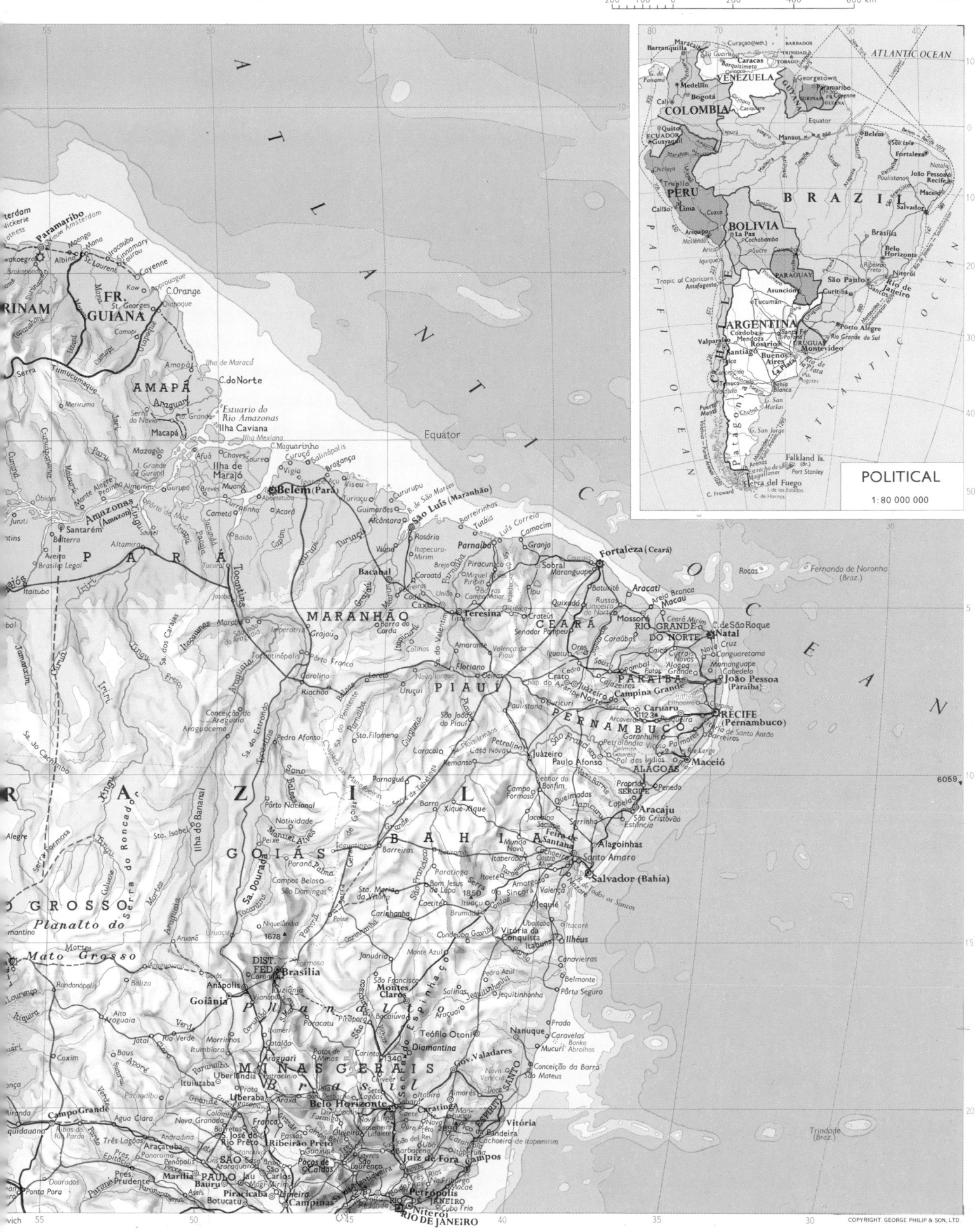

1:16 000 000

200 100 0 200 400 600 km

POLITICAL

1:80 000 000

ATLANTIC OCEAN

BARBADOS

Barranquilla Curaçao (Neth.) TRINIDAD TOBAGO
Maracaibo La Guaira Caracas Georgetown Paramaribo Cayenne
COLOMBIA VENEZUELA GUIANA FR. GUIANA
Medellín Bogotá Orinoco Casiquiare
Quito Equator Manaus Belém São Luís
ECUADOR Guayaquil Fortaleza
Trujillo Amazon Natal
PERU João Pessoa Recife
Callao Lima Cuzco B R A Z I L Maceió
Arequipa BOLIVIA Salvador
La Paz Cochabamba Brasília
Mollendo Sucre Belo Horizonte
Arica PARAGUAY São Paulo Rio de
Tropic of Capricorn Asunción Curitiba Janeiro
Antofagasta Tucumán Porto Alegre
ARGENTINA Rio Grande do Sul
Valparaíso Córdoba URUGUAY Montevideo
Santiago Mendoza Rosário Buenos La Plata
Concepción Bahía Aires Bahía Blanca
PACIFIC OCEAN Patagonia G. San Matías
Puerto Montt Chubut G. San Jorge
ATLANTIC OCEAN
Falkland Is. (Br.) Port Stanley
C. Froward Tierra del Fuego Estr. de Magallanes
Arenas C. de Hornos

A T L A N T I C

ATLANTIC

Amsterdam
Nieuw Nickerie
SURINAM Paramaribo New Amsterdam
Moengo Mana
Wakoegron Albina St. Laurent Cayenne
Brokopondo Approuague
FR. GUIANA C. Orange
Serra St. Georges Oiapoque
Tumucumaque Camopi
AMAPÁ
Araguari
Serra Macapá
do Navio Estuário do
Rio Amazonas
Mazagão Ilha Caviana
Óbidos Afuá Chaves Soure Curuçá Salinópolis
Santarém I. Grande de Gurupá Ilha Mexiana Vigia Bragança
Amazonas Ilha de Marajó Muaná Viseu
Breves Belém (Pará) Capanema
PARÁ Cametá Cururupu B. de São Marcos
Altamira Tucuruí São Luís (Maranhão)
Alcântara Luís Correia Camocim
Barreirinhas Tutóia Granja
Parnaíba Sobral Fortaleza (Ceará)
Rosário Marangupe Aracati
Bacabal Piracuruca Baturité Macau
MARANHÃO Caxias Teresina CEARÁ Quixadá RIO GRANDE
Imperatriz Crateús DO NORTE Natal
Grajaú Floriano PIAUÍ Crato PARAÍBA João Pessoa (Paraíba)
Carolina PERNAMBUCO Campina Grande Caruaru RECIFE (Pernambuco)
Juazeiro Petrolina ALAGOAS Maceió
Pedro Afonso Paulo Afonso SERGIPE Penedo
GOIÁS B A H I A Feira de Santana Aracaju
Barreiras Santo Amaro Salvador (Bahia)
Bom Jesus da Lapa Valença Jequié
Vitória da Conquista Ilhéus
DIST. FED. Brasília Canavieiras
Anápolis Montes Claros Belmonte
Goiânia Diamantina Pôrto Seguro
Planalto do Teófilo Otoni Prado
Mato Grosso Gov. Valadares Nanuque Caravelas
MINAS GERAIS Conceição da Barra
Campo Grande Belo Horizonte Vitória
Uberlândia Juiz de Fora Campos
SÃO PAULO Petrópolis
Marília Campinas RIO DE JANEIRO Niterói
Bauru Piracicaba Cabo Frio

COPYRIGHT. GEORGE PHILIP & SON, LTD.

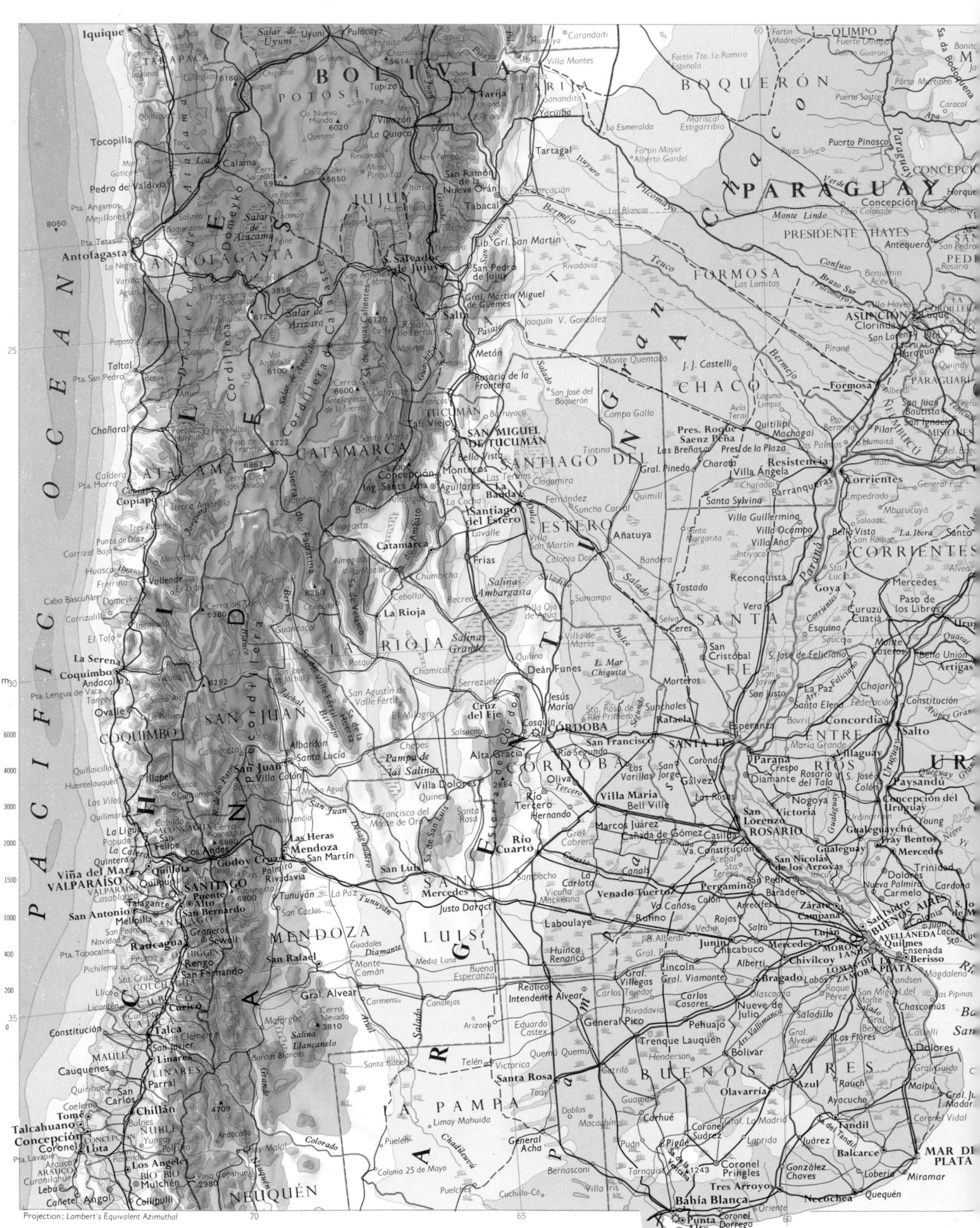

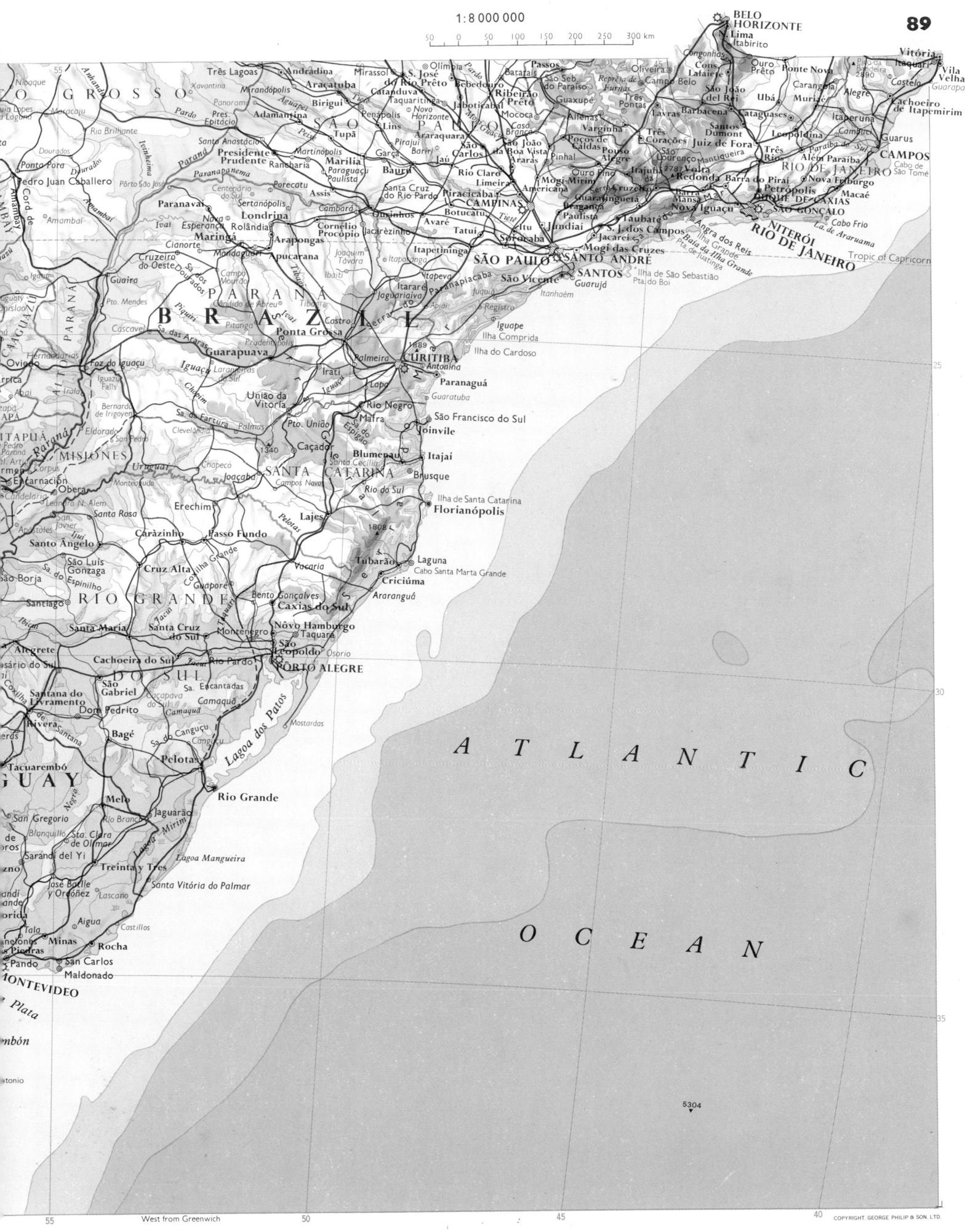

1:8 000 000

50 0   50 100 150 200 250 300 km

BELO
HORIZONTE

ATLANTIC

OCEAN

West from Greenwich

Tropic of Capricorn

1:16 000 000

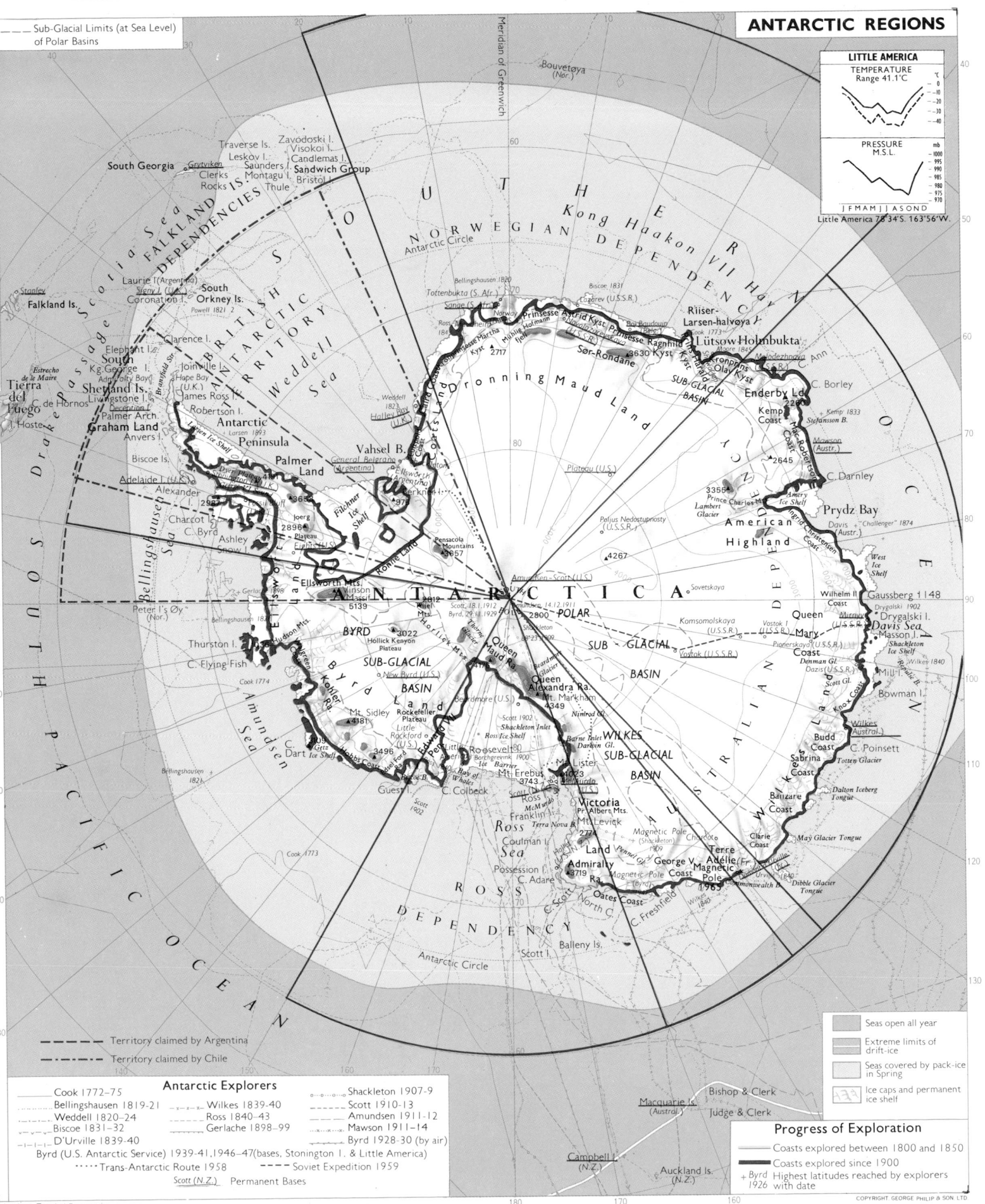

1 : 20 000 000

200   0   200   400   600   800 km

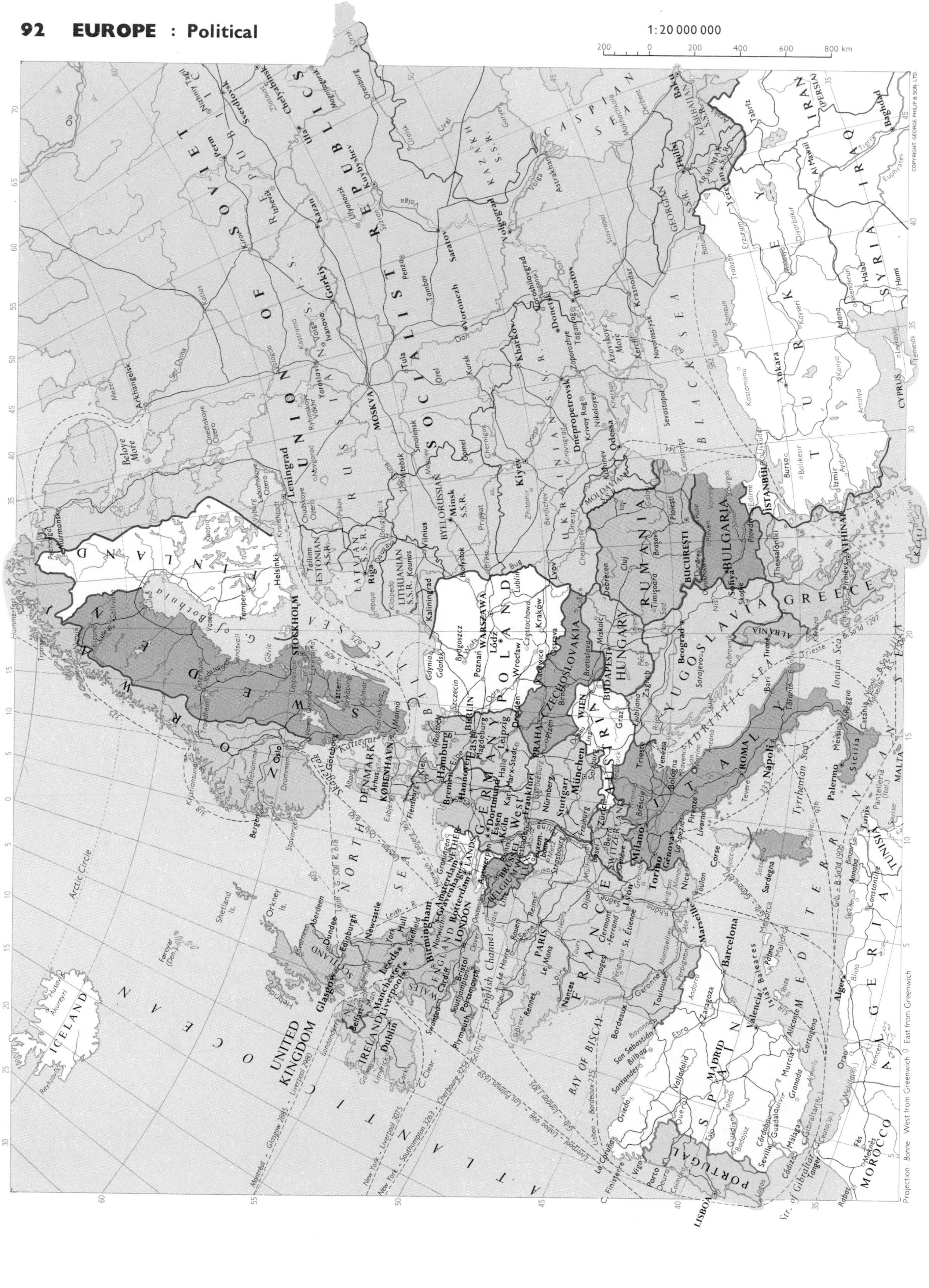

UNION OF SOVIET SOCIALIST REPUBLICS

R U S S I A N   S.F.S.R.

FINLAND

NORWAY

SWEDEN

DENMARK

GERMANY East / West

POLAND

CZECHOSLOVAKIA

AUSTRIA

HUNGARY

RUMANIA

BULGARIA

YUGOSLAVIA

GREECE

ALBANIA

ITALY

SWITZERLAND

FRANCE

SPAIN

PORTUGAL

UNITED KINGDOM

IRELAND

ENGLAND

SCOTLAND

WALES

ICELAND

NETHERLANDS

BELGIUM

LUXEMBOURG

ESTONIAN S.S.R.

LATVIAN S.S.R.

LITHUANIAN S.S.R.

BYELORUSSIAN S.S.R.

UKRAINIAN S.S.R.

MOLDAVIAN

GEORGIAN S.S.R.

ARMENIAN S.S.R.

AZERBAIJAN S.S.R.

KAZAKH S.S.R.

TURKEY

IRAN (PERSIA)

IRAQ

SYRIA

CYPRUS

MALTA

MOROCCO

ALGERIA

TUNISIA

ATLANTIC OCEAN

NORTH SEA

BALTIC SEA

BLACK SEA

CASPIAN SEA

MEDITERRANEAN SEA

Tyrrhenian Sea

Adriatic Sea

Ionian Sea

Aegean Sea

Gulf of Bothnia

Bay of Biscay

English Channel

Arctic Circle

MOSKVA   Leningrad   Gorkiy   Kazan   Kuybyshev   Saratov   Volgograd   Rostov   Kharkov   Kiyev   Odessa   Minsk   Vilnius   Riga   Tallinn   Helsinki   STOCKHOLM   Oslo   KØBENHAVN   Göteborg   Malmö

WARSZAWA   Łódź   Kraków   Wrocław   Poznań   Gdańsk   Szczecin

BERLIN   Hamburg   Bremen   Hannover   Köln   Dortmund   Essen   Frankfurt   Stuttgart   München   Nürnberg   Leipzig   Dresden   Magdeburg

PRAHA   Bratislava   WIEN   BUDAPEST   BUCUREȘTI   Sofiya   Beograd   Zagreb   Sarajevo   Skopje

ROMA   Milano   Torino   Genova   Venezia   Firenze   Napoli   Bologna   Palermo   Catania   Bari   Sicilia   Sardegna   Corse

PARIS   Marseille   Lyon   Toulouse   Bordeaux   Nantes   Nice   Rennes   Le Havre

MADRID   Barcelona   Valencia   Sevilla   Zaragoza   Bilbao   Málaga   Córdoba   Granada   Cartagena   Alicante   Baleares   Mallorca

LISBOA   Porto

LONDON   Birmingham   Manchester   Leeds   Liverpool   Sheffield   Glasgow   Edinburgh   Newcastle   Bristol   Cardiff   Belfast   Dublin

Amsterdam   Rotterdam   BRUSSEL

ISTANBUL   Ankara   İzmir   ATHENS

Reykjavík   Akureyri

Baku   Yerevan   Tbilisi

Baghdad   Mosul

Projection Bonne   West from Greenwich 0 East from Greenwich

1 : 20 000 000

200   0   200   400   600   800 km

Projection: Bonne

COPYRIGHT GEORGE PHILIP & SON LTD.

West from Greenwich East from Greenwich

Seas and Oceans

ATLANTIC OCEAN
NORWEGIAN SEA
NORTH SEA
BALTIC SEA
White Sea
BLACK SEA
CASPIAN SEA
ADRIATIC SEA
AEGEAN SEA
Ionian Sea
Tyrrhenian Sea
Ligurian Sea
MEDITERRANEAN SEA
Sea of Azov
English Channel
Bay of Biscay
Gulf of Bothnia
Gulf of Finland
Gulf of Riga
Gulf of Lions
Str. of Otranto
Str. of Messina
Str. of Bonifacio
Str. of Gibraltar

Mountains and Regions

Ural Mountains
Timan
Obshchiy Syrt
Volga Uplands
Central Russian Uplands
UKRAINE
Pripyat Marshes
Carpathians
Transylvanian Alps
Wallachia
Plain of Hungary
Balkans
Balkan Peninsula
Rhodope
Pindus Mts.
Morea
Anatolia
Kurdistan
Armenia
Caucasus
Crimea
Finland
Lapland
Scandinavia
Kjølen
Iceland
British Isles
Ireland
Great Britain
Shetland Is.
Orkney Is.
Hebrides
Faroe Is.
Brittany
Netherlands
Jutland
Harz
Erz Geb.
Sudeten
Bohemian For.
Dinaric Alps
Apennines
Alps
Jura
Vosges
Ardennes
Central Massif
Cevennes
Pyrenees
Cantabrian Mts.
Old Castile
New Castile
Iberian Peninsula
Sierra Morena
Andalusia
Sa. Nevada
Maritime Alps
Corsica
Sardinia
Sicily
Malta
Calabria
Balearic Is.
Atlas
Plateau of the Shotts

Rivers and Lakes

Ob
Pechora
Mezen
N. Dvina
Volga
Kama
Onega
L. Onega
L. Ladoga
Chudskoye
Neva
Dvina
Dnieper
Dniester (Dnestr)
Bug
Don
Donets
Oka
Rybinsk Res.
Tsimlyansk Res.
Manych
Ural
Terek
Kura
Rioni
Euphrates
Kizil Irmak
Sakarya
Danube
Prut
Tisza
Drava
Save
Morava
Vardar
Wisła (Vistula)
Odra (Oder)
Elbe
Weser
Rhine
Ems
Maas
Seine
Loire
Garonne
Gironde
Dordogne
Rhône
Saône
Po
Tiber
Duero (Douro)
Tajo (Tagus)
Guadiana
Guadalquivir
Ebro
L. Vänern
L. Vättern
L. Mälaren
Gotland
Öland

Heights (in metres)

1617
2123
2469
2119
1974
3734
1085
1343
1142
4807
2265
2914
5165
5663
2211
3770
1766
5121
4061
2914
1272
3263
3478
4404
2661
1886
1766
951
28

1 : 2 000 000

10   0   10   20   30   40   50   60   70   80 km

East from Greenwich

West from Greenwich

SCILLY ISLES
On same Scale

Isles of Scilly

St. Ives
Penzance
Land's End
St. Mary's

Projection - Conical with two standard parallels.

ENGLISH   CHANNEL

F   R   A   N   C   E

Dieppe
Le Tréport
St-Valery
-en-Caux
Fécamp
Étretat
C. d'Antifer
C. de la Hève   Le Havre
Rouen
Yvetot
Caudebec
Seine
Lillebonne
Trouville
Honfleur
Pont l'Evêque
Lisieux
Bernay
Elbeuf
Louviers
Caen
Bayeux
Arromanches
Vierville
St-Lô
Carentan
Isigny
Quinéville
Valognes
Volognes
Barfleur
Cherbourg
C. de la Hague
Barneville
Périers
Coutances

Alderney
Guernsey
St. Peter Port
Sark
Channel   Islands
Jersey
St. Helier

Channel Islands

Cap de la Hague

CORNWALL
DEVON
SOMERSET
DORSET
WILTS
HANTS
BERKS
GLOUCESTER
WORCESTER
HEREFORD
WARWICK
OXFORD
BUCKS
HERTFORD
BEDFORD
NORTHAMPTON
CAMBRIDGE
SUFFOLK
ESSEX
KENT
SURREY
EAST SUSSEX
WEST SUSSEX
ISLE OF WIGHT

London
Birmingham
Bristol
Cardiff
Swansea
Plymouth
Exeter
Torquay
Bournemouth
Southampton
Portsmouth
Brighton
Hastings
Dover
Folkestone
Margate
Ramsgate
Canterbury
Maidstone
Ashford
Colchester
Ipswich
Cambridge
Bedford
Luton
Reading
Oxford
Gloucester
Cheltenham
Worcester
Coventry
Northampton
Newport
Weston-super-Mare
Weymouth
Poole

m
1000   400   200   100   50   0

1:2 000 000

10 0 10 20 30 40 50 60 70 80 km

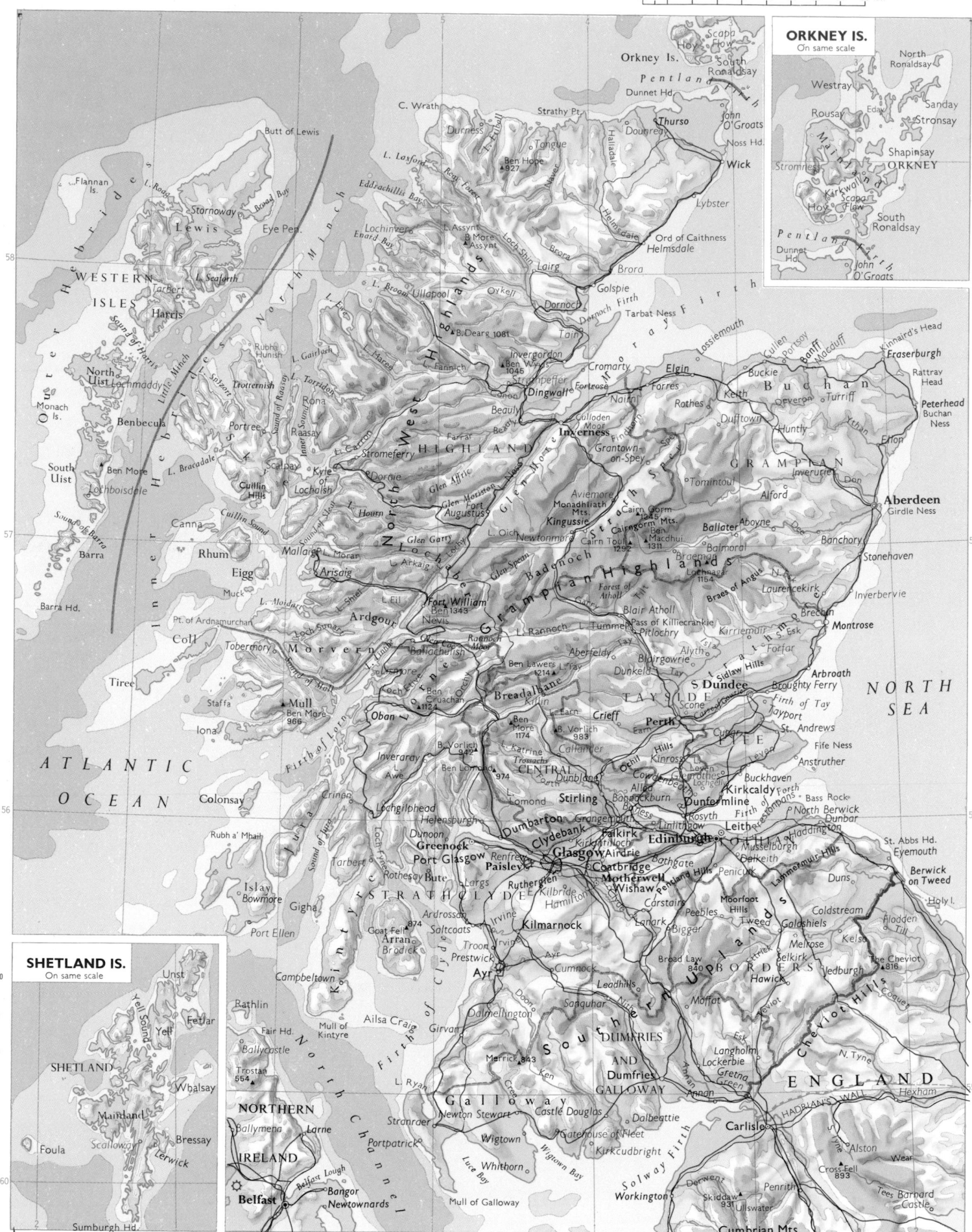

ORKNEY IS.
On same scale

SHETLAND IS.
On same scale

Projection: Conical with two standard parallels.

West from Greenwich

1 : 2 000 000

10 0 10 20 30 40 50 60 70 80 km

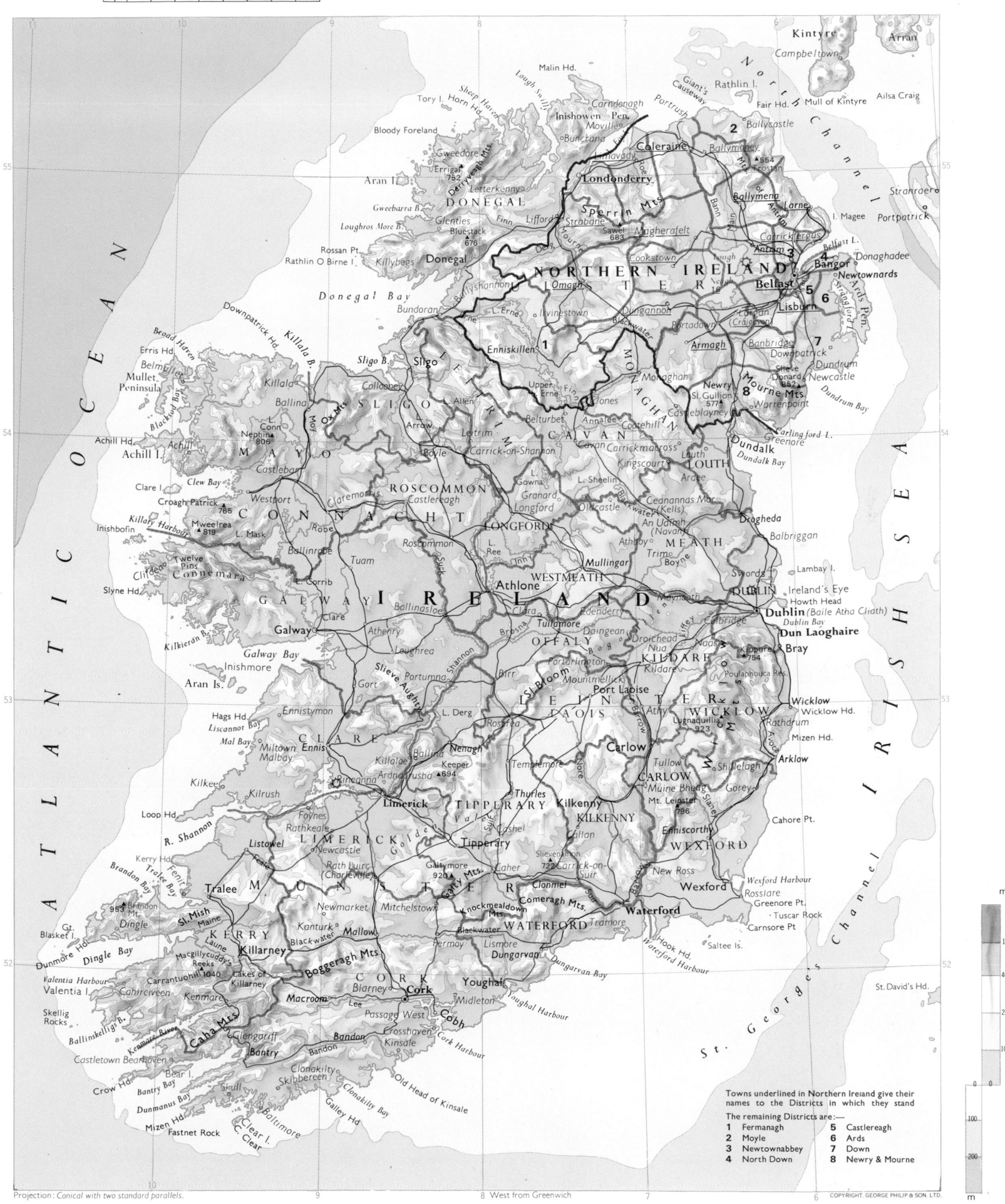

Towns underlined in Northern Ireland give their
names to the Districts in which they stand

The remaining Districts are:—

1	Fermanagh	5	Castlereagh
2	Moyle	6	Ards
3	Newtownabbey	7	Down
4	North Down	8	Newry & Mourne

Projection : Conical with two standard parallels.

West from Greenwich

COPYRIGHT. GEORGE PHILIP & SON LTD.

1:4 000 000

50   50   100   150 km

Orkney Is.

Westray
N. Ronaldsay
Sanday
Stronsay
Mainland
Hoy Kirkwall
South Ronaldsay
Pentland Firth
Thurso
Wick

Shetland Is.

Unst
Yell
Mainland
Foula
Lerwick
Fair I.

ATLANTIC

OCEAN

St. Kilda

Outer Hebrides

Lewis
Harris
North Uist
Benbecula
South Uist
Barra

Stornoway
North Minch

Inner Hebrides

Coll
Tiree

Skye
Portree
Rhum
Eigg
Muck
Staffa Iona
Mull
Colonsay
Islay
Jura
Firth of Lorne

Cape Wrath
Thurso
Pentland Firth
Wick
L. Shin
Laing
Golspie
Ullapool
North West Highlands
Dingwall
Inverness
L. Ness
Kingussie
Fort William
Ben Nevis
1343
Ballachulish
Oban
Loch Linnhe

Moray Firth
Nairn
Elgin
Lossiemouth
Banff
Fraserburgh
Peterhead
Aberdeen
Stonehaven

Grampian Mts.
Ballater
Balmoral
Blair Atholl
Forfar
Montrose
Arbroath
L. Tay
Crieff
Perth
Dundee
Firth of Tay
St. Andrews
Cupar

SCOTLAND

Helensburgh
Greenock
Rothesay
Campbeltown
Arran
Kilmarnock
Saltcoats
Irvine
Prestwick
Ayr

Stirling
Alloa
Kinross
Kirkcaldy
Dunfermline
Firth of Forth
Edinburgh
Falkirk
Dunbar
Haddington
Glasgow
Paisley
Dumbarton
Hamilton Motherwell
Peebles
Galashiels
St. Boswells
Selkirk Jedburgh
Berwick-on-Tweed
Sanquhar
Nith
Moffat Hawick
Cheviot Hills
Alnwick

NORTH

SEA

Malin Hd.
Tory I.
Aran
Portrush
Coleraine
Antrim Mts.
Larne
Belfast
Bangor

Derryveagh Mts.
Letterkenny
Lifford
Ballymena
Antrim
L. Neagh
Lisburn

Londonderry

Donegal
Donegal Bay
Killala Bay
Erris Hd.
Ballina
Sligo
Enniskillen
NORTHERN IRELAND
Omagh
Blackwater
Upper
Lr. L. Erne
Clones
Monaghan
Armagh
Downpatrick
Dundrum
Newry
Mourne Mts.
Greenore
Dundalk

Achill I.
Clare
Castlebar
Westport
L. Conn
L. Mask
Connemara
Galway
Galway Bay

Cavan
Longford
Roscommon
Athlone
Mullingar
Ceanannus Mor
L. Corrib
Athenry
IRELAND
Tullamore
Birr
Port Laoise
Nenagh

Boyne
Drogheda
Balbriggan
Dublin
(Baile Atha Cliath)
Dun Laoghaire
Bray
Naas
Wicklow Mts.
Wicklow
Arklow

Limerick
Golden Vale
Tipperary
Thurles
Rath Luirc
Clonmel
Carrick-on-Suir
Mallow
Blackwater
Fermoy
Dungarvan
Youghal
Carlow
Kilkenny
Enniscorthy
New Ross
Wexford
Waterford
Rosslare
Carnsore Pt.

Ennis
Kilrush
Listowel
Tralee
Killarney
Macgillycuddy's Reeks
Carrantuohill
1040
Castletown Bere
C. Clear
Bantry
Bandon
Blarney
Cork
Cobh
Cork Harbour
Kinsale

Loop Hd.
Shannon

NORTH CHANNEL
Mull of Kintyre
Campbeltown
Firth of Clyde

Dumfries
Wigtown
Kirkcudbright
Mull of Galloway
Solway Firth
Stranraer

Carlisle
Penrith
Cumbrian Mts.
Scafell
978
Windermere
Kendal

Whitehaven
St. Bee's Hd.
Workington
Barrow

ISLE OF MAN
Douglas

IRISH SEA

Anglesey
Beaumaris
Holyhead
Caernarfon Bay
Conway
Caernarfon
1085
Snowdon
Pwllheli
Ruthin
Denbigh
Rhyl

Newcastle
Tynemouth
South Shields
Gateshead
Sunderland
Durham
Hartlepool
Stockton
Darlington
Middlesbrough
N. York Moors
Whitby
Northallerton
Scarborough
Flamborough Hd.

Blackpool
Preston
Blackburn
Burnley
Morecambe Bay
Lancaster
Ripon
York
Beverley
Keighley
Pennine Range

Liverpool
Birkenhead
St. Helens
Salford
Manchester
Stockport
Warrington
Crewe
Wrexham
Macclesfield
Chesterfield
Sheffield
Rotherham
Doncaster
Barnsley
Wakefield
Huddersfield
Oldham
Bolton
Halifax
Bradford
Leeds
Hull
Scunthorpe
Grimsby
Spurn Hd.
Humber
Lincoln

Mansfield
Nottingham
Derby
Stoke-on-Trent
ENGLAND
Stafford
Burton-upon-Trent
Grantham
Sleaford
Boston
The Wash
Skegness

Dolgellau
Cardigan Bay
Aberystwyth
Welshpool
Montgomery
Shrewsbury
W. Cambrian Mts.
E. Cambrian Mts.
Wolverhampton
Walsall
Kidderminster
Birmingham
Coventry
Leicester
Oakham
Rugby
Peterborough
Market Harborough
The Fens
Kings Lynn
Wisbech
Ouse
Norwich
Gt. Yarmouth
Lowestoft

Cardigan
Rhayader
Llandrindod Wells
Knighton
Hereford
Worcester
Leamington
Warwick
Stratford-on-Avon
Northampton
Bedford
Wellingborough
Buckingham
Huntingdon
Cambridge
Bury St. Edmunds
Ipswich
Colchester
Harwich
The Naze

St. David's Hd.
Fishguard
Haverfordwest
Milford Haven
Pembroke
Carmarthen
Llanelli
Swansea
Port Talbot
Brecon
Merthyr Tydfil
Rhondda
Newport
Cardiff
Cheltenham
Gloucester
Monmouth
Cotswolds
Oxford
Aylesbury
Hertford
St. Albans
Watford
LONDON
Luton
Chelmsford
Southend
Thames
Chatham
Gillingham
Margate
Canterbury
Maidstone
The Weald
NORTH DOWNS
Dover
Folkestone

Bristol
Bath
Trowbridge
Swindon
Reading
Slough
Windsor
Guildford
Redgate
Ashford
Weston-super-Mare
Wells
Salisbury Plain
Salisbury
Winchester
Chichester
SOUTH DOWNS
Lewes
Hastings
Eastbourne
Worthing
Brighton
Newhaven

Bristol Channel
Lundy I.
Ilfracombe
Hartland Point
Barnstaple
Exmoor
Taunton
Yeovil
Dorchester
Axminster
Bournemouth
Poole
Weymouth
Newport
Isle of Wight
Needles
Southampton
Portsmouth

Bude
Dartmoor
Exeter
Devonport
Plymouth
Torquay
Dartmouth
Start Pt.
St. Austell
Truro
Camborne
Penzance
Falmouth
Land's End
Lizard
Scilly Is.

ENGLISH   CHANNEL

Dieppe

St. George's Channel

Carnsore Pt.

WALES

m
1000
600
400
200
100
0
100
200
400
m

West from Greenwich | East from Greenwich

Projection: Conical with two standard parallels

COPYRIGHT. GEORGE PHILIP & SON. LTD.

58
56
54
52
50
60
59

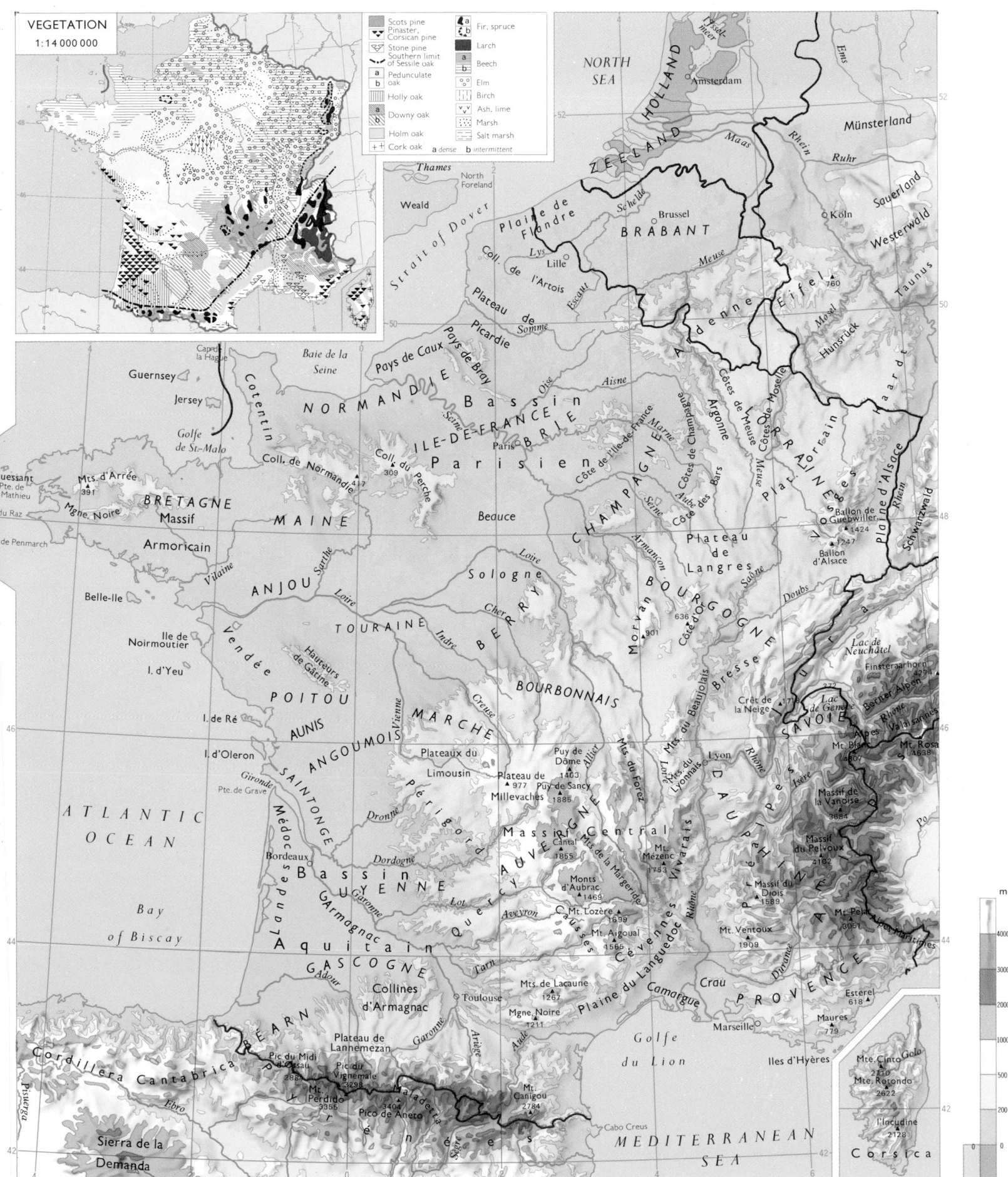

1:5 000 000

50   0   50   100   150   200 km

VEGETATION
1:14 000 000

Scots pine
Pinaster,
Corsican pine
Stone pine
Southern limit
of Sessile oak
a Pedunculate
b oak
Holly oak
a Downy oak
Holm oak
+ Cork oak

a
b Fir, spruce
a Larch
b
a Beech
b
Elm
Birch
Ash, lime
Marsh
Salt marsh
a dense **b** intermittent

NORTH
SEA

Amsterdam

HOLLAND

IJssel-
meer

Ems

Münsterland

ZEELAND

Maas

Rhein

Ruhr

Thames

North
Foreland

Weald

Strait of Dover

Plaine de
Flandre

Schelde

Brussel

BRABANT

Meuse

Sauerland

Köln

Westerwald

Lys

Coll.
de
l'Artois

Lille

Escaut

Ardenne

Eifel

760

Hunsrück

Taunus

Plateau
de
Somme

Picardie

Pays de Bray

Oise

Aisne

Meuse

Argonne

Côtes de Meuse

Moselle

Moselle

LORRAINE

Plat. de

Plaine d'Alsace

Baie de la
Seine

Pays de Caux

NORMANDIE

Bassin

Seine

ILE-DE-FRANCE

BRIE

Marne

CHAMPAGNE

Côtes de Champagne

Aube des Bars

Plateau
de
Langres

Schwarzwald

Guernsey

Cap de
la Hague

Cotentin

Golfe
de St-Malo

Coll. de Normandie

Coll. du Perche

Paris

Parisien

Côte de Ile-de-France

Serre

Côte des Bars

Aube

Ballon de
Guebwiller
1424

Ballon
d'Alsace
1247

Jersey

417

309

Beauce

Armançon

BOURGOGNE

Saône

Doubs

Rhein

Ouessant
Pte. de
St. Mathieu
du Raz

Mts. d'Arrée
391

BRETAGNE

Mgne. Noire
Massif

MAINE

Beauce

Morvan
636

Côte-d'Or

Bresse

Lac de
Neuchâtel

Finsteraarhorn
4274

Berner Alpen

de Penmarch

Armoricain

ANJOU

Sarthe

Loire

Sologne

BERRY

901

BOURBONNAIS

JURA

Crêt de
la Neige
1718

Lac de
Genève

SAVOIE

Rhône

Valais

Mt. Rosa
4638

Belle-Ile

Vilaine

Vendée

TOURAINE

Cher

Indre

Creuse

Lyon

Alpes

Isère

Mt. Blanc
4807

Ile de
Noirmoutier

Hauteurs
de Gâtine

MARCHE

Mts. du Beaujolais

Valaisannes

I. d'Yeu

POITOU

Vienne

Plateaux du
Limousin

Puy de
Dôme
1463

Allier

Mts. du Forez

Mts. du Lyonnais

Massif de
la Vanoise
3684

46

AUNIS

ANGOUMOIS

Plateau de
977

Puy de Sancy
1885

Po

I. de Ré

SAINTONGE

Périgord

Millevaches

Mts. de la Margeride

Vivarais

Massif
du Pelvoux
4102

I. d'Oléron

Gironde
Pte. de Grave

Dronne

Massif Central

Cantal
1855

Mt.
Mézenc
1753

DAUPHINÉ

ATLANTIC
OCEAN

Médoc

Dordogne

AUVERGNE

QUERCY

Lot

Monts
d'Aubrac
1469

Mt. Lozère
1699

Causses

Massif du
Diois
1589

Mt. Pelat
3051

Bordeaux

Bassin

GUYENNE

Garonne

Aveyron

Mt. Aigoual
1565

CÉVENNES

Mt. Ventoux
1909

Bay
of Biscay

AU

Armagnac

Tarn

Mt.
Durance

Esterel
618

44

Aquitain

Adour

GASCOGNE

Garonne

Mts. de Lacaune
1267

Plaine du Languedoc

Crau

Camargue

PROVENCE

Alpes Maritimes

Collines
d'Armagnac

Toulouse

Mgne. Noire
1211

Aude

Marseille

Maures
779

Cordillera Cantabrica

BÉARN

Plateau de
Lannemezan

Garonne

Ariège

Golfe
du Lion

Iles d'Hyères

Mte. Cinto Golo
2710

Pisuerga

Pic du Midi
d'Ossau
2885

Pic du
Vignemale
3298

Mt.
Canigou
2784

Mte. Rotondo
2622

Ebro

Mt.
Perdido
3355

Maladetta
3404

Pico de Aneto

Pyrénées

Cabo Creus

MEDITERRANEAN

Corsica

l'Incudine
2128

Sierra de la
Demanda

42

SEA

Projection: *Conical with two standard parallels*

m

4000
3000
2000
1000
500
200
0

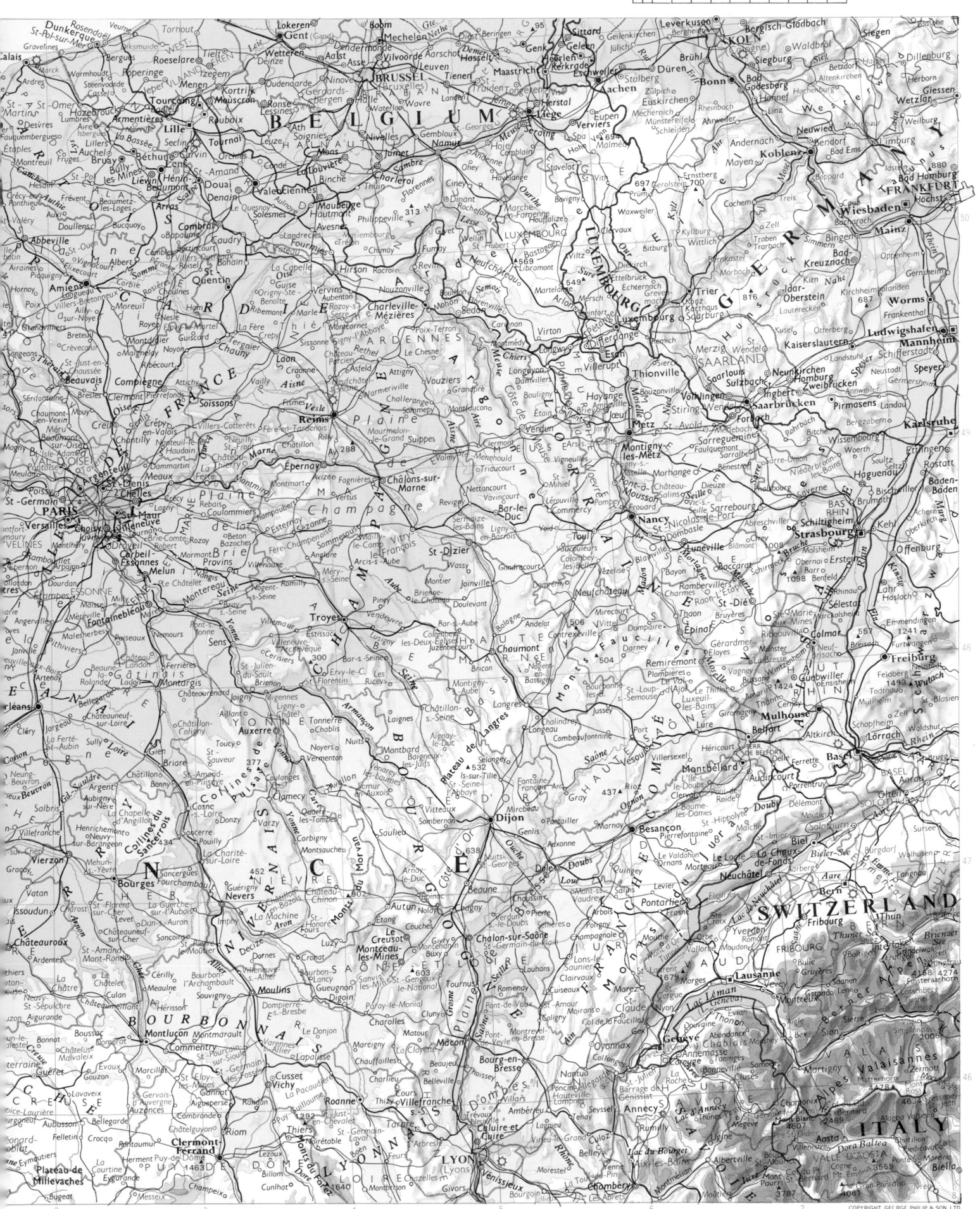

1 : 2 500 000

10 0 10 20 30 40 50 60 70 80 90 100 km

COPYRIGHT GEORGE PHILIP & SON LTD.

1 : 2 500 000

10 0 10 20 30 40 50 60 70 80 90 100 km

COPYRIGHT. GEORGE PHILIP & SON. LTD.

1:5 000 000

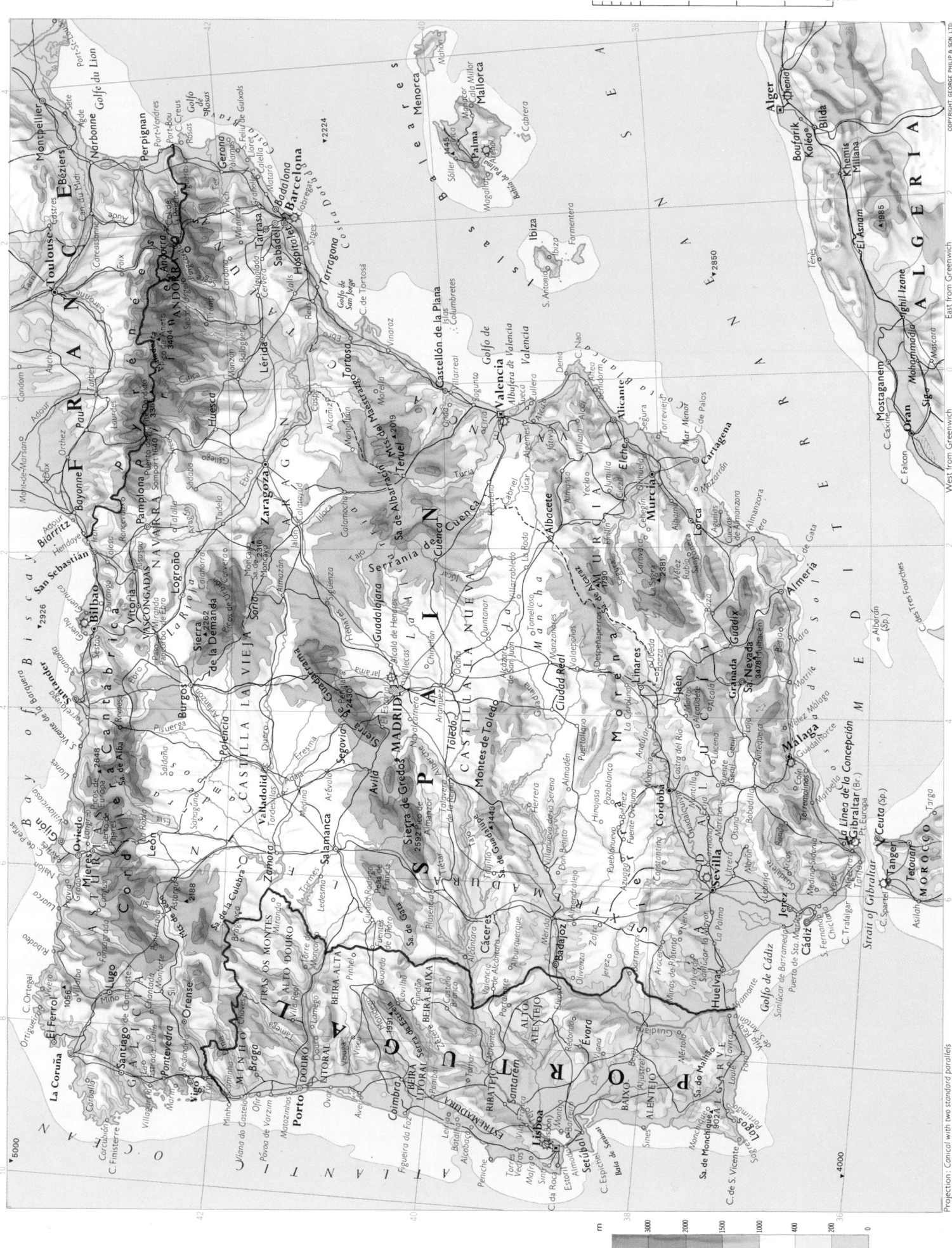

1:2 000 000

10 0 10 20 30 40 50 60 70 80 km

NORTH
SEA

NETHERLANDS

WESTFRIESCHE EILANDEN
Texel Vlieland Terschelling Ameland Schiermonnikoog
Waddenzee

Den Helder
FRIESLAND
Leeuwarden Groningen
Harlingen Sneek
Bolsward Workum
Staveren Heerenveen Assen
Den Oever DRENTHE
IJsselmeer Meppel Emmen
Noordoost Hoogeveen
Polder Urk

Alkmaar Hoorn Kampen Zwolle
Heiloo Enkhuizen
Zaandam OVERIJSSEL
Haarlem AMSTERDAM Almelo Enschede
Hilversum Deventer Hengelo
Leiden UTRECHT Apeldoorn GELDERLAND
s'GRAVENHAGE Zeist Amersfoort
(The Hague) Arnhem Münster
Delft Gouda
Hoek van Holland ROTTERDAM Nijmegen
Vlaardingen Dordrecht Kleve
Schiedam 's-Hertogenbosch NORDRHEIN
ZUID BRABANT Goch Wesel
Breda Tilburg Venlo Dorsten
Roosendaal Eindhoven Recklinghausen DORTMUND
Bergen-op-Zoom Krefeld Gelsenkirchen Bochum
Middelburg ANTWERPEN Roermond Oberhausen ESSEN
Vlissingen Antwerpen Duisburg Mülheim
Westerschelde Mönchen- DÜSSELDORF
Brugge Gladbach Neuss Wuppertal
Oostende Mechelen Solingen Remscheid
(Ostend) Ghent (Gand) Hasselt KÖLN
BRUSSEL Genk Heerlen Aachen Bonn
(Bruxelles) Leuven Maastricht Düren
BRABANT Tongeren
Kortrijk HAINAUT Liège Verviers RHEINLAND
Lille Namur Koblenz
BELGIUM
Roubaix Mons Charleroi Dinant PFALZ
Tournai La Louvière Wiesbaden
Douai Maubeuge Mainz
PAS-DE-CALAIS ARDENNES
Arras LUXEMBOURG Bastogne Bad Kreuznach
FRANCE Bitburg
PICARDIE LUXEMBOURG
St-Quentin Luxembourg Trier Idar-Oberstein
Sedan Esch Saarburg
Charleville- Arlon SAAR Kaiserslautern
Mézières Thionville Saarbrücken Neunkirchen
Reims Verdun Metz Homburg
MOSELLE Zweibrücken
Epernay MEUSE

East from Greenwich

Projection: Conical with two standard parallels

COPYRIGHT. GEORGE PHILIP & SON. LTD.

Projection : Conical with two standard parallels

East from Greenwich

1:5 000 000

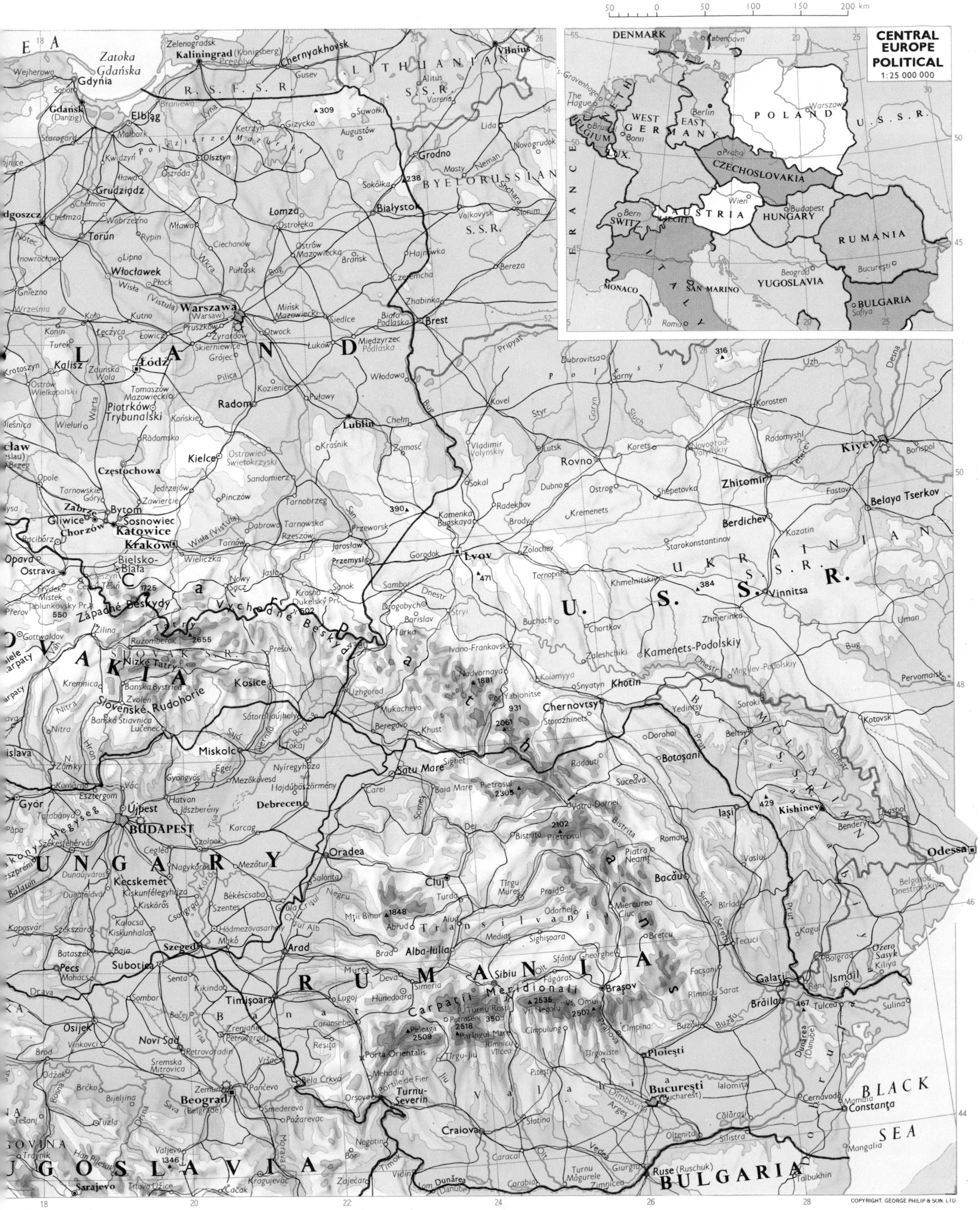

50 0 50 100 150 200 km

CENTRAL EUROPE POLITICAL
1:25 000 000

COPYRIGHT. GEORGE PHILIP & SON. LTD.

SWITZERLAND

Brenner

Lyon

Grenoble

DAUPHINÉ

PROVENCE

Marseille
Toulon

Aix
Nice
MONACO
Monte Carlo
Cannes

LIGURIAN SEA

CORSE
(CORSICA)
(Fr.) Ajaccio

Mt. Cinto
2710

Asinara
C. Falcone

Sássari

Alghero

Bosa

Nuoro

SARDEGNA (SARDINIA)

Mt. Gennargentu
1834

Oristano

Iglésias

Cágliari

C. Spartivento

Torino
(Turin)

PIEMONTE

Génova
(Genoa)

La Spézia

Livorno
(Leghorn)

Pisa

Firenze
(Florence)

TOSCANA
Siena

Arezzo

UMBRIA

Perúgia

Terni

ROMA (Rome)

Ostia

Ánzio

Latina

MOLISE

Campobasso

Caserta

Napoli
(Naples)

Salerno

BASILICATA

TYRRHENIAN SEA

Como
Bergamo
Milano
(Milan)

LOMBARDIA

Novara
Pavia
Piacenza
Cremona

Parma
Ferrara

Reggio
Módena
Bologna
ROMAGNA

Ravenna

Forlì
Cesena
Rímini

Pésaro

MARCHE
Ancona

Ascoli Piceno

L'Aquila

ABRUZZI

Pescara

Chieti

Térmoli

Fóggia

Cerignola
Barletta
Andria

Bari

PUGLIA

Tàranto

Golfo di Táranto

Cosenza

CALABRIA

Catanzaro

Pizzo

Palmi

Réggio

Str. di Messina

Messina

Milazzo

Palermo

Trápani

Marsala

Caltanissetta

Catánia

Siracusa
(Syracuse)

Ragusa

Etna
3340

MEDITE

Gozo
Comino

Valletta

MALTA

Trento
TRENTINO
ALTO ADIGE
Bolzano

VENETO
Verona
Vicenza
Padova
(Padua)

Venézia
(Venice)

Trieste

FRIULI
VENEZIA
GIULIA
Udine

Klagenfurt

Ljubljana

Zagreb

Rijeka

ADRIATIC SEA

Split

AFRICA

Projection: Conical with two standard parallels

S.E. EUROPE
POLITICAL
1:25 000 000

FRANCE
SWITZ
LIECHT
AUSTRIA
HUNGARY
RUMANIA
U.S.S.R.

Wien
Budapest
Bucureşti

Venézia
Trieste
SAN MARINO
ITALY
YUGOSLAVIA
Beograd
Sofija
BULGARIA

Corse
(Fr.)

Roma

Napoli

Tiranë
ALBANIA
GREECE
Thessaloniki
Athínai

TURKEY

AEGEAN SEA

MALTA

Sicilia

MEDITERRANEAN SEA

Kríti

1:5 000 000

50   0   50   100   150   200 km

U.S.S.R.

RUMANIA

Transilvania

Carpatii Meridionali

Bucureşti (Bucharest)

Constanţa

Mamaia

B L A C K

S E A

Nos Kaliakra

Varna

Burgas

BULGARIA

Sofiya (Sofia)

Plovdiv

Rhodopi Planina

TURKEY

Edirne

İstanbul Üsküdar

Marmara denizi

GOSLAVIA

Sarajevo

Beograd (Belgrade)

Craiova

Pleven

SERBIA

Titograd (Podgorica)

Skopje

MAKEDONIJA

Bitola (Monastir)

ALBANIA

Tiranë

Shkumbini

Durrësi

THRAKI

Alexandroúpolis

Thessaloniki

Marmara

İmralı

Bursa

TURKEY

Anadolu

İzmir (Smyrna)

Thásos

Samothráki

Límnos

Lésvos

Áthos

Khíos

Samos

G R E E C E

ÍPIROS

Kérkira (Corfu)

Ioánnina

THESSALIA

Lárisa

Vólos

Olympus

Kozáni

Skíros

Évvoia

Khalkís

STEREA ELLAS

Athínai (Athens)

Piraiévs (Piraeus)

Ándros

Tínos

Míkonos

Náxos

Ikaría

Pátmos

KIKLÁDHES

D O D E K A N I S O S

Ródhos

Kárpathos

Kásos

Brindisi

Lecce

I O N I A N

S E A

Patrai

Pírgos

PELOPÓNNISOS

Kalamata

Kíthira

Andikíthira

K R I T I

Khaniá

Réthimnon

Iráklion

Ierápetra

Ákra Líthinon

M E D I T E R R A N E A N   S E A

East from Greenwich

COPYRIGHT. GEORGE PHILIP & SON. LTD.

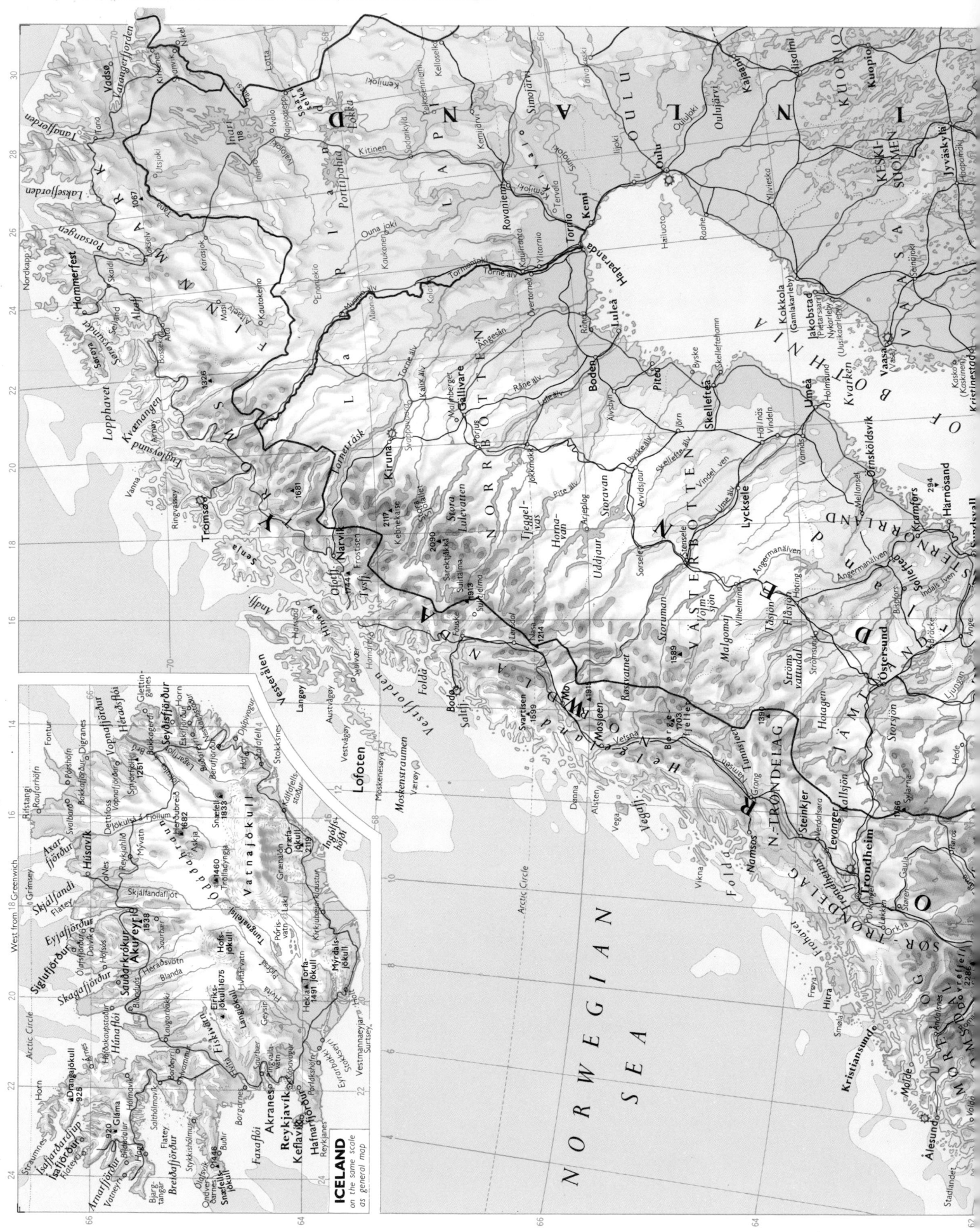

ICELAND
on the same scale
as general map

1 : 5 000 000

50   0   50   100   150   200 km

Projection: Conical with two standard parallels   East from Greenwich

m   2000   1500   1000   400   200   0

m

Selected place names (reading across the map):

Heinola · Kotka · Lovisa · Lahti · Kundo · Rakvere
Tampere · Hämeenlinna · Hyvinkää · HELSINKI (Helsingfors) · Tallinn
TURUN · PORI · Turku (Åbo) · Porkkala · Paldiski · ESTONIAN S.S.R.
Pori · Rauma · Naantali · Hango (Hanko) · Kärdla · Haapsalu · Pärnu · Viljandi · Valga
Uusikaupunki · Pärainen · Hiiumaa (Dagö) · Saaremaa (Ösel) · Kingisepp
Kokemäenjoki · Åland (Ahvenanmaa) · Ruhnu · Rīgas Jūras Līcis (Gulf of Riga)
Mariehamn (Maarianhamina) · Gotska Sandön · RIGA · Valmiera · Cesis
Ventspils · Kuldiga · Tukums · LATVIAN S.S.R.
Söderhamn · Gävle · Sandviken · STOCKHOLM · Uppsala · Gotland · Liepaja · Jelgava · Bauska · LITHUANIAN S.S.R.
Hudiksvall · Falun · Borlänge · Västerås · Eskilstuna · Nyköping · Visby · Klaipeda · Šiauliai · VILNIUS
Mora · Örebro · Katrineholm · Norrköping · Linköping · Västervik · Oskarshamn · Öland · Telšiai · Kaunas · Grodno
Hagfors · Karlstad · Mariestad · Jönköping · Nässjö · Växjö · Kalmar · Soviets'k · Kaliningrad · Chernyakhovsk
Arvika · Vänersborg · Borås · Ljungby · Karlskrona · Karlshamn · Bornholm · Gusev · Suwałki · Białystok
Kongsvinger · Trollhättan · Alingsås · HALLAND · Kristianstad · Gdynia · Elbląg · Olsztyn · Łomża
OSLO · Drammen · GÖTEBORG · Varberg · Halmstad · Helsingborg · MALMÖ · Ystad · Zatoka Gdańska · GDAŃSK · Grudziądz · Toruń · Ostrołęka
Lillehammer · Moss · Halden · Strömstad · Falkenberg · KØBENHAVN · Trelleborg · Rügen · Słupsk · Chojnice · BYDGOSZCZ
Gjøvik · Kongsberg · Skien · Frederikshavn · Hjørring · Ålborg · Randers · Århus · Odense · Nykøbing · Rostock · SZCZECIN
Arendal · Grimstad · Lillesand · Thisted · Viborg · Silkeborg · Horsens · Vejle · Kolding · Odense · Svendborg · Lübeck · Schwerin
Kristiansand · Mandal · Esbjerg · Herning · Ribe · Åbenrå · Flensburg · Kiel · HAMBURG · Wismar · GERMANY
Stavanger · Sandnes · Eigersund (Egersund) · Farsund · Limfjorden · Tønder · Bremerhaven · Bremen · Oldenburg · NETHERLANDS
Haugesund · Kopervik · Bokn · Skagerrak · Kattegat · Nordfriesische Inseln · Wilhelmshaven · Emden · Groningen

DENMARK

BALTIC SEA

GULF OF FINLAND

KORPI · VÄSTMANLAND · SÖDERMANLAND · ÖSTERGÖTLAND · SMÅLAND · BLEKINGE · SKÅNE
TELEMARK · AUST-AGDER · VEST-AGDER · ROGALAND · HORDALAND · SOGN OG FJORDANE
BUSKERUD · OPPLAND · HEDMARK · KOPPARBERG · GÄVLEBORG
HALLAND · BOHUSLÄN · ÄLVSBORG · SKARABORG · JÖNKÖPING · KRONOBERG · KALMAR
POLAND · WEST GERMANY · R.S.F.S.R.

1:40 000 000

400 0 400 800 1200 1600 km

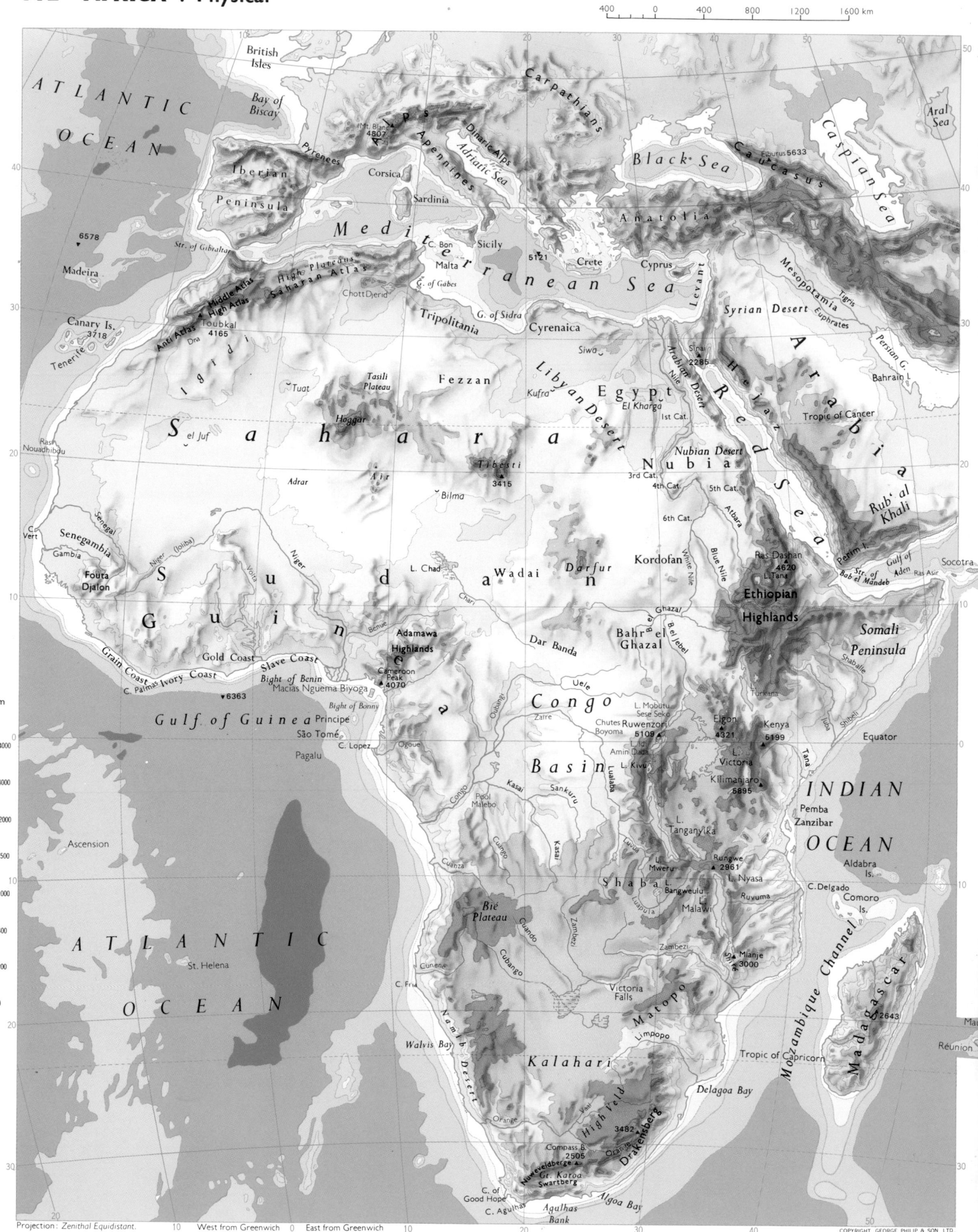

ATLANTIC OCEAN

British Isles

Bay of Biscay

Carpathians

Black Sea

Caucasus Elburus 5633

Aral Sea

Caspian Sea

Iberian Peninsula

Mt Blanc 4807

Pyrenees

Apennines

Dinaric Alps

Adriatic Sea

Corsica

Sardinia

Anatolia

6578

Madeira

Str. of Gibraltar

C. Bon

Sicily

Malta

5121

Crete

Cyprus

Mediterranean Sea

Levant

Mesopotamia

Tigris

Euphrates

Persian G.

Bahrain I.

Canary Is.
3718

Tenerife

Middle Atlas
High Atlas

Anti Atlas Toubkal
4165

High plateaus

Saharan Atlas

Chott Djerid

G. of Gabes

Tripolitania

G. of Sidra

Cyrenaica

Siwa

Egypt

Syrian Desert

Arabia

Dra

Igidi

S el Juf

Tuat

Tasili Plateau

Fezzan

Hoggar

Kufra

Libyan Desert

El Kharga

1st Cat.

Sinai
2285

Arabian Desert

Nile

Tropic of Cancer

Rub' al Khali

Adrar

Aïr

Tibesti
3415

Bilma

Nubian Desert

3rd Cat.

Nubia

4th Cat.

5th Cat.

Atbara

Perim I.

Str. of
Bab el Mandeb

Gulf of Aden

Ras Asir

Socotra

Ras Nouadhibou

Sahara

6th Cat.

White Nile

Blue Nile

Ras Dashan
4620

L. Tana

C. Vert

Senegal

Senegambia

Gambia

Foura Djalon

Niger (Joliba)

Sudan

Yobe

Niger

L. Chad

Wadai

Darfur

Kordofan

Ethiopian Highlands

Somali Peninsula

Shabelle

Guinea

Benue

Chari

Dar Banda

Bahr el Ghazal

Bahr el Ghazal

Grain Coast

Gold Coast

Ivory Coast

Slave Coast

Bight of Benin

Adamawa Highlands

Cameroon Peak
4070

Dar Banda

Bahr el Jebel

C. Palmas

Macias Nguema Biyogo

6363

Bight of Bonny

Uele

Ubangi

Congo

Uele

L. Mobutu Sese Seko

Zaïre

Chutes Boyoma

Ruwenzori
5109

Elgon
4321

Turkana

Kenya
5199

Equator

Gulf of Guinea

Príncipe

São Tomé

C. Lopez

Pagalu

Ogooué

Pool Malebo

Kasai

Congo

Lualaba

Amin Dada

L. Kivu

Basin

Sankuru

L. Victoria

Kilimanjaro
5895

INDIAN

Pemba

Zanzibar

OCEAN

Ascension

Cuango

Cuilo

Kasai

L. Tanganyika

Aldabra Is.

L. Mweru

Rungwe
2961

Shaba

L. Bangweulu

L. Nyasa

Ruvuma

C. Delgado

Comoro Is.

St. Helena

ATLANTIC

OCEAN

Cuanza

Bié Plateau

Cuango

Zambezi

Luangwa

Malawi

Mlanje
3000

Mozambique Channel

Madagascar
2643

Cunene

Victoria Falls

Zambezi

Mau

Réunion

Namib Desert

Walvis Bay

C. Frio

Limpopo

Matopo

Kalahari

Tropic of Capricorn

High Veld

3482

Drakensberg

Delagoa Bay

Orange

Vaal

Compass B.
2505

Nieuveldberge

Gt. Karoo

Swartberg

C. of Good Hope

C. Agulhas

Agulhas Bank

Algoa Bay

m

4000
3000
2000
1500
1000
400
200
0

0
200
1000
2000
4000
6000

m

1:40 000 000

400 0 400 800 1200 1600 km

ATLANTIC OCEAN

UNITED KINGDOM London

Bay of Biscay

NETH. GERMANY E. POLAND Warszawa

BELG. Praha CZECHOSLOVAKIA Kiyev

Paris FRANCE Wien HUNGARY Volgograd

SWITZ. AUSTRIA RUMANIA U. S. S. R.

ITALY YUGOSLAVIA Odessa

Corse BULGARIA Black Sea Caspian Sea

Madrid SPAIN Roma GREECE İstanbul Ankara Baku Aral Sea

Lisboa Sardegna Athínai TURKEY Al Mawsil Tehrān

PORTUGAL Kriti CYPRUS Halab SYRIA Baghdād Esfahān

Tanger Alger Annaba Tunis MALTA Tel Aviv-Yafo Dimashq IRAN

Casablanca Constantine Sfax El Iskandarîya Jerusalem Al Basrah

Rabat Fès Oran ISRAEL JORDAN KUWAIT Persian Gulf

Marrakech Tarâbulus EL QÂHIRA El Suweis Bahrein QATAR

Islas Canarias Ghadames El Faiyûm SAUDI-ARABIA

Tenerife LIBYA Sahrâ' EGYPT Aswân Tropic of Cancer

El Aaiun In Salah Ghat Al Madînah Makkah

Dakhla Marzuq Al Jawf Wadi-Halfa Es Sahrâ En Nûbiya Bûr Sûdân

MOROCCO ALGERIA Dongola YEMEN

Ras Nouadhibou S a h a r a Esh Shimâliya Atbara Mitsiwa

MAURITANIA Agades Omdurmân Kassala Asmera SOUTH YEMEN

Nouakchott Tombouctou El Khartûm Al 'Adan Socotra

Gao NIGER CHAD SUDAN L. Tana DJIBOUTI Ras Asir

St. Louis Niamey Darfûr El Fâsher El Obeid Kordofan Berbera Hafun

Dakar SENEGAL Sokoto Kano Ndjamena Abéché Addis Abeba Hargeisa

GAMBIA MALI UPPER VOLTA Kaduna Lac Tchad ETHIOPIA SOMALI REP

GUINEA BISSAU Bamako Ouagadougou Maiduguri CENTRAL AFRICA Mongalla

Conakry SIERRA LEONE Bauchi NIGERIA Bangui Equator

Freetown Kankan GHANA Ibadan CAMEROON UGANDA Mogadishu

LIBERIA IVORY COAST Lagos Enugu Yaoundé Douala KENYA Kismayu

Monrovia Bouaké Accra Port Harcourt GABON ZAÏRE Nairobi

Abidjan Gulf of Guinea EQUATORIAL GUINEA Libreville Kisangani Mombasa

São Tomé Brazzaville Kinshasa TANZANIA Dodoma Dar-es-Salaam

Pagalu Pointe Noire Cabinda Luanda Zanzibar Pemba

Ascension ANGOLA Huambo ZAMBIA L. Nyasa Arch. des Comores

ATLANTIC OCEAN Benguela Lubumbashi Lusaka MOÇAMBIQUE MADAGASCAR

St. Helena Moçâmedes Livingstone Salisbury Beira Tananarive

NAMIBIA (SOUTH WEST AFRICA) Windhoek BOTSWANA RHODESIA Bulawayo Quelimane MAURITIUS

Walvis baai Kalahari Gaborone Tropic of Capricorn Réunion

Lüderitz TRANSVAAL Pretoria Maputo Lourenço Marques

INDIAN OCEAN

SOUTH AFRICA Johannesburg Kimberley O.-V. Bloemfontein Durban NATAL

Cape Town CAPE PROVINCE East London

Kaap die Goeie Hoop (Cape of Good Hope) Port Elizabeth

LES. Lesotho
O.-V. Oranje-Vrystaat
SWAZ. Swaziland

Projection: Zenithal Equidistant. 10 West from Greenwich 0 East from Greenwich 10

COPYRIGHT. GEORGE PHILIP & SON. LTD.

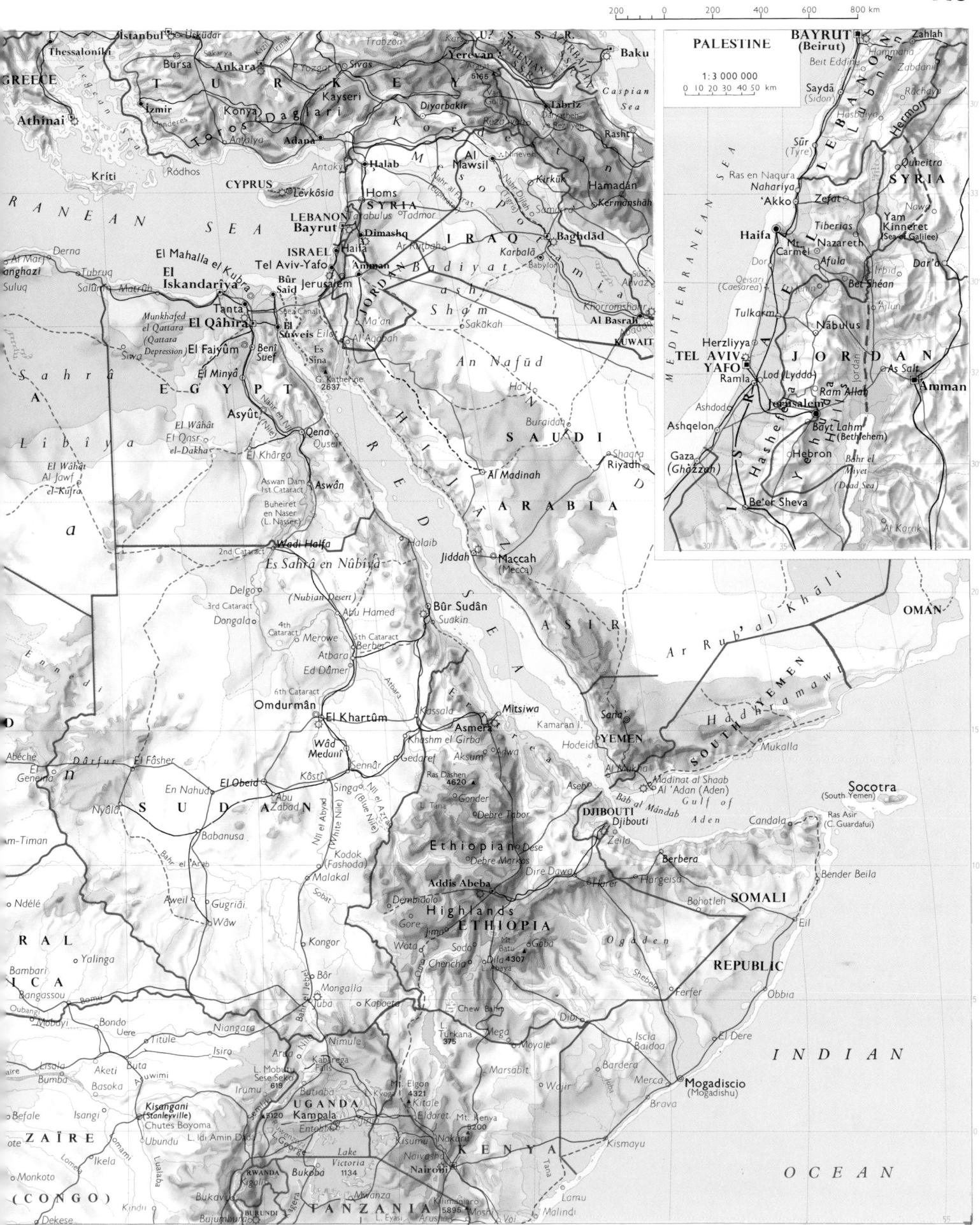

1:20 000 000

200   0   200   400   600   800 km

PALESTINE

1:3 000 000

0 10 20 30 40 50 km

BAYRUT
(Beirut)

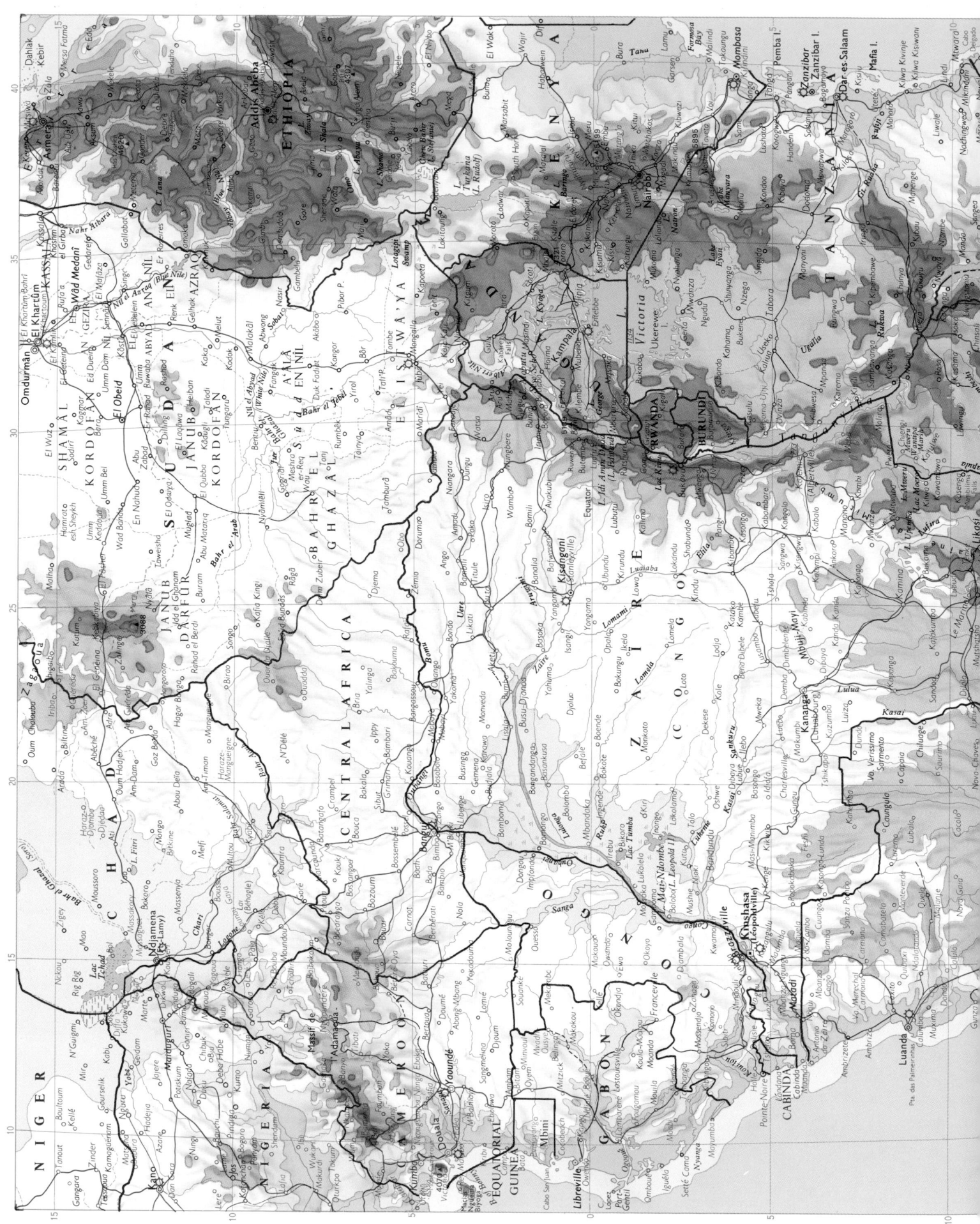

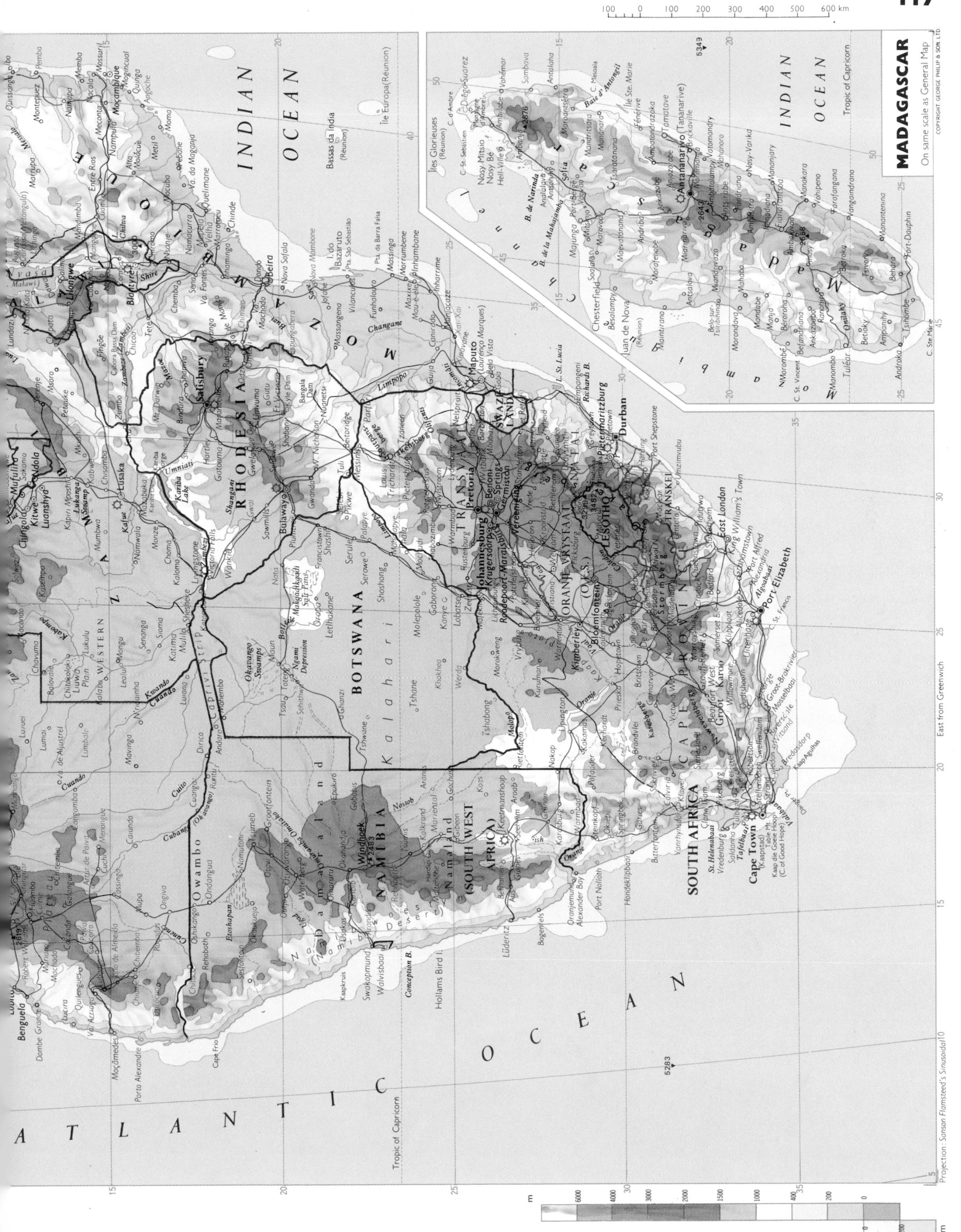

1:15 000 000

100   0   100   200   300   400   500   600 km

MADAGASCAR
On same scale as General Map

COPYRIGHT GEORGE PHILIP & SON, LTD.

INDIAN OCEAN

Tropic of Capricorn

5349 ▼

2876 ▲

2643

2658

INDIAN OCEAN

Îles Glorieuses (Réunion)

Juan de Nova (Réunion)

Chesterfield

C. Ste. Marie

C. St. Sébastien

C. d'Ambre

Diégo-Suarez

Vohémar

Antalaha

Sambava

Antananarivo (Tananarive)

Tamatave

Fianarantsoa

Morombe

Tuléar

Port-Dauphin

Bassas da India

Île Europa (Réunion)

INDIAN OCEAN

MALAWI

Nyasa (Malawi)

Lilongwe

Blantyre

RHODESIA

Salisbury

Bulawayo

Beira

MOZAMBIQUE

Maputo (Lourenço Marques)

Zambezi

Limpopo

BOTSWANA

Kalahari

Okavango Swamps

Ngami Depression

Kariba Lake

Lusaka

Livingstone

Kitwe

Ndola

ZAMBIA

Caprivi Strip

WESTERN

Benguela

ATLANTIC OCEAN

Tropic of Capricorn

Cape Frio

Porto Alexandre

Moçâmedes

Walvisbaai

Swakopmund

Conception B.

Hollams Bird I.

Lüderitz

NAMIBIA (SOUTH WEST AFRICA)

Windhoek

5283

Namib Desert

Namaland

Namaqualand

Great Karroo

Orange

SOUTH AFRICA

Cape Town

Kaap die Goeie Hoop (C. of Good Hope)

Kaap Agulhas

Table Mt.

Port Elizabeth

East London

TRANSKEI

LESOTHO

Drakensberg

Durban

Pietermaritzburg

NATAL

SWAZILAND

ORANJE-VRYSTAAT (O.F.S.)

Bloemfontein

Kimberley

TRANSVAAL

Pretoria

Johannesburg

Benoni

Springs

Germiston

Krugersdorp

Roodepoort-Maraisburg

Vereeniging

CAPE PROVINCE

Stormberg

ATLANTIC OCEAN

East from Greenwich

Projection: Sanson Flamsteed's Sinusoidal

5283 ▼

m
6000 4000 3000 2000 1500 1000 400 200 0

m
200 0

1:50 000 000

1:50 000 000

500 0 500 1000 1500 2000 km

East from Greenwich

Projection Bonne

1:20 000 000

200   0   200   400   600   800 km

O C E A N

Mys Dezhneva
(East C.)

St. Lawrence I.
(U.S.A.)

60

Severnaya
Zemlya

Ostrov
Shmidt
Mys Arkticheskiy
Ostrov
Komsomolets
Ostrov Oktyabrskoy
Revolyutsii
Ostrov
Pioner
965
Ostrov Bolshevik

Chukotskoye
More

Koryakskiy Khrebet

Proliv Vilkutskogo

L a p t e v   Novosibirskiye Ostrova

Ostrov
Henrietta
Ostrova Delong

3800

East Siberian Sea

Ostrov Vrangelya

Sredinnyy

Bering

Sea

Poluostrov
Byrranga
Gory
Poluostrov
Taymyr
1146

S e a

Ostrov Faddeyevskiy
Ostrov
Novaya Sibir

Ostrov
Medvezhi

Verkhoyansk
2389

Khrebet Cherskogo

Poluostrov
Kamchatka

Nordvik
Tiksi

Petropavlovsk-
Kamchatsky

Arctic Circle

962

Y A K U T

A.S.S.R.

Vilyuysk
Yakutsk

S O C I A L I S T   R E P U B L I C

Sea
of
Okhotsk

Sakhalin

Olekminsk

Krasnoyarsk

Bratsk

Kirensk

Komsomolsk

Khabarovsk

Hokkaidō
Sapporo
Hakodate

Nizhneudinsk

Chita
Ulan Ude
Angarsk
Irkutsk

Blagoveshchensk

Birobidzhan

40

Ulaanbaatar
(Ulan Bator)

Harbin

Tsitsihar

Kiamusze

Ussuriysk
Vladivostok

Sea   of   JAPAN

Honshū

M O N G O L I A

Changchun

Kirin

Chongjin

J a p a n

Niigata

G O B I

Shenyang
(Mukden)
Anshan
Fushun

Wŏnsan

North

Pyongyang
Lü-ta

Peiping
(Peking)

Paotow
Changkiakow
(Kalgan)

Sŏul
South

Inch'ŏn
Taejŏn

Pusan

Boundaries of U.S.S.R.
Boundaries of S.S.R.
Boundaries of A.S.S.R.

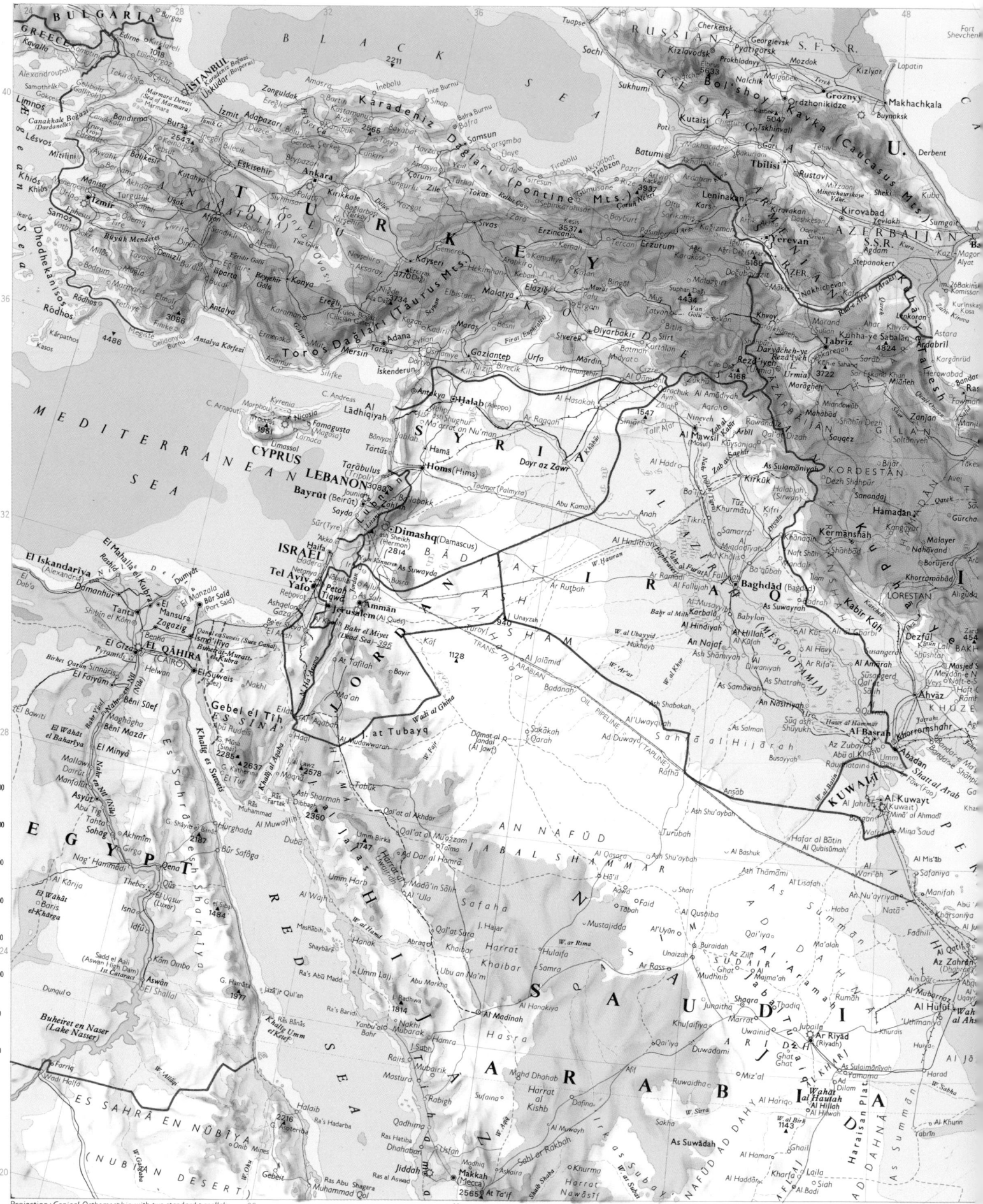

Projection: Conical Orthomorphic with two standard parallels

1:10 000 000

100   0   100   200   300   400 km

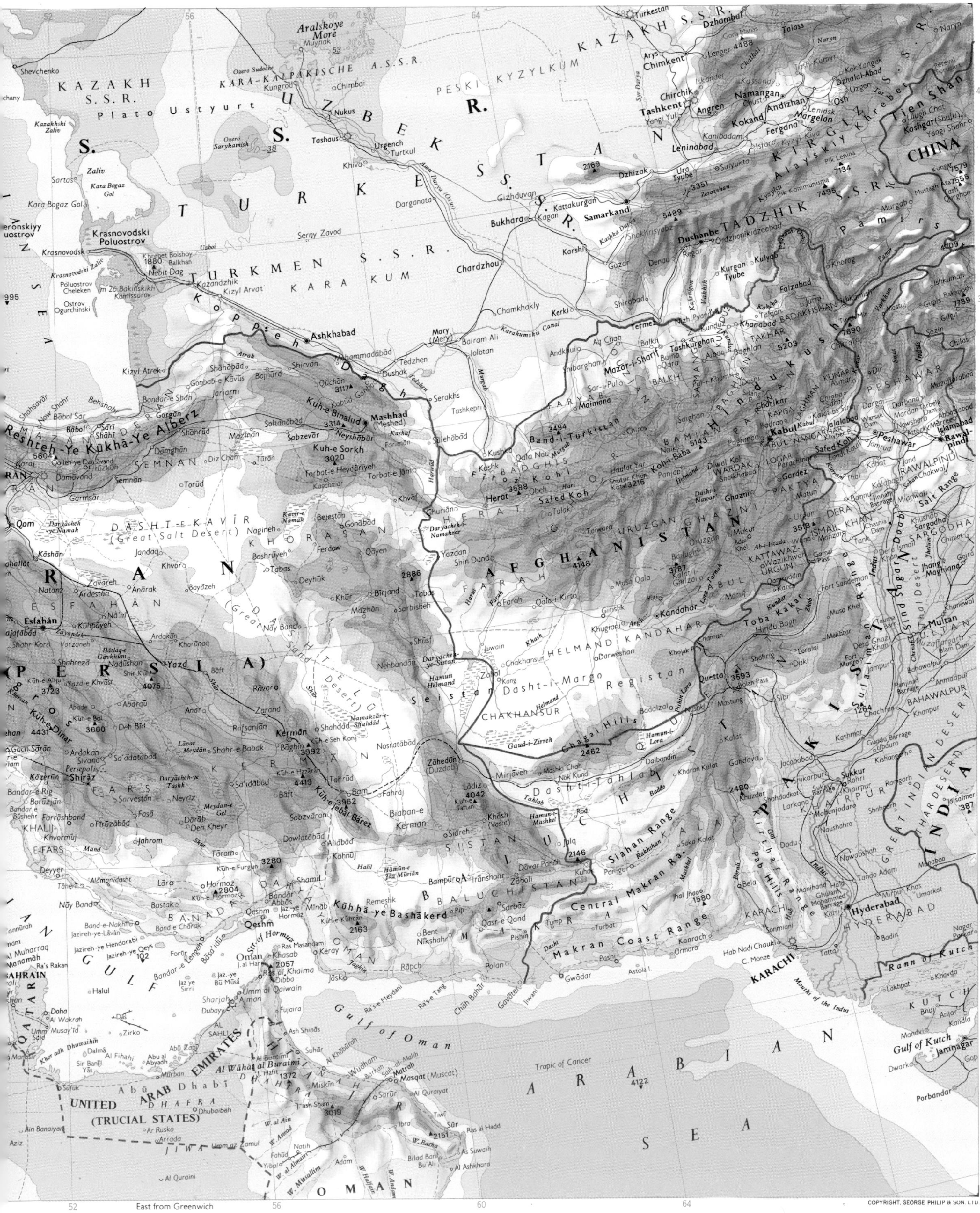

KAZAKH S.S.R.
KARA-KALPAKISCHE A.S.S.R.
Plato Ustyurt
Aralskoye More
Muynak
Ozero Sudoche
Kungrad
Chimbai
Nukus
PESKI KYZYLKUM
KAZAKH S.S.R.
Turkestan
Dzhambul
Gora Kogar
Talass
Talas
Naryn
Chirchik
Chimkent
Lenger 4488
Chu
Arys
Tashkent
Angren
Namangan
Andizhan
Osh
Kok Yangak
Kashgar (Shufu)
Tien Shan
Ulugh Chat
7579
CHINA
7555

Shevchenko
Kazakhskiy Zaliv
S.S.R.
S.
Zaliv
Kara Bogaz Gol
Sartass
chany
Ozera Sarykamish
Tashaus
Urgench
Turtkul
Khiva
Darganata
Gizhduvan
Dzhizak
Ura Tyube
3351
Sulyukta
KIRGIZ
S.S.R.
Pik Lenina
Kommunizma
7134
Pik
7495
Mustagh Ata 7555
Gez

UZBEK S.S.R.
TURKESTAN
Amu Darya (Oxus)
Bukhara
Kagan
Samarkand
5489
Karshi
Guzar
Kurgan Tyube
Khorog
TADZHIK S.S.R.
Dushanbe
Ordzhonikidzeabad
Pamirs
4409

Krasnovodski Poluostrov
Krasnovodsk
m Zal. Balkhan
Nebit Dag
1880
Kizyl Arvat
Serny Zavod
Chardzhou
Kerki
Shirabad
Termez
Kunduz
Khanabad
BADAKHSHAN
7690
Ishkuman
7789

TURKMEN S.S.R.
KARA KUM
Kazandzhik
Kopet Dagh
Ashkhabad
Muhammadabad
Mary (Merv)
Bairam Ali
Iolotan
Karakumskii Canal
Andkhoy
Aq Chah
Balkh
Mazar-i-Sharif
Tashkurghan
TAKHAR
5203
PESHAWAR
Chitral

Ashkhabad
Airak
Shahabad
Shirvan
Bojnurd
Quchan
3117
Kuh-e Binalud
3314
Mashhad (Meshed)
Tashkepri
Serakhs
Herat
FARYAB
Maimana
BALKH
HINDU KUSH
KUNAR
Jalalabad
PESHAWAR
Peshawar
RAWALPINDI
Rawalpindi

Reshteh-Ye Kukha-Ye Alberz
5604
Bandar-e Shah
Gonbad-e Kavus
Jajarm
Soltanabad
Kuh-e Sorkh
3020
Sabzevar
Neyshabur
Turbat-e Heydariyeh
Torbat-e Jam
BADGHIS
Firoza
Qala Nau
3588
Qeh
3494
Band-i-Turkistan
5143
BAMIAN
Koh-i-Baba
Charikar
KAPISA
Kabul
KABUL
NANGARHAR
Khyber Pass
Safed Koh
LOGAR
Safed Koh
Attock
Islamabad

DASHT-E KAVIR
(Great Salt Desert)
SEMNAN
Damavand
Semnan
Garmsar
Diz Chah
Naginah
Bejestan
Gonabad
Ferdows
KHORASAN
Boshruyeh
Khur
Deyhuk
Tabas
Yazdan
Daryacheh-ye Namaksar
HERAT
Ghurian
Shin Dand
Obeh
Safed Koh
Taiwara
URUZGAN
GHAZNI
Gardez
PAKTYA
WARDAK
Ghazni
Urgun
DERA ISMAIL KHAN
Bannu
Salt Range
Sargodha

IRAN
(PERSIA)
Qom
Daryacheh-ye Namak
Kashan
Natanz
Ardestan
Anarak
Bayazeh
Esfahan
Na'in
Khvor
2886
FARAH
4148
Musa Qala
3787
Ghazni
ZABUL
Muqur
3518
KATTAWAZ-WAZIKHWA
URGUN
Fort Sandeman
Duki
Moghiana

Shahr Kord
Vorzaneh
Ardakan
Khoransq
Nay Band
Mazhan
Sarbisheh
D (Great Sand Desert)
Nehbandan
Daryacheh-ye Sistan
Juwain
Qala-i-Kirta
Chakhansur
HELMAND
KANDAHAR
Kandahar
Spin Baldak
Toba Kakar
Hirdu Bagh
Chaman
Quetta
3693
Bolan Pass
1264
BAHAWALPUR
Khanpur
Guddu Barrage
Jacobabad

Kuh-e Dinar
3723
Abade
Yazd-e Khvast
4075
Ravar
Zarand
Namakzar-e Shahdad
Shahdad
Seh Koni
Bam
Nosratabad
Zabol
Seistan
Hamun Helmand
Dasht-i-Margo
Registan
Chagai Hills
2462
CHAKHANSUR
Gaud-i-Zirreh
Hamun-i-Lora
Nushki
Kalat
2480
Khuzdar
Sukkur
Rohri
KHAIRPUR
Shikarpur
Larkana
Mohenjodaro
Nawabshah

Kerman
3992
Baghin
KERMAN
Sirjan
Sa'idabad
Zahedan
Duzdab
Ladiz
4042
Kuh-e Taftan
Mirjaveh
Khash (Vasht)
2146
Siahan Range
Makran Ra
KALAT
Pab Hills
Bela
Sonmiani
KARACHI
Hyderabad
HYDERABAD
GREAT INDIAN DESERT

Kuh-e Jebal Barez
3962
Sabzvaran
Biaban-e Kerman
Siareh
SISTAN
Jaz Murian
Bampur
Iranshahr
Zaboli
Davar Panah
Panjgur
BALUCHISTAN
Central Makran Range
Turbat
Pasni
Gwadar
KARACHI
C. Monze
Cape Monze
Mouths of the Indus
Thatta
Rann of Kutch

Shiraz
FARS
Sarvestan
Neyriz
Darab
Jahrom
Kuh-e Furglun
3280
Kuhha-ye Bashakerd
2163
Rapch
Jask
Gulf of Oman
INDIA
387
Jaisalmer
Umarkot
Mirpur Khas
KUTCH
Gulf of Kutch
Jamnagar
Porbandar

BANDAR
Hormoz
2804
Bandar-e Abbas
Minab
Qeshm
Qeshm
Ras Masandam
J. al Harf
2057
Ras al Khaima
Dibba
OMAN
Chah Bahar
Gwatar
Jiwani

GULF
Bushehr
Deyyer
Nay Band
Lar
Bastak
Bandar-e Lengeh
Sharjah
Ajman
Dubayy
Fujaira
ARABIAN SEA

KHALIJ-E FARS
Khvormuj
Mand
Tahert
Aldamavdasht
BANDAR
Band-e Nakhilu
Jazireh-ye Qeys
102
Lavan
Jaz ye Sirri
Bu Musa
Umm al Qaiwain
Ash Shinas
Sohar
Khaburah
Suwaiq
Masqat (Muscat)
Matrah
ARABIAN SEA
4122

BAHRAIN
Al Muharraq
Manamah
Doha
Al Wakrah
QATAR
Halul
Das
Zirko
Abu al Abyadh
Murban
Al Burami
Al Wahat al Buraimi
1372
DHAHIRAH
Wadham
Sib
Al Masna'h
Sarur
Rustaq
Izki
Tropic of Cancer
Nizwa
Ibra
Sur
2151
Ras al Hadd

UNITED ARAB EMIRATES
(TRUCIAL STATES)
Abu Dhabi
DHAFRA
Dhubaibah
Ain Banaiyan
JIWA
SAHIL
JA'ALAN
3019
OMAN
Bilad Bani
Bu Ali

ARABIAN SEA

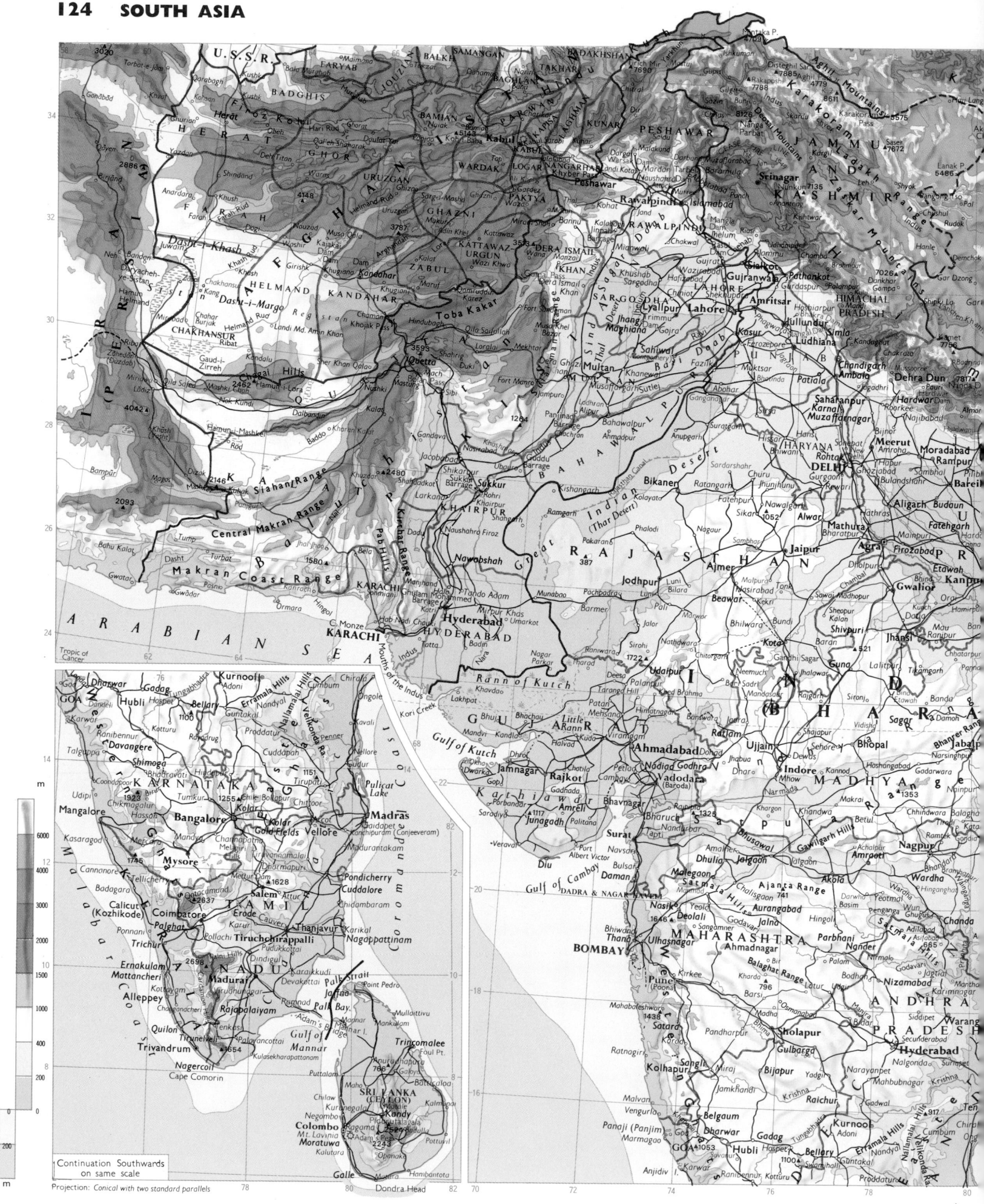

Continuation Southwards on same scale

Projection: Conical with two standard parallels

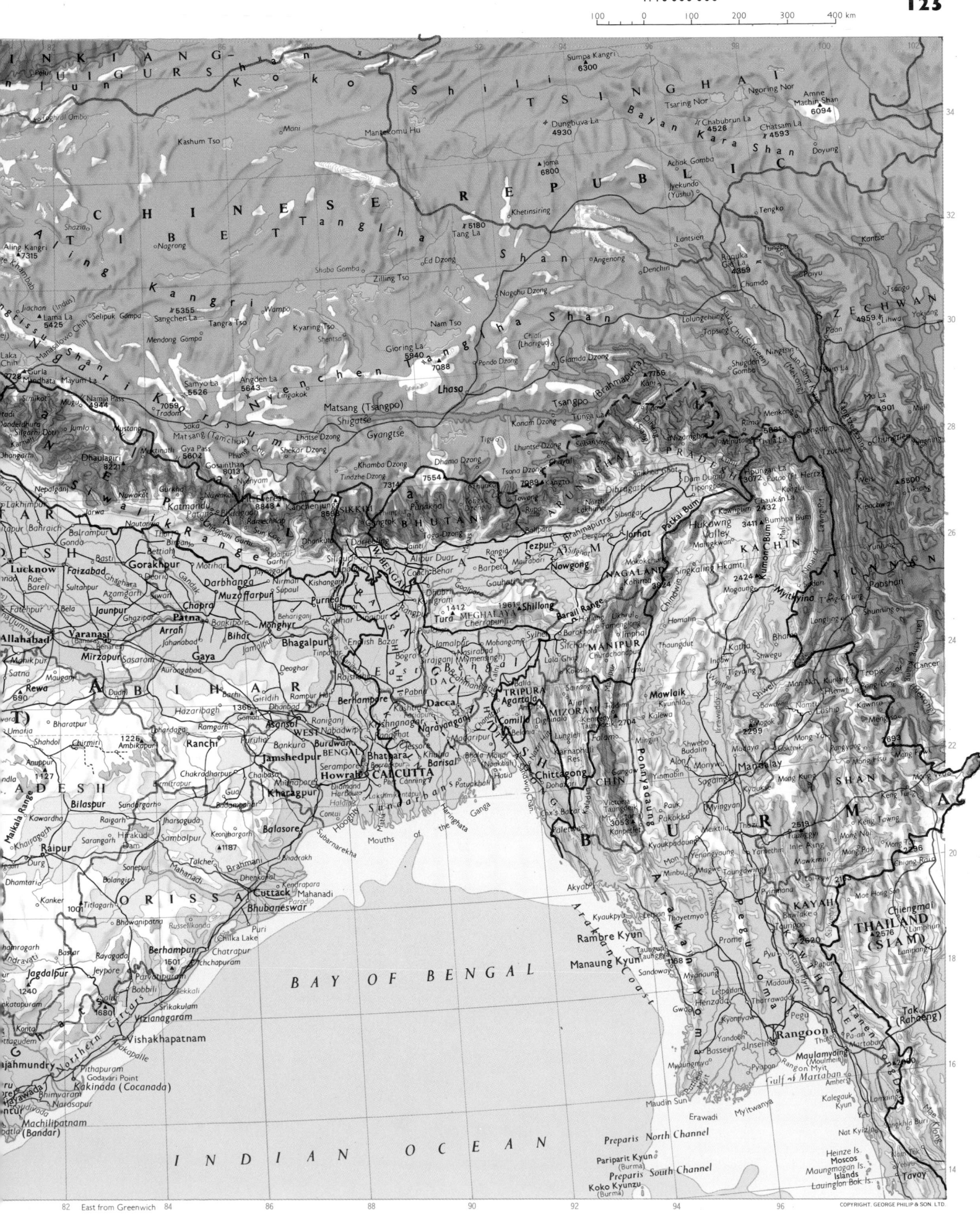

1:10 000 000

100   0   100   200   300   400 km

INKIANG-

niuiGURS
Koko Shili

CHINESE   REPUBLIC

TSINGHAI

Sumpa Kangri
6300

Ngoring Nor

Amne
Machin Shan
6094

34

Dungbuya La
4930

Bayan
Kara
Shan

Jr Chabubrun La
4526

Chatsam La
4593

Doyung

T   I   B   E   T

Tanglha

5180

Tang La

Khetinsiring

Jyekundo
(Yushu)

Lantsien

Tengko

SZECHWAN

32

4959

Yokiang

Nenchen Tanglha Shan

Nam Tso

Lhasa

Tsangpo (Brahmaputra)

30

BAY OF BENGAL

INDIAN   OCEAN

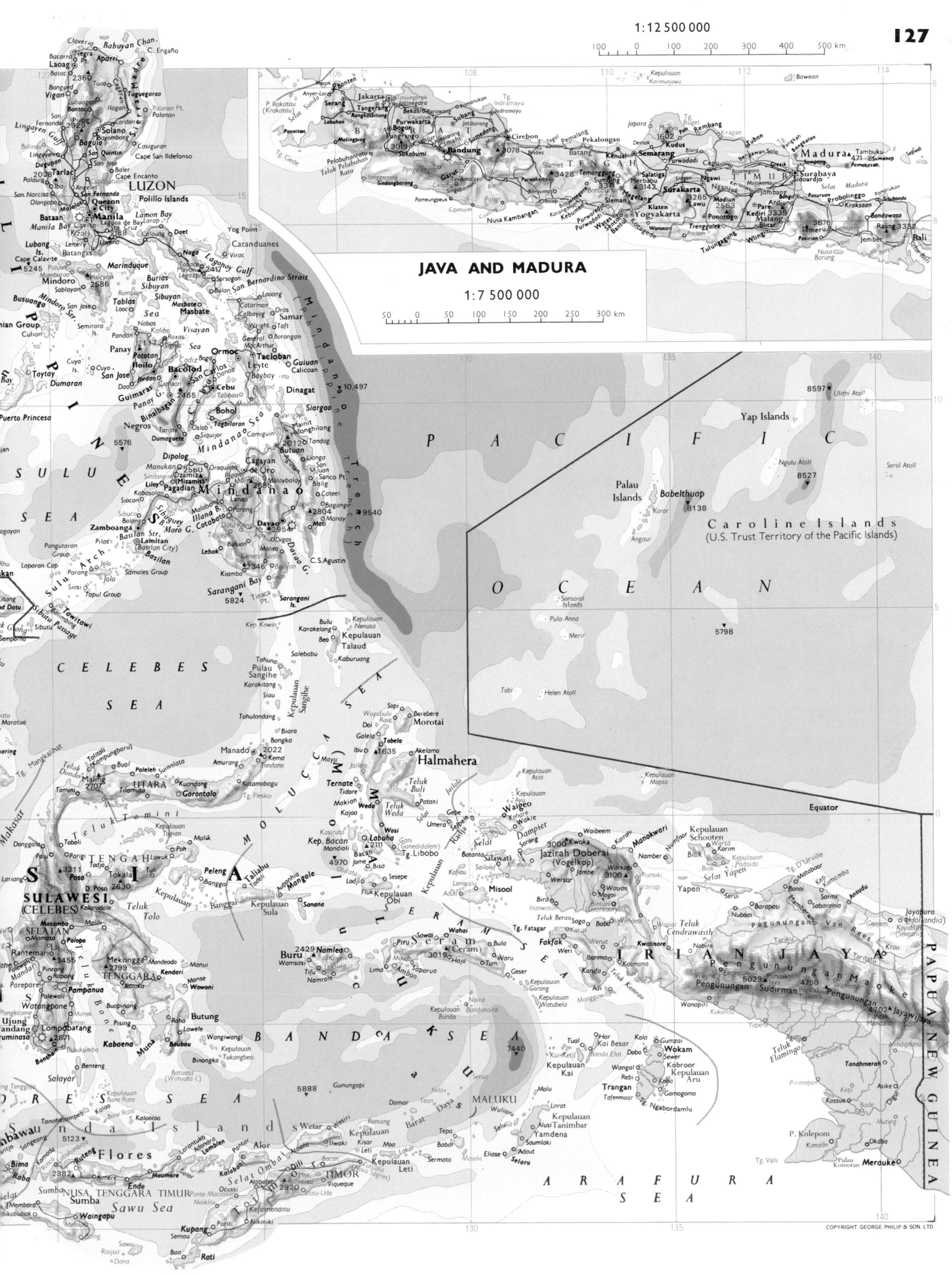

1 : 12 500 000

100   0   100   200   300   400   500 km

JAVA AND MADURA

1 : 7 500 000

50   0   50   100   150   200   250   300 km

LUZON

PHILIPPINE

SULU
SEA

CELEBES
SEA

SULAWESI
(CELEBES)

PACIFIC

OCEAN

Caroline Islands
(U.S. Trust Territory of the Pacific Islands)

Equator

Yap Islands

Palau
Islands

MOLUCCA SEA

Halmahera

SERAM SEA

BANDA SEA

MALUKU

ARAFURA
SEA

IRIAN JAYA

PAPUA NEW GUINEA

NUSA TENGGARA TIMUR

Sawu Sea

COPYRIGHT GEORGE PHILIP & SON, LTD

1:10 000 000

MALAYA AND SINGAPORE

1:6 000 000

Projection: Conical with two standard parallels

East from Greenwich

COPYRIGHT. GEORGE PHILIP & SON. LTD.

1:20 000 000

200 0 200 400 600 800 km

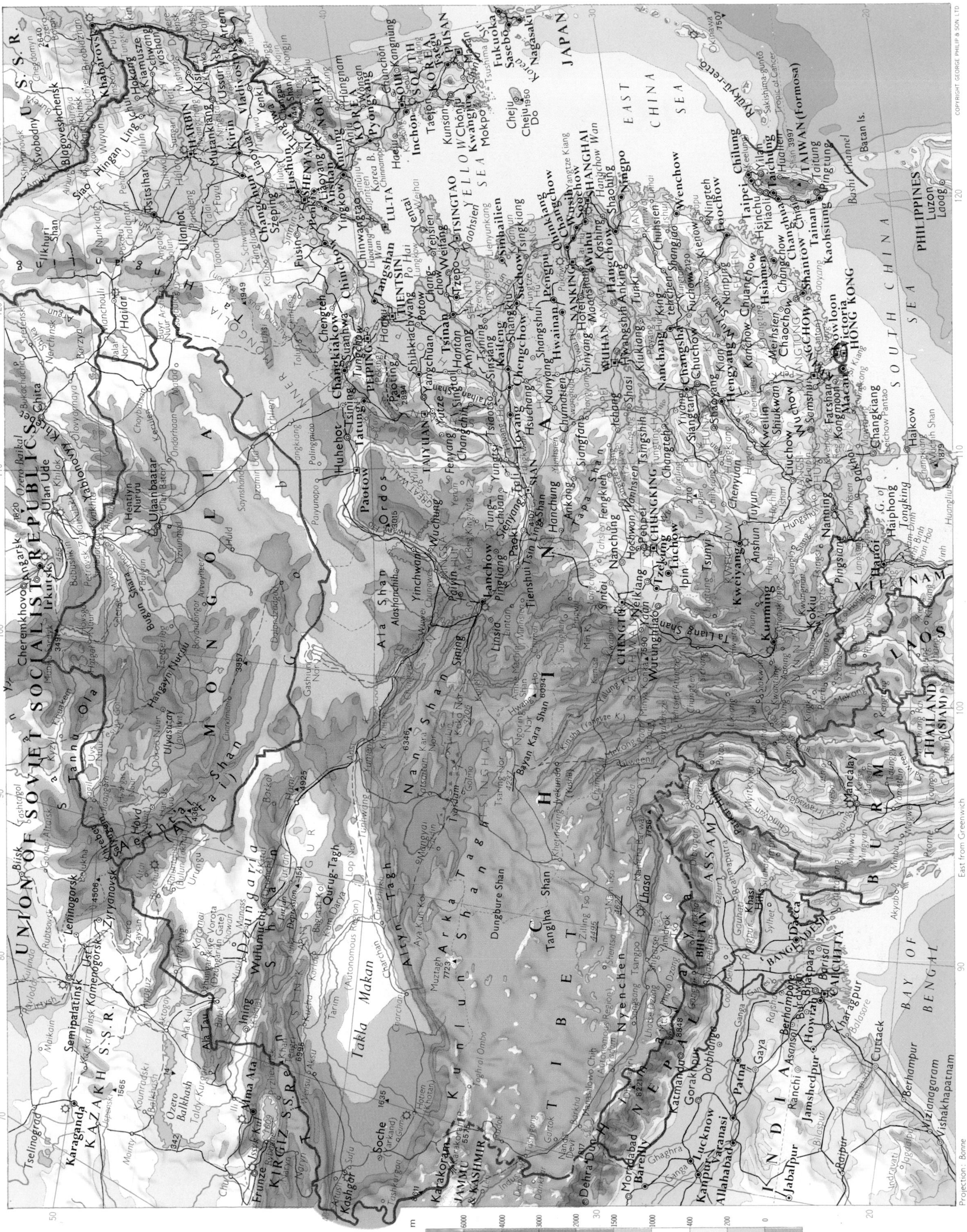

U.S.S.R.

UNION OF SOVIET SOCIALIST REPUBLICS

MONGOLIA

INNER MONGOLIA

KAZAKH S.S.R.

KIRGIZ S.S.R.

SINKIANG

Takla Makan

Tarim

JAMMU and KASHMIR

TIBET

Kunlun Shan

Nan Shan

Altyn Tagh

Tsinghai

Tangla Shan

C H I N A

HARBIN

PEIPING

TIENTSIN

TAIYUAN

SIAN

Ordos

Paotow

Lanchow

NORTH KOREA

SOUTH KOREA

PYONGYANG

SEOUL

PUSAN

JAPAN

Fukuoka

Nagasaki

YELLOW SEA

EAST CHINA SEA

SHANGHAI

NANKING

WUHAN

CHUNGKING

CHENGTU

Kweiyang

Kunming

SZECHWAN

HONG KONG

Macao

KWANGCHOW

Swatow

TAIWAN (Formosa)

Taipei

Kaohsiung

SOUTH CHINA SEA

PHILIPPINES

Luzon

BURMA

THAILAND (SIAM)

LAOS

VIETNAM

Hanoi

Haiphong

NEPAL

Katmandu

BHUTAN

BANGLADESH

CALCUTTA

Dacca

I N D I A

BAY OF BENGAL

Lhasa

Tropic of Cancer

East from Greenwich

Projection: Bonne

COPYRIGHT GEORGE PHILIP & SON, LTD

m 6000 4000 3000 2000 1500 1000 400 200 0

1:10 000 000

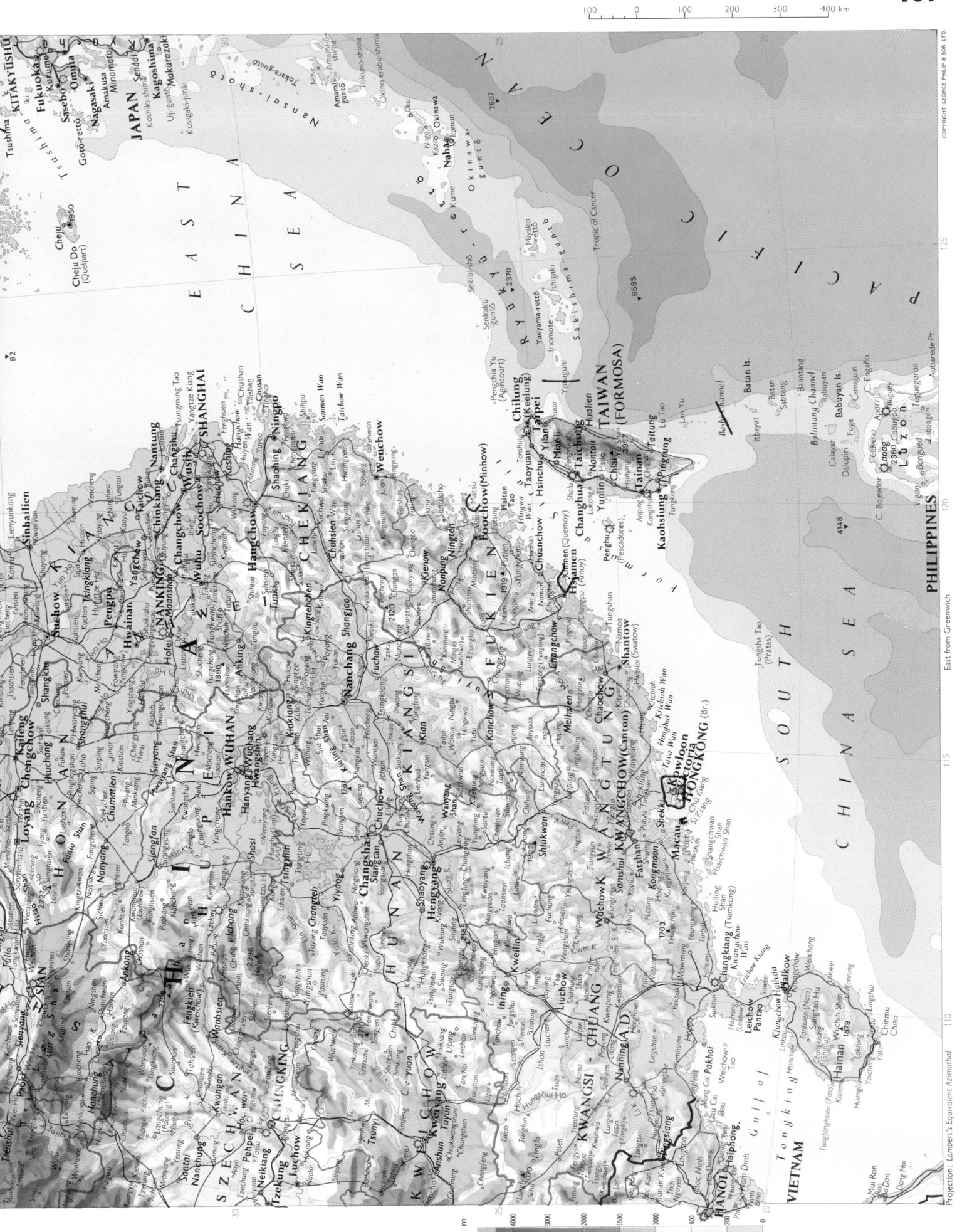

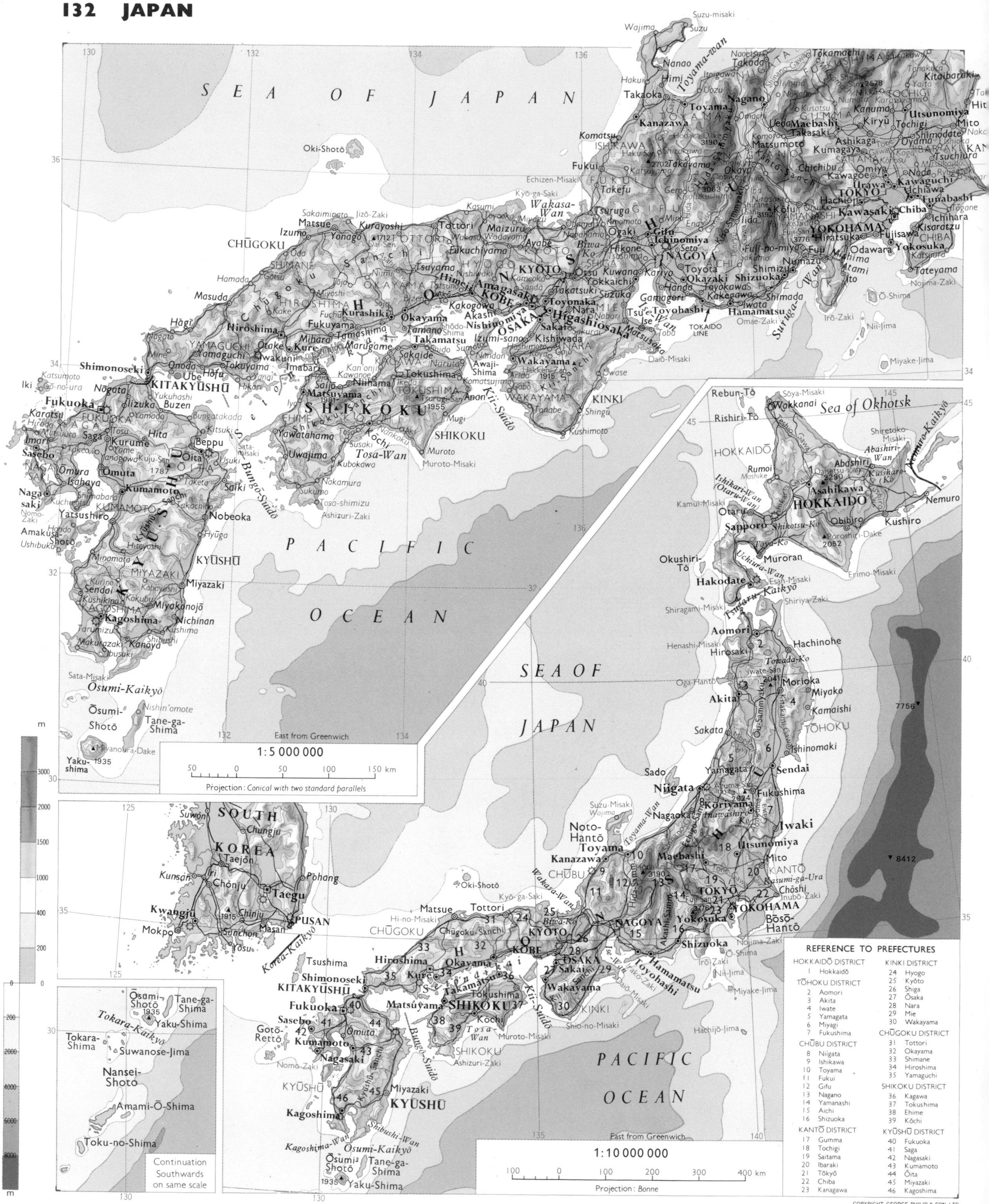

Main map

SEA OF JAPAN

Suzu-misaki
Wajima · Suzu
Nanao · Toyama-wan · Takada
Himi · Takaoka · Toyama · Nagano · Kitaibaraki
Komatsu · Kanazawa · ISHIKAWA · Ueda · Maebashi · Kiryu · Tochigi · Utsunomiya
Fukui · Matsumoto · Takasaki · Ashikaga · Mito · Shimodate
Takayama · Chichibu · Omiya · Tsuchiura
Echizen-Misaki · FUKUI · TOKYO · YOKOHAMA · Chiba · Ichihara
Kasumi · Wakasa-Wan · Gifu · Ichinomiya · NAGOYA · Kofu · Hachioji · Kawasaki
Sakaiminato · Jizō-Zaki · Tsuruga · Otsu · Kuwana · Kariya · Fuji-no-miya · Fuji · Odawara · Yokosuka
Matsue · Tottori · Maizuru · KYOTO · Okazaki · Toyokawa · Shizuoka · Shimizu · Atami · Tateyama
Izumo · Yonago · Ayabe · Kobe · Toyonaka · Higashiosaka · Tsu · Ise · Hamamatsu · Ō-Shima · Nojima-Zaki
CHŪGOKU · Fukuchiyama · OSAKA · Sakai · Kishiwada · Iwata · TOKAIDO LINE · Omae-Zaki · Irō-Zaki
Hamada · Tsuyama · Himeji · Amagasaki · Nishinomiya · Suzuka · Daiō-Misaki · Miyake-Jima
Masuda · Kurashiki · Okayama · Takatsuki · MIE · Owase
Hiroshima · Fukuyama · Kakogawa · Takamatsu · Wakayama
Hagi · Otake · Mihara · Tamashima · Tokushima · WAKAYAMA · Shingū
YAMAGUCHI · Yamaguchi · Iwakuni · Imabari · Naruto · KINKI · Tanabe
Shimonoseki · Onoda · Ube · Hōfu · Tokuyama · Marugame · SHIKOKU · Kushimoto
KITAKYŪSHŪ · Matsuyama · Kii-Suidō · Muroto
Iki · Nōgata · Buzen · Saijo · Niihama · Kōchi · Tosa-Wan · Muroto-Misaki
Fukuoka · Iizuka · EHIME · Uwajima · Kubokawa
Karatsu · SAGA · Kurume · Hita · Kitsuki · Nakamura
Imari · Saga · Beppu · Oita · Tosa-shimizu
Sasebo · Isahaya · Ōita · Saiki · Ashizuri-Zaki
Nagasaki · Ōmuta · Kumamoto · Nobeoka
Yatsushiro · KUMAMOTO · Hyūga
Amakusa-Shoto · Minamata · KYŪSHŪ
MIYAZAKI · Miyakonojō · Miyazaki
Sendai · Kobayashi · Nichinan
Kagoshima · KAGOSHIMA · Kanoya
Makurazaki · Kushikino
Sata-Misaki
Osumi-Kaikyō
Ōsumi-Shoto · Tane-ga-Shima
Yaku-shima · Nishin'omote
Miyanoura-Dake

PACIFIC OCEAN

SEA OF JAPAN

Inset: Hokkaido (1:5 000 000)

Sea of Okhotsk
Rebun-Tō · Sōya-Misaki · Wakkanai
Rishiri-Tō
HOKKAIDO
Rumoi · Mashike · Asahikawa · Abashiri · Abashiri-Wan
Otaru · Ishikari-Wan (Otaru-Wan) · Daisetsu-zan · Kussharo-Ko
Kamui-Misaki · Sapporo · Shikotsu-Ko · Obihiro · Kushiro
Okushiri-Tō · Uchiura-Wan · Muroran · Horoshiri-Dake · Nemuro
Hakodate · Esan-Misaki · Erimo-Misaki
Shiragami-Misaki · Shiriya-Zaki
Tsugaru-Kaikyō
Aomori · Hachinohe
Henashi-Misaki · Hirosaki · Towada-Ko
Oga-Hantō · Iwate-San · Morioka · Miyako
Akita · Kamaishi
TŌHOKU
Sakata · Ishinomaki
Sado · Yamagata · Sendai
Niigata · Kōriyama · Fukushima
Nagaoka · Inawashiro · Iwaki
Suzu-Misaki · Noto-Hantō · Toyama · Maebashi · Utsunomiya
Wajima · Toyama-wan · KANTO
Noto-Hantō · Kanazawa · Mito · Kasumi-ga-Ura
CHŪBU · TOKYO · YOKOHAMA · Chōshi · Inubō-Zaki
Yokosuka · Bōsō-Hantō
NAGOYA · Shizuoka · Ō-Shima
Hamamatsu · Toyohashi · Nojima-Zaki · Miyake-Jima
KINKI · Irō-Zaki · Hachijō-Jima

Elevation scale (left)

m
3000
2000
1500
1000
400
200
0
200
2000
4000
6000
8000
m

1:5 000 000
50 0 50 100 150 km
Projection: Conical with two standard parallels

East from Greenwich

Lower map (1:10 000 000)

SOUTH KOREA
Suwŏn · Chungju
Taejŏn
Kunsan · Chŏnju · Pohang
Kwangju · Chinju · Taegu
Mokpo · Sunchŏn · PUSAN
Masan · Tosu
Tsushima · Korea-Kaikyō
Shimonoseki · CHŪGOKU · Matsue · Tottori
KITAKYŪSHŪ · Hiroshima · Okayama · KOBE · OSAKA · NAGOYA · Shizuoka
Fukuoka · Kure · KYOTO · Sakai · Hamamatsu
Sasebo · Kumamoto · Takamatsu · Tokushima · Wakayama · Toyohashi
Nagasaki · SHIKOKU · Matsuyama · Kōchi · KINKI
Gotō-Rettō · Ōmuta · Tosa-Wan · Muroto-Misaki
Kagoshima · Miyazaki · KYŪSHŪ
Oki-Shoto · Wakasa-Wan · CHŪBU · TOKYO · YOKOHAMA · Yokosuka
Kyō-ga-Saki · Kii-Suidō · Shio-no-Misaki · Nojima-Zaki

PACIFIC OCEAN

1:10 000 000
100 0 100 200 300 400 km
Projection: Bonne

East from Greenwich

Inset: Nansei-Shoto (Continuation Southwards on same scale)

Ōsumi-Shoto · Tane-ga-Shima
Tokara-Kaikyō · Yaku-Shima
Tokara-Shima · Suwanose-Jima
Nansei-Shoto
Amami-Ō-Shima
Toku-no-Shima

REFERENCE TO PREFECTURES

HOKKAIDŌ DISTRICT
1 Hokkaidō

TŌHOKU DISTRICT
2 Aomori
3 Akita
4 Iwate
5 Yamagata
6 Miyagi
7 Fukushima

CHŪBU DISTRICT
8 Niigata
9 Ishikawa
10 Toyama
11 Fukui
12 Gifu
13 Nagano
14 Yamanashi
15 Aichi
16 Shizuoka

KANTO DISTRICT
17 Gumma
18 Tochigi
19 Saitama
20 Tōkyō
21 Tōkyō
22 Chiba
23 Kanagawa

KINKI DISTRICT
24 Hyogo
25 Kyōto
26 Shiga
27 Ōsaka
28 Nara
29 Mie
30 Wakayama

CHŪGOKU DISTRICT
31 Tottori
32 Okayama
33 Shimane
34 Hiroshima
35 Yamaguchi

SHIKOKU DISTRICT
36 Kagawa
37 Tokushima
38 Ehime
39 Kōchi

KYŪSHŪ DISTRICT
40 Fukuoka
41 Saga
42 Nagasaki
43 Kumamoto
44 Ōita
45 Miyazaki
46 Kagoshima

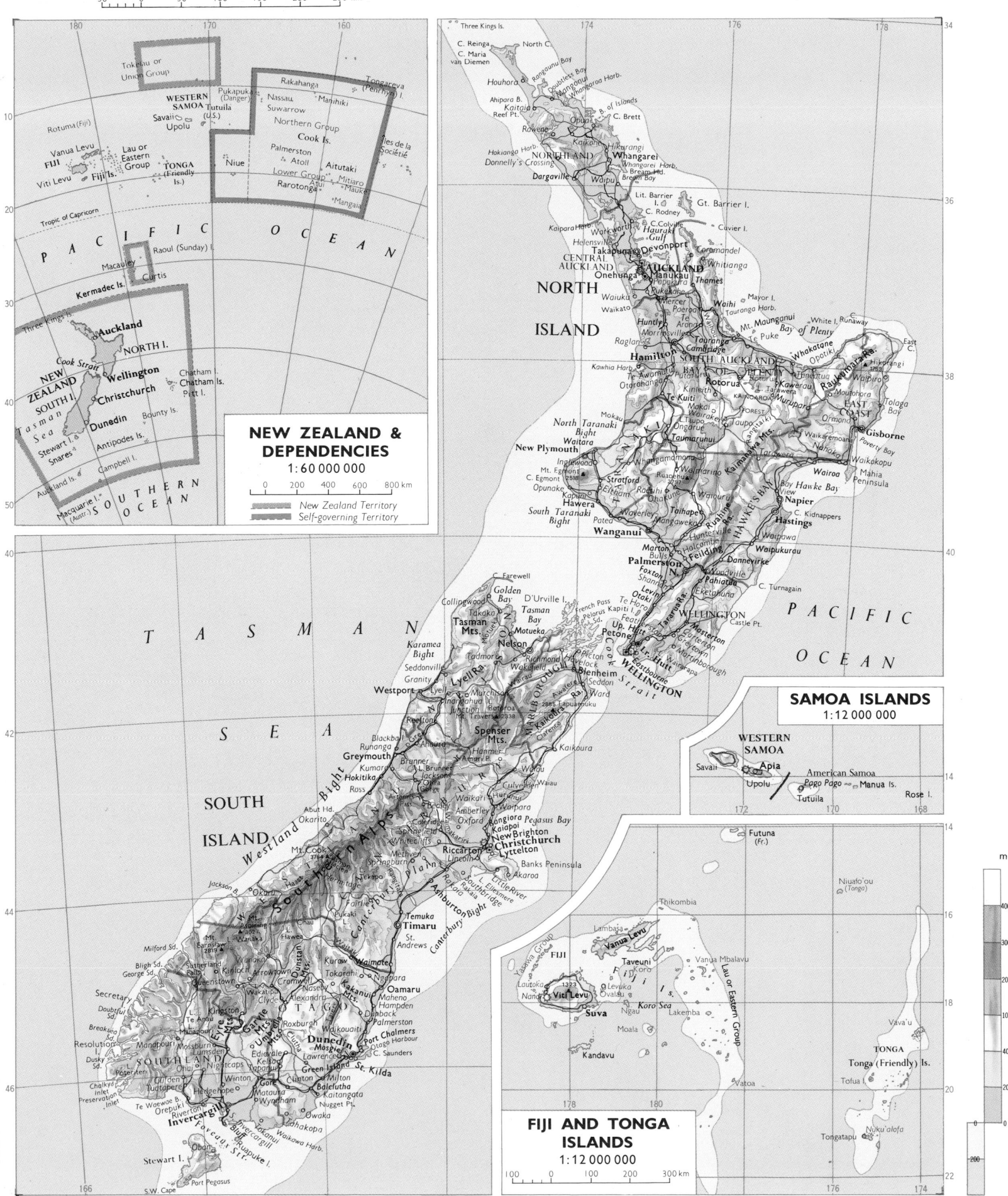

1:6 000 000

50 0 50 100 150 200 250 km

NEW ZEALAND & DEPENDENCIES
1:60 000 000

0 200 400 600 800 km

New Zealand Territory
Self-governing Territory

SAMOA ISLANDS
1:12 000 000

WESTERN SAMOA
Savaii Apia
Upolu
American Samoa Is.
Pago Pago Manua Is.
Tutuila Rose I.

FIJI AND TONGA ISLANDS
1:12 000 000

100 0 100 200 300 km

NORTH ISLAND

SOUTH ISLAND

TASMAN SEA

PACIFIC OCEAN

SOUTHERN ALPS

Projection: Conical with two standard parallels

COPYRIGHT. GEORGE PHILIP & SON. LTD.

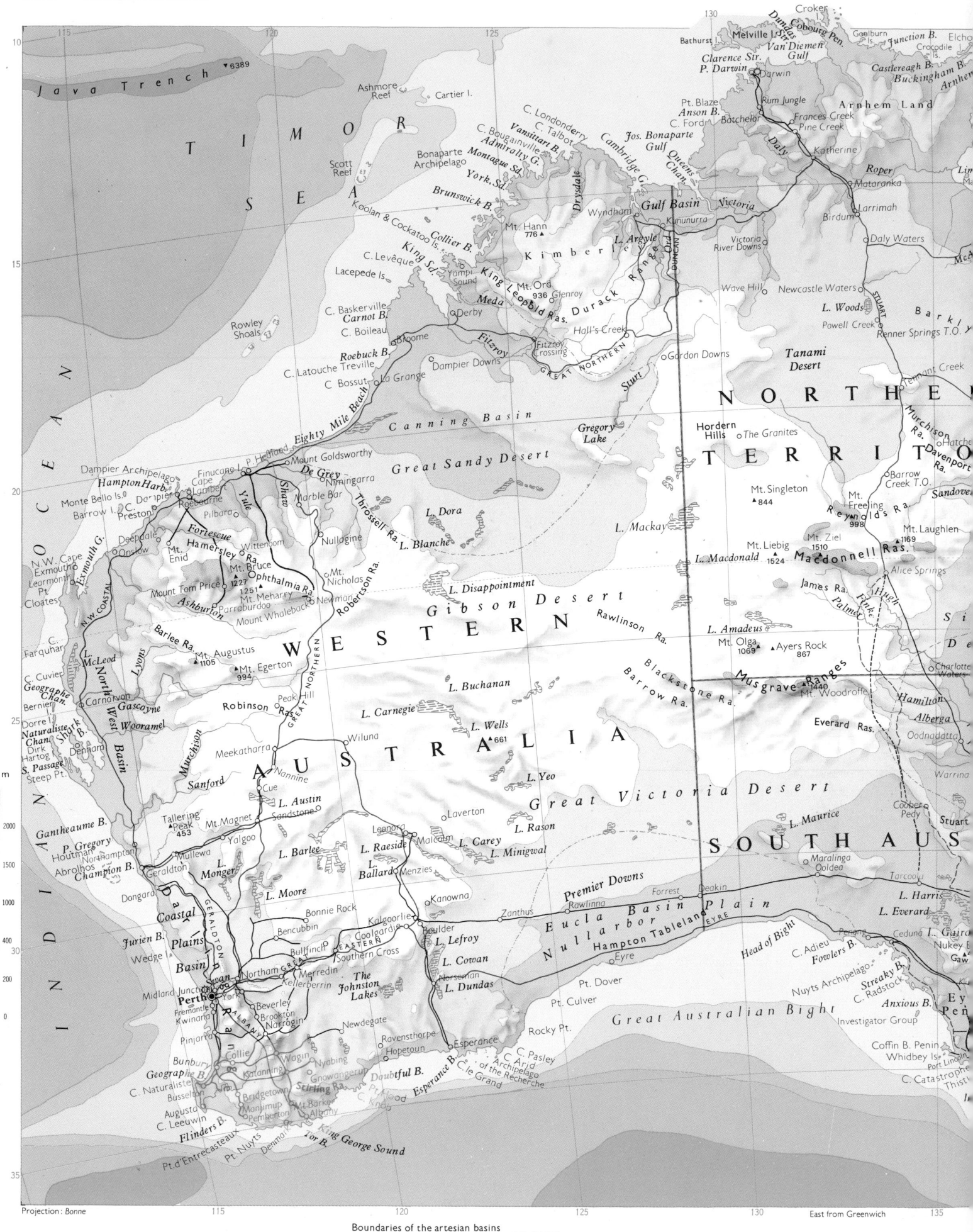

Projection: Bonne
East from Greenwich

Boundaries of the artesian basins

1:12 000 000

100   0   100   200   300   400   500 km

AUSTRALASIA
POLITICAL
1:80 000 000

200 0   400   800   1200   1600 Km

INDONESIA

IRIAN
JAYA

NEW GUINEA

PAPUA

NORTHERN
TERRITORY

WESTERN
AUSTRALIA

SOUTH
AUSTRALIA

QUEENSLAND

NEW
SOUTH
WALES

Brisbane

Sydney
Canberra

VICTORIA

Melbourne

TASMANIA

Hobart

PACIFIC
OCEAN

NEW
ZEALAND

Auckland
Wellington
Christchurch
Dunedin

Wessel Is.
Co. Is.
Wilberforce
Melville B.
Nhulunbuy
P. Bradshaw
Caledon B.
Grey
Mud B.
angula
Groote Eylandt
C. Beatrice
Edward Pellew Group
Vanderlin I.

Thursday I.   Banks I.
Prince of Wales I.   C. York
Newcastle B.

Arnhem & Gove Pen.

Gulf of
Carpentaria

Mornington   C. van
I.   Diemen
Wellesley Is.
Bentinck I.

P. Musgrave
Duifken Pt.
Albatross B. Weipa

Shelburne   B.
C. Grenville
Temple B.
Weymouth
Direction

Coral
Sea
Basin

Cape York
Wenlock
Holroyd
Coleman
Archer

Peninsula

McIlwraith Ra.

Coen

Normanby

C. Flattery
C. Bedford
Cooktown

Great Barrier Reef

Princess Charlotte B.
Bathurst B.
C. Melville Osprey Rf.

CORAL SEA ISLANDS

Lihou Reef
& Cays

Mellish
Reef

Mitchell

Normanton
Burketown
Camooweal

Gilbert

Leichhardt

Croydon

Georgetown
Forsayth
Einasleigh

Chillagoe
Mareeba
Mitchell
Mossman
Trinity Bay
Cairns
Atherton
Bartle Frere
Innisfail

Ravenshoe

Hinchinbrook I.
Ingham
Palm Is.
Halifax B.

TERRITORY

Marion
Reef

Île Chesterfield

Îles Avon

Mount Isa
Mary
Kathleen
Kajabbi
Cloncurry
Julia Cr.
Richmond
Hughenden

Selwyn Range
Selwyn
Duchess
Dajarra

Flinders

Georgina

Urandangi

QUEENSLAND

Charters
Towers
Mt. Dalrymple 1277
Netherdale

Townsville
Ayr
Home Hill
Bowen

C. Cleveland
C. Bowling Green

Proserpine
Whitsunday I.
Cumberland Is.
Collinsville
Mackay

Swain
Rfs.

Frederick
Reef

Kenn Reef

Wreck Reef
Bird I.

Bellona Rfs.

Boulia
Winton
Muttaburra
Aramac
Clermont
Emerald

Denham Ra.
Peak Ra.

C. Palmerston

C. Townshend
Townshend I.

Cato I.

Diamantina

Bedourie

Longreach
Ilfracombe Barcaldine
Jundah

CAPRICORN
Alpha

Springsure
Mt. Acland
975

Theodore

Yeppoon
Rockhampton
Keppel B.

C. Capricorn
Curtis I.
P. Curtis
Gladstone
Biloela

Bustard Head
Burnett
Bundaberg
Hervey Bay
Childers
Maryborough

Sandy C.
Fraser I.

Tropic of Capricorn

4681

Birdsville

Eyre Cr.

L. Machattie
L. Yamma
Yamma

Blackall
Yaraka
Windorah
Adavale
Augathella
Injune

Charleville
Quilpie

Wyandra

Mitchell
Roma

Expedition Ra.
Wardoon
Taroom

Gayndah
Gympie
Murgon
Wondai
Kingaroy
Nanango

Nambour
Bribie I.
Moreton B.
Caboolture

L. Gregory
L. Blanche
Tibooburra

Thargomindah

Cunnamulla
St. George

Moonie
Dalby

Toowoomba
Ipswich
Brisbane
Southport
N. Stradbroke I.

Leigh Creek
Copley

Warrego

BALONNE

Paroo

Dirranbandi

Goondiwindi
Mungindi

Warwick
Stanthorpe

Murwillumbah
Sutherland Pt.
C. Byron

St. Mary's Pk.
1165
Hawker

Bourke
Walgett

Barwon

Gwydir
Moree

Inverell
Warialda

Glen
Innes

Tenterfield
Casino
Lismore
Ballina

Clarence
Grafton

FLINDERS Ranges

L. Frome
L. Callabonna

NEW   SOUTH

Cobar
Nyngan

Narrabri

Gunnedah

Tamworth

Armidale

New England Range

Coffs Harbour
Macleay

Broken Hill
Wilcannia

BARRIER Ra.
Main Barrier Ra.

Menindee
Darling

Gilgandra

Liverpool
Plains

Liverpool Ra.
1585

Kempsey
Taree
Port Macquarie

Peterborough
Burra

Ivanhoe

Condobolin
Parkes
Forbes

Dubbo
Wellington

Mudgee

Muswellbrook
Sugarloaf Pt.

VICTORIA

Adelaide

Broken Hill

Murray River

Wentworth
Mildura

Hillston
Hay
Roto
Cargelligo

Orange
Bathurst
Cowra
Young

Singleton
Cessnock
Maitland

P. Stephens
5944
Newcastle
Hawkesbury R.

Gawler
Elizabeth

Loxton

Balranald

Griffith
Leeton

Cootamundra
Junee

Lithgow
Katoomba

SYDNEY
& Port Jackson

Murray
Swan Hill
Kerang

Deniliquin

Murrumbidgee
Irrigation Area

Wagga Wagga

Yass
Goulburn

Wollongong
Shellharbour
Nowra
Jervis B.

Murray River Basin
Wimmera

Echuca
Shepparton
Benalla

Tumut   CAP.
Canberra   TERR.

Batemans B.

Murray Mouth

Bordertown
Horsham
Stawell
Bendigo
Castlemaine
Maryborough

Mt. Bogong
1986

Hume
2230

Cooma
Mt. Kosciusko

Bega

Tasman
Sea

Twofold B.

Naracoorte
Penola

Ararat
Ballarat

Australian Alps
Gippsland

Bombala

Disaster B.
Mallacoota Inlet

Millicent
Mt. Gambier

Hamilton
Geelong
MELBOURNE
Colac
Moe Sale
Morwell Traralgon

Snowy

C. Northumberland
Discovery B.
C. Bridgewater
Port Fairy
Warrnambool
C. Otway
Port Phillip B.
Wonthaggi

Ninety Mile Beach
Corner Inlet
C. Everard

Ararat   Castlemaine
Ballarat
Geelong
Colac
C. Otway

Australian Alps
MELBOURNE
Gippsland
Moe Sale
Morwell Traralgon
Yallourn
Orbost

Port Phillip B.
Phillip I.
Wonthaggi

Corner Inlet
Wilsons Promontory

Grindy Mile
Beach

Snowy

King I.

Bass Strait

Cape Barren I.
Hunter I.
C. Grim
C. Portland

Flinders I.
Furneaux
Group
Clarke I.

Sandy C. Ulverstone
Burnie
Devonport
Zeehan
Macquarie Harb.
Queenstown
New Norfolk

Mt. Ossa
1617
Strahan
Great L.

Scottsdale
Ben Lomond
St. Marys
Launceston
1573
Freycinet
Penin.

TASMANIA

Low Rocky Pt.

Hobart
Huonville

Tasman Penin.
C. Arthur
Storm B.

P. Davey
S.E. Cape

Bruny I.

on same scale

COPYRIGHT. GEORGE PHILIP & SON. LTD

1:4 500 000

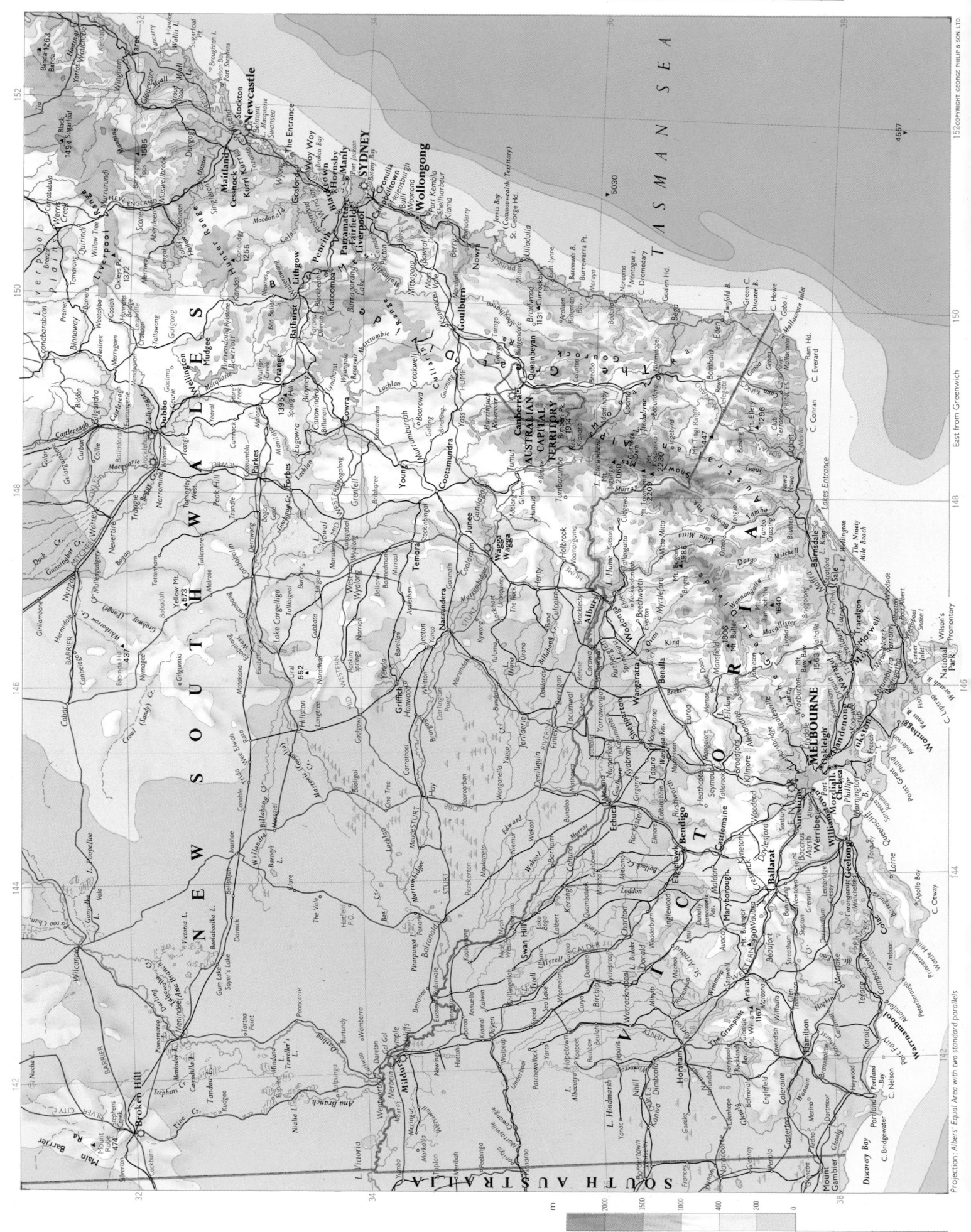

Projection: Albers' Equal Area with two standard parallels

152 COPYRIGHT GEORGE PHILIP & SON, LTD.

Index

The number printed in bold type against each index entry indicates the map page where the feature will be found. The geographical coordinates which follow the name are sometimes only approximate but are close enough for the place name to be located.

An open square □ signifies that the name refers to an administrative subdivision of a country while a solid square ■ follows the name of a country.

The alphabetical order of names composed of two or more words is governed primarily by the first word and then by the second. This rule applies even if the second word is a description or its abbreviation, R.,L.,I. for example. Names composed of a proper name (St. Lawrence) and a description (Gulf of) are positioned alphabetically by the proper name. If the same place name occurs twice or more times in the index and all are in the same country, each is followed by the name of the administrative subdivision in which it is located. The names are placed in the alphabetical order of the subdivisions. If the same place name occurs twice or more in the index and the places are in different countries they will be followed by their country names, the latter governing the alphabetical order. In a mixture of these situations the primary order is fixed by the alphabetical sequence of the countries and the secondary order by that of the country subdivisions.

Aachen Al Madīnah

A

Aachen	**105**	50 47N	6 4 E
Aadorf	**13**	47 30N	8 55 E
Aalsmeer	**105**	52 17N	4 43 E
Aalst, Neth.	**54**	50 57N	4 20 E
Aalst, Neth.	**105**	51 23N	5 29 E
Aalten	**105**	51 56N	6 35 E
Aarau	**106**	47 23N	8 4 E
Aare, R.	**106**	47 33N	8 14 E
Aarschot	**105**	50 59N	4 49 E
Aba	**114**	5 10N	7 19 E
Abadan	**122**	30 22N	48 20 E
Abade	**123**	31 8N	52 40 E
Abadla	**114**	31 2N	2 45W
Abaetetuba	**87**	1 40 S	48 50W
Abai	**89**	25 58 S	55 54W
Abakan	**121**	53 40N	91 10 E
Aballetuba	**87**	1 40 S	51 15W
Abamasagi L.	**53**	50 28N	87 15W
Abarqū	**123**	31 10N	53 20 E
Abashiri	**132**	44 0N	144 15 E
Abaya L.	**115**	6 30N	37 50 E
Abbaye, Pt.	**72**	46 58N	88 4W
Abbeville, France	**101**	50 6N	1 49 E
Abbeville, La., U.S.A.	**75**	30 0N	92 7W
Abbeville, S.C., U.S.A.	**73**	34 12N	82 21W
Abbey	**56**	50 44N	108 45W
Abbotabad	**124**	34 10N	73 15 E
Abbotsford, B.C., Can.	**63**	49 5N	122 20W
Abbotsford, Que., Can.	**71**	45 25N	72 53W
Abbotsford, U.S.A.	**74**	44 55N	90 20W
Abbott Corners	**43**	45 3N	72 48W
Abéché	**115**	13 50N	20 35 E
Åbenrå	**111**	55 3N	9 25 E
Abeokuta	**114**	7 3N	3 19 E
Aberaeron	**95**	52 15N	4 16W
Aberayron = Aberaeron	**95**	52 15N	4 16W
Abercorn = Mbala	**116**	8 46 S	31 17 E
Abercrombie, R.	**136**	33 54 S	149 8 E
Aberdare	**95**	51 43N	3 27W
Aberdaron	**95**	52 48N	4 41W
Aberdeen, Austral.	**136**	32 9 S	150 56 E
Aberdeen, Can.	**56**	52 20N	106 8W
Aberdeen, U.K.	**96**	57 9N	2 6W
Aberdeen, Ohio, U.S.A.	**77**	38 39N	83 46W
Aberdeen, S.D., U.S.A.	**74**	45 30N	98 30W
Aberdeen, Wash., U.S.A.	**80**	47 0N	123 50W
Aberdovey	**95**	52 33N	4 3W
Aberfeldy	**96**	56 37N	3 50W
Aberfoyle	**49**	43 28N	80 9W
Abernathy	**75**	33 49N	101 49W
Abernethy	**56**	50 45N	103 25W
Aberystwyth	**95**	52 25N	4 6W
Abidjan	**114**	5 26N	3 58W
Abilene, Kans., U.S.A.	**74**	39 0N	97 16W
Abilene, Texas, U.S.A.	**75**	32 22N	99 40W
Abingdon, Can.	**49**	43 5N	79 41W
Abingdon, U.K.	**95**	51 40N	1 17W
Abingdon, Ill., U.S.A.	**76**	40 53N	90 23W
Abingdon, Va., U.S.A.	**73**	36 46N	81 56W
Abitau L.	**55**	60 27N	107 15W
Abitau, R.	**55**	59 53N	109 3W
Abitibi L.	**34**	48 40N	79 40W
Abitibi, R.	**53**	51 3N	80 55W
Abkhaz A.S.S.R. □	**120**	43 0N	41 0 E
Abkit	**121**	64 10N	157 10 E
Åbo = Turku	**111**	60 27N	22 14 E
Abohar	**124**	30 10N	74 10 E
Abomey	**114**	7 10N	2 5 E
Abondance	**103**	46 18N	6 42 E
Abong Mbang	**116**	4 0N	13 8 E
Aboyne	**96**	57 4N	2 48W
Abqaiq	**122**	26 0N	49 45 E
Abra Pampa	**88**	22 43 S	65 42W
Abrantes	**104**	39 24N	8 7W
Abreojos, Pta.	**82**	26 50N	113 40W
Abreschviller	**101**	48 39N	7 6 E
Abrets, Les	**103**	45 32N	5 35 E
Abrolhos, Arquipélago dos	**87**	18 0 S	38 30W
Abrud	**107**	46 19N	23 5 E
Abruzzi □	**108**	42 15N	14 0 E
Absaroka Ra.	**78**	44 40N	110 0W
Abū al Khasib	**122**	30 25N	48 0 E
Abū 'Ali	**122**	27 20N	49 27 E
Abū Dhabī	**123**	24 28N	54 36 E
Abu Hamed	**115**	19 32N	33 13 E
Abu Kamal	**122**	34 30N	41 0 E
Abu Markha	**122**	25 4N	38 22 E
Abû Zabad	**115**	12 25N	29 10 E
Abukumagawa	**132**	37 30N	140 30 E
Abunã	**86**	9 40 S	65 20W
Abuná, R.	**86**	9 41 S	65 20W
Abut Hd.	**133**	43 7 S	170 15 E
Acacías	**86**	3 59N	73 46W
Acadia	**59**	50 58N	114 4W
Acadia Valley	**6P**	51 8N	110 13W
Acadie, L', R.	**45**	45 29N	73 16W
Acajutla	**84**	13 36N	89 50W
Acámbaro	**82**	20 0N	100 40W
Acaponeta	**82**	22 30N	105 20W
Acapulco de Juárez	**83**	16 51N	99 56W
Acarai, Serra	**87**	1 50N	57 50W
Acarigua	**86**	9 33N	69 12W
Acatlan	**83**	18 10N	98 3W
Acayucán	**83**	17 59N	94 58W
Accomac	**72**	37 43N	75 40W
Accra	**114**	5 35N	0 6W
Accrington	**94**	53 46N	2 22W
Acebal	**88**	33 20 S	60 50W
Aceh □	**126**	4 0N	97 30 E
Achaguas	**86**	7 46N	68 14W
Achalpur	**124**	21 22N	77 32 E
Achill	**97**	53 56N	9 55W
Achill Hd.	**97**	53 59N	10 15W
Achill I.	**97**	53 58N	10 5W
Achill Sd.	**97**	53 53N	9 55W
Achinsk	**121**	56 20N	90 20 E
Ackerman	**75**	33 20N	89 8W
Ackley	**76**	42 33N	93 3W
Acklin's I.	**85**	22 30N	74 0W
Acland, Mt.	**135**	24 50 S	148 20 E
Acme	**61**	51 33N	113 30W
Aconcagua	**88**	32 50 S	70 0W
Aconcagua □	**88**	32 15 S	70 30W
Aconcagua, Cerro	**88**	32 39 S	70 0W
Aconquija, Mt.	**88**	27 0 S	66 0W
Açores, Is. dos	**12**	38 44N	29 0W
Acre = 'Akko	**115**	32 35N	35 4 E
Acre □	**86**	9 1 S	71 0W
Acre, R.	**86**	10 45 S	68 25W
Actinolite	**70**	44 34N	77 20W
Acton	**49**	43 38N	80 3W
Acton Vale	**41**	45 39N	72 34W
Ad Dammam	**122**	26 20N	50 5 E
Ad Dar al Hamrā	**122**	27 20N	37 45 E
Ad Dawhah	**123**	25 15N	51 35 E
Ad Dilam	**122**	23 55N	47 10 E
Ada, Minn., U.S.A.	**74**	47 20N	96 30W
Ada, Ohio, U.S.A.	**77**	40 46N	83 49W
Ada, Okla., U.S.A.	**75**	34 50N	96 45W
Adair C.	**17**	71 50N	71 0W
Adaja, R.	**104**	41 15N	4 50W
Adam	**123**	22 15N	57 28 E
Adamaoua, Massif de l'	**114**	7 20N	12 20 E
Adamawa Highlands = Adamaoua	**114**	7 20N	12 20 E
Adamello, Mt.	**108**	46 10N	10 34 E
Adaminaby	**136**	36 0 S	148 45 E
Adams, Mass., U.S.A.	**71**	42 38N	73 8W
Adams, N.Y., U.S.A.	**71**	43 50N	76 3W
Adams, Wis., U.S.A.	**74**	43 59N	89 50W
Adam's Bridge	**124**	9 15N	79 40 E
Adams Center	**71**	43 51N	76 1W
Adams L.	**63**	51 10N	119 40W
Adams Mt.	**80**	46 10N	121 28W
Adam's Peak	**124**	6 55N	80 45 E
Adams, R.	**63**	51 25N	119 27W
Adamsville	**43**	45 17N	72 47W
Adana	**122**	37 0N	35 16 E
Adapazari	**122**	40 48N	30 25 E
Adare, C.	**91**	71 0 S	171 0 E
Adavale	**135**	25 52 S	144 32 E
Adda, R.	**108**	45 25N	9 30 E
Addie	**61**	48 55N	116 10W
Addis Ababa = Addis Abeba	**115**	9 2N	38 42 E
Addis Abeba	**115**	9 2N	38 42 E
Addison, Ill., U.S.A.	**77**	41 56N	87 59W
Addison, N.Y., U.S.A.	**70**	42 9N	77 15W
Addison, Vt., U.S.A.	**71**	44 6N	73 18W
Addu Atoll	**119**	0 30 S	73 0 E
Addyston	**77**	39 8N	84 43W
Adel, Ga., U.S.A.	**73**	31 10N	83 28W
Adel, Iowa, U.S.A.	**76**	41 37N	94 1W
Adelaide, Austral.	**135**	34 52 S	138 30 E
Adelaide, Bahamas	**84**	25 0N	77 31W
Adelaide I.	**91**	67 15 S	68 30W
Adelaide Pen.	**65**	68 15N	97 30W
Adelanto	**81**	34 35N	117 22W
Adélie, Terre	**91**	67 0 S	140 0 E
Aden	**115**	12 50N	45 0 E
Aden, G. of	**115**	13 0N	50 0 E
Adi	**127**	4 15 S	133 30 E
Adieu, C.	**134**	32 0 S	132 10 E
Adige, R.	**108**	45 9N	11 25 E
Adilabad	**124**	19 33N	78 35 E
Adin	**78**	41 10N	121 0W
Adin Khel	**124**	32 45N	68 5 E
Adirondack Mts.	**71**	44 0N	74 15W
Adlavik Is.	**36**	55 2N	58 45W
Admiral	**56**	49 43N	108 1W
Admiral's Beach	**37**	47 1N	53 39W
Admiralty B.	**91**	62 0 S	59 0W
Admiralty G.	**134**	14 20 S	125 55 E
Admiralty I., Can.	**65**	69 25N	101 10W
Admiralty I., U.S.A.	**67**	57 40N	134 35W
Admiralty In.	**65**	72 30N	86 0W
Admiralty Inlet	**78**	48 0N	122 40W
Admiralty Ra.	**91**	72 0 S	164 0 E
Adonara	**127**	8 15 S	123 5 E
Adoni	**124**	15 33N	77 18W
Adour, R.	**102**	43 32N	1 32W
Adra	**104**	36 43N	3 3W
Adrano	**108**	37 40N	14 49 E
Adrar	**114**	27 51N	0 11W
Adrian, Mich., U.S.A.	**77**	41 55N	84 0W
Adrian, Mo., U.S.A.	**76**	38 24N	94 21W
Adrian, Tex., U.S.A.	**75**	35 19N	102 37W
Adriatic Sea	**108**	43 0N	16 0 E
Adua	**127**	1 45 S	129 50 E
Advocate Harbour	**39**	45 20N	64 47W
Adwa, Ethiopia	**115**	14 15N	38 52 E
Adwa, Si Arab.	**122**	27 15N	42 35 E
Adzhar A.S.S.R. □	**120**	42 0N	42 0 E
Ægean Sea	**109**	37 0N	25 0 E
Aerht'ai Shan	**129**	46 40N	92 45 E
Afars Issas, Terr. of ■	**115**	11 30N	42 15 E
Affric, R.	**96**	57 15N	4 50W
Afghanistan ■	**124**	33 0N	65 0 E
Afif	**122**	23 53N	42 56 E
Afognak I.	**67**	58 10N	152 50W
Africa	**112**	10 0N	20 0 E
Afton	**71**	42 14N	75 31W
Afuá	**87**	0 15 S	50 10W
Afula	**115**	32 37N	35 17 E
Afyon Karahisar	**122**	38 45N	30 33 E
Agadès	**114**	16 58N	7 59 E
Agadir	**114**	30 28N	9 35W
Agano, R.	**132**	37 50N	139 30 E
Agapa	**121**	71 27N	89 15 E
Agartala	**125**	23 50N	91 23 E
Agassiz	**63**	49 14N	121 46W
Agattu I.	**67**	52 25N	172 30 E
Agawa, R.	**53**	47 23N	84 40W
Agde	**102**	43 19N	3 28 E
Agde, C. d'	**102**	43 16N	3 28 E
Agen	**102**	44 12N	0 38 E
Aghil Mts.	**124**	36 0N	77 0 E
Aghil Pass	**124**	36 15N	76 35 E
Agincourt	**50**	43 47N	79 17W
Aginskoye	**121**	51 6N	114 32 E
Agly, R.	**102**	42 46N	3 3 E
Agnes L.	**52**	48 15N	91 20W
Agon	**100**	49 2N	1 34W
Agout, R.	**102**	43 47N	1 41 E
Agra	**124**	27 17N	77 58 E
Agrado	**86**	2 15N	75 46W
Ağri Daği	**122**	39 50N	44 15 E
Agri, R.	**108**	40 17N	16 15 E
Agrigento	**108**	37 19N	13 33 E
Agrínion	**109**	38 37N	21 27 E
Agua Caliente, Mexico	**82**	26 30N	108 20W
Agua Caliente, U.S.A.	**81**	32 29N	116 59W
Agua Caliente Springs	**81**	32 56N	116 19W
Agua Clara	**87**	20 25 S	52 45W
Agua Hechicero	**81**	32 26N	116 14W
Agua Prieta	**82**	31 20N	109 32W
Aguadas	**86**	5 40N	75 38W
Aguadilla	**85**	18 27N	67 10W
Aguadulce	**84**	8 15N	80 32W
Aguanaval, R.	**82**	23 45N	103 10W
Aguanga	**81**	33 27N	116 51W
Aguanus, R.	**38**	50 13N	62 5W
Aguapey, R.	**88**	29 7 S	56 36W
Aguaray Guazú, R.	**88**	24 47 S	57 19W
Aguarico, R.	**86**	0 0	77 30W
Aguas Blancas	**88**	24 15 S	69 55W
Aguas Calientes, Sierra de	**88**	25 26 S	67 27W
Aguascalientes	**82**	22 0N	102 12W
Aguascalientes □	**82**	22 0N	102 20W
Aguilares	**88**	27 26 S	65 35W
Aguilas	**104**	37 23N	1 35W
Aguja, C. de la	**86**	11 18N	74 12W
Aguja, Pta.	**86**	6 0 S	81 0W
Agulhas Basin	**16**	45 0 S	25 0 E
Agulhas, Kaap	**117**	34 52 S	20 0 E
Agung	**126**	8 20 S	115 28 E
Agusan, R.	**127**	9 20N	125 50 E
Ahaggar	**114**	23 0N	6 30 E
Ahar	**122**	38 35N	47 0 E
Ahaura	**133**	42 20 S	171 32 E
Ahimanawa Ra.	**14**	39 5 S	176 30 E
Ahipara B.	**133**	35 5 S	173 5 E
Ahiri	**124**	19 30N	80 0 E
Ahlen	**105**	51 45N	7 52 E
Ahmadabad (Ahmedabad)	**124**	23 0N	72 40 E
Ahmadnagar (Ahmednagar)	**124**	19 7N	74 46 E
Ahmadpur	**124**	29 12N	71 10 E
Ahome	**82**	25 55N	109 11W
Ahsā, Wahatā al	**122**	25 50N	49 0 E
Ahuachapán	**84**	13 54N	89 52W
Ahvāz	**122**	31 20N	48 40 E
Ahvenanmaa	**111**	60 15N	20 0 E
Aibaq	**123**	36 15N	68 5 E
Aichi-ken □	**132**	35 0N	137 15 E
Aignay-le-Duc	**101**	47 40N	4 43 E
Aigre	**102**	45 54N	0 1 E
Aigua	**89**	34 13 S	54 46W
Aiguebelle, Parc	**40**	48 30N	78 45W
Aigueperse	**102**	46 3N	3 13 E
Aigues-Mortes	**103**	43 35N	4 12 E
Aiguilles	**103**	44 47N	6 51 E
Aiguillon	**102**	44 18N	0 21 E
Aiguillon, L'	**102**	46 20N	1 16W
Aigurande	**102**	46 27N	1 49 E
Aihun	**130**	49 55N	127 30 E
Aija	**86**	9 50 S	77 45W
Aijal	**125**	23 40N	92 44 E
Aiken	**73**	33 34N	81 50W
Aillant-sur-Tholon	**101**	47 52N	3 20 E
Aillik	**36**	55 11N	59 18W
Ailly-sur-Noye	**101**	49 45N	2 20 E
Ailsa Craig	**46**	43 8N	81 33W
Ailsa Craig, I.	**96**	55 15N	5 7W
Aim	**121**	59 0N	133 55 E
Aimere	**127**	8 45 S	121 3 E
Aimogasta	**88**	28 33 S	66 50W
Aimorés	**87**	19 30 S	41 4W
Aimorés, Serra dos	**87**	17 50 S	40 30W
Ain □	**103**	46 5N	5 20 E
Ain Banaiyan	**123**	23 0N	51 0 E
Ain Dār	**122**	25 55N	49 10 E
Ain, R.	**103**	45 52N	5 11 E
Ainslie, L.	**39**	46 8N	61 11W
Ainsworth	**74**	42 33N	99 52W
Aion	**121**	69 50N	169 0 E
Aipe	**86**	3 13N	75 15W
Aïr	**114**	18 30N	8 0 E
Air Force I.	**65**	67 58N	74 5W
Airaines	**101**	49 58N	1 55 E
Aird, The, C.	**96**	57 26N	4 30W
Airdrie, Can.	**61**	51 18N	114 2W
Airdrie, U.K.	**96**	55 53N	3 57W
Aire	**101**	50 37N	2 22 E
Aire, R., France	**101**	49 18N	5 0 E
Aire, R., U.K.	**94**	53 42N	1 30W
Aire-sur-l'Adour	**102**	43 42N	0 15W
Airvault	**100**	46 50N	0 8W
Aishihik	**67**	61 40N	137 46W
Aisne □	**101**	49 42N	3 40 E
Aisne, R.	**101**	49 26N	2 50 E
Aitkin	**52**	46 32N	93 43W
Aitush	**129**	39 54N	75 40 E
Aiud	**107**	46 19N	23 44 E
Aix-en-Provence	**103**	43 32N	5 27 E
Aix-la-Chapelle = Aachen	**105**	50 47N	6 4 E
Aix-les-Bains	**103**	45 41N	5 53 E
Aix-sur-Vienne	**102**	45 48N	1 8 E
Aiyansh	**54**	55 17N	129 2W
Aiyina	**109**	37 45N	23 26 E
Aíyion	**109**	38 15N	22 5 E
Aizenay	**100**	46 44N	1 38W
Ajaccio	**103**	41 55N	8 40 E
Ajaccio, G. d'	**103**	41 52N	8 40 E
Ajalpán	**83**	18 22N	97 15W
Ajanta Ra.	**124**	20 28N	75 50 E
Ajax	**51**	43 50N	79 1W
'Ajlun	**115**	32 18N	35 47 E
Ajman	**123**	25 25N	55 30 E
Ajmer	**124**	26 28N	74 37 E
Ajo	**79**	32 18N	112 54W
Ak Dağ	**122**	36 30N	30 0 E
Akaroa	**133**	43 49 S	172 59 E
Akaroa Harb.	**15**	43 54 S	172 59 E
Akashi	**132**	34 45N	135 0 E
Akelamo	**127**	1 35N	129 40 E
Akershus Fylke □	**111**	60 10N	11 15 E
Aketi	**116**	2 38N	23 47 E
Akhelóös, R.	**109**	39 5N	21 25 E
Akhisar	**122**	38 56N	27 48 E
Akiak	**67**	60 50N	161 12W
Akimiski I.	**34**	52 50N	81 30W
Akita	**132**	39 45N	140 0 E
Akita-ken □	**132**	39 40N	140 30 E
'Akko	**115**	32 35N	35 4 E
Akkol	**120**	43 36N	70 45 E
Aklavik	**64**	68 12N	135 0W
Akola	**124**	20 42N	77 2 E
Akpatok I.	**36**	60 25N	68 8W
Akranes	**110**	64 19N	22 6W
Akron, Can.	**53**	48 55N	84 7W
Akron, Colo., U.S.A.	**74**	40 13N	103 15W
Akron, Ind., U.S.A.	**77**	41 2N	86 1W
Akron, Ohio, U.S.A.	**70**	41 7N	81 31W
Akrotíri, Ákra	**109**	40 26N	25 27W
Aksaray	**122**	38 25N	34 2 E
Aksarka	**120**	66 31N	67 50 E
Aksehir	**122**	38 18N	31 30 E
Aksenovo Zilovskoye	**121**	53 20N	117 40 E
Aksu	**129**	41 4N	80 5 E
Aksum	**115**	14 5N	38 40 E
Aktogay	**120**	44 25N	76 44 E
Aktyubinsk	**120**	50 17N	57 10 E
Akulurak	**67**	62 40N	164 35W
Akun I.	**67**	54 15N	165 30W
Akureyri	**110**	65 40N	18 6W
Akutan I.	**67**	53 30N	166 0W
Al Amādiyah	**122**	37 5N	43 30 E
Al Amārah	**122**	31 55N	47 15 E
Al 'Aqabah	**122**	29 37N	35 0 E
Al Ashkhara	**123**	21 50N	59 30 E
Al Badi	**122**	22 0N	46 35 E
Al Basrah	**122**	30 30N	47 50 E
Al Dīwaniyah	**122**	32 0N	45 0 E
Al Fallujah	**122**	33 20N	43 55 E
Al Fāw	**122**	30 0N	48 30 E
Al Hadithan	**122**	34 0N	41 13 E
Al Hāmad	**122**	31 30N	39 30 E
Al Hamar	**122**	22 23N	46 6 E
Al Hariq	**122**	23 29N	46 27 E
Al Hasakah	**122**	36 35N	40 45 E
Al Havy	**122**	32 5N	46 5 E
Al Hillah, Iraq	**122**	32 30N	44 25 E
Al Hillah, Si Arab.	**122**	23 35N	46 50 E
Al Hilwah	**122**	23 24N	46 48 E
Al Hindiyah	**122**	32 30N	44 10 E
Al Hūfuf	**122**	25 25N	49 45 E
Al Ittihad = Madinat al Shaab	**115**	12 50N	45 0 E
Al Jahrah	**122**	29 25N	47 40 E
Al Jalāmid	**122**	31 20N	39 45 E
Al Jawf	**115**	24 10N	23 24 E
Al Jubail	**122**	27 0N	49 50 E
Al Khābūrah	**123**	23 57N	57 5 E
Al Kūt	**122**	32 30N	46 0 E
Al Kuwayt	**122**	29 20N	48 0 E
Al Lādhiqiyah	**122**	35 30N	35 45 E
Al Madīnah	**122**	24 35N	39 52 E

Al Majma'ah **Ambato**

Al Majma'ah **122** 25 57N 45 22 E
Al Manamāh **123** 26 10N 50 30 E
Al Marj **115** 32 25N 20 30 E
Al Mawsil **122** 36 15N 43 5 E
Al Miqdadīyah **122** 34 0N 45 0 E
Al Mubarraz **122** 25 30N 49 40 E
Al Muharraq **123** 26 15N 50 40 E
Al Musayyib **122** 32 40N 44 25 E
Al Muwaylih **122** 27 40N 35 30 E
Al Qāmishli **122** 37 10N 41 10 E
Al Qatif **122** 26 35N 50 0 E
Al Quaisūmah **122** 28 10N 46 20 E
Al Quraiyat **123** 23 17N 58 53 E
Al Qurnah **122** 31 1N 47 25 E
Al 'Ula **122** 26 35N 38 0 E
Al Uqayr **122** 25 40N 50 15 E
Al' Uwayqilah **122** 30 30N 42 10 E
Al 'Uyūn **122** 26 30N 43 50 E
Al Wakrah **123** 25 10N 51 40 E
Al Warī 'ah **122** 27 50N 47 30 E
Ala Shan **129** 40 0N 104 0 E
Alabama □ **73** 33 0N 87 0W
Alabama, R. **73** 31 30N 87 35W
Alabaster **46** 44 10N 83 33W
Alagôa Grande **87** 7 3S 35 35W
Alagôas □ **87** 9 0S 36 0W
Alagoinhas **87** 12 0S 38 20W
Alajuela **84** 10 2N 84 8W
Alameda, Can. **57** 49 16N 102 17W
Alameda, Calif., U.S.A. **80** 37 46N 122 15W
Alameda, Idaho, U.S.A. **78** 43 2N 112 30W
Alameda, N. Mex., U.S.A. **79** 35 10N 106 43W
Alamitos, Sierra de los **82** 26 30N 102 20W
Alamo **81** 37 21N 115 10W
Alamo Crossing **81** 34 16N 113 33W
Alamogordo **79** 32 59N 106 0W
Alamos **82** 27 0N 109 0W
Alamosa **79** 37 30N 106 0W
Åland **111** 60 15N 20 0 E
Ålands hav **111** 60 10N 19 30 E
Alanson **46** 45 27N 84 47W
Alanya **122** 36 38N 32 0 E
Alapayevsk **120** 57 52N 61 42 E
Alashanchih **130** 38 58N 105 14 E
Alaska □ **67** 65 0N 150 0W
Alaska, G. of **67** 58 0N 145 0W
Alaska Highway **54** 60 0N 130 0W
Alaska Pen. **67** 56 0N 160 0W
Alaska Range **67** 62 50N 151 0W
Alatyr **120** 54 45N 46 35 E
Alausí **86** 2 0S 78 50W
Alava, C. **78** 48 10N 124 40W
Alba **108** 44 41N 8 1 E
Alba-Iulia **107** 46 8N 23 39 E
Albacete **104** 39 0N 1 50W
Albanel **41** 48 53N 72 27W
Albanel, L. **36** 50 55N 73 12W
Albania ■ **109** 41 0N 20 0 E
Albany, Austral. **134** 35 1S 117 58 E
Albany, Ga., U.S.A. **73** 31 40N 84 10W
Albany, Ind., U.S.A. **77** 40 18N 85 13W
Albany, Minn., U.S.A. **74** 45 37N 94 38W
Albany, Mo., U.S.A. **76** 40 15N 94 20W
Albany, N.Y., U.S.A. **71** 42 35N 73 47W
Albany, Oreg., U.S.A. **78** 44 41N 123 0W
Albany, Tex., U.S.A. **75** 32 45N 99 20W
Albany, Wis., U.S.A. **76** 42 43N 89 26W
Albany, R. **34** 52 17N 81 31W
Albardón **88** 31 20S 68 30W
Albarracín, Sierra de **104** 40 30N 1 30W
Albatross B. **135** 12 45S 141 30 E
Albemarle **73** 35 27N 80 15W
Albemarle Sd. **73** 36 0N 76 30W
Alberche, R. **104** 40 10N 4 30W
Alberdi **88** 26 14S 58 20W
Alberga, R. **134** 26 50S 133 40 E
Alberni **54** 49 20N 124 50W
Albert, Can. **35** 45 51N 64 38W
Albert, France **101** 50 0N 2 38 E
Albert Canyon **63** 51 8N 117 41W
Albert L. **78** 42 40N 120 8W
Albert Lea **74** 43 32N 93 20W
Albert, L. = Mobutu Sese Seko, L. **116** 1 30N 31 0 E
Albert Nile, R. **116** 3 16N 31 38 E
Albert Park **58** 50 24N 104 38W
Albert Town **85** 22 37N 74 33 E
Alberta □ **54** 54 40N 115 0W
Alberta Beach **60** 53 40N 114 21W
Alberti **88** 35 1S 60 16W
Alberton, Ont., Can. **49** 43 11N 80 5W
Alberton, P.E.I., Can. **39** 46 50N 64 0W
Albertville **103** 45 40N 6 22 E
Albertville = Kalemie **116** 5 55S 29 9 E
Alberz, Reshteh-Ye Kūkhā-Ye **123** 36 0N 52 0 E
Albi **102** 43 56N 2 9 E
Albia **76** 41 0N 92 50W
Albina **87** 5 37N 54 15W
Albion, Idaho, U.S.A. **78** 42 21N 113 37W
Albion, Ill., U.S.A. **77** 38 23N 88 4W
Albion, Ind., U.S.A. **77** 41 24N 85 25W
Albion, Mich., U.S.A. **77** 42 15N 84 45W
Albion, Nebr., U.S.A. **74** 41 47N 98 0W
Albion, Pa., U.S.A. **70** 41 53N 80 21W
Ålborg **111** 57 2N 9 54 E
Albreda **63** 52 35N 119 10W
Albuquerque **79** 35 5N 106 47W
Albuquerque, Cayos de **84** 12 10N 81 50W
Alburg **43** 44 58N 73 19W
Alburquerque **104** 39 15N 6 59W
Alcalá de Henares **104** 40 28N 3 22W
Alcalá la Real **104** 37 27N 3 57W
Alcamo **108** 37 59N 12 55 E
Alcañiz **104** 41 2N 0 8W
Alcântara **87** 2 20S 44 30W
Alcántara **104** 39 41N 6 57W
Alcantara L. **55** 60 57N 108 9W
Alcaraz, Sierra de **104** 38 40N 2 20W
Alcaudete **104** 37 35N 4 5W
Alcázar de San Juan **104** 39 24N 3 12W
Alcira **104** 39 9N 0 30W
Alcoa **73** 35 50N 84 0W
Alcobaça **104** 39 32N 9 0W
Alcova **78** 42 37N 106 52W
Alcoy **104** 38 43N 0 30W
Aldabra Is. **16** 9 22S 46 28 E
Aldama **83** 22 25N 98 4W
Aldan **121** 58 40N 125 30 E
Aldan, R. **121** 62 30N 135 10 E
Aldeburgh **95** 52 9N 1 35 E
Alder **78** 45 27N 112 3W
Alder Pk. **80** 35 53N 12 22W
Alderney, I. **100** 49 42N 2 12W
Aldershot, N.S., Can. **39** 45 6N 64 31W
Aldershot, Ont., Can. **48** 43 18N 79 51W
Aldershot, U.K. **95** 51 15N 0 43W
Aldersyde **54** 50 40N 113 53W
Aledo **76** 41 10N 90 50W
Alegre **89** 20 50S 41 30W
Alegrete **89** 29 40S 56 0W
Aleisk **120** 52 40N 83 0 E
Alejandro Selkirk, I. **15** 33 50S 80 15W
Aleksandrov Gay. **120** 50 15N 48 35 E
Aleksandrovsk-Sakhaliniskiy **121** 50 50N 142 20 E
Aleksandrovskiy Zavod **121** 50 40N 117 50 E
Aleksandrovskoye **120** 60 35N 77 50 E
Além Paraíba **89** 21 52S 42 41W
Alemania, Argent. **88** 25 40S 65 30W
Alemania, Chile **88** 25 10S 69 55W
Alençon **100** 48 27N 0 4 E
Alentejo, Alto- **104** 39 0N 7 40W
Alentejo, Baixo- **104** 38 0N 8 30W
Alenuihaha Chan. **67** 20 25N 156 0W
Aleppo **122** 36 10N 37 15 E
Aléria **103** 42 5N 9 26 E
Alert **65** 83 2N 60 0W
Alert B. **62** 50 30N 127 35W
Alès **103** 44 9N 4 5 E
Alessándria **108** 44 54N 8 37 E
Ålesund **111** 62 28N 6 12 E
Alet-les-Bains **102** 43 0N 2 14 E
Aleutian Is. **67** 52 0N 175 0W
Aleutian Ra. **67** 55 0N 155 0W
Alex Graham, Mt. **63** 52 4N 122 52W
Alexander **74** 47 51N 103 40W
Alexander Arch. **67** 57 0N 135 0W
Alexander B. **117** 28 36S 16 33 E
Alexander City **73** 32 58N 85 57W
Alexander I. **91** 69 0S 70 0W
Alexandra, Austral. **136** 37 8S 145 40 E
Alexandra, N.Z. **133** 45 14S 169 25 E
Alexandra Falls **54** 60 29N 116 18W
Alexandretta = Iskenderun **129** 36 32N 36 10 E
Alexandria, B.C., Can. **63** 52 35N 122 27W
Alexandria, Ont., Can. **47** 45 19N 74 38W
Alexandria, S. Afr. **117** 33 38S 26 28 E
Alexandria, Ind., U.S.A. **77** 40 18N 85 40W
Alexandria, Ky., U.S.A. **77** 38 58N 84 23W
Alexandria, La., U.S.A. **75** 31 20N 92 30W
Alexandria, Minn., U.S.A. **74** 45 50N 95 20W
Alexandria, Mo., U.S.A. **76** 40 27N 91 28W
Alexandria, S.D., U.S.A. **74** 43 40N 97 45W
Alexandria, Va., U.S.A. **72** 38 47N 77 1W
Alexandria = El Iskandarîya **115** 31 0N 30 0 E
Alexandria Bay **71** 44 20N 75 52W
Alexandrina, L. **135** 35 25S 139 10 E
Alexandroúpolis **109** 40 50N 25 54 E
Alexis **76** 41 4N 90 33W
Alexis Creek **62** 52 10N 123 20W
Alexis, R. **36** 52 33N 56 8W
Alfenas **89** 21 40S 44 0W
Alford **96** 57 13N 2 42W
Alfred, Me., U.S.A. **71** 43 28N 70 40W
Alfred, N.Y., U.S.A. **70** 42 15N 77 45W
Alfreton **94** 53 6N 1 22W
Alftanes **110** 64 29N 22 10W
Alga **120** 49 53N 57 20 E
Alganac **70** 42 36N 82 34W
Algarve **104** 37 15N 8 10W
Algeciras **104** 36 9N 5 28W
Algemesí **104** 39 11N 0 27W
Alger **114** 36 42N 3 8 E
Algeria ■ **114** 35 10N 3 11 E
Alghero **108** 40 34N 8 20 E
Algiers = Alger **114** 36 42N 3 8 E
Algoabaai **117** 33 50S 25 45 E
Algoma, Oreg., U.S.A. **78** 42 25N 121 54W
Algoma, Wis., U.S.A. **72** 44 35N 87 27W
Algona **76** 43 1N 94 10W
Algonac **46** 42 37N 82 32W
Algonquin **77** 42 10N 88 18W
Algonquin Prov. Pk. **47** 45 50N 78 30W
Alhama de Murcia **104** 37 51N 1 25W
Alhambra, Can. **61** 52 20N 114 40W
Alhambra, Calif., U.S.A. **81** 34 8N 118 10W
Alhambra, Ill., U.S.A. **76** 38 52N 89 45W
Ali al Gharbi **122** 32 30N 46 45 E
Ali Khel **124** 33 56N 69 35 E
Aliābād **123** 28 10N 57 35 E
Aliakmon, R. **109** 40 10N 22 0 E
Alicante **104** 38 23N 0 30W
Alice, Can. **47** 45 47N 77 14W
Alice, U.S.A. **75** 27 47N 98 1W
Alice Arm **54** 55 29N 129 31W
Alice Springs **134** 23 40S 135 50 E
Alicedale **124** 33 15S 26 4 E
Aliceville **73** 33 9N 88 10W
Alida **57** 49 25N 101 55W
Aligarh **124** 27 55N 78 10 E
Aligudarz **122** 33 25N 49 45 E
Aling Kangri,Range **125** 31 45N 84 45 E
Alingsås **111** 57 56N 12 31 E
Alipur **124** 29 25N 70 55 E
Alipur Duar **125** 26 30N 89 35 E
Aliquippa **70** 40 38N 80 18W
Aliwal North **117** 30 45S 26 45 E
Alix **61** 52 24N 113 11W
Aljustrel **104** 37 55N 8 10W
Alkmaar **105** 52 37N 4 45 E
All American Canal **79** 32 45N 115 0W
Allahabad **125** 25 25N 81 58 E
Allakaket **67** 66 30N 152 45W
Allakh Yun **121** 60 50N 137 5 E
Allan **56** 51 53N 106 4W
Allanburg **49** 43 5N 79 12W
Allanche **102** 45 14N 2 57 E
Allanwater **52** 50 14N 90 10W
Allard, L. **38** 50 32N 63 31W
Allardville **39** 47 28N 65 29W
Allassac **102** 45 15N 1 29 E
Allegan **77** 42 32N 85 52W
Allegany **70** 41 30N 78 30W
Allegheny Mts. **72** 38 0N 80 0W
Allegheny, R. **70** 41 14N 79 50W
Allegheny Res. **70** 42 0N 78 55W
Allègre **102** 45 12N 3 41 E
Allen, Bog of **97** 53 15N 7 0W
Allen, L. **97** 54 30N 8 5W
Allende **82** 28 20N 100 50W
Allentown **71** 40 36N 75 30W
Alleppey **124** 9 30N 76 28 E
Allevard **103** 45 24N 6 5 E
Alliance, Can. **61** 52 26N 111 47W
Alliance, Nebr., U.S.A. **74** 42 10N 102 50W
Alliance, Ohio, U.S.A. **70** 40 53N 81 7W
Allier □ **102** 46 25N 3 0 E
Allier, R. **101** 46 57N 3 4 E
Alliford Bay **62** 53 12N 131 58W
Allison **76** 42 45N 92 48W
Allison Harbour **62** 51 2N 127 29W
Alliston **46** 44 9N 79 52W
Alloa **96** 56 7N 3 49W
Allos **103** 44 15N 6 38 E
Alluviaq, Fj. **36** 59 27N 65 10W
Alma, N.B., Can. **39** 45 36N 64 57W
Alma, Ont., Can. **49** 43 44N 80 30W
Alma, Qué., Can. **41** 48 35N 71 40W
Alma, Kans., U.S.A. **74** 39 1N 96 22W
Alma, Mich., U.S.A. **46** 43 25N 84 40W
Alma, Nebr., U.S.A. **74** 40 10N 99 25W
Alma, Wis., U.S.A. **74** 44 19N 91 54W
Alma Ata **120** 43 15N 76 57 E
Almada **104** 38 40N 9 9W
Almadén **104** 38 49N 4 52W
Almanor, L. **78** 40 15N 121 11W
Almansa **104** 38 51N 1 5W
Almanzor, Pico de **104** 40 15N 5 18W
Almanzora, R. **104** 37 22N 2 21W
Almazán **104** 41 30N 2 30W
Almeirim **87** 1 30S 52 0W
Almelo **105** 52 22N 6 42 E
Almendralejo **104** 38 41N 6 26W
Almería **104** 36 52N 2 32W
Almirante **84** 9 10N 82 30W
Almont **46** 42 53N 83 2W
Almonte **47** 45 14N 76 12W
Almora **124** 29 38N 79 4 E
Alnwick **94** 55 25N 1 42W
Alo Tau, mts. **129** 45 30N 80 40 E
Alon **125** 22 12N 95 5 E
Alonsa **55** 50 50N 99 0W
Alor, I. **127** 8 15S 124 30 E
Alor Setar **128** 6 7N 100 22 E
Alpaugh **80** 35 53N 119 29W
Alpena **46** 45 6N 83 24W
Alpes-de-Haute-Provence □ **103** 44 8N 6 10 E
Alpes-Maritimes □ **103** 43 55N 7 10 E
Alpha, Austral. **135** 23 39S 146 37 E
Alpha, U.S.A. **76** 41 11N 90 23W
Alphen **105** 51 29N 4 58 E
Alphonse, I. **16** 7 0S 52 45 E
Alpi Craie **101** 45 40N 7 0 E
Alpine, Ariz., U.S.A. **79** 33 57N 109 4W
Alpine, Calif., U.S.A. **81** 32 50N 116 46W
Alpine, Tex., U.S.A. **75** 30 25N 103 35W
Alps **106** 47 0N 8 0 E
Alsace **101** 48 15N 7 25 E
Alsask **56** 51 21N 109 59W
Alsásua **104** 42 54N 2 10W
Alsdorf **105** 50 53N 6 10 E
Alsten **110** 65 58N 12 40 E
Alta **110** 69 57N 23 10 E
Alta Gracia **88** 31 40S 64 30W
Alta Lake **63** 50 10N 123 0W
Alta Sierra **81** 35 42N 118 33W
Alta Vista **48** 45 23N 75 40W
Altaelva **110** 69 46N 23 45 E
Altafjorden **110** 70 5N 23 5 E
Altagracia **86** 10 45N 71 30W
Altai **129** 48 6N 87 2 E
Altai = Aerhatai Shan **129** 46 40N 92 45 E
Altamaha, R. **73** 31 50N 82 0W
Altamira, Brazil **87** 3 0S 52 10W
Altamira, Chile **88** 25 47S 69 51W
Altamira, Colomb. **86** 2 3N 75 47W
Altamira, Mexico **83** 22 24N 97 55W
Altamont, Ill., U.S.A. **77** 39 4N 88 45W
Altamont, N.Y., U.S.A. **71** 42 43N 74 3W
Altanbulag **130** 50 16N 106 30 E
Altar **82** 30 40N 111 50W
Altario **61** 51 55N 110 9W
Altata **82** 24 30N 108 0W
Altavista **72** 37 9N 79 22W
Altkirch **101** 47 37N 7 15 E
Alto Araguaia **87** 17 15S 53 20W
Alto Cuchumatanes **82** 15 30N 91 10W
Alto del Inca **88** 24 10S 68 10W
Alto Molocue **117** 15 50S 37 35 E
Alto Paraná □ **89** 25 0S 54 50W
Alto Uruguay, R. **89** 27 0S 53 30W
Alton, Can. **49** 43 54N 80 5W
Alton, U.S.A. **76** 38 55N 90 5W
Altona, Austral. **136** 37 51S 144 50 E
Altona, Man., Can. **57** 49 6N 97 33W
Altona, Ont., Can. **50** 43 58N 79 12W
Altona, Ger. **106** 53 32N 9 56 E
Altoona, Iowa, U.S.A. **76** 41 39N 93 28W
Altoona, Pa., U.S.A. **70** 40 32N 78 24W
Alturas **78** 41 36N 120 37W
Altus **75** 34 30N 99 25W
Altyn Tagh **129** 39 0N 90 0 E
Alunite **81** 35 59N 114 55W
Alusi **127** 7 35S 131 40 E
Alva **75** 36 50N 98 50W
Alvarado, Mexico **83** 18 40N 95 50W
Alvarado, U.S.A. **75** 32 25N 97 15W
Alvaro Obregón, Presa **82** 27 55N 109 52W
Alvear **88** 29 5S 56 30W
Alvena **56** 52 31N 106 1W
Alvesta **111** 56 54N 14 35 E
Alvin **75** 29 23N 95 12W
Alvinston **46** 42 49N 81 52W
Älvkarleby **111** 60 32N 17 40 E
Älvsborgs län □ **111** 58 30N 12 30 E
Älvsbyn **110** 65 40N 20 0 E
Alwar **124** 27 38N 76 34 E
Alyangula **135** 13 55S 136 30 E
Alyaskitovyy **121** 64 45N 141 30 E
Alzada **74** 45 3N 104 22W
Am Timan **115** 11 0N 20 10 E
Amadeus, L. **134** 24 54S 131 0 E
Amadi **116** 3 40N 26 40 E
Amadia **122** 37 6N 43 30 E
Amadjuak **65** 64 0N 72 39W
Amadjuak L. **65** 65 0N 71 8W
Amadore **70** 43 12N 82 36W
Amaga **86** 6 3N 75 42W
Amagasaki **132** 34 42N 135 20 E
Amakusa-Shotō **132** 32 15N 130 10 E
Amål **111** 59 2N 12 40 E
Amalfi **86** 6 55N 75 4W
Amalner **124** 21 5N 75 5 E
Amambaí **89** 23 5S 55 13W
Amambaí, R. **89** 23 22S 53 56W
Amambay □ **89** 23 0S 56 0W
Amambay, Cordillera de **89** 20 30S 56 0W
Amami-guntō **131** 28 0N 129 0 E
Amanda Park **80** 47 28N 123 55W
Amangeldy **120** 50 10N 65 10 E
Amapá **87** 2 5N 50 50W
Amapá □ **87** 1 40N 52 0W
Amara **122** 31 57N 47 12 E
Amarante **87** 6 14S 42 50W
Amaranth **57** 50 36N 98 43W
Amaravati = Amraoti **124** 20 55N 77 45 E
Amargosa **87** 13 2S 39 36W
Amargosa, R. **81** 36 14N 116 51W
Amargosa Ra., mts **81** 36 25N 116 40W
Amarillo **75** 35 14N 101 46W
Amaro, Mt. **108** 42 5N 14 6 E
Amarpur **125** 23 30N 91 45 E
Amasra **122** 41 45N 32 30 E
Amasya **122** 40 40N 35 50 E
Amatignak I. **67** 51 19N 179 10W
Amatitlán **84** 14 29N 90 38W
Amazon, R. **87** 2 0S 53 30W
Amazonas □, Brazil **86** 4 20S 64 0W
Amazonas □, Colomb. **86** 1 0S 72 0W
Amazonas □, Venez. **86** 3 30N 66 0W
Amazonas, R. **87** 2 0S 53 30W
Ambala **124** 30 23N 76 56 E
Ambalavao **117** 21 50S 46 56 E
Ambam **116** 2 20N 11 15 E
Ambanja **117** 13 40S 48 27 E
Ambarchik **121** 69 40N 162 20 E
Ambato **86** 1 5S 78 42W

Ambato, Sierra de — Aquiles Serdán

Ambato, Sierra de 88 28 25N 66 10W
Ambatolampy 117 19 20S 47 35E
Ambatondrazaka 117 17 55S 48 28E
Ambeno 127 9 20S 124 30E
Amberg 106 49 25N 11 52E
Ambergris Cay 83 18 0N 88 0W
Ambérieu-en-Bugey 103 45 57N 5 20E
Amberley 133 43 9S 172 44E
Ambert 102 45 33N 3 44E
Ambikapur 125 23 15N 83 15E
Ambilobé 117 13 10S 49 3E
Ambleside 94 54 26N 2 58W
Ambo 86 10 5S 76 10W
Ambon 127 3 35S 128 20E
Ambositra 117 20 31S 47 25E
Amboy, Calif., U.S.A. 81 34 33N 115 51W
Amboy, Ill., U.S.A. 76 41 44N 89 20W
Amboy, N.J., U.S.A. 71 40 31N 74 18W
Ambre, C. d' 117 12 40S 49 10E
Ambre, Mt. d' 117 12 30S 49 10E
Ambridge 70 40 36N 80 15W
Ambriz 116 7 48S 13 8E
Ambrizete 116 7 10S 12 52E
Ambrose 56 48 57N 103 29W
Amchitka I. 67 51 30N 179 0W
Amchitka P. 67 51 30N 179 0W
Amderma 120 69 45N 61 30E
Ameca 82 20 30N 104 0W
Ameca, R. 82 20 40N 105 15W
Amecameca 83 19 10N 98 57W
Ameland 105 53 27N 5 45E
Amélie-les-Bains-Palalda 102 42 29N 2 41E
Amen 121 68 45N 180 0E
American Falls 78 42 46N 112 56W
American Falls Res. 78 43 0N 112 50W
American Highland 91 73 0S 75 0E
American Samoa 133 14 20S 170 40W
Americana 89 22 45S 47 20W
Americus 73 32 0N 84 10W
Amersfoort 105 52 9N 5 23E
Amery 55 56 34N 94 3W
Ames 76 42 0N 93 40W
Amesbury 71 42 50N 70 52W
Amesdale 55 50 2N 92 55W
Ameson 34 49 50N 84 35W
Amet Sound 39 45 47N 63 10W
Amga, R. 121 61 0N 132 0E
Amgu 121 45 45N 137 15E
Amgun, R. 121 52 50N 138 0E
Amherst, Burma 125 16 2N 97 20E
Amherst, Can. 39 45 48N 64 8W
Amherst, Mass., U.S.A. 71 42 21N 72 30W
Amherst, Ohio, U.S.A. 70 41 23N 82 15W
Amherst, Tex., U.S.A. 75 34 0N 102 24W
Amherst I. 47 44 8N 76 43W
Amherstburg 46 42 6N 83 6W
Amiata Mte. 108 42 54N 11 40E
Amiens 101 49 54N 2 16E
Amirante Is. 16 6 0S 53 0E
Amisk 61 52 33N 111 4W
Amisk L. 55 54 35N 102 15W
Amistati, Presa 82 29 24N 101 0W
Amite 75 30 47N 90 31W
Amlia I. 67 52 5N 173 30W
Amlwch 94 53 24N 4 21W
'Ammān 115 32 0N 35 52E
Amne Machin Shan 129 34 25N 99 40E
Amnéville 101 49 16N 6 9E
Amoret 76 38 15N 94 35W
Amorgós 109 36 50N 25 57E
Amos 40 48 35N 78 5W
Amoy = Hsiamen 131 24 25N 118 4E
Amoy Hsiamen 131 24 25N 118 4E
Amozoc 83 19 2N 98 3W
Ampanihy 117 24 40S 44 45E
Amqui 38 48 28N 67 27W
Amraoti 124 20 55N 77 45E
Amreli 124 21 35N 71 17E
Amritsar 124 31 35N 74 57E
Amroha 124 28 53N 78 30E
Amsterdam, Neth. 105 52 23N 4 54E
Amsterdam, U.S.A. 71 42 58N 74 10W
Amsterdam, I. 16 37 30S 77 30E
Amu Darya, R. 120 37 50N 65 0E
Amuay 86 11 50N 70 10W
Amukta I. 67 52 29N 171 20W
Amund Ringnes I. 65 78 20N 96 25W
Amundsen Gulf 64 71 0N 124 0W
Amundsen Sea 91 72 0S 115 0W
Amuntai 126 2 28S 115 25E
Amur, R. 121 53 30N 122 30E
Amurang 127 1 5N 124 40E
Amuri Pass 133 42 31S 172 11E
Amurzet 121 47 50N 131 5E
Amyot 53 48 29N 84 57W
An Nafūd 122 28 15N 41 0E
An Najaf 122 32 3N 44 15E
An Nasiriyah 122 31 0N 46 15E
An Nhon (Binh Dinh) 128 13 55N 109 7E
An Nu'ayriyah 122 27 30N 48 30E
An Uaimh, Ireland 97 53 39N 6 40W
An Uaimh, Ireland 97 53 39N 6 40W
Ana Branch, R. 136 32 20S 143 0E
Anaco 86 9 27N 64 28W
Anaconda 78 46 7N 113 0W
Anacortes 80 48 30N 122 40W
Anadarko 75 35 4N 98 15W
Anadolu 122 38 0N 29 0E
Anadyr 121 64 35N 177 20E
Anadyr, R. 121 66 50N 171 0E
Anadyrskiy Zaliv 121 64 0N 180 0E
Anah 122 34 25N 42 0E
Anaheim 81 33 50N 118 0W
Anahim Lake 62 52 28N 125 18W
Anáhuac 82 27 14N 100 9W
Anakapalle 125 17 42N 83 06E
Analalava 117 14 35S 48 0E
Anama Bay 57 51 58N 98 4W
Anambas, Kepulauan 126 3 20N 106 30E
Anamoose 74 47 55N 100 20W
Anamosa 76 42 7N 91 30W
Anamur 122 36 8N 32 58E
Anan 132 33 54N 134 40E
Anantnag 124 33 45N 75 10E
Anápolis 87 16 15S 48 50W
Anar 123 30 55N 55 13E
Anārak 123 33 25N 53 40E
Anatolia = Anadolu 122 38 0N 29 0E
Anatone 78 46 9N 117 4W
Añatuya 88 28 20S 62 50W
Anaunethad L. 55 60 55N 104 25W
Ancaster 48 43 13N 79 59W
Ancenis 100 47 21N 1 10W
Anchor Bay 80 38 48N 123 34W
Anchorage 67 61 10N 149 50W
Ancien Cadet 44 45 19N 74 2W
Ancienne-Lorette 42 46 48N 71 21W
Ancohuma, Nevada 86 16 0S 68 50W
Ancon 82 8 57N 79 33W
Ancón 86 11 50S 77 10W
Ancona 108 43 37N 13 30E
Ancud 90 42 0S 73 50W
Ancud, G. de 90 42 0S 73 0W
Andacollo, Argent. 88 37 10S 70 42W
Andacollo, Chile 88 30 15S 71 10W
Andalgalá 88 27 40S 66 30W
Åndalsnes 110 62 35N 7 43E
Andalucía 104 37 35N 5 0W
Andalusia 73 31 25N 86 30W
Andalusia = Andalucía 104 37 35N 5 0W
Andaman Is. 128 12 30N 92 30E
Andaman Sea 128 13 0N 96 0E
Andaman Str. 128 12 15N 92 20E
Andara 117 18 2S 21 9E
Andelot 101 46 51N 5 56E
Andelys, Les 100 49 15N 1 25E
Anderlues 105 50 25N 4 16E
Andernach 105 50 24N 7 25E
Andernos-les-Bains 102 44 44N 1 6W
Anderson, Calif., U.S.A. 78 40 30N 122 19W
Anderson, Ind., U.S.A. 77 40 5N 85 40W
Anderson, Mo., U.S.A. 75 36 43N 94 29W
Anderson, S.C., U.S.A. 73 34 32N 82 40W
Anderson L. 63 50 37N 122 25W
Anderson, R. 64 69 42N 129 0W
Andes, mts. 86 20 0S 68 0W
Andfjorden 110 69 10N 16 20E
Andhra Pradesh □ 124 15 0N 80 0E
Andikíthira 109 35 52N 23 15E
Andizhan 120 41 10N 72 0E
Andkhui 123 36 52N 65 8E
Ando 136 36 43S 149 16E
Andorra ■ 104 42 30N 1 30E
Andorra La Vella 104 42 31N 1 32E
Andover, Can. 39 46 45N 67 42W
Andover, U.K. 95 51 13N 1 29W
Andover, N.Y., U.S.A. 70 42 11N 77 48W
Andover, Ohio, U.S.A. 70 41 35N 80 35W
Andreanof Is. 67 51 0N 178 0W
Andreville 41 47 41N 69 44W
Andrew 60 53 53N 112 21W
Andrews, S.C., U.S.A. 73 33 29N 79 30W
Andrews, Tex., U.S.A. 75 32 18N 102 33W
Ándria 108 41 13N 16 17E
Andriba 117 17 30S 46 58E
Androka 117 24 58S 44 2E
Andros 109 37 50N 24 50E
Andros I. 84 24 30N 78 0W
Andros Town 84 24 43N 77 47W
Andújar 104 38 3N 4 5W
Anegada I. 85 18 45N 64 20W
Aneroid 56 49 43N 107 18W
Aneto, Pico de 104 42 37N 0 40E
Ang Thong 128 14 35N 100 31E
Anga 121 60 35N 132 0E
Angamos, Punta 88 23 1S 70 32W
Angangki 130 47 9N 123 48E
Angara, R. 121 58 30N 97 0E
Angarsk 121 52 30N 104 0E
Ånge 110 62 31N 15 35E
Ange-Gardien 42 45 22N 72 57W
Ángel de la Guarda, I. 82 29 30N 113 30W
Ängelholm 111 56 15N 12 58E
Angels Camp 80 38 8N 120 30W
Ångermanälven 110 62 40N 18 0E
Angers, Can. 40 45 31N 75 29W
Angers, France 100 47 30N 0 35W
Angerville 101 48 19N 2 0E
Ångesån 110 66 50N 22 15E
Angikuni L. 55 62 0N 100 0W
Angkor 128 13 22N 103 50E
Anglesey, I. 94 53 17N 4 20W
Anglet 102 43 29N 1 31W
Angleton 75 29 12N 95 23W
Angliers 40 47 33N 79 14W
Anglure 101 48 35N 3 50E
Angmagssalik 17 65 40N 37 20W
Ango 116 4 10N 26 5E
Angoche, I. 117 16 20S 39 50E
Angol 88 37 56S 72 45W
Angola, Ind., U.S.A. 77 41 40N 85 0W
Angola, N.Y., U.S.A. 70 42 38N 79 2W
Angola ■ 117 12 0S 18 0E
Angoon 67 57 40N 134 40W
Angoulême 102 45 39N 0 10E
Angoumois 102 45 50N 0 25E
Angra dos Reis 89 23 0S 44 10W
Angran 120 80 59N 69 3E
Anguilla, I. 85 18 14N 63 5W
Anguille Mts. 37 48 0N 59 11W
Angus 46 44 19N 79 53W
Angus, Braes of 96 56 51N 3 0W
Angusville 57 50 44N 101 1W
Anhanduí, R. 89 21 46S 52 9W
Anholt 111 56 42N 11 33E
Anhwa 131 28 18N 111 25E
Ani 131 28 50N 115 29E
Aniak 67 61 58N 159 50W
Animas 79 31 58N 108 58W
Anin 128 15 36N 97 50E
Anita 76 41 27N 94 46W
Anjen 131 26 42N 113 19E
Anjidiv I. 124 14 40N 74 10E
Anjou, Can. 43 45 36N 73 33W
Anjou, France 100 47 20N 0 15W
Anjozorobe 117 18 22S 47 52E
Anju 130 39 40N 125 45E
Ankang 131 32 38N 109 5E
Ankara 122 40 0N 32 54E
Ankazoabo 117 22 18S 44 31E
Ankazobé 117 18 20S 47 10E
Ankeny 76 41 44N 93 36W
Anki 131 25 1N 118 4E
Anking 131 30 34N 117 1E
Ankoro 116 6 45S 26 55E
Anlu 131 31 12N 113 38E
Ann Arbor 46 42 17N 83 45W
Ann C., Antarct. 91 66 30S 50 30E
Ann C., U.S.A. 71 42 39N 70 37W
Anna, Ill., U.S.A. 75 37 28N 89 10W
Anna, Ohio, U.S.A. 77 40 24N 84 11W
Annaba 114 36 50N 7 46E
Annacis I. 66 49 10N 122 57W
Annaheim 56 52 19N 104 49W
Annalee, R. 97 54 3N 7 15W
Annalera Telegraph Office 136 41 16S 143 59E
Annam = Trung-Phan 128 16 30N 107 30E
Annamitique, Chaîne 128 17 0N 106 0E
Annan 96 55 0N 3 17W
Annan, R. 96 54 58N 3 18W
Annapolis Royal 39 44 44N 65 32W
Annecy 103 45 55N 6 8E
Annecy, L. d' 103 45 52N 6 10E
Annemasse 103 46 12N 6 16E
Annette 67 55 2N 131 35W
Annieopsquotch Mts. 37 48 20N 57 30W
Annieville 66 49 11N 122 55W
Anning 129 24 58N 102 30E
Anniston 73 33 45N 85 50W
Annobón = Pagalu 112 1 35S 3 35E
Annonay 103 45 15N 4 40E
Annonciation, L', Can. 34 46 25N 74 55W
Annonciation, L', Qué., Can. 40 46 25N 74 55W
Annot 103 43 58N 6 38E
Annotto Bay 84 18 17N 77 3W
Annville 71 40 18N 76 32W
Anoka 74 45 10N 93 26W
Anola 57 49 53N 96 38W
Anping 131 23 0N 120 6E
Ansbach 106 49 17N 10 34E
Anse-au-Clair, L' 37 51 25N 57 5W
Anse au Loup, L' 37 51 32N 56 50W
Anse, L' 52 46 47N 88 28W
Anserma 86 5 13N 75 48W
Anshun 131 26 2N 105 57E
Ansi 130 40 21N 96 10E
Ansley 74 41 19N 99 24W
Anson 75 32 46N 99 54W
Anson B. 134 13 20S 130 6E
Ansonia, Conn., U.S.A. 71 41 21N 73 6W
Ansonia, Ohio, U.S.A. 77 40 13N 84 38W
Ansonville 34 48 46N 80 43W
Anstruther 96 56 14N 2 40W
Anstruther, E. and W. 96 56 14N 2 40W
Ansudu 127 2 11S 139 22E
Anta 130 46 18N 125 34E
Antabamba 86 14 40S 73 0W
Antakya 122 36 14N 36 10E
Antalaha 117 14 57S 50 20E
Antalya 122 36 52N 30 45E
Antalya Körfezi 122 36 15N 31 30E
Antananarivo 117 18 55S 47 35E
Antarctic Pen. 91 67 0S 60 0W
Antarctica 91 90 0S 0 0
Antequera, Parag. 88 24 8S 57 7W
Antequera, Spain 104 37 5N 4 33W
Antero Mt. 79 38 45N 106 15W
Anthony, Kans., U.S.A. 75 37 8N 98 2W
Anthony, N. Mex., U.S.A. 79 32 1N 106 37W
Anti Atlas, Mts. 114 30 30N 6 30W
Antibes 103 43 34N 7 6E
Antibes, C. d' 103 43 31N 7 7E
Anticosti, Í. d' 38 49 30N 63 0W
Antifer, C. d' 100 49 41N 0 10E
Antigo 74 45 8N 89 5W
Antigonish 39 45 38N 61 58W
Antigua 84 14 34N 90 41W
Antigua Bahama, Canal de la 84 22 10N 77 30W
Antigua, I. 85 17 0N 61 50W
Antilla 84 20 40N 75 50W
Antimony 79 38 7N 112 0W
Antioch 80 38 7N 121 45W
Antioche, Pertuis d' 102 46 6N 1 20W
Antioquia 86 6 40N 75 55W
Antioquia □ 86 7 0N 75 30W
Antipodes Is. 14 49 45S 178 40E
Antler, Can. 57 49 34N 101 27W
Antler, U.S.A. 57 48 58N 101 18W
Antler, R. 57 49 8N 101 0W
Antlers 75 34 15N 95 35W
Antofagasta 88 23 50S 70 30W
Antofagasta □ 88 24 0S 69 0W
Antofagasta de la Sierra 88 26 5S 67 20W
Antofallá 88 25 30S 68 5W
Antofalla, Salar de 88 25 40S 67 45W
Anton 75 33 49N 102 5W
Anton Chico 79 35 12N 105 5W
Antongil, B. d' 117 15 30S 49 50E
Antonina 89 25 26S 48 42W
Antonito 79 37 4N 106 1W
Antrain 100 48 28N 1 30W
Antrim 97 54 43N 6 13W
Antrim □ 97 54 42N 6 20W
Antrim Co. 97 54 58N 6 20W
Antrim, Mts. of 97 54 57N 6 8W
Antsalova 117 18 40S 44 37E
Antsirabé 117 19 55S 47 2E
Antsohihy 117 14 50S 47 50E
Antung 130 40 10N 124 18E
Antwerp, N.Y., U.S.A. 71 44 12N 75 36W
Antwerp, Ohio, U.S.A. 77 41 11N 84 45W
Antwerp = Antwerpen 105 51 13N 4 25E
Antwerpen 105 51 13N 4 25E
Antwerpen □ 105 51 15N 4 40E
Anupgarh 124 29 10N 73 10E
Anuradhapura 124 8 22N 80 28E
Anvers I. 91 64 30S 63 40W
Anvik 67 62 37N 160 20W
Anxious B. 134 33 24S 134 45E
Anyang 130 36 7N 114 26E
Anyer-Lor 127 6 6S 105 56E
Anyi 131 35 0N 110 44E
Anyuan 131 24 59N 115 31E
Anza 81 33 35N 116 39W
Anzhero-Sudzhensk 120 56 10N 83 40E
Ánzio 108 41 28N 12 37E
Aomori 132 40 45N 140 45E
Aomori-ken □ 132 40 45N 140 45E
Aosta 108 45 43N 7 20E
Apa, R. 88 22 6S 58 2W
Apache, Ariz., U.S.A. 79 31 46N 109 6W
Apache, Okla., U.S.A. 75 34 53N 98 22W
Apalachee B. 73 30 0N 84 0W
Apalachicola 73 29 40N 85 0W
Apaporis, R. 86 0 30S 70 30W
Aparri 127 18 22N 121 38E
Aparurén 86 5 6N 62 8W
Apatzingán 82 19 0N 102 20W
Apeldoorn 105 52 13N 5 57E
Apenam 126 8 35S 116 13E
Apennines 93 44 20N 10 20E
Apia 86 5 5N 75 58W
Apia 133 13 50S 171 50W
Apiacás, Serra dos 86 9 50S 57 0W
Apiaí 86 24 31S 48 50W
Apizaco 83 19 26N 98 9W
Aplao 86 16 0S 72 40W
Apo, Mt. 127 6 53N 125 14E
Apohaqui 39 45 42N 65 36W
Apollo Bay 136 38 45S 143 40E
Apolo 86 14 30S 68 30W
Apostle Is. 52 47 0N 90 30W
Apóstoles 89 28 0S 56 0W
Apoteri 86 4 2N 58 32W
Appalachian Mts. 72 38 0N 80 0W
Appalachicola, R. 73 30 0N 85 0W
Appennini 108 41 0N 15 0E
Appingedam 105 53 19N 6 51E
Apple Hill 47 45 13N 74 46W
Apple Valley 81 34 30N 117 11W
Appleby, Can. 48 43 23N 79 46W
Appleby, U.K. 94 54 35N 2 29W
Appleton 72 44 17N 88 25W
Appleton City 76 38 11N 94 2W
Approuague 87 4 20N 52 0W
Apsley 47 44 45N 78 6W
Apt 103 43 53N 5 24E
Apucarana 89 23 55S 51 33W
Apulia = Puglia 108 41 0N 16 30E
Apure □ 86 7 10N 68 50W
Apure, R. 86 8 0N 69 20W
Apurimac, R. 86 12 10S 73 30W
Apurito, R. 86 7 50N 67 0W
Aq Chah 123 37 0N 66 5E
'Aqaba, Khalij al 122 28 15N 33 20E
'Aqrah 122 36 46N 43 45E
Aqsu 129 41 10N 80 15E
Aquanish 38 50 14N 62 2W
Aquidauana 87 20 30S 55 50W
Aquila, L' 108 42 21N 13 24E
Aquiles Serdán 82 28 37N 105 54W

Aquin Assis

Aquin	**85**	18 16N	73 24W
Ar Ramadi	**122**	33 25N	43 20E
Ar Raqqah	**122**	36 0N	38 55E
Ar Rass	**122**	25 50N	43 40E
Ar Rifai	**122**	31 50N	46 10E
Ar Riyād	**122**	24 41N	46 42E
Ar Rub 'al Khālī	**115**	21 0N	51 0E
Ar Ruṭbah	**122**	33 0N	40 15E
Ara L.	**53**	50 33N	87 28W
Arab, Shatt al	**122**	30 0N	48 31E
Arabelo	**86**	4 55N	64 13W
Arabia	**118**	25 0N	45 0E
Arabian Sea	**118**	16 0N	65 0E
Aracajú	**87**	10 55S	37 4W
Aracataca	**86**	10 38N	74 9W
Aracati	**87**	4 30S	37 44W
Araçatuba	**89**	21 10S	50 30W
Aracena	**104**	37 53N	6 38W
Aracruz	**87**	19 49S	40 16W
Araçuai	**87**	16 52S	42 4W
Arad	**107**	46 10N	21 20E
Arafura Sea	**127**	10 0S	135 0E
Aragón	**104**	41 25N	1 0W
Aragón, R.	**104**	42 35N	0 50W
Aragua □	**86**	10 0N	67 10W
Aragua de Barcelona	**86**	9 28N	64 49W
Araguacema	**87**	8 50S	49 20W
Araguaia, R.	**87**	7 0S	49 15W
Araguari	**87**	18 38S	48 11W
Araguari, R.	**87**	1 0N	51 40W
Arak	**114**	25 20N	3 45E
Arāk	**122**	34 0N	49 40E
Arakan Coast	**125**	19 0N	94 0E
Arakan Yoma	**125**	20 0N	94 30E
Araks, R. = Aras, Rud-e	**122**	39 10N	47 10E
Aral Sea = Aralskoye More	**120**	44 30N	60 0E
Aralsk	**120**	46 50N	61 20E
Aralskoye More	**120**	44 30N	60 0E
Aramac	**135**	22 58S	145 14E
Aran, I.	**97**	55 0N	8 30W
Aran Is.	**97**	53 5N	9 42W
Aranjuez	**104**	40 1N	3 40W
Aranos	**117**	24 9S	19 7E
Aransas Pass	**75**	27 55N	97 9W
Aranyaprathet	**128**	13 41N	102 30E
Aranzazu	**86**	5 16N	75 30W
Arapahoe	**74**	40 22N	99 53W
Arapawa I.	**15**	41 13S	174 20E
Arapey Grande, R.	**88**	30 55S	57 49W
Arapkir	**122**	39 5N	38 30E
Arapongas	**89**	23 29S	51 28W
Arapuni	**14**	38 3S	175 37E
Araranguá	**89**	29 0S	49 30W
Araraquara	**87**	21 50S	48 0W
Araras	**89**	5 15S	60 35W
Ararás, Serra dos	**89**	25 0S	53 10W
Ararat	**136**	37 16S	143 0E
Ararat, Mt. = Ağri Daği	**122**	39 50N	44 15E
Araruama, Lagoa de	**89**	22 53S	42 12W
Aras, Rud-e	**122**	39 10N	47 10E
Arauca	**86**	7 0N	70 40W
Arauca □	**86**	6 40N	71 0W
Arauca, R.	**86**	7 30N	69 0W
Arauco	**88**	37 16S	73 25W
Arauco □	**88**	37 40S	73 25W
Arauquita	**86**	7 2N	71 25W
Araure	**86**	9 34N	69 13W
Araxá	**87**	19 35S	46 55W
Araya, Pen. de	**86**	10 40N	64 0W
Arbatax	**108**	39 57N	9 42E
Arbeláez	**86**	4 17N	74 26W
Arbīl	**122**	36 15N	44 5E
Arbois	**101**	46 55N	5 46E
Arbor Vitae	**52**	48 54N	94 18W
Arborfield	**56**	53 6N	103 39W
Arborg	**57**	50 54N	97 13W
Arbresle, L'	**103**	45 50N	4 26E
Arbroath	**96**	56 34N	2 35W
Arbuckle	**80**	39 3N	122 2W
Arc	**101**	47 28N	5 34E
Arcachon	**102**	44 40N	1 10W
Arcachon, Bassin d'	**102**	44 42N	1 10W
Arcade	**70**	42 34N	78 25W
Arcadia, Can.	**39**	43 50N	66 4W
Arcadia, Fla., U.S.A.	**73**	27 20N	81 50W
Arcadia, Ind., U.S.A.	**77**	40 10N	86 1W
Arcadia, Iowa, U.S.A.	**76**	42 5N	95 3W
Arcadia, La., U.S.A.	**75**	32 34N	92 53W
Arcadia, Nebr., U.S.A.	**74**	41 29N	99 4W
Arcadia, Pa., U.S.A.	**70**	40 46N	78 54W
Arcadia, Wis., U.S.A.	**74**	44 13N	91 29W
Arcanum	**77**	39 59N	84 33W
Arcata	**78**	40 55N	124 4W
Arcen	**131**	51 29N	6 11E
Archangel = Arkhangelsk	**120**	64 40N	41 0E
Archbald	**71**	41 30N	75 31W
Archbold	**77**	41 31N	84 18W
Archer, R.	**135**	13 25S	142 50E
Archerwill	**56**	52 26N	103 51W
Arcis-sur-Aube	**101**	48 32N	4 10E
Arco	**78**	43 45N	113 16W
Arcola, Can.	**57**	49 40N	102 30W
Arcola, U.S.A.	**77**	39 41N	88 19W
Arcos	**104**	41 12N	2 16W
Arcot	**124**	12 53N	79 20E
Arcoverde	**87**	8 25S	37 4W
Arctic B.	**65**	73 1N	85 7W
Arctic Ocean	**17**	78 0N	160 0W
Arctic Red, R.	**67**	66 0N	132 0W
Arctic Red River	**64**	67 15N	134 0W
Arctic Village	**67**	68 5N	145 45W
Arda, R.	**109**	41 40N	25 40E
Ardabrīl	**122**	38 15N	48 18E
Ardakan	**123**	30 20N	52 5E
Ardbeg	**46**	45 38N	80 5W
Ardèche □	**103**	44 42N	4 16E
Ardee	**97**	53 51N	6 32W
Arden, Man., Can.	**57**	50 17N	99 16W
Arden, Ont., Can.	**47**	44 43N	76 56W
Arden, U.S.A.	**81**	36 1N	115 14W
Ardennes	**106**	49 30N	5 10E
Ardennes □	**101**	49 35N	4 40E
Ardentes	**101**	46 45N	1 50E
Ardestān	**123**	33 20N	52 25E
Ardgour	**96**	56 45N	5 25W
Ardlethan	**136**	34 22S	146 53E
Ardmore, Can.	**60**	54 20N	110 29W
Ardmore, Okla., U.S.A.	**75**	34 10N	97 5W
Ardmore, Pa., U.S.A.	**71**	39 58N	75 18W
Ardmore, S.D., U.S.A.	**74**	43 0N	103 40W
Ardnacrusha	**97**	52 43N	8 38W
Ardnamurchan Pt.	**96**	56 44N	6 14W
Ardoise, L'	**39**	45 37N	60 45W
Ardres	**101**	50 50N	2 0E
Ardrossan	**96**	55 39N	4 50W
Ards □	**97**	54 35N	5 30W
Ards Pen.	**97**	54 30N	5 25W
Arecibo	**85**	18 29N	66 42W
Areia Branca	**87**	5 0S	37 0W
Arena de la Ventana, Punta	**82**	24 4N	109 52W
Arena, Pt.	**80**	38 57N	123 44W
Arenales, Cerro	**90**	47 5S	73 40W
Arenas, Pta.	**86**	10 20N	62 39W
Arendal	**111**	58 28N	8 46E
Arendonk	**105**	51 19N	5 5E
Arenzville	**76**	39 53N	90 22W
Arequipa	**86**	16 20S	71 30W
Arès	**102**	44 47N	1 8W
Arévalo	**104**	41 3N	4 43W
Arezzo	**108**	43 28N	11 50E
Argelès-Gazost	**102**	43 0N	0 6W
Argelès-sur-Mer	**102**	42 34N	3 1E
Argent-sur-Sauldre	**101**	47 33N	2 25E
Argenta, Can.	**54**	50 20N	116 55W
Argenta, U.S.A.	**77**	39 59N	88 49W
Argentan	**100**	48 45N	0 1W
Argentário, Mte.	**108**	42 23N	11 11E
Argentat	**102**	45 6N	1 56E
Argenteuil	**101**	48 57N	2 14E
Argenteuil □	**43**	45 50N	74 30W
Argentia	**37**	47 18N	53 58W
Argentina	**86**	0 34N	74 17W
Argentina ■	**90**	35 0S	66 0W
Argentino, L.	**90**	50 10S	73 0W
Argenton-sur-Creuse	**102**	46 36N	1 30E
Argentré	**100**	48 5N	0 40W
Argeş, R.	**107**	44 30N	25 50E
Arghandab, R.	**124**	32 15N	66 23E
Argolikós Kólpos	**109**	37 20N	22 52E
Argonne	**101**	49 0N	5 20E
Argos	**109**	37 40N	22 43E
Argos	**77**	41 14N	86 15W
Argostólion	**109**	38 12N	20 33E
Arguello, Pt.	**81**	34 34N	120 40W
Argun, R.	**121**	53 20N	121 28E
Argus Pk.	**81**	35 52N	117 26W
Argyle, Can.	**57**	50 11N	97 27W
Argyle, U.S.A.	**74**	48 23N	96 49W
Århus	**111**	56 8N	10 11E
Ariake-wan	**132**	31 30N	131 10E
Arica, Chile	**86**	18 32S	70 20W
Arica, Colomb.	**86**	2 0S	71 50W
Arica, Peru	**86**	1 30S	75 30W
Arichat	**39**	45 31N	61 1W
Arid, C.	**134**	34 1S	123 10E
Ariège □	**102**	42 56N	1 30E
Ariège, R.	**102**	43 30N	1 25E
Arima	**85**	10 38N	61 17W
Arinos, R.	**86**	11 15S	57 0W
Ario de Rosales	**82**	19 12N	101 42W
Aripuanã	**86**	9 25S	60 30W
Aripuanã, R.	**86**	7 30S	60 25W
Ariquemes	**86**	9 55S	63 6W
Arisaig	**96**	56 55N	5 50W
Arismendi	**86**	8 29N	68 22W
Ariss	**49**	43 35N	80 22W
Aristazabal, I.	**62**	52 40N	129 10W
Arivaca	**79**	31 37N	111 25W
Arizaro, Salar de	**88**	24 40S	67 50W
Arizona	**88**	35 45S	65 25W
Arizona □	**79**	34 20N	111 30W
Arizpe	**82**	30 20N	110 11W
Arjeplog	**110**	66 3N	18 2E
Arjona	**86**	10 14N	75 22W
Arjuno	**127**	7 49S	112 19E
Arka	**121**	60 15N	142 0E
Arka Tagh	**129**	36 30N	90 0E
Arkadelphia	**75**	34 5N	93 0W
Arkaig, L.	**96**	56 58N	5 10W
Arkansas □	**75**	35 0N	92 30W
Arkansas City	**75**	37 4N	97 3W
Arkansas, R.	**75**	35 20N	93 30W
Arkell	**49**	43 32N	80 10W
Arkhangelsk	**120**	64 40N	41 0E
Arklow	**97**	52 48N	6 10W
Arkona	**46**	43 4N	81 50W
Arkticheskiy, Mys	**121**	81 10N	95 0E
Arlanc	**102**	45 25N	3 42E
Arlanzón, R.	**104**	42 12N	4 0W
Arlberg Pass	**106**	49 9N	10 12E
Arlee	**78**	47 10N	114 4W
Arles	**103**	43 41N	4 40E
Arlington, Oreg., U.S.A.	**78**	45 48N	120 6W
Arlington, S.D., U.S.A.	**74**	44 25N	97 4W
Arlington, Wash., U.S.A.	**80**	48 11N	122 4W
Arlington Heights	**77**	42 5N	87 59W
Arlon	**105**	49 42N	5 49E
Armadale	**50**	43 50N	79 15W
Armagh, Can.	**41**	46 41N	70 32W
Armagh, U.K.	**97**	54 22N	6 40W
Armagh □	**97**	54 18N	6 37W
Armagh Co.	**97**	54 16N	6 35W
Armagnac	**102**	43 44N	0 10E
Armançon, R.	**101**	47 59N	3 30E
Armavir	**120**	45 2N	41 7E
Armenia	**86**	4 35N	75 45W
Armentières	**101**	50 40N	2 50E
Armero	**86**	4 58N	74 54W
Armidale, Austral.	**135**	30 30S	151 40E
Armidale, Can.	**39**	44 37N	63 38W
Armour	**74**	43 20N	98 25W
Arms	**34**	49 34N	86 3W
Armstead	**78**	45 0N	112 56W
Armstrong, B.C., Can.	**63**	50 25N	119 10W
Armstrong, Ont., Can.	**52**	50 18N	89 4W
Armstrong, U.S.A.	**75**	26 59N	97 48W
Arnarfjörður	**110**	65 48N	23 40W
Arnaud, R.	**36**	59 59N	69 46W
Arnay-le-Duc	**101**	47 10N	4 27E
Arnes	**110**	66 1N	21 31W
Arnett	**75**	36 9N	99 44W
Arnhem	**105**	51 58N	5 55E
Arnhem B.	**134**	12 20S	136 10E
Arnhem, C.	**135**	12 20S	137 0E
Arnhem Ld.	**134**	13 10S	135 0E
Arno, R.	**108**	43 44N	10 20E
Arnold, Calif., U.S.A.	**80**	38 15N	120 20W
Arnold, Nebr., U.S.A.	**74**	41 29N	100 10W
Arnold, Pa., U.S.A.	**70**	40 36N	79 44W
Arnot	**55**	55 56N	96 41W
Arnøy	**110**	70 9N	20 40E
Arnprior	**47**	45 26N	76 21W
Arntfield	**40**	48 12N	79 15W
Aroa	**86**	10 26N	68 54W
Aroab	**117**	26 41S	19 39E
Arpajon, Cantal, France	**102**	44 54N	2 28E
Arpajon, Seine et Oise, France	**101**	48 37N	2 12E
Arrah	**125**	25 35N	84 32E
Arraiján	**84**	8 56N	79 36W
Arran	**57**	51 53N	101 43W
Arran, I.	**96**	55 34N	5 12W
Arrandale	**54**	54 57N	130 0W
Arras	**101**	50 17N	2 46E
Arreau	**102**	42 54N	0 22E
Arrecifes	**88**	34 06S	60 9W
Arrée, Mts. d'	**100**	48 26N	3 55W
Arriaga, Chiapas, Mexico	**83**	16 15N	93 52W
Arriaga, San Luís de Potosi, Mexico	**82**	21 55N	101 23W
Arromanches-les-Bains	**100**	49 20N	0 38W
Arrou	**100**	48 6N	1 8E
Arrow L.	**97**	54 3N	8 20W
Arrow Park	**63**	50 6N	117 57W
Arrow Rock Res.	**78**	43 45N	115 50W
Arrowhead	**63**	50 40N	117 55W
Arrowhead, L.	**81**	34 16N	117 10W
Arrowtown	**133**	44 57S	168 50E
Arrowwood	**61**	50 44N	113 9W
Arroyo Grande	**81**	35 9N	120 32W
Ars	**102**	46 13N	1 30W
Ars-sur-Moselle	**101**	49 5N	6 4E
Arsenault L.	**55**	55 6N	108 32W
Arshan	**130**	46 59N	120 0E
Árta	**109**	39 8N	21 2E
Arteaga	**82**	18 50N	102 20W
Artenay	**101**	48 5N	1 50E
Artesia	**75**	32 55N	104 25W
Artesia Wells	**75**	28 17N	99 18W
Artesian	**74**	44 2N	97 54W
Arthez-de-Béarn	**102**	43 29N	0 38W
Arthur, Can.	**49**	43 50N	80 32W
Arthur, U.S.A.	**77**	39 43N	88 28W
Arthurette	**39**	46 47N	67 29W
Arthur's Pass	**133**	42 54S	171 35E
Arthur's Town	**85**	24 38N	75 42W
Artigas	**88**	30 20S	56 30W
Artillery L.	**55**	63 9N	107 52W
Artois	**101**	50 20N	2 30E
Arts Bogd Uul, mts.	**130**	44 40N	102 20E
Artvin	**122**	41 14N	41 44E
Aru, Kepulauan	**127**	6 0S	134 30E
Arua	**116**	3 1N	30 58E
Aruanã	**87**	15 0S	51 10W
Aruba I.	**85**	12 30N	70 0W
Arudy	**102**	43 7N	0 28W
Arunachal Pradesh □	**125**	28 0N	95 0E
Arundel	**40**	45 58N	74 37W
Arusha	**116**	3 20S	36 40E
Aruwimi, R.	**116**	1 30N	25 0E
Arvada	**78**	44 43N	106 6W
Arvayheer	**130**	46 15N	102 45E
Arve, R.	**103**	46 11N	6 8E
Arvert, L.	**38**	52 18N	61 45W
Arvida	**41**	48 25N	71 14W
Arvidsjaur	**110**	65 35N	19 10E
Arvika	**111**	59 40N	12 36E
Arvilla	**60**	53 59N	114 0W
Arvin	**81**	35 12N	118 50W
Arys	**120**	42 26N	68 48E
Arzamas	**120**	55 27N	43 55E
As Salt	**115**	32 2N	35 43E
As Samāwah	**122**	31 15N	45 15E
As Shatrah	**122**	31 30N	46 10E
As Sulaimānīyah	**122**	35 35N	45 29E
As Suwaih	**123**	22 10N	59 33E
As Suwayda	**122**	32 40N	36 30E
As Suwayrah	**122**	32 55N	45 0E
Asadabad	**122**	34 50N	48 10E
Asahi-dake, mt.	**132**	43 42N	142 54E
Asahigawa	**132**	43 45N	142 30E
Asahikawa	**132**	43 45N	142 30E
Asamankese	**114**	5 50N	0 40W
Asansol	**125**	23 40N	87 1E
Asbestos	**35**	45 47N	71 58W
Asbury Park	**71**	40 15N	74 1W
Ascensión	**82**	31 6N	107 59W
Ascensión, B. de la	**83**	19 50N	87 20W
Ascension, I.	**13**	8 0S	14 15W
Aschaffenburg	**106**	49 58N	9 8E
Áscoli Piceno	**108**	42 51N	13 34E
Ascope	**86**	7 46S	79 8W
Ascotán	**88**	21 45S	68 17W
Aseb	**115**	13 0N	42 40E
Asfeld	**101**	49 27N	4 5E
Ash Fork	**79**	35 14N	112 32W
Ash Grove	**75**	37 21N	93 36W
Ash Shām, Bādiyat	**122**	31 30N	40 0E
Ash Shāmīyah	**122**	31 55N	44 35E
Ashan	**130**	41 3N	122 58E
Ashburn	**73**	31 42N	83 40W
Ashburton	**133**	43 53S	171 48E
Ashburton, R., Austral.	**134**	21 40S	114 56E
Ashburton, R., N.Z.	**15**	44 2S	171 50E
Ashby-de-la-Zouch	**94**	52 45N	1 29W
Ashcroft	**63**	50 40N	121 20W
Ashdod	**115**	31 49N	34 35E
Asheboro	**73**	35 43N	79 46W
Ashern	**57**	51 11N	98 21W
Asherton	**75**	28 25N	99 43W
Asheville	**73**	35 39N	82 30W
Asheweig, R.	**34**	54 17N	87 12W
Ashford, U.K.	**95**	51 8N	0 53E
Ashford, U.S.A.	**78**	46 45N	122 2W
Ashgrove	**49**	43 36N	79 53W
Ashikaga	**132**	36 28N	139 29E
Ashizuri-Zaki	**132**	32 35N	132 50E
Ashkhabad	**120**	38 0N	57 50E
Ashland, U.S.A.	**76**	39 53N	90 0W
Ashland, Kans., U.S.A.	**75**	37 13N	99 43W
Ashland, Ky., U.S.A.	**72**	38 25N	82 40W
Ashland, Me., U.S.A.	**35**	46 34N	68 26W
Ashland, Mont., U.S.A.	**78**	45 41N	106 12W
Ashland, Nebr., U.S.A.	**74**	41 5N	96 27W
Ashland, Ohio, U.S.A.	**70**	40 52N	82 20W
Ashland, Oreg., U.S.A.	**78**	42 10N	122 38W
Ashland, Pa., U.S.A.	**71**	40 45N	76 22W
Ashland, Va., U.S.A.	**72**	37 46N	77 30W
Ashland, Wis., U.S.A.	**52**	46 40N	90 52W
Ashley, Ill., U.S.A.	**76**	38 20N	89 11W
Ashley, Ind., U.S.A.	**77**	41 32N	85 4W
Ashley, Mich., U.S.A.	**77**	43 11N	84 29W
Ashley, N.D., U.S.A.	**74**	46 3N	99 23W
Ashley, Pa., U.S.A.	**71**	41 12N	75 55W
Ashmont	**60**	54 7N	111 35W
Ashmore Reef	**134**	12 14S	123 5E
Ashquelon	**115**	31 42N	34 55E
Ashtabula	**70**	41 52N	80 50W
Ashton	**78**	44 6N	111 30W
Ashton-u.-Lyne	**94**	53 30N	2 8E
Ashuanipi, L.	**38**	52 45N	66 15W
Ashun	**131**	25 10N	106 0E
Asia	**118**	45 0N	75 0E
Asia, Kepulauan	**127**	1 0N	131 13E
Asifabad	**124**	19 30N	79 24E
Asinara, G. dell'	**108**	41 0N	8 30E
Asinara I.	**108**	41 5N	8 15E
Asino	**120**	57 0N	86 0E
Asir	**115**	18 40N	42 30E
Asir, Ras	**115**	11 55N	51 10E
Askersund	**111**	58 53N	14 55E
Askja	**110**	65 3N	16 48W
Askov	**52**	46 12N	92 51W
Asmar	**123**	35 10N	71 27E
Asmara = Asmera	**115**	15 19N	38 55E
Asmera	**115**	15 19N	38 55E
Aso	**132**	33 0N	130 42E
Aspen, Can.	**39**	45 18N	62 3W
Aspen, U.S.A.	**79**	39 12N	106 56W
Aspen Grove	**63**	49 57N	120 37W
Aspermont	**75**	33 11N	100 15W
Aspiring, Mt.	**133**	44 23S	168 46E
Aspres	**103**	44 32N	5 44E
Asquith	**56**	52 8N	107 13W
Assam □	**125**	25 45N	92 30E
Assen	**105**	53 0N	6 35E
Assigny, L.	**38**	52 0N	65 20W
Assiniboia	**56**	49 40N	105 59W
Assiniboine, R.	**58**	49 53N	97 8W
Assinica L.	**34**	50 30N	75 20W
Assis	**89**	22 40S	50 20W

Baganga Barkah

Baganga 127 7 34N 126 33 E
Bagdad 81 34 35N 115 53W
Bagdarin 121 54 26N 113 36 E
Bagé 89 31 20 S 54 15W
Baggs 78 41 8N 107 46W
Baghdād 122 33 20N 44 30 E
Bāghīn 123 30 12N 56 45 E
Baghlan 124 36 12N 69 0 E
Baghlan □ 123 36 0N 68 30 E
Bagley 74 47 30N 95 22W
Bagnell Dam 76 38 14N 92 36W
Bagnères-de-Bigorre 102 43 5N 0 9 E
Bagnères-de-Luchon 102 42 47N 0 38 E
Bagnoles-de-l'Orne 100 48 32N 0 25W
Bagnols-les-Bains 102 44 30N 3 40 E
Bagnols-sur-Cèze 103 44 10N 4 36 E
Bagot □ 45 45 35N 72 45W
Bagotville 41 48 22N 70 54W
Bagrash Kol 129 42 0N 87 0 E
Baguio 127 16 26N 120 34 E
Bahama, Canal Viejo de 84 22 10N 77 30W
Bahama Is. 85 24 40N 74 0W
Bahamas ■ 85 24 0N 74 0W
Bahau 128 2 48N 102 26 E
Bahawalpur 124 29 37N 71 40 E
Bahawalpur □ 124 29 5N 71 3 E
Bahía = Salvador 87 13 0 S 38 30W
Bahía Blanca 88 38 35 S 62 13W
Bahía de Caráquez 86 0 40 S 80 27W
Bahía Honda 84 22 54N 83 10W
Bahía, Islas de la 84 16 45N 86 15W
Bahía Laura 90 48 10 S 66 30W
Bahía Negra 86 20 5 S 58 5W
Bahr el 'Arab, R. 115 10 0N 26 0 E
Bahr el Ghazâl □ 116 7 0N 28 0 E
Bahr el Jebel 115 7 30N 30 30 E
Bahra 122 21 25N 39 32 E
Bahraich 125 27 38N 81 50 E
Bahrain ■ 123 26 0N 50 35 E
Bahramabad 123 30 28N 56 2 E
Bahu Kalat 123 25 50N 61 20 E
Baia-Mare 107 47 40N 23 17 E
Baie Comeau 38 49 12N 68 10W
Baie de l'Abri 35 50 3N 67 0W
Baie-des-Sables 38 48 43N 67 54W
Baie-du-Poste 41 50 24N 73 56W
Baie-du-Renard 38 49 17N 61 50W
Baie Johan Beetz 35 50 18N 62 50W
Baie-St-Paul 41 47 28N 70 32W
Baie-Ste-Anne 39 47 3N 64 58W
Baie-Ste-Catherine 41 48 6N 69 44W
Baie-Ste-Claire 38 49 54N 64 30W
Baie Trinité 38 49 25N 67 20W
Baie Verte, N.B., Can. 39 46 1N 64 6W
Baie Verte, Newf., Can. 37 49 55N 56 12W
Baieville 41 46 8N 72 43W
Baignes 102 45 28N 0 25W
Baigneux-les-Juifs 101 47 31N 4 39 E
Ba'iji 122 35 0N 43 30 E
Baikal, L. 121 53 0N 108 0 E
Baile Atha Cliath = Dublin 97 53 20N 6 18W
Bailleul 101 50 44N 2 41 E
Bain-de-Bretagne 100 47 50N 1 40W
Bainbridge, Ga., U.S.A. 73 30 53N 84 34W
Bainbridge, Ind., U.S.A. 77 39 46N 86 49W
Bainbridge, N.Y., U.S.A. 71 42 17N 75 29W
Bainbridge, Ohio, U.S.A. 77 39 14N 83 16W
Baing 127 10 14 S 120 34 E
Bainsville 43 45 10N 74 25W
Bainville 74 48 8N 104 10W
Baird 75 32 25N 99 25W
Baird Inlet 67 64 49N 164 18W
Baird Mts. 67 67 10N 160 15W
Baird Pen. 65 68 55N 76 4W
Bairnsdale 136 37 48 S 147 36 E
Baissoklyn 130 47 55N 102 20 E
Baitadi 125 29 35N 80 25 E
Baja 107 46 12N 18 59 E
Baja California 82 32 10N 115 12W
Baja, Pta. 82 29 50N 116 0W
Bajo Boquete 85 8 49N 82 27W
Bakala 116 6 15N 20 20 E
Baker, Calif., U.S.A. 81 35 16N 116 8W
Baker, Mont., U.S.A. 74 46 22N 104 12W
Baker, Nev., U.S.A. 78 38 59N 114 7W
Baker, Oreg., U.S.A. 78 44 50N 117 55W
Baker Is. 14 0 10N 176 35 E
Baker, L. 65 64 0N 96 0W
Baker Lake 65 64 20N 96 3W
Baker Mt. 63 48 50N 121 49W
Baker's Dozen Is. 36 56 45N 78 45W
Bakersfield, Calif., U.S.A. 81 35 25N 119 0W
Bakersfield, Vt., U.S.A. 71 44 46N 72 48W
Bakhtiari □ 122 32 0N 49 0 E
Bakinskikh Komissarov 122 39 20N 49 15 E
Bakkafjörðr 110 66 2N 14 48W
Bakkagerði 110 65 31N 13 49W
Bakony Forest = Bakony Hegység 107 47 10N 17 30 E
Bakony Hegység 107 47 10N 17 30 E
Bakouma 116 5 40N 22 56 E
Baku 120 40 25N 49 45 E
Bala, Can. 46 45 1N 79 37W
Bala, U.K. 94 52 54N 3 36W
Bala, L. = Tegid, L. 94 52 53N 3 38W
Balabac I. 126 8 0N 117 0 E
Balabac, Selat 126 7 53N 117 5 E
Balabakk 122 34 0N 36 10 E
Balabalangan, Kepulauan 126 2 20 S 117 30 E
Balaghat 124 21 49N 80 12 E
Balaghat Ra. 124 18 50N 76 30 E
Balaguer 104 41 50N 0 50 E
Balakovo 120 52 4N 47 55 E
Balancán 83 17 48N 91 32W
Balasore 125 21 35N 87 3 E
Balaton 107 46 50N 17 40 E
Balboa 84 9 0N 79 30W
Balboa Hill 84 9 6N 79 44W
Balbriggan 97 53 35N 6 10W
Balcarce 88 38 0 S 58 10W
Balcarres 56 50 50N 103 35W
Balchik 109 43 28N 28 11 E
Balclutha 133 46 15 S 169 45 E
Bald Knob 75 35 20N 91 35W
Baldock L. 55 56 33N 97 57W
Baldur 57 49 23N 99 15W
Baldwin, Fla., U.S.A. 72 30 15N 82 10W
Baldwin, Mich., U.S.A. 72 43 54N 85 53W
Baldwinsville 71 43 10N 76 19W
Baleares, Islas 104 39 30N 3 0 E
Balearic Is. = Baleares, Islas 104 39 30N 3 0 E
Baler 127 15 46N 121 34 E
Balfate 84 15 48N 86 25W
Balgonie 56 50 29N 104 16W
Bali □ 126 8 20 S 115 0 E
Bali, I. 126 8 20 S 115 0 E
Bali, Selat 127 8 30 S 114 35 E
Balikesir 122 39 35N 27 58 E
Balikpapan 126 1 10 S 116 55 E
Balimbing 127 5 10N 120 3 E
Baling 128 5 41N 100 55 E
Balintang Chan. 131 19 50N 122 0 E
Balintang Is. 131 19 55N 122 0 E
Balipara 125 26 50N 92 45 E
Baliston Spa 71 43 0N 73 52W
Baliza 87 16 0 S 52 20W
Balkan Mts. = Stara Planina 109 43 15N 23 0 E
Balkan Pen. 93 42 0N 22 0 E
Balkh = Wazirabad 123 36 44N 66 47 E
Balkh □ 123 36 30N 67 0 E
Balkhash 120 46 50N 74 50 E
Balkhash, Ozero 120 40 0N 74 50 E
Balla 125 24 10N 91 35 E
Ballachulish 96 56 40N 5 10W
Balladoran 136 31 52 S 148 39 E
Ballarat 136 37 33 S 143 50 E
Ballard, L. 134 29 20 S 120 10 E
Ballater 96 57 2N 3 2W
Ballenas, Canal de las 82 29 10N 113 45W
Balleny Is. 91 66 30 S 163 0 E
Ballina, Austral. 135 28 50 S 153 31 E
Ballina, Mayo, Ireland 97 54 7N 9 10W
Ballina, Tipp., Ireland 97 52 49N 8 27W
Ballinafad 49 43 42N 80 1W
Ballinasloe 97 53 20N 8 12W
Ballinger 75 31 45N 99 58W
Ballinrobe 97 53 36N 9 13W
Ballinskelligs 97 51 50N 10 17W
Ballinskelligs B. 97 51 46N 10 11W
Ballivian 88 22 41 S 62 10W
Ballycastle 97 55 12N 6 15W
Ballymena 97 54 53N 6 18W
Ballymena □ 97 54 53N 6 18W
Ballymoncy 97 55 5N 6 30W
Ballymoney □ 97 55 5N 6 23W
Ballyshannon 97 54 30N 8 10W
Balmaceda 90 46 0 S 71 50W
Balmertown 52 51 4N 93 41W
Balmoral, Austral. 136 37 15 S 141 48 E
Balmoral, Can. 57 50 15N 97 19W
Balmoral, U.K. 96 57 3N 3 13W
Balmorhea 75 31 2N 103 41W
Balonne, R. 135 28 47 S 147 56 E
Balovale 117 13 30 S 23 15 E
Balpunga 136 33 46 S 141 45 E
Balrampur 125 27 30N 82 20 E
Balranald 136 34 38 S 143 33 E
Balsam 51 43 59N 79 4W
Balsam L. 70 44 35N 78 50W
Balsas 83 18 0N 99 40W
Balsas, R. 82 18 30N 101 20W
Balta 74 48 12N 100 7W
Baltic Sea 111 56 0N 20 0 E
Baltimore, Can. 70 44 2N 78 10W
Baltimore, Ireland 97 51 29N 9 22W
Baltimore, U.S.A. 72 39 18N 76 37W
Baluchistan □ 124 27 30N 65 0 E
Balygychan 121 63 56N 154 12 E
Bam 123 29 7N 58 14 E
Bamako 114 12 34N 7 55W
Bambari 116 5 40N 20 35 E
Bamberg, Ger. 106 49 54N 10 53 E
Bamberg, U.S.A. 73 33 19N 81 1W
Bambili 116 3 40N 26 0 E
Bamfield 62 48 45N 125 10W
Bamian □ 124 35 0N 67 0 E
Bampūr 123 27 15N 60 21 E
Bampur, R. 123 27 20N 59 30 E
Ban Ban 128 19 31N 103 15 E
Ban Bua Chum 128 15 11N 101 12 E
Ban Bua Yai 128 15 33N 102 26 E
Ban Houei Sai 128 20 22N 100 32 E
Ban Kantang 128 7 25N 99 31 E
Ban Khe Bo 128 19 10N 104 39 E
Ban Khun Yuam 128 18 49N 97 57 E
Ban Me Thuot 128 12 40N 108 3 E
Ban Phai 128 16 4N 102 44 E
Ban Takua Pa 128 8 55N 98 25 E
Ban Thateng 128 15 25N 106 27 E
Banadar Daryay Oman □ 123 25 30N 56 0 E
Banadia 86 6 54N 71 49W
Banalia 116 1 32N 25 5 E
Banam 128 11 20N 105 17 E
Bananal, I. do 87 11 30 S 50 30W
Banaras = Varanasi 125 25 22N 83 8 E
Banat □ 107 45 45N 21 15 E
Banbridge 97 54 21N 6 17W
Banbridge □ 97 54 21N 6 16W
Banbury 95 52 4N 1 21W
Banchory 96 57 3N 2 30W
Bancroft 47 45 3N 77 51W
Bancroft = Chililabombwe 117 12 18 S 27 43 E
Band-i-Turkistan, Ra. 123 35 2N 64 0 E
Banda 124 25 30N 80 26 E
Banda Aceh 126 5 35N 95 20 E
Banda Banda, Mt. 136 31 10 S 152 28 E
Banda Elat 127 5 40 S 133 5 E
Banda, Kepulauan 127 4 37 S 129 50 E
Banda, La 88 27 45 S 64 10W
Banda, Punta 82 31 47N 116 50W
Banda Sea 127 6 0 S 130 0 E
Bandar = Masulipatnam 125 16 12N 81 12 E
Bandār 'Abbās 123 [illegible] 15N 56 15 E
Bandar-e Būshehr 123 28 55N 50 55 E
Bandar-e Chārak 123 26 45N 54 20 E
Bandar-e Deylam 122 30 5N 50 10 E
Bandar-e Lengeh 123 26 35N 54 58 E
Bandar-e Ma'shur 122 30 35N 49 10 E
Bandar-e-Nakhīlū 123 26 58N 53 30 E
Bandar-e Rīg 123 29 30N 50 45 E
Bandar-e Shāh 123 37 0N 54 10 E
Bandar-e-Shāhpūr 122 30 30N 49 5 E
Bandar-i-Pahlavi 122 37 30N 49 30 E
Bandar Maharani = Muar 128 2 3N 102 34 E
Bandar Penggaram = Batu Pahat 128 1 50N 102 56 E
Bandar Seri Begawan 126 4 52N 115 0 E
Bandawe 117 11 58 S 34 5 E
Bandeira, Pico da 89 20 26 S 41 47W
Bandera, Argent. 88 28 55 S 62 20W
Bandera, U.S.A. 75 29 45N 99 3W
Banderas, Bahía de 82 20 40N 105 30W
Bandi-San 132 37 36N 140 4 E
Bandirma 122 40 20N 28 0 E
Bandon 97 51 44N 8 45W
Bandon, R. 97 51 40N 8 11W
Bandundu 116 3 15 S 17 22 E
Bandung 127 6 36 S 107 48 E
Banes 85 21 0N 75 42W
Banff, Can. 61 51 10N 115 34W
Banff, U.K. 96 57 40N 2 32W
Banff Nat. Park 61 51 30N 116 15W
Bang Hieng, R. 128 16 24N 105 40 E
Bang Lamung 128 13 3N 100 56 E
Bang Saphan 128 11 14N 99 28 E
Bangala Dam 117 21 7 S 31 25 E
Bangalore 124 12 59N 77 40 E
Bangassou 116 4 55N 23 55 E
Banggai 127 1 40 S 123 30 E
Banggi, P. 126 7 50N 117 0 E
Banghāzī 115 32 11N 20 3 E
Bangil 127 7 36 S 112 50 E
Bangka, Pulau, Celebes, Indon. 127 1 50N 125 5 E
Bangka, Pulau, Sumatera, Indon. 126 2 0 S 105 50 E
Bangka, Selat, Indon. 126 2 30 S 105 30 E
Bangka, Selat, Indon. 126 3 30 S 105 30 E
Bangkalan 127 7 2 S 112 46 E
Bangkinang 126 0 18N 100 5 E
Bangko 126 2 5 S 102 9 E
Bangkok = Krung Thep 128 13 45N 100 31 E
Bangladesh ■ 125 24 0N 90 0 E
Bangor, Me., U.S.A. 35 44 48N 68 42W
Bangor, Mich., U.S.A. 77 42 18N 86 7W
Bangor, Pa., U.S.A. 71 40 51N 75 13W
Bangor, N.I., U.K. 97 54 40N 5 40W
Bangor, Wales, U.K. 94 53 13N 4 9W
Bangued 127 17 40N 120 37 E
Bangui 116 4 23N 18 35 E
Bangweulu, L. 116 11 0 S 30 0 E
Bangweulu Swamp 116 11 20 S 30 15 E
Bani 85 18 16N 70 22W
Bāniyas 122 35 10N 36 0 E
Banja Luka 108 44 49N 17 26 E
Banjak, Kepulauan 126 2 10N 97 10 E
Banjar 127 7 24 S 108 30 E
Banjarmasin 126 3 20 S 114 35 E
Banjarnegara 127 7 24 S 109 42 E
Banjul 114 13 28N 16 40W
Bankipore 125 25 35N 85 10 E
Banks I., B.C., Can. 62 53 20N 130 0W
Banks I., N. W. Terr., Can. 64 73 15N 121 30W
Banks I., P.N.G. 135 10 10 S 142 15 E
Banks Peninsula 133 43 45 S 173 15 E
Bankura 125 23 11N 87 18 E
Bann, R. 97 55 2N 6 35W
Bann R. 97 54 30N 6 31W
Bannalec 100 47 57N 3 42W
Banning, Can. 34 48 44N 91 56W
Banning, U.S.A. 81 33 58N 116 58W
Banningville = Bandundu 116 3 15 S 17 22 E
Bannockburn, Can. 47 44 39N 77 33W
Bannockburn, U.K. 96 56 5N 3 55W
Bannu 124 33 0N 70 18 E
Banon 103 44 2N 5 38 E
Banská Bystrica 107 48 46N 19 14 E
Banská Stiavnica 107 48 25N 18 55 E
Banswara 124 23 32N 74 24 E
Banten 127 6 5 S 106 8 E
Bantry 97 51 40N 9 28W
Bantry, B. 97 51 35N 9 50W
Bantul 127 7 55 S 110 19 E
Banu 124 35 35N 69 5 E
Banyuls 102 42 29N 3 8 E
Banyumas 127 7 32 S 109 18 E
Banyuwangi 127 8 13 S 114 21 E
Banzare Coast 91 66 30 S 125 0 E
Bapatla 125 15 55N 80 30 E
Bapaume 101 50 7N 2 50 E
Baqūbah 122 33 45N 44 50 E
Baquedano 88 23 20 S 69 52W
Bar 109 42 8N 19 8 E
Bar Harbor 35 44 15N 68 20W
Bar-le-Duc 101 48 47N 5 10 E
Bar-sur-Aube 101 48 14N 4 40 E
Bar-sur-Seine 101 48 7N 4 20 E
Barabai 126 2 32 S 115 34 E
Barabinsk 120 55 20N 78 20 E
Baraboo 74 43 28N 89 46W
Barachois-de-Malbaie 38 48 37N 64 17W
Barachois Pond Prov. Park 37 48 28N 58 15W
Baracoa 85 20 20N 74 30W
Baradero 88 33 52 S 59 29W
Baraga 52 46 49N 88 29W
Barahona 85 18 13N 71 7W
Barail Range 125 25 15N 93 20 E
Barakhola 125 25 0N 92 45 E
Baralzon L. 55 60 0N 98 3W
Baramula 124 34 15N 74 20 E
Baran 124 25 9N 76 40 E
Baranoa 86 10 48N 74 55W
Baranof I. 67 57 0N 135 10W
Baranovichi 120 53 10N 26 0 E
Barão de Melgaço 86 11 50 S 60 45W
Barapasi 127 2 15 S 137 5 E
Barat Daya,Kepuluan 127 7 30 S 128 0 E
Barataria B. 75 29 15N 89 45W
Baraya 86 3 10N 75 4W
Barbacena 89 21 15 S 43 56W
Barbacoas, Colomb. 86 1 45N 78 0W
Barbacoas, Venez. 86 9 29N 66 58W
Barbados ■ 85 13 0N 59 30W
Barbara L. 53 49 20N 87 47W
Barbeau Pk. 65 81 54N 75 1W
Barbel, L. 38 51 55N 68 13W
Barberton, S. Afr. 117 25 42 S 31 2 E
Barberton, U.S.A. 70 41 0N 81 40W
Barbourville 73 36 57N 83 52W
Barbuda I. 85 17 30N 61 40W
Barca, La 82 20 20N 102 40W
Barcaldine 135 23 33 S 145 13 E
Barce = Al Marj 115 32 25N 20 40 E
Barcelona, Spain 104 41 21N 2 10 E
Barcelona, Venez. 86 10 10N 64 40W
Barcelonette 103 44 23N 6 40 E
Barcelos 86 1 0 S 63 0W
Barclay 52 49 47N 92 43W
Barcoo, R. 135 28 29 S 137 46 E
Bardai 114 21 25N 17 0 E
Bardas Blancas 88 35 49 S 69 45W
Bardera 115 2 20N 42 27 E
Bardoux, L. 38 51 9N 67 50W
Bardsey, I. 94 52 46N 4 47W
Bardstown 77 37 50N 85 29W
Bareilly 124 28 22N 79 27 E
Barentin 100 49 33N 0 58 E
Barenton 100 48 38N 0 50W
Barents Sea 17 73 0N 39 0 E
Barfleur 100 49 40N 1 17W
Barge, La 78 42 12N 110 4W
Barguzin 121 53 37N 109 37 E
Barham 136 35 36 S 144 8 E
Barhi 125 24 15N 85 25 E
Bari 108 41 6N 16 52 E
Bari Doab 124 30 20N 73 0 E
Baria = Phuoc Le 128 10 39N 107 19 E
Barinas 86 8 36N 70 15W
Barinas □ 86 8 10N 69 50W
Baring 76 40 15N 92 12W
Baring C. 64 70 0N 117 30W
Baringo 116 0 47N 36 16 E
Baringo, L. 116 0 47N 36 16 E
Barinitas 86 8 45N 70 25W
Barisal 125 22 30N 90 20 E
Barisan, Bukit 126 3 30 S 102 15 E
Barito, R. 126 2 50 S 114 50 E
Barjac 103 44 20N 4 22 E
Barjols 103 43 34N 6 2 E
Bark L 47 45 27N 77 51W
Bark L. 34 46 58N 82 25W
Barkah 123 23 40N 58 0 E

Barker **Bédarieux**

Barker 70 43 20N 78 35W
Barkha 129 31 0N 81 10 E
Barkley Sound 62 48 50N 125 10W
Barkly Tableland 135 19 50 S 138 40 E
Barkol 129 43 37N 93 2 E
Barksdale 75 29 47N 100 2W
Barlee, L. 134 29 15 S 119 30 E
Barlee Ra. 134 23 30 S 116 0 E
Barlett 80 36 29N 118 2W
Barletta 108 41 20N 16 17 E
Barlow L. 55 62 00N 103 0W
Barmedman 136 34 9 S 147 21 E
Barmer 124 25 45N 71 20 E
Barmouth 94 52 44N 4 3W
Barnard Castle 94 54 33N 1 55W
Barnaul 120 53 20N 83 40 E
Barne Inlet 91 80 15 S 160 0 E
Barnes Icecap 65 70 0N 73 15W
Barnesville 73 33 6N 84 9W
Barnet, Can. 66 49 17N 122 55W
Barnet, U.K. 95 51 37N 0 15W
Barneveld, Neth. 105 52 7N 5 36 E
Barneveld, U.S.A. 71 43 16N 75 14W
Barneville 100 49 23N 1 46W
Barney, Mt. 135 28 17 S 152 44 E
Barnhart 75 31 10N 101 8W
Barnsley 94 53 33N 1 29W
Barnstaple 95 51 5N 4 3W
Barnston I. 66 49 12N 122 42W
Barnsville 74 46 43N 96 28W
Barnwell 61 49 46N 112 15W
Baro 114 8 35N 6 18 E
Baroda = Vadodara 124 22 20N 73 10 E
Barons 61 50 0N 113 5W
Barpeta 125 26 20N 91 10 E
Barques, Pte. aux 46 44 5N 82 55W
Barquísimeto 86 9 58N 69 13W
Barr 101 48 25N 7 28 E
Barra 87 11 5 S 43 10W
Barra de Navidad 82 19 12N 104 41W
Barra do Corda 87 5 30 S 45 10W
Barra do Piraí 89 22 30 S 43 50W
Barra Falsa, Pta. da 117 22 58 S 35 37 E
Barra Hd. 96 56 47N 7 40W
Barra, I. 96 57 0N 7 30W
Barra Mansa 89 22 35 S 44 12W
Barra, Sd. of 96 57 4N 7 25W
Barrackpur 125 22 44N 88 30 E
Barranca, Lima, Peru 86 10 45 S 77 50W
Barranca, Loreto, Peru 86 4 50 S 76 50W
Barrancabermeja 86 7 0N 73 50W
Barrancas, Colomb. 86 10 57N 72 50W
Barrancas, Venez. 86 8 55N 62 5W
Barrancos 104 38 10N 6 58W
Barranqueras 88 27 30 S 59 0W
Barranquilla, Atlántico, Colomb. 86 11 0N 74 50W
Barranquilla, Vaupés, Colomb. 86 1 39N 72 19W
Barras 86 1 45 S 73 13W
Barraute 40 48 26N 77 38W
Barre 71 44 15N 72 30W
Barreal 88 31 33 S 69 28W
Barreiras 87 12 8 S 45 0W
Barreirinhas 87 2 30 S 42 50W
Barreiro 104 38 40N 9 6W
Barreiros 87 8 49 S 35 12W
Barrême 103 43 57N 6 23 E
Barren I. 128 12 17N 95 50 E
Barren Is. 67 58 45N 152 0W
Barretos 87 20 30 S 48 35W
Barrhead 60 54 10N 114 24W
Barrie 46 44 24N 79 40W
Barriefield 47 44 14N 76 28W
Barrière 63 51 12N 120 7W
Barrington, Austral. 135 31 58 S 151 55 E
Barrington, Can. 43 45 6N 73 35W
Barrington, Ill., U.S.A. 77 42 8N 88 5W
Barrington, R.I., U.S.A. 71 41 43N 71 20W
Barrington L. 55 56 55N 100 15W
Barrington Passage 39 43 30N 65 38W
Barrington Tops. 136 32 6 S 151 28 E
Barrow 67 71 16N 156 50W
Barrow Creek T.O. 134 21 30 S 133 55 E
Barrow I. 134 20 45 S 115 20 E
Barrow-in-Furness 94 54 8N 3 15W
Barrow, Pt. 67 71 22N 156 30W
Barrow Ra. 134 26 0 S 127 40 E
Barrow Strait 65 74 20N 95 0W
Barrows 57 52 50N 101 27W
Barry, U.K. 95 51 23N 3 19W
Barry, U.S.A. 76 39 42N 91 2W
Barry's Bay 47 45 29N 77 41W
Barsi 124 18 10N 75 50 E
Barsoi 125 25 48N 87 57 E
Barstow, Calif., U.S.A. 81 34 58N 117 2W
Barstow, Tex., U.S.A. 87 31 30N 103 25W
Bartica 86 6 25N 58 40W
Bartle Frere, Mt. 135 17 27 S 145 50 E
Bartlesville 75 36 50N 95 58W
Bartlett 75 30 46N 97 30W
Bartlett, L. 54 63 5N 118 20W
Bartletts Harbour 37 50 57N 57 0W
Barton-upon-Humber 94 53 41N 0 27W
Bartonville, Can. 48 43 14N 79 48W
Bartonville, U.S.A. 76 40 39N 89 39W
Bartow 73 27 53N 81 49W
Barú, I. de 86 10 15N 75 35W
Baruun Urt 130 46 46N 113 15 E
Bas-Rhin □ 101 48 40N 7 30 E
Bāsa'idū 123 26 35N 55 20 E
Basankusa 116 1 5N 19 50 E
Bascuñán, C. 88 28 52 S 71 35W
Basel (Basle) 106 47 35N 7 35 E
Bashaw 61 52 35N 112 58W
Bashi Channel 131 21 15N 122 0 E
Bashkir A.S.S.R. □ 120 54 0N 57 0 E
Basilan, I. 127 6 35N 122 0 E
Basilan, Selat 127 6 50N 122 0 E
Basildon 95 51 34N 0 29 E
Basilicata □ 108 40 30N 16 0 E
Basim 124 20 3N 77 0 E
Basin 78 44 22N 108 2W
Basin L. 56 52 38N 105 17W
Basingstoke 95 51 15N 1 5W
Baskatong Res. 34 46 46N 75 50W
Baskerville C. 134 17 10 S 122 15 E
Basle = Basel 106 47 35N 7 35 E
Basoka 116 1 16N 23 40 E
Basongo 116 4 15 S 20 20 E
Basque Provinces = Vascongadas 104 42 50N 2 45W
Basra = Al Basrah 122 30 30N 47 50 E
Bass River 39 45 25N 63 47W
Bass Rock 96 56 5N 2 40W
Bassano 61 50 48N 112 20W
Bassano, del Grappa 108 45 45N 11 45 E
Bassas da India 117 22 0 S 39 0 E
Basse-Terre, I. 85 16 0N 61 40W
Bassée, La 101 50 31N 2 49 E
Bassein 125 16 30N 94 30 E
Basseterre 85 17 17N 62 43W
Bassett, Nebr., U.S.A. 74 42 37N 99 30W
Bassett, Va., U.S.A. 73 36 48N 79 59W
Bassigny 101 48 0N 5 10 E
Bassin-de-la-Chaudière 42 46 44N 71 16W
Basswood L. 52 48 6N 91 52W
Bastak 123 27 15N 54 25 E
Bastar 125 19 25N 81 40 E
Basti 125 26 52N 82 55 E
Bastia 103 42 40N 9 30 E
Bastide, La 102 44 35N 3 55 E
Bastille, L. 38 51 46N 61 11W
Bastion, C. = Chinmu Chiao 131 18 10N 109 35 E
Bastogne 105 50 1N 5 43 E
Bastrop 75 30 5N 97 22W
Bata, Eq. Guin. 116 1 57N 9 50 E
Bata, Rumania 114 46 1N 22 4 E
Bataan 127 14 40N 120 25 E
Bataan Pen. 127 14 38N 120 30 E
Batabanó 84 22 40N 82 20W
Batabanó, G. de 85 22 30N 82 30W
Batac 127 18 3N 120 34 E
Batagoy 121 67 38N 134 38 E
Batalha 104 39 40N 8 50W
Batamay 121 63 30N 129 15 E
Batan I. 131 20 58N 122 5 E
Batan Is. 131 20 25N 121 59 E
Batanes Is. 129 20 30N 122 0 E
Batang 127 6 55 S 109 40 E
Batangafo 116 7 25N 18 20 E
Batangas 127 13 35N 121 10 E
Batanta, I. 127 0 55N 130 40 E
Bataszék 107 46 10N 18 44 E
Batatais 89 20 54 S 47 37W
Batavia, Ind., U.S.A. 77 41 55N 88 17W
Batavia, N.Y., U.S.A. 70 43 0N 78 10W
Batavia, Ohio, U.S.A. 77 39 5N 84 11W
Batchawana B. 53 46 53N 84 30W
Batchawana Bay 53 46 55N 84 37W
Bateman's B. 135 35 40 S 150 12 E
Batemans Bay 136 35 44 S 150 11 E
Batesburg 73 33 54N 81 32W
Batesville, Ark., U.S.A. 75 35 48N 91 40W
Batesville, Ind., U.S.A. 77 39 18N 85 13W
Batesville, Miss., U.S.A. 75 34 17N 89 58W
Batesville, Tex., U.S.A. 75 28 59N 99 38W
Bath, N.B., Can. 39 46 31N 67 36W
Bath, Ont., Can. 47 44 11N 76 47W
Bath, U.K. 95 51 22N 2 22W
Bath, Maine, U.S.A. 35 43 50N 69 49W
Bath, N.Y., U.S.A. 70 42 20N 77 17W
Bathgate, U.K. 96 55 54N 3 38W
Bathgate, U.S.A. 57 48 53N 97 29W
Bathurst, Austral. 136 33 25 S 149 31 E
Bathurst, Can. 35 47 37N 65 43W
Bathurst B. 135 14 16 S 144 25 E
Bathurst, C. 64 70 34N 128 0W
Bathurst, Gambia = Banjul 114 13 28N 16 40W
Bathurst I., Austral. 134 11 30 S 130 10 E
Bathurst I., Can. 65 76 0N 100 30W
Bathurst In. 64 68 10N 108 50W
Bathurst Inlet 64 66 50N 108 1W
Batiscan 41 46 30N 72 15W
Batiscan, L. 41 47 22N 71 55W
Batiscan, R. 41 46 16N 72 15W
Batman 122 37 55N 41 5 E
Batna 114 35 34N 6 15 E
Baton Rouge 75 30 30N 91 5W
Batopilas 82 27 45N 107 45W
Batouri 116 4 30N 14 25 E
Battambang 128 13 7N 103 12 E
Batticaloa 124 7 43N 81 45 E
Battle, Can. 61 52 58N 110 52W
Battle, U.K. 95 50 55N 0 30 E
Battle Creek 77 42 20N 85 6W
Battle Ground 80 45 47N 122 32W
Battle Harbour 36 52 16N 55 35W
Battle Lake 74 46 20N 95 43W
Battle Mountain 78 40 45N 117 0W
Battle, R. 56 52 43N 108 15W
Battleford 56 52 45N 108 15W
Batu Gajah 128 4 28N 101 3 E
Batu, Kepulauan 126 0 30 S 98 25 E
Batu, Mt. 115 6 55N 39 45 E
Batu Pahat 128 1 50N 102 56 E
Batuata, P. 127 6 30 S 122 20 E
Batulaki 127 5 40N 125 30 E
Batumi 120 41 30N 41 30 E
Baturaja 126 4 11 S 104 15 E
Baturité 87 4 28 S 38 45W
Baturité, Serra de 87 4 25 S 39 0W
Baubau 127 5 25 S 123 50 E
Bauchi 114 10 22N 9 48 E
Baud 100 47 52N 3 1W
Baudette 52 48 46N 94 35W
Baugé 100 47 31N 0 8W
Bauld, C. 37 51 38N 55 26W
Baule, La 100 47 18N 2 23W
Baume les Dames 101 47 22N 6 22 E
Bauru 89 22 10 S 49 0W
Baús 87 18 22 S 52 47W
Bautzen 106 51 11N 14 25 E
Baux, Les 103 43 45N 4 51 E
Bavaria = Bayern 106 49 7N 11 30 E
Bavispe, R. 82 29 30N 109 11W
Baw Baw, Mt. 136 37 49 S 146 19 E
Bawdwin 125 23 5N 97 50 E
Bawean 126 5 46 S 112 35 E
Bawku 114 11 3N 0 19W
Bawlake 125 19 11N 97 21 E
Bawlf 61 52 55N 112 28W
Baxley 73 31 43N 82 23W
Baxter, Iowa, U.S.A. 76 41 49N 93 9W
Baxter, Minn., U.S.A. 52 46 20N 94 16W
Baxter Springs 75 37 3N 94 45W
Bay Bulls 37 47 19N 52 50W
Bay City, Mich., U.S.A. 46 43 35N 83 51W
Bay City, Oreg., U.S.A. 78 45 45N 123 58W
Bay City, Tex., U.S.A. 75 28 59N 95 55W
Bay de Verde 37 48 5N 52 54W
Bay, Laguna de 127 14 20N 121 11 E
Bay L'Argent 37 47 33N 54 54W
Bay Port 46 43 51N 83 23W
Bay Roberts 37 47 36N 53 16W
Bay St. Louis 75 30 18N 89 22W
Bay Shore 71 40 44N 73 15W
Bay Springs 75 31 58N 89 18W
Bay View 133 39 25 S 176 50 E
Bayamo 84 20 20N 76 40W
Bayamón 85 18 24N 66 10W
Bayan 130 47 20N 107 55 E
Bayan Agt 130 48 32N 101 16 E
Bayan Kara Shan 129 34 0N 98 0 E
Bayan-Ovoo 130 47 55N 112 0 E
Bayan-Uul 130 49 6N 112 12 E
Bayanaul 120 50 45N 75 45 E
Bayandalay 130 43 30N 103 29 E
Bayandelger 130 47 45N 108 7 E
Bayantsogt 130 47 58N 105 1 E
Bayanzürh 130 47 48N 107 15 E
Bayard 74 41 48N 103 17W
Baybay 127 10 40N 124 55 E
Bayburt 122 40 15N 40 20 E
Bayern □ 106 49 7N 11 30 E
Bayeux 100 49 17N 0 42W
Bayfield, Can. 46 43 34N 81 42W
Bayfield, U.S.A. 52 46 50N 90 48W
Bayir 122 30 45N 36 55 E
Baykal, Oz. 121 53 0N 108 0 E
Baykit 121 61 50N 95 50 E
Baykonur 120 47 48N 65 50 E
Bayombong 127 16 30N 121 10 E
Bayon 101 48 30N 6 20 E
Bayonne 102 43 30N 1 28W
Bayovar 86 5 50 S 81 0W
Bayram-Ali 120 37 37N 62 10 E
Bayreuth 106 49 56N 11 35 E
Bayrūt 115 33 53N 35 31 E
Bays, L. of 46 45 15N 79 4W
Bayside 47 44 7N 77 30W
Baysville 46 45 9N 79 7W
Bayt Lahm 115 31 43N 35 12 E
Baytown 75 29 42N 94 57W
Baza 104 37 30N 2 47W
Bazaruto, I. do 117 21 40 S 35 28 E
Bazas 102 44 27N 0 13W
Bazin, R. 40 47 29N 75 22W
Beach 74 46 57N 104 0W
Beach City 70 40 38N 81 35W
Beach Grove 66 49 2N 123 3W
Beachburg 47 45 44N 76 51W
Beachville 46 43 5N 80 49W
Beachy Head 95 50 44N 0 16 E
Beacon 71 41 32N 73 58W
Beaconia 57 50 25N 96 31W
Beaconsfield, Austral. 135 41 11 S 146 48 E
Beaconsfield, Can. 44 45 26N 73 50W
Beagle, Canal 90 55 0 S 68 30W
Beale, C. 62 48 47N 125 13W
Bealey 133 43 2 S 171 36 E
Beamsville 70 43 12N 79 28W
Bear I. 97 51 38N 9 50W
Bear I. (Nor.) 17 74 30N 19 0 E
Bear L., Alta., Can. 60 55 9N 119 4W
Bear L., B.C., Can. 54 56 10N 126 52W
Bear L., Man., Can. 55 55 8N 96 0W
Bear L., Ont., Can. 70 45 28N 79 34W
Bear L., U.S.A. 78 42 0N 111 20W
Bear, R. 80 38 56N 121 36W
Bear River 39 44 34N 65 39W
Bearcreek 78 45 11N 109 6W
Beardmore 53 49 36N 87 57W
Beardmore Glacier 91 84 30 S 170 0 E
Beardstown 76 40 0N 90 25W
Bearhaven 97 51 40N 9 54W
Béarn, Can. 40 47 17N 79 20W
Béarn, France 102 43 28N 0 36W
Bearpaw Mt. 78 48 15N 109 55W
Bearskin Lake 34 53 58N 91 2W
Beata, C. 85 17 40N 71 30W
Beata, I. 85 17 34N 71 31W
Beatrice 74 40 20N 96 40W
Beatrice, C. 135 14 20 S 136 55 E
Beatton, R. 54 56 15N 120 45W
Beatton River 54 57 26N 121 20W
Beatty, Can. 56 52 54N 104 48W
Beatty, U.S.A. 80 36 58N 116 46W
Beattyville 77 37 35N 83 42W
Beaucaire 103 43 48N 4 39 E
Beauce, Plaines de 101 48 10N 1 45 E
Beauceville 41 46 13N 70 46W
Beauchêne, L. 40 46 35N 78 55W
Beaufort, Austral. 136 37 25 S 143 25 E
Beaufort, Malay. 126 5 30N 115 40 E
Beaufort, N.C., U.S.A. 73 34 45N 76 40W
Beaufort, S.C., U.S.A. 73 32 25N 80 40W
Beaufort Sea 64 72 0N 140 0W
Beaufort-West 117 32 18 S 22 36 E
Beaugency 101 47 47N 1 38 E
Beauharnois 44 45 20N 73 52W
Beauharnois □ 44 45 15N 74 0W
Beauharnois, Canal de 44 45 19N 73 54W
Beaujeu 103 46 10N 4 35 E
Beaujolais 103 46 0N 4 25 E
Beaulac 41 45 50N 71 23W
Beaulieu, Can. 42 46 51N 71 8W
Beaulieu, France 103 46 41N 1 37W
Beaulieu, R. 54 62 3N 113 11W
Beauly 96 57 29N 4 27W
Beauly, R. 96 57 26N 4 28W
Beaumaris 94 53 16N 4 7W
Beaumetz-les-Loges 101 50 15N 2 40 E
Beaumont, Alta., Can. 60 53 21N 113 25W
Beaumont, Newf., Can. 37 49 37N 55 41W
Beaumont, Qué., Can. 42 46 50N 71 1W
Beaumont, France 102 44 45N 0 46 E
Beaumont, Calif., U.S.A. 81 33 56N 116 58W
Beaumont, Tex., U.S.A. 75 30 5N 94 8W
Beaumont-le-Roger 100 49 4N 0 47 E
Beaumont-sur-Oise 101 49 9N 2 17 E
Beaune 101 47 2N 4 50 E
Beaune-la-Rolande 101 48 4N 2 25 E
Beauport 42 46 52N 71 11W
Beaupré 41 47 3N 70 54W
Beauséjour 57 50 5N 96 35W
Beausset, Le 103 43 10N 5 46 E
Beauvais 101 49 25N 2 8 E
Beauval 55 55 9N 107 37W
Beauvoir, Deux Sèvres, France 102 46 12N 0 30W
Beauvoir, Vendée, France 100 46 55N 2 1W
Beaver, Alaska, U.S.A. 67 66 20N 147 30W
Beaver, Okla., U.S.A. 75 36 52N 100 31W
Beaver, Pa., U.S.A. 70 40 40N 80 18W
Beaver, Utah, U.S.A. 79 38 20N 112 45W
Beaver Brook Station 39 47 8N 65 36W
Beaver City 74 40 13N 99 50W
Beaver Creek 64 63 0N 141 0W
Beaver Dam 74 43 28N 88 50W
Beaver Falls 70 40 44N 80 20W
Beaver I. 46 45 40N 85 31W
Beaver, R. 54 59 52N 124 20W
Beaver, R 34 55 55N 87 48W
Beaver, R. 55 55 26N 107 45W
Beaverdell 63 49 27N 119 6W
Beaverhill L., Alta., Can. 60 53 27N 112 32W
Beaverhill L., Man., Can. 55 54 5N 94 50W
Beaverhill L., N.W.T., Can. 55 63 2N 111 22W
Beaverlodge 60 55 11N 119 29W
Beavermouth 63 51 32N 117 23W
Beaverstone, R. 34 54 59N 89 25W
Beaverton, Can. 46 44 26N 79 9W
Beaverton, Mich., U.S.A. 46 43 53N 84 29W
Beaverton, Oreg., U.S.A. 80 45 29N 122 48W
Beaverville 77 40 57N 87 39W
Beawar 124 26 3N 74 18 E
Bebedouro 89 21 0 S 48 25W
Beccles 95 52 27N 1 33 E
Bečej 109 45 36N 20 3 E
Béchar 114 31 38N 2 18 E
Becharof L. 67 58 0N 156 30W
Bechuanaland = Botswana 117 23 0 S 24 0 E
Beckley 72 37 50N 81 8W
Bécon 100 47 30N 0 50W
Bédarieux 102 43 37N 3 10 E

Bédarrides **Beuil**

Place	Page	Lat.	Long.
Bédarrides	**103**	44 2N	4 54 E
Beddington Cr.	**59**	51 9N	114 3W
Bedford, N.S., Can.	**39**	44 44N	63 40W
Bedford, Qué., Can.	**43**	45 7N	72 59W
Bedford, S. Afr.	**117**	32 40 S	26 10 E
Bedford, U.K.	**95**	52 8N	0 29W
Bedford, Ind., U.S.A.	**77**	38 50N	86 30W
Bedford, Iowa, U.S.A.	**76**	40 40N	94 41W
Bedford, Ky., U.S.A.	**77**	38 36N	85 19W
Bedford, Ohio, U.S.A.	**70**	41 23N	81 32W
Bedford, Pa., U.S.A.	**70**	40 1N	78 30W
Bedford, Va., U.S.A.	**72**	37 25N	79 30W
Bedford □	**95**	52 4N	0 28W
Bedford Basin	**39**	44 42N	63 38W
Bedford, C.	**135**	15 14 S	145 21 E
Bednesti	**54**	53 50N	123 10W
Bedourie	**135**	24 30 S	139 30 E
Beebe Plain	**41**	45 1N	72 9W
Beech Forest	**136**	38 37 S	143 37 E
Beech Fork, R.	**77**	37 55N	85 50W
Beech Grove	**77**	39 40N	86 2W
Beecher	**77**	41 21N	87 38W
Beechey Hd.	**63**	48 10N	123 30W
Beechey Point	**67**	70 27N	149 18W
Beechworth	**136**	36 22 S	146 43 E
Beechy	**56**	50 53N	107 24W
Beemunnel	**136**	31 40 S	147 51 E
Be'er Sheva'	**115**	31 15N	34 48 E
Beeston	**94**	52 55N	1 11W
Beeton	**46**	44 5N	79 47W
Beetz, L.	**38**	50 34N	62 42W
Beeville	**75**	28 27N	97 44W
Befale	**116**	0 25N	20 45 E
Befandriana	**117**	21 55 S	44 0 E
Bega	**136**	36 41 S	149 51 E
Béhagle = Lai	**114**	9 25N	16 30 E
Behara	**117**	24 55 S	46 20 E
Behbehan	**122**	30 30N	50 15 E
Behshahr	**123**	36 45N	53 35 E
Beilen	**105**	52 52N	6 27 E
Beira	**117**	19 50 S	34 52 E
Beira-Alta	**104**	40 35N	7 35W
Beira-Baixa	**104**	40 2N	7 30W
Beira-Litoral	**104**	40 5N	8 30W
Beirut = Bayrūt	**115**	33 53N	35 31 E
Beiseker	**61**	51 23N	113 32W
Beitbridge	**117**	22 12 S	30 0 E
Beja	**104**	38 2N	7 53W
Béjaïa	**114**	36 42N	5 2 E
Bejestān	**123**	34 30N	58 5 E
Bekasi	**127**	6 20 S	107 0 E
Békéscsaba	**107**	46 40N	21 10 E
Bekok	**128**	2 20N	103 7 E
Bela, India	**125**	25 50N	82 0 E
Bela, Pak.	**124**	26 12N	66 20 E
Bela Crkva	**109**	44 55N	21 27 E
Bela Vista, Brazil	**89**	22 12 S	56 20W
Bela Vista, Mozam.	**117**	26 10 S	32 44 E
Bélâbre	**102**	46 34N	1 8 E
Bélair	**42**	46 51N	71 26W
Bélanger	**44**	45 36N	73 43W
Belanger, R.	**57**	53 27N	97 41W
Belawan	**126**	3 33N	98 32 E
Belaya Tserkov	**120**	49 45N	30 10 E
Belbutte	**56**	53 22N	107 49W
Belcher, C.	**17**	75 0N	160 0W
Belcher Chan.	**65**	77 15N	95 0W
Belcher Is.	**36**	56 15N	78 45W
Belcourt	**40**	48 24N	77 21W
Belden	**80**	40 2N	121 17W
Belém (Pará)	**87**	1 20 S	48 30W
Belén, Argent.	**88**	27 40 S	67 5W
Belén, Colomb.	**86**	1 26N	75 56W
Belén, Parag.	**88**	23 30 S	57 6W
Belen	**79**	34 40N	106 50W
Bélesta	**102**	42 55N	1 56 E
Belfair	**80**	47 27N	122 50W
Belfast, S. Afr.	**117**	25 42 S	30 2 E
Belfast, U.K.	**97**	54 35N	5 56W
Belfast, Maine, U.S.A.	**35**	44 30N	69 0W
Belfast, N.Y., U.S.A.	**70**	42 21N	78 9W
Belfast □	**97**	54 35N	5 56W
Belfast, L.	**97**	54 40N	5 50W
Belfield	**74**	46 54N	103 11W
Belfort	**101**	47 38N	6 50 E
Belfort □	**101**	47 38N	6 52 E
Belfountain	**49**	43 48N	80 1W
Belfry	**78**	45 10N	109 2W
Belgaum	**124**	15 55N	74 35 E
Belgium ■	**105**	51 30N	5 0 E
Belgorod	**120**	50 35N	36 35 E
Belgrade	**78**	45 50N	111 10W
Belgrade = Beograd	**109**	44 50N	20 37 E
Belhaven	**73**	35 34N	76 35W
Beli Drim, R.	**109**	42 25N	20 34 E
Belinga	**116**	1 10N	13 2 E
Belinyu	**126**	1 35 S	105 50 E
Belitung, P.	**126**	3 10 S	107 50 E
Belize ■	**83**	17 0N	88 30W
Belize City	**83**	17 25N	88 0W
Belize Inlet	**62**	51 8N	127 20W
Bell I., Newf., Can.	**37**	47 38N	52 58W
Bell I., Newf., Can.	**37**	50 46N	55 35W
Bell Irving, R.	**54**	56 12N	129 5W
Bell L.	**52**	49 48N	90 58W
Bell Peninsula	**65**	63 50N	82 0W
Bell, R.	**40**	49 48N	77 38W
Bell Ville	**88**	32 40 S	62 40W
Bella Bella	**62**	52 10N	128 10W
Bella Coola	**62**	52 25N	126 40W
Bella Unión	**88**	30 15 S	57 40W
Bella Vista, Corrientes, Argent.	**88**	28 33 S	59 0W
Bella Vista, Tucuman, Argent.	**88**	27 10 S	65 25W
Bellaire, Mich., U.S.A.	**46**	44 59N	85 13W
Bellaire, Ohio, U.S.A.	**70**	40 1N	80 46W
Bellary	**124**	15 10N	76 56 E
Bellburns	**37**	50 20N	57 32W
Belle	**76**	38 17N	91 43W
Belle Fourche	**74**	44 43N	103 52W
Belle Fourche, R.	**74**	44 25N	105 0W
Belle Glade	**73**	26 43N	80 38W
Belle-Ile	**100**	47 20N	3 10W
Belle Isle	**37**	51 57N	55 25W
Belle-Isle-en-Terre	**100**	48 33N	3 23W
Belle Isle, Str. of	**37**	51 30N	56 30W
Belle, La, Fla., U.S.A.	**73**	26 45N	81 22W
Belle, La, Mo., U.S.A.	**76**	40 7N	91 55W
Belle Plaine, Iowa, U.S.A.	**76**	41 51N	92 18W
Belle Plaine, Minn., U.S.A.	**74**	44 35N	93 48W
Belle Rive	**77**	38 14N	88 45W
Belle River	**46**	42 18N	82 43W
Belle Rivière	**44**	45 37N	74 6W
Belle-Vallée	**43**	45 4N	73 26W
Bellechasse□	**42**	46 47N	71 14W
Belledonne	**103**	45 11N	6 0 E
Belledune	**35**	47 55N	65 50W
Bellefontaine	**77**	40 20N	83 45W
Bellefonte	**70**	40 56N	77 45W
Bellegarde, Ain, France	**103**	46 4N	5 49 E
Bellegarde, Creuse, France	**101**	45 59N	2 19 E
Bellegarde, Loiret, France	**101**	48 0N	2 26 E
Belleoram	**37**	47 31N	55 25W
Bellerive	**43**	45 15N	74 10W
Belleterre	**40**	47 25N	78 41W
Belleville, Can.	**47**	44 10N	77 23W
Belleville, Rhône, France	**103**	46 7N	4 45 E
Belleville, Vendée, France	**100**	46 48N	1 28W
Belleville, Ill., U.S.A.	**77**	38 30N	90 0W
Belleville, Kans., U.S.A.	**74**	39 51N	97 38W
Belleville, N.Y., U.S.A.	**71**	43 46N	76 10W
Bellevue, Can.	**61**	49 35N	114 22W
Bellevue, Idaho, U.S.A.	**78**	43 25N	144 23W
Bellevue, Iowa, U.S.A.	**76**	42 16N	90 26W
Bellevue, Mich., U.S.A.	**77**	42 27N	85 1W
Bellevue, Ohio, U.S.A.	**70**	41 20N	82 48W
Bellevue, Pa., U.S.A.	**70**	40 29N	80 3W
Bellevue, Wash., U.S.A.	**80**	47 37N	122 12W
Belley	**103**	45 46N	5 41 E
Bellflower	**76**	39 0N	91 21W
Bellin (Payne Bay)	**36**	60 0N	70 0W
Bellingham	**80**	48 45N	122 27W
Bellingshausen Sea	**91**	66 0 S	80 0W
Bellinzona	**106**	46 11N	9 1 E
Belliveau Cove	**39**	44 23N	66 4W
Bello	**86**	6 20N	75 33W
Bellona Reefs	**135**	21 26 S	159 0 E
Bellows Falls	**71**	43 10N	72 30W
Bells Corners	**48**	45 19N	75 50W
Bellsite	**57**	52 35N	101 4W
Belluno	**108**	46 8N	12 6 E
Bellville, Ohio, U.S.A.	**70**	40 38N	82 32W
Bellville, Tex., U.S.A.	**75**	29 58N	96 18W
Bellwood	**70**	40 36N	78 21W
Belly, R.	**61**	49 46N	113 2W
Belmar	**71**	40 10N	74 2W
Bélmez	**104**	38 17N	5 17W
Belmond	**76**	42 51N	93 37W
Belmont, Austral.	**136**	33 4 S	151 42 E
Belmont, Man., Can.	**57**	49 25N	99 27W
Belmont, N.S., Can.	**39**	45 25N	63 23W
Belmont, Ont., Can.	**46**	42 53N	81 5W
Belmont, U.S.A.	**70**	42 14N	78 3W
Belmont Park	**63**	48 27N	123 27W
Belmonte	**87**	16 0 S	39 0W
Belmopan	**83**	17 18N	88 30W
Belmullet	**97**	54 13N	9 58W
Belo Horizonte	**87**	19 55 S	43 56W
Belo-sur-Tsiribihana	**117**	19 40 S	43 30 E
Beloeil	**45**	45 34N	73 12W
Belogorsk	**121**	51 0N	128 20 E
Beloit, Kans., U.S.A.	**74**	39 32N	98 9W
Beloit, Wis., U.S.A.	**76**	42 35N	89 0W
Belomorsk	**120**	64 35N	34 30 E
Belonia	**125**	23 15N	91 30 E
Belot, L.	**64**	66 53N	126 16W
Belovo	**120**	54 30N	86 0 E
Beloye Ozero	**120**	45 15N	46 50 E
Belozersk	**120**	60 0N	37 30 E
Belterra	**87**	2 45 S	55 0W
Belton, S.C., U.S.A.	**73**	34 31N	82 39W
Belton, Tex., U.S.A.	**75**	31 4N	97 30W
Belturbet	**97**	54 6N	7 28W
Belukha	**120**	49 50N	86 50 E
Beluran	**126**	5 48N	117 35 E
Belvès	**102**	44 46N	1 0 E
Belvidere, Ill., U.S.A.	**77**	42 15N	88 55W
Belvidere, N.J., U.S.A.	**71**	40 48N	75 5W
Belwood	**49**	43 47N	80 19W
Belwood, L.	**49**	43 46N	80 20W
Belyando, R.	**135**	21 38 S	146 50 E
Belyj Jar	**120**	58 26N	84 39 E
Belyy, Ostrov	**120**	73 30N	71 0 E
Belzoni	**75**	33 12N	90 30W
Bement	**77**	39 55N	88 34W
Bemidji	**74**	47 30N	94 50W
Ben Cruachan, Mt.	**96**	56 26N	5 8W
Ben Dearg, mt.	**96**	56 54N	3 49W
Ben Hope, mt.	**96**	58 24N	4 36W
Ben Lawers, mt.	**96**	56 33N	4 13W
Ben Lomond	**135**	41 38 S	147 42 E
Ben Lomond, mt.	**96**	56 12N	4 39W
Ben Macdhui	**96**	57 4N	3 40W
Ben Mhor	**96**	57 16N	7 21W
Ben More, Mull, U.K.	**96**	56 26N	6 2W
Ben More, Perth, U.K.	**96**	56 23N	4 31W
Ben More Assynt	**96**	58 7N	4 51W
Ben Nevis, mt.	**96**	56 48N	5 0W
Ben Vorlich, Strathclyde, U.K.	**96**	56 17N	4 47W
Ben Vorlich, Tayside, U.K.	**96**	56 22N	4 15W
Ben Wyvis, mt.	**96**	57 40N	4 35W
Bena	**52**	47 19N	94 8W
Bena Dibele	**116**	4 4 S	22 50 E
Benalla	**136**	36 30 S	146 0 E
Benambra, Mt.	**136**	36 31 S	147 34 E
Benares = Varanasi	**125**	25 22N	83 8 E
Benavides	**75**	27 35N	98 28W
Benbecula, I.	**96**	57 26N	7 21W
Bencubbin	**134**	30 48 S	117 52 E
Bend	**78**	44 2N	121 15W
Bendale	**50**	43 46N	79 14W
Bender Beila	**115**	9 30N	50 48 E
Bendigo	**136**	36 40 S	144 15 E
Bénestroff	**101**	48 54N	6 45 E
Benet	**102**	46 22N	0 35W
Benevento	**108**	41 7N	14 45 E
Benfeld	**101**	48 22N	7 34 E
Bengal, Bay of	**125**	15 0N	00 90 E
Bengawan Solo	**127**	7 5 S	112 25 E
Benghazi = Banghāzī	**115**	32 11N	20 3 E
Bengkalis	**126**	1 30N	102 10 E
Bengkulu	**126**	3 50 S	102 12 E
Bengkulu □	**126**	3 48 S	102 16 E
Bengough	**56**	49 25N	105 10W
Benguela	**117**	12 37 S	13 25 E
Beni	**116**	0 30N	29 27 E
Beni, R.	**86**	10 30 S	66 0W
Benî Suêf	**115**	29 5N	31 6 E
Beniah L.	**54**	63 23N	112 17W
Benicia	**80**	38 3N	122 9W
Benidorm	**104**	38 33N	0 9W
Benin ■	**114**	10 0N	2 0 E
Benin, Bight of	**114**	5 0N	3 0 E
Benin City	**114**	6 20N	5 31 E
Benjamin Aceval	**88**	24 58 S	57 34W
Benjamin Constant	**86**	4 40 S	70 15W
Benjamin Hill	**82**	30 10N	111 10W
Benkelman	**74**	40 7N	101 32W
Bennett	**67**	59 56N	134 53W
Bennettsville	**73**	34 38N	79 39W
Bennington	**71**	42 52N	73 12W
Benny	**46**	46 47N	81 38W
Benoa	**126**	8 50 S	115 20 E
Bénodet	**100**	47 53N	4 7W
Benoit's Cove	**37**	49 1N	58 7W
Benoni	**117**	26 11 S	28 18 E
Benque Viejo	**83**	17 5N	89 8W
Benson, Can.	**56**	49 27N	103 1W
Benson, U.S.A.	**79**	31 59N	110 19W
Bent	**123**	26 20N	59 25 E
Benteng	**127**	6 10 S	120 30 E
Bentinck I.	**135**	17 3 S	139 35 E
Bentley	**61**	52 28N	114 4W
Bento Gonçalves	**89**	29 10 S	51 31W
Benton, Ark., U.S.A.	**75**	34 30N	92 35W
Benton, Calif., U.S.A.	**80**	37 48N	118 32W
Benton, Ill., U.S.A.	**76**	38 0N	88 55W
Benton Harbor	**77**	42 10N	86 28W
Bentong	**128**	3 31N	101 55 E
Benue, R.	**114**	7 50N	6 30 E
Beo	**127**	4 25N	126 50 E
Beograd	**109**	44 50N	20 37 E
Beowawe	**78**	40 45N	116 30W
Beppu	**132**	33 15N	131 30 E
Berber	**115**	18 0N	34 0 E
Berbera	**115**	10 30N	45 2 E
Berbérati	**116**	4 15N	15 40 E
Berbice, R.	**86**	5 20N	58 10W
Berck-sur-Mer	**101**	50 25N	1 36 E
Berdsk	**120**	54 47N	83 2 E
Berea, Kentucky, U.S.A.	**72**	37 35N	84 18W
Berea, Ohio, U.S.A.	**70**	41 21N	81 50W
Berebere	**127**	2 25N	128 45 E
Berens I.	**57**	52 18N	97 18W
Berens, R.	**57**	52 25N	96 55W
Berens River	**57**	52 25N	97 0W
Beresford	**39**	47 42N	65 42W
Bereziuk, L.	**36**	54 0N	76 18W
Berezniki	**120**	59 24N	56 46 E
Berezovo	**120**	64 0N	65 0 E
Bergama	**122**	39 8N	27 15 E
Bérgamo	**108**	45 42N	9 40 E
Bergen, Norway	**111**	60 23N	5 20 E
Bergen, U.S.A.	**70**	43 5N	77 56W
Bergen-Binnen	**105**	52 40N	4 43 E
Bergen-op-Zoom	**105**	51 30N	4 18 E
Bergerac	**102**	44 51N	0 30 E
Bergisch-Gladbach	**105**	50 59N	7 9 E
Bergland	**52**	46 35N	89 34W
Bergues	**101**	50 58N	2 24 E
Bergum	**105**	53 13N	5 59 E
Berhala, Selat	**126**	1 0 S	104 15 E
Berhampore	**125**	24 2N	88 27 E
Berhampur	**125**	19 15N	84 54 E
Bering Sea	**14**	58 0N	167 0 E
Bering Str.	**67**	66 0N	170 0W
Beringovskiy	**121**	63 3N	179 19 E
Berisso	**88**	34 40 S	58 0W
Berja	**104**	36 50N	2 56W
Berkeley	**80**	37 52N	122 20W
Berkeley Springs	**72**	39 38N	78 12W
Berkner I.	**91**	79 30 S	50 0W
Berkshire □	**95**	51 30N	1 20W
Berkshire Downs	**95**	51 30N	1 30W
Berlaar	**105**	51 7N	4 39 E
Berland, R.	**60**	54 0N	116 50W
Berlin, Ger.	**106**	52 32N	13 24 E
Berlin, Md., U.S.A.	**72**	38 19N	75 12W
Berlin, N.H., U.S.A.	**71**	44 29N	71 10W
Bermejo, R., Formosa, Argent.	**88**	26 30 S	58 50W
Bermejo, R., San Juan, Argent.	**88**	30 0 S	68 0W
Bermen, L.	**36**	53 35N	68 55W
Bermuda, I.	**10**	32 45N	65 0W
Bern (Berne)	**106**	46 57N	7 28 E
Bernalillo	**79**	35 17N	106 37W
Bernam, R.	**128**	3 45N	101 5 E
Bernard L.	**46**	45 45N	79 23W
Bernardo de Irigoyen	**89**	26 15 S	53 40W
Bernasconi	**88**	37 55 S	63 44W
Bernay	**100**	49 5N	0 35 E
Bernburg	**106**	51 40N	11 42 E
Berne	**77**	40 39N	84 57W
Berne = Bern	**106**	46 57N	7 28 E
Bernier B.	**65**	71 5N	88 15W
Bernier I.	**134**	24 50 S	113 12 E
Bernierville	**41**	46 6N	71 34W
Beroroha	**117**	21 40 S	45 10 E
Beroun	**106**	49 57N	14 5 E
Berowra	**136**	33 35 S	151 12 E
Berre	**103**	43 28N	5 11 E
Berre, Étang de	**103**	43 27N	5 5 E
Berrien Springs	**77**	41 57N	86 20W
Berrigan	**136**	35 38 S	145 49 E
Berry, France	**101**	47 0N	2 0 E
Berry, U.S.A.	**77**	38 31N	84 23W
Berry Cr.	**61**	50 50N	111 37W
Berry Is.	**84**	25 40N	77 50W
Berryessa, L.	**80**	38 31N	122 6W
Berryville	**75**	36 23N	93 35W
Berthaund	**74**	40 21N	105 5W
Berthierville	**41**	46 5N	73 10W
Berthold	**74**	48 19N	101 45W
Bertincourt	**101**	50 5N	2 58 E
Bertoua	**116**	4 30N	13 45 E
Bertrand, Can.	**39**	47 45N	65 4W
Bertrand, U.S.A.	**74**	40 35N	99 38W
Berufjörður	**110**	64 48N	14 29W
Berwick, N.B., Can.	**39**	45 47N	65 36W
Berwick, N.S., Can.	**39**	45 3N	64 44W
Berwick, U.S.A.	**71**	41 4N	76 17W
Berwick-upon-Tweed	**94**	55 47N	2 0W
Berwyn	**60**	56 9N	117 44W
Berwyn Mts.	**94**	52 54N	3 26W
Besalampy	**117**	16 43 S	44 29 E
Besançon	**101**	47 9N	6 0 E
Besar	**126**	2 40 S	116 0 E
Beserah	**128**	3 50N	103 21 E
Besnard L.	**55**	55 25N	106 0W
Bessèges	**103**	44 18N	4 8 E
Bessemer	**74**	46 27N	90 0W
Bessin	**100**	49 21N	1 0W
Bessines-sur-Gartempe	**100**	46 6N	1 22 E
Bet She'an	**115**	32 30N	35 30 E
Bete Grise B.	**53**	47 26N	87 53W
Bethanien	**117**	26 31 S	17 8 E
Bethany, Can.	**47**	44 11N	78 34W
Bethany, Ill., U.S.A.	**77**	39 39N	88 45W
Bethany, Mo., U.S.A.	**76**	40 18N	94 0W
Bethel, Alaska, U.S.A.	**67**	60 50N	161 50W
Bethel, Ohio, U.S.A.	**77**	38 58N	84 5W
Bethel, Pa., U.S.A.	**70**	40 20N	80 2W
Bethel, Vt., U.S.A.	**71**	43 50N	72 37W
Bethesda	**50**	43 58N	79 21W
Bethlehem, S. Afr.	**117**	28 14 S	28 18 E
Bethlehem, U.S.A.	**71**	40 39N	75 24W
Bethlehem = Bayt Lahm	**115**	31 43N	35 12 E
Bethulie	**117**	30 30 S	25 59 E
Bethune	**56**	50 43N	105 13W
Béthune	**101**	50 30N	2 38 E
Béthune, R.	**100**	49 56N	1 5 E
Betijoque	**86**	9 23N	70 44W
Betioky	**117**	23 48 S	44 20 E
Beton Bazoches	**101**	48 42N	3 15 E
Betong	**128**	5 45N	101 5 E
Betroka	**117**	23 16 S	46 0 E
Betsiamites	**41**	48 56N	68 40W
Betsiamites, R.	**41**	48 56N	68 38W
Bettendorf	**76**	41 32N	90 30W
Bettiah	**125**	26 48N	84 33 E
Bettles	**67**	66 54N	150 50W
Betul	**124**	21 48N	77 59 E
Betung	**126**	2 0 S	103 10 E
Beuil	**103**	44 6N	7 0 E

Beulah Blåvands Huk

Beulah, Can. 55 50 16N 101 02W
Beulah, U.S.A. 74 47 18N 101 47W
Beverley, Austral. 134 32 9S 116 56E
Beverley, U.K. 94 53 52N 0 26W
Beverly, Can. 54 53 36N 113 21W
Beverly, Mass., U.S.A. 71 42 32N 70 50W
Beverly, Wash., U.S.A. 78 46 55N 119 59W
Beverly Hills 81 34 4N 118 29W
Beverwijk 105 52 28N 4 38E
Bevin, L. 43 45 57N 74 35W
Bewdley 47 44 5N 78 19W
Beynat 102 45 8N 1 44E
Beyneu 120 45 10N 55 3E
Beypazarı 122 40 10N 31 48E
Beyşehir Gölü 122 37 40N 31 45E
Bezhitsa 120 53 19N 34 17E
Béziers 102 43 20N 3 12E
Bezwada = Vijayawada 125 16 31N 80 39E
Bhachau 124 23 20N 70 16E
Bhadrakh 125 21 10N 86 30E
Bhadravati 124 13 49N 76 15E
Bhagalpur 125 25 10N 87 0E
Bhakra Dam 124 31 30N 76 45E
Bhamo 125 24 15N 97 15E
Bhandara 124 21 5N 79 42E
Bhanrer Ra. 124 23 40N 79 45E
Bharat = India 124 24 0N 78 0E
Bharatpur 124 27 15N 77 30E
Bhatpara 125 22 50N 88 25E
Bhaunagar = Bhavnagar 124 21 45N 72 10E
Bhavnagar 124 21 45N 72 10E
Bhawanipatna 125 19 55N 83 30E
Bhilsa = Vidisha 124 23 28N 77 53E
Bhilwara 124 25 25N 74 38E
Bhima, R. 124 17 20N 76 30E
Bhimvaram 125 16 30N 81 30E
Bhind 124 26 30N 78 46E
Bhiwandi 124 19 15N 73 0E
Bhiwani 124 28 50N 76 9E
Bhola 125 22 45N 90 35E
Bhopal 124 23 20N 77 53E
Bhubaneswar 125 20 15N 85 50E
Bhuj 124 23 15N 69 49E
Bhusaval 124 21 15N 69 49E
Bhutan ■ 125 27 25N 89 50E
Biafra, B. of = Bonny, Bight of 116 3 30N 9 20E
Biak 127 1 0S 136 0E
Biała Podlaska 107 52 4N 23 6E
Białystok 107 53 10N 23 10E
Biaro 127 2 5N 125 26E
Biarritz 102 43 29N 1 33W
Bibby I. 55 61 55N 93 0W
Biberach 106 48 5N 9 49E
Bic 41 48 20N 68 41W
Bic, Île du 41 48 24N 68 52W
Bicester 95 51 53N 1 9W
Biche, L. la 60 54 50N 112 3W
Biche, La, R. 54 59 57N 123 50W
Bickerton West 39 45 6N 61 44W
Bicknell, Ind., U.S.A. 77 38 50N 87 20W
Bicknell, Utah, U.S.A. 79 38 16N 111 35W
Bida 114 9 3N 5 58E
Bidar 124 17 55N 77 35E
Biddeford 35 43 30N 70 28W
Bideford 95 51 1N 4 13W
Bidor 128 4 6N 101 15E
Bié Plateau 117 12 0S 16 0E
Bieber 78 41 4N 121 6W
Biel (Bienne) 106 47 8N 7 14E
Bielé Karpaty 107 49 5N 18 0E
Bielefeld 106 52 2N 8 31E
Biella 108 45 33N 8 3E
Bielsko-Biała 107 49 50N 19 8E
Bien Hoa 128 10 57N 106 49E
Bienfait 56 49 10N 102 50W
Bienne = Biel 106 47 8N 7 14E
Bienville, L. 36 55 5N 72 40W
Big B. 36 55 43N 60 35W
Big Bar Creek 63 51 12N 122 7W
Big Basswood L. 46 46 25N 83 23W
Big Bay 53 46 49N 87 44W
Big Bear City 81 34 16N 116 51W
Big Bear L. 81 34 15N 116 56W
Big Beaver 56 49 10N 105 10W
Big Beaver House 34 52 59N 89 50W
Big Belt Mts. 78 46 50N 111 30W
Big Bend Nat. Park 75 29 15N 103 15W
Big Bend Res. 61 52 59N 115 30W
Big Black, R. 75 32 35N 90 30W
Big Blue, R., Ind., U.S.A. 77 39 12N 85 56W
Big Blue, R., Kans., U.S.A. 74 40 20N 96 40W
Big Cr. 63 51 42N 122 41W
Big Creek, Can. 63 51 43N 123 2W
Big Creek, U.S.A. 80 37 11N 119 14W
Big Cypress Swamp 73 26 12N 81 10W
Big Delta 67 64 15N 145 0W
Big Falls 52 48 11N 93 48W
Big Fork 52 47 45N 93 39W
Big Fork, R. 52 48 31N 93 43W
Big Horn 78 46 11N 107 25W
Big Horn Dam 61 52 20N 116 20W
Big Horn Mts. = Bighorn Mts. 78 44 30N 107 30W
Big Horn R. 78 45 30N 108 10W
Big I., N.W.T., Can. 65 62 43N 70 43W
Big I., Ont., Can. 52 49 9N 94 40W
Big L. 59 53 37N 113 42W
Big Lake 75 31 12N 101 25W
Big Moose 71 43 49N 74 58W
Big Muddy L. 56 49 9N 104 51W
Big Muddy, R 76 38 0N 89 0W
Big Muddy, R. 74 48 25N 104 45W
Big Pine 80 37 12N 118 17W
Big Piney 78 42 32N 110 3W
Big Pond 39 45 57N 60 32W
Big Quill L. 56 51 55N 104 22W
Big, R., Can. 36 54 50N 58 55W
Big, R., U.S.A. 76 38 27N 90 37W
Big Rapids 72 43 42N 85 27W
Big Rideau L. 47 44 40N 76 15W
Big River 56 53 50N 107 0W
Big Run 70 40 57N 78 55W
Big Sable Pt. 72 44 5N 86 30W
Big Salmon 67 61 50N 136 0W
Big Sand L. 55 57 45N 99 45W
Big Sandy 78 48 12N 110 9W
Big Sandy Cr. 74 38 52N 103 11W
Big Sandy L., Can. 56 54 27N 104 6W
Big Sandy L., U.S.A. 52 46 45N 93 20W
Big Sioux, R. 74 44 20N 96 53W
Big Snowy Mt. 78 46 50N 109 15W
Big Spring 75 32 10N 101 25W
Big Springs 74 41 4N 102 3W
Big Stone City 74 45 20N 96 30W
Big Stone Gap 73 36 52N 82 45W
Big Stone L. 74 45 30N 96 35W
Big Sur 80 36 15N 121 48W
Big Trout L., Ont., Can. 34 53 40N 90 0W
Big Trout L., Ont., Can. 47 45 46N 78 37W
Big Valley 61 52 2N 112 46W
Biganos 102 44 39N 0 59W
Bigfork 78 48 3N 114 2W
Biggar 56 52 4N 108 0W
Biggs 80 39 24N 121 43W
Bighorn Mts. 78 44 30N 107 30W
Bigniba, R. 40 49 18N 77 20W
Bigot, L. 38 50 50N 65 39W
Bigsby I 52 49 4N 94 34W
Bigstick L. 56 50 16N 109 20W
Bigstone L. 57 53 42N 95 44W
Bigtimber 78 45 53N 110 0W
Bihać 108 44 49N 15 57E
Bihar 125 25 5N 85 40E
Bihar □ 125 25 0N 86 0E
Bihé Plateau 117 12 0S 16 0E
Bihor, Munţii 107 46 29N 22 47E
Bijagós, Arquipélago dos 114 11 15N 16 10W
Bijapur, Mad. P., India 125 18 50N 80 50E
Bijapur, Mysore, India 124 16 50N 75 55E
Bijār 122 35 52N 47 35E
Bijeljina 109 44 46N 19 17E
Bijnor 124 29 27N 78 11E
Bikaner 124 28 2N 73 18E
Bikin 121 46 50N 134 20E
Bikini, atoll 14 12 0N 167 30E
Bikoro 116 0 48S 18 15E
Bilād Banī Bū 'Alt 123 22 0N 59 20E
Bilara 124 26 14N 73 53E
Bilaspur 125 22 2N 82 15E
Bilauk Taungdan 128 13 0N 99 0E
Bilbao 104 43 16N 2 56W
Bíldudalur 110 65 41N 23 36W
Bilecik 122 40 5N 30 5E
Bilibino 121 68 3N 166 20E
Bilir 121 65 40N 131 20E
Bill 74 43 18N 105 18W
Billabong Creek 136 35 5S 144 2E
Billingham 94 54 36N 1 18W
Billings 78 45 43N 108 29W
Billiton Is = Belitung 126 3 10S 107 50E
Billom 102 45 43N 3 20E
Bilma 114 18 50N 13 30E
Biloxi 75 30 30N 89 0W
Bima 127 8 22S 118 49E
Bimberi Peak, mt. 136 35 44S 148 51E
Bimbo 116 4 15N 18 33E
Bina-Etawah 124 24 13N 78 14E
Binalbagan 127 10 12N 122 50E
Binalong 136 34 40S 148 39E
Binatang 126 2 10N 111 40E
Binbrook 49 43 7N 79 48W
Binche 105 50 26N 4 10E
Bindura 117 17 18S 31 18E
Bingen 105 49 57N 7 53E
Bingerville 114 5 18N 3 49W
Bingham 35 45 5N 69 50W
Bingham Canyon 78 40 31N 112 10W
Binghamton 71 42 9N 75 54W
Bingöl 122 39 20N 41 0E
Binh Dinh = An Nhon 128 13 55N 109 7E
Binh Son 128 15 20N 108 40E
Binjai 126 3 50N 98 30E
Binnaway 136 31 28S 149 24E
Binongko 127 5 55S 123 55E
Binscarth 57 50 37N 101 17W
Bint 123 26 22N 59 25E
Bintan 126 1 0N 104 0E
Bintulu 126 3 10N 113 0E
Binzert = Bizerte 114 37 15N 9 50E
Bío-Bío □ 88 37 35S 72 0W
Bir 124 19 0N 75 54E
Bir Mogreïn, (Fort Trinquet) 114 25 10N 11 25W
Bira 127 2 3S 132 2E
Birch Cliff, Ont., Can. 49 43 41N 79 18W
Birch Cliff, Ont., Can. 50 43 41N 79 17W
Birch Cove 39 44 42N 63 41W
Birch Hills 56 52 59N 105 25W
Birch I. 57 52 26N 99 54W
Birch Island 63 51 37N 119 54W
Birch L., Alta., Can. 60 53 19N 111 35W
Birch L., N.W.T., Can. 54 62 4N 116 33W
Birch L., Ont., Can. 52 51 23N 92 18W
Birch L., Sask., Can. 56 53 27N 108 10W
Birch L., U.S.A. 52 47 48N 91 43W
Birch Manor 48 45 26N 75 46W
Birch Mts. 54 57 30N 113 10W
Birch River 57 52 24N 101 6W
Birch Run 46 43 15N 83 48W
Birchip 136 35 56S 142 55E
Birchy Bay 37 49 21N 54 44W
Bird 55 56 30N 94 13W
Bird City 74 39 48N 101 33W
Bird Cove 37 51 3N 56 56W
Bird I. 135 22 10S 155 28E
Birds 77 38 50N 87 40W
Birds Hill 58 49 59N 97 0W
Birdseye 77 38 19N 86 42W
Birdsville 135 25 51S 139 20E
Birdum 134 15 39S 133 13E
Birecik 122 37 0N 38 0E
Bireuen 126 5 14N 96 39E
Birigui 89 21 18S 50 16W
Birjand 123 32 57N 59 10E
Birken 63 50 28N 122 37W
Birkenhead 94 53 24N 3 1W
Bîrlad 107 46 15N 27 38E
Birmingham, U.K. 95 52 30N 1 55W
Birmingham, U.S.A. 46 42 33N 83 15W
Birmingham, Ala., U.S.A. 73 33 31N 86 50W
Birmingham, Iowa, U.S.A. 76 40 53N 91 57W
Birmitrapur 125 22 30N 84 10E
Birobidzhan 121 48 50N 132 50E
Biron 38 48 12N 66 16W
Birr 97 53 7N 7 55W
Birsay 56 51 6N 106 59W
Birsk 120 55 25N 55 30E
Birtle 57 50 30N 101 5W
Birur 124 13 30N 75 55E
Bisa 127 1 10S 127 40E
Bisbee 79 31 30N 110 0W
Biscay, B. of 12 45 0N 2 0W
Biscayne B. 73 25 40N 80 12W
Bischwiller 101 48 41N 7 50E
Biscoe I. 91 66 0S 67 0W
Biscostasing 53 47 18N 82 9W
Biscotasi L. 53 47 22N 82 1W
Biscucuy 86 9 22N 69 59W
Bishop, Calif., U.S.A. 80 37 20N 118 26W
Bishop, Tex., U.S.A. 75 27 35N 97 49W
Bishop Auckland 94 54 40N 1 40W
Bishop, Mt. 66 49 26N 122 56W
Bishop's Falls 37 49 2N 55 30W
Bishop's Stortford 95 51 52N 0 11E
Bishopton 41 45 35N 71 35W
Biskra 114 34 50N 5 44E
Bislig 127 8 15N 126 27E
Bismarck, Can. 49 43 3N 79 30W
Bismarck, Mo., U.S.A. 76 37 46N 90 38W
Bismarck, N.Dak., U.S.A. 74 46 49N 100 49W
Bismarck Arch. 14 2 30S 150 0E
Bison 74 45 34N 102 28W
Bison L. 60 57 12N 116 8W
Bispfors 110 63 1N 16 39E
Bissagos = Bijagós 114 11 15N 16 10W
Bissau 114 11 45N 15 45W
Bissett 57 51 2N 95 41W
Bistcho L. 54 59 45N 118 50W
Bistrița 107 47 9N 24 35E
Bistrița, R. 107 47 10N 24 30E
Bitam 116 2 5N 11 25E
Bitche 101 48 58N 7 25E
Bitlis 122 38 20N 42 3E
Bitola (Bitolj) 109 41 5N 21 10E
Bitter Creek 78 41 39N 108 36W
Bitter L. 56 50 7N 109 48W
Bitterfontein 117 31 0S 18 32E
Bittern L., Alta., Can. 61 53 3N 113 5W
Bittern L., Sask., Can. 56 53 56N 105 45W
Bitteroot, R. 78 46 30N 114 20W
Bitterroot Range 78 46 0N 114 20W
Bitterwater 80 36 23N 121 0W
Bitumount 54 57 26N 111 40W
Biu 114 10 40N 12 3E
Biwa-Ko 132 35 15N 135 45E
Biwabik 74 47 33N 92 19W
Biysk 120 52 40N 85 0E
Bizard, Île 44 45 29N 73 54W
Bizerte (Binzert) 114 37 15N 9 50E
Bjargtangar 110 65 30N 24 30W
Bjelovar 108 45 56N 16 49E
Bjorkdale 56 52 43N 103 39W
Blache, L. de la 41 50 5N 69 29W
Black B. 52 48 40N 88 25W
Black Creek 62 49 49N 125 7W
Black Diamond 61 50 45N 114 14W
Black Hills 74 44 0N 103 50W
Black Horse 49 43 59N 79 49W
Black I. 57 51 12N 96 30W
Black L., Can. 55 59 12N 105 15W
Black L., U.S.A. 46 45 28N 84 15W
Black Lake 41 46 1N 71 22W
Black Mesa, Mt. 75 36 57N 102 55W
Black Mt. 66 49 23N 123 13W
Black Mt. = Mynydd Du 95 51 45N 3 45W
Black Mts. 95 51 52N 3 5W
Black Pines 63 50 57N 120 15W
Black, R., Can. 46 44 42N 79 19W
Black, R., Ark., U.S.A. 75 36 15N 90 45W
Black, R., Mich., U.S.A. 46 43 3N 82 37W
Black, R., Minn., U.S.A. 52 48 32N 93 51W
Black, R., N.Y., U.S.A. 71 43 59N 76 40W
Black, R., Wis., U.S.A. 74 44 18N 90 52W
Black Range, Mts. 79 33 30N 107 55W
Black River, Jamaica 84 18 0N 77 50W
Black River, U.S.A. 46 44 53N 83 18W
Black Rock Pt. 36 60 2N 64 10W
Black Sea 92 43 30N 35 0E
Black Sturgeon L. 52 49 20N 88 53W
Black Sugarloaf, Mt. 136 31 18S 151 35E
Black Warrior, R. 73 33 0N 87 45W
Blackall 135 24 25S 145 45E
Blackball 133 42 22S 171 26E
Blackburn 94 53 44N 2 30W
Blackburn Hamlet 48 45 26N 75 33W
Blackburn, Mt. 67 61 5N 142 3W
Blackduck 52 47 43N 94 32W
Blackfalds 61 52 23N 113 47W
Blackfoot, Can. 60 53 17N 110 10W
Blackfoot, U.S.A. 78 43 13N 112 12W
Blackfoot, R. 78 47 0N 113 35W
Blackhead 37 47 32N 52 39W
Blackhead Road 37 47 33N 52 43W
Blackheath 49 43 4N 79 49W
Blackie 61 50 36N 113 37W
Blackmud Cr. 59 53 27N 113 33W
Blackpool, Can. 43 45 1N 73 28W
Blackpool, U.K. 94 53 48N 3 3W
Blackriver 70 44 46N 83 17W
Blacks Harbour 39 45 3N 66 49W
Blacksburg 72 37 17N 80 23W
Blacksod B. 97 54 6N 10 0W
Blackstone 72 37 6N 78 0W
Blackstone, R. 54 61 5N 122 55W
Blackstone Ra. 134 26 00S 129 00E
Blackville 39 46 44N 65 50W
Blackwater 54 53 20N 123 0W
Blackwater, R., Cork, Ireland 97 52 5N 9 3W
Blackwater, R., Limerick, Ireland 97 51 55N 7 50W
Blackwater, R., Meath, Ireland 97 53 46N 7 0W
Blackwater, R., U.K. 97 54 31N 6 35W
Blackwater, R., U.S.A. 76 38 59N 92 59W
Blackwell 75 36 55N 97 20W
Blackwells Corner 81 35 37N 119 47W
Bladworth 56 51 22N 106 8W
Blaenau Ffestiniog 94 53 0N 3 57W
Blagnac 102 43 38N 1 24E
Blagoveshchensk 121 50 20N 127 30E
Blaine 66 48 59N 122 43W
Blaine Lake 56 52 51N 106 52W
Blainville, Can. 44 45 40N 73 52W
Blainville, France 101 48 33N 6 23E
Blair, Can. 49 43 23N 80 23W
Blair, U.S.A. 74 41 38N 96 10W
Blair Athol 135 22 42S 147 31E
Blair Atholl 96 56 46N 3 50W
Blairgowrie 96 56 36N 3 20W
Blairmore 61 49 40N 114 25W
Blairs Mills 70 40 17N 77 45W
Blairsden 80 39 47N 120 37W
Blairsville 70 40 27N 79 15W
Blairville 49 43 14N 79 2W
Blake Pt. 52 48 12N 88 27W
Blakely 73 31 22N 85 0W
Blakesburg 76 40 58N 92 38W
Blâmont 101 48 35N 6 50E
Blanc, Le 102 46 37N 1 3E
Blanc, Mont 103 45 48N 6 50E
Blanca, Bahía 90 39 10S 61 30W
Blanca Peak 79 37 35N 105 29W
Blanchard 75 35 8N 97 40W
Blanchardville 76 42 48N 89 52W
Blanche L., S. Austral., Austral. 134 29 15S 139 40E
Blanche L., W. Austral., Austral. 135 22 25S 123 17E
Blanche, R. 48 45 30N 75 33W
Blanchester 77 39 17N 83 59W
Blanco 75 30 7N 98 30W
Blanco, C., C. Rica 84 9 34N 85 8W
Blanco, C., Peru 86 4 10S 81 10W
Blanco, C., U.S.A. 78 42 50N 124 40W
Blanco, R. 88 31 54S 69 42W
Blanda 110 65 20N 19 40W
Blandford Forum 95 50 52N 2 10W
Blanding 79 37 35N 109 30W
Blandinsville 76 40 33N 90 52W
Blankenberge 105 51 20N 3 9E
Blanquefort 102 44 55N 0 38W
Blanquilla, La 86 11 51N 64 37W
Blanquillo 89 32 53S 55 37W
Blantyre 117 15 45S 35 0E
Blarney 97 51 57N 8 35W
Blåvands Huk 111 55 33N 8 4E

Bowden **Bruce Crossing**

Bowden	**61**	51 55N	114 2W
Bowdle	**74**	45 30N	99 40W
Bowen	**135**	20 0S	148 16E
Bowen Island	**63**	49 23N	123 20W
Bowie, Ariz., U.S.A.	**79**	32 15N	109 30W
Bowie, Tex., U.S.A.	**75**	33 33N	97 50W
Bowland, Forest of	**94**	54 0N	2 30W
Bowling Green, Ky., U.S.A.	**72**	37 0N	86 25W
Bowling Green, Mo., U.S.A.	**76**	39 21N	91 12W
Bowling Green, Ohio, U.S.A.	**77**	41 22N	83 40W
Bowling Green, C.	**135**	19 19S	147 25E
Bowman	**74**	46 12N	103 21W
Bowman, I.	**91**	65 0S	104 0E
Bowman L.	**52**	51 10N	91 25W
Bowmanville	**47**	43 55N	78 41W
Bowmore	**96**	55 45N	6 18W
Bowness	**59**	51 5N	114 10W
Bowral	**136**	34 26S	150 27E
Bowron Lake Prov. Park	**63**	53 10N	121 5W
Bowron, R.	**63**	54 3N	121 50W
Bowser	**62**	49 27N	124 40W
Bowser L.	**54**	56 30N	129 30W
Bowsman	**57**	52 14N	101 12W
Bowstring L.	**52**	47 34N	93 52W
Bowyer I.	**66**	49 26N	123 16W
Boxelder Creek	**78**	47 20N	108 30W
Boxtel	**105**	51 36N	5 9E
Boyacá □	**86**	5 30N	72 30W
Boyce	**75**	31 25N	92 39W
Boyd L.	**36**	52 46N	76 42W
Boyer-Nord, R.	**42**	46 44N	70 58W
Boyer, R., Alta., Can.	**54**	58 27N	115 57W
Boyer, R., Qué., Can.	**42**	46 53N	70 52W
Boyer-Sud, R.	**42**	46 44N	70 58W
Boyle, Can.	**60**	54 35N	112 49W
Boyle, Ireland	**97**	53 58N	8 19W
Boylston	**39**	45 26N	61 30W
Boyne	**49**	43 29N	79 50W
Boyne City	**46**	45 13N	85 1W
Boyne, R.	**97**	53 40N	6 34W
Boynton Beach	**73**	26 31N	80 3W
Bozeman	**78**	45 40N	111 0W
Bozouls	**102**	44 28N	2 43E
Bozoum	**116**	6 25N	16 35E
Brabant □	**105**	50 46N	4 30E
Brabant L.	**55**	55 58N	104 5W
Brač	**108**	43 20N	16 40E
Bracadale, L.	**96**	57 20N	6 30W
Bracciano, L. di	**108**	42 8N	12 11E
Bracebridge	**46**	45 2N	79 19W
Brach	**114**	27 31N	14 20E
Bracieux	**101**	47 30N	1 30E
Bräcke	**110**	62 45N	15 26E
Bracken	**56**	49 11N	108 6W
Brackendale	**63**	49 48N	123 8W
Brackenridge	**70**	40 38N	79 44W
Brackettville	**75**	29 21N	100 20W
Brad	**107**	46 10N	22 50E
Braddock	**70**	40 24N	79 51W
Bradenton	**73**	27 25N	82 35W
Bradford, Can.	**46**	44 7N	79 34W
Bradford, U.K.	**94**	53 47N	1 45W
Bradford, Ill., U.S.A.	**76**	41 11N	89 39W
Bradford, Ohio, U.S.A.	**77**	40 8N	84 27W
Bradford, Pa., U.S.A.	**70**	41 58N	78 41W
Bradford, Vt., U.S.A.	**71**	43 59N	72 9W
Bradley, Ark., U.S.A.	**75**	33 7N	93 39W
Bradley, Calif., U.S.A.	**80**	35 52N	120 48W
Bradley, Ill., U.S.A.	**77**	41 9N	87 52W
Bradley, S.D., U.S.A.	**74**	45 10N	97 40W
Bradore Bay	**37**	51 27N	57 18W
Bradshaw	**135**	15 21S	130 16E
Bradwell	**56**	51 57N	106 14W
Brady	**75**	31 8N	99 25W
Braedale	**49**	43 8N	79 14W
Braeside	**47**	45 28N	76 24W
Braga	**104**	41 35N	8 25W
Bragado	**88**	35 2S	60 27W
Bragança, Brazil	**87**	1 0S	47 2W
Bragança, Port.	**104**	41 48N	6 50W
Bragança Paulista	**89**	22 55S	46 32W
Bragg Creek	**61**	50 57N	114 35W
Brahmanbaria	**125**	23 50N	91 15E
Brahmani, R.	**125**	21 0N	85 15E
Brahmaputra, R.	**125**	26 30N	93 30E
Brahmaur	**124**	32 28N	76 32E
Braich-y-Pwll	**94**	52 47N	4 46W
Braidwood	**136**	35 27S	149 49E
Brăila	**107**	45 19N	27 59E
Brainerd	**52**	46 20N	94 10W
Braintree, U.K.	**95**	51 53N	0 34E
Braintree, U.S.A.	**71**	42 11N	71 0W
Bralorne	**63**	50 50N	123 45W
Bramalea	**50**	43 44N	79 43W
Brampton	**50**	43 45N	79 45W
Branch	**37**	46 53N	53 57W
Branchton	**49**	43 18N	80 15W
Branco, R.	**86**	0 0	61 15W
Brandenburg, Ger.	**106**	52 24N	12 33E
Brandenburg, U.S.A.	**77**	38 0N	86 10W
Brandon, Can.	**57**	49 50N	99 57W
Brandon, U.S.A.	**71**	43 48N	73 4W
Brandon B.	**97**	52 17N	10 8W
Brandon, Mt.	**97**	52 15N	10 15W
Brandsen	**88**	35 10S	58 15W
Brandvlei	**117**	30 25S	20 30E
Branford	**71**	41 15N	72 48W
Braniewo	**107**	54 25N	19 50E
Bransfield Str.	**91**	63 0S	59 0W
Brańsk	**107**	52 45N	22 50E
Branson, Colo., U.S.A.	**75**	37 4N	103 53W
Branson, Mo., U.S.A.	**75**	36 40N	93 18W
Brant □	**49**	43 10N	80 20W
Brantford	**49**	43 10N	80 15W
Brantôme	**102**	45 22N	0 39E
Brantville	**39**	47 22N	64 58W
Bras d'or, L.	**39**	45 50N	60 50W
Brasiléia	**86**	11 0S	68 45W
Brasília	**87**	15 47S	47 55E
Braşov	**107**	45 38N	25 35E
Brasschaat	**105**	51 19N	4 27E
Brassey, Barisan	**126**	5 0N	117 15E
Brasstown Bald, Mt.	**73**	34 54N	83 45W
Bratislava	**106**	48 10N	17 7E
Bratsk	**121**	56 10N	101 30E
Brattleboro	**71**	42 53N	72 37W
Braunschweig	**106**	52 17N	10 28E
Brava	**115**	1 20N	44 8E
Bravo del Norte, R.	**82**	30 30N	105 0W
Brawley	**81**	32 58N	115 30W
Bray	**97**	53 12N	6 6W
Bray, Pays de	**101**	49 15N	1 40E
Bray-sur-Seine	**101**	48 25N	3 14E
Braymer	**76**	39 35N	93 48W
Brazeau, R.	**61**	52 55N	115 14W
Brazil	**77**	39 32N	87 8W
Brazil ■	**86**	5 0N	20 0W
Brazilian Highlands	**87**	18 0S	46 30W
Brazo Sur, R.	**88**	25 30S	58 0W
Brazos, R.	**75**	30 30N	96 20W
Brazzaville	**116**	4 9S	15 12E
Brčko	**109**	44 54N	18 46E
Breadalbane	**96**	56 30N	4 15W
Breaksea Sd.	**133**	45 35S	166 35E
Bream Bay	**133**	35 56S	174 28E
Bream Head	**133**	35 51S	174 36E
Breas	**88**	25 29S	70 24W
Brebes	**127**	6 52S	109 3E
Brechin, Can.	**46**	44 32N	79 10W
Brechin, U.K.	**96**	56 44N	2 40W
Breckenridge, Colo., U.S.A.	**78**	39 30N	106 2W
Breckenridge, Mich., U.S.A.	**46**	43 24N	84 29W
Breckenridge, Minn., U.S.A.	**74**	46 20N	96 36W
Breckenridge, Mo., U.S.A.	**76**	39 46N	93 48W
Breckenridge, Tex., U.S.A.	**75**	32 48N	98 55W
Breckland	**98**	52 30N	0 40E
Brecon	**95**	51 57N	3 23W
Brecon Beacons	**95**	51 53N	3 27W
Breda	**105**	51 35N	4 45E
Bredasdorp	**117**	34 33S	20 2E
Bredenbury	**57**	50 57N	102 3W
Bregenz	**106**	47 30N	9 45E
Bréhal	**100**	48 53N	1 30W
Bréhat, I. de	**100**	48 51N	3 0W
Breiðafjörður	**110**	65 15N	23 15W
Breil	**103**	43 56N	7 31E
Bremen	**106**	53 4N	8 47E
Bremerhaven	**106**	53 34N	8 35E
Bremerton	**80**	47 30N	122 38W
Brenham	**75**	30 5N	96 27W
Brenner Pass	**106**	47 0N	11 30E
Brent, Can.	**47**	46 2N	78 29W
Brent, U.K.	**95**	51 33N	0 18W
Brentwood	**59**	51 7N	114 9W
Bréscia	**108**	45 33N	10 13E
Breslau	**49**	43 28N	80 25W
Breslau = Wrocław.	**106**	51 5N	17 5E
Bresle, R.	**100**	50 4N	1 21E
Bresles	**101**	49 25N	2 13E
Bressanone	**108**	46 43N	11 40E
Bressay I.	**96**	60 10N	1 5W
Bresse, La	**101**	48 0N	6 53E
Bresse, Plaine de	**101**	46 50N	5 10E
Bressuire	**100**	46 51N	0 30W
Brest, France	**100**	48 24N	4 31W
Brest, U.S.S.R.	**120**	52 10N	23 40E
Bretagne	**100**	48 0N	3 0W
Bretçu	**107**	46 7N	26 18E
Breteuil, Eur, France	**100**	48 50N	0 53E
Breteuil, Oise, France	**101**	49 38N	2 18E
Breton	**61**	53 7N	114 28W
Breton, Le, L.	**38**	51 53N	60 9W
Breton, Pertuis	**102**	46 17N	1 25W
Breton Sd.	**75**	29 40N	89 12W
Brett, C.	**133**	35 10S	174 20E
Brevard	**73**	35 19N	82 42W
Brevort	**46**	46 2N	85 2W
Brewer	**35**	44 43N	68 50W
Brewer, Mt.	**80**	36 44N	118 28W
Brewster, N.Y., U.S.A.	**71**	41 23N	73 37W
Brewster, Wash., U.S.A.	**78**	48 10N	119 51W
Brewster, Kap	**17**	70 7N	22 0W
Brewton	**73**	31 9N	87 2W
Bria	**116**	6 30N	21 58E
Briançon	**103**	44 54N	6 39E
Briare	**101**	47 38N	2 45E
Bribie I.	**135**	27 0S	152 58E
Brickaville	**117**	18 49S	49 4E
Bricon	**101**	48 5N	5 0E
Briçonnet, L.	**38**	51 27N	60 10W
Bricquebec	**100**	49 29N	1 39W
Bridge River	**54**	50 50N	122 40W
Bridgehampton	**71**	40 56N	72 19W
Bridgeman	**77**	41 57N	86 33W
Bridgend	**95**	51 30N	3 35W
Bridgenorth	**47**	44 23N	78 23W
Bridgeport, B.C., Can.	**66**	49 12N	123 8W
Bridgeport, Ont., Can.	**46**	43 29N	80 29W
Bridgeport, Calif., U.S.A.	**80**	38 14N	119 15W
Bridgeport, Conn., U.S.A.	**71**	41 12N	73 12W
Bridgeport, Mich., U.S.A.	**46**	43 22N	83 53W
Bridgeport, Nebr., U.S.A.	**74**	41 42N	103 10W
Bridgeport, Tex., U.S.A.	**75**	33 15N	97 45W
Bridger	**78**	45 20N	108 58W
Bridgeton	**72**	39 29N	75 10W
Bridgetown, Austral.	**134**	33 58S	116 7E
Bridgetown, Barbados	**85**	13 0N	59 30W
Bridgetown, Can.	**39**	44 55N	65 18W
Bridgeview Survey	**48**	43 18N	79 54W
Bridgewater, Can.	**39**	44 25N	64 31W
Bridgewater, Mass., U.S.A.	**71**	41 59N	70 56W
Bridgewater, S.D., U.S.A.	**74**	43 34N	97 29W
Bridgewater, C.	**136**	38 23S	141 23E
Bridgnorth	**95**	52 33N	2 25W
Bridgton	**71**	44 5N	70 41W
Bridgwater	**95**	51 7N	3 0W
Bridlington	**94**	54 6N	0 11W
Bridport	**95**	50 43N	2 45W
Brie-Comte-Robert	**101**	48 40N	2 35E
Brie, Plaine de	**101**	48 35N	3 10E
Briec	**100**	48 6N	4 0W
Brienne-le-Château	**101**	48 24N	4 30E
Brienon	**101**	48 0N	3 35E
Briercrest	**56**	50 10N	105 16W
Briey	**101**	49 14N	5 57E
Brig	**106**	46 18N	7 59E
Brigg	**94**	53 33N	0 30W
Briggsdale	**74**	40 40N	104 20W
Brigham City	**78**	41 30N	112 1W
Brighouse	**66**	49 10N	123 8W
Bright	**136**	36 42S	146 56E
Brighton, Can.	**47**	44 2N	77 44W
Brighton, U.K.	**95**	50 50N	0 9W
Brighton, Colo., U.S.A.	**74**	39 59N	104 50W
Brighton, Ill., U.S.A.	**76**	39 2N	90 8W
Brighton, Iowa, U.S.A.	**76**	41 10N	91 49W
Brighton, Pa., U.S.A.	**70**	40 42N	80 19W
Brightsand L.	**56**	53 36N	108 53W
Brignogan-Plage	**100**	48 40N	4 20W
Brignoles	**103**	43 25N	6 5E
Brilliant, Can.	**63**	49 19N	117 38W
Brilliant, U.S.A.	**70**	40 15N	80 39W
Brimfield	**76**	40 50N	89 53W
Brimley	**46**	46 25N	84 41W
Brimstone	**49**	43 48N	80 0W
Brindisi	**109**	40 39N	17 55E
Brinkley	**75**	34 55N	91 15W
Brinnon	**80**	47 41N	122 54W
Brion I.	**39**	47 46N	61 26W
Brionne	**100**	49 11N	0 43E
Brioude	**102**	45 18N	3 23E
Briouze	**100**	48 42N	0 23W
Brisbane, Austral.	**135**	27 25S	153 2E
Brisbane, Can.	**49**	43 44N	80 4W
Bristol, N.B., Can.	**39**	46 28N	67 35W
Bristol, Qué., Can.	**40**	45 32N	76 28W
Bristol, U.K.	**95**	51 26N	2 35W
Bristol, Conn., U.S.A.	**71**	41 44N	72 57W
Bristol, R.I., U.S.A.	**71**	41 40N	71 15W
Bristol, S.D., U.S.A.	**74**	45 25N	97 43W
Bristol B.	**67**	58 0N	160 0W
Bristol Channel	**95**	51 18N	4 30W
Bristol I.	**91**	58 45S	28 0W
Bristol L.	**79**	34 23N	116 50W
Bristow	**75**	35 55N	96 28W
Britannia Beach	**63**	49 38N	123 12W
British Antarctic Territory	**91**	66 0S	45 0W
British Columbia □	**54**	55 0N	125 15W
British Guiana = Guyana	**86**	5 0N	59 0W
British Honduras = Belize	**83**	17 0N	88 30W
British Isles	**93**	55 0N	4 0W
British Mts.	**64**	68 50N	140 0W
Britstown	**117**	30 37S	23 30E
Britt, Can.	**46**	45 46N	80 34W
Britt, U.S.A.	**76**	43 6N	93 48W
Brittany = Bretagne	**100**	48 0N	3 0W
Britton	**74**	45 50N	97 47W
Brive-la-Gaillarde	**102**	45 10N	1 32E
Brlik	**120**	44 0N	74 5E
Brno	**106**	49 10N	16 35E
Broach, L.	**38**	50 45N	67 59W
Broad B.	**96**	58 14N	6 16W
Broad Haven	**97**	54 20N	9 55W
Broad Law, Mt.	**96**	55 30N	3 22W
Broad, R.	**73**	34 30N	81 26W
Broad Sd.	**135**	22 0S	149 45E
Broadback, R.	**36**	51 21N	78 52W
Broadford	**136**	37 14S	145 4E
Broads, The	**94**	52 45N	1 30E
Broadsound Ra.	**135**	22 50S	149 30E
Broadus	**74**	45 28N	105 27W
Broadview	**56**	50 22N	102 35W
Brochet, Man., Can.	**55**	57 53N	101 40W
Brochet, Québec, Can.	**34**	47 12N	72 42W
Brochet, L.	**55**	58 36N	101 35W
Brochet, L. du	**41**	49 40N	69 37W
Brock	**56**	51 26N	108 43W
Brock I.	**64**	77 52N	114 19W
Brock, R.	**40**	50 0N	75 5W
Brock Road	**51**	43 53N	79 5W
Brocken	**106**	51 48N	10 40E
Brockport	**70**	43 12N	77 56W
Brockton	**71**	42 8N	71 2W
Brockville	**47**	44 35N	75 41W
Brockway	**74**	47 18N	105 46W
Brockwayville	**70**	41 14N	78 48W
Brocton	**70**	42 25N	79 26W
Brod	**109**	41 35N	21 17E
Broderick	**56**	51 30N	106 55W
Brodeur	**45**	45 22N	72 59W
Brodeur Pen.	**65**	72 30N	88 10W
Brodhead	**76**	42 37N	89 22W
Brodick	**96**	55 34N	5 9W
Brogan	**78**	44 14N	117 32W
Broglie	**100**	49 0N	0 30E
Broken Bay	**136**	33 30S	151 15E
Broken Bow, Nebr., U.S.A.	**74**	41 25N	99 35W
Broken Bow, Okla., U.S.A.	**75**	34 2N	94 43W
Broken Hill	**136**	31 58S	141 29E
Broken, R.	**136**	36 24S	145 24E
Bromhead	**55**	49 18N	103 40W
Bromley	**95**	51 20N	0 5E
Bromont	**41**	45 17N	72 39W
Bromptonville	**41**	45 28N	71 57W
Bronaugh	**76**	37 41N	94 28W
Brønderslev	**111**	57 16N	9 57E
Bronson	**77**	41 52N	85 12W
Bronte, Can.	**49**	43 24N	79 43W
Bronte, U.S.A.	**75**	31 54N	100 18W
Bronte Cr.	**49**	43 24N	79 43W
Brookdale	**57**	50 3N	99 34W
Brookfield, Can.	**39**	45 15N	63 17W
Brookfield, Ill., U.S.A.	**77**	41 50N	87 51W
Brookfield, Mo., U.S.A.	**76**	39 50N	92 55W
Brookhaven	**75**	31 40N	90 25W
Brookings, Oreg., U.S.A.	**78**	42 4N	124 10W
Brookings, S.D., U.S.A.	**74**	44 20N	96 45W
Brooklands	**58**	49 55N	97 12W
Brooklin	**51**	43 55N	78 55W
Brooklyn, Can.	**39**	44 3N	64 42W
Brooklyn, Iowa, U.S.A.	**76**	41 44N	92 27W
Brooklyn, N.Y., U.S.A.	**71**	40 45N	73 58W
Brookmere	**63**	49 52N	120 53W
Brookport	**43**	45 15N	72 50W
Brooks	**61**	50 35N	111 55W
Brooks B.	**62**	50 15N	127 55W
Brooks L.	**55**	61 55N	106 35W
Brooks Ra.	**67**	68 40N	147 0W
Brookston	**77**	40 36N	86 52W
Brooksville, Fla., U.S.A.	**73**	28 32N	82 21W
Brooksville, Ky., U.S.A.	**77**	38 41N	84 4W
Brookton	**134**	32 22S	116 57E
Brookville, Ind., U.S.A.	**77**	39 25N	85 0W
Brookville, Pa., U.S.A.	**70**	41 10N	79 6W
Broom, L.	**96**	57 55N	5 15W
Broome	**134**	18 0S	122 15E
Broons	**100**	48 20N	2 16W
Brora	**58**	50 35N	104 41W
Brora, R.	**96**	58 4N	3 52W
Brosna, R.	**97**	53 8N	8 0W
Brossard	**45**	45 26N	73 29W
Brothers	**78**	43 56N	120 39W
Brougham	**51**	43 55N	79 6W
Broughton	**77**	37 56N	88 27W
Broughton I.	**62**	50 48N	126 42W
Broughton Island	**65**	67 33N	63 0W
Broughty Ferry	**96**	56 29N	2 50W
Browerville	**74**	46 3N	94 50W
Brown City	**46**	43 13N	82 59W
Brown Willy, Mt.	**95**	50 35N	4 34W
Brownfield	**75**	33 10N	102 15W
Browning, Can.	**56**	49 27N	102 38W
Browning, Ill., U.S.A.	**76**	40 7N	90 22W
Browning, Mo., U.S.A.	**76**	40 3N	93 12W
Browning, Mont., U.S.A.	**78**	48 35N	113 0W
Brownlee	**56**	50 43N	106 1W
Browns Flats	**39**	45 28N	66 8W
Browns Line	**50**	43 36N	79 32W
Brownsburg, Can.	**43**	45 41N	74 25W
Brownsburg, U.S.A.	**77**	39 50N	86 26W
Brownstown	**77**	38 53N	86 3W
Brownsville, Oreg., U.S.A.	**78**	44 29N	123 0W
Brownsville, Tenn., U.S.A.	**75**	35 35N	89 15W
Brownsville, Tex., U.S.A.	**75**	25 56N	97 25W
Brownwood	**75**	31 45N	99 0W
Brownwood, L.	**75**	31 35N	99 15W
Bruas	**128**	4 31N	100 46E
Bruay-en-Artois	**101**	50 29N	2 33E
Bruce	**61**	53 10N	112 2W
Bruce Crossing	**52**	46 38N	89 9W

Bruce L **Cáceres**

Bruce L.	**52**	50 49N	93 20W
Bruce Mines	**34**	46 20N	83 45W
Bruce, Mt.	**134**	22 37S	118 8E
Bruce Mts.	**65**	71 12N	72 15W
Bruce Pen.	**46**	45 0N	81 30W
Bruck a.d. Leitha	**106**	48 1N	16 47E
Bruderheim	**60**	53 47N	112 56W
Brue, R.	**95**	51 10N	2 59W
Bruges = Brugge	**105**	51 13N	3 13E
Brugge	**105**	51 13N	3 13E
Brühl	**105**	50 49N	6 51E
Brûlé	**60**	53 15N	117 58W
Brûlé, L.	**38**	52 30N	63 40W
Brûlon	**100**	47 58N	0 15W
Brumado	**87**	14 14S	41 40W
Brumath	**101**	48 43N	7 40E
Brundidge	**73**	31 43N	85 45W
Bruneau	**78**	42 57N	115 55W
Bruneau, R.	**78**	42 45N	115 50W
Brunei = Bandar Seri Begawan	**126**	4 52N	115 0E
Brunei ■	**126**	4 50N	115 0E
Brunette I.	**37**	47 16N	55 55W
Brunkild	**57**	49 36N	97 35W
Brunner	**133**	42 27S	171 20E
Brunner, L.	**133**	42 27S	171 20E
Bruno, Can.	**56**	52 20N	105 30W
Bruno, U.S.A.	**52**	46 17N	92 44W
Brunsbüttelkoog	**106**	53 52N	9 13E
Brunswick, Ga., U.S.A.	**73**	31 10N	81 30W
Brunswick, Md., U.S.A.	**72**	39 20N	77 38W
Brunswick, Me., U.S.A.	**35**	43 53N	69 50W
Brunswick, Mo., U.S.A.	**76**	39 26N	93 10W
Brunswick, Ohio, U.S.A.	**70**	41 15N	81 50W
Brunswick = Braunschweig	**106**	52 17N	10 28E
Brunswick B.	**134**	15 15S	124 50E
Brunswick L.	**53**	48 58N	83 23W
Brunswick, Pen. de	**90**	53 30S	71 30W
Bruny I.	**135**	43 20S	147 15E
Brus Laguna	**84**	15 47N	84 35W
Brush	**74**	40 17N	103 33W
Brushton	**71**	44 50N	74 62W
Brusque	**89**	27 5S	49 0W
Brussel	**105**	50 51N	4 21E
Brussels, Can.	**70**	43 45N	81 25W
Brussels, Ont., Can.	**46**	43 44N	81 15W
Brussels = Bruxelles	**105**	50 51N	4 21E
Bruxelles	**105**	50 51N	4 21E
Bruyères	**101**	48 10N	6 40E
Bryan, Ohio, U.S.A.	**77**	41 30N	84 30W
Bryan, Texas, U.S.A.	**75**	30 40N	96 27W
Bryansk	**120**	53 13N	34 25E
Bryne	**111**	58 44N	5 38E
Bryson	**40**	45 41N	76 37W
Bryson City	**73**	35 28N	83 25W
Bryte	**80**	38 35N	121 33W
Buapinang	**127**	4 40S	121 30E
Buayan	**127**	5 3N	125 28E
Bucaramanga	**86**	7 0N	73 0W
Buchan	**96**	57 32N	2 8W
Buchan Ness	**96**	57 29N	1 48W
Buchanan, Can.	**56**	51 40N	102 45W
Buchanan, Liberia	**114**	5 57N	10 2W
Buchanan, U.S.A.	**77**	41 50N	86 22W
Buchanan, L., Austral.	**134**	25 33S	123 2E
Buchanan, L., U.S.A.	**75**	30 50N	98 25W
Buchans	**37**	48 50N	56 52W
Buchans Junction	**37**	48 51N	56 28W
Bucharest = Bucureşti	**107**	44 27N	26 10E
Buchon, Pt.	**80**	35 15N	120 54W
Buck L.	**61**	52 59N	114 46W
Buck Lake	**61**	52 57N	114 47W
Buckeye	**79**	33 28N	112 40W
Buckhannon	**72**	39 2N	80 10W
Buckhaven	**96**	56 10N	3 2W
Buckhorn L.	**47**	44 29N	78 23W
Buckie	**96**	57 40N	2 58W
Buckingham, Can.	**40**	45 37N	75 24W
Buckingham, U.K.	**95**	52 0N	0 59W
Buckingham □	**95**	51 50N	0 55W
Buckingham B.	**134**	12 10S	135 40E
Buckland, Alaska, U.S.A.	**67**	66 0N	161 5W
Buckland, Ohio, U.S.A.	**77**	40 37N	84 16W
Buckland Newton	**70**	50 50N	2 57W
Buckley, Ill., U.S.A.	**77**	40 35N	88 2W
Buckley, Wash., U.S.A.	**78**	47 10N	122 2W
Bucklin, Kans., U.S.A.	**75**	37 37N	99 40W
Bucklin, Mo., U.S.A.	**76**	39 47N	92 53W
Bucks L.	**80**	39 54N	121 12W
Bucquoy	**101**	50 9N	2 43E
Buctouche	**39**	46 30N	64 45W
Bucureşti	**107**	44 27N	26 10E
Bucyrus	**77**	40 48N	83 0W
Budacul, Munte	**99**	47 5N	25 40E
Budalin	**125**	22 20N	95 10E
Budapest	**107**	47 29N	19 5E
Budaun	**124**	28 5N	79 10E
Budd Coast	**91**	67 0S	112 0E
Bude	**95**	50 49N	4 33W
Búdir	**110**	64 49N	23 23W
Budjala	**116**	2 50N	19 40E
Buea	**114**	4 10N	9 9E
Buellton	**81**	34 37N	120 12W
Buena Vista, Colo., U.S.A.	**79**	38 56N	106 6W
Buena Vista, Va., U.S.A.	**72**	37 47N	79 23W
Buena Vista L.	**81**	35 15N	119 21W
Buenaventura	**82**	29 50N	107 30W
Buenaventura, B. de	**86**	3 48N	77 17W
Buenos Aires, Argent.	**88**	34 30S	58 20W
Buenos Aires, Colomb.	**86**	1 36N	73 18W
Buenos Aires, C. Rica	**84**	9 10N	83 20W
Buenos Aires □	**88**	36 30S	60 0W
Buenos Aires, Lago	**90**	46 35S	72 30W
Buesaco	**86**	1 23N	77 9W
Buffalo, Can.	**55**	50 49N	110 42W
Buffalo, Mo., U.S.A.	**76**	37 40N	93 5W
Buffalo, N.Y., U.S.A.	**49**	42 55N	78 50W
Buffalo, Okla., U.S.A.	**75**	36 55N	99 42W
Buffalo, S.D., U.S.A.	**75**	45 39N	103 31W
Buffalo, Wyo., U.S.A.	**78**	44 25N	106 50W
Buffalo Center	**67**	64 2N	145 50W
Buffalo Creek	**63**	51 44N	121 9W
Buffalo Head Hills	**54**	57 25N	115 55W
Buffalo L.	**61**	52 27N	112 54W
Buffalo Narrows	**55**	55 51N	108 29W
Buffalo Pound L.	**56**	50 39N	105 30W
Buffalo, R.	**54**	60 5N	115 5W
Buford	**73**	34 5N	84 0W
Bug, R.	**107**	51 20N	23 40E
Buga	**86**	4 0N	77 0W
Bugeat	**102**	45 36N	1 55E
Buggs I. L.	**73**	36 20N	78 30W
Bugsuk, I.	**126**	8 15N	117 15E
Bugue, Le	**102**	44 55N	0 56E
Bugun Shara	**130**	49 0N	104 0E
Buguruslan	**120**	53 39N	52 26E
Buhl, Idaho, U.S.A.	**78**	42 35N	114 54W
Buhl, Minn., U.S.A.	**74**	47 30N	92 46W
Buick	**75**	37 38N	91 2W
Builth Wells	**95**	52 10N	3 26W
Buina Qara	**123**	36 20N	67 0E
Buis-les-Baronnies	**103**	44 17N	5 16E
Buit, L.	**38**	50 59N	63 13W
Buitenpost	**105**	53 15N	6 9E
Bujnurd	**123**	37 35N	57 15E
Bujumbura (Usumbura)	**116**	3 16S	29 18E
Bukachacha	**121**	52 55N	116 50E
Bukama	**116**	9 10S	25 50E
Bukavu	**116**	2 20S	28 52E
Bukene	**116**	4 15S	32 48E
Bukhara	**120**	39 48N	64 25E
Bukittinggi	**126**	0 20S	100 20E
Bukoba	**116**	1 20S	31 49E
Bukuru	**114**	9 42N	8 48E
Bulak	**129**	45 2N	82 5E
Bulan	**127**	12 40N	123 52E
Bulandshahr	**124**	28 28N	77 58E
Bulawayo	**117**	20 7S	28 32E
Buldir I.	**67**	52 20N	175 55E
Bulgan	**130**	48 35N	103 34E
Bulgaria ■	**109**	42 35N	25 30E
Buli, Teluk	**127**	1 5N	128 25E
Buliluyan, C.	**126**	8 20N	117 15E
Bulkley, R.	**54**	55 15N	127 40W
Bulkur	**121**	71 50N	126 30E
Bull, R.	**62**	49 18N	115 18W
Bull Shoals L.	**75**	36 40N	93 5W
Buller, Mt.	**136**	37 10S	146 28E
Bullfinch	**134**	30 58S	119 3E
Bullhead City	**81**	35 11N	114 33W
Bullocks Corners	**48**	43 17N	79 59W
Bulls	**133**	40 10S	175 24E
Bully-les-Mines	**101**	50 27N	2 44E
Bulnes	**88**	36 42S	72 19W
Bulsar	**124**	20 40N	72 58E
Bulu Karakelong	**127**	4 35N	126 50E
Buluan	**127**	9 0N	125 30E
Bulukumba	**127**	5 33S	120 11E
Bulun	**121**	70 37N	127 30E
Bulun Tokhai = Puluntohai	**129**	47 2N	87 29E
Bulyea	**56**	50 59N	104 52W
Bumba	**116**	2 13N	22 30E
Bumble Bee	**79**	34 8N	112 18W
Bumhpa Bum	**125**	26 51N	97 14E
Buna	**116**	2 58N	39 30E
Bunaiyin	**122**	23 10N	51 8E
Bunaloo	**136**	35 47S	144 35E
Bunbury	**134**	33 20S	115 35E
Buncrana	**97**	55 8N	7 28W
Bundaberg	**135**	24 54S	152 22E
Bundi	**124**	25 30N	75 35E
Bundoran	**97**	54 24N	8 17W
Bundure	**136**	35 10S	146 1E
Bungendore	**136**	35 14S	149 30E
Bungō-Suidō	**132**	33 0N	132 15E
Bunguran N. Is.	**126**	4 45N	108 0E
Bungwahl	**136**	32 25S	153 0E
Bunia	**116**	1 35N	30 20E
Bunji	**124**	35 45N	74 40E
Bunju	**126**	3 35N	117 50E
Bunker Hill, Ill., U.S.A.	**76**	39 3N	89 57W
Bunker Hill, Ind., U.S.A.	**77**	40 40N	86 6W
Bunkerville	**79**	36 47N	114 6W
Bunkie	**75**	31 1N	92 12W
Bunnell	**73**	29 28N	81 12W
Buntok	**126**	1 40S	114 58E
Buntzen L.	**66**	49 21N	122 52W
Búoareyri	**110**	65 2N	14 13W
Buol	**127**	1 15N	121 32E
Buorkhaya, Mys	**121**	71 50N	133 10E
Bûr Sa'îd	**115**	31 16N	32 18E
Bûr Sûdân	**115**	19 32N	37 9E
Bura	**116**	1 4S	39 58E
Buraidah	**122**	26 20N	44 8E
Buraimī, Al Wāhāt al	**123**	24 15N	55 43E
Buras	**75**	29 20N	89 33W
Burbank	**81**	34 9N	118 23W
Burcher	**136**	33 30S	147 16E
Burchun	**129**	48 0N	86 7E
Burdett	**61**	49 50N	111 32W
Burdur	**122**	37 45N	30 22E
Burdwan	**125**	23 16N	87 54E
Bure, R.	**94**	52 38N	1 45E
Burford	**49**	43 7N	80 27W
Burgan	**122**	29 0N	47 57E
Burgas	**109**	42 33N	27 29E
Burgenland □	**106**	47 20N	16 20E
Burgeo	**37**	47 37N	57 38W
Burgersdorp	**117**	31 0S	26 20E
Burgos	**104**	42 21N	3 41W
Burgsvik	**111**	57 3N	18 19E
Burgundy = Bourgogne	**101**	47 0N	4 30E
Burhou Rocks	**100**	49 45N	2 15W
Burias, I.	**127**	12 55N	123 5E
Burica, Punta	**84**	8 3N	82 51W
Burin	**37**	47 1N	55 14W
Burin Peninsula	**37**	47 0N	55 40W
Buriram	**128**	15 0N	103 0E
Burkburnett	**75**	34 7N	98 35W
Burke	**78**	47 31N	115 56W
Burke Chan.	**62**	52 10N	127 30W
Burketown	**135**	17 45S	139 33E
Burkettsville	**77**	40 21N	84 39W
Burk's Falls	**46**	45 37N	79 24W
Burleigh Falls	**47**	44 33N	78 12W
Burley	**78**	42 37N	113 55W
Burlingame	**80**	37 35N	122 21W
Burlington, Newf., Can.	**37**	49 45N	56 1W
Burlington, Ont., Can.	**48**	43 18N	79 45W
Burlington, Colo., U.S.A.	**74**	39 21N	102 18W
Burlington, Ill., U.S.A.	**77**	42 43N	88 33W
Burlington, Iowa, U.S.A.	**76**	40 50N	91 5W
Burlington, Kans., U.S.A.	**74**	38 15N	95 47W
Burlington, Ky., U.S.A.	**77**	39 2N	84 43W
Burlington, N.C., U.S.A.	**73**	36 7N	79 27W
Burlington, N.J., U.S.A.	**71**	40 5N	74 50W
Burlington, Vt., U.S.A.	**71**	44 27N	73 14W
Burlington, Wash., U.S.A.	**80**	48 29N	122 19W
Burlington, Wis., U.S.A.	**72**	42 41N	88 18W
Burlington Beach	**48**	43 18N	79 48W
Burlyu-Tyube	**120**	46 30N	79 10E
Burma ■	**125**	21 0N	96 30E
Burnaby	**66**	49 15N	123 0W
Burnaby I.	**62**	52 25N	131 19W
Burnaby L.	**66**	49 14N	122 56W
Burnet	**75**	30 45N	98 11W
Burnett, R.	**135**	24 45S	152 23E
Burney	**78**	40 56N	121 41W
Burnham	**70**	40 37N	77 34W
Burnhamthorpe	**50**	43 37N	79 36W
Burnie	**135**	41 4S	145 56E
Burnley	**94**	53 47N	2 15W
Burns, Oreg., U.S.A.	**78**	43 40N	119 4W
Burns, Wyo., U.S.A.	**74**	41 13N	104 18W
Burns Lake	**54**	54 20N	125 45W
Burnside, R.	**64**	66 51N	108 4W
Burnt Island	**37**	47 36N	58 53W
Burnt L.	**36**	53 35N	64 4W
Burnt Paw	**67**	67 2N	142 43W
Burnt, R.	**70**	44 40N	78 42W
Burnt River	**47**	44 41N	78 42W
Burntwood L.	**55**	55 22N	100 26W
Burntwood, R.	**55**	56 8N	96 34W
Burquitlam	**66**	49 16N	122 54W
Burra	**135**	33 40S	138 55E
Burragorang, L.	**136**	33 52S	150 37E
Burrard Inlet	**66**	49 18N	123 15W
Burrendong Res.	**136**	32 45S	149 10E
Burrewarra Pt.	**136**	35 50S	150 15E
Burrinjuck Dam	**136**	35 0S	148 34E
Burrinjuck Res.	**136**	35 0S	148 36E
Burro, Serranías del	**82**	29 0N	102 0W
Burrows L.	**53**	49 57N	86 44W
Burruyacú	**88**	26 30S	64 40W
Bursa	**122**	40 15N	29 5E
Burstall	**56**	50 39N	109 54W
Burt L.	**46**	45 27N	84 40W
Burton	**63**	50 0N	117 53W
Burton L.	**36**	54 45N	78 20W
Burton-upon-Trent	**94**	52 48N	1 39W
Burtts Corner	**39**	46 3N	66 52W
Buru, I.	**127**	3 30S	126 30E
Burujird	**122**	33 58N	48 41E
Burundi ■	**116**	3 15S	30 0E
Burung	**126**	0 21N	108 25E
Burwash	**46**	46 14N	80 51W
Burwash Landing	**67**	61 21N	139 0W
Burwell	**74**	41 49N	99 8W
Burwell, Mt.	**66**	49 27N	123 1W
Bury, Can.	**41**	45 28N	71 30W
Bury, U.K.	**94**	53 36N	2 19W
Bury St. Edmunds	**95**	52 15N	0 42E
Buryat A.S.S.R. □	**121**	53 0N	110 0E
Busayyah	**122**	30 0N	46 10E
Busby	**54**	53 55N	114 0W
Bushell	**55**	59 31N	108 45W
Bushnell, Ill., U.S.A.	**74**	40 32N	90 30W
Bushnell, Nebr., U.S.A.	**74**	41 18N	103 50W
Businga	**116**	3 16N	20 59E
Buskerud fylke □	**111**	60 13N	9 0E
Busra	**122**	32 30N	36 25E
Bussang	**101**	47 50N	6 50E
Busselton	**134**	33 42S	115 15E
Bussum	**105**	52 16N	5 10E
Bustard Hd.	**135**	24 0S	151 48E
Busto Arsizio	**108**	45 40N	8 50E
Busu-Djanoa	**116**	1 50N	21 5E
Busuangal, I.	**127**	12 10N	120 0E
Buta	**116**	2 50N	24 53E
Butare	**116**	2 31S	29 52E
Bute Inlet	**62**	50 40N	124 53W
Butedale	**62**	53 8N	128 42W
Butembo	**116**	0 9N	29 18E
Butiaba	**116**	1 50N	31 20E
Butler, Ind., U.S.A.	**77**	41 26N	84 52W
Butler, Ky., U.S.A.	**77**	38 47N	84 22W
Butler, Mo., U.S.A.	**76**	38 17N	94 18W
Butler, Pa., U.S.A.	**70**	40 52N	79 52W
Butte, Mont., U.S.A.	**78**	46 0N	112 31W
Butte, Nebr., U.S.A.	**74**	42 56N	98 54W
Butte Creek, R.	**80**	39 12N	121 56W
Butterworth	**128**	5 24N	100 23E
Buttle L.	**62**	49 42N	125 33W
Button B.	**55**	58 45N	94 23W
Button Is.	**36**	60 38N	64 40W
Buttonville	**50**	43 51N	79 21W
Buttonwillow	**81**	35 24N	119 28W
Butuan	**127**	8 57N	125 33E
Butung, I.	**127**	5 0S	122 45E
Buxton	**94**	53 16N	1 54W
Buxy	**101**	46 44N	4 40E
Buyaga	**121**	59 50N	127 0E
Buyr Nuur	**130**	47 50N	117 35E
Büyük Menderes, R.	**122**	37 45N	27 40E
Buzançais	**100**	46 54N	1 25E
Buzău	**107**	45 10N	26 50E
Buzău, R.	**107**	45 10N	27 20E
Buzen	**132**	33 35N	131 5E
Buzi, R.	**117**	19 52S	34 30E
Buzuluk	**120**	52 48N	52 12E
Buzzards Bay	**71**	41 45N	70 38W
Byam Martin I.	**64**	75 15N	104 15W
Bydgoszcz	**107**	53 10N	18 0E
Byelorussian S.S.R. □	**120**	53 30N	27 0E
Byers	**74**	39 46N	104 13W
Byesville	**70**	39 56N	81 32W
Byhalia	**75**	34 53N	89 41W
Bylas	**79**	33 11N	110 9W
Bylot I.	**65**	73 13N	78 34W
Byng Inlet	**46**	45 46N	80 33W
Byrd Land = Marie Byrd Land	**91**	79 30S	125 0W
Byrd Sub-Glacial Basin	**91**	82 0S	120 0W
Byron	**76**	42 8N	89 15W
Byron B.	**35**	54 42N	57 40W
Byron, C.	**135**	28 38S	153 40E
Byrranga, Gory	**121**	75 0N	100 0E
Byske	**110**	64 57N	21 11E
Byske, R.	**110**	65 20N	20 0E
Bytom	**107**	50 25N	19 0E

C

Ca Mau = Quan Long	**128**	9 7N	105 8E
Ca Mau, Mui = Bai Bung	**128**	8 35N	104 42E
Caacupé	**88**	25 23N	57 5W
Caamano Sd.	**62**	52 55N	129 25W
Caatingas	**87**	7 0S	52 30W
Caazapá	**88**	26 8S	56 19W
Caazapá □	**89**	26 10S	56 0W
Cabanatuan	**127**	15 30N	121 5E
Cabane-Ronde	**45**	45 47N	73 33W
Cabano	**41**	47 40N	68 56E
Cabazon	**81**	33 55N	116 47W
Cabedelo	**87**	7 0S	34 50W
Cabery	**77**	41 0N	88 12W
Cabildo	**88**	32 30S	71 5W
Cabimas	**86**	10 30N	71 25W
Cabinda	**116**	5 40S	12 11E
Cabinda □	**116**	5 0S	12 30E
Cabinet Mts.	**78**	48 0N	115 30W
Cabo Blanco	**90**	47 56S	65 47W
Cabo Frio	**89**	22 51S	42 3W
Cabo Pantoja	**86**	1 0S	75 10W
Cabonga Réservoir	**40**	47 20N	76 40W
Cabool	**75**	37 10N	92 8W
Cabora Bassa Dam	**117**	15 20S	32 50E
Caborca (Heroica)	**82**	30 40N	112 10W
Cabot Hd.	**70**	45 14N	81 18W
Cabot, Mt.	**71**	44 30N	71 25W
Cabot Strait	**35**	47 15N	59 40W
Cabrera, I.	**104**	39 6N	2 59E
Cabri	**56**	50 35N	108 25W
Cabriel, R.	**104**	39 20N	1 20W
Cabruta	**86**	7 50N	66 10W
Caburan	**127**	6 3N	125 45E
Çabuyaro	**86**	4 18N	72 49W
Čačak	**109**	43 54N	20 20E
Cáceres, Brazil	**86**	16 5S	57 40W

Cáceres Canyon Creek

Cáceres, Colomb. 86 7 35N 75 20W
Cáceres, Spain 104 39 26N 6 23W
Cache B. 34 46 26N 80 1W
Cache Bay 46 46 22N 80 0W
Cache Cr. 80 38 45N 121 43W
Cache Creek 63 50 48N 121 19W
Cachi 88 25 5S 66 10W
Cachimbo, Serra do 87 9 30S 55 0W
Cáchira 86 7 21N 73 17W
Cachoeira 87 12 30S 39 0W
Cachoeira de Itapemirim 89 20 51S 41 7W
Cachoeira do Sul 89 30 3S 52 53W
Cacolo 116 10 9S 19 21E
Caconda 117 13 48S 15 8E
Cadboro Bay 63 48 28N 123 17W
Caddo 75 34 8N 96 18W
Cader Idris 94 52 43N 3 56W
Cadereyta Jiménez 83 25 40N 100 0W
Cadillac, Qué., Can. 40 48 14N 78 23W
Cadillac, Sask., Can. 56 49 44N 107 44W
Cadillac, France 102 44 38N 0 20W
Cadillac, U.S.A. 46 44 16N 85 25W
Cadiz 127 11 30N 123 15E
Cádiz 104 36 30N 6 20W
Cadiz 70 40 13N 81 0W
Cádiz, G. de 104 36 40N 7 0W
Cadomin 61 53 2N 117 20W
Cadotte, R. 60 56 43N 117 10W
Cadours 102 43 44N 1 2E
Caen 100 49 10N 0 22W
Caergwrle 95 53 6N 3 3W
Caernarfon 94 53 8N 4 17W
Caernarfon B. 94 53 4N 4 40W
Caernarvon = Caernarfon 94 53 8N 4 17W
Cæsarea = Qesari 115 32 30N 34 53E
Caeté 87 20 0S 43 40W
Caetité 87 13 50S 42 50W
Cafayate 88 26 2S 66 0W
Cagayan de Oro 127 8 30N 124 40E
Cagayan, R. 127 18 25N 121 42E
Cágliari 108 39 15N 9 6E
Cágliari, G. di 108 39 8N 9 10E
Cagnes-sur-Mer 103 43 40N 7 9E
Caguas 85 18 14N 66 4W
Caha Mts. 97 51 45N 9 40W
Cahir 97 52 23N 7 56W
Cahirciveen 97 51 57N 10 13W
Cahore Pt. 97 52 34N 6 11W
Cahors 102 44 27N 1 27E
Cahuapanas 86 5 15S 77 0W
Caibarién 84 22 30N 79 30W
Caicara 86 7 38N 66 10W
Caicó 87 6 20S 37 0W
Caicos Is. 85 21 40N 71 40W
Caicos Passage 85 22 45N 72 45W
Caihaique 90 45 30S 71 45W
Cains, R. 39 46 40N 65 47W
Cainsville 49 43 9N 80 15W
Caird Coast 91 75 0S 25 0W
Cairn Gorm 96 57 7N 3 40W
Cairn Toul 96 57 3N 3 44W
Cairngorm Mts. 96 57 6N 3 42W
Cairns 135 16 57S 145 45E
Cairnside 43 45 7N 73 54W
Cairo, Ga., U.S.A. 73 30 52N 84 12W
Cairo, Illinois, U.S.A. 75 37 0N 89 10W
Cairo = El Qahîra 115 30 1N 31 14E
Caistorville 49 43 3N 79 44W
Caithness, Ord of, C. 96 58 35N 3 37W
Caiundo 117 15 50S 17 52E
Caiza 86 20 2S 65 40W
Cajamarca 86 7 5S 78 28W
Cajarc 102 44 29N 1 50E
Cajàzeiros 87 7 0S 38 30W
Calabar 114 4 57N 8 20E
Calabogie 47 45 18N 76 43W
Calabozo 86 9 0N 67 20W
Calábria □ 108 39 24N 16 30E
Calafate 90 50 25S 72 25W
Calahorra 104 42 18N 1 59W
Calais, France 101 50 57N 1 56E
Calais, U.S.A. 35 45 5N 67 20W
Calais, Pas de 78 50 57N 1 20E
Calalaste, Sierra de 88 25 0S 67 0W
Calama, Brazil 86 8 0S 62 50W
Calama, Chile 88 22 30S 68 55W
Calamar, Bolívar, Colomb. 86 10 15N 74 55W
Calamar, Vaupés, Colomb. 86 1 58N 72 32W
Calamian Group 127 11 50N 119 55E
Calamocha 104 40 50N 1 17W
Calanaque 86 0 5S 64 0W
Calang 126 4 30N 95 43E
Calapan 127 13 25N 121 7E
Calatayud 104 41 20N 1 40W
Calauag 127 13 55N 122 15E
Calavite, Cape 127 13 26N 120 10E
Calayan, I. 131 19 20N 121 30E
Calca 86 13 10S 72 0W
Calcutta 125 22 36N 88 24E
Caldas □ 86 5 15N 75 30W
Calder, R. 94 53 44N 1 21W
Caldera 88 27 5S 70 55W
Caldiran 122 39 7N 44 0E
Caldwell, Idaho, U.S.A. 78 43 45N 116 42W
Caldwell, Kans., U.S.A. 75 37 5N 97 37W
Caldwell, Texas, U.S.A. 75 30 30N 96 42W
Caledon, Can. 49 43 52N 80 0W
Caledon, S. Afr. 117 34 14S 19 26E
Caledon B. 135 12 45S 137 0E
Caledon East 49 43 52N 79 52W
Caledon, R. 117 30 0S 26 46E
Caledonia, N.S., Can. 39 44 22N 65 2W
Caledonia, N.S., Can. 39 45 17N 62 33W
Caledonia, Ont., Can. 49 43 7N 79 58W
Caledonia, Mo., U.S.A. 76 37 45N 90 46W
Caledonia, N.Y., U.S.A. 70 42 57N 77 54W
Calella 104 41 37N 2 40E
Calera, La 88 32 50S 71 10W
Calexico 81 32 40N 115 33W
Calf of Man 94 54 4N 4 48W
Calgary 59 51 0N 114 10W
Calgary International Airport 59 51 4N 114 1W
Calhoun 73 34 30N 84 55W
Cali 86 3 25N 76 35W
Calicoan, I. 127 10 59N 125 50E
Calicut, (Kozhikode) 124 11 15N 75 43E
Caliente 79 37 43N 114 34W
California, Mo., U.S.A. 76 38 37N 92 30W
California, Pa., U.S.A. 70 40 4N 79 55W
California □ 78 37 25N 120 0W
California, Baja 82 32 10N 115 12W
California, Baja, T.N. □ 82 30 0N 115 0W
California, Baja, T.S. □ 82 25 50N 111 50W
California City 81 35 7N 117 57W
California, Golfo de 82 27 0N 111 0W
California Hot Springs 81 35 51N 118 41W
California, Lr. = California, Baja 82 25 50N 111 50W
Calilegua 88 23 45S 64 42W
Calingasta 88 31 15S 69 30W
Calipatria 81 33 8N 115 30W
Calistoga 80 38 36N 122 32W
Calixa-Lavallée 45 45 45N 73 17W
Calkiní 83 20 21N 90 3W
Callabonna, L. 135 29 40S 140 5E
Callac 100 48 25N 3 27W
Callan 97 52 33N 7 25W
Callander 46 46 13N 79 22W
Callao 86 12 0S 77 0W
Callaway 74 41 20N 99 56W
Callender 76 42 22N 94 17W
Calles 83 23 2N 98 42W
Calling L. 60 55 15N 113 20W
Calling Lake 60 55 15N 113 12W
Calmar, Can. 60 53 16N 113 49W
Calmar, U.S.A. 76 43 11N 91 52W
Calpella 80 39 14N 123 12W
Calpine 80 39 40N 120 27W
Calstock 53 49 47N 84 9W
Caltagirone 108 37 13N 14 30E
Caltanissetta 108 37 30N 14 3E
Caluire-et-Cuire 103 45 49N 4 51E
Calulo 116 10 1S 14 56E
Calumbo 116 9 0S 13 20E
Calumet City 77 41 37N 87 32W
Calvados □ 100 49 5N 0 15W
Calvert 75 30 59N 96 50W
Calvert C. 62 51 25N 127 53W
Calvert I. 62 51 30N 128 0W
Calvi 108 42 34N 8 45E
Calvillo 82 21 51N 102 43W
Calvinia 117 31 28S 19 45E
Calwa 80 36 42N 119 46W
Cam Lam 128 11 54N 109 10E
Cam, R. 95 52 21N 0 16E
Cam Ranh 128 11 54N 109 12E
Camabatela 116 8 20S 15 26E
Camachigama, L. 40 47 50N 76 19W
Camacho 82 24 25N 102 18W
Camaguán 86 8 6N 67 36W
Camagüey 84 21 20N 78 0W
Camaná 86 16 30S 72 50W
Camanche 76 41 47N 90 15W
Camano I. 63 48 10N 122 30W
Camaquã, R. 89 30 50S 52 50W
Camaret 100 48 16N 4 37W
Camargo 86 20 38S 65 15E
Camargue 103 43 34N 4 34E
Camarillo 81 34 13N 119 2W
Camarón, C. 84 16 0N 85 0W
Camarones, Argent. 90 44 50S 65 40W
Camarones, Chile 86 19 0S 69 58W
Camas 80 45 35N 122 24W
Camas Valley 78 43 0N 123 46W
Cambará 89 23 2S 50 5W
Cambay 124 22 23N 72 33E
Cambay, G. of 124 20 45N 72 30E
Cambo-les-Bains 102 43 22N 1 23W
Cambodia ■ 128 12 15N 105 0E
Camborne 95 50 13N 5 18W
Cambrai 101 50 11N 3 14E
Cambria, Calif., U.S.A. 80 35 44N 121 6W
Cambria, N.Y., U.S.A. 49 43 11N 78 49W
Cambrian Mts. 95 52 25N 3 52W
Cambridge, N.B., Can. 39 45 50N 65 58W
Cambridge, Ont., Can. 49 43 23N 80 15W
Cambridge, Jamaica 84 18 18N 77 54W
Cambridge, N.Z. 133 37 54S 175 29E
Cambridge, U.K. 95 52 13N 0 8E
Cambridge, Idaho, U.S.A. 78 44 36N 116 52W
Cambridge, Ill., U.S.A. 76 41 18N 90 12W
Cambridge, Iowa, U.S.A. 76 41 54N 93 32W
Cambridge, Mass., U.S.A. 72 42 20N 71 8W
Cambridge, Md., U.S.A. 72 38 33N 76 2W
Cambridge, Minn., U.S.A. 74 45 34N 93 15W
Cambridge, Nebr., U.S.A. 74 40 20N 100 12W
Cambridge, N.Y., U.S.A. 71 43 2N 73 22W
Cambridge, Ohio, U.S.A. 70 40 1N 81 22W
Cambridge Bay 64 69 10N 105 0W
Cambridge City 77 39 49N 85 10W
Cambridge Gulf 134 14 45S 128 0E
Cambridge Springs 70 41 47N 80 4W
Cambridgeshire □ 95 52 12N 0 7E
Cambuci 89 21 35S 41 55W
Camden, Ala., U.S.A. 73 31 59N 87 15W
Camden, Ark., U.S.A. 75 33 40N 92 50W
Camden, Me., U.S.A. 35 44 14N 69 6W
Camden, N.J., U.S.A. 72 39 57N 75 1W
Camden, Ohio, U.S.A. 77 39 38N 84 39W
Camden, S.C., U.S.A. 73 34 17N 80 34W
Camden, B. 67 71 0N 145 0W
Camdenton 76 38 1N 92 45W
Camembert 100 48 53N 0 10E
Cameron, Ariz., U.S.A. 79 35 55N 111 31W
Cameron, La., U.S.A. 75 29 50N 93 18W
Cameron, Mo., U.S.A. 76 39 42N 94 14W
Cameron, Tex., U.S.A. 75 30 53N 97 0W
Cameron Falls 52 49 8N 88 19W
Cameron Highlands 128 4 27N 101 22E
Cameron Hills 54 59 48N 118 0W
Cameron L. 53 49 1N 84 17W
Cameroon ■ 114 3 30N 12 30E
Cameroun, Mt. 116 4 45N 8 55E
Cametá 87 2 0S 49 30W
Camiguin, I. 131 19 55N 122 0E
Caminha 104 41 50N 8 50W
Camino 80 38 47N 120 40W
Camlachie 70 43 3N 82 9W
Cammal 70 41 24N 77 28W
Camocim 87 2 55S 40 50W
Camooweal 135 19 56S 138 7E
Camopi, R. 87 3 12N 52 17W
Camp Borden 46 44 18N 79 56W
Camp Crook 74 45 36N 103 59W
Camp Nelson 81 36 8N 118 39W
Camp Point 76 40 3N 91 4W
Camp Wood 75 29 47N 100 0W
Campagna 108 40 40N 15 5E
Campana 88 34 10S 58 55W
Campana, I. 90 48 20S 75 10W
Campania □ 108 40 50N 14 45E
Campania I. 62 53 5N 129 25W
Campbell 80 37 17N 121 57W
Campbell Island 62 52 8N 128 12W
Campbell L. 55 63 14N 106 55W
Campbell, R. 66 49 1N 122 47W
Campbell River 62 50 5N 125 20W
Campbellford 47 44 18N 77 48W
Campbell's Bay 40 45 44N 76 36W
Campbellsburg, Ind., U.S.A. 77 38 39N 86 16W
Campbellsburg, Ky., U.S.A. 77 38 31N 85 12W
Campbellsville 72 37 23N 85 12W
Campbellton, Alta., Can. 54 53 32N 113 15W
Campbellton, N.B., Can. 39 47 57N 66 43W
Campbellton, Newf., Can. 37 49 17N 54 56W
Campbelltown 136 34 4S 150 49E
Campbellville 49 43 29N 79 59W
Campbeltown 96 55 25N 5 36W
Campeche 83 19 50N 90 32W
Campeche □ 83 19 50N 90 32W
Campeche, Golfo de 83 19 30N 93 0W
Camperdown 136 38 14S 143 9E
Camperville 57 51 59N 100 9W
Campina Grande 87 7 20S 35 47W
Campinas 89 22 50S 47 0W
Campinho 87 14 30S 39 10W
Campo 116 2 15N 9 58E
Campo Beló 87 21 0S 45 30W
Campo Formoso 87 10 30S 40 20W
Campo Grande 87 20 25S 54 40W
Campo Maior 87 4 50S 42 12W
Campoalegre 86 2 41N 75 20W
Campobasso 108 41 34N 14 40E
Campos 89 21 50S 41 20W
Campos Belos 87 13 10S 46 45W
Campos Novos 89 27 21S 51 20W
Campsie Fells 98 56 2N 4 20W
Campton 77 37 44N 83 33W
Camptonville 80 39 27N 121 3W
Campuya, R. 86 1 10S 74 0W
Camrose 61 53 0N 112 50W
Camsall L. 55 72 32N 106 47W
Camsell Portage 55 59 37N 109 15W
Can Tho 128 10 2N 105 46E
Canaan 71 42 1N 73 20W
Canaan, R. 39 45 55N 65 47W
Canaan Station 39 46 15N 65 4W
Canada ■ 22 60 0N 100 0W
Canada B. 37 50 43N 56 8W
Canadian 75 35 56N 100 25W
Canadian Pacific Irrigation Canal 59 51 0N 114 0W
Canadian, R. 75 36 0N 98 45W
Canakkale 122 40 8N 26 30E
Canakkale Boğazi 109 40 0N 26 0E
Canal de l'Est 101 48 45N 5 35E
Canal Flats 61 50 10N 115 48W
Canal latéral à la Garonne 102 44 25N 0 15E
Canalejas 88 35 15S 66 34W
Canals 88 33 35S 62 40W
Canandaigua 70 42 55N 77 18W
Cananea 82 31 0N 110 20W
Canarias, Islas 114 29 30N 17 0W
Canarreos, Arch. de los 84 21 35N 81 40W
Canary Is. = Canarias, Islas 114 29 30N 17 0W
Canatlán 82 24 31N 104 47W
Canaveral, C. 73 28 28N 80 31W
Canavieiras 87 15 39S 39 0W
Canberra 136 35 15S 149 8E
Canboro 49 42 59N 79 41W
Canby, Calif., U.S.A. 78 41 26N 120 58W
Canby, Minn., U.S.A. 74 44 44N 96 15W
Canby, Ore., U.S.A. 80 45 16N 122 42W
Cancale 100 48 40N 1 50W
Candala 115 11 30N 49 58E
Candé 100 47 34N 1 0W
Candelaria 89 27 29S 55 44W
Candiac 45 45 23N 73 31W
Candle L. 56 53 50N 105 18W
Cando, Can. 56 52 23N 108 14W
Cando, U.S.A. 74 48 30N 99 14W
Canelones 88 34 32S 56 10W
Canet-Plage 102 42 41N 3 2E
Cañete, Chile 88 37 50S 73 30W
Cañete, Cuba 85 20 36N 74 43W
Cañete, Peru 86 13 0S 76 30W
Canfield 49 42 58N 79 45W
Cangamba 117 13 40S 19 54E
Cangas 104 42 16N 8 47W
Canguaretama 87 6 20S 35 5W
Canguçu 89 31 22S 52 43W
Canicado 117 24 2S 33 2E
Canim, L. 63 51 45N 120 50W
Canim Lake 63 51 47N 120 54W
Canipaan 126 8 33N 117 15E
Canisteo 70 42 17N 77 37W
Canisteo, R. 70 42 15N 77 30W
Cañitas 82 23 36N 102 43W
Cankırı 122 40 40N 33 30E
Canlaon, Mt. 127 9 27N 118 25E
Canmore 61 51 7N 115 18W
Canna I. 96 57 3N 6 33W
Cannanore 124 11 53N 75 27E
Cannelton 77 37 55N 86 45W
Cannes 103 43 32N 7 0E
Canning 39 45 9N 64 25W
Canning Basin 134 19 50S 124 0E
Cannington 70 44 20N 79 2W
Cannock 94 52 42N 2 2W
Cannock Chase, hills 98 52 43N 2 0W
Cannon Ball, R. 74 46 20N 101 20W
Caño Colorado 86 2 18N 68 22W
Canoe 63 50 45N 119 13W
Canoe L. 55 55 10N 108 15W
Canol 67 65 15N 126 50W
Canon City 74 39 30N 105 20W
Canonba 136 31 21S 147 22E
Canora 57 51 40N 102 30W
Canourgue, Le 102 44 26N 3 13E
Canowindra 136 33 35S 148 38E
Canrobert 45 45 21N 72 56W
Canso 39 45 20N 61 0W
Cantabrian Mts. = Cantábrica 104 43 0N 5 10W
Cantábrica, Cordillera 104 43 0N 5 10W
Cantal □ 102 45 4N 2 45E
Cantaura 86 9 19N 64 21W
Canterbury, Can. 39 45 53N 67 29W
Canterbury, U.K. 95 51 17N 1 5E
Canterbury □ 133 43 45S 171 19E
Canterbury Bight 133 44 16S 171 55E
Canterbury Plains 133 43 55S 171 22E
Cantic 43 45 4N 73 21W
Cantil 81 35 18N 117 58W
Canton, Ga., U.S.A. 73 34 13N 84 29W
Canton, Ill., U.S.A. 76 40 30N 90 0W
Canton, Mass., U.S.A. 71 42 8N 71 8W
Canton, Miss., U.S.A. 75 32 40N 90 1W
Canton, Mo., U.S.A. 76 40 10N 91 33W
Canton, N.Y., U.S.A. 71 44 32N 75 3W
Canton, Ohio, U.S.A. 70 40 47N 81 22W
Canton, Okla., U.S.A. 75 36 5N 98 36W
Canton, S.D., U.S.A. 74 43 20N 96 35W
Canton = Kwangchow 131 23 10N 113 10E
Canton I. 14 2 30S 172 0W
Canton L. 75 36 12N 98 40W
Canuck 56 49 12N 108 13W
Canudos 86 7 13S 58 5W
Canulloit 79 31 58N 106 36W
Canuta 44 45 42N 74 9W
Canutama 86 6 30S 64 20W
Canwood 56 53 22N 106 36W
Canyon, Can. 67 47 25N 84 36W
Canyon, Texas, U.S.A. 75 35 0N 101 57W
Canyon, Wyo., U.S.A. 78 44 43N 110 36W
Canyon Creek 60 55 22N 115 5W

Canyonlands Nat. Park

Canyonlands Nat. Park 79 38 25N 109 30W
Canyonville 78 42 55N 123 14W
Caopacho, L. 38 52 0N 66 9W
Caopacho, R. 38 51 18N 66 18W
Caotibi, L. 38 50 45N 67 34W
Cap-aux-Meules 39 47 23N 61 52W
Cap-aux Meules, Î. du 39 47 23N 61 54W
Cap-Chat 38 49 6N 66 40W
Cap-de-la-Madeleine 41 46 22N 72 31W
Cap-des-Rosiers 38 48 52N 64 13W
Cap d'Espoir 38 48 26N 64 20W
Cap Haïtien 85 19 40N 72 20W
Cap-Pelé 39 46 13N 64 18W
Cap-St-Ignace 41 47 2N 70 28W
Capac 46 43 1N 82 56W
Capaia 116 8 27S 20 13E
Capanaparo, R. 86 7 0N 67 30W
Caparo, R. 86 7 30N 70 30W
Capatárida 86 11 11N 70 37W
Capbreton 102 43 39N 1 26W
Capdenac 102 44 34N 2 5E
Cape Barren I. 135 40 25S 148 15E
Cape Breton Highlands Nat. Park 39 46 50N 60 40W
Cape Breton I. 39 46 0N 60 30W
Cape Broyle 37 47 6N 52 57W
Cape Charles 72 37 15N 75 59W
Cape Coast 114 5 5N 1 15W
Cape Dorset 65 64 14N 76 32W
Cape Dyer 65 66 40N 61 22W
Cape Fear, R. 73 34 30N 78 25W
Cape Girardeau 75 37 20N 89 30W
Cape May 72 39 1N 74 53W
Cape Montague 35 46 5N 62 25W
Cape Province □ 117 32 0S 23 0E
Cape Ray 37 47 38N 59 17W
Cape Scott Prov. Park 62 50 45N 128 20W
Cape Tormentine 39 46 8N 63 47W
Cape Town (Kaapstad) 117 33 55S 18 22E
Cape Verde Is. 12 17 10N 25 20W
Cape Vincent 71 44 9N 76 21W
Cape York Peninsula 135 33 34S 115 33E
Capela 87 10 30S 37 0W
Capelle, La 101 49 59N 3 50E
Capendu 102 43 11N 2 31E
Capestang 102 43 20N 3 2E
Capilano L. 66 49 23N 123 7W
Capilano, R. 66 49 19N 123 7W
Capim, R. 87 3 0S 48 0W
Capitachouane, R. 40 47 36N 76 54W
Capitan 79 33 40N 105 41W
Capitola 80 36 59N 121 57W
Caplan 39 48 6N 65 40W
Capraia, I. 108 43 2N 9 50E
Capreol 46 46 43N 80 56W
Caprera, I. 108 41 12N 9 28E
Capri, I. 108 40 34N 14 15E
Capricorn, C. 135 23 30S 151 13E
Caprivi Strip 117 18 0S 23 0E
Captain's Flat 136 35 35S 149 27E
Captieux 102 44 18N 0 16W
Capulin 75 36 48N 103 59W
Caquetá □ 86 1 0N 74 0W
Caquetá, R. 86 1 0N 76 20W
Cáqueza 86 4 25N 73 57W
Carabobo 86 10 10N 68 5W
Caracal 107 44 8N 24 22E
Caracaraí 86 1 50N 61 8W
Caracas 86 10 30N 66 55W
Caracol, Piauí, Brazil 87 9 15S 43 45W
Caracol, Rondonia, Brazil 86 9 15S 64 20W
Carajás, Serra dos 87 6 0S 51 30W
Caramanta 86 5 33N 75 38W
Caramat 53 49 37N 86 9W
Carangola 89 20 50S 42 5W
Caransebeş 107 45 28N 22 18E
Carantec 100 48 40N 3 55W
Caraquet 39 47 48N 64 57W
Caratasca, Laguna 84 15 30N 83 40W
Caratunk 35 45 13N 69 55W
Caraúbas 87 7 43S 36 31W
Caravaca 104 38 8N 1 52W
Caravelas 87 17 45S 39 15W
Caraveli 86 15 45S 73 25W
Caràzinho 89 28 0S 53 0W
Carballo 104 43 13N 8 41W
Carberry 57 49 50N 99 25W
Carbó 82 29 42N 110 58W
Carbon 61 51 30N 113 9W
Carbonara, C. 108 39 8N 9 30E
Carbondale, Can. 60 53 45N 113 32W
Carbondale, Colo, U.S.A. 78 39 30N 107 10W
Carbondale, Ill., U.S.A. 76 37 45N 89 10W
Carbondale, Pa., U.S.A. 71 41 37N 75 30W
Carbonear 37 47 42N 53 13W
Carbonia 108 39 10N 8 30E
Carcajou 54 57 47N 117 6W
Carcasse, C. 85 18 30N 74 28W
Carcassonne 102 43 13N 2 20E
Carcross 22 60 13N 134 45W
Cardamom Hills 124 9 30N 77 15E
Cárdenas, Cuba 84 23 0N 81 30W
Cárdenas, San Luis Potosí, Mexico 84 22 0N 99 41W
Cárdenas, Tabasco, Mexico 83 17 59N 93 21W
Cardiff 95 51 28N 3 11W
Cardiff-by-the-Sea 81 33 1N 117 17W
Cardigan 95 52 6N 4 41W
Cardigan B. 95 52 30N 4 30W
Cardinal 47 44 47N 75 23W
Cardinal L. 60 56 14N 117 44W
Cardón 86 11 37N 70 14W
Cardona, Spain 104 41 56N 1 40E
Cardona, Uruguay 88 33 53S 57 18W
Cardross 56 49 50N 105 40W
Cardston 61 49 15N 113 20W
Careen L. 55 57 0N 108 11W
Carei 107 47 40N 22 29E
Carentan 100 49 19N 1 15W
Carey, Idaho, U.S.A. 78 43 19N 113 58W
Carey, Ohio, U.S.A. 77 40 58N 83 22W
Carey, L. 134 29 0S 122 15E
Carey L. 55 62 12N 102 55W
Cargados Garajos, Is. 16 17 0S 59 0E
Cargèse 103 42 7N 8 35E
Carhaix-Plouguer 100 48 18N 3 36W
Carheil, L. 38 52 40N 67 5W
Carhué 88 37 10S 62 50W
Cariaco 86 10 29N 63 33W
Caribbean Sea 85 15 0N 75 0W
Cariboo Mts. 63 53 0N 121 0W
Cariboo, R. 63 53 3N 121 20W
Caribou, Can. 55 53 15N 121 55W
Caribou, U.S.A. 35 46 55N 68 0W
Caribou I. 53 47 22N 85 49W
Caribou Is. 54 61 55N 113 15W
Caribou L., Man., Can. 55 59 21N 96 10W
Caribou L., Ont., Can. 52 50 25N 89 5W
Caribou Mts. 54 59 12N 115 40W
Caribou, R., Man., Can. 55 59 20N 94 44W
Caribou, R., N.W.T., Can. 54 61 27N 125 45W
Carichic 82 27 56N 107 3W
Carignan, Can. 45 45 27N 73 19W
Carignan, France 101 49 38N 5 10E
Carillo 82 26 50N 103 55W
Carinhanha 87 14 15S 44 0W
Caripito 86 10 8N 63 6W
Caritianas 86 9 20S 63 0W
Carleton, N.-S., Can. 39 44 0N 65 56W
Carleton, N.B., Can. 39 48 5N 66 4W
Carleton Place 47 45 8N 76 9W
Carlin 78 40 50N 116 5W
Carlingford, L. 97 54 0N 6 5W
Carlinville 76 39 20N 89 55W
Carlisle, Can. 49 43 23N 79 59W
Carlisle, U.K. 94 54 54N 2 55W
Carlisle, Ky., U.S.A. 77 38 18N 84 1W
Carlisle, Pa., U.S.A. 70 40 12N 77 10W
Carlitte, Pic 102 42 35N 1 43E
Carlos Casares 88 35 53S 61 20W
Carlos Tejedor 88 35 25S 62 25W
Carlota, La 88 33 30S 63 20W
Carlow 97 52 50N 6 58W
Carlow □ 97 52 43N 6 50W
Carlsbad, Calif., U.S.A. 81 33 11N 117 25W
Carlsbad, N. Mex., U.S.A. 75 32 20N 104 7W
Carlton, Minn., U.S.A. 52 46 40N 92 25W
Carlton, Wash., U.S.A. 63 48 14N 120 5W
Carlyle, Can. 57 49 40N 102 20W
Carlyle, U.S.A. 74 38 38N 89 23W
Carlyle Resr. 76 38 37N 89 21W
Carmacks 67 62 5N 136 16W
Carman 57 49 30N 98 0W
Carmangay 61 50 10N 113 10W
Carmanville 37 49 23N 54 19W
Carmarthen 95 51 52N 4 20W
Carmarthen B. 95 51 40N 4 30W
Carmaux 102 44 3N 2 10E
Carmel, Calif., U.S.A. 80 36 38N 121 55W
Carmel, Ind., U.S.A. 77 39 59N 86 8W
Carmel, N.Y., U.S.A. 71 41 25N 73 38W
Carmel Mt. 115 32 45N 35 3E
Carmel Valley 80 36 29N 121 43W
Carmelo 88 34 0S 58 10W
Carmen, Colomb. 86 9 43N 75 8W
Carmen, Parag. 89 27 13S 56 12W
Carmen de Patagones 90 40 50S 63 0W
Carmen, I. 82 26 0N 111 20W
Carmen, R. 82 30 42N 106 29W
Carmensa 88 35 15S 67 40W
Carmi, Can. 63 49 36N 119 8W
Carmi, U.S.A. 77 38 6N 88 10W
Carmichael 80 38 38N 121 19W
Carmona 104 37 28N 5 42W
Carnarvon, Austral. 134 24 51S 113 42E
Carnarvon, S. Afr. 117 30 56S 22 8E
Carnation 80 47 39N 121 55W
Carndonagh 97 55 15N 7 16W
Carnduff 57 49 10N 101 50W
Carnegie 70 40 24N 80 4W
Carnegie, L. 134 26 5S 122 30E
Carniche, Alpi 108 46 34N 13 0E
Carnon 102 43 32N 3 59E
Carnot 116 4 59N 15 56E
Carnot B. 134 17 20S 121 30E
Carnsore Pt. 97 52 10N 6 20W
Carnwood 61 53 11N 114 38W
Caro 46 43 29N 83 27W
Carolina 87 7 10S 47 30W
Carolina, La 104 38 17N 3 38W
Caroline 61 52 5N 114 45W
Caroline I. 15 9 15S 150 3W
Caroline Is. 14 8 0N 150 0E
Carollton 76 39 22N 93 30W
Carolside 54 51 20N 111 40W
Carolville 76 41 42N 91 34W
Carolville Res. 76 41 50N 91 40W
Caron 56 50 30N 105 50W
Caron, L. 38 50 57N 67 44W
Caroni, R. 86 6 0N 62 40W
Carora 86 10 11N 70 5W
Carp 71 45 20N 76 5E
Carpathians, Mts. 107 46 20N 26 0E
Carpaţii Meridionali 107 45 30N 25 0E
Carpentaria, G. of 135 14 0S 139 0E
Carpenter L. 63 50 53N 122 37W
Carpentersville 77 42 6N 88 17W
Carpentras 103 44 3N 5 2E
Carpinteria 81 34 25N 119 31W
Carpolac 136 36 43S 141 18E
Carrabelle 73 29 52N 84 40W
Carragana 56 52 35N 103 6W
Carraipia 86 11 16N 72 22W
Carrara 108 44 5N 10 7E
Carrauntohill, Mt. 97 52 0N 9 49W
Carriacou, I. 85 12 30N 61 28W
Carrick-on-Shannon 97 53 57N 8 7W
Carrick-on-Suir 97 52 22N 7 30W
Carrickfergus 97 54 43N 5 50W
Carrickfergus □ 97 54 43N 5 49W
Carrickmacross 97 54 0N 6 43W
Carrington 74 47 30N 99 7W
Carrizal 86 12 1N 72 11W
Carrizal Bajo 88 28 5S 71 20W
Carrizalillo 88 29 0S 71 30W
Carrizo Cr. 75 36 30N 103 40W
Carrizo Springs 75 28 28N 99 50W
Carrizozo 79 33 40N 105 57W
Carroll 76 42 2N 94 55W
Carrollton, Ga., U.S.A. 73 33 36N 85 5W
Carrollton, Ill., U.S.A. 74 39 20N 90 25W
Carrollton, Ky., U.S.A. 77 38 40N 85 10W
Carrollton, Mo., U.S.A. 76 39 19N 93 24W
Carrollton, Ohio, U.S.A. 70 40 31N 81 9W
Carron L. 96 57 22N 5 35W
Carron R. 96 57 30N 5 30W
Carrot, R. 57 53 50N 101 17W
Carrot River 56 53 17N 103 35W
Carrouges 100 48 34N 0 10W
Carruthers 56 52 52N 109 16W
Çarşamba 122 41 15N 36 45E
Carson 74 46 27N 101 29W
Carson City, U.S.A. 46 43 11N 84 51W
Carson City, Nev., U.S.A. 80 39 12N 119 46W
Carson, R. 80 39 12N 119 20W
Carson Sink 78 39 50N 118 40W
Carsonville 72 43 25N 82 39W
Carstairs, Can. 61 51 34N 114 6W
Carstairs, U.K. 96 55 42N 3 41W
Cartagena, Colomb. 86 10 25N 75 33W
Cartagena, Spain 104 37 38N 0 59W
Cartago, Colomb. 86 4 45N 75 55W
Cartago, C. Rica 84 9 50N 84 0W
Carteret 100 49 23N 1 47W
Cartersville 73 34 11N 84 48W
Carterton 133 41 2S 175 31E
Carterville 76 37 46N 89 5W
Carthage, Ark., U.S.A. 75 34 4N 92 32W
Carthage, Ill., U.S.A. 76 40 25N 91 10W
Carthage, Mo., U.S.A. 75 37 10N 94 20W
Carthage, N.Y., U.S.A. 71 43 59N 75 37W
Carthage, S.D., U.S.A. 74 44 14N 97 38W
Carthage, Texas, U.S.A. 75 32 8N 94 20W
Cartier 46 46 42N 81 33W
Cartier I. 134 12 31S 123 29E
Cartwright, Man., Can. 57 49 6N 99 20W
Cartwright, Newf., Can. 36 53 41N 56 58W
Cartwright Sd. 62 53 10N 132 38W
Caruaru 87 8 15S 35 55W
Carúpano 86 10 45N 63 15W
Caruthersville 75 36 10N 89 40W
Carvin 101 50 30N 2 57E
Carvoeiro 86 1 30S 61 59W
Casa Agapito 86 2 3N 73 58W
Casa Grande 79 32 53N 111 51W
Casa Nova 87 9 10S 41 5W
Casablanca, Chile 88 33 20S 71 25W
Casablanca, Moroc. 114 33 36N 7 36W
Casale Monferrato 108 45 8N 8 28E
Casanare, R. 86 6 30N 71 20W
Casas Grandes 82 30 22N 108 0W
Cascade, Idaho, U.S.A. 78 44 30N 116 2W
Cascade, Iowa, U.S.A. 76 42 18N 91 1W
Cascade, Mont., U.S.A. 78 47 16N 111 46W
Cascade Locks 80 45 44N 121 54W
Cascade Ra. 80 45 0N 121 30W
Caserta 108 41 5N 14 20E
Caseville 46 43 56N 83 16W
Casey 41 47 53N 74 11W
Cashel, Can. 50 43 55N 79 19W
Cashel, Ireland 97 52 31N 7 53W
Cashmere 78 47 31N 120 30W
Casigua 86 11 2N 71 1W
Casiguran 127 16 15N 122 15E
Casilda 88 33 10S 61 10W
Casino 135 28 52S 153 3E
Casiquiare, R. 86 2 45N 66 20W
Caslan 60 54 38N 112 31W
Casma 86 9 30S 78 20W
Casmalia 81 34 50N 120 32W
Caspe 104 41 14N 0 1W
Casper 78 42 52N 106 27W
Caspian Sea 120 43 0N 50 0E
Casquets 100 49 46N 2 15W
Cass City 46 43 34N 83 15W
Cass Lake 52 47 23N 94 38W
Cass, R. 46 43 23N 83 59W
Cassel 101 50 48N 2 30E
Casselman 47 45 19N 75 5W
Casselton 74 47 0N 97 15W
Cassiar 54 59 16N 129 40W
Cassiar Mts. 54 59 30N 130 30W
Cassils 54 50 29N 112 15W
Cassinga 117 15 5S 16 23E
Cassiporé, C. 87 3 50N 51 5W
Cassis 103 43 14N 5 32E
Cassopolis 77 41 55N 86 1W
Cassville, Mo., U.S.A. 75 36 45N 93 59W
Cassville, Wisc., U.S.A. 76 42 43N 90 59W
Castaic 81 34 30N 118 38W
Castanheiro 86 0 17S 65 38W
Casteljaloux 102 44 19N 0 6E
Castellammare del Golfo 108 38 2N 12 53E
Castellammare di Stábia 108 40 47N 14 29E
Castellane 103 43 50N 6 31E
Castelli 88 36 7S 57 47W
Castellón de la Plana 104 39 58N 0 3W
Castelnau-de-Médoc 102 45 2N 0 48W
Castelnaudary 102 43 20N 1 58E
Castelo 89 20 53S 41 42E
Castelo Branco 104 39 50N 7 31W
Castelsarrasin 102 44 2N 1 7E
Castelvetrano 108 37 40N 12 46E
Casterton 136 37 30S 141 30E
Castets 102 43 52N 1 6W
Castilla La Nueva 104 39 45N 3 20W
Castilla La Vieja 104 41 55N 4 0W
Castille = Castilla 104 40 0N 3 30W
Castilletes 86 11 51N 71 19W
Castillón 82 28 20N 103 38W
Castillon-en-Couserans 102 42 56N 1 1E
Castillon-la-Bataille 102 44 51N 0 2W
Castillonès 102 44 39N 0 37E
Castillos 89 34 12S 53 52W
Castle Dale 78 39 11N 111 1W
Castle Douglas 96 54 57N 3 57W
Castle Mountain 61 51 16N 115 55W
Castle Point 133 40 54N 176 15E
Castle Rock, Can. 63 52 32N 122 29W
Castle Rock, Colo., U.S.A. 74 39 26N 104 50W
Castle Rock, Wash., U.S.A. 80 46 20N 122 58W
Castlebar 97 53 52N 9 17W
Castleblayney 97 54 7N 6 44W
Castlegar 63 49 20N 117 40W
Castlegate 78 39 45N 110 57W
Castlemaine 136 37 2S 144 12E
Castlereagh 97 53 47N 8 30W
Castlereagh □ 97 54 33N 5 33W
Castlereagh B. 134 12 10S 135 10E
Castlereagh, R. 135 30 12S 147 32E
Castleton 71 42 33N 73 44W
Castletown 94 54 4N 4 40W
Castletown Bearhaven 97 51 40N 9 54W
Castor 61 52 15N 111 50W
Castor, R. 36 53 24N 78 58W
Castres 102 43 37N 2 13E
Castricum 105 52 33N 4 40E
Castries 85 14 0N 60 50W
Castro, Brazil 89 24 45S 50 0W
Castro, Chile 90 42 30S 73 50W
Castro Alves 87 12 46S 39 26W
Castro del Río 104 37 41N 4 29W
Castroville, Calif., U.S.A. 80 36 46N 121 45W
Castroville, Tex, U.S.A. 75 29 20N 98 53W
Casummit Lake 52 51 29N 92 22W
Cat I., Bahamas 85 24 30N 75 30W
Cat I., U.S.A. 75 30 15N 89 7W
Cat L. 52 51 40N 91 50W
Catacamas 84 14 54N 85 56W
Catacaos 86 5 20S 80 45W
Cataguases 89 21 23S 42 39W
Catahoula L. 75 31 30N 92 5W
Catalão 87 18 10S 47 57W
Çatalca 122 41 9N 28 28E
Catalina 37 48 31N 53 4W
Catalonia = Cataluña 104 41 40N 1 15E
Cataluña 104 41 40N 1 15E
Catamarca 88 28 30S 65 50W
Catamarca □ 88 28 30S 65 50W
Catanduanas, Is. 127 13 50N 124 20E
Catanduva 89 21 5S 48 58W
Catánia 108 37 31N 15 4E
Catanzaro 108 38 54N 16 38E
Catarman 127 12 28N 124 1E
Catastrophe C. 134 34 59S 136 0E
Cateau, Le 101 50 6N 3 30E
Cateel 127 7 47N 126 24E
Cathcart 49 43 6N 80 31W
Cathedral Mt. 66 49 28N 123 1W
Cathedral Prov. Park 63 49 5N 120 0W
Cathlamet 80 46 15N 123 29W
Catine 99 46 30N 0 15W
Catismiña 86 4 5N 63 52W
Cativá 84 9 21N 79 49W
Catlettsburg 72 38 23N 82 38W

Catlin Charleswood

Catlin	77	40 4N	87 42W
Cato I.	135	23 15S	155 32E
Catoche, C.	83	21 40N	87 0W
Catrimani	86	0 27N	61 41W
Catskill	71	42 14N	73 52W
Catskill Mts.	71	42 15N	74 15W
Cattaraugus	70	42 22N	78 52W
Cauca □	86	2 30N	76 50W
Cauca, R.	86	7 25N	75 30W
Caucasia	86	8 0N	75 12W
Caucasus Mts. = Bolshoi Kavkas	120	42 50N	44 0E
Cauchy, L.	38	50 36N	60 46W
Caudebec-en-Caux	100	49 30N	0 42E
Caudry	101	50 7N	3 22E
Caughnawaga	44	45 25N	73 41W
Caulfield	66	49 21N	123 15W
Caulnes	100	48 18N	2 10W
Caungula	116	8 15S	18 50E
Cáuquenes	88	36 0S	72 30W
Caura, R.	86	6 20N	64 30W
Causapscal	38	48 19N	67 12W
Causapscal, Parc Prov. de	38	48 15N	67 0W
Caussade	102	44 10N	1 33E
Cauterets	102	42 52N	0 8W
Caution C.	62	51 10N	127 47W
Cauvery, R.	124	12 0N	77 45E
Caux, Pays de	100	49 38N	0 35E
Cavaillon	103	43 50N	5 2E
Cavalaire-sur-Mer	103	43 10N	6 33E
Cavalerie, La	102	44 0N	3 10E
Cavalier	57	48 50N	97 39W
Cavallo, I. de	103	41 22N	9 16E
Cavan	97	54 0N	7 22W
Cavan □	97	53 58N	7 10W
Cave City	72	37 13N	85 57W
Cavers	34	48 55N	87 41W
Caviana, Ilha	87	0 15N	50 0W
Cavite	127	14 20N	120 55E
Cawasachouane, L.	40	47 27N	77 45W
Caxias	86	5 0S	43 27W
Caxias do Sul	89	29 10S	51 10W
Cay Sal Bank	84	23 45N	80 0W
Cayambe	86	0 3N	78 22W
Cayce	73	33 59N	81 2W
Caycuse	62	48 53N	124 22W
Cayenne	87	5 0N	52 18W
Cayes, Les	85	18 15N	73 46W
Cayeux-sur-Mer.	101	50 10N	1 30E
Cayey	67	18 7N	66 10W
Cayley	61	50 27N	113 51W
Caylus	102	44 15N	1 47E
Cayman Brac, I.	84	19 43N	79 49W
Cayman Is.	84	19 40N	79 50W
Cayo	83	17 10N	89 0W
Cayo Romano, I.	85	22 0N	77 30W
Cayuga, Can.	49	42 59N	79 50W
Cayuga, Ind., U.S.A.	77	39 57N	87 38W
Cayuga, N.Y., U.S.A.	71	42 54N	76 44W
Cayuga L.	71	42 45N	76 45W
Cazaux et de Sanguinet, Étang de	102	44 29N	1 10W
Cazaville	43	45 5N	74 22W
Cazères	102	43 13N	1 5E
Cazombo	117	12 0S	22 48E
Cazorla	86	8 1N	67 0W
Ceanannas Mor	97	53 42N	6 53W
Ceará □	87	5 0S	40 0W
Ceará Mirim	87	5 38S	35 25W
Cebaco, I.	84	7 33N	81 9W
Cebollar	88	29 10S	66 35W
Cebú	127	10 18N	123 54E
Cebú, I.	127	10 15N	123 40E
Cedar City	79	37 41N	113 3W
Cedar Creek Res.	75	32 15N	96 0W
Cedar Falls, Iowa, U.S.A.	76	42 39N	92 29W
Cedar Falls, Wash., U.S.A.	80	47 25N	121 45W
Cedar Grove	77	39 22N	84 56W
Cedar Key	73	29 9N	83 5W
Cedar L., Man., Can.	57	53 20N	100 10W
Cedar L., Ont., Can.	47	46 2N	78 30W
Cedar Lake	77	41 20N	87 25W
Cedar Mills	49	43 55N	79 48W
Cedar Point	77	41 44N	83 21W
Cedar, R.	76	41 17N	91 21W
Cedar Rapids	76	42 0N	91 38W
Cedar Springs	77	43 13N	85 33W
Cedar Valley	49	43 46N	80 10W
Cedarburg	72	43 18N	87 55W
Cedartown	73	34 1N	85 15W
Cedarvale	54	55 1N	128 22W
Cedarville, Calif., U.S.A.	78	41 37N	120 13W
Cedarville, Ill., U.S.A.	76	42 23N	89 38W
Cedarville, Mich., U.S.A.	46	46 0N	84 22W
Cedarville, Ohio, U.S.A.	77	39 44N	83 49W
Cedral	82	23 50N	100 42W
Cèdres, Les	44	45 18N	74 3W
Cedro	87	6 34S	39 3W
Cedros, I. de	82	28 10N	115 20W
Ceduna	134	32 7S	133 46E
Ceepeecee	54	49 52N	126 42W
Cefalù	108	38 3N	14 1E
Cegléd	107	47 11N	19 47E
Cehegín	104	38 6N	1 48W
Ceiba, La	84	15 40N	86 50W
Celaya	82	20 31N	100 37W
Celbridge	97	53 20N	6 33W
Celebes I. = Sulawesi	127	2 0S	120 0E
Celebes Sea	127	3 0N	123 0E
Celina	77	40 32N	84 31W
Celje	108	46 16N	15 18E
Celle	106	52 37N	10 4E
Cement	75	34 56N	98 8W
Cenis, Col du Mt.	103	45 15N	6 55E
Cenon	102	44 50N	0 33W
Centennial	58	49 54N	97 9W
Center, N.D., U.S.A.	74	47 9N	101 17W
Center, Texas, U.S.A.	75	31 50N	94 10W
Center Point	76	42 12N	91 46W
Centerfield	78	39 9N	111 56W
Centerville, Ala., U.S.A.	73	32 55N	87 7W
Centerville, Calif., U.S.A.	80	36 44N	119 30W
Centerville, Iowa, U.S.A.	76	40 45N	92 57W
Centerville, Mich., U.S.A.	77	41 55N	85 32W
Centerville, Miss., U.S.A.	75	31 10N	91 3W
Centerville, Pa., U.S.A.	70	40 3N	79 59W
Centerville, S.D., U.S.A.	74	43 10N	96 58W
Centerville, Tenn., U.S.A.	73	35 46N	87 29W
Centerville, Tex., U.S.A.	75	31 15N	95 56W
Central □	96	56 0N	4 30W
Central African Empire ■	116	7 0N	20 0E
Central Butte	56	50 48N	106 31W
Central City, Ky., U.S.A.	72	37 20N	87 7W
Central City, Nebr., U.S.A.	74	41 8N	98 0W
Central, Cordillera, C. Rica	84	10 10N	84 5W
Central, Cordillera, Dom. Rep.	85	19 15N	71 0W
Central Islip	71	40 49N	73 13W
Central Lake	46	45 4N	85 16W
Central Makran Range	124	26 30N	64 15E
Central Patricia	52	51 30N	90 9W
Central Russian Uplands	93	54 0N	36 0E
Central Siberian Plateau	121	65 0N	105 0E
Centralia, Ill., U.S.A.	76	38 32N	89 5W
Centralia, Mo., U.S.A.	76	39 12N	92 6W
Centralia, Wash., U.S.A.	80	46 46N	122 59W
Centreville, N.B., Can.	39	46 26N	67 43W
Centreville, N.S., Can.	39	44 33N	66 1W
Ceram I. = Seram I.	127	3 10S	129 0E
Ceram Sea = Seram Sea	127	2 30S	128 30E
Cerbère	102	42 26N	3 10E
Cerbicales, Îles	103	41 33N	9 22E
Cereal	61	51 25N	110 48W
Ceres, Argent.	88	29 55S	61 55W
Ceres, S. Afr.	117	33 21S	19 18E
Ceres, U.S.A.	80	37 35N	120 57W
Céret	102	42 30N	2 42E
Cereté	86	8 53N	75 48W
Cerf, L. de	40	46 16N	75 30W
Cerfontaine	105	50 11N	4 26E
Cerignola	108	41 17N	15 53E
Cérilly	102	46 37N	2 50E
Cerisiers	101	48 8N	3 30E
Cerizay	100	46 50N	0 40W
Çerkeş	122	40 40N	32 58E
Cerknica	108	45 48N	14 21E
Cernavodă	107	44 22N	28 3E
Cernay	101	47 44N	7 10E
Cerralvo, I.	82	24 20N	109 45E
Cerritos	82	22 20N	100 20W
Cerro	79	36 47N	105 36W
Cerro de Punta, Mt.	67	18 10N	67 0W
Cerro Gordo	77	39 53N	88 44W
Cervera	104	41 40N	1 16E
Cervera del Río Alhama	104	42 2N	1 58W
Cervione	103	42 20N	9 29E
César □	86	9 0N	73 30W
Cesena	108	44 9N	12 14E
Česke Budějovice	106	48 55N	14 25E
Český TěV5n	107	49 45N	18 39E
Cessnock	136	32 50S	151 21E
Cetinje	109	42 23N	18 59E
Ceuta	114	35 52N	5 18W
Cévennes, mts.	102	44 10N	3 50E
Ceylon	56	49 27N	104 36W
Ceylon = Sri Lanka ■	124	7 30N	80 50E
Cha Pa.	128	22 20N	103 47E
Chaati I.	62	53 7N	132 30W
Chabeuil	103	44 54N	5 1E
Chablais	103	46 20N	6 36E
Chablis	101	47 47N	3 48E
Chacabuco	88	34 40S	60 27W
Chachapoyas	86	6 15S	77 50W
Chachran	124	28 55N	70 30E
Chaco □	88	25 0S	61 0W
Chaco Austral	90	27 30S	61 40W
Chaco Boreal	88	22 30S	60 10W
Chaco Central	90	24 0S	61 0W
Chad ■	114	12 30N	17 15E
Chad, L. = Tchad, L.	114	13 30N	14 30E
Chadan	121	51 17N	91 35E
Chadileuvú, R.	88	37 0S	65 55W
Chadron	74	42 50N	103 0W
Chafurray	86	3 10N	73 14W
Chagai	123	29 30N	63 0E
Chagai Hills	124	29 30N	63 0E
Chagda	121	58 45N	130 30E
Chagny	101	46 57N	4 45E
Chagos Arch.	16	6 0S	72 0E
Chágres, R.	84	9 5N	79 40W
Chāh Bahār	123	25 20N	60 40E
Chahar Buriak	124	30 15N	62 0E
Chāhr-e Babak	123	30 10N	55 20E
Chaibasa	125	22 42N	85 49E
Chaillé-les-Marais	102	46 25N	1 2W
Chaise-Dieu, La	102	45 20N	3 40E
Chaize-le-Vicomté, La	100	46 40N	1 18W
Chajari	88	30 42N	58 0W
Chakhansur	124	31 10N	62 0E
Chakonipau, L.	36	56 18N	68 30W
Chakradharpur	125	22 45N	85 40E
Chakwal	124	32 50N	72 45E
Chala	86	15 48S	74 20W
Chalainor	130	49 31N	117 30E
Chalais	102	45 16N	0 3E
Chalantun = Putehachi	130	48 4N	122 45E
Chalcatongo	83	17 4N	97 34W
Chalchihuites	82	23 29N	103 53W
Chaleur B.	39	47 55N	65 30W
Chalfant	80	37 32N	118 21W
Chalhuanca	86	14 15S	73 5W
Chaling	131	26 47N	113 35E
Chalisgaon	124	20 30N	75 10E
Chalk River	47	46 1N	77 27W
Chalky Inlet	133	46 3S	166 31E
Challans	100	46 50N	1 52W
Challapata	86	19 0S	66 50W
Challerange	101	49 18N	4 46E
Challis	78	44 32N	114 25W
Chalon-sur-Saône	101	46 48N	4 50E
Chalonnes	100	47 20N	0 45W
Châlons-sur-Marne	101	48 58N	4 20E
Châlus	102	45 39N	0 58E
Chaman	124	30 58N	66 25E
Chamba, India	124	32 35N	76 10E
Chamba, Tanz.	117	11 37S	37 0E
Chambal, R.	124	26 0N	76 55E
Chamberlain	74	43 50N	99 21W
Chambers	79	35 13N	109 30W
Chambersburg	72	39 53N	77 41W
Chambéry	103	45 34N	5 55E
Chambeshi, R.	116	10 20S	31 58E
Chambly	45	45 27N	73 17W
Chambly □	45	45 30N	73 30W
Chambly, Bassin de	45	45 27N	73 17W
Chambois	100	48 48N	0 6E
Chambon-Feugerolles, Le	103	45 24N	4 18E
Châmbon, Le	103	45 35N	4 26E
Chambord	41	48 25N	72 6W
Chamboulive	102	45 26N	1 42E
Chamdo	129	31 21N	97 2E
Chamela	82	19 32N	105 5W
Chamical	88	30 22S	66 27W
Chamois	76	38 41N	91 46W
Chamonix	103	45 55N	6 51E
Chamouchouane, R.	41	48 37N	72 20W
Champagne, Can.	54	60 49N	136 30W
Champagne, France	101	49 0N	4 40E
Champagnole	101	46 45N	5 55E
Champaign	77	40 8N	88 14W
Champain, L.	43	44 45N	73 15W
Champaubert	101	48 50N	3 45E
Champdeniers	102	46 29N	0 25W
Champdoré, L.	36	55 55N	65 49W
Champeix	102	45 37N	3 8E
Champerico	84	14 18N	91 55W
Champigny	42	46 47N	71 21W
Champion, Can.	61	50 14N	113 9W
Champion, U.S.A.	53	46 31N	87 58W
Champion B.	134	28 44S	114 36E
Champlain, Can.	35	46 27N	72 24W
Champlain, U.S.A.	43	44 59N	73 27W
Champlain, L.	71	44 30N	73 20W
Champneuf	40	48 35N	77 30W
Champotón	83	19 20N	90 50W
Chan-chŏsujigjin	130	40 21N	127 20E
Chañaral	88	26 15S	70 50W
Chance Harbour	39	45 7N	66 21W
Chanda	124	19 57N	79 25E
Chandalar	67	67 30N	148 35W
Chandeleur Sd.	75	29 58N	88 40W
Chandigarh	124	30 30N	76 58E
Chandler, Can.	38	48 18N	64 46W
Chandler, Ariz., U.S.A.	79	33 20N	111 56W
Chandler, Okla., U.S.A.	75	35 43N	97 20W
Chandmani	129	45 22N	98 2E
Chandpur	125	22 8N	90 55E
Changanacheri	124	9 25N	76 31E
Changane, R.	117	23 30S	33 50E
Changchow, Fukien, China	131	24 32N	117 44E
Changchow, Shantung, China	130	36 55N	118 3E
Changchun	130	43 58N	125 19E
Change Islands	37	49 40N	54 25W
Changhua	131	24 2N	120 30E
Changkiakow	130	40 52N	114 45E
Changkiang	131	21 7N	110 21E
Changkiang (Shihlu)	131	19 25N	108 57E
Changkwansai Ling	130	44 40N	129 0E
Changlo	131	24 0N	115 33E
Changning	131	26 25N	112 15E
Changpai Shan, mts.	130	42 25N	129 0E
Changping	130	40 15N	116 15E
Changpu	131	24 2N	117 31E
Changsha	131	28 5N	113 1E
Changshow	131	29 49N	107 10E
Changshu	131	31 33N	120 45E
Changtai	131	24 34N	117 50E
Changteh	131	29 12N	111 43E
Changting	131	25 52N	116 20E
Changwu	130	42 21N	122 45E
Changyeh	129	38 56N	100 37E
Chankiang (Tsamkong)	131	21 7N	110 21E
Channapatna	124	12 40N	77 15E
Channel Is.	100	49 30N	2 40W
Channel Islands	81	33 30N	119 0W
Channel-Port aux Basques	37	47 30N	59 9W
Channing, Mich., U.S.A.	72	46 9N	88 1W
Channing, Tex., U.S.A.	75	35 45N	102 20W
Chantada	104	42 36N	7 46W
Chanthaburi	128	12 38N	102 12E
Chantilly	101	49 12N	2 29E
Chantonnay	100	46 40N	1 3W
Chantrey Inlet	65	67 48N	96 20W
Chanute	75	37 45N	85 25W
Chanyi	129	25 56N	104 1E
Chao Phraya, R.	128	13 32N	100 36E
Chaoan	131	23 41N	116 38E
Chaochow	131	23 45N	116 32E
Chaohwa	131	32 16N	105 41E
Chaoping	131	24 1N	110 59E
Chaotung	129	27 19N	103 42E
Chaoyan	130	37 23N	120 29E
Chaoyang, Kwangtung, China	131	23 10N	116 30E
Chaoyang, Liaoning, China	130	41 46N	120 16E
Chap Kuduk	120	48 45N	55 5E
Chapais	40	49 47N	74 51W
Chapala, Lago de	82	20 10N	103 20W
Chapayevo	120	50 25N	51 10E
Chapayevsk	120	53 0N	49 40E
Chapeau	40	45 54N	77 4W
Chapecó	89	27 14S	52 41W
Chapel Hill	73	35 53N	79 3W
Chapelle-d'Angillon, La	101	47 21N	2 25E
Chapelle Glain, La	100	47 38N	1 11W
Chapleau	53	47 50N	83 24W
Chaplin, Can.	56	50 28N	106 40W
Chaplin, U.S.A.	76	39 46N	90 24W
Chaplin L.	56	50 22N	106 36W
Chapman, Mt.	63	51 56N	118 20W
Chapra	125	25 48N	84 50E
Chara	121	56 54N	118 12E
Charadai	88	27 35S	60 0W
Charagua	86	19 45S	63 10W
Charak	123	26 46N	54 18E
Charalá	86	6 17N	73 10W
Charaña	86	17 30S	69 35W
Charapita	86	0 37S	74 21W
Charata	88	27 13S	61 14W
Charcas	82	23 10N	101 20W
Charchan	129	38 4N	85 16E
Charcoal L.	55	58 49N	102 22W
Charcot I.	91	70 0S	75 0W
Chard, Can.	55	55 55N	111 10W
Chard, U.K.	95	50 52N	2 59W
Chardara	120	41 16N	67 59E
Chardon	70	41 34N	81 17W
Chardzhou	120	39 6N	63 34E
Charente-Maritime □	102	45 30N	0 35W
Charente □	102	45 50N	0 16E
Charente, R.	102	45 41N	0 30W
Charette	41	46 27N	72 56W
Chari, R.	114	13 0N	15 20E
Charikar	124	35 0N	69 10E
Charité, La	101	47 10N	3 0E
Chariton	76	41 1N	93 19W
Chariton R.	76	39 19N	92 58W
Charity I.	46	44 3N	83 27W
Charkhlikh	129	39 16N	88 17E
Charlemagne	45	45 43N	73 29W
Charleroi	105	50 24N	4 27E
Charlerol	70	40 8N	79 54W
Charles, C.	72	37 10N	75 52W
Charles City	76	43 2N	92 41W
Charles L.	55	59 50N	110 33W
Charles Town	72	39 20N	77 50W
Charlesbourg	42	46 51N	71 16W
Charleston, Ill., U.S.A.	77	39 30N	88 10W
Charleston, Miss., U.S.A.	75	34 2N	90 3W
Charleston, Mo., U.S.A.	75	36 52N	89 20W
Charleston, S.C., U.S.A.	73	32 47N	79 56W
Charleston, W. Va., U.S.A.	73	38 24N	81 36W
Charleston L.	47	44 32N	76 0W
Charleston Park	81	36 17N	115 37W
Charleston Pk., mt.	81	36 16N	115 42W
Charlestown	77	38 29N	85 40W
Charlesville	116	5 27S	20 59E
Charleswood	58	49 51N	97 17W

Charleville Chinmu Chiao

Charleville	135	26 24 S	146 15 E
Charleville-Mézières	101	49 44 N	4 40 E
Charleville = Rath Luirc	97	52 21 N	8 40 W
Charlevoix	46	45 19 N	85 14 W
Charlevoix, L.	46	45 15 N	85 8 W
Charlieu	103	46 10 N	4 10 E
Charlo	39	47 59 N	66 17 W
Charlotte, Mich., U.S.A.	77	42 36 N	84 48 W
Charlotte, N.C., U.S.A.	73	35 16 N	80 46 W
Charlotte Amalie	85	18 22 N	64 56 W
Charlotte Harb.	73	26 45 N	82 10 W
Charlotte L.	62	52 12 N	125 19 W
Charlotte Waters	134	25 56 S	134 54 E
Charlottesville	72	38 1 N	78 30 W
Charlottetown	39	46 14 N	63 8 W
Charlton, Austral.	136	36 16 S	143 24 E
Charlton, U.S.A.	74	40 59 N	93 20 W
Charlton I.	36	52 0 N	79 20 W
Charmes	101	48 22 N	6 17 E
Charnwood Forest	98	52 43 N	1 18 W
Charny	42	46 43 N	71 15 W
Charolles	103	46 27 N	4 16 E
Charost	101	47 0 N	2 7 E
Charron L.	57	52 44 N	95 15 W
Charroux	102	46 9 N	0 25 E
Charters Towers	135	20 5 S	146 13 E
Chartre, La	100	47 42 N	0 34 E
Chartres	100	48 29 N	1 30 E
Chascomús	88	35 30 S	58 0 W
Chase	63	50 50 N	119 41 W
Chasm	63	51 13 N	121 30 W
Chasseneuil-sur-Bonnieure	102	45 52 N	0 29 E
Châtaigneraie, La	100	46 38 N	0 45 W
Château-Chinon	101	47 4 N	3 56 E
Château-du-Loir	100	47 40 N	0 25 E
Château Gontien	100	47 50 N	0 42 W
Château-la-Vallière	100	47 30 N	0 20 E
Château-Landon	101	48 8 N	2 40 E
Château, Le	102	45 52 N	1 12 W
Château Porcien	101	49 31 N	4 13 E
Château Renault	100	47 36 N	0 56 E
Château-Salins	101	48 50 N	6 30 E
Château-Thierry	101	49 3 N	3 20 E
Châteaubourg	100	48 7 N	1 25 W
Châteaubriant	100	47 43 N	1 23 W
Châteaudun	100	48 3 N	1 20 E
Châteaugiron	100	48 3 N	1 30 W
Châteauguay	44	45 23 N	73 45 W
Châteauguay □	44	45 11 N	73 45 W
Châteauguay-Centre	44	45 21 N	73 45 W
Châteauguay, L.	36	56 26 N	70 3 W
Châteauguay, R.	44	45 23 N	73 45 W
Châteaulin	100	48 11 N	4 8 W
Châteaumeillant	102	46 35 N	2 12 E
Châteauneuf	100	48 35 N	1 15 E
Châteauneuf-du-Faou	100	48 11 N	3 50 W
Châteauneuf-sur-Charente	102	45 36 N	0 3 W
Châteauneuf-sur-Cher	101	46 52 N	2 18 E
Châteauneuf-sur-Loire	101	47 52 N	2 13 E
Châteaurenard	103	43 53 N	4 51 E
Châteauroux	101	46 50 N	1 40 E
Châteauvert, L.	41	47 39 N	73 56 W
Châtelaillon-Plage	102	46 5 N	1 5 W
Châtelaudren	100	48 33 N	2 59 W
Chatelet	105	50 24 N	4 32 E
Châtelet, Le, Cher, France	102	46 40 N	2 20 E
Châtelet, Le, Seine-et-Marne, France	101	48 30 N	2 47 E
Châtelguyon	102	45 55 N	3 4 E
Châtellerault	100	46 50 N	0 30 E
Châtelus-Malvaleix	102	46 18 N	2 1 E
Chatham, N.B., Can.	39	47 2 N	65 28 W
Chatham, Ont., Can.	46	42 24 N	82 11 W
Chatham, U.K.	95	51 22 N	0 32 E
Chatham, Alaska, U.S.A.	67	57 30 N	135 0 W
Chatham, Ill., U.S.A.	76	39 40 N	89 42 W
Chatham, La., U.S.A.	75	32 22 N	92 26 W
Chatham, Mich., U.S.A.	53	46 20 N	86 56 W
Chatham, N.Y., U.S.A.	71	42 21 N	73 32 W
Chatham Head	39	47 0 N	65 33 W
Chatham Is.	14	44 0 S	176 40 W
Chatham Reach	66	49 15 N	122 44 W
Chatham Str.	54	57 0 N	134 40 W
Châtillon, Loiret, France	101	47 36 N	2 44 E
Châtillon, Marne, France	101	49 5 N	3 43 E
Châtillon-Coligny	101	47 50 N	2 51 E
Châtillon-en-Bazois	101	47 3 N	3 39 E
Châtillon-en-Diois	103	44 41 N	5 29 E
Châtillon-sur-Seine	101	47 50 N	4 33 E
Châtillon-sur-Sèvre	100	46 56 N	0 45 W
Chatrapur	125	19 22 N	85 2 E
Châtre, La	102	46 35 N	1 59 E
Chats, L. des	47	45 30 N	76 20 W
Chatsworth, Can.	46	44 27 N	80 54 W
Chatsworth, U.S.A.	77	40 45 N	88 18 W
Chattahoochee	73	30 43 N	84 51 W
Chattanooga	73	35 2 N	85 17 W
Chaudes-Aigues	102	44 51 N	3 1 E
Chaudière, R.	41	46 45 N	71 17 W
Chauffailles	103	46 13 N	4 20 E
Chaukan La	125	27 0 N	97 15 E
Chaulnes	101	49 48 N	2 47 E
Chaumont, France	101	48 7 N	5 8 E
Chaumont, U.S.A.	71	44 4 N	76 9 W
Chaumont-en-Vexin	101	49 16 N	1 53 E
Chaumont-sur-Loire	100	47 29 N	1 11 E
Chaunay	102	46 13 N	0 9 E
Chauny	101	49 37 N	3 12 E
Chausey, Îs.	100	48 52 N	1 49 W
Chaussin	101	46 59 N	5 22 E
Chautauqua	70	42 17 N	79 30 W
Chauvin	61	52 45 N	110 10 W
Chaux de Fonds, La	106	47 7 N	6 50 E
Chaves, Brazil	87	0 15 S	49 55 W
Chaves, Port.	104	41 45 N	7 32 W
Chavigny, L.	36	58 12 N	75 8 W
Chavuma	117	13 10 S	22 55 E
Chazelles-sur-Lyon	103	45 39 N	4 22 E
Chazy	71	44 52 N	73 28 W
Cheam View	63	49 15 N	121 40 W
Cheb (Eger)	106	50 9 N	12 20 E
Chebanse	77	41 0 N	87 54 W
Cheboksary	120	56 8 N	47 30 E
Cheboygan	46	45 38 N	84 29 W
Checheng	131	34 4 N	115 33 E
Checheno-Ingush, A.S.S.R. □	120	43 30 N	45 29 E
Checleset B.	62	50 5 N	127 35 W
Checotah	75	35 31 N	95 30 W
Chedabucto B.	39	45 25 N	61 8 W
Chedoke	48	43 14 N	79 53 W
Cheepash, R.	53	51 3 N	80 59 W
Cheepay, R.	53	51 25 N	83 26 W
Cheeseman L.	52	49 27 N	89 20 W
Chef-Boutonne	102	46 7 N	0 4 W
Chef, R. du	41	49 21 N	73 25 W
Chefornak	67	60 10 N	164 15 W
Chegdomyn	121	51 7 N	132 52 E
Chegga	114	25 15 N	5 40 W
Chehalis	80	46 44 N	122 59 W
Cheju	131	33 28 N	126 30 E
Cheju Do	131	33 29 N	126 34 E
Chekiang □	131	29 30 N	120 0 E
Chelan, Can.	55	52 38 N	103 22 E
Chelan, U.S.A.	78	47 49 N	120 0 W
Chelan, L.	63	48 5 N	120 30 W
Cheleken	120	39 26 N	53 7 E
Chelforó	90	39 0 S	66 40 W
Chelkar	120	47 40 N	59 32 E
Chelkar Tengiz, Solonchak	120	48 0 N	62 30 E
Chelles	101	48 52 N	2 33 E
Chełm	107	51 8 N	23 30 E
Chełmno	107	53 20 N	18 30 E
Chelmsford	95	51 44 N	0 29 E
Chełmża	107	53 10 N	18 39 E
Chelsea, Austral.	136	38 5 S	145 8 E
Chelsea, Can.	48	45 30 N	75 47 W
Chelsea, Mich., U.S.A.	77	42 19 N	84 1 W
Chelsea, Okla., U.S.A.	75	36 35 N	95 35 W
Chelsea, Vermont, U.S.A.	71	43 59 N	72 27 W
Cheltenham, Can.	49	43 45 N	79 55 W
Cheltenham, U.K.	95	51 55 N	2 5 W
Chelyabinsk	120	55 10 N	61 24 E
Chelyuskin, C.	118	77 30 N	103 0 E
Chemainus	63	48 55 N	123 48 W
Chemillé	100	47 14 N	0 45 W
Chemnitz = Karl-Marx-Stadt	106	50 50 N	12 55 E
Chemor	128	4 44 N	101 6 E
Chemult	78	43 14 N	121 54 W
Chemung	71	42 2 N	76 37 W
Chen, Gora	121	65 10 N	141 20 E
Chenab, R.	124	30 40 N	73 30 E
Chenango Forks	71	42 15 N	75 51 W
Chencha	115	6 15 N	37 32 E
Chêne, R. du	44	45 33 N	73 54 W
Chénéville	40	45 53 N	75 3 W
Cheney	78	47 38 N	117 34 W
Chenfeng	131	25 25 N	105 51 E
Chengan	131	28 30 N	107 30 E
Chengchow	131	34 47 N	113 46 E
Chengho	131	27 25 N	118 46 E
Chenghsien	131	29 30 N	120 40 E
Chengkiang	129	24 58 N	102 59 E
Chengkung	131	27 8 N	108 57 E
Chengpu	131	26 12 N	110 5 E
Chengteh	130	41 0 N	117 55 E
Chengtu	129	30 45 N	104 0 E
Chenhsien	131	25 46 N	112 59 E
Chenil, L.	38	51 51 N	59 41 W
Chenkán	83	19 8 N	90 58 W
Chenki	131	28 1 N	110 2 E
Chenning	131	25 57 N	105 51 E
Chenoa	77	40 45 N	88 42 W
Chentung	130	46 2 N	123 1 E
Chenyuan, Kansu, China	130	35 59 N	107 2 E
Chenyuan, Kweichow, China	131	27 0 N	108 20 E
Cheo Reo = Hau Bon	128	13 25 N	108 28 E
Cheom Ksan	128	14 13 N	104 56 E
Chepén	86	7 10 S	79 15 W
Chepes	88	31 20 S	66 35 W
Chepo	84	9 10 N	79 6 W
Chequamegon B.	74	46 40 N	90 30 W
Cher □	101	47 10 N	2 30 E
Chér, R.	101	47 10 N	2 10 E
Cheraw	73	34 42 N	79 54 W
Cherbourg	100	49 39 N	1 40 W
Cherdyn	120	60 24 N	56 29 E
Cheremkhovo	121	53 32 N	102 40 E
Cherepanovo	120	54 15 N	83 30 E
Cherepovets	120	59 5 N	37 55 E
Cherhill	60	53 49 N	114 41 W
Cherkassy	120	49 30 N	32 0 E
Cherlak	120	54 15 N	74 55 E
Chernigov	120	51 28 N	31 20 E
Chernogorsk	121	54 5 N	91 10 E
Chernovtsy	120	48 0 N	26 0 E
Chernoye	121	70 30 N	89 10 E
Chernyakhovsk	120	54 29 N	21 48 E
Chernyshevskiy	121	62 40 N	112 30 E
Cherokee, Iowa, U.S.A.	74	42 40 N	95 30 W
Cherokee, Okla., U.S.A.	75	36 45 N	98 25 W
Cherokees, L. O'The	75	36 50 N	95 12 W
Cherquenco	90	38 35 S	72 0 W
Cherrapunji	125	25 17 N	91 47 E
Cherry Creek, Can.	63	50 43 N	120 40 W
Cherry Creek, Nev., U.S.A.	78	39 50 N	114 58 W
Cherry Creek, N.Y., U.S.A.	70	42 18 N	79 6 W
Cherry Valley	81	33 59 N	116 57 W
Cherryvale	75	37 20 N	95 33 W
Cherryville	63	50 15 N	118 37 W
Cherrywood	51	43 52 N	79 8 W
Cherskiy	121	68 45 N	161 18 E
Cherskogo Khrebet	121	65 0 N	143 0 E
Cherwell, R.	95	51 46 N	1 18 W
Chesaning	46	43 11 N	84 7 W
Chesapeake Bay	72	38 0 N	76 12 W
Chesha B. = Cheshskaya G.	120	67 20 N	47 0 E
Cheshire □	94	53 14 N	2 30 W
Chesil Beach	98	50 37 N	2 33 W
Cheslatta	62	53 48 N	125 48 W
Cheslatta L.	62	53 49 N	125 20 W
Chesley	46	44 17 N	81 5 W
Chesne, Le	101	49 30 N	4 45 E
Chester, Can.	39	44 33 N	64 15 W
Chester, U.K.	94	53 12 N	2 53 W
Chester, Calif., U.S.A.	78	40 22 N	121 22 W
Chester, Ill., U.S.A.	76	37 58 N	89 50 W
Chester, Mont., U.S.A.	78	48 31 N	111 0 W
Chester, N.Y., U.S.A.	71	41 22 N	74 16 W
Chester, Pa., U.S.A.	72	39 54 N	75 20 W
Chester, S.C., U.S.A.	73	34 44 N	81 13 W
Chesterfield	94	53 14 N	1 26 W
Chesterfield I.	117	16 20 S	43 58 E
Chesterfield, Îles	135	19 52 S	158 15 E
Chesterfield In.	65	63 25 N	90 45 W
Chesterfield Inlet	65	63 30 N	90 45 W
Chesterville	47	45 6 N	75 14 W
Chesuncook L.	35	46 0 N	69 10 W
Chéticamp	39	46 37 N	60 59 W
Chetumal	83	18 30 N	88 20 W
Chetumal, Bahía de	83	18 40 N	88 10 W
Chetwynd	54	55 45 N	121 45 W
Chevanceaux	102	45 18 N	0 14 W
Cheviot	77	39 10 N	84 37 W
Cheviot Hills	94	55 20 N	2 30 W
Cheviot, The	94	55 29 N	2 8 W
Chew Bahir	115	4 40 N	30 50 E
Chewelah	63	48 17 N	117 43 W
Cheyenne, Okla., U.S.A.	75	35 35 N	99 40 W
Cheyenne, Wyo., U.S.A.	74	41 9 N	104 49 W
Cheyenne, R.	74	44 50 N	101 0 W
Cheyenne Wells	74	38 51 N	102 23 W
Cheylard, Le	103	44 55 N	4 25 E
Chezacut	62	52 24 N	124 1 W
Chhang	126	12 15 N	104 14 E
Chhatarpur	124	24 55 N	79 43 E
Chhindwara	124	22 2 N	78 59 E
Chhlong	128	12 15 N	105 58 E
Chi, R.	128	15 11 N	104 43 E
Chiai	131	23 29 N	120 25 E
Chiang Mai	128	18 47 N	98 59 E
Chianie	117	15 35 S	13 40 E
Chiapa de Corzo	83	16 42 N	93 0 W
Chiapa, R.	83	16 42 N	93 0 W
Chiapas □	83	17 0 N	92 45 W
Chiautla	83	18 18 N	98 34 W
Chiba	132	35 30 N	140 7 E
Chiba-ken □	132	35 30 N	140 20 E
Chibemba	117	15 48 S	14 8 E
Chibougamau	41	49 56 N	74 24 W
Chibougamau L.	41	49 50 N	74 20 W
Chibougamau, Parc Prov. de	41	49 15 N	73 45 W
Chibougamau, R.	40	49 42 N	75 57 W
Chic-Chocs, Mts.	38	48 55 N	66 0 W
Chic-Chocs, Parc Prov. des	38	48 55 N	66 20 W
Chicago	77	41 53 N	87 40 W
Chicago Heights	77	41 29 N	87 37 W
Chichagof I.	54	58 0 N	136 0 W
Chichén Itzá	83	20 40 N	88 32 W
Chichester	95	50 50 N	0 47 W
Chichibu	132	36 5 N	139 10 E
Chichirin	130	50 35 N	123 45 E
Chichiriviche	86	10 56 N	68 16 W
Chichow	130	38 30 N	115 25 E
Chickasha	75	35 0 N	98 0 W
Chicken Hd.	94	58 10 N	6 15 W
Chiclana de la Frontera	104	36 26 N	6 9 W
Chiclayo	86	6 42 S	79 50 W
Chico	80	39 45 N	121 54 W
Chico, R., Chubut, Argent.	78	44 0 S	67 0 W
Chico, R., Santa Cruz, Argent.	90	49 30 S	69 30 W
Chicoa	117	15 35 S	32 20 E
Chicobi, L.	40	48 53 N	78 30 W
Chicontepec	83	20 58 N	98 10 W
Chicopee	71	42 6 N	72 37 W
Chicot	44	45 36 N	73 56 W
Chicoutimi	35	48 28 N	71 5 W
Chicoutimi, Parc Prov. de	41	48 30 N	70 20 W
Chidambaram	124	11 20 N	79 45 E
Chidley C.	36	60 23 N	64 26 W
Chiefs Pt.	46	44 41 N	81 18 W
Chiengi	116	8 45 S	29 10 E
Chiese, R.	108	45 45 N	10 35 E
Chieti	108	42 22 N	14 10 E
Chignecto B.	39	45 30 N	64 40 W
Chignecto, Cape	39	45 20 N	64 57 W
Chignik	67	56 15 N	158 27 W
Chigorodó	86	7 41 N	76 42 W
Chigoubiche, L.	41	49 7 N	73 30 W
Chiguana	88	21 0 S	67 50 W
Chihfeng	130	42 18 N	118 57 E
Chihing	131	25 2 N	113 45 E
Chihkiang, Hunan, China	131	27 21 N	109 45 E
Chihkiang, Hupei, China	131	30 25 N	111 30 E
Chihkin	131	26 30 N	105 45 E
Chihli, G. of (Po Hai)	130	38 30 N	119 0 E
Chihsien (Weihwei)	131	35 29 N	114 1 E
Chihuahua	82	28 40 N	106 3 W
Chihuahua □	82	28 40 N	106 3 W
Chihuatlán	82	19 14 N	104 35 W
Chik Ballapur	124	13 25 N	77 45 E
Chikmagalur	124	13 15 N	75 45 E
Chilac	83	18 20 N	97 24 W
Chilako, R.	62	53 53 N	122 57 W
Chilanko Forks	62	52 7 N	124 5 W
Chilanko, R.	62	52 7 N	123 41 W
Chilapa	83	17 40 N	99 20 W
Chilas	124	35 25 N	74 5 E
Chilaw	124	7 30 N	79 50 E
Chilco	62	54 3 N	123 49 W
Chilcotin, R.	63	51 44 N	122 23 W
Childers	135	25 15 S	152 17 E
Childress	75	34 30 N	100 15 W
Chile ■	90	35 0 S	71 15 W
Chilecito	88	29 0 S	67 40 W
Chilete	86	7 10 S	78 50 W
Chilhowee	76	38 36 N	93 51 W
Chililabombwe (Bancroft)	117	12 18 S	27 43 E
Chilka L.	125	19 40 N	85 25 E
Chilko, L.	62	51 20 N	124 10 W
Chilko, R.	62	52 6 N	123 40 W
Chillagoe	135	17 14 S	144 33 E
Chillán	88	36 40 S	72 10 W
Chillicothe, Ill., U.S.A.	76	40 55 N	89 32 W
Chillicothe, Mo., U.S.A.	76	39 45 N	93 30 W
Chillicothe, Ohio, U.S.A.	72	39 20 N	82 58 W
Chilliwack	63	49 10 N	122 0 W
Chiloé, I. de	90	42 50 S	73 45 W
Chilpancingo	83	17 30 N	99 40 W
Chiltern Hills	95	51 44 N	0 42 W
Chilton	72	44 1 N	88 12 W
Chiluage	116	9 15 S	21 42 E
Chilung	131	25 3 N	121 45 E
Chilwa, L. (Shirwa)	117	15 15 S	35 40 E
Chimacum	78	48 1 N	122 53 W
Chimai	129	33 35 N	102 10 E
Chimaltitán	82	21 46 N	103 50 W
Chimán	84	8 45 N	78 40 W
Chimay	105	50 3 N	4 20 E
Chimbay	120	42 57 N	59 47 E
Chimborazo	86	1 20 S	78 55 W
Chimbote	86	9 0 S	78 35 W
Chimkent	120	42 18 N	69 36 E
Chin □	125	22 0 N	93 0 E
Chin Chai	131	31 58 N	115 59 E
China	82	25 40 N	99 20 W
China ■	129	30 0 N	110 0 E
China Lake	81	35 44 N	117 37 W
Chinacates	82	25 0 N	105 14 W
Chinacota	86	7 37 N	72 36 W
Chinandega	84	12 30 N	87 0 W
Chinati Pk.	75	30 0 N	104 25 W
Chincha Alta	86	13 20 S	76 0 W
Chinchaga, R.	60	58 53 N	118 20 W
Chinchón	104	40 9 N	3 26 W
Chinchorro, Banco	83	18 35 N	87 20 W
Chinchow	130	41 10 N	121 2 E
Chincoteague	72	37 58 N	75 21 W
Chinde	117	18 45 S	36 30 E
Chindwin, R.	125	21 26 N	95 15 E
Ching Ho, R.	131	34 30 N	109 0 E
Chinghai □	129	36 0 N	97 0 E
Chingola	117	12 31 S	27 53 E
Chinguar	117	12 18 S	16 45 E
Chiniot	124	31 45 N	73 0 E
Chinipas	82	27 22 N	108 32 W
Chinkiang	131	32 2 N	119 29 E
Chinle	79	36 14 N	109 38 W
Chinmu Chiao	131	18 10 N	109 35 E

Chinnampo	**130**	38 52N	125 28E
Chino	**81**	34 1N	117 41W
Chino Valley	**79**	34 54N	112 28W
Chinon	**100**	47 10N	0 15E
Chinook, Can.	**61**	51 28N	110 59W
Chinook, U.S.A.	**78**	48 35N	109 19W
Chinook Valley	**60**	56 29N	117 39W
Chinsali	**116**	10 30S	32 2E
Chinwangtao	**130**	40 0N	119 31E
Chióggia	**108**	45 13N	12 15E
Chip L.	**60**	53 40N	115 23W
Chip Lake	**54**	53 35N	115 35W
Chipai L.	**34**	52 56N	87 53W
Chipata (Ft. Jameson)	**117**	13 38S	32 28E
Chipewyan L.	**55**	58 0N	98 27W
Chipley	**73**	30 45N	85 32W
Chipman, Alta., Can.	**60**	53 42N	112 38W
Chipman, N.B., Can.	**39**	46 6N	65 53W
Chipman L.	**53**	49 58N	86 15W
Chippawa	**49**	43 5N	79 2W
Chippenham	**95**	51 27N	2 7W
Chippewa Falls	**74**	44 55N	91 22W
Chippewa, R.	**74**	44 45N	91 55W
Chiputneticook Lakes	**39**	45 37N	67 40W
Chiquian	**86**	10 10S	77 0W
Chiquimula	**84**	14 51N	89 37W
Chiquinquirá	**86**	5 37N	73 50W
Chirala	**124**	15 50N	80 20E
Chiras	**123**	35 14N	65 40E
Chirchik	**120**	41 29N	69 35E
Chiricahua Pk.	**79**	31 53N	109 14W
Chirikof I.	**67**	55 50N	155 40W
Chiriquí, Golfo de	**84**	8 0N	82 10W
Chiriquí, Lago de	**84**	9 10N	82 0W
Chiriquí, Vol.	**84**	8 55N	82 35W
Chirmiri	**125**	23 15N	82 20E
Chiromo	**117**	16 30S	35 7E
Chirripó Grande, cerro	**84**	9 29N	83 29W
Chisamba	**117**	14 55S	28 20E
Chisapani Garhi	**125**	27 30N	84 2E
Chishan	**131**	22 44N	120 31E
Chisholm, Can.	**60**	54 55N	114 10W
Chisholm, U.S.A.	**52**	47 29N	92 53W
Chisos Mts.	**75**	29 20N	103 15W
Chistopol	**120**	55 25N	50 38E
Chita, Colomb.	**86**	6 11N	72 28W
Chita, U.S.S.R.	**121**	52 0N	113 25E
Chitado	**117**	17 10S	14 8E
Chitek	**56**	53 48N	107 45W
Chitek L., Man., Can.	**57**	52 25N	99 25W
Chitek L., Sask., Can.	**56**	53 45N	107 47W
Chitembo	**117**	13 30S	16 50E
Chitina	**67**	61 30N	144 30W
Chitokoloki	**117**	13 43S	23 4E
Chitorgarh	**124**	24 52N	74 43E
Chitral	**124**	35 50N	71 56E
Chitré	**85**	7 59N	80 27W
Chittagong	**125**	22 19N	91 55E
Chittagong □	**125**	24 5N	91 25E
Chittoor	**124**	13 15N	79 5E
Chiusi	**108**	43 1N	11 58E
Chivasso	**108**	45 10N	7 52E
Chivilcoy	**88**	35 0S	60 0W
Chkalov = Orenburg	**120**	52 0N	55 5E
Chloride	**81**	35 25N	114 12W
Choahsien	**130**	37 48N	114 46E
Chocó □	**86**	6 0N	77 0W
Chocontá	**86**	5 9N	73 41W
Choele Choel	**90**	39 11S	65 40W
Choelquoit L.	**62**	51 42N	124 12W
Choiceland	**56**	53 29N	104 29W
Choiseul I.	**14**	7 0S	156 40E
Choisy	**44**	45 29N	74 13W
Choisy-le-Roi	**101**	48 45N	2 24E
Choix	**82**	26 40N	108 10W
Chojnice	**107**	53 42N	17 40E
Chokurdakh	**121**	70 38N	147 55E
Cholame	**80**	35 44N	120 18W
Cholet	**100**	47 4N	0 52W
Choluteca	**84**	13 20N	87 14W
Choluteca, R.	**84**	13 5N	87 20W
Choma	**117**	16 48S	26 59E
Chomedey	**44**	45 32N	73 45W
Chomutov	**106**	50 28N	13 23E
Chŏnan	**130**	36 48N	127 9E
Chonburi	**128**	13 21N	101 1E
Chone	**86**	0 40S	80 0W
Chongjin	**130**	41 47N	129 50E
Chŏngju	**130**	36 39N	127 27E
Chŏnju	**130**	35 50N	127 4E
Chonos, Arch. de los	**90**	45 0S	75 0W
Chopim, R.	**89**	25 35S	53 5W
Chorley	**94**	53 39N	2 39W
Chorolque, Cerro	**88**	20 59S	66 5W
Chorrera, La	**84**	8 50N	79 50W
Chŏrwŏn	**130**	38 15N	127 10E
Chorzów	**107**	50 18N	19 0E
Chos-Malal	**88**	37 15S	70 5W
Choshi	**132**	35 45N	140 45E
Choszczno	**106**	53 7N	15 25E
Choteau	**78**	47 50N	112 10W
Chotila	**124**	22 30N	71 15E
Chow Hu	**131**	31 35N	117 30E
Chowchilla	**80**	37 11N	120 12W
Choybalsan	**130**	48 3N	114 28E
Choyr	**130**	46 24N	108 30E
Chrisman	**77**	39 48N	87 41W
Christchurch, N.Z.	**133**	43 33S	172 47E
Christchurch, U.K.	**95**	50 44N	1 47W
Christian I.	**46**	44 50N	80 12W
Christiana	**117**	27 52S	25 8E
Christiansted	**85**	17 45N	64 42W
Christie B.	**55**	62 32N	111 10W
Christies Corners	**49**	43 16N	80 2W
Christina, L.	**63**	49 3N	118 12W
Christina, R.	**60**	56 40N	111 3W
Christmas I., Ind. Oc.	**16**	10 0S	105 40E
Christmas I., Pac. Oc.	**15**	1 58N	157 27W
Christopher Lake	**56**	53 32N	105 48W
Chu	**120**	43 36N	73 42E
Chu Chua	**63**	51 22N	120 10W
Chu Kiang	**131**	22 15N	113 45E
Chu, R.	**128**	19 53N	105 45E
Chuanchow	**131**	24 57N	118 31E
Chuanhsien	**131**	25 50N	111 12E
Chūbu □	**132**	36 45N	137 30E
Chubut, R.	**90**	43 0S	70 0W
Chuchi L.	**54**	55 12N	124 30W
Chuchow	**131**	27 56N	113 3E
Chuchow (Lishui)	**131**	28 30N	119 50E
Chugach Mts.	**67**	62 0N	146 0W
Chugiak	**67**	61 7N	149 10W
Chuginadak I.	**67**	52 50N	169 45W
Chūgoku □	**132**	35 0N	133 0E
Chūgoku-Sanchi	**132**	35 0N	133 0E
Chugwater	**74**	41 48N	104 47W
Chuho = Shangchih	**130**	45 10N	127 59E
Chuhsien, Chekiang, China	**130**	28 57N	118 58E
Chuhsien, Shantung, China	**131**	35 31N	118 45E
Chuhsien, Szechwan, China	**131**	30 51N	107 1E
Chukai	**128**	4 13N	103 25E
Chuki, Chekiang, China	**131**	29 30N	120 4E
Chuki, Hupei, China	**131**	32 26N	110 0E
Chukotskiy Khrebet	**121**	68 0N	175 0E
Chukotskiy, Mys	**121**	66 10N	169 3E
Chukotskoye More	**121**	68 0N	175 0W
Chula	**76**	39 55N	93 29W
Chula Vista	**81**	32 39N	117 8W
Chulucanas	**86**	5 0S	80 0W
Chumatien	**131**	33 0N	114 4E
Chumbicha	**88**	29 0S	66 10W
Chumikan	**121**	54 40N	135 10E
Chumphon	**128**	10 35N	99 14E
Chunchŏn	**130**	37 58N	127 44E
Chungan	**131**	27 45N	118 0E
Chunghsien	**131**	30 17N	108 4E
Chungking	**131**	29 30N	106 30E
Chungsiang	**131**	31 14N	112 42E
Chunya	**116**	8 30S	33 27E
Chuquibamba	**86**	15 47N	72 44W
Chuquicamata	**88**	22 15S	69 0W
Chuquisaca □	**88**	23 30S	63 30W
Chur	**106**	46 52N	9 32E
Churachandpur	**125**	24 20N	93 40E
Church House	**54**	50 20N	125 10W
Churchbridge	**57**	50 54N	101 54W
Churchill	**55**	58 47N	94 11W
Churchill, C.	**55**	58 46N	93 12W
Churchill Falls	**36**	53 36N	64 19W
Churchill L., Ont., Can.	**52**	50 50N	91 10W
Churchill L., Sask., Can.	**55**	55 55N	108 20W
Churchill Pk.	**54**	58 10N	125 10W
Churchill, R., Man., Can.	**55**	58 47N	94 12W
Churchill, R., Newf., Can.	**36**	53 19N	60 10W
Churchill, R., Sask., Can.	**55**	58 47N	94 12W
Churdan	**76**	42 9N	94 29W
Churu	**124**	28 20N	75 0E
Churubusco	**77**	41 14N	85 19W
Churuguaro	**86**	10 49N	69 32W
Chusan	**131**	30 0N	122 20E
Chushul	**124**	33 40N	78 40E
Chusnan	**131**	32 14N	110 30E
Chusovoy	**120**	58 15N	57 40E
Chute-à-Blondeau	**43**	45 35N	74 28W
Chute-aux-Outardes	**41**	49 7N	68 24W
Chute-des-Passes	**41**	49 52N	71 16W
Chuting	**131**	27 28N	113 1E
Chuvash A.S.S.R. □	**120**	55 30N	48 0E
Chwangho	**130**	39 41N	123 2E
Cibola	**81**	33 17N	114 9W
Cicero	**72**	41 48N	87 48W
Ciechanów	**107**	52 52N	20 38E
Ciego de Avila	**84**	21 50N	78 50W
Ciénaga	**86**	11 1N	74 15W
Ciénaga de Oro	**86**	8 53N	75 37W
Cienfuegos	**84**	22 10N	80 30W
Cierp	**102**	42 55N	0 40E
Cieszyn	**107**	49 45N	18 35E
Cieza	**104**	38 17N	1 23W
Cijulang	**127**	7 42S	108 27E
Cikampek	**127**	6 23S	107 28E
Cilacap	**127**	7 43S	109 0E
Cilician Gates P.	**122**	37 20N	34 52E
Cilician Taurus	**122**	36 40N	34 0E
Cima	**81**	35 14N	115 30W
Cimarron, Kans., U.S.A.	**75**	37 50N	100 20W
Cimarron, N. Mex., U.S.A.	**75**	36 30N	104 52W
Cimarron, R.	**75**	37 10N	102 10W
Cimone, Mte.	**108**	44 10N	10 40E
Cîmpina	**107**	45 10N	25 45E
Cîmpulung	**107**	45 17N	25 3E
Cinca, R.	**104**	42 20N	0 9E
Cinch, R.	**73**	36 0N	84 15W
Cincinnati, Iowa, U.S.A.	**76**	40 38N	92 56W
Cincinnati, Ohio, U.S.A.	**77**	39 10N	84 26W
Cinto, Mt.	**103**	42 24N	8 54E
Ciotat, La	**103**	43 12N	5 36E
Circle, Alaska, U.S.A.	**67**	65 50N	144 10W
Circle, Montana, U.S.A.	**74**	47 26N	105 35W
Circleville, Ohio, U.S.A.	**72**	39 35N	82 57W
Circleville, Utah, U.S.A.	**79**	38 12N	112 24W
Cirebon	**127**	6 45S	108 32E
Cirencester	**95**	51 43N	1 59W
Cirey-sur-Vezouze	**101**	48 35N	6 57E
Cisco	**75**	32 25N	99 0W
Cisne	**77**	38 31N	88 26W
Cisneros	**86**	6 33N	75 4W
Cissna Park	**77**	40 34N	87 54W
Citlaltépetl, mt.	**83**	19 0N	97 20W
City View, Ont., Can.	**48**	45 21N	75 45W
City View, Sask., Can.	**58**	50 28N	104 37W
Ciudad Acuña	**82**	29 20N	101 10W
Ciudad Altamirano	**82**	18 20N	100 40W
Ciudad Bolívar	**86**	8 5N	63 30W
Ciudad Camargo	**82**	27 41N	105 10W
Ciudad de Valles	**83**	22 0N	98 30W
Ciudad del Carmen	**83**	18 20N	97 50W
Ciudad Delicias = Delicias	**82**	28 10N	105 30W
Ciudad Guerrero	**82**	28 33N	107 28W
Ciudad Guzmán	**82**	19 40N	103 30W
Ciudad Juárez	**82**	31 40N	106 28W
Ciudad Madero	**83**	22 19N	97 50W
Ciudad Mante	**83**	22 50N	99 0W
Ciudad Obregón	**82**	27 28N	109 59W
Ciudad Piar	**86**	7 27N	63 19W
Ciudad Real	**104**	38 59N	3 55W
Ciudad Rodrigo	**104**	40 35N	6 32W
Ciudad Trujillo = Sto. Domingo	**85**	18 30N	70 0W
Ciudad Victoria	**83**	23 41N	99 9W
Civitanova Marche	**108**	43 18N	13 41E
Civitavécchia	**108**	42 6N	11 46E
Civray	**102**	46 10N	0 17E
Çivril	**122**	38 20N	29 55E
Cizre	**122**	37 19N	42 10E
Clacton-on-Sea	**95**	51 47N	1 10E
Clairambault, L.	**36**	54 29N	69 0W
Claire	**41**	47 15N	68 40W
Claire, L.	**54**	58 35N	112 5W
Claire, Le	**76**	41 36N	90 21W
Clairemont	**75**	33 9N	100 44W
Clairmont	**60**	55 16N	118 47W
Clairton	**70**	40 18N	79 54W
Clairvaux-les-Lacs	**103**	46 35N	5 45E
Clallam Bay	**80**	48 15N	124 16W
Clamecy	**101**	47 28N	3 30E
Clandonald	**60**	53 34N	110 44W
Clanton	**73**	32 48N	86 36W
Clanwilliam, Can.	**57**	50 22N	99 49W
Clanwilliam, S. Afr.	**117**	32 11S	18 52E
Clapperton I.	**46**	46 0N	82 14W
Clappisons Corners	**48**	43 18N	79 55W
Clara	**97**	53 20N	7 38W
Claraville	**81**	35 24N	118 20W
Clare, Austral.	**136**	33 50S	138 37E
Clare, U.S.A.	**46**	43 47N	84 45W
Clare □	**97**	52 20N	7 38W
Clare I.	**97**	53 48N	10 0W
Clare, I.	**97**	53 48N	10 0W
Clare, R.	**97**	53 20N	9 0W
Claremont, Can.	**51**	43 58N	79 7W
Claremont, U.S.A.	**71**	43 23N	72 20W
Claremore	**75**	36 40N	95 20W
Claremorris	**97**	53 45N	9 0W
Clarence	**76**	39 45N	92 16W
Clarence I.	**91**	61 30S	53 50W
Clarence, I.	**90**	54 0S	72 0W
Clarence, R., Austral.	**135**	29 25S	153 22E
Clarence, R., N.Z.	**133**	42 10S	173 56E
Clarence Str., Austral.	**134**	12 0S	131 0E
Clarence Str., U.S.A.	**54**	55 40N	132 10W
Clarence Town	**85**	23 6N	74 59W
Clarenceville	**43**	45 4N	73 15W
Clarendon, Can.	**39**	45 29N	66 26W
Clarendon, Ark., U.S.A.	**75**	34 41N	91 20W
Clarendon, Tex., U.S.A.	**75**	34 58N	100 54W
Clarenville	**37**	48 10N	54 1W
Claresholm	**61**	50 0N	113 45W
Clarie Coast	**91**	67 0S	135 0E
Clarinda	**74**	40 45N	95 0W
Clarion, Iowa, U.S.A.	**76**	42 41N	93 46W
Clarion, Pa., U.S.A.	**70**	41 12N	79 22W
Clarion, R.	**70**	41 19N	79 10W
Clark	**74**	44 55N	97 45W
Clark Fork	**78**	48 9N	116 9W
Clark Fork, R.	**78**	48 0N	115 40W
Clark Hill Res.	**73**	33 45N	82 20W
Clark, Pt.	**46**	44 4N	81 45W
Clarkdale	**79**	34 53N	112 3W
Clarke City	**38**	50 12N	66 38W
Clarke, I.	**135**	40 32S	148 10E
Clarke L.	**56**	54 24N	106 54W
Clarkefield	**136**	37 30S	44 40E
Clark's Fork, R.	**78**	45 0N	109 30W
Clark's Harbour	**39**	43 25N	65 38W
Clarks Summit	**71**	41 31N	75 44W
Clarksburg	**72**	39 18N	80 21W
Clarksdale	**75**	34 12N	90 33W
Clarkson	**50**	43 31N	79 37W
Clarkston	**78**	46 28N	117 2W
Clarksville, Ark., U.S.A.	**75**	35 29N	93 27W
Clarksville, Iowa, U.S.A.	**76**	42 47N	92 40W
Clarksville, Mich., U.S.A.	**77**	42 50N	85 15W
Clarksville, Ohio, U.S.A.	**77**	39 24N	83 59W
Clarksville, Tenn., U.S.A.	**73**	36 32N	87 20W
Clarksville, Tex., U.S.A.	**75**	33 37N	94 59W
Clatskanie	**80**	46 9N	123 12W
Claude, Can.	**49**	43 47N	79 54W
Claude, U.S.A.	**75**	35 8N	101 22W
Claveria	**127**	18 37N	121 15E
Clay	**80**	38 17N	121 10W
Clay Center	**74**	39 27N	97 9W
Clay City, Ind., U.S.A.	**77**	39 17N	87 7W
Clay City, Ky., U.S.A.	**77**	37 52N	83 55W
Clay L.	**52**	50 3N	93 30W
Clayette, La	**103**	46 17N	4 19E
Claypool	**79**	33 27N	110 55W
Claysville	**70**	40 5N	80 25W
Clayton, Idaho, U.S.A.	**78**	44 12N	114 31W
Clayton, Ind., U.S.A.	**77**	39 41N	86 31W
Clayton, N. Mex., U.S.A.	**75**	36 30N	103 10W
Cle Elum	**78**	47 15N	120 57W
Clear L.	**80**	39 5N	122 47W
Clear C.	**97**	51 26N	9 30W
Clear I.	**97**	51 26N	9 30W
Clear, L.	**47**	45 26N	77 12W
Clear Lake, S.D., U.S.A.	**74**	44 48N	96 41W
Clear Lake, Wash., U.S.A.	**78**	48 27N	122 15W
Clear Lake City	**76**	43 8N	93 23W
Clear Lake Res.	**78**	41 55N	121 10W
Clear, R.	**60**	56 11N	119 42W
Clearfield, Iowa, U.S.A.	**76**	40 48N	94 29W
Clearfield, Pa., U.S.A.	**72**	41 0N	78 27W
Clearfield, Utah, U.S.A.	**78**	41 10N	112 0W
Clearlake Highlands	**80**	38 57N	122 38W
Clearmont	**78**	43 43N	106 29W
Clearwater, Can.	**63**	51 38N	120 2W
Clearwater, U.S.A.	**73**	27 58N	82 45W
Clearwater Cr.	**54**	61 36N	125 30W
Clearwater L.	**63**	52 15N	120 13W
Clearwater, Mts.	**78**	46 20N	115 30W
Clearwater Prov. Park	**57**	54 0N	101 0W
Clearwater, R., Alta., Can.	**60**	56 44N	111 23W
Clearwater, R., Alta., Can.	**61**	52 22N	114 57W
Clearwater, R., B.C., Can.	**63**	51 38N	120 3W
Cleburne	**75**	32 18N	97 25W
Clee Hills	**98**	52 26N	2 35W
Cleethorpes	**94**	53 33N	0 2W
Cleeve Cloud	**95**	51 56N	2 0W
Cleeve Hill	**95**	51 54N	2 0W
Clelles	**103**	44 50N	5 38E
Clementsport	**39**	44 40N	65 37W
Clendale	**77**	39 16N	84 28W
Clerks Rocks	**91**	56 0S	36 30W
Clermont, Austral.	**135**	22 49S	147 39E
Clermont, Can.	**41**	47 41N	70 14W
Clermont-en-Argonne	**101**	49 5N	5 4E
Clermont-Ferrand	**102**	45 46N	3 4E
Clermont-l'Hérault	**102**	43 38N	3 26E
Clerval	**101**	47 25N	6 30E
Cléry-Saint-André	**101**	47 50N	1 46E
Cleveland, U.K.	**94**	54 29N	1 0W
Cleveland, Miss., U.S.A.	**75**	33 43N	90 43W
Cleveland, Ohio, U.S.A.	**70**	41 28N	81 43W
Cleveland, Okla., U.S.A.	**75**	36 21N	96 33W
Cleveland, Tenn., U.S.A.	**73**	35 9N	84 52W
Cleveland, Tex., U.S.A.	**75**	30 18N	95 0W
Cleveland □	**94**	54 35N	1 8E
Cleveland, C.	**135**	19 11S	147 1E
Cleveland Heights	**70**	41 32N	81 30W
Clevelândia	**89**	26 24S	52 23W
Cleves	**77**	39 10N	84 45W
Clevvaux	**105**	50 4N	6 2E
Clew Bay	**97**	53 54N	9 50W
Clewiston	**73**	26 44N	80 50W
Clifden, Ireland	**97**	53 30N	10 2W
Clifden, N.Z.	**133**	46 1S	167 42E
Cliff	**79**	33 0N	108 44W
Cliffdell	**80**	46 44N	120 42W
Clifton, Ariz., U.S.A.	**79**	33 8N	109 23W
Clifton, Ill., U.S.A.	**77**	40 56N	87 56W
Clifton, Tex., U.S.A.	**75**	31 46N	97 35W
Clifton Forge	**72**	37 49N	79 51W
Climax	**56**	49 10N	108 20W
Clingmans Dome	**73**	35 35N	83 30W
Clint	**79**	31 37N	106 11W
Clinton, B.C., Can.	**63**	51 6N	121 35W
Clinton, Ont., Can.	**46**	43 37N	81 32W
Clinton, N.Z.	**133**	46 12S	169 23E

Clinton **Concots**

Clinton, Ark., U.S.A.	**75**	35 37N	92 30W
Clinton, Ill., U.S.A.	**74**	40 8N	89 0W
Clinton, Ind., U.S.A.	**77**	39 40N	87 22W
Clinton, Iowa, U.S.A.	**76**	41 50N	90 12W
Clinton, Mass., U.S.A.	**71**	42 26N	71 40W
Clinton, Mo., U.S.A.	**76**	38 20N	93 46W
Clinton, N.C., U.S.A.	**73**	35 5N	78 15W
Clinton, Okla., U.S.A.	**75**	35 30N	99 0W
Clinton, S.C., U.S.A.	**73**	34 30N	81 54W
Clinton, Tenn., U.S.A.	**73**	36 6N	84 10W
Clinton, Wash., U.S.A.	**80**	47 59N	122 22W
Clinton, Wis., U.S.A.	**77**	42 34N	88 52W
Clinton Colden L.	**64**	64 58N	107 27W
Clinton Creek	**64**	64 25N	140 37W
Clintonville	**74**	44 35N	88 46W
Clisson	**100**	47 5N	1 16W
Clive	**61**	52 28N	113 27W
Clive L.	**54**	63 13N	118 54W
Clodomira	**88**	27 35S	64 14W
Clonakilty	**97**	51 37N	8 53W
Clonakilty B.	**97**	51 33N	8 50W
Cloncurry	**135**	20 40S	140 28E
Clones	**97**	54 10N	7 13W
Clonmel	**97**	52 22N	7 42W
Cloquet	**52**	46 40N	92 30W
Cloquet, R.	**52**	46 52N	92 35W
Clorinda	**88**	25 16S	57 45W
Cloud Peak	**78**	44 30N	107 10W
Cloudcroft	**79**	33 0N	105 48W
Clova	**40**	48 7N	75 22W
Clover Pt.	**63**	48 24N	123 21W
Cloverdale, B.C., Can.	**66**	49 7N	122 44W
Cloverdale, N.B., Can.	**39**	46 17N	67 22W
Cloverdale, Calif., U.S.A.	**80**	38 49N	123 0W
Cloverdale, Ind., U.S.A.	**77**	39 31N	86 47W
Cloverport	**77**	37 50N	86 38W
Clovis, Calif., U.S.A.	**80**	36 54N	119 45W
Clovis, N. Mex., U.S.A.	**75**	34 20N	103 10W
Cloyne	**47**	44 49N	77 11W
Clucluz L.	**62**	53 53N	123 33W
Cluj	**107**	46 47N	23 38E
Cluny	**103**	46 26N	4 38E
Cluses	**103**	46 5N	6 35E
Clutha, R.	**133**	46 20S	169 49E
Clwyd □	**94**	53 5N	3 20W
Clwyd, R.	**94**	53 12N	3 30W
Clyde, Alta., Can.	**60**	54 9N	113 39W
Clyde, N.W.T., Can.	**65**	70 30N	68 30W
Clyde, Ont., Can.	**49**	43 22N	80 14W
Clyde, N.Z.	**133**	45 12S	169 20E
Clyde, N.Y., U.S.A.	**70**	43 8N	76 52W
Clyde, Ohio, U.S.A.	**76**	41 18N	82 59W
Clyde, Firth of	**96**	55 20N	5 0W
Clyde, R., Can.	**39**	43 35N	65 27W
Clyde, R., U.K.	**96**	55 46N	4 58W
Clyde River	**39**	43 38N	65 29W
Clydebank	**96**	55 54N	4 25W
Clymer	**70**	42 3N	79 39W
Coachella	**81**	33 44N	116 13W
Coachella Canal	**81**	32 43N	114 57W
Coachman's Cove	**35**	50 6N	56 20W
Coacoachou, L.	**38**	50 25N	60 14W
Coahoma	**75**	32 17N	101 20W
Coahuayana, R.	**82**	18 41N	103 45W
Coahuayutla	**82**	18 19N	101 42W
Coahuila □	**82**	27 0N	112 30W
Coal City	**77**	41 17N	88 17W
Coal Creek	**61**	49 30N	114 59W
Coal Harbour	**62**	50 36N	127 35W
Coal, R.	**54**	59 39N	126 57W
Coalcomán	**82**	18 40N	103 10W
Coaldale	**61**	49 45N	112 35W
Coalgate	**75**	34 35N	96 13W
Coalhurst	**61**	49 45N	112 56W
Coalinga	**80**	36 10N	120 21W
Coalmont	**63**	49 32N	120 42W
Coalspur	**54**	53 15N	117 0W
Coalville, U.K.	**94**	52 43N	1 21W
Coalville, U.S.A.	**78**	40 58N	111 24W
Coamo	**67**	18 5N	66 22W
Coari	**86**	4 8S	63 7W
Coast Mts.	**62**	52 0N	126 0W
Coast Range	**80**	40 0N	124 0W
Coastal Plains Basin	**134**	30 10S	115 30E
Coatbridge	**96**	55 52N	4 2W
Coatepec	**83**	19 27N	96 58W
Coatepeque	**84**	14 46N	91 55W
Coatesville	**72**	39 59N	75 55W
Coaticook	**41**	45 10N	71 46W
Coats I.	**65**	62 30N	83 0W
Coats Land	**91**	77 0S	25 0W
Coatzacoalcos	**83**	18 7N	94 35W
Cobalt	**34**	47 25N	79 42W
Cobán	**84**	15 30N	90 21W
Cobar	**136**	31 27S	145 48E
Cobaz, L.	**38**	51 15N	60 21W
Cobden	**47**	45 38N	76 53W
Cóbh	**97**	51 50N	8 18W
Cobija	**86**	11 0S	68 50W
Cobleskill	**71**	42 40N	74 30W
Coboconk	**47**	44 39N	78 48W
Cobourg	**47**	43 58N	78 10W
Cobourg Pen.	**134**	11 20S	132 15E
Cobram	**136**	35 54S	145 40E
Cobre	**78**	41 6N	114 25W
Cóbué	**117**	12 0S	34 58E
Coburg	**106**	50 15N	10 58E
Coburg I.	**65**	75 57N	79 26W
Coca, R.	**86**	0 25S	77 5W
Cocagne	**39**	46 20N	64 37W
Cocha, La	**88**	27 50S	65 40W
Cochabamba	**86**	17 15S	66 20W
Coche, I.	**86**	10 47N	63 56W
Cochenour	**52**	51 5N	93 48W
Cochilha Grande de Albardão	**89**	28 30S	51 30W
Cochin China = Nam-Phan	**128**	10 30N	106 0E
Cochise	**79**	32 6N	109 58W
Cochran	**73**	32 25N	83 23W
Cochrane, Alta., Can.	**61**	51 11N	114 30W
Cochrane, Ont., Can.	**34**	49 0N	81 0W
Cochrane, L.	**90**	47 10S	72 0W
Cochrane, R.	**55**	57 53N	101 34W
Cockatoo I.	**134**	16 6S	123 37E
Cockburn	**136**	32 5S	141 0E
Cockburn, Canal	**90**	54 30S	72 0W
Cockburn, C.	**65**	74 52N	79 24W
Cockburn I.	**46**	45 55N	83 22W
Coco Chan.	**128**	13 50N	93 25E
Coco, Pta.	**86**	2 58N	77 43W
Coco, R. (Wanks)	**84**	14 10N	85 0W
Coco Solo	**84**	9 22N	79 53W
Cocoa	**73**	28 22N	80 40W
Cocobeach	**116**	0 59N	9 34E
Cocos, Is.	**16**	12 10S	96 50E
Cocos (Keeling) Is.	**11**	12 12S	96 54E
Cod, C.	**72**	42 8N	70 10W
Cod I.	**36**	57 47N	61 47W
Codajás	**86**	3 40S	62 0W
Codera, C.	**86**	10 35N	66 4W
Coderre	**56**	50 11N	106 31W
Codette	**56**	53 16N	104 0W
Codó	**87**	4 30S	43 55W
Codroy	**37**	47 53N	59 24W
Codroy Pond	**37**	48 4N	58 52W
Cody	**78**	44 35N	109 0W
Coe Hill	**47**	44 52N	77 50W
Coelemu	**88**	36 30S	72 48W
Coen	**135**	13 52S	143 12E
Coesfeld	**105**	51 56N	7 10E
Coetivy Is.	**16**	7 8S	56 16E
Coeur d'Alene	**78**	47 45N	116 51W
Coffeyville	**75**	37 0N	95 40W
Coffs Harbour	**135**	30 16S	153 5E
Cofre de Perote, Cerro	**83**	19 30N	97 10W
Coghinas, R.	**108**	40 55N	8 48E
Cognac	**102**	45 41N	0 20W
Cohagen	**78**	47 2N	106 45W
Cohasset	**52**	47 18N	93 39W
Cohoes	**71**	42 47N	73 42W
Cohuna	**136**	35 45S	144 15E
Coiba I.	**84**	7 30N	81 40W
Coig, R.	**90**	51 0S	70 20W
Coimbatore	**124**	11 2N	76 59E
Coimbra	**104**	40 15N	8 27W
Coín	**104**	36 40N	4 48W
Coin-Rond	**45**	45 38N	73 13W
Cojedes □	**86**	9 20N	68 20W
Cojimies	**86**	0 20N	80 0W
Cojutepequé	**84**	13 41N	88 54W
Cokeville	**78**	42 4N	111 0W
Colac	**136**	38 21S	143 35E
Colbinabbin	**136**	36 38S	144 48E
Colborne	**47**	44 0N	77 53W
Colby	**74**	39 27N	101 2W
Colchagua □	**88**	34 30S	71 0W
Colchester	**95**	51 54N	0 55E
Cold L.	**60**	54 33N	110 5W
Cold Lake	**60**	54 27N	110 10W
Coldstream	**96**	55 39N	2 14W
Coldwater, Can.	**46**	44 42N	79 40W
Coldwater, Kans., U.S.A.	**75**	37 18N	99 24W
Coldwater, Mich., U.S.A.	**77**	41 57N	85 0W
Coldwater, Ohio, U.S.A.	**77**	40 29N	84 38W
Coldwater, L.	**77**	41 48N	84 59W
Coldwell	**34**	48 45N	86 30W
Cole Camp	**76**	38 28N	93 12W
Colebrook, Can.	**66**	49 6N	122 52W
Colebrook, U.S.A.	**71**	44 54N	71 29W
Coleman, Can.	**61**	49 40N	114 30W
Coleman, Mich., U.S.A.	**46**	43 46N	84 35W
Coleman, Tex., U.S.A.	**75**	31 52N	99 30W
Coleman, R.	**135**	15 6S	141 38E
Coleraine, Austral.	**136**	37 36S	141 40E
Coleraine, Can.	**50**	43 49N	79 41W
Coleraine, U.K.	**97**	55 8N	6 40E
Coleraine, U.S.A.	**52**	47 17N	93 27W
Coleraine □	**97**	55 8N	6 40E
Coleridge, L.	**133**	43 17S	171 30E
Colesberg	**117**	30 45S	25 5E
Colesburg	**76**	42 38N	91 12W
Coleville, Can.	**56**	51 43N	109 15W
Coleville, U.S.A.	**80**	38 44N	119 30W
Colfax, Calif., U.S.A.	**80**	39 6N	120 57W
Colfax, Ill., U.S.A.	**77**	40 34N	88 37W
Colfax, Ind., U.S.A.	**77**	40 12N	86 40W
Colfax, La., U.S.A.	**75**	31 35N	92 39W
Colfax, Wash., U.S.A.	**78**	46 57N	117 28W
Colhué Huapi, L.	**90**	45 30S	69 0W
Colima	**82**	19 10N	103 40W
Colima □	**82**	19 10N	103 40W
Colima, Nevado de	**82**	19 30N	103 40W
Colina	**88**	33 13S	70 45W
Colinas	**87**	6 0S	44 10W
Colinet	**37**	47 13N	53 33W
Colinton, Austral.	**136**	35 50S	149 10E
Colinton, Can.	**60**	54 37N	113 15W
Coll, I.	**96**	56 40N	6 35W
Collaguasi	**88**	21 5S	68 45W
Collbran	**79**	39 16N	107 58W
College Bridge	**39**	45 59N	64 33W
College Heights	**61**	52 28N	113 45W
College Park	**73**	33 42N	84 27W
Collette	**35**	46 40N	65 30W
Colleymount	**62**	54 2N	126 19W
Collie	**134**	33 22S	116 8E
Collier B.	**134**	16 10S	124 15E
Collingwood, Can.	**46**	44 29N	80 13W
Collingwood, N.Z.	**133**	40 25S	172 40E
Collingwood Corner	**39**	45 37N	63 56W
Collins, Can.	**52**	50 17N	89 27W
Collins, U.S.A.	**76**	37 54N	93 37W
Collinson Pen	**65**	69 58N	101 24W
Collinsville, Austral.	**135**	20 30S	147 56E
Collinsville, U.S.A.	**76**	38 40N	89 59W
Collipulli	**88**	37 55S	72 30W
Collonges	**103**	46 9N	5 52E
Collooney	**97**	54 11N	8 28W
Colmar	**101**	48 5N	7 20E
Colmars	**103**	44 11N	6 39E
Colmor	**75**	36 18N	104 36W
Colne	**94**	53 51N	2 11W
Colnett, Cabo	**82**	31 0N	116 20W
Colo, R.	**136**	33 25S	150 52E
Cologne = Koln	**105**	50 56N	9 58E
Colombey-les-Belles	**101**	48 32N	5 54E
Colombey-les-Deux Églises	**101**	48 20N	4 50E
Colombia	**86**	3 24N	79 49W
Colombia ■	**86**	3 45N	73 0W
Colombier	**41**	48 52N	68 51W
Colombo	**124**	6 56N	79 58E
Colombus, Kans., U.S.A.	**75**	37 15N	94 30W
Colombus, Nebr., U.S.A.	**74**	41 30N	97 25W
Colombus, N.Mex., U.S.A.	**79**	31 54N	107 43W
Colome	**74**	43 20N	99 44W
Colón, Argent.	**88**	32 12S	58 30W
Colón, Cuba	**84**	22 42N	80 54W
Colón, Panama	**84**	9 20N	80 0W
Colonel Hill	**85**	22 50N	74 21W
Colonia del Sacramento	**89**	34 25S	57 50W
Colonia Dora	**88**	28 34S	62 59W
Colonia Las Heras	**90**	46 30S	69 0W
Colonia Sarmiento	**90**	45 30S	68 15W
Colonial Hts.	**72**	37 19N	77 25W
Colonial Village	**49**	43 12N	78 59W
Colonsay	**56**	51 59N	105 52W
Colonsay, I.	**96**	56 4N	6 12W
Colorado □	**68**	37 40N	106 0W
Colorado Aqueduct	**81**	34 17N	114 10W
Colorado City	**75**	32 25N	100 50W
Colorado Desert	**68**	34 20N	116 0W
Colorado, I.	**84**	9 12N	79 50W
Colorado Plateau	**79**	36 40N	110 30W
Colorado, R., Argent.	**88**	37 30S	69 0W
Colorado, R., Ariz., U.S.A.	**79**	33 30N	114 30W
Colorado, R., Calif., U.S.A.	**79**	34 0N	114 33W
Colorado, R., Tex., U.S.A.	**75**	29 40N	96 30W
Colorado Springs	**74**	38 55N	104 50W
Colotepec	**83**	15 47N	97 3W
Colotlán	**82**	22 6N	103 16W
Colquitz	**63**	48 29N	123 24W
Colton, Calif., U.S.A.	**81**	34 4N	117 20W
Colton, N.Y., U.S.A.	**71**	44 34N	74 58W
Colton, Wash., U.S.A.	**78**	46 41N	117 6W
Columa	**80**	38 49N	120 53W
Columbia, Ill., U.S.A.	**76**	38 26N	90 12W
Columbia, La., U.S.A.	**75**	32 7N	92 5W
Columbia, Miss., U.S.A.	**75**	31 16N	89 50W
Columbia, Mo., U.S.A.	**76**	38 58N	92 20W
Columbia, Pa., U.S.A.	**71**	40 2N	76 30W
Columbia, S.C., U.S.A.	**73**	34 0N	81 0W
Columbia, Tenn., U.S.A.	**73**	35 40N	87 0W
Columbia, C.	**17**	83 0N	70 0W
Columbia City	**77**	41 8N	85 30W
Columbia, District of □	**72**	38 55N	77 0W
Columbia Falls	**78**	48 25N	114 16W
Columbia Heights	**74**	45 5N	93 10W
Columbia L.	**61**	50 15N	115 52W
Columbia, Mt.	**63**	52 8N	117 20W
Columbia Plateau	**78**	47 30N	118 30W
Columbia, R.	**78**	45 49N	120 0W
Columbiana	**70**	40 53N	80 40W
Columbiaville	**46**	43 9N	83 25W
Columbretes, Is.	**104**	39 50N	0 50E
Columbus, Can.	**51**	43 59N	78 55W
Columbus, Ga., U.S.A.	**73**	32 30N	84 58W
Columbus, Ind., U.S.A.	**72**	39 14N	85 55W
Columbus, Miss., U.S.A.	**73**	33 30N	88 26W
Columbus, Mont., U.S.A.	**78**	45 45N	109 14W
Columbus, N.D., U.S.A.	**56**	48 52N	102 48W
Columbus, Ohio, U.S.A.	**77**	39 57N	83 1W
Columbus, Tex., U.S.A.	**75**	29 42N	96 33W
Columbus, Wis., U.S.A.	**74**	43 20N	89 2W
Columbus Grove	**77**	40 55N	84 4W
Columbus Junction	**76**	41 17N	91 22W
Colusa	**80**	39 15N	122 1W
Colville	**63**	48 33N	117 54W
Colville, C.	**133**	36 29S	175 21E
Colville Lake	**64**	67 2N	126 7W
Colville, R.	**67**	69 15N	152 0W
Colwood	**63**	48 26N	123 29W
Colwyn Bay	**94**	53 17N	3 44W
Com-Est	**44**	45 27N	74 7W
Comácchio	**108**	44 41N	12 10E
Comalcalco	**83**	18 16N	93 13W
Comallo	**90**	41 0S	70 5W
Comanche, Okla., U.S.A.	**75**	34 27N	97 58W
Comanche, Tex., U.S.A.	**75**	31 55N	98 35W
Comayagua	**84**	14 25N	87 37W
Combahee, R.	**73**	32 45N	80 50W
Combeaufontaine	**101**	47 38N	5 54E
Comber	**46**	42 14N	82 33W
Combermere	**47**	45 22N	77 37W
Comblain	**105**	50 29N	5 35E
Combles	**101**	50 0N	2 50E
Combourg	**100**	48 25N	1 46W
Combronde	**102**	45 58N	3 5E
Come by Chance	**37**	47 51N	54 0W
Comeragh Mts.	**97**	52 17N	7 35W
Comilla	**125**	23 28N	91 10E
Comino I.	**108**	36 0N	14 22E
Comitán	**83**	16 18N	92 9W
Commanda	**46**	45 57N	79 36W
Commentry	**102**	46 20N	2 46E
Commerce, Ga., U.S.A.	**73**	34 10N	83 25W
Commerce, Tex., U.S.A.	**75**	33 15N	95 50W
Commercy	**101**	48 40N	5 34E
Commissaires, L. des	**41**	48 10N	72 16W
Commissioner I.	**57**	52 10N	97 16W
Committee B.	**65**	68 30N	86 30W
Commonwealth B.	**91**	67 0S	144 0E
Communism Pk. = Kommunisma, Pk.	**123**	38 40N	72 20E
Como	**108**	45 48N	9 5E
Como, L. di	**108**	46 5N	9 17E
Comodoro Rivadavia	**90**	45 50S	67 40W
Comores, Arch. des	**11**	10 0S	50 0E
Comores, Is.	**11**	12 10S	44 15E
Comorin, C.	**124**	8 3N	77 40E
Comoro Is.	**11**	12 10S	44 15E
Comox	**62**	49 42N	124 55W
Compeer	**61**	51 52N	110 0W
Compiègne	**101**	49 24N	2 50E
Compostela	**82**	21 15N	104 53W
Comprida, I.	**89**	24 50S	47 42W
Compton, Can.	**41**	45 14N	71 49W
Compton, U.S.A.	**81**	33 54N	118 13W
Côn Dao	**128**	8 45N	106 45E
Conakry	**114**	9 29N	13 49W
Conatlán	**82**	24 30N	104 42W
Concarneau	**100**	47 52N	3 56W
Conceição da Barra	**87**	18 35S	39 45W
Conceição do Araguaia	**87**	8 0S	49 2W
Concepción, Argent.	**88**	27 20S	65 35W
Concepción, Boliv.	**86**	15 50S	61 40W
Concepción, Chile	**88**	36 50S	73 0W
Concepción, Colomb.	**86**	0 5N	75 37W
Concepción, Mexico	**83**	18 15N	90 5W
Concepción, Parag.	**88**	23 30S	57 20W
Concepción, Venez.	**86**	10 48N	71 46W
Concepción □	**88**	37 0S	72 30W
Concepcion, C.	**68**	34 30N	120 34W
Concepción del Oro	**82**	24 40N	101 30W
Concepción del Uruguay	**88**	32 35S	58 20W
Concepción, L.	**86**	17 20S	61 10W
Concepción, Punta	**82**	26 55N	111 50W
Concepción, R.	**82**	30 32N	113 2W
Conception B., Can.	**37**	47 45N	53 0W
Conception B., Namibia	**117**	23 55S	14 22E
Conception I.	**85**	23 52N	75 9W
Conception, La	**40**	46 9N	74 42W
Conchas Dam	**75**	35 25N	104 10W
Conche	**37**	50 48N	55 58W
Concho	**79**	34 32N	109 43W
Concho, R.	**75**	31 30N	100 8W
Conchos, R., Chihnahua, Mexico	**82**	29 20N	105 0W
Conchos, R., Tamaulipas, Mexico	**83**	25 0N	97 32W
Concon	**88**	32 56S	71 33W
Conconully	**63**	48 31N	119 45W
Concord, Can.	**50**	43 48N	79 29W
Concord, Calif., U.S.A.	**80**	37 59N	122 2W
Concord, Mich., U.S.A.	**77**	42 11N	84 38W
Concord, N.C., U.S.A.	**73**	35 28N	80 35W
Concord, N.H., U.S.A.	**71**	43 12N	71 30W
Concórdia, Argent.	**88**	31 20S	58 2W
Concórdia, Brazil	**86**	4 36S	66 36W
Concordia, Colomb.	**86**	2 39N	72 47W
Concordia, Mexico	**82**	23 18N	106 2W
Concordia, U.S.A.	**76**	38 59N	93 34W
Concordia, Kans., U.S.A.	**74**	39 35N	97 40W
Concordia, La	**83**	16 8N	92 38W
Concots	**102**	44 26N	1 40E

Concrete **Craon**

Concrete 63 48 35N 121 49W
Condamine, R. 135 27 7S 149 48E
Condat 102 45 21N 2 46E
Condé 101 50 26N 3 34E
Conde 74 45 13N 98 5W
Condé-sur-Noireau 100 48 51N 0 33W
Condeúba 87 15 0S 42 0W
Condie Res. 58 50 34N 104 43W
Condobolin 136 33 4S 147 6E
Condom 102 43 57N 0 22E
Condon 78 45 15N 120 8W
Conejos 82 26 14N 103 53W
Conemaugh, R. 70 40 24N 79 0W
Conestogo 49 43 32N 80 30W
Conflans-en-Jarnisy 101 49 10N 5 52E
Confolens 102 46 2N 0 40E
Confuso, R. 88 24 10S 59 0W
Congleton 94 53 10N 2 12W
Congnarauya 36 58 35N 68 1W
Congo ■ 116 1 0S 16 0E
Congo Basin 112 0 10S 24 30E
Congo (Kinshasa) ■ = Zaïre ■ 116 1 0S 16 0E
Congo, R. = Zaïre, R. 116 1 30N 28 0E
Congonhas 89 20 30S 43 52W
Congress 79 34 11N 112 56W
Congucu 113 31 25S 52 30W
Coniston 46 46 29N 80 51W
Conjeevaram = Kanchipuram 124 12 52N 79 45E
Conklin 60 55 38N 111 5W
Conn, L. 97 54 3N 9 15W
Connacht 97 53 23N 8 40W
Conneaut 70 41 55N 80 32W
Connecticut □ 71 41 40N 72 40W
Connecticut, R. 71 41 17N 72 21W
Connell 78 46 45N 118 58W
Connemara 97 53 29N 9 45W
Conner, La 78 48 22N 122 27W
Connersville 77 39 40N 85 10W
Connolsville 70 40 5N 79 32W
Connors 41 47 10N 68 52W
Conoble 136 32 55S 144 42E
Conon, R. 96 57 33N 4 45W
Cononaco, R. 86 1 20S 76 30W
Conquest 56 51 32N 107 14W
Conquet, Le 100 48 21N 4 46W
Conrad, Iowa, U.S.A. 76 42 14N 92 52W
Conrad, Mont., U.S.A. 78 48 11N 112 0W
Conroe 75 30 15N 95 28W
Consecon 47 44 0N 77 31W
Conselheiro Lafaiete 89 20 40S 43 48W
Conshohocken 71 40 5N 75 18W
Consort 61 52 1N 110 46W
Constanța 107 44 14N 28 38E
Constantina 104 37 51N 5 40W
Constantine, Alg. 114 36 25N 6 42E
Constantine, U.S.A. 77 41 50N 85 40W
Constitución, Chile 88 35 20S 72 30W
Constitución, Uruguay 88 31 0S 58 10W
Consul 56 49 20N 109 30W
Contact 78 41 50N 114 56W
Contai 125 21 54N 87 55E
Contamana 86 7 10S 74 55W
Contas, R. 87 13 5S 41 53W
Contes 103 43 49N 7 19E
Contin L. 57 53 25N 95 10W
Continental 77 41 6N 84 16W
Contoocook 71 43 13N 71 45W
Contrecoeur 43 45 51N 73 14W
Contres 100 47 24N 1 26E
Contrexéville 101 48 6N 5 53E
Contwoyto L. 64 65 42N 110 50W
Convención 86 8 28N 73 21W
Converse 77 40 34N 85 52W
Convoy 77 40 55N 84 43W
Conway, Ark., U.S.A. 75 35 5N 92 30W
Conway, N.H., U.S.A. 71 43 58N 71 8W
Conway, S.C., U.S.A. 73 33 49N 79 2W
Conway = Conwy 94 53 17N 3 50W
Conway, R. = Conwy 94 53 10N 3 50W
Conwy 94 53 17N 3 50W
Conwy, R. 94 53 18N 3 50W
Coober Pedy 134 29 1S 134 43E
Cooch Behar 125 26 22N 89 29E
Cook 52 47 49N 92 39W
Cook, Bahia 90 55 10S 70 0W
Cook Inlet 67 59 0N 151 0W
Cook Is. 15 20 0S 160 0W
Cook, Mt. 133 43 36S 170 9E
Cook Strait 133 41 15S 174 29E
Cookeville 73 36 12N 85 30W
Cooking L. 60 53 26N 113 2W
Cook's Harbour 37 51 36N 55 52W
Cookshire 41 45 25N 71 38W
Cookstown 97 54 40N 6 43W
Cookstown □ 97 54 40N 6 43W
Cooksville 50 43 36N 79 35W
Cooktown 135 15 30S 145 16E
Coolah 136 31 48S 149 41E
Coolamon 136 34 46S 147 8E
Coolgardie 134 30 55S 121 8E
Coolidge 79 33 1N 111 35W
Coolidge Dam 79 33 10N 110 30W
Cooma 136 36 12S 149 8E
Coombs 62 49 18N 124 25W
Coon Rapids 76 41 53N 94 41W
Coonabarabran 136 31 14S 149 18E
Coonamble 135 30 56S 148 27E
Coondapoor 124 13 42N 74 40E
Cooper 75 33 20N 95 40W
Cooper, R. 73 33 0N 79 55W
Cooperstown, N.D., U.S.A. 74 47 30N 98 14W
Cooperstown, N.Y., U.S.A. 71 42 42N 74 57W
Coopersville 77 43 4N 85 57W
Coorong, The 135 35 50S 139 20E
Coos Bay 78 43 26N 124 7W
Cootamundra 136 34 36S 148 1E
Cootehill 97 54 5N 7 5W
Copahué, Paso 88 37 49S 71 8W
Copainalá 83 17 8N 93 11W
Copán 84 14 50N 89 9W
Cope 74 39 44N 102 50W
Copenhagen = København 111 55 41N 12 34E
Copetown 49 43 14N 80 4W
Copiapó 88 27 15S 70 20E
Copiapó, R. 88 27 19S 70 56W
Copp L. 54 60 14N 114 40W
Copper Center 67 62 10N 145 25W
Copper Cliff 46 46 28N 81 4W
Copper Harbor 53 47 31N 87 55W
Copper Mountain 54 49 20N 120 30W
Copper R. 67 61 30N 144 30W
Coppermine 64 67 50N 115 5W
Coppermine, R. 64 67 49N 115 4W
Copperopolis 80 37 58N 120 38W
Coquet, R. 94 55 18N 1 45W
Coquille 78 43 15N 124 6W
Coquimbo 88 30 0S 71 20W
Coquimbo □ 88 31 0S 71 0W
Coquitlam, R. 66 49 13N 122 48W
Corabia 107 43 48N 24 30E
Coracora 86 15 5S 73 45W
Coral Harbour 65 64 8N 83 10W
Coral Rapids 34 50 20N 81 40W
Coral Sea 135 15 0S 150 0E
Coral Sea Islands Terr. 135 20 0S 155 0E
Corangamite, L. 136 38 0S 143 30E
Coraopolis 70 40 30N 80 10W
Corato 108 41 12N 16 22E
Corbeil-Essonnes 101 48 36N 2 26E
Corbie 101 49 54N 2 30E
Corbières, mts. 102 42 55N 2 35E
Corbigny 101 47 16N 3 40E
Corbin, Can. 43 45 3N 73 41W
Corbin, U.S.A. 72 37 0N 84 3W
Corby, Lincs., U.K. 95 52 49N 0 31W
Corby, Northants., U.K. 95 52 29N 0 41W
Corcoran 80 36 6N 119 35W
Corcubión 104 42 56N 9 12W
Cord. de Caravaya 86 14 0S 70 30W
Cordele 73 31 55N 83 49W
Cordell 75 35 18N 99 0W
Cordes 102 44 5N 1 57E
Cordillera Oriental 86 5 0N 74 0W
Córdoba, Argent. 88 31 20S 64 10W
Córdoba, Mexico 83 18 50N 97 0W
Córdoba, Spain 104 37 50N 4 50W
Córdoba □, Argent. 88 31 22S 64 15W
Córdoba □, Colomb. 86 8 20N 75 40W
Córdoba, Sierra de 88 31 10S 64 25W
Cordon 127 16 42N 121 32E
Cordova, Ala., U.S.A. 73 33 45N 87 12W
Cordova, Alaska, U.S.A. 67 60 36N 145 45W
Cordova, Ill., U.S.A. 76 41 41N 90 19W
Corfu = Kerkira 109 39 38N 19 50E
Coricudgy, Mt. 136 32 51S 150 24E
Corigliano Cálabro 108 39 36N 16 31E
Corinth, Ky., U.S.A. 77 38 30N 84 34W
Corinth, Miss., U.S.A. 73 34 54N 88 30W
Corinth, N.Y., U.S.A. 71 43 15N 73 50W
Corinto, Brazil 87 18 20S 44 30W
Corinto, Nic. 84 12 30N 87 10W
Cork 97 51 54N 8 30W
Cork □ 97 51 50N 8 50W
Cork Harbour 97 51 46N 8 16W
Corlay 100 48 20N 3 5W
Çorlu 122 41 11N 27 49E
Cormack 37 49 18N 57 23W
Cormack L. 54 60 56N 121 37W
Cormorant 57 54 14N 100 35W
Cormorant L. 57 54 15N 100 50W
Corn Is. 85 12 0N 83 0W
Cornelio 82 29 55N 111 8W
Cornélio Procópio 89 23 7S 50 40W
Cornell, U.S.A. 74 45 10N 91 8W
Cornell, U.S.A. 77 40 58N 88 43W
Corner Brook 37 48 57N 57 58W
Corner Inlet 136 38 45S 146 20E
Corning, Can. 56 49 58N 102 58W
Corning, Ark., U.S.A. 75 36 27N 90 34W
Corning, Calif., U.S.A. 78 39 56N 122 9W
Corning, Iowa, U.S.A. 76 40 57N 94 40W
Corning, N.Y., U.S.A. 70 42 10N 77 3W
Cornwall, Can. 39 46 14N 63 13W
Cornwall, Ont., Can. 47 45 2N 74 44W
Cornwall □ 95 50 26N 4 40W
Cornwall I. 65 77 37N 94 38W
Cornwallis I. 65 75 8N 95 0W
Coro 86 11 25N 69 41W
Coroatá 87 4 20S 44 0W
Corocoro 86 17 15S 69 19W
Coroico 86 16 0S 67 50W
Coromandel 133 36 45S 175 31E
Coromandel Coast 124 12 30N 81 0E
Corona, Calif., U.S.A. 81 33 49N 117 36W
Corona, N. Mex., U.S.A. 79 34 15N 105 32W
Coronach 56 49 7N 105 31W
Coronada B. 84 9 0N 83 40W
Coronadas, Is. de 81 32 25N 117 15W
Coronado 81 32 45N 117 9W
Coronado, Bahía de 84 9 0N 83 40W
Coronation 61 52 5N 111 27W
Coronation Gulf 64 68 25N 112 0W
Coronation I., Antarct. 91 60 45S 46 0W
Coronation I., U.S.A. 54 55 52N 134 20W
Coronda 88 31 58S 60 56W
Coronel 88 37 0S 73 10W
Coronel Bogado 88 27 11S 56 18W
Coronel Dorrego 88 38 40S 61 10W
Coronel Oviedo 88 25 24S 56 30W
Coronel Pringles 88 38 0S 61 30W
Coronel Suárez 88 37 30S 62 0W
Coronel Vidal 88 37 28S 57 45W
Coronie 87 5 55N 56 25W
Corowa 136 35 58S 146 21E
Corozal, Belize 83 18 30N 88 30W
Corozal, Colomb. 86 9 19N 75 18W
Corozal, Pan. C. Z. 84 8 59N 79 34W
Corps 103 44 50N 5 56E
Corpus 89 27 10S 55 30W
Corpus Christi 75 27 50N 97 28W
Corpus Christi L. 75 28 5N 97 54W
Corque 86 18 10S 67 50W
Corrèze □ 102 45 20N 1 45E
Corrib, L. 97 53 25N 9 10W
Corrientes 88 27 30S 58 45W
Corrientes □ 88 28 0S 57 0W
Corrientes, C., Colomb. 86 5 30N 77 34W
Corrientes, C., Cuba 84 21 43N 84 30W
Corrientes, C., Mexico 82 20 25N 105 42W
Corrientes, R., Argent. 88 30 21S 59 33W
Corrientes, R., Colomb. 86 3 15S 75 58W
Corrigan 75 31 0N 94 48W
Corry 70 41 55N 79 39W
Corse, C. 103 43 1N 9 25E
Corse-du-Sud □ 103 41 45N 9 0E
Corse, Î 103 42 0N 9 0E
Corsica = Corse 103 42 0N 9 0E
Corsicana 75 32 5N 96 30W
Corté 103 42 19N 9 11E
Cortez 79 37 24N 108 35W
Cortland 71 42 35N 76 11W
Cortona 108 43 16N 12 0E
Çorum 122 40 30N 35 5E
Corumbá, Goias, Brazil 87 16 0S 48 50W
Corumbá, Mato Grosso, Brazil 86 19 0S 57 30W
Coruña, La 104 43 20N 8 25W
Corunna, Can. 46 42 53N 82 26W
Corunna, U.S.A. 46 42 59N 84 7W
Corunna = La Coruña 104 43 20N 8 25W
Coruripe 87 10 5S 36 10W
Corvallis 78 44 36N 123 15W
Corvette, L. de la 36 53 25N 74 3W
Corwhin 49 43 31N 80 6W
Corydon, Ind., U.S.A. 77 38 13N 86 7W
Corydon, Iowa, U.S.A. 76 40 42N 93 22W
Corydon, Ky., U.S.A. 77 37 44N 87 43W
Cosalá 82 24 28N 106 40W
Cosamaloapán 83 18 23N 95 50W
Cosenza 108 39 17N 16 14E
Coshocton 70 40 17N 81 51W
Cosne-s.-Loire 101 47 24N 2 54E
Coso Junction 81 36 3N 117 57W
Coso Pk. 81 36 13N 117 44W
Cosquín 88 31 15S 64 30W
Cossé-le-Vivien 100 47 57N 0 54W
Costa Blanca 104 38 25N 0 10W
Costa Brava 104 41 30N 3 0E
Costa del Sol 104 36 30N 4 30W
Costa Dorada 104 40 45N 1 15E
Costa Mesa 81 33 39N 117 55W
Costa Rica 82 31 20N 112 40W
Costa Rica ■ 84 10 0N 84 0W
Costebelle, L. 38 50 19N 62 23W
Costilla 79 37 0N 105 30W
Cosumnes, R. 80 38 14N 121 25W
Cotabato 127 7 14N 124 15E
Cotagaita 88 20 45S 65 30W
Côte d'Azur 103 43 25N 6 50E
Côte d'Or 101 47 10N 4 50E
Côte d'Or □ 101 47 30N 4 50E
Côte-Rouge 44 45 33N 74 6W
Côte-St. André, La 103 45 24N 5 15E
Côte-St-Luce 44 45 28N 73 40W
Côte-St-Vincent 44 45 36N 74 8W
Coteau des Prairies 74 44 30N 97 0W
Coteau-du-Lac 44 45 18N 74 11W
Coteau du Missouri, Plat. du 68 47 0N 101 0W
Coteau Landing 43 45 15N 74 13W
Coteau Sta. 71 45 17N 74 14W
Cotentin 100 49 30N 1 30W
Côtes de Meuse 101 49 15N 5 22E
Côtes-du-Nord □ 100 48 25N 2 40W
Cotonou 114 6 20N 2 25E
Cotopaxi, Vol. 86 0 30S 78 30W
Cotswold Hills 95 51 42N 2 10W
Cottage Grove 78 43 48N 123 2W
Cottam 46 42 8N 82 45W
Cottbus 106 51 44N 14 20E
Cottonwood, Can. 54 53 5N 121 50W
Cottonwood, U.S.A. 79 34 48N 112 1W
Coubre, Pte. de la 102 45 42N 1 15W
Couches 101 46 53N 4 30E
Coudersport 70 41 45N 77 40W
Coudres, Île aux 41 47 24N 70 23W
Couëron 100 47 13N 1 44W
Couesnon, R. 100 48 20N 1 15W
Couhé-Vérac 102 46 18N 0 12E
Coulanges 101 47 30N 3 30E
Coulee City 78 47 44N 119 12W
Coulman I. 91 73 35S 170 0E
Coulommiers 101 48 50N 3 3E
Coulonge, R. 40 45 52N 76 46W
Coulonges 102 46 58N 0 35W
Coulterville, Calif., U.S.A. 80 37 42N 120 12W
Coulterville, Ill., U.S.A. 76 38 11N 89 36W
Council 67 64 55N 163 45W
Council Bluffs 74 41 20N 95 50W
Council Grove 74 38 41N 96 30W
Coupeaux, L. 38 51 27N 63 58W
Coupeville 80 48 13N 122 41W
Courantyne, R. 86 5 0N 57 45W
Courçon 102 46 15N 0 50W
Cours 103 46 7N 4 19E
Courseulles 100 49 20N 0 29W
Courtenay 62 49 45N 125 0W
Courtice 49 43 55N 78 46W
Courtine, La 102 45 43N 2 16E
Courtland, Can. 46 42 51N 80 38W
Courtland, U.S.A. 80 38 20N 121 34W
Courtright 46 42 49N 82 28W
Courville, Can. 42 46 53N 71 10W
Courville, France 100 48 28N 1 15E
Coutances 100 49 3N 1 28W
Couterne 100 48 30N 0 25W
Coutras 102 45 3N 0 8W
Coutts 61 49 0N 111 57W
Couture, L. 36 60 7N 75 20W
Couvin 105 50 3N 4 29E
Cove I. 46 45 17N 81 44W
Coventry 95 52 25N 1 31W
Coventry L. 55 61 15N 106 15W
Covey Hill 43 45 1N 73 46W
Covilhã 104 40 17N 7 31W
Covina 81 34 5N 117 52W
Covington, Ga., U.S.A. 73 33 36N 83 50W
Covington, Ind., U.S.A. 77 40 9N 87 24W
Covington, Ky., U.S.A. 77 39 5N 84 30W
Covington, Mich., U.S.A. 52 46 30N 88 35W
Covington, Ohio, U.S.A. 77 40 8N 84 20W
Covington, Okla., U.S.A. 75 36 21N 97 36W
Covington, Tenn., U.S.A. 75 35 34N 89 39W
Cow Head 37 49 55N 57 48W
Cowal, L. 136 33 40S 147 25E
Cowan 57 52 5N 100 45W
Cowan, L. 134 31 45S 121 45E
Cowan L., Can. 56 54 0N 107 0W
Cowan L., Sask., Can. 55 54 0N 107 15W
Cowansville 43 45 14N 72 46W
Cowden 77 39 15N 88 52W
Cowdenbeath 96 56 7N 3 20W
Cowes 95 50 45N 1 18W
Cowichan L. 62 48 53N 124 17W
Cowley 61 49 34N 114 5W
Cowlitz, R 80 46 5N 122 53W
Cowra 136 33 49S 148 42E
Cox I. 62 50 48N 128 36W
Coxim 87 18 30S 54 55W
Cox's Bazar 125 21 26N 91 59E
Cox's Cove 37 49 7N 58 5W
Coyame 82 29 28N 105 6W
Coyote Wells 81 32 44N 115 58W
Coyuca de Benitez 83 17 1N 100 8W
Coyuca de Catalán 82 18 58N 100 41W
Cozad 74 40 55N 99 57W
Cozumel 83 20 31N 86 55W
Cozumel, Isla de 83 20 30N 86 40W
Craboon 136 32 3S 149 30E
Crabtree 43 45 58N 73 28W
Cracroft Is. 62 50 32N 126 25W
Cradock 117 32 8S 25 36E
Crafton 70 40 25N 80 4W
Craig, Alaska, U.S.A. 67 55 30N 133 5W
Craig, Colo., U.S.A. 78 40 32N 107 44W
Craigavon = Portadown 97 54 27N 6 26W
Craigavon □ 97 54 28N 6 25W
Craigavon = Lurgan 97 54 28N 6 20W
Craigflower 63 48 27N 123 26W
Craigmyle 61 51 40N 112 15W
Craik 56 51 3N 105 49W
Craiova 107 44 21N 23 48E
Crampel 116 7 8N 19 81E
Cranberry Portage 55 54 35N 101 23W
Cranbrook 61 49 30N 115 46W
Crandon 74 45 30N 88 55W
Crane, Oregon, U.S.A. 78 43 21N 118 39W
Crane, Texas, U.S.A. 75 31 26N 102 27W
Crane I. 41 47 4N 70 33W
Crane L. 56 50 5N 109 5W
Crane River 57 51 30N 99 14W
Cranston 71 41 47N 71 27W
Craon 100 47 50N 0 58W

Craonne Dâmboviţa, R

Craonne 101 49 27N 3 46E
Crapaud 39 46 14N 63 30W
Crater, L. 78 42 55N 122 3W
Crateús 87 5 10S 40 50W
Crato 87 7 10S 39 25W
Crau 103 43 32N 4 40E
Crauford, C. 65 73 44N 84 51W
Craven 56 50 42N 104 49W
Craven, L. 36 54 20N 76 56W
Crawford 74 42 40N 103 25W
Crawfordsville 77 40 2N 86 51W
Crawley 95 51 7N 0 10W
Crazy Mts. 78 46 14N 110 30W
Crean L. 56 54 5N 106 9W
Crèche, La 102 46 23N 0 19W
Crécy-en-Brie 101 48 50N 2 53E
Crécy-en-Ponthieu 101 50 15N 1 53E
Crécy-sur-Serre 101 49 40N 3 32E
Credit, R. 50 43 33N 79 35W
Crediton 46 43 17N 81 33W
Cree L. 55 57 30N 106 30W
Cree, R., Can. 55 58 57N 105 47W
Cree, R., U.K. 96 54 51N 4 24W
Creede 79 37 56N 106 59W
Creel 82 27 45N 107 38W
Creelman 56 49 49N 103 18W
Creemore 46 44 19N 80 6W
Creighton 74 42 30N 97 52W
Creil 101 49 15N 2 34E
Cremona, Can. 61 51 33N 114 29W
Cremona, Italy 108 45 8N 10 2E
Crépy 101 49 37N 3 32E
Crépy-en-Valois 101 49 14N 2 54E
Cres 108 44 58N 14 25E
Cresbard 74 45 13N 98 57W
Crescent, Okla., U.S.A. 75 35 58N 97 36W
Crescent, Oreg., U.S.A. 78 43 30N 121 37W
Crescent Beach 66 49 3N 122 53W
Crescent City 78 41 45N 124 12W
Crescent Spur 63 53 34N 120 42W
Crespo 88 32 2S 60 19W
Cressman 34 47 40N 72 55W
Cressy 136 38 2S 143 40E
Crest 103 44 44N 5 2E
Crested Butte 79 38 57N 107 0W
Crestline, Calif., U.S.A. 81 34 14N 117 18W
Crestline, Ohio, U.S.A. 70 40 46N 82 45W
Creston, Can. 61 49 10N 116 31W
Creston, Calif., U.S.A. 80 35 32N 120 33W
Creston, Iowa, U.S.A. 76 41 0N 94 20W
Creston, Wash., U.S.A. 78 47 47N 118 36W
Creston, Wyo., U.S.A. 78 41 46N 107 50W
Crestone 79 35 2N 106 0W
Crestview, Calif., U.S.A. 80 37 46N 118 58W
Crestview, Fla., U.S.A. 73 30 45N 86 35W
Creswick 136 37 25S 143 51E
Crete 74 40 38N 96 58W
Crete, La 54 58 11N 116 24W
Creus, C. 104 42 20N 3 19E
Creuse □ 102 46 0N 2 0E
Creuse, R. 102 47 0N 0 34E
Creusot, Le 101 46 50N 4 24E
Crèvecœur-le-Grand 101 49 37N 2 5E
Crewe 94 53 6N 2 28W
Criciúma 89 28 40S 49 23W
Cridersville 77 40 39N 84 9W
Crieff 96 56 22N 3 50W
Crillon, Mt. 54 58 39N 137 14W
Crimea = Krymskaya 120 45 0N 34 0E
Crimson Lake 61 52 27N 115 2W
Crimson Lake Prov. Park 61 52 28N 114 54W
Crinan 96 56 6N 5 34W
Cristóbal 84 9 10N 80 0W
Crişul Alb, R. 107 46 25N 21 40E
Crişul Negru, R. 107 46 38N 22 26E
Crittenden 77 38 47N 84 36W
Crna Gora □ 109 42 40N 19 20E
Crna Gora, Mts. 109 42 10N 21 30E
Crna, R. 109 41 20N 21 59E
Croagh Patrick, mt. 97 53 46N 9 40W
Crocker 76 37 57N 92 16W
Crocker, Barisan 126 5 0N 116 30E
Crockett 75 31 20N 95 30W
Crocodile Is. 134 11 43S 135 8E
Crocq 102 45 52N 2 21E
Crofton 63 48 52N 123 38W
Croisic, Le 100 47 18N 2 30W
Croisic, Pte. du. 100 47 19N 2 31W
Croix, La, L. 52 48 20N 92 15W
Croker, C. 46 44 58N 80 59W
Croker, I. 134 11 12S 132 32E
Cromarty, Can. 55 58 3N 94 9W
Cromarty, U.K. 96 57 40N 4 2W
Cromer, Can. 57 49 44N 101 14W
Cromer, U.K. 94 52 56N 1 18E
Cromwell, N.Z. 133 45 3S 169 14E
Cromwell, U.S.A. 52 46 42N 92 51W
Cronat 101 46 43N 3 40E
Cronulla 136 34 3S 151 8E
Crooked I. 85 22 50N 74 10W
Crooked Island Passage 85 23 0N 74 30W
Crooked L. 37 48 24N 56 17W
Crooked, R., Can. 54 54 10N 122 35W
Crooked, R., U.S.A. 78 44 30N 121 0W
Crooked River 56 52 51N 103 44W
Crookston, Minn., U.S.A. 74 47 50N 96 40W
Crookston, Nebr., U.S.A. 74 42 56N 100 45W
Crooksville 72 39 45N 82 8W
Crookwell 136 34 28S 149 24E
Crosby, Minn., U.S.A. 52 46 28N 93 57W
Crosby, N.D., U.S.A. 56 48 55N 103 18W
Crosby, Pa., U.S.A. 70 41 45N 78 23W
Crosbyton 75 33 37N 101 12W
Cross City 73 29 35N 83 5W
Cross Creek 39 46 19N 66 43W
Cross Fell 94 54 44N 2 29W
Cross L. 55 54 45N 97 30W
Cross Plains 75 32 8N 99 7W
Cross, R. 95 4 46N 8 20E
Cross Sound 67 58 20N 136 30W
Cross Timbers 76 38 1N 93 14W
Crosse, La, Kans., U.S.A. 74 38 33N 99 20W
Crosse, La, Wis., U.S.A. 74 43 48N 91 13W
Crossett 75 33 10N 91 57W
Crossfield 61 51 25N 114 0W
Crosshaven 97 51 48N 8 19W
Crossville 77 38 10N 88 4W
Croswell 46 43 16N 82 37W
Croton-on-Hudson 71 41 12N 73 55W
Crotone 108 39 5N 17 6E
Crow Agency 78 45 40N 107 30W
Crow Hd. 97 51 34N 10 9W
Crow, R. 54 59 41N 124 20W
Crow Wing R. 52 46 19N 94 20W
Crowell 75 33 59N 99 45W
Crowes 136 38 43S 143 24E
Crowley 75 30 15N 92 20W
Crowley, L. 80 37 53N 118 42W
Crown Point 77 41 24N 87 23W
Crows Landing 80 37 23N 121 6W
Crowsnest Pass 61 49 40N 114 40W
Croydon, Austral. 135 18 13S 142 14E
Croydon, U.K. 95 51 18N 0 5W
Crozet Basin 16 46 0S 52 0E
Crozet, Île 16 46 27S 52 0E
Crozon 100 48 15N 4 30W
Cruz, C. 84 19 50N 77 50W
Cruz del Eje 88 30 45S 64 50W
Cruz, La, Colomb. 86 1 35N 76 58W
Cruz, La, C. Rica 84 11 4N 85 39W
Cruz, La, Mexico 82 23 55N 106 54W
Cruzeiro 89 22 50S 45 0W
Cruzeiro do Oeste 89 23 46S 53 4W
Cruzeiro do Sul 86 7 35S 72 35W
Cry L. 54 58 45N 128 5W
Crystal Bay, Can. 48 45 22N 75 51W
Crystal Bay, U.S.A. 80 39 15N 120 0W
Crystal City, Can. 57 49 9N 98 57W
Crystal City, Mo., U.S.A. 76 38 15N 90 23W
Crystal City, Tex., U.S.A. 75 28 40N 99 50W
Crystal Falls 72 46 9N 88 11W
Crystal Lake 77 41 14N 88 19W
Crystal River 73 28 54N 82 35W
Crystal Springs 75 31 59N 90 25W
Csongrád 107 46 43N 20 12E
Ctesiphon 122 33 9N 44 35E
Cu Lao Hon 128 10 54N 108 18E
Cuamba = Nova Freixo 117 14 45S 36 22E
Cuando, R. 117 14 0S 19 30E
Cuango 116 6 15S 16 35E
Cuarto, R. 88 33 25S 63 2W
Cuatrociénegas de Carranza 82 26 59N 102 5W
Cuauhtémoc 82 28 25N 106 52W
Cuba, Mo., U.S.A. 76 38 4N 91 24W
Cuba, N. Mex., U.S.A. 79 36 0N 107 0W
Cuba, N.Y., U.S.A. 70 42 12N 78 18W
Cuba ■ 84 22 0N 79 0W
Cuba City 77 42 36N 90 26W
Cubango, R. 117 16 15S 17 45E
Cuchi 117 14 37S 17 10E
Cuchumatanes, Sierra de los 84 15 35N 91 25W
Cucurpe 82 30 20N 110 43W
Cucurrupí 86 4 23N 76 56W
Cúcuta 86 7 54N 72 31W
Cudahy 77 42 54N 87 50W
Cuddalore 124 11 46N 79 45E
Cuddapah 124 14 30N 78 47E
Cudworth 56 52 30N 105 44W
Cue 134 27 25S 117 54E
Cuenca, Ecuador 86 2 50S 79 9W
Cuenca, Spain 104 40 5N 2 10W
Cuenca, Serranía de 104 39 55N 1 50W
Cuencamé 82 24 53N 103 41W
Cuernavaca 83 18 50N 99 20W
Cuero 75 29 5N 97 17W
Cuers 103 43 14N 6 5E
Cuervo 75 35 5N 104 25W
Cuevas del Almanzora 104 37 18N 1 58W
Cuevo 88 20 25N 63 30W
Cuhimbre 86 0 10S 75 23W
Cuiabá 87 15 30S 56 0W
Cuiabá, R. 87 16 50S 56 30W
Cuidad Bolivar 86 8 21N 70 34W
Cuilco 84 15 24N 91 58W
Cuillin Hills 96 57 14N 6 15W
Cuillin Sd. 96 57 4N 6 20W
Cuima 117 13 0S 15 45E
Cuiseaux 103 46 30N 5 22E
Cuito, R. 117 16 50S 19 30E
Cuitzeo, L. 82 19 55N 101 5W
Cuivre, R. 76 38 55N 90 44W
Culan 102 46 34N 2 20E
Cŭlaraşi 101 44 14N 27 23E
Culbertson 74 48 9N 104 30W
Culcairn 136 35 41S 147 3E
Culebra, I. 67 18 19N 65 17W
Culebra, Sierra de la 104 41 55N 6 20W
Culiacán 82 24 50N 107 40W
Culiacán, R. 82 24 30N 107 42W
Culion, I. 127 11 54N 120 1E
Cullarin Range 136 34 30S 149 30E
Cullen 96 57 45N 2 50W
Cullera 104 39 9N 0 17W
Cullman 73 34 13N 86 50W
Culloden Moor 96 57 29N 4 7W
Cullom 77 40 53N 88 16W
Culoz 103 45 47N 5 46E
Culpeper 72 38 29N 77 59W
Culuene, R. 87 12 15S 53 10W
Culver 77 41 13N 86 25W
Culver, Pt. 134 32 54S 124 43E
Culverden 133 42 47S 172 49E
Cumaná 86 10 30N 64 5W
Cumberland, B.C., Can. 62 49 40N 125 0W
Cumberland, Ont., Can. 47 45 29N 75 24W
Cumberland, Qué., Can. 71 45 30N 75 24W
Cumberland, Iowa, U.S.A. 76 41 16N 94 52W
Cumberland, Md., U.S.A. 72 39 40N 78 43W
Cumberland, Wis., U.S.A. 74 45 32N 92 3W
Cumberland House 57 53 58N 102 16W
Cumberland I. 73 30 52N 81 30W
Cumberland Is. 135 20 35S 149 10E
Cumberland L. 57 54 3N 102 18W
Cumberland Pen. 65 67 0N 64 0W
Cumberland Plat. 73 36 0N 84 30W
Cumberland, R. 73 36 15N 87 0W
Cumberland Sound 65 65 30N 67 0W
Cumbria □ 94 54 35N 2 55W
Cumbrian Mts. 94 54 30N 3 0W
Cumbum 124 15 40N 79 10E
Cummings Mt. 81 35 2N 118 34W
Cumnock 49 43 46N 80 27W
Cumpas 82 30 0N 109 48W
Cumshewa Inlet 62 53 3N 131 50W
Cumuruxatiba 87 17 6S 39 13W
Cuñaré 86 0 49N 72 32W
Cuncumén 88 31 53S 70 38W
Cundinamarca □ 86 5 0N 74 0W
Cunene, R. 117 17 0S 15 0E
Cúneo 108 44 23N 7 31E
Cunlhat 102 45 38N 3 32E
Cunnamulla 135 28 2S 145 38E
Cupar, Can. 56 50 57N 104 10W
Cupar, U.K. 96 56 20N 3 0W
Cupica 86 6 50N 77 30W
Cupica, Golfo de 86 6 25N 77 30W
Curaçao, I. 85 12 10N 69 0W
Curanilahue 88 37 29S 73 28W
Curaray, R. 86 1 30S 75 30W
Curatabaca 86 6 19N 62 51W
Curbarado 86 7 3N 76 54W
Curepto 88 35 8S 72 1W
Curiapo 86 8 33N 61 5W
Curicó 88 34 55S 71 20W
Curicó □ 88 34 50S 71 15W
Curiplaya 86 0 16N 74 52W
Curitiba 89 25 20S 49 10W
Curlwaa 136 34 2S 141 59E
Currais Novos 87 6 13S 36 30W
Curralinho 87 1 35S 49 30W
Curran 46 44 41N 83 47W
Currant 78 38 51N 115 32W
Current, R. 75 37 15N 91 10W
Currie 78 40 16N 114 45W
Currituck Sd. 73 36 20N 75 50W
Currockbilly Mt. 136 35 25S 150 0E
Curtis 74 40 41N 100 32W
Curtis, I. 135 23 35S 151 10E
Curtis, Pt. 135 23 53S 151 21E
Curuapanema, R. 87 7 0S 54 30W
Curuçá 87 0 35S 47 50W
Curuguaty 89 24 19S 55 49W
Curundu 84 8 59N 79 38W
Curupira, Serra 86 1 25N 64 30W
Cururupu 87 1 50S 44 50W
Curuzú Cuatiá 88 29 50S 58 5W
Curvelo 87 18 45S 44 27W
Cushing 43 45 36N 74 28W
Cushing, Mt. 54 57 35N 126 57W
Cusihuiriáchic 82 28 10N 106 50W
Cusset 102 46 8N 3 28E
Cusson, Pte. 36 60 23N 77 46W
Custer 74 43 45N 103 38W
Cut Bank 61 48 40N 112 15W
Cut Knife 56 52 45N 109 1W
Cutbank 56 51 18N 106 51W
Cutbank, R. 60 54 43N 118 32W
Cuthbert 73 31 47N 84 47W
Cutler 80 36 31N 119 17W
Cuttack 125 20 25N 85 57E
Cuvier, C. 134 23 14S 113 22E
Cuvier I. 133 36 27S 175 50E
Cuxhaven 106 53 51N 8 41E
Cuyabeno 86 0 16S 75 53W
Cuyahoga Falls 70 41 8N 81 30W
Cuyahoga, R. 70 41 20N 81 35W
Cuyo 127 10 50N 121 5E
Cuyuni, R. 87 7 0N 59 30W
Cuzco 86 13 32S 72 0W
Cuzco, Mt. 86 20 0S 66 50W
Cynthia 60 53 17N 115 25W
Cynthiana 77 38 23N 84 10W
Cypress Hills 55 49 40N 109 30W
Cypress Hills Prov. Park 56 49 40N 109 30W
Cypress River 57 49 34N 99 5W
Cyprus ■ 122 35 0N 33 0E
Cyrville 48 45 25N 75 38W
Czar 61 52 27N 110 50W
Czech S.R. □ 106 49 30N 15 0E
Czechoslovakia ■ 106 49 0N 17 0E
Czeremcha 107 52 32N 23 20E
Częstochowa 107 50 49N 19 7E

D

Da Lat 128 11 56N 108 25E
Da Nang 128 16 4N 108 13E
Da, R. 128 21 15N 105 20E
Dabajuro 86 11 2N 70 40W
Dabie 106 53 27N 14 45E
Dabrowa Tarnówska 107 50 10N 20 59E
Dacca 125 23 43N 90 26E
Dacca □ 125 24 0N 90 25E
Dadanawa 86 3 0N 59 30W
Dade City 73 28 20N 82 12W
Dadra and Nagar Haveli □ 124 20 5N 73 0E
Dadu 124 26 45N 67 45E
Daet 127 14 2N 122 55E
Dafter 46 46 21N 84 27W
Dagestan, A.S.S.R. □ 120 42 30N 47 0E
Daggett 81 34 43N 116 52W
Dagupan 127 16 3N 120 20E
Dagus Mines 70 41 20N 78 36W
Dahlgren 77 38 12N 88 41W
Dahlonega 73 34 35N 83 59W
Dahomey ■ = Benin ■ 114 8 0N 2 0E
Daingean 97 53 18N 7 15W
Daintree 97 16 20S 145 20E
Daiō-Misaki 132 34 15N 136 45E
Dairen = Lu-ta 130 39 0N 121 31E
Dakar 114 14 34N 17 29W
Dakhla 114 23 50N 15 53W
Dakhla, El Wâhât el- 115 25 30N 28 50E
Dakota City, Iowa, U.S.A. 76 42 43N 94 12W
Dakota City, Nebr., U.S.A. 74 42 27N 96 28W
Đakovica 109 42 22N 20 26E
Dalälven, L. 111 61 27N 17 15E
Dalandzadgad 130 43 37N 104 30E
Dalarö 111 59 8N 18 24E
Dalat 128 12 3N 108 32E
Dalbandin 124 29 0N 64 23E
Dalbeattie 96 54 55N 3 50W
Dalby 135 27 10S 151 17E
Dale 77 38 10N 86 59W
Dalesville 43 45 42N 74 24W
Daleville 77 40 7N 85 33W
Dalhart 75 36 10N 102 30W
Dalhousie 39 48 5N 66 26W
Dalhousie East 39 44 43N 64 48W
Dalhousie Station 43 45 18N 74 27W
Dalhousie West 39 44 43N 65 13W
Dalj 86 45 28N 18 58E
Dalkeith, Can. 43 45 27N 74 32W
Dalkeith, U.K. 96 55 54N 3 5W
Dall I. 54 54 59N 133 25W
Dallas, Oregon, U.S.A. 78 45 0N 123 15W
Dallas, Texas, U.S.A. 75 32 50N 96 50W
Dallas Center 76 41 41N 93 58W
Dallas City 76 40 38N 91 10W
Dalles, Les 43 45 59N 73 31W
Dalmacija 108 43 20N 17 0E
Dalmatia = Dalmacija 108 43 20N 17 0E
Dalmeny 56 52 20N 106 46W
Dalneretchensk 121 45 50N 133 40E
Daloa 114 7 0N 6 30W
Dalrymple, Mt. 135 21 1S 148 39E
Dalton, Can. 53 48 11N 84 1W
Dalton, Ga., U.S.A. 127 34 45N 85 0W
Dalton, Mass., U.S.A. 71 42 28N 73 11W
Dalton, Nebr., U.S.A. 74 41 27N 103 0W
Dalton Post 54 66 42N 137 0W
Dalupuri, I. 131 19 2N 121 8E
Dalvík 110 65 58N 18 32W
Daly City 80 37 42N 122 28W
Daly L. 55 56 32N 105 39W
Daly, R. 134 13 21S 130 18E
Daly Waters 134 16 15S 133 24E
Dam 87 4 45N 55 0W
Daman 124 20 25N 72 57E
Daman □ 124 20 25N 72 58E
Damar, I. 127 7 15S 128 30E
Damaraland 117 21 0S 17 0E
Damascus 49 43 55N 80 29W
Damascus = Dimashq 122 33 30N 36 18E
Damävand 123 35 56N 52 10E
Damävand, Qolleh-ye 123 35 45N 52 10E
Damba 116 6 44S 15 29E
Dâmboviţa, R. 107 44 40N 26 0E

Dame Marie Deva

Dame Marie 85 18 36N 74 26W
Dāmghān 123 36 10N 54 17 E
Damin 123 27 30N 60 40 E
Damman 122 26 25N 50 2 E
Dammarie 101 48 20N 1 30 E
Dammartin 101 49 3N 2 41 E
Damme 105 52 32N 8 12 E
Damoh 124 23 50N 79 28 E
Dampier 134 20 41 S 116 42 E
Dampier Arch. 134 20 38 S 116 32 E
Dampier Downs 134 18 24 S 123 5 E
Dampier, Selat 127 0 40 S 131 0 E
Damville 100 48 51N 1 5 E
Damvillers 101 49 20N 5 21 E
Dana 127 11 0 S 122 52 E
Dana, Lac 36 50 53N 77 20W
Dana, Mt 80 37 54N 119 12W
Danao 127 10 31N 124 1 E
Danbury 71 41 23N 73 29W
Danby L. 79 34 17N 115 0W
Dandeldhura 125 29 20N 80 35 E
Dandeli 124 15 5N 74 30 E
Dandenong 136 38 0 S 145 15 E
Danforth, Can. 50 43 43N 79 15W
Danforth, U.S.A. 35 45 39N 67 57W
Dang Raek 128 14 40N 104 0 E
Danger Is. 15 10 53 S 165 49W
Danger Pt. 117 34 40 S 19 17 E
Daniel 78 42 56N 110 2W
Daniel's Harbour 37 50 13N 57 35W
Danielson 71 41 50N 71 52W
Danielson Prov. Park 56 51 16N 106 50W
Dankhar Gompa 124 32 10N 78 10 E
Danli 84 14 4N 86 35W
Dannemora, Sweden 111 60 12N 17 51 E
Dannemora, U.S.A. 71 44 41N 73 44W
Dannevirke 133 40 12 S 176 8 E
Dansalan 127 8 2N 124 30 E
Danskin 62 53 59N 125 47W
Dansville 70 42 32N 77 41W
Danube, R. 106 45 0N 28 20W
Danvers 71 42 34N 70 55 E
Danville, Ill., U.S.A. 77 40 10N 87 40W
Danville, Ind., U.S.A. 77 39 46N 86 32W
Danville, Ky., U.S.A. 77 37 40N 84 45W
Danville, Va., U.S.A. 73 36 40N 79 20W
Danzig = Gdansk 107 54 22N 18 40 E
Dão 127 10 30N 122 6 E
Daoulas 100 48 22N 4 17W
Dar al Hamrā, Ad 122 27 22N 37 43 E
Dar es Salaam 116 6 50 S 39 12 E
Dar'ā 115 32 36N 36 7 E
Dārāb 123 28 50N 54 30 E
Darband 124 34 30N 72 50 E
Darbhanga 125 26 15N 86 8 E
Darby 78 46 2N 114 7W
D'Arcy 54 50 35N 122 30W
Dardanelle 80 38 2N 119 50W
Dardanelles = Canakkale Bğazi 122 40 0N 26 20 E
Dardenelle 75 35 12N 93 9W
Dargai 124 34 25N 71 45 E
Dargan Ata 120 40 40N 62 20 E
Dargaville 133 35 57 S 173 52 E
Darhan 130 49 27N 105 57 E
Darién 84 9 7N 79 46W
Darién, G. del 86 9 0N 77 0W
Darién, Serranía del 86 8 30N 77 30W
Darjeeling 125 27 3N 88 18 E
Dark Cove 37 48 47N 54 13W
Darling, R. 136 34 4 S 141 54 E
Darling Ra. 134 32 30 S 116 0 E
Darlington, U.K. 94 54 33N 1 33W
Darlington, S.C., U.S.A. 73 34 18N 79 50W
Darlington, Wis., U.S.A. 76 42 43N 90 7W
Darlington Point 136 34 37 S 146 1 E
Darłowo 106 54 25N 16 25 E
Darmstadt 106 49 51N 8 40 E
Darnétal 100 49 25N 1 10 E
Darney 101 48 5N 6 0 E
Darnick 136 32 48 S 143 38 E
Darnley B. 67 69 30N 123 30W
Darnley, C. 91 68 0 S 69 0 E
Darrington 63 48 14N 121 37W
Dart, R. 95 50 24N 3 36W
Dartmoor 95 50 36N 4 0W
Dartmouth, Can. 39 44 40N 63 30W
Dartmouth, U.K. 95 50 21N 3 35W
Dartmouth, R. 38 48 53N 64 34W
Darvel Bay 127 4 50N 118 20 E
Darwha 124 20 15N 77 45 E
Darwin, Austral. 134 12 25 S 130 51 E
Darwin, U.S.A. 81 36 15N 117 35W
Daryacheh-ye-Sistan 123 31 0N 61 0 E
Dashinchilen 130 48 0N 105 59 E
Dasht-e Kavīr 123 34 30N 55 0 E
Dasht-e Lūt 123 31 30N 58 0 E
Dasht-i-Khash 124 32 0N 62 0 E
Dasht-i-Margo 124 30 40N 62 30 E
Dasht, R. 124 25 40N 62 20 E
Dasserat, L. 40 48 16N 79 25W
Datia 124 25 39N 78 27 E
Datteln 105 51 39N 7 23 E
Daugavpils 120 55 53N 26 32 E
Daulat Yar 123 34 30N 65 45 E
Daulnay 39 47 25N 65 28W
Dauphin 57 51 9N 100 5W
Dauphin I. 73 30 16N 88 10W
Dauphin L. 57 51 20N 99 45W
Dauphiné 103 45 15N 5 25 E
Davangere 124 14 25N 75 50 E
Davao 127 7 0N 125 40 E
Davao, G. of 127 6 30N 125 48 E
Dāvar Panāh 123 27 25N 62 15 E
Davenport, Calif., U.S.A. 80 37 1N 122 12W
Davenport, Iowa, U.S.A. 76 41 30N 90 40W
Davenport, Wash., U.S.A. 78 47 40N 118 5W
Davenport Ra. 134 20 28 S 134 0 E
Daventry 95 52 16N 1 10W
David 84 8 30N 82 30W
David City 74 41 18N 97 10W
David, R. 43 45 58N 72 54W
Davidson 56 51 16N 105 59W
Davis 80 38 33N 121 45W
Davis Dam 81 35 11N 114 35W
Davis Inlet 36 55 50N 60 59W
Davis Mts. 75 30 42N 104 15W
Davis Str. 65 65 0N 58 0W
Davison 46 43 2N 83 31W
Davisson, L. 80 46 30N 122 20W
Davos 106 46 48N 9 49 E
Davy L. 55 58 53N 108 18W
Dawson, Can. 64 64 10N 139 30W
Dawson, Ga., U.S.A. 73 31 45N 84 28W
Dawson, N.D., U.S.A. 74 46 56N 99 45W
Dawson B. 57 52 53N 100 49W
Dawson Creek 54 55 45N 120 15W
Dawson, I. 90 53 50 S 70 50W
Dawson Inlet 55 61 50N 93 25W
Dawson, R. 135 23 25 S 150 10 E
Daylesford 136 37 21 S 144 9 E
Dayr az Zawr 122 35 20N 40 5 E
Daysland 61 52 50N 112 20W
Dayton, Iowa, U.S.A. 76 42 14N 94 6W
Dayton, Ky., U.S.A. 77 39 7N 84 28W
Dayton, Nev., U.S.A. 80 39 15N 119 34W
Dayton, Ohio, U.S.A. 72 39 45N 84 10W
Dayton, Pa., U.S.A. 70 40 54N 79 18W
Dayton, Tenn., U.S.A. 73 35 30N 85 1W
Dayton, Wash., U.S.A. 78 46 20N 118 10W
Daytona Beach 73 29 14N 81 0W
Dayville 78 44 33N 119 37W
De Aar 117 30 39 S 24 0 E
De Beaujeu 43 45 19N 74 20W
De Forest 76 43 15N 89 20W
De Funiak Springs 73 30 42N 86 10W
De Grau 37 48 29N 59 9W
De Grey 134 20 12 S 119 12 E
De Land 73 29 1N 81 19W
De Leon 75 32 9N 98 35W
De Léry 45 45 15N 73 26W
De Long Mts. 67 68 10N 163 0W
De Long, Ostrova 121 76 40N 149 20 E
De Morhiban, L. 38 51 50N 62 54W
De Pere 72 44 28N 88 1W
De Queen 75 34 3N 94 24W
De Quincy 75 30 30N 93 27W
De Ridder 75 30 48N 93 15W
De Smet 74 44 25N 97 35W
De Soto 76 38 7N 90 33W
De Tour 46 45 59N 83 56W
De Witt, Ark., U.S.A. 75 34 19N 91 20W
De Witt, Iowa, U.S.A. 76 41 49N 90 33W
De Witt, Mich., U.S.A. 77 42 50N 84 33W
Deacon 58 49 51N 96 56W
Dead Sea = Miyet, Bahr el 115 31 30N 35 30 E
Deadwood L. 54 59 10N 128 30W
Deakin 134 30 46 S 129 58 E
Deal 95 51 13N 1 25 E
Dean Chan. 62 52 30N 127 15W
Dean, Forest of 95 51 50N 2 35W
Deán Funes 88 30 20 S 64 20W
Dean, R. 62 52 49N 126 58W
Dearborn, U.S.A. 46 42 18N 83 15W
Dearborn, U.S.A. 76 39 32N 94 46W
Dease Arm 106 66 52N 119 37W
Dease L. 54 58 40N 130 5W
Dease Lake 54 58 25N 130 6W
Dease, R. 54 59 56N 128 32W
Death Valley 81 36 27N 116 52W
Death Valley Junc. 81 36 21N 116 30W
Death Valley Nat. Monument 81 36 30N 117 0W
Deauville 100 49 23N 0 2 E
Debar 109 41 21N 20 37 E
Debden 56 53 30N 106 50W
Debec 39 46 4N 67 41W
Debert 39 45 26N 63 28W
Debolt 60 55 12N 118 1W
Debre Markos 115 10 20N 37 40 E
Debre Tabor 115 11 50N 38 26 E
Debrecen 107 47 33N 21 42 E
Decatur, Ala., U.S.A. 73 34 35N 87 0W
Decatur, Ga., U.S.A. 73 33 47N 84 17W
Decatur, Ill., U.S.A. 76 39 50N 89 0W
Decatur, Ind., U.S.A. 72 40 52N 85 28W
Decatur, Ind., U.S.A. 77 40 50N 84 56W
Decatur, Mich., U.S.A. 77 42 7N 85 58W
Decatur, Texas, U.S.A. 75 33 15N 97 35W
Decazeville 102 44 34N 2 15 E
Deccan 124 14 0N 77 0 E
Decelles, Rés 40 47 42N 78 8W
Déception, B. 36 62 8N 74 41W
Deception I. 91 63 0 S 60 15W
Deception L. 55 56 33N 104 13W
Decize 101 46 50N 3 28 E
Deckerville 46 43 33N 82 46W
Decorah 74 43 20N 91 50W
Dedham 71 42 14N 71 10W
Dee, R., Scot., U.K. 96 57 4N 2 7W
Dee, R., Wales, U.K. 94 53 15N 3 7W
Deep B. 54 61 15N 116 35W
Deep Cove 66 49 20N 122 56W
Deep River 76 41 35N 92 22W
Deepdale 134 26 22 S 114 20 E
Deepwater 76 38 18N 93 46W
Deer I. 67 54 55N 162 20W
Deer, L. 37 49 6N 57 35W
Deer Lake, Newf., Can. 37 49 11N 57 27W
Deer Lake, Ontario, Can. 55 52 36N 94 20W
Deer Lodge 78 46 25N 112 40W
Deer Park, Ohio, U.S.A. 77 39 13N 84 23W
Deer Park, Wash., U.S.A. 78 47 55N 117 21W
Deer Pond 37 48 30N 54 45W
Deer, R. 55 58 23N 94 13W
Deer River 52 47 21N 93 44W
Deering 67 66 5N 162 50W
Deesa 124 24 18N 72 10 E
Defiance 77 41 20N 84 20W
Dégelis 41 47 30N 68 35W
Deggendorf 106 48 49N 12 59 E
Deh Bīd 123 30 39N 53 11 E
Deh Kheyr 123 28 45N 54 40 E
Deh Titan 124 33 45N 63 50 E
Dehkareqan 122 37 50N 45 55 E
Dehra Dun 124 30 20N 78 4 E
Deinze 105 50 59N 3 32 E
Dej 107 47 10N 23 52 E
Dekalb 77 41 55N 88 45W
Dekese 116 3 24 S 21 24 E
Del Mar 81 32 58N 117 16W
Del Norte 79 37 47N 106 27W
Del Rio, Mexico 82 29 22N 100 54W
Del Rio, U.S.A. 75 29 15N 100 50W
Delagua 75 32 35N 104 40W
Delano 81 35 48N 119 13W
Delaronde L. 56 54 3N 107 3W
Delavan, Ill., U.S.A. 76 40 22N 89 33W
Delavan, Wis., U.S.A. 77 42 40N 88 39W
Delaware 77 40 20N 83 0W
Delaware □ 72 39 0N 75 40W
Delaware, R. 71 39 20N 75 25W
Delburne 61 52 12N 113 14W
Delft 105 52 1N 4 22 E
Delgado, C. 116 10 45 S 40 40 E
Delgo 115 20 6N 30 40 E
Delhi, Can. 46 42 51N 80 30W
Delhi, India 124 28 38N 77 17 E
Delhi, U.S.A. 71 42 17N 74 56W
Delia 61 51 38N 112 23W
Delice, R. 122 39 45N 34 15 E
Delicias 82 28 10N 105 30W
Delicias, Laguna 82 28 7N 105 40W
Delisle 56 51 55N 107 8W
Dell City 79 31 58N 105 19W
Dell Rapids 74 43 53N 96 44W
Delle 101 47 30N 7 2 E
Delmar, Iowa, U.S.A. 76 42 0N 90 37W
Delmar, N.Y., U.S.A. 71 42 37N 73 47W
Delmiro 87 9 24 S 38 6W
Deloraine 57 49 15N 100 29W
Delorme, L. 36 54 31N 69 52W
Delphi 77 40 37N 86 40W
Delphos 77 40 51N 84 17W
Delray Beach 73 26 27N 80 4W
Delson 45 45 22N 73 33W
Delta, Colo., U.S.A. 79 38 44N 108 5W
Delta, Utah, U.S.A. 78 39 21N 112 29W
Delta □ 66 49 7N 123 0W
Delta Amacuro □ 86 8 30N 61 30W
Delta Beach 57 50 11N 98 19W
Demak 127 6 50 S 110 40 E
Demanda, Sierra de la 104 42 15N 3 0W
Demba 116 5 28 S 22 15 E
Dembidolo 115 8 34N 34 50 E
Demer, R. 105 51 0N 5 8 E
Demerais, L. 34 47 35N 77 0W
Demerara, R. 86 7 0N 58 0W
Deming, N.Mex., U.S.A. 79 32 10N 107 50W
Deming, Wash., U.S.A. 80 48 49N 122 13W
Demini, R. 86 0 46N 62 56W
Demmit 54 55 20N 119 50W
Demopolis 73 32 30N 87 48W
Dempo, Mt. 126 4 10 S 103 15 E
Den Burg 105 53 3N 4 47 E
Den Haag = 's Gravenhage 105 52 7N 4 17 E
Den Helder 105 52 57N 4 45 E
Den Oever 105 52 56N 5 2 E
Denain 101 50 20N 3 22 E
Denair 80 37 32N 120 48W
Denau 120 38 16N 67 54 E
Denbigh, Can. 47 45 8N 77 15W
Denbigh, U.K. 94 53 12N 3 26W
Dendang 126 3 7 S 107 56 E
Denham 134 25 56 S 113 31 E
Denham Ra. 135 21 55 S 147 46 E
Denholm 55 52 40N 108 0W
Denia 104 38 49N 0 8 E
Deniliquin 136 35 30 S 144 58 E
Denison, Iowa, U.S.A. 74 42 0N 95 18W
Denison, Texas, U.S.A. 75 33 50N 96 40W
Denison Range 135 28 30 S 136 5 E
Denizli 122 37 42N 29 2 E
Denman Island 62 49 33N 124 48W
Denmark 134 34 59 S 117 18 E
Denmark ■ 111 55 30N 9 0 E
Denmark Str. 12 66 0N 30 0W
Dennison 70 40 21N 81 21W
Denpasar 126 8 45 S 115 5 E
Denton, Mont., U.S.A. 78 47 25N 109 56W
Denton, Texas, U.S.A. 75 33 12N 97 10W
Denver, Colo., U.S.A. 74 39 45N 105 0W
Denver, Ind., U.S.A. 77 40 52N 86 5W
Denver, Iowa, U.S.A. 76 42 40N 92 20W
Denver City 75 32 58N 102 48W
Denzil 56 52 14N 109 39W
Deoghar 125 24 30N 86 59 E
Deolali 124 19 50N 73 50 E
Deoria 125 26 31N 83 48 E
Deosai, Mts. 124 35 40N 75 0 E
Departure Bay 62 49 13N 123 57W
Depew 70 42 55N 78 43W
Deposit 71 42 5N 75 23W
Depot Harbour 70 45 18N 80 5W
Deputatskiy 121 69 18N 139 54 E
Dera Ghazi Khan 124 30 5N 70 43 E
Dera Ismail Khan 124 31 50N 70 50 E
Dera Ismail Khan □ 124 32 30N 70 0 E
Derbent 120 42 5N 48 15 E
Derby, Austral. 134 17 18 S 123 38 E
Derby, U.K. 94 52 55N 1 28W
Derby, Conn., U.S.A. 71 41 20N 73 5W
Derby, N.Y., U.S.A. 70 42 40N 78 59W
Derby, Ohio, U.S.A. 77 39 46N 83 13W
Derby □ 94 52 55N 1 28W
Derg, L. 97 53 0N 8 20W
Derg, R. 97 54 42N 7 26W
Dergaon 125 26 45N 94 0 E
Derna 115 32 40N 22 35 E
Dernieres Isles 75 29 0N 90 45W
Deroche 63 49 12N 122 4W
Derrynane 49 43 56N 80 35W
Derryveagh Mts. 97 55 0N 8 40W
Derval 100 47 40N 1 41W
Derwent 60 53 41N 110 58W
Derwent, R., Cumb., U.K. 94 54 42N 3 22W
Derwent, R., Derby, U.K. 94 52 53N 1 17W
Derwent, R., N. Yorks., U.K. 94 53 45N 0 57W
Derwentwater, L. 94 53 34N 3 9W
Des Moines, Iowa, U.S.A. 76 41 35N 93 37W
Des Moines, N. Mex., U.S.A. 75 36 50N 103 51W
Des Moines, R. 74 40 23N 91 25W
Des Plaines 77 42 3N 87 52W
Des Plaines, R. 77 41 23N 88 15W
Desaguadero, R., Argent. 88 33 28 S 67 15W
Desaguadero, R., Boliv. 86 17 30 S 68 0W
Desbarats 46 46 20N 83 56W
Desbiens 41 48 25N 71 57W
Descanso 81 32 12N 116 58W
Descanso, Pta. 81 32 21N 117 3W
Deschaillons 41 46 32N 72 7W
Deschambault 41 46 39N 71 56W
Descharme, R. 55 56 51N 109 13W
Deschênes, Ont., Can. 48 45 25N 75 49W
Deschênes, Qué., Can. 40 45 23N 75 48W
Deschênes, L. 48 45 22N 75 51W
Deschutes, R. 78 45 30N 121 0W
Dese 115 11 5N 39 40 E
Deseado, R. 90 40 0 S 69 0W
Desemboque 82 30 30N 112 27W
Deseronto 47 44 12N 77 3W
Desert Center 81 33 45N 115 27W
Desert Hot Springs 81 33 58N 116 30W
Désirade, I. 85 16 18N 61 3W
Deskenatlata L. 54 60 55N 112 3W
Desmarais 60 55 56N 113 49W
Desmaraisville 40 49 32N 76 9W
Desméloizes 40 48 57N 79 29W
Desolación, I. 90 53 0 S 74 0W
Desolation Sound Prov. Marine Park 62 50 5N 124 25W
Despeñaperros, Paso 104 38 24N 3 30W
Dessau 106 51 49N 12 15 E
Destruction Bay 64 61 15N 138 48W
Desvrès 101 50 40N 1 48 E
Detmold 106 51 55N 8 50 E
Detour Pt. 72 45 37N 86 35W
Detroit, Mich., U.S.A. 46 42 13N 83 22W
Detroit, Tex., U.S.A. 75 33 40N 95 10W
Detroit Lakes 74 46 50N 95 50W
Dettifoss 110 65 49N 16 24W
Deurne, Belg. 105 51 12N 4 24 E
Deurne, Neth. 105 51 27N 5 49 E
Deutsche Bucht 106 54 10N 7 51 E
Deux-Loutres, L. aux 38 51 31N 62 28W
Deux Montagnes 44 45 32N 73 53W
Deux Montagnes □ 44 45 40N 74 0W
Deux Montagnes, Lac des 44 45 28N 73 59W
Deux-Sèvres □ 100 46 35N 0 20W
Deva 107 45 53N 22 55 E

Devakottai **Dover Plains**

Devakottai **124** 9 55N 78 45 E
Devastation Chan. **62** 53 40N 128 50W
Deventer **105** 52 15N 6 10 E
Devenyns, L. **41** 47 5N 73 50W
Deveron, R. **96** 57 40N 2 31W
Devils Den **80** 35 46N 119 58W
Devils Lake **74** 48 5N 98 50W
Devils Paw, mt. **54** 58 47N 134 0W
Devizes **95** 51 21N 2 0W
Devon **60** 53 24N 113 44W
Devon I. **65** 75 47N 88 0W
Devonport, Austral. **135** 41 10 S 146 22 E
Devonport, N.Z. **133** 36 49 S 174 49 E
Devonport, U.K. **95** 50 23N 4 11W
Devonshire □ **95** 50 50N 3 40W
Dewas **124** 22 59N 76 3 E
Dewberry **60** 53 35N 110 32W
Dewittville **43** 45 7N 74 5W
Dewsbury **94** 53 42N 1 38W
Dexter, U.S.A. **77** 42 20N 83 53W
Dexter, Mo., U.S.A. **75** 36 50N 90 0W
Dexter, N. Mex., U.S.A. **75** 33 15N 104 25W
Deyhūk **123** 33 15N 57 30 E
Deyyer **123** 27 55N 51 55 E
Dezadeash L. **54** 60 28N 136 58W
Dezfūl **122** 32 20N 48 30 E
Dezh Shāhpūr **122** 35 30N 46 25 E
Dezhneva, Mys **121** 66 10N 169 3 E
Dhaba **122** 27 25N 35 40 E
Dhahran **122** 26 9N 50 10 E
Dhamtari **125** 20 42N 81 35 E
Dhanbad **125** 23 50N 86 30 E
Dhangarhi **125** 28 55N 80 40 E
Dhankuta **125** 26 55N 87 20 E
Dhar **124** 22 35N 75 26 E
Dharmapuri **124** 12 10N 78 10 E
Dhaulagiri Mt. **125** 28 45N 83 45 E
Dhenkanal **125** 20 45N 85 35 E
Dhidhimótikhon **109** 41 22N 26 29 E
Dhikti, Mt. **109** 35 8N 25 29 E
Dhirfis, Mt. **109** 38 40N 23 54 E
Dhodhekánisos **109** 36 35N 27 0 E
Dholpur **124** 26 45N 77 59 E
Dhrol **124** 22 40N 70 25 E
Dhubaibah **123** 23 25N 54 35 E
Dhubri **125** 26 2N 90 2 E
Dhulia **124** 20 58N 74 50 E
Di Linh, Cao Nguyen **128** 11 30N 108 0 E
Diable, Mt. **80** 37 53N 121 56W
Diablo Heights **84** 8 58N 79 34W
Diablo Range **80** 37 0N 121 5W
Diagonal **76** 40 49N 94 20W
Diamante **88** 32 5 S 60 40W
Diamante, R. **88** 34 31 S 66 56W
Diamantina **87** 18 5 S 43 40W
Diamantina, R. **135** 22 25 S 142 20 E
Diamantino **87** 14 30 S 56 30W
Diamond City **61** 49 48N 112 51W
Diamond Harbour **125** 22 11N 88 14 E
Diamond Mts. **78** 40 0N 115 58W
Diamond Springs **80** 38 42N 120 49W
Diamondville **78** 41 51N 110 30W
Diana B. **36** 61 20N 70 0W
Diaole, Î. du. **87** 5 15N 52 45W
Dibai (Dubai) **123** 25 15N 55 20 E
Dibaya **116** 6 20 S 22 0 E
Dibaya Lubue **116** 4 12 S 19 54 E
Dibba **123** 25 45N 56 16 E
Dibega **122** 35 50N 43 46 E
Dibi **115** 4 10N 41 52 E
Dibrugarh **125** 27 29N 94 55 E
Dibulla **86** 11 17N 73 19W
Dickersonville **49** 43 14N 78 53W
Dickeyville **76** 42 38N 90 36W
Dickinson **74** 46 50N 102 40W
Dickson **73** 36 5N 87 22W
Dickson City **71** 41 29N 75 40W
Didsbury **61** 51 35N 114 10W
Die **103** 44 47N 5 22 E
Diefenbaker L. **55** 51 0N 106 55W
Diego Garcia, I. **16** 9 50 S 75 0 E
Diégo Suarez **117** 12 25 S 49 20 E
Diekirch **105** 49 52N 6 10 E
Diélette **100** 49 33N 1 52W
Diên Biên Phu **128** 21 20N 103 0 E
Diepenbeek **105** 50 54N 5 25 E
Dieppe, Can. **39** 46 6N 64 45W
Dieppe, France **100** 49 54N 1 4 E
Dieren **105** 52 3N 6 6 E
Dierks **75** 34 9N 94 0W
Diest **105** 50 58N 5 4 E
Dieterich **77** 39 4N 88 23W
Dieulefit **103** 44 32N 5 4 E
Dieuze **101** 48 30N 6 40 E
Differdange **105** 49 81N 5 54 E
Digby **39** 44 38N 65 50W
Digby Neck **39** 44 30N 66 5W
Digges **55** 58 40N 94 0W
Digges Is. **36** 62 40N 77 50W
Dighinala **125** 23 15N 92 5 E
Dighton **74** 38 30N 100 26W
Digne **103** 44 5N 6 12 E
Digoin **102** 46 29N 3 58 E
Digos **127** 6 45N 125 20 E
Digranes **110** 66 4N 14 44 E
Dihang, R. **125** 27 30N 96 30 E
Dijlah **122** 37 0N 42 30 E
Dijon **101** 47 20N 5 0 E
Diksmuide **105** 51 2N 2 52 E
Dikson **120** 73 40N 80 5 E
Dila **115** 6 14N 38 22 E
Dilam **122** 23 55N 47 10 E
Dildo **37** 47 34N 53 33W
Dili **127** 8 39 S 125 34 E
Dilke **56** 50 52N 105 15W
Dillard **76** 37 44N 91 13W
Dilley **75** 28 40N 99 12W
Dillingham **67** 59 5N 158 30W
Dillon, Can. **55** 55 56N 108 56W
Dillon, Mont., U.S.A. **78** 45 9N 112 36W
Dillon, S.C., U.S.A. **73** 34 26N 79 20W
Dillon, R. **55** 55 56N 108 56W
Dillsboro **77** 39 1N 85 4W
Dilolo **12** 10 28 S 22 18 E
Dimas **82** 23 43N 106 47W
Dimashq **122** 33 30N 36 18 E
Dimbelenge **116** 4 30N 23 0 E
Dimboola **136** 36 28 S 142 0 E
Dimitriya Lapteva, Proliv **121** 73 0N 140 0 E
Dimitrovgrad **109** 42 5N 25 35 E
Dimmitt **75** 34 36N 102 16W
Dinagat I. **127** 10 10N 125 40 E
Dinajpur **125** 25 33N 88 43 E
Dinan **100** 48 28N 2 2W
Dinant **105** 50 16N 4 55 E
Dinar **122** 38 5N 30 15 E
Dinara Planina, mts. **108** 44 0N 16 30 E
Dinard **100** 48 38N 2 6W
Dinaric Alps **93** 44 0N 17 30 E
Dindigul **124** 10 25N 78 0 E
Dingle **97** 52 9N 10 17W
Dingle B. **97** 52 3N 10 20W
Dingmans Ferry **71** 41 13N 74 55W
Dingwall, Can. **39** 46 54N 60 28W
Dingwall, U.K. **96** 57 36N 4 26W
Dinorwic **52** 49 41N 92 30W
Dinorwic L. **52** 49 37N 92 33W
Dinosaur National Monument **78** 40 30N 108 45W
Dinosaur Prov. Park **61** 50 47N 111 30W
Dinsmore **56** 51 20N 107 26W
Dinuba **80** 36 37N 119 22W
Dionne, L. **38** 49 26N 67 55W
Dipolog **127** 8 36N 123 20 E
Dir **124** 35 08N 71 59 E
Dire Dawa **115** 9 35N 41 45 E
Direction, C. **135** 12 51 S 143 32 E
Diriamba **84** 11 51N 86 19W
Dirico **117** 17 50 S 20 42 E
Dirk Hartog I. **134** 25 50 S 113 5 E
Dirranbandi **135** 28 33 S 148 17 E
Disappointment, C. **78** 46 20N 124 0W
Disappointment L. **134** 23 20 S 122 40 E
Disaster B. **135** 37 15 S 150 0 E
Discovery B. **136** 38 10 S 140 40 E
Disko **17** 69 45N 53 30W
Disko Bugt **65** 69 10N 52 0W
Disko I. **65** 69 30N 54 30W
Disraëli **41** 45 54N 71 21W
Disteghil Sar **124** 36 20N 75 5 E
Distrito Federal □ **86** 10 30N 66 55W
Diu, I. **124** 20 45N 70 58 E
Diver **34** 46 44N 79 30W
Dives, R. **100** 49 18N 0 7W
Dives-sur-Mer **100** 49 18N 0 8W
Divide **78** 45 48N 112 47W
Dix, R. **77** 37 49N 84 44W
Dixie **78** 45 37N 115 27W
Dixie Mt. **80** 39 55N 120 16W
Dixon, Calif., U.S.A. **80** 38 27N 121 49W
Dixon, Ill., U.S.A. **76** 41 50N 89 30W
Dixon, Iowa, U.S.A. **76** 41 45N 90 47W
Dixon, Mo., U.S.A. **76** 37 59N 92 6W
Dixon, Mont., U.S.A. **78** 47 19N 114 25W
Dixon, N. Mex., U.S.A. **79** 36 15N 105 57W
Dixon Entrance **54** 54 30N 132 0W
Dixonville **60** 56 32N 117 40W
Dixville **41** 45 4N 71 46W
Diyarbakir **122** 37 55N 40 18 E
Djakarta = Jakarta **127** 6 9 S 106 49 E
Djambala **116** 2 20 S 14 30 E
Djawa = Jawa **127** 7 0 S 110 0 E
Djelfa **114** 34 40N 3 15 E
Djema **116** 6 9N 25 15 E
Djibouti **115** 11 30N 43 5 E
Djibouti ■ **115** 11 30N 42 15 E
Djirlange **128** 11 44N 108 15 E
Djolu **116** 0 45N 22 5 E
Djoum **116** 2 41N 12 35 E
Djugu **116** 1 55N 30 35 E
Djúpivogur **110** 64 39N 14 17W
Dmitriya Lapteva, Proliv **121** 73 0N 140 0 E
Dneiper, R. = Dnepr **120** 52 29N 35 10 E
Dnepr, R. **120** 50 0N 31 0 E
Dneprodzerzhinskoye Vdkhr. **121** 49 0N 34 0 E
Dnepropetrovsk **120** 48 30N 35 0 E
Dnestr, R. **120** 48 30N 26 30 E
Dniester = Dnestr **120** 48 30N 26 30 E
Doaktown **39** 46 33N 66 8W
Doba **114** 8 40N 16 50 E
Dobbyn **135** 19 44 S 139 59 E
Doberai, Jazirah **127** 1 25 S 133 0 E
Dobie, R. **52** 51 41N 90 29W
Doblas **88** 37 5 S 64 0W
Dobo **127** 5 45 S 134 15 E
Dobruja, reg. **107** 44 30N 28 30 E
Dodecanese = Dhodhekánisos **109** 36 35N 27 0 E
Dodge Center **74** 44 1N 92 57W
Dodge City **75** 37 42N 100 0W
Dodge L. **55** 59 50N 105 36W
Dodgeville **76** 42 55N 90 8W
Dodoma **116** 6 8 S 35 45 E
Dodsland **56** 51 50N 108 45W
Dodson **78** 48 23N 108 4W
Doesburg **105** 52 1N 6 9 E
Doetinchem **105** 51 59N 6 18 E
Dog Creek **63** 51 35N 122 14W
Dog L., Man., Can. **54** 51 2N 98 31W
Dog L., Ont., Can. **52** 48 40N 89 30W
Dog L., Ont., Can. **53** 48 17N 84 8W
Dog, R. **52** 48 32N 89 39W
Dogi **124** 32 20N 62 50 E
Dohad **124** 22 50N 74 15 E
Dohazari **125** 22 10N 92 5 E
Doheny **34** 47 4N 72 35W
Doherty **34** 46 35N 79 44W
Doi, I. **127** 2 21N 127 49 E
Doi Luang **128** 18 20N 101 30 E
Doig, R., Alta., Can. **54** 56 57N 120 0W
Doig, R., B.C., Can. **54** 56 25N 120 40W
Dojran **109** 41 10N 22 45 E
Dokkum **105** 53 20N 5 59 E
Dol **100** 48 34N 1 47W
Dolak, Pulau = Kolepom, P. **127** 8 0 S 138 30 E
Doland **74** 44 55N 98 5W
Dolbeau **41** 48 53N 72 18W
Dole **101** 47 7N 5 31 E
Dolgellau **94** 52 44N 3 53W
Dolgelly = Dolgellau **94** 52 44N 3 53W
Dolisie **116** 4 0 S 13 10 E
Dollard **56** 49 37N 108 35W
Dollard-des-Ormeaux **44** 45 29N 73 49W
Dollarton **66** 49 18N 122 57W
Dolomites = Dolomiti **108** 46 30N 11 40 E
Dolomiti **108** 46 30N 11 40 E
Dolores, Argent. **88** 36 20 S 57 40W
Dolores, Mexico **82** 28 53N 108 27W
Dolores, Uruguay **88** 33 34 S 58 15W
Dolores, Colo., U.S.A. **79** 37 30N 108 30W
Dolores, Tex., U.S.A. **75** 27 40N 99 38W
Dolores, R. **75** 38 30N 108 55W
Dolphin and Union Str. **64** 69 5N 114 45W
Dolphin C. **90** 51 10 S 50 0W
Dom Pedrito **89** 31 0 S 54 40W
Dombarovskiy **120** 50 46N 59 32 E
Dombås **111** 62 6N 9 4 E
Dombasle **101** 49 8N 5 10 E
Dombe Grande **117** 12 56 S 13 8 E
Dombes **103** 46 3N 5 0 E
Dome Creek **63** 53 44N 121 1W
Domel, I = Letsok-aw-kyun **128** 11 30N 98 25 E
Domérat **102** 46 21N 2 32 E
Domeyko **88** 29 0 S 71 30W
Domeyko, Cordillera **88** 24 30 S 69 0W
Domfront **100** 48 37N 0 40W
Dominador **88** 24 21 S 69 20W
Dominica I. **85** 15 20N 61 20W
Dominica Passage **85** 15 10N 61 20W
Dominican Rep. ■ **85** 19 0N 70 30W
Dominion **39** 46 13N 60 1W
Dominion, C. **65** 65 30N 74 28W
Dominion City **57** 49 9N 97 9W
Dominion L. **38** 52 40N 61 45W
Domme **102** 44 48N 1 12 E
Domodossóla **106** 46 6N 8 19 E
Dompaire **101** 48 14N 6 14 E
Dompierre-sur-Besbre **102** 46 31N 3 41 E
Domrémy **101** 48 26N 5 40 E
Don Benito **104** 38 53N 5 51W
Don Martín, Presa de **82** 27 30N 100 50W
Don Mills **50** 43 42N 79 21W
Don Pedro Res. **80** 37 43N 120 24W
Don Pen. **62** 52 25N 128 12W
Don, R., Can. **50** 43 39N 79 21W
Don, R., Eng., U.K. **94** 53 41N 0 51W
Don, R., Scot., U.K. **96** 57 14N 2 5W
Don, R., U.S.S.R. **120** 49 35N 41 40 E
Donaghadee **97** 54 38N 5 32W
Donald, Austral. **136** 36 23 S 143 0 E
Donald, Can. **63** 51 29N 117 10W
Donalda **61** 52 35N 112 34W
Donaldsonville **75** 30 2N 91 0W
Donalsonville **73** 31 3N 84 52W
Donan **58** 49 57N 97 6W
Donau, R. **107** 47 55N 17 20 E
Donauwörth **106** 48 42N 10 47 E
Doncaster **94** 53 31N 1 9W
Dondo, Angola **110** 9 45 S 14 25 E
Dondo, Mozam. **116** 19 33 S 34 46 E
Dondo, Teluk **127** 0 29N 120 45 E
Dondra Head **124** 5 55N 80 40 E
Donegal **97** 54 39N 8 8W
Donegal □ **97** 54 53N 8 0W
Donegal B. **97** 54 30N 8 35W
Donetsk **120** 48 0N 37 45 E
Dongara **134** 29 14 S 114 57 E
Dongen **105** 51 38N 4 56 E
Donges **100** 47 18N 2 4W
Donggala **127** 0 30 S 119 40 E
Dongou **116** 2 0N 18 5 E
Doniphan **75** 36 40N 90 50W
Donjon, Le **102** 46 22N 3 48 E
Donken **52** 46 58N 88 51W
Donkin **39** 46 11N 59 52W
Donna **110** 66 6N 12 30 E
Donna **75** 26 12N 98 2W
Donnaconna **41** 46 41N 71 41W
Donnelly **60** 55 44N 117 6W
Donnelly's Crossing **133** 35 42 S 173 38 E
Donora **70** 40 11N 79 50W
Donovans **37** 47 32N 52 50W
Donzère-Mondragon **103** 44 28N 4 43 E
Donzy **101** 47 20N 3 6 E
Doon, R. **96** 55 26N 4 41W
Dor (Tantura) **115** 32 37N 34 55 E
Dora Báltea, R. **108** 45 42N 7 25 E
Dora, L. **134** 22 0 S 123 0 E
Dorada, La **86** 5 30N 74 40W
Doran L. **55** 61 13N 108 6W
Dorat, Le **102** 46 14N 1 5 E
Dorchester, Can. **39** 45 54N 64 31W
Dorchester, U.K. **95** 50 42N 2 28W
Dorchester, C. **65** 65 27N 77 27W
Dorchester Crossing **39** 46 10N 64 34W
Dordogne □ **102** 45 5N 0 40 E
Dordogne, R. **102** 45 2N 0 36W
Dordrecht **105** 51 48N 4 39 E
Doré L. **55** 54 46N 107 17W
Doré Lake **55** 54 38N 107 54W
Doré, Le, L. **38** 51 17N 61 23W
Dore, Mt. **102** 45 32N 2 50 E
Dore, R. **102** 45 59N 3 28 E
Dori **114** 14 3N 0 2W
Dorion, Ont., Can. **52** 48 47N 88 39W
Dorion, Qué., Can. **44** 45 23N 74 3W
Dorion-Vaudreuil **71** 45 25N 75 4W
Dornes **101** 46 48N 3 18 E
Dornoch **96** 57 52N 4 0W
Dornoch Firth **96** 57 52N 4 0W
Dorohoi **107** 47 56N 26 30 E
Döröö Nuur **129** 48 0N 93 0 E
Dorre I. **134** 25 13 S 113 12 E
Dorris **78** 41 59N 121 58W
Dorset, Can. **46** 45 14N 78 54W
Dorset, U.S.A. **70** 41 41N 8 42W
Dorset □ **95** 50 48N 2 25W
Dorsten **105** 51 40N 6 55 E
Dortmund **105** 51 32N 7 28 E
Dörtyol **122** 36 52N 36 12 E
Doruma **116** 4 42N 27 33 E
Dorval **44** 45 27N 73 44W
Dorval Airport **44** 45 28N 73 44W
Dos Bahías, C. **90** 44 58 S 65 32W
Dos Cabezas **79** 32 10N 109 37W
Dos Palos **80** 36 59N 120 37W
Doshi **123** 35 35N 68 50 E
Dosquet **41** 46 28N 71 32W
Dot **54** 50 12N 121 25W
Dothan **73** 31 10N 85 25W
Doting Cove **37** 49 27N 53 57W
Doty **80** 46 38N 123 17W
Douai **101** 50 21N 3 4 E
Douala **116** 4 0N 9 45 E
Douarnenez **100** 48 6N 4 21W
Doubs □ **101** 47 10N 6 20 E
Doubs, R. **101** 46 53N 5 1 E
Doubtful B. **134** 34 15 S 119 28 E
Doubtful Sd. **133** 45 20 S 166 49 E
Doubtless B. **133** 34 55 S 173 26 E
Doucet **34** 48 15N 76 35W
Doudeville **100** 49 43N 0 47 E
Doué **100** 47 11N 0 20W
Douglas, Can. **47** 45 31N 76 56W
Douglas, U.K. **94** 54 9N 4 29W
Douglas, Alaska, U.S.A. **67** 58 23N 134 32W
Douglas, Ariz., U.S.A. **79** 31 21N 109 30W
Douglas, Ga., U.S.A. **73** 31 32N 82 52W
Douglas, Wyo., U.S.A. **74** 42 45N 105 20W
Douglas Chan. **62** 53 40N 129 20W
Douglas I. **66** 49 13N 122 47W
Douglas Pt. **46** 44 19N 81 37W
Douglas Prov. Park **56** 51 3N 106 28W
Douglastown, N.B., Can. **38** 48 46N 64 24W
Douglastown, N.B., Can. **39** 47 1N 65 30W
Douglasville **73** 33 46N 84 43W
Doulevant **101** 48 22N 4 53 E
Doullens **101** 50 10N 2 20 E
Doumé **116** 4 15N 13 25 E
Dounreay **96** 58 40N 3 28W
Dourados **89** 22 9 S 54 50W
Dourados, R. **89** 21 58 S 54 18W
Dourdan **101** 48 30N 2 0 E
Douro Litoral □ **104** 41 10N 8 20W
Douro, R. **104** 41 1N 8 16W
Douvaine **103** 46 19N 6 16 E
Douville **45** 45 36N 72 59W
Dove Creek **79** 37 53N 108 59W
Dove, R., N. Yorks, U.K. **94** 54 20N 0 55W
Dove, R., Staffs., U.K. **94** 52 51N 1 36W
Dover, U.K. **95** 51 7N 1 19 E
Dover, Del., U.S.A. **72** 39 10N 75 31W
Dover, Ky., U.S.A. **77** 38 43N 83 52W
Dover, N.H., U.S.A. **71** 43 5N 70 51W
Dover, N.J., U.S.A. **71** 40 53N 74 34W
Dover, Ohio, U.S.A. **70** 40 32N 81 30W
Dover-Foxcroft **35** 45 14N 69 14W
Dover Plains **71** 41 43N 73 35W

Dover, Pt Eatonia

Dover, Pt.	134	32 32 S	125 32 E
Dover, Str. of	93	51 0 N	1 30 E
Dovey, R.	95	52 32 N	4 0 W
Dovrefjell	110	62 15 N	9 33 E
Dowa	117	13 38 S	33 58 E
Dowager I.	62	52 25 N	128 22 W
Dowagiac	77	42 0 N	86 8 W
Dowlatabad	123	28 20 N	50 40 E
Down □	97	54 20 N	6 0 W
Downers Grove	77	41 49 N	88 1 W
Downey	78	42 29 N	112 3 W
Downeys	49	43 29 N	80 14 W
Downham Market	95	52 36 N	0 22 E
Downieville	80	39 34 N	120 50 W
Downing	76	40 29 N	92 22 W
Downpatrick	97	54 20 N	5 43 W
Downpatrick Hd.	97	54 20 N	9 21 W
Downsview	50	43 43 N	79 29 W
Downton, Mt.	62	52 42 N	124 52 W
Doyle	80	40 2 N	120 6 W
Doyles	37	47 50 N	59 12 W
Doylestown	71	40 21 N	75 10 W
Dozois, Rés	40	47 30 N	77 5 W
Drachten	105	53 7 N	6 5 E
Dragoman, P.	109	43 0 N	22 57 E
Dragon	43	45 29 N	74 16 W
Dragon's Mouth	86	11 0 N	61 50 W
Draguignan	103	43 30 N	6 27 E
Drain	78	43 45 N	123 17 W
Drake, Can.	56	51 45 N	105 1 W
Drake, U.S.A.	74	47 56 N	100 31 W
Drake Passage	91	58 0 S	68 0 W
Drakensberg	117	31 0 S	25 0 E
Dráma	109	41 9 N	24 10 E
Drammen	111	59 42 N	10 12 E
Drangajökull	110	66 9 N	22 15 W
Drava, R.	107	45 50 N	18 0 E
Draveil	101	48 41 N	2 25 E
Drayton	46	43 46 N	80 40 W
Drayton Harb.	66	48 58 N	122 46 W
Drayton Plains	77	42 42 N	83 23 W
Drayton Valley	60	53 12 N	114 58 W
Drenthe □	105	52 52 N	6 40 E
Dresden, Can.	46	42 35 N	82 11 W
Dresden, Ger.	106	51 2 N	13 45 E
Dreux	100	48 44 N	1 23 E
Drexel	77	39 45 N	84 18 W
Driffield	94	54 0 N	0 25 W
Driftwood, Can.	34	49 8 N	81 23 E
Driftwood, U.S.A.	70	41 22 N	78 9 W
Driggs	78	43 50 N	111 8 W
Drina, R.	109	44 30 N	19 10 E
Drinkwater	56	50 18 N	105 8 W
Dröbak	111	59 39 N	10 48 E
Drocourt	46	45 46 N	80 21 W
Drogheda	97	53 45 N	6 20 W
Droichead Nua	97	53 11 N	6 50 W
Droitwich	95	52 16 N	2 10 W
Drôme □	103	44 38 N	5 15 E
Drôme, R.	103	44 46 N	4 46 E
Dromedary, C.	136	36 17 S	150 10 E
Dromore	136	32 25 S	143 55 E
Drowning, R.	53	50 54 N	84 34 W
Drumbo	49	43 16 N	80 35 W
Drumheller	61	51 25 N	112 40 W
Drummond, Can.	39	47 2 N	67 41 W
Drummond, Mich., U.S.A.	46	46 1 N	83 50 W
Drummond, Mont., U.S.A.	78	46 46 N	113 4 W
Drummond, Wis., U.S.A.	52	46 20 N	91 15 W
Drummond I.	46	46 0 N	83 40 W
Drummond Ra.	135	23 45 S	147 10 E
Drummondville	41	45 55 N	72 25 W
Drumquin	49	43 32 N	79 47 W
Drumright	75	35 59 N	96 38 W
Druzhina	121	68 14 N	145 18 E
Dry Tortugas	84	24 38 N	82 55 W
Dryberry L.	52	49 33 N	93 53 W
Dryden, Can.	52	49 47 N	92 50 W
Dryden, U.S.A.	75	30 3 N	102 3 W
Drygalski I.	91	66 0 S	92 0 E
Drysdale, R.	134	13 59 S	126 51 E
Du Bois	70	41 8 N	78 46 W
Du Gas, L.	38	51 55 N	75 12 W
Du Gué, R.	36	57 21 N	70 45 W
Du Quoin	76	38 0 N	89 10 W
Duanesburg	71	42 45 N	74 11 W
Dubā	122	27 10 N	35 40 E
Dubai = Dubayy	123	25 18 N	55 20 E
Dubawnt, L.	55	63 4 N	101 42 W
Dubawnt, R.	55	63 33 N	100 6 W
Dubayy	123	25 18 N	55 20 E
Dubbo	136	32 11 S	148 35 E
Duberger	42	46 49 N	71 18 W
Dublin, Can.	70	43 32 N	81 18 W
Dublin, Ireland	97	53 20 N	6 18 W
Dublin, Ga., U.S.A.	73	32 30 N	83 0 W
Dublin, Tex., U.S.A.	75	32 0 N	98 20 W
Dublin □	97	53 24 N	6 20 W
Dublin, B.	97	53 24 N	6 20 W
Dubois, Idaho, U.S.A.	78	44 7 N	112 9 W
Dubois, Ind., U.S.A.	77	38 26 N	86 48 W
Dubreuilville	53	48 21 N	84 32 W
Dubrovnik	109	42 39 N	18 6 E
Dubrovskoye	121	58 55 N	111 0 E
Dubuc	57	50 41 N	102 28 W
Dubuque	76	42 30 N	90 41 W
Duchesne	78	40 14 N	110 22 W
Duchess, Austral.	135	21 20 S	139 50 E
Duchess, Can.	61	50 43 N	111 55 W
Ducie I.	15	24 47 S	124 40 W
Duck Bay	57	52 10 N	100 9 W
Duck Lake	56	52 50 N	106 16 W
Duck, Mt.	55	51 27 N	100 35 W
Duck Mt. Prov. Parks	57	51 45 N	101 0 W
Duckwall ,Mt.	80	37 58 N	120 7 W
Dudhi	125	24 15 N	83 10 E
Dudinka	121	69 30 N	86 0 E
Dudley	95	52 30 N	2 5 W
Duero, R.	104	41 37 N	4 25 W
Duffel	105	51 6 N	4 30 E
Dufferin □	49	43 55 N	80 15 W
Duffin, R.	51	43 49 N	79 2 W
Dufrost, Pte.	36	60 4 N	77 39 W
Dugald	58	49 53 N	96 51 W
Dugger	77	39 4 N	87 16 W
Dugi Otok	108	44 0 N	15 0 E
Duhak	123	33 20 N	57 30 E
Duifken Pt.	135	12 33 S	141 38 E
Duisburg	105	51 27 N	6 42 E
Duitama	86	5 50 N	73 2 W
Duke I.	54	54 50 N	131 20 W
Dukhan	123	25 25 N	50 50 E
Duki	124	30 14 N	68 25 E
Dulawan	127	7 5 N	124 20 E
Dulce, Golfo	84	8 40 N	83 20 W
Dulce, R.	88	29 30 S	63 0 W
Duluth	52	46 48 N	92 10 W
Dum Duma	125	27 40 N	95 40 E
Dumaguete	127	9 17 N	123 15 E
Dumai	126	1 35 N	101 20 E
Dumaran I.	127	10 33 N	119 50 E
Dumaring	127	1 46 N	118 10 E
Dumas, Ark., U.S.A.	75	33 52 N	91 30 W
Dumas, Tex., U.S.A.	75	35 50 N	101 58 W
Dūmat al Jandal	122	29 55 N	39 40 E
Dumbarton	96	55 58 N	4 35 W
Dumbell L.	38	52 28 N	65 45 W
Dumfries	96	55 4 N	3 37 W
Dumfries & Galloway □	96	54 30 N	4 0 W
Dumoine L.	40	46 55 N	77 55 W
Dumoine, R.	40	46 13 N	77 51 W
Dun Laoghaire, (Dunleary)	97	53 17 N	6 9 W
Dun-le-Palestel	102	46 18 N	1 39 E
Dun-sur-Auron	101	46 53 N	2 33 E
Dunaföldvár	107	46 50 N	18 57 E
Dunback	133	45 23 S	170 36 E
Dunbar	96	56 0 N	2 32 W
Dunbarton	51	43 50 N	79 7 W
Dunblane	96	56 10 N	3 58 W
Duncan, Can.	63	48 45 N	123 40 W
Duncan, Ariz., U.S.A.	79	32 46 N	109 6 W
Duncan, Okla., U.S.A.	75	34 25 N	98 0 W
Duncan Dam	63	50 15 N	116 56 W
Duncan L.	54	62 51 N	113 58 W
Duncan, L.	54	53 29 N	77 58 W
Duncan, L.B.C.	34	50 20 N	116 57 W
Duncan Pass.	128	11 0 N	92 30 E
Duncan Town	84	22 15 N	75 45 W
Duncannon	70	40 23 N	77 2 W
Dunchurch	46	45 39 N	79 51 W
Dundalk, Can.	46	44 10 N	80 24 W
Dundalk, Ireland	97	53 55 N	6 45 W
Dundalk, B.	97	53 55 N	6 15 W
Dundarave	66	49 20 N	123 10 W
Dundas, Can.	48	43 17 N	79 59 W
Dundas, Greenl.	65	77 0 N	69 0 W
Dundas I.	54	54 30 N	130 50 W
Dundas, L.	134	32 35 S	121 50 E
Dundas Pen.	64	74 50 N	111 36 W
Dundas Str.	134	11 15 S	131 35 E
Dundee, Can.	43	45 0 N	74 30 W
Dundee, S. Afr.	117	28 11 S	30 15 E
Dundee, U.K.	96	56 29 N	3 0 W
Dundee, U.S.A.	77	41 57 N	83 40 W
Dundrum	97	54 17 N	5 50 W
Dundrum B.	97	54 12 N	5 40 W
Dundurn	56	51 49 N	106 30 W
Dundurn Camp	56	51 51 N	106 34 W
Dunedin, N.Z.	133	45 50 S	170 33 E
Dunedin, U.S.A.	73	28 1 N	82 45 W
Dunedin, R.	54	59 30 N	124 5 W
Dunfermline	96	56 5 N	3 28 W
Dungannon, Can.	46	43 51 N	81 36 W
Dungannon, U.K.	97	54 30 N	6 47 W
Dungannon □	97	54 30 N	6 55 W
Dungarvan	97	52 6 N	7 40 W
Dungarvan Bay	97	52 5 N	7 35 W
Dungarvan Harb.	97	52 5 N	7 35 W
Dungarvon, R.	39	46 49 N	65 54 W
Dungbure Shan	129	35 0 N	90 0 E
Dungeness	95	50 54 N	0 59 E
Dungog	136	32 22 S	151 40 E
Dungu	116	2 32 N	28 22 E
Dunham	43	45 8 N	72 48 W
Dunière, Parc Prov. de	38	48 45 N	66 41 W
Dunières	103	45 13 N	4 20 E
Dunkeld	96	56 34 N	3 36 W
Dunkerque	101	51 2 N	2 20 E
Dunkery Beacon	95	51 15 N	3 37 W
Dunkirk	70	42 30 N	79 18 W
Dunkirk = Dunkerque	101	51 2 N	2 20 E
Dunkley	63	53 17 N	122 28 W
Dunlap	74	41 50 N	95 30 W
Dunmanus B.	97	51 31 N	9 50 W
Dunmore, Can.	61	49 58 N	110 36 W
Dunmore, U.S.A.	71	41 27 N	75 38 W
Dunmore Town	84	25 30 N	76 39 W
Dunn	73	35 18 N	78 36 W
Dunnellon	73	29 4 N	82 28 W
Dunnet Hd.	96	58 38 N	3 22 W
Dunning	74	41 52 N	100 4 W
Dunnville	46	42 54 N	79 36 W
Dunoon	96	55 57 N	4 56 W
Dunrankin, R.	53	48 47 N	82 51 W
Duns	96	55 47 N	2 20 W
Dunseith	74	48 49 N	100 2 W
Dunsmuir	78	41 10 N	122 10 W
Dunstable	95	51 53 N	0 31 W
Dunstan Mts.	133	44 53 S	169 35 E
Dunster	63	53 8 N	119 50 W
Dunûrea, R.	107	45 0 N	29 40 E
Dunvegan	60	55 55 N	118 36 W
Dunvegan L.	55	60 8 N	107 10 W
Dunville	37	47 16 N	53 54 W
Duparquet	40	48 30 N	79 14 W
Duparquet, L.	40	48 28 N	79 16 W
Dupree	74	45 4 N	101 35 W
Dupuy	40	48 50 N	79 21 W
Dupuyer	78	48 11 N	112 31 W
Duque de Caxias	89	22 45 S	43 19 W
Duquesne	70	40 22 N	79 55 W
Durack Ra.	134	16 50 S	127 40 E
Durance, R.	103	43 55 N	4 45 E
Durand, Ill., U.S.A.	76	42 26 N	89 20 W
Durand, Mich., U.S.A.	77	42 54 N	83 58 W
Durango, Mexico	82	24 3 N	104 39 W
Durango, Spain	104	43 13 N	2 40 W
Durango, U.S.A.	79	37 10 N	107 50 W
Durango □	82	25 0 N	105 0 W
Durant, Iowa, U.S.A.	76	41 36 N	90 54 W
Durant, Okla., U.S.A.	75	34 0 N	96 25 W
Durazno	88	33 25 S	56 38 W
Durban, France	102	43 0 N	2 49 E
Durban, S. Afr.	117	29 49 S	31 1 E
Düren	105	50 48 N	6 30 E
Durg	125	21 15 N	81 22 E
Durham, Can.	46	44 10 N	80 49 W
Durham, U.K.	94	54 47 N	1 34 W
Durham, Calif., U.S.A.	80	39 39 N	121 48 W
Durham, N.C., U.S.A.	73	36 0 N	78 55 W
Durham □, Can.	51	43 57 N	79 5 W
Durham □, U.K.	94	54 42 N	1 45 W
Durham Bridge	39	46 7 N	66 36 W
Durmitor Mt.	109	43 10 N	19 0 E
Durocher, L.	38	50 52 N	61 12 W
Durrës	109	41 19 N	19 28 E
Durtal	100	47 40 N	0 18 W
D'Urville Island	133	40 50 S	173 55 E
Duryea	71	41 20 N	75 45 W
Dusey, R.	53	51 11 N	86 21 W
Dushak	120	37 20 N	60 10 E
Dushanbe	120	38 33 N	68 48 E
Dusky Sd.	133	45 47 S	166 30 E
Düsseldorf	105	51 15 N	6 46 E
Dutch Harbour	67	53 54 N	166 35 W
Dutton	46	42 39 N	81 30 W
Duval	56	51 9 N	104 59 W
Duvernay	44	45 35 N	73 40 W
Duwadami	122	24 35 N	44 15 E
Duzdab = Zāhedān	123	29 30 N	60 50 E
Dwarka	124	22 18 N	69 8 E
Dwight, Can.	47	45 20 N	79 1 W
Dwight, U.S.A.	77	41 5 N	88 25 W
Dyer	77	37 24 N	86 13 W
Dyer's B.	70	45 9 N	81 24 W
Dyersburg	75	36 2 N	89 20 W
Dyersville	76	42 29 N	91 8 W
Dyfed □	95	52 0 N	4 30 W
Dyment	52	49 37 N	92 18 W
Dysart	56	50 57 N	104 2 W
Dzerzhinsk	120	53 40 N	27 7 E
Dzhailma	120	51 30 N	61 50 E
Dzhalinda	121	53 40 N	124 0 E
Dzhambul	120	42 54 N	71 22 E
Dzhardzhan	121	68 10 N	123 5 E
Dzhelinde	121	70 0 N	114 20 E
Dzhetygara	120	52 11 N	61 12 E
Dzhezkazgan	120	47 10 N	67 40 E
Dzhizak	120	40 6 N	67 50 E
Dzhugdzur, Khrebet	121	57 30 N	138 0 E
Dzhungarskiye Vorota	120	45 0 N	82 0 E
Dzibilchaltún	83	21 5 N	89 36 W
Dzilam de Bravo	83	21 24 N	88 53 W
Dzungaria	129	44 10 N	88 0 E
Dzuunbulag	130	46 58 N	115 30 E
Dzuunmod	130	47 45 N	106 58 E

E

Eabamet, L.	53	51 30 N	87 46 W
Eads	74	38 30 N	102 46 W
Eagle, Alaska, U.S.A.	67	64 44 N	141 29 W
Eagle, Colo., U.S.A.	78	39 45 N	106 55 W
Eagle Butt	74	45 1 N	101 12 W
Eagle Cr.	56	52 20 N	107 30 W
Eagle Creek, R.	77	38 36 N	85 46 W
Eagle Grove	76	42 37 N	93 53 W
Eagle I.	57	53 40 N	98 55 W
Eagle L., B.C., Can.	62	51 55 N	124 23 W
Eagle L., Ont., Can.	52	49 42 N	93 13 W
Eagle L., Calif., U.S.A.	78	40 35 N	120 50 W
Eagle L., Me., U.S.A.	35	46 23 N	69 22 W
Eagle Lake, Can.	47	45 8 N	78 29 W
Eagle Lake, U.S.A.	75	29 35 N	96 21 W
Eagle Mountain	81	33 52 N	115 26 W
Eagle Nest	79	36 33 N	105 13 W
Eagle Pass	75	28 45 N	100 35 W
Eagle Pk.	80	38 10 N	119 25 W
Eagle, R.	36	53 36 N	57 26 W
Eagle River, Can.	52	49 47 N	93 12 W
Eagle River, Mich., U.S.A.	52	47 24 N	88 18 W
Eagle River, Wis., U.S.A.	74	45 55 N	89 17 W
Eaglehawk	136	36 43 S	144 16 E
Eaglehead L.	52	49 2 N	89 12 W
Eaglesham	60	55 47 N	117 53 W
Eagleville	76	40 28 N	93 59 W
Ealing	95	51 30 N	0 19 W
Ear Falls	52	50 38 N	93 13 W
Earl Grey	56	50 57 N	104 43 W
Earle	75	35 18 N	90 26 W
Earlimart	81	35 53 N	119 16 W
Earls Cove	62	49 45 N	124 0 W
Earltown	39	45 35 N	63 8 W
Earlville	77	41 35 N	88 55 W
Earn, L.	96	56 23 N	4 14 W
Earn, R.	96	56 20 N	3 19 W
Earnslaw, Mt.	133	44 32 S	168 27 E
Earth	75	34 18 N	102 30 W
Easley	73	34 52 N	82 35 W
East Angus	41	45 30 N	71 40 W
East Aurora	70	42 46 N	78 38 W
East, B.	75	29 2 N	89 16 W
East Bathurst	35	47 35 N	65 40 W
East Bay	39	46 1 N	60 25 W
East Bengal	125	24 0 N	90 0 E
East Brady	70	40 59 N	79 36 W
East Broughton Station	41	46 14 N	71 5 W
East C.	133	37 42 S	178 35 E
East Chezzetcook	39	44 43 N	63 14 W
East Chicago	77	41 40 N	87 30 W
East China Sea	131	30 5 N	126 0 E
East Coulee	61	51 23 N	112 27 W
East Detroit	46	42 28 N	82 56 W
East Don, R.	50	43 39 N	79 21 W
East Dubuque	76	42 29 N	90 39 W
East Falkland	90	51 30 S	58 30 W
East Farnham	43	45 14 N	72 46 W
East Florenceville	35	46 26 N	67 36 W
East Fork, R.	77	38 33 N	87 14 W
East Franklin	43	44 59 N	72 48 W
East Grand Forks	74	47 55 N	97 5 W
East Greenwich	71	41 39 N	71 27 W
East Harbour	66	49 22 N	123 16 W
East Hartford	71	41 45 N	72 39 W
East Helena	78	46 37 N	111 58 W
East Humber, R.	50	43 48 N	79 35 W
East Indies	126	0 0	120 0 E
East Jordan	46	45 10 N	85 7 W
East Kildonan	58	49 55 N	97 5 W
East Lansing	77	42 44 N	84 29 W
East Liverpool	70	40 39 N	80 35 W
East London	117	33 0 S	27 55 E
East Los Angeles	81	34 1 N	118 9 W
East Moline	76	41 31 N	90 25 W
East P.	39	46 27 N	61 58 W
East Palestine	70	40 50 N	80 32 W
East Peoria	76	40 40 N	89 34 W
East Pine	54	55 48 N	120 5 W
East Point	73	33 40 N	84 28 W
East Providence	71	41 48 N	71 22 W
East Retford	94	53 19 N	0 55 W
East St. Louis	76	38 37 N	90 9 W
East Sd.	63	48 45 N	123 0 W
E. Siberian Sea	121	73 0 N	160 0 E
East Stroudsburg	71	41 1 N	75 11 W
East Suffolk □	95	52 15 N	1 20 E
East Sussex □	95	50 55 N	0 20 E
East Tawas	46	44 17 N	83 31 W
East Thurlow I.	62	50 24 N	125 25 W
East Trout L.	56	54 22 N	105 5 W
East Troy	77	42 47 N	88 24 W
East Walker, R.	80	38 52 N	119 10 W
East York	50	43 42 N	79 20 W
Eastbourne, N.Z.	133	41 19 S	174 55 E
Eastbourne, U.K.	95	50 46 N	0 18 E
Eastcap Cr.	66	49 27 N	123 6 W
Eastend	56	49 32 N	108 50 W
Eastern Ghats	124	15 0 N	80 0 E
Eastern Passage	39	44 37 N	63 30 W
Easterville	57	53 8 N	99 49 W
Easthampton	71	42 15 N	72 41 W
Eastland	75	32 26 N	98 45 W
Eastleigh	95	50 58 N	1 21 W
Eastmain (East Main)	36	52 20 N	78 30 W
Eastmain, R.	36	52 27 N	72 26 W
Eastman, Can.	41	45 18 N	72 19 W
Eastman, Ga., U.S.A.	73	32 13 N	83 20 W
Eastman, Wis., U.S.A.	76	43 10 N	91 1 W
Easton, Md., U.S.A.	72	38 47 N	76 7 W
Easton, Pa., U.S.A.	71	40 41 N	75 15 W
Easton, Wash., U.S.A.	80	47 14 N	121 8 W
Eastport	35	44 57 N	67 0 W
Eastsound	80	48 42 N	122 55 W
Eastview	34	45 27 N	75 40 W
Eaton, Colo., U.S.A.	74	40 35 N	104 42 W
Eaton, Ohio, U.S.A.	77	39 45 N	84 38 W
Eaton Rapids	77	42 31 N	84 39 W
Eatonia	56	51 13 N	109 25 W

Eatonton
Emmeloord

Eatonton 73 33 22N 83 24W
Eatonville, Can. 41 47 20N 69 41W
Eatonville, U.S.A. 80 46 52N 122 16W
Eau Claire, S.C., U.S.A. 73 34 5N 81 2W
Eau Claire, Wis., U.S.A. 74 44 46N 91 30W
Eau-Claire, L. à l' 38 52 36N 65 50W
Eau Claire, L. à l' 36 56 10N 74 25W
Eauze 102 43 53N 0 7E
Ebbw Vale 95 51 47N 3 12W
Ebeltoft 111 56 12N 10 41E
Ebensburg 70 40 29N 78 43W
Eberswalde 106 52 49N 13 50E
Eboli 108 40 39N 15 2E
Ebolowa 116 2 55N 11 10E
Eboulements, Les 41 47 28N 70 21W
Ebro, R. 104 41 49N 1 5W
Écueillé 100 47 10N 1 19E
Echaneni 121 27 33S 32 6E
Echelles, Les 103 45 27N 5 45E
Echo Bay 46 46 29N 84 4W
Echo Bay (Port Radium) 64 66 05N 117 55W
Echoing, R. 55 55 51N 92 5W
Échouani, L. 40 47 46N 75 42W
Echternach 105 49 49N 6 3E
Echuca 136 36 3S 144 46E
Ecija 104 37 30N 5 10W
Eckville 61 52 21N 114 22W
Eclipse Sd. 65 72 38N 79 0W
Écommoy 100 47 50N 0 17E
Écorce, L. de l' 40 47 5N 76 24W
Ecorces, L. des 43 46 0N 74 32W
Ecorse 77 42 14N 83 10W
Écos 101 49 9N 1 35E
Écouché 100 48 42N 0 10W
Ecuador ■ 86 2 0S 78 0W
Ecueils, Pte. aux 36 59 47N 77 50W
Ecum Secum 39 44 58N 62 8W
Ed Damer 115 17 27N 34 0E
Edam, Can. 56 53 11N 108 46W
Edam, Neth. 105 52 31N 5 3E
Eday, I. 96 59 11N 2 47W
Edberg 61 52 47N 112 47W
Eddrachillis B. 96 58 16N 5 10W
Eddystone 95 50 11N 4 16W
Eddyville 76 41 9N 92 38W
Ede 105 52 4N 5 40E
Édea 116 3 51N 10 9E
Edehon L. 55 60 25N 97 15W
Eden, Austral. 136 37 3S 149 55E
Eden, Can. 57 50 23N 99 28W
Eden, N.Y., U.S.A. 70 42 39N 78 55W
Eden, Tex., U.S.A. 75 31 16N 99 50W
Eden, Wyo., U.S.A. 78 42 2N 109 27W
Eden L. 55 56 38N 100 15W
Eden Mills 49 43 35N 80 9W
Eden, R. 94 54 57N 3 2W
Edenderry 97 53 21N 7 3W
Edenton 73 36 5N 76 36W
Edgar 74 40 25N 98 0W
Edgartown 71 41 22N 70 28W
Edge Hill 95 52 7N 1 28W
Edge I. 17 77 45N 22 30E
Edgefield 73 33 43N 81 59W
Edgeley, Can. 50 43 48N 79 31W
Edgeley, U.S.A. 74 46 27N 98 41W
Edgemont 74 43 15N 103 53W
Edgeøya 17 77 45N 22 30E
Edgerton, Can. 61 52 45N 110 27W
Edgerton, Ohio, U.S.A. 77 41 27N 84 45W
Edgerton, Wis., U.S.A. 76 42 50N 89 4W
Edgewater 61 50 42N 116 5W
Edgewood, Can. 63 49 47N 118 8W
Edgewood, U.S.A. 77 38 55N 88 40W
Edgington 70 45 24N 79 46W
Edhessa 109 40 48N 22 5E
Edievale 133 45 49S 169 22E
Edina 76 40 6N 92 10W
Edinburg, Ill., U.S.A. 76 39 39N 89 23W
Edinburg, Ind., U.S.A. 77 39 21N 85 58W
Edinburg, Tex., U.S.A. 75 26 22N 98 10W
Edinburgh 96 55 57N 3 12W
Edirne 109 41 40N 26 45E
Edison, Calif., U.S.A. 81 35 21N 118 52W
Edison, Wash., U.S.A. 80 48 33N 122 27W
Edmeston 71 42 42N 75 15W
Edmond 75 35 37N 97 30W
Edmonds, Can. 66 49 13N 122 57W
Edmonds, U.S.A. 80 47 47N 122 22W
Edmonton 59 53 30N 113 30W
Edmore 46 43 25N 85 3W
Edmund L. 55 54 45N 93 17W
Edmundston 39 47 23N 68 20W
Edna 75 29 0N 96 40W
Edna Bay 54 55 55N 133 40W
Edremit 122 39 40N 27 0E
Edsel Ford Ra. 91 77 0S 143 0W
Edson 60 53 35N 116 28W
Eduardo Castex 88 35 50S 64 25W
Edward I. 52 48 22N 88 37W
Edward, L. = Idi Amin Dada, L. 116 0 25S 29 40E
Edward, R. 136 35 0S 143 30E
Edward VII Pen. 91 80 0S 160 0W
Edwards 81 34 55N 117 51W
Edwards Plat. 75 30 30N 101 5W
Edwards, R. 76 41 10N 90 59W
Edwardsburg 77 41 48N 86 6W
Edwardsport 77 38 49N 87 15W
Edwardsville, Ill., U.S.A. 76 38 49N 89 57W
Edwardsville, Pa., U.S.A. 71 41 15N 75 56W
Edzo 54 62 49N 116 4W
Eek 67 60 10N 162 0W
Eekloo 105 51 11N 3 33E
Eel, R., Ind., U.S.A. 77 39 7N 86 58W
Eel, R., Ind., U.S.A. 77 40 45N 86 22W
Eel River Crossing 39 48 1N 66 25W
Eernegem 105 51 8N 3 2E
Effingham 77 39 8N 88 30W
Égadi, Ísole 108 37 55N 12 10E
Eganville 47 45 32N 77 5W
Egeland 74 48 42N 99 6W
Egenolf L. 55 59 3N 100 0W
Eger 107 47 53N 20 27E
Egersund = Eigersund 111 58 26N 6 1E
Egerton, Mt. 134 24 42S 117 44E
Egg L. 55 55 5N 105 30W
Eggertsville 49 42 58N 78 46W
Égletons 102 45 24N 2 3E
Eglington I. 64 75 48N 118 30W
Egmont 62 49 45N 123 56W
Egmont B. 39 46 29N 64 6W
Egmont, C. 133 39 16S 173 45E
Egmont, Mt. 133 39 17S 174 5E
Eğridir Gölü 122 37 53N 30 50E
Egua 86 5 5N 68 0W
Éguzon 102 46 27N 1 33E
Egvekinot 121 66 19N 179 50W
Egypt ■ 115 28 0N 31 0E
Ehime-ken □ 132 33 30N 132 40E
Eholt 63 49 10N 118 34W
Ehrenburg 81 33 36N 114 31W
Eidsvoll 111 60 19N 11 14E
Eifel 105 50 10N 6 45E
Eigersund 111 58 26N 6 1E
Eigg, I. 96 56 54N 6 10W
Eighty Mile Beach 134 19 30S 120 40E
Eil 115 8 0N 49 50E
Eil, L. 96 56 50N 5 15W
Eilat 122 29 30N 34 56E
Eildon, L. 136 37 10S 146 0E
Eileen L. 55 62 16N 107 37W
Einasleigh 135 18 32S 144 5E
Eindhoven 105 51 26N 5 30E
Eiríksjökull 110 64 46N 20 24W
Eirunepé 86 6 35S 70 0W
Eisenach 106 50 58N 10 18E
Eisenerz 106 47 32N 14 54E
Ejido 86 8 33N 71 14W
Ejutla 83 16 34N 96 44W
Ekalaka 74 45 55N 104 30W
Eketahuna 133 40 38S 175 43E
Ekibastuz 120 51 40N 75 22E
Ekimchan 121 53 0N 133 0W
Ekwan Pt. 34 53 16N 82 7W
Ekwan, R. 34 53 12N 82 15W
El Baúl 86 8 57N 68 17W
El Bluff 84 11 59N 83 40W
El Cajon 81 32 49N 117 0W
El Callao 86 7 25N 61 50W
El Campo 75 29 10N 96 20W
El Carmen 86 1 16N 66 52W
El Centro 81 32 50N 115 40W
El Cerro 86 17 30S 61 40W
El Cocuy 86 6 25N 72 27W
El Compadre 81 32 20N 116 14W
El Cuy 90 39 55S 68 25W
El Cuyo 83 21 30N 87 40W
El Dátil 82 30 7N 112 15W
El Dere 115 3 50N 47 8E
El Diaz 83 21 1N 87 17W
El Dificul 86 9 51N 74 14W
El Díos 82 20 40N 87 20W
El Diviso 86 1 22N 78 14W
El Djouf 114 20 0N 11 30E
El Dorado, Colomb. 86 1 11N 71 52W
El Dorado, Ark., U.S.A. 75 33 10N 92 40W
El Dorado, Kans., U.S.A. 75 37 55N 96 56W
El Dorado, Venez. 86 6 55N 61 30W
El Dorado Springs 76 37 54N 93 59W
El Escorial 104 40 35N 4 7W
El Faiyûm 115 29 19N 30 50E
El Fâsher 115 13 33N 25 26E
El Ferrol 104 43 29N 3 14W
El Fuerte 82 26 30N 108 40W
El Iskandarîya 115 31 0N 30 0E
El Khârga 115 25 30N 30 33E
El Khartûm 115 15 31N 32 35E
El Ladhiqiya 122 35 20N 35 30E
El Mahalla el Kubra 115 31 0N 31 0E
El Mansûra 122 31 0N 31 19E
El Mantico 86 7 27N 62 32W
El Miamo 86 7 39N 61 46W
El Milagro 88 30 59S 65 59W
El Minyâ 115 28 7N 30 33E
El Monte 81 34 4N 118 2W
El Obeid 115 13 8N 30 10E
El Oro = Sta. María del Oro 82 25 50N 105 20W
El Oro de Hidalgo 83 19 48N 100 8W
El Palmar 86 7 58N 61 53W
El Palmito, Presa 82 25 40N 105 3W
El Pao 86 9 38N 68 8W
El Paso, Ill., U.S.A. 76 40 44N 89 1W
El Paso, Tex., U.S.A. 79 31 50N 106 30W
El Paso Robles 80 35 38N 120 41W
El Pilar 86 10 32N 63 9W
El Portal 80 37 44N 119 49W
El Porvenir, Mexico 82 31 15N 105 51W
El Porvenir, Venez. 86 4 42N 71 19W
El Progreso 84 15 26N 87 51W
El Pueblito 82 29 3N 105 4W
El Qahira 115 30 1N 31 14E
El Qasr 115 25 44N 28 42E
El Reno 75 35 30N 98 0W
El Rio 81 34 14N 119 10W
El Salado 86 8 56N 73 55W
El Salto 82 23 47N 105 22W
El Salvador ■ 84 13 50N 89 0W
El Sauce 84 13 0N 86 40W
El Suweis 115 29 58N 32 31E
El Temblador 86 8 59N 62 44W
El Tigre 86 8 55N 64 15W
El Tocuyo 86 9 47N 69 48W
El Tofo 88 29 22S 71 18W
El Tránsito 88 28 52S 70 17W
El Turbio 90 51 30S 72 40W
El Vigia 86 8 38N 71 39W
El Wak 116 2 49N 40 56E
Elaho, R. 62 50 7N 123 23W
Elat 127 5 40S 133 5E
Eläzig 122 38 37N 39 22E
Elba 73 31 27N 86 4W
Elba, I. 108 42 48N 10 15E
Elbasani 109 41 9N 20 9E
Elbe 80 46 45N 121 49W
Elbe, R. 106 53 15N 10 7E
Elberfeld 77 38 10N 87 27W
Elbert, Mt. 79 39 12N 106 36W
Elberta, Mich., U.S.A. 72 44 35N 86 14W
Elberta, N.Y., U.S.A. 49 43 16N 78 52W
Elberton 73 34 7N 82 51W
Elbeuf 100 49 17N 1 2E
Elblag 107 54 10N 19 25E
Elbow 56 51 7N 106 35W
Elbow, R. 59 51 3N 114 2W
Elbrus, Mt. 120 43 30N 42 30E
Elburg 105 52 26N 5 50E
Elburn 77 41 54N 88 28W
Elburz Mts. = Alborz 123 36 0N 52 0E
Elche 104 38 15N 0 42W
Elcho I. 134 11 55S 135 45E
Eldon, Iowa, U.S.A. 76 40 50N 92 12W
Eldon, Mo., U.S.A. 76 38 20N 92 38W
Eldora 76 42 20N 93 5W
Eldorado, Argent. 89 26 28S 54 43W
Eldorado, Ont., Can. 47 44 35N 77 31W
Eldorado, Sask., Can. 55 59 35N 108 30W
Eldorado, Mexico 82 24 0N 107 30W
Eldorado, Ill., U.S.A. 77 37 50N 88 25W
Eldorado, Tex., U.S.A. 75 30 52N 100 35W
Eldorado Park 50 43 39N 79 46W
Eldoret 116 0 30N 35 25E
Eldred 70 41 57N 78 24W
Eldridge 76 41 39N 90 35W
Electra 75 34 0N 99 0W
Eleele 67 21 54N 159 35W
Elephant Butte Res. 79 33 45N 107 30W
Elephant I. 91 61 0S 55 0W
Eleuthera I. 84 25 0N 76 20W
Elfin Cove 67 58 11N 136 20W
Elfrida 48 43 10N 79 47W
Elgin, B.C., Can. 66 49 4N 122 49W
Elgin, Man., Can. 57 49 27N 100 16W
Elgin, N.B., Can. 35 45 48N 65 10W
Elgin, Ont., Can. 47 44 36N 76 13W
Elgin, Ont., Can. 71 44 37N 76 15W
Elgin, U.K. 96 57 39N 3 20W
Elgin, Ill., U.S.A. 77 42 0N 88 20W
Elgin, N.D., U.S.A. 74 46 24N 101 46W
Elgin, Nebr., U.S.A. 74 41 58N 98 3W
Elgin, Nev., U.S.A. 79 37 27N 114 36W
Elgin, Oreg., U.S.A. 78 45 37N 118 0W
Elgin, Texas, U.S.A. 75 30 21N 97 22W
Elgon, Mt. 116 1 10N 34 30E
Eliase 127 8 10S 130 55E
Elida 75 33 56N 103 41W
Elie 55 49 48N 97 52W
Elim 67 64 35N 162 20W
Elisabethville = Lubumbashi 117 11 32S 27 38E
Elista 120 46 16N 44 14E
Elizabeth, Austral. 135 34 42S 138 41E
Elizabeth, Ill., U.S.A. 76 42 19N 90 13W
Elizabeth, N.J., U.S.A. 71 40 37N 74 12W
Elizabeth City 73 36 18N 76 16W
Elizabethton 73 36 20N 82 13W
Elizabethtown, Ill., U.S.A. 77 37 27N 88 18W
Elizabethtown, Ky., U.S.A. 72 37 40N 85 54W
Elizabethtown, N.Y., U.S.A. 71 44 13N 73 36W
Elizabethtown, Pa., U.S.A. 71 40 8N 76 36W
Elk City 75 35 25N 99 25W
Elk Creek 80 39 36N 122 32W
Elk Grove 80 38 25N 121 22W
Elk Island Nat. Park 60 53 35N 112 59W
Elk Lake 34 47 40N 80 25W
Elk Lakes Prov. Pzrk 61 50 30N 115 10W
Elk Point 60 53 54N 110 55W
Elk, R. 61 49 11N 115 14W
Elk Rapids 46 44 54N 85 25W
Elk River, Idaho, U.S.A. 78 46 50N 116 8W
Elk River, Minn., U.S.A. 74 45 17N 93 34W
Elkader 76 42 51N 91 24W
Elkford 61 49 52N 114 53W
Elkhart, Ind., U.S.A. 77 41 42N 85 55W
Elkhart, Kans., U.S.A. 75 37 3N 101 54W
Elkhart, R. 77 41 41N 85 58W
Elkhorn, Can. 57 49 59N 101 14W
Elkhorn, U.S.A. 77 42 40N 88 33W
Elkhorn, R. 74 42 0N 98 15W
Elkhovo 109 42 10N 26 40E
Elkin 73 36 17N 80 50W
Elkins 72 38 53N 79 53W
Elko, Can. 61 49 20N 115 10W
Elko, U.S.A. 78 40 50N 115 50W
Elkton 46 43 49N 83 11W
Ellef Ringnes I. 65 78 30N 102 2W
Ellen, Mt. 79 38 4N 110 56W
Ellendale, Can. 39 44 41N 63 33W
Ellendale, U.S.A. 74 46 3N 98 30W
Ellensburg 78 47 0N 120 30W
Ellenville 71 41 42N 74 23W
Ellerslie 59 53 26N 113 30W
Ellery, Mt. 136 37 28S 148 40E
Ellesmere I. 65 79 30N 80 0W
Ellesmere, L. 15 43 46S 172 27E
Ellesworth Land 91 74 0S 85 0W
Ellettsville 77 39 14N 86 38W
Ellice Is. 14 8 0S 176 0E
Ellinwood 74 38 27N 98 37W
Elliot L. 57 52 54N 95 18W
Elliot Lake 46 46 25N 82 35W
Ellis 74 39 0N 99 39W
Elliston 37 48 38N 53 3W
Ellisville 73 31 38N 89 12W
Ellon 96 57 21N 2 5W
Ellore = Eluru 125 16 48N 81 8E
Ells, R. 60 57 18N 111 40W
Ellsworth 74 38 47N 98 15W
Ellsworth Land 91 76 0S 89 0W
Ellwood City 70 40 52N 80 19W
Elm Grove 58 49 47N 96 49W
Elma, Can. 57 49 52N 95 55W
Elma, U.S.A. 80 47 0N 123 30W
Elmer 76 39 57N 92 39W
Elmhurst 77 41 52N 87 58W
Elmira, Ont., Can. 49 43 36N 80 33W
Elmira, P.E.I., Can. 35 46 30N 61 59W
Elmira, U.S.A. 70 42 8N 76 49W
Elmore, Austral. 136 36 30S 144 37E
Elmore, Calif., U.S.A. 81 33 7N 115 49W
Elmore, Minn., U.S.A. 77 41 29N 83 18W
Elmsdale 39 44 58N 63 30W
Elmvale 46 44 35N 79 52W
Elmwood, Can. 70 44 14N 81 3W
Elmwood, U.S.A. 76 40 47N 89 58W
Elmworth 60 55 3N 119 37W
Elnora, Can. 61 51 59N 113 12W
Elnora, U.S.A. 77 38 53N 87 5W
Elora 49 43 41N 80 26W
Elorza 86 7 3N 69 31W
Eloy 79 32 46N 111 46W
Éloyes 101 48 6N 6 36E
Elphin 47 44 55N 76 37W
Elphinstone 57 50 32N 100 30W
Elrose 56 51 12N 108 0W
Elsa 64 63 55N 135 29W
Elsas 53 48 32N 82 55W
Elsie, Mich., U.S.A. 46 43 5N 84 23W
Elsie, Oreg., U.S.A. 80 45 52N 123 35W
Elsinore, Cal., U.S.A. 81 33 40N 117 15W
Elsinore, Utah, U.S.A. 79 38 40N 112 2W
Elson 80 47 32N 123 4W
Elsona 66 49 12N 122 57W
Elst 105 51 55N 5 51E
Eltham 133 39 26S 174 19E
Eluru 125 16 48N 81 8E
Elvas 104 38 50N 7 17W
Elven 100 47 44N 2 36W
Elverum 111 60 53N 11 34E
Elvire, Mt. 136 29 22S 119 33E
Elwood, Ill., U.S.A. 77 41 24N 88 7W
Elwood, Ind., U.S.A. 77 40 20N 85 50W
Elwood, Nebr., U.S.A. 74 40 38N 99 51W
Ely, U.K. 95 52 24N 0 16E
Ely, Minn., U.S.A. 52 47 54N 91 52W
Ely, Nev., U.S.A. 78 39 10N 114 50W
Elyria 70 41 22N 82 8W
Emba 120 48 50N 58 8E
Emba, R. 120 48 0N 56 0E
Embarcación 88 23 10S 64 0W
Embarras Portage 55 58 27N 111 28W
Embarrass, R. 77 38 39N 87 37W
Embro 46 43 9N 80 54W
Embrun 103 44 34N 6 30E
Embu 116 0 32S 37 38E
Emden 105 53 22N 7 12E
Emerald 135 23 32S 148 10E
Emeril 36 47 26N 75 47W
Emerson 57 49 0N 97 10W
Emery 79 38 59N 111 17W
Emery Park 79 32 10N 110 59W
Emi Koussi, Mt. 114 20 0N 18 55E
Emilia-Romagna □ 108 44 33N 10 40E
Eminence 77 38 22N 85 11W
Emlenton 70 41 11N 79 41W
Emmeloord 105 52 44N 5 46E

Emmen **Eyre Pen**

Emmen **105** 52 48N 6 57 E
Emmerich **105** 51 50N 6 12 E
Emmetsburg **76** 43 3N 94 40W
Emmett, Idaho, U.S.A. **78** 43 51N 116 33W
Emmett, Mich., U.S.A. **46** 42 59N 82 46W
Emo **52** 48 38N 93 50W
Empalme **82** 28 1N 110 49W
Empangeni **117** 28 50S 31 52 E
Empedrado **88** 28 0S 58 46W
Emporia, Kans., U.S.A. **74** 38 25N 96 16W
Emporia, Va., U.S.A. **73** 36 41N 77 32W
Emporium **70** 41 30N 78 17W
Empress **61** 50 57N 110 0W
Ems, R. **105** 52 37N 7 16 E
Emsdale **46** 45 32N 79 19W
Emsdetten **105** 52 11N 7 31 E
En Nahud **115** 12 45N 28 25 E
Enambú **86** 1 1N 70 17W
Enard B. **96** 58 5N 5 20W
Encantadas, Serra **89** 30 40S 53 0W
Encanto, Cape **127** 15 44N 121 40 E
Encarnación **89** 27 15S 56 0W
Encarnación de Diaz **82** 21 30N 102 20W
Encinal **75** 28 3N 99 25W
Encinillas **82** 33 3N 117 17W
Encinitas **81** 33 3N 117 17W
Encino **79** 34 38N 105 40W
Encounter B. **135** 35 45S 138 45 E
Endako **62** 54 6N 125 2W
Endau **128** 2 40N 103 38 E
Endau, R. **128** 2 30N 103 30 E
Ende **127** 8 45S 121 30 E
Endeavour **56** 52 10N 102 39W
Endeavour Str. **135** 10 45S 142 0 E
Enderbury I. **15** 3 8S 171 5W
Enderby **63** 50 35N 119 10W
Enderby Land **91** 66 0S 53 0 E
Enderlin **74** 46 45N 97 41W
Endicott, N.Y., U.S.A. **71** 42 6N 76 2W
Endicott, Wash., U.S.A. **78** 47 0N 117 45W
Endicott Mts. **67** 68 0N 152 30W
Enez **109** 40 45N 26 5 E
Enfield, Can. **39** 44 56N 63 32W
Enfield, U.K. **95** 51 39N 0 4W
Enfield, U.S.A. **77** 38 6N 88 20W
Engadin **106** 46 45N 10 10 E
Engadine **46** 46 4N 85 38W
Engano, C. **85** 18 30N 68 20W
Engaño, C. **127** 18 35N 122 23 E
Engels **120** 51 28N 46 6 E
Engemann L. **55** 58 0N 106 55W
Enggano, I. **126** 5 20S 102 40 E
Enghien **105** 50 37N 4 2 E
Engkilili **126** 1 3N 111 42 E
England **75** 34 30N 91 58W
England □ **94** 53 0N 2 0W
Englee **37** 50 45N 56 5W
Englefeld **56** 52 10N 104 39W
Englefield, C. **65** 69 49N 85 34W
Englehart **34** 47 49N 79 52W
Engler L. **55** 59 8N 106 52W
Englewood, U.S.A. **77** 39 53N 84 18W
Englewood, Colo., U.S.A. **74** 39 40N 105 0W
Englewood, Kans., U.S.A. **75** 37 7N 99 59W
English **77** 38 20N 86 28W
English B. **66** 49 17N 123 11W
English Bazar **125** 24 58N 88 21 E
English Channel **95** 50 0N 2 0W
English Company Is. **135** 12 0S 137 0 E
English Harbour East **37** 47 38N 54 54W
English, R., Ont., Can. **52** 50 35N 93 30W
English, R., Ont., Can. **52** 49 12N 91 5W
English, R., U.S.A. **76** 41 29N 91 32W
English River **52** 49 20N 91 0W
Engteng (Yungting) **131** 24 46N 116 45 E
Enid **75** 36 26N 97 52W
Enilda **60** 55 25N 116 18W
Eniwetok **15** 11 30N 152 16 E
Enkhuizen **105** 52 42N 5 17 E
Enna **108** 37 34N 14 15 E
Ennadai **55** 61 8N 100 53W
Ennadai L. **55** 61 0N 101 0W
Ennedi, reg. **115** 19 20N 28 0 E
Ennis, Ireland **97** 52 51N 8 59W
Ennis, Mont., U.S.A. **78** 45 27N 111 48W
Ennis, Texas, U.S.A. **75** 32 15N 96 40W
Enniscorthy **97** 52 30N 6 35W
Enniskillen **97** 54 20N 7 40W
Ennistimon **97** 52 56N 9 18W
Ennotville **49** 43 39N 80 20W
Enns, R. **106** 48 8N 14 27 E
Enontekiö **110** 68 23N 23 37 E
Enriquillo, L. **85** 18 20N 72 5W
Enschede **105** 52 13N 6 53 E
Ensenada, Argent. **88** 34 55S 57 55W
Ensenada, Mexico **82** 31 50N 116 50W
Enshih **131** 30 18N 109 27 E
Ensisheim **101** 47 50N 7 20 E
Entebbe **116** 0 4N 32 28 E
Enterprise, Can. **54** 60 47N 115 45W
Enterprise, Oreg., U.S.A. **78** 45 30N 117 11W
Enterprise, Utah, U.S.A. **79** 37 37N 113 36W
Entiako L. **62** 53 13N 125 31W
Entrance **54** 53 25N 117 50W
Entre Ríos, Boliv. **88** 21 30S 64 25W
Entre Ríos, Mozam. **117** 14 57S 37 20 E
Entre Ríos □ **88** 30 30S 58 30W
Entrecasteaux, Pt. d' **134** 34 50S 115 56 E
Entwistle **54** 53 30N 115 0W
Enugu **114** 6 30N 7 30 E
Enumclaw **80** 47 12N 122 0W
Envermeu **100** 49 53N 1 15 E
Envigado **86** 6 10N 75 35W
Eólie o Lípari, Is. **108** 38 30N 14 50 E
Epe **105** 52 21N 5 59 E
Épernay **101** 49 3N 3 56 E
Épernon **101** 48 35N 1 40 E
Ephesus **122** 38 0N 27 30 E
Ephraim **78** 39 30N 111 37W
Ephrata **78** 47 28N 119 32W
Épinac-les-Mines **101** 46 59N 4 31 E
Épinal **101** 48 19N 6 27 E
Epiphanie, L' **43** 45 51N 73 29W
Epping **95** 51 42N 0 8 E
Epukiro **117** 21 30S 19 0 E
Equality **77** 37 44N 88 20W
Equatorial Guinea ■ **116** 2 0S 78 0W
Équeurdreville-Hainneville **100** 49 40N 1 40W
Er Rif **114** 35 1N 4 1W
Eramosa **49** 43 37N 80 13W
Ercha **121** 69 45N 147 20 E
Erciyas Daği **122** 38 30N 35 30 E
Erdene **130** 44 30N 111 10 E
Erdenedalay **130** 46 3N 105 1 E
Erebus, Mt. **91** 77 35S 167 0 E
Erechim **89** 27 35S 52 15W
Ereğli **122** 41 15N 31 30 E
Eresma, R. **104** 41 13N 4 30W
Erewadi Myitwanya **125** 15 30N 95 0 E
Erfurt **106** 50 58N 11 2 E
Erg Chech, dist. **114** 50 59N 11 0 E
Ergani **122** 38 26N 39 49 E
Ergene, R. **109** 41 20N 27 0 E
Erhlien **130** 43 42N 112 2 E
Erhtao Kiang **130** 42 40N 127 10 E
Eriboll, L. **96** 58 28N 4 41W
Eric **36** 51 56N 65 45W
Eric L. **38** 51 55N 65 36W
Érice **108** 38 4N 12 34 E
Erie, Mich., U.S.A. **77** 41 47N 83 31W
Erie, Pa., U.S.A. **70** 42 10N 80 7W
Erie □ **49** 42 58N 78 56W
Erie Canal **70** 43 15N 78 0W
Erie, L. **46** 42 15N 81 0W
Erieau **46** 42 16N 81 57W
Eriksdale **57** 50 52N 98 7W
Erímanthos **109** 37 57N 21 50 E
Erimo-misaki **132** 41 50N 143 15 E
Erin **49** 43 45N 80 7W
Erindale **50** 43 32N 79 39W
Erith **54** 53 25N 116 46W
Eritrea □ **115** 14 0N 41 0 E
Erlandson, L. **36** 57 3N 68 28W
Erlangen **106** 49 35N 11 0 E
Ermenak **122** 36 44N 33 0 E
Ermoúpolis = Siros **109** 37 28N 24 57 E
Ernakulam **124** 9 59N 76 19 E
Erne, Lough **97** 54 26N 7 46W
Erne, R. **97** 54 30N 8 16W
Ernée **100** 48 18N 0 56W
Erode **124** 11 24N 77 45 E
Erquy **100** 48 38N 2 29W
Erquy, Cap d' **100** 48 39N 2 29W
Erramala Hills **124** 15 30N 78 15 E
Errigal, Mt. **97** 55 2N 8 8W
Erris Hd. **97** 54 19N 10 0W
Erskine, Can. **61** 52 20N 112 53W
Erskine, U.S.A. **74** 47 37N 96 0W
Erstein **101** 48 25N 7 38 E
Ervy-le-Châtel **101** 48 2N 3 55 E
Erwin **73** 36 10N 82 28W
Erzgebirge **106** 50 25N 13 0 E
Erzin **121** 50 15N 95 10 E
Erzincan **122** 39 46N 39 30 E
Erzurum **122** 39 57N 41 15 E
Es Sînâ' **115** 29 0N 34 0 E
Esan-misaki **132** 41 40N 141 10 E
Esbjerg **111** 55 29N 8 29 E
Escalante **79** 37 47N 111 37W
Escalante, R. **79** 37 45N 111 0W
Escalón **82** 26 40N 104 20W
Escambia, R. **73** 30 45N 87 15W
Escanaba **72** 45 44N 87 5W
Esch **105** 51 37N 5 17 E
Eschweiler **105** 50 49N 6 14 E
Escobal **84** 9 6N 80 1W
Escondida, La **82** 24 6N 99 55W
Escondido **81** 33 9N 117 4W
Escoumins, Les **41** 48 21N 69 24W
Escuinapa **82** 22 50N 105 50W
Escuintla **84** 14 20N 90 48W
Escuminac **35** 48 0N 67 0W
Escutillas = Ceba **86** 6 33N 70 24W
Esfahãn □ **123** 33 0N 53 0 E
Esh Sham = Dimashq **122** 33 30N 36 18 E
Esk, R., Dumfries, U.K. **96** 54 58N 3 4W
Esk, R., N. Yorks., U.K. **94** 54 27N 0 36W
Esker **36** 53 53N 66 25W
Eskifjördur **110** 65 3N 13 55W
Eskilstuna **111** 59 22N 16 32 E
Eskimo Ls. **67** 69 15N 132 17W
Eskimo Pt. **55** 61 10N 94 3W
Eskişehir **122** 39 50N 30 35 E
Esla, R. **104** 41 45N 5 50W
Esmeralda, La **88** 22 16S 62 33W
Esmeraldas **86** 1 0N 79 40W
Esnagami L. **53** 50 19N 86 51W
Esnagi L. **53** 48 36N 84 33W
Espada, Pta. **86** 12 5N 71 7W
Espalion **102** 44 32N 2 47 E
Espanola **46** 46 15N 81 46W
Esparta **84** 9 59N 84 40W
Espenberg, C. **67** 66 35N 163 40W
Esperance **134** 33 45S 121 55 E
Esperance B. **134** 33 48S 121 55 E
Esperanza, Argent. **88** 31 29S 61 3W
Esperanza, Can. **62** 49 52N 126 43W
Esperanza Inlet **62** 49 51N 126 55W
Esperanza, La, Argent. **88** 24 9S 64 52W
Esperanza, La, Boliv. **86** 14 20S 62 0W
Esperanza, La, Cuba **84** 22 46N 83 44W
Esperanza, La, Hond. **84** 14 15N 88 10W
Espéraza **102** 42 56N 2 14 E
Espichel, C. **104** 38 22N 9 16W
Espigão, Serra do **89** 26 35S 50 30W
Espinal **86** 4 9N 74 53W
Espinilho, Serra do **89** 28 30S 55 0W
Espino **86** 8 34N 66 1W
Espíritu Santo, B. del **83** 19 15N 79 40W
Espíritu Santo, I. **82** 24 30N 110 23W
Espita **83** 21 1N 88 19W
Espungabera **117** 20 29S 32 45 E
Esquel **90** 42 40S 71 20W
Esquimalt **63** 48 26N 123 25W
Esquina **88** 30 0S 59 30W
Essaouira **114** 31 32N 9 42W
Essarts, Les **100** 46 47N 1 12W
Essen, Belg. **105** 51 28N 4 28 E
Essen, Ger. **105** 51 28N 6 59 E
Essequibo, R. **86** 5 45N 58 50W
Essex, Can. **46** 42 10N 82 49W
Essex, Calif., U.S.A. **81** 34 44N 115 15W
Essex, Ill., U.S.A. **77** 41 10N 88 11W
Essex, N.Y., U.S.A. **71** 44 17N 73 21W
Essex □ **95** 51 48N 0 30 E
Essexville **46** 43 37N 83 50W
Esslingen **106** 48 43N 9 19 E
Essondale **66** 49 14N 122 48W
Essonne □ **101** 48 30N 2 20 E
Est, I.del' **39** 47 37N 61 23W
Estados, I. de los **90** 54 40S 64 30W
Estagel **102** 42 47N 2 40 E
Estância **87** 11 16S 37 26W
Estancia **79** 34 50N 106 1W
Estats, Pic d' **102** 42 40N 1 40 E
Estcourt **41** 47 28N 69 14W
Esteli **84** 13 9N 86 22W
Estelline, S.D., U.S.A. **74** 44 39N 96 52W
Estelline, Texas, U.S.A. **75** 34 35N 100 27W
Esterhazy **57** 50 37N 102 5W
Esternay **101** 48 44N 3 33 E
Estevan **56** 49 10N 102 59W
Estevan Group **62** 53 3N 129 38W
Estevan Sd. **62** 53 5N 129 34W
Estherville **74** 43 25N 94 50W
Estissac **101** 48 16N 3 48 E
Eston **56** 51 8N 108 40W
Estonian S.S.R. □ **120** 48 30N 25 30 E
Estoril **104** 38 42N 9 23W
Estrada, La **104** 42 43N 8 27W
Estrêla, Serra da **104** 40 10N 7 45W
Estremadura **104** 39 0N 9 0W
Estrondo, Serra do **87** 7 20S 48 0W
Esztergom **107** 47 47N 18 44 E
Étables-sur-Mer **100** 48 38N 2 51W
Étain **101** 49 13N 5 38 E
Etamamu **38** 50 18N 59 59W
Étampes **101** 48 26N 2 10 E
Étang **101** 46 52N 4 10 E
Étang-du-Nord **39** 47 22N 61 57W
Étaples **101** 50 30N 1 39 E
Etawah **124** 26 48N 79 6 E
Etawah, R. **73** 34 20N 84 15W
Etawney L. **55** 57 50N 96 50W
Etchemin, R. **42** 46 46N 71 14W
Ethel **80** 46 32N 122 46W
Ethelbert **57** 51 32N 100 25W
Ethiopia ■ **115** 8 0N 40 0 E
Ethiopian Highlands **112** 10 0N 37 0 E
Etive, L. **96** 56 30N 5 12W
Etna, Mt. **108** 37 45N 15 0 E
Etobicoke **50** 43 42N 79 34W
Etobicoke Cr. **50** 43 35N 79 32W
Etolin I. **54** 56 5N 132 20W
Etoshapan **117** 18 40S 16 30 E
Etowah **73** 35 20N 84 30W
Étrépagny **100** 49 18N 1 36 E
Étretat **100** 49 42N 0 12 E
Étroits, Les **41** 47 24N 68 54W
Ettelbrüch **105** 49 50N 6 5 E
Ettrick Water **96** 55 31N 2 55W
Etzatlán **82** 20 48N 104 5W
Etzikom **61** 49 29N 111 6W
Etzna **83** 19 35N 90 15W
Eu **100** 50 3N 1 26 E
Euabalong West **136** 33 3S 146 23 E
Euboea = Évvoia **109** 38 40N 23 40 E
Eucla Basin **134** 31 19S 126 9 E
Euclid **70** 41 32N 81 31W
Eucumbene, L. **136** 36 2S 148 40 E
Eudistes, L. des **38** 50 30N 65 15W
Eudora **75** 33 5N 91 17W
Eufaula, Ala., U.S.A. **73** 31 55N 85 11W
Eufaula, Okla., U.S.A. **75** 35 20N 95 33W
Eufaula, L. **75** 35 15N 95 28W
Eugene **78** 44 0N 123 8W
Eugenia, Punta **82** 27 50N 115 5W
Eugowra **136** 33 22S 148 24 E
Eunice, La., U.S.A. **75** 30 35N 92 28W
Eunice, N. Mex., U.S.A. **75** 32 30N 103 10W
Eupen **105** 50 37N 6 3 E
Euphrates = Furat, Nahr al **122** 33 30N 43 0 E
Eure □ **100** 49 6N 1 0 E
Eure-et-Loir □ **100** 48 22N 1 30 E
Eureka, Can. **65** 80 0N 85 56W
Eureka, Calif., U.S.A. **78** 40 50N 124 0W
Eureka, Ill., U.S.A. **76** 40 43N 89 16W
Eureka, Kans., U.S.A. **75** 37 50N 96 20W
Eureka, Mo., U.S.A. **76** 38 30N 90 38W
Eureka, Mont., U.S.A. **61** 48 53N 115 6W
Eureka, Nev., U.S.A. **78** 39 32N 116 2W
Eureka, S.D., U.S.A. **74** 45 49N 99 38W
Eureka, Utah, U.S.A. **78** 40 0N 112 0W
Eureka River **60** 56 27N 118 44W
Euroa **136** 36 44S 145 35 E
Europa, Île **117** 22 20S 40 22 E
Europa, Picos de **104** 43 10N 5 0W
Europa Pt. **104** 36 2N 6 32W
Europe **93** 20 0N 20 0 E
Europoort **105** 51 57N 4 10 E
Eustis **73** 28 54N 81 36W
Eutsuk L. **62** 53 20N 126 45W
Évain **40** 48 14N 79 8W
Evans **74** 40 25N 104 43W
Evans L. **36** 50 50N 77 0W
Evans Mills **71** 44 6N 75 48W
Evans P. **74** 41 0N 105 35W
Evansburg **60** 53 36N 114 59W
Evansdale **76** 42 30N 92 17W
Evanston, Ill., U.S.A. **77** 42 0N 87 40W
Evanston, Wy., U.S.A. **78** 41 10N 111 0W
Evansville, Ill., U.S.A. **76** 38 5N 89 56W
Evansville, Ind., U.S.A. **77** 38 0N 87 35W
Evansville, Wis., U.S.A. **76** 42 47N 89 18W
Evart **46** 43 54N 85 8W
Évaux-les-Bains **102** 46 12N 2 29 E
Eveleth **74** 47 29N 92 30W
Evensk **121** 61 57N 159 14 E
Everard, C. **136** 37 49S 149 17 E
Everard, L. **134** 31 30S 135 0 E
Everard Ras. **134** 27 5S 132 28 E
Everest, Mt. **125** 28 5N 86 58 E
Everett, Pa., U.S.A. **70** 40 2N 78 24W
Everett, Wash., U.S.A. **80** 48 0N 122 10W
Everglades **73** 26 0N 80 30W
Evergreen **73** 31 28N 86 55W
Everrett Mts. **65** 62 45N 67 12W
Everson **78** 48 57N 122 22W
Everton **49** 43 40N 80 9W
Evesham **95** 52 6N 1 57W
Evian-les-Bains **103** 46 24N 6 35 E
Evinayong **116** 1 50N 10 35 E
Évisa **103** 42 15N 8 48 E
Évora **104** 38 33N 7 57W
Évreux **100** 49 0N 1 8 E
Évron **100** 48 23N 1 58W
Évvoia **109** 38 30N 24 0 E
Ewe, L. **96** 57 49N 5 38W
Ewen **52** 46 32N 89 17W
Ewing, Mo., U.S.A. **76** 40 6N 91 43W
Ewing, Nebr., U.S.A. **74** 42 18N 98 22W
Ewo **116** 0 48S 14 45 E
Exaltación **86** 13 10S 65 20W
Excelsior Springs **76** 39 20N 94 10W
Excideuil **102** 45 20N 1 4 E
Exe, R. **95** 50 38N 3 27W
Exeter, Can. **46** 43 21N 81 29W
Exeter, U.K. **95** 50 43N 3 31W
Exeter, Calif., U.S.A. **80** 36 17N 119 9W
Exeter, Nebr., U.S.A. **74** 40 43N 97 30W
Exeter, N.H., U.S.A. **71** 43 0N 70 58W
Exira **76** 41 35N 94 52W
Exmes **100** 48 45N 0 10 E
Exmoor **95** 51 10N 3 59W
Exmouth, Austral. **134** 22 6S 114 0 E
Exmouth, U.K. **95** 50 37N 3 26W
Exmouth G. **134** 22 15S 114 15 E
Expedition Range **135** 24 30S 149 12 E
Exploits, B. of **37** 49 20N 55 0W
Exshaw **61** 51 3N 115 9W
Extremadura **104** 39 30N 6 5W
Exuma Sound **84** 24 30N 76 20W
Eyasi, L. **116** 3 30S 35 0 E
Eyeberry L. **55** 63 8N 104 43W
Eyebrow **56** 50 48N 106 9W
Eyehill Cr., Alta., Can. **61** 52 14N 110 0W
Eyehill Cr., Sask., Can. **56** 52 40N 109 39W
Eyemouth **96** 55 53N 2 5W
Eygurande **102** 45 40N 2 26 E
Eyjafjorður **110** 66 15N 18 30W
Eymet **102** 44 40N 0 25 E
Eymoutiers **102** 45 40N 1 45 E
Eyrarbakki **110** 63 52N 21 9W
Eyre **134** 32 15S 126 18 E
Eyre Cr. **135** 26 40S 139 0 E
Eyre, L. **135** 29 30S 137 26 E
Eyre Mts. **133** 45 25S 168 25 E
Eyre Pen. **134** 33 30S 137 17 E

Fabens Flat Bay

F

Fabens 79 31 30N 106 8W
Fabre 40 47 12N 79 22W
Fabreville 44 45 34N 73 51W
Fabriano 108 43 20N 12 52 E
Fabrizia 101 38 29N 16 19 E
Facatativá 86 4 49N 74 22W
Facture 102 44 39N 0 58W
Faddeyevski, Ostrov 121 76 0N 150 0 E
Fadhili 122 26 55N 49 10 E
Faenza 108 44 17N 11 53 E
Făgăraş 107 45 48N 24 58 E
Fagatogo 133 14 17 S 170 41W
Fagernes 111 60 59N 9 14 E
Fagersta 111 60 1N 15 46 E
Fagnano, L. 90 54 30 S 68 0W
Fagnières 101 48 58N 4 20 E
Fahraj 123 29 0N 59 0 E
Fahsien 131 21 19N 110 33 E
Fahūd 123 22 18N 56 28 E
Faid 122 27 1N 42 52 E
Faillon, L. 40 48 21N 76 39W
Fair Harbour 62 50 4N 127 10W
Fair Hd. 97 55 14N 6 10W
Fair Isle 98 59 30N 1 40W
Fair Oaks 80 38 39N 121 16W
Fair Play 76 37 38N 93 35W
Fairbank 79 31 44N 110 12W
Fairbanks 67 64 59N 147 40W
Fairborn 77 39 42N 84 2W
Fairbury, U.S.A. 77 40 45N 88 31W
Fairbury, Nebr., U.S.A. 74 40 5N 97 5W
Fairfax, Ohio, U.S.A. 77 39 5N 83 37W
Fairfax, Okla., U.S.A. 75 36 37N 96 45W
Fairfield, Austral. 136 33 53 S 150 57 E
Fairfield, Ala., U.S.A. 73 33 30N 87 0W
Fairfield, Calif., U.S.A. 80 38 14N 122 1W
Fairfield, Conn., U.S.A. 71 41 8N 73 16W
Fairfield, Idaho, U.S.A. 78 43 27N 114 52W
Fairfield, Ill., U.S.A. 77 38 20N 88 20W
Fairfield, Iowa, U.S.A. 76 41 0N 91 58W
Fairfield, Mont., U.S.A. 78 47 40N 112 0W
Fairfield, Ohio, U.S.A. 77 39 21N 84 34W
Fairfield, Texas, U.S.A. 75 31 40N 96 0W
Fairfield Plain 49 43 3N 80 24W
Fairford 57 51 37N 98 38W
Fairgrove 46 43 31N 83 33W
Fairhope 73 30 35N 87 50W
Fairlie 133 44 5 S 170 49 E
Fairmead 80 37 5N 120 10W
Fairmont, Minn., U.S.A. 74 43 37N 94 30W
Fairmont, W. Va., U.S.A. 72 39 29N 80 10W
Fairmont Hot Springs 54 50 20N 115 56W
Fairmount 81 34 45N 118 26W
Fairplay 79 39 9N 105 40W
Fairport, Can. 51 43 49N 79 5W
Fairport, N.Y., U.S.A. 70 43 8N 77 29W
Fairport, Ohio, U.S.A. 70 41 45N 81 17W
Fairvale 39 45 25N 66 0W
Fairview, Can. 39 44 40N 63 38W
Fairview, Alta., Can. 60 56 5N 118 25W
Fairview, Mich., U.S.A. 46 44 44N 84 3W
Fairview, N. Dak., U.S.A. 74 47 49N 104 7W
Fairview, Okla., U.S.A. 75 36 19N 98 30W
Fairview, Utah, U.S.A. 78 39 50N 111 0W
Fairweather, Mt. 67 58 55N 137 45W
Faith 74 45 2N 102 4W
Faizabad, Afghan. 123 37 7N 70 33 E
Faizabad, India 125 26 45N 82 10 E
Fajardo 85 18 20N 65 39W
Fakfak 127 3 0 S 132 15 E
Fakiya 87 42 10N 27 4 E
Falaise 100 48 54N 0 12W
Falcón □ 86 11 0N 69 50W
Falcon Dam 75 26 50N 99 20W
Falcon I. 52 49 23N 94 45W
Falconbridge 46 46 35N 80 45W
Falconer 70 42 7N 79 13W
Falfurrias 75 27 8N 98 8W
Falher 60 55 44N 117 15W
Falkenberg, Can. 70 45 9N 79 21W
Falkenberg, Sweden 111 56 54N 12 30 E
Falkirk 96 56 0N 3 47W
Falkland, N.S., Can. 39 44 37N 63 34W
Falkland, Ont., Can. 49 43 10N 80 26W
Falkland Is. 90 51 30 S 59 0W
Falkland Is. Dep. 91 57 0 S 40 0W
Falkland Sd. 90 52 0 S 60 0W
Falköping 111 58 12N 13 33 E
Fall Brook 79 33 25N 117 12W
Fall River 71 41 45N 71 5W
Fall River Mills 78 41 1N 121 30W
Fallbrook 81 33 23N 117 15W
Fallon, Mont., U.S.A. 74 46 52N 105 8W
Fallon, Nev., U.S.A. 78 39 31N 118 51W
Falls City, Nebr., U.S.A. 74 40 0N 95 40W
Falls City, Oreg., U.S.A. 78 44 54N 123 29W
Falls Creek 70 41 8N 78 49W
Falmouth, Jamaica 84 18 30N 77 40W
Falmouth, U.K. 95 50 9N 5 5W
Falmouth, U.S.A. 77 38 40N 84 20W
Falmouth B. 95 50 7N 5 3 E
False Cr. 66 49 15N 123 8W
Falso, C. 84 15 12N 83 21W
Falsterbo 111 55 23N 12 50 E
Falun 111 60 37N 15 37 E
Famagusta 122 35 8N 33 55 E
Famatina, Sierra, de 88 29 5 S 68 0W
Family L. 57 51 54N 95 27W
Famoso 81 35 37N 119 12W
Fancheng 131 31 2N 118 13 E
Fandriana 117 20 14 S 47 21 E
Fangcheng 131 33 16N 112 59 E
Fankiatun 130 43 50N 125 6 E
Fannich, L. 96 57 40N 5 0W
Fanning I. 15 3 51N 159 22W
Fanny Bay 62 49 27N 124 48W
Fano 108 43 50N 13 0 E
Fanshaw 54 57 11N 133 30W
Fao (Al Fāw) 122 30 0N 48 30 E
Far Mt. 62 52 47N 125 20W
Faraday Seamount Group 12 50 0N 27 0W
Faradje 116 3 50N 29 45 E
Farafangana 117 22 49 S 47 50 E
Farah 124 32 20N 62 7 E
Farah □ 124 32 25N 62 10 E
Fareham 95 50 52N 1 11W
Farewell, Alaska, U.S.A. 67 62 30N 154 0W
Farewell, Mich., U.S.A. 46 43 52N 84 55W
Farewell, C. 133 40 29 S 172 43 E
Farewell C. = Farvel, K. 17 59 48N 43 55W
Farfán 86 0 16N 76 41W
Fargeville, La 71 44 12N 75 58W
Fargo 74 47 0N 97 0W
Faribault 74 44 15N 93 19W
Faride, L. 38 50 58N 59 55W
Faridpur 125 18 14N 79 34 E
Farimān 123 35 40N 60 0 E
Farmer City 77 40 15N 88 39W
Farmers Rapids 48 45 30N 75 45W
Farmersburg 77 39 15N 87 23W
Farmerville 75 32 48N 92 23W
Farmington, Calif., U.S.A. 80 37 56N 121 0W
Farmington, Ill., U.S.A. 76 40 42N 90 0W
Farmington, Iowa, U.S.A. 76 40 38N 91 44W
Farmington, Mo., U.S.A. 76 37 47N 90 25W
Farmington, N. Mex., U.S.A. 79 36 45N 108 28W
Farmington, N.H., U.S.A. 71 43 25N 71 7W
Farmington, Utah, U.S.A. 78 41 0N 111 58W
Farmington, R. 71 41 51N 72 38W
Farmland 77 40 15N 85 5W
Farmville 72 37 19N 78 22W
Farnborough 95 51 17N 0 46W
Farne Is. 94 55 38N 1 37W
Farnham 45 45 17N 72 59W
Farnham Centre 43 45 15N 72 50W
Farnham, Mt. 54 45 20N 72 55W
Faro, Brazil 87 2 0 S 56 45W
Faro, Can. 64 62 11N 133 22W
Faro, Port. 104 37 2N 7 55W
Fårö 111 58 0N 19 10 E
Faroe Is. 93 62 0N 7 0W
Farquhar, C. 134 23 38 S 113 36 E
Farquhar Is. 16 11 0 S 52 0 E
Farrand, C. 65 71 45N 90 0W
Farrāshband 123 28 57N 52 5 E
Farrell 70 41 13N 80 29W
Fars □ 123 29 30N 55 0 E
Fársala 109 39 17N 22 23 E
Farsund 111 58 5N 6 55 E
Fartura, Serra da 89 26 21 S 52 52W
Farvel, Kap 17 59 48N 43 55W
Farwell 75 34 25N 103 0W
Faryab 124 28 7N 57 14 E
Fasā 123 29 0N 53 32 E
Fastnet Rock 97 51 22N 9 37W
Fatehgarh 124 27 25N 79 35 E
Fatehpur, Raj., India 124 28 0N 75 4 E
Fatehpur, Ut. P., India 125 27 8N 81 7 E
Fati 131 23 10N 113 10 E
Fatima 39 47 24N 61 53W
Fatkeng 131 23 58N 113 29 E
Fatshan 131 23 0N 113 4 E
Faucilles, Monts 101 48 5N 5 50 E
Faulkton 74 45 4N 99 8W
Faulquemont 101 49 3N 6 36 E
Fauquembergues 101 50 36N 2 5 E
Fauquier, B.C., Can. 63 49 52N 118 5W
Fauquier, Ont., Can. 53 49 18N 82 3W
Fauresmith 117 29 44 S 25 17 E
Fauske 110 67 17N 15 25 E
Faust 60 55 19N 115 38W
Favara 108 37 19N 13 39 E
Favignana 108 37 56N 12 18 E
Favone 103 41 47N 9 26 E
Favourable Lake 34 52 50N 93 39W
Fawcett 60 54 32N 114 5W
Fawn, R. 34 52 22N 88 20W
Fawnskin 81 34 16N 116 56W
Faxaflói 110 64 29N 23 0W
Fayence 103 43 38N 6 42 E
Fayette, Ala., U.S.A. 73 33 40N 87 50W
Fayette, Iowa, U.S.A. 76 42 51N 91 48W
Fayette, Mo., U.S.A. 76 39 10N 92 40W
Fayette, Ohio, U.S.A. 77 41 40N 84 20W
Fayette, La. 72 40 22N 86 52W
Fayetteville, Ark., U.S.A. 75 36 0N 94 5W
Fayetteville, N.C., U.S.A. 73 35 0N 78 58W
Fayetteville, Tenn., U.S.A. 73 35 20N 86 50W
Fazilka 124 30 27N 74 2 E
F'Derik 114 22 40N 12 45W
Fé, La 84 22 2N 84 15W
Feale, R. 97 52 26N 9 28W
Fear, C. 73 33 45N 78 0W
Feather Falls 80 39 36N 121 16W
Feather, R. 78 39 30N 121 20W
Featherston 133 41 6 S 175 20 E
Fécamp 100 49 45N 0 22 E
Federación 88 31 0 S 57 55W
Federal 48 45 20N 75 42W
Fehmarn 106 54 26N 11 10 E
Fehmarn Bælt 106 54 35N 11 20 E
Feilding 133 40 13 S 175 35 E
Feira 117 15 35 S 30 16 E
Feldkirch 106 47 15N 9 37 E
Felicity 77 38 51N 84 6W
Felipe Carrillo Puerto 83 19 38N 88 3W
Felixstowe 95 51 58N 1 22W
Felletin 102 45 53N 2 11 E
Felton 80 37 3N 122 4W
Femunden 110 62 10N 11 53 E
Fen Ho, R. 130 35 25N 110 30 E
Fenelon Falls 47 44 32N 78 45W
Fénérive 117 17 22 S 49 25 E
Fengcheng, Heilungkiang, China 130 45 41N 128 54 E
Fengcheng, Kiangsi, China 131 28 2N 115 46 E
Fengcheng, Liaoning, China 130 40 28N 124 4 E
Fengfeng 130 36 40N 114 24 E
Fenghsien 131 33 56N 106 41 E
Fenghwa 131 29 37N 121 29 E
Fengkieh (Kweichow) 131 31 0N 109 33 E
Fenglo 131 31 30N 112 29 E
Fengsiang 131 34 27N 107 30 E
Fengsin 131 28 41N 115 11 E
Fengtai 130 39 57N 116 21 E
Fengtu 131 29 58N 107 59 E
Fengy 131 23 48N 106 50 E
Fengyi 131 25 31N 100 13 E
Fengyuan 131 24 10N 120 45 E
Fenit 97 52 17N 9 51W
Fennimore 76 42 58N 90 41W
Feno, C. de 103 41 58N 8 33 E
Fens, The 94 52 45N 0 2 E
Fenton, Can. 55 53 0N 105 35W
Fenton, U.S.A. 46 42 47N 83 44W
Fenwick 49 43 1N 79 22W
Fenyang 130 37 19N 111 46 E
Feodosiya 120 45 2N 35 28 E
Ferdows 123 33 58N 58 2 E
Fère-Champenoise 101 48 45N 4 0 E
Fère-en-Tardenois 101 49 10N 3 30 E
Fère, La 101 49 40N 3 20 E
Ferfer 115 5 18N 45 20 E
Fergana 120 40 23N 71 46 E
Fergus 49 43 43N 80 24W
Fergus Falls 74 46 25N 96 0W
Ferguson, Can. 34 47 50N 73 30W
Ferguson, U.S.A. 76 38 45N 90 18W
Ferintosh 61 52 46N 112 58W
Ferland, Ont., Can. 52 50 19N 88 27W
Ferland, Sask., Can. 56 49 27N 106 57W
Fermanagh (□) 97 54 21N 7 40W
Ferme-Neuve 40 46 42N 75 27W
Fermoy 97 52 4N 8 18W
Fernández 88 27 55 S 63 50W
Fernandina Beach 73 30 40N 81 30W
Fernando de Noronha, I. 87 4 0 S 33 10W
Fernando do Noronho □ 87 4 0 S 33 10W
Fernando Póo = Macias Nguema Biyoga 113 3 30N 8 40 E
Ferndale, U.S.A. 46 42 26N 83 6W
Ferndale, Calif., U.S.A. 78 40 37N 124 12W
Ferndale, Wash., U.S.A. 80 48 51N 122 41W
Fernie 61 49 30N 115 5W
Fernley 78 39 42N 119 20W
Feronia 46 46 22N 79 19W
Ferozepore 124 30 55N 74 40 E
Ferrara 108 44 50N 11 36 E
Ferreñafe 86 6 35 S 79 50W
Ferret, C. 102 44 38N 1 15W
Ferrette 101 47 30N 7 20 E
Ferriday 75 31 35N 91 33W
Ferrières 101 48 5N 2 48 E
Ferron 78 39 3N 111 3W
Ferryland 37 47 2N 52 53W
Ferrysburg 77 43 5N 86 13W
Ferté Bernard, La 100 48 10N 0 40 E
Ferté, La 101 48 57N 3 6 E
Ferté-Mace, La 100 48 35N 0 21W
Ferté-St. Aubin, La 101 47 42N 1 57 E
Ferté-Vidame, La 100 48 37N 0 53 E
Fertile 74 47 37N 96 18W
Fès 114 34 0N 5 0W
Feshi 116 6 0 S 18 10 E
Fessenden 74 47 42N 99 44W
Festus 76 38 13N 90 24W
Fethiye 122 36 36N 29 10 E
Fetlar, I. 96 60 36N 0 52W
Feuilles, B. aux 36 58 55N 69 20W
Feuilles, R. 36 58 47N 70 4W
Feurs 103 45 45N 4 13 E
Ffestiniog 94 52 58N 3 56W
Fiambala 88 27 45 S 67 37W
Fianarantsoa 117 21 20 S 46 45 E
Fichtelgebirge 106 50 10N 12 0 E
Field 46 46 31N 80 1W
Fife □ 96 56 13N 3 2W
Fife L. 56 49 14N 105 53W
Fife Ness 96 56 17N 2 35W
Figeac 102 44 37N 2 2 E
Figueira da Foz 104 40 7N 8 54W
Figueras 104 42 18N 2 58 E
Fiji ■ 133 17 20 S 179 0 E
Fiji Is. 133 17 20 S 179 0 E
Filadelfia 88 22 25 S 60 0W
Filchner Ice Shelf 91 78 0 S 60 0W
File Axe, L. 41 50 18N 73 34W
Filer 78 42 30N 114 35W
Filey 94 54 13N 0 18W
Filiatrá 109 37 9N 21 35 E
Filipstad 111 59 43N 14 9 E
Fillmore, Can. 56 49 50N 103 25W
Fillmore, U.S.A. 81 34 23N 118 58W
Fils, L. du 40 46 37N 78 7W
Filyos çayi 122 41 35N 32 10 E
Finch 47 45 11N 75 7W
Findhorn, R. 96 57 38N 3 38W
Findlater 56 50 47N 105 24W
Findlay 77 41 0N 83 41W
Finger L. 62 53 33N 124 18W
Fingõe 117 15 12 S 31 50 E
Finike 122 36 21N 30 10 E
Finistère □ 100 48 20N 4 0W
Finisterre, C. 104 42 50N 9 19W
Finke, R. 134 24 54 S 134 16 E
Finland 52 48 51N 93 55W
Finland ■ 111 64 0N 27 0 E
Finland, G. of 111 60 0N 26 0 E
Finlay, R. 54 56 50N 125 10W
Finley, Austral. 136 35 38 S 145 35 E
Finley, U.S.A. 74 47 35N 97 50W
Finmark 52 48 35N 89 45W
Finn, R. 97 54 50N 7 55W
Finnmark fylke □ 110 69 30N 25 0 E
Finucanel I. 134 20 19 S 118 30 E
Fiora, R. 108 42 25N 11 35 E
Fire River 53 48 47N 83 36W
Firebag, R. 60 57 45N 111 21W
Firebaugh 80 36 52N 120 27W
Firedrake L. 55 61 25N 104 30W
Firenze 108 43 47N 11 15 E
Firmi 102 44 32N 2 19 E
Firminy 103 45 23N 4 18 E
Fīroz Kohi 124 34 45N 63 0 E
Firozabad 124 27 10N 78 25 E
First Narrows 66 49 19N 123 8W
Fīrūzābād 123 28 52N 52 35 E
Fīrūzkūh 123 35 50N 52 40 E
Firvale 62 52 27N 126 13W
Fish Cr. 59 50 54N 114 1W
Fish Pt. 46 43 43N 83 38W
Fish, R. 117 27 40 S 17 30 E
Fisher B. 57 51 35N 97 13W
Fisher Bay 57 51 29N 97 18W
Fisher Branch 57 51 5N 97 13W
Fisher Str. 65 63 15N 83 30W
Fishguard 95 51 59N 4 59W
Fishing L. 57 52 10N 95 24W
Fiskivötn 110 64 50N 20 45W
Fismes 101 49 20N 3 40 E
Fitchburg 71 42 35N 71 47W
Fitz Hugh Sd. 63 51 40N 127 55W
Fitz Roy 90 47 10 S 67 0W
Fitzgerald, Can. 54 59 51N 111 36W
Fitzgerald, U.S.A. 73 31 45N 83 10W
Fitzpatrick 34 47 29N 72 46W
Fitzroy Crossing 134 18 9 S 125 38 E
Fitzroy, R. 134 17 25 S 124 0 E
Fitzwilliam I. 46 45 30N 81 45W
Fiume = Rijeka 108 45 20N 14 21 E
Five Islands 39 45 23N 64 6W
Five Points 80 36 26N 120 6W
Fizi 116 4 17 S 28 55 E
Flagler 74 39 20N 103 4W
Flagstaff 79 35 10N 111 40W
Flagstone 54 49 4N 115 10W
Flaherty, I. 36 56 15N 79 15W
Flåm 111 60 52N 7 14 E
Flambeau, R. 74 45 40N 90 50W
Flamboro Centre 49 43 22N 79 56W
Flamborough Hd. 94 54 8N 0 4W
Flaming Gorge Dam 78 40 50N 109 25W
Flaming Gorge L. 78 41 15N 109 30W
Flamingo, Teluk 127 5 30 S 138 0 E
Flanagan 77 40 53N 88 52W
Flanders 52 48 44N 92 5W
Flandre 106 51 10N 3 15 E
Flandre Occidental □ 105 51 0N 3 0 E
Flandreau 74 44 5N 96 38W
Flanigan 80 40 10N 119 53W
Flannan Is. 96 58 9N 7 52W
Flåsjön 110 64 5N 15 50 E
Flat Bay 37 48 24N 58 36W

Flat L Frederick Sd

Flat L. 60 54 38N 112 54W
Flat, R., Can. 54 61 51N 128 0W
Flat, R., U.S.A. 77 42 56N 85 15W
Flat River 75 37 50N 90 30W
Flat Rock, Ill., U.S.A. 77 38 54N 87 40W
Flat Rock, Mich., U.S.A. 46 42 6N 83 18W
Flatbush 60 54 42N 114 9W
Flatey, Barðastrandarsýsla, Iceland 110 66 10N 17 52W
Flatey, Suður-þingeyjarsýsla, Iceland 110 65 22N 22 56W
Flathead L. 78 47 50N 114 0W
Flatrock, R. 77 38 46N 85 10W
Flattery, C. 80 48 21N 124 43W
Flavy-le-Martel 101 49 43N 3 12E
Flaxcombe 56 51 29N 109 36W
Flaxton 57 48 52N 102 24W
Flèche, La 100 47 42N 0 5W
Fleetwood 94 53 55N 3 1W
Fleming 57 50 4N 101 31W
Flemingsburg 77 38 25N 83 45W
Flemington 70 41 7N 77 28W
Flensburg 106 54 46N 9 28E
Flers 100 48 47N 0 33W
Flesherton 46 44 16N 80 33W
Fletton 95 52 34N 0 13W
Fleur de Lys 37 50 7N 56 8W
Fleur-de-May, L. 38 52 0N 65 5W
Fleurance 102 43 52N 0 40E
Flin Flon 55 54 46N 101 53W
Flinders I. 135 40 0S 148 0E
Flint, U.K. 94 53 15N 3 7W
Flint, U.S.A. 46 43 5N 83 40W
Flint, I. 15 11 26S 151 48W
Flint L. 53 49 52N 85 53W
Flint, R. 73 31 20N 84 10W
Flixecourt 101 50 0N 2 5E
Flodden 94 55 37N 2 8W
Floodwood 52 46 55N 92 55W
Flora, Ill., U.S.A. 72 38 40N 88 30W
Flora, Ind., U.S.A. 77 40 33N 86 31W
Florac 102 44 20N 3 37E
Floradale 49 43 37N 80 35W
Florala 73 31 0N 86 20W
Florence, Can. 39 46 16N 60 16W
Florence, Ala., U.S.A. 73 34 50N 87 50W
Florence, Ariz., U.S.A. 79 33 0N 111 25W
Florence, Colo., U.S.A. 74 38 26N 105 0W
Florence, Ky., U.S.A. 77 39 0N 84 38W
Florence, Oreg., U.S.A. 78 44 0N 124 3W
Florence, S.C., U.S.A. 73 34 5N 79 50W
Florence = Firenze 108 43 47N 11 15E
Florensac 102 43 23N 3 28E
Flores, Azores 93 39 13N 31 13W
Flores, Guat. 84 16 50N 89 40W
Flores I. 62 49 20N 126 10W
Flores, I. 127 8 35S 121 0E
Flores Sea 126 6 30S 124 0E
Floresville 75 29 10N 98 10W
Floriano 87 6 50S 43 0W
Florianópolis 89 27 30S 48 30W
Florida, Cuba 84 21 32N 78 14W
Florida, Uruguay 89 34 7S 56 10W
Florida □ 73 28 30N 82 0W
Florida B. 85 25 0N 81 20W
Florida Keys 85 25 0N 80 40W
Florida, Strait of 85 25 0N 80 0W
Florissant 76 38 48N 90 20W
Florø 111 61 35N 5 1E
Flower Sta. 47 45 10N 76 41W
Flower's Cove 37 51 14N 56 46W
Floydada 75 33 58N 101 18W
Fluk 127 1 42S 127 38E
Flushing 46 43 4N 83 51W
Flushing = Vlissingen 105 51 26N 3 34E
Foam Lake 56 51 40N 103 32W
Fogo 37 49 43N 54 17W
Fogo, C. 37 49 40N 54 0W
Fogo I. 37 49 40N 54 5W
Foins, L. aux 40 47 5N 78 11W
Foix 102 42 58N 1 38E
Folda, Nord-Trøndelag, Norway 110 64 41N 10 50E
Folda, Nordland, Norway 110 67 38N 14 50E
Folette, La 73 36 23N 84 9W
Foley I. 65 68 32N 75 5W
Foleyet 53 48 15N 82 25W
Folkestone 95 51 5N 1 11E
Folkston 73 30 55N 82 0W
Follett 75 36 30N 100 12W
Folsom 80 38 41N 121 7W
Folsom Res. 80 38 42N 121 9W
Fond-du-Lac 55 59 19N 107 12W
Fond du lac 74 43 46N 88 26W
Fond-du-Lac, R. 55 59 17N 106 0W
Fonda, Iowa, U.S.A. 76 42 35N 94 51W
Fonda, N.Y., U.S.A. 71 42 57N 74 23W
Fonseca, G. de 84 13 10N 87 40W
Fontaine 39 46 51N 64 58W
Fontaine-Française 101 47 32N 5 21E
Fontaine, La 77 40 40N 85 43W
Fontainebleau 101 48 24N 2 40E
Fontas, R. 54 58 14N 121 48W
Fonte Boa 86 2 25S 66 0W
Fontenay-le-Comte 102 46 28N 0 48W
Fonteneau, L. 38 51 55N 61 30W
Fontenelle 35 48 54N 64 33W
Fontur 110 66 23N 14 32W
Foochow (Minhow) 131 26 2N 119 25E
Foothills 61 53 4N 116 47W
Forbach 101 49 10N 6 52E
Forcalquier 103 43 58N 5 47E
Ford City, Calif., U.S.A. 81 35 9N 119 27W
Ford City, Pa., U.S.A. 70 40 47N 79 31W
Fording 61 50 12N 114 52W
Fordongianus 102 40 0N 8 50E
Fordyce 75 33 50N 92 20W
Forel 17 66 52N 36 55W
Foremost 61 49 26N 111 25W
Forest, Can. 46 43 6N 82 0W
Forest, U.S.A. 75 32 21N 89 27W
Forest City, Iowa, U.S.A. 74 43 12N 93 39W
Forest City, N.C., U.S.A. 73 35 23N 81 50W
Forest City, Pa., U.S.A. 71 41 39N 75 29W
Forest Grove, Can. 63 51 46N 121 5W
Forest Grove, U.S.A. 80 45 31N 123 4W
Forest Hill 50 43 42N 79 25W
Forest Lawn 59 51 2N 113 58W
Forestburg 61 52 35N 112 1W
Foresthill 80 39 1N 120 49W
Forestville, Can. 41 48 48N 69 2W
Forestville, Calif., U.S.A. 80 38 28N 122 54W
Forestville, Wis., U.S.A. 72 44 41N 87 29W
Forez, Mts. du 102 45 40N 3 50E
Forfar 96 56 40N 2 53W
Forges-les-Eaux 101 49 37N 1 30E
Forget 56 49 39N 102 52W
Forillon, Parc National 38 48 46N 64 12W
Fork River 57 51 31N 100 1W
Forks 80 47 56N 124 23W
Forli 108 44 14N 12 2E
Forman 74 46 9N 97 43W
Formby Pt. 94 53 33N 3 7W
Formentera, I. 104 38 40N 1 30E
Formiguères 102 42 37N 2 5E
Formosa 88 26 15S 58 10W
Formosa = Taiwan 131 23 30N 121 0E
Formosa = Taiwan ■ 131 24 0N 121 0E
Formosa □ 88 26 5S 58 10W
Formosa Bay 116 2 40S 40 20E
Formosa Str. 131 24 40N 120 0E
Forres 96 57 37N 3 38W
Forrest City 75 35 0N 90 50W
Forreston 76 42 8N 89 35W
Forsyth, Ga., U.S.A. 73 33 4N 83 55W
Forsyth, Mont., U.S.A. 78 46 14N 106 37W
Forsythe 40 48 14N 76 26W
Fort Albany 34 52 15N 81 35W
Fort Amador 84 8 56N 79 32W
Fort Apache 79 33 50N 110 0W
Fort Assiniboine 60 54 20N 114 45W
Fort Atkinson 77 42 56N 88 50W
Fort Augustus 96 57 9N 4 40W
Fort Babine 54 55 22N 126 37W
Fort Benton 78 47 50N 110 40W
Fort Bragg 78 39 28N 123 50W
Fort Bridger 78 41 22N 110 20W
Fort Chimo 36 58 6N 68 25W
Fort Chipewyan 55 58 42N 111 8W
Fort Clayton 84 9 0N 79 35W
Fort Collins 74 40 30N 105 4W
Fort-Coulonge 40 45 50N 76 45W
Fort Covington 43 44 59N 74 30W
Fort-Dauphin 117 25 2S 47 0E
Fort Davis, Pan. C. Z. 84 9 17N 79 56W
Fort Davis, U.S.A. 75 30 38N 103 53W
Fort-de-France 85 14 36N 61 2W
Fort Defiance 79 35 47N 109 4W
Fort Dodge 74 42 29N 94 10W
Fort Edward 71 43 16N 73 35W
Fort Frances 52 48 36N 93 24W
Fort Fraser 62 54 4N 124 33W
Fort Garland 79 37 28N 105 30W
Fort Garry 58 49 50N 97 9W
Fort George 36 53 50N 79 0W
Fort George, R. 34 53 50N 77 0W
Fort Good-Hope 67 66 14N 128 40W
Fort Grahame 54 56 30N 124 35W
Fort Hancock 79 31 19N 105 56W
Fort Hauchuca 79 31 32N 110 30W
Fort Hertz (Putao) 125 27 28N 97 30E
Fort Hope 53 51 30N 88 0W
Fort Irwin 81 35 16N 116 34W
Fort Jameson = Chipata 117 13 38S 32 38E
Fort Kent 35 47 12N 68 30W
Fort Klamath 78 42 45N 122 0W
Fort Knox 77 38 50N 85 0W
Fort Langley 63 49 10N 122 35W
Fort Laramie 74 42 15N 104 30W
Fort Lauderdale 73 26 10N 80 5W
Fort Leonard Wood 76 37 46N 92 11W
Fort Liard 54 60 20N 123 30W
Fort Liberté 85 19 42N 71 51W
Fort Lupton 74 40 8N 104 48W
Fort Mackay 60 57 12N 111 41W
Fort McKenzie 36 57 20N 69 0W
Fort Macleod 61 49 45N 113 30W
Fort McMurray 60 56 44N 111 23W
Fort McPherson 67 67 30N 134 55W
Fort Madison 74 40 39N 91 20W
Fort Meade 73 27 45N 81 45W
Fort Morgan 74 40 10N 103 50W
Fort Myers 73 26 30N 81 50W
Fort Nelson 54 58 50N 122 38W
Fort Nelson, R. 54 59 32N 124 0W
Fort Norman 67 64 57N 125 30W
Fort Payne 73 34 25N 85 44W
Fort Peck 78 48 1N 106 30W
Fort Peck Dam 78 48 0N 106 20W
Fort Peck L. 78 47 40N 107 0W
Fort Pierce 74 27 29N 80 19W
Fort Pierre 74 44 25N 100 25W
Fort Plain 71 42 56N 74 39W
Fort Portal 116 0 40N 30 20E
Fort Providence 54 61 21N 117 40W
Fort Qu'Appelle 56 50 45N 103 50W
Fort Randall 67 55 10N 162 48W
Fort Randolph 84 9 23N 79 53W
Fort Recovery 77 40 25N 84 47W
Fort Resolution 54 61 10N 113 40W
Fort Ross, Can. 65 72 0N 94 14W
Fort Ross, U.S.A. 80 38 32N 123 13W
Fort Rouge 58 49 52N 97 9W
Fort Rupert 62 50 42N 127 23W
Fort Rupert (Rupert House) 36 51 30N 78 40W
Fort St. James 54 54 30N 124 10W
Fort St. John 54 56 15N 120 50W
Fort Sandeman 124 31 20N 69 25E
Fort Saskatchewan 60 53 40N 113 15W
Fort Scott 75 37 50N 94 40W
Fort Selkirk 67 62 43N 137 22W
Fort Severn 34 56 0N 87 40W
Fort Sherman 84 9 22N 79 56W
Fort Shevchenko 120 44 30N 50 10W
Fort Simpson 54 61 45N 121 23W
Fort Smith, Can. 54 60 0N 111 51W
Fort Smith, U.S.A. 75 35 25N 94 25W
Fort Stanton 79 33 33N 105 36W
Fort Stockton 75 30 48N 103 2W
Fort Sumner 75 34 24N 104 8W
Fort Thomas, Ariz., U.S.A. 79 33 2N 109 59W
Fort Thomas, Ky., U.S.A. 77 39 5N 84 27W
Fort Valley 73 32 33N 83 52W
Fort Vermilion 54 58 24N 116 0W
Fort Victoria 117 20 8S 30 55E
Ft. Walton Beach 73 30 25N 86 40W
Fort Wayne 72 41 5N 85 10W
Fort Whyte 58 49 49N 97 13W
Fort William 96 56 48N 5 8W
Fort William = Thunder Bay 34 48 20N 89 10W
Fort Worth 75 32 45N 97 25W
Fort Yates 74 46 8N 100 38W
Fort Yukon 67 66 35N 145 12W
Fortaleza 87 3 35S 38 35W
Forte Coimbra 86 19 55S 57 48W
Forteau 36 51 28N 56 58W
Forth, Firth of 96 56 5N 2 55W
Forth, R. 96 56 9N 4 18W
Fortín Corrales 86 22 21S 60 35W
Fortín Guachalla 86 22 22S 62 23W
Fortin, L. 38 50 50N 67 46W
Fortín Rojas Silva 88 22 40S 59 3W
Fortín Siracuas 86 21 3S 61 46W
Fortín Teniente Montania 88 22 1S 59 45W
Fortrose 96 57 35N 4 10W
Fortuna, Cal., U.S.A. 78 48 38N 124 8W
Fortuna, N.D., U.S.A. 56 48 55N 103 48W
Fortune 37 47 4N 55 50W
Fortune B. 37 47 30N 55 22W
Forty Mile 67 64 20N 140 30W
Forūr 123 26 20N 54 30E
Fos do Jordão 86 9 30S 72 14W
Fos-sur-Mer 103 43 26N 4 56E
Fosheim Pen. 65 80 0N 85 0W
Fossil 78 45 0N 120 9W
Fosston, Can. 56 52 12N 103 49W
Fosston, U.S.A. 74 47 33N 95 39W
Foster, Can. 41 45 17N 72 30W
Foster, U.S.A. 77 38 48N 84 13W
Foster, R. 55 55 47N 105 49W
Fostoria 72 41 8N 83 25W
Fougamou 116 1 38S 11 39E
Fougères 100 48 21N 1 14W
Foul Pt. 124 8 35N 81 25E
Foula, I. 96 60 10N 2 5W
Fountain, Colo., U.S.A. 74 38 42N 104 40W
Fountain, Utah, U.S.A. 78 39 41N 111 50W
Fountain Springs 81 35 54N 118 51W
Four Mts., Is. of the 67 52 0N 170 30W
Fourchambault 101 47 0N 3 3E
Fourchu 39 45 43N 60 17W
Fourmies 101 50 1N 4 2E
Fourmont, L. 38 52 5N 60 27W
Fournier, L. 38 51 33N 65 25W
Fours 101 46 50N 3 42E
Fourteen Island Lake 43 45 54N 74 2W
Fouta Djalon 114 11 20N 12 10W
Foux, Cap-à- 85 19 43N 73 27W
Foveaux Str. 133 46 42S 168 10E
Fowler, Calif., U.S.A. 80 36 41N 119 41W
Fowler, Colo., U.S.A. 74 38 10N 104 0W
Fowler, Ind., U.S.A. 77 40 37N 87 19W
Fowler, Kans., U.S.A. 75 37 28N 100 7W
Fowler, Mich., U.S.A. 77 43 0N 84 45W
Fowlerton 75 28 26N 98 50W
Fowlerville 77 42 40N 84 4W
Fowliang 131 27 8N 117 12E
Fowling 131 29 39N 107 29E
Fox Creek 60 54 24N 116 48W
Fox Is. 67 52 30N 166 0W
Fox, R., Can. 55 56 3N 93 18W
Fox, R., U.S.A. 76 40 21N 91 28W
Fox Valley 56 50 30N 109 25W
Foxe Basin 65 66 0N 77 0W
Foxe Chan. 65 65 0N 80 0W
Foxe Pen. 65 65 0N 76 0W
Foxpark 78 41 4N 106 6W
Foxton 133 40 29S 175 18E
Foxville 53 50 4N 81 38W
Foyle, Lough 97 55 6N 7 8W
Foynes 97 52 30N 9 5W
Foz do Gregório 86 6 47S 71 0W
Foz do Iguaçu 89 25 30S 54 30W
Frackville 71 40 46N 76 15W
Framlingham 71 42 18N 71 26W
Franca 87 20 25S 47 30W
Francavilla Fontana 109 40 32N 17 35E
France ■ 99 47 0N 3 0E
Frances Creek 134 13 25S 132 3E
Frances L. 54 61 23N 129 30W
Frances, R. 54 60 16N 129 10W
Francés Viejo, C. 85 19 40N 70 0W
Francesville 77 40 59N 86 53W
Franceville 116 1 40S 13 32E
Franche Comté 101 46 30N 5 50E
Francis 56 50 6N 103 52W
Francis Harbour 35 52 34N 55 44W
Francisco I. Madero, Coahuila, Mexico 82 25 48N 103 18W
Francisco I. Madero, Durango, Mexico 82 24 32N 104 22W
Francistown 117 21 7S 27 33E
François 37 47 35N 56 45W
François L. 62 54 0N 125 30W
François, Le 85 14 38N 60 57W
Franeker 105 53 12N 5 33E
Frankford, Can. 47 44 12N 77 36W
Frankford, U.S.A. 76 39 29N 91 19W
Frankfort, Ind., U.S.A. 77 40 20N 86 33W
Frankfort, Kans., U.S.A. 74 39 42N 96 26W
Frankfort, Ky., U.S.A. 77 38 12N 84 52W
Frankfort, Mich., U.S.A. 72 44 38N 86 14W
Frankfort, Ohio, U.S.A. 77 39 24N 83 11W
Frankfurt am Main 106 50 7N 8 40E
Frankfurt an der Oder 106 52 50N 14 31E
Fränkische Alb 106 49 20N 11 30E
Franklin, Ill., U.S.A. 76 39 37N 90 3W
Franklin, Ind., U.S.A. 77 39 29N 86 3W
Franklin, Ky., U.S.A. 73 36 40N 86 30W
Franklin, La., U.S.A. 75 29 45N 91 30W
Franklin, Mass., U.S.A. 71 42 4N 71 23W
Franklin, Nebr., U.S.A. 74 40 9N 98 55W
Franklin, N.H., U.S.A. 71 43 28N 71 39W
Franklin, N.J., U.S.A. 71 41 9N 74 38W
Franklin, Ohio, U.S.A. 77 39 34N 84 18W
Franklin, Pa., U.S.A. 70 41 22N 79 45W
Franklin, Tenn., U.S.A. 73 35 54N 86 53W
Franklin, Va., U.S.A. 73 36 40N 76 58W
Franklin, Vt., U.S.A. 43 44 59N 72 55W
Franklin, W. Va., U.S.A. 72 38 38N 79 21W
Franklin, Wis., U.S.A. 77 42 53N 88 1W
Franklin □ 64 71 0N 99 0W
Franklin B. 67 69 45N 126 0W
Franklin Centre 43 45 2N 73 55W
Franklin D. Roosevelt L. 78 48 30N 118 16W
Franklin I. 91 76 10S 168 30E
Franklin, L. 78 40 20N 115 26W
Franklin Mts. 64 65 0N 125 0W
Franklin Park 77 41 56N 87 51W
Franklin River 62 49 7N 124 48W
Franklin Str. 65 72 0N 96 0W
Franklinton 75 30 53N 90 10W
Franklinville 70 42 21N 78 28W
Franks Peak 78 43 50N 109 5W
Frankston 136 38 8S 145 8E
Franquelin 38 49 18N 67 54W
Frantsa Josifa, Zemlya 120 79 0N 62 0E
Franz 53 48 25N 84 30W
Franz Josef Fd. 17 73 20N 22 0E
Franz Josef Land = Frantsa Josifa 120 76 0N 62 0E
Fraser 46 42 32N 82 57W
Fraser I. 135 25 15S 153 10E
Fraser Lake 62 54 0N 124 50W
Fraser, R., B.C., Can. 66 49 7N 123 11W
Fraser, R., Newf., Can. 36 56 39N 62 10W
Fraserburgh 96 57 41N 2 0W
Fraserdale 53 49 55N 81 37W
Fraserwood 57 50 38N 97 13W
Frasne 101 46 50N 6 10E
Frater 34 47 20N 84 25W
Fray Bentos 88 33 10S 58 15W
Frazer L. 52 49 15N 88 40W
Fredericia 111 55 34N 9 45E
Frederick, Md., U.S.A. 72 39 25N 77 23W
Frederick, Okla., U.S.A. 75 34 22N 99 0W
Frederick, S.D., U.S.A. 74 45 55N 98 29W
Frederick Reef 135 20 58S 154 23E
Frederick Sd. 54 57 10N 134 0W

Fredericksburg Gatun

Fredericksburg, Tex., U.S.A.	75	30 17N	98 55W
Fredericksburg, Va., U.S.A.	72	38 16N	77 29W
Frederickstown	75	37 35N	90 15W
Fredericton	39	45 57N	66 40W
Fredericton Junc.	39	45 41N	66 40W
Frederikshåb	17	62 0N	49 30W
Frederikshavn	111	57 28N	10 31E
Frederiksted	85	17 43N	64 53W
Fredonia, Ariz., U.S.A.	79	36 59N	112 36W
Fredonia, Kans., U.S.A.	75	37 34N	95 50W
Fredonia, N.Y., U.S.A.	70	42 26N	79 20W
Fredrikstad	111	59 13N	10 57E
Freeburg	76	38 19N	91 56W
Freehold	71	40 15N	74 18W
Freel Pk.	80	38 52N	119 53W
Freeland	71	41 3N	75 48W
Freeling, Mt.	134	22 35S	133 06E
Freels, C.	37	49 15N	53 30W
Freelton	49	43 24N	80 2W
Freeman, Calif., U.S.A.	81	35 35N	117 53W
Freeman, Mo., U.S.A.	76	38 37N	94 30W
Freeman, S.D., U.S.A.	74	43 25N	97 20W
Freeman, R.	60	54 19N	114 47W
Freeport, Bahamas	85	25 45N	88 30E
Freeport, N.S., Can.	39	44 15N	66 20W
Freeport, Ont., Can.	49	43 25N	80 25W
Freeport, Ill., U.S.A.	76	42 18N	89 40W
Freeport, Tex., U.S.A.	75	28 55N	95 22W
Freetown	114	8 30N	13 10W
Frégate, L.	36	53 15N	74 45W
Fréhel, C.	100	48 40N	2 20W
Freiberg	106	50 55N	13 20E
Freire	90	39 0S	72 50W
Freirina	88	28 30S	70 27W
Freising	106	48 24N	11 47E
Freistadt	106	48 30N	14 30E
Fréjus	103	43 25N	6 44E
Frelighsburg	43	45 3N	72 50W
Fremantle	134	32 1S	115 47E
Fremont, Calif., U.S.A.	80	37 32N	122 57W
Fremont, Ind., U.S.A.	77	41 44N	84 56W
Fremont, Mich., U.S.A.	72	43 29N	85 59W
Fremont, Nebr., U.S.A.	74	41 30N	96 30W
Fremont, Ohio, U.S.A.	77	41 20N	83 5W
Fremont, L.	78	43 0N	109 50W
Fremont, R.	79	38 15N	110 20W
French Camp	80	37 53N	121 16W
French Cr.	70	41 30N	80 2W
French Guiana ■	87	4 0N	53 0W
French I.	136	38 20S	145 22E
French Lick	77	38 33N	86 37W
French, R., Ont., Can.	46	46 2N	80 34W
French, R., Ont., Can.	53	50 40N	80 59W
French River	46	46 2N	80 34W
French Terr. of Afars & Issas □ = Djibouti	115	11 30N	42 15E
Frenchburg	77	37 57N	83 38W
Frenchglen	78	42 56N	119 0W
Frenchman Butte	56	53 35N	109 38W
Frenchman Creek, R.	74	40 34N	101 35W
Frenchman, R.	78	49 25N	108 20W
Fresco, R.	87	7 15S	51 30W
Freshfield, C.	91	68 25S	151 10E
Fresnillo	82	23 10N	103 0W
Fresno	80	36 47N	119 50W
Fresno Res.	78	48 47N	110 0W
Frévent	101	50 15N	2 17E
Freycinet Pen.	135	42 10S	148 25E
Fría, La	86	8 13N	72 15W
Friant	80	36 59N	119 43W
Frías	88	28 40S	65 5W
Fribourg	106	48 0N	7 52E
Friday Harbor	80	48 32N	123 1W
Friedberg	10	50 19N	8 45E
Friedrichshafen	106	47 39N	9 29E
Friendly (Tonga) Is.	133	19 50S	174 30W
Friesland □	105	53 5N	5 50E
Frigate, L.	34	53 15N	74 45W
Frijoles	84	9 11N	79 48W
Frikson	57	50 30N	99 55W
Frio, C.	117	18 0S	12 0E
Frio, R.	75	29 40N	99 40W
Friona	75	34 40N	102 42W
Fritch	75	35 40N	101 35W
Friuli-Venezia Giulia □	108	46 0N	13 0E
Frobisher	57	49 12N	102 26W
Frobisher B.	65	63 0N	67 0W
Frobisher Bay	65	63 44N	68 31W
Frobisher L.	55	56 20N	108 15W
Frog L.	60	53 55N	110 20W
Frohavet	110	64 5N	9 35E
Froid	74	48 20N	104 29W
Fromberg	78	45 19N	108 58W
Frome	95	51 16N	2 17W
Frome, L.	135	30 45S	139 45E
Fromentine	100	46 53N	2 9W
Front Range	78	40 0N	105 10W
Front Royal	72	38 55N	78 10W
Frontera	83	18 30N	92 40W
Frontier	56	49 12N	108 34W
Frontignan	102	43 27N	3 45E
Frosinone	108	41 38N	13 20E
Frostburg	72	39 43N	78 57W
Frostisen	110	68 14N	17 10E
Frouard	101	48 47N	6 8E
Fröya I.	110	63 45N	8 45E
Fruges	101	50 30N	2 8E
Fruitland	48	43 13N	79 43W
Fruitvale	63	49 7N	117 33W
Frunze	120	42 54N	74 36E
Frutal	87	20 0S	49 0W
Fry L.	52	51 14N	91 19W
Frýdek-Místek	107	49 40N	18 20E
Fuchin	130	47 10N	132 0E
Fuchow, Kiangsi, China	131	27 50N	116 14E
Fuchow, Liaoning, China	130	39 45N	121 45E
Fuchun K.	131	30 1N	120 1E
Fuchung	131	24 25N	110 16E
Fucino, L.	102	42 0N	13 30E
Fuente Ovejuna	104	38 15N	5 25W
Fuentes de Oñoro	104	40 33N	6 52W
Fuerte Olimpo	88	21 0S	58 0W
Fuerte, R.	82	26 0N	109 0W
Fuga, I.	131	19 55N	121 10E
Fugløysund	110	70 15N	20 20E
Fujaira	123	25 7N	56 18E
Fuji-no-miya	132	35 20N	138 40E
Fuji-San	132	35 22N	138 44E
Fujisawa	132	35 22N	139 29E
Fukien □	131	26 0N	117 30E
Fukow	131	34 11N	114 36E
Fukuchiyama	132	35 25N	135 9E
Fukui	132	36 0N	136 10E
Fukui-ken □	132	36 0N	136 12E
Fukuoka	132	33 30N	130 30E
Fukuoka-ken □	132	33 30N	131 0E
Fukushima-ken □	132	37 30N	140 15E
Fukuyama	132	34 35N	133 20E
Fulda	106	50 32N	9 41E
Fulda, R.	106	50 37N	9 40E
Fulford Harbour	63	48 47N	123 27W
Fullerton, Calif., U.S.A.	81	33 52N	117 58W
Fullerton, Nebr., U.S.A.	74	41 25N	98 0W
Fulton, Can.	49	43 8N	79 40W
Fulton, Ill., U.S.A.	76	41 52N	90 11W
Fulton, Ind., U.S.A.	77	40 57N	86 16W
Fulton, Mo., U.S.A.	76	38 50N	91 55W
Fulton, N.Y., U.S.A.	71	43 20N	76 22W
Fumay	101	50 0N	4 40E
Fumel	102	44 30N	0 58E
Funabashi	132	35 45N	140 0E
Funafuti, I.	14	8 30S	179 0E
Funchal	114	32 45N	16 55W
Fundación	86	10 31N	74 11W
Fundão	104	40 8N	7 30W
Fundy, B. of	39	45 0N	66 0W
Fundy Nat. Park	39	45 35N	65 10W
Funes	86	1 0N	77 28W
Fungchun	131	23 27N	111 30E
Funing	131	23 45N	105 30E
Furat, Nahr al	122	33 30N	43 0E
Furbero	83	20 22N	97 31W
Furnas, Reprêsa de	89	20 50S	45 0W
Furneaux Group	135	40 10S	147 50E
Furness	94	54 14N	3. 8W
Furness, Pen.	94	54 12N	3 10W
Fürth	106	49 29N	11 0E
Fury and Hecla Str.	65	69 56N	84 0W
Fusagasugá	86	4 21N	74 22W
Fuse	132	34 40N	135 37E
Fushun	130	41 50N	123 55E
Fusin	130	42 12N	121 33E
Fusui	131	22 35N	107 58E
Futing	131	27 15N	120 10E
Futsing	131	25 46N	119 29E
Futuna I.	14	14 25S	178 20E
Fuyang Ho	131	38 14N	116 5E
Fuyuan	130	48 9N	134 3E
Fwaka	117	12 5S	29 25E
Fyekundo = Yushu	129	33 6N	96 48E
Fylde	94	53 50N	2 58W
Fyn	111	55 20N	10 30E
Fyne, L.	96	56 0N	5 20W

G

Gabarouse	39	45 50N	60 9W
Gabela	116	11 0S	14 37E
Gaberones = Gaborone	117	24 37S	25 57E
Gabès	114	33 53N	10 2E
Gabès, Golfe de	114	34 0N	10 30E
Gabon ■	116	0 10S	10 0E
Gaborone	117	24 37S	25 57E
Gabriels	71	44 26N	74 12W
Gabriola I.	63	49 9N	123 47W
Gabrovo	109	42 52N	25 27E
Gacé	100	48 49N	0 20E
Gach Sārān	123	30 15N	50 45E
Gadag	124	15 30N	75 45E
Gadarwara	124	22 50N	78 50E
Gadhada	124	22 0N	71 35E
Gadsden, Ala., U.S.A.	73	34 1N	86 0W
Gadsden, Ariz., U.S.A.	79	32 35N	114 47W
Gadwal	124	16 10N	77 50E
Gaffney	73	35 10N	81 31W
Gagetown	39	45 46N	66 10W
Gagnoa	114	6 4N	5 55W
Gagnon	38	51 50N	68 5W
Gagnon, L., N.W.T., Can.	55	62 3N	110 27W
Gagnon, L., Qué., Can.	40	46 7N	75 7W
Gail	75	32 48N	101 25W
Gaillac	102	43 54N	1 54E
Gaillarbois, L.	38	52 0N	67 27W
Gaillon	100	49 10N	1 20E
Gaines	70	41 45N	77 35W
Gainesville, Fla., U.S.A.	73	29 38N	82 20W
Gainesville, Ga., U.S.A.	73	34 17N	83 47W
Gainesville, Mo., U.S.A.	75	36 35N	92 26W
Gainesville, Tex., U.S.A.	75	33 40N	97 10W
Gainsborough	94	53 23N	0 46W
Gairdner L.	134	31 30S	136 0E
Gairloch L.	96	57 43N	5 45W
Galahad	61	52 31N	111 56W
Galán, Cerro	88	25 55S	66 52W
Galangue	117	13 48S	16 3E
Galápagos, Is.	15	0 0	89 0W
Galas, R.	128	4 55N	101 57E
Galashiels	96	55 37N	2 50W
Galaţi	107	45 27N	28 2E
Galatina	109	40 10N	18 10E
Galax	73	36 42N	80 57W
Galdhøpiggen	111	61 38N	8 18E
Galeana	82	24 50N	100 4W
Galela	127	1 50N	127 55E
Galena, Alaska, U.S.A.	67	64 42N	157 0W
Galena, Ill., U.S.A.	76	42 25N	90 26W
Galeota Point	85	10 8N	61 0W
Galera, Pta. de la	86	10 48N	71 16W
Galesburg, Ill., U.S.A.	76	40 57N	90 23W
Galesburg, Mich., U.S.A.	77	42 17N	85 26W
Galeton, Can.	53	51 8N	80 55W
Galeton, U.S.A.	70	41 43N	77 40W
Galicia	104	42 43N	8 0W
Galien	77	41 48N	86 30W
Galilee, S. of = Kinneret, L.	115	32 49N	35 36E
Galion	70	40 43N	82 48W
Galissonnière, La, L.	38	51 25N	62 0W
Galiuro Mts.	79	32 40N	110 30W
Gallatin, Mo., U.S.A.	76	39 55N	93 58W
Gallatin, Tenn., U.S.A.	73	36 24N	86 27W
Galle	124	6 5N	80 10E
Gallego	82	29 49N	106 22W
Gállego, R.	104	42 23N	0 30W
Gallegos, R.	90	51 50S	71 0W
Galley Hd.	97	51 32N	8 56W
Gallinas, Pta.	86	12 28N	71 40W
Gallipoli	109	40 8N	18 0E
Gallipoli = Gelibolu	109	40 28N	26 43E
Gallipolis	72	38 50N	82 10W
Gallitzin	70	40 28N	78 32W
Gällivare	110	67 9N	20 40E
Galloway	96	55 0N	4 25W
Galloway, Mull of	96	54 38N	4 50W
Gallup	79	35 30N	108 54W
Galoya	124	8 10N	80 55E
Galt, Can.	49	43 22N	80 19W
Galt, Calif., U.S.A.	80	38 15N	121 18W
Galt, Mo., U.S.A.	76	40 8N	93 23W
Galty Mts.	97	52 22N	8 10W
Galtymore, Mt.	97	52 22N	8 12W
Galva	76	41 10N	90 0W
Galveston, Ind., U.S.A.	77	40 35N	86 11W
Galveston, Tex., U.S.A.	75	29 15N	94 48W
Galveston B.	75	29 30N	94 50W
Gálvez	88	32 0S	61 20W
Galway	97	53 16N	9 4W
Galway □	97	53 16N	9 3W
Galway B.	97	53 10N	9 20W
Gamarra	86	8 20N	73 45W
Gambell	67	63 55N	171 50W
Gambia ■	114	13 25N	16 0W
Gambia, R.	114	13 20N	15 45W
Gambier I.	63	49 30N	123 23W
Gamboa	84	9 8N	79 42W
Gamboma	116	1 55S	15 52E
Gameleira	87	7 50S	50 0W
Gamerco	79	35 33N	108 56W
Gammelgarn	87	57 24N	18 49E
Gammon, R.	57	51 24N	95 44W
Gan	102	43 12N	0 27W
Gan (Addu Atoll)	119	0 10S	71 10E
Ganado, Ariz., U.S.A.	79	35 46N	109 41W
Ganado, Tex., U.S.A.	75	29 4N	96 31W
Gananoque	47	44 20N	76 10W
Ganaveh	123	29 35N	50 35E
Gand	105	51 2N	3 37E
Gandak, R.	125	27 0N	84 8E
Gandava	124	28 32N	67 32E
Gander	37	48 58N	54 35W
Gander L.	37	48 58N	54 35W
Gander, R.	37	49 16N	54 30W
Gand = Gent	105	51 2N	3 37E
Gandhi Sagar	124	24 40N	75 40E
Gandi	114	12 55N	5 49E
Ganedidalem = Gani	127	0 48S	128 14E
Gang Ranch	63	51 33N	122 20W
Ganga, R.	125	25 0N	88 0E
Ganganagar	124	29 56N	73 56E
Gangaw	125	22 5N	94 15E
Ganges	102	43 56N	3 42E
Ganges = Ganga, R.	125	25 0N	88 0E
Ganges, Mouth of the	125	21 30N	90 0E
Gangtok	125	27 20N	88 37E
Gannat	102	46 7N	3 11E
Gannett Pk.	78	43 15N	109 47W
Gannvalley	74	44 3N	98 57W
Gantheaume B.	134	27 40S	114 10E
Gao	114	16 15N	0 5W
Gao Bang	128	22 37N	106 18E
Gap	103	44 33N	6 5E
Gar Dzong	124	32 20N	79 55E
Garachiné	84	8 0N	78 12W
Garanhuns	87	8 50S	36 30W
Garber	75	36 30N	97 36W
Garberville	78	40 11N	123 50W
Gard □	103	44 2N	4 10E
Garda, L. di	108	45 40N	10 40E
Gardanne	103	43 27N	5 27E
Garde L.	55	62 50N	106 13W
Garden City, Kans., U.S.A.	75	38 0N	100 45W
Garden City, Mo., U.S.A.	76	38 34N	94 12W
Garden City, Tex., U.S.A.	75	31 52N	101 28W
Garden Grove	81	33 47N	117 55W
Garden I.	46	45 49N	85 30W
Gardez	124	33 31N	68 59E
Gardiner, Can.	34	49 19N	81 2W
Gardiner, Mont., U.S.A.	78	45 3N	110 53W
Gardiner, N. Mex., U.S.A.	75	36 55N	104 29W
Gardiner Ls.	60	57 32N	112 30W
Gardiners I.	71	41 4N	72 5W
Gardner, Ill., U.S.A.	77	41 12N	88 17W
Gardner, Mass., U.S.A.	71	42 35N	72 0W
Gardner Canal	62	53 27N	128 8W
Gardnerville	80	38 59N	119 47W
Gareloi I.	67	51 49N	178 50W
Garey	81	34 53N	120 19W
Garfield, Utah, U.S.A.	78	40 45N	112 15W
Garfield, Wash., U.S.A.	78	47 3N	117 8W
Gargano, Mte.	108	41 43N	15 43E
Gargans, Mt.	102	45 37N	1 39E
Gargantua, C.	34	47 35N	85 0W
Garibaldi	54	49 56N	123 15W
Garibaldi, Mt.	63	49 51N	123 0W
Garibaldi Prov. Park	63	49 50N	122 40W
Garies	117	30 32S	17 59E
Garigliano, R.	108	41 13N	13 44E
Garland	78	41 47N	112 10W
Garm	120	39 0N	70 20E
Garmsār	123	35 20N	52 25E
Garneau, L.	38	51 43N	63 22W
Garner	76	43 4N	93 37W
Garners Corners	48	43 12N	79 57W
Garnett	74	38 18N	95 12W
Garnish	37	47 14N	55 22W
Garonne, R.	102	45 2N	0 36W
Garoua	114	9 19N	13 21E
Garrett	77	41 21N	85 8W
Garrigues	102	43 40N	3 30E
Garrison, Ky., U.S.A.	77	38 36N	83 10W
Garrison, Mont., U.S.A.	78	46 37N	112 56W
Garrison, N.D., U.S.A.	74	31 50N	94 28W
Garrison, Tex., U.S.A.	75	47 39N	101 27W
Garrison Res.	74	47 30N	102 0W
Garry, Glen	96	57 3N	5 7W
Garry L., Can.	65	65 58N	100 18W
Garry L., U.K.	96	57 5N	4 52W
Garry, R.	96	56 47N	3 47W
Garsen	116	2 20S	40 5E
Garson L.	60	56 19N	110 2W
Garson, R..	55	56 20N	110 1W
Gartempe, R.	102	46 47N	0 49E
Gartok	129	31 59N	80 30E
Garupá	87	1 25S	51 35W
Garut	127	7 14S	107 53E
Garvie Mts.	133	45 30S	168 50E
Gary	77	41 35N	87 20W
Garzón	86	2 10N	75 40W
Gas City	77	40 29N	85 36W
Gasan Kuli	120	37 40N	54 20E
Gascogne	102	43 45N	0 20E
Gasconade	76	38 40N	91 33W
Gasconade R.	76	38 41N	91 33W
Gascons	38	48 11N	64 51W
Gascony = Gascogne	102	43 45N	0 20E
Gascoyne, R.	134	24 52S	113 37E
Gashiun Nor	129	42 20N	100 40E
Gashua	114	12 54N	11 0E
Gaspé	38	48 52N	64 30W
Gaspé, Baie de	38	48 46N	64 17W
Gaspé, C.	38	48 48N	64 7W
Gaspé Pen.	38	48 45N	65 40W
Gaspé, Péninsule de	38	48 30N	65 30W
Gaspésie, Parc Prov. de la	38	48 55N	65 50W
Gassaway	72	38 42N	80 43W
Gastonia	73	35 17N	81 10W
Gastre	90	42 10S	69 15W
Gata, C. de	104	36 41N	2 13W
Gata, Sierra de	104	40 20N	6 20W
Gataga, R.	54	58 35N	126 59W
Gateshead	94	54 57N	1 37W
Gateshead I.	65	70 36N	100 26W
Gatesville	75	31 29N	97 45W
Gatico	88	22 40S	70 20W
Gâtinais	101	48 5N	2 40E
Gâtine, Hauteurs de	102	46 35N	0 45W
Gatineau, Ont., Can.	48	45 29N	75 39W
Gatineau, Qué., Can.	40	45 29N	75 38W
Gatineau, Parc de la	40	45 40N	76 0W
Gatineau, R.	48	45 27N	75 42W
Gatooma	117	18 20S	29 52E
Gatun	84	9 16N	79 55W

Gatun Dam Gobles

Gatun Dam	**84**	9 16N	79 55W
Gatun, L.	**84**	9 7N	79 56W
Gatun Locks	**84**	9 16N	79 55W
Gaud-i-Zirreh	**124**	29 45N	62 0E
Gauer L.	**55**	57 0N	97 50W
Gauhati	**125**	26 10N	91 45E
Gaula, R.	**110**	62 57N	11 0E
Gaultois	**37**	47 36N	55 54W
Gaussberg, Mt.	**91**	66 45S	89 0E
Gausta, Mt.	**111**	59 48N	8 40E
Gavarnie	**102**	42 44N	0 3W
Gavāter	**123**	25 10N	61 23E
Gaviota	**81**	34 29N	120 13W
Gavle	**111**	60 41N	17 13E
Gävleborgs Lan □	**111**	61 20N	16 15E
Gavray	**100**	48 55N	1 20W
Gawilgarh Hills	**124**	21 15N	76 45E
Gawler	**135**	34 30S	138 42E
Gawler Ranges	**134**	32 30S	135 45E
Gaya	**125**	24 47N	85 4E
Gaylord	**46**	45 1N	84 35W
Gayndah	**135**	25 35S	151 39E
Gayot, L.	**36**	55 43N	70 50W
Gaza	**115**	31 30N	34 28E
Gaziantep	**122**	37 6N	37 23E
Gdansk	**107**	54 22N	18 40E
Gdanska, Zatoka	**107**	54 30N	19 20E
Gdynia	**107**	54 35N	18 33E
Geary	**39**	45 46N	66 29W
Gebe, I.	**127**	0 5N	129 25E
Gedaref	**115**	14 2N	35 28E
Gèdre	**102**	42 47N	0 2E
Gedser	**111**	54 35N	11 55E
Geel	**105**	51 10N	4 59E
Geelong	**136**	38 10S	144 22E
Geikie I.	**52**	50 0N	88 35W
Geikie, R.	**55**	57 45N	103 52W
Geita	**116**	2 48S	32 12E
Gela	**108**	37 6N	14 18E
Gelderland □	**105**	52 5N	6 10E
Geldermalsen	**105**	51 53N	5 17E
Geldrop	**105**	51 25N	5 32E
Geleen	**105**	50 57N	5 49E
Gelibolu	**109**	40 28N	26 43E
Gelsenkirchen	**105**	51 30N	7 5E
Gem	**61**	50 57N	112 11W
Gemas	**128**	2 37N	102 36E
Gembloux	**105**	50 34N	4 43E
Gemena	**116**	3 20N	19 40E
Gemerek	**122**	39 15N	36 10E
Gemert	**105**	51 33N	5 41E
Gemlik	**122**	40 28N	29 13E
Gençay	**102**	46 23N	0 23E
General Acha	**88**	37 20S	64 38W
General Alvear, B. A., Argent.	**88**	36 0S	60 0W
General Alvear, Mend., Argent.	**88**	35 0S	67 40W
General Artigas	**88**	26 52S	56 16W
General Belgrano	**88**	36 0S	58 30W
General Cabrera	**88**	32 53S	63 58W
General Cepeda	**82**	25 23N	101 27W
General Guido	**88**	36 40S	57 50W
General Juan Madariaga	**88**	37 0S	57 0W
General La Madrid	**88**	37 30S	61 10W
General MacArthur	**127**	11 18N	125 28E
General Martin Miguel de Güemes	**88**	24 50S	65 0W
General Paz	**88**	27 45S	57 36W
General Paz, L.	**90**	44 0S	72 0W
General Pico	**88**	35 45S	63 50W
General Pinedo	**88**	27 15S	61 30W
General Pinto	**88**	34 45S	61 50W
General Roca	**90**	30 0S	67 40W
General Santos	**127**	6 12N	125 14E
General Treviño	**83**	26 14N	99 29W
General Trías	**82**	28 21N	106 22W
General Viamonte	**88**	35 1S	61 3W
General Villegas	**88**	35 0S	63 0W
Genesee, Can.	**60**	53 21N	114 20W
Genesee, Idaho, U.S.A.	**78**	46 31N	116 59W
Genesee, Mich., U.S.A.	**70**	43 7N	83 38W
Genesee, Pa., U.S.A.	**70**	42 0N	77 54W
Genesee, R.	**70**	41 35N	78 0W
Geneseo, Ill., U.S.A.	**76**	41 25N	90 10W
Geneseo, Kans., U.S.A.	**74**	38 32N	98 8W
Geneseo, N.Y., U.S.A.	**70**	42 49N	77 49W
Geneva, Can.	**43**	45 36N	74 20W
Geneva, Ala., U.S.A.	**73**	31 2N	85 52W
Geneva, Ill., U.S.A.	**77**	41 53N	88 18W
Geneva, Nebr., U.S.A.	**74**	40 35N	97 35W
Geneva, N.Y., U.S.A.	**70**	42 53N	77 0W
Geneva, Ohio, U.S.A.	**70**	41 49N	80 58W
Geneva = Genève	**106**	46 12N	6 9E
Geneva, L.	**77**	42 38N	88 30W
Geneva, L. = Léman, Lac	**106**	46 26N	6 30E
Genève	**106**	46 12N	6 9E
Geneve	**77**	40 36N	84 57W
Genil, R.	**104**	37 12N	3 50W
Génissiat, Barrage de	**103**	46 1N	5 48E
Genk	**105**	50 58N	5 32E
Genlis	**101**	47 15N	5 12E
Gennargentu, Mt. del	**108**	40 0N	9 10E
Gennes	**100**	47 20N	0 17W
Genoa, Ill., U.S.A.	**77**	42 6N	88 42W
Genoa, Nebr., U.S.A.	**74**	41 31N	97 44W
Genoa, Nev., U.S.A.	**80**	39 2N	119 50W
Genoa, N.Y., U.S.A.	**71**	42 40N	76 32W
Genoa = Génova	**108**	44 24N	8 57E
Genoa City	**77**	42 30N	88 20W
Génova	**108**	44 24N	8 56E
Génova, Golfo di	**108**	44 0N	9 0E
Gent	**105**	51 2N	3 37E
Genteng	**127**	7 25S	106 23E
Geographe B.	**134**	33 30S	113 20E
Geographe Chan.	**134**	24 30S	113 0E
George, Can.	**35**	46 12N	62 32W
George, S. Afr.	**117**	33 58S	22 29E
George B.	**39**	45 45N	61 45W
George, L., N.S.W., Austral.	**136**	35 10S	149 25E
George, L., S. Austral., Austral.	**136**	37 25S	140 0E
George, L., Uganda	**116**	0 5N	30 10E
George, L., Fla., U.S.A.	**73**	29 15N	81 35W
George, L., N.Y., U.S.A.	**71**	43 30N	73 30W
George, R., Qué., Can.	**35**	58 49N	66 10W
George, R., Qué., Can.	**36**	49 21N	67 59W
George River = Port Nouveau-Québec	**36**	58 32N	65 54W
George Sound	**133**	44 52S	167 25E
George Town, Bahamas	**84**	23 33N	75 47W
George Town, Malay.	**128**	5 25N	100 19E
George V Coast	**91**	67 0S	148 0E
George West	**75**	28 18N	98 5W
Georgetown, Austral.	**135**	18 17S	143 33E
Georgetown, Ont., Can.	**49**	43 40N	79 56W
Georgetown, P.E.I., Can.	**39**	46 13N	62 24W
Georgetown, Cay. Is.	**84**	19 20N	81 24W
Georgetown, Guyana	**86**	6 50N	58 12W
Georgetown, Calif., U.S.A.	**80**	38 54N	120 50W
Georgetown, Colo., U.S.A.	**78**	39 46N	105 49W
Georgetown, Ill., U.S.A.	**77**	39 59N	87 38W
Georgetown, Ky., U.S.A.	**77**	38 13N	84 33W
Georgetown, Ohio, U.S.A.	**72**	38 50N	83 50W
Georgetown, S.C., U.S.A.	**73**	33 22N	79 15W
Georgetown, Tex., U.S.A.	**75**	30 40N	97 45W
Georgia □	**72**	32 0N	82 0W
Georgia, Str. of	**62**	49 25N	124 0W
Georgian B.	**46**	45 15N	81 0W
Georgian S.S.R. □	**120**	41 0N	45 0E
Georgievsk	**120**	44 12N	43 28E
Georgina I.	**46**	44 22N	79 17W
Georgina, R.	**135**	23 30S	139 47E
Georgiu-Dezh	**120**	51 3N	39 20E
Gera	**106**	50 53N	12 5E
Geraardsbergen	**105**	50 45N	3 53E
Geral de Goias, Serra	**87**	12 0S	46 0W
Geral, Serra	**89**	26 25S	50 0W
Gerald	**76**	38 24N	91 21W
Geraldine	**78**	47 45N	110 18W
Geraldton, Austral.	**134**	28 48S	114 32E
Geraldton, Can.	**53**	49 44N	86 59W
Gérardmer	**101**	48 3N	6 50E
Gerdine, Mt.	**67**	61 32N	152 30W
Gerede	**122**	40 45N	32 10E
Gerik	**128**	5 25N	100 8E
Gering	**74**	41 51N	103 40W
Gerlach	**78**	40 43N	119 27W
Germain, Grand L.	**38**	51 12N	66 41W
Germansen Landing	**54**	55 43N	124 40W
Germantown	**77**	39 38N	84 22W
Germany, East ■	**106**	52 0N	12 0E
Germany, West ■	**106**	52 0N	9 0E
Germiston	**117**	26 11S	28 10E
Gerona	**104**	41 58N	2 46E
Gerrard	**63**	50 30N	117 17W
Gers □	**102**	43 35N	0 38E
Gerze	**122**	41 45N	35 10E
Geser	**127**	3 50S	130 35E
Gethsémani	**36**	50 13N	60 40W
Gettysburg, Pa., U.S.A.	**72**	39 47N	77 18W
Gettysburg, S.D., U.S.A.	**74**	45 3N	99 56W
Getz Ice Shelf	**91**	75 0S	130 0W
Gévaudan	**102**	44 40N	3 40E
Gevelsberg	**105**	51 21N	7 7E
Gex	**103**	46 21N	6 3E
Geyser	**78**	47 17N	110 30W
Geyserville	**80**	38 42N	122 54W
Geysir	**110**	64 19N	20 18W
Ghaghara, R.	**125**	26 0N	84 20E
Ghail	**122**	21 40N	46 20E
Ghana ■	**114**	6 0N	1 0W
Ghanzi	**117**	21 50S	21 45E
Ghardaïa	**114**	32 31N	3 37E
Gharyān	**114**	32 10N	13 0E
Ghāt	**114**	24 59N	10 19E
Ghat Ghat	**122**	24 40N	46 15E
Ghawdex = Gozo, I.	**108**	36 0N	14 13E
Ghaziabad	**124**	28 42N	77 35E
Ghazipur	**125**	25 38N	83 35E
Ghazni	**124**	33 30N	68 17E
Ghazni □	**124**	33 0N	68 0E
Ghent = Gand	**105**	51 4N	3 43E
Ghisonaccia	**103**	42 1N	9 26E
Ghizao	**124**	33 30N	65 59E
Ghorat □	**124**	34 0N	64 20E
Ghost River	**52**	50 12N	91 30W
Ghugus	**124**	20 0N	79 0E
Ghuriān	**124**	34 17N	61 25E
Gia Lai = Pleiku	**128**	14 3N	108 0E
Gia Nghia	**128**	12 0N	107 42E
Giant Forest	**80**	36 36N	118 43W
Giant's Causeway	**97**	55 15N	6 30W
Giarre	**108**	37 44N	15 10E
Gibara	**84**	21 0N	76 20W
Gibbon	**74**	40 49N	98 45W
Gibbons	**60**	53 50N	113 20W
Gibeon	**117**	25 7S	17 45E
Gibraltar	**104**	36 7N	5 22W
Gibraltar, Str. of	**104**	35 55N	5 40W
Gibson City	**77**	40 28N	88 22W
Gibson Des.	**134**	24 0S	126 0E
Gibsonburg	**77**	41 23N	83 19W
Gibsons	**63**	49 24N	123 32W
Gibsonville	**80**	39 46N	120 54W
Gida. G.	**17**	72 30N	77 0E
Giddings	**75**	30 11N	96 58W
Gien	**101**	47 40N	2 36E
Giessen	**106**	50 34N	8 40E
Giffard	**42**	46 51N	71 12W
Gift Lake	**60**	55 53N	115 49W
Gifu	**132**	35 30N	136 45E
Gifu-ken □	**132**	36 0N	137 0E
Gig Harbor	**80**	47 20N	122 35W
Giganta, Sa. de la	**82**	25 30N	111 30W
Gigha, I.	**96**	55 42N	5 45W
Gignac	**102**	43 39N	3 32E
Gijón	**104**	43 32N	5 42W
Gil I.	**62**	53 12N	129 15W
Gila Bend	**79**	33 0N	112 46W
Gila Bend Mts.	**79**	33 15N	113 0W
Gila, R.	**79**	33 5N	108 40W
Gilbert Is.	**14**	1 0S	176 0E
Gilbert, Mt.	**62**	50 52N	124 16W
Gilbert Plains	**57**	51 9N	100 28W
Gilbert, R.	**135**	16 35S	141 15E
Gilford I.	**62**	50 40N	126 30W
Gilgandra	**136**	31 43S	148 39E
Gilgit	**124**	35 50N	74 15E
Gillam	**55**	56 20N	94 40W
Gillespie	**76**	39 7N	89 49W
Gillette	**74**	44 20N	105 38W
Gillies Bay	**62**	49 42N	124 29W
Gillingham	**95**	51 23N	0 34E
Gilman, Ill., U.S.A.	**77**	40 46N	88 0W
Gilman, Mo., U.S.A.	**76**	40 8N	93 53W
Gilmer	**75**	32 44N	94 55W
Gilmour	**47**	44 48N	77 37W
Gilroy	**80**	37 1N	121 37W
Gimli	**55**	50 40N	97 10W
Gimont	**102**	43 38N	0 52E
Gióna, Óros	**109**	38 38N	22 14E
Giong, Teluk	**127**	4 50N	118 20E
Giovi, P. dei	**103**	44 30N	8 55E
Gippsland	**135**	37 45S	147 15E
Girard, Ill., U.S.A.	**76**	39 27N	89 48W
Girard, Kans., U.S.A.	**75**	37 30N	94 50W
Girard, Ohio, U.S.A.	**70**	41 10N	80 42W
Girard, Pa., U.S.A.	**70**	42 1N	80 21W
Girardot	**86**	4 18N	74 48W
Girardville	**41**	49 0N	72 32W
Girdle Ness	**96**	57 9N	2 2W
Giresun	**122**	40 45N	38 30E
Giridih	**125**	24 10N	86 21E
Girishk	**124**	31 47N	64 24E
Giromagny	**101**	47 44N	6 50E
Gironde □	**102**	44 45N	0 30W
Gironde, R.	**102**	45 27N	0 53W
Girouxville	**60**	55 45N	117 20W
Girvan	**96**	55 15N	4 50W
Gisborne	**133**	38 39S	178 5E
Gisborne L.	**37**	47 48N	54 49W
Gisenyi	**116**	1 41S	29 30E
Gisors	**101**	49 15N	1 40E
Giurgiu	**107**	43 52N	25 57E
Givet	**101**	50 8N	4 49E
Givors	**103**	45 35N	4 45E
Givry	**101**	46 41N	4 46E
Gizhiga	**121**	62 0N	150 27E
Gizhiginskaya, Guba	**121**	61 0N	158 0E
Gizycko	**107**	54 2N	21 48E
Gjirokastër	**109**	40 7N	20 16E
Gjoa Haven	**65**	68 38N	95 53W
Gjøvik	**111**	60 47N	10 43E
Glace Bay	**39**	46 11N	59 58W
Glacier B.	**54**	58 30N	136 10W
Glacier Nat. Park	**63**	51 15N	117 30W
Glacier National Park	**61**	48 35N	113 40W
Glacier Peak Mt.	**63**	48 7N	121 7W
Glacier Str.	**65**	76 12N	79 15W
Gladewater	**75**	32 30N	94 58W
Gladmar	**56**	49 10N	104 27W
Gladstone, Austral.	**136**	23 52S	151 16E
Gladstone, Can.	**57**	50 13N	98 57W
Gladstone, Mich., U.S.A.	**72**	45 52N	87 1W
Gladstone, Mo., U.S.A.	**76**	39 13N	94 35W
Gladwin	**46**	43 59N	84 29W
Gladys L.	**54**	59 50N	133 0W
Gláma	**110**	65 48N	23 0W
Glåma, R.	**111**	60 30N	12 8E
Glamis	**81**	33 0N	115 4W
Glamorgan (□)	**95**	51 37N	3 35W
Glamorgan, Vale of	**98**	50 45N	3 15W
Glan	**127**	5 45N	125 20E
Glanville	**76**	41 17N	89 15W
Glasco, Kans., U.S.A.	**74**	39 25N	97 50W
Glasco, N.Y., U.S.A.	**71**	42 3N	73 57W
Glasgow, U.K.	**96**	55 52N	4 14W
Glasgow, Ky., U.S.A.	**72**	37 2N	85 55W
Glasgow, Mo., U.S.A.	**76**	39 14N	92 51W
Glasgow, Mont., U.S.A.	**78**	48 12N	106 35W
Glaslyn	**56**	53 22N	108 21W
Glastonbury, U.K.	**95**	51 9N	2 42W
Glastonbury, U.S.A.	**71**	41 42N	72 27W
Glauchau	**106**	50 50N	12 33E
Glazov	**120**	58 9N	52 40E
Gleichen	**54**	50 50N	113 0W
Glen	**71**	44 7N	71 10W
Glen Affric	**96**	57 15N	5 0W
Glen Almond	**40**	45 42N	75 29W
Glen Canyon Dam	**79**	37 0N	111 25W
Glen Canyon Nat. Recreation Area	**79**	37 30N	111 0W
Glen Coe	**98**	56 40N	5 0W
Glen Cove	**71**	40 51N	73 37W
Glen Cross	**49**	43 59N	80 3W
Glen Ewen	**57**	49 12N	102 1W
Glen Garry	**96**	57 3N	5 7W
Glen Gordon	**43**	45 10N	74 32W
Glen Innes	**135**	29 40S	151 39E
Glen Lyon	**71**	41 10N	76 7W
Glen Mor	**96**	57 12N	4 37E
Glen Moriston	**96**	57 10N	4 58W
Glen Morris	**49**	43 16N	80 21W
Glen Robertson	**43**	45 22N	74 30W
Glen Thompson	**136**	37 38S	142 35E
Glen Ullin	**74**	46 48N	101 46W
Glen Williams	**49**	43 40N	79 55W
Glénans, Îs. de	**100**	47 42N	4 0W
Glenavon	**56**	50 12N	103 8W
Glenboro	**57**	49 33N	99 17W
Glenbrook	**133**	33 46S	150 37E
Glenburnie	**136**	37 51S	140 50E
Glencairn	**58**	50 26N	104 33W
Glenchristie	**49**	43 28N	80 17W
Glencoe, Can.	**46**	42 45N	81 43W
Glencoe, U.S.A.	**74**	44 45N	94 10W
Glendale, Alta., Can.	**59**	51 2N	114 9W
Glendale, N.S., Can.	**39**	45 49N	61 18W
Glendale, Ariz., U.S.A.	**79**	33 40N	112 8W
Glendale, Calif., U.S.A.	**81**	34 7N	118 18W
Glendale, Oreg., U.S.A.	**78**	42 44N	123 29W
Glendive	**74**	47 7N	104 40W
Glendo	**74**	42 30N	105 0W
Glendon	**60**	54 15N	111 10W
Glendora	**81**	34 8N	117 52W
Gleneagle	**48**	45 32N	75 48W
Glenelg, R.	**136**	38 4S	140 59E
Glenella	**57**	50 33N	99 11W
Glengariff	**97**	51 45N	9 33W
Glengarry □	**43**	45 15N	74 30W
Glenmoor Res.	**59**	50 59N	114 8W
Glenmora	**75**	31 1N	92 34W
Glenn	**80**	39 31N	122 1W
Glennie	**46**	44 32N	83 39W
Glennie's Creek	**136**	32 30S	151 8E
Glenns Ferry	**78**	43 0N	115 15W
Glenrock	**78**	42 53N	105 55W
Glenroy	**134**	26 23S	28 17E
Glens Falls	**71**	43 20N	73 40W
Glenties	**97**	54 48N	8 18W
Glenville	**72**	38 56N	80 50W
Glenwood, Alta., Can.	**61**	49 21N	113 31W
Glenwood, Newf., Can.	**37**	49 0N	54 47W
Glenwood, Ark., U.S.A.	**75**	34 20N	93 30W
Glenwood, Hawaii, U.S.A.	**67**	19 29N	155 10W
Glenwood, Iowa, U.S.A.	**74**	41 7N	95 41W
Glenwood, Minn., U.S.A.	**74**	45 38N	95 21W
Glenwood, Wash., U.S.A.	**80**	46 1N	121 17W
Glenwood Sprs.	**78**	39 39N	107 15W
Glettinganes	**110**	65 30N	13 37W
Gliwice	**107**	50 22N	18 41E
Globe	**79**	33 25N	110 53W
Głogów	**106**	51 37N	16 5E
Gloria, La	**86**	8 37N	73 48W
Glorieuses, Îs.	**117**	11 30S	47 20E
Glossop	**94**	53 27N	1 56W
Gloucester, Can.	**48**	45 21N	75 39W
Gloucester, U.K.	**95**	51 52N	2 15W
Gloucester, U.S.A.	**71**	42 38N	70 39W
Gloucestershire □	**95**	51 44N	2 10W
Gloversville	**71**	43 5N	74 18W
Glovertown	**35**	48 40N	54 03W
Glückstadt	**106**	53 46N	9 28E
Gmünd	**106**	48 45N	15 0E
Gmunden	**106**	47 55N	13 48E
Gniezno	**107**	52 30N	17 35E
Gnowangerup	**134**	33 58S	117 59E
Go Cong	**128**	10 22N	106 40E
Goa	**124**	15 33N	73 59E
Goa □	**124**	15 33N	73 59E
Goalen Hd.	**136**	36 33S	150 4E
Goalpara	**125**	26 10N	90 40E
Goat Fell	**96**	55 37N	5 11W
Goba, Ethiopia	**115**	7 1N	39 59E
Goba, Mozam.	**117**	26 15S	32 13E
Gobabis	**117**	22 15S	19 0E
Gobi, desert	**129**	44 0N	111 0E
Gobles, Can.	**49**	43 9N	80 34W

Gobles **Great Central**

Gobles, U.S.A. 77 42 22N 85 53W
Gochas 117 24 59S 19 25E
Godavari Point 125 17 0N 82 20E
Godavari, R. 125 19 5N 79 0E
Godbout 38 49 20N 67 38W
Godbout, R. 38 49 19N 67 36W
Goderich 46 43 45N 81 41W
Goderville 100 49 38N 0 22E
Godfrey 76 38 57N 90 11W
Godham 65 60 55N 60 40W
Godhavn 17 69 15N 53 38W
Godhra 124 22 49N 73 40E
Godoy Cruz 88 32 56S 68 52W
Gods L. 55 54 40N 94 15W
Gods, R. 55 56 22N 92 51W
Godthåb 17 64 10N 51 46W
Goeie Hoop, Kaap die 117 34 24S 18 30E
Goéland, L. du 41 49 47N 71 43W
Goéland, L.au 40 49 50N 76 48W
Goeree 105 51 50N 4 0E
Goes 105 51 30N 3 55E
Goetzville 46 46 3N 84 5W
Gogama 53 47 35N 81 43W
Gogebic, L. 52 46 30N 89 34W
Gogriâl 115 8 30N 28 0E
Goiânia 87 16 35S 49 20W
Goiás 87 15 55S 50 10W
Goiás □ 87 12 10S 48 0W
Goirle 105 51 31N 5 4E
Gojra 124 31 10N 72 40E
Gokteik 125 22 26N 97 0E
Golchikha 17 71 45N 84 0E
Golconda 78 40 58N 117 32W
Gold Beach 78 42 25N 124 25W
Gold Creek 67 62 45N 149 45W
Gold Hill 78 42 28N 123 2W
Gold River 62 49 40N 126 10E
Golden, Can. 63 51 20N 117 59W
Golden, Colo., U.S.A. 74 39 42N 105 30W
Golden, Ill., U.S.A. 76 40 7N 91 1W
Golden Bay 133 40 40S 172 50E
Golden Ears Prov. Park 63 49 30N 122 25W
Golden Gate 78 37 54N 122 30W
Golden Hinde, mt. 62 49 40N 125 44W
Golden Lake 47 45 34N 77 21W
Golden Prairie 56 50 13N 109 37W
Golden Vale 97 52 33N 8 17W
Goldendale 78 45 53N 120 48W
Goldfield 79 37 45N 117 13W
Goldfields 55 59 28N 108 29W
Goldpines 55 50 45N 93 05W
Goldsand L. 55 57 2N 101 8W
Goldsboro 73 35 24N 77 59W
Goldsmith 75 32 0N 102 40W
Goldthwaite 75 31 25N 98 32W
Goleniów 106 53 35N 14 50E
Goleta 81 34 27N 119 50W
Golfito 84 8 41N 83 5W
Goliad 75 28 40N 97 22W
Golmo 129 36 30N 95 10E
Golo, R. 103 42 31N 9 32E
Golspie 96 57 58N 3 58W
Goma 116 2 11S 29 18E
Gombe 114 10 19N 11 2E
Gomel 120 52 28N 31 0E
Gómez Palacio 82 25 40N 104 40W
Gomogomo 127 6 25S 134 53E
Gomoh 125 23 52N 86 10E
Gonābād 123 34 15N 58 45E
Gonaïves 85 19 20N 72 50W
Gonâve, G. de la 85 19 29N 72 42W
Gonâve, I. de la 85 18 45N 73 0W
Gonda 125 27 9N 81 58E
Gondab-e Kāvūs 123 37 20N 55 25E
Gonder 115 12 23N 37 30E
Gondia 124 21 30N 80 10E
Gondrecourt-le-Château 101 48 26N 5 30E
Gonno-Altaysk 120 51 50N 86 5E
Gonzales, Calif., U.S.A. 80 36 35N 121 30W
Gonzales, Tex., U.S.A. 75 29 30N 97 30W
González Chaves 88 38 02S 60 05W
Goobang Cr. 136 33 20S 147 50E
Good Hart 46 45 34N 85 7W
Good Hope, C. of = Goeie Hoop 117 34 24S 18 30E
Good Hope Mt. 62 51 9N 124 10W
Good Spirit L. 56 51 34N 102 40W
Gooderham 47 44 54N 78 21W
Goodeve 56 51 4N 103 10W
Gooding 78 43 0N 114 50W
Goodland 74 39 22N 101 44W
Goodnight 75 35 4N 101 13W
Goodsoil 55 54 24N 109 13W
Goodsprings 79 35 51N 115 30W
Goodwater 56 49 24N 103 42W
Goodwood 39 44 37N 63 40W
Goole 94 53 42N 0 52W
Goolgowi 136 33 58S 145 41E
Goolma 136 32 18S 149 10E
Goondiwindi 135 28 30S 150 21E
Goose Bay 36 53 15N 60 20W
Goose Cove 37 51 18N 55 38W
Goose I. 62 51 57N 128 26W
Goose L., Can. 57 54 28N 101 30W
Goose L., U.S.A. 78 42 0N 120 30W
Goose R. 36 53 20N 60 35W
Gop 124 22 5N 69 50E
Gorakhpur 125 26 47N 83 32E
Gorda 80 35 53N 121 26W
Gorda, Punta 84 14 10N 83 10W
Gordon, Can. 58 50 0N 97 21W
Gordon, Nebr., U.S.A. 74 42 49N 102 6W
Gordon, Wis., U.S.A. 52 46 15N 91 48W
Gordon Downs 134 18 48S 128 40E
Gordon Hd. 63 48 29N 123 18W
Gordon L., Alta., Can. 60 56 30N 110 25W
Gordon L., N.W.T., Can. 54 63 5N 113 11W
Gordonville 49 43 54N 80 33W
Gore, Ethiopia 115 8 12N 35 32E
Gore, N.Z. 133 46 5S 168 58E
Gore Bay 46 45 57N 82 28W
Gorey 97 52 41N 6 18W
Gorgān 123 36 55N 54 30E
Gorgona, I. 86 3 0N 78 10W
Gorham 71 44 23N 71 10W
Gorham Mt. 71 43 42N 70 37W
Gorin 76 40 22N 92 1W
Gorinchem 105 51 50N 4 59E
Gorízia 108 45 56N 13 37E
Gorki = Gorkiy 120 56 20N 44 0E
Gorkiy 120 57 20N 44 0E
Görlitz 106 51 10N 14 59E
Gorman, Calif., U.S.A. 81 34 47N 118 51W
Gorman, Tex., U.S.A. 75 32 15N 98 43W
Gormley 50 43 56N 79 23W
Gorna Oryakhovitsa 109 43 7N 25 40E
Gorno Filinskoye 120 60 5N 70 0E
Gorong, Kepulauan 127 4 5S 131 15E
Gorontalo 127 0 35N 123 13E
Gorron 100 48 25N 0 50W
Gort 97 53 4N 8 50W
Gorzów Wielkopolski 106 52 43N 15 15E
Gosainthan, Mt. 125 28 20N 85 45E
Goschen I. 62 53 48N 130 33W
Gosford 136 33 23N 151 18E
Goshen, Can. 39 45 23N 61 59W
Goshen, Calif., U.S.A. 80 36 21N 119 25W
Goshen, Ind., U.S.A. 77 41 36N 85 46W
Goshen, N.Y., U.S.A. 71 41 23N 74 21W
Goslar 106 51 55N 10 23E
Gospič 108 44 35N 15 23E
Gosport, U.K. 95 50 48N 1 8W
Gosport, U.S.A. 77 39 21N 86 40W
Göta Kanal 111 58 35N 14 15E
Götaland, reg. 111 58 0N 14 0E
Göteborg 111 57 43N 11 59E
Göteborg & Bohus □ 111 58 20N 11 50E
Gotha 106 50 56N 10 42E
Gothenburg 74 40 58N 100 8W
Gothenburg & Goteborg 111 57 43N 11 59E
Gotō-rettō 132 32 55N 129 5E
Gotska Sandön 111 58 24N 19 15E
Göttingen 106 51 31N 9 55E
Gottwaldov (Zlin) 107 49 14N 17 40E
Gouda 105 52 1N 4 42E
Gough I. 13 40 10S 9 45W
Gough L. 61 52 2N 112 28W
Gouin Rés. 40 48 35N 74 40W
Goulais, R. 53 46 43N 84 27W
Goulburn, Austral. 136 34 44S 149 44E
Goulburn, N.S.W., Austral. 136 32 22S 149 31E
Goulburn Is. 134 11 40S 133 20E
Goulburn, R. 136 36 6S 144 55E
Goulds 37 47 29N 52 46W
Goundam 114 16 25N 3 45W
Gourdon 102 44 44N 1 23E
Gournay-en-Bray 101 49 29N 1 44E
Gourock Ra. 136 36 0S 149 25E
Gouverneur 71 44 18N 75 30W
Gouzon 102 46 12N 2 14E
Govan 56 51 20N 105 0W
Gove 135 12 25S 136 55E
Governador Valadares 87 18 15S 41 57W
Governor's Harbour 84 25 10N 76 14W
Gowanda 70 42 29N 78 58W
Gower, The 95 51 35N 4 10W
Gowna, L. 97 53 52N 7 35W
Gowrie 76 42 17N 94 17W
Goya 88 29 10S 59 10W
Goyelle, L. 38 50 47N 60 45W
Goyllarisquizga 86 10 19S 76 31W
Gozo, I. 108 36 0N 14 13E
Graaff-Reinet 117 32 13S 24 32E
Grabill 77 41 13N 84 57W
Gračac 108 44 18N 15 57E
Graçay 101 47 10N 1 50E
Grace 78 42 38N 111 46W
Gracefield 40 46 6N 76 3W
Graceville 74 45 36N 96 23W
Gracias a Dios, C. 84 15 0N 83 20W
Grado 104 43 23N 6 4W
Grady 75 34 52N 103 15W
Graénalon, L. 110 64 10N 17 20W
Grafton, Austral. 135 29 38S 152 58E
Grafton, Ill., U.S.A. 76 38 58N 90 26W
Grafton, N.Dak., U.S.A. 74 48 30N 97 25W
Grafton, C. 135 16 51S 146 0E
Graham, Can. 52 49 20N 90 30W
Graham, N.C., U.S.A. 73 36 5N 79 22W
Graham, Tex., U.S.A. 75 33 7N 98 38W
Graham Bell, Os. 120 80 5N 70 0E
Graham I., B.C., Can. 62 53 40N 132 30W
Graham I., N.W.T., Can. 65 77 25N 90 30W
Graham L. 60 56 35N 114 33W
Graham Land 91 65 0S 64 0W
Graham Mt. 79 32 46N 109 58W
Graham, R. 54 56 31N 122 17W
Grahamdale 57 51 23N 98 30W
Grahamstown 117 33 19S 26 31E
Grainland 56 50 59N 106 33W
Grajaú 87 5 50S 46 30W
Gramat 102 44 48N 1 43E
Grampian □ 96 57 0N 3 0W
Gramsh 96 40 52N 20 12E
Gran Chaco 130 25 0S 61 0W
Gran Paradiso 108 49 33N 7 17E
Gran Sabana, La 86 5 30N 61 30W
Gran Sasso d'Italia, Mt. 102 42 25N 13 30E
Granada, Nic. 84 11 58N 86 0W
Granada, Spain 104 37 10N 3 35W
Granada, U.S.A. 74 38 5N 102 13W
Granard 97 53 47N 7 30W
Granbury 75 32 28N 97 48W
Granby 41 45 25N 72 45W
Granby, R. 63 49 2N 118 27W
Grand Bahama I. 84 26 40N 78 30W
Grand Bank 37 47 6N 55 48W
Grand Bassam 114 5 10N 3 49W
Grand Bay 39 45 18N 66 12W
Grand Bend 46 43 19N 81 45W
Grand Blanc 46 42 56N 83 38W
Grand-Bourg 85 15 53N 61 19W
Grand Bruit 37 47 40N 58 14W
Grand Calumet, Île du 40 45 44N 76 41W
Grand Canal = Yun Ho 129 35 0N 117 0E
Grand Canyon National Park 79 36 15N 112 20W
Grand Cayman 84 19 20N 81 20W
Grand Centre 60 54 25N 110 13W
Grand Cess 114 4 40N 8 12W
Grand-Combe, La 103 44 13N 4 2E
Grand Coulee, Can. 56 50 26N 104 49W
Grand Coulee, U.S.A. 78 47 48N 119 1W
Grand Coulee Dam 78 48 0N 118 50W
Grand Falls 39 48 56N 55 40W
Grand Forks, Can. 63 49 0N 118 30W
Grand Forks, U.S.A. 74 48 0N 97 3W
Grand Fougeray, Le 100 47 44N 1 43W
Grand Harbour 39 44 41N 66 46W
Grand Haven 77 43 3N 86 13W
Grand I., Can. 57 52 51N 100 0W
Grand I., Mich., U.S.A. 53 46 30N 86 40W
Grand I., N.Y., U.S.A. 49 43 2N 78 59W
Grand Island 74 40 59N 98 25W
Grand Isle 75 29 15N 89 58W
Grand Junction, Colo., U.S.A. 79 39 0N 108 30W
Grand Junction, Iowa, U.S.A. 76 42 2N 94 14W
Grand L., N.B., Can. 39 45 57N 66 7W
Grand L., Newf., Can. 35 48 45N 57 45W
Grand L., Newf., Can. 36 53 40N 60 30W
Grand L., Newf., Can. 37 49 0N 57 30W
Grand L., Louis., U.S.A. 75 29 55N 92 45W
Grand L., Mich., U.S.A. 46 45 18N 83 30W
Grand L., Ohio, U.S.A. 77 40 32N 84 25W
Grand Lac 34 47 35N 77 35W
Grand Lake 78 40 20N 105 54W
Grand le Pierre 37 47 41N 54 47W
Grand Ledge 77 42 45N 84 45W
Grand-Lieu, Lac de 100 47 6N 1 40W
Grand Manan I. 39 44 45N 66 52W
Grand Marais, Can. 52 47 45N 90 25W
Grand Marais, U.S.A. 53 46 39N 85 59W
Grand Mère 41 46 36N 72 40W
Grand Motte, La 103 48 35N 1 4E
Grand Piles 41 46 40N 72 40W
Grand Portage 52 47 58N 89 41W
Grand Pressigny, Le 100 46 55N 0 48E
Grand, R., Can. 49 42 51N 79 34W
Grand, R., Mich., U.S.A. 77 43 4N 86 15W
Grand, R., Mo., U.S.A. 78 39 23N 93 27W
Grand, R., S.D., U.S.A. 78 45 45N 101 30W
Grand Rapids, Can. 57 53 12N 99 19W
Grand Rapids, Mich., U.S.A. 77 42 57N 85 40W
Grand Rapids, Minn., U.S.A. 52 47 15N 93 29W
Grand River 76 40 49N 93 58W
Grand Teton 78 43 54N 111 57W
Grand Valley, Can. 49 43 54N 80 19W
Grand Valley, U.S.A. 78 39 30N 108 2W
Grand View 57 51 10N 100 42W
Grande 87 11 30S 44 30W
Grande-Anse 39 47 48N 65 11W
Grande, B. 90 50 30S 68 20W
Grande Baie 41 48 19N 70 52W
Grande Baleine, R. de la 36 55 16N 77 47W
Grande Cache 60 53 53N 119 8W
Grande-Cascapédia 38 48 15N 65 54W
Grande, Coxilha 89 28 18S 51 30W
Grande de Santiago, R. 82 21 20N 105 50W
Grande-Entrée 39 47 30N 61 40W
Grande, Île 43 45 52N 73 14W
Grande, La 78 45 15N 118 0W
Grande, La, R. 36 53 50N 79 0W
Grande-Ligne 43 45 14N 73 22W
Grande Pointe 58 49 46N 97 3W
Grande Prairie 60 55 10N 118 50W
Grande, R., Jujuy, Argent. 88 23 9S 65 52W
Grande, R., Mendoza, Argent. 88 36 52S 69 45W
Grande R. 86 18 35S 63 0W
Grande, R., Brazil 87 20 0S 50 0W
Grande, R., U.S.A. 75 29 20N 100 40W
Grande-Rivière 38 48 26N 64 30W
Grande, Serra 87 4 30S 41 20W
Grande-Vallée 38 49 14N 65 8W
Grandes-Bergeronnes 41 48 16N 69 35W
Grandfalls 75 31 21N 102 51W
Grandmesnil, L. 38 51 19N 67 33W
Grandoe Mines 54 56 29N 129 54W
Grandpré 101 49 20N 4 50E
Grandview, Mo., U.S.A. 76 38 53N 94 32W
Grandview, Wash., U.S.A. 78 46 13N 119 58W
Grandview Heights 77 39 58N 83 2W
Grandville 77 42 54N 85 46W
Grandvilliers 101 49 40N 1 57E
Graneros 88 34 5S 70 45W
Granet, L. 40 47 47N 77 31W
Grange, La, Austral. 134 18 45S 121 43E
Grange, La, U.S.A. 80 37 42N 120 27W
Grange, La, Ga., U.S.A. 73 33 4N 85 0W
Grange, La, Ky., U.S.A. 72 38 20N 85 20W
Grange, La, Mo., U.S.A. 76 40 3N 91 35W
Grange, La, Tex., U.S.A. 75 29 54N 96 52W
Grangemouth 96 56 1N 3 43W
Granger 78 46 25N 120 5W
Grangeville 78 45 57N 116 4W
Granite, Pk. 78 45 8N 109 52W
Granite City 76 38 45N 90 3W
Granite Falls 74 44 45N 95 35W
Granite Mtn. 81 33 5N 116 28W
Granite Pt. 37 50 31N 56 17W
Granity 133 41 39S 171 51E
Granja 87 3 17S 40 50W
Granollers 104 41 39N 2 18E
Grant, Can. 34 50 6N 86 18W
Grant, U.S.A. 74 40 53N 101 42W
Grant City 76 40 30N 94 25W
Grant, Mt. 80 38 34N 118 48W
Grant, Pt. 136 38 32S 145 6E
Grant Range Mts. 79 38 30N 115 30W
Grantham 94 52 55N 0 39W
Grantown-on-Spey 96 57 19N 3 36W
Grants 79 35 14N 107 57W
Grants Pass 78 42 30N 123 22W
Grantsburg 74 45 46N 92 44W
Grantsville 78 40 35N 112 32W
Granville, France 100 48 50N 1 35W
Granville, N.D., U.S.A. 74 48 18N 100 48W
Granville, N.Y., U.S.A. 72 43 24N 73 16W
Granville L. 55 56 18N 100 30W
Grapeland 75 31 30N 95 25W
Gras, L. de 64 64 30N 110 30W
Grass, R. 55 56 3N 96 33W
Grass Range 78 47 0N 109 0W
Grass River Prov. Park 55 54 40N 100 50W
Grass Valley, Calif., U.S.A. 80 39 18N 121 0W
Grass Valley, Oreg., U.S.A. 78 45 28N 120 48W
Grasse 103 43 38N 6 56E
Grasset, L. 40 49 55N 78 10W
Grassie 49 43 9N 79 37W
Grassy Lake 61 49 49N 111 43W
Grate's Cove 35 48 8N 53 0W
Gratis 77 39 38N 84 32W
Gratz 77 38 28N 84 57W
Graulhet 102 43 45N 1 58E
Grave, Pte. de 102 45 34N 1 4W
Gravelbourg 56 49 50N 106 35W
Gravelines 101 51 0N 2 10E
's-Gravenhage 105 52 7N 4 17E
Gravenhurst 46 44 52N 79 20W
Gravesend 95 51 25N 0 22E
Gravois, Pointe-à 85 16 15N 73 45W
Gravone, R. 103 41 58N 8 45E
Gray 101 47 27N 5 35E
Grayling 46 44 40N 84 42W
Grayling, R. 54 59 21N 125 0W
Grays Harbor 78 46 55N 124 8W
Grays L. 78 43 8N 111 30W
Grays River 80 46 21N 123 37W
Grayson 56 50 45N 102 40W
Grayville 77 38 16N 88 0W
Graz 106 47 4N 15 27E
Greasy L. 54 62 55N 122 12W
Great Abaco I. 84 26 15N 77 10W
Great Australia Basin 135 26 0S 140 0E
Great Australian Bight 134 33 30S 130 0E
Great Barrier I. 133 36 11S 175 25E
Great Barrier Reef 135 19 0S 149 0E
Great Barrington 71 42 11N 73 22W
Great Basin 68 40 0N 116 30W
Great Bear L. 64 65 30N 120 0W
Great Bear, R. 64 65 0N 124 0W
Great Bena 71 41 57N 75 45W
Great Bend 74 38 25N 98 55W
Great Blasket, I. 97 52 5N 10 30W
Great Britain 93 54 0N 2 15W
Great Burnt L. 37 48 20N 56 20W
Great Central 62 49 20N 125 10W

Great Central L   Gunisao, R

Great Central L. 62 49 22N 125 10W
Great Coco I. 128 14 10N 93 25 E
Great Divide 135 23 0 S 146 0 E
Great Duck I. 46 45 40N 82 57W
Great Exuma I. 84 23 30N 75 50W
Great Falls, Can. 57 50 27N 96 1W
Great Falls, U.S.A. 78 47 27N 111 12W
Great Guana Cay 84 24 0N 76 20W
Great Harbour Deep 37 50 25N 56 25W
Great I. 55 58 53N 96 35W
Great Inagua I. 85 21 0N 73 20W
Gt. Indian Desert = Thar Desert 124 28 0N 72 0 E
Great Jarvis 35 47 39N 57 12W
Great Karoo = Groot Karoo 117 32 30 S 23 0 E
Great Lake 135 41 50 S 146 30 E
Great Lakes 55 44 0N 82 0W
Great Orme's Head 94 53 20N 3 52W
Great Ouse, R. 94 52 20N 0 8 E
Great Ruaha, R. 116 7 30 S 35 0 E
Gt. St. Bernard P. 106 45 50N 7 10 E
Great Salt Lake 78 41 0N 112 30W
Great Salt Lake Desert 78 40 20N 113 50W
Great Salt Plains Res. 75 36 40N 98 15W
Great Sandy Desert 134 21 0 S 124 0 E
Great Sandy I. = Fraser I. 135 25 15 S 153 0 E
Great Sitkin I. 67 52 0N 176 10W
Great Slave L. 54 61 23N 115 38W
Great Stour, R. 95 51 21N 1 15 E
Gt. Victoria Des. 134 29 30 S 126 30 E
Great Wall 130 38 30N 109 30 E
Great Whale, R. 34 55 20N 75 30W
Great Whernside, mt. 85 54 9N 1 59W
Great Yarmouth 94 52 40N 1 45 E
Greater Antilles 85 17 40N 74 0W
Greater Manchester □ 94 53 30N 2 15W
Gredos, Sierra de 104 40 20N 5 0W
Greece ■ 109 40 0N 23 0 E
Greece's Point 43 45 36N 74 30W
Greeley, Colo., U.S.A. 74 40 30N 104 40W
Greeley, Nebr., U.S.A. 74 41 36N 98 32W
Greely Fd. 65 80 30N 85 0W
Green B., Can. 37 49 45N 55 55W
Green B., U.S.A. 72 45 0N 87 30W
Green Bay 72 44 30N 88 0W
Green C. 136 37 13 S 150 1 E
Green City 76 40 16N 92 57W
Green Cove Springs 73 29 59N 81 40W
Green Cr. 48 45 28N 75 34W
Green Island 133 45 55 S 170 26 E
Green Lake 56 54 17N 107 47W
Green Park 49 43 52N 80 27W
Green, R. 39 47 18N 68 9W
Green R., Ky., U.S.A. 77 37 54N 87 30W
Green R., Utah, U.S.A. 79 39 0N 110 6W
Green R., Wyo., U.S.A. 78 43 2N 110 2W
Green R., Wyo., U.S.A. 78 41 44N 109 28W
Green River 50 43 53N 79 11W
Greenbank 80 48 6N 122 34W
Greenbush, Mich., U.S.A. 46 44 35N 83 19W
Greenbush, Minn., U.S.A. 57 48 46N 96 10W
Greencastle 77 39 40N 86 48W
Greene, U.S.A. 76 42 54N 92 48W
Greene, N.Y., U.S.A. 71 42 20N 75 45W
Greenfield, Calif., U.S.A. 80 36 19N 121 15W
Greenfield, Calif., U.S.A. 81 35 15N 119 0W
Greenfield, Ill., U.S.A. 76 39 21N 90 12W
Greenfield, Ind., U.S.A. 77 39 47N 85 51W
Greenfield, Iowa, U.S.A. 76 41 18N 94 28W
Greenfield, Mass., U.S.A. 71 42 38N 72 38W
Greenfield, Miss., U.S.A. 75 37 28N 93 50W
Greenfield, Ohio, U.S.A. 77 39 21N 83 23W
Greenfield Park 45 45 29N 73 29W
Greenfields 49 43 18N 80 29W
Greenhills 77 39 16N 84 32W
Greening 34 48 10N 74 55W
Greenland 17 66 0N 45 0W
Greenland Sea 17 73 0N 10 0W
Greenock 96 55 57N 4 46W
Greenore 97 54 2N 6 8W
Greenore Pt. 97 52 15N 6 20W
Greenough Pt. 46 44 58N 81 26W
Greenport 71 41 5N 72 23W
Greensboro, Ga., U.S.A. 73 33 34N 83 12W
Greensboro, N.C., U.S.A. 73 36 7N 79 46W
Greensburg, Ind., U.S.A. 77 39 20N 85 30W
Greensburg, Kans., U.S.A. 75 37 38N 99 20W
Greensburg, Pa., U.S.A. 70 40 18N 79 31W
Greentown 77 40 29N 85 58W
Greenup 77 39 15N 88 10W
Greenville, Ala., U.S.A. 73 31 50N 86 37W
Greenville, Calif., U.S.A. 80 40 8N 121 0W
Greenville, Ill., U.S.A. 76 38 53N 89 22W
Greenville, Ind., U.S.A. 77 38 22N 85 59W
Greenville, Me., U.S.A. 35 45 30N 69 32W
Greenville, Mich., U.S.A. 77 43 12N 85 14W
Greenville, Miss., U.S.A. 75 33 25N 91 0W
Greenville, N.C., U.S.A. 73 35 37N 77 26W
Greenville, Ohio, U.S.A. 77 40 5N 84 38W
Greenville, Pa., U.S.A. 70 41 23N 80 22W
Greenville, S.C., U.S.A. 73 34 54N 82 24W
Greenville, Tenn., U.S.A. 73 36 13N 82 51W
Greenville, Tex., U.S.A. 75 33 5N 96 5W
Greenwater L. 52 48 34N 90 26W
Greenwater Lake 56 52 30N 103 31W
Greenwater Lake Prov. Park 56 52 32N 103 30W
Greenwich, U.K. 95 51 28N 0 0
Greenwich, N.Y., U.S.A. 71 43 2N 73 36W
Greenwich, Ohio, U.S.A. 70 41 1N 82 32W
Greenwood, B.C., Can. 63 49 10N 118 40W
Greenwood, Ont., Can. 51 43 56N 79 3W
Greenwood, Ind., U.S.A. 77 39 37N 86 7W
Greenwood, Miss., U.S.A. 75 33 30N 90 4W
Greenwood, S.C., U.S.A. 73 34 13N 82 13W
Gregory 74 43 14N 99 20W
Gregory, L. 135 28 55 S 139 0 E
Gregory Lake 134 20 10 S 127 30 E
Gregory Ra. 135 19 30 S 143 40 E
Greifswald 106 54 6N 13 23 E
Gremikha 120 67 50N 39 40 E
Grenada 75 33 45N 89 50W
Grenada I. ■ 85 12 10N 61 40W
Grenade 102 43 47N 1 17 E
Grenadines 85 12 40N 61 20W
Grenen 111 57 44N 10 40 E
Grenfell, Austral. 136 33 52 S 148 8 E
Grenfell, Can. 56 50 30N 102 56W
Grenoble 103 45 12N 5 42 E
Grenora 74 48 38N 103 54W
Grenville 43 45 37N 74 36W
Grenville, C. 135 12 0 S 143 13 E
Grenville Chan. 62 53 40N 129 46W
Gréoux-les-Bains 103 43 45N 5 52 E
Gresham 80 45 30N 122 31W
Gresik 127 9 13 S 112 38 E
Gretna, Can. 57 49 1N 97 34W
Gretna, U.S.A. 75 30 0N 90 2W
Gretna Green 96 55 0N 3 3W
Grevenmacher 105 49 41N 6 26 E
Greves, Les 43 45 59N 73 11W
Grey, C. 135 13 0 S 136 35 E
Grey Is. 37 50 50N 55 35W
Grey, Pt. 66 49 16N 123 16W
Grey, R., Can. 37 47 34N 57 6W
Grey, R., N.Z. 133 42 27 S 171 12 E
Grey Range 135 27 0 S 143 30 E
Grey Res. 37 48 20N 56 30W
Grey River 37 47 35N 57 6W
Greybull 78 44 30N 108 3W
Greytown, N.Z. 133 41 5 S 175 29 E
Greytown, S. Afr. 117 29 1 S 30 36 E
Gribbell I. 62 53 23N 129 0W
Gridley 80 39 27N 121 47W
Griffin 73 33 17N 84 14W
Griffith, Austral. 136 34 18 S 146 2 E
Griffith, Can. 47 45 15N 77 10W
Griffith I. 46 44 50N 80 55W
Griffith Mine 55 50 47N 93 25W
Grijalva, R. 82 16 20N 92 20W
Grim, C. 135 40 45 S 144 45 E
Grimari 116 5 43N 20 0 E
Grimes 80 39 4N 121 54W
Grimsby, Can. 49 43 12N 79 34W
Grimsby, U.K. 94 53 35N 0 5W
Grimsby Beach 49 43 12N 79 32W
Grimsey 110 66 33N 18 0W
Grimshaw 60 56 10N 117 40W
Grimstad 111 58 22N 8 35 E
Grindstone I. 47 44 43N 76 14W
Grindstone Island 35 47 25N 62 0W
Grinnell 76 41 45N 92 43W
Grise Fiord 65 76 25N 82 57W
Grisolles 102 43 49N 1 19 E
Grita, La 86 8 8N 71 59W
Griz Nez, C. 101 50 50N 1 35 E
Groais I. 37 50 55N 55 35W
Grodno 120 53 42N 23 52 E
Grodzisk Wlkp. 106 52 15N 16 22 E
Groesbeck 75 31 32N 96 34W
Groix 100 47 38N 3 29W
Groix, I. de 100 47 38N 3 28W
Grójec 107 51 50N 20 58 E
Gronau 105 52 13N 7 2 E
Grong 110 64 25N 12 8 E
Groningen 105 53 15N 6 35 E
Groningen □ 105 53 16N 6 40 E
Gronlid 56 53 6N 104 28W
Groom 75 35 12N 100 59W
Groot-Brakrivier 117 34 2 S 22 18 E
Groot Karoo 117 32 35 S 23 0 E
Groot Namakwaland = Namaland 117 26 0 S 18 0 E
Groote Eylandt 135 14 0 S 136 50 E
Grootfontein 117 19 31 S 18 6 E
Gros C. 54 61 59N 113 32W
Gros-Morne 38 49 15N 65 34W
Gros Morne Nat. Park 37 49 40N 57 50W
Grosne, R. 103 46 30N 4 40 E
Gross Glockner 106 47 5N 12 40 E
Grossa, Pta. 87 1 20N 50 0W
Grosse I. 46 42 8N 83 9W
Grosse Isle 57 50 4N 97 27W
Grossenhain 106 51 17N 13 32 E
Grosses-Roches 38 48 57N 67 5W
Grosseto 108 42 45N 11 7 E
Groswater B. 36 54 20N 57 40W
Groton 71 41 22N 72 12W
Grouard Mission 60 55 33N 116 9W
Grouin, Pointe du 100 48 43N 1 51W
Groundhog, R. 53 48 45N 82 20W
Grouse Creek 78 41 51N 113 57W
Grove City, Ohio, U.S.A. 77 39 53N 83 6W
Grove City, Pa., U.S.A. 70 41 10N 80 5W
Grovedale 60 55 3N 118 52W
Groveland 80 37 50N 120 14W
Grover City 81 35 7N 120 37W
Grover Hill 77 41 1N 84 29W
Groveton, N.H., U.S.A. 71 44 34N 71 30W
Groveton, Tex., U.S.A. 75 31 5N 95 4W
Groznyy 120 43 20N 45 45 E
Grudziadz 107 53 30N 18 47 E
Gruissan 102 43 8N 3 7 E
Grünau 117 27 45 S 18 26 E
Grundy Center 76 42 22N 92 45W
Grundy Prov. Pk. 46 45 58N 80 30W
Grunthal 57 49 24N 96 51W
Gruver 75 36 19N 101 20W
Gryazi 120 52 30N 39 58 E
Gryazovets 120 58 50N 40 20 E
Grytviken 91 53 50 S 37 10W
Gua 125 22 18N 85 20 E
Guacanayabo, G. de 84 20 40N 77 20W
Guacara 86 10 14N 67 53W
Guachípas 88 25 40 S 65 30W
Guachiría, R. 86 5 30N 71 30W
Guadalajara, Mexico 82 20 40N 103 20W
Guadalajara, Spain 104 40 37N 3 12W
Guadalcanal, I. 14 9 32 S 160 12 E
Guadales 88 34 30 S 67 55W
Guadalete, R. 104 36 45N 5 47W
Guadalhorce, R. 104 36 50N 4 42W
Guadalquivir, R. 104 38 0N 4 0W
Guadalupe, Mexico 81 32 4N 116 32W
Guadalupe, U.S.A. 81 34 59N 120 33W
Guadalupe Bravos 82 31 20N 106 10W
Guadalupe de los Reyes 82 25 23N 104 15W
Guadalupe Pk. 79 31 50N 105 30W
Guadalupe, R., Mexico 81 32 6N 116 51W
Guadalupe, R., U.S.A. 75 29 25N 97 30W
Guadalupe, Sierra de 104 39 28N 5 30W
Guadalupe y Calvo 82 26 6N 106 58W
Guadarrama, Sierra de 104 41 0N 4 0W
Guadeloupe, I. 85 16 20N 61 40W
Guadeloupe, La 41 45 57N 70 56W
Guadeloupe Passage 85 16 50N 68 15W
Guadiana, R. 104 37 45N 7 35W
Guadix 104 37 18N 3 11W
Guafo, Boca del 90 43 35 S 74 0W
Guaina 86 5 9N 63 36W
Guainía □ 86 2 30N 69 00W
Guaíra 89 24 5 S 54 10W
Guaira, La 86 10 36N 66 56W
Guaitecas, Islas 90 44 0 S 74 30W
Guajará-Mirim 86 10 50 S 65 20W
Guajira, La □ 86 11 30N 72 30W
Guajira, Pen. de la 85 12 0N 72 0W
Gualan 84 15 8N 89 22W
Gualeguay 88 33 10 S 59 20W
Gualeguaychú 88 33 3 S 58 31W
Guam I. 14 13 27N 144 45 E
Guama 86 10 16N 68 49W
Guamareyes 86 0 30 S 73 0W
Guaminí 88 37 1 S 62 28W
Guampí, Sierra de 86 6 0N 65 35W
Guamuchil 82 25 25N 108 3W
Guanabacoa 84 23 8N 82 18W
Guanabara □ 89 23 0 S 43 25W
Guanacaste 84 10 40N 85 30W
Guanacaste, Cordillera del 84 10 40N 85 4W
Guanacevío 82 25 40N 106 0W
Guanajay 84 22 56N 82 42W
Guanajuato 82 21 0N 101 20W
Guanajuato □ 82 20 40N 101 20W
Guanare 86 8 42N 69 12W
Guanare, R. 86 8 50N 68 50W
Guandacol 88 29 30 S 68 40W
Guane 84 22 10N 84 0W
Guanica 67 17 58N 66 55W
Guanipa, R. 86 9 20N 63 30W
Guanta 86 10 14N 64 36W
Guantánamo 85 20 10N 75 20W
Guapí 86 2 36N 77 54W
Guápiles 84 10 10N 83 46W
Guaporé 89 12 0 S 64 0W
Guaporé, R. 86 13 0 S 63 0W
Guaqui 86 16 41 S 68 54W
Guarapari 89 20 40 S 40 30W
Guarapuava 87 25 20 S 51 30W
Guaratinguetá 89 22 49 S 45 9W
Guaratuba 89 25 53 S 48 38W
Guarda 104 40 32N 7 20W
Guardafui, C. = Asir, Ras 115 11 55N 51 10 E
Guaria □ 88 25 45N 56 30W
Guárico □ 86 8 40N 66 35W
Guarujá 89 24 2 S 46 25W
Guarus 89 21 30 S 41 20W
Guasave 82 25 34N 108 27W
Guasdualito 86 7 15N 70 44W
Guasipati 86 7 28N 61 54W
Guatemala 84 14 40N 90 30W
Guatemala ■ 84 15 40N 90 30W
Guatire 86 10 28N 66 32W
Guaviare, R. 86 3 30N 71 0W
Guaxupé 89 21 10 S 47 5W
Guayabal 86 4 43N 71 37W
Guayama 85 17 59N 66 7W
Guayaquil 86 2 15 S 79 52W
Guayaquil, G. de 86 3 10 S 81 0W
Guaymallen 88 32 50 S 68 45W
Guaymas 82 27 50N 111 0W
Guchil 128 5 35N 102 10 E
Guchin-Us 130 45 28N 102 10 E
Gudbransdal 111 61 33N 10 0 E
Guddu Barrage 71 28 30N 69 50 E
Gudivada 125 16 30N 81 15 E
Gudur 124 14 12N 79 55 E
Guebwiller 101 47 55N 7 12 E
Guecho 104 43 21N 2 59W
Guéguen, L. 40 48 6N 77 13W
Guelph 49 43 35N 80 20W
Guéméné-Penfao 100 47 38N 1 50W
Guéméné-sur-Scorff 100 48 4N 3 13W
Güemes 88 24 50 S 65 0W
Guer 100 47 54N 2 8W
Guérande 100 47 20N 2 26W
Guerche, La 100 47 57N 1 16W
Guerche-sur-l'Aubois, La 101 46 58N 2 56 E
Guéret 102 46 11N 1 51 E
Guérigny 101 47 6N 3 10 E
Guerneville 80 38 30N 123 0W
Guernica 104 43 19N 2 40W
Guernsey, Can. 56 51 53N 105 11W
Guernsey, U.S.A. 74 42 19N 104 45W
Guernsey I. 100 49 30N 2 35W
Guerrero □ 83 17 30N 100 0W
Gueugnon 103 45 36N 4 3 E
Gueydan 75 30 3N 92 30W
Guhra 123 27 36N 56 8 E
Guia Lopes da Laguna 89 21 26 S 56 7W
Guiana Highlands 86 5 0N 60 0W
Guibes 117 26 41 S 16 49 E
Guigues 40 47 28N 79 26W
Guija 117 34 35 S 33 15 E
Guildford 95 51 14N 0 34W
Guilford 35 45 12N 69 25W
Guillaume-Delisle, L. 36 56 15N 76 17W
Guillaumes 103 44 5N 6 52 E
Guillestre 103 44 39N 6 40 E
Guilvinec 100 47 48N 4 17W
Guimarães 87 2 9 S 44 35W
Guimaras I. 127 10 35N 122 37 E
Guinda 80 38 50N 122 12W
Guinea ■ 114 10 20N 10 0W
Guinea Bissau ■ 114 12 0N 15 0W
Guinea, Gulf of 114 3 0N 2 30 E
Guinea, Port. = Guinea Bissau 114 12 0N 15 0W
Güines 84 22 50N 82 0W
Guines, L. 38 52 8N 61 25W
Guingamp 100 48 34N 3 10W
Guipavas 100 48 26N 4 29W
Güiria 86 10 32N 62 18W
Guiscard 101 49 40N 3 0 E
Guise 101 49 52N 3 35 E
Guivan 127 11 5N 125 55 E
Gujan-Mestras 102 44 38N 1 4W
Gujarat □ 124 23 20N 71 0 E
Gujranwala 124 32 10N 74 12 E
Gujrat 124 32 40N 74 2 E
Gukhothae 128 17 2N 99 50 E
Gulargambone 136 31 20 S 148 30 E
Gulbahar 123 35 5N 69 10 E
Gulbargâ 124 17 20N 76 50 E
Gulf Basin 134 15 20 S 129 0 E
Gulfport 75 30 28N 89 3W
Gulgong 136 32 20 S 149 30 E
Gulkana 67 62 15N 145 48W
Gull L., Can. 61 52 34N 114 0W
Gull L., U.S.A. 52 46 30N 94 21W
Gull Lake 56 50 10N 108 29W
Gull, R. 52 49 45N 89 0W
Gulpaigan 122 33 26N 50 20 E
Gulshad 120 46 45N 74 25 E
Gulu 116 2 48N 32 17 E
Gum Lake 136 32 42 S 143 9 E
Guma 129 37 37N 78 18 E
Gumma-ken □ 132 36 30N 138 20 E
Gummersbach 105 51 2N 7 32 E
Gümüsane 122 40 30N 39 30 E
Gumzai 127 5 28 S 134 42 E
Guna 124 24 40N 77 19 E
Gundagai 136 35 3 S 148 6 E
Gundih 127 7 10 S 110 56 E
Gungu 116 5 43 S 19 20 E
Gunisao L. 57 53 33N 96 15W
Gunisao, R. 57 53 56N 97 53W

Gunnedah Harry S. Truman Res

Gunnedah 135 30 59S 150 15E
Gunning 136 34 47S 149 14E
Gunnison, Colo., U.S.A. 79 38 32N 106 56W
Gunnison, Utah, U.S.A. 78 39 11N 111 48W
Gunnison, R. 79 38 50N 108 30W
Guntakal 124 15 11N 77 27E
Guntersville 73 34 18N 86 16W
Guntur 125 16 23N 80 30E
Gunung-Sitoli 126 1 15N 97 30E
Gunungapi 127 6 45S 126 30E
Gunungsugih 126 4 58S 105 7E
Gunworth 55 51 20N 108 10W
Gupis 124 36 15N 73 20E
Gürchañ 122 34 55N 49 25E
Gurdaspur 124 32 5N 75 25E
Gurdon 75 33 55N 93 10W
Gurgaon 124 28 33N 77 10E
Gurkha 125 28 5N 84 40E
Gurnee 77 42 22N 87 55W
Gurun 128 5 49N 100 27E
Gürün 122 38 41N 37 22E
Gurupá 87 1 20S 51 45W
Gurupá, I. Grande de 87 1 0S 51 45W
Gurupi, R. 87 3 20S 47 20W
Gurvandzagal 130 49 35N 115 2E
Guryev 120 47 5N 52 0E
Gusau 114 12 18N 6 31E
Gusinoczersk 130 51 16N 106 27E
Gustavus 67 58 25N 135 58W
Gustine 80 37 21N 121 0W
Güstrow 106 53 47N 12 12E
Guthega Dam 136 36 20S 148 27E
Guthrie 75 35 55N 97 30W
Guthrie Center 76 41 41N 94 30W
Guttenberg 76 42 46N 91 10W
Guyana ■ 86 5 0N 59 0W
Guyenne 102 44 30N 0 40E
Guymon 75 36 45N 101 30W
Guysborough 39 45 23N 61 30W
Guzmán, Laguna de 82 31 25N 107 25W
Gwa 125 17 30N 94 40E
Gwādar 124 25 10N 62 18E
Gwalior 124 26 12N 78 10E
Gwanda 117 20 55S 29 0E
Gweebarra B. 97 54 52N 8 21W
Gweedore 97 55 4N 8 15W
Gwelo 117 19 28S 29 45E
Gwent □ 95 51 45N 2 55W
Gwinn 53 46 15N 87 29W
Gwydir, R. 135 29 27S 149 48E
Gwynedd □ 94 53 0N 4 0W
Gya La 125 28 45N 84 45E
Gyangtse 125 28 50N 89 33E
Gydanskiy P-ov. 120 70 0N 78 0E
Gympie 135 26 11S 152 38E
Gyoda 132 36 10N 139 30E
Gyöngyös 107 47 48N 20 15E
Györ 107 47 41N 17 40E
Gypsum Pt. 54 61 53N 114 35W
Gypsumville 57 51 45N 98 40W

H

Ha Nam = Phu-Ly 128 20 35N 105 50E
Haapamäki 110 62 18N 24 28E
Haarlem 105 52 23N 4 39E
Haast, R. 133 43 50S 169 2E
Hab Nadi Chauki 124 25 0N 66 50E
Haba 122 27 10N 47 0E
Habana, La 84 23 8N 82 22W
Habaswein 116 1 2N 39 30E
Habay 54 58 50N 118 44W
Hachijō-Jima 132 33 5N 139 45E
Hachinohe 132 40 30N 141 29E
Hachiōji 132 35 30N 139 30E
Hackensack 52 46 56N 94 29W
Hackett 54 52 9N 112 28W
Hadd, Ras al 123 22 35N 59 50E
Haddington 96 55 57N 2 48W
Hadhramaut = Hadramawt 115 15 30N 49 30E
Hadramawt 115 15 30N 49 30E
Hadrians Wall 94 55 0N 2 30W
Haeju 130 38 3N 125 45E
Hafar al Bātin 122 28 25N 46 50E
Hafford 56 52 43N 107 21W
Hafizabad 124 32 5N 73 40E
Haflong 125 25 10N 93 5E
Hafnarfjörður 110 64 4N 21 57W
Haft-Gel 122 31 30N 49 32E
Hagemeister I. 67 58 42N 161 0W
Hagen 105 51 21N 7 29E
Hagensborg 62 52 23N 126 32W
Hagerman 75 33 5N 104 22W
Hagerstown, Ind., U.S.A. 77 39 55N 85 10W
Hagerstown, Md., U.S.A. 72 39 39N 77 46W
Hagersville 49 42 58N 80 3W
Hagetmau 102 43 39N 0 37W
Hagfors 111 60 3N 13 45E
Hagi, Iceland 110 65 28N 23 25W
Hagi, Japan 132 34 30N 131 30E
Hags Hd. 97 52 57N 9 30W
Hague, C. de la 100 49 44N 1 56W
Hague, The = s'-Gravenhage 105 52 7N 4 17E
Haguenau 101 48 49N 7 47E
Haicheng 130 40 56N 122 51E
Haifa 115 32 46N 35 0E
Haihang 131 20 55N 110 3E
Haik'ou 131 20 5N 110 20E
Haikow 131 20 0N 110 20E
Hā'il 122 27 28N 42 2E
Hailar 130 49 12N 119 37E
Hailar Ho 130 49 30N 118 30E
Hailey 78 43 30N 114 15W
Haileybury 34 47 30N 79 38W
Hailun 130 47 24N 127 0E
Hailuoto 110 65 3N 24 45E
Haimen 131 31 48N 121 8E
Hainan, I. 131 19 0N 110 0E
Hainan Str. = Ch'iungcho Haihsia 131 20 10N 110 15E
Hainaut □ 105 50 30N 4 0E
Haines, Alaska, U.S.A. 67 59 20N 135 36W
Haines, Oreg., U.S.A. 78 44 51N 117 59W
Haines City 73 28 6N 81 35W
Haines Junction 67 60 45N 137 30W
Haining 131 30 23N 120 30E
Haiphong 128 20 47N 106 35E
Haitan Tao 131 25 30N 119 45E
Haiti ■ 85 19 0N 72 30W
Haiyen 131 30 28N 120 57E
Haiyuan 130 36 32N 105 31E
Haja 127 3 19S 129 37E
Hajdúböszörmény 107 47 40N 21 30E
Haji Langar 124 35 50N 79 20E
Hajnówka 107 52 45N 23 32E
Hajr 123 24 0N 56 34E
Hakken-Zan 132 34 10N 135 54E
Hakodate 132 41 45N 140 44E
Hala 124 25 43N 68 20E
Halab = Aleppo 122 36 10N 37 15E
Halabjah 122 35 10N 45 58E
Halaib 115 22 5N 36 30E
Halawa 67 21 9N 156 47W
Halberstadt 106 51 53N 11 2E
Halbrite 56 49 30N 103 33W
Halcombe 133 40 8S 175 30E
Halcyon, Mt. 127 13 0N 121 30E
Haldia 125 22 5N 88 3E
Haldimand-Norfolk □ 49 42 57N 79 50W
Haldwani 124 29 25N 79 30E
Hale, Mich., U.S.A. 46 44 18N 83 48W
Hale, Mo., U.S.A. 76 39 36N 93 20W
Haleakala Crater 67 20 43N 156 12W
Haleyville 73 34 15N 87 40W
Half Island Cove 39 45 21N 61 12W
Halfway 78 44 56N 117 8W
Halfway, R. 54 56 12N 121 32W
Haliburton 47 45 3N 78 30W
Halifax, Can. 39 44 38N 63 35W
Halifax, U.K. 94 53 43N 1 51W
Halifax B. 135 18 50S 147 0E
Halil, R. 123 27 40N 58 30E
Halkirk 61 52 17N 112 9W
Hall Beach 65 68 46N 81 12W
Hall Land 17 81 20N 60 0W
Hall Pen. 65 63 30N 66 0W
Halland 111 56 55N 12 50E
Halle 105 51 29N 12 0E
Hallebourg 53 49 40N 83 31W
Hallettsville 75 29 28N 96 57W
Halley Bay 91 75 31S 26 36W
Halliday 74 47 20N 102 25W
Halliday L. 55 61 21N 108 56W
Hallingdal, R. 111 60 34N 9 12E
Hällnäs 110 64 19N 19 36E
Hallock 57 48 47N 97 0W
Hall's Creek 134 18 16S 127 46E
Hallstead 71 41 56N 75 45W
Halmahera, I. 127 0 40N 128 0E
Halmstad 111 56 41N 12 52E
Hals 111 56 59N 10 18E
Halstad 74 47 21N 96 41W
Halton □ 48 43 30N 79 53W
Hamā 122 35 5N 36 40E
Hamada 132 34 50N 132 10E
Hamadān 122 34 52N 48 32E
Hamadān □ 122 35 0N 49 0E
Hamamatsu 132 34 45N 137 45E
Hamar 111 60 48N 11 7E
Hamarøy 110 68 5N 15 38E
Hambantota 124 6 10N 81 10E
Hamber Prov. Park 63 52 20N 118 0W
Hamburg, Ger. 106 53 32N 9 59E
Hamburg, Ark., U.S.A. 75 33 15N 91 47W
Hamburg, Iowa, U.S.A. 74 40 37N 95 38W
Hamburg, N.Y., U.S.A. 70 42 44N 78 50W
Hamburg, Pa., U.S.A. 71 40 33N 76 0W
Hame 111 61 30N 24 0E
Hämeenlinna 111 61 0N 24 28E
Hameln 106 52 7N 9 24E
Hamer 71 42 38N 76 11W
Hamersley Ra. 134 22 0S 117 45E
Hamhung 130 40 0N 127 30E
Hamilton, Austral. 136 37 45S 142 2E
Hamilton, Can. 48 43 15N 79 50W
Hamilton, N.Z. 133 37 47S 175 19E
Hamilton, U.K. 96 55 47N 4 2W
Hamilton, Alas., U.S.A. 67 62 55N 164 0W
Hamilton, Ill., U.S.A. 76 40 24N 91 21W
Hamilton, Ind., U.S.A. 77 41 33N 84 56W
Hamilton, Mo., U.S.A. 96 39 45N 93 59W
Hamilton, Mont., U.S.A. 78 46 20N 114 6W
Hamilton, N.Y., U.S.A. 71 42 49N 75 31W
Hamilton, Ohio, U.S.A. 77 39 20N 84 35W
Hamilton, Tex., U.S.A. 75 31 40N 98 5W
Hamilton, Wash., U.S.A. 63 48 31N 121 59W
Hamilton Beach 48 43 17N 79 47W
Hamilton City 80 39 45N 122 1W
Hamilton Harbour 48 43 18N 79 50W
Hamilton Inlet 35 54 0N 57 30W
Hamilton, R. 134 26 40S 134 20E
Hamilton Sound 37 49 35N 54 15W
Hamilton-Wentworth □ 48 43 15N 79 49W
Hamiota 57 50 11N 100 38W
Hamlet 73 34 56N 79 40W
Hamlin, N.Y., U.S.A. 70 43 17N 77 55W
Hamlin, Tex., U.S.A. 75 32 58N 100 8W
Hamm 105 51 40N 7 58E
Hammenton 72 39 40N 74 47W
Hammerfest 110 70 39N 23 41E
Hammond, Can. 71 45 26N 75 15W
Hammond, Ill., U.S.A. 77 39 48N 88 36W
Hammond, Ind., U.S.A. 77 41 40N 87 30W
Hammond, La., U.S.A. 75 30 32N 90 30W
Hammond B. 46 45 31N 84 0W
Hampden, Can. 37 49 33N 56 51W
Hampden, N.Z. 133 45 18S 170 50E
Hampshire □ 95 51 3N 1 20W
Hampshire Downs 95 51 10N 1 10W
Hampstead 39 45 37N 66 5W
Hampton, N.B., Can. 39 45 32N 65 51W
Hampton, Ont., Can. 47 43 58N 78 45W
Hampton, Ark., U.S.A. 75 33 35N 92 29W
Hampton, Iowa, U.S.A. 76 42 43N 93 12W
Hampton, N.H., U.S.A. 71 42 56N 70 48W
Hampton, S.C., U.S.A. 73 32 52N 81 2W
Hampton, Va., U.S.A. 72 37 4N 76 18W
Hampton Harbour 134 20 30S 116 30E
Hampton Tableland 134 32 0S 127 0E
Hamra 122 24 2N 38 55E
Hamun Helmand 123 31 15N 61 15E
Hamun-i-Lora 124 29 38N 64 58E
Hamun-i-Mashkel 124 28 30N 63 0E
Han K., Hupei, China 131 31 40N 112 20E
Han K., Kwangtung, China 131 23 45N 116 35E
Han Kiang R. 131 31 40N 112 20E
Han Pijesak 109 44 0N 19 0E
Hana 67 20 45N 155 59W
Hanau 106 50 8N 8 56E
Hanbagd 130 43 12N 107 10E
Hanceville 63 51 55N 123 2W
Hancheng 130 35 14N 110 22E
Hanchow Wan 131 35 0N 119 0E
Hancock, Mich., U.S.A. 52 47 10N 88 40W
Hancock, Minn., U.S.A. 74 45 26N 95 46W
Hancock, Pa., U.S.A. 71 41 57N 75 19W
Handa 132 34 53N 137 0E
Handel 56 52 4N 108 42W
Handeni 116 5 25S 38 2E
Handlová 69 48 45N 18 35E
Handshur 130 48 29N 118 2E
Haney 63 49 12N 122 40W
Hanford 80 36 25N 119 39W
Hangchow 131 30 12N 120 1E
Hangchow Wan 131 30 30N 121 30E
Hangchwang 131 34 34N 117 27E
Hangö (Hanko) 111 59 59N 22 57E
Hanh 130 51 32N 100 35E
Hankinson 74 46 9N 96 58W
Hanko = Hangö 111 59 59N 22 57E
Hankow 131 30 35N 114 20E
Hanksville 79 38 19N 110 45W
Hanku 130 39 16N 117 50E
Hanlan 50 43 39N 79 39W
Hanle 124 32 42N 79 4E
Hanley 56 51 38N 106 26W
Hanmer, Can. 46 46 39N 80 56W
Hanmer, N.Z. 133 42 32S 172 50E
Hann, Mt. 134 16 0S 126 0E
Hanna 61 51 40N 111 54W
Hannaford 74 47 23N 98 18W
Hannah 57 48 58N 98 42W
Hannah B. 34 51 40N 80 0W
Hannibal 76 39 42N 91 22W
Hannon 48 43 11N 79 50W
Hannover 106 52 23N 9 43E
Hanoi 128 21 5N 105 55E
Hanover, Can. 46 44 9N 81 2W
Hanover, U.S.A. 77 38 43N 85 28W
Hanover, N.H., U.S.A. 71 43 43N 72 17W
Hanover, Ohio, U.S.A. 70 40 5N 82 17W
Hanover, Pa., U.S.A. 72 39 46N 76 59W
Hanover = Hannover 106 52 23N 9 43E
Hanover, I. 90 51 0S 74 50W
Hansi 124 29 10N 75 57E
Hanson Range 134 27 0S 136 30E
Hantan 130 36 42N 114 30E
Hant's Harbour 37 48 1N 53 16W
Hantsport 39 45 4N 64 11W
Hanuy Gol 130 48 20N 101 30E
Hanwood 136 34 22S 146 2E
Hanyang 131 30 32N 114 10E
Haparanda 110 65 52N 24 8E
Happy 75 34 47N 101 50W
Happy Camp 78 41 52N 123 30W
Happy Valley 36 53 15N 60 20W
Hapur 124 28 45N 77 45E
Haql 122 29 10N 35 0E
Har 127 5 16S 133 14E
Har-Ayrag 130 45 47N 109 16E
Har Us Nuur 129 48 0N 92 0E
Hara Narinula, (Lang Shan) 130 41 30N 107 0E
Haraa Gol 129 49 0N 106 0E
Harad 122 24 15N 49 0E
Haradh 122 24 15N 49 0E
Haran 122 36 48N 39 0E
Harbin 130 45 46N 126 51E
Harbor Beach 46 43 50N 82 38W
Harbor Springs 46 45 28N 85 0W
Harbour Breton 37 47 29N 55 50W
Harbour Deep 35 50 25N 56 30W
Harbour Grace 37 47 40N 53 22W
Harburg 106 53 27N 9 58E
Harcourt 39 46 27N 65 15W
Hardangerfjorden. 111 60 15N 6 0E
Hardap Dam 117 24 32S 17 50E
Hardenberg 105 52 34N 6 37E
Harderwijk 105 52 21N 5 38E
Hardin, Ill., U.S.A. 76 39 9N 90 37W
Hardin, Mont., U.S.A. 78 45 50N 107 35W
Harding 117 30 22S 29 55E
Hardinsburg 77 37 47N 86 28W
Hardinxveld 105 51 49N 4 53E
Hardisty 61 52 40N 111 18W
Hardman 78 45 12N 119 49W
Hardoi 124 27 26N 80 15E
Hardwar 124 29 58N 78 16E
Hardwick 71 44 30N 72 20W
Hardwicke I. 62 50 27N 125 50W
Hardwicke Island 62 50 26N 125 55W
Hardwood Ridge 39 46 10N 66 1W
Hardy 75 36 20N 91 30W
Hardy, Pen. 90 55 30S 68 20W
Hare B. 37 51 15N 55 45W
Hare Bay 37 48 51N 54 1W
Harelbeke 105 50 52N 3 20E
Harer 115 9 20N 42 8E
Harfleur 100 49 30N 0 10E
Hargeisa 115 9 30N 44 2E
Hargshamn 111 60 12N 18 30E
Hari, R., Afghan. 124 34 20N 64 30E
Hari, R., Indon. 126 1 10S 101 50E
Haringhata, R. 125 22 0N 89 58E
Harirūd 123 35 0N 61 0E
Harlan, Iowa, U.S.A. 74 41 37N 95 20W
Harlan, Tenn., U.S.A. 73 36 58N 83 20W
Harlech 94 52 52N 4 7W
Harlem 78 48 29N 108 39W
Harley 49 43 4N 80 29W
Harlingen, Neth. 105 53 11N 5 25E
Harlingen, U.S.A. 75 26 20N 97 50W
Harlowton 78 46 30N 109 54W
Harmon L. 52 49 56N 90 13W
Harmony 49 43 54N 78 50W
Harney Basin 78 43 30N 119 0W
Harney L. 78 43 0N 119 0W
Harney Pk. 74 43 52N 103 33W
Harnösand 110 62 38N 18 5E
Haro, C. 82 27 50N 110 55W
Haro Str. 63 48 30N 123 15W
Harp L. 36 55 5N 61 50W
Harpe, La 76 40 30N 91 0W
Harper Mt. 67 64 15N 143 57W
Harput 122 38 48N 39 15E
Harrat al Kishb 122 22 30N 40 15E
Harrat al Uwairidh 122 26 50N 38 0E
Harricana, R. 40 50 56N 79 32W
Harriman 73 36 0N 84 35W
Harrington Harbour 38 50 31N 59 30W
Harris, Can. 56 51 44N 107 35W
Harris, U.K. 96 57 50N 6 55W
Harris L. 134 31 10S 135 10E
Harris Pt. 46 43 6N 82 9W
Harris, Sd. of 96 57 44N 7 6W
Harrisburg, Can. 49 43 14N 80 13W
Harrisburg, Ill., U.S.A. 77 37 42N 88 30W
Harrisburg, Nebr., U.S.A. 74 41 36N 103 46W
Harrisburg, Oreg., U.S.A. 78 44 25N 123 10W
Harrisburg, Pa., U.S.A. 70 40 18N 76 52W
Harrison, Ark., U.S.A. 75 36 10N 93 4W
Harrison, Idaho, U.S.A. 78 47 30N 116 51W
Harrison, Mich., U.S.A. 46 44 1N 84 48W
Harrison, Nebr., U.S.A. 74 42 42N 103 52W
Harrison, Ohio, U.S.A. 77 39 16N 84 49W
Harrison B. 67 70 25N 151 0W
Harrison, C. 36 54 55N 57 55W
Harrison Grove 49 43 18N 78 58W
Harrison Hot Springs 63 49 18N 121 47W
Harrison L. 63 49 33N 121 50W
Harrisonburg 72 38 28N 78 52W
Harrisonville 76 38 39N 94 21W
Harriston 46 43 57N 80 53W
Harrisville 46 44 40N 83 19W
Harrodsburg, Ind., U.S.A. 77 39 1N 86 33W
Harrodsburg, Ky., U.S.A. 77 37 46N 84 51W
Harrogate 94 53 59N 1 32W
Harrow, Can. 46 42 2N 82 55W
Harrow, U.K. 95 51 35N 0 15W
Harrowsmith 47 44 24N 76 40W
Harry S. Truman Res 76 38 14N 93 30W

Harstad 110 68 48N 16 30E
Hart 72 43 42N 86 21W
Hartell 61 50 36N 114 14W
Hartford, Conn., U.S.A. 71 41 47N 72 41W
Hartford, Ky., U.S.A. 72 37 26N 86 50W
Hartford, Mich., U.S.A. 77 42 13N 86 10W
Hartford, S.D., U.S.A. 74 43 40N 96 58W
Hartford, Wis., U.S.A. 74 43 18N 88 25W
Hartford City 77 40 22N 85 20W
Hartland, Can. 39 46 20N 67 32W
Hartland, U.S.A. 77 43 6N 88 21W
Hartland Pt. 95 51 2N 4 32W
Hartlepool 94 54 42N 1 11W
Hartley 117 18 10S 30 7E
Hartley Bay 62 53 25N 129 15W
Hartney 57 49 30N 100 35W
Hartselle 73 34 25N 86 55W
Hartshorne 75 34 51N 95 30W
Hartsville 73 34 23N 80 2W
Hartwell 73 34 21N 82 52W
Harty 53 49 29N 82 41W
Harvard 77 42 25N 88 37W
Harvard, Mt. 79 39 0N 106 5W
Harvey, Can. 39 45 43N 67 1W
Harvey, Ill., U.S.A. 77 41 40N 87 40W
Harvey, N.D., U.S.A. 74 47 50N 99 58W
Harwich 95 51 56N 1 18E
Harwood 70 44 7N 78 11W
Haryana □ 124 29 0N 76 10E
Harz 106 51 40N 10 40E
Hasa 122 26 0N 49 0E
Hasbaiya 115 33 25N 35 41E
Hashefela 115 31 30N 34 43E
Haskell, Okla., U.S.A. 75 35 51N 95 40W
Haskell, Tex., U.S.A. 75 33 10N 99 45W
Hasparren 102 43 24N 1 18W
Hassan 122 13 0N 76 5E
Hasselt, Belg. 105 50 56N 5 21E
Hasselt, Neth. 105 52 36N 6 6E
Hassi Messaoud 114 31 43N 6 8E
Hassi Taguenza 88 29 8N 0 23W
Hastings, Can. 47 44 18N 77 57W
Hastings, N.Z. 133 39 39S 176 52E
Hastings, U.K. 95 50 51N 0 36E
Hastings, Mich., U.S.A. 77 42 40N 85 20W
Hastings, Minn., U.S.A. 74 44 41N 92 51W
Hastings, Nebr., U.S.A. 74 40 34N 98 22W
Hastings, Pa., U.S.A. 70 40 40N 78 45W
Hastings Road 66 49 16N 122 56W
Hat Nhao 128 14 46N 106 32E
Hatch 79 32 45N 107 8W
Hatches Creek 134 20 56S 135 12E
Hatchet L. 55 58 36N 103 40W
Hatfield Post Office 136 33 54N 143 49E
Hathras 124 27 36N 78 6E
Hatia 125 22 30N 91 5E
Hato de Corozal 86 6 11N 71 45W
Hato Mayor 85 18 46N 69 15W
Hattem 105 52 28N 6 4E
Hatteras, C. 73 35 10N 75 30W
Hattiesburg 75 31 20N 89 20W
Hatton 55 50 2N 109 50W
Hattonford 60 53 46N 115 42W
Hatvan 107 47 40N 19 45E
Hau Bon (Cheo Reo) 128 13 25N 108 28E
Haubstadt 77 38 12N 87 34W
Hauchinango 82 20 12N 97 45W
Haugesund 111 59 23N 5 13E
Haultain, R. 55 55 51N 106 46W
Hauraki Gulf 133 36 35S 175 5E
Haut Atlas 114 32 0N 7 0W
Haut-Rhin □ 101 48 0N 7 15E
Hauta Oasis 122 23 40N 47 0E
Hautah, Wahāt al 122 23 40N 47 0E
Haute-Corse □ 103 42 30N 9 30E
Haute-Garonne □ 102 43 28N 1 30E
Haute-Loire □ 102 45 5N 3 50E
Haute-Marne □ 101 48 10N 5 20E
Haute-Saône □ 101 47 45N 6 10E
Haute-Savoie □ 103 46 0N 6 20E
Haute-Vienne □ 102 45 50N 1 10E
Hauterive 41 49 10N 68 16W
Hautes-Alpes □ 103 44 42N 6 20E
Hautes-Pyrénées □ 102 43 0N 0 10E
Hauteville-Lompnes 103 45 59N 5 35E
Hautmont 101 50 15N 3 55E
Hauts-de-Seine □ 101 48 52N 2 15E
Havana 76 40 19N 90 3W
Havana = La Habana 84 23 8N 82 22W
Havasu, L. 81 34 18N 114 28W
Havel, R. 106 52 40N 12 15E
Havelange 105 50 23N 5 15E
Havelock, N.B., Can. 39 46 2N 65 24W
Havelock, Ont., Can. 47 44 26N 77 53W
Havelock, Qué., Can. 43 45 3N 73 45W
Havelock, N.Z. 133 41 17S 173 48E
Havelock I. 128 11 55N 93 2E
Haverfordwest 95 51 48N 4 59W
Haverhill 71 42 50N 71 2W
Havering 95 51 33N 0 20E
Haverstraw 71 41 12N 73 58W
Havlíčkův Brod 106 49 36N 15 33E
Havre 78 48 40N 109 34W
Havre -St.-Pierre 38 50 18N 63 33W
Havre-Aubert 39 47 12N 61 56W
Havre Aubert, Î. 39 47 13N 61 57W
Havre-aux-Maisons, Î. 39 47 25N 61 47W
Havre, Le 100 49 30N 0 5E
Havza 122 41 0N 35 35E
Haw, R. 73 37 43N 80 52W
Hawaii □ 67 20 30N 157 0W
Hawaii I. 67 20 0N 155 0W
Hawaiian Is. 67 20 30N 156 0W
Hawarden, Can. 56 51 25N 106 36W
Hawarden, U.S.A. 74 43 2N 96 28W
Hawea Lake 133 44 28S 169 19E
Hawera 133 39 35S 174 19E
Hawesville 77 37 54N 86 45W
Hawick 96 55 25N 2 48W
Hawk Junction 53 48 5N 84 38W
Hawk Lake 52 49 48N 93 59W
Hawk Point 76 38 58N 91 8W
Hawke B. 133 39 25N 177 20E
Hawke, C. 136 32 13S 152 34E
Hawker 94 31 59S 138 22E
Hawkes Bay 37 50 36N 57 10W
Hawke's Bay □ 133 39 45S 176 35E
Hawkesbury 43 45 37N 74 37W
Hawkesbury I. 62 53 37N 129 3W
Hawkesbury River 136 33 50S 151 44W
Hawkestone 70 44 31N 79 27W
Hawkinsville 73 32 17N 83 30W
Hawley 74 46 58N 96 20W
Hawthorne 78 38 31N 118 37W
Haxtun 74 40 40N 102 39W
Hay, Austral. 136 34 30S 144 51E
Hay, U.K. 95 52 4N 3 9W
Hay, C. 64 74 25N 113 0W
Hay Cove 39 45 45N 60 44W
Hay I. 46 44 53N 80 58W
Hay L. 54 58 50N 118 50W
Hay Lakes 61 53 12N 113 2W
Hay, R., Austral. 135 24 10S 137 20E
Hay, R., Can. 54 60 0N 116 56W
Hay River 54 60 51N 115 44W
Hay Springs 74 42 40N 102 38W
Hayange 101 49 20N 6 2E
Haycock 67 65 10N 161 20W
Hayden, Ariz., U.S.A. 79 33 2N 110 54W
Hayden, Colo., U.S.A. 78 40 30N 107 22W
Haye Descartes, La 100 46 58N 0 42E
Haye-du-Puits, La 100 49 17N 1 33W
Hayes 74 44 22N 101 1W
Hayes Pen. 17 75 30N 65 0W
Hayes, R. 55 57 3N 92 12W
Haymana 122 39 30N 32 35E
Haynesville 75 33 0N 93 7W
Hays, Can. 61 50 6N 111 48W
Hays, U.S.A. 74 38 55N 99 25W
Haysboro 59 50 59N 114 5W
Haysville 77 38 28N 86 55W
Hayward, Calif., U.S.A. 80 37 40N 122 5W
Hayward, Wis., U.S.A. 74 46 2N 91 30W
Hayward's Heath 95 51 0N 0 5W
Hazard 72 37 18N 83 10W
Hazaribagh 125 23 58N 85 26E
Hazebrouck 101 50 42N 2 31E
Hazelmere 66 49 2N 122 43W
Hazelton, Can. 54 55 20N 127 42W
Hazelton, U.S.A. 74 46 30N 100 15W
Hazen 78 39 37N 119 2W
Hazenmore 56 49 42N 107 8W
Hazlehurst 73 31 50N 82 35W
Hazlet 56 50 24N 108 36W
Hazleton, Ind., U.S.A. 77 38 29N 87 34W
Hazleton, Pa., U.S.A. 71 40 58N 76 0W
Hazrat Imam 123 37 15N 68 50E
Head of Bay d'Espoir 37 47 56N 55 45W
Head of Bight 134 31 30S 131 25E
Head of St. Margarets Bay 39 44 41N 63 55W
Headingley 58 49 53N 97 24W
Healdsburg 80 38 33N 122 51W
Healdton 75 34 16N 97 31W
Healesville 136 37 35S 145 30E
Heanor 94 53 1N 1 20W
Heard I. 16 53 0S 74 0E
Hearne 75 30 54N 96 35W
Hearne B. 55 60 10N 99 10W
Hearne L. 54 62 20N 113 10W
Hearst 53 49 40N 83 41W
Heart, R. 74 46 40N 101 30W
Heart's Content 37 47 54N 53 27W
Heath Pt. 38 49 8N 61 40W
Heath Steele 39 47 17N 66 5W
Heatherton, Newf., Can. 37 48 17N 58 45W
Heatherton, N.S., Can. 39 45 35N 61 47W
Heavener 75 34 54N 94 36W
Hebbronville 75 27 20N 98 40W
Heber 81 32 44N 115 32W
Heber Springs 75 35 29N 91 59W
Hebert 56 50 30N 107 10W
Hebgen, L. 78 44 50N 111 15W
Hebrides, U.K. 96 57 30N 7 0W
Hebrides, Inner Is., U.K. 96 57 20N 6 40W
Hebrides, Outer Is., U.K. 96 57 50N 7 25W
Hebron, Newf., Can. 36 58 12N 62 38W
Hebron, N.S., Can. 39 43 53N 66 5W
Hebrón 115 31 32N 35 6E
Hebron, Ind., U.S.A. 77 41 19N 87 17W
Hebron, N.D., U.S.A. 74 46 56N 102 2W
Hebron, Nebr., U.S.A. 74 40 15N 97 33W
Hebron Fd. 36 58 9N 62 45W
Hecate I. 62 51 42N 128 0W
Hecate Str. 62 53 10N 130 30W
Hecks Corner 43 45 4N 73 12W
Hecla 74 45 56N 98 8W
Hecla I. 57 51 10N 96 43W
Hédé 100 48 18N 1 49W
Hede 110 62 23N 13 30E
Hedemora 111 60 18N 15 58E
Hedley, Can. 63 49 22N 120 4W
Hedley, U.S.A. 75 34 53N 100 39W
Hedley B. 64 73 0N 108 0W
Hedmark □ 111 61 17N 11 40E
Hedrick 76 41 11N 92 19W
Heemstede 105 52 22N 4 37E
Heerenveen 105 52 57N 5 55E
Heerlen 105 50 55N 6 0E
Heidelberg 106 49 23N 8 41E
Heilbron 117 27 16S 27 59E
Heilbronn 106 49 8N 9 13E
Heilungkiang □ 130 47 30N 129 0E
Heinola 111 61 13N 26 24E
Heinsburg 55 53 50N 110 30W
Heinze Is. 128 14 25N 97 45E
Heisler 61 52 41N 112 13W
Hejaz = Hijāz 122 26 0N 37 30E
Hekimhan 122 38 50N 38 0E
Hekla 110 63 56N 19 35W
Helena, Ark., U.S.A. 75 34 30N 90 35W
Helena, Mont., U.S.A. 78 46 40N 112 0W
Helendale 81 34 45N 117 19W
Helene L. 56 53 33N 108 12W
Helensburgh, Austral. 136 34 11S 151 1E
Helensburgh, U.K. 96 56 0N 4 44W
Helensville 133 36 41S 174 29E
Helgeland 110 66 20N 13 30E
Helgoland, I. 106 54 10N 7 51E
Heligoland = Helgoland 106 54 10N 7 51E
Hell-Ville 117 13 25S 48 16E
Hellick Kenyon Plateau 91 82 0S 110 0W
Hellin 104 38 31N 1 40W
Helmand □ 124 31 20N 64 0E
Helmand, R. 124 34 0N 67 0E
Helmond 105 51 29N 5 41E
Helmsdale 96 58 7N 3 40W
Helmsdale, R. 96 58 10N 3 50W
Helper 78 39 44N 110 56W
Helsingborg 111 56 3N 12 42E
Helsingfors = Helsinki 111 60 15N 25 3E
Helsingør 111 56 2N 12 35E
Helsinki (Helsingfors) 111 60 15N 25 3E
Helvellyn 94 54 31N 3 1W
Hemet 81 33 45N 116 59W
Hemford 39 44 30N 64 47W
Hemingford 74 42 21N 103 4W
Hemmingford 43 45 3N 73 35W
Hemphill 75 31 21N 93 49W
Hempstead 75 30 5N 96 5W
Hemse 111 57 15N 18 22E
Henares, R. 104 40 55N 3 0W
Hendaye 102 43 23N 1 47W
Henderson, Argent. 88 36 18S 61 43W
Henderson, Ky., U.S.A. 77 37 50N 87 38W
Henderson, Nev., U.S.A. 81 36 2N 115 0W
Henderson, Pa., U.S.A. 73 35 25N 88 40W
Henderson, Tex., U.S.A. 75 32 5N 94 49W
Henderson, Mt. 62 54 16N 128 4W
Hendersonville 73 35 21N 82 28W
Hendrix Lake 63 52 5N 120 48W
Hengelo 105 52 16N 6 48E
Henghsien 131 22 36N 109 16E
Hengshan 130 27 10N 112 45E
Hengyang 131 26 51N 112 30E
Hénin-Beaumont 101 50 25N 2 58E
Henley Harbour 37 52 2N 55 51W
Henlopen, C. 72 38 48N 75 5W
Hennebont 100 47 49N 3 19W
Hennepin 76 41 15N 89 21W
Hennessy 75 36 8N 97 53W
Henribourg 55 53 25N 105 38W
Henrichemont 101 47 20N 2 21E
Henrietta 75 33 50N 98 15W
Henrietta Maria C. 34 55 9N 82 20W
Henry 76 41 5N 89 20W
Henry Kater, C. 65 69 8N 66 30W
Henryetta 75 35 30N 96 0W
Henrysburg 43 45 5N 73 27W
Henryville 43 45 8N 73 11W
Hensall 46 43 26N 81 30W
Hentiyn Nuruu 130 48 30N 108 30E
Henty 136 35 30N 147 0E
Henzada 125 17 38N 95 35E
Heppner 78 45 27N 119 34W
Hepworth 46 44 37N 81 9W
Héraðsflói 110 65 42N 14 12W
Héraðsvötn 110 65 25N 19 5W
Herāt 124 34 20N 62 7E
Herāt □ 124 35 0N 62 0E
Hérault □ 102 43 34N 3 15E
Hérault, R. 102 43 20N 3 32E
Herbert I. 67 52 49N 170 10W
Herbert Inlet 62 49 20N 125 58W
Herbiers, Les 100 46 52N 1 0W
Herbignac 100 47 27N 2 18W
Hercegnovi 109 42 30N 18 33E
Herculaneum 76 38 16N 90 23W
Herðubreið 110 65 11N 16 21W
Herdman 43 45 2N 74 6W
Hereford, U.K. 95 52 4N 2 42W
Hereford, U.S.A. 75 34 50N 102 28W
Hereford and Worcester □ 95 52 10N 2 30W
Hereford, Mt. 41 45 5N 71 36W
Herentals 105 51 12N 4 51E
Hereward 49 43 50N 80 19W
Herford 106 52 7N 8 40E
Héricourt 101 47 32N 6 55E
Herington 74 38 43N 97 0W
Heriot Bay 62 50 7N 125 13W
Hérisson 102 46 32N 2 42E
Herjehogna 111 61 43N 12 7E
Herkimer 71 43 0N 74 59W
Herlong 80 40 8N 120 8W
Herm I. 100 49 30N 2 28W
Herman 74 45 51N 96 8W
Hermandez 80 36 24N 120 46W
Hermann 74 38 40N 91 25W
Herment 102 45 45N 2 24E
Hermidale 136 31 30S 146 42E
Hermiston 78 45 50N 119 16W
Hermitage, Can. 37 47 33N 55 56W
Hermitage, N.Z. 133 43 44S 170 5E
Hermitage, U.S.A. 76 37 56N 93 19W
Hermitage B. 35 47 33N 56 10W
Hermite, Is. 90 55 50S 68 0W
Hermon, Mt. 115 33 20N 36 0E
Hermon, Mt. = Sheikh, J. ash 115 33 20N 36 0E
Hermosillo 82 29 10N 111 0W
Hernad, R. 107 48 20N 21 15E
Hernandarias 89 25 20S 54 40W
Hernando, Argent. 88 32 28S 63 40W
Hernando, U.S.A. 75 34 50N 89 59W
Herne 105 51 33N 7 12E
Herne Bay 95 51 22N 1 8E
Herning 111 56 8N 8 58E
Heroica Nogales 82 31 14N 110 56W
Heron Bay 53 48 40N 86 25W
Hérons, Ile aux 44 45 25N 73 35W
Herreid 74 45 53N 100 5W
Herrera 104 39 12N 4 50W
Herrero, Punta 83 19 17N 87 27W
Herrin 76 37 50N 89 0W
Herring Cove 39 44 34N 63 34W
Herschel 56 51 38N 108 21W
Herschel I. 67 69 35N 139 5W
Herstal 105 50 40N 5 38E
Hertford 95 51 47N 0 4W
Hertford □ 95 51 51N 0 5W
's-Hertogenbosch 105 51 42N 5 17E
Hervey B. 135 25 0S 152 52E
Hervey Is. 15 19 30S 159 0W
Hervey Junction 34 46 50N 72 29W
Herzliyya 115 32 10N 34 50E
Hesdin 101 50 21N 2 0E
Hespeler 49 43 26N 80 19W
Hesperia 81 34 25N 117 18W
Hesse = Hessen 106 50 40N 9 20E
Hessel 46 46 1N 84 28W
Hessen □ 106 50 40N 9 20E
Hetch Hetchy Aqueduct 80 37 36N 121 25W
Hettinger 74 46 8N 102 38W
Hève, C. de la 100 49 30N 0 5E
Hewett, C. 65 70 16N 67 45W
Hexham 94 54 58N 2 7W
Heyfield 136 37 59S 146 47E
Heysham 94 54 5N 2 53W
Heywood 136 38 8S 141 37E
Hi-no-Misaki 132 35 26N 132 38E
Hi Vista 81 34 44N 117 46W
Hiawatha, Kans., U.S.A. 74 39 55N 95 33W
Hiawatha, Utah, U.S.A. 78 39 37N 111 1W
Hibben I. 62 53 0N 132 18W
Hibbing 52 47 30N 93 0W
Hickman 75 36 35N 89 8W
Hickmans Harbour 37 48 6N 53 44W
Hickory 73 35 46N 81 17W
Hicksville, N.Y., U.S.A. 71 40 46N 73 30W
Hicksville, Ohio, U.S.A. 77 41 18N 84 46W
Hida-Sammyaku 132 36 30N 137 40E
Hida-sammyaku 132 36 30N 137 40E
Hidalgo 77 39 9N 88 9W
Hidalgo □ 82 20 30N 99 10W
Hidalgo del Parral 82 26 58N 105 40W
Hidalgo, Presa M. 82 26 30N 108 35W
Hifung 131 22 59N 115 17E
Higashiōsaka 132 34 40N 135 37E
Higbee 76 39 19N 92 31W
Higgins 75 36 9N 100 1W
Higgins Corner 80 39 2N 121 5W
Higgins L. 46 44 30N 84 45W
Higginsville 76 39 4N 93 43W
Higgs I. L. 73 36 20N 78 30W
High Atlas = Haut Atlas 114 32 30N 5 0W
High I., Newf., Can. 35 56 40N 61 10W
High I., Newf., Can. 36 52 28N 55 40W
High Island 75 29 32N 94 22W
High Level 54 58 31N 117 8W
High Point 73 35 57N 79 58W
High Prairie 60 55 30N 116 30W
High River 61 50 30N 113 50W
High Springs 73 29 50N 82 40W
High Wycombe 95 51 37N 0 45W
Highland, U.S.A. 77 41 33N 87 28W
Highland, Ill., U.S.A. 76 38 44N 89 41W

Highland Huanglui

Highland, Wis., U.S.A. 76 43 6N 90 21W
Highland □ 96 57 30N 5 0W
Highland Creek 50 43 47N 79 10W
Highland Park 59 51 6N 114 4W
Highland Pk., Ill., U.S.A. 77 42 10N 87 50W
Highland Pk., Mich., U.S.A. 70 42 25N 83 6W
Highmore 74 44 35N 99 26W
Highridge 60 54 3N 114 8W
Highrock L. 55 57 5N 105 32W
Higley 79 33 27N 111 46W
Higüay 85 18 37N 68 42W
Higüero, Pta. 85 18 22N 67 16W
Hiko 80 37 30N 115 13W
Hikone 132 35 15N 136 10 E
Hikurangi 133 37 55 S 178 4 E
Hilda 61 50 28N 110 3W
Hilden 39 45 18N 63 18W
Hildesheim 106 52 9N 9 55 E
Hill 47 45 40N 74 45W
Hill City, Idaho, U.S.A. 78 43 20N 115 2W
Hill City, Kans., U.S.A. 74 39 25N 99 51W
Hill City, Minn., U.S.A. 52 46 57N 93 35W
Hill City, S.D., U.S.A. 74 43 58N 103 35W
Hill Island L. 55 60 30N 109 50W
Hill Spring 61 49 17N 113 38W
Hilla, Iraq 122 32 30N 44 27 E
Hilla, Si Arab. 122 23 35N 46 50 E
Hillegom 105 52 18N 4 35 E
Hillhurst 59 51 3N 114 7W
Hillingdon 95 51 33N 0 29W
Hillman 46 45 5N 83 52W
Hillmond 56 53 26N 109 41W
Hillsboro, Ill., U.S.A. 76 39 9N 89 29W
Hillsboro, Iowa, U.S.A. 76 40 50N 91 42W
Hillsboro, Kans., U.S.A. 74 38 28N 97 10W
Hillsboro, Mo., U.S.A. 76 38 14N 90 34W
Hillsboro, N. Mex., U.S.A. 79 33 0N 107 35W
Hillsboro, N.D., U.S.A. 74 47 23N 97 9W
Hillsboro, N.H., U.S.A. 71 43 8N 71 56W
Hillsboro, Ohio, U.S.A. 77 39 12N 83 37W
Hillsboro, Oreg., U.S.A. 80 45 31N 123 0W
Hillsboro, Tex., U.S.A. 75 32 0N 97 10W
Hillsborough 85 12 28N 61 28W
Hillsborough B. 39 46 8N 63 5W
Hillsburgh 49 43 47N 80 9W
Hillsdale, Can. 58 50 25N 104 37W
Hillsdale, Mich., U.S.A. 77 41 55N 84 40W
Hillsdale, N.Y., U.S.A. 71 42 11N 73 30W
Hillsport 53 49 27N 85 34W
Hillston 136 33 30 S 145 31 E
Hilo 67 19 44N 155 5W
Hilonghilong, mt. 127 9 10N 125 45 E
Hilton 70 43 16N 77 48W
Hilton Beach 46 46 15N 83 53W
Hilversum 105 52 14N 5 10 E
Himachal Pradesh □ 124 31 30N 77 0 E
Himalaya, mts. 124 29 0N 84 0 E
Himatnagar 124 23 37N 72 57 E
Himeji 132 34 50N 134 40 E
Himi 132 36 50N 137 0 E
Hims = Homs 122 34 40N 36 45 E
Hinako, Kepulauan 126 0 50N 97 20 E
Hinche 85 19 9N 72 1W
Hinckley, U.K. 95 52 33N 1 21W
Hinckley, U.S.A. 78 39 18N 112 41W
Hindmarsh L. 136 36 5 S 141 55 E
Hinds L. 37 48 58N 57 0W
Hindu Kush 124 36 0N 71 0 E
Hindubagh 124 30 56N 67 57 E
Hindupur 124 13 49N 77 32 E
Hines Creek 60 56 20N 118 40W
Hingan 131 25 39N 110 43 E
Hinganghat 124 20 30N 78 59 E
Hingham 78 48 40N 110 29W
Hingi 131 25 4N 105 2 E
Hingkwo 131 26 15N 115 13 E
Hingning 131 24 2N 115 55 E
Hingol, R. 124 25 30N 65 30 E
Hingoli 124 19 41N 77 15 E
Hinlopenstretet 17 79 35N 18 40 E
Hinnøy 110 68 40N 16 28 E
Hinojosa 104 38 30N 5 17W
Hinsdale 78 48 26N 107 2W
Hinton, Can. 60 53 26N 117 34W
Hinton, U.S.A. 72 37 40N 80 51W
Hirakud Dam 125 21 32N 83 45 E
Hiratsuka 132 35 19N 139 21 E
Hirosaki 132 40 34N 140 28 E
Hiroshima 132 34 30N 132 30 E
Hiroshima-ken □ 132 34 50N 133 0 E
Hirson 101 49 55N 4 4 E
Hispaniola, I. 83 19 0N 71 0W
Hissar 124 29 12N 75 45 E
Hita 132 33 20N 130 58 E
Hitachi 132 16 40N 140 35 E
Hitchcock 56 49 14N 103 7W
Hitchin 95 51 57N 0 16W
Hitoyoshi 132 32 13N 130 45 E
Hitra 110 63 30N 8 45 E
Hiungyao 130 40 10N 122 9 E
Hixon 63 53 25N 122 35W
Hjalmar L. 55 61 33N 109 25W
Hjälmaren 111 59 18N 15 40 E
Hjørring 111 57 29N 9 59 E
Ho Chi Minh, Phanh Bho 128 10 58N 106 40 E
Hoa Binh 128 20 50N 105 20 E
Hoa Da (Phan Ri) 128 11 16N 108 40 E
Hoadley 54 52 45N 114 30W
Hoai Nhon (Bon Son) 128 14 28N 109 1 E
Hoare B. 65 65 17N 62 0W
Hobart, Austral. 135 42 50 S 147 21 E
Hobart, Ind., U.S.A. 77 41 32N 87 15W
Hobart, Okla., U.S.A. 75 35 0N 99 5W
Hobbs 75 32 40N 103 3W
Hobo 86 2 35N 75 30W
Hoboken, Belg. 105 51 11N 4 21 E
Hoboken, U.S.A. 71 40 45N 74 4W
Hobro 111 56 39N 9 46 E
Hobson L. 63 52 35N 120 15W
Hoburgen 111 56 55N 18 7 E
Hochatown 75 34 11N 94 39W
Hochih 131 24 43N 107 43 E
Hochwan 131 30 0N 106 15 E
Hodeïda 115 14 50N 43 0 E
Hodges Hill 37 49 4N 55 53W
Hodgeville 56 50 7N 106 58W
Hodgson 57 51 13N 97 36W
Hódmezóvásárhely 107 46 28N 20 22 E
Hodonín 106 48 50N 17 0 E
Hoëdic, I. 100 47 21N 2 52W
Hoek van Holland 105 52 0N 4 7 E
Hof, Ger. 106 50 18N 11 55 E
Hof, Iceland 110 64 33N 14 40W
Höfðakaupstaður 110 65 50N 20 19W
Hofei 131 31 52N 117 15 E
Hofeng 131 29 55N 110 5 E
Hofsjökull 110 64 49N 18 48W
Hofsós 110 65 53N 19 26W
Hōfu 132 34 3N 131 34 E
Hofuf 122 25 20N 49 40 E
Hog I. 46 45 48N 85 22W
Hogansville 73 33 14N 84 50W
Hogeland 56 48 51N 108 40W
Hogsty Reef 85 21 41N 73 48W
Hoh, R. 80 47 45N 124 29W
Hohenlimburg 105 51 21N 7 35 E
Hohenwald 73 35 35N 87 30W
Hohpi 130 35 59N 114 13 E
Hôi An 128 15 30N 108 19 E
Hoi Xuan 128 20 25N 105 9 E
Hoiping 131 22 30N 112 12 E
Hoisington 74 38 33N 98 50W
Hokang 130 47 36N 130 28 E
Hokiang 131 28 50N 105 50 E
Hokianga Harbour 133 35 31 S 173 22 E
Hokitika 133 42 42 S 171 0 E
Hokkaidō 132 43 30N 143 0 E
Hokow 128 22 39N 103 57 E
Hokowchen 130 40 16N 111 4 E
Holan Shan 130 38 40N 105 50 E
Holberg 62 50 40N 128 0W
Holbrook, Austral. 136 35 42 S 147 18 E
Holbrook, U.S.A. 79 35 0N 110 0W
Holden, Can. 60 53 13N 112 11W
Holden, Mo., U.S.A. 76 38 43N 94 0W
Holden, Wash., U.S.A. 63 48 12N 120 47W
Holden Fillmore 78 39 0N 112 26W
Holdenville 75 35 5N 96 25W
Holderness 94 53 45N 0 5W
Holdfast 56 50 58N 105 25W
Holdrege 55 40 25N 99 30W
Holgate 77 41 15N 84 8W
Holguín 84 20 50N 76 20W
Holinshead L. 52 49 39N 89 40W
Hollams Bird I. 117 24 40 S 14 30 E
Holland, U.K. 94 52 50N 0 10W
Holland, U.S.A. 77 42 47N 86 7W
Holland Landing 70 44 7N 79 30W
Hollandia = Jayapura 127 2 28 S 140 38 E
Hollidaysburg 70 40 26N 78 25W
Hollis 75 34 45N 99 55W
Hollister, Calif., U.S.A. 80 36 51N 121 24W
Hollister, Idaho, U.S.A. 70 42 21N 114 36W
Holly, U.S.A. 46 42 48N 83 38W
Holly, Colo., U.S.A. 74 38 7N 102 7W
Holly Hill 73 29 15N 81 3W
Holly Springs 75 34 45N 89 25W
Hollywood, Calif., U.S.A. 68 34 7N 118 25W
Hollywood, Fla., U.S.A. 73 26 0N 80 9W
Holman 64 70 44N 117 44W
Hólmavík 110 65 42N 21 40W
Holmsund 110 63 41N 20 20 E
Holroyd, R. 135 14 10 S 141 36 E
Holsteinsborg 65 66 40N 53 30W
Holt 110 63 33N 19 48W
Holton 36 54 31N 57 12W
Holtville 81 32 50N 115 27W
Holy Cross 67 62 10N 159 52W
Holy I., England, U.K. 94 55 42N 1 48W
Holy I., Wales, U.K. 94 53 17N 4 37W
Holyhead 94 53 18N 4 38W
Holyhead B. 94 53 20N 4 35W
Holyoke, Colo., U.S.A. 74 40 39N 102 18W
Holyoke, Mass., U.S.A. 71 42 14N 72 37W
Holyrood 37 47 27N 53 8W
Homalin 125 24 55N 95 0 E
Homathko, R. 62 51 0N 124 56W
Hombori 114 15 20N 1 38W
Homburg 105 49 19N 7 21 E
Home B. 65 68 40N 67 10W
Home Hill 135 19 43 S 147 25 E
Homedale 78 43 42N 116 59W
Homer, Can. 49 43 10N 79 11W
Homer, Alaska, U.S.A. 67 59 40N 151 35W
Homer, Ill, U.S.A. 77 40 4N 87 57W
Homer, La., U.S.A. 75 32 50N 93 4W
Homer, Mich., U.S.A. 77 42 9N 84 49W
Homestead, Can. 60 55 31N 119 22W
Homestead, Fla., U.S.A. 73 25 29N 80 27W
Homestead, Idaho, U.S.A. 70 45 3N 116 58W
Homewood, Calif., U.S.A. 80 39 4N 120 8W
Homewood, Ill., U.S.A. 77 41 34N 87 40W
Hominy 75 36 26N 96 24W
Homs (Hims) 122 34 40N 36 45 E
Hon Chong 128 10 16N 104 38 E
Honan □ 131 33 50N 113 15 E
Honcut 80 39 20N 121 32W
Honda 86 5 12N 74 45W
Hondeklipbaai 117 30 19 S 17 17 E
Hondo, Can. 60 55 4N 114 2W
Hondo, U.S.A. 75 29 22N 99 6W
Hondo, R. 83 18 25N 88 21W
Honduras ■ 84 14 40N 86 30W
Honduras, Golfo de 84 16 50N 87 0W
Hönefoss 111 60 10N 10 12 E
Honesdale 71 41 34N 75 17W
Honey Harbour 46 44 52N 79 49W
Honey L. 80 40 13N 120 14W
Honfleur 100 49 25N 0 13 E
Hong Kong ■ 131 22 11N 114 14 E
Hongha, R. 128 22 0N 104 0 E
Honghai B. 131 22 45N 115 15 E
Hongkong ■ 131 22 11N 114 14 E
Honguedo, Détroit d' 38 49 15N 64 0W
Honiton 95 50 48N 3 11W
Honolulu 67 21 19N 157 52W
Honshū 132 36 0N 138 0 E
Hood Mt. 78 45 30N 121 50W
Hood, Pt. 134 34 23 S 119 34 E
Hood River 78 45 45N 121 37W
Hoodsport 80 47 24N 123 7W
Hoogeveen 105 52 44N 6 30 E
Hoogezand 105 53 11N 6 45 E
Hooghly, R. 125 21 59N 88 10 E
Hooglede 105 50 59N 3 5 E
Hook Hd. 97 52 8N 6 57W
Hooker 75 36 55N 101 10W
Hooker L. 52 50 35N 91 1W
Hoonah 67 58 15N 135 30W
Hooper Bay 67 61 30N 166 10W
Hoopeston 77 40 30N 87 40W
Hoorn 105 52 38N 5 4 E
Hoosick Falls 71 42 54N 73 21W
Hoover Dam 81 36 0N 114 45W
Hooversville 70 40 8N 78 57W
Hop Bottom 71 41 41N 75 47W
Hope, B.C., Can. 63 49 25N 121 25 E
Hope, Ont., Can. 50 43 53N 79 31W
Hope, Ariz., U.S.A. 81 33 43N 113 42W
Hope, Ark., U.S.A. 75 33 40N 93 30W
Hope, Ind., U.S.A. 77 39 18N 85 46W
Hope, N.D., U.S.A. 74 47 21N 97 42W
Hope Bay 91 65 0 S 55 0W
Hope I., B.C., Can. 62 50 55N 127 53W
Hope I., Ont., Can. 46 44 55N 80 11W
Hope Pt. 67 68 20N 166 50W
Hope Town 73 26 30N 76 30W
Hopedale 36 55 28N 60 13W
Hopelchén 83 19 46N 89 50W
Hopes Advance, C. 36 61 4N 69 34W
Hopetoun 136 33 57 S 120 7 E
Hopetown 117 29 34 S 24 3 E
Hopewell 39 45 29N 62 42W
Hopewell Cape 39 45 51N 64 35W
Hoping 131 24 31N 115 2 E
Hopkins, Mich., U.S.A. 77 42 37N 85 46W
Hopkins, Mo., U.S.A. 76 40 31N 94 45W
Hopkins, R. 136 37 55 S 142 40 E
Hopkinsville 73 36 52N 87 26W
Hopland 80 39 0N 123 7W
Hoppo 131 21 32N 109 6 E
Hoquiam 80 46 50N 123 55W
Hordaland fylke □ 111 60 25N 6 15 E
Hordern Hills 134 20 40 S 130 20 E
Horlick Mts. 91 84 0 S 102 0W
Hormoz 123 27 35N 55 0 E
Hormuz, I. 123 27 8N 56 28 E
Hormuz Str. 123 26 30N 56 30 E
Horn, Austria 106 48 39N 15 40 E
Horn, Isafjarðarsýsla, Iceland 110 66 28N 22 28W
Horn, Suður-Múlasýsla, Iceland 110 65 10N 13 31W
Horn, Cape = Hornos, C. de 90 55 50 S 67 30W
Horn Head 97 55 13N 8 0W
Horn, I. 73 30 17N 88 40W
Horn Mts. 54 62 15N 119 15W
Horn, R. 54 61 30N 118 1W
Hornaday, R. 64 69 19N 123 48W
Hornavan 110 66 15N 17 30 E
Hornbeck 75 31 22N 93 20W
Hornbrook 78 41 58N 122 37W
Hornby 49 43 34N 79 50W
Horncastle 94 53 13N 0 8W
Hornell 70 42 23N 77 41W
Hornell L. 54 62 20N 119 25W
Hornepayne 53 49 14N 84 48W
Hornings Mills 46 44 9N 80 12W
Hornitos 80 37 30N 120 14W
Hornos, Cabo de 90 55 50 S 67 30 E
Hornoy 101 49 50N 1 54 E
Hornsby 136 33 42 S 151 2 E
Hornsea 94 53 55N 0 10W
Hornu 105 50 26N 3 50 E
Horoshiri Dake 132 42 40N 142 40 E
Horqueta 88 23 15 S 56 55W
Horse Cr. 74 41 33N 104 45W
Horse Is. 37 50 15N 55 50W
Horsefly 63 52 20N 121 25W
Horsefly L. 63 52 25N 121 0W
Horsens 111 55 52N 9 51 E
Horseshoe Bay 66 49 22N 123 17W
Horseshoe Dam 79 33 45N 111 35W
Horsham, Austral. 136 36 44 S 142 13 E
Horsham, U.K. 95 51 4N 0 20W
Horten 111 59 25N 10 32 E
Horton 74 39 42N 95 30W
Horton, R. 67 69 56N 126 52W
Horwood 37 49 27N 54 32W
Horwood, L. 53 48 5N 82 20W
Hose, Pegunungan 126 2 5N 114 6 E
Hoshangabad 124 22 45N 77 45 E
Hoshiarpur 124 31 30N 75 58 E
Hosmer 74 45 36N 99 29W
Hospet 124 15 15N 76 20 E
Hospitalet de Llobregat 104 41 21N 2 6 E
Hospitalet, L' 102 42 36N 1 47 E
Hoste, I. 90 55 0 S 69 0W
Hostens 102 44 30N 0 40W
Hot 128 18 8N 98 29 E
Hot Creek Ra. 78 39 0N 116 0W
Hot Springs, Ark, U.S.A. 75 34 30N 93 0W
Hot Springs, S.D., U.S.A. 74 43 25N 103 30W
Hotagen, L. 110 63 50N 14 30 E
Hotchkiss 79 38 55N 107 47W
Hotchkiss, R. 60 57 2N 117 28W
Hotien (Khotan) 129 37 6N 79 59 E
Hoting 110 64 8N 16 15 E
Hottah L. 64 65 4N 118 30W
Hotte, Massif de la 85 18 30N 73 45W
Houat, I. 100 47 24N 2 58W
Houck 79 35 15N 109 15W
Houdan 101 48 48N 1 35 E
Houffalize 105 50 8N 5 48 E
Houghton 52 47 9N 88 39W
Houghton L. 46 44 20N 84 40W
Houghton Lake Heights 46 44 18N 84 51W
Houghton-le-Spring 94 54 51N 1 28W
Houhora 133 34 49 S 173 9 E
Houlton 35 46 5N 68 0W
Houma 75 29 35N 90 50W
Hourtin 102 45 11N 1 4W
Houston, Can. 54 54 25N 126 30W
Houston, Mo., U.S.A. 75 37 20N 92 0W
Houston, Tex., U.S.A. 75 29 50N 95 20W
Hovd (Jargalant) 129 48 2N 91 37 E
Hove 95 50 50N 0 10W
Hövsgöl Nuur 130 51 0N 100 30 E
Howard, Kans., U.S.A. 75 37 30N 96 16W
Howard, Penn., U.S.A. 70 41 0N 77 40W
Howard, S.D., U.S.A. 74 44 2N 97 30W
Howard L. 55 62 15N 105 57W
Howe 78 43 48N 113 0W
Howe, C. 136 37 30 S 150 0 E
Howe I. 47 44 16N 76 17W
Howe Sd. 63 49 35N 123 15W
Howell 46 42 38N 83 56W
Howick 43 45 11N 73 51W
Howley 37 49 12N 57 2W
Howrah 125 22 37N 88 27 E
Howth Hd. 97 53 21N 6 0W
Hoy I. 96 58 50N 3 15W
Høyanger 111 61 25N 6 50 E
Hpungan Pass 125 27 30N 96 55 E
Hrádec Králové 106 50 15N 15 50 E
Hron, R. 107 48 0N 18 4 E
Hrvatska 108 45 20N 16 0 E
Hsaichwan Shan 131 21 34N 112 30 E
Hsaio Shan 131 34 0N 111 30 E
Hsenwi 125 23 22N 97 55 E
Hsiamen 131 24 30N 118 7 E
Hsinchow 131 19 37N 109 17 E
Hsinchu 131 24 48N 120 58 E
Hsinhsing 131 22 45N 112 11 E
Hua Hin 128 12 34N 99 58 E
Huachacalla 82 18 45 S 68 17W
Huachinera 82 30 9N 108 55W
Huachipato 88 36 45 S 73 09W
Huacho 86 11 10 S 77 35W
Huachón 86 10 35 S 76 0W
Huacrachuco 86 8 35 S 76 50W
Huaian 131 33 28N 119 5 E
Huain 131 36 26N 119 12 E
Huajuapan 83 17 50N 98 0W
Hualien 131 24 0N 121 30 E
Huallaga, R. 86 5 30 S 76 10W
Hualpai Pk. 79 35 8N 113 58W
Huancabamba 86 5 10 S 79 15W
Huancané 86 15 10 S 69 50W
Huancapi 86 13 25 S 74 0W
Huancavelica 86 12 50 S 75 5W
Huancayo 86 12 5 S 75 0W
Huanglui 131 18 30N 108 46 E

Huangnipo **Incomáti, R**

Huangnipo 131 27 40N 105 10 E
Huánuco 86 9 55 S 76 15W
Huaraz 86 9 30 S 77 32W
Huarmey 86 10 5 S 78 5W
Huasamota 82 22 30N 104 30W
Huascarán 86 9 0 S 77 30W
Huasco 88 28 24 S 71 15W
Huasco, R. 88 28 27 S 71 13W
Huasna 81 35 6N 120 24W
Huatabampo 82 26 50N 109 50W
Huauchinango 83 20 11N 98 3W
Huautla 82 18 20N 96 50W
Huautla de Jiménez 83 18 8N 96 51W
Huay Namota 82 21 56N 104 30W
Huayllay 86 11 03 S 76 21W
Hubbard, Can. 56 51 8N 103 22W
Hubbard, Iowa, U.S.A. 76 42 18N 93 18W
Hubbard, Tex., U.S.A. 75 31 50N 96 50W
Hubbard L. 46 44 49N 83 34W
Hubbards 39 44 38N 64 4W
Hubbart Pt. 55 59 21N 94 41W
Hubbell 52 47 11N 88 26W
Hubli-Dharwar 124 15 22N 75 15 E
Huchow 131 30 57N 120 1 E
Huchuetenango 82 15 25N 91 30W
Huddersfield 94 53 38N 1 49W
Hudiksvall 111 61 43N 17 10 E
Hudson, Ont., Can. 52 50 6N 92 09W
Hudson, Qué., Can. 44 45 27N 74 9W
Hudson, Mass., U.S.A. 71 42 23N 71 35W
Hudson, Mich., U.S.A. 77 41 50N 84 20W
Hudson, N.Y., U.S.A. 71 42 15N 73 46W
Hudson, Wis., U.S.A. 74 44 57N 92 45W
Hudson, Wyo., U.S.A. 78 42 54N 108 37W
Hudson B. 55 59 0N 91 0W
Hudson Bay, Can. 65 60 0N 86 0W
Hudson Bay, Sask., Can. 57 52 51N 102 23W
Hudson Falls 71 43 18N 73 34W
Hudson Heights 44 45 28N 74 10W
Hudson Hope 54 56 0N 121 54W
Hudson, R. 71 40 42N 74 2W
Hudson Str. 65 62 0N 70 0W
Hudsonville 77 42 52N 85 52W
Hudwin L. 57 53 12N 95 41W
Hué 128 16 30N 107 35 E
Huehuetenango 84 15 20N 91 28W
Huejúcar 82 22 21N 103 13W
Huelgoat 100 48 22N 3 46W
Huelva 104 37 18N 6 57W
Huentelauquén 88 31 38 S 71 33W
Huerta, Sa. de la 88 31 10 S 67 30W
Huesca 104 42 8N 0 25W
Huétamo 82 18 36N 100 54W
Hugh, R. 134 25 1 S 134 10 E
Hughenden 135 20 52 S 144 10 E
Hughes 67 66 0N 154 20W
Hugo, Colo., U.S.A. 74 39 12N 103 27W
Hugo, Okla., U.S.A. 75 34 0N 95 30W
Hugoton 75 37 18N 101 22W
Huhehot 130 40 52N 111 36 E
Huichapán 83 20 24N 99 40W
Huila □ 86 2 30N 75 45W
Huila, Nevado del 86 3 0N 76 0W
Huiling Shan 131 21 35N 111 57 E
Huinan 130 42 40N 126 5 E
Huinca Renancó 88 34 51 S 64 22W
Huixtla 83 15 9N 92 28W
Huiya 122 24 40N 49 15 E
Huizen 105 52 18N 5 14 E
Hukawng Valley 125 26 30N 96 30 E
Hukow 131 29 38N 116 25 E
Hulaifa 122 25 58N 41 0 E
Hulan 130 46 0N 126 44 E
Hulbert 46 46 21N 85 9W
Huld 130 45 5N 105 30 E
Hulin 130 45 45N 133 0 E
Hull, Can. 48 45 25N 75 44W
Hull, U.K. 94 53 45N 0 20W
Hull, U.S.A. 76 39 43N 91 13W
Hull, R. 94 53 55N 0 23W
Hulst 105 51 17N 4 2 E
Huma 130 51 44N 126 42 E
Humacao 67 18 9N 65 50W
Humahuaca 88 23 10 S 65 25W
Humaitá 86 7 35 S 62 40W
Humaita 88 27 2 S 58 31W
Humansville 76 37 48N 93 35W
Humber 49 43 54N 79 49W
Humber B. 50 43 38N 79 28W
Humber Bay 50 43 38N 79 27W
Humber, R., Can. 50 43 38N 79 28W
Humber, R., U.K. 94 53 40N 0 10W
Humberside □ 94 53 50N 0 30W
Humberstone 70 42 53N 79 16W
Humble 75 29 59N 95 10W
Humboldt, Can. 56 52 15N 105 9W
Humboldt, Iowa, U.S.A. 76 42 42N 94 15W
Humboldt, Minn., U.S.A. 57 48 53N 97 7W
Humboldt, Tenn., U.S.A. 73 35 50N 88 55W
Humboldt Gletscher 65 79 30N 62 0W
Humboldt, R. 78 40 55N 116 0W
Hume, Calif., U.S.A. 80 36 48N 118 54W
Hume, Kans., U.S.A. 76 38 5N 94 35W
Hume, L. 136 36 0 S 147 0 E
Humeston 76 40 51N 93 30W
Humphreys, Mt. 80 37 17N 118 40W
Humphreys Pk. 79 35 24N 111 38W
Humptulips 80 47 14N 123 57W
Huna Floi 110 65 50N 20 50W
Hunan □ 131 27 30N 111 30 E
Hunchun 130 42 49N 130 31 E
Hundred and Fifty Mile House 63 52 7N 121 57W
Hundred Mile House 63 51 38N 121 18W
Hunedoara 107 45 40N 22 50 E
Hung Ho, R. 131 32 25N 115 35 E
Hungary ■ 107 47 20N 19 20 E
Hungary, Plain of 93 47 0N 20 0 E
Hunghai Wan 131 22 45N 115 15 E
Hunghu (Sinti) 131 29 49N 113 30 E
Hungkiang 131 27 0N 109 49 E
Hŭngnam 130 39 55N 127 45 E
Hungshui Ho, R. 131 23 24N 110 12 E
Hungtze Hu 131 33 20N 118 35 E
Hunsrück, mts. 105 49 30N 7 0 E
Hunstanton 94 52 57N 0 30 E
Hunstsville 77 40 26N 83 48W
Hunter, N.D., U.S.A. 74 47 12N 97 17W
Hunter, N.Y., U.S.A. 71 42 13N 74 13W
Hunter, C. 65 71 42N 72 30W
Hunter, I. 135 40 30 S 144 54 E
Hunter I. 62 51 55N 128 0W
Hunter, R. 136 32 52 S 151 46 E
Hunter Ra. 136 32 45 S 150 15 E
Hunterville 133 39 56 S 175 35 E
Huntingburg 77 38 20N 86 58W
Huntingdon, Can. 43 45 6N 74 10W
Huntingdon, U.K. 95 52 20N 0 11W
Huntingdon, N.Y., U.S.A. 71 40 52N 73 25W
Huntingdon, Pa., U.S.A. 70 40 28N 78 1W
Huntingdon □ 43 45 5N 74 15W
Huntington, Ind., U.S.A. 77 40 52N 85 30W
Huntington, Oreg., U.S.A. 78 44 22N 117 21W
Huntington, Ut., U.S.A. 78 39 24N 111 1W
Huntington, W. Va., U.S.A. 72 38 20N 82 30W
Huntington Beach 81 33 40N 118 0W
Huntington Park 79 33 58N 118 15W
Huntington, Resr. 77 40 49N 85 25W
Huntley 77 42 10N 88 26W
Huntly, N.Z. 133 37 34 S 175 11 E
Huntly, U.K. 96 57 27N 2 48W
Huntsville, Can. 46 45 20N 79 14W
Huntsville, Ala., U.S.A. 73 34 45N 86 35W
Huntsville, Mo., U.S.A. 76 39 26N 92 33W
Huntsville, Tex., U.S.A. 75 30 45N 95 35W
Huonville 135 43 0 S 147 5 E
Hupei □ 131 31 5N 113 5 E
Hupel 63 50 37N 118 44W
Hurd C. 70 45 15N 81 40W
Hurley, N. Mex., U.S.A. 79 32 45N 108 7W
Hurley, Wis., U.S.A. 52 46 26N 90 10W
Huron, Calif., U.S.A. 80 36 12N 120 6W
Huron, Ohio, U.S.A. 70 41 22N 82 34W
Huron, S.D., U.S.A. 74 44 30N 98 20W
Huron B. 52 46 57N 88 9W
Huron, L. 46 45 0N 83 0W
Hurons, R. des 45 45 28N 73 16W
Hurricane 79 37 10N 113 12W
Hurstbridge 136 37 40 S 145 10 E
Hurunui, R. 133 42 54 S 173 18 E
Húsavík 110 66 3N 17 21W
Huskvarna 111 57 47N 14 15 E
Huslia 67 65 40N 156 30W
Hussar 61 51 3N 112 41W
Hutag 130 49 25N 102 34 E
Hutchinson, Kans., U.S.A. 75 38 3N 97 59W
Hutchinson, Minn, U.S.A. 74 44 50N 94 22W
Huto Ho 130 38 30N 113 45 E
Hutsonville 77 39 6N 87 40W
Hutte Sauvage, L. de la 36 56 15N 64 45W
Huttig 75 33 5N 92 10W
Huttonsville 49 43 38N 79 48W
Huy 105 50 31N 5 15 E
Hvammsfjörður 110 65 4N 22 5W
Hvammur 110 65 13N 21 49W
Hvar, I. 108 43 11N 16 28 E
Hvítá, Arnessýsla, Iceland 110 64 0N 20 58W
Hvítá, Mýrasýsla, Iceland 110 64 40N 21 5W
Hvítárvatn 110 63 37N 19 50W
Hwachwan 130 47 1N 130 50 E
Hwai Ho 131 32 20N 114 30 E
Hwainan 131 32 44N 117 1 E
Hwaiyang 131 33 50N 115 2 E
Hwan Ho 130 37 10N 117 30 E
Hwang-ho, R. 130 40 50N 107 30 E
Hwangan 131 31 30N 114 40 E
Hwangshih 131 30 27N 115 0 E
Hwangyen 131 28 34N 121 12 E
Hwanjen 130 41 24N 125 26 E
Hwateh 130 41 58N 113 58 E
Hwatien 130 43 0N 126 52 E
Hweian 131 25 2N 118 56 E
Hweichang 131 25 33N 115 41 E
Hweihsien 131 35 30N 113 46 E
Hweilai 131 23 0N 116 15 E
Hweimin 130 37 36N 117 30 E
Hweining 130 35 45N 105 0 E
Hweitseh 129 26 32N 103 6 E
Hwokiu 131 32 23N 116 16 E
Hyannis 74 42 0N 101 45W
Hyas 57 51 54N 102 16W
Hyattsville 72 38 59N 76 55W
Hydaburg 67 55 15N 132 45W
Hyde In. 65 75 2N 80 0W
Hyderabad, India 124 17 10N 78 29 E
Hyderabad, Pak. 124 25 23N 68 36 E
Hyderabad □ 124 25 3N 68 24 E
Hyères 103 43 8N 6 9 E
Hyères, Is. d' 103 43 0N 6 28 E
Hyesan 130 41 20N 128 10 E
Hyland, R. 54 59 52N 128 12W
Hymers 52 48 18N 89 43W
Hyndman Pk. 78 43 50N 114 0W
Hyōgo-ken □ 132 35 15N 135 0 E
Hyrum 78 41 35N 111 56W
Hysham 78 46 21N 107 11W
Hythe, Can. 60 55 20N 119 33W
Hythe, U.K. 95 51 4N 1 5 E
Hyvinkä 111 60 38N 24 50 E

I

Iaco, R. 86 10 25 S 70 30W
Ialomiţa, R. 107 44 45N 27 57 E
Ian L. 62 53 50N 132 45W
Iaşi 107 47 10N 27 40 E
Iauaretê 86 0 30N 69 5W
Iba 127 15 22N 120 0 E
Ibadan 114 7 22N 3 58 E
Ibagué 86 4 27N 73 14W
Ibar, R. 109 43 15N 20 40 E
Ibaraki-ken □ 132 36 10N 140 10 E
Ibarra 86 0 21N 78 7W
Ibera, Laguna 88 28 30 S 57 9W
Iberia 76 38 5N 92 18W
Iberian Peninsula 93 40 0N 5 0W
Iberville 45 45 19N 73 17W
Iberville □ 45 45 15N 73 10W
Iberville, Lac d' 36 55 55N 73 15W
Iberville, Mt. d' 36 58 50N 63 50W
Ibiá 87 19 30 S 46 30W
Ibicuy 88 33 55 S 59 10W
Ibiracu 87 19 50 S 40 30W
Ibiza 104 38 54N 1 26 E
Ibiza, I. 104 39 0N 1 30 E
Ibo 117 12 22 S 40 32 E
Ibonma 127 3 22 S 133 31 E
Ibotirama 87 12 13 S 43 12W
Ibu 127 1 35N 127 25 E
Ica 86 14 0 S 75 30W
Ica, R. 86 2 55 S 69 0W
Icabarú 86 4 20N 61 45W
Içana 86 1 21N 69 0W
Iceland, I. ■ 110 65 0N 19 0W
Icha 121 55 30N 156 0 E
Ichang 131 30 48N 111 29 E
Ichchapuram 125 19 10N 84 40 E
Ichihara 132 35 28N 140 5 E
Ichikawa 132 35 44N 139 55 E
Ichilo, R. 86 16 30 S 64 45W
Ichinomiya 132 35 18N 136 48 E
Ichun, Heilungkiang, China 129 47 42N 129 8 E
Ichun, Kiangsi, China 131 27 51N 114 12 E
Ichun, Shensi, China 130 35 24N 109 9 E
Ichung 131 25 30N 112 29 E
Ichwan 130 36 9N 109 58 E
Icy C. 17 70 25N 162 0W
Icy Str. 54 58 20N 135 30W
Ida 77 41 55N 83 34W
Ida Grove 74 42 20N 95 25W
Idabel 75 33 53N 94 50W
Idaho □ 78 44 10N 114 0W
Idaho City 78 43 50N 115 52W
Idaho Falls 78 43 30N 112 10W
Idaho Springs 78 39 49N 105 30W
Idar-Oberstein 105 49 43N 7 19 E
Idhi Oros 109 35 15N 24 45 E
Idhra 109 37 20N 23 28 E
Idi 126 4 55N 97 45 E
Idi Amin Dada, L. 116 0 25 S 29 40 E
Idiofa 116 4 55 S 19 42 E
Idria 80 36 25N 120 41W
Idutywa 117 32 8 S 28 18 E
Ieper 105 50 51N 2 53 E
Ierápetra 109 35 0N 25 44 E
Ierzu 108 39 48N 9 32 E
Ifanadiana 117 21 29 S 47 39 E
Ife 114 7 30N 4 31 E
Igarapava 87 20 3 S 47 47W
Igarapé Açu 87 1 4 S 47 33W
Igarka 121 67 30N 87 20 E
Igatimi 89 24 5 S 55 30W
Iggesund 111 61 39N 17 10 E
Iglésias 108 39 19N 8 27 E
Igloolik 65 69 20N 81 30W
Ignace 52 49 30N 91 40W
Igornachoix Bay 37 50 40N 57 25W
Iguaçu, Cat. del 89 25 41N 54 26W
Iguaçu, R. 89 25 30 S 53 10W
Iguala 83 18 20N 99 40W
Igualada 104 41 37N 1 37 E
Iguape, R. 89 24 40 S 48 0W
Iguassu = Iguaçu 89 25 41N 54 26W
Iguatu 87 6 20 S 39 18W
Iguéla 116 2 0 S 9 16 E
Ihing 131 31 21N 119 51 E
Ihosy 117 22 24 S 46 8 E
Ihsien 130 41 45N 121 3 E
Ihwang 131 27 30N 116 2 E
Ii 110 65 15N 25 30 E
Iida 132 35 35N 138 0 E
Iijoki 110 65 20N 26 15 E
Iisalmi 110 63 32N 27 10 E
Iizuka 132 33 38N 130 42 E
IJmuiden 105 52 28N 4 35 E
IJsselmeer 105 52 45N 5 20 E
IJsselstein 105 52 1N 5 2 E
Ijuí, R. 89 27 58 S 55 20W
Ikamatua 99 42 15 S 171 41 E
Ikaria, I. 109 37 35N 26 10 E
Ikela 116 1 0 S 23 35 E
Iki 132 33 45N 129 42 E
Ilan 130 46 14N 129 33 E
Ilanskiy 121 56 14N 96 3 E
Ile-à-la Crosse 55 55 27N 107 53W
Île-à-la-Crosse, Lac 55 55 40N 107 45W
Île-aux-Noix 43 45 8N 73 17W
Île-Bizard 44 45 29N 73 53W
Île-Bouchard, L' 100 47 7N 0 26 E
Île-Cadieux 44 45 25N 74 1W
Île de France □ 101 49 0N 2 20 E
Ile d'Orleans, Chenal de l' 42 46 58N 71 0W
Île-Perrot 44 45 23N 73 57W
Île-Perrot-Sud 44 45 21N 73 54W
Île-Sainte-Thérèse 43 45 22N 73 15W
Ile-sur-le-Doubs, L' 101 47 26N 6 34 E
Ilebo 116 4 17 S 20 47 E
Ilek 120 51 32N 53 21 E
Ilek, R. 120 51 30N 53 22 E
Îles, L. des 40 46 20N 75 18W
Ilford 55 56 4N 95 35W
Ilfracombe, Austral. 135 23 30 S 144 30 E
Ilfracombe, U.K. 95 51 13N 4 8W
Ilheus 87 14 49 S 39 2W
Iliamna L. 67 59 35N 155 30W
Ilich 120 40 50N 68 27 E
Ilico 88 34 50 S 72 20W
Iliff 74 40 50N 103 3W
Ilio Pt. 67 21 13N 157 16W
Iliodhrómia 109 39 12N 23 50 E
Ilion 71 43 0N 75 3W
Iliysk 120 44 10N 77 20 E
Ilkeston 94 52 59N 1 19W
Ilkhuri Shan 130 51 30N 124 0 E
Ilkley 92 53 56N 1 49W
Illana B. 127 7 35N 123 45 E
Illapel 88 32 0 S 71 10W
Ille 102 42 40N 2 37 E
Ille-et-Vilaine □ 100 48 10N 1 30W
Iller, R. 106 47 53N 10 10 E
Illimani, Mte. 86 16 30 S 67 50W
Illinois □ 69 40 15N 89 30W
Illinois R. 76 38 5N 90 28W
Illiopolis 76 39 51N 89 15W
Illukotat, R. 36 60 48N 78 11W
Ilo 86 17 40 S 71 20W
Iloilo 127 10 45N 122 33 E
Ilorin 114 8 30N 4 35 E
Ilwaco 80 46 19N 124 3W
Ilwaki 127 7 55 S 126 30 E
Imabari 132 34 4N 133 0 E
Iman = Dalneretchensk 121 45 50N 133 40 E
Imandra, Oz. 120 67 45N 33 0 E
Imari 132 33 15N 129 52 E
Imbler 78 45 31N 118 0W
Imeni Poliny Osipenko 121 55 25N 136 29 E
Imeri, Serra 86 0 50N 65 25W
Imienpo 130 45 0N 128 16 E
Imlay 78 40 45N 118 9W
Imlay City 46 43 0N 83 2W
Immingham 94 53 37N 0 12W
Immokalee 73 26 25N 81 20W
Imola 108 44 20N 11 42 E
Imperatriz 87 5 30 S 47 29W
Impéria 108 43 52N 8 0 E
Imperial, Can. 56 51 21N 105 28W
Imperial, Calif., U.S.A. 81 32 52N 115 34W
Imperial, Nebr., U.S.A. 74 40 38N 101 39W
Imperial Beach 81 32 35N 117 8W
Imperial Dam 81 32 50N 114 30W
Imperial Res. 81 32 53N 114 28W
Imperial Valley 81 32 55N 115 30W
Impfondo 116 1 40N 18 0 E
Imphal 125 24 48N 93 56 E
Imphy 101 46 56N 3 15 E
Imuruan B. 127 10 40N 119 10 E
In Salah 114 27 10N 2 32 E
Ina 132 35 50N 138 0 E
Inangahua Junc. 133 41 52 S 171 59 E
Inanwatan 127 2 10 S 132 5 E
Iñapari 86 11 0 S 69 40W
Inari 110 68 54N 27 5 E
Inari, L. 110 69 0N 28 0 E
Inawashir-Ko 132 37 28N 140 2 E
Inca 104 39 43N 2 54 E
Incaguasi 88 29 12 S 71 5W
Ince Burnu 122 42 2N 35 0 E
Inchŏn 130 37 32N 126 45 E
Incomáti, R. 117 25 15 S 32 35 E

Incudine, Mte. l' Jacmel

Incudine, Mte. l' **103** 41 50N 9 12 E
Indalsälven **110** 62 36N 17 30 E
Indaw **125** 24 15N 96 5 E
Independence, Calif., U.S.A. **80** 36 51N 118 7W
Independence, Iowa, U.S.A. **76** 42 27N 91 52W
Independence, Kans., U.S.A. **75** 37 10N 95 50W
Independence, Ky., U.S.A. **77** 38 57N 84 33W
Independence, Mo., U.S.A. **76** 39 3N 94 25W
Independence, Oreg., U.S.A. **78** 44 53N 123 6W
Independence Fjord **17** 82 10N 29 0W
Independence Mts. **78** 41 30N 116 2W
Independencia, La **83** 16 31N 91 47W
Index **80** 47 50N 121 33W
India ■ **119** 20 0N 80 0 E
Indian Arm **66** 49 23N 122 53W
Indian Cabins **54** 59 52N 117 2W
Indian Harbour **36** 54 27N 57 13W
Indian Head **56** 50 30N 103 35W
Indian L. **52** 50 14N 94 5W
Indian Ocean **11** 5 0S 75 0 E
Indian Springs **68** 36 35N 115 40W
Indiana **70** 40 38N 79 9W
Indiana □ **72** 40 0N 86 0W
Indianapolis **77** 39 42N 86 10W
Indianola, Iowa, U.S.A. **76** 41 20N 93 38W
Indianola, Miss., U.S.A. **75** 33 27N 90 40W
Indiga **120** 67 50N 48 50 E
Indigirka, R. **121** 69 0N 147 0 E
Indio **81** 33 46N 116 15W
Indonesia ■ **126** 5 0S 115 0 E
Indore **124** 22 42N 75 53 E
Indramaju **127** 6 21S 108 20 E
Indramaju, Tg. **127** 6 20S 108 20 E
Indravati, R. **125** 19 0N 81 15 E
Indre □ **101** 47 12N 1 39 E
Indre-et-Loire □ **100** 47 12N 0 40 E
Indre, R. **100** 47 2N 1 8 E
Indus, R. **124** 28 40N 70 10 E
Industry **76** 40 20N 90 36W
İnebolu **122** 41 55N 33 40 E
Infiernillo, Presa del **82** 18 9N 102 0W
Ingelmunster **105** 50 56N 3 16 E
Ingende **116** 0 12S 18 57 E
Ingenio Santa Ana **88** 27 25S 65 40W
Ingersoll **46** 43 4N 80 55W
Ingham **135** 18 43S 146 10 E
Ingleborough, mt. **94** 54 11N 2 23W
Inglefield G. **65** 77 30N 67 0W
Inglega **136** 31 20S 147 50 E
Inglewood, Queensland, Austral. **136** 28 25S 151 8 E
Inglewood, Vic., Austral. **136** 36 29S 143 53 E
Inglewood, Can. **49** 43 47N 79 56W
Inglewood, N.Z. **133** 39 9S 174 14 E
Inglewood, U.S.A. **81** 33 58N 118 21W
Ingólfshöfði **110** 63 48N 16 39W
Ingolstadt **106** 48 45N 11 26 E
Ingomar, Can. **39** 43 34N 65 22W
Ingomar, U.S.A. **78** 46 43N 107 37W
Ingonish **39** 46 42N 60 18W
Ingonish Beach **39** 46 38N 60 25W
Inhambane **117** 23 54S 35 30 E
Inhaminga **117** 18 26S 35 0 E
Inharrime **117** 24 30S 35 0 E
Ining **131** 25 8N 109 57 E
Ining (Kuldja) **129** 43 57N 81 20 E
Inirida, R. **86** 3 0N 68 40W
Inishbofin I. **97** 53 35N 10 12W
Inishmore, I. **97** 53 8N 9 45W
Inishowen, Pen. **97** 55 14N 7 15W
Injune **135** 25 46S 148 32 E
Inkerman **39** 47 40N 64 49W
Inklin **54** 58 56N 133 5W
Inklin, R. **54** 58 50N 133 10W
Inkom **78** 42 51N 112 7W
Inkpen Beacon **95** 51 22N 1 28W
Inle Aing **125** 20 30N 96 58 E
Inn, R. **106** 48 35N 13 28 E
Inner Hebrides, Is. **96** 57 0N 6 30W
Inner Mongolia □ **130** 44 50N 117 40 E
Inner Sound **96** 57 30N 5 55W
Innerkip, Can. **70** 43 12N 80 41W
Innerkip, Ont., Can. **46** 43 13N 80 42W
Innetalling I. **36** 56 0N 79 0W
Innisfail, Austral. **135** 17 33S 146 5 E
Innisfail, Can. **61** 52 0N 113 57W
Innisfree **60** 53 22N 111 32W
Innsbruck **106** 47 16N 11 23 E
Inongo **116** 1 35S 18 30 E
Inosu **86** 12 22N 71 38W
Inoucdjouac (Port Harrison) **36** 58 27N 78 6W
Inowrocław **107** 52 50N 18 20 E
Inquisivi **86** 16 50S 66 45W
Intata Reach **62** 53 38N 125 30W
Intendente Alvear **88** 35 12S 63 32W
Interior **74** 43 46N 101 59W
Interlaken **101** 46 41N 7 50 E
International Falls **52** 48 36N 93 25W
Interview I. **128** 12 55N 92 42 E
Inthanon, Mt. **128** 18 35N 98 29 E
Intiyaco **88** 28 50S 60 0W
Inútil, B. **90** 53 30S 70 15W
Inuvik **67** 68 16N 133 40W
Inveraray **96** 56 13N 5 5W
Inverbervie **96** 56 50N 2 17W
Invercargill **133** 46 24S 168 24 E
Inverell **135** 29 45S 151 8 E
Invergordon **96** 57 41N 4 10W
Invermay **56** 51 48N 103 9W
Invermere **61** 50 30N 116 2W
Inverness, Can. **39** 46 15N 61 19W
Inverness, U.K. **96** 57 29N 4 12W
Inverness, U.S.A. **73** 28 50N 82 20W
Inverurie **96** 57 15N 2 21W
Investigator Group **134** 34 45S 134 20 E
Investigator Str. **135** 35 30S 137 0 E
Invona **70** 40 46N 78 35W
Inwood **57** 50 30N 97 30W
Inyo Range **79** 37 0N 118 0W
Inyokern **81** 35 37N 117 54W
Inza **120** 53 55N 46 25 E
Ioánnina (Janinà) □ **109** 39 39N 20 57 E
Ioco **66** 49 18N 122 53W
Iola **75** 38 0N 95 20W
Iona **39** 45 58N 60 48W
Iona I. **96** 56 20N 6 25W
Ione, Calif., U.S.A. **80** 38 20N 121 0W
Ione, Wash., U.S.A. **63** 48 44N 117 29W
Ionia **77** 42 59N 85 7W
Ionian Is. = Ionioi Nisoi **109** 38 40N 20 0 E
Ionian Sea **109** 37 30N 17 30 E
Iónioi Nísoi **109** 38 40N 20 8 E
Íos, I. **109** 36 41N 25 20 E
Iowa □ **74** 42 18N 93 30W
Iowa City **76** 41 40N 91 35W
Iowa Falls **76** 42 30N 93 15W
Iowa, R. **76** 41 10N 91 1W
Ipameri **87** 17 44S 48 9W
Ipiales **86** 0 50N 77 37W
Ipin **129** 28 48N 104 33 E
Ípiros □ **109** 39 30N 20 30 E
Ipixuna **86** 7 0S 71 40W
Ipoh **128** 4 35N 101 5 E
Ippy **116** 6 5N 21 7 E
Ipswich, Austral. **135** 27 35S 152 46 E
Ipswich, U.K. **95** 52 4N 1 9 E
Ipswich, N.H., U.S.A. **71** 42 40N 70 50W
Ipswich, S.D., U.S.A. **74** 45 28N 99 20W
Ipu **87** 4 23S 40 44W
Iquique **86** 20 19S 70 5W
Iquitos **86** 3 45S 73 10W
Iracoubo **87** 5 30N 53 10W
Iráklion **109** 35 20N 25 12 E
Irala **89** 25 55S 54 35W
Iran ■ **123** 33 0N 53 0 E
Iran, Pegunungan **126** 2 20N 114 50 E
Iran, Plateau of **101** 33 00N 55 0 E
Irānshahr **123** 27 75N 60 40 E
Irapa **86** 10 34N 62 35W
Irapuato **82** 20 40N 101 40W
Iraq ■ **122** 33 0N 44 0 E
Irati **89** 25 25S 50 38W
Irbid **115** 32 35N 35 48 E
Irebu **116** 0 40S 17 55 E
Ireland ■ **97** 53 0N 8 0W
Ireland's Eye **97** 53 25N 6 4W
Irentala Steppe **130** 43 45N 112 15 E
Iret **121** 60 10N 154 5 E
Irian Jaya □ **127** 4 0S 137 0 E
Iringa **116** 7 48S 35 43 E
Iriomote **131** 24 25N 123 58 E
Iriona **84** 15 57N 85 11W
Irish Republic ■ **97** 53 0N 8 0 E
Irish Sea **94** 54 0N 5 0W
Irish Town **124** 40 55S 145 9 E
Irkutsk **121** 52 10N 104 20 E
Irma **61** 52 55N 111 14W
Irmak **122** 39 58N 33 25 E
Iroise, Mer d' **100** 48 15N 4 45W
Iron Bridge **46** 46 17N 83 14W
Iron Knob **135** 32 46S 137 8 E
Iron Mountain **72** 45 49N 88 4W
Iron River, Mich., U.S.A. **74** 46 6N 88 40W
Iron River, Wis., U.S.A. **52** 46 34N 91 24W
Iron Springs **61** 49 56N 112 41W
Ironbridge **95** 52 38N 2 29W
Irondale **70** 44 51N 78 30W
Ironside **48** 45 27N 75 45W
Ironton, Mo., U.S.A. **75** 37 40N 90 40W
Ironton, Ohio, U.S.A. **72** 38 35N 82 40W
Ironwood **52** 46 30N 90 10W
Iroquois **47** 44 51N 75 19W
Iroquois Falls **34** 48 46N 80 41W
Iroquois, R. **77** 41 5N 87 49W
Irrawaddy, R. **125** 15 50N 95 6 E
Irshih **130** 47 8N 119 57 E
Irtysh, R. **120** 53 36N 75 30 E
Irumu **116** 1 32N 29 53 E
Irún **104** 43 20N 1 52W
Irvine, Can. **61** 49 57N 110 16W
Irvine, U.K. **96** 55 37N 4 40W
Irvine, U.S.A. **72** 37 42N 83 58W
Irvine, R. **96** 55 35N 4 40W
Irvinestown **97** 54 28N 7 38W
Irvington **77** 37 53N 86 17W
Irymple **136** 34 14S 142 8 E
Is-sur-Tille **101** 47 30N 5 10 E
Isaac, R. **135** 22 55S 149 20 E
Isabel **74** 45 27N 101 22W
Isabela, Dom. Rep. **85** 19 58N 71 2W
Isabela, Pto Rico **67** 18 30N 67 01W
Isabela, Cord. **84** 13 30N 85 25W
Isabela, I. **82** 21 51N 105 55W
Isachsen **65** 78 47N 103 30W
Ísafjarðardjúp **110** 66 10N 23 0W
Ísafjörður **110** 66 5N 23 9W
Isangi **116** 0 52N 24 10 E
Isar, R. **106** 48 40N 12 30 E
Isbergues **101** 50 36N 2 24 E
Íschia, I. **108** 40 45N 13 51 E
Iscuandé **86** 2 28N 77 59W
Ise **132** 34 25N 136 45 E
Ise-Wan **132** 34 43N 136 43 E
Isère □ **103** 45 15N 5 40 E
Isère, R. **102** 45 15N 5 30 E
Iserlohn **105** 51 22N 7 40 E
Ishan **130** 24 30N 108 41 E
Ishigaki **131** 24 26N 124 10 E
Ishikari-Wan **132** 43 20N 141 20 E
Ishikawa-ken □ **132** 36 30N 136 30 E
Ishim **120** 56 10N 69 18 E
Ishim, R. **120** 57 45N 71 10 E
Ishinomaki **132** 38 32N 141 20 E
Ishkuman **124** 36 30N 73 50 E
Ishpeming **53** 46 30N 87 40W
Isigny-sur-Mer **100** 49 19N 1 6W
Isil Kul **120** 54 55N 71 16 E
Isili **102** 39 45N 9 6 E
Isiolo **116** 0 24N 37 33 E
Isiro **116** 2 53N 27 58 E
İskenderun **122** 36 32N 36 10 E
Iskut, R. **54** 56 45N 131 49W
Isla, La **86** 6 51N 76 56W
Isla, R. **96** 56 32N 3 20W
Islamabad **124** 33 40N 73 0 E
Island Falls, Can. **53** 49 35N 81 20W
Island Falls, U.S.A. **35** 46 0N 68 25W
Island L., Can. **55** 53 47N 94 25W
Island L., U.S.A. **52** 47 7N 92 10W
Island Pond, Can. **37** 48 25N 56 23W
Island Pond, U.S.A. **71** 44 50N 71 50W
Island, R. **54** 60 25N 121 12W
Islands, B. of, Can. **37** 49 11N 58 15W
Islands, B. of, N.Z. **133** 35 20S 174 20 E
Islay **60** 53 24N 110 33W
Islay, I. **96** 55 46N 6 10W
Islay Sound **96** 55 45N 6 5W
Isle-Adam, L' **101** 49 6N 2 14 E
Isle aux Morts **37** 47 35N 59 0W
Isle-Jourdain, L', Gers, France **102** 43 36N 1 5 E
Isle-Jourdain, L', Vienne, France **100** 46 13N 0 31 E
Isle L. **60** 53 38N 114 44W
Isle of Wight □ **95** 50 40N 1 20W
Isle Pierre **62** 53 57N 123 16W
Isle Royale **52** 48 0N 88 50W
Isle Royale Nat. Park **52** 48 0N 89 0W
Isle-sur-la-Sorgue, L' **103** 43 55N 5 2 E
Isle Verte, L' **41** 48 1N 69 20W
Isle Vista **81** 34 27N 119 52W
Isles, L. des **52** 49 10N 89 40W
Islet, L' **35** 47 4N 70 23W
Isleta **79** 34 58N 106 46W
Isleton **80** 38 10N 121 37W
Islington **50** 43 38N 79 32W
Ismâ'ilîya **122** 30 37N 32 18 E
Ismay **74** 46 33N 104 44W
Isparta **122** 37 47N 30 30 E
Íspica **108** 36 47N 14 53 E
Israel ■ **115** 32 0N 34 50 E
Issoire **102** 45 32N 3 15 E
Issoudun, Can. **41** 46 35N 71 38W
Issoudun, France **101** 46 57N 2 0 E
Issyk-Kul, Ozero **120** 42 25N 77 15 E
İstanbul **122** 41 0N 29 0 E
Istiaía **86** 38 57N 23 10 E
Istmina **86** 5 10N 76 39W
Istokpoga, L. **73** 27 22N 81 14W
Istra **108** 45 10N 14 0 E
Istres **103** 43 31N 4 59 E
Istria = Istra **108** 45 10N 14 0 E
Itá **88** 25 29N 57 21W
Itabaiana **87** 7 18S 35 19W
Itaberaba **87** 12 32S 40 18W
Itabira **87** 19 37S 43 13W
Itabirito **89** 20 15S 43 48W
Itabuna **87** 14 48S 39 16W
Itaete **87** 13 0S 41 5W
Itaituba **87** 4 10S 55 50W
Itajaí **89** 27 0S 48 45W
Itajubá **89** 22 24S 45 30W
Italy ■ **108** 42 0N 13 0 E
Itambe, mt. **87** 18 30S 43 15W
Itapecuru, R. **87** 3 20S 44 15W
Itaperuna **87** 21 10S 42 0W
Itapetininga **89** 23 36S 48 7W
Itapeva **89** 23 59S 48 59W
Itapicuru, R., Bahia, Brazil **87** 10 50S 38 40W
Itapicuru, R., Maranhão, Brazil **87** 5 40S 44 30W
Itapuá □ **89** 26 40S 55 40W
Itaquari **89** 20 12S 40 25W
Itaquatiana **86** 2 58S 58 30W
Itaquí **88** 29 0S 56 30W
Itararé **89** 24 6S 49 23W
Itatí **88** 27 16S 58 15W
Itatuba **86** 5 40S 63 20W
Itbayat I. **131** 20 45N 121 50 E
Itchen, R. **95** 50 57N 1 20W
Ithaca, Mich., U.S.A. **46** 43 18N 84 36W
Ithaca, N.Y., U.S.A. **71** 42 25N 76 30W
Itháki **109** 38 25N 20 43 E
Ito **132** 34 58N 139 5 E
Itomamo, L. **41** 49 11N 70 28W
Itoman **131** 26 7N 127 40 E
Itonamas, R. **86** 13 0S 64 25W
Itu **89** 23 10S 47 15W
Ituaçu **87** 13 50S 41 18W
Ituango **86** 7 4N 75 45W
Ituiutaba **87** 19 0S 49 25W
Ituliho **129** 50 40N 121 30 E
Itumbiara **87** 18 20S 49 10W
Ituna **56** 51 10N 103 30W
Itung **130** 43 25N 125 21 E
Iturbe **88** 23 0S 65 25W
Iturup, Ostrov **121** 45 0N 148 0 E
Ituyuro, R. **88** 22 40S 63 50W
Iuka **77** 38 37N 88 47W
Ivalo **110** 68 38N 27 35 E
Ivalojoki **110** 68 30N 27 0 E
Ivanhoe, Austral. **136** 32 56S 144 20 E
Ivanhoe, U.S.A. **80** 36 23N 119 13W
Ivanhoe L. **55** 60 25N 106 30W
Ivano-Frankovsk, (Stanislav) **120** 49 0N 24 40 E
Ivanovo **120** 52 7N 25 29 E
Ivinheima, R. **89** 21 48S 54 15W
Iviza = Ibiza **104** 39 0N 1 30 E
Ivory Coast ■ **114** 7 30N 5 0W
Ivrea **108** 45 30N 7 52 E
Ivugivik, (N.D. d'Ivugivic) **36** 62 24N 77 55W
Iwahig **126** 8 35N 117 32 E
Iwakuni **132** 34 15N 132 8 E
Iwata **132** 34 49N 137 59 E
Iwate-ken □ **132** 39 30N 141 30 E
Iwo **114** 7 39N 4 9 E
Ixiamas **86** 13 50S 68 5W
Ixtepec **83** 16 40N 95 10W
Ixtlán de Juárez **83** 17 23N 96 28W
Ixtlán del Rio **82** 21 5N 104 28W
Iyang **131** 28 36N 112 20 E
Izabal, L. **84** 15 30N 89 10W
Izamal **83** 20 56N 89 1W
Izegem **105** 50 55N 3 12 E
Izhevsk **120** 56 51N 53 14 E
Izmail **120** 45 22N 28 46 E
İzmir (Smyrna) **122** 38 25N 27 8 E
İzmit **122** 40 45N 29 50 E
Izumisano **132** 34 40N 135 43 E
Izumo **132** 35 20N 132 55 E

J

Jaab L. **53** 51 10N 82 58W
Jabalpur **124** 23 9N 79 58 E
Jablah **122** 35 20N 36 0 E
Jablanica, Mt. **109** 41 20N 20 30 E
Jablonec **106** 50 43N 15 10 E
Jaboticabal **89** 21 15S 48 17W
Jaburu **86** 5 30S 64 0W
Jaca **104** 42 35N 0 33W
Jacala **83** 21 1N 99 11W
Jacareí **89** 23 20S 46 0W
Jacarèzinho **89** 23 5S 50 0W
Jáchal **88** 30 5S 69 0W
Jack Lane B. **35** 55 45N 60 35W
Jackfish **34** 48 45N 87 0W
Jackfish L. **56** 53 9N 108 29W
Jackman **35** 45 35N 70 17W
Jacksboro **75** 33 14N 98 15W
Jackson, Ala., U.S.A. **73** 31 32N 87 53W
Jackson, Calif., U.S.A. **80** 38 25N 120 47W
Jackson, Ky., U.S.A. **72** 37 35N 83 22W
Jackson, Mich., U.S.A. **77** 42 18N 84 25W
Jackson, Minn., U.S.A. **74** 43 35N 95 0W
Jackson, Miss., U.S.A. **75** 32 20N 90 10W
Jackson, Mo., U.S.A. **75** 37 25N 89 42W
Jackson, Ohio, U.S.A. **72** 39 0N 82 40W
Jackson, Tenn., U.S.A. **73** 35 40N 88 50W
Jackson, Wyo., U.S.A. **78** 43 30N 110 49W
Jackson Bay, Can. **54** 50 32N 125 57W
Jackson Bay, N.Z. **133** 43 58S 168 42 E
Jackson Center **77** 40 27N 84 4W
Jackson, L. **78** 43 55N 110 40W
Jacksons **133** 42 46S 171 32 E
Jackson's Arm **37** 49 52N 56 47W
Jacksonville, Ala., U.S.A. **73** 33 49N 85 45W
Jacksonville, Calif., U.S.A. **80** 37 52N 120 24W
Jacksonville, Fla., U.S.A. **73** 30 15N 81 38W
Jacksonville, Ill., U.S.A. **76** 39 42N 90 15W
Jacksonville, N.C., U.S.A. **73** 34 50N 77 29W
Jacksonville, Oreg., U.S.A. **78** 42 13N 122 56W
Jacksonville, Tex., U.S.A. **75** 31 58N 95 12W
Jacksonville Beach **73** 30 19N 81 26W
Jacmel **85** 18 20N 72 40W

Jacob Lake Jundiaí

Jacob Lake 79 36 45N 112 12W
Jacobabad 124 28 20N 68 29E
Jacobina 87 11 11S 40 30W
Jacobs 52 50 15N 89 50W
Jacques-Cartier 41 45 31N 73 29W
Jacques Cartier, Dét. de 36 50 0N 63 30W
Jacques-Cartier, L. 41 47 35N 71 13W
Jacques-Cartier, Mt. 38 48 57N 66 0W
Jacques Cartier Pass 35 49 50N 62 30W
Jacques-Cartier, R. 41 46 40N 71 45W
Jacquet River 39 47 55N 66 0W
Jacuí, R. 89 30 2S 51 15W
Jacuipe, R. 87 12 30S 39 5W
Jacumba 81 32 37N 116 11W
Jacundá, R. 87 1 57S 50 26W
Jaén, Peru 86 5 25S 78 40W
Jaén, Spain 104 37 44N 3 43W
Jaffna 124 9 45N 80 2E
Jagadhri 124 30 10N 77 20E
Jagdalpur 125 19 3N 82 6E
Jagersfontein 117 29 44S 25 27E
Jagraon 124 30 50N 75 25E
Jagtial 124 18 50N 79 0E
Jaguariaíva 89 24 10S 49 50W
Jaguaribe, R. 87 6 0S 38 35W
Jagüey 84 22 35N 81 7W
Jagungal, Mt. 136 36 12S 148 28E
Jahrom 122 28 30N 53 31E
Jainti 125 26 45N 89 40E
Jaipur 124 27 0N 76 10E
Jakarta 127 6 9S 106 49E
Jakobshavn 65 68 0N 51 0W
Jakobstad (Pietarsaari) 110 63 40N 22 43E
Jal 75 32 8N 103 8W
Jala 123 27 30N 62 40E
Jalalabad 124 34 30N 70 29E
Jalama 81 34 29N 120 29W
Jalapa, Guat. 84 14 45N 89 59W
Jalapa, Mexico 83 19 30N 96 50W
Jalas, Jabal al 122 27 30N 36 30E
Jalgaon, Maharashtra, India 124 21 2N 76 31E
Jalgaon, Maharashtra, India 124 21 0N 75 42E
Jalisco □ 82 20 0N 104 0W
Jalna 124 19 48N 75 57E
Jalón, R. 104 41 20N 1 40W
Jalpa 82 21 38N 102 58W
Jalpaiguri 125 26 32N 88 46E
Jalq 123 27 35N 62 33E
Jaluit I. 14 6 0N 169 30E
Jamaica 76 41 51N 94 18W
Jamaica, I. ■ 84 18 10N 77 30W
Jamalpur, Bangla. 125 24 52N 90 2E
Jamalpur, India 125 25 18N 86 28E
Jamanxim, R. 87 6 30S 55 50W
Jambe 127 1 15S 132 10E
Jambi 126 1 38S 103 30E
Jamdena, I. = Yamdena 127 7 45S 131 20E
James B. 53 51 30N 80 0W
James, R. 74 44 50N 98 0W
James Ranges 134 24 10S 132 0E
James River 39 45 35N 62 7W
James Ross I. 91 63 58S 50 94W
Jameson, C. 65 72 5N 74 14W
Jamesport 76 39 58N 93 48W
Jamestown, Austral. 135 33 10S 138 32E
Jamestown, Ind., U.S.A. 77 39 56N 86 38W
Jamestown, Ky., U.S.A. 72 37 0N 85 5W
Jamestown, Mo., U.S.A. 76 38 48N 92 30W
Jamestown, N.D., U.S.A. 74 47 0N 98 45W
Jamestown, N.Y., U.S.A. 70 42 5N 79 18W
Jamestown, Ohio, U.S.A. 77 39 39N 83 44W
Jamestown, Penn., U.S.A. 70 41 22N 80 27W
Jamestown, Tenn., U.S.A. 73 36 25N 85 0W
Jamiltepec 83 16 17N 97 49W
Jamkhandi 124 16 30N 75 15E
Jammu 124 32 43N 74 54E
Jammu & Kashmir □ 124 34 25N 77 0E
Jamnagar 124 22 30N 70 0E
Jamshedpur 125 22 44N 86 20E
Jämtlands län □ 110 62 40N 13 50E
Jan L. 55 54 56N 102 55W
Jan Mayen Is. 17 71 0N 11 0W
Jand 124 33 30N 72 0E
Jandaq 122 34 3N 54 22E
Janesville 76 42 39N 89 1W
Jani Khel 123 32 45N 68 25E
Janos 82 30 45N 108 10W
Jansen 56 51 54N 104 45W
Januária 87 15 25S 44 25W
Janville 101 48 10N 1 50E
Janzé 100 47 55N 1 28W
Jaoho 130 47 12N 134 15E
Jaora 124 23 40N 75 10E
Japan ■ 132 36 0N 136 0E
Japan, Sea of 132 40 0N 135 0E
Japara 127 6 30S 110 40E
Japen, I. = Yapen 127 1 50S 136 0E
Japurá 86 1 48S 66 30W
Japurá, R. 86 3 8S 64 46W
Jaque 86 7 27N 78 15W
Jaques-Cartier, Détroit de 38 50 0N 63 30W
Jara, La 79 37 16N 106 0W
Jarales 79 34 39N 106 51W
Jarama, R. 104 40 50N 3 20W
Jarbridge 78 41 56N 115 27W
Jardim 88 21 28S 56 9W
Jardines de la Reina, Is. 84 20 50N 78 50W
Jargalant 130 47 2N 115 1E
Jargalant (Kobdo) 129 48 0N 91 43E
Jargeau 101 47 50N 2 7E
Jarjarni 123 37 5N 56 20E
Jarnac 102 45 40N 0 11W
Jarny 101 49 9N 5 53E
Jarosław 107 50 2N 22 42E
Jarvis 46 42 53N 80 6W
Jarvis I. 15 0 15S 159 55W
Jarvis River 52 48 7N 89 21W
Jarwa 125 27 45N 82 30E
Jasin 128 2 20N 102 26E
Jäsk 123 25 38N 57 45E
Jasło 107 49 45N 21 30E
Jasonville 77 39 10N 87 13W
Jasper, Alta., Can. 61 52 55N 118 5W
Jasper, Ont., Can. 47 44 50N 75 56W
Jasper, Ont., Can. 71 44 52N 75 57W
Jasper, Ala., U.S.A. 73 33 48N 87 16W
Jasper, Fla., U.S.A. 73 30 31N 82 58W
Jasper, Ind., U.S.A. 77 38 24N 86 56W
Jasper, La., U.S.A. 75 30 59N 93 58W
Jasper, Minn., U.S.A. 74 43 52N 96 22W
Jasper Nat. Park 61 52 50N 118 8W
Jasper Place 54 53 33N 113 25W
Jászberény 107 47 30N 19 55E
Jataí 87 17 50S 51 45W
Jatibarang 127 6 28S 108 18E
Jatinegara 127 6 13S 106 52E
Játiva 104 39 0N 0 32W
Jatobal 87 4 35S 49 33W
Jaú 89 22 10S 48 30W
Jauja 86 11 45S 75 30W
Jaunpur 125 25 46N 82 44E
Java = Jawa 127 7 0S 110 0E
Java Sea 126 4 35S 107 15E
Javhlant = Ulyasutay 129 47 42N 13 10E
Javron 100 48 25N 0 25W
Jawa 127 7 0S 110 0E
Jay 75 36 17N 94 46W
Jayapura 127 2 28S 140 38E
Jayawijaya, Pengunungan 127 7 0S 139 0E
Jaydot 55 49 15N 110 15W
Jaynagar 125 26 43N 86 9E
Jayton 75 33 17N 100 35W
Jazminal 82 24 56N 101 25W
Jean 81 35 47N 115 20W
Jean Marie River 54 61 32N 120 38W
Jean Rabel 85 19 50N 73 30W
Jeanerette 75 29 52N 91 38W
Jeanette L. 52 51 5N 92 5W
Jeanne-d'Arc 48 45 32N 75 38W
Jeannette 70 40 20N 79 36W
Jedburgh 96 55 28N 2 33W
Jedrzejów 107 50 35N 20 15E
Jedway 62 52 17N 131 14W
Jefferson, Iowa, U.S.A. 76 42 3N 94 25W
Jefferson, Ohio, U.S.A. 70 41 40N 80 46W
Jefferson, Tex., U.S.A. 75 32 45N 94 23W
Jefferson, Wis., U.S.A. 77 43 0N 88 49W
Jefferson City, Mo., U.S.A. 76 38 34N 92 10W
Jefferson City, Tenn., U.S.A. 73 36 8N 83 30W
Jefferson, Mt., Nev., U.S.A. 78 38 51N 117 0W
Jefferson, Mt., Oreg., U.S.A. 78 44 45N 121 50W
Jeffersontown 77 38 17N 85 44W
Jeffersonville, Ind., U.S.A. 77 38 20N 85 42W
Jeffersonville, Ohio, U.S.A. 77 39 38N 83 34W
Jega 114 12 15N 4 23E
Jelenia Góra 106 50 50N 15 45E
Jelgava 111 56 41N 22 49E
Jellicoe 53 49 40N 87 30W
Jemaja 126 3 5N 105 45E
Jemappes 105 50 27N 3 54E
Jember 127 8 11S 113 41E
Jembongan, I. 126 6 45N 117 20E
Jemeppe 105 50 37N 5 30E
Jemseg 39 45 50N 66 7W
Jena, Ger. 106 50 56N 11 33E
Jena, U.S.A. 75 31 41N 92 7W
Jenhwai 131 28 5N 106 10E
Jenin 115 32 28N 35 18E
Jenkins 72 37 13N 82 41W
Jenner 80 38 27N 123 7W
Jennings, La., U.S.A. 75 30 10N 92 45W
Jennings, Mo., U.S.A. 76 38 43N 90 16W
Jennings, R. 54 59 38N 132 5W
Jequié 87 13 51S 40 5W
Jequitinhonha 87 16 30S 41 0W
Jequitinhonha, R. 87 15 51S 38 53W
Jerantut 128 3 56N 102 22E
Jérémie 85 18 40N 74 10W
Jerez de García Salinas 82 22 39N 103 0W
Jerez de la Frontera 104 36 41N 6 7W
Jerez de los Caballeros 104 38 20N 6 45W
Jerez, Punta 83 22 58N 97 40W
Jerico Springs 76 37 37N 94 1W
Jerilderie 136 35 20S 145 41E
Jermyn 71 41 31N 75 31W
Jerome, Can. 53 47 37N 82 14W
Jerome, U.S.A. 79 34 50N 112 0W
Jersey City 71 40 41N 74 8W
Jersey, I. 100 49 13N 2 7W
Jersey Shore 70 41 17N 77 18W
Jerseyside 37 47 16N 53 58W
Jerseyville, Can. 49 43 12N 80 7W
Jerseyville, U.S.A. 76 39 5N 90 20W
Jerusalem 115 31 47N 35 10E
Jervis B. 136 35 8S 150 46E
Jervis Inlet 62 50 0N 123 57W
Jesselton = Kota Kinabalu 126 6 0N 116 12E
Jessore 125 23 10N 89 10E
Jesup, U.S.A. 73 31 30N 82 0W
Jesup, U.S.A. 76 42 29N 92 4W
Jesús Carranza 83 17 28N 95 1W
Jesus, Île 44 45 35N 73 45W
Jesús María 88 30 59S 64 5W
Jetmore 75 38 10N 99 57W
Jewell 76 42 20N 93 39W
Jewett, Ohio, U.S.A. 70 40 22N 81 2W
Jewett, Tex., U.S.A. 75 31 20N 96 8W
Jewett City 71 41 36N 72 0W
Jeypore 125 18 50N 82 38E
Jhal Jhao 124 26 20N 65 35E
Jhalawar 124 24 35N 76 10E
Jhang Maghiana 124 31 15N 72 15E
Jhansi 124 25 30N 78 36E
Jharsaguda 125 21 50N 84 5E
Jhelum 124 33 0N 73 45E
Jhelum, R. 124 31 50N 72 10E
Jhunjhunu 124 28 10N 75 20E
Jicarón, I. 84 7 10N 81 50W
Jiddah 122 21 29N 39 16E
Jido 125 29 2N 94 58E
Jihchao 131 35 18N 119 28E
Jihlava 106 49 28N 15 35E
Jihlava R. 106 49 21N 15 38E
Jiloca, R. 104 41 0N 1 20W
Jima 115 7 40N 36 55E
Jiménez 82 27 10N 105 0W
Jindabyne 136 36 25S 148 35E
Jindabyne L. 136 36 20N 148 38E
Jinja 116 0 25N 33 12E
Jinnah Barrage 124 32 58N 71 33E
Jinné 130 51 32N 121 25E
Jinotega 84 13 6N 85 59W
Jinotepe 84 11 50N 86 10W
Jiparaná (Machado), R. 86 8 45S 62 20W
Jipijapa 86 1 0S 80 40W
Jiquilpán 82 19 57N 102 42W
Jis rash Shughur 122 35 49N 36 18E
Jitra 128 6 16N 100 25E
Jiu, R. 107 44 50N 23 20E
Joaçaba 89 27 5S 51 31W
João de Almeida 117 15 10S 13 50E
João Pessoa 87 7 10S 34 52W
Joaquín V. González 88 25 10S 64 0W
Jobourg, Nez de 100 49 41N 1 57W
Jodhpur 124 26 23N 73 2E
Joe Batt's Arm 37 49 44N 54 10W
Jœuf 101 49 12N 6 1E
Jofane 117 21 15S 34 18E
Joffre, Mt. 61 50 32N 115 13W
Joggins 39 45 42N 64 27W
Jogjakarta = Yogyakarta 127 7 49S 110 22E
Jogues, Ont., Can. 53 49 36N 83 45W
Jogues, Qué., Can. 43 45 29N 72 49W
Johannesburg, S. Afr. 117 26 10S 28 8E
Johannesburg, U.S.A. 81 35 22N 117 38W
John Days, R. 78 45 0N 120 0W
John o' Groats 96 58 39N 3 3W
Johnnie 81 36 25N 116 5W
Johnson 75 37 35N 101 48W
Johnson City, Ill., U.S.A. 76 37 49N 88 56W
Johnson City, Tenn., U.S.A. 73 36 18N 82 21W
Johnson City, Tex., U.S.A. 75 30 15N 98 24W
Johnson Cy. 71 42 9N 67 0W
Johnsonburg 70 41 30N 78 40W
Johnsondale 81 35 58N 118 32W
Johnson's Crossing 54 60 29N 133 18W
Johnston I. 15 17 10N 169 8E
Johnston Lakes 134 32 20S 120 45E
Johnstone Str. 62 50 28N 126 0W
Johnstown, N.Y., U.S.A. 71 43 1N 74 20W
Johnstown, Pa., U.S.A. 70 40 19N 78 53W
Johor □ 128 2 5N 103 20E
Johor Baharu 128 1 45N 103 47E
Joigny 101 48 0N 3 20E
Joinvile 89 26 15S 48 55E
Joinville 101 48 27N 5 10E
Joinville I. 91 63 15N 55 30W
Joir, R. 38 51 59N 60 12W
Jojutla 83 18 37N 99 11W
Jokkmokk 110 66 35N 19 50E
Jökulsá á Brú 110 65 40N 14 16W
Jökulsá! Fjöllum 110 65 30N 16 15W
Jökulsa R. 110 65 30N 16 15W
Jolan 80 35 58N 121 9W
Joliet 77 41 30N 88 0W
Joliette 41 46 3N 73 24W
Joliette, Parc. Prov. de 41 46 30N 74 0W
Jolo I. 127 6 0N 121 0E
Jome, I. 127 1 16S 127 30E
Jones C. 34 54 33N 79 35W
Jones Sound 65 76 0N 89 0W
Jonesboro, Ark., U.S.A. 75 35 50N 90 45W
Jonesboro, Ill., U.S.A. 75 37 26N 89 18W
Jonesboro, La., U.S.A. 75 32 15N 92 41W
Jonesburg 76 38 51N 91 18W
Jonesport 35 44 32N 67 38W
Jonesville, Ind., U.S.A. 77 39 5N 85 54W
Jonesville, Mich, U.S.A. 77 41 59N 84 40W
Jönköping 111 57 45N 14 10E
Jönköpings län □ 111 57 30N 14 30E
Jonquière 41 48 27N 71 14W
Jonzac 102 45 27N 0 28W
Joplin 75 37 0N 94 25W
Jordan, Phil. 127 10 41N 122 38E
Jordan, U.S.A. 78 47 25N 106 58W
Jordan ■ 122 31 0N 36 0E
Jordan Falls 39 43 49N 65 14W
Jordan Harbour 49 43 11N 79 23W
Jordan, L. 39 44 5N 65 14W
Jordan, R. 115 32 10N 35 32E
Jordan Valley 78 43 0N 117 2W
Jorhat 125 26 45N 94 20E
Jörn 110 65 4N 20 1E
Jorquera, R. 88 28 3S 69 58W
Jos 114 9 53N 8 51E
José Batlle y OrdóPez 89 33 20S 55 10W
Joseph 78 45 27N 117 13W
Joseph City 79 35 0N 110 16W
Joseph, L. 46 45 10N 79 44W
Joseph, Lac 38 52 45N 65 18W
Joseph, Petit lac 38 52 36N 65 5W
Joshua Tree 81 34 8N 116 19W
Joshua Tree Nat. Mon. 81 33 56N 116 5W
Josselin 100 47 57N 2 33W
Jostedal 111 61 35N 7 15E
Jotunheimen 111 61 35N 8 25E
Jounieh 122 33 59N 35 30E
Jourdanton 75 28 54N 98 32W
Joussard 60 55 22N 115 57W
Jouzjan □ 123 36 10N 66 0E
Jovellanos 84 22 40N 81 10W
Joy B. 36 61 30N 72 0W
Joyeuse 103 44 29N 4 16E
Juan Aldama 82 24 20N 103 23W
Juan Bautista 79 36 55N 121 33W
Juan Bautista Alberdi 88 34 26S 61 48W
Juan de Fuca Str. 80 48 15N 124 0W
Juan de Nova, I. 117 17 3S 42 45E
Juan Fernández, Arch. de 15 33 50S 80 0W
Juan José Castelli 88 25 57S 60 37W
Juan L. Lacaze 88 34 26S 57 25W
Juan Perez Sd. 62 52 32N 131 30W
Juárez, Argent. 88 37 40S 59 43W
Juárez, Mexico 82 27 37N 100 44W
Juárez, U.S.A. 81 32 20N 115 57W
Juárez, Sierra de 82 32 0N 116 0W
Juàzeiro 87 9 30S 40 30W
Juàzeiro do Norte 87 7 10S 39 18W
Jûbâ 115 4 57N 31 35E
Juba, R. 115 1 30N 42 35E
Jubaila 122 24 55N 46 25E
Jubilee L. 37 48 3N 55 11W
Juby, C. 114 28 0N 12 59W
Júcar, R. 104 40 8N 2 13W
Júcaro 84 21 37N 78 51W
Juchitán 83 16 27N 95 5W
Judaea = Yehuda 115 31 35N 34 57E
Jude I. 37 47 15N 54 49W
Judique 39 45 52N 61 30W
Judith Gap 78 46 48N 109 46W
Judith Pt. 71 41 20N 71 30W
Judith, R. 78 47 30N 109 30W
Juian 131 27 45N 120 38E
Juigalpa 84 12 6N 85 26W
Juillac 102 45 20N 1 19E
Juiz de Fora 87 21 43S 43 19W
Jujuy 88 24 10S 65 25W
Jujuy □ 88 23 20S 65 40W
Jukao 131 32 24N 120 35E
Julesberg 74 41 0N 102 20W
Juli 86 16 10S 69 25W
Julia Creek 135 20 39S 141 44E
Juliaca 86 15 25S 70 10W
Julian 81 33 4N 116 38W
Julian L. 36 54 25N 77 57W
Julianehåb 17 60 43N 46 0W
Julimes 82 28 25N 105 27W
Jullundur 124 31 20N 75 40E
Jumbo Pk. 81 36 12N 114 11W
Jumento, Cayos 85 23 0N 75 40E
Jumet 105 50 27N 4 25E
Jumilla 104 38 28N 1 19W
Jumla 125 29 15N 82 13E
Jumna, R. = Yamuna 125 27 0N 78 30E
Junagadh 124 21 30N 70 30E
Junction, Tex., U.S.A. 75 30 29N 99 48W
Junction, Utah, U.S.A. 79 38 10N 112 15W
Junction B. 134 11 52S 133 55E
Junction City, Kans., U.S.A. 74 39 4N 96 55W
Junction City, Oreg., U.S.A. 78 44 20N 123 12W
Jundah 135 24 46S 143 2E
Jundiaí 89 23 10S 47 0W

Juneau Kasenga

Juneau 67 58 26N 134 30W
Junee 136 34 53S 147 35E
Juniata, R. 70 40 30N 77 40W
Junín 88 34 33S 60 57W
Junín de los Andes 90 39 45S 71 0W
Juniper 39 46 33N 67 13W
Junkuren, R. 130 47 40N 113 0E
Junta, La 75 38 0N 103 30W
Juntura 78 43 44N 118 4W
Jupiter, R. 38 49 29N 63 37W
Jura 101 46 35N 6 5E
Jura □ 101 46 47N 5 45E
Jura, I. 96 56 0N 5 50W
Jura, Sd. of 96 55 57N 5 45W
Jurado 86 7 7N 77 46W
Jurien B. 134 30 17S 115 0E
Jurm 123 36 50N 70 45E
Juruá, R. 86 2 30S 66 0W
Juruena, R. 86 7 20S 58 3W
Juruti 87 2 9S 56 4W
Juskatla 62 53 37N 132 18W
Jussey 101 47 50N 5 55E
Justo Daract 88 33 52S 65 12W
Juticalpa 84 14 40N 85 50W
Jutland 93 56 0N 8 0E
Juvigny-sous-Andaine 100 48 32N 0 30W
Juvisy 101 48 43N 2 23E
Juwain 124 31 45N 61 30E
Juzennecourt 101 48 10N 5 0E
Jylland 111 56 15N 9 20E
Jyväskylä 110 62 14N 25 44E

K

K2, Mt. 124 36 0N 77 0E
Ka Lae (South C.) 67 18 55N 155 41W
Kaaia, Mt. 67 21 31N 158 9W
Kaap die Goeie Hoop 117 34 24S 18 30E
Kaap Plato 117 28 30S 24 0E
Kaapkruis 117 21 43S 14 0E
Kaapstad = Cape Town 117 33 56S 18 27E
Kabaena, I. 127 5 15S 122 0E
Kabale 116 1 15S 30 0E
Kabalo 116 6 0S 27 0E
Kabambare 116 4 41S 27 39E
Kabanjahe 126 8 2N 98 27E
Kabardino-Balkar, A.S.S.R. □ 120 43 30N 43 30E
Kabarega Falls 116 2 15N 31 38E
Kabasalan 127 7 47N 122 44E
Kabetogama L. 52 48 28N 92 59W
Kabinakagami L. 53 48 54N 84 25W
Kabinakagami, R. 53 50 25N 84 20W
Kabinda 116 6 23S 24 28E
Kabompo, R. 117 13 50S 24 10E
Kabongo 116 7 22S 25 33E
Kabūd Gonbad 123 37 5N 59 45E
Kabul 124 34 28N 69 18E
Kabul □ 124 34 0N 68 30E
Kaburuang 127 3 50N 126 30E
Kabwe 117 14 30S 28 29E
Kachin □ 125 26 0N 97 0E
Kachiry 120 53 10N 75 50E
Kaçkar 122 40 45N 41 30E
Kadan Kyun 128 12 30N 98 20E
Kadina 135 34 0S 137 43E
Kadoka 74 43 50N 101 31W
Kaduna 114 10 30N 7 21E
Kaedi 114 16 9N 13 28W
Kaegudeck L. 37 48 7N 55 12W
Kaelé 114 10 15N 14 15E
Kaena Pt. 67 21 35N 158 17W
Kaesŏng 130 37 58N 126 35E
Kāf 122 31 25N 37 20E
Kafakumba 116 9 38S 23 46E
Kafirévs, Akra 109 38 9N 24 8E
Kafiristan 123 35 0N 70 30E
Kafue, R. 117 15 30S 26 0E
Kafulwe 116 9 0S 29 1E
Kagaki L. 52 49 13N 93 52W
Kagamil I. 67 53 0N 169 40W
Kagan 120 39 43N 64 33E
Kagawa-ken □ 132 34 15N 134 0E
Kagawong L. 46 45 54N 82 15W
Kagianagami L. 53 50 57N 87 50W
Kagiano L. 53 49 16N 86 26W
Kağizman 122 40 5N 43 10E
Kagoshima 132 31 36N 130 40E
Kagoshima-ken □ 132 30 0N 130 0E
Kagoshima-Wan 132 31 0N 130 40E
Kahajan, R. 126 2 10S 114 0E
Kahama 116 4 8S 32 30E
Kahemba 116 7 18S 18 55E
Kahniah, R. 54 58 15N 120 55W
Kahnūj 123 27 55N 57 40E
Kahoka 76 40 25N 91 42W
Kahoolawe, I. 67 20 33N 156 35W
Kahuku & Pt. 67 21 41N 157 57W
Kahului 67 20 54N 156 28W
Kai, Kepulauan 127 5 55S 132 45W
Kaiapoi 133 42 24S 172 40E
Kaifeng 131 34 49N 114 30E
Kaihwa 131 29 0N 118 21E
Kaikohe 133 35 25S 173 49E
Kaikoura 133 42 25S 173 43E
Kaikoura Pen. 133 42 25S 173 43E
Kaikoura Ra. 133 41 59S 173 41E
Kailua 67 19 39N 156 0W
Kaimana 127 3 30S 133 45E
Kaimanawa Mts. 133 39 15S 175 56E
Kaingaroa Forest 133 38 30S 176 30E
Kainji Res. 114 10 1N 4 40E
Kaipara Harb. 133 36 25S 174 14E
Kaiping 130 40 28N 122 10E
Kaipokok B. 36 54 54N 59 47W
Kaironi 127 0 47S 133 40E
Kaiserslautern 105 49 30N 7 43E
Kaitaia 133 35 8S 173 17E
Kaitangata 133 46 17S 169 51E
Kaitung 130 44 58N 123 2E
Kaiwi Channel 67 21 13N 157 30W
Kaiyüan 130 42 40N 124 30E
Kaiyuh Mts. 67 63 40N 159 0W
Kajaani 110 64 17N 27 46E
Kajabbi 135 20 0S 140 1E
Kajan, R. 126 2 40N 116 40E
Kajang 128 2 59N 101 48E
Kajeli 127 3 20S 127 10E
Kajoa, I. 127 0 1N 127 28E
Kajuagung 126 32 8S 104 46E
Kakabeka Falls 52 48 24N 89 37W
Kakamas 117 28 45S 20 33E
Kakamega 116 0 20N 34 46E
Kakanui Mts. 133 45 10S 170 30E
Kake 67 57 0N 134 0W
Kakegawa 132 34 45N 138 1E
Kakinada = Cocanada 125 16 50N 82 11E
Kakisa L. 54 60 56N 117 43W
Kakisa, R. 54 61 3N 117 10W
Kaktovik 67 70 8N 143 50W
Kakwa, R. 60 54 37N 118 28W
Kalabagh 124 33 0N 71 28E
Kalabáka 109 39 42N 21 39E
Kalabo 117 14 58S 22 33E
Kaladan, R. 125 21 30N 92 45E
Kaladar 47 44 37N 77 5W
Kalahari, Des. 117 24 0S 22 0E
Kalakan 121 55 15N 116 45E
Kalama 80 46 0N 122 55W
Kalamata 109 37 3N 22 10E
Kalamazoo 77 42 20N 85 35W
Kalamazoo, R. 77 42 40N 86 12W
Kalao, I. 127 7 21S 121 0E
Kalaotoa, I. 127 7 20S 121 50E
Kalasin 128 16 26N 103 30E
Kalat 124 29 8N 66 31E
Kalat □ 124 27 0N 64 30E
Kalat-i-Ghilzai 123 32 15N 66 58E
Kalaupapa 67 21 12N 156 59W
Kalegauk Kyun 125 15 33N 97 35E
Kalemie 116 5 55S 29 9E
Kalewa 125 22 41N 95 32E
Kálfafellsstaður 110 64 11N 15 53W
Kalgoorlie 134 30 40S 121 22E
Kalianda 126 5 50S 105 45E
Kalibo 127 11 43N 122 22E
Kalima 116 2 33S 26 32E
Kalimantan Barat □ 126 0 0 110 30E
Kalimantan Selatan □ 126 4 10S 115 30E
Kalimantan Tengah □ 126 2 0S 113 30E
Kalimantan Timur □ 126 1 30N 116 30E
Kálimnos, I. 109 37 0N 27 0E
Kalinin 120 56 55N 35 55E
Kaliningrad 120 54 42N 20 32E
Kalispell 78 48 10N 114 22W
Kalisz 107 51 45N 18 8E
Kaliua 116 5 5S 31 48E
Kalkaska 46 44 44N 85 11W
Kalkrand 117 24 1S 17 35E
Kallia 118 31 46N 35 30E
Kallsjön 110 63 38N 13 0E
Kalmar 111 56 40N 16 20E
Kalmthout 105 51 23N 4 29E
Kalmyk A.S.S.R. □ 120 46 5N 46 1E
Kalmykovo 120 49 0N 51 35E
Kalocsa 107 46 32N 19 0E
Kalomo 117 17 0S 26 30E
Kalona 76 41 29N 91 43W
Kaluga 120 54 35N 36 10E
Kalundborg 111 55 41N 11 5E
Kalutara 124 6 35N 80 0E
Kalyani 86 17 53N 76 59E
Kam Keut 128 18 20N 104 48E
Kama, R. 120 60 0N 53 0E
Kamaishi 132 39 20N 142 0E
Kamalino 67 21 50N 160 14W
Kamaran 115 15 28N 42 35E
Kamchatka, P-ov. 121 57 0N 160 0E
Kamen 120 53 50N 81 30E
Kamenets-Podolskiy 120 48 45N 26 10E
Kamenjak, Rt. 108 44 47N 13 55E
Kamensk-Uralskiy 120 56 25N 62 2E
Kamenskoye 121 62 45N 165 30E
Kamiah 78 46 12N 116 2W
Kamilukuak, L. 55 62 22N 101 40W
Kamina 116 8 45S 25 0E
Kaminak L. 55 62 10N 95 0W
Kaministikwia 52 48 32N 89 35W
Kamloops L. 63 50 45N 120 40W
Kamouraska 41 47 34N 69 52W
Kampala 116 0 20N 32 30E
Kampar 128 4 18N 101 9E
Kampar, R. 126 0 30N 102 0E
Kampen 105 52 33N 5 53E
Kampsville 76 39 18N 90 37W
Kampuchea ■ = Cambodia 128 12 15N 105 0E
Kamrau, Teluk 127 3 30S 133 45E
Kamsack 57 51 34N 101 54W
Kamuchawie L. 55 56 18N 101 59W
Kamyshin 120 50 10N 45 30E
Kanaaupscow 36 54 2N 76 30W
Kanaaupscow, R. 36 53 39N 77 9W
Kanab 79 37 3N 112 29W
Kanab Creek 79 37 0N 112 40W
Kanaga I. 67 51 45N 177 22W
Kanagawa-ken □ 132 35 20N 139 20E
Kanairiktok, R., Can. 35 54 30N 62 30W
Kanairiktok, R., Newf., Can. 36 55 2N 60 18W
Kanakanak 67 59 0N 158 58W
Kananchen 130 45 45N 121 55E
Kananga 116 5 55S 22 18E
Kanarraville 79 37 34N 113 12W
Kanaskat 80 47 19N 121 54W
Kanata 47 45 20N 75 59W
Kanawha, R. 72 39 40N 82 0W
Kanazawa 132 36 30N 136 38E
Kanchanaburi 128 14 8N 99 31E
Kanchenjunga, Mt. 125 27 50N 88 10E
Kanchipuram (Conjeeveram) 124 12 52N 79 45E
Kanchow 131 25 58N 114 55E
Kanchwan 130 36 29N 109 24E
Kanda Kanda 116 6 52S 23 48E
Kandahar 124 31 32N 65 30E
Kandahar □ 124 31 0N 65 0E
Kandalaksha 120 67 9N 32 30E
Kandalu 124 29 55N 63 20E
Kandangan 126 2 50S 115 20E
Kandi 114 11 7N 2 55E
Kandira 122 41 5N 30 10E
Kandla 124 23 0N 70 10E
Kandos 136 32 45S 149 58E
Kandy 124 7 18N 80 43E
Kane 70 41 39N 78 53W
Kane Basin 65 79 1N 73 0W
Kane Bassin 17 79 30N 68 0W
Kanen 131 18 46N 108 33E
Kaneohe 67 21 25N 157 48W
Kang 124 30 55N 61 55E
Kangar 128 6 27N 100 12E
Kangaroo Flat 136 36 45S 144 20E
Kangaroo I. 135 35 45S 137 0E
Kangavar 122 34 40N 48 0E
Kangean, Kepulauan 126 6 55S 115 23E
Kangerdlugsuaé 17 68 10N 32 20W
Kangnŭng 130 37 45N 128 54E
Kango 116 0 11N 10 5E
Kangshan 131 22 43N 120 14E
Kangtissu Shan 125 31 0N 82 0E
Kangto, Mt. 125 27 50N 92 35E
Kaniapiskau L. 36 54 10N 69 55W
Kaniapiskau, R. 36 57 40N 69 30E
Kanin Nos, Mys 120 68 45N 43 20E
Kanin, P-ov. 120 68 0N 45 0E
Kaniva 136 36 22S 141 18E
Kankakee 77 41 6N 87 50W
Kankakee, R. 77 41 13N 87 0W
Kankan 114 10 30N 9 15W
Kanker 125 20 10N 81 40E
Kankunskiy 121 57 37N 126 8E
Kannapolis 73 35 32N 80 37W
Kannauj 124 27 3N 79 26E
Kannod 124 22 45N 76 40E
Kano 114 12 2N 8 30E
Kanowha 76 42 57N 93 47W
Kanowit 126 2 14N 112 20E
Kanowna 134 30 32S 121 31E
Kanoya 132 31 25N 130 50E
Kanpetlet 125 21 10N 93 59E
Kanpur 124 26 35N 80 20E
Kansas 77 39 33N 87 56W
Kansas □ 74 38 40N 98 0W
Kansas City, Kans., U.S.A. 76 39 0N 94 40W
Kansas City, Mo., U.S.A. 76 39 3N 94 30W
Kansas, R. 74 39 15N 96 20W
Kansk 121 56 20N 95 37E
Kansu □ 129 35 30N 104 30E
Kantishna 67 63 31N 151 5W
Kantse 129 31 30N 100 29E
Kanturk 97 52 10N 8 55W
Kanuma 132 36 44N 139 42E
Kanyu 131 34 56N 119 8E
Kaoan 131 28 20N 115 17E
Kaohsiung 131 22 35N 120 16E
Kaoko Otavi 117 18 12S 13 45E
Kaolack 114 14 5N 16 8W
Kaomi 130 36 25N 119 45E
Kaoping 130 35 57N 113 0E
Kaoyu Ho 131 32 50N 119 10E
Kapaa 67 22 5N 159 19W
Kapanga 116 8 30S 22 40E
Kapela, Mts. 108 44 40N 15 40E
Kapellen 105 51 19N 4 25E
Kapfenberg 106 47 26N 15 18E
Kapikotongwa, R. 53 50 39N 86 43W
Kapiri Mposhi 117 13 59S 28 43E
Kapiskau 34 52 50N 82 1W
Kapiskau, R. 34 52 47N 81 55W
Kapit 126 2 0N 113 5E
Kapiti I. 133 40 50S 174 56E
Kapoeta 115 4 50N 33 35E
Kaposvár 107 46 25N 17 47E
Kaposvar Cr. 56 50 31N 101 55W
Kapowsin 80 46 59N 122 13W
Kapuas Hulu, Pegunungan 126 1 30N 113 30E
Kapuas, R. 126 0 20N 111 40E
Kapuskasing 53 49 25N 82 30W
Kapuskasing, R. 53 49 49N 82 0W
Kaputir 116 2 5N 35 28E
Kara 120 69 10N 65 25E
Kara Bogaz Gol, Zaliv 120 41 0N 53 30E
Kara Kalpak A.S.S.R. □ 120 43 0N 60 0E
Kara Kum 120 39 30N 60 0E
Kara Nor 129 38 45N 98 0E
Kara Sea 120 75 0N 70 0E
Karabutak 120 49 59N 60 14E
Karachi, Austral. 136 36 58S 148 45E
Karachi, Pak. 124 24 53N 67 0E
Karad 124 17 15N 74 10E
Karadeniz Boğazı 122 41 10N 29 5E
Karadeniz Dağlari 122 41 30N 35 0E
Karagajly 120 49 26N 76 0E
Karaganda 120 49 50N 73 0E
Karaginskiy, Ostrov 121 58 45N 164 0E
Karaikkudi 124 10 0N 78 45E
Karaj 123 35 4N 51 0E
Karakas 120 48 20N 83 30E
Karakitang 127 3 14N 125 28E
Karakoram 124 35 20N 76 0E
Karakoram Pass 124 35 20N 78 0E
Karakorum 130 47 30N 102 20E
Karalon 121 57 5N 115 50E
Karamai 129 45 57N 84 30E
Karaman 122 37 14N 33 13E
Karambu 126 3 53S 116 6E
Karamea Bight 133 41 22S 171 40E
Karanganjar 127 7 38S 109 37E
Karasburg 117 28 0S 18 44E
Karasino 120 66 50N 86 50E
Karasjok 110 69 27N 25 30E
Karasuk 120 53 44N 78 2E
Karatau 120 43 10N 70 28E
Karatau, Khrebet 120 43 30N 69 30E
Karatsu 132 33 30N 130 0E
Karawa 116 3 18N 20 17E
Karawanken 108 46 30N 14 40E
Karazhal 120 48 2N 70 49E
Karbalā 122 32 47N 44 3E
Karcag 107 47 19N 21 1E
Kardhítsa 109 39 23N 21 54E
Kareeberge 117 30 50S 22 0E
Karelian A.S.S.R. □ 120 65 30N 32 30E
Karema 116 6 49S 30 24E
Karen 128 12 49N 92 53E
Kargānrūd 122 37 55N 49 0E
Kargasok 120 59 3N 80 53E
Kargat 120 55 10N 80 15E
Kariba Dam 117 16 30S 28 35E
Kariba Gorge 117 16 30S 28 35E
Kariba Lake 117 16 40S 28 25E
Karibib 117 21 0S 15 56E
Karikal 124 10 59N 79 50E
Karikkale 122 39 55N 33 30E
Karimata, Kepulauan 126 1 40S 109 0E
Karimata, Selat 126 2 0S 108 20E
Karimnagar 124 18 26N 79 10E
Karimundjawa, Kepulauan 126 5 50S 110 30E
Kariya 132 34 58N 137 1E
Karl-Marx-Stadt 106 50 50N 12 55E
Karlovac 108 45 31N 15 36E
Karlovy Vary 106 50 13N 12 51E
Karlsborg 111 58 33N 14 33E
Karlshamn 111 56 10N 14 51E
Karlskoga 111 59 22N 14 33E
Karlskrona 111 56 10N 15 35E
Karlsruhe 106 49 3N 8 23E
Karlstad, Sweden 111 59 23N 13 30E
Karlstad, U.S.A. 74 48 38N 96 30W
Karnal 124 29 42N 77 2E
Karnali, R. 125 29 0N 82 0E
Karnaphuli Res. 125 22 40N 92 20E
Karnataka □ 124 13 15N 77 0E
Karnes City 75 28 53N 97 53W
Karnische Alpen 106 46 36N 13 0E
Kârnten □ 106 46 52N 13 30E
Karonga 116 9 57S 33 55E
Kárpathos, I. 109 35 37N 27 10E
Kars 122 40 40N 43 5E
Karsakpay 120 47 55N 66 40E
Karshi 120 38 53N 65 48E
Kartaly 120 53 3N 60 40E
Karthaus 70 41 8N 78 9W
Karufa 127 3 50S 133 20E
Karungu 116 0 50S 34 10E
Karur 124 10 59N 78 2E
Karwar 124 14 55N 74 13E
Kas Kong 128 11 27N 102 12E
Kasai, R. 116 8 20S 22 0E
Kasama 116 10 16S 31 9E
Kasanga 116 8 30S 31 10E
Kasangulu 116 4 15S 15 15E
Kasaragod 124 12 30N 74 58E
Kasba L. 55 60 20N 102 10W
Kaschmar 123 35 16N 58 26E
Kasempa 117 13 30S 25 44E
Kasenga 116 10 20S 28 45E

Kashabowie Kiangyin

Kashabowie 52 48 40N 90 26W
Kāshān 123 34 5N 51 30E
Kashgar 129 39 46N 75 52E
Kashing 131 30 45N 120 41E
Kaskaskia, R. 76 37 58N 89 57W
Kaskattama, R. 55 57 3N 90 4W
Kaskinen (Kaskö) 110 62 22N 21 15E
Kaskö (Kaskinen) 110 62 22N 21 15E
Kaslo 63 49 55N 116 55W
Kasmere L. 55 59 34N 101 10W
Kasongo 116 4 30S 26 33E
Kasongo Lunda 116 6 35S 17 0E
Kásos, I. 109 35 20N 26 55E
Kassala 115 15 23N 36 26E
Kassala □ 116 15 20N 36 26E
Kassel 106 51 19N 9 32E
Kassue 127 6 58S 139 21E
Kastamonu 122 41 25N 33 43E
Kastoría 109 40 30N 21 19E
Kasulu 116 4 37S 30 5E
Kasur 124 31 5N 74 25E
Kata 121 58 46N 102 40E
Katako Kombe 116 3 25S 24 20E
Katalla 67 60 10N 144 35W
Katangi 124 21 56N 79 50E
Katangli 121 51 42N 143 14E
Katanning 134 33 40S 117 33E
Katha 125 24 10N 96 30E
Katherina, Gebel 115 28 30N 33 57E
Katherine 134 14 27S 132 20E
Kathiawar, dist. 124 22 20N 71 0E
Katiet 126 2 21S 99 44E
Katihar 125 25 34N 87 36E
Katima Mulilo 117 17 28S 24 13E
Katimik L. 57 52 53N 99 21W
Katmai Nat. Monument 67 58 30N 155 0W
Katmai, vol. 67 58 20N 154 59W
Katmandu 125 27 45N 85 12E
Katompi 116 6 2S 26 23E
Katoomba 136 33 41S 150 19E
Katowice 107 50 17N 19 5E
Katrine L. 96 56 15N 4 30W
Katrineholm 111 59 9N 16 12E
Katsina 114 7 10N 9 20E
Katsuura 132 35 15N 140 20E
Kattawaz 124 32 48N 68 23E
Kattawaz-Urgun □ 124 32 10N 68 20E
Kattegat 111 57 0N 11 20E
Katwijk-aan-Zee 105 52 12N 4 24E
Kau Tao 128 10 6N 99 48E
Kauai Chan. 67 21 45N 158 50W
Kauai, I. 67 19 30N 155 30W
Kaufman 75 32 35N 96 20W
Kaukauna 72 44 20N 88 13W
Kaukonen 110 67 31N 24 53E
Kauliranta 110 66 27N 23 41E
Kaunas 120 54 54N 23 54E
Kaupulehu 67 19 43N 155 53W
Kautokeino 110 69 0N 23 4E
Kavacha 121 60 16N 169 51E
Kavali 124 14 55N 80 1E
Kaválla 109 40 57N 24 28E
Kavanayén 86 5 38N 61 48W
Kaw = Caux 87 4 30N 52 15W
Kawagama L., Can. 70 45 18N 78 45W
Kawagama L., Ont., Can. 47 45 18N 78 45W
Kawagoe 132 35 55N 139 29E
Kawaguchi 132 35 52N 138 45E
Kawaihae 67 20 3N 155 50W
Kawaihoa Pt. 67 21 47N 160 12W
Kawaikini, Mt. 67 22 0N 159 30W
Kawambwa 116 9 48S 29 3E
Kawana 132 35 5N 135 27E
Kawardha 125 22 0N 81 17E
Kawasaki 132 35 35N 138 42E
Kawene 52 48 45N 91 15W
Kawerau 133 38 7S 176 42E
Kawhia Harbour 133 38 5S 174 51E
Kawinawl 57 52 50N 99 30W
Kawthaung 128 10 5N 98 36E
Kawthoolei □ = Kawthuk 125 18 0N 97 30E
Kawthuk □ 125 18 0N 97 30E
Kayah □ 125 19 15N 97 15E
Kayak I. 67 60 0N 144 30W
Kaycee 78 43 45N 106 46W
Kayenta 79 36 46N 110 15W
Kayes 114 14 25N 11 30W
Kayseri 122 38 45N 35 30E
Kaysville 78 41 2N 111 58W
Kazachinskoye 121 56 16N 107 36E
Kazachye 121 70 52N 135 58E
Kazakh S.S.R. □ 120 50 0N 58 0E
Kazan 120 55 48N 49 3E
Kazan, R. 55 64 2N 95 30W
Kazanluk 109 42 38N 25 35E
Kāzerūn 123 29 38N 51 40E
Kazumba 116 6 25S 22 5E
Kazvin 122 36 15N 50 0E
Kazym, R. 120 63 40N 68 30E
Kéa 109 37 35N 24 22E
Keaau 67 19 37N 155 3W
Keams Canyon 79 35 53N 110 9W
Keanae 67 20 52N 156 9W
Kearney, Can. 46 45 33N 79 13W
Kearney, U.S.A. 76 39 22N 94 22W
Kearney, Nebr., U.S.A. 74 40 45N 99 3W
Keban 122 38 50N 38 50E
Kebnekaise, mt. 110 67 54N 18 33E
Kebumen 127 7 42S 109 40E
Kechika, R. 54 59 41N 127 12W
Kecskemét 107 46 57N 19 35E
Kedah □ 128 5 50N 100 40E
Kedgwick 39 47 40N 67 20W
Kediri 127 7 51S 112 1E
Keefers 54 50 0N 121 40W
Keele, R. 67 64 15N 127 0W
Keeler 80 36 29N 117 52W
Keeley L. 55 54 54N 108 8W
Keeling Is. = Cocos Is. 16 12 12S 96 54E
Keelung = Chilung 131 25 3N 121 45E
Keene, Can. 47 44 15N 78 10W
Keene, Calif., U.S.A. 81 35 13N 118 33W
Keene, N.H., U.S.A. 71 42 57N 72 17W
Keeper, Mt. 97 52 46N 8 17W
Keer-Weer, C. 135 14 0S 141 32E
Keeseville 71 44 29N 73 30W
Keetmanshoop 117 26 35S 18 8E
Keewatin, Can. 52 49 46N 94 34W
Keewatin, U.S.A. 52 47 23N 93 0W
Keewatin □ 55 63 20N 94 40W
Keewatin, R. 55 56 29N 100 46W
Keezhik L. 52 51 45N 88 30W
Kefallinía, I. 109 38 28N 20 30E
Kefamenanu 127 9 28S 124 38E
Keflavík 110 64 2N 22 35W
Keg River 54 57 54N 117 7W
Kegashka 38 50 9N 61 18W
Kégashka, L. 38 50 20N 61 25W
Keglo, B. 36 58 40N 66 0W
Keighley 94 53 52N 1 54W
Keith 96 57 33N 2 58W
Keith Arm 64 64 20N 122 15W
Keithsburg 76 41 6N 90 56W
Kejimkujik Nat. Park 39 44 25N 65 25W
Kekri 124 26 0N 75 10E
Kël 121 69 30N 124 10E
Kelang 128 3 2N 101 26E
Kelantan □ 128 5 10N 102 0E
Kelantan, R. 128 6 13N 102 14E
Kellé 116 0 8S 14 38E
Keller 78 48 2N 118 44W
Kellerberrin 134 31 36S 117 38E
Kellett C. 64 72 0N 126 0W
Kellett Str. 64 75 45N 117 30W
Kelleys I. 70 41 35N 82 42W
Kelligrews 37 47 30N 53 1W
Kelliher 56 51 16N 103 44W
Kellogg 78 47 30N 116 5W
Kelloselkä 110 66 56N 28 53E
Kells = Ceanannas Mor 97 53 42N 6 53W
Kelowna 63 49 50N 119 25W
Kelsey Bay 62 50 25N 126 0W
Kelseyville 80 38 59N 122 50W
Kelso, N.Z. 133 45 54S 169 15E
Kelso, U.K. 96 55 36N 2 27W
Kelso, U.S.A. 80 46 10N 122 57W
Keluang 128 2 3N 103 18E
Kelvin I. 52 49 51N 88 40W
Kelvington 56 52 10N 103 30W
Kelwood 57 50 37N 99 28W
Kem 120 65 0N 34 38E
Kema 127 1 22N 125 8E
Kemah 122 39 32N 39 5E
Kemano 62 53 35N 128 0W
Kemerovo 120 55 20N 85 50E
Kemi 110 65 44N 24 34E
Kemi älv = Kemijoki 110 65 47N 24 32E
Kemijärvi 110 66 43N 27 22E
Kemijoki 110 65 47N 24 32E
Kemmerer 78 41 52N 110 30W
Kemmuna = Comino, I. 108 36 0N 14 20E
Kemp Coast 91 69 0S 55 0E
Kemp L. 75 33 45N 99 15W
Kempsey 135 31 1S 152 50E
Kempt, L. 41 47 25N 74 22W
Kempten 106 47 42N 10 18E
Kempton 77 40 56N 86 14W
Kemptown 39 45 28N 63 5W
Kemptville 47 45 0N 75 38W
Ken L. 96 55 0N 4 8W
Kenai 67 60 35N 151 20W
Kenai Mts. 67 60 0N 150 0W
Kenaston 56 51 30N 106 17W
Kendal, Indon. 127 6 56S 110 14E
Kendal, U.K. 94 54 19N 2 44W
Kendall 136 31 35S 152 44E
Kendallville 77 41 25N 85 15W
Kendari 127 3 50S 122 30E
Kendawangan 126 2 32S 110 17E
Kendrapara 125 20 35N 86 30E
Kendrick 78 46 43N 116 41W
Keng Tawng 125 20 45N 98 18E
Keng Tung 125 21 0N 99 30E
Kenge 116 4 50S 16 55E
Kenhardt 117 29 19S 21 12E
Kenho 130 50 43N 121 30E
Kenitra 114 34 15N 6 40W
Kenmare, Ireland 97 51 52N 9 35W
Kenmare, U.S.A. 74 48 40N 102 4W
Kenmare, R. 97 51 40N 10 0W
Kenmore 136 34 44S 149 45E
Kenn Reef 135 21 12S 155 46E
Kennaway 70 45 9N 78 11W
Kennebec 74 43 56N 99 54W
Kennebecasis, R. 39 45 19N 66 4W
Kennedy, B.C., Can. 66 49 10N 122 53W
Kennedy, Sask., Can. 57 50 1N 102 21W
Kennedy I. 62 54 3N 130 11W
Kennedy L. 62 49 3N 125 32W
Kennedy, Mt. 64 81 2N 78 55W
Kennedy Taungdeik 125 23 35N 94 4E
Kennet, R. 95 51 24N 1 7W
Kennetcook 39 45 11N 63 44W
Kennett 75 36 7N 90 0W
Kennewick 78 46 11N 119 2W
Keno Hill 96 63 57N 135 18W
Kénogami 41 48 25N 71 15W
Kénogami, L. 41 48 20N 71 23W
Kenogami, R. 53 51 6N 84 28W
Kenora 52 49 47N 94 29W
Kenosha 77 42 33N 87 48W
Kensington, P.E.I., Can. 39 46 28N 63 34W
Kensington, Qué., Can. 43 45 1N 74 18W
Kensington, U.S.A. 74 39 48N 99 2W
Kent, Ohio, U.S.A. 70 41 8N 81 20W
Kent, Oreg., U.S.A. 78 45 11N 120 45W
Kent, Tex., U.S.A. 75 31 5N 104 12W
Kent, Wash., U.S.A. 80 47 23N 122 14W
Kent □ 95 51 12N 0 40E
Kent Junction 39 46 35N 65 20W
Kent Pen. 64 68 30N 107 0W
Kent, Vale of 98 51 12N 0 30E
Kentau 120 43 32N 68 36E
Kentland 77 40 45N 87 25W
Kenton 77 40 40N 83 35W
Kentucky □ 72 37 20N 85 0W
Kentucky Dam 72 37 2N 88 15W
Kentucky L. 73 36 0N 88 0W
Kentucky, R. 77 38 41N 85 11W
Kentville 39 45 6N 64 29W
Kentwood 75 31 0N 90 30W
Kenville 57 52 0N 101 20W
Kenya ■ 116 2 20N 38 0E
Kenya, Mt. 116 0 10S 37 18E
Keokuk 76 40 25N 91 24W
Keosauqua 76 40 44N 91 58W
Keota 76 41 22N 91 57W
Kepi 127 6 32S 139 19E
Keppel B. 135 23 21S 150 55E
Kepsut 122 39 40N 28 15E
Kepuhi 67 22 13N 159 21W
Kepulauan, R. 127 5 30S 139 0E
Kepulauan Sunda, Ketjil Barat □ 126 8 50S 117 30E
Kepulauan Sunda, Ketjil Timor □ 127 9 30S 122 0E
Kerala □ 124 11 0N 76 15E
Kerang 136 35 40S 143 55E
Keray 123 26 15N 57 30E
Kerch 120 45 20N 36 20E
Keremeos 63 49 13N 119 50W
Kerguelen I. 16 48 15S 69 10E
Kericho 116 0 22S 35 15E
Kerinci 126 2 5S 101 0E
Kerki 120 37 50N 65 12E
Kérkira 109 39 38N 19 50E
Kermadec Is. 14 31 8S 175 16W
Kermān 123 30 15N 57 1E
Kerman 80 36 43N 120 4W
Kermān □ 123 30 0N 57 0E
Kermānshāh 122 34 23N 47 0E
Kermānshāh □ 122 34 0N 46 30E
Kermit 75 31 56N 103 3W
Kern, R. 81 35 16N 119 18W
Kernville 81 35 45N 118 26W
Kerrobert 73 52 0N 109 11W
Kerrville 75 30 1N 99 8W
Kerry □ 97 52 7N 9 35W
Kerry Hd. 97 52 26N 9 56W
Kersley 63 52 49N 122 25W
Kertosono 127 7 38S 112 9E
Kerulen, R. 130 48 48N 117 0E
Kesagami L. 34 50 23N 80 15W
Kesagami, R. 34 51 4N 79 45W
Keski Suomen □ 110 62 45N 25 15E
Kessel-Lo 105 50 53N 4 43E
Kestenga 120 66 0N 31 50E
Keswick, Can. 46 44 15N 79 28W
Keswick, U.K. 94 54 35N 3 9W
Ketapang 126 1 55S 110 0E
Ketchikan 67 55 25N 131 40W
Ketchum 78 43 50N 114 27W
Kettering, U.K. 95 52 24N 0 44W
Kettering, U.S.A. 77 39 41N 84 10W
Kettle Falls 63 48 41N 118 2W
Kettle Pt. 46 43 13N 82 1W
Kettle, R., B.C., Can. 63 48 41N 118 7W
Kettle, R., Man., Can. 55 56 23N 94 34W
Kettle R. 82 46 22N 92 53W
Kettleman City 80 36 1N 119 58W
Kevin 61 48 45N 111 58W
Kewanee 76 41 18N 90 0W
Kewanna 77 41 1N 86 25W
Kewaunee 72 44 27N 87 30W
Keweenaw B. 52 46 56N 88 23W
Keweenaw Pen. 72 47 30N 88 0W
Keweenaw Pt. 72 47 26N 87 40W
Key Harbour 46 45 50N 80 45W
Key West 84 24 40N 82 0W
Keyesport 76 38 45N 89 17W
Keyport 71 40 26N 74 12W
Keyser 72 39 26N 79 0W
Keystone, S.D., U.S.A. 74 43 54N 103 27W
Keystone, W. Va., U.S.A. 72 37 30N 81 30W
Keytesville 76 39 26N 92 56W
Kezhma 121 59 15N 100 57E
Khabarovo 120 69 30N 60 30E
Khabarovsk 121 48 20N 135 0E
Khaibar 122 25 38N 39 28E
Khairpur 124 27 32N 68 49E
Khairpur □ 124 23 30N 69 8E
Khakhea 117 24 48S 23 22E
Khalij-e-Fars □ 123 28 20N 51 45E
Khalkís 109 38 27N 23 42E
Khalmer-Sede = Tazovskiy 120 67 30N 78 30E
Khalmer Yu 120 67 58N 65 1E
Khalturin 120 58 40N 48 50E
Khan Tengri 129 42 25N 80 10E
Khanabad 123 36 45N 69 5E
Khānaqin 122 34 23N 45 25E
Khandwa 124 21 49N 76 22E
Khandyga 121 62 30N 134 50E
Khanewal 124 30 20N 71 55E
Khaniá 109 35 30N 24 4E
Khanion Kólpos 109 35 33N 23 55E
Khanka, Oz. 120 45 0N 132 30E
Khanty-Mansiysk 120 61 0N 69 0E
Kharagpur 125 22 20N 87 25E
Kharan Kalat 124 28 34N 65 21E
Kharānaq 123 32 20N 54 45E
Kharda 124 18 40N 75 40E
Kharfa 122 22 0N 46 35E
Kharg, Jazireh 122 29 15N 50 28E
Khargon 124 21 45N 75 35E
Kharkov 120 49 58N 36 20E
Kharsaniya 122 27 10N 49 10E
Khartoum = El Khartûm 115 15 31N 32 35E
Khasab 123 26 14N 56 15E
Khāsh 124 28 15N 61 5E
Khashm el Girba 115 14 59N 35 58E
Khaskovo 109 41 56N 25 30E
Khatanga 121 72 0N 102 20E
Khatanga, Zaliv 17 66 0N 112 0E
Khatyrka 121 62 3N 175 15E
Khavar □ 122 37 20N 46 0E
Khed Brahma 124 24 7N 73 5E
Khedive 56 49 37N 104 31W
Khemmarat 128 16 10N 105 15E
Khenmarak Phouminville 126 11 40N 102 58E
Kherson 120 46 35N 32 35E
Khetinsiring 129 32 52N 92 21E
Khilok 121 51 30N 110 45E
Khingan, mts. 118 47 0N 119 30E
Khíos 109 38 27N 26 9E
Khíos, I. 109 38 20N 26 0E
Khiva 120 41 30N 60 18E
Khiyāv 122 38 30N 47 45E
Khlong, R. 128 15 30N 98 50E
Khmelnitsky 107 49 23N 27 0E
Khmer Republic ■ = Cambodia 128 12 15N 105 0E
Khoi 122 38 40N 45 0E
Khojak P. 124 30 55N 66 30E
Kholm 120 57 10N 31 15E
Kholmsk 121 35 5N 139 48E
Khomayn 122 33 40N 50 7E
Khon Kaen 128 16 30N 102 47E
Khong 128 13 55N 105 56E
Khong, R. 128 15 0N 106 50E
Khonh Hung (Soc Trang) 128 9 37N 105 50E
Khonu 121 66 30N 143 25E
Khoper, R. 120 52 0N 43 20E
Khorasan □ 123 34 0N 58 0E
Khorat = Nakhon Ratchasima 128 14 59N 102 12E
Khorat, Cao Nguyen 128 15 30N 102 50E
Khorat Plat. 128 15 30N 102 50E
Khorog 120 37 30N 71 36E
Khorramābād 122 33 30N 48 25E
Khorromshahr 122 30 29N 48 15E
Khotan = Hotien 129 37 6N 79 59E
Khu Khan 128 14 42N 104 12E
Khufaifiya 122 24 50N 44 35E
Khugiani 124 31 28N 66 14E
Khulna 125 22 45N 89 34E
Khulna □ 125 22 45N 89 35E
Khūr 123 32 55N 58 18E
Khurais 122 24 55N 48 5E
Khurma 122 21 58N 42 3E
Khush 124 32 55N 62 10E
Khushab 124 32 20N 72 20E
Khuzdar 124 27 52N 66 30E
Khuzestan □ 122 31 0N 50 0E
Khvor 123 33 45N 55 0E
Khvormūj 123 28 40N 51 30E
Khvoy 122 38 35N 45 0E
Khwaja Muhammad 123 36 0N 70 0E
Khyber Pass 124 34 10N 71 8E
Kiahsien 130 38 10N 110 8E
Kiama 136 34 40S 150 50E
Kiamusze 130 46 45N 130 30E
Kian 131 27 1N 114 58E
Kianghwa 131 25 26N 111 29E
Kiangling 131 30 28N 113 16E
Kiangpeh 131 29 40N 106 30E
Kiangshan 131 28 51N 118 38E
Kiangsi □ 131 27 20N 115 40E
Kiangsu □ 131 33 0N 119 50E
Kiangyin 131 31 51N 120 0E

Kiangyu Kokand

Kiangyu 131 31 41N 104 26 E
Kiaochow Wan 130 36 10N 120 15 E
Kiaohsien 130 36 20N 120 0 E
Kiawang 131 34 23N 117 28 E
Kibangou 116 3 18 S 12 22 E
Kibombo 116 3 57 S 25 53 E
Kibondo 116 3 35 S 30 45 E
Kibwesa 116 6 30 S 29 58 E
Kibwezi 116 2 27 S 37 57 E
Kichiga 121 59 50N 163 5 E
Kichow 131 30 0N 115 30 E
Kicking Horse Pass 63 51 28N 116 16W
Kidderminster 95 52 24N 2 13W
Kidnappers, C. 133 39 38 S 177 5 E
Kiel 106 54 16N 10 8 E
Kielce 107 50 58N 20 42 E
Kieler Bucht 106 54 30N 10 30 E
Kienhinghsien 131 26 50N 116 50 E
Kienhsien 131 34 30N 108 16 E
Kienko 131 31 50N 105 30 E
Kienning 131 27 4N 118 21 E
Kienow 131 27 0N 118 16 E
Kienshui 129 23 57N 102 45 E
Kiensi 131 26 58N 106 0 E
Kienteh 131 29 30N 119 28 E
Kienyang, Fukien, China 131 27 30N 118 0 E
Kienyang, Hunan, China 131 27 10N 109 50 E
Kiev = Kiyev 120 50 30N 30 28 E
Kifri 122 34 45N 45 0 E
Kigali 116 1 5 S 30 4 E
Kiglapait Mts. 36 57 6N 61 22W
Kigoma-Ujiji 116 5 30 S 30 0 E
Kihsien 130 36 20N 110 35 E
Kii-Suido 132 33 40N 135 0 E
Kijik 67 60 20N 154 20W
Kikiang 131 28 58N 106 44 E
Kikinda 109 45 50N 20 30 E
Kikino 60 54 27N 112 8W
Kikkatla 62 53 47N 130 25W
Kikládhes □ 109 37 0N 25 0 E
Kikládhes, Is. 109 37 20N 24 30 E
Kikwit 116 5 5 S 18 45 E
Kilauea 67 22 13N 159 25W
Kilauea Crater 67 19 24N 155 17W
Kilbride, Newf., Can. 37 47 32N 52 45W
Kilbride, Ont., Can. 49 43 25N 79 56W
Kilbuck Mts. 67 60 30N 160 0W
Kildala Arm 62 53 50N 128 29W
Kildare 97 53 10N 6 50W
Kildare □ 97 53 10N 6 50W
Kilembe 116 0 15N 30 3 E
Kilgore 75 32 22N 94 55W
Kilimanjaro, Mt. 116 3 7 S 37 20 E
Kilindini 116 4 4 S 39 40 E
Kilis 122 36 50N 37 10 E
Kilkee 97 52 41N 9 40W
Kilkenny 97 52 40N 7 17W
Kilkenny □ 97 52 35N 7 15W
Kilkieran B. 97 53 18N 9 45W
Killala 97 54 13N 9 12W
Killala B. 97 54 20N 9 12W
Killala L. 53 49 5N 86 32W
Killaloe 97 52 48N 8 28W
Killaloe Sta. 47 45 33N 77 25W
Killaly 56 50 45N 102 50W
Killam 61 52 47N 111 51W
Killarney, Man., Can. 34 49 10N 99 40W
Killarney, Ont., Can. 55 45 55N 81 30W
Killarney, Ireland 97 52 2N 9 30W
Killarney, L's. of 97 52 0N 9 30W
Killarney Prov. Park 46 46 2N 81 35W
Killary Harb. 97 53 38N 9 52W
Killbuck 70 40 29N 81 58W
Killdeer, Can. 56 49 6N 106 22W
Killdeer, U.S.A. 74 47 26N 102 48W
Killeen 75 31 7N 97 45W
Killiecrankie P. 96 56 44N 3 46W
Killinek I. 36 60 24N 64 37W
Killíni, Mts. 109 37 54N 22 25 E
Killowen 43 45 36N 74 15W
Killybegs 97 54 38N 8 26W
Kilmar 43 45 46N 74 37W
Kilmarnock 96 55 36N 4 30W
Kilmore 136 37 25 S 144 53 E
Kilosa 116 6 48 S 37 0 E
Kilrush 97 52 39N 9 30W
Kilwa Kisiwani 116 8 58 S 39 32 E
Kilwa Kivinje 116 8 45 S 39 25 E
Kim 75 37 18N 103 20W
Kimba 134 33 8 S 136 23 E
Kimball, Nebr., U.S.A. 74 41 17N 103 40W
Kimball, S.D., U.S.A. 74 43 47N 98 57W
Kimberley, Austral. 134 16 20 S 127 0 E
Kimberley, Can. 61 49 40N 115 59W
Kimberley, S. Afr. 117 28 43 S 24 46 E
Kimberly 78 42 33N 114 25W
Kimbo 49 43 7N 79 36W
Kimchaek 130 40 40N 129 10 E
Kimiwan L. 60 55 45N 116 55W
Kimsquit 62 52 45N 126 57W
Kinabalu, mt. 126 6 0N 116 0 E
Kinaskan L. 54 57 38N 130 8W
Kincaid 56 49 40N 107 0W
Kincald 76 39 35N 89 25W
Kincardine 46 44 10N 81 40W
Kinchwan 130 42 28N 126 6 E
Kinde 46 43 56N 83 0W
Kindersley 56 51 30N 109 10W
Kindia 114 10 0N 12 52W
Kindu 116 2 55 S 25 50 E
King City, Can. 50 43 56N 79 32W
King City, U.S.A. 76 40 3N 94 31W
King City, Calif., U.S.A. 80 36 11N 121 8W
King Frederick VI Land 17 63 0N 43 0W
King Frederick VIII Land 17 77 30N 25 0W
King George B. 90 51 30 S 60 30W
King George I. 91 60 0 S 60 0W
King George Is. 36 57 20N 78 25W
King George Sd. 134 35 5 S 118 0 E
King I., Austral. 135 39 50 S 144 0 E
King I., Can. 62 52 10N 127 40W
King I. = Kadah Kyun 128 12 30N 98 20 E
King Leopold Ranges 134 17 20 S 124 20 E
King Sd. 134 16 50 S 123 20 E
King William I. 65 69 10N 97 25W
King William's Town 117 32 51 S 27 22 E
Kingaroy 135 26 32 S 151 51 E
Kingcome Inlet 62 50 56N 126 29W
Kingfisher 75 35 50N 97 55W
Kinghorn 50 43 55N 79 34W
Kingku 129 23 49N 100 30 E
Kingman, U.S.A. 77 39 58N 87 18W
Kingman, Ariz., U.S.A. 81 35 12N 114 2W
Kingman, Kans., U.S.A. 75 37 41N 98 9W
Kingmen 131 31 10N 112 15 E
Kingning 131 27 55N 119 30 E
Kingpeng 130 43 10N 117 25 E
Kings B. 17 78 0N 15 0 E
Kings Canyon National Park 80 37 0N 118 35W
King's Lynn 94 52 45N 0 25 E
Kings Mountain 73 35 13N 81 20W
King's Peak 78 40 46N 110 27W
King's Point 37 49 35N 56 11W
Kings, R. 80 36 10N 119 50W
Kingsburg 80 36 35N 119 36W
Kingsbury 77 41 31N 86 42W
Kingscourt 97 53 55N 6 48W
Kingsey Falls 41 45 51N 72 4W
Kingsgate 61 49 1N 116 11W
Kingsley 74 42 37N 95 58W
Kingsley Dam 74 41 20N 101 40W
Kingsmere L. 56 54 6N 106 27W
Kingsport 73 36 33N 82 36W
Kingston, N.S., Can. 39 44 59N 64 57W
Kingston, Ont., Can. 47 44 14N 76 30W
Kingston, Jamaica 84 18 0N 76 50W
Kingston, N.Z. 133 45 20 S 168 43 E
Kingston, Mich., U.S.A. 46 43 29N 83 11W
Kingston, Mo., U.S.A. 76 39 38N 94 2W
Kingston, N.Y., U.S.A. 71 41 55N 74 0W
Kingston, Pa., U.S.A. 71 41 19N 75 58W
Kingston, R.I., U.S.A. 71 41 29N 71 30W
Kingston, Wash., U.S.A. 80 47 48N 122 30W
Kingston Mines 76 40 34N 89 47W
Kingston Pk. 81 35 45N 115 54W
Kingstown 85 13 10N 61 10W
Kingstree 73 33 40N 79 48W
Kingsville, Can. 46 42 2N 82 45W
Kingsville, U.S.A. 75 27 30N 97 53W
Kingtai 130 37 4N 103 59 E
Kingtehchen (Fowliang) 131 29 8N 117 21 E
Kingtzekwan 131 33 25N 111 10 E
Kingussie 96 47 5N 4 2W
Kingyang 130 36 6N 107 49 E
Kinhsien 130 36 6N 107 49 E
Kinhwa 131 29 5N 119 32 E
Kinistino 56 52 57N 105 2W
Kinkala 116 4 18 S 14 49 E
Kinkora 39 46 19N 63 36W
Kinleith 133 38 20 S 175 56 E
Kinloch 133 44 51 S 168 20 E
Kinmen (Quemoy) Is. 131 24 25N 118 24 E
Kinmount 47 44 48N 78 45W
Kinmundy 77 38 46N 88 51W
Kinnaird 63 49 17N 117 39W
Kinnaird's Hd. 96 57 40N 2 0W
Kino 82 28 45N 111 59W
Kinoje Ls. 53 51 35N 81 48W
Kinoje, R. 34 52 8N 81 25W
Kinping 128 22 56N 103 15 E
Kinross 96 56 13N 3 25W
Kinsale, Can. 51 43 56N 79 2W
Kinsale, Ireland 97 51 42N 8 31W
Kinsale Harbour 97 51 40N 8 30W
Kinsale Old Hd. 97 51 37N 8 32W
Kinsha (Yangtze) 129 32 30N 98 30 E
Kinshasa 116 4 20 S 15 15 E
Kinsiang 131 35 4N 116 25 E
Kinsley 75 37 57N 99 30W
Kinston 73 35 18N 77 35W
Kintap 126 3 51 S 115 13 E
Kintyre, Mull of 96 55 17N 5 4W
Kintyre, pen. 96 55 30N 5 35W
Kinushseo, R. 34 55 15N 83 45W
Kinuso 60 55 20N 115 25W
Kinzua 70 41 52N 78 58W
Kinzua Dam 70 41 53N 79 0W
Kioshan 131 32 50N 114 0 E
Kiosk 47 46 6N 78 53W
Kiowa, Kans., U.S.A. 75 37 3N 98 30W
Kiowa, Okla., U.S.A. 75 34 45N 95 50W
Kipahigan L. 55 55 20N 101 55W
Kiparissia 109 37 15N 21 40 E
Kiparissiakós Kólpos 109 37 25N 21 25 E
Kipawa 40 46 47N 78 59W
Kipawa L. 40 46 50N 79 0W
Kipawa, Parc de 40 47 0N 78 50W
Kipawa Res. Prov. Park 34 47 0N 78 30W
Kipembawe 116 7 38 S 33 27 E
Kipili 116 7 28 S 30 32 E
Kipling 56 50 6N 102 38W
Kipnuk 67 59 55N 164 7W
Kippens 37 48 33N 58 38W
Kippure, Mt. 97 53 11N 6 23W
Kipushi 117 11 48 S 27 12 E
Kirensk 121 57 50N 107 55 E
Kirgiz S.S.R. □ 120 42 0N 75 0 E
Kiri 116 1 29 S 19 25 E
Kirikkale 122 39 51N 33 32 E
Kirin 130 43 58N 126 31 E
Kirin □ 130 43 50N 125 45 E
Kirkcaldy 96 56 7N 3 10W
Kirkcudbright 96 54 50N 4 3W
Kirkee 124 18 34N 73 56 E
Kirkenes 110 69 40N 30 5 E
Kirkfield 47 44 34N 78 59W
Kirkfield Park 58 49 53N 97 17W
Kirkintilloch 96 55 57N 4 10W
Kirkjubæjarklaustur 110 63 47N 18 4W
Kirkland, Can. 44 45 27N 73 52W
Kirkland, U.S.A. 77 42 5N 88 51W
Kirkland, Ariz., U.S.A. 79 34 29N 112 46W
Kirkland, Wash., U.S.A. 78 47 40N 122 10W
Kirkland Lake 34 48 9N 80 2W
Kırklareli 109 41 44N 27 15 E
Kirklin 77 40 12N 86 22W
Kirksville 76 40 8N 92 35W
Kirkūk 122 35 30N 44 21 E
Kirkwall, Can. 49 43 21N 80 10W
Kirkwall, U.K. 96 58 59N 2 59W
Kirkwood 76 38 35N 90 24W
Kirov, R.S.F.S.R., U.S.S.R. 120 58 35N 49 40 E
Kirov, R.S.F.S.R., U.S.S.R. 120 58 35N 49 40 E
Kirovabad 120 40 45N 46 10 E
Kirovograd 120 48 35N 32 20 E
Kirovsk 120 67 48N 33 50 E
Kirriemuir 55 51 56N 110 20W
Kirşehir 122 39 14N 34 5 E
Kirthar Range 124 27 0N 67 0 E
Kiruna 110 67 52N 20 15 E
Kirundu 116 0 50 S 25 35 E
Kiryū 132 36 24N 139 20 E
Kisalaya 84 14 40N 84 3W
Kisangani 116 0 35N 25 15 E
Kisar, I. 127 8 5 S 127 10 E
Kisaran 126 2 47N 99 29 E
Kisaratzu 132 35 25N 139 59 E
Kisbey 56 49 39N 102 40W
Kiselevsk 120 54 5N 86 6 E
Kishanganj 125 26 3N 88 14 E
Kishangarh 124 27 50N 70 30 E
Kishinev 120 47 0N 28 50 E
Kishiwada 132 34 28N 135 22 E
Kishow 131 28 16N 109 47 E
Kishtwar 124 33 20N 75 48 E
Kishwaukee, R. 77 42 12N 89 8W
Kisi 130 45 21N 131 0 E
Kisii 116 0 40 S 34 45 E
Kisiju 116 7 23 S 39 19 E
Kiska I. 67 52 0N 177 30 E
Kiskatinaw, R. 54 56 8N 120 10W
Kiskitto L. 57 54 16N 98 30W
Kiskittogisu L. 57 54 13N 98 20W
Kiskörös 107 46 37N 19 20 E
Kiskunfelégyháza 107 46 42N 19 53 E
Kiskunhalas 107 46 28N 19 37 E
Kismayu 113 0 20 S 42 30 E
Kiso-Gawa 132 35 20N 137 0 E
Kiso-Sammyaku 132 35 30N 137 45 E
Kissimmee 73 28 18N 81 22W
Kissimmee, R. 73 27 20N 81 0W
Kississing L. 55 55 10N 101 10W
Kisumu 116 0 3 S 34 45 E
Kit Carson 74 38 48N 102 45W
Kita 114 13 5N 9 25W
Kitab 120 39 7N 66 52 E
Kitai 129 44 0N 89 27 E
Kitaibaraki 132 36 50N 140 45 E
Kitakami-Gawa 132 39 30N 141 15 E
Kitakyūshū 132 33 50N 130 50 E
Kitale 116 1 0N 35 12 E
Kitchener 49 43 27N 80 29W
Kitchigami, R. 34 50 35N 78 5W
Kitchioh 131 22 57N 116 2 E
Kitega = Citega 116 3 30 S 29 58 E
Kitgum Matidi 116 3 17N 32 52 E
Kithira 109 36 9N 23 0 E
Kithira, I. 109 36 15N 23 0 E
Kithnos 109 37 26N 24 27 E
Kíthnos, I. 109 37 25N 24 25 E
Kitimat 62 54 3N 128 38W
Kitimat Arm 62 53 55N 128 42W
Kitimat Ranges 62 54 0N 129 15W
Kitinen, R. 110 67 34N 26 40 E
Kitscoty 60 53 20N 110 20W
Kittanning 70 40 49N 79 30W
Kittatinny Mts. 71 41 0N 75 0W
Kittertoksoak, I. 36 58 50N 65 50W
Kittery 71 43 7N 70 42W
Kitui 116 1 17 S 38 0 E
Kitwe 117 12 54 S 28 7 E
Kityang 131 23 30N 116 29 E
Kiuchuan 129 39 51N 98 30 E
Kiukiang 131 29 37N 116 2 E
Kiuling Shan, mts. 131 28 30N 114 30 E
Kiungchow 131 19 57N 110 17 E
Kiungchow Haihsia 131 20 40N 110 0 E
Kivalina 67 67 45N 164 40W
Kivalo 110 66 18N 26 0 E
Kivitoo 65 67 56N 64 52W
Kivu, L. 116 1 48 S 29 0 E
Kiyang 131 26 36N 111 42 E
Kiyev 120 50 30N 30 28 E
Kiyuanshan 131 28 6N 117 46 E
Kizil Kiya 120 40 20N 72 35 E
Kizlyar 120 43 51N 46 40 E
Kizyl-Arvat 120 38 58N 56 15 E
Klabat, Teluk 126 1 30 S 105 40 E
Kladno 106 50 10N 14 7 E
Klagenfurt 106 46 38N 14 20 E
Klaipeda 120 55 43N 21 10 E
Klamath Falls 78 42 20N 121 50W
Klamath Mts. 78 41 20N 123 0W
Klamath, R. 78 41 40N 123 30W
Klang = Kelang 128 3 1N 101 33 E
Klappan, R. 54 58 0N 129 43W
Klarälven 111 60 32N 13 15 E
Klaten 127 7 43 S 110 36 E
Klatovy 106 49 23N 13 18 E
Klawak 54 55 35N 133 0W
Klawer 117 31 44 S 18 36 E
Kleczkowski, L. 38 50 48N 63 27W
Kleena Kleene 62 52 0N 124 50W
Klein 78 46 26N 108 31W
Kleinburg 50 43 50N 79 38W
Kleindale 62 49 38N 123 58W
Klemtu 54 52 35N 128 55W
Klerksdorp 117 26 51 S 26 38 E
Kletskaïa Kletskiy 120 49 20N 43 0 E
Kletskiy 120 49 20N 43 0 E
Kleve 105 51 46N 6 10 E
Klickitat 78 45 50N 121 10W
Klickitat, R. 80 45 42N 121 17W
Klin 120 56 28N 36 48 E
Klinaklini, R. 62 51 21N 125 40W
Kłodzko 106 50 28N 16 38 E
Klondike 64 64 0N 139 26W
Klotz, L. 36 60 32N 73 40W
Kluane L. 64 61 15N 138 40W
Kluang = Keluang 128 1 59N 103 20 E
Knaresborough 94 54 1N 1 29W
Knee L., Man., Can. 55 55 3N 94 45W
Knee L., Sask., Can. 55 55 51N 107 0W
Knewstubb L. 62 53 33N 124 55W
Knight Inlet 62 50 45N 125 40W
Knighton 95 52 21N 3 2W
Knights Ferry 80 37 50N 120 40W
Knight's Landing 80 38 50N 121 43W
Knightstown 77 39 49N 85 32W
Knob, C. 134 34 32 S 119 16 E
Knockmealdown Mts. 97 52 16N 8 0W
Knokke 105 51 20N 3 17 E
Knossos 109 35 18N 25 10 E
Knowlton 41 45 13N 72 31W
Knox 77 41 18N 86 36W
Knox, C. 62 54 11N 133 5W
Knox City 75 33 26N 99 38W
Knox Coast 91 66 30 S 108 0 E
Knoxville, Iowa, U.S.A. 76 41 20N 93 5W
Knoxville, Pa., U.S.A. 73 41 57N 77 26W
Knoxville, Tenn., U.S.A. 73 35 58N 83 57W
Knud Rasmussen Land 65 79 0N 60 0W
Ko Chang 128 12 0N 102 20 E
Ko Kut 128 11 40N 102 32 E
Ko Phangan 128 9 45N 100 10 E
Ko Phra Thong 128 9 6N 98 15 E
Ko Samui 128 9 30N 100 0 E
Koartac (Notre Dame de Koartac) 36 61 5N 69 36 E
Koba, Aru, Indon. 127 6 37 S 134 37 E
Koba, Bangka, Indon. 126 2 26 S 106 14 E
Kobarid 108 46 15N 13 30 E
Kobayashi 132 31 56N 130 59 E
Kōbe 132 34 45N 135 10 E
København 111 55 41N 12 34 E
Koblenz 105 50 21N 7 36 E
Kobroor, Kepulauan 127 6 10 S 134 30 E
Kobuk 67 66 55N 157 0W
Kobuk, R. 67 66 55N 157 0W
Kočani 109 41 55N 22 25 E
Kočevje 108 45 39N 14 50 E
Kōchi 132 33 30N 133 35 E
Kōchi-ken □ 132 33 40N 133 30 E
Kodiak 67 57 30N 152 45W
Kodiak I. 67 57 30N 152 45W
Kodiang 128 6 21N 100 18 E
Koes 117 26 0 S 19 15 E
Köflach 91 47 4N 15 4 E
Kōfu 132 35 40N 138 30 E
Kogaluk, R. 36 56 12N 61 44W
Koh-i-Baba, mts. 124 34 30N 67 0 E
Kohat 124 33 40N 71 29 E
Kohima 125 25 35N 94 10 E
Kohler Ra. 91 77 0N 110 0W
Kojabuti 127 2 36 S 140 37 E
Kokand 120 40 30N 70 57 E

Kokanee Glacier Prov. Park

Kweiyang

Kokanee Glacier Prov. Park 63 49 47N 117 10W
Kokas 127 2 42S 132 26E
Kokchetav 120 53 20N 69 10E
Kokemäenjoki 111 61 32N 21 44E
Kokiu 129 23 30N 103 0E
Kokkola (Gamlakarleby) 110 63 50N 23 8E
Koko Kyunzu 128 14 10N 93 25E
Koko-Nor 129 37 0N 100 0E
Koko Shili 125 35 20N 91 0E
Kokomo 72 40 30N 86 6W
Kokoura 121 71 35N 144 50E
Kokstad 117 30 32S 29 29E
Kola 120 68 45N 33 8E
Kola, I. 127 5 35S 134 30E
Kola Pen. = Kolskiy P-ov. 120 67 30N 38 0E
Kolagede 127 7 54S 110 26E
Kolaka 127 4 3S 121 46E
Kolar 124 13 12N 78 15E
Kolar Gold Fields 124 12 58N 78 16E
Kolari 110 67 20N 23 48E
Kolarovgrad 109 43 27N 26 42E
Kolayat 124 27 50N 72 50E
Koldewey I. 17 77 0N 18 0W
Kolding 111 55 30N 9 29E
Kole 116 3 16S 22 42E
Kolepom, Pulau 127 8 0S 138 30E
Kolguyev, Ostrov 120 69 20N 48 30E
Kolhapur 124 16 43N 74 15E
Kolín 106 50 2N 15 9E
Köln 105 50 56N 9 58E
Koło 107 52 14N 18 40E
Kołobrzeg 106 54 10N 15 35E
Kolomna 120 55 8N 38 45E
Kolonodale 127 2 3S 121 25E
Kolosib 125 24 15N 92 45E
Kolpashevo 120 58 20N 83 5E
Kolskiy Poluostrov 120 67 30N 38 0E
Kolwezi 116 10 40S 25 25E
Kolyma, R. 121 64 40N 153 0E
Kolymskoye, Okhotsko 121 63 0N 157 0E
Komandorskiye Ostrava 121 55 0N 167 0E
Komárno 107 47 49N 18 5E
Komi, A.S.S.R. □ 120 64 0N 55 0E
Kommunizma, Pik 120 39 0N 72 2E
Komodo 127 8 37S 119 20E
Komono 116 3 15S 13 20E
Komoran, Pulau 127 8 18S 138 45E
Komotiri 109 41 9N 25 26E
Kompong Cham 128 11 54N 105 30E
Kompong Chhnang 128 12 20N 104 35E
Kompong Speu 128 11 26N 104 32E
Kompong Thom 128 12 35N 104 51E
Komsomolets, Ostrov 121 80 30N 95 0E
Komsomolsk 121 50 30N 137 0E
Konawa 75 34 59N 96 46W
Kondoa 116 4 55S 35 50E
Kondratyevo 121 57 30N 98 30E
Kong 114 8 54N 4 36W
Kong Christian IX.s Land 17 68 0N 36 0W
Kong Christian X.s Land 17 74 0N 29 0W
Kong Frederik VIII.s Land 17 78 30N 26 0W
Kong Frederik VI.s Kyst 17 63 0N 43 0W
Kong, Koh 128 11 20N 103 0E
Kong Oscar Fjord 17 72 20N 24 0W
Kongmoon 131 22 35N 113 1E
Kongolo 116 5 22S 27 0E
Kongsberg 111 59 39N 9 39E
Kongsvinger 111 60 12N 12 2E
Konin 107 52 12N 18 15E
Konjic 109 43 42N 17 58E
Konosha 120 61 0N 40 5E
Konotop 120 51 12N 33 7E
Konskie 107 51 15N 20 23E
Konstanz 106 47 39N 9 10E
Kontagora 114 10 23N 5 27E
Kontum 128 14 24N 108 0E
Konya 122 37 52N 32 35E
Konza 116 1 45S 37 0E
Koo-wee-rup 136 38 13S 145 28E
Koocanusa, L. 61 49 20N 115 15W
Koog 17 52 27N 4 49E
Koolan I. 134 16 0S 123 45E
Kooloonong 136 34 48S 143 10E
Koorakee 136 34 27S 142 56E
Koorawatha 136 34 2S 148 33E
Kooskia 78 46 9N 115 59W
Koostatak 55 51 26N 97 26W
Kootenai, R. 78 48 30N 115 30W
Kootenay L. 63 49 45N 116 50W
Kootenay Nat. Park 61 51 0N 116 0W
Kootingal 89 31 1S 151 3E
Kopaonik Planina 109 43 10N 21 50E
Kópavogur 110 64 6N 21 55W
Koper 108 45 31N 13 44E
Kopervik 111 59 17N 5 17E
Kopeysk 120 55 7N 61 37E
Köping 111 59 31N 16 3E
Kopka, R. 52 50 4N 89 1W
Kopparberg 111 59 52N 15 0E
Kopparbergs län □ 67 61 20N 14 15E
Koppeh Dāgh 123 38 0N 58 0E
Korab, mt. 109 41 44N 20 40E
Korça 109 40 37N 20 50E
Korčula, I. 108 42 57N 17 0E
Kordestān □ 122 36 0N 47 0E
Kordestan, reg. 122 37 30N 42 0E
Korea, South ■ 130 36 0N 128 0E
Korea Strait 118 34 0N 129 30E
Korea,North ■ 130 40 0N 127 0E
Korhogo 114 9 29N 5 28W
Korim 127 0 58S 136 10E
Korinthiakós Kólpos 109 38 16N 22 30E
Kórinthos 109 37 56N 22 55E
Kōriyama 132 37 24N 140 23E
Korla 129 41 45N 86 4E
Kormack 53 47 38N 82 59W
Koro, I. 133 17 19S 179 23E
Koroc, R. 36 58 50N 65 50W
Korogwe 116 5 5S 38 25E
Koroit 136 38 18S 142 24E
Koror 127 7 20N 134 28E
Körös, R. 107 46 45N 20 20E
Korsakov 121 46 30N 142 42E
Korshunovo 121 58 37N 110 10E
Korsör 111 55 20N 11 9E
Kortrijk 105 50 50N 3 17E
Koryakskiy Khrebet 121 61 0N 171 0E
Kos 109 36 52N 27 19E
Kos, I. 109 36 50N 27 15E
Kosciusko 75 33 3N 89 34W
Kosciusko, I. 54 56 0N 133 40W
Kosciusko, Mt. 136 36 27S 148 16E
Koshkonong, L. 77 42 53N 88 58W
Košice 107 48 42N 21 15E
Kosŏnf 130 38 40N 128 22E
Kosovska-Mitrovica 109 42 54N 20 52E
Kosścian 106 52 5N 16 40E
Kôstî 115 13 8N 32 43E
Kostroma 120 57 50N 41 58E
Kostrzyn 106 52 24N 17 14E
Koszalin 106 54 12N 16 8E
Kota 124 25 14N 75 49E
Kota Baharu 128 6 7N 102 14E
Kota Kinabalu 126 6 0N 116 12E
Kota Tinggi 128 1 44N 103 53E
Kotaagung 126 5 38S 104 29E
Kotabaru 126 3 20S 116 20E
Kotabumi 126 4 49S 104 46E
Kotamobagu 127 0 57N 124 31E
Kotaneelee, R. 54 60 11N 123 42W
Kotawaringin 126 2 28S 111 27E
Kotcho L. 54 59 7N 121 12W
Kotelnich 120 58 20N 48 10E
Kotelnikovo 120 47 45N 43 15E
Kotelnyy, Ostrov 121 75 10N 139 0E
Kotka 111 60 28N 26 58E
Kotlas 120 61 15N 47 0E
Kotor 109 42 25N 18 47E
Kotri 124 25 22N 68 22E
Kottayam 124 9 35N 76 33E
Kotturu 124 14 45N 76 10E
Kotuy, R. 121 70 30N 103 0E
Kotzebue 67 66 50N 162 40W
Kotzebue Sd. 67 66 30N 164 0W
Kouango 116 5 0N 20 10E
Kouchibouguac Nat. Park 39 46 50N 65 20W
Koudougou 114 12 10N 2 20W
Kouilou, R. 116 4 10S 12 5E
Kouki 116 7 22N 17 3E
Koula Moutou 116 1 15S 12 25E
Koulen 128 13 50N 104 40E
Koulikoro 114 12 40N 7 50W
Koumradskiy 120 47 20N 75 0E
Kountze 75 30 20N 94 22W
Kouts 77 41 18N 87 2W
Kovel 120 51 10N 24 20E
Kovic, B. 36 61 35N 77 36W
Kowkash 53 50 20N 87 12W
Kowloon 131 22 20N 114 15E
Kowpangtze 130 41 24N 121 56E
Koyan, Pegunungan 126 3 15N 114 30E
Koyiu 131 23 2N 112 28E
Koyuk 67 64 55N 161 20W
Koyukuk, R. 67 65 45N 156 30W
Koza 131 26 20N 127 47E
Kozan 122 37 35N 35 50E
Kozàni 109 40 19N 21 47E
Kozhikode = Calicut 124 11 15N 75 43E
Kra Buri 128 10 22N 98 46E
Kra, Isthmus of = Kra, Kho Khot 128 10 15N 99 30E
Kra, Kho Khot 128 10 15N 99 30E
Kragan 127 6 43S 111 38E
Kragerø 111 58 52N 9 25E
Kragujevac 109 44 2N 20 56E
Krakatau = Rakata, Pulau 126 6 10S 105 20E
Kraków 107 50 4N 19 57E
Kraksaan 127 7 43S 113 23E
Kraljevo 109 43 44N 20 41E
Kramer 79 35 0N 117 38W
Kramfors 110 62 55N 17 48E
Kraskino 121 42 44N 130 48E
Krasnoarmeysk 120 50 32N 45 50E
Krasnodar 120 45 5N 38 50E
Krasnoïarsk 121 56 8N 93 0E
Krasnoperekopsk 120 46 0N 33 54E
Krasnoselkupsk 120 65 20N 82 10E
Krasnoturinsk 120 59 46N 60 12E
Krasnoufimsk 120 56 57N 57 46E
Krasnouralsk 120 58 21N 60 3E
Krasnovodsk 120 40 0N 52 52E
Krasnoyarsk 121 56 8N 93 0E
Kraśnik 107 50 55N 22 5E
Kratie 128 12 32N 106 10E
Kravanh, Chuor Phnum 128 12 0N 103 32E
Krawang 127 6 19N 107 18E
Krefeld 105 51 20N 6 22E
Kremenchug 120 49 5N 33 25E
Kremmling 78 40 10N 106 30W
Kremnica 107 48 45N 18 50E
Kribi 116 2 57N 9 56E
Krishna, R. 124 16 30N 77 0E
Krishnanagar 125 23 24N 88 33E
Kristiansand 111 58 9N 8 1E
Kristianstad 111 56 2N 14 9E
Kristianstad □ 111 56 15N 14 0E
Kristiansund 110 63 7N 7 45E
Kristiinankaupunki 110 62 16N 21 21E
Kristinehamn 111 59 18N 14 13E
Kristinestad 110 62 16N 21 21E
Kríti, I. 109 35 15N 25 0E
Krivoy Rog 120 47 51N 33 20E
Krk, I. 108 45 8N 14 40E
Kroeng Krai 128 14 55N 98 30E
Kronobergs län □ 111 56 45N 14 30E
Kronprins Harald Kyst 91 70 0S 35 1E
Kronprins Olav Kyst 91 69 0S 42 0E
Kronprinsesse Märtha Kyst 91 73 30S 10 0W
Kronshtadt 120 60 5N 29 35E
Kroonstad 117 27 43S 27 19E
Kropotkin 121 45 25N 40 35E
Krosno 107 49 35N 21 56E
Krotoszyn 107 51 42N 17 23E
Krugersdorp 117 26 5S 27 46E
Krung Thep 128 13 45N 100 35E
Kruševac 109 43 35N 21 28E
Kruzof I. 54 57 10N 135 40W
Krydor 56 52 47N 107 4W
Krymskaya 120 45 0N 34 0E
Kuala 126 2 46N 105 47E
Kuala Kangsar 128 4 46N 100 56E
Kuala Kerai 128 5 30N 102 12E
Kuala Kubu Baharu 128 3 34N 101 39E
Kuala Lipis 128 4 10N 102 3E
Kuala Lumpur 128 3 9N 101 41E
Kuala Sedili Besar 128 1 55N 104 5E
Kuala Trengganu 128 5 20N 103 8E
Kualakahi Chan 67 22 2N 159 53W
Kualakapuas 126 2 55S 114 20E
Kualakurun 126 1 10S 113 50E
Kualapembuang, Indon. 126 2 52S 111 45E
Kualapembuang, Indon. 126 3 14S 112 38E
Kuandang 127 0 56N 123 1E
Kuantan 128 3 49N 103 20E
Kuba 120 41 21N 48 32E
Kucha 129 41 50N 82 30E
Kuchen 131 33 29N 117 27E
Kuching 126 1 33N 110 25E
Kuda 124 23 10N 71 15E
Kudat 126 6 55N 116 55E
Kudus 127 6 48S 110 51E
Kudymkar 120 59 1N 54 39E
Kufra, El Wâhât el 115 24 17N 23 15E
Kufstein 106 47 35N 12 11E
Kugaluk, B. 36 59 10N 78 40W
Kugmallit B. 67 69 0N 134 0W
Kugong, I. 36 56 18N 79 50W
Kūh-e-Aliju 123 31 30N 51 41E
Kūh-e-Dinar 123 30 10N 51 0E
Kūh-e-Hazārān 123 29 35N 57 20E
Kūh-e-Jebāl Bārez 123 29 0N 58 0E
Kūh-e-Sorkh 123 35 30N 58 45E
Kūh-e-Taftan 123 28 40N 61 0E
Kūhak 123 27 12N 63 10E
Kūhhā-ye-Bashākerd 123 26 45N 59 0E
Kūhhā-ye Sabalān 123 38 15N 47 45E
Kūhpāyeh 123 32 44N 52 20E
Kuinre 105 52 47N 5 51E
Kuiu I. 67 56 40N 134 15W
Kukukus L. 52 49 47N 91 41W
Kulai 128 1 44N 103 35E
Kulasekharapattanam 124 8 20N 78 0E
Kuldja = Ining 129 43 57N 81 20E
Kulm 74 46 22N 98 58W
Kulsary 120 46 59N 54 1E
Kulu 130 37 12N 115 2E
Kulunda 120 52 45N 79 15E
Kulunkai 130 42 46N 121 55E
Kulwin 136 35 0S 142 42E
Kulyab 120 37 55N 69 50E
Kum Darya 129 41 0N 89 0E
Kum Tekei 120 43 10N 79 30E
Kuma, R. 120 44 55N 45 57E
Kumagaya 132 36 9N 139 22E
Kumamoto 132 32 45N 130 45E
Kumamoto-ken □ 132 32 30N 130 40E
Kumanovo 109 42 9N 21 42E
Kumara 133 42 37S 171 12E
Kumasi 114 6 41N 1 38W
Kumba 116 4 36N 9 24E
Kume-guntō 131 26 8N 126 45E
Kumla 111 59 8N 15 10E
Kumon Bum 125 26 30N 97 15E
Kumukahi, C. 67 19 31N 154 49W
Kunar 124 34 30N 71 3E
Kunashir, Ostrov 121 44 0N 146 0E
Kunch 124 26 0N 79 10E
Kunduz 123 36 50N 68 50E
Kunduz □ 123 36 50N 68 50E
Kungan 131 30 0N 112 2E
Kungchuling 130 43 31N 124 58E
Kunghit I. 62 52 6N 131 3W
Kungho 129 36 28N 100 45E
Kungrad 120 43 6N 58 54E
Kungsbacka 111 57 30N 12 5E
Kungur 120 57 25N 56 57E
Kungyifow 131 22 24N 112 41E
Kunhsien 131 32 30N 111 17E
Kuningan 127 6 59S 108 29E
Kunlong 125 23 20N 98 50E
Kunlun Shan 129 36 0N 86 30E
Kunming 129 25 11N 102 37E
Kunsan 130 35 59N 126 45E
Kunshan 131 31 16N 121 0E
Kununurra 134 15 40S 128 39E
Kuopio 110 62 53N 27 35E
Kuopion Lääni □ 110 63 25N 27 10E
Kupa, R. 108 45 30N 16 10E
Kupang 127 10 19S 123 39E
Kupreanof I. 67 56 50N 133 30W
Kupyansk 120 49 45N 37 35E
Kurashiki 132 34 40N 133 50E
Kurayoshi 132 35 26N 133 50E
Kure 132 34 14N 132 32E
Kurgaldzhino 120 50 35N 70 20E
Kurgan, R.S.F.S.R., U.S.S.R. 120 55 26N 65 18E
Kurgan, R.S.F.S.R., U.S.S.R. 121 64 5N 172 50W
Kurigram 125 25 49N 89 39E
Kurilskiye Ostrova 121 45 0N 150 0E
Kurnool 124 15 45N 78 0E
Kuroki 56 51 52N 103 29W
Kurow 133 44 4S 170 29E
Kurri Kurri 136 32 50S 151 28E
Kursk 120 51 42N 36 11E
Kuršumlija 109 43 9N 21 19E
Kurtalān 122 37 55N 41 40E
Kuruman 117 27 28S 23 28E
Kurume 132 33 15N 130 30E
Kurunegala 124 7 30N 80 18E
Kurya 121 61 15N 108 10E
Kusagaki 131 30 54N 129 28E
Kusawa L. 54 60 20N 136 13W
Kushan 130 39 58N 123 30E
Kushih 131 32 12N 115 43E
Kushiro 132 43 0N 144 25E
Kushirogawa 132 43 0N 144 30E
Kushk 124 34 55N 62 30E
Kushka 120 35 20N 62 18E
Kushtia 125 23 55N 89 5E
Kuskokwim Bay 67 59 50N 162 56W
Kuskokwim Mts. 67 63 0N 156 0W
Kuskokwim, R. 67 61 48N 157 0W
Kustanay 120 53 10N 63 35E
Kutahya 122 39 30N 30 2E
Kutaisi 120 42 19N 42 40E
Kutaradja = Banda Aceh 126 5 35N 95 20E
Kutatjane 126 3 45N 97 50E
Kutch, G. of 124 22 50N 69 15E
Kutch, Rann of 124 24 0N 70 0E
Kutno 107 52 15N 19 23E
Kutu 116 2 40S 18 11E
Kuwait = Al Kuwayt 122 29 30N 47 30E
Kuwait ■ 122 29 30N 47 30E
Kuyang 130 41 8N 110 1E
Kuybyshev 120 55 27N 78 19E
Kuyung 131 32 0N 119 8E
Kvænangen 110 69 55N 21 15E
Kvarken 111 63 30N 21 0E
Kvarner 108 44 50N 14 10E
Kvarnerič 108 44 43N 14 37E
Kwadacha, R. 54 57 28N 125 38W
Kwakoegron 87 5 25N 55 25W
Kwando, R. 117 16 48S 22 45E
Kwangan 131 30 35N 106 40E
Kwangchow 131 23 10N 113 10E
Kwangchow Wan. 131 21 0N 111 0E
Kwangju 130 35 9N 126 55E
Kwangnan 129 24 10N 105 0E
Kwangping 130 36 40N 114 41E
Kwangshui 131 31 45N 114 0E
Kwangsi-Chuang □ 131 23 30N 108 55E
Kwangtseh 131 27 30N 117 25E
Kwangtsi 131 30 2N 115 46E
Kwangtung 131 23 35N 114 0E
Kwangyuan 131 32 30N 105 49E
Kwanhsien 129 30 59N 103 40E
Kwantung 129 25 12N 101 37E
Kwanyun 131 34 28N 119 29E
Kwataboahegan, R. 53 51 9N 80 50W
Kwatisore 127 3 7S 139 59E
Kweichih 131 30 40N 117 30E
Kweichow = Fengkieh 131 31 0N 109 33E
Kweichow □ 131 27 20N 107 0E
Kweihsien 131 22 59N 109 44E
Kweihwa = Mingki 131 26 10N 117 14E
Kweiki 131 28 10N 117 8E
Kweilin 131 25 16N 110 15E
Kweiping 131 23 12N 110 0E
Kweishun = Tsingsing 131 38 1N 114 4E
Kweitung 131 26 0N 113 35E
Kweiyang, Hunan, China 131 25 50N 112 25E

Name	Map	Lat °	Lat ′		Long °	Long ′	
Kweiyang, Kweichow, China	131	26	30	N	106	35	E
Kwethluk	67	60	45	N	161	34	W
Kwidzyn	107	54	45	N	18	58	E
Kwigillingok	67	59	50	N	163	10	W
Kwiguk	67	63	45	N	164	35	W
Kwinana	134	32	15	S	115	47	E
Kwinitsa	62	54	19	N	129	22	W
Kwo Ho	131	33	20	N	116	50	E
Kwohwa	131	23	10	N	107	0	E
Kwoyang	131	33	35	N	116	15	E
Kyabram	136	36	19	S	145	4	E
Kyaikto	128	17	20	N	97	3	E
Kyakhta	121	50	30	N	106	25	E
Kyargas Nuur	129	49	0	N	93	0	E
Kyaukpadaung	125	20	52	N	95	8	E
Kyaukpyu	125	19	28	N	93	30	E
Kyaukse	125	21	36	N	96	10	E
Kyburz	80	38	47	N	120	18	W
Kyle	56	50	50	N	108	2	W
Kyle Dam	117	20	15	S	31	0	E
Kyle of Lochalsh	96	57	17	N	5	43	W
Kyneton	136	37	10	S	144	29	E
Kynoch Inlet	62	52	45	N	128	0	W
Kyō-ga-Saki	132	35	45	N	135	15	E
Kyoga, L.	116	1	35	N	33	0	E
Kyongju	130	35	50	N	129	13	E
Kyongpyaw	125	17	12	N	95	10	E
Kyōto	132	35	0	N	135	45	E
Kyōto-fu □	132	35	15	N	135	30	E
Kyrenia	122	35	20	N	33	20	E
Kystatyam	121	67	20	N	123	10	E
Kytalktakh	121	65	30	N	123	40	E
Kyulyunken	121	64	10	N	137	5	E
Kyunhla	125	23	25	N	95	15	E
Kyuquot	62	50	3	N	127	25	W
Kyūshū	132	33	0	N	131	0	E
Kyushu, I.	132	32	30	N	131	0	E
Kyūshū-Sanchi	132	32	45	N	131	40	E
Kyustendil	109	42	25	N	22	41	E
Kyusyur	121	70	39	N	127	15	E
Kywong	136	34	58	S	146	44	E
Kyzyl	121	51	50	N	94	30	E
Kyzyl-Kiya	120	40	16	N	72	8	E
Kyzyl Orda	120	44	56	N	65	30	E
Kyzyl Rabat	120	37	45	N	74	55	E
Kyzylkum	120	42	30	N	65	0	E
Kzyl-orda	120	44	48	N	65	28	E

L

Name	Map	Lat °	Lat ′		Long °	Long ′	
La Broquerie	57	49	25	N	96	30	W
La Havre, R.	39	44	14	N	64	20	W
La Push	80	47	55	N	124	38	W
Laau Pt.	67	21	57	N	159	40	W
Labastide	102	43	28	N	2	39	E
Labastide-Murat	102	44	39	N	1	33	E
Labe, R.	106	50	3	N	15	20	E
Laberge, L.	54	61	11	N	135	12	W
Labis	128	2	22	N	103	2	E
Laboa	127	8	6	S	122	50	E
Labouheyre	102	44	13	N	0	55	W
Laboulaye	88	34	10	S	63	30	W
Labrador City	38	52	57	N	66	55	W
Labranzagrande	86	5	33	N	72	34	W
Lábrea	86	7	15	S	64	51	W
Labrède	102	44	41	N	0	32	W
Labrie	42	46	48	N	70	56	W
Labrieville	41	49	18	N	69	34	W
Labuan, I.	126	5	15	N	115	38	W
Labuha	127	0	30	S	127	30	E
Labuhan	127	6	26	S	105	50	E
Labuhanbajo	127	8	28	S	120	1	E
Labuk, Telok	126	6	10	N	117	50	E
Lac Allard	38	50	33	N	63	24	W
Lac-Alouette	43	45	49	N	73	58	W
Lac-au-Saumon	38	48	25	N	67	22	W
Lac-aux-Sables	41	46	51	N	72	24	W
Lac Bouchette	41	48	16	N	72	11	W
Lac-Brière	43	45	50	N	73	58	W
Lac Carré	41	46	7	N	74	29	W
Lac-des-Écorces	40	46	34	N	75	22	W
Lac du Bonnet	57	50	15	N	96	4	W
Lac du Flambeau	74	46	1	N	89	51	W
Lac Édouard	41	47	40	N	72	16	W
Lac-Etchemin	41	46	24	N	70	30	W
Lac la Biche	60	54	45	N	111	58	W
Lac la Hache	63	51	49	N	121	27	W
Lac la Martre	64	63	8	N	117	16	W
Lac-l'Achigan	43	45	57	N	73	59	W
Lac-Lapierre	43	45	56	N	73	47	W
Lac-Marois	43	45	51	N	74	8	W
Lac-Meach	48	45	32	N	75	51	W
Lac-Mégantic	41	45	35	N	70	53	W
Lac-Millette	43	45	58	N	74	12	W
Lac-Rémi	40	46	1	N	74	46	W
Lac-St-Charles	42	46	54	N	71	23	W
Lac-Ste-Marie	40	45	57	N	75	57	W
Lac Seul	55	50	28	N	92	0	W
Lacadie	45	45	19	N	73	21	W
Lacanau, Étang de	102	44	58	N	1	7	W
Lacanau Médoc	102	44	59	N	1	5	W
Lacantum, R.	83	16	36	N	90	40	W
Lacaune	102	43	43	N	2	40	E
Lacaune, Mts. de	102	43	43	N	2	50	E
Laccadive Is. = Lakshadweep Is.	118	10	0	N	72	30	E
Lacepede Is.	134	16	55	S	122	0	E
Lacey	80	47	7	N	122	49	W
Lachenaie	45	45	42	N	73	33	W
Lachine	44	45	30	N	73	40	W
Lachlan, R.	136	34	22	S	143	55	E
Lachute	43	45	39	N	74	21	W
Lackawanna	70	42	49	N	78	50	W
Laclu	52	49	46	N	94	41	W
Lacolle	43	45	5	N	73	22	W
Lacombe	61	52	30	N	113	44	W
Lacon	76	41	2	N	89	24	W
Lacona, U.S.A.	76	41	11	N	93	23	W
Lacona, N.Y., U.S.A.	71	43	37	N	76	5	W
Laconia	71	43	32	N	71	30	W
Lacq	102	43	25	N	0	35	W
Lacrosse	78	46	51	N	117	58	W
Ladd	76	41	23	N	89	13	W
Laddonia	76	39	15	N	91	39	W
Lādiz	123	28	55	N	61	15	E
Ladner	66	49	5	N	123	4	W
Ladon	101	48	0	N	2	30	E
Ladozhskoye Ozero	120	61	15	N	30	30	E
Ladrone Is. = Mariana Is.	14	17	0	N	145	0	E
Lady Ann Str.	65	75	40	N	79	50	W
Lady Beatrix L.	34	52	0	N	76	50	W
Ladysmith, Can.	62	49	0	N	123	49	W
Ladysmith, S. Afr.	117	28	32	S	29	46	E
Ladysmith, U.S.A.	74	45	27	N	91	4	W
Lae	14	6	40	S	147	2	E
Læsø	111	57	15	N	10	53	E
Lafayette, U.S.A.	77	40	25	N	86	54	W
Lafayette, Colo., U.S.A.	74	40	0	N	105	2	W
Lafayette, Ga., U.S.A.	73	34	44	N	85	15	W
Lafayette, La., U.S.A.	75	30	18	N	92	0	W
Lafayette, Tenn., U.S.A.	73	36	35	N	86	0	W
Laferté	34	48	37	N	78	48	W
Laferte, R.	54	61	53	N	117	44	W
Lafia	114	8	30	N	8	34	E
Laflamme, R.	40	49	17	N	77	9	W
Laflèche	43	45	30	N	73	28	W
Lafleche	56	49	45	N	106	40	W
Lafontaine	43	45	48	N	74	1	W
Laforce	40	47	32	N	78	44	W
Laforest	34	47	4	N	81	12	W
Lagan, R.	97	54	35	N	5	55	W
Lagarfljót	110	65	40	N	14	18	W
Lagarto, Serra do	89	23	0	S	57	15	W
Lågen, R.	111	61	30	N	10	20	E
Laghman □	123	34	20	N	70	0	E
Laghouat	114	33	50	N	2	59	E
Lagnieu	103	45	55	N	5	20	E
Lagny	101	48	52	N	2	40	E
Lagonoy Gulf	127	13	50	N	123	50	E
Lagoon	63	48	25	N	123	28	W
Lagos, Nigeria	114	6	25	N	3	27	E
Lagos, Port.	104	37	5	N	8	41	W
Lagos de Moreno	82	21	21	N	101	55	W
Lagrange	77	41	39	N	85	25	W
Laguépie	102	44	8	N	1	57	E
Laguna, Brazil	89	28	30	S	48	50	W
Laguna, U.S.A.	79	35	3	N	107	28	W
Laguna Beach	81	33	31	N	117	52	W
Laguna Dam	79	32	55	N	114	30	W
Laguna Limpia	88	26	32	S	59	45	W
Laguna Madre	83	27	0	N	97	20	W
Lagunas, Chile	88	21	0	S	69	45	W
Lagunas, Peru	86	5	10	S	75	35	W
Lagunillas	86	10	8	N	71	16	W
Laha	130	48	9	N	124	30	E
Lahad Datu	127	5	0	N	118	30	E
Lahaina	67	20	52	N	156	41	W
Lahat	126	3	45	S	103	30	E
Lahewa	126	1	22	N	97	12	E
Lahijan	122	37	10	N	50	6	E
Lahn, R.	106	50	52	N	8	35	E
Laholm	111	56	30	N	13	2	E
Lahontan Res.	78	39	28	N	118	58	W
Lahore	124	31	32	N	74	22	E
Lahore □	124	31	55	N	74	5	E
Lahti	111	60	58	N	25	40	E
Lai (Béhagle)	114	9	25	N	16	30	E
Lai Chau	128	22	5	N	103	3	E
Laichow Wan	130	37	30	N	119	30	E
Laidlaw	63	49	20	N	121	36	W
Laifeng	131	29	30	N	109	30	E
L'Aigle	100	48	46	N	0	38	E
Laignes	101	47	50	N	4	20	E
Laila	122	22	10	N	46	40	E
Laillahue, Mt.	86	17	0	S	69	30	W
Laipin	131	23	45	N	109	10	E
Laird	56	52	43	N	106	35	W
Lairg	96	58	1	N	4	24	W
Lais	126	3	35	S	102	0	E
Laiyang	130	37	0	N	120	42	E
Laja, R.	82	20	55	N	100	46	W
Lajes	89	27	48	S	50	20	W
Lakar	127	8	15	S	128	17	E
Lake Alma	56	49	9	N	104	12	W
Lake Alpine	80	38	29	N	120	0	W
Lake Andes	74	43	10	N	98	32	W
Lake Anse	72	46	42	N	88	25	W
Lake Arthur	75	30	8	N	92	40	W
Lake Bluff	77	42	17	N	87	50	W
Lake Bronson	57	48	44	N	96	49	W
Lake Cargelligo	136	33	15	S	146	22	E
Lake Charles	75	30	15	N	93	10	W
Lake City, Colo, U.S.A.	79	38	3	N	107	27	W
Lake City, Fla., U.S.A.	73	30	10	N	82	40	W
Lake City, Iowa, U.S.A.	77	42	12	N	94	42	W
Lake City, Mich., U.S.A.	46	44	20	N	85	10	W
Lake City, Minn., U.S.A.	74	44	28	N	92	21	W
Lake City, Pa., U.S.A.	70	42	2	N	80	20	W
Lake City, S.C., U.S.A.	73	33	51	N	79	44	W
Lake Cowichan	62	48	49	N	124	3	W
Lake District	98	54	30	N	3	10	W
Lake Forest	77	42	15	N	87	50	W
Lake Geneva	77	42	36	N	88	26	W
Lake George	71	43	25	N	73	43	W
Lake Harbour	65	62	30	N	69	50	W
Lake Havasu City	81	34	25	N	114	29	W
Lake Hill	63	48	28	N	123	22	W
Lake Hughes	81	34	41	N	118	26	W
Lake Isabella	81	35	38	N	118	28	W
Lake Lenore	56	52	24	N	104	59	W
Lake Linden	52	47	11	N	88	26	W
Lake Louise	61	51	30	N	116	10	W
Lake Mead Nat. Rec. Area	81	36	0	N	114	30	W
Lake Michigan Beach	77	42	13	N	86	25	W
Lake Mills, U.S.A.	77	43	5	N	88	55	W
Lake Mills, Iowa, U.S.A.	74	43	23	N	93	33	W
Lake Nebagamon	52	46	30	N	91	42	W
Lake Odesse	77	42	47	N	85	8	W
Lake of the Woods	69	49	0	N	95	0	W
Lake Orion	77	42	47	N	83	14	W
Lake Providence	75	32	49	N	91	12	W
Lake River	34	54	22	N	82	31	W
Lake St. Peter	47	45	18	N	78	2	W
Lake Superior Prov. Park	53	47	45	N	84	45	W
Lake Traverse	34	45	56	N	78	4	W
Lake Tyers	136	37	52	S	148	5	E
Lake Victoria Res.	136	34	0	S	141	17	E
Lake View	50	43	34	N	79	33	W
Lake Villa	77	42	25	N	88	5	W
Lake Village	75	33	20	N	91	19	W
Lake Wales	73	27	55	N	81	32	W
Lake Worth	73	26	36	N	80	3	W
Lakefield, Ont., Can.	47	44	25	N	78	16	W
Lakefield, Qué., Can.	43	45	45	N	74	15	W
Lakeland	73	28	0	N	82	0	W
Lakemba, I.	133	18	13	S	178	47	W
Lakeport, Calif., U.S.A.	80	39	1	N	122	56	W
Lakeport, Mich., U.S.A.	46	43	7	N	82	30	W
Lakes Entrance	136	37	50	S	148	0	E
Lakeside, Ariz., U.S.A.	79	34	12	N	109	59	W
Lakeside, Calif., U.S.A.	81	32	52	N	116	55	W
Lakeside, Nebr., U.S.A.	74	42	5	N	102	24	W
Lakeview, Ont., Can.	48	45	21	N	75	50	W
Lakeview, Qué., Can.	43	45	53	N	74	34	W
Lakeview, Sask., Can.	58	50	25	N	104	38	W
Lakeview, Mich., U.S.A.	46	43	27	N	85	17	W
Lakeview, N.Y., U.S.A.	72	42	43	N	78	57	W
Lakeview, Oreg., U.S.A.	78	42	15	N	120	22	W
Lakewood, Calif., U.S.A.	81	33	51	N	118	8	W
Lakewood, N.J., U.S.A.	71	40	5	N	74	13	W
Lakewood, Ohio, U.S.A.	70	41	28	N	81	50	W
Laki	110	64	4	N	18	14	W
Lakin	75	37	58	N	101	18	W
Lakitusaki, R.	34	54	21	N	82	25	W
Lakonikós Kólpos	109	36	40	N	22	40	E
Lakor, I.	127	8	15	S	128	17	E
Lakota	74	48	0	N	98	22	W
Laksefjorden	110	70	45	N	26	50	E
Lakselv	110	70	2	N	24	56	E
Lakshadweep Is.	118	10	0	N	72	30	E
Lalín	104	42	40	N	8	5	W
Lalinde	102	44	50	N	0	44	E
Lamaline	37	46	52	N	55	49	W
Lamar, Colo., U.S.A.	74	38	9	N	102	35	W
Lamar, Mo., U.S.A.	75	37	30	N	94	20	W
Lamas	86	6	28	S	76	31	W
Lamastre	103	44	59	N	4	35	E
Lamatientze	130	46	46	N	124	46	E
Lamballe	100	48	29	N	2	31	W
Lambaréné	116	0	20	S	10	12	E
Lambay I.	97	53	30	N	6	0	W
Lambayeque □	86	6	45	S	80	0	W
Lambert	74	47	44	N	104	39	W
Lambert Land	17	79	12	N	20	30	W
Lambesc	103	43	39	N	5	16	E
Lambeth	46	42	54	N	81	18	W
Lambi Kyun, (Sullivan I.)	128	10	50	N	98	20	E
Lambton	41	45	50	N	71	5	W
Lambton, C.	64	71	5	N	123	9	W
Lambton Mills	50	43	39	N	79	31	W
Lame Deer	78	45	45	N	106	40	W
Lamego	104	41	5	N	7	52	W
Lamèque	39	47	45	N	64	38	W
Lamesa	75	32	45	N	101	57	W
Lamia	109	38	55	N	22	41	E
Lamitan	127	6	40	N	122	10	E
Lammermuir Hills	96	55	50	N	2	40	W
Lamming Mills	63	53	20	N	120	15	W
Lamoille	78	40	47	N	115	31	W
Lamon Bay	127	14	30	N	122	20	E
Lamoni	76	40	37	N	93	56	W
Lamont, Can.	60	53	46	N	112	50	W
Lamont, U.S.A.	76	42	35	N	91	40	W
Lamont, Calif., U.S.A.	81	35	15	N	118	55	W
Lampa	86	15	10	S	70	30	W
Lampang	128	18	18	N	99	31	E
Lampasas	75	31	5	N	98	10	W
Lampaul	100	48	28	N	5	7	W
Lampazos de Naranjo	82	27	2	N	100	32	W
Lampedusa, I.	108	35	36	N	12	40	E
Lampeter	95	52	6	N	4	6	W
Lampman	56	49	25	N	102	50	W
Lamprey	55	58	33	N	94	8	W
Lampung □	126	1	48	S	115	0	E
Lamu	116	2	10	S	40	55	E
Lamy	79	35	30	N	105	58	W
Lan Tsan Kiang (Mekong)	119	18	0	N	104	15	E
Lan Yu, I.	131	22	0	N	121	30	E
Lanark, Can.	47	45	1	N	76	22	W
Lanark, U.K.	96	55	40	N	3	48	W
Lancashire □	94	53	40	N	2	30	W
Lancaster, N.B., Can.	35	45	17	N	66	10	W
Lancaster, Ont., Can.	47	45	8	N	74	30	W
Lancaster, Ont., Can.	71	45	10	N	74	30	W
Lancaster, Qué., Can.	43	45	8	N	74	30	W
Lancaster, U.K.	94	54	3	N	2	48	W
Lancaster, Calif., U.S.A.	81	34	47	N	118	8	W
Lancaster, Ky., U.S.A.	77	37	40	N	84	40	W
Lancaster, Minn., U.S.A.	57	48	52	N	96	48	W
Lancaster, Mo., U.S.A.	76	40	31	N	92	32	W
Lancaster, N.H., U.S.A.	71	44	27	N	71	33	W
Lancaster, N.Y., U.S.A.	70	42	53	N	78	43	W
Lancaster, Pa., U.S.A.	71	40	4	N	76	19	W
Lancaster, S.C., U.S.A.	73	34	45	N	80	47	W
Lancaster, Wis., U.S.A.	76	42	48	N	90	43	W
Lancaster Sd.	65	74	13	N	84	0	W
Lancer	56	50	48	N	108	53	W
Lanchow	130	36	4	N	103	44	E
Lanciano	108	42	15	N	14	22	E
Lándana	116	5	11	S	12	5	E
Landau	105	49	12	N	8	7	E
Landeck	106	47	9	N	10	34	E
Landen	105	50	45	N	5	3	E
Landerneau	100	48	28	N	4	17	W
Landes □	102	43	57	N	0	48	W
Landes, Les	102	44	20	N	1	0	W
Landis	56	52	12	N	108	27	W
Landivisiau	100	48	31	N	4	6	W
Landrecies	101	50	7	N	3	40	E
Landrienne	40	48	30	N	77	50	W
Land's End, Can.	17	76	10	N	123	0	W
Land's End, U.K.	95	50	4	N	5	43	W
Landshut	106	48	31	N	12	10	E
Landskrona	111	56	53	N	12	50	E
Lanesboro	71	41	57	N	75	34	W
Lanett	73	33	0	N	85	15	W
Lanfeng	131	34	50	N	114	58	E
Lang Bay	62	49	45	N	124	21	W
Langara I.	62	54	14	N	133	1	W
Langchung (Paoning)	131	31	30	N	106	0	E
Langdon	74	48	47	N	98	24	W
Langeac	102	45	7	N	3	29	E
Langenburg	57	50	51	N	101	43	W
Langfeng	130	48	4	N	121	10	E
Langford	63	48	27	N	123	29	W
Langham	56	52	22	N	106	58	W
Langholm	96	55	9	N	2	59	W
Langjökull	110	64	39	N	20	12	W
Langkawi, P.	128	6	25	N	99	45	E
Langkon	126	6	30	N	116	40	E
Langlade, Can.	34	48	14	N	76	10	W
Langlade, St. P. & M.	37	46	50	N	56	20	W
Langley	66	49	7	N	122	39	W
Langlois	78	42	54	N	124	26	W
Langogne	102	44	43	N	3	50	E
Langon	102	44	33	N	0	16	W
Langoya	110	68	45	N	15	10	E
Langres	101	47	52	N	5	20	E
Langres, Plateau de	101	47	45	N	5	20	E
Langruth	57	50	23	N	98	40	W
Langsa	126	4	30	N	97	57	E
Langson	128	21	52	N	106	42	E
Langstaff	50	43	50	N	79	25	W
Langtry	75	29	50	N	101	33	W
Languedoc	102	43	58	N	4	0	E
Lanigan	56	51	51	N	105	2	W
Lannemezan	102	43	8	N	0	23	E
Lannilis	100	48	35	N	4	32	W
Lannion	100	48	46	N	3	29	W
Lanoraie	43	45	58	N	73	13	W
Lanouaille	102	45	24	N	1	9	E
Lansdale	71	40	14	N	75	18	W
Lansdowne	47	44	24	N	76	1	W
Lansdowne House	34	52	14	N	87	53	W
Lansford	71	40	48	N	75	55	W
Lansing, Can.	50	43	45	N	79	25	W
Lansing, U.S.A.	77	42	47	N	84	40	W
Lanslebourg	103	45	17	N	6	52	E
Lantuna	127	8	19	S	124	8	E
Lanus	88	34	44	S	58	27	W
Lanz I.	62	50	49	N	128	41	W
Lanzville	62	49	15	N	124	5	W
Lao Cai	128	22	30	N	103	57	E
Laoag	127	18	7	N	120	34	E
Laoang	127	12	32	N	125	8	E
Laois □	97	53	0	N	7	20	W

Laon Lewisburg

Laon	101	49 33N	3 35E
Laona	72	45 32N	88 41W
Laos ■	128	17 45N	105 0E
Lapa	89	25 46S	49 44W
Lapalisse	102	46 15N	3 44E
Laparan Cap, I.	127	6 0N	120 0E
Lapeer	46	43 3N	83 20W
Lapi □	110	67 0N	27 0E
Lapland = Lappland	110	68 7N	24 0E
Laporte	71	41 27N	76 30W
Lappland	110	68 7N	24 0E
Laprairie	44	45 20N	73 30W
Laprairie □	43	45 20N	73 30W
Laprida	88	37 34S	60 45W
Laptev Sea	121	76 0N	125 0E
Lapush	78	47 56N	124 33W
Lār	123	27 40N	54 14E
Lara □	86	10 10N	69 50W
Laragne-Monteglin	103	44 18N	5 49E
Laramie	74	41 15N	105 29W
Laramie Mts.	74	42 0N	105 30W
Laranjeiras do Sul	89	25 23S	52 23W
Larantuka	127	8 5S	122 55E
Larap	127	14 18N	122 39E
Larat, I.	127	7 0S	132 0E
Larder Lake	34	48 5N	79 40W
Laredo	75	27 34N	99 29W
Laredo Sd.	62	52 30N	128 53W
Laren	105	52 16N	5 14E
Largentière	103	44 34N	4 18E
Largs	96	55 48N	4 51W
Lariang	127	1 35S	119 25E
Larimore	74	47 55N	97 35W
Lárisa	109	39 38N	22 28E
Lark Harbour	37	49 6N	58 23W
Lark, R.	95	52 26N	0 18E
Larnaca	122	35 0N	33 35E
Lárnax	122	35 0N	33 35E
Larne	97	54 52N	5 50W
Larne □	97	54 55N	5 55W
Larned	74	38 15N	99 10W
Laroquebrou	102	44 58N	2 12E
Larrimah	134	15 35S	133 12E
Larrys River	39	45 13N	61 23W
Larsen Ice Shelf	91	67 0S	62 0W
Larus L.	52	51 17N	94 40W
Larvik	111	59 4N	10 0E
Laryak	120	61 15N	80 0E
Larzac, Causse du	102	44 0N	3 17E
Las Animas	75	38 8N	103 18W
Las Bonitas	86	7 50N	65 40W
Las Brenãs	88	27 5S	61 7W
Las Cascadas	84	9 5N	79 41W
Las Chimeneas	81	32 12N	116 5W
Las Cruces	79	32 25N	106 50W
Las Flores	88	36 0S	59 0W
Las Heras, Mendoza, Argent.	89	32 51S	68 49W
Las Heras, Santa Cruz, Argent.	90	46 30S	69 0W
Las Lajas	90	38 30S	70 25W
Las Lajitas	86	6 55N	65 39W
Las Lomitas	88	24 35S	60 50W
Las Mercedes	86	9 7N	66 24W
Las Palmas	88	27 8S	58 45W
Las Palmas □	114	28 10N	15 28W
Las Palmas, R.	81	32 8N	116 33W
Las Piedras	89	34 35S	56 20W
Las Plumas	90	43 40S	67 15W
Las Rosas	88	32 30S	61 40W
Las Tablas	84	7 49N	80 14W
Las Termas	88	27 29S	64 52W
Las Tres Marías, Is.	82	20 12N	106 30W
Las Varillas	88	32 0S	62 50W
Las Vegas, Nev., U.S.A.	81	36 10N	115 5W
Las Vegas, N.M., U.S.A.	79	35 35N	105 10W
Lasalle	44	45 26N	73 38W
Lascano	89	33 35S	54 18W
Lascaux	102	45 5N	1 10E
Lashburn	56	53 10N	109 40W
Lashio	125	22 56N	97 45E
Lasqueti	62	49 30N	124 21W
Lasqueti I.	62	49 29N	124 16W
Lassay	100	48 27N	0 30W
Lassen, Pk.	78	40 35N	121 40W
Last Mountain L.	56	51 5N	105 14W
Lastchance Cr.	80	40 2N	121 15W
Lastoursville	116	0 55S	12 38E
Lastovo, I.	108	42 46N	16 55E
Latacunga	86	0 50S	78 35W
Latakia = Al Lādhiquiyah	122	35 30N	35 45E
Latchford	34	47 20N	79 50W
Lathrop	76	39 33N	94 20W
Lathrop Wells	81	36 39N	116 24W
Latina	108	41 26N	12 53E
Lating	130	39 23N	118 55E
Laton	80	36 26N	119 41W
Latouche	67	60 0N	148 0W
Latouche Treville, C.	134	18 27S	121 49E
Latrobe, Austral.	136	38 8S	146 44E
Latrobe, U.S.A.	70	40 19N	79 21W
Latulipe	40	47 26N	79 2W
Lau (Eastern) Group	133	17 0S	178 30W
Lauchhammer	106	51 35N	13 40E
Lauenburg	106	53 23N	10 33E
Laugarbakki	110	65 20N	20 55W
Launceston, Austral.	135	41 24S	147 8E
Launceston, U.K.	95	50 38N	4 21W
Laune, R.	97	52 5N	9 40W
Launglon Bok	128	13 50N	97 54E
Laura	135	15 32S	144 32E
Laurel, Ont., Can.	49	43 57N	80 13W
Laurel, Qué., Can.	43	45 51N	74 28W
Laurel, U.S.A.	77	39 31N	85 11W
Laurel, Miss., U.S.A.	75	31 50N	89 0W
Laurel, Mont., U.S.A.	78	45 46N	108 49W
Laurencekirk	96	56 50N	2 30W
Laurens	73	34 32N	82 2W
Laurentian Plat.	36	52 0N	70 0W
Laurentides	43	45 51N	73 46W
Laurentides, Parc Prov. des	41	47 45N	71 15W
Laurie I.	91	60 0S	46 0W
Laurie L.	55	56 35N	101 57W
Laurier	57	50 53N	99 33W
Laurier-Station	41	46 32N	71 38W
Laurierville	41	46 18N	71 39W
Laurinburg	73	34 50N	79 25W
Laurium	52	47 14N	88 26W
Lausanne	106	46 32N	6 38E
Laut Kecil, Kepulauan	126	4 45S	115 40E
Laut, Kepulauan	126	4 45N	108 0E
Lautoka	133	17 37S	177 27E
Lauzon	42	46 48N	71 10W
Lava Hot Springs	78	42 38N	112 1W
Laval, Can.	44	45 35N	73 45W
Laval, France	100	48 4N	0 48W
Laval-des-Rapides	44	45 33N	73 42W
Laval-Ouest	44	45 33N	73 52W
Laval-sur-le-Lac	44	45 32N	73 52W
Lavalle	88	28 15S	65 15W
Lavaltrie	43	45 53N	73 17W
Lavandou, Le	103	43 8N	6 22E
Lavant Sta.	47	45 3N	76 42W
Lavardac	102	44 12N	0 20E
Lavaur	102	43 42N	1 49E
Lavaveix	102	46 5N	2 8E
Lavelanet	102	42 57N	1 51E
Laverendrye Prov. Park	34	46 15N	17 15W
Laverlochère	40	47 26N	79 18W
Laverne	75	36 43N	99 58W
Laverton	134	28 44S	122 29E
Lavieille, L.	47	45 51N	78 14W
Lavillètte	39	47 16N	65 18W
Lavoy	60	53 27N	111 52W
Lavras	89	21 20S	45 0W
Lavrentiya	121	65 35N	171 0W
Lávrion	109	37 40N	24 4E
Lawas	126	4 55N	115 40E
Lawele	127	5 16S	123 3E
Lawn	37	46 57N	55 35W
Lawrence, Austral.	89	29 30S	153 8E
Lawrence, U.S.A.	77	39 50N	86 2W
Lawrence, Kans., U.S.A.	74	39 0N	95 10W
Lawrence, Mass., U.S.A.	71	42 40N	71 9W
Lawrence Station	39	45 26N	67 11W
Lawrenceburg, Ind., U.S.A.	77	39 5N	84 50W
Lawrenceburg, Ky., U.S.A.	77	38 2N	84 54W
Lawrenceburg, Tenn., U.S.A.	73	35 12N	87 19W
Lawrencetown	39	44 53N	65 10W
Lawrenceville, U.S.A.	77	38 44N	87 41W
Lawrenceville, Ga., U.S.A.	73	33 55N	83 59W
Laws	80	37 24N	118 20W
Lawson	76	39 26N	94 12W
Lawton, U.S.A.	75	34 33N	98 25W
Lawton, U.S.A.	77	42 10N	85 50W
Lawu Mt.	127	7 40S	111 13E
Laxford, L.	96	58 25N	5 10W
Laytonville	78	39 44N	123 29W
Lazio □	108	42 10N	12 30E
Lea, R.	95	51 40N	0 3W
Leach I.	53	47 28N	84 57W
Lead	74	44 20N	103 40W
Leader	56	50 50N	109 30W
Leadhills	96	55 25N	3 47W
Leadville	79	39 17N	106 23W
Leaf L.	57	53 1N	102 8W
Leaf, R., Can.	36	58 47N	70 4W
Leaf, R., U.S.A.	75	31 45N	89 20W
Leakey	75	29 45N	99 45W
Leaksville	73	36 30N	79 49W
Lealui	117	15 10S	23 2E
Leamington, Can.	46	42 3N	82 36W
Leamington, N.Z.	14	37 55S	175 29E
Leamington, U.K.	95	52 18N	1 32W
Leamington, U.S.A.	78	39 37N	112 17W
Leandro Norte Alem	89	27 34S	55 15W
Learmonth	134	22 40S	114 10E
Leaside	50	43 42N	79 22W
Leask	56	53 5N	106 45W
Leavenworth, Mo., U.S.A.	74	39 25N	95 0W
Leavenworth, Wash., U.S.A.	78	47 44N	120 37W
Leavenworthth	77	38 12N	86 21W
Leawood	76	38 57N	94 37W
Lebak	127	6 32N	124 5E
Lebam	80	46 34N	123 33W
Lebanon, Ill., U.S.A.	76	38 38N	89 49W
Lebanon, Ind., U.S.A.	77	40 3N	86 20W
Lebanon, Kans., U.S.A.	74	39 50N	98 35W
Lebanon, Ky., U.S.A.	72	37 35N	85 15W
Lebanon, Mo., U.S.A.	76	37 40N	92 40W
Lebanon, N.H., U.S.A.	71	43 38N	72 15W
Lebanon, Ohio, U.S.A.	77	39 26N	84 13W
Lebanon, Oreg., U.S.A.	78	44 31N	122 57W
Lebanon, Pa., U.S.A.	71	40 20N	76 28W
Lebanon, Tenn., U.S.A.	73	36 15N	86 20W
Lebanon ■	122	34 0N	36 0E
Lebanon Junction	77	37 50N	85 44W
Lebbeke	105	51 0N	4 8E
Lebec	81	34 46N	118 59W
Lebel-sur-Quévillon	40	49 3N	76 59W
Lebrija	104	36 53N	6 5W
Lebu	88	37 40S	73 47W
Lecce	109	40 20N	18 10E
Lecco	108	45 50N	9 27E
Lectoure	102	43 56N	0 38E
Łeczyca	107	52 5N	19 45E
Ledbury	95	52 3N	2 25W
Leduc	60	53 15N	113 30W
Lee, Mass., U.S.A.	71	42 17N	73 18W
Lee, Nev., U.S.A.	78	40 35N	115 36W
Lee, R.	97	51 51N	9 2W
Lee Vining	80	37 58N	119 7W
Leech L., Can.	56	51 5N	102 28W
Leech L., U.S.A.	52	47 9N	94 23W
Leedey	75	35 53N	99 24W
Leeds, U.K.	94	53 48N	1 34W
Leeds, U.S.A.	73	33 32N	86 30W
Leek	94	53 7N	2 2W
Lee's Summit	76	38 55N	94 23W
Leesburg, U.S.A.	77	39 21N	83 33W
Leesburg, Fla., U.S.A.	73	28 47N	81 52W
Leesville	75	31 12N	93 15W
Leetonia	70	40 53N	80 45W
Leeuwarden	105	53 15N	5 48E
Leeuwin, C.	134	34 20S	115 9E
Leeward Is.	85	16 30N	63 30W
Lefebvre	41	47 12N	69 49W
Lefors	75	35 30N	100 50W
Lefroy	46	44 16N	79 34W
Lefroy, L.	134	31 21S	121 40E
Legal	60	53 55N	113 45W
Légère	39	47 25N	64 56W
Leghorn = Livorno	108	43 32N	10 18E
Legnica	106	51 12N	16 10E
Leh	124	34 15N	77 35E
Lehi	78	40 20N	112 0W
Lehighton	71	40 50N	75 44W
Lehua, I.	67	22 1N	160 6W
Leicester	95	52 39N	1 9W
Leicester □	95	52 40N	1 10W
Leichhardt, R.	135	17 35S	139 49E
Leichow = Haihang	131	20 55N	110 3E
Leichow Pantao	131	20 30N	110 0E
Leiden	105	52 9N	4 30E
Leie, R.	105	51 2N	3 45E
Leigh Creek	135	30 28S	138 24E
Leigh, R.	136	37 50S	144 0E
Leine, R.	106	52 35N	9 40E
Leinster □	97	53 0N	7 10W
Leinster Downs	70	27 52S	120 34E
Leinster, Mt.	97	52 38N	6 47W
Leipzig	106	51 20N	12 23E
Leiria	104	39 46N	8 53W
Leishan	131	25 55N	108 15E
Leith	96	55 59N	3 10W
Leith Hill	95	51 10N	0 23W
Leitrim, Can.	48	45 20N	75 36W
Leitrim, Ireland	97	54 0N	8 5W
Leitrim □	97	54 8N	8 0W
Leiyang	131	26 27N	112 50E
Lejeune	41	47 46N	68 34W
Lek, R.	105	51 54N	4 38E
Leksula	127	3 46S	126 31E
Leland	75	33 25N	90 52W
Leland Lakes	55	60 0N	110 59W
Leleque	90	42 15S	71 0W
Lelystad	105	52 30N	5 25E
Léman, Lac	106	46 26N	6 30E
Lemay	76	38 20N	90 16W
Lemberg	56	50 44N	103 12W
Lemery	127	13 58N	120 56E
Lemesós	122	34 42N	33 1E
Lemhi Ra.	78	44 30N	113 30W
Lemieux	41	46 18N	72 7W
Lemieux Is.	65	63 40N	64 20W
Lemieux, L.	40	50 19N	74 38W
Lemmer	105	52 51N	5 43E
Lemmon	74	45 59N	102 10W
Lemoine, L.	40	48 0N	78 0W
Lemon Grove	81	32 45N	117 2W
Lemont	77	41 40N	88 0W
Lemoore	80	36 23N	119 46W
Lemoyne	45	45 30N	73 30W
Lempdes	102	45 22N	3 17E
Lemvig	111	56 33N	8 20E
Lena, R.	121	64 30N	127 0E
Lencloître	100	46 50N	0 20E
Lengau de Vaca, Punta	88	30 14S	71 38W
Lenggong	128	5 6N	100 58E
Leninabad	120	40 17N	69 37E
Leninakan	120	41 0N	42 50E
Leningrad	120	59 55N	30 20E
Leninogorsk	120	50 20N	83 30E
Leninsk-Kuznetskiy	120	55 10N	86 10E
Leninskoye	121	47 56N	132 38E
Lenmalu	127	1 58S	130 0E
Lennoxville	41	45 22N	71 51W
Lenoir	73	35 55N	81 36W
Lenoir City	73	35 40N	84 20W
Lenora	74	39 39N	100 1W
Lenore L.	56	52 30N	104 59W
Lenox, U.S.A.	76	40 53N	94 34W
Lenox, Mass., U.S.A.	71	42 20N	73 18W
Lens	101	50 26N	2 50E
Lensk (Mukhtuya)	121	60 48N	114 55E
Lentini	108	37 18N	15 0E
Lenwood	81	34 53N	117 7W
Leoben	106	47 22N	15 5E
Leola	74	45 47N	98 58W
Leominster, U.K.	95	52 15N	2 43W
Leominster, U.S.A.	71	42 32N	71 45W
Léon	102	43 53N	1 18W
León, Mexico	82	21 7N	101 30W
León, Nic.	84	12 20N	86 51W
León, Spain	104	42 38N	5 34W
Leon	76	40 40N	93 40W
León □	104	42 40N	5 55W
León, Montañas de	104	42 30N	6 18W
Leonardtown	72	38 19N	76 39W
Leongatha	136	38 30S	145 58E
Leonora	134	28 49S	121 19E
Léopold II, Lac = Mai-Ndombe	116	2 0S	18 0E
Leopoldina	89	21 28S	42 40W
Leopoldsburg	105	51 7N	5 13E
Léopoldville = Kinshasa	116	4 20S	15 15E
Leoti	74	38 31N	101 19W
Leoville	56	53 39N	107 33W
Lepellé, R.	36	59 58N	72 24W
Lepikha	121	64 45N	125 55E
Lepreau	39	45 10N	66 28W
Lerdo	82	25 32N	103 32W
Lérida	104	41 37N	0 39E
Lérins, Is. de	103	43 31N	7 3E
Lérouville	101	48 50N	5 30E
Leroy	56	52 0N	104 44W
Leroy, L.	36	55 10N	67 15W
Lerwick	96	60 10N	1 10W
Léry	44	45 21N	73 48W
Leskov, I.	91	56 0S	28 0W
Leskovac	109	43 0N	21 58E
Leslie, U.S.A.	77	42 27N	84 26W
Leslie, Ark., U.S.A.	75	35 50N	92 35W
Leslieville	61	52 23N	114 36W
Lesneven	100	48 35N	4 20W
Lesotho ■	117	29 40S	28 0E
Lesozavodsk	121	45 30N	133 20E
Lesparre-Médoc	102	45 18N	0 57W
Lessay	100	49 14N	1 30W
Lesse, R.	105	50 15N	4 54E
Lesser Antilles	85	12 30N	61 0W
Lesser Slave L.	60	55 30N	115 25W
Lesser Slave Lake Prov. Park	60	55 26N	114 49W
Lessines	105	50 42N	3 50E
Lester	80	47 12N	121 29W
Lestock	56	51 19N	103 59W
Lésvos, I.	109	39 0N	26 20E
Leszno	106	51 50N	16 30E
Letchworth	95	51 58N	0 13W
Lethbridge, Alta., Can.	61	49 45N	112 45W
Lethbridge, Newf., Can.	37	48 22N	53 52W
Leti	127	8 10S	127 40E
Leti, Kepulauan	127	8 10S	128 0E
Leticia	86	4 0S	70 0W
Letsôk-aw-Kyun (Domel I.)	128	11 30N	98 25E
Letterkenny	97	54 57N	7 42W
Leucadia	81	33 4N	117 18W
Leucate	102	42 56N	3 3E
Leucate, Étang de	102	42 50N	3 0E
Leuser, G.	126	4 0N	96 51E
Leuven (Louvain)	105	50 52N	4 42E
Leuze	105	50 36N	3 37E
Levack	46	46 38N	81 23W
Levan	78	39 37N	111 32W
Levanger	110	63 45N	11 19E
Levelland	75	33 38N	102 17W
Leven	96	56 12N	3 0W
Leven, L.	96	56 12N	3 22W
Levens	103	43 50N	7 12E
Leveque C.	134	16 20S	123 0E
Levering	46	45 38N	84 47W
Leverkusen	105	51 2N	6 59E
Levet	101	46 56N	2 22E
Levick, Mt.	91	75 0S	164 0E
Levie	103	41 40N	9 7E
Levier	101	46 58N	6 8E
Levin	133	40 37S	175 18E
Lévis	42	46 48N	71 9W
Levis, L.	54	62 37N	117 58W
Levittown	71	40 10N	74 51W
Levkás, I.	109	38 40N	20 43E
Levkôsia = Nicosia	122	35 10N	33 25E
Levroux	101	47 0N	1 38E
Lewellen	74	41 22N	102 5W
Lewes, U.K.	95	50 53N	0 2E
Lewes, U.S.A.	72	38 45N	75 8W
Lewis, Butt of	96	58 30N	6 12W
Lewis Hills	37	48 48N	58 30W
Lewis, I.	96	58 10N	6 40W
Lewis, R.	80	45 51N	122 48W
Lewis Range	78	48 0N	113 15W
Lewisburg, U.S.A.	77	39 51N	84 33W

Lewisburg **Lobstick L**

Lewisburg, Pa., U.S.A. **70** 40 57N 76 57W
Lewisburg, Tenn., U.S.A. **73** 35 29N 86 46W
Lewisport **77** 37 56N 86 54W
Lewisporte **37** 49 15N 55 3W
Lewiston, Idaho, U.S.A. **78** 46 30N 117 0W
Lewiston, Mich., U.S.A. **46** 44 53N 84 18W
Lewiston, N.Y., U.S.A. **49** 43 12N 79 2W
Lewiston, Utah, U.S.A. **78** 41 58N 111 56W
Lewistown, Ill., U.S.A. **76** 40 24N 90 9W
Lewistown, Mont., U.S.A. **78** 47 0N 109 25W
Lewistown, Pa., U.S.A. **70** 40 37N 77 33W
Lewisville **39** 46 6N 64 46W
Lexington, Ill., U.S.A. **77** 40 37N 88 47W
Lexington, Ky., U.S.A. **77** 38 6N 84 30W
Lexington, Mich., U.S.A. **46** 43 15N 82 30W
Lexington, Miss., U.S.A. **75** 33 8N 90 2W
Lexington, Mo., U.S.A. **76** 39 7N 93 55W
Lexington, N.C., U.S.A. **73** 35 50N 80 13W
Lexington, Nebr., U.S.A. **74** 40 48N 99 45W
Lexington, Ohio, U.S.A. **70** 40 39N 82 35W
Lexington, Oreg., U.S.A. **78** 45 29N 119 46W
Lexington, Tenn., U.S.A. **73** 35 38N 88 25W
Leyte, I. **127** 11 0N 125 0 E
Lezay **102** 46 17N 0 0 E
Lèze, R. **102** 43 28N 1 25 E
Lézignan-Corbières **102** 43 13N 2 43 E
Lezoux **102** 45 49N 3 21 E
Lhasa **129** 29 50N 91 3 E
Lhatse Dzong **129** 29 10N 87 45 E
Lhokseumawe **126** 5 20N 97 10 E
Liang Liang **127** 5 58N 121 30 E
Lianga **127** 8 38N 126 6 E
Liangpran, Gunong **126** 1 0N 114 23 E
Liangsiang **130** 39 55N 116 15 E
Liao Ho, R. **130** 41 0N 121 55 E
Liaocheng **130** 36 30N 115 59 E
Liaochung **130** 41 35N 122 45 E
Liaoning □ **130** 41 40N 122 30 E
Liaotung **130** 40 10N 123 0 E
Liaotung Wan **130** 40 0N 120 45 E
Liaoyang **130** 41 15N 123 10 E
Liaoyüan **130** 42 55N 125 10 E
Liard, R. **54** 61 51N 121 18W
Libby **78** 48 20N 115 10W
Libenge **116** 3 40N 18 55 E
Liberal, Kans., U.S.A. **75** 37 4N 101 0W
Liberal, Mo., U.S.A. **75** 37 35N 94 30W
Liberec **106** 50 47N 15 7 E
Liberia **84** 10 40N 85 30W
Liberia ■ **114** 6 30N 9 30W
Libertad **86** 8 20N 69 37W
Libertad, La **84** 16 47N 90 7W
Liberty, Can. **56** 51 8N 105 26W
Liberty, U.S.A. **77** 39 38N 84 56W
Liberty, Mo., U.S.A. **76** 39 15N 94 24W
Liberty, N.Y., U.S.A. **71** 41 48N 74 45W
Liberty, Tex., U.S.A. **75** 30 5N 94 50W
Liberty Center **77** 41 27N 84 1W
Libertyville **77** 42 18N 87 57W
Lîbîya, Sahrâ' **112** 27 35N 25 0 E
Libourne **102** 44 55N 0 14W
Libreville **116** 0 25N 9 26 E
Libya ■ **114** 28 30N 17 30 E
Licantén **88** 34 55 S 72 0W
Licata **108** 37 6N 13 55 E
Lichfield **94** 52 40N 1 50W
Lichtenburg **117** 26 8 S 26 8 E
Lida **79** 37 30N 117 30W
Liddon Gulf **64** 75 3N 113 0W
Lidköping **111** 58 31N 13 14 E
Liechtenstein ■ **106** 47 8N 9 35 E
Liège **105** 50 38N 5 35 E
Liège □ **105** 50 32N 5 35 E
Lienhua **131** 26 58N 113 59 E
Lienkiang **131** 26 11N 119 30 E
Lienshankwan **130** 41 0N 123 59 E
Lienyunkang **131** 34 45N 119 30 E
Lienz **106** 46 50N 12 46 E
Liepāja **120** 56 30N 21 0 E
Lier **105** 51 7N 4 34 E
Lieshankwan **130** 40 56N 124 51 E
Liévin **101** 50 24N 2 47 E
Lièvre, R. **40** 45 31N 75 26W
Liffey, R. **97** 53 21N 6 20W
Lifford **97** 54 50N 7 30W
Liffré **100** 48 12N 1 30W
Ligny-en-Barrois **101** 48 36N 5 20 E
Ligny-le-Châtel **101** 47 54N 3 45 E
Ligua, La **88** 32 30 S 71 16W
Liguria □ **108** 44 30N 9 0 E
Ligurian Sea **108** 43 20N 9 0 E
Lihou Reefs and Cays **135** 17 25 S 151 40 E
Lihue **67** 21 59N 159 24W
Likasi **116** 10 55 S 26 48 E
Likati **116** 3 20N 24 0 E
Likely **63** 52 37N 121 35W
Likiang **129** 26 50N 100 15 E
Likunpu **130** 36 31N 106 12 E
Liling **131** 27 47N 113 30 E
Lille **101** 50 38N 3 3 E
Lille Bælt **111** 55 30N 9 45 E
Lillebonne **100** 49 30N 0 32 E
Lillehammer **111** 61 8N 10 30 E
Lillers **101** 50 35N 2 28 E
Lillesand **111** 58 15N 8 23 E
Lillestrøm **111** 59 58N 11 5 E
Lillian L. (Daré, Le, L.) **38** 51 17N 61 23W
Lillooet **63** 50 44N 121 57W
Lillooet L. **63** 50 18N 122 35W
Lillooet, R. **63** 49 15N 121 57W
Lilongwe **117** 14 0 S 33 48 E
Liloy **127** 8 4N 122 39 E
Lima, Austral. **136** 36 44 S 146 10 E
Lima, Indon. **127** 3 37 S 128 4 E
Lima, Peru **86** 12 0 S 77 0W
Lima, Mont., U.S.A. **78** 44 41N 112 38W
Lima, Ohio, U.S.A. **77** 40 42N 84 5W
Limages **71** 45 20N 75 16W
Limassol **122** 34 42N 33 1 E
Limavady **97** 55 3N 6 58W
Limavady □ **97** 55 0N 6 55W
Limay Mahuida **88** 37 10 S 66 45W
Limay, R. **90** 39 40 S 69 45W
Limbang **126** 4 42N 115 6 E
Limbour **48** 45 29N 75 45W
Limbourg □ **105** 51 2N 5 25 E
Limburg □ **108** 51 20N 5 55 E
Limehouse **49** 43 38N 79 58W
Limeira **89** 22 35 S 47 28W
Limerick, Can. **56** 49 39N 106 16W
Limerick, Ireland **97** 52 40N 8 38W
Limerick □ **97** 52 30N 8 50W
Limestone **70** 42 2N 78 39W
Limestone B. **57** 53 50N 98 53W
Limestone, R. **55** 56 31N 94 7W
Limfjorden **111** 56 55N 9 0 E
Limia, R. **104** 41 55N 8 8W
Limko **131** 20 57N 109 43 E
Limmen Bight **134** 14 40 S 135 35 E
Límnos, I. **109** 39 50N 25 5 E
Limoeiro do Norte **87** 5 5 S 38 0W
Limoges, Can. **47** 45 20N 75 15W
Limoges, France **102** 45 50N 1 15 E
Limón **85** 10 0N 83 2W
Limon, Panama **84** 9 20N 79 45W
Limon, U.S.A. **74** 39 18N 103 38W
Limon B. **84** 9 22N 79 56W
Limousin **102** 46 0N 1 0 E
Limousin, Plateau du **102** 46 0N 1 0 E
Limoux **102** 43 4N 2 12 E
Limpopo, R. **117** 23 15 S 32 5 E
Limuru **116** 1 2 S 36 35 E
Linares **88** 35 50 S 71 40W
Linàres **86** 1 23N 77 31W
Linares, Mexico **83** 24 50N 99 40W
Linares, Spain **104** 38 10N 3 40W
Linares □ **88** 36 0 S 71 0W
Linaria **60** 54 19N 114 8W
Linch'eng **130** 37 26N 114 34 E
Lincheng **131** 37 20N 114 30 E
Lincoln, Argent. **88** 34 55N 61 30W
Lincoln, Can. **49** 43 10N 79 29W
Lincoln, N.Z. **133** 43 38 S 172 30 E
Lincoln, U.K. **94** 53 14N 0 32W
Lincoln, Calif., U.S.A. **80** 38 54N 121 17W
Lincoln, Ill., U.S.A. **76** 40 10N 89 20W
Lincoln, Kans., U.S.A. **74** 39 6N 98 9W
Lincoln, Maine, U.S.A. **35** 45 27N 68 29W
Lincoln, Mich., U.S.A. **46** 44 41N 83 25W
Lincoln, N. Mex., U.S.A. **79** 33 30N 105 26W
Lincoln, Nebr., U.S.A. **74** 40 50N 96 42W
Lincoln □ **94** 53 14N 0 32W
Lincoln Park **77** 42 15N 83 11W
Lincoln Sea **17** 84 0N 55 0W
Lincoln Wolds **94** 53 20N 0 5W
Lincolnton **73** 35 30N 81 15W
Lincolnville **39** 45 30N 61 33W
Lind **78** 47 0N 118 33W
Linda **80** 39 6N 121 34W
Lindell Beach **63** 49 2N 122 1W
Linden, Can. **61** 51 36N 113 28W
Linden, Guyana **86** 6 0N 58 10W
Linden, U.S.A. **77** 40 11N 86 54W
Linden, Calif., U.S.A. **80** 38 1N 121 5W
Linden, Mich., U.S.A. **46** 42 49N 83 47W
Linden, Tex., U.S.A. **75** 33 0N 94 20W
Lindi **116** 9 58 S 39 38 E
Lindsay, Can. **47** 44 22N 78 43W
Lindsay, Calif., U.S.A. **80** 36 14N 119 6W
Lindsay, Okla., U.S.A. **75** 34 51N 97 37W
Lindsborg **74** 38 35N 97 40W
Línea de la Concepción, La **104** 36 15N 5 23W
Lineville **76** 40 35N 93 31W
Linfen **130** 36 0N 111 30 E
Lingayer **127** 16 1N 120 14 E
Lingayer G. **127** 16 10N 120 15 E
Lingen **105** 52 32N 7 21 E
Lingga, Kepulauan **126** 0 10 S 104 30 E
Linghsien, Hunan, China **130** 26 26N 113 45 E
Linghsien, Shantung, China **130** 37 21N 116 34 E
Lingle **74** 42 10N 104 18W
Lingling **131** 26 15N 111 40 E
Linglo **131** 24 20N 105 25 E
Lingshan **131** 22 26N 109 17 E
Lingshih **130** 36 55N 111 45 E
Lingshui **131** 18 27N 110 0 E
Lingt'ai **131** 35 4N 107 37 E
Linguéré **114** 15 25N 15 5W
Linh Cam **128** 18 31N 105 31 E
Linhai **131** 28 50N 121 8 E
Linho **130** 40 50N 107 30 E
Linhsien **130** 37 57N 110 57 E
Lini **131** 35 5N 118 20 E
Linière **41** 46 4N 70 32W
Link L. **62** 52 25N 127 40W
Linkian **130** 41 57N 126 59 E
Linkiang **129** 46 2N 133 56 E
Linköping **111** 58 28N 15 36 E
Linkow **130** 45 16N 130 18 E
Linlithgow **96** 55 58N 3 38W
Linn **76** 38 29N 91 51W
Linn, Mt. **78** 40 0N 123 0W
Linneus **76** 39 53N 93 11W
Linney Head **95** 51 37N 5 4W
Linnhe, L. **96** 56 36N 5 25W
Linping **131** 24 25N 114 32 E
Lins **89** 21 40 S 49 44W
Linsi **130** 43 30N 118 5 E
Linsia **129** 35 50N 103 0 E
Lintan **129** 34 37N 103 40 E
Lintao **130** 35 16N 103 38 E
Lintien **129** 46 8N 124 58 E
Lintlaw **56** 52 4N 103 14W
Linton, Ont., Can. **50** 43 56N 79 40W
Linton, Qué., Can. **41** 47 15N 72 16W
Linton, Ind., U.S.A. **77** 39 0N 87 10W
Linton, N. Dak., U.S.A. **74** 46 21N 100 12W
Lintsing **130** 36 50N 115 45 E
Lintung **130** 43 59N 119 8 E
Linwood **46** 43 35N 80 43W
Linwu **131** 25 25N 112 10 E
Linxe **102** 43 56N 1 13W
Linyi **130** 37 10N 116 50 E
Linz, Austria **106** 48 18N 14 18 E
Linz, Ger. **106** 50 33N 7 18 E
Lion-d'Angers, Le **100** 47 37N 0 43W
Lion, G. du **102** 43 0N 4 0 E
Lion's Head **34** 44 58N 81 15W
Lioyang **131** 33 30N 106 0 E
Lípari, Is. **108** 38 40N 15 0 E
Lipetsk **120** 52 45N 39 35 E
Liping **131** 26 12N 109 0 E
Lipo **131** 25 33N 107 45 E
Lippe, R. **105** 51 40N 7 20 E
Lipscomb **75** 36 16N 100 28W
Lipton **56** 50 54N 103 51W
Liptrap C. **136** 38 50 S 145 55 E
Lira **116** 2 17N 32 57 E
Liria **104** 39 37N 0 35W
Lisala **116** 2 12N 21 38 E
Lisboa **104** 38 42N 9 10W
Lisbon, N. Dak., U.S.A. **74** 46 30N 97 46W
Lisbon, N.H., U.S.A. **71** 44 13N 71 52W
Lisbon, Ohio, U.S.A. **70** 40 45N 80 42W
Lisbon = Lisboa **104** 38 42N 9 10W
Lisburn **97** 54 30N 6 9W
Lisburn □ **97** 54 30N 6 5W
Lisburne, C. **67** 68 50N 166 0W
Liscannor **97** 52 57N 9 24W
Liscannor, B. **97** 52 57N 9 24W
Liscomb **35** 45 2N 62 0W
Lishih **130** 37 30N 111 7 E
Lishui **131** 28 27N 119 54 E
Lisianski I. **14** 25 30N 174 0W
Lisieux **100** 49 10N 0 12 E
Lisle-sur-Tarn **102** 43 52N 1 49 E
Lismore, Austral. **135** 37 58 S 143 21 E
Lismore, Ireland **97** 52 8N 7 58W
Lisse **105** 52 16N 4 33 E
Lista, Norway **111** 58 7N 6 39 E
Lista, Sweden **111** 59 19N 16 16 E
Lister, Mt. **91** 78 0 S 162 0 E
Listowel, Can. **46** 43 44N 80 58W
Listowel, Ireland **97** 52 27N 9 30W
Lit-et-Mixe **102** 44 2N 1 15W
Litang, China **131** 23 6N 109 2 E
Litang, Malay. **127** 5 27N 118 31 E
Litchfield, Calif., U.S.A. **80** 40 24N 120 23W
Litchfield, Conn., U.S.A. **71** 41 44N 73 12W
Litchfield, Ill., U.S.A. **76** 39 10N 89 40W
Litchfield, Minn., U.S.A. **74** 45 5N 94 40W
Lithgow **136** 33 25 S 150 8 E
Líthinon, Ákra **109** 34 55N 24 44 E
Lithuania S.S.R. □ **120** 55 30N 24 0 E
Litoměrice **106** 50 33N 14 10 E
Little Abaco I. **73** 26 50N 77 30W
Little Abitibi, R. **53** 50 29N 81 32W
Little America **91** 79 0N 160 0W
Little Andaman I. **128** 10 40N 92 15 E
Little Barrier I. **133** 36 12 S 175 8 E
Little Bay **37** 49 36N 55 57W
Little Belt Mts. **78** 46 50N 111 0W
Little Blue, R. **74** 40 18N 97 45W
Little Bow, R. **61** 49 53N 112 29W
Little Burnt Bay **37** 49 25N 55 5W
Little Cadotte, R. **60** 56 41N 117 6W
Little Cayman, I. **84** 19 41N 80 3W
Little Churchill, R. **55** 57 30N 95 22W
Little Coco I. **128** 14 0N 93 15 E
Little Colorado, R. **79** 36 0N 111 31W
Little Corners **49** 43 20N 80 17W
Little Current **46** 45 55N 82 0W
Little Current, R. **53** 50 57N 84 36W
Little Dover **39** 45 15N 61 3W
Little Falls, Minn., U.S.A. **74** 45 58N 94 19W
Little Falls, N.Y., U.S.A. **71** 43 3N 74 50W
Little Fork, R. **52** 48 31N 93 35W
Little Fort **63** 51 26N 120 13W
Lit. Grand Rapids **57** 52 0N 95 29W
Lit. Humboldt, R. **78** 41 20N 117 27W
Lit. Inagua I. **85** 21 40N 73 50W
Little Lake **81** 35 58N 117 58W
Little Longlac **34** 49 42N 86 58W
Little Marais **74** 47 24N 91 8W
Little Mecatiná I. **35** 50 30N 59 25W
Little Minch **96** 57 35N 6 45W
Lit. Missouri R. **74** 46 40N 103 50W
Little Narrows **39** 45 59N 60 59W
Little Ouse, R. **95** 52 25N 0 50 E
Little Pic, R. **53** 48 48N 86 37W
Little Quill L. **56** 51 55N 104 5W
Little Red, R. **75** 35 40N 92 15W
Little River **133** 43 45 S 172 49 E
Little Rock **75** 34 41N 92 10W
Little Rouge, R. **51** 43 48N 79 8W
Little Sable Pt. **72** 43 40N 86 32W
Little Sioux, R. **67** 42 20N 95 55W
Little Smoky, R. **60** 54 44N 117 11W
Little Snake, R. **78** 40 45N 108 15W
Little Valley **70** 42 15N 78 48W
Little Wabash, R. **77** 38 40N 88 20W
Little Whale, R. **34** 55 50N 75 0W
Little White, R. **46** 46 23N 83 20W
Little York **76** 41 1N 90 45W
Littlefield **75** 33 57N 102 17W
Littlefork **74** 48 24N 93 35W
Littlehampton **95** 50 48N 0 32W
Littleton **71** 44 19N 71 47W
Liuan **131** 31 49N 116 29 E
Liucheng **131** 24 5N 109 3 E
Liuchow **131** 24 10N 109 10 E
Liupa **131** 33 40N 107 0 E
Liupan Shan **130** 35 40N 106 10 E
Liuwa Plain **117** 14 20 S 22 30 E
Livarot **100** 49 0N 0 9 E
Live Oak, Calif., U.S.A. **80** 39 17N 121 40W
Live Oak, Fla., U.S.A. **73** 30 17N 83 0W
Lively **46** 46 26N 81 9W
Livermore **80** 37 41N 121 47W
Livermore, Mt. **75** 30 45N 104 8W
Liverpool, Austral. **136** 33 54 S 150 58 E
Liverpool, Can. **39** 44 5N 64 41W
Liverpool, U.K. **94** 53 25N 3 0W
Liverpool Bay, Can. **67** 70 0N 128 0W
Liverpool Bay, U.K. **98** 53 30N 3 20W
Liverpool, C. **65** 73 38N 78 6W
Liverpool Plains **136** 31 15 S 150 15 E
Liverpool Ra. **136** 31 50 S 150 30 E
Livingston, Guat. **84** 15 50N 88 50W
Livingston, U.S.A. **76** 42 54N 90 26W
Livingston, Calif., U.S.A. **80** 37 23N 120 43W
Livingston, Mont., U.S.A. **78** 45 40N 110 40W
Livingstone **75** 30 44N 94 54W
Livingstone I. **91** 63 0 S 60 15W
Livingstone (Maramba) **117** 17 46 S 25 52 E
Livingstonia **116** 10 38 S 34 5 E
Livny **120** 52 30N 37 30 E
Livonia **46** 42 25N 83 23W
Livorno **108** 43 32N 10 18 E
Livramento **89** 30 55 S 55 30W
Livron-sur-Drôme **103** 44 46N 4 51 E
Liwale **116** 9 48 S 37 58 E
Lizard Pt. **95** 49 57N 5 11W
Ljubljana **108** 46 4N 14 33 E
Ljungan, R. **110** 62 30N 14 30 E
Ljungby **111** 56 49N 13 55 E
Ljusdal **111** 61 46N 16 3 E
Ljusnan, R. **111** 62 0N 15 20 E
Ljusne **111** 61 13N 17 7 E
Llancanelo, Salina **88** 35 40 S 69 8W
Llandovery **95** 51 59N 3 49W
Llandrindod Wells **95** 52 15N 3 23W
Llandudno **94** 53 19N 3 51W
Llanelli **95** 51 41N 4 11W
Llanes **104** 43 25N 4 50W
Llangollen **94** 52 58N 3 10W
Llanidloes **95** 52 28N 3 31W
Llano Estacado **68** 34 0N 103 0W
Llano R. **75** 30 50N 99 0W
Llanos **86** 3 25N 71 35W
Llaoyang **130** 41 14N 123 6 E
Llera **83** 23 19N 99 1W
Llico **88** 34 46 S 72 5W
Llobregat, R. **104** 41 19N 2 9 E
Lloret de Mar **104** 41 41N 2 53 E
Lloyd L. **55** 57 22N 108 57W
Lloydminster **56** 53 17N 110 0W
Lloyds, R. **37** 48 35N 57 15W
Lloydtown **50** 43 59N 79 42W
Llullaillaco, volcán **88** 24 30 S 68 30W
Lo Ho **131** 34 15N 111 10 E
Loa **79** 38 18N 111 46W
Loa, R. **88** 21 30 S 70 0W
Lobatse **117** 25 12 S 25 40 E
Lobería **88** 38 10 S 58 40W
Lobito **117** 12 18 S 13 35 E
Lobos **88** 35 2 S 59 0W
Lobos, I. **82** 21 27N 97 13W
Lobstick L. **36** 54 0N 65 12W

Loc Binh Lufkin

Loc Binh 128 21 46N 106 54 E
Loc Ninh 128 11 50N 106 34 E
Locarno 106 46 10N 8 47 E
Lochaber 96 56 55N 5 0W
Lochdale 66 49 17N 122 58W
Loche, La 55 56 29N 109 26W
Loche, La, L. 55 56 40N 109 30W
Lochem 105 52 9N 6 26 E
Loches 100 47 7N 1 0 E
Lochgelly 96 56 7N 3 18W
Lochgilphead 96 56 2N 5 37W
Lochnagar, Mt. 96 56 57N 3 14W
Lochwan 130 35 59N 109 30 E
Lochy, R. 96 56 52N 5 3W
Lock Haven 70 41 7N 77 31W
Lockeford 80 38 10N 121 9W
Lockeport 39 43 47N 65 4W
Lockerbie 96 55 7N 3 21W
Lockhart 75 29 55N 97 40W
Lockport, U.S.A. 77 41 35N 88 3W
Lockport, N.Y., U.S.A. 70 43 12N 78 42W
Locminé 100 47 54N 2 51W
Locronan 100 48 7N 4 15W
Loctudy 100 47 50N 4 12W
Locust Cr. 76 39 40N 93 17W
Lod 115 31 57N 34 54 E
Loddon, R. 136 35 31 S 143 51 E
Lodève 102 43 44N 3 19 E
Lodge Grass 78 45 21N 107 27W
Lodgepole, Can. 61 53 6N 115 19W
Lodgepole, U.S.A. 74 41 12N 102 40W
Lodgepole Cr. 74 41 20N 104 30W
Lodhran 124 29 32N 71 30 E
Lodi 80 38 12N 121 16W
Lodja 116 3 30 S 23 23 E
Lodji 127 1 38 S 127 28 E
Lodwar 116 3 10N 35 40 E
Łodz 107 51 45N 19 27 E
Lofoten Is. 110 68 30N 15 0 E
Logan, Kans., U.S.A. 74 39 40N 99 35W
Logan, Ohio, U.S.A. 72 39 25N 82 22W
Logan, Utah, U.S.A. 78 41 45N 111 50W
Logan I. 52 50 7N 88 27W
Logan, Mount 38 48 53N 66 38W
Logan, Mt . 67 60 41N 140 22W
Logan Pass 61 48 41N 113 44W
Logandale 81 36 36N 114 29W
Logansport, U.S.A. 77 40 45N 86 22W
Logansport, La., U.S.A. 72 31 58N 93 58W
Loggieville 39 47 4N 65 23W
Logroño 104 42 28N 2 32W
Logy Bay 37 47 38N 52 40W
Lohardaga 125 23 27N 84 45 E
Loho 131 33 33N 114 5 E
Lohrville 76 42 17N 94 33W
Loikaw 125 19 40N 97 17 E
Loimaa 111 60 50N 23 5 E
Loir-et-Cher □ 101 47 40N 1 20 E
Loire □ 103 45 40N 4 5 E
Loire-Atlantique □ 100 47 25N 1 40W
Loire, R. 100 47 16N 2 10W
Loiret □ 101 47 58N 2 10 E
Loja, Ecuador 86 3 59 S 79 16W
Loja, Spain 104 37 10N 4 10W
Lokandu 116 2 30 S 25 45 E
Lokchong 131 25 15N 113 0 E
Lokeren 105 51 6N 3 59 E
Lokitaung 116 4 12N 35 48 E
Lokka 110 67 49N 27 45 E
Løkken 110 63 8N 9 45 E
Lokoja 114 7 47N 6 45 E
Lokolama 116 2 35 S 19 50 E
Loktung 131 18 41N 109 5 E
Lokwei 131 19 12N 110 30 E
Lola, Mt. 80 39 26N 120 22W
Loliondo 116 2 2 S 35 39 E
Lolland 111 54 45N 11 30 E
Lolo 78 46 50N 114 8W
Lom 109 43 48N 23 20 E
Loma 78 47 59N 110 29W
Loma Linda 81 34 3N 117 16W
Lomami, R. 116 1 0 S 24 40 E
Lomas de Zamóra 88 34 45 S 58 25W
Lombard, U.S.A. 77 41 53N 88 1W
Lombard, Mont., U.S.A. 78 46 7N 111 28W
Lombardia □ 108 45 35N 9 45 E
Lombardy = Lombardia 108 45 35N 9 45 E
Lombez 102 43 29N 0 55 E
Lomblen, I. 127 8 30 S 123 32 E
Lombok, I. 126 8 35 S 116 20 E
Lomé 114 6 9N 1 20 E
Lomela 116 2 5 S 23 52 E
Lomela, R. 116 1 30 S 22 50 E
Lometa 75 31 15N 98 25W
Lomie 116 3 13N 13 38 E
Lommel 105 51 14N 5 19 E
Lomond 61 50 24N 112 36W
Lomond, L. 96 56 8N 4 38W
Lompobatang, mt. 127 5 24 S 119 56 E
Lompoc 81 34 41N 120 32W
Łomza 107 53 10N 22 2 E
Loncoche 90 39 20 S 72 50W
Londa 124 15 30N 74 30 E
Londe, La 103 43 8N 6 14 E
Londinières 100 49 50N 1 25 E
London, Can. 46 42 59N 81 15W
London, U.K. 95 51 30N 0 5W
London, Ky., U.S.A. 72 37 11N 84 5W
London, Ohio, U.S.A. 77 39 54N 83 28W
London □ 95 51 30N 0 5W
London Mills 76 40 43N 90 11W
Londonderry, Can. 39 45 29N 63 36W
Londonderry, U.K. 97 55 0N 7 20W
Londonderry, C. 134 13 45 S 126 55 E
Londonderry, Co. 97 55 0N 7 20W
Londonderry, I. 90 55 0 S 71 0W
Londrina 89 23 0 S 51 10W
Lone Butte 63 51 33N 121 12W
Lone Pine, Can. 60 54 18N 115 7W
Lone Pine, U.S.A. 80 36 35N 118 2W
Lone Rock 56 53 3N 109 53W
Lonely I. 46 45 34N 81 28W
Long Beach, Can. 62 49 1N 125 40W
Long Beach, Calif., U.S.A. 81 33 46N 118 12W
Long Beach, N.Y., U.S.A. 71 40 35N 73 40W
Long Beach, Wash., U.S.A. 80 46 20N 124 1W
Long Branch, Can. 50 43 35N 79 32W
Long Branch, U.S.A. 71 40 19N 74 0W
Long Cr. 56 49 7N 102 59W
Long Eaton 94 52 54N 1 16W
Long I., Bahamas 85 23 20N 75 10W
Long I., Newf., Can. 37 47 34N 55 59W
Long I., N.W.T., Can. 36 54 50N 79 20W
Long I., U.S.A. 71 40 50N 73 20W
Long I. Sd. 71 41 10N 73 0W
Long L., Alta., Can. 60 54 22N 112 46W
Long L., Ont., Can. 53 49 30N 86 50W
Long L., U.S.A. 71 43 57N 74 25W
Long Lake, Can. 39 44 36N 63 38W
Long Lake, U.S.A. 46 44 25N 83 52W
Long Mynd 98 52 35N 2 50W
Long Pine 74 42 33N 99 50W
Long Pt., Man., Can. 57 53 2N 98 25W
Long Pt., Newf., Can. 37 48 47N 58 46W
Long Pt., Ont., Can. 46 42 38N 80 8W
Long Pt., Ont., Can. 46 42 35N 80 2W
Long Point B. 46 42 40N 80 10W
Long Pt. Bay 70 42 40N 80 20W
Long Range Mts 37 48 0N 58 30W
Long Range Mts. 37 49 30N 57 30W
Long Reach 39 45 28N 66 5W
Long Str. 17 70 0N 175 0 E
Long Xuyen 128 10 19N 105 28 E
Longeau 101 47 47N 5 20 E
Longford 97 53 43N 7 50W
Longford □ 97 53 42N 7 45W
Longhawan 126 2 15N 114 55 E
Longiram 126 0 5 S 115 45 E
Longlac 53 49 45N 86 25W
Longlegged L. 52 50 46N 94 8W
Longmont 74 40 10N 105 4W
Longnawan 126 21 50N 114 55 E
Longreach 135 23 28 S 144 14 E
Longs Peak 78 40 20N 105 50W
Longué 100 47 22N 0 8W
Longue-Pointe-de-Mingan 38 50 16N 64 9W
Longueuil, Can. 71 45 32N 73 28W
Longueuil, Qué., Can. 45 45 32N 73 30W
Longueuil-St-Hubert 43 45 29N 73 26W
Longuyon 101 49 27N 5 35 E
Longview, Can. 61 50 32N 114 10W
Longview, Tex., U.S.A. 75 32 30N 94 45W
Longview, Wash., U.S.A. 80 46 9N 122 58W
Longwy 101 49 30N 5 45 E
Loning 131 34 28N 111 42 E
Löningen 105 54 43N 7 44 E
Lonoke 75 34 48N 91 57W
Lonouaille 102 46 30N 1 35 E
Lons-le-Saunier 101 46 40N 5 31 E
Lønsdal 110 66 46N 15 26 E
Looc 127 12 20N 112 5 E
Loogootee 77 38 41N 86 55W
Lookout, C., Can. 34 55 18N 83 56W
Lookout, C., U.S.A. 73 34 30N 76 30W
Loomis 55 49 15N 108 45W
Loon L. 55 44 50N 77 15W
Loon Lake 56 54 2N 109 10W
Loon, R., Alta., Can. 60 57 8N 115 3W
Loon, R., Man., Can. 55 55 53N 101 59W
Loop Hd. 97 52 34N 9 55W
Lop Nor 129 40 20N 90 10 E
Lopatina, G. 121 50 0N 143 30 E
Lopei 130 47 40N 131 12 E
Lopez C. 116 0 47 S 8 40 E
Lopez I. 63 48 30N 122 54W
Lopphavet 110 70 27N 21 15 E
Lora, R. 124 32 0N 67 15 E
Lorain 70 41 20N 82 55W
Loraine 76 40 9N 91 13W
Loralai 124 30 29N 68 30 E
Lorca 104 37 41N 1 42W
Lord Howe I. 14 31 33 S 159 6 E
Lord Selkirk 58 49 56N 97 11W
Lord's Cove 37 46 53N 55 40W
Lordsburg 79 32 15N 108 45W
Loreburn 56 51 13N 106 36W
Loreto, Brazil 87 7 5 S 45 30W
Loreto, Italy 108 43 26N 13 36 E
Loreto, Mexico 82 26 1N 111 21W
Lorette 57 49 44N 96 52W
Loretteville 42 46 51N 71 21W
Lorgues 103 43 28N 6 22 E
Lorica 86 9 14N 75 49W
Lorient 100 47 45N 3 23W
Lorimor 76 41 7N 94 3W
Lorne, Austral. 136 38 33 S 143 59 E
Lorne, Can. 39 47 53N 66 8W
Lorne, U.K. 96 56 26N 5 10W
Lorne, Firth of 96 56 20N 5 40W
Lorne Park 50 43 32N 79 36W
Lorraine, Can. 44 45 41N 73 47W
Lorraine, France 101 49 0N 6 0 E
Lorrainville 40 47 21N 79 23W
Los Alamos, Calif., U.S.A. 81 34 44N 120 17W
Los Alamos, N. Mex., U.S.A. 79 35 57N 106 17W
Los Altos 80 37 23N 122 7W
Los Andes 88 32 50 S 70 40W
Los Angeles 88 37 28 S 72 23W
Los Angeles 81 34 0N 118 10W
Los Angeles Aqueduct 81 35 25N 118 0W
Los Banos 80 37 8N 120 56W
Los Blancos 88 23 45 S 62 30W
Los Gatos 80 37 15N 121 59W
Los Lamentos 82 30 36N 105 50W
Los Lunas 79 34 55N 106 47W
Los Mochis 82 25 45N 109 5W
Los Olivos 81 34 40N 120 7W
Los Palacios 84 22 35N 83 15W
Los Reyes 82 19 21N 99 7W
Los Roques, Is. 85 11 50N 66 45W
Los Testigos, Is. 86 11 23N 63 6W
Los Vilos 88 32 0 S 71 30W
Loshing 131 24 45N 108 58 E
Loshkalakh 121 62 45N 147 20 E
Lošinj, I. 108 44 30N 14 30 E
Lossiemouth 96 57 43N 3 17W
Lost River 43 45 50N 74 33W
Lot □ 102 44 39N 1 40 E
Lot-et-Garonne □ 102 44 22N 0 30 E
Lot, R. 102 44 18N 0 20 E
Lota 88 37 5 S 73 10W
Lothiers 101 46 42N 1 33 E
Loting 131 22 46N 111 34 E
Lott Cr. 59 51 0N 114 13W
Loudéac 100 48 11N 2 47W
Loudon 73 35 35N 84 22W
Loudonville 70 40 40N 82 15W
Loudun 100 47 0N 0 5 E
Loué 100 47 59N 0 9W
Loue, R. 100 47 4N 6 10 E
Loughborough 94 52 46N 1 11W
Lougheed 61 52 44N 111 33W
Lougheed I. 64 77 26N 105 6W
Loughrea 97 53 11N 8 33W
Loughros More, B. 97 54 48N 8 30W
Louhans 103 46 38N 5 12 E
Louis Creek 63 51 8N 120 7W
Louis Trichardt 117 23 0 S 29 55 E
Louis XIV, Pte. 36 54 37N 79 45W
Louisa 72 38 5N 82 40W
Louisa, L. 43 45 46N 74 25W
Louisbourg 39 45 55N 60 0W
Louisbourg Nat. Historic Park 39 45 58N 60 20W
Louisburg 76 38 37N 94 41W
Louisdale 39 45 36N 61 4W
Louise I. 62 52 55N 131 40W
Louiseville 41 46 20N 72 56W
Louisiade Arch. 14 11 10 S 153 0 E
Louisiana 76 39 25N 91 0W
Louisiana □ 75 30 50N 92 0W
Louisville, Ky., U.S.A. 77 38 15N 85 45W
Louisville, Miss., U.S.A. 75 33 7N 89 3W
Loulay 102 46 3N 0 30W
Loulé 104 37 9N 8 0W
Lount L. 55 50 10N 94 20W
Loup City 74 41 19N 98 57W
Loupe, La 100 48 29N 1 1 E
Loups Marins, Lacs des 36 56 30N 73 45W
Lourdes, Can. 37 48 39N 59 0W
Lourdes, France 102 43 6N 0 3W
Lourdus-du-Blanc-Sablon 37 51 24N 57 12W
Lourenço-Marques = Maputo 117 25 58 S 32 32 E
Louroux Béconnais, Le 100 47 30N 0 55W
Louth, Ireland 97 53 47N 6 33W
Louth, U.K. 94 53 23N 0 0W
Louth □ 97 53 55N 6 30W
Louvière, La 105 50 27N 4 10 E
Louviers 100 49 12N 1 10 E
Love 56 53 29N 104 10W
Loveland, U.S.A. 77 39 16N 84 16W
Loveland, Colo., U.S.A. 74 40 27N 105 4W
Lovell 78 44 51N 108 20W
Lovelock 78 40 17N 118 25W
Loverna 56 51 40N 110 0W
Loves Park 76 42 19N 89 3W
Loviisa = Lovisa 111 60 31N 26 20 E
Lovilia 76 41 8N 92 55W
Loving 75 32 17N 104 4W
Lovington, U.S.A. 77 39 43N 88 38W
Lovington, N.Mex., U.S.A. 75 33 0N 103 20W
Low 40 45 50N 76 0W
Low, C. 65 63 7N 85 18W
Low L. 36 55 54N 67 5W
Low Rocky Pt. 135 42 59 S 145 29 E
Lowa 116 1 25 S 25 47 E
Lowden 76 41 52N 90 56W
Lowe Farm 57 49 21N 97 35W
Lowell, Ind., U.S.A. 77 41 18N 87 25W
Lowell, Mass., U.S.A. 71 42 38N 71 19W
Lowell, Mich., U.S.A. 77 42 56N 85 20W
Lower Arrow L. 63 49 40N 118 5W
Lower Capilano 66 49 19N 123 7W
Lower Hutt 133 41 10 S 174 55 E
Lower L. 78 41 17N 120 3W
Lower Lake 80 38 56N 122 36W
Lower Manitou L. 52 49 15N 93 0W
Lower Neguac 35 47 20N 65 10W
Lower Nicola 63 50 12N 120 54W
Lower Post 54 59 58N 128 30W
Lower Red L. 52 48 0N 94 50W
Lower Sackville 35 44 45N 63 43W
Lower Seal, L. 34 56 30N 74 23W
Lower West Pubnico 39 43 38N 65 48W
Lower Wood Harbour 39 43 31N 65 44W
Lowestoft 95 52 29N 1 44 E
Łowicz 107 52 6N 19 55 E
Lowry City 76 38 8N 93 44W
Lowther 53 49 32N 83 2W
Lowville 71 43 48N 75 30W
Loxton 135 34 28 S 140 31 E
Loyalton 80 39 41N 120 14W
Loyalty Is. 14 21 0 S 167 30 E
Loyang 131 34 41N 112 28 E
Loyauté, Îles 14 21 0 S 167 30 E
Loyüan 131 26 25N 119 33 E
Loyung 131 24 25N 109 25 E
Lozère □ 102 44 35N 3 30 E
Lu-ta 130 39 0N 121 31 E
Lü-ta (Dairen-P. Arthur) 130 39 0N 121 31 E
Lü-Tao 131 22 47N 121 20 E
Luabo 85 18 30 S 36 10 E
Luacano 116 11 15 S 21 37 E
Lualaba, R. 116 5 45 S 26 50 E
Luan 127 6 10N 124 25 E
Luan Chau 128 21 38N 103 24 E
Luanda 116 8 58 S 13 9 E
Luang Prabang 128 19 45N 102 10 E
Luangwa, R. 117 14 25 S 30 25 E
Luanshya 117 13 3 S 28 28 E
Luapula, R. 116 12 0 S 28 50 E
Luarca 104 43 32N 6 32W
Luashi 116 10 50 S 23 36 E
Lubalo 116 9 10 S 19 15 E
Lubang Is. 127 13 50N 120 12 E
Lubbock 75 33 40N 101 55W
Lübeck 106 53 52N 10 41 E
Lubefu 116 4 47 S 24 27 E
Lubicon L. 60 56 23N 115 56W
Lubicon Lake 60 56 22N 115 52W
Lublin 107 51 12N 22 38 E
Lubny 120 50 3N 32 58 E
Lubok Antu 126 1 3N 111 50 E
Lubuagan 127 17 21N 121 10 E
Lubudi 116 6 50 S 21 20 E
Lubuhanbilik 126 2 33N 100 14 E
Lubuk Linggau 126 3 15 S 102 55 E
Lubuk Sikaping 126 0 10N 100 15 E
Lubumbashi 117 11 32 S 27 28 E
Lubutu 116 0 45 S 26 30 E
Luc-en-Diois 103 44 36N 5 28 E
Luc, Le 103 43 23N 6 21 E
Lucan 46 43 11N 81 24W
Lucania, Mt. 67 60 48N 141 25W
Lucca 108 43 50N 10 30 E
Luce Bay 96 54 45N 4 48W
Lucea 84 18 25N 78 10W
Lucedale 73 30 55N 88 34W
Lucena, Phil. 127 13 56N 121 37 E
Lucena, Spain 104 37 27N 4 31W
Lučenec 107 48 18N 19 42 E
Lucerne, Can. 63 52 52N 118 33W
Lucerne, Calif., U.S.A. 80 39 6N 122 48W
Lucerne, Wash., U.S.A. 63 48 12N 120 36W
Lucerne = Luzern 106 47 3N 8 18 E
Lucerne Valley 81 34 27N 116 57W
Lucero 82 30 49N 106 30W
Luceville 41 48 32N 68 22W
Luchow 131 28 57N 105 26 E
Lucira 117 14 0 S 12 35 E
Luck L. 56 51 5N 107 5W
Luckenwalde 106 52 5N 13 11 E
Luckey 77 41 27N 83 29W
Lucknow, Can. 46 43 57N 81 31W
Lucknow, India 125 26 50N 81 0 E
Lucky Lake 56 50 59N 107 8W
Luçon 102 46 28N 1 10W
Lüdenscheid 105 51 13N 7 37 E
Lüderitz 117 26 41 S 15 8 E
Ludhiana 124 30 57N 75 56 E
Ludington 72 43 58N 86 27W
Ludlow, Can. 39 46 29N 66 21W
Ludlow, U.K. 95 52 23N 2 42W
Ludlow, Calif., U.S.A. 81 34 43N 116 10W
Ludlow, Vt., U.S.A. 71 43 25N 72 40W
Ludvika 111 60 8N 15 14 E
Ludwigsburg 106 48 53N 9 11 E
Ludwigshafen 106 49 27N 8 27 E
Luebo 116 5 21 S 21 17 E
Luepa 86 5 43N 61 31W
Lufira R. 116 9 30 S 27 0 E
Lufkin 75 31 25N 94 40W

M

Madre del Sur, Sierra **Manitoba, L**

Madre del Sur, Sierra **83** 17 30N 100 0W
Madre, Laguna **83** 25 0N 97 30W
Madre Occidental, Sierra **82** 27 0N 107 0W
Madre Oriental, Sierra **82** 25 0N 100 0W
Madre, Sierra, Mexico **83** 16 0N 93 0W
Madre, Sierra, Phil. **127** 17 0N 122 0E
Madrid, Spain **104** 40 25N 3 45W
Madrid, U.S.A. **76** 41 53N 93 49W
Madsen **52** 50 58N 93 55W
Madura, Selat **127** 7 30S 113 20E
Madurai **124** 9 55N 78 10E
Madurantakam **124** 12 30N 79 50E
Mae Hong Son **128** 19 16N 98 8E
Mae Sot **128** 16 43N 98 34E
Maebashi **132** 36 24N 139 4E
Maesteg **95** 51 36N 3 40W
Maestra, Sierra **84** 20 15N 77 0W
Maestrazgo, Mts. del **104** 40 30N 0 25W
Maevatanana **117** 16 56N 46 49E
Mafeking, Can. **57** 52 40N 101 10W
Mafeking, S. Afr. **117** 25 50S 25 38E
Maffra **136** 37 53S 146 58E
Mafia I. **116** 7 45S 39 50E
Mafra, Brazil **89** 26 10N 50 0W
Mafra, Port. **104** 38 55N 9 20W
Magadan **121** 59 30N 151 0E
Magadi **116** 1 54S 36 19E
Magaguadavic **39** 45 42N 67 12W
Magaguadavic L. **39** 45 43N 67 12W
Magaguadavic, R. **39** 45 7N 66 54W
Magallanes, Estrecho de **90** 52 30S 75 0W
Magangué **86** 9 14N 74 45W
Magdalen Is. = Madeleine, Is. de la **35** 47 30N 61 40W
Magdalena, Argent. **88** 35 5S 57 30W
Magdalena, Boliv. **86** 13 13S 63 57W
Magdalena, Mexico **82** 30 50N 112 0W
Magdalena, U.S.A. **79** 34 10N 107 20W
Magdalena □ **86** 10 0N 74 0W
Magdalena, B. **82** 24 30N 112 10W
Magdalena, I. **82** 24 40N 112 15W
Magdalena, Llano de la **82** 25 0N 111 30W
Magdalena, mt. **126** 4 25N 117 55E
Magdalena, R., Colomb. **86** 8 30N 74 0W
Magdalena, R., Mexico **82** 30 50N 112 0W
Magdeburg **106** 52 8N 11 36E
Magee **75** 31 53N 89 45W
Magee, I. **97** 54 48N 5 44W
Magelang **127** 7 29S 110 13E
Magellan's Str. **90** 52 30S 75 0W
Magellan's Str. = Magallanes, Est. de **90** 52 30S 75 0W
Maggiore, L. **108** 46 0N 8 35E
Magherafelt **97** 54 44N 6 37W
Magherafelt □ **97** 54 50N 6 40W
Magnac-Laval **102** 46 13N 1 11E
Magnetawan **46** 45 40N 79 39W
Magnetic Pole, 1976, (South) **91** 68 48S 139 30E
Magnetic Pole, 1976(North) **17** 76 12N 100 12W
Magnitogorsk **120** 53 27N 59 4E
Magnolia, Ark., U.S.A. **75** 33 18N 93 12W
Magnolia, Miss., U.S.A. **75** 31 8N 90 28W
Magny-en-Vexin **101** 49 9N 1 47E
Magog **41** 45 18N 72 9W
Magosa = Famagusta **122** 35 8N 33 55E
Magpie **38** 50 19N 64 30W
Magpie L. **38** 51 0N 64 41W
Magpie, R., Ont., Can. **53** 47 56N 84 50W
Magpie, R., Qué., Can. **38** 50 19N 64 27W
Magrath **61** 49 25N 112 50W
Maguarinho, C. **87** 0 15S 48 30W
Maguse L. **55** 61 40N 95 10W
Maguse Pt. **55** 61 20N 93 50W
Maguse River **55** 61 20N 94 25W
Magwe **125** 20 10N 95 0E
Mahābād **122** 36 50N 45 45E
Mahabo **117** 20 23S 44 40E
Mahagi **116** 2 20N 31 0E
Mahajamba, B. de la **117** 15 24S 47 5E
Mahakam, R. **126** 1 0N 114 40E
Mahalapye **117** 23 1S 26 51E
Mahallāt **123** 33 55N 50 30E
Mahanadi R. **125** 20 33N 85 0E
Mahanoro **117** 19 54S 48 48E
Mahanoy City **71** 40 48N 76 10W
Maharashtra □ **124** 19 30N 75 30E
Mahatta River **62** 50 22N 127 47W
Mahbubnagar **124** 16 45N 77 59E
Mahd Dhahab **122** 25 55N 45 30E
Mahdia **114** 35 28N 11 0E
Mahé, I. **16** 5 0S 55 30E
Mahenge **116** 8 45S 36 35E
Maheno **133** 45 10S 170 50E
Mahia Pen. **133** 39 9S 177 55E
Mahnomen **74** 47 22N 95 57W
Mahomet **77** 40 12N 88 24W
Mahón **104** 39 50N 4 18E
Mahone Bay **35** 44 30N 64 20W
Mahood Falls **63** 51 50N 120 38W
Mahood L. **63** 51 50N 120 23W
Mahukona **67** 20 11N 155 52W
Mai-Ndombe, L. **116** 2 0S 18 0E
Maicasagi, R. **40** 49 58N 76 33W
Maîche **101** 47 16N 6 48E
Maicuru, R. **87** 1 0S 54 30W
Maidenhead **95** 51 31N 0 42W
Maidstone, Can. **56** 53 5N 109 20W
Maidstone, U.K. **95** 51 16N 0 31E
Maiduguri **114** 12 0N 13 20E
Maignelay **101** 49 32N 2 30E
Maigualida, Sierra **86** 5 30N 65 10W
Maijdi **125** 22 48N 91 10E
Maikala Ra. **125** 22 0N 81 0E
Maillardville **66** 49 15N 122 52W
Mailly-le-Camp **101** 48 41N 4 12E
Maimana **124** 35 53N 64 38E
Main-à-Dieu **39** 46 0N 59 51W
Main Barrier Ra. **136** 31 10S 141 20E
Main Brook **37** 51 11N 56 1W
Main Centre **56** 50 35N 107 21W
Main Channel **70** 45 22N 81 45W
Main, R., Ger. **106** 50 13N 11 0E
Main, R., U.K. **97** 54 49N 6 20W
Maine **100** 48 0N 0 0E
Maine □ **35** 45 20N 69 0W
Maine-et-Loire □ **100** 47 31N 0 30W
Maine, R. **97** 52 10N 9 40W
Maingkwan **125** 26 15N 96 45E
Mainit, L. **127** 9 31N 125 30E
Mainland, I., Orkneys, U.K. **96** 59 0N 3 10W
Mainland, I., Shetlands, U.K. **96** 60 15N 1 22W
Maintenon **101** 48 35N 1 35E
Maintirano **117** 18 3S 44 1E
Mainz **106** 50 0N 8 17E
Maipú **88** 37 0S 58 0W
Maipures **86** 5 11N 67 49W
Maiquetía **86** 10 36N 66 57W
Mairabari **125** 26 30N 92 30E
Maisí **85** 20 17N 74 9W
Maisi, C. **85** 20 10N 74 10W
Maisonnette **39** 47 49N 65 0W
Maisse **101** 48 24N 2 21E
Maitland, Austral. **136** 32 44S 151 36E
Maitland, Can. **39** 45 19N 63 30W
Maitland Bridge **39** 44 27N 65 12W
Maitland, R. **70** 43 45N 81 33W
Maíz, Islas del **84** 12 15N 83 4W
Maizuru **132** 35 25N 135 22E
Majagual **86** 8 33N 74 38W
Majalengka **127** 6 55S 108 14E
Majene **127** 3 27S 118 57E
Major **56** 51 52N 109 37W
Majorca, I. = Mallorca, I. **104** 39 30N 3 0E
Majunga **117** 15 40S 46 25E
Makale **127** 3 6S 119 51E
Makamik **34** 48 45N 79 0W
Makapuu Hd. **67** 21 19N 157 39W
Makarikari = Makgadikgadi **117** 20 40S 25 45E
Makarovo **121** 57 40N 107 45E
Makasar = Ujung Pandang **127** 5 10S 119 20E
Makasar, Selat **127** 1 0S 118 20E
Makat **120** 47 39N 53 19E
Makedhona □ **109** 40 39N 22 0E
Makedonija □ **109** 41 53N 21 40E
Makena **67** 20 39N 156 27W
Makeyevka **120** 48 0N 38 0E
Makgadikgadi Salt Pans **117** 20 40S 25 45E
Makhachkala **120** 43 0N 47 15E
Makian, I. **127** 0 12N 127 20E
Makin, I. **14** 3 30N 174 0E
Makindu **116** 2 7S 37 40E
Makinsk **120** 52 37N 70 26E
Makkah **122** 21 30N 39 54E
Makkovik **36** 55 10N 59 10W
Maklakovo **121** 58 16N 92 29E
Makó **107** 46 14N 20 33E
Makokibatan L. **53** 51 17N 87 20W
Makoua **116** 0 5S 15 50E
Makrai **124** 22 2N 77 0E
Makran **123** 26 13N 61 30E
Makran Coast Range **124** 25 40N 4 0E
Maksimkin Yar **120** 58 58N 86 50E
Mākū **122** 39 15N 44 31E
Makumbi **116** 5 50S 20 43E
Makurazaki **132** 31 15N 130 20E
Makurdi **114** 7 43N 8 28E
Mal B. **97** 52 50N 9 30W
Mala, Pta. **84** 7 28N 80 2W
Malabang **127** 7 36N 124 3E
Malabar Coast **124** 11 0N 75 0E
Malacca = Melaka **128** 2 15N 102 15E
Malacca, Str. of **128** 3 0N 101 0E
Malachi **52** 49 56N 94 59W
Malad City **78** 42 15N 112 20E
Maladetta, Mt. **104** 42 40N 0 30E
Málaga **86** 6 42N 72 44W
Malaga **75** 32 12N 104 2W
Málaga □ **104** 36 38N 4 58W
Malagasy Rep. ■ = Madagascar ■ **117** 20 0S 47 0E
Malakal **115** 9 33N 31 50E
Malakand **124** 34 40N 71 55E
Malakoff **75** 32 10N 95 55W
Malakwa **54** 50 55N 118 50W
Malamyzh **121** 50 0N 136 50E
Malang **127** 7 59S 112 35E
Malanje **116** 9 30S 16 17E
Mälaren **111** 59 30N 17 10E
Malargüe **88** 35 40S 69 30W
Malartic **40** 48 9N 78 9W
Malartic, L. **40** 48 15N 78 5W
Malatya **122** 38 25N 38 20E
Malawi ■ **117** 13 0S 34 0E
Malawi, L. (Lago Niassa) **117** 12 30S 34 30E
Malay Pen. **128** 7 25N 100 0E
Malaya □ **128** 4 0N 102 0E
Malaybalay **127** 8 5N 125 15E
Malayer **122** 34 19N 48 51E
Malaysia ■ **126** 5 0N 110 0E
Malaysia, Western □ **128** 5 0N 102 0E
Malazgirt **122** 39 10N 42 33E
Malbaie, La **41** 47 40N 70 10W
Malbork **107** 54 3N 19 10E
Malcolm **134** 28 51S 121 25E
Malcolm I. **62** 50 38N 127 0W
Maldegem **105** 51 14N 3 26E
Malden, Mass., U.S.A. **71** 42 26N 71 5W
Malden, Mo., U.S.A. **75** 36 35N 90 0W
Maldive Is. ■ **16** 2 0N 73 0W
Maldonado **89** 35 0S 55 0W
Maldonado, Punta **83** 16 19N 98 35W
Malé Karpaty **106** 48 30N 17 20E
Malea, Ákra **109** 36 28N 23 7E
Malegaon **124** 20 30N 74 30E
Malesherbes **101** 48 15N 2 24E
Malestroit **100** 47 49N 2 25W
Malgomaj L. **110** 64 40N 16 30E
Malhão, Sa. do **104** 37 25N 8 0W
Malheur L. **78** 43 19N 118 42W
Malheur, R. **78** 43 55N 117 55W
Mali ■ **114** 15 0N 10 0W
Mali Kyun, I. **128** 13 0N 98 20E
Mali, R. **125** 26 20N 97 40E
Malibu **81** 34 2N 118 41W
Maligne L. **61** 52 40N 117 31W
Malik **127** 0 39S 123 16E
Malili **127** 2 42S 121 23E
Malin Hd. **97** 55 18N 7 16W
Malinau **126** 3 35N 116 30E
Malindi **116** 3 12S 40 5E
Maling, Mt. **127** 1 0N 121 0E
Malingping **127** 6 45S 106 2E
Malita **127** 6 19N 125 39E
Mallacoota **136** 37 40S 149 40E
Mallacoota Inlet **136** 37 40S 149 40E
Mallaig, Can. **60** 54 13N 111 22W
Mallaig, U.K. **96** 57 0N 5 50W
Mallard **76** 42 56N 94 41W
Mallee **136** 35 10S 142 20E
Mallemort **103** 43 44N 5 11E
Mallorca, I. **104** 39 30N 3 0E
Mallorytown, Can. **71** 44 29N 75 53W
Mallorytown, Ont., Can. **47** 44 29N 75 53W
Mallow **97** 52 8N 8 40W
Malmberget **110** 67 11N 20 40E
Malmö **111** 55 36N 12 59E
Malmöhus län □ **111** 55 45N 13 30E
Malolos **127** 14 50N 121 2E
Malone **71** 44 50N 74 19W
Malott **63** 48 19N 119 39W
Malpelo I. **86** 4 3N 80 35W
Malta, Idaho, U.S.A. **78** 42 15N 113 30W
Malta, Mont., U.S.A. **78** 48 20N 107 55W
Malta ■ **108** 35 50N 14 30E
Maltahöhe **117** 24 55S 17 0E
Malton, Ont., Can. **49** 43 42N 79 38W
Malton, Ont., Can. **50** 43 42N 79 38W
Malton, U.K. **94** 54 9N 0 48W
Maluku □ **127** 3 0S 128 0E
Maluku, Is. **127** 1 0S 127 0E
Maluku, Kepulauan **127** 3 0S 128 0E
Malung **57** 48 45N 95 45W
Malvan **124** 16 2N 73 30E
Malvern, Can. **50** 43 48N 79 14W
Malvern, U.K. **95** 52 7N 2 19W
Malvern, Ark., U.S.A. **75** 34 22N 92 50W
Malvern, Ohio, U.S.A. **70** 40 31N 31 12W
Malvern Hills **95** 52 0N 2 19W
Malvinas Is. = Falkland Is. **86** 51 30S 59 0W
Mama **121** 58 18N 112 54E
Mamaia **107** 44 18N 28 37E
Mamanguape **87** 6 50S 35 4W
Mamasa **127** 2 55S 119 20E
Mamberamo, R. **127** 2 0S 137 50E
Mameigwess L., Can. **34** 52 35N 87 50W
Mameigwess L., Ont., Can. **52** 49 34N 91 49W
Mamers **100** 48 21N 0 22E
Mammamattawa **34** 50 25N 84 23W
Mammoth **79** 32 46N 110 43W
Mamoi **131** 26 0N 119 25E
Mamoré, R. **87** 9 55S 65 20W
Mamou **114** 10 15N 12 0W
Mampawah **126** 0 30N 109 5E
Mamuju **127** 2 50S 118 50E
Man **114** 7 30N 7 40W
Man, I. of **94** 54 15N 4 30W
Man Na **125** 23 27N 97 19E
Man O' War Peak **35** 56 58N 61 40W
Mana, Fr. Gui. **87** 5 45N 53 55W
Mana, U.S.A. **67** 22 3N 159 45W
Manaar, Gulf of **124** 8 30N 79 0E
Manacacías, R. **86** 4 23N 72 4W
Manacapuru **86** 3 10S 60 50W
Manacor **104** 39 32N 3 12E
Managua **84** 12 0N 86 20W
Managua, L. **84** 12 20N 86 30W
Manakara **117** 22 8S 48 1E
Manamāh, Al **123** 26 11N 50 35E
Mananara **117** 16 10S 49 30E
Mananjary **117** 21 13S 48 20E
Manantenina **117** 24 17S 47 19E
Manaos = Manaus **86** 3 0S 60 0W
Manapouri **133** 45 34S 167 39E
Manapouri, L. **133** 45 32S 167 32E
Manas, R. **125** 26 12N 90 40E
Manasalowo Chih **129** 30 45N 81 20E
Manasir **123** 24 30N 51 10E
Manasquan **71** 40 7N 74 3W
Manass **129** 44 20N 86 21E
Manassa **79** 37 12N 105 58W
Manati **67** 18 26N 66 29W
Manaung Kyun **125** 18 45N 93 40E
Manaus **86** 3 0S 60 0W
Manawan L. **55** 55 24N 103 14W
Manay **127** 7 17N 126 33E
Mancelona **46** 44 54N 85 5W
Mancha, La **104** 39 10N 2 54W
Manche □ **100** 49 10N 1 20W
Manchester, U.K. **94** 53 30N 2 15W
Manchester, U.S.A. **77** 42 9N 84 2W
Manchester, Calif., U.S.A. **80** 38 58N 123 41W
Manchester, Conn., U.S.A. **71** 41 47N 72 30W
Manchester, Ga., U.S.A. **73** 32 53N 84 32W
Manchester, Iowa, U.S.A. **76** 42 28N 91 27W
Manchester, Ky., U.S.A. **72** 37 15N 83 45W
Manchester, N.H., U.S.A. **71** 42 58N 71 29W
Manchester, N.Y., U.S.A. **70** 42 56N 77 16W
Manchester Depot **71** 43 10N 73 5W
Manchester L. **55** 61 28N 107 29W
Manchouli **129** 49 46N 117 24E
Mand, R. **123** 28 20N 52 30E
Manda **116** 10 30S 34 40E
Mandabé **117** 21 0S 44 55E
Mandaguari **89** 23 32S 51 42W
Mandal **111** 58 2N 7 25E
Mandal Gobi **130** 45 47N 106 15E
Mandalay **125** 22 0N 96 10E
Mandalgovi **130** 45 40N 106 22E
Mandali **122** 33 52N 45 28E
Mandan **74** 46 50N 101 0W
Mandar, Teluk **127** 3 35S 119 4E
Mandasaur **124** 24 3N 75 8E
Mandawai (Katingan), R. **126** 1 30S 113 0E
Mandelieu-la-Napoule **103** 43 34N 6 57E
Mandi **124** 31 39N 76 58E
Mandimba **117** 14 20S 35 40E
Mandioli **127** 0 40S 127 20E
Mandla **125** 22 39N 80 30E
Mandritsara **117** 15 50S 48 49E
Mandvi **124** 22 51N 69 22E
Mandya **124** 12 30N 77 0E
Manfredónia **108** 41 40N 15 55E
Mangabeiras, Chapada das **87** 10 0S 46 30W
Mangaia, I. **133** 21 55S 157 55W
Mangalia **107** 43 50N 28 35E
Mangalore **124** 12 55N 74 47E
Manggar **126** 2 50S 108 10E
Manggawitu **127** 4 8S 133 32E
Mangla Dam **124** 33 32N 73 50E
Mangoche **117** 14 25S 35 16E
Mangole I. **127** 1 50S 125 55E
Mangonui **133** 35 1S 173 32E
Mangueira, Lagoa da **89** 33 0S 52 50W
Mangum **75** 34 50N 99 30W
Mangyai **129** 38 6N 91 37E
Mangyshlak P-ov. **120** 43 40N 52 30E
Manhattan, U.S.A. **77** 41 26N 87 59W
Manhattan, Kans., U.S.A. **74** 39 10N 96 40W
Manhattan, Nev., U.S.A. **78** 38 31N 117 3W
Manhuaçu **87** 20 15S 42 2W
Maní **86** 4 49N 72 17W
Manicoré **86** 6 0S 61 10W
Manicouagan L. **38** 51 25N 68 15W
Manicouagan, R. **41** 49 30N 68 30W
Manicouagan, Rés. **36** 51 5N 68 40W
Manifah **122** 27 30N 49 0E
Manigotagan **57** 51 6N 96 8W
Manigotagan L. **57** 50 52N 95 37W
Manihiki I. **15** 10 24S 161 1W
Manila, Phil. **127** 14 40N 121 3E
Manila, U.S.A. **78** 41 0N 109 44W
Manila B. **127** 14 0N 120 0E
Manipur □ **125** 24 30N 94 0E
Manipur, R. **125** 23 45N 93 40E
Manisa **122** 38 38N 27 30E
Manistee **72** 44 15N 86 20W
Manistee, R. **46** 44 15N 86 21W
Manistique **72** 45 59N 86 18W
Manito **76** 40 25N 89 47W
Manito L. **56** 52 43N 109 43W
Manitoba □ **57** 55 30N 97 0W
Manitoba, L. **57** 51 0N 98 45W

Manitou Masi

Manitou, Man., Can. 57 49 15N 98 32W
Manitou, Qué., Can. 38 50 18N 65 15W
Manitou Beach 77 41 58N 84 19W
Manitou I. 53 47 22N 87 30W
Manitou Is. 72 45 8N 86 0W
Manitou L., Ont., Can. 46 45 51N 82 0W
Manitou L., Ont., Can. 55 49 15N 93 0W
Manitou L., Qué., Can. 36 50 55N 65 17W
Manitou, R. 38 50 18N 65 15W
Manitoulin I. 46 45 40N 82 30W
Manitouwadge 53 49 8N 85 48W
Manitowaning 46 45 46N 81 49W
Manitowoc 72 44 8N 87 40W
Maniwaki 40 46 23N 75 58W
Manizales 86 5 5N 75 32W
Manja 117 21 26S 44 20E
Manjacaze 117 24 45S 34 0E
Manjhand 124 25 50N 68 10E
Manjil 122 36 46N 49 30E
Manjimup 134 34 15S 116 6E
Manjra, R. 124 18 20N 77 20E
Mankato, Kans., U.S.A. 74 39 49N 98 11W
Mankato, Minn., U.S.A. 74 44 8N 93 59W
Mankota 56 49 25N 107 5W
Manlius 58 50 0N 97 2W
Manly 136 33 48S 151 17E
Manmad 124 20 18N 74 28E
Manna 126 4 25S 102 55E
Mannar 124 9 1N 79 54E
Mannar, G. of 124 8 30N 79 0E
Mannar I. 124 9 5N 79 45E
Mannheim, Can. 49 43 24N 80 33W
Mannheim, Ger. 106 49 28N 8 29E
Manning, Can. 60 56 53N 117 39W
Manning, Oreg., U.S.A. 80 45 45N 123 13W
Manning, S.C., U.S.A. 73 33 40N 80 9W
Manning Park 63 49 4N 120 47W
Manning Prov. Park 63 49 5N 120 45W
Manning, R. 136 31 52S 152 43E
Mannington 72 39 35N 80 25W
Mannville 60 53 20N 111 10W
Manokwari 127 0 54S 134 0E
Manombo 117 22 57S 43 28E
Manono 116 7 15S 27 25E
Manor 57 49 36N 102 5W
Manosque 103 43 49N 5 47E
Manotick 47 45 13N 75 41W
Manouane L. 36 50 45N 70 45W
Manouane, L. 41 47 33N 74 6W
Manresa 104 41 48N 1 50E
Mans, Le 100 48 0N 0 10E
Mansa 116 11 13S 28 55E
Manseau 41 46 22N 72 0W
Mansel I. 36 62 0N 79 50W
Mansfield, Austral. 136 37 4S 146 6E
Mansfield, U.K. 94 53 8N 1 12W
Mansfield, La., U.S.A. 75 32 2N 93 40W
Mansfield, Mass., U.S.A. 71 42 2N 71 12W
Mansfield, Ohio, U.S.A. 70 40 45N 82 30W
Mansfield, Pa., U.S.A. 70 41 48N 77 4W
Mansfield, Wash., U.S.A. 78 47 51N 119 44W
Mansle 102 45 52N 0 9E
Manso, R. 87 14 0S 52 0W
Manson 76 42 32N 94 32W
Manson Creek 54 55 37N 124 25W
Manta 86 1 0S 80 40W
Mantalingajan, Mt. 126 8 55N 117 45E
Manteca 80 37 50N 121 12W
Mantecal 86 7 34N 69 17W
Manteno 77 41 15N 87 50W
Manteo 73 35 55N 75 41W
Mantes-la-Jolie 101 49 0N 1 41E
Manthani 124 18 40N 79 35E
Manthelan 100 47 9N 0 47E
Manti 78 39 23N 111 32W
Mantiqueira, Serra da 89 22 0S 44 0W
Manton 46 44 23N 85 25W
Mántova 108 45 10N 10 47E
Mänttä 110 62 0N 24 40E
Mantua 70 41 15N 81 14W
Mantua = Mántova 108 45 10N 10 47E
Manu 86 12 10S 71 0W
Manua Is. 133 14 13S 169 35W
Manucan 127 8 14N 123 3E
Manuel Alves, R. 87 11 19S 48 28W
Manuels 39 47 3N 64 59W
Manui I. 127 3 35S 123 5E
Manville 74 42 48N 104 36W
Many 75 31 36N 93 28W
Many Island L. 61 50 8N 110 3W
Manyara L. 116 3 40S 35 50E
Manyberries 61 49 24N 110 42W
Manyoni 116 5 45S 34 55E
Manzai 124 32 20N 70 15E
Manzanares 104 39 0N 3 22W
Manzanillo, Cuba 84 20 20N 77 10W
Manzanillo, Mexico 82 19 0N 104 20W
Manzanillo, Pta. 84 9 30N 79 40W
Manzano Mts. 79 34 30N 106 45W
Maoke, Pengunungan 126 3 40S 137 30E
Mapastepec 83 15 26N 92 54W
Mapia, Kepulauan 127 0 50N 134 20E
Mapimí 82 25 50N 103 31W
Mapimí, Bolsón de 82 27 30N 103 15W
Maple 50 43 51N 79 31W
Maple Bay 63 48 48N 123 37W
Maple Creek 56 49 55N 109 29W
Maple Falls 63 48 56N 122 5W
Maple Grove 44 45 19N 73 50W
Maple, R. 77 42 58N 84 56W
Maple Valley 80 47 25N 122 3W
Maples, The 49 43 52N 80 10W
Mapleton 78 44 4N 123 58W
Maplewood 74 38 33N 90 18W
Mapuera, R. 86 0 30S 58 25W
Maputo 117 25 58S 32 32E
Maqnā 122 28 25N 34 50E
Maquinchao 90 41 15S 68 50W
Maquoketa 76 42 4N 90 40W
Mar Chiquita, L. 88 30 40S 62 50W
Mar del Plata 88 38 0S 57 30W
Mar, Serra do 89 25 30S 49 0W
Maraã 86 1 43S 65 25W
Marabá 87 5 20S 49 5W
Maracá, I. de 87 2 10N 50 30W
Maracaibo 86 10 40N 71 37W
Maracaibo, Lago de 86 9 40N 71 30W
Maracaju 89 21 38S 55 9W
Maracay 86 10 15N 67 36W
Marāgheh 122 37 30N 46 12E
Marajó, Ilha de 87 1 0S 49 30W
Maralal 116 1 0N 36 38E
Marana 79 32 30N 111 9W
Marand 122 38 30N 45 45E
Marandellas 117 18 5S 31 42E
Maranguape 87 3 55S 38 50W
Maranhão = São Luis 87 2 31S 44 16W
Maranhão □ 87 5 0S 46 0W
Marañ n, R. 86 4 50S 75 35W
Maranoa R. 135 27 50S 148 37E
Maraş 122 37 37N 36 53E
Marathon 53 48 44N 86 23W
Marathón 109 38 11N 23 58E
Marathon, U.S.A. 76 42 52N 94 59W
Marathon, N.Y., U.S.A. 71 42 25N 76 3W
Marathon, Tex., U.S.A. 75 30 15N 103 15W
Maratua, I. 127 2 10N 118 35E
Marbella 104 36 30N 4 57W
Marble 52 47 19N 93 18W
Marble Bar 134 21 9S 119 44E
Marble Falls 75 30 30N 98 15W
Marblehead, Can. 63 50 15N 116 58W
Marblehead, U.S.A. 71 42 29N 70 51W
Marblemount 63 48 32N 121 26W
Marbleton 41 45 37N 71 35W
Marburg 106 50 49N 8 44E
Marceau, L. 38 51 25N 66 41W
Marcelin 56 52 55N 106 47W
Marceline 76 39 43N 92 57W
March 95 52 33N 0 5E
Marché 102 46 0N 1 20E
Marche □ 108 43 22N 13 10E
Marche-en-Famenne 105 50 14N 5 19E
Marchin 105 50 28N 5 14E
Marcigny 103 46 17N 4 2E
Marcillac-Vallon 102 44 29N 2 27E
Marcillat 102 46 12N 2 38E
Marck 101 50 57N 1 57E
Marckolsheim 101 48 10N 7 30E
Marconi 58 49 55N 97 6W
Marcos Juárez 88 32 42S 62 5W
Marcus I. 14 24 0N 153 45E
Marcy Mt. 71 44 7N 73 55W
Mardan 124 34 20N 72 0E
Marden 49 43 36N 80 18W
Mardin 122 37 20N 40 36E
Maree L. 96 57 40N 5 30W
Mareeba 135 16 59S 145 28E
Marek 127 4 41S 120 24E
Marek = Stanke Dimitrov 109 42 17N 23 9E
Marelan 43 45 38N 74 33W
Maremma 108 42 45N 11 15E
Maremma, reg. 108 42 30N 11 0E
Marengo, Can. 56 51 29N 109 47W
Marengo, U.S.A. 76 41 42N 92 5W
Marenisco 52 46 23N 89 40W
Mareuil-sur-Lay 102 46 32N 1 14W
Marfa 75 30 15N 104 0W
Margaree Forks 39 46 20N 61 5W
Margaree Harbour 35 46 26N 61 8W
Margaret Bay 62 51 20N 127 20W
Margaret L. 54 58 56N 115 25W
Margarita 84 9 20N 79 55W
Margarita, Isla de 86 11 0N 64 0W
Margate 95 51 23N 1 24E
Margeride, Mts. de la 102 44 43N 3 38E
Margo 56 51 49N 103 20W
Marguerite 63 52 30N 122 25W
Mari, A.S.S.R. □ 120 56 30N 48 0E
Maria 38 48 10N 65 59W
María Elena 88 22 18S 69 40W
María Grande 88 31 45S 59 55W
Maria, I. 134 14 52S 135 45E
Maria I. 134 42 35S 148 0E
Maria van Diemen, C. 133 34 29S 172 40E
Marian L. 54 63 0N 116 15W
Mariana Is. 14 17 0N 145 0E
Mariana Trench 14 13 0N 145 0W
Marianao 84 23 8N 82 24W
Marianna, Ark., U.S.A. 75 34 48N 90 48W
Marianna, Fla., U.S.A. 73 30 45N 85 15W
Marias, R. 78 48 26N 111 40W
Mariato, Punta 84 7 12N 80 52W
Maribor 108 46 36N 15 40E
Maricopa, Ariz., U.S.A. 79 33 5N 112 2W
Maricopa, Calif., U.S.A. 81 35 7N 119 27W
Maricourt 36 56 34N 70 49W
Marie Galante, I. 85 15 56N 61 16W
Marie L. 60 54 38N 110 18W
Mariehamn (Maarianhamina) 111 60 5N 19 57E
Marienberg 105 52 30N 6 35E
Marienbourg 105 50 6N 4 31E
Mariental 117 24 36S 18 0E
Marienville 70 41 27N 79 8W
Mariestad 111 58 43N 13 50E
Marietta, Ga., U.S.A. 73 34 0N 84 30W
Marietta, Ohio, U.S.A. 72 39 27N 81 27W
Marieville 45 45 26N 73 10W
Marignane 103 43 25N 5 13E
Mariinsk 120 56 10N 87 20E
Marilia 89 22 0S 50 0W
Marín 104 42 23N 8 42W
Marina 80 36 41N 121 48W
Marinduque, I. 127 13 25N 122 0E
Marine City 46 42 45N 82 29W
Marinel, Le 116 10 25S 25 17E
Marinette, Ariz., U.S.A. 79 33 41N 112 16W
Marinette, Wis., U.S.A. 72 45 4N 87 40W
Maringá 89 23 35S 51 50W
Marion, Ala., U.S.A. 73 32 33N 87 20W
Marion, Ill., U.S.A. 76 37 45N 88 55W
Marion, Ind., U.S.A. 77 40 35N 85 40W
Marion, Iowa, U.S.A. 76 42 2N 91 36W
Marion, Kans., U.S.A. 74 38 25N 97 2W
Marion, Mich., U.S.A. 46 44 7N 85 8W
Marion, N.C., U.S.A. 73 35 42N 82 0W
Marion, Ohio, U.S.A. 77 40 38N 83 8W
Marion, S.C., U.S.A. 73 34 11N 79 22W
Marion, Va., U.S.A. 73 36 51N 81 29W
Marion I. 16 47 0S 38 0E
Marion, L. 73 33 30N 80 15W
Marion Reef 135 19 10S 152 17E
Maripa 86 7 26N 65 9W
Mariposa 80 37 31N 119 59W
Mariscal Estigarribia 88 22 3S 60 40W
Maritsa, R. 109 42 15N 24 0E
Marjan 123 32 5N 68 20E
Markdale 46 44 19N 80 39W
Marked Tree 75 35 35N 90 24W
Markerville 61 52 7N 114 10W
Market Drayton 94 52 55N 2 30W
Market Harborough 95 52 29N 0 55W
Markham 50 43 52N 79 16W
Markham I. 17 84 0N 0 45W
Markham L. 55 62 30N 102 35W
Markham Mts. 91 83 0S 164 0E
Markleeville 80 38 42N 119 47W
Markovo 121 64 40N 169 40E
Markstay 46 46 29N 80 32W
Marksville 75 31 10N 92 2W
Marl 105 51 39N 7 4E
Marlbank 47 44 26N 77 6W
Marlboro, Can. 54 53 30N 116 50W
Marlboro, U.S.A. 71 42 19N 71 33W
Marlborough □ 133 41 45S 173 33E
Marlborough Downs 95 51 25N 1 55W
Marle 101 49 43N 3 47E
Marlin 75 31 25N 96 50W
Marlow 75 34 40N 97 58W
Marmagao 124 15 25N 73 56E
Marmande 102 44 30N 0 10E
Marmara denizi 122 40 45N 28 15E
Marmara, I. 109 40 35N 27 38E
Marmara, Sea of = Marmara denizi 122 40 45N 28 15E
Marmaris 122 36 50N 28 14E
Marmarth 74 46 21N 103 52W
Marmion L. 52 48 55N 91 30W
Marmolada, Mte. 108 46 25N 11 55E
Marmora 47 44 28N 77 41W
Marnay 101 47 20N 5 48E
Marne □ 101 49 0N 4 10E
Marne, R. 101 48 53N 2 25E
Marnoo 136 36 40S 142 54E
Maroa 86 2 43N 67 33W
Maroantsetra 117 15 26S 49 44E
Maroni, R. 87 4 0N 52 0W
Marovoay 117 16 6S 46 39E
Marquesas Is. = Marquises 15 9 30S 140 0W
Marquette, Can. 57 50 4N 97 44W
Marquette, U.S.A. 53 46 30N 87 21W
Marquette I. 46 45 58N 84 18W
Marquette, L. 41 48 54N 73 54W
Marquise 101 50 50N 1 40E
Marquises, Is. 15 9 30S 140 0W
Marrakech 114 31 40N 8 0W
Marrat 122 25 0N 45 35E
Marree 135 29 39S 138 1E
Marromeu 117 18 40S 36 25E
Marrupa 117 13 8S 37 30E
Mars, Le 74 43 0N 96 0W
Marsabit 116 2 18N 38 0E
Marsala 108 37 48N 12 25E
Marsaxlokk (Medport) 108 35 47N 14 32E
Marsden 56 52 51N 109 49W
Marseillan 102 43 23N 3 31E
Marseille 103 43 18N 5 23E
Marseilles 77 41 20N 88 43W
Marseilles = Marseille 103 43 18N 5 23E
Marsh I. 75 29 35N 91 50W
Marshall, Can. 56 53 11N 109 47W
Marshall, Ark., U.S.A. 75 35 58N 92 40W
Marshall, Ill., U.S.A. 77 39 23N 87 42W
Marshall, Mich., U.S.A. 77 42 17N 84 59W
Marshall, Minn., U.S.A. 74 44 25N 95 45W
Marshall, Mo., U.S.A. 76 39 8N 93 15W
Marshall, Tex., U.S.A. 75 32 29N 94 20W
Marshall Is. 14 9 0N 171 0E
Marshalltown 76 42 5N 92 56W
Marshfield, Mo., U.S.A. 75 37 20N 92 58W
Marshfield, Wis., U.S.A. 74 44 42N 90 10W
Marsoui 38 49 13N 66 4W
Marstrand 111 57 53N 11 35E
Marsville 49 43 50N 80 13W
Mart 75 31 34N 96 51W
Martaban 125 16 30N 97 35E
Martagne 100 46 59N 0 57W
Martapura 126 3 22S 114 56E
Martelange 105 49 49N 5 43E
Marten River 46 46 44N 79 49W
Martensdale 76 41 23N 93 45W
Martensville 56 52 17N 106 40W
Martha's Vineyard 71 41 25N 70 35W
Martigné Ferchaud 100 47 50N 1 20W
Martigues 103 43 24N 5 4E
Martin, S.D., U.S.A. 74 43 11N 101 45W
Martin, Tenn., U.S.A. 75 36 23N 88 51W
Martin, L. 73 32 45N 85 50W
Martinborough 133 41 14S 175 29E
Martinez 80 38 1N 122 8W
Martinique, I. 85 14 40N 61 0W
Martinique Passage 85 15 15N 61 0W
Martinópolis 89 22 11S 51 12W
Martins Ferry 71 40 5N 80 46W
Martinsburg, Pa., U.S.A. 70 40 18N 78 21W
Martinsburg, W. Va., U.S.A. 72 39 30N 77 57W
Martinsville, Ill., U.S.A. 77 39 20N 87 53W
Martinsville, Ind., U.S.A. 77 39 29N 86 23W
Martinsville, N.Y., U.S.A. 49 43 2N 78 50W
Martinsville, Va., U.S.A. 73 36 41N 79 52W
Marton 133 40 4S 175 23E
Martos 104 37 44N 3 58W
Martre, L., La 64 63 0N 118 0W
Marudi 126 4 10N 114 25E
Maruf 124 31 30N 67 0E
Marugame 132 34 15N 133 55E
Marvejols 102 44 33N 3 19E
Marvine Mt. 79 38 44N 111 40W
Marwar 124 25 43N 73 45E
Marwayne 60 53 32N 110 20W
Mary 120 37 40N 61 50E
Mary Frances L. 55 63 19N 106 13W
Mary Kathleen 135 20 35S 139 48E
Maryborough, Queens., Austral. 135 25 31S 152 37E
Maryborough, Vic., Austral. 136 37 0S 143 44E
Maryborough = Port Laoise 97 53 2N 7 20W
Maryen, L. 38 51 20N 60 28W
Maryfield 57 49 50N 101 35W
Maryhill 49 43 32N 80 23W
Maryland □ 72 39 10N 76 40W
Maryport 94 54 43N 3 30W
Mary's Harbour 36 52 18N 55 51W
Marystown 37 47 10N 55 10W
Marysvale 79 38 25N 112 17W
Marysville, B.C., Can. 61 49 35N 116 0W
Marysville, N.B., Can. 39 45 59N 66 35W
Marysville, Calif., U.S.A. 80 39 14N 121 40W
Marysville, Kans., U.S.A. 74 39 50N 96 38W
Marysville, Mich., U.S.A. 46 42 55N 82 29W
Marysville, Ohio, U.S.A. 77 40 15N 83 20W
Marysville, Wash., U.S.A. 80 48 3N 122 11W
Maryville, U.S.A. 76 40 21N 94 52W
Maryville, Tenn., U.S.A. 73 35 50N 84 0W
Marzo, Punta 86 6 50N 77 42W
Marzuq 114 25 53N 14 10E
Masaka 116 0 21S 31 45E
Masalima, Kepulauan 126 5 10S 116 50E
Masamba 127 2 30S 120 15E
Masan 130 35 11N 128 32E
Masandam, Ras 123 26 30N 56 30E
Masasi 116 10 45S 38 52E
Masaya 84 12 0N 86 7W
Mascarene Is. 16 22 0S 55 0E
Mascota 82 20 30N 104 50W
Mascouche 44 45 45N 73 36W
Mascouche, R. 44 45 41N 73 37W
Mascoutah 76 38 29N 89 48W
Masela 127 8 9S 129 51E
Maseme 85 18 46S 25 3E
Maseru 117 29 18S 27 30E
Mashābih 122 25 35N 36 30E
Mashhad 123 36 20N 59 35E
Mashike 132 43 31N 141 30E
Mashki Chah 124 29 5N 62 30E
Mashkode 34 47 2N 84 7W
Masi 110 69 26N 23 50E

Mendota Mindanao Trench

Mendota, Ill., U.S.A. 76 41 35N 89 5W
Mendoza 88 32 50S 68 52W
Mendoza □ 88 33 0S 69 0W
Mene Grande 86 9 49N 70 56W
Menemen 122 38 18N 27 10E
Menfi 108 37 36N 12 57E
Meng-so 128 22 33N 99 31E
Meng Wang 128 22 18N 100 31E
Menggala 126 4 20S 105 15E
Mengshan 131 24 2N 110 32E
Mengtsz 129 23 20N 103 20E
Mengyin 130 35 40N 117 55E
Menihek 36 54 28N 56 36W
Menihek L. 36 54 0N 67 0W
Menin 105 50 47N 3 7E
Menindee 136 32 20S 142 25E
Ménistouc, L. 38 52 52N 66 29W
Menlo Park 80 37 27N 122 12W
Menominee 72 45 9N 87 39W
Menominee, R. 72 45 30N 87 50W
Menomonee Falls 77 43 11N 88 7W
Menomonie 74 44 50N 91 54W
Menor, Mar 104 37 43N 0 48W
Menorca, I. 104 40 0N 4 0E
Mentawai, Kepulauan 126 2 0S 99 0E
Menton 103 43 50N 7 29E
Mentone 77 41 10N 86 2W
Mentor 70 41 40N 81 21W
Menzies 134 29 40S 120 58E
Meoqui 82 28 17N 105 29W
Meota 56 53 2N 108 27W
Meppel 105 52 42N 6 12E
Meppen 105 52 41N 7 20E
Mequon 77 43 14N 87 59W
Mer Rouge 75 32 47N 91 48W
Merabéllou, Kólpos 109 35 10N 25 50E
Merak 127 5 55S 106 1E
Meramec, R. 76 38 23N 91 21W
Merano (Meran) 108 46 40N 11 10E
Merasheen I. 37 47 25N 54 15W
Merauke 127 8 29S 140 24E
Merbabu, Mt. 127 7 30S 110 40E
Merbein 136 34 10S 142 2E
Merca 115 1 48N 44 50E
Mercara 124 12 30N 75 45E
Merced 80 37 18N 120 30W
Merced Pk. 80 37 36N 119 24W
Mercedes, Buenos Aires, Argent. 88 34 40S 59 30W
Mercedes, Corrientes, Argent. 88 29 10S 58 5W
Mercedes, San Luis, Argent. 88 33 5S 65 21W
Mercedes, Uruguay 88 33 12S 58 0W
Merceditas 88 28 20S 70 35W
Mercer, N.Z. 133 37 16S 175 5E
Mercer, U.S.A. 76 40 31N 93 32W
Mercer, Pa., U.S.A. 70 41 14N 80 13W
Mercier 44 45 19N 73 45W
Mercoal 60 53 10N 117 5W
Mercury 81 36 40N 116 0W
Mercy C. 65 65 0N 62 30W
Merdrignac 100 48 11N 2 27W
Meredith C. 90 52 15S 60 40W
Meredith, L. 75 35 30N 101 35W
Meredosia 76 39 50N 90 34W
Méréville 101 48 20N 2 5E
Mergui Arch. 128 12 30N 98 35E
Mergui Arch. = Myeik Kyunzu 128 11 30N 97 30E
Mérida, Mexico 83 20 50N 89 40W
Mérida, Spain 104 38 55N 6 25W
Mérida, Venez. 86 8 36N 71 8W
Mérida □ 86 8 30N 71 10W
Mérida, Cord. de 86 9 0N 71 0W
Meriden 71 41 33N 72 47W
Meridian, Calif., U.S.A. 80 39 9N 121 55W
Meridian, Idaho, U.S.A. 78 43 41N 116 25W
Meridian, Miss., U.S.A. 73 32 20N 88 42W
Meridian, Tex., U.S.A. 75 31 55N 97 37W
Merigomish 39 45 38N 62 26W
Merimula 136 36 54S 149 54E
Meringur 136 34 20S 141 19E
Merirumã 87 1 15N 54 50W
Merivale 48 45 19N 75 43W
Merkel 75 32 30N 100 0W
Merksem 105 51 16N 4 25E
Merlebach 101 49 5N 6 52E
Merlerault, Le 100 48 41N 0 16E
Merowe 115 18 29N 31 46E
Merredin 134 31 28S 118 18E
Merrick, Mt. 96 55 8N 4 30W
Merrickville 47 44 55N 75 50W
Merrill, Mich., U.S.A. 46 43 25N 84 20W
Merrill, Oregon, U.S.A. 78 42 2N 121 37W
Merrill, Wis., U.S.A. 74 45 11N 89 41W
Merriton 70 43 12N 79 13W
Merritt 63 50 10N 120 45W
Merry I. 36 55 29N 77 31W
Merrygoen 136 31 51S 149 12E
Merryville 75 30 47N 93 31W
Mersch 105 49 44N 6 7E
Merseburg 106 51 20N 12 0E
Mersey, R., Can. 39 44 2N 64 43W
Mersey, R., U.K. 94 53 20N 2 56W
Merseyside □ 94 53 25N 2 55W
Mersin 122 36 51N 34 36E
Mersing 128 2 25N 103 50E
Merthyr Tydfil 95 51 45N 3 23W
Mertoa 136 36 33S 142 29E
Mértola 104 37 40N 7 40E
Merton 49 43 25N 79 44W
Mertzon 75 31 17N 100 48W
Méru 101 49 13N 2 8E
Meru 116 0 3N 37 40E
Merville, Can. 62 49 48N 125 3W
Merville, France 101 50 38N 2 38E
Mervin 56 53 20N 108 53W
Méry-sur-Seine 101 48 31N 3 54E
Merzig 105 49 26N 6 37E
Mesa 79 33 20N 111 56W
Mesa, La, Colomb. 86 4 38N 74 28W
Mesa, La, Calif., U.S.A. 81 32 48N 117 5W
Mesa, La, N. Mex., U.S.A. 79 32 6N 106 48W
Mesgouez, L. 36 51 20N 75 0W
Meshed = Mashhad 123 36 20N 59 35E
Meshoppen 71 41 36N 76 3W
Mesick 72 44 24N 85 42W
Mesilinka, R. 54 56 6N 124 30W
Mesilla 79 32 20N 106 50W
Meslay-du-Maine 100 47 58N 0 33W
Mesolóngion 109 38 27N 21 28E
Mesopotamia, reg. 122 33 30N 44 0E
Mess Cr. 54 57 55N 131 14W
Messac 100 47 49N 1 50W
Messeix 102 45 37N 2 33E
Messina, Italy 108 38 10N 15 32E
Messina, S. Afr. 117 22 20S 30 12E
Messina, Str. di 108 38 5N 15 35E
Messine 40 46 14N 76 2W
Messíni 109 37 4N 22 1E
Messiniakós, Kólpos 109 36 45N 22 5E
Mesta, R. 109 41 30N 24 0E
Meta 76 38 19N 92 10W
Meta □ 86 3 30N 73 0W
Meta, R. 86 6 20N 68 5W
Metagama 34 47 0N 81 55W
Metaline Falls 63 48 52N 117 22W
Metamora 76 40 47N 89 22W
Metán 88 25 30S 65 0W
Metchosin 54 48 15N 123 37W
Meteghan 39 44 11N 66 10W
Methuen 71 42 43N 71 10W
Methven 133 43 38S 171 40E
Methy L. 55 56 28N 109 30W
Metil 117 16 24S 39 0E
Métis-sur-Mer 38 48 40N 67 59W
Metlakatla 67 55 10N 131 33W
Metropolis 75 37 10N 88 47W
Mettur Dam 124 11 45N 77 45E
Metz 101 49 8N 6 10E
Meulaboh 126 4 11N 96 3E
Meulan 101 49 0N 1 52E
Meung-sur-Loire 101 47 50N 1 40E
Meureudu 126 5 19N 96 10E
Meurthe-et-Moselle □ 101 48 52N 6 0E
Meurthe, R. 101 48 47N 6 9E
Meuse □ 101 49 8N 5 25E
Meuse, R. 105 50 45N 5 41E
Mexborough 94 53 29N 1 18W
Mexia 75 31 38N 96 32W
Mexiana, I. 87 0 0 49 30W
Mexicali 82 32 40N 115 30W
México 83 19 20N 99 10W
Mexico, Me., U.S.A. 71 44 33N 70 30W
Mexico, Mo., U.S.A. 76 39 10N 91 55W
Mexico ■ 82 20 0N 100 0W
México □ 82 19 20N 99 10W
Mexico, G. of 83 25 0N 90 0W
Meymac 102 45 32N 2 10E
Meyrargues 103 43 38N 5 32E
Meyronne 56 49 39N 106 50W
Meyrueis 102 44 12N 3 27E
Meyssac 102 45 3N 1 40E
Mèze 102 43 27N 3 36E
Mezen 120 65 50N 44 20E
Mezen, R. 120 64 34N 46 30E
Mézidon 100 49 5N 0 1W
Mézilhac 103 44 49N 4 21E
Mézin 102 44 4N 0 16E
Mezökövesd 107 47 49N 20 35E
Mézos 102 44 5N 1 10W
Mezötúr 107 47 0N 20 41E
Mezquital 82 23 29N 104 23W
Mhow 124 22 33N 75 50E
Miahuatlán 83 16 21N 96 36W
Miami, Ariz., U.S.A. 79 33 25N 111 0W
Miami, Fla., U.S.A. 73 25 52N 80 15W
Miami, Tex., U.S.A. 75 35 44N 100 38W
Miami Beach 73 25 49N 80 6W
Miami, R. 72 39 20N 84 40W
Miamisburg 77 39 40N 84 11W
Miandowāb 122 37 0N 46 5E
Miandrivazo 117 19 50S 45 56E
Mīāneh 122 37 30N 47 40E
Mianwali 124 32 38N 71 28E
Miao Tao 130 38 10N 120 50E
Miaoli 131 24 33N 120 42E
Miarinarivo 117 18 57S 46 55E
Miass 120 54 59N 60 6E
Mica Creek 63 52 2N 118 35W
Mica Dam 63 52 5N 118 32W
Mica Res. 54 51 55N 118 00W
Michaudville 43 45 50N 73 4W
Michelson, Mt. 67 69 20N 144 20W
Michigan □ 69 44 40N 85 40W
Michigan Center 46 42 14N 84 20W
Michigan City 77 41 42N 86 56W
Michigan, L. 72 44 0N 87 0W
Michih 130 37 58N 110 0E
Michipicoten 53 47 55N 84 55W
Michipicoten B. 53 47 53N 84 53W
Michipicoten I. 53 47 40N 85 50W
Michoacan □ 82 19 0N 102 0W
Michurinsk 120 52 58N 40 27E
Micmac Lake 39 44 41N 63 33W
Micronesia 14 17 0N 160 0E
Mid Glamorgan □ 95 51 40N 3 25W
Midai, P. 126 3 0N 107 47E
Midale 56 49 25N 103 20W
Midas 78 41 14N 116 56W
Middelburg, Neth. 105 51 30N 3 36E
Middelburg, S. Afr. 117 31 30S 25 0E
Middle Alkali L. 78 41 30N 120 3W
Middle Andaman I. 128 12 30N 92 30E
Middle Brook 35 48 40N 54 20W
Middle Church 58 49 59N 97 4W
Middle Fork Feather, R. 80 39 35N 121 25W
Middle Lake 56 52 29N 105 18W
Middle Musquodoboit 39 45 3N 63 9W
Middle, R. 76 41 26N 93 30W
Middle Raccoon, R. 76 41 35N 93 35W
Middleboro 71 41 56N 70 52W
Middleburg, N.Y., U.S.A. 71 42 36N 74 19W
Middleburg, Pa., U.S.A. 70 40 46N 77 5W
Middlebury, Ind., U.S.A. 77 41 41N 85 42W
Middlebury, Vt., U.S.A. 71 44 0N 73 9W
Middleport 72 39 0N 82 5W
Middlesbrough 94 54 35N 1 14W
Middlesex, Belize 83 17 2N 88 31W
Middlesex, U.S.A. 71 40 36N 74 30W
Middleton, Can. 39 44 57N 65 4W
Middleton, U.S.A. 76 43 6N 89 30W
Middleton I. 67 59 30N 146 28W
Middletown, Calif., U.S.A. 80 38 45N 122 37W
Middletown, Conn., U.S.A. 71 41 37N 72 40W
Middletown, N.Y., U.S.A. 71 41 28N 74 28W
Middletown, Ohio, U.S.A. 77 39 30N 84 21W
Middletown, Pa., U.S.A. 71 40 12N 76 44W
Middleville 77 42 43N 85 28W
Middlewood 39 44 14N 64 34W
Midi, Canal du 102 43 45N 1 21E
Midland, Man., Can. 58 49 54N 97 11W
Midland, Ont., Can. 46 44 45N 79 50W
Midland, Calif., U.S.A. 81 33 52N 114 48W
Midland, Mich., U.S.A. 46 43 37N 84 17W
Midland, Pa., U.S.A. 70 40 39N 80 27W
Midland, Tex., U.S.A. 75 32 0N 102 3W
Midland Junction 134 31 50S 115 58E
Midleton 97 51 52N 8 12W
Midlothian 75 32 30N 97 0W
Midnapore, Can. 59 50 55N 114 5W
Midnapore, India 125 22 25N 87 21E
Midvale 78 40 39N 111 58W
Midway 63 49 1N 118 48W
Midway Is. 14 28 13N 177 22W
Midway Wells 81 32 41N 115 7W
Midwest 78 43 27N 106 11W
Mie-ken □ 132 34 30N 136 10E
Miedzychód 106 52 35N 15 53E
Miedzyrzec Podlaski 107 51 58N 22 45E
Miélan 102 43 27N 0 19E
Mienchih 131 34 47N 111 49E
Mienhsien 131 33 11N 106 35E
Mienyang, Hupei, China 131 30 10N 113 20E
Mienyang, Szechwan, China 131 31 18N 104 26E
Miercurea Ciuc 107 46 21N 25 48E
Mieres 104 43 18N 5 48W
Miette Hotsprings 60 53 8N 117 46W
Migennes 101 47 58N 3 31E
Miguel Alemán, Presa 83 18 15N 96 40W
Miguel Alves 87 4 11S 42 55W
Mihara 132 34 24N 133 5E
MiIntown 70 40 34N 77 24W
Mikardo 46 44 34N 83 28W
Mikínai 109 37 43N 22 46E
Mikindani 116 10 15S 40 2E
Mikkeli 111 61 43N 27 25E
Mikkeli □ 110 62 0N 28 0E
Mikkwa, R. 60 58 25N 114 46W
Míkonos, I. 109 37 30N 25 25E
Mikura-Jima 132 33 52N 139 36E
Milaca 74 45 45N 93 40W
Milagro 86 2 0S 79 30W
Milan, U.S.A. 46 42 5N 83 40W
Milan, Ill., U.S.A. 76 41 27N 90 34W
Milan, Mo., U.S.A. 76 40 10N 93 5W
Milan, Tenn., U.S.A. 73 35 55N 88 45W
Milan = Milano 108 45 28N 9 10E
Milano 108 45 28N 9 10E
Milâs 122 37 20N 27 50E
Milazzo 108 38 13N 15 13E
Milbank 74 45 17N 96 38W
Milden 56 51 29N 107 32W
Mildmay 46 44 3N 81 7W
Mildura 136 34 13S 142 9E
Miles, Austral. 135 26 40S 150 23E
Miles, U.S.A. 75 31 39N 100 11W
Miles City 74 46 30N 105 50W
Milestone 56 49 59N 104 31W
Milford, U.S.A. 77 42 35N 83 36W
Milford, U.S.A. 77 41 40N 87 43W
Milford, Conn., U.S.A. 71 41 13N 73 4W
Milford, Del., U.S.A. 72 38 52N 75 27W
Milford, Mass., U.S.A. 71 42 8N 71 30W
Milford, Pa., U.S.A. 71 41 20N 74 47W
Milford, Utah, U.S.A. 79 38 20N 113 0W
Milford Haven 95 51 43N 5 2W
Milford Haven, B. 95 51 40N 5 10W
Milford Sd. 133 44 34S 167 47E
Milford Station 39 45 3N 63 26W
Milk, R., Can. 61 49 0N 110 33W
Milk, R., U.S.A. 78 48 40N 107 15W
Milk River 61 49 10N 112 5W
Mill City 78 44 45N 122 28W
Mill Cr. 59 53 33N 113 29W
Mill Grove 48 43 20N 79 58W
Mill, I. 91 66 0S 101 30E
Mill Shoals 77 38 15N 88 21W
Mill Valley 80 37 54N 122 32W
Mill Village 39 44 9N 64 39W
Millau 102 44 8N 3 4E
Millbridge 47 44 41N 77 36W
Millbrook 47 44 10N 78 29W
Mille 73 33 7N 83 15W
Mille Îles, R. des 44 45 42N 73 32W
Mille Isles 43 45 49N 74 14W
Mille Lacs, L. 52 46 10N 93 30W
Mille Lacs, L. des 52 48 45N 90 35W
Milledgeville 76 41 58N 89 46W
Millen 73 32 50N 81 57W
Miller 74 44 35N 98 59W
Millerand 39 47 13N 61 59W
Millersburg, U.S.A. 77 41 32N 85 42W
Millersburg, Mich., U.S.A. 46 45 20N 84 4W
Millersburg, Ohio, U.S.A. 70 40 32N 81 52W
Millersburg, Pa., U.S.A. 70 40 32N 76 58W
Millerton 71 41 57N 73 32W
Millerton, L. 80 37 0N 119 42W
Millertown 37 48 49N 56 33W
Millet 61 53 6N 113 28W
Millevaches, Plat. de 102 45 45N 2 0E
Millicent 135 37 34S 140 21E
Milliken 50 43 49N 79 18W
Millington 46 43 17N 83 32W
Millinocket 35 45 45N 68 45W
Mills L. 54 61 30N 118 20W
Millsboro 70 40 0N 80 0W
Millstream 39 48 2N 67 2W
Milltown, N.B., Can. 39 45 10N 67 18W
Milltown, Newf., Can. 37 47 54N 55 46W
Milltown Malbay 97 52 51N 9 25W
Millview 39 44 43N 63 40W
Millville, Can. 39 46 8N 67 12W
Millville, U.S.A. 72 39 22N 75 0W
Millwood Res. 75 33 45N 94 0W
Milly 101 48 24N 2 20E
Milnesville 50 43 55N 79 16W
Milnor 74 46 19N 97 29W
Milo 61 50 34N 112 53W
Milolii 67 22 8N 159 42W
Milos 109 36 44N 24 25E
Milot 41 48 54N 71 49W
Milroy 77 39 30N 85 28W
Milton, N.S., Can. 39 44 4N 64 45W
Milton, Ont., Can. 49 43 31N 79 53W
Milton, N.Z. 133 46 7S 169 59E
Milton, U.S.A. 76 40 41N 92 10W
Milton, U.S.A. 77 42 47N 88 56W
Milton, Calif., U.S.A. 80 38 3N 120 51W
Milton, Fla., U.S.A. 73 30 38N 87 0W
Milton, Pa., U.S.A. 70 41 0N 76 53W
Milton-Freewater 78 45 57N 118 24W
Milton Heights 49 43 31N 79 56W
Milton Keynes 95 52 3N 0 42W
Milton West 70 43 33N 79 53W
Milverton 46 43 34N 80 55W
Milwaukee 77 43 9N 87 58W
Milwaukie 80 45 27N 122 39W
Mimico Cr. 50 43 37N 79 30W
Miminegash 39 46 53N 64 14W
Miminiska L. 52 51 35N 88 37W
Mimizan 102 44 12N 1 13W
Mimosa 49 43 44N 80 13W
Min K. 131 26 0N 119 20E
Mina 79 38 21N 118 9W
Mina Pirquitas 88 22 40S 66 40W
Mina Saud 122 28 45N 48 20E
Minā'al Ahmadī 122 29 5N 48 10E
Mīnāb 123 27 10N 57 1E
Minago, R. 57 54 33N 98 59W
Minaki 52 49 59N 94 40W
Minamata 132 32 10N 130 30E
Minas Basin 39 45 20N 64 12W
Minas Channel 39 45 15N 64 45W
Minas de Rio Tinto 104 37 42N 6 22W
Minas Gerais □ 87 18 50S 46 0W
Minas, Sierra de las 84 15 9N 89 31W
Minatitlán 83 17 58N 94 35W
Minbu 125 20 10N 95 0E
Mindanao, I. 127 8 0N 125 0E
Mindanao Sea 127 9 0N 124 0E
Mindanao Trench 127 8 0N 128 0E

Mindemoya Monroe

Mindemoya 46 45 44N 82 10W
Minden, Can. 47 44 55N 78 43W
Minden, Ger. 106 52 18N 8 54 E
Minden, La., U.S.A. 75 32 40N 93 20W
Minden, Nev., U.S.A. 80 38 57N 119 48W
Mindiptana 127 5 45 S 140 22 E
Mindona, L. 136 33 6 S 142 6 E
Mindoro, I. 127 13 0N 121 0 E
Mindoro Strait 127 12 30N 120 30 E
Mindouli 116 4 12 S 14 28 E
Mine Centre 52 48 45N 92 37W
Mine, L. 38 50 51N 64 43W
Minegan, Îles de 38 50 12N 63 35W
Minehead 95 51 12N 3 29W
Mineola 75 32 40N 95 30W
Mineral King 80 36 27N 118 36W
Mineral Point 76 42 52N 90 11W
Mineral Wells 75 32 50N 98 5W
Minersville, Pa., U.S.A. 71 40 40N 76 17W
Minersville, Utah, U.S.A. 79 38 14N 112 58W
Minerva 70 40 43N 81 8W
Minette 73 30 54N 87 43W
Minetto 71 43 24N 76 28W
Mingan 38 50 20N 64 0W
Mingan = Pangkiang 130 43 4N 112 30 E
Mingan, R. 38 50 18N 63 59W
Mingechaurskoye Vdkhr. 120 40 56N 47 20 E
Mingin 125 22 50N 94 30 E
Mingki (Kweihwa) 131 26 10N 117 14 E
Minho □ 104 41 25N 8 20W
Minho, R. 104 41 58N 8 40W
Minhow = Foochow 131 26 2N 119 12 E
Minhsien 131 34 26N 104 2 E
Minidoka 78 42 47N 113 34W
Minier 76 40 26N 89 19W
Minilya 134 23 55 S 114 0 E
Minipi, L. 38 52 25N 60 45W
Miniss L. 52 50 48N 90 50W
Minitonas 57 52 5N 101 2W
Mink L. 54 61 54N 117 40W
Minkiang 131 32 30N 114 10 E
Minneapolis, Kans., U.S.A. 74 39 11N 97 40W
Minneapolis, Minn., U.S.A. 74 44 58N 93 20W
Minnedosa 57 50 14N 99 50W
Minnesota □ 74 46 40N 94 0W
Minnitaki L. 52 49 57N 91 55W
Miño, R. 104 41 58N 8 40W
Minonk 76 40 54N 89 2W
Minooka 77 41 27N 88 16W
Minorca = Menorca 104 40 0N 4 0 E
Minot 74 48 10N 101 15W
Minquiers, Les 100 48 58N 2 8W
Minsk 120 53 52N 27 30 E
Minsk Mazowiecki 107 52 10N 21 33 E
Minster 77 40 24N 84 23W
Minstrel Island 62 50 37N 126 18W
Mintaka Pass 124 37 0N 74 58 E
Minto, Can. 39 46 5N 66 5W
Minto, U.S.A. 67 64 55N 149 20W
Minto, L. 36 57 13N 75 0W
Minton 56 49 10N 104 35W
Mintsing 131 26 8N 118 57 E
Minturn 78 39 45N 106 25W
Minusinsk 121 53 50N 91 20 E
Minutang 125 28 15N 96 30 E
Minvoul 116 2 9N 12 8 E
Minya Konka, mt. 129 29 36N 101 50 E
Mio 46 44 39N 84 8W
Mios Num, I. 127 1 30 S 135 10 E
Miquelon, Can. 40 49 25N 76 27W
Miquelon, St. P. & M. 37 47 3N 56 20W
Miquelon, I. 37 47 1N 56 20W
Miquelon, St. Pierre et, □ 37 47 8N 56 24W
Mira 39 46 2N 59 58W
Mira, R. 39 46 2N 59 58W
Mirabel 44 45 40N 74 10W
Mirabel Airport 44 45 41N 74 2W
Miraflores 82 23 21N 109 45W
Miraflores Locks 84 8 59N 79 36W
Miraj 124 16 50N 74 45 E
Miram Shah 124 33 0N 70 0 E
Miramar 88 38 15 S 57 50W
Miramas 103 43 33N 4 59 E
Mirambeau 102 45 23N 0 35W
Miramichi B. 39 47 15N 65 0W
Miramichi, Little S.W., R. 39 46 58N 65 38W
Miramichi, N.W., R. 39 46 57N 65 55W
Miramichi, S.W., R. 39 46 58N 65 38W
Miramont-de-Guyenne 102 44 37N 0 21 E
Miranda 87 20 10 S 56 15W
Miranda de Ebro 104 42 41N 2 57W
Mirando City 75 27 28N 98 59W
Mirandópolis 89 21 9 S 51 6W
Miraporvos, I. 85 22 9N 74 30W
Mirassol 89 20 46 S 49 28W
Mirebeau, Côte d'Or, France 101 47 25N 5 20 E
Mirebeau, Vienne, France 100 46 49N 0 10 E
Mirecourt 101 48 20N 6 10 E
Miri 126 4 18N 114 0 E
Mirim, Lagoa 89 32 45 S 52 50W
Mirimire 86 11 10N 68 43W
Mirny 91 66 0 S 95 0 E
Mirnyy 121 62 33N 113 53 E
Mirond L. 55 55 6N 102 47W
Mirool 136 34 24 S 147 5 E
Mirpur Khas 124 25 30N 69 0 E
Mirror 61 52 30N 113 7W
Miryang 130 35 34N 128 42 E
Mirzapur 125 25 10N 82 45 E
Misantla 83 19 56N 96 50W
Miscou Centre 39 47 57N 64 34W
Miscou I. 39 47 57N 64 31W
Miscouche 39 46 26N 63 52W
Misehkow, R. 52 51 26N 89 11W
Mish'āb, Ra'as al 122 28 15N 48 43 E
Mishan 129 45 31N 132 2 E
Mishawaka 77 41 40N 86 8W
Mishima 132 35 10N 138 52 E
Misión 81 32 6N 116 53W
Misión, La 82 32 5N 116 50W
Misiones □, Argent. 89 27 0 S 55 0W
Misiones □, Parag. 88 27 0 S 56 0W
Miskīn 123 23 44N 56 52 E
Miskitos, Cayos 84 14 26N 82 50W
Miskolc 107 48 7N 20 50 E
Misoöl, I. 127 2 0 S 130 0 E
Misrâtah 114 32 18N 15 3 E
Missanabie 53 48 20N 84 6W
Missinaibi L. 53 48 23N 83 40W
Missinaibi Lake Prov. Park 53 48 25N 83 30W
Missinaibi, R. 53 50 43N 81 29W
Mission, S.D., U.S.A. 74 43 21N 100 36W
Mission, Tex., U.S.A. 75 26 15N 98 30W
Mission City 63 49 10N 122 15W
Missipuskiow, R. 56 53 53N 103 18W
Missisa L. 34 52 20N 85 7W
Missisicabi, R. 36 51 14N 79 31W
Missisquoi □ 45 45 5N 73 0W
Missisquoi, B. 43 45 2N 73 9W
Mississagi Prov. Park 46 46 30N 82 40W
Mississagi, R. 46 46 15N 83 9W
Mississauga 50 43 32N 79 35W
Mississinewa, R. 77 40 46N 86 3W
Mississippi, Delta of the 75 29 15N 90 30W
Mississippi L. 47 45 5N 76 10W
Mississippi, R. 75 35 29N 89 15W
Mississippi Sd. 75 30 25N 89 0W
Missoula 78 47 0N 114 0W
Missouri □ 74 38 25N 92 30W
Missouri, Little, R. 78 46 0N 111 35W
Missouri, R. 72 40 20N 95 40W
Mist 80 45 59N 123 15W
Mistake B. 55 62 8N 93 0W
Mistanipisipou, R. 38 51 32N 61 50W
Mistaouac, L. 40 49 25N 78 41W
Mistassibi Nord-Est., R. 41 49 31N 71 56W
Mistassibi, R. 41 48 53N 72 13W
Mistassini 41 48 53N 72 12W
Mistassini L. 36 51 0N 73 40W
Mistassini, Parc. Prov. de 41 50 20N 74 0W
Mistassini, R. 41 48 42N 72 20W
Mistastin L. 35 55 57N 63 20W
Mistatim 56 52 52N 103 22W
Mistretta 108 37 56N 14 20 E
Misty L. 55 58 53N 101 40W
Mitchell, Austral. 135 26 29 S 147 58 E
Mitchell, Can. 46 43 28N 81 12W
Mitchell, Ind., U.S.A. 77 38 42N 86 25W
Mitchell, Nebr., U.S.A. 74 41 58N 103 45W
Mitchell, Oreg., U.S.A. 78 44 31N 120 8W
Mitchell, S.D., U.S.A. 74 43 40N 98 0W
Mitchell Corners, Ont., Can. 49 43 55N 78 53W
Mitchell Corners, Qué., Can. 43 45 2N 73 1W
Mitchell I. 66 49 12N 123 5W
Mitchell L. 63 52 52N 120 37W
Mitchell, Mt. 73 35 40N 82 20W
Mitchell, R. 135 15 12 S 141 35 E
Mitchelstown 97 52 16N 8 18W
Mitchelton 97 27 25 S 152 59 E
Mitchinamécus, Rés. 40 47 19N 75 9W
Mitiaro, I. 133 19 49 S 157 43W
Mitilini = Lesvos 109 39 0N 26 20 E
Mitla 83 16 55N 96 24W
Mito 132 36 20N 140 30 E
Mitsinjo 117 16 1 S 45 52 E
Mitsiwa Channel 115 15 30N 40 0 E
Mitta Mitta, R. 136 36 14 S 147 10 E
Mittagong 136 34 28 S 150 29 E
Mitú 86 1 8N 70 3W
Mituas 86 3 52N 68 49W
Mitumba, Chaîne des 116 10 0 S 26 20 E
Mitwaba 116 8 2N 27 17 E
Mitzick 116 0 45N 11 40 E
Mixteco, R. 83 18 11N 98 30W
Miyagi-Ken □ 132 38 15N 140 45 E
Miyake-Jima 132 34 0N 139 30 E
Miyako 132 39 40N 141 75 E
Miyako-rettō 131 24 47N 125 20 E
Miyakonojō 132 31 32N 131 5 E
Miyazaki 132 31 56N 131 30 E
Miyazaki-ken □ 132 32 0N 131 30 E
Miyazu 132 35 35N 135 10 E
Miyet, Bahr el 115 31 30N 35 30 E
Miyun 130 40 25N 116 50 E
Mizamis = Ozamiz 127 8 15N 123 50 E
Mizen Hd., Cork, Ireland 97 51 27N 9 50W
Mizen Hd., Wick., Ireland 97 52 52N 6 4W
Mizoram □ 125 23 0N 92 40 E
Mjölby 111 58 20N 15 10 E
Mjøsa 111 60 40N 11 0 E
Mkushi 117 14 25 S 29 15 E
Mladá Boleslav 106 50 27N 14 53 E
Mława 107 53 9N 20 25 E
Mo i Rana 110 66 15N 14 7 E
Moa, I. 127 8 0 S 128 0 E
Moab 79 38 40N 109 35W
Moabi 116 2 24 S 10 59 E
Moala, I. 133 18 36 S 179 53 E
Moama 136 36 3 S 144 45 E
Moamba 136 25 34 S 32 16 E
Moapo 81 36 45N 114 37W
Moba 116 7 0 S 29 48 E
Mobaye 116 4 25N 21 5 E
Mobayi 116 4 15N 21 8 E
Moberley 76 39 25N 92 25W
Moberly, R. 54 56 12N 120 55W
Mobert 34 48 41N 85 40W
Mobile 73 30 41N 88 3W
Mobile B. 73 30 30N 88 0W
Mobile, Pt. 73 30 15N 88 0W
Mobridge 74 45 40N 100 28W
Mobutu Sese Seko, L. 116 1 30N 31 0 E
Moçambique 117 15 3 S 40 42 E
Mochudi 117 24 27 S 26 7 E
Mocimboa da Praia 116 11 25 S 40 20 E
Moclips 80 47 14N 124 10W
Moç"medes □ 117 16 35 S 12 30 E
Mocoa 86 1 15N 76 45W
Mococa 89 21 28 S 47 0W
Mocorito 82 25 20N 108 0W
Moctezuma 82 30 12N 106 26W
Moctezuma, R. 83 21 59N 98 34W
Mocuba 117 16 54 S 37 25 E
Modane 103 45 12N 6 40 E
Módena 108 44 39N 10 55 E
Modena 79 37 55N 113 56W
Modesto 80 37 43N 121 0W
Módica 108 36 52N 14 45 E
Modjokerto 127 7 29 S 112 25 E
Moe 135 38 12 S 146 19 E
Moei, R. 128 17 25N 98 10 E
Moëlan-sur-Mer 100 47 49N 3 38W
Moengo 87 5 45N 54 20W
Moffat, Can. 49 43 31N 80 3W
Moffat, U.K. 96 55 20N 3 27W
Mogadiscio = Mogadishu 115 2 2N 45 25 E
Mogadishu 115 2 2N 45 25 E
Mogami-gawa, R. 132 38 45N 140 0 E
Mogaung 125 25 20N 97 0 E
Mogi das Cruzes 89 23 45 S 46 20W
Mogi-Guaçu, R. 89 20 53 S 48 10W
Mogi-Mirim 89 22 20 S 47 0W
Mogilev 120 53 55N 30 18 E
Mogilla 136 36 41 S 149 38 E
Mogincual 117 15 35 S 40 25 E
Mogocha 121 53 40N 119 50 E
Mogoi 127 1 55 S 133 10 E
Mogok 125 23 0N 96 40 E
Mogollon 79 33 25N 108 55W
Mogollon Mesa 79 35 0N 111 0W
Mohács 107 45 58N 18 41 E
Mohall 74 48 46N 101 30W
Mohammadābād 123 37 30N 59 5 E
Mohave Desert 79 35 0N 117 30W
Mohave L. 81 35 25N 114 36W
Mohawk, Ariz., U.S.A. 79 32 45N 113 50W
Mohawk, Mich., U.S.A. 52 47 18N 88 26W
Mohembo 117 18 15 S 21 43 E
Mohican, C. 67 60 10N 167 30W
Möhne, R. 105 51 29N 8 10 E
Moho 129 53 15N 122 27 E
Mohon 101 49 45N 4 44 E
Mohoro 116 8 6 S 39 8 E
Moidart, L. 96 56 47N 5 40W
Moille, La 76 41 32N 89 17W
Moine, R, La 76 39 58N 90 32W
Mointy 120 47 40N 73 45 E
Moira, R. 47 44 21N 77 24W
Moirans 103 45 20N 5 33 E
Moirans-en-Montagne 103 46 26N 5 43 E
Moisie 38 50 12N 66 1W
Moisie, R. 38 50 14N 66 5W
Moissac 102 44 7N 1 5 E
Mojave 81 35 8N 118 8W
Mojave Desert 81 35 0N 116 30W
Mojikit L. 52 50 40N 88 15W
Mojo 88 21 48 S 65 33W
Mojo, I. 126 8 10 S 117 40 E
Mokai 133 38 32 S 175 56 E
Mokane 76 38 41N 91 53W
Mokelumne Hill 80 38 18N 120 43W
Mokelumne, R. 80 38 23N 121 25W
Mokokchung 125 26 15N 94 30 E
Mokpo 131 34 50N 126 30 E
Mol 105 51 11N 5 5 E
Molchanovo 120 57 40N 83 50 E
Mold 94 53 10N 3 10W
Moldavian S.S.R.□ 120 47 0N 28 0 E
Molde 110 62 45N 7 9 E
Molepolole 117 24 28 S 25 28 E
Molfetta 108 41 12N 16 35 E
Moline 76 41 30N 90 30W
Molinos 88 25 28 S 66 15W
Moliro 116 8 12 S 30 30 E
Molise □ 108 41 45N 14 30 E
Mollendo 86 17 0 S 72 0W
Mölndal 111 57 40N 12 3 E
Molokai, I. 67 21 8N 157 0W
Molong 136 33 5 S 148 54 E
Molopo, R. 117 25 40 S 24 30 E
Molotov, Mys 121 81 10N 95 0 E
Moloundou 116 2 8N 15 15 E
Molsheim 101 48 33N 7 29 E
Molson L. 57 54 22N 95 32W
Molu, I. 127 6 45 S 131 40 E
Molucca Sea 127 4 0 S 124 0 E
Moluccas = Maluku, Is. 127 1 0 S 127 0 E
Moma 117 16 47 S 39 4 E
Mombasa 116 4 2 S 39 43 E
Momchilgrad 109 41 33N 25 23 E
Momence 77 41 10N 87 40W
Mompós 86 9 14N 74 26W
Møn 111 54 57N 12 15 E
Mon, R. 125 20 25N 94 30 E
Mona, Canal de la 85 18 30N 67 45W
Mona, I. 85 18 5N 67 54W
Mona Passage 85 18 0N 67 40W
Mona, Punta 84 9 37N 82 36W
Monach Is. 96 57 32N 7 40W
Monaco ■ 103 43 46N 7 23 E
Monadhliath Mts. 96 57 10N 4 4W
Monagas □ 86 9 20N 63 0W
Monaghan 97 54 15N 6 58W
Monaghan □ 97 54 10N 7 0W
Monahans 75 31 35N 102 50W
Monarch 61 49 48N 113 7W
Monarch Mt. 54 51 55N 125 57W
Monaro Ra. 136 36 20 S 149 0 E
Monashee Prov. Park 63 50 30N 118 15W
Monastier-sur-Gazeille, Le 102 44 57N 3 59 E
Monastir = Bitola 109 41 5N 21 21 E
Moncayo, Sierra del 104 41 48N 1 50W
Mönchengladbach 105 51 12N 6 23 E
Monchique 104 37 19N 8 38W
Monchique, Sa. de, 104 37 18N 8 39W
Monck 49 43 58N 80 29W
Monclova 82 26 50N 101 30W
Moncontour 100 48 22N 2 38W
Moncouche, L. 41 48 45N 70 42W
Moncton 39 46 7N 64 51W
Mondego, R. 104 40 28N 8 0W
Mondeodo 127 3 21 S 122 9 E
Mondonac, L. 41 47 24N 73 58W
Mondoví 108 44 23N 7 56 E
Mondovi 74 44 37N 91 40W
Mondragon 103 44 13N 4 44 E
Monessen 70 40 9N 79 50W
Monestier-de-Clermont 103 44 55N 5 38 E
Monet 34 48 10N 75 40W
Monêtier-les-Bains, Le 103 44 58N 6 30 E
Monett 75 36 55N 93 56W
Monflanquin 102 44 32N 0 47 E
Monforte 104 39 6N 7 25W
Mong Cai 128 21 27N 107 54 E
Möng Hsu 125 21 54N 98 30 E
Möng Kung 125 21 35N 97 35 E
Mong Lang 128 20 29N 97 52 E
Möng Nai 125 20 32N 97 55 E
Möng Pai 125 19 40N 97 15 E
Mong Pawk 125 22 4N 99 16 E
Mong Ton 125 20 25N 98 45 E
Mong Wa 125 21 26N 100 27 E
Mong Yai 125 22 28N 98 3 E
Mongalla 115 5 8N 31 55 E
Monger, L. 134 29 25 S 117 5 E
Monghyr 125 25 23N 86 30 E
Mongolia 49 43 56N 79 13W
Mongolia ■ 129 47 0N 103 0 E
Mongolia, Inner, □ 130 44 15N 117 0 E
Mongoumba 116 3 33N 18 40 E
Mongpang 128 23 5N 100 25 E
Mongu 117 15 16 S 23 12 E
Monistrol-St.-Loire 103 45 17N 4 11 E
Monitor 61 51 58N 110 34W
Monk 55 47 7N 69 59W
Monkey River 83 16 22N 88 29W
Monkoto 116 1 38 S 20 35 E
Monkstown 37 47 35N 54 26W
Monkton 46 43 35N 81 5W
Monmouth, U.K. 95 51 48N 2 43W
Monmouth, U.S.A. 76 40 50N 90 40W
Monmouth Mt. 62 51 0N 123 47W
Mono, L. 80 38 0N 119 9W
Mono Mills 49 43 57N 79 58W
Mono, Punta del 84 12 0N 83 30W
Mono Road Station 49 43 51N 79 51W
Monolith 81 35 7N 118 22W
Monon 77 40 52N 86 53W
Monona, Iowa, U.S.A. 76 43 3N 91 24W
Monona, Wis., U.S.A. 76 43 4N 89 20W
Monongahela 70 40 12N 79 56W
Monópoli 108 40 57N 17 18 E
Monroe, Iowa, U.S.A. 76 41 31N 93 6W
Monroe, La., U.S.A. 75 32 32N 92 4W
Monroe, Mich., U.S.A. 46 41 55N 83 26W
Monroe, N.C., U.S.A. 73 35 2N 80 37W
Monroe, N.Y., U.S.A. 71 41 19N 74 11W
Monroe, Ohio, U.S.A. 77 39 27N 84 22W
Monroe, Utah, U.S.A. 79 38 45N 112 5W

Monroe Mouchalagane, R

Monroe, Wash., U.S.A. 80 47 51N 121 58W
Monroe, Wis., U.S.A. 76 42 38N 89 40W
Monroe City 76 39 40N 91 40W
Monroe, Res. 77 39 1N 86 31W
Monroeville, U.S.A. 77 40 59N 84 52W
Monroeville, Ala., U.S.A. 73 31 33N 87 15W
Monrovia, Liberia 114 6 18N 10 47W
Monrovia, U.S.A. 79 34 7N 118 1W
Mons 105 50 27N 3 58E
Monse 127 4 0S 123 10E
Monségur 102 44 38N 0 4E
Mont-Carmel 41 47 26N 69 52W
Mont-de-Marsan 102 43 54N 0 31W
Mont d'Or, Tunnel 101 46 45N 6 18E
Mont-Dore, Le 102 45 35N 2 50E
Mont-Gabriel 43 45 55N 74 10W
Mont-Joli 41 48 37N 68 10W
Mont Laurier 40 46 35N 75 30W
Mont-Louis 38 49 15N 65 44W
Mont Luis 35 42 31N 2 6E
Mont-Rolland 43 45 57N 74 7W
Mont-Royal 44 45 31N 73 39W
Mont-St-Grégoire 45 45 20N 73 10W
Mont-St-Hilaire 43 45 34N 73 12W
Mont St-Pierre 38 49 13N 65 49W
Mont-St-Michel, Le 100 48 40N 1 30W
Mont-Tremblant 40 46 13N 74 36W
Mont Tremblant Prov. Park 41 46 30N 74 30W
Montagnac 102 43 29N 3 28E
Montagu, I. 82 58 30S 26 15W
Montague, Can. 39 46 10N 62 39W
Montague, Calif., U.S.A. 78 41 47N 122 30W
Montague, Mass., U.S.A. 71 42 31N 72 33W
Montague, I. 82 31 40N 144 46W
Montague I. 67 60 0N 147 0W
Montague Sd. 134 14 28S 125 20E
Montaigu 100 46 59N 1 18W
Montalbán 104 40 50N 0 45W
Montalvo 81 34 15N 119 12W
Montaña 86 6 0S 73 0W
Montana □ 68 47 0N 110 0W
Montañita 86 1 30N 75 28W
Montargis 101 48 0N 2 43E
Montauban 102 44 0N 1 21E
Montauk 71 41 3N 71 57W
Montbard 101 47 38N 4 20E
Montbéliard 101 47 31N 6 48E
Montbrison 103 45 36N 4 3E
Montcalm □ 43 45 59N 73 45W
Montcalm, Pic de 102 42 40N 1 25E
Montceau-les-Mines 101 46 40N 4 23E
Montcerf 40 46 32N 76 3W
Montcevelles, L. 38 51 7N 60 38W
Montclair 71 40 53N 74 49W
Montcornet 101 49 40N 4 0E
Montcuq 102 44 21N 1 13E
Montdidier 101 49 38N 2 35E
Monte Albán 83 17 2N 96 45W
Monte Alegre 87 2 0S 54 0W
Monte Bello Is. 134 20 30S 115 45E
Monte-Carlo 103 43 46N 7 23E
Monte Caseros 88 30 10S 57 50W
Monte Comán 88 34 40S 68 0W
Monte Cristi 85 19 52N 71 39W
Monte, Le 76 38 47N 93 27W
Monte Libano 93 8 5N 75 29W
Monte Lindo, R. 88 25 30S 58 40W
Monte Quemado 88 25 53S 62 41W
Monte Rio 80 38 28N 123 0W
Monte Sant' Angelo 108 41 42N 15 59E
Monte Santu, C. di 108 40 5N 9 42E
Monte Visto 79 37 40N 106 8W
Monteagudo 89 27 14S 54 8W
Montebello 40 45 40N 74 55W
Montebourg 100 49 30N 1 20W
Montecito 81 34 26N 119 40W
Montecristi 86 1 0S 80 40W
Montego B. 84 18 30N 78 0W
Montelíbano 86 8 5N 75 29W
Montélimar 103 44 33N 4 45E
Montello 74 43 49N 89 21W
Montemorelos 83 25 11N 99 42W
Montendre 102 45 16N 0 26W
Montenegro 89 29 39S 51 29W
Montepuez 117 13 8S 38 59E
Montereau 101 48 22N 2 57E
Monterey, U.S.A. 77 41 11N 86 30W
Monterey, Calif., U.S.A. 80 36 35N 121 57W
Monterey, B. 80 36 50N 121 55W
Montería 86 8 46N 75 53W
Monteros 88 27 11S 65 30W
Monterrey 82 25 40N 100 30W
Montes Claros 87 16 30S 43 50W
Montesano 80 47 0N 123 39W
Monteverde 116 8 45S 16 45E
Montevideo 89 34 50S 56 11W
Montezuma, U.S.A. 76 41 32N 92 35W
Montezuma, U.S.A. 77 39 47N 87 22W
Montfaucon, Haute-Loire, France 103 45 11N 4 20E
Montfaucon, Meuse, France 101 49 16N 5 8E
Montfort 43 45 53N 74 20W
Montfort-l'Amaury 101 48 47N 1 49E
Montfort-sur-Meu 100 48 8N 1 58W
Montgenèvre 103 44 56N 6 42E
Montgomery, Can. 59 51 4N 114 10W
Montgomery, U.K. 95 52 34N 3 9W
Montgomery, U.S.A. 77 41 44N 88 21W
Montgomery, Ala., U.S.A. 73 32 20N 86 20W
Montgomery, W. Va., U.S.A. 72 38 9N 81 21W
Montgomery = Sahiwal 124 30 45N 73 8E
Montgomery City 76 38 59N 91 30W
Montguyon 102 45 12N 0 12W
Monticello, Can. 49 43 59N 80 24W
Monticello, U.S.A. 76 40 7N 91 43W
Monticello, U.S.A. 76 42 13N 91 11W
Monticello, Ark., U.S.A. 75 33 40N 91 48W
Monticello, Fla., U.S.A. 73 30 35N 83 50W
Monticello, Ill., U.S.A. 77 40 1N 88 34W
Monticello, Ind., U.S.A. 77 40 40N 86 45W
Monticello, Iowa, U.S.A. 74 42 18N 91 18W
Monticello, Ky., U.S.A. 73 36 52N 84 50W
Monticello, Minn., U.S.A. 74 45 17N 93 52W
Monticello, Miss., U.S.A. 75 31 35N 90 8W
Monticello, N.Y., U.S.A. 71 41 37N 74 42W
Monticello, Utah, U.S.A. 79 37 55N 109 27W
Montier 101 48 30N 4 45E
Montignac 102 45 4N 1 10E
Montigny-les-Metz 101 49 7N 6 10E
Montigny-sur-Aube 101 47 57N 4 45E
Montijo 104 38 52N 6 39W
Montilla 104 37 36N 4 40W
Montivideo 74 44 55N 95 40W
Montlhéry 101 48 39N 2 15E
Montluçon 102 46 22N 2 36E
Montmagny 41 46 58N 70 34W
Montmartre 56 50 14N 103 27W
Montmédy 101 49 30N 5 20E
Montmélian 103 45 30N 6 4E
Montmirail 101 48 51N 3 30E
Montmoreau-St.-Cybard 102 45 23N 0 8E
Montmorency 42 46 53N 71 11W
Montmorency, R. 42 46 53N 71 7W
Montmorillon 102 46 26N 0 50E
Montmort 101 48 55N 3 49E
Monto 135 24 52S 151 12E
Montoro 104 38 1N 4 27W
Montour Falls 70 42 20N 76 51W
Montpelier, Idaho, U.S.A. 78 42 15N 111 20W
Montpelier, Ind., U.S.A. 77 40 33N 85 17W
Montpelier, Ohio, U.S.A. 77 41 34N 84 40W
Montpelier, Vt., U.S.A. 71 44 15N 72 38W
Montpellier 102 43 37N 3 52E
Montpezat-de-Quercy 102 44 15N 1 30E
Montpon-Ménestrol 102 45 2N 0 11E
Montréal, Can. 44 45 31N 73 34W
Montréal, France 102 43 13N 2 8E
Montreal I. 53 47 19N 84 44W
Montréal, Île de 44 45 30N 73 40W
Montreal L. 56 54 20N 105 45W
Montreal Lake 56 54 3N 105 46W
Montréal-Nord 44 45 36N 73 38W
Montreal, R. 53 47 14N 84 39W
Montredon-Labessonnié 102 43 45N 2 18E
Montréjeau 102 43 6N 0 35E
Montrésor 100 47 10N 1 10E
Montreuil 101 50 27N 1 45E
Montreuil-Bellay 100 47 8N 0 9W
Montreuil, L. 40 50 12N 77 40W
Montreux 106 46 26N 6 55E
Montrevault 100 47 17N 1 2W
Montrevel-en-Bresse 103 46 21N 5 8E
Montrichard 100 47 20N 1 10E
Montrose, B.C., Can. 63 49 5N 117 35W
Montrose, Ont., Can. 49 43 3N 79 8W
Montrose, U.K. 96 56 43N 2 28W
Montrose, Col., U.S.A. 79 38 30N 107 52W
Montrose, Mich., U.S.A. 46 43 11N 83 54W
Montrose, Pa., U.S.A. 71 41 50N 75 55W
Montrose, L. 76 38 18N 93 50W
Monts, Pte des 38 49 20N 67 12W
Montsalvy 102 44 41N 2 30E
Montsauche 101 47 13N 4 0E
Montserrat, I. 85 16 40N 62 10W
Monveda 116 2 52N 21 30E
Mônywa 125 22 7N 95 11E
Monze 117 16 17S 27 29E
Monze, C. 124 24 47N 66 37E
Monzón 104 41 52N 0 10E
Moonbeam 53 49 20N 82 10W
Moonie, R. 136 27 45S 150 0E
Moorcroft 74 44 17N 104 58W
Moore, L. 134 29 50S 117 35E
Moore Pt. 51 43 48N 79 3W
Moorefield 72 39 5N 78 59W
Moores Mill 39 45 18N 67 17W
Moores Res. 71 44 45N 71 50W
Mooresville, U.S.A. 77 39 37N 86 22W
Mooresville, N.C., U.S.A. 73 35 36N 80 45W
Moorfoot Hills 96 55 44N 3 8W
Moorhead 74 47 0N 97 0W
Mooroopna 136 36 25S 145 22E
Moorpark 81 34 17N 118 53W
Moose Creek 47 45 15N 74 58W
Moose Factory 53 51 16N 80 40W
Moose Heights 63 53 4N 122 31W
Moose Hill 52 48 15N 89 29W
Moose I. 57 51 42N 97 10W
Moose Jaw 56 50 24N 105 30W
Moose Jaw, R. 56 50 34N 105 18W
Moose L. 57 53 46N 100 8W
Moose Lake, Can. 57 53 43N 100 20W
Moose Lake, U.S.A. 52 46 27N 92 48W
Moose Mountain Cr. 56 49 13N 102 12W
Moose Mtn. Prov. Park 57 49 48N 102 25W
Moose, R. 53 51 20N 80 25W
Moose River 53 50 48N 81 17W
Moosehead L. 35 45 40N 69 40W
Moosomin 57 50 9N 101 40W
Moosonee 53 51 17N 80 39W
Moosup 71 41 44N 71 52W
Mopeia 117 17 30S 35 40E
Mopti 114 14 30N 4 0W
Moquegua 86 17 15S 70 46W
Mora, Sweden 111 61 2N 14 38E
Mora, Minn., U.S.A. 74 45 52N 93 19W
Mora, N. Mex., U.S.A. 79 35 58N 105 21W
Moradabad 124 28 50N 78 50E
Morafenobe 117 17 50S 44 53E
Morales 86 2 45N 76 38W
Moramanga 117 18 56S 48 12E
Moran, Kans., U.S.A. 75 37 53N 94 35W
Moran, Mich., U.S.A. 46 46 0N 84 50W
Moran, Wyo., U.S.A. 78 43 53N 110 37W
Morant Cays 84 17 22N 76 0W
Morant Pt. 84 17 55N 76 12W
Morar L. 96 56 57N 5 40W
Moratuwa 124 6 45N 79 55E
Morava, R. 106 49 50N 16 50E
Moravatio 82 19 51N 100 25W
Moravia 76 40 50N 92 50W
Morawhanna 86 8 30N 59 40W
Moray Firth 96 57 50N 3 30W
Morbihan □ 100 47 55N 2 50W
Morcenx 102 44 0N 0 55W
Mordelles 100 48 5N 1 52W
Morden 57 49 15N 98 10W
Mordialloc 136 38 1S 145 6E
Mordovian S.S.R. □ 120 54 20N 44 30E
Mordvinske A S S R 96 54 20N 44 30E
More L. 96 58 18N 4 52W
Møre og Romsdal □ 110 63 0N 9 0E
Moreau, R. 74 45 15N 102 45W
Morecambe 94 54 5N 2 52W
Morecambe B. 94 54 7N 3 0W
Moree 135 29 28S 149 54E
Morehead 72 38 12N 83 22W
Morehead City 73 34 46N 76 44W
Moreira 86 0 34S 63 26W
Morelia 82 19 40N 101 11W
Morell 39 46 25N 62 42W
Morella 104 40 35N 0 5W
Morelos 82 26 42N 107 40W
Morelos □ 83 18 40N 99 10W
Morena, Sierra 104 38 20N 4 0W
Morenci, U.S.A. 77 41 43N 84 13W
Morenci, Ariz., U.S.A. 79 33 7N 109 20W
Mores, I. 73 26 15N 77 35W
Moresby I. 62 52 30N 131 40W
Morestel 103 45 40N 5 28E
Moret 101 48 22N 2 58E
Moreton B. 135 27 10S 153 10E
Moreton, I. 135 27 10S 153 25E
Moreuil 101 49 46N 2 30E
Morez 103 46 31N 6 2E
Morgan 78 41 3N 111 44W
Morgan City 75 29 40N 91 15W
Morgan Hill 80 37 8N 121 39W
Morganfield 72 37 40N 87 55W
Morganton 73 35 46N 81 48W
Morgantown, U.S.A. 77 39 22N 86 16W
Morgantown, W. Va., U.S.A. 72 39 39N 79 58W
Morgat 100 48 15N 4 32W
Morhange 101 48 55N 6 38E
Moriarty 79 35 3N 106 2W
Morice L. 62 53 50N 127 40W
Morice, R. 62 54 12N 127 5W
Morichal 86 2 10N 70 34W
Morichal Largo, R. 86 8 55N 63 0W
Morin-Heights 43 45 54N 74 15W
Morinville 60 53 49N 113 41W
Morioka 132 39 45N 141 8E
Moris 82 28 8N 108 32W
Moriston, Glen 96 57 10N 5 0W
Moriston, R. 96 57 10N 5 0W
Morlaàs 102 43 21N 0 18W
Morlaix 100 48 36N 3 52W
Mormant 101 48 37N 2 52E
Mornington 136 38 15S 145 5E
Mornington I. 135 16 30S 139 30E
Mornington, I. 90 49 50S 75 30W
Moro G. 127 6 30N 123 0E
Morocco 77 40 57N 87 27W
Morocco ■ 114 32 0N 5 50W
Morococha 86 11 40S 76 5W
Morogoro 116 6 50S 37 40E
Morokweng 117 26 12S 23 45E
Moroleón 82 20 8N 101 32W
Morombé 117 21 45S 43 22E
Moron 88 34 39S 58 37W
Morón 84 22 0N 78 30W
Morón de la Frontera 104 37 6N 5 28W
Morondava 117 20 17S 44 17E
Morongo Valley 81 34 3N 116 37W
Morotai, I. 127 2 10N 128 30E
Moroto 116 2 28N 34 42E
Morpeth 94 55 11N 1 41W
Morrilton 75 35 10N 92 45W
Morrin 61 51 40N 112 47W
Morrinhos 87 17 45S 49 10W
Morrinsville 133 37 40S 175 32E
Morris, Can. 57 49 25N 97 22W
Morris, Ill., U.S.A. 77 41 20N 88 20W
Morris, Minn., U.S.A. 74 45 33N 95 56W
Morris L. 39 44 39N 63 30W
Morris, R. 57 49 21N 97 21W
Morrisburg 47 44 55N 75 7W
Morrison 76 41 47N 90 0W
Morrisonville 76 39 25N 89 27W
Morriston 49 43 27N 80 7W
Morristown, U.S.A. 77 39 40N 85 42W
Morristown, Ariz., U.S.A. 79 33 54N 112 45W
Morristown, N.J., U.S.A. 71 40 48N 74 30W
Morristown, S.D., U.S.A. 74 45 57N 101 44W
Morristown, Tenn., U.S.A. 73 36 18N 83 20W
Morro Bay 80 35 27N 120 54W
Morro, Pta. 88 27 6S 71 0W
Morrosquillo, Golfo de 85 9 35N 75 40W
Morrow 77 39 21N 84 8W
Morrumbene 117 23 31S 35 16E
Morse 56 50 25N 107 3W
Morson 52 49 6N 94 19W
Mortagne 102 45 28N 0 49W
Mortagne-au-Perche 100 48 31N 0 33E
Mortagne, R. 101 48 30N 6 30E
Mortain 100 48 40N 0 57W
Morteau 101 47 3N 6 35E
Morteros 88 30 50S 62 0W
Mortes, R. das 87 11 45S 50 44W
Mortlach 56 50 27N 106 4W
Mortlake 136 38 5S 142 50E
Morton, U.S.A. 76 40 37N 89 28W
Morton, Tex., U.S.A. 75 33 39N 102 49W
Morton, Wash., U.S.A. 80 46 33N 122 17W
Morvan, Mts. du 101 47 5N 4 0E
Morven, dist. 96 56 38N 5 44W
Morvern 96 56 38N 5 44W
Morwell 136 38 10S 146 22E
Moscos Is. 128 14 0N 97 30E
Moscow 78 46 45N 116 59W
Moscow = Moskva 120 55 45N 37 35E
Mosel, R. 105 50 22N 7 36E
Moselle □ 101 48 59N 6 33E
Moselle, R. 105 50 22N 7 36E
Moses Inlet 62 51 47N 127 23W
Moses Lake 78 47 16N 119 17W
Mosgiel 133 45 53S 170 21E
Mosher 53 48 42N 84 12W
Moshi 116 3 22S 37 18E
Mosjøen 110 65 51N 13 12E
Moskenesøya 110 67 58N 13 0E
Moskenstraumen 110 67 47N 13 0E
Moskva 120 55 45N 37 35E
Mosley Cr. 62 51 18N 124 50W
Mosquera 86 2 35N 78 30W
Mosquero 75 35 48N 103 57W
Mosquitia 84 15 20N 84 10W
Mosquito B. 36 61 10N 78 0W
Mosquitos, Golfo de los 84 9 15N 81 10W
Moss 111 59 27N 10 40E
Moss Vale 136 34 32S 150 25E
Mossaka 116 1 15S 16 45E
Mossbank 56 49 56N 105 56W
Mossburn 133 45 41S 168 15E
Mosselbaai 117 34 11S 22 8E
Mossendjo 116 2 55S 12 42E
Mossman 135 16 28S 145 23E
Mossoró 87 5 10S 37 15W
Mossuril 117 14 58S 40 42E
Mossy, R. 56 54 5N 102 58W
Most 106 50 31N 13 38E
Mosta 108 35 54N 14 24E
Mostaganem 114 35 54N 0 5E
Mostar 109 43 22N 17 50E
Mostardas 89 31 2S 50 51W
Mosul = Al Mawsil 122 36 20N 43 5E
Mosun 131 23 35N 109 30E
Motagua, R. 84 15 44N 88 14W
Motala 111 58 32N 15 1E
Mothe-Achard, La 100 46 37N 1 40W
Mothe, La, Rés. 41 48 46N 71 9W
Motherwell 96 55 48N 4 0W
Motihari 125 26 37N 85 1E
Motocurunya 86 4 24N 64 5W
Motozintea de Mendoza 83 15 21N 92 14W
Mott 74 46 25N 102 14W
Motte-Chalançon, La 103 44 30N 5 21E
Motte, L. la 40 48 20N 78 2W
Motte, La 103 44 20N 6 3E
Motueka 133 41 7S 173 1E
Motul 83 21 0N 89 20W
Mouchalagane, R. 36 50 56N 68 41W

Moucontant Myanaung

Place	Page	Lat.	Long.
Moucontant	100	46 43N	0 36W
Moúdhros	109	39 50N	25 18E
Mouila	116	1 50S	11 0E
Moulamein Cr.	136	35 6S	144 3E
Mould Bay	64	76 12N	119 25W
Moule, Le	85	16 20N	61 22W
Moulins	102	46 35N	3 19E
Moulmein	125	16 30N	97 40E
Moulton, U.S.A.	76	40 41N	92 41W
Moulton, Tex., U.S.A.	75	29 35N	97 8W
Moultrie	73	31 11N	83 47W
Moultrie, L.	73	33 25N	80 10W
Mound City, Mo., U.S.A.	74	40 2N	95 25W
Mound City, S.D., U.S.A.	74	45 46N	100 3W
Moundsville	70	39 53N	80 43W
Mount Airy	73	36 31N	80 37W
Mount Albert, Can.	70	44 10N	79 20W
Mount Albert, Ont., Can.	46	44 8N	79 19W
Mount Angel	78	45 4N	122 46W
Mount Assiniboine Prov. Park	61	50 53N	115 39W
Mount Ayr	76	40 43N	94 14W
Mount Baker	63	48 50N	121 40W
Mount Barker	134	34 38S	117 40E
Mount Brydges	46	42 54N	81 29W
Mount Carleton Prov. Park	39	47 25N	66 55W
Mount Carmel, Can.	37	47 9N	53 29W
Mount Carmel, Ill., U.S.A.	77	38 20N	87 48W
Mount Carmel, Pa., U.S.A.	71	40 46N	76 25W
Mount Carroll	76	42 6N	89 59W
Mount Clemens	46	42 35N	82 50W
Mount Darwin	117	16 47S	31 38E
Mount Dennis	50	43 41N	79 29W
Mount Desert I.	35	44 25N	68 25W
Mount Dora	73	28 49N	81 32W
Mount Eden	77	38 3N	85 9W
Mount Edgecumbe	67	57 8N	135 22W
Mount Enid	134	21 42S	116 26E
Mount Forest	46	43 59N	80 43W
Mount Gambier	136	37 50S	140 46E
Mount Goldsworthy	134	20 25S	119 39E
Mount Hamilton	48	43 14N	79 51W
Mount Henry	77	42 21N	88 16W
Mount Hope, Can.	48	43 9N	79 55W
Mount Hope, U.S.A.	72	37 52N	81 9W
Mount Horeb	76	43 0N	89 42W
Mount Hotham	136	37 2S	146 52E
Mount Isa	135	20 42S	139 26E
Mount Joy	71	40 6N	76 30W
Mount Laguna	81	32 52N	116 25W
Mount Lavinia	124	6 50N	79 50E
Mount Lofty Ra.	135	34 35S	139 5E
Mount McKinley Nat. Pk.	67	64 0N	150 0W
Mount Magnet	134	28 2S	117 47E
Mount Maunganui	133	37 40S	176 14E
Mount Morgan	135	23 40S	150 25E
Mount Moriah	37	48 58N	58 2W
Mount Morris, Mich., U.S.A.	46	43 8N	83 42W
Mount Morris, N.Y., U.S.A.	70	42 43N	77 50W
Mount Nicholas	134	22 54S	120 27E
Mount Olive	76	39 4N	89 44W
Mount Olivet	77	38 32N	84 2W
Mount Orab	77	39 5N	83 56W
Mount Pearl	37	47 31N	52 47W
Mount Pleasant, Alta., Can.	59	51 4N	114 5W
Mount Pleasant, Ont., Can.	49	43 5N	80 19W
Mount Pleasant, Iowa, U.S.A.	76	41 0N	91 35W
Mount Pleasant, Mich., U.S.A.	46	43 35N	84 47W
Mount Pleasant, Pa., U.S.A.	70	40 9N	79 31W
Mount Pleasant, S.C., U.S.A.	73	32 45N	79 48W
Mount Pleasant, Tenn., U.S.A.	73	35 31N	87 11W
Mount Pleasant, Tex., U.S.A.	75	33 5N	95 0W
Mount Pleasant, Ut., U.S.A.	78	39 40N	111 29W
Mount Pocono	71	41 8N	75 21W
Mount Pulaski	76	40 1N	89 17W
Mount Rainier Nat. Park.	80	46 50N	121 43W
Mount Revelstoke Nat. Park	63	51 5N	118 30W
Mount Robson	54	52 56N	119 15W
Mount Robson Prov. Park	63	53 0N	119 0W
Mount Royal	58	50 27N	104 40W
Mount Seymour Prov. Park	66	49 24N	122 55W
Mount Shasta	78	41 20N	122 18W
Mount Signal	81	32 39N	115 37W
Mount Singleton	136	32 30S	151 3E
Mount Sterling, Ill., U.S.A.	76	40 0N	90 40W
Mount Sterling, Ky., U.S.A.	77	38 0N	84 0W
Mount Sterling, Ohio, U.S.A.	77	39 43N	83 16W
Mount Stewart	39	46 22N	62 52W
Mount Tolmie	63	48 28N	123 20W
Mount Tom Price	134	22 50S	117 40E
Mount Uniacke	39	44 54N	63 50W
Mount Union	70	40 22N	77 51W
Mount Vernon, Can.	49	43 6N	80 24W
Mount Vernon, Ill., U.S.A.	77	38 19N	88 55W
Mount Vernon, Ind., U.S.A.	77	38 17N	88 57W
Mount Vernon, Iowa, U.S.A.	76	41 55N	91 23W
Mount Vernon, N.Y., U.S.A.	71	40 57N	73 49W
Mount Vernon, Ohio, U.S.A.	72	40 20N	82 30W
Mount Vernon, Wash., U.S.A.	63	48 25N	122 20W
Mount Vernon, Wash., U.S.A.	80	48 27N	122 18W
Mount Washington	77	38 3N	85 33W
Mount Whaleback	134	23 18S	119 44E
Mount Zion	77	39 46N	88 53W
Mountain Center	81	33 42N	116 44W
Mountain City, Nev., U.S.A.	78	41 54N	116 0W
Mountain City, Tenn., U.S.A.	73	36 30N	81 50W
Mountain Grove	75	37 5N	92 20W
Mountain Home, Ark., U.S.A.	75	36 20N	92 25W
Mountain Home, Idaho, U.S.A.	78	43 11N	115 45W
Mountain Iron	74	47 30N	92 37W
Mountain Park.	61	52 50N	117 15W
Mountain Pass	81	35 29N	115 35W
Mountain View, Can.	61	49 8N	113 36W
Mountain View, Ark., U.S.A.	75	35 52N	92 10W
Mountain View, Calif., U.S.A.	79	37 26N	122 5W
Mountain Village	67	62 10N	163 50W
Mountainair	79	34 35N	106 15W
Mountmellick	97	53 7N	7 20W
Mountnorris	97	54 15N	6 29W
Moura	86	1 25S	61 45W
Moure, La	74	46 27N	98 17W
Mourenx	102	43 23N	0 36W
Mourmelon-le-Grand	101	49 8N	4 22E
Mourne Mts.	97	54 10N	6 0W
Mourne, R.	97	54 45N	7 39W
Mouscron	105	50 45N	3 12E
Mouthe	101	46 44N	6 12E
Moûtiers	103	45 29N	6 31E
Moutong	127	0 28N	121 13E
Mouy	101	49 18N	2 20E
Movas	82	28 10N	109 25W
Moville	97	55 11N	7 3W
Moweaqua	76	39 37N	89 1W
Mowming	131	21 50N	110 32E
Mowping	130	37 25N	121 34E
Moy, R.	97	54 5N	8 50W
Moyahua	82	21 16N	103 10W
Moyale	116	3 30N	39 0E
Moyie	54	49 17N	115 50W
Moyie Springs	61	48 43N	116 11W
Moyle □	97	55 10N	6 15W
Moyobamba	86	6 0S	77 0W
Mozambique = Moçambique	117	15 3S	40 42E
Mozambique ■	117	19 0S	35 0E
Mozambique Chan.	117	20 0S	39 0E
Mozdok	120	43 45N	44 48E
Mozyr	120	52 0N	29 15E
Mpanda	116	6 23S	31 40E
Mpika	117	11 51S	31 25E
Mpwapwa	116	6 30S	36 30E
Msoro	117	13 35S	31 50E
Mtwara	116	10 20S	40 20E
Muaná	87	1 25S	49 15W
Muang Chiang Rai	128	19 52N	99 50E
Muang Kalasin	128	16 26N	103 30E
Muang Lampang	128	18 16N	99 32E
Muang Lamphun	128	18 40N	98 53E
Muang Nan	128	18 52N	100 42E
Muang Phetchabun	128	16 23N	101 12E
Muang Phichit	128	16 29N	100 21E
Muang Ubon	128	15 15N	104 50E
Muang Yasothon	128	15 50N	104 10E
Muar	128	2 3N	102 34E
Muar, R.	128	2 15N	102 48E
Muarabungo	126	1 40S	101 10E
Muaradjuloi	126	0 12S	114 3E
Muaraenim	126	3 40S	103 50E
Muarakaman	126	0 2S	116 45E
Muaratebo	126	1 30S	102 26E
Muaratembesi	126	1 42S	103 2E
Muaratewe	126	0 50S	115 0E
Mubairik	122	23 22N	39 8E
Mubende	116	0 33N	31 22E
Mucajaí, Serra do	86	2 23N	61 10W
Muchalat Inlet	62	49 38N	126 15W
Muchikan	129	53 2N	120 27E
Muck, I.	96	56 50N	6 15W
Mucuri	87	18 0S	40 0W
Mud B.	66	49 5N	122 53W
Mud L.	78	40 15N	120 15W
Muddy L.	56	52 19N	109 6W
Muddy, R.	79	38 30N	110 55W
Mudgee	136	32 32S	149 31E
Mudhnib	122	25 50N	44 18E
Mudjatik, R.	55	56 1N	107 36W
Muenster	56	52 12N	105 0W
Muerto, Mar	83	16 10N	94 10W
Mufulira	117	12 32S	28 15E
Muğla	122	37 15N	28 28E
Mugu	125	29 45N	82 30E
Mühlig-Hofmann-fjella	91	72 30S	5 0E
Mui Bai Bung	128	8 35N	104 42E
Mui Ron	128	18 7N	106 27E
Muine Bheag	97	52 42N	6 59W
Mukah	126	2 55N	112 5E
Mukalla	115	14 33N	49 2E
Mukden = Shenyang	130	41 35N	123 30E
Mukomuko	126	2 20S	101 10E
Muktsar	124	30 30N	74 30E
Mukur	124	32 50N	67 50E
Mukutawa, R.	57	53 10N	97 24W
Mukwonago	77	42 52N	88 20W
Mulanay	127	13 30N	122 30E
Mulatas, Arch. de las	84	6 51N	78 31W
Mulberry Grove	76	38 55N	89 16W
Mulchén	88	37 45S	72 20W
Mulde, R.	106	50 55N	12 42E
Muldraugh	77	37 56N	85 59W
Mule Creek	74	43 19N	104 8W
Mulegé	82	26 53N	112 1W
Muleshoe	75	34 17N	102 42W
Mulgrave	39	45 38N	61 31W
Mulhacén	104	37 4N	3 20W
Mülheim	105	51 26N	6 53W
Mulhouse	101	47 40N	7 20E
Mull I.	96	56 27N	6 0W
Mull, Sound of	96	56 30N	5 50W
Mullaittvu	124	9 15N	80 55E
Mullen	74	42 5N	101 0W
Mullens	72	37 34N	81 22W
Muller, Pegunungan	126	0 30N	113 30E
Mullet Pen.	97	54 10N	10 2W
Mullett L.	46	45 30N	84 30W
Mullewa	134	28 29S	115 30E
Mullin	75	31 33N	98 38W
Mullingar	97	53 31N	7 20W
Mullins	73	34 12N	79 15W
Mullion Creek	136	33 9S	148 7E
Multan	124	30 15N	71 30E
Multan □	124	30 29N	72 29E
Mulvane	75	37 30N	97 15W
Mulwala	136	35 59S	146 0E
Mumbwa	117	15 0S	27 0E
Mun	128	15 17N	103 0E
Muna, I.	127	5 0S	122 30E
Muna Sotuta	83	20 29N	89 43W
München	106	48 8N	11 33E
Munchen-Gladbach = Mönchengladbach	105	51 12N	6 23E
Muncho Lake	54	59 0N	125 50W
Muncie	77	40 10N	85 20W
Mundala, Puncak	127	4 30S	141 0E
Mundare	60	53 35N	112 20W
Munday	75	33 26N	99 39W
Münden	106	51 25N	9 42E
Mundo Novo	87	11 50S	40 29W
Mungbere	116	2 36N	28 28E
Mungindi	135	28 58S	149 1E
Munhango R.	117	11 30S	19 30E
Munich = München	106	48 8N	11 35E
Munising	53	46 25N	86 39W
Muñoz Gamero, Pen.	90	52 30S	73 5E
Munroe L.	55	59 13N	98 35W
Munson	61	51 34N	112 45W
Munster	101	48 2N	7 8E
Münster, Ger.	105	52 59N	10 5E
Münster, Switz.	106	46 30N	8 17E
Munster □	97	52 20N	8 40W
Muntok	126	2 5S	105 10E
Muon Pak Beng	128	19 51N	101 4E
Muong La	128	20 52N	102 5E
Muonio	110	67 57N	23 40E
Muonio älv	110	67 48N	23 25E
Mur-de-Bretagne	100	48 12N	3 0W
Mûr, R.	106	47 7N	13 55E
Murallón, Cuerro	90	49 55S	73 30W
Murang'a	116	0 45S	37 9E
Murashi	120	59 30N	49 0E
Murat	102	45 7N	2 53E
Murchison I.	52	50 0N	88 21W
Murchison, R.	134	26 45S	116 15E
Murchison Ra.	134	20 0S	134 10E
Murcia	104	38 2N	1 10W
Murcia □	104	37 50N	1 30W
Murdo	74	43 56N	100 43W
Murdochville	38	48 58N	65 30W
Murdock	58	49 56N	97 4W
Mure, La	103	44 55N	5 48E
Mures R.	107	46 0N	22 0E
Muret	102	43 30N	1 20E
Murfreesboro	73	35 50N	86 21W
Murgab	120	38 10N	73 59E
Murgon	135	26 15S	151 54E
Muriaé	89	21 8S	42 23W
Muriel L.	60	54 9N	110 40W
Müritz-see	106	53 25N	12 40E
Murjo Mt.	127	6 36S	110 53E
Murmansk	120	68 57N	33 10E
Muro	103	42 34N	8 54E
Muro, C. de	103	41 44N	8 37E
Murom	120	55 35N	42 3E
Muroran	132	42 25N	141 0E
Muroto-Misaki	132	33 15N	134 10E
Murphy	78	43 11N	116 33W
Murphy L.	63	52 3N	121 15W
Murphys	80	38 8N	120 28W
Murphysboro	76	37 50N	89 20W
Murray, U.S.A.	76	41 3N	93 57W
Murray, Ky., U.S.A.	73	36 40N	88 20W
Murray, Utah, U.S.A.	78	40 41N	111 58W
Murray Bridge	135	35 6S	139 14E
Murray Harbour	39	46 0N	62 28W
Murray, L.	73	34 8N	81 30W
Murray, R., S. Australia, Austral.	136	35 20S	139 22E
Murray, R., W. Australia, Austral.	135	32 33S	115 45E
Murray, R., Can.	54	56 11N	120 45W
Murray River	39	46 1N	62 37W
Murraysburg	117	31 58S	23 47E
Murrayville, Austral.	136	35 16S	141 11E
Murrayville, U.S.A.	76	39 35N	90 15W
Murree	124	33 56N	73 28E
Murrieta	81	33 33N	117 13W
Murrumbidgee, R.	136	34 40S	143 0E
Murrumburrah	136	34 32S	148 22E
Murrurundi	136	31 42S	150 51E
Murtle L.	63	52 8N	119 38W
Murtoa	136	36 35S	142 28E
Murwara	125	23 46N	80 28E
Murwillumbah	135	28 18S	153 27E
Mürzzuschlag	106	47 36N	15 41E
Muş	122	38 45N	41 30E
Musa Khel	124	30 29N	69 52E
Musa Qala (Musa Kala)	124	32 20N	64 50E
Musaffargarh	124	30 10N	71 10E
Musala, I.	126	1 41N	98 28E
Musalla, mt.	109	42 13N	23 37E
Musan	130	42 12N	129 12E
Muscat = Masqat	123	23 37N	58 36E
Muscatine	76	41 25N	91 5W
Muscoda	76	43 11N	90 27W
Musgrave Harbour	37	49 27N	53 58W
Musgrave Ras.	134	26 0S	132 0E
Mushaboom	39	44 51N	62 32W
Mushie	116	2 56S	17 4E
Musi, R.	126	2 55S	103 40E
Muskeg B.	52	48 59N	95 5W
Muskeg L.	52	49 0N	90 2W
Muskeg, R.	54	60 20N	123 20W
Muskeg River	60	53 55N	118 39W
Muskego	77	42 54N	88 8W
Muskegon	46	43 15N	86 17W
Muskegon Hts.	77	43 12N	86 17W
Muskegon, R.	72	43 25N	86 0W
Muskogee	75	35 50N	95 25W
Muskoka, L.	46	45 0N	79 25W
Muskwa L.	60	56 9N	114 38W
Muskwa, R., Alta., Can.	60	56 15N	113 48W
Muskwa, R., B.C., Can.	54	58 47N	122 48W
Musoma	116	1 30S	33 48E
Musquanousse, L.	38	50 22N	61 5W
Musquaro	38	50 10N	61 3W
Musquaro, L.	36	50 38N	61 5W
Musquash	39	45 11N	66 19W
Musquodoboit Harbour	39	44 50N	63 9W
Mussel Inlet	62	52 53N	128 7W
Musselburgh	96	55 57N	3 3W
Musselshell, R.	78	46 30N	108 15W
Mussidan	102	45 2N	0 22E
Mussooree	124	30 27N	78 6E
Mustafa Kemalpaşa	122	40 3N	28 25E
Mustajidda	122	26 30N	41 50E
Mustang	125	29 10N	83 55E
Musters, L.	90	45 20S	69 25W
Muswellbrook	135	32 16S	150 56E
Mut	122	36 40N	33 28E
Mutan Kiang	130	46 18N	129 31E
Mutankiang	130	44 35N	129 30E
Mutis	86	1 4N	77 25W
Mutshatsha	116	10 35S	24 20E
Muttaburra	135	22 38S	144 29E
Mutton Bay	35	50 50N	59 2W
Muxima	116	9 25S	13 52E
Muy, Le	103	43 28N	6 34E
Muy Muy	84	12 39N	85 36W
Muya	121	56 27N	115 39E
Muzaffarabad	124	34 25N	73 30E
Muzaffarnagar	124	29 26N	77 40E
Muzaffarpur	125	26 7N	85 32E
Muzhi	120	65 25N	64 40E
Muzillac	100	47 35N	2 30W
Muzo	86	5 32N	74 6W
Muzon C.	54	54 40N	132 40W
Muztagh P.	129	36 30N	87 22E
Mwanza, Congo	116	7 55S	26 43E
Mwanza, Tanz.	116	2 30S	32 58E
Mwaya	116	9 32S	33 55E
Mweelrea, Mt.	97	53 37N	9 48W
Mweka	116	4 50S	21 40E
Mwenga	116	3 1S	28 21E
Mweru, L.	116	9 0S	29 0E
Mwinilunga	117	11 43S	24 25E
My Tho	128	10 29N	106 23E
Myall, R.	136	32 30S	152 15E
Myanaung	125	18 25N	95 10E

Name	Page	Lat.	Long.
Myaungmya	125	16 30N	95 0 E
Mycenæ	109	37 44N	22 45 E
Myerstown	71	40 22N	76 18W
Myingyan	125	21 30N	95 30 E
Myitkyina	125	25 30N	97 26 E
Mymensingh	125	24 45N	90 24 E
Myndmere	74	46 23N	97 7W
Myogi	128	21 24N	96 28 E
Mýrdalsjökull	110	63 40N	19 6W
Myrnam	60	53 40N	111 14W
Myrtle Beach	73	33 43N	78 50W
Myrtle Creek	78	43 0N	123 9W
Myrtle Point	78	43 0N	124 4W
Myrtleford	136	36 34 S	146 44 E
Mysore	124	12 17N	76 41 E
Mysore □ = Karnataka	124	13 15N	77 0 E
Mystery Lake	60	54 10N	114 55W
Mystic, U.S.A.	76	40 47N	92 57W
Mystic, Conn., U.S.A.	71	41 21N	71 58W
Myton	78	40 10N	110 2W
Mývatn	110	65 36N	17 0W

N

Name	Page	Lat.	Long.
Naab, R.	106	49 10N	12 0 E
Naaldwijk	105	51 59N	4 13 E
Naalehu	67	19 4N	155 35W
Naantali	111	60 29N	22 2 E
Naas	97	53 12N	6 40W
Nabadwip	125	23 34N	88 20 E
Nabas	127	11 47N	122 6 E
Naberezhnyye Chelny	120	55 42N	52 19 E
Nabesna	67	62 33N	143 10W
Nabire	127	3 15 S	136 27 E
Nabisipi, R.	36	50 14N	62 13W
Nablus = Nābulus	115	32 14N	35 15 E
Nābulus	115	32 14N	35 15 E
Nacala-Velha	117	14 32 S	40 34 E
Nacaome	84	13 31N	87 30W
Nachako Res.	62	53 42N	127 30W
Naches	78	46 48N	120 49W
Naches, R.	80	46 38N	120 31W
Nachi	131	28 50N	105 25 E
Nachicapau, L.	36	56 40N	68 5W
Nachingwea	116	10 49 S	38 49 E
Nachvak Fd.	36	59 3N	63 45W
Nacimento Res.	80	35 46N	120 53W
Nackawic	39	45 59N	67 17W
Nacmine	61	51 28N	112 47W
Naco, Mexico	82	31 20N	109 56W
Naco, U.S.A.	79	31 24N	109 58W
Nacogdoches	75	31 33N	95 30W
Nácori Chico	82	29 39N	109 1W
Nacozari	82	30 30N	109 50W
Nadern Harb.	62	54 0N	132 36W
Nadiad	124	22 41N	72 56 E
Nadina L.	62	53 53N	127 2W
Nadina, R.	62	53 58N	126 30W
Nadūshan	123	32 2N	53 35 E
Nadym	120	63 35N	72 42 E
Nadym, R.	120	65 30N	73 0 E
Naft Shāh	122	34 0N	45 30 E
Nafūd ad Dahy	122	22 0N	45 0 E
Naga, Japan	131	26 34N	127 43 E
Naga, Phil.	127	13 38N	123 15 E
Naga Hills	130	26 0N	94 30 E
Nagagami L.	53	49 25N	85 1W
Nagagami, R.	53	49 40N	84 40W
Nagagamisis L.	53	49 28N	84 40W
Nagaland □	125	26 0N	94 30 E
Nagano	132	36 40N	138 10 E
Nagano-ken □	132	36 15N	138 0 E
Nagaoka	132	37 27N	138 50 E
Nagappattinam	124	10 46N	79 51 E
Nagar Parkar	124	24 30N	70 35 E
Nagas Pt.	62	52 12N	131 22W
Nagasaki	132	32 47N	129 50 E
Nagasaki-ken □	132	32 50N	129 40 E
Nagasin L.	53	47 48N	83 37W
Nagaur	124	27 15N	73 45 E
Nagercoil	124	8 12N	77 33 E
Nagineh	123	34 20N	57 15 E
Nago	131	26 36N	128 0 E
Nagoya	132	35 10N	136 50 E
Nagpur	124	21 8N	79 10 E
Nagua	85	19 23N	69 50W
Nagykanizsa	106	46 28N	17 0 E
Nagykörös	107	46 55N	19 48 E
Naha	131	26 12N	127 40 E
Nahanni Butte	54	61 2N	123 20W
Nahanni Nat. Pk.	54	61 15N	125 0W
Nahariya	115	33 1N	35 5 E
Nahāvand	122	34 10N	48 30 E
Nahlin	54	58 55N	131 38W
Naicá	82	27 53N	105 31W
Naicam	56	52 30N	104 30W
Naikoon Prov. Park	62	53 55N	131 55W
Nain	36	56 34N	61 40W
Nā'in	123	32 54N	53 0 E
Nainpur	124	22 30N	80 10 E
Naintré	100	46 46N	0 29 E
Naira, I.	127	4 28 S	130 0 E
Nairn, Can.	46	46 20N	81 35W
Nairn, U.K.	96	57 35N	3 54W
Nairobi	116	1 17 S	36 48 E
Naivasha	116	0 40 S	36 30 E
Najac	102	44 14N	1 58 E
Najafābād	123	32 40N	51 15 E
Najd	122	26 30N	42 0 E
Najibabad	124	29 40N	78 20 E
Najin	130	42 12N	130 15 E
Nakamura	132	33 0N	133 0 E
Nakano Shima	132	29 50N	130 0 E
Nakelele Pt.	67	21 2N	156 35W
Nakhi Mubarak	122	24 10N	38 10 E
Nakhichevan A.S.S.R. □	120	39 14N	45 30 E
Nakhodka	121	43 10N	132 45 E
Nakhon Phanom	128	17 23N	104 43 E
Nakhon Ratchasima (Khorat)	128	14 59N	102 12 E
Nakhon Sawan	128	15 35N	100 10 E
Nakhon Si Thammarat	128	8 29N	100 0 E
Nakina, B.C., Can.	54	59 12N	132 52W
Nakina, Ont., Can.	53	50 10N	86 40W
Naknek	67	58 45N	157 0W
Nakskov	111	54 50N	11 8 E
Naktong, R.	130	35 7N	128 57 E
Nakuru	116	0 15 S	35 5 E
Nakusp	63	50 20N	117 45W
Nal, R.	124	27 0N	65 50 E
Nalayh	129	47 43N	107 22 E
Nalchik	120	43 30N	43 33 E
Nalgonda	124	17 6N	79 15 E
Nallamalai Hills	124	15 30N	78 50 E
Nalón, R.	104	43 35N	6 10W
Nam Dinh	128	20 25N	106 5 E
Nam-Phan	128	10 30N	106 0 E
Nam Phong	128	16 42N	102 52 E
Nam Tha	128	20 58N	101 30 E
Nam Tso	129	30 40N	90 30 E
Nama	131	23 45N	108 1 E
Namacurra	117	17 30 S	36 50 E
Namakan L.	52	48 27N	92 35W
Namaland	117	26 0 S	18 0 E
Naman	131	25 0N	118 30 E
Namangan	120	41 0N	71 40 E
Namapa	117	13 43 S	39 50 E
Namber	127	1 2 S	134 57 E
Nambour	135	26 32 S	152 58 E
Namcha Barwa	129	29 40N	95 10 E
Nameh	126	2 34N	116 21 E
Namew L., Can.	57	54 10N	102 0W
Namew L., Sask., Can.	55	54 14N	101 56W
Namib Desert = Namib Woestyn	117	22 30 S	15 0 E
Namib-Woestyn	117	22 30 S	15 0 E
Namibia □	117	22 0 S	18 9 E
Namiquipa	82	29 15N	107 25W
Namja Pass	125	30 0N	82 25 E
Namlea	127	3 10 S	127 5 E
Namoa tao	131	23 30N	117 0 E
Nampa	78	43 40N	116 40W
Nampula	117	15 6 S	39 7 E
Namrole	127	3 46 S	126 46 E
Namsen, R.	110	64 40N	12 45 E
Namsos	110	64 28N	11 0 E
Namtu	125	23 5N	97 28 E
Namu	62	51 52N	127 50W
Namur, Belg.	105	50 27N	4 52 E
Namur, Can.	40	45 54N	74 56W
Namur □	105	50 17N	5 0 E
Namutoni	117	18 49 S	16 55 E
Namwala	117	15 44 S	26 30 E
Namyung	131	25 15N	114 5 E
Nan Shan	129	38 30N	99 0 E
Nanaimo	62	49 10N	124 0W
Nanam	130	41 44N	129 40 E
Nanango	135	26 40 S	152 0 E
Nanao	132	37 0N	137 0 E
Nanchang, Hupei, China	131	31 50N	111 50 E
Nanchang, Kiangsi, China	131	28 34N	115 48 E
Nancheng	131	27 30N	116 28 E
Nancheng = Hanchung	131	33 10N	107 2 E
Nanchung	131	30 47N	105 59 E
Nanchwan	131	29 10N	107 15 E
Nancy	101	48 42N	6 12 E
Nanda Devi, Mt.	129	30 30N	80 30 E
Nander	124	19 10N	77 20 E
Nandi	133	17 25 S	176 50 E
Nandurbar	124	21 20N	74 15 E
Nandyal	124	15 30N	78 30 E
Nanga Eboko	116	4 41N	12 22 E
Nanga Parbat, mt.	124	35 10N	74 35 E
Nangapinoh	126	0 20 S	111 14 E
Nangarhar □	124	34 20N	70 0 E
Nangatajap	126	1 32 S	110 34 E
Nangfeng	131	27 10N	116 20 E
Nangis	101	48 33N	3 0 E
Nanika L.	62	53 47N	127 38W
Nanisivik	65	73 2N	84 33W
Nankang	131	25 42N	114 35 E
Nankiang	131	32 20N	106 50 E
Nanking	131	32 10N	118 50 E
Nannine	134	26 51 S	118 18 E
Nanning	131	22 48N	108 20 E
Nanpi	130	38 0N	116 40 E
Nanping, Fukien, China	131	26 45N	118 5 E
Nanping, Szechwan, China	131	33 20N	103 56 E
Nanpu	131	31 17N	105 59 E
Nansei-Shotō, Japan	132	26 0N	128 0 E
Nansei-Shotō, Japan	132	29 0N	129 0 E
Nansen Sd.	65	81 0N	91 0W
Nant	102	44 1N	3 18 E
Nantan	131	25 0N	107 35 E
Nantes	100	47 12N	1 33W
Nanteuil-le-Haudouin	101	49 9N	2 48 E
Nantiat	102	46 1N	1 11 E
Nanticoke	71	41 12N	76 1W
Nanton	61	50 21N	113 46W
Nantou	131	23 57N	120 35 E
Nantua	103	46 10N	5 35 E
Nantucket I.	69	41 16N	70 3W
Nantung	131	32 0N	120 50 E
Nanuque	87	17 50 S	40 21W
Nanyang	131	33 0N	112 32 E
Nanyuan	130	39 45N	116 30 E
Nanyuki	116	0 2N	37 4 E
Nao, C. de la	104	38 44N	0 14 E
Naococane L.	36	52 50N	70 45W
Naoetsu	132	37 12N	138 10 E
Napa	80	38 18N	122 17W
Napa, R.	80	38 10N	122 19W
Napamute	67	61 30N	158 45W
Napanee	47	44 15N	77 0W
Napanoch	71	41 44N	74 2W
Napartokh B.	36	58 1N	62 19W
Naperville	77	41 46N	88 9W
Napier	133	39 30 S	176 56 E
Napierville	45	45 11N	73 25W
Napierville □	44	45 10N	73 30W
Napinka	57	49 19N	100 50W
Naples, Fla., U.S.A.	73	26 10N	81 45W
Naples, N.Y., U.S.A.	70	42 35N	77 25W
Naples = Nápoli	108	40 50N	14 5 E
Napo □	86	0 30 S	77 0W
Napo, R.	86	3 5 S	73 0W
Napoleon, N. Dak., U.S.A.	74	46 32N	99 49W
Napoleon, Ohio, U.S.A.	77	41 24N	84 7W
Nápoli	108	40 50N	14 5 E
Nappanee	77	41 27N	86 0W
Nara, Japan	132	34 40N	135 49 E
Nara, Mali	114	15 25N	7 20W
Nara-ken □	132	34 30N	136 0 E
Nara Visa	75	35 39N	103 10W
Naracoorte	136	36 58 S	140 45 E
Naradhan	136	33 34 S	146 17 E
Narasapur	125	16 26N	81 50 E
Narathiwat	128	6 40N	101 55 E
Narayanganj	125	23 31N	90 33 E
Narayanpet	124	16 45N	77 30 E
Narbonne	102	43 11N	3 0 E
Nardò	109	40 10N	18 0 E
Narin	124	36 5N	69 0 E
Narinda, B. de	117	14 55 S	47 30 E
Narino □	86	1 30N	78 0W
Narmada, R.	124	22 40N	77 30 E
Narooma	136	36 14 S	150 4 E
Narrabri	135	30 19 S	149 46 E
Narrandera	136	34 42 S	146 31 E
Narraway, R.	60	55 44N	119 55W
Narriah	136	33 56 S	146 43 E
Narrogin	134	32 58 S	117 14 E
Narromine	136	32 12 S	148 12 E
Narsinghpur	124	22 54N	79 14 E
Narva	120	59 10N	28 5 E
Narvik	110	68 28N	17 26 E
Naryan-Mar	120	68 0N	53 0 E
Narym	120	59 0N	81 58 E
Narymskoye	120	49 10N	84 15 E
Naryn	120	41 26N	75 58 E
Nasa, mt.	110	66 32N	15 23 E
Naseby	133	45 1 S	170 10 E
Naselle	80	46 22N	123 49W
Naser, Buheirat en	115	23 0N	32 30 E
Nash Creek	39	47 56N	66 6W
Nashua, Iowa, U.S.A.	76	42 55N	92 34W
Nashua, Mont., U.S.A.	78	48 10N	106 25W
Nashua, N.H., U.S.A.	71	42 50N	71 25W
Nashville, Ark., U.S.A.	75	33 56N	93 50W
Nashville, Ga., U.S.A.	73	31 13N	83 15W
Nashville, Ill., U.S.A.	76	38 21N	89 23W
Nashville, Ind., U.S.A.	77	39 12N	86 14W
Nashville, Mich., U.S.A.	77	42 36N	85 5W
Nashville, Tenn., U.S.A.	73	36 12N	86 46W
Nashwaak Bridge	39	46 14N	66 37W
Nashwaaksis	39	45 59N	66 38W
Nasik	124	20 2N	73 50 E
Nasirabad, Bangla.	125	24 42N	90 30 E
Nasirabad, India	124	26 15N	74 45 E
Naskaupi, R.	36	53 47N	60 51W
Nass, R.	54	55 0N	129 40W
Nassau, Bahamas	84	25 0N	77 30W
Nassau, U.S.A.	71	42 30N	73 34W
Nassau, Bahia	90	55 20 S	68 0W
Nasser, L. = Naser, Buheirat en	115	23 0N	32 30 E
Nässjö	111	57 38N	14 45 E
Nastapoka, Is.	36	56 55N	76 50W
Nastapoka, R.	36	56 55N	76 33W
Nastopoka Is.	34	57 0N	77 0W
Nata	131	19 37N	109 17 E
Natā	122	27 15N	48 35 E
Nata	117	2 0 S	34 25 E
Natagaima	86	3 37N	75 6W
Natal, Brazil	87	5 47 S	35 13W
Natal, Can.	61	49 43N	114 51W
Natal, Indon.	126	0 35N	99 0 E
Natal □	117	28 30 S	30 30 E
Natalkuz L.	62	53 36N	125 20W
Natanz	123	33 30N	51 55 E
Natashquan	38	50 14N	61 46W
Natashquan-Est, R.	38	51 20N	61 40W
Natashquan Pt.	38	50 8N	61 40W
Natashquan, R.	38	50 7N	61 50W
Natchez	75	31 35N	91 25W
Natchitoches	75	31 47N	93 4W
Nathdwara	124	24 55N	73 50 E
Natick	71	42 16N	71 19W
Natih	123	22 25N	56 30 E
Nation, R.	54	55 30N	123 32W
National City	80	32 45N	117 7W
National Mills	55	52 52N	101 40W
Natividad, I. de	82	27 50N	115 10W
Natkyizin	128	14 57N	97 59 E
Natoma	74	39 14N	99 0W
Natron L.	116	2 20 S	36 0 E
Natrona	70	40 39N	79 43W
Natuna Besar, Kepulauan	126	4 0N	108 15 E
Natuna Selatan, Kepulauan	126	2 45N	109 0 E
Natural Bridge	71	44 5N	75 30W
Naturaliste, C.	134	33 32 S	115 0 E
Naturaliste Channel	134	25 20 S	113 0 E
Naubinway	46	46 7N	85 27W
Naucelle	102	44 13N	2 20 E
Naugatuck	71	41 28N	73 4W
Naughton	46	46 24N	81 12W
Naumburg	106	51 10N	11 48 E
Nauru I.	14	0 25N	166 0 E
Naushahra	124	34 0N	72 0 E
Nauta	86	4 20 S	73 35W
Nautanwa	125	27 20N	83 25 E
Nautla	83	20 20N	96 50W
Nauvoo	76	40 33N	91 23W
Nava	82	28 25N	100 46W
Navalcarnero	104	40 17N	4 5W
Navan = An Uaimh	97	53 39N	6 40W
Navarino, I.	90	55 0 S	67 30W
Navarra □	104	42 40N	1 40W
Navarre, France	102	43 15N	1 20 E
Navarre, U.S.A.	70	40 43N	81 31W
Navarrenx	102	43 20N	0 47W
Navarro	80	39 10N	123 32W
Navasota	75	30 20N	96 5W
Navassa I.	85	18 30N	75 0W
Naver, R.	96	58 34N	4 15W
Navidad	88	33 57 S	71 50W
Navin	58	49 51N	97 0W
Navoi	120	40 9N	65 22 E
Navojoa	82	27 0N	109 30W
Navolato	82	24 47N	107 42W
Návpaktos	109	38 23N	21 42 E
Návplion	109	37 33N	22 50 E
Navsari	124	20 57N	72 59 E
Nawabshah	124	26 15N	68 25 E
Nawakot	125	28 0N	85 10 E
Nawalgarh	124	27 50N	75 15 E
Náxos	109	37 8N	25 25 E
Nay	102	43 10N	0 18W
Nāy Band	123	27 20N	52 40 E
Naya	86	3 13N	77 22W
Naya, R.	86	3 13N	77 22W
Nayakhan	121	62 10N	159 0 E
Nayarit □	82	22 0N	105 0W
Nazare	87	13 0 S	39 0W
Nazaré da Mata	87	7 44 S	35 14W
Nazareth	115	32 42N	35 17 E
Nazas	82	25 10N	104 0W
Nazas, R.	82	25 20N	104 4W
Naze, The	95	51 43N	1 19 E
Nazir Hat	125	22 35N	91 55 E
Nazko	62	53 1N	123 37W
Nazko, R.	62	53 7N	123 34W
Ncheu	117	14 50 S	34 37 E
Ndélé	116	8 25N	20 36 E
Ndendeé	116	2 29 S	10 46 E
Ndjamena	114	12 4N	15 8 E
Ndjolé	116	0 10 S	10 45 E
Ndola	117	13 0 S	28 34 E
Neagh, Lough	97	54 35N	6 25W
Neah Bay	80	48 25N	124 40W
Near Is.	67	53 0N	172 0W
Neath	95	51 39N	3 49W
Neath, R.	98	51 46N	3 35W
Nebraska □	74	41 30N	100 0W
Nebraska City	74	40 40N	95 52W
Nébrodi, Monti	108	37 55N	14 45 E
Necedah	74	44 2N	90 7W
Nechako, R.	63	53 30N	122 44W
Neche	57	48 59N	97 39W
Neches, R.	75	31 80N	94 20W
Neckar, R.	106	48 43N	9 15 E
Necochea	88	38 30 S	58 50W
Needles	81	34 50N	114 35W
Needles, The	95	50 48N	1 19W
Ñeembucú □	88	27 0 S	58 0W
Neemuch (Nimach)	124	24 30N	74 50 E
Neenah	72	44 10N	88 30W
Neepawa	57	50 15N	99 30W
Negaunee	53	46 30N	87 36W
Negeri Sembilan □	128	2 50N	102 10 E
Negoiu, Vf.	107	43 35N	24 31 E
Negombo	124	7 12N	79 50 E
Negotin	109	44 16N	22 37 E
Negra, La	88	23 46 S	70 18W
Negra Pt.	127	18 40N	120 50 E

Noss Hd Okehampton

Noss Hd. 96 58 29N 3 4W
Nossob, R. 117 25 15S 20 30E
Nosy Bé, I. 117 13 25S 48 15E
Nosy Mitsio, I. 117 12 54S 48 36E
Nosy Varika 117 20 35S 48 32E
Notigi Dam 55 56 40N 99 10W
Notikewin 54 56 55N 117 50W
Notikewin, R. 60 57 2N 117 38W
Notituchow 131 24 25N 107 20E
Noto 108 36 52N 15 4E
Noto-Hanto 132 37 0N 137 0E
Notre-Dame, N.B., Can. 39 46 18N 64 46W
Notre-Dame, Qué., Can. 45 45 28N 73 28W
Notre Dame B. 37 49 45N 55 30W
Notre Dame de Koartac 36 60 55N 69 40W
Notre-Dame-de-la-Doré 41 48 43N 72 39W
Notre-Dame-de-l'Île-Perrot 44 45 23N 73 56W
Notre Dame de Lourdes 57 49 32N 98 33W
Notre-Dame-de-Stanbridge 43 45 8N 73 2W
Notre-Dame-des-Bois 41 45 24N 71 4W
Notre-Dame-des-Laurentides 42 46 55N 71 18W
Notre-Dame-du-Bon-Conseil 41 46 0N 72 21W
Notre Dame du Lac 46 46 18N 80 11W
Notre-Dame-du-Lac 41 47 36N 68 48W
Notre-Dame-du-Laus 40 46 5N 75 37W
Notre-Dame-du-Nord 40 47 36N 79 30W
Notre-Dame-du-Portage 41 47 46N 69 37W
Notre-Dame, Les 38 48 10N 68 0W
Nottawasaga B. 46 44 35N 80 15W
Nottaway, R. 36 51 22N 78 55W
Nottingham 94 52 57N 1 10W
Nottingham □ 94 53 10N 1 0W
Nottingham I. 65 63 20N 77 55W
Nottingham Island 65 63 6N 77 50W
Nottoway, R. 72 37 0N 77 45W
Notukeu Cr. 56 49 56N 106 29W
Nouadhibou 114 21 0N 17 0W
Nouakchott 114 18 20N 15 50W
Nouméa 14 22 17S 166 30E
Noupoort 117 31 10S 24 57E
Nouveau Comptoir (Paint Hills) 36 53 0N 78 49W
Nouveau-Quebec, Reg. 36 56 0N 71 0W
Nouvelle 39 48 8N 66 19W
Nouvelle France, C. de 36 62 27N 73 42W
Nouvelle, R. 39 48 7N 66 19W
Nouzonville 101 49 48N 4 44E
Nova Chaves 116 10 50S 21 15E
Nova Cruz 87 6 28S 35 25W
Nova Esperança 89 23 8S 52 13W
Nova Friburgo 89 22 10S 42 30W
Nova Gaia 116 10 10S 17 35E
Nova Iguaçu 89 22 45S 43 28W
Nova Iorque 87 7 0S 44 5W
Nova Lima 89 19 59S 43 51W
Nova Lisboa = Huambo 117 12 42S 15 54E
Nova Mambone 117 21 0S 35 3E
Nova Preixo 117 14 45S 36 22E
Nova Scotia □ 35 45 10N 63 0W
Nova Sofala 117 20 7S 34 48E
Nova Venécia 87 18 45S 40 24W
Nova Zembla I. 65 72 11N 74 50W
Novalorque 87 6 48S 44 0W
Novar 46 45 27N 79 15W
Novara 108 45 27N 8 36E
Novato 80 38 6N 122 35W
Novaya Lyalya 120 58 50N 60 35E
Novaya Sibir, O. 121 75 10N 150 0E
Novaya Zemlya 120 75 0N 56 0E
Nové Zámky 107 48 2N 18 8E
Novelty 76 40 1N 92 12W
Novgorod 120 58 30N 31 25E
Novi-Pazar 109 43 25N 27 15E
Novi Sad 109 45 18N 19 52E
Novinger 76 40 14N 92 43W
Nôvo Hamburgo 89 29 37S 51 7W
Novo Luso 127 4 3S 126 6E
Novoataysk 120 53 30N 84 0E
Novocherkassk 120 47 27N 40 5E
Novokazalinsk 120 45 40N 61 40E
Novokuznetsk 120 54 0N 87 10E
Novomoskovsk 120 54 5N 38 15E
Novorossiysk 120 44 43N 37 52E
Novosibirsk 120 55 0N 83 5E
Novosibirskiye Ostrava 121 75 0N 140 0E
Novska 108 45 19N 17 0E
Novyy Port 120 67 40N 72 30E
Now Shahr 123 36 40N 51 40E
Nowgong 125 26 20N 92 50E
Nowingi 136 34 33S 142 15E
Nowra 136 34 53S 150 35E
Nowy Sącz 107 49 40N 20 41E
Nowy Tomyśl 106 52 19N 16 10E
Noxen 71 41 25N 76 4W
Noxon 78 48 0N 115 54W
Noyant 100 47 30N 0 6E
Noyers 101 47 40N 4 0E
Noyes, I. 54 55 30N 133 40W
Noyon 101 49 34N 3 0E
Nriquinha 117 16 0S 21 25E
Nsanje 117 16 55S 35 12E
Nuanetsi 117 21 15S 30 48E
Nubian Desert 115 21 30N 33 30E
Nûbîya, Es Sahrâ En 115 21 30N 33 30E
Ñuble □ 88 37 0S 72 0W
Nuboai 127 2 10S 136 30E
Nudo Ausangate, Mt. 86 13 45S 71 10W
Nudo de Vilcanota 86 14 30S 70 0W
Nueces, R. 75 28 18N 98 39W
Nueltin L. 55 60 30N 99 30W
Nueva Antioquia 86 6 5N 69 26W
Nueva Casas Grandes 82 30 25N 107 55W
Nueva Esparta □ 86 11 0N 64 0W
Nueva Gerona 84 21 53N 82 49W
Nueva Imperial 90 38 45S 72 58W
Nueva Palmira 88 33 52S 58 20W
Nueva Rosita 82 28 0N 101 20W
Nueva San Salvador 84 13 40N 89 25W
Nuéve de Julio 88 35 30S 61 0W
Nuevitas 84 21 30N 77 20W
Nuevo, Golfo 90 43 0S 64 30W
Nuevo Guerrero 83 26 34N 99 15W
Nuevo Laredo 83 27 30N 99 40W
Nuevo León □ 82 25 0N 100 0W
Nuevo Rocafuerte 86 0 55S 76 50W
Nugget Pt. 133 46 27S 169 50E
Nugssuaq Pen. 65 70 30N 53 0W
Nuhaka 133 39 3S 177 45E
Nuhurowa, I. 127 5 30S 132 45E
Nuits-St.-Georges 101 47 10N 4 56E
Nukey Bluff, Mt. 134 32 32S 135 40E
Nukus 120 42 20N 59 40E
Nulato 67 64 40N 158 10W
Nulki L. 62 53 55N 124 7W
Nulla Nulla 136 33 47S 141 28E
Nullagine 134 21 53S 120 6E
Nullarbor Plain 134 30 45S 129 0E
Numan 114 9 29N 12 3E
Numata 132 36 45N 139 4E
Numazu 132 35 7N 138 51E
Numfoor, I. 127 1 0S 134 50E
Numurkah 136 36 0S 145 26E
Nunaksaluk I. 36 55 49N 60 20W
Nuneaton 95 52 32N 1 29W
Nungan 130 44 29N 125 10E
Nungesser L. 52 51 28N 93 30W
Nunivak I. 67 60 0N 166 0W
Nunkiang 129 49 11N 125 12E
Nunkun, Mt. 124 33 57N 76 8E
Nunspeet 105 52 21N 5 45E
Nuorgam 108 70 5N 27 51E
Nuquí 86 5 42N 77 17W
Nurcoung 136 36 45S 141 42E
Nuremburg = Nürnberg 106 49 26N 11 5E
Nuri 82 28 2N 109 22W
Nürnberg 106 49 26N 11 5E
Nusa Barung 127 8 22S 113 20E
Nusa Kambangan 127 7 47S 109 0E
Nusa Tenggara □ 126 7 30S 117 0E
Nusa Tenggara Barat 126 8 50S 117 30E
Nusa Tenggara Timur 127 9 30S 122 0E
Nushki 124 29 35N 65 65E
Nut L. 56 52 22N 103 42W
Nutak 36 57 28N 61 52W
Nuvuk Is. 36 62 24N 78 3W
Nuwakot 125 28 10N 83 55E
Nuweveldberge 117 32 10S 21 45E
Nuyts Arch. 134 32 12S 133 20E
Nuyts, Pt. 134 35 4S 116 38E
Nyaake (Webo) 114 4 52N 7 37W
Nyabing 134 33 30S 118 7E
Nyack 71 41 5N 73 57W
Nyagyn 120 62 8N 63 36E
Nyah West 136 35 11S 143 21E
Nyahanga 116 2 20S 33 37E
Nyahururu 116 0 2N 36 27E
Nyâlâ 115 12 2N 24 58E
Nyarling, R. 54 60 41N 113 23W
Nyasa, L. = Malawi, L. 117 12 0S 34 30E
Nybro 111 56 44N 15 55E
Nyda 120 66 40N 73 10E
Nyenchen Tanglha Shan 129 30 30N 95 0E
Nyeri 116 0 23S 36 56E
Nyíregyháza 107 48 0N 21 47E
Nykarleby (Uusikaarlepyy) 110 63 32N 22 31E
Nykøbing 111 54 56N 11 52E
Nylstroom 117 24 42S 28 22E
Nynäshamn 111 58 54N 17 57E
Nyngan 136 31 30S 147 8E
Nyons 103 44 22N 5 10E
Nysa 107 50 40N 17 22E
Nysa, R. 106 52 4N 14 46E
Nyssa 78 43 56N 117 2W
Nyurba 121 63 17N 118 20E
Nzega 116 4 10S 33 12E

O

O-Shima 132 34 44N 139 24E
Oacoma 74 43 50N 99 26W
Oahe 74 44 33N 100 29W
Oahe Dam 74 44 28N 100 25W
Oahe Res 74 45 30N 100 15W
Oahu I. 67 21 30N 158 0W
Oak Bay, B.C., Can. 63 48 26N 123 18W
Oak Bay, N.B., Can. 39 45 14N 67 12W
Oak Bluff 58 49 46N 97 19W
Oak Creek, U.S.A. 77 42 52N 87 55W
Oak Creek, Colo., U.S.A. 78 40 15N 106 59W
Oak Harb. 80 48 20N 122 38W
Oak Hill, Can. 39 45 20N 67 20W
Oak Hill, U.S.A. 72 38 0N 81 7W
Oak I. 52 46 57N 90 51W
Oak Lake 57 49 46N 100 38W
Oak Lawn 77 41 43N 87 44W
Oak Park 72 41 55N 87 45W
Oak Point 57 50 30N 98 1W
Oak Ridge 73 36 1N 84 5W
Oak Ridges 50 43 57N 79 28W
Oak River 57 50 8N 100 26W
Oak View 81 34 24N 119 18W
Oakbank 58 49 57N 96 51W
Oakdale, Calif., U.S.A. 80 37 49N 120 56W
Oakdale, La., U.S.A. 75 30 50N 92 38W
Oakengates 94 52 42N 2 29W
Oakes 74 46 14N 98 4W
Oakesdale 78 47 11N 117 9W
Oakford 76 40 6N 89 58W
Oakham 94 52 40N 0 43W
Oakhurst 80 37 19N 119 40W
Oakland, Can. 49 43 2N 80 20W
Oakland, Calif., U.S.A. 80 37 50N 122 18W
Oakland, Ill., U.S.A. 77 39 39N 88 2W
Oakland City 77 38 20N 87 20W
Oakleigh 136 37 54S 145 6E
Oakley 78 42 14N 113 55W
Oakridge 78 43 47N 122 31W
Oaktown 77 38 52N 87 27W
Oakville, Can. 50 43 27N 79 41W
Oakville, U.S.A. 80 46 50N 123 14W
Oakville, R. 49 43 27N 79 41W
Oakwood, Ohio, U.S.A. 77 39 43N 84 11W
Oakwood, Ohio, U.S.A. 77 41 6N 84 23W
Oakwood, Tex., U.S.A. 75 31 35N 95 47W
Oamaru 133 45 5S 170 59E
Oasis, Calif., U.S.A. 81 33 28N 116 6W
Oasis, Nev., U.S.A. 80 37 29N 117 55W
Oates Coast 91 69 0S 160 0E
Oatman 81 35 1N 114 19W
Oaxaca 83 17 2N 96 40W
Oaxaca □ 83 17 0N 97 0W
Ob, R. 120 62 40N 66 0E
Oba 53 49 4N 84 7W
Oba L. 53 48 40N 84 16W
Obakamiga L. 53 49 9N 85 9W
Obalski, L. 40 48 43N 77 58W
Obamsca, L. 40 50 24N 78 16W
Oban, N.Z. 133 46 55S 168 10E
Oban, U.K. 96 56 25N 5 30W
Obatanga Prov. Park 53 48 20N 85 10W
Obatogamau L. 34 49 34N 74 26W
Obbia 115 5 25N 48 30E
Obed 60 53 30N 117 10W
Obedjwan 40 48 40N 74 56W
Obeh 124 34 28N 63 10E
Obera 89 27 21S 55 2W
Oberhausen 105 51 28N 6 50E
Oberlin, Kans., U.S.A. 74 39 52N 100 31W
Oberlin, La., U.S.A. 75 30 42N 92 42W
Oberlin, Ohio, U.S.A. 70 41 15N 82 10W
Obernai 101 48 28N 7 30E
Oberon 136 33 45S 149 52E
Obi, Kepulauan 127 1 30S 127 30E
Óbidos 87 1 50S 55 30W
Obihiro 132 42 25N 143 12E
Objat 102 45 16N 1 24E
Oblong 77 39 0N 87 55W
Obluchye 121 49 10N 130 50E
Obo 116 5 20N 26 32E
Obonga L. 52 49 57N 89 22W
Oboyan 120 51 20N 36 28E
Obozerskaya 120 63 20N 40 15E
Observatory Inlet 54 55 25N 129 45W
Obshchi Syrt 93 52 0N 53 0E
Obskaya Guba 120 70 0N 73 0E
Ocala 73 29 11N 82 5W
Ocampo 82 28 9N 108 8W
Ocaña 104 39 55N 3 30W
Ocanomowoc 74 43 7N 88 30W
Ocate 75 36 12N 104 59W
Occidental, Cordillera 86 5 0N 76 0W
Ocean City, N.J., U.S.A. 72 39 18N 74 34W
Ocean City, Wash., U.S.A. 80 47 4N 124 10W
Ocean Falls 62 52 18N 127 48W
Ocean I. 14 0 45S 169 50E
Ocean Park, Can. 66 49 2N 122 52W
Ocean Park, U.S.A. 80 46 30N 124 2W
Oceanlake 78 45 0N 124 0W
Oceano 81 35 6N 120 37W
Oceanport 71 40 20N 74 3W
Oceanside 81 33 13N 117 26W
Ochil Hills 96 56 14N 3 40W
Ochre River 57 51 4N 99 47W
Ocilla 73 31 35N 83 12W
Ocmulgee, R. 73 32 0N 83 19W
Oconee, R. 73 32 30N 82 55W
Oconomowoc 77 43 6N 88 30W
Oconto 72 44 52N 87 53W
Oconto Falls 72 44 52N 88 10W
Ocós 84 14 31N 92 11W
Ocosingo 83 18 4N 92 15W
Ocotal 84 13 41N 86 41W
Ocotlán 82 20 21N 102 42W
Octave 79 34 10N 112 43W
Octeville 100 49 38N 1 40W
Octyabrskoy Revolyutsii, Os. 121 79 30N 97 0E
Ocumare del Tuy 86 10 7N 66 46W
Ocussi 127 9 20S 124 30E
Odanah 52 46 38N 90 41W
Ódáoahraun 110 65 5N 17 0W
Odawara 132 35 20N 139 6E
Odda 111 60 3N 6 35E
Odei, R. 55 56 6N 96 54W
Odell 77 41 0N 88 31W
Ödemiş 122 38 15N 28 0E
Odense 111 55 22N 10 23E
Oder, R. 106 53 0N 14 12E
Odessa, Ont., Can. 47 44 17N 76 43W
Odessa, Sask., Can. 56 50 17N 103 47W
Odessa, U.S.A. 76 39 0N 93 57W
Odessa, Tex., U.S.A. 75 31 51N 102 23W
Odessa, Wash., U.S.A. 78 47 25N 118 35W
O'Donnell 75 33 0N 101 48W
Odorheiul Secuiesc 107 46 21N 25 21E
Odra, R. 106 52 40N 14 28E
Odžak 109 45 3N 18 18E
Odzi 117 19 0S 32 20E
Oeiras 87 7 0S 42 8W
Oelrichs 74 43 11N 103 14W
O'Fallon 76 38 50N 90 43W
Ofanto, R. 108 41 8N 15 50E
Offaly □ 97 53 15N 7 30W
Offenbach 106 50 6N 8 46E
Offranville 100 49 52N 1 0E
Ofotfjorden 110 68 27N 16 40E
Ogahalla 53 50 6N 85 51W
Ōgaki 132 35 21N 136 37E
Ogallala 74 41 12N 101 40W
Ogascanane, L. 40 47 5N 78 25W
Ogbomosho 114 8 1N 3 29E
Ogden, Can. 59 51 0N 114 0W
Ogden, Iowa, U.S.A. 76 42 3N 94 0W
Ogden, Utah, U.S.A. 78 41 13N 112 1W
Ogdensburg 71 44 40N 75 27W
Ogeechee, R. 73 32 30N 81 32W
Ogema 56 49 35N 104 55W
Ogilby 81 32 49N 114 50W
Ogilvie Mts. 64 65 0N 140 0W
Oglesby 76 41 21N 89 3W
Oglio, R. 108 45 15N 10 15E
Ogmore Vale 95 51 35N 3 32W
Ognon, R. 101 47 16N 5 28E
Ogoki 53 51 38N 85 58W
Ogoki L. 53 50 50N 87 10W
Ogoki, R. 53 51 38N 85 57W
Ogoki Res. 52 50 45N 88 15W
Ogooué, R. 116 1 0S 10 0E
Ogowe, R. = Ogooué, R. 116 1 0S 10 0E
Ohai 133 44 55S 168 0E
Ohakune 133 39 24S 175 24E
Ohau, L. 133 44 15S 169 53E
Oheida 76 41 4N 90 13W
Ohey 105 50 26N 5 8E
O'Higgins □ 88 34 15S 71 1W
Ohio □ 72 40 20N 83 0W
Ohio City 77 40 46N 84 37W
Ohio, R. 72 38 0N 86 0W
Ohre, R. 106 50 10N 12 30E
Ohridsko, Jezero 109 41 8N 20 52E
Ohsweken 49 43 4N 80 7W
Oil City 70 41 26N 79 40W
Oil Springs 46 42 47N 82 7W
Oildale 81 35 25N 119 1W
Oise □ 101 49 28N 2 30E
Oise, R. 101 49 53N 3 50E
Oisterwijk 105 51 35N 5 12E
Oita 132 33 14N 131 36E
Oita-ken □ 132 33 15N 131 30E
Oiticica 87 5 3S 41 5W
Ojai 81 34 28N 119 16W
Ojinaga 82 29 34N 104 25W
Ojocaliente 82 30 25N 106 30W
Ojos del Salado 88 27 0S 68 40W
Oka 44 45 28N 74 5W
Oka, R. 120 56 20N 43 59E
Oka-sur-le-Lac 44 45 28N 74 6W
Okahandja 117 22 0S 16 59E
Okak 36 57 33N 61 58W
Okak Is. 36 57 30N 61 30W
Okanagan L. 63 50 0N 119 30W
Okanagan Mission 63 49 45N 119 30W
Okanagan Mountain Prov. Park 63 49 45N 119 30W
Okanogan 63 48 22N 119 35W
Okanogan, R. 78 48 40N 119 24W
Okarito 133 43 15S 170 9E
Okaukuejo 117 19 10S 16 0E
Okavango, R. = Cubango, R. 117 16 15S 18 0E
Okavango Swamp 117 19 30S 23 0E
Okawville 76 38 26N 89 33W
Okaya 132 36 0N 138 10E
Okayama 132 34 40N 133 54E
Okayama-ken □ 132 35 0N 133 50E
Okazaki 132 34 57N 137 10E
Okeechobee 73 27 16N 80 46W
Okeechobee L. 73 27 0N 80 50W
Okefenokee Swamp 73 30 50N 82 15W
Okehampton 95 50 44N 4 1W

Okha Otago □

Okha **121** 53 40N 143 0 E
Okhotsk **121** 59 20N 143 10 E
Okhotsk, Sea of **121** 55 0N 145 0 E
Okhotskiy Perevoz **121** 61 52N 135 35 E
Okhotsko Kolymskoy **121** 63 0N 157 0 E
Oki no Erabu **131** 27 15N 128 45 E
Oki-Shotō **132** 36 15N 133 15 E
Okiep **117** 29 39 S 17 53 E
Okinawa **131** 26 40N 128 0 E
Okinawa-guntō **131** 26 0N 127 30 E
Oklahoma □ **75** 35 20N 97 30W
Oklahoma City **75** 35 25N 97 30W
Okmulgee **75** 35 38N 96 0W
Okolona, U.S.A. **75** 34 0N 88 45W
Okolona, U.S.A. **77** 38 8N 85 41W
Okondja **116** 0 35 S 13 45 E
Oku **131** 26 35N 127 50 E
Okuru **133** 43 55 S 168 55 E
Okushiri-Tō **132** 42 15N 139 30 E
Ola **75** 35 2N 93 10W
Ólafsfjörður **110** 66 4N 18 39W
Ólafsvík **110** 64 53N 23 43W
Olancha **81** 36 15N 118 1W
Olancha Pk. **81** 36 15N 118 7W
Olanchito **85** 15 30N 86 30W
Öland **111** 56 45N 16 50 E
Olargues **102** 43 34N 2 53 E
Olascoaga **88** 35 15 S 60 39W
Olathe **74** 38 50N 94 50W
Olavarría **88** 36 55 S 60 20W
Ólbia **108** 40 55N 9 30 E
Old Bahama Chan. **84** 22 10N 77 30W
Old Baldy Pk = San Antonio, Mt. **81** 34 17N 117 38W
Old Castile = Castilla la Vieja **104** 41 55N 4 0W
Old Castle **97** 53 46N 7 10W
Old Chelsea **48** 45 30N 75 49W
Old Crow **64** 67 30N 140 5 E
Old Dale **81** 34 8N 115 47W
Old Factory **34** 52 36N 78 43W
Old Forge, N.Y., U.S.A. **71** 43 43N 74 58W
Old Forge, Pa., U.S.A. **71** 41 20N 75 46W
Old Fort, R. **55** 58 36N 110 24W
Old Harbor **67** 57 12N 153 22W
Old Perlican **37** 48 5N 53 1W
Old Speckle, Mt. **71** 44 35N 70 57W
Old Town **35** 45 0N 68 50W
Old Wives L. **56** 50 5N 106 0W
Oldcastle **97** 53 46N 7 10W
Oldenburg **105** 53 10N 8 10 E
Oldham **94** 53 33N 2 8W
Oldman, R. **61** 49 57N 111 42W
Olds **61** 51 50N 114 10W
Olean **70** 42 8N 78 25W
O'Leary **39** 46 42N 64 13W
Olekma, R. **121** 58 0N 121 30 E
Olekminsk **121** 60 40N 120 30 E
Olema **80** 38 3N 122 47W
Olenek **121** 68 20N 112 30 E
Olenek, R. **121** 71 0N 123 50 E
Oléron, I. d' **102** 45 55N 1 15W
Oleśnica **107** 51 13N 17 22 E
Olga **121** 43 50N 135 0 E
Olga, L. **40** 49 47N 77 15W
Olga, Mt. **134** 25 20 S 130 40 E
Olgastretet **17** 78 35N 25 0 E
Olifants, R. **117** 24 5 S 31 20 E
Ólimbos, Óros **109** 40 6N 22 23 E
Olimpia **89** 20 44 S 48 54W
Olimpo □ **88** 20 30 S 58 45W
Olin **76** 42 0N 91 9W
Oliva **88** 32 0 S 63 38W
Olive Hill **77** 38 18N 83 13W
Olivehurst **80** 39 6N 121 34W
Oliveira **87** 20 50 S 44 50W
Olivenza **104** 38 41N 7 9W
Oliver **63** 49 13N 119 30W
Oliver L. **55** 56 56N 103 22W
Ollagüe **88** 21 15 S 68 10W
Olmos, L. **88** 33 25 S 63 19W
Olney, Ill., U.S.A. **77** 38 40N 88 0W
Olney, Tex., U.S.A. **75** 33 25N 98 45W
Olomane, R. **36** 50 14N 60 37W
Olomouc **106** 49 38N 17 12 E
Olongapo **127** 14 50N 120 18 E
Oloron-Ste.-Marie **102** 43 11N 0 38W
Olovyannaya **121** 50 50N 115 10 E
Olsztyn **107** 53 48N 20 29 E
Olt, R. **107** 43 50N 24 40 E
Oltenița **107** 44 7N 26 42 E
Olton **75** 34 16N 102 7W
Oltu **122** 40 35N 41 50 E
Olympia, Greece **109** 37 39N 21 39 E
Olympia, U.S.A. **80** 47 0N 122 58W
Olympic Mts. **80** 47 50N 123 45W
Olympic Nat. Park **80** 47 48N 123 30W
Olympus, Mt. **80** 47 52N 123 40W
Olympus, Mt. = Ólimbos, Óros **109** 40 6N 22 23 E
Olyphant **71** 41 27N 75 36W
Omachi **132** 36 30N 137 50 E
Omagh **97** 54 36N 7 20W
Omagh □ **97** 54 35N 7 15W
Omaha **74** 41 15N 96 0W
Omak **63** 48 24N 119 31W
Omak L. **63** 48 16N 119 23W
Oman ■ **122** 23 0N 58 0 E
Oman, G. of **123** 24 30N 58 30 E
Omaruru **117** 21 26 S 16 0 E
Omate **86** 16 45 S 71 0W
Ombai, Selat **127** 8 30 S 124 50 E
Omboué **116** 1 35 S 9 15 E
Ombrone, R. **108** 42 48N 11 15 E
Omdurmân **115** 15 40N 32 28 E
Omemee **47** 44 18N 78 33W
Ometepe, Isla de **84** 11 32N 85 35W
Ometepec **83** 16 39N 98 23W
Omineca, R. **54** 56 3N 124 16W
Ōmiya **132** 35 54N 139 38 E
Ommanney B. **65** 73 0N 101 0W
Ommen **105** 52 31N 6 26 E
Omsk **120** 55 0N 73 38 E
Omsukchan **121** 62 32N 155 48 E
Omu **130** 43 48N 128 10 E
Omul, Vf. **107** 45 27N 25 29 E
Omura **132** 33 8N 130 0 E
Omuramba, R. **117** 19 10 S 19 20 E
Ōmuta **132** 33 0N 130 26 E
Onaga **74** 39 32N 96 12W
Onakawana **53** 50 36N 81 27W
Onalaska **74** 43 53N 91 14W
Onaman L. **53** 50 0N 87 26W
Onaman, R. **53** 49 59N 88 0W
Onamia **74** 46 4N 93 38W
Onancock **72** 37 42N 75 49W
Onang **127** 3 2 S 118 55 E
Onanole **57** 50 37N 99 58W
Onaping **46** 46 37N 81 25W
Onaping L. **53** 47 3N 81 30W
Onaping, R. **46** 46 37N 81 18W
Onarga **77** 40 43N 88 1W
Onatchiway, L. **41** 49 3N 71 5W
Onavas **82** 28 28N 109 30W
Onawa **74** 42 2N 96 2W
Onaway **46** 45 21N 84 11W
Oncocua **117** 16 30 S 13 40 E
Onda **104** 39 55N 0 17W
Öndörhaan **129** 47 19N 110 39 E
Ondorhaan **130** 47 22N 110 31 E
Ondverdarnes **110** 64 52N 24 0W
One Tree **136** 34 13 S 144 42 E
Onega **120** 64 0N 38 10 E
Onega, G. of = Onezhskaya G. **120** 64 30N 37 0 E
Onega, L. = Onezhskoye Oz. **120** 62 0N 35 30 E
Onehunga **133** 36 55N 174 30 E
Oneida **71** 43 5N 75 40W
Oneida L. **71** 43 12N 76 0W
O'Neill **74** 42 30N 98 38W
Onekotan, Ostrov **121** 49 59N 154 0 E
Oneonta, Ala., U.S.A. **73** 33 58N 86 29W
Oneonta, N.Y., U.S.A. **71** 42 26N 75 5W
Onezhskoye Ozero **120** 62 0N 35 30 E
Ongarue **133** 38 42 S 175 19 E
Ongiyn Gol **130** 45 56N 103 0 E
Ongole **124** 15 33N 80 2 E
Onida **74** 44 42N 100 5W
Onilahy, R. **117** 23 30 S 44 0 E
Onion Lake **56** 53 43N 110 0W
Onitsha **114** 6 6N 6 42 E
Onoda **132** 33 59N 131 11 E
Onondaga **49** 43 7N 80 7W
Onoway **60** 53 42N 114 12W
Onslow **134** 21 40 S 115 0 E
Onslow B. **73** 34 30N 77 0W
Onstwedde **105** 52 2N 7 4 E
Ontake-San **132** 35 53N 137 29 E
Ontario, Calif., U.S.A. **81** 34 2N 117 40W
Ontario, Oreg., U.S.A. **78** 44 1N 117 1W
Ontario □ **34** 52 0N 88 10W
Ontario, L. **48** 43 40N 78 0W
Ontonagon **52** 46 52N 89 19W
Onyx **81** 35 41N 118 14W
Oodnadatta **134** 27 33 S 135 30 E
Ooglaamie **17** 72 1N 157 0W
Ookala **67** 20 1N 155 17W
Ooldea **134** 30 27 S 131 50 E
Oona River **62** 53 57N 130 16W
Oostende **105** 51 15N 2 50 E
Oosterhout **105** 51 39N 4 52 E
Oosterschelde **105** 51 33N 4 0 E
Ootacamund **124** 11 30N 76 44 E
Ootmarsum **105** 52 24N 6 54 E
Ootsa L. **62** 53 50N 126 20W
Ootsa Lake **62** 53 50N 126 5W
Opala, U.S.S.R. **121** 52 15N 156 15 E
Opala, Zaïre **116** 1 11 S 24 45 E
Opanake **124** 6 35N 80 40 E
Opasatica, L. **40** 48 5N 79 18W
Opasatika **53** 49 30N 82 50W
Opasatika L. **53** 49 4N 83 6W
Opasatika, R. **53** 50 25N 82 25W
Opasquia **55** 53 16N 93 34W
Opataca, L. **40** 50 22N 74 55W
Opava **107** 49 57N 17 58 E
Opawica, L. **40** 49 35N 75 55W
Opelousas **75** 30 35N 92 0W
Opémisca L. **36** 50 0N 75 0W
Opémisca, L. **40** 49 56N 74 52W
Opeongo L. **47** 45 42N 78 23W
Opheim **56** 48 52N 106 30W
Ophir **67** 63 10N 156 40W
Ophthalmia Ra. **134** 23 15 S 119 30 E
Opinaca L. **36** 52 39N 76 20W
Opinaca, R. **36** 52 15N 78 2W
Opiscoteo, L. **36** 53 10N 68 10W
Opiskotish, L. **36** 53 10N 67 50W
Opladen **105** 51 4N 7 2 E
Opocopa, L. **38** 52 38N 66 35W
Opole **107** 50 42N 17 58 E
Oporto = Porto **104** 41 8N 8 40W
Opotiki **133** 38 1 S 177 19 E
Opp **73** 31 19N 86 13W
Oppland fylke □ **111** 61 15N 9 30 E
Opua **133** 35 19 S 174 9 E
Opunake **133** 39 26 S 173 52 E
Oquawka **76** 40 56N 90 57W
Oracle **79** 32 45N 110 46W
Oradea **107** 47 2N 21 58 E
Öræfajökull **110** 64 2N 16 39W
Orai **124** 25 58N 79 30 E
Oraison **103** 43 55N 5 55 E
Oran, Alg. **114** 35 37N 0 39W
Oran, Argent. **88** 23 10 S 64 20W
Orange, Austral. **136** 33 15 S 149 7 E
Orange, France **103** 44 8N 4 47 E
Orange, Calif., U.S.A. **81** 33 47N 117 51W
Orange, Mass., U.S.A. **71** 42 35N 72 15W
Orange, Tex., U.S.A. **75** 30 10N 93 50W
Orange, Va., U.S.A. **72** 38 17N 78 5W
Orange, C. **87** 4 20N 51 30W
Orange Cove **80** 36 38N 119 19W
Orange Free State □ **117** 28 30 S 27 0 E
Orange Grove **75** 27 57N 97 57W
Orange, R. = Oranje, R. **117** 28 30 S 18 0 E
Orange Walk **83** 18 6N 88 33W
Orangeburg **73** 33 35N 80 53W
Orangeville, Can. **49** 43 55N 80 5W
Orangeville, U.S.A. **76** 42 28N 89 39W
Oranienburg **106** 52 45N 13 15 E
Oranje, R. **117** 28 30 S 18 0 E
Oranje Vrystaat □ **117** 28 30 S 27 0 E
Oranjemund (Orange Mouth) **117** 28 32 S 16 29 E
Orapa **117** 21 13 S 25 25 E
Oras **127** 12 9N 125 22 E
Orb, R. **102** 43 17N 3 17 E
Orbec **100** 49 1N 0 23 E
Orbetello **108** 42 26N 11 11 E
Orbost **136** 37 40 S 148 29 E
Orcas **63** 48 36N 122 57W
Orchies **101** 50 28N 3 14 E
Orchila, Isla **85** 11 48N 66 10W
Orchy, Bridge of **96** 56 30N 4 46W
Orchy, Glen **96** 56 27N 4 52W
Orcutt **81** 34 52N 120 27W
Ord, Mt. **134** 17 20 S 125 34 E
Ord, R. **134** 15 33 S 128 35 E
Orderville **79** 37 18N 112 43W
Ordos **130** 39 25N 108 45 E
Ordu **122** 40 55N 37 53 E
Ordway **74** 38 15N 103 42W
Ordzhonikidze **120** 43 0N 44 35 E
Örebro **111** 59 20N 15 18 E
Örebro län □ **111** 59 27N 15 0 E
Oregon, U.S.A. **77** 41 38N 83 25W
Oregon, Ill., U.S.A. **76** 42 1N 89 20W
Oregon, Wis., U.S.A. **76** 42 56N 89 23W
Oregon □ **78** 44 0N 120 0W
Oregon City **80** 45 21N 122 35W
Orel **120** 52 57N 36 3 E
Orem **78** 40 27N 111 45W
Orenburg **120** 51 45N 55 6 E
Orense **104** 42 19N 7 55W
Orepuki **133** 46 19 S 167 46 E
Orford Ness **95** 52 6N 1 31 E
Orgon **103** 43 47N 5 3 E
Orhon Gol **129** 49 30N 106 0 E
Orient **76** 41 12N 94 25W
Orient Bay **34** 49 20N 88 10W
Oriente **88** 38 44 S 60 37W
Origny-Ste.-Benoîte **101** 49 50N 3 30 E
Orihuela **104** 38 7N 0 55W
Orillia **46** 44 40N 79 24W
Orinoco, Delta del **85** 8 30N 61 0W
Orinoco, R. **86** 5 45N 67 40W
Orion, Can. **55** 49 28N 110 49W
Orion, U.S.A. **76** 41 21N 90 23W
Orissa □ **125** 21 0N 85 0 E
Oristano **108** 39 54N 8 35 E
Oristano, Golfo di **108** 39 50N 8 22 E
Orizaba **83** 18 50N 97 10W
Orkanger **110** 63 18N 9 52 E
Orkla, R. **110** 63 18N 9 51 E
Orkney □ **96** 59 0N 3 0W
Orkney Is. **96** 59 0N 3 0W
Orland, U.S.A. **77** 41 47N 85 12W
Orland, Calif., U.S.A. **80** 39 46N 122 12W
Orlando **73** 28 30N 81 25W
Orléanais **101** 48 0N 2 0 E
Orléans **101** 47 54N 1 52 E
Orleans **71** 44 49N 72 10W
Orléans, Î. d' **42** 46 54N 70 58W
Ormara **124** 25 16N 64 33 E
Ormiston **56** 49 44N 105 24W
Ormoc **127** 11 0N 124 37 E
Ormond, N.Z. **133** 38 33 S 177 56 E
Ormond, U.S.A. **73** 29 13N 81 5W
Ormstown **43** 45 8N 74 0W
Ornans **101** 47 7N 6 10 E
Orne □ **100** 48 40N 0 0 E
Örnsköldsvik **110** 63 17N 18 40 E
Oro Grande **81** 34 36N 117 20W
Oro, R. **82** 26 8N 105 58W
Orocué **86** 4 48N 71 20W
Orogrande **79** 32 20N 106 4W
Oromocto **39** 45 54N 66 29W
Oromocto, L. **39** 45 36N 67 0W
Oron, R. **121** 69 21N 95 43 E
Orono **47** 43 59N 78 37W
Oroquieta **127** 8 32N 123 44 E
Orós **87** 6 15 S 38 55W
Orosei **108** 40 20N 9 40 E
Orotukan **121** 62 16N 151 42 E
Oroville, Calif., U.S.A. **80** 39 31N 121 30W
Oroville, Wash., U.S.A. **63** 48 58N 119 30W
Oroville, Res. **80** 39 33N 121 29W
Orr **52** 48 3N 92 48W
Orrick **76** 39 13N 94 7W
Orrville **70** 40 50N 81 46W
Orsainville **42** 46 51N 71 14W
Orsha **120** 54 30N 30 25 E
Orsk **120** 51 12N 58 34 E
Orşova **107** 44 41N 22 25 E
Ortegal, C. **104** 43 43N 7 52W
Orthez **102** 43 29N 0 48W
Ortigueira **104** 43 40N 7 50W
Orting **80** 47 6N 122 12W
Ortles, mt. **108** 46 31N 10 33 E
Ortón, R. **86** 10 50 S 67 0W
Ortona **108** 42 21N 14 24 E
Oruro **86** 18 0 S 67 19W
Orvault **100** 47 17N 1 38W
Orvieto **108** 42 43N 12 8 E
Orwell **70** 41 32N 80 52W
Orwell, R. **95** 52 2N 1 12 E
Oryakhovo **109** 43 40N 23 57 E
Osa, Pen. de **84** 8 0N 84 0W
Osage, Iowa, U.S.A. **74** 43 15N 92 50W
Osage, Wyo., U.S.A. **74** 43 59N 104 25W
Osage City **74** 38 43N 95 51W
Osage, R. **76** 38 15N 92 30W
Ōsaka **132** 34 30N 135 30 E
Osaka-fu □ **132** 34 40N 135 30 E
Osawatomie **74** 38 30N 94 55W
Osawin, R. **53** 49 45N 85 19W
Osborne **74** 39 30N 98 45W
Osborne Corners **49** 43 13N 80 16W
Osceola, Ark., U.S.A. **75** 35 40N 90 0W
Osceola, Iowa, U.S.A. **76** 41 0N 93 20W
Osceola, Mo., U.S.A. **76** 38 3N 93 42W
Oscoda-Au-Sable **46** 44 26N 83 20W
Osgood **77** 39 8N 85 18W
Osgoode **47** 45 8N 75 36W
Osh **120** 40 37N 72 49 E
Oshawa **51** 43 50N 78 50W
Oshawa Cr. **51** 43 52N 78 50W
Oshikango **117** 17 9 S 16 10 E
Oshkosh, Nebr., U.S.A. **72** 41 27N 102 20W
Oshkosh, Wis., U.S.A. **72** 44 3N 88 35W
Oshogbo **114** 7 48N 4 37 E
Oshwe **116** 3 25 S 19 28 E
Osijek **109** 45 34N 18 41 E
Oskaloosa **76** 41 18N 92 40W
Oskarshamn **111** 57 15N 16 27 E
Oskélanéo **40** 48 5N 75 15W
Osler **56** 52 22N 106 33W
Oslo **111** 59 55N 10 45 E
Oslob **127** 9 31N 123 26 E
Oslofjorden **111** 59 20N 10 35 E
Osmanabad **124** 18 5N 76 10 E
Osmaniye **122** 37 5N 36 10 E
Osnabrück **105** 52 16N 8 2 E
Osnaburgh L. **52** 51 12N 90 9W
Osorio **89** 29 53 S 50 17W
Osorno **90** 40 25 S 73 0W
Osorno, Vol. **90** 41 0N 72 30W
Osoyoos **63** 49 0N 119 30W
Osoyoos L. **63** 49 0N 119 27W
Ospika, R. **54** 56 20N 124 0W
Osprey Reef **135** 13 52 S 146 36 E
Ospringe **49** 43 42N 80 7W
Oss **105** 51 46N 5 32 E
Ossa, Mt. **135** 41 52 S 146 3 E
Ossa, Oros **109** 39 47N 22 42 E
Ossabaw I. **73** 31 45N 81 8W
Ossineke **46** 44 55N 83 26W
Ossining **71** 41 9N 73 50W
Ossipee **71** 43 41N 71 9W
Ossokmanuan L. **36** 53 25N 65 0W
Ossora **121** 59 20N 163 13 E
Ostaboningue, L. **40** 47 9N 78 53W
Ostend = Oostende **105** 51 15N 2 50 E
Österdalälven **111** 61 30N 13 45 E
Östergötlands Län □ **111** 58 35N 15 45 E
Östersund **110** 63 10N 14 38 E
Østfold fylke □ **111** 59 25N 11 25 E
Ostfriesische Inseln **106** 53 45N 7 15 E
Ostfriesland **105** 53 27N 7 30 E
Ostia **108** 41 40N 12 20 E
Ostrava **107** 49 51N 18 18 E
Ostróda **107** 53 42N 19 58 E
Ostrołeka **107** 53 4N 21 38 E
Ostrów Mazowiecka **107** 52 50N 21 51 E
Ostrów Wielkopolski **107** 51 36N 17 44 E
Ostrowiec-Swietokrzyski **107** 50 55N 21 22 E
O'Sullivan L. **53** 50 25N 87 2W
Osumi-Kaikyō **132** 30 55N 131 0 E
Osumi-Shotō **132** 30 30N 130 45 E
Osuna **104** 37 14N 5 8W
Oswego **71** 43 29N 76 30W
Oswestry **94** 52 52N 3 3W
Otago □ **133** 45 20 S 169 20 E

Otago Harb **Panhandle**

Otago Harb. **133** 45 47S 170 42E
Otake **132** 34 12N 132 13E
Otaki **133** 40 45S 175 10E
Otaru **132** 43 10N 141 0E
Otaru-Wan **132** 43 25N 141 1E
Otavalo **86** 0 20N 78 20W
Otavi **117** 19 40S 17 24E
Otelnuk L. **36** 56 9N 68 12W
Othello **78** 46 53N 119 8W
Otira Gorge **133** 42 53S 171 33E
Otis **74** 40 12N 102 58W
Otish, Mts. **36** 52 22N 70 30W
Otjiwarongo **117** 20 30S 16 33E
Otorohanga **133** 38 12S 175 14E
Otoskwin, R. **34** 52 13N 88 6W
Otosquen **57** 53 17N 102 1W
Otranto **109** 40 9N 18 28E
Otranto, C.d' **109** 40 7N 18 30E
Otranto, Str. of **109** 40 15N 18 40E
Otsego **77** 42 27N 85 42W
Ottawa, Can. **48** 45 27N 75 42W
Ottawa, Ill., U.S.A. **77** 41 20N 88 55W
Ottawa, Kans., U.S.A. **74** 38 40N 95 10W
Ottawa, Ohio, U.S.A. **77** 41 1N 84 3W
Ottawa-Carleton □ **48** 45 23N 75 40W
Ottawa International Airport **48** 45 19N 75 40W
Ottawa Is. **23** 59 35N 80 16W
Ottawa, R. **44** 45 20N 73 55W
Otter L. **55** 55 35N 104 39W
Otter Lake **46** 43 13N 83 28W
Otter Rapids, Ont., Can. **53** 50 11N 81 39W
Otter Rapids, Sask., Can. **55** 55 38N 104 44W
Otterbein **77** 40 29N 87 6W
Otterburn Park **45** 45 32N 73 13W
Otterville, Can. **46** 42 55N 80 36W
Otterville, U.S.A. **76** 38 42N 93 0W
Ottoville **77** 40 57N 84 22W
Ottumwa **76** 41 0N 92 25W
Otway, Bahia **90** 53 30S 74 0W
Otway, C. **136** 38 52S 143 30E
Otwock **107** 52 5N 21 20E
Ötztaler Alpen **106** 46 58N 11 0E
Ou, R. **128** 20 4N 102 13E
Ou-Sammyaku **132** 39 20N 140 35E
Ouachita Mts. **75** 34 50N 94 30W
Ouachita, R. **75** 33 0N 92 15W
Ouadda **116** 8 15N 22 20E
Ouagadougou **114** 12 25N 1 30W
Ouanda Djallé **116** 8 55N 22 53E
Ouango **116** 4 19N 22 30E
Ouareau, L., Rés. **41** 46 17N 74 9W
Ouargla **114** 31 59N 5 25E
Ouasiemsca, R. **41** 49 0N 72 30W
Oubangi, R. **116** 1 0N 17 50E
Ouche, R. **101** 47 11N 5 10E
Oude Rijn, R. **105** 52 12N 4 24E
Oudenaarde **105** 50 50N 3 37E
Oudenbosch **105** 51 35N 4 32E
Oudon **100** 47 22N 1 19W
Oudon, R. **100** 47 47N 1 2W
Oudtshoorn **117** 33 35S 22 14E
Ouessant, Île d' **100** 48 28N 5 6W
Ouesso **116** 1 37N 16 5E
Ouest, Pte. **38** 49 52N 64 40W
Ougrée **105** 50 36N 5 32E
Ouimet **34** 48 43N 88 35W
Ouistreham **100** 49 17N 0 18W
Oulu **110** 65 1N 25 29E
Oulu □ **110** 65 10N 27 20E
Oulujärvi **110** 64 25N 27 0E
Oulujoki **110** 64 45N 26 30E
Ouray **79** 38 3N 107 48W
Ouricuri **87** 7 53S 40 5W
Ourinhos **89** 23 0S 49 54W
Ouro Fino **89** 22 16S 46 25W
Ouro Prêto **89** 20 20S 43 30W
Ourthe, R. **105** 50 29N 5 35E
Ouse, Great, R. **94** 52 12N 0 7E
Ouse, Little, R. **95** 52 25N 0 20E
Ouse, R., Sussex, U.K. **95** 50 58N 0 3E
Ouse, R., Yorks., U.K. **94** 54 3N 0 7E
Oust **102** 42 52N 1 13E
Oust, R. **100** 48 8N 2 49W
Oustic **49** 43 42N 80 15W
Outaouais, R. **48** 45 28N 75 38W
Outardes **41** 50 20N 69 10W
Outardes, R. **41** 49 24N 69 30W
Outer Hebrides, Is. **96** 57 30N 7 40W
Outer I., Can. **36** 51 10N 58 35W
Outer I., U.S.A. **52** 47 5N 90 30W
Outjo **117** 20 5S 16 7E
Outlook, Can. **56** 51 30N 107 0W
Outlook, U.S.A. **56** 48 53N 104 46W
Outreau **101** 50 40N 1 36E
Outremount **44** 45 31N 73 37W
Ouyen **136** 35 1S 142 22E
Ouzouer-le-Marché **100** 47 54N 1 32E
Ovalau, I. **133** 17 40S 178 48E
Ovalle **88** 30 33S 71 18W
Ovamboland = Owambo **117** 17 20S 16 30E
Ovar **104** 40 51N 8 40W
Ovejas **86** 9 32N 75 14W
Ovens, R. **136** 36 2S 146 12E
Overflakkee **105** 51 44N 4 10E
Overflowing, R. **57** 53 8N 101 5W
Overijssel □ **105** 52 25N 6 35E
Overland **76** 38 41N 90 23W
Overland Park **76** 38 58N 94 40W
Overton **81** 36 32N 114 31W
Övertorneå **110** 66 23N 23 40E
Ovid, Colo., U.S.A. **74** 41 0N 102 17W
Ovid, Mich., U.S.A. **46** 43 1N 84 22W
Oviedo **104** 43 25N 5 50W
Ovruch **120** 51 25N 28 45E
Owaka **133** 46 27S 169 40E
Owambo **117** 17 20S 16 30E
Owase **132** 34 7N 136 5E
Owatonna **74** 44 3N 93 17W
Owego **71** 42 6N 76 17W
Owen Sound **46** 44 35N 80 55W
Owendo **116** 0 17N 9 30E
Owens L. **81** 36 20N 118 0W
Owens, R. **80** 36 32N 117 59W
Owensboro **77** 37 40N 87 5W
Owensville, U.S.A. **77** 38 16N 87 41W
Owensville, Mo., U.S.A. **76** 38 20N 91 30W
Owenton **77** 38 32N 84 50W
Owikeno L. **62** 51 40N 126 50W
Owingsville **77** 38 9N 83 46W
Owl, R. **55** 57 51N 92 44W
Owosso **77** 43 0N 84 10W
Owyhee **78** 42 0N 116 3W
Owyhee, R. **78** 43 10N 117 37W
Owyhee Res. **78** 43 30N 117 30W
Ox Mts. **97** 54 6N 9 0W
Oxbow **57** 49 14N 102 10W
Oxelösund **111** 58 43N 17 15E
Oxford, Can. **39** 45 44N 63 52W
Oxford, N.Z. **133** 43 18S 172 11E
Oxford, U.K. **95** 51 45N 1 15W
Oxford, U.S.A. **76** 41 43N 91 47W
Oxford, Mich., U.S.A. **46** 42 49N 83 16W
Oxford, Mich., U.S.A. **77** 42 49N 83 16W
Oxford, Miss., U.S.A. **75** 34 22N 89 30W
Oxford, N.C., U.S.A. **73** 36 19N 78 36W
Oxford, Ohio, U.S.A. **77** 39 30N 84 40W
Oxford □ **95** 51 45N 1 15W
Oxford L. **55** 54 51N 95 37W
Oxleys Pk. **136** 31 51S 150 22E
Oxnard **81** 34 10N 119 14W
Oya **126** 2 55N 111 55E
Oyama **63** 50 7N 119 22W
Oyem **116** 1 42N 11 43E
Oyen **61** 51 22N 110 28W
Oykell, R. **96** 57 55N 4 26W
Oymyakon **121** 63 25N 143 10E
Oyo **114** 7 46N 3 56E
Oyonnax **103** 46 16N 5 40E
Oyster B. **71** 40 52N 73 32W
Oyster River **62** 49 53N 125 7W
Ozaka **132** 34 40N 135 30E
Ozamis (Mizamis) **127** 8 15N 123 50E
Ozark, Ala., U.S.A. **73** 31 29N 85 39W
Ozark, Ark., U.S.A. **75** 35 30N 93 50W
Ozark, Mo., U.S.A. **75** 37 0N 93 15W
Ozark Plateau **75** 37 20N 91 40W
Ozarks, L. of **76** 38 10N 93 0W
Ozette, L. **80** 48 6N 124 38W
Ozona **75** 30 43N 101 11W
Ozuluama **83** 21 40N 97 50W

P

Pa-an **125** 16 45N 97 40E
Pa Sak, R. **128** 15 30N 101 0E
Paan (Batang) **129** 30 0N 99 3E
Paarl **117** 33 45S 18 56E
Paatsi, R. **110** 68 55N 29 0E
Paauilo **67** 20 3N 155 22W
Pab Hills **124** 26 30N 66 45E
Pabna **124** 24 1N 89 18E
Pabos Mills **38** 48 19N 64 42W
Pacajá, R. **87** 1 56S 50 50W
Pacasmayo **86** 7 20S 79 35W
Pacaudière, La **101** 46 11N 3 52E
Pacho **86** 5 8N 74 10W
Pachpadra **124** 25 58N 72 10E
Pachuca **83** 20 10N 98 40W
Pachung **131** 31 58N 106 40E
Pacific, Can. **54** 54 48N 128 28W
Pacific, U.S.A. **76** 38 29N 90 45W
Pacific Grove **80** 36 38N 121 58W
Pacific Ocean **14** 10 0N 140 0W
Pacific Rim Nat. Park **62** 48 40N 124 45W
Pacifica **80** 37 36N 122 30W
Packenham **47** 45 22N 76 25W
Packwood **80** 46 36N 121 40W
Pacofi **54** 53 0N 132 30W
Pacquet **37** 50 0N 55 53W
Pacy-sur-Eure **100** 49 1N 1 23E
Padaido, Kepulauan **127** 1 5S 138 0E
Padalarang **127** 7 50S 107 30E
Padang **126** 1 0S 100 20E
Padang, I. **126** 1 0S 100 10E
Padangsidimpuan **126** 1 30N 99 15E
Paddockwood **56** 53 30N 105 30W
Paderborn **106** 51 42N 8 44E
Padlei **55** 62 10N 97 5W
Padloping Island **65** 67 0N 63 0W
Pádova **108** 45 24N 11 52E
Padre I. **75** 27 0N 97 20W
Padstow **95** 50 33N 4 57W
Padua = Pádova **108** 45 24N 11 52E
Paducah, Ky., U.S.A. **72** 37 0N 88 40W
Paducah, Tex., U.S.A. **75** 34 3N 100 16W
Paeroa **133** 37 23S 175 41E
Pag, I. **108** 44 30N 14 50E
Pagadian **127** 7 55N 123 30E
Pagai Selatan, I. **126** 3 0S 100 15W
Pagai Utara, I. **126** 2 35S 100 0E
Pagalu, I. **112** 1 35S 3 35E
Pagaralam **126** 4 0S 103 17E
Pagastikós Kólpos **109** 39 15N 23 12E
Pagatan **126** 3 33S 115 59E
Page **74** 47 11N 97 37W
Pagny-sur-Moselle **101** 48 59N 6 2E
Pago Pago **133** 14 16S 170 43W
Pagosa Springs **79** 37 16N 107 4W
Pagwa River **53** 50 2N 85 14W
Pagwachuan, R. **53** 50 12N 84 43W
Pahala **67** 20 25N 156 0W
Pahang □ **128** 3 40N 102 20E
Pahang, R. **128** 3 30N 103 9E
Pahiatua **133** 40 27S 175 50E
Pahoa **67** 19 30N 154 57W
Pahokee **73** 26 50N 80 30W
Pahrump **81** 36 15N 116 0W
Paia **67** 20 54N 156 22W
Paicheng **130** 45 50N 122 53E
Paicines **80** 36 44N 121 17W
Paignton **95** 50 26N 3 33W
Päijänne **111** 61 30N 25 30E
Pailin **128** 12 46N 102 36E
Pailolo Chan. **67** 21 5N 156 42W
Paimbœuf **100** 47 17N 2 0W
Paimpol **100** 48 48N 3 4W
Paimpont, L. **38** 50 28N 61 34W
Painan **126** 1 15S 100 40E
Painesdale **52** 47 2N 88 41W
Painesville **70** 41 42N 81 18W
Paint l. **55** 55 28N 97 57W
Paint Rock **75** 31 30N 99 56W
Painted Desert **79** 36 40N 111 30W
Paintsville **72** 37 50N 82 50W
Paipa **86** 5 47N 73 7W
Paisley, Can. **46** 44 18N 81 16W
Paisley, U.K. **96** 55 51N 4 27W
Paisley, U.S.A. **78** 42 43N 120 40W
Paita **86** 5 5S 81 0W
Paix, Îles de la **44** 45 20N 73 51W
Paiyin **130** 36 45N 104 4E
Paiyü Shan, mts. **130** 37 20N 107 30E
Paiyunopo **130** 41 46N 109 58E
Pajares **104** 39 57N 1 48W
Pak Lay **128** 18 15N 101 27E
Pakanbaru **126** 0 30N 101 15E
Pakaraima, Sierra **86** 6 0N 60 0W
Pakashkan L. **52** 49 21N 90 15W
Pakenham **71** 45 18N 76 18W
Pakhoi **131** 21 30N 109 10E
Pakistan ■ **124** 30 0N 70 0E
Pakokku **125** 21 30N 95 0E
Pakonghow **131** 23 50N 113 0E
Pakowi L. **61** 49 20N 111 0W
Pakse **128** 15 5N 105 52E
Paktya □ **124** 33 0N 69 15E
Pakwash L. **52** 50 45N 93 30W
Pala **81** 33 22N 117 5W
Palacios **75** 28 44N 96 12W
Palagruza **108** 42 24N 16 15E
Palais, Le **100** 47 20N 3 10W
Palam **124** 19 0N 77 0E
Palamós **104** 41 50N 3 10E
Palampur **124** 32 10N 76 30E
Palana **121** 59 10N 160 10E
Palanan **127** 17 8N 122 29E
Palanpur **124** 24 10N 72 25E
Palapye **117** 22 30S 27 7E
Palatine **77** 42 7N 88 3W
Palatka **73** 29 40N 81 40W
Palau Is. **14** 7 30N 134 30E
Palauig **127** 15 26N 119 54E
Palauk **128** 13 10N 98 40E
Palavas **102** 43 32N 3 56E
Palawan, I. **126** 10 0N 119 0E
Palayancottai **124** 8 45N 77 45E
Palchewoflock **136** 35 20S 142 15E
Paleleh **127** 1 10N 121 50E
Palembang **126** 3 0S 104 50E
Palencia **104** 42 1N 4 34W
Palermo, Can. **49** 43 26N 79 47W
Palermo, Colomb. **86** 2 54N 75 26W
Palermo, Italy **108** 38 8N 13 20E
Palermo, U.S.A. **78** 39 30N 121 37W
Palestine, Asia **115** 32 0N 35 0E
Palestine, U.S.A. **75** 31 42N 95 35W
Paletwa **125** 21 30N 92 50E
Palghat **124** 10 46N 76 42E
Palgrave **49** 43 57N 79 50W
Pali **124** 25 50N 73 20E
Palinyuch'i (Tapanshang) **130** 43 40N 118 20E
Palisade **74** 40 35N 101 10W
Palitana **124** 21 32N 71 49E
Palizada **83** 18 18N 92 8W
Palk Bay **124** 9 30N 79 30E
Palk Strait **124** 10 0N 80 0E
Palm Beach **73** 26 46N 80 0W
Palm Desert **81** 33 43N 116 22W
Palm Is. **135** 18 40S 146 35E
Palm Springs **81** 33 51N 116 35W
Palma, Canary Is. **93** 28 40N 17 50W
Palma, Mozam. **116** 10 46S 40 29E
Palma, Bahia de **104** 39 30N 2 39E
Palma, La, Panama **84** 8 15N 78 0W
Palma, La, Spain **104** 37 21N 6 38W
Palma, R. **87** 10 10N 71 50W
Palma Soriano **84** 20 15N 76 0W
Palmares **87** 8 41S 35 36W
Palmarito **86** 7 37N 70 10W
Palmarolle **40** 48 40N 79 12W
Palmas **89** 26 29S 52 0W
Palmas, C. **114** 4 27N 7 46W
Pálmas, G. di **108** 39 0N 8 30E
Palmdale **81** 34 36N 118 7W
Palmeira dos Índios **87** 9 25S 36 37W
Palmer, Alaska, U.S.A. **67** 61 35N 149 10W
Palmer, Mass., U.S.A. **71** 42 9N 72 21W
Palmer Arch **91** 64 15S 65 0W
Palmer Lake **74** 39 10N 104 52W
Palmer Pen. **91** 73 0S 60 0W
Palmer, R., N. Terr., Austral. **134** 24 30S 133 0E
Palmer, R., Queens., Austral. **134** 16 5S 142 43E
Palmerston, Can. **70** 43 50N 80 40W
Palmerston, Ont., Can. **46** 43 50N 80 51W
Palmerston, N.Z. **133** 45 29S 170 43E
Palmerston, C. **135** 21 32S 149 29E
Palmerston North **133** 40 21S 175 39E
Palmerton **71** 40 47N 75 36W
Palmetto **73** 27 33N 82 33W
Palmi **108** 38 21N 15 51E
Palmira, Argent. **88** 32 59S 68 25W
Palmira, Colomb. **86** 3 32N 76 16W
Palms **46** 43 37N 82 47W
Palmyra, U.S.A. **77** 42 52N 88 36W
Palmyra, Ill., U.S.A. **76** 39 26N 90 0W
Palmyra, Mo., U.S.A. **76** 39 45N 91 30W
Palmyra, N.Y., U.S.A. **70** 34 5N 77 18W
Palmyra = Tadmor **122** 34 30N 37 55E
Palni Hills **124** 10 14N 77 33E
Palo Alto **80** 37 25N 122 8W
Palo Verde **81** 33 26N 114 45W
Paloe **127** 8 20S 121 43E
Paloma, La **88** 30 35S 71 0W
Palomar **53** 48 10N 82 16W
Palopo **127** 3 0S 120 16E
Palos, Cabo de **104** 37 38N 0 40W
Palos Verdes **81** 33 48N 118 23W
Palos Verdes, Pt. **81** 33 43N 118 26W
Palouse **78** 46 59N 117 5W
Palu, Indon. **127** 1 0S 119 59E
Palu, Turkey **122** 38 45N 40 0E
Paluan **127** 13 35N 120 29E
Pamamaroo, L. **136** 32 17S 142 28E
Pamanukan **127** 6 16S 107 49E
Pamekasan **127** 7 10S 113 29E
Pameungpeuk **127** 7 38S 107 44E
Pamiencheng **130** 43 16N 124 4E
Pamiers **102** 43 7N 1 39E
Pamirs, Ra. **120** 37 40N 73 0E
Pamlico, R. **73** 35 25N 76 40W
Pamlico Sd. **73** 35 20N 76 0W
Pampa **75** 35 35N 100 58W
Pampa de las Salinas **88** 32 1S 66 58W
Pampa, La □ **88** 36 50S 66 0W
Pampanua **127** 4 22S 120 14E
Pampas, Argent. **88** 34 0S 64 0W
Pampas, Peru **86** 12 20S 74 50W
Pamplona, Colomb. **86** 7 23N 72 39W
Pamplona, Spain **104** 42 48N 1 38W
Pana **76** 39 25N 89 10W
Panaca **79** 37 51N 114 50W
Panache, L. **46** 46 15N 81 20W
Panaitan, I. **127** 6 35S 105 10E
Panaji (Panjim) **124** 15 25N 73 50E
Panamá **84** 9 0N 79 25W
Panama ■ **84** 8 48N 79 55W
Panama Canal **84** 9 10N 79 56W
Panama Canal Zone **84** 9 10N 79 56W
Panama City **73** 30 10N 85 41W
Panamá, Golfo de **84** 8 4N 79 20W
Panamint Mts. **79** 36 15N 117 20W
Panamint Springs **81** 36 20N 117 28W
Panão **86** 9 55S 75 55W
Panarukan **127** 7 40S 113 52E
Panay, G. **127** 11 0N 122 30E
Panay I. **127** 11 10N 122 30E
Pancake Ra. **79** 38 30N 116 0W
Pančevo **109** 44 52N 20 41E
Pancorbo, Paso **104** 42 32N 3 5W
Pandan **127** 11 45N 122 10E
Pandangpanjang **126** 0 40S 100 20E
Pandeglang **127** 6 25S 106 0E
Pandharpur **124** 17 41N 75 20E
Pando **89** 34 30S 56 0W
Panfilov **120** 44 30N 80 0E
Pang-Long **125** 23 11N 98 45E
Pangani **116** 5 25S 38 58E
Pangi **116** 3 10S 26 35E
Pangkalanberandan **126** 4 1N 98 20E
Pangkalansusu **126** 4 2N 98 42E
Pangkiang (Mingan) **130** 43 4N 112 30E
Pangkoh **126** 3 5S 114 8E
Pangmar **56** 49 39N 104 40W
Pangong Tso, L. **124** 34 0N 78 20E
Pangrango **127** 6 46S 107 1E
Panguitch **79** 37 52N 112 30W
Pangutaran Group **127** 6 18N 120 34E
Panhandle **75** 35 23N 101 23W

Panjgur **Pelican Rapids**

Panjgur	124	27 0N	64 5E
Panjim = Panaji	124	15 25N	73 50E
Panjinad Barrage	124	29 22N	71 15E
Pankadjene	127	4 46S	119 34E
Pankal Pinang	126	2 0S	106 0E
Panna	124	24 40N	80 15E
Panny, R.	60	57 8N	114 51W
Panora	76	41 41N	94 22W
Panorama	89	21 21S	51 51W
Panshan	130	41 15N	122 0E
Panshih	130	42 59N	126 0E
Pantano	79	32 0N	110 32W
Pantar, I.	127	8 28S	124 10E
Pantelleria, I.	108	36 52N	12 0E
Pantjo	127	8 42S	118 40E
Pantukan	127	7 17N	125 58E
Panuco	83	22 0N	98 25W
Paochang	130	41 46N	115 30E
Paocheng	131	33 12N	107 0E
Paokang	131	31 57N	111 21E
Paoki	131	34 25N	107 15E
Paoko	131	34 22N	107 12E
Paola	74	38 36N	94 50W
Paoli	77	31 33N	86 28W
Paonia	79	38 56N	107 37W
Paoshan	125	25 7N	99 9E
Paoteh	130	39 0N	110 45E
Paoting	130	38 50N	115 30E
Paotow	130	40 45N	110 0E
Paotsing	131	28 35N	109 35E
Paoua	116	7 25N	16 30E
Papá	107	47 22N	17 30E
Papagayo, Golfo de	84	10 4N	85 50W
Papagayo, R., Brazil	82	12 30S	58 10W
Papagayo, R., Mexico	83	16 36N	99 43W
Papaikou	67	19 47N	155 6W
Papakura	133	37 4S	174 59E
Papaloapan, R.	82	18 2N	96 51W
Papantla	83	20 45N	97 21W
Papar	126	5 45N	116 0E
Papenburg	105	53 7N	7 25E
Papigochic, R.	82	29 9N	109 40W
Papineau-Labelle, Parc Prov.	40	46 10N	75 15W
Papineauville	40	45 37N	75 1W
Paposo	88	25 0S	70 30W
Papua New Guinea ■	14	8 0S	145 0E
Papudo	88	32 29S	71 27W
Papun	125	18 0N	97 30E
Pará = Belém	87	1 20S	48 30W
Pará □	87	3 20S	52 0W
Paracatú	87	17 10S	46 50W
Paracel Is.	126	16 49N	111 2E
Paradip	125	20 15N	86 35E
Paradis	40	48 15N	76 35W
Paradise, Calif., U.S.A.	80	39 46N	121 37W
Paradise, Mich., U.S.A.	46	46 38N	85 3W
Paradise, Mont., U.S.A.	78	47 27N	114 54W
Paradise, Nev., U.S.A.	81	36 4N	115 7W
Paradise Hill	56	53 32N	109 28W
Paradise, R.	36	53 27N	57 19W
Paradise Valley, Can.	61	53 2N	110 17W
Paradise Valley, U.S.A.	78	41 30N	117 28W
Parado	127	8 42S	118 30E
Paragould	75	36 5N	90 30W
Paragua, La	86	6 50N	63 20W
Paragua, R.	86	6 30N	63 30W
Paraguaçu Paulista	89	22 22S	50 35W
Paraguaçu, R.	87	12 45S	38 54W
Paraguai, R.	86	16 0S	57 52W
Paraguaipoa	86	11 21N	71 57W
Paraguana, Pen. de	86	12 0N	70 0W
Paraguarí	88	25 36S	57 0W
Paraguarí □	88	26 0S	57 10W
Paraguay ■	88	23 0S	57 0W
Paraguay, R.	88	27 18S	58 38W
Paraíba = Joéo Pessoa	82	7 10S	35 0W
Paraiba □	87	7 0S	36 0W
Paraíba do Sul, R.	89	21 37S	41 3W
Parainen	111	60 18N	22 18E
Paraiso	83	19 3S	52 59W
Paraiso	83	18 24N	93 14W
Parakou	114	9 25N	2 40E
Paramaribo	87	5 50N	55 10W
Paramillo, Nudo del	86	7 4N	75 55W
Paramushir, Ostrov	121	40 24N	156 0E
Paraná	88	32 0S	60 30W
Paranã	87	12 30S	47 40W
Paraná □	89	24 30S	51 0W
Paraná, R.	88	33 43S	59 15W
Paranã, R.	87	22 25S	53 1W
Paranaguá	89	25 30S	48 30W
Paranaíba, R.	87	18 0S	49 12W
Paranapanema, R.	89	22 40S	53 9W
Paranapiacaba, Serra do	89	24 31S	48 35W
Paranavaí	89	23 4S	52 28W
Parang, Jolo, Phil.	127	5 55N	120 54E
Parang, Mindanao, Phil.	127	7 23N	124 16E
Paratinga	87	12 40S	43 10W
Paray-le-Monial	103	46 27N	4 7E
Parbhani	124	19 8N	76 52E
Parchim	106	53 25N	11 50E
Pardee Res.	80	38 16N	120 51W
Pardo, R., Bahia, Brazil	87	15 40S	39 0W
Pardo, R., Mato Grosso, Brazil	87	21 0S	53 25W
Pardo, R., São Paulo, Brazil	87	20 45S	48 0W
Pardubice	106	50 3N	15 45E
Pare	127	7 43S	112 12E
Pare Pare	127	4 0S	119 45E
Parecis, Serra dos	86	13 0S	60 0W
Paren	121	62 45N	163 0E
Parent	40	47 55N	74 35W
Parent, Lac.	40	48 31N	77 1W
Parentis-en-Born	102	44 21N	1 4W
Parepare	127	4 0S	119 40E
Parfuri	117	22 28S	31 17E
Parham, Can.	71	44 40N	76 40W
Parham, Ont., Can.	47	44 39N	76 43W
Paria, Golfo de	86	10 20N	62 0W
Paria, Pen. de	86	10 50N	62 30W
Pariaguán	86	8 51N	64 43W
Pariaman	126	0 47S	100 11E
Paricutín, Cerro	82	19 28N	102 15W
Parigi	127	0 50S	120 5E
Parika	86	6 50N	58 20W
Parima, Serra	86	2 30N	64 0W
Parinari	86	4 35S	74 25W
Parîngul-Mare, mt.	107	45 20N	23 37E
Parintins	87	2 40S	56 50W
Pariparit Kyun	125	14 55S	93 45E
Paris, Can.	49	43 12N	80 25W
Paris, France	101	48 50N	2 20E
Paris, U.S.A.	76	39 29N	92 0W
Paris, Idaho, U.S.A.	78	42 13N	111 30W
Paris, Ill., U.S.A.	77	39 36N	87 42W
Paris, Ky., U.S.A.	77	38 12N	84 12W
Paris, Tenn., U.S.A.	73	36 20N	88 20W
Paris, Tex., U.S.A.	75	33 40N	95 30W
Parish	71	43 24N	76 9W
Pariti	127	9 55S	123 30E
Park	80	48 45N	122 18W
Park City	78	40 42N	111 35W
Park Falls	74	45 58N	90 27W
Park Head	70	44 36N	81 10W
Park Range	78	40 0N	106 30W
Park Rapids	74	46 56N	95 0W
Park Ridge	77	42 2N	87 51W
Park River	74	48 25N	97 50W
Park Royal	66	49 20N	123 8W
Park View	79	36 45N	106 37W
Parker, Can.	49	43 46N	80 35W
Parker, Ariz., U.S.A.	81	34 8N	114 16W
Parker, S.D., U.S.A.	74	43 25N	97 7W
Parker Dam	81	34 13N	114 5W
Parkersburg, U.S.A.	76	42 35N	92 47W
Parkersburg, W. Va., U.S.A.	72	39 18N	81 31W
Parkerview	56	51 21N	103 18W
Parkes, A.C.T., Austral.	135	35 18S	149 8E
Parkes, N.S.W., Austral.	136	33 9S	148 11E
Parkfield	80	35 54N	120 26W
Parkhill	46	43 15N	81 38W
Parkland	80	47 9N	122 26W
Parks L.	53	49 27N	87 38W
Parkside	56	53 10N	106 33W
Parkston	74	43 25N	98 0W
Parksville	62	49 20N	124 21W
Parma, Italy	108	44 50N	10 20E
Parma, Idaho, U.S.A.	78	43 49N	116 59W
Parma, Ohio, U.S.A.	70	41 25N	81 42W
Parnaguá	87	10 10S	44 10W
Parnaíba, Piauí, Brazil	87	3 0S	41 40W
Parnaíba, São Paulo, Brazil	87	19 34S	51 14W
Parnaíba, R.	87	3 35S	43 0W
Parnassós, mt.	109	38 17N	21 30E
Pärnu	120	58 12N	24 33E
Paroo Chan.	135	30 50S	143 35E
Paroo, R.	135	30 0S	144 5E
Paropamisus Range = Fīroz Kohi	123	34 45N	63 0E
Páros, I.	109	37 5N	25 12E
Parowan	79	37 54N	112 56W
Parpaillon, mts.	103	44 30N	6 40E
Parral	88	36 10S	72 0W
Parramatta	136	33 48S	151 1E
Parras	82	25 30N	102 20W
Parrett, R.	95	51 7N	2 58W
Parris I.	73	32 20N	80 30W
Parrsboro	39	45 30N	64 25W
Parry	55	49 47N	104 41W
Parry, C.	67	70 20N	123 38W
Parry Is.	64	77 0N	110 0W
Parry Sound	46	45 20N	80 0W
Parshall	74	47 56N	102 11W
Parsnip, R.	54	55 10N	123 2W
Parson	63	51 5N	116 37W
Parsons	75	37 20N	95 10W
Parsons Pond	37	49 59N	57 37W
Parson's Pond	37	50 2N	57 43W
Parthenay	100	46 38N	0 16W
Partridge Pt.	37	50 10N	56 10W
Partridge, R.	53	51 19N	80 18W
Paru, R.	87	0 20S	53 30W
Paruro	86	13 45S	71 50W
Parvatipuram	125	18 50N	83 25E
Parwan □	124	35 0N	69 0E
Pas-de-Calais □	101	50 30N	2 30E
Pasadena, Can.	37	49 1N	57 36W
Pasadena, Calif., U.S.A.	81	34 5N	118 9W
Pasadena, Tex., U.S.A.	75	29 45N	95 14W
Pasaje	86	3 10S	79 40W
Pasaje, R.	88	25 35S	64 57W
Pascagoula	75	30 30N	88 30W
Pascagoula, R.	75	30 40N	88 35W
Pasco	78	46 10N	119 0W
Pasco, Cerro de	86	10 45S	76 10W
Pasfield L.	55	58 24N	105 20W
Pasir Mas	128	6 2N	102 8E
Pasir Puteh	128	5 50N	102 24E
Pasirian	127	8 13S	113 8E
Pasley, C.	134	33 52S	123 35E
Pasni	124	25 15N	63 27E
Paso Cantinela	81	32 33N	115 47W
Paso de Indios	90	43 55S	69 0W
Paso de los Libres	88	29 44S	57 10W
Paso de los Toros	88	32 36S	56 37W
Paso Robles	79	35 40N	120 45W
Paspébiac	39	48 3N	65 17W
Pass Island	37	47 30N	56 12W
Passage Pt.	64	73 29N	115 16W
Passage West	97	51 52N	8 20W
Passaic	71	40 50N	74 8W
Passau	106	48 34N	13 27E
Passero, C.	108	36 42N	15 8E
Passo Fundo	89	28 10S	52 30W
Passos	87	20 45S	46 37W
Passy	101	45 55N	6 41E
Pastaza, R.	86	2 45S	76 50W
Pasteur, L.	38	50 13N	66 58W
Pasto	86	1 13N	77 17W
Pasuruan	127	7 40S	112 53E
Patagonia, Argent.	90	45 0S	69 0W
Patagonia, U.S.A.	79	31 35N	110 45W
Patan	124	23 54N	72 14E
Patan (Lalitapur)	125	27 40N	85 20E
Patani	127	0 20N	128 50E
Pataokiang	130	41 58N	126 30E
Patay	101	48 2N	1 40E
Patchewollock	136	35 22S	142 12E
Patchogue	71	40 46N	73 1W
Patea	133	39 45S	174 30E
Paternò	108	37 34N	14 53E
Paternoster, Kepulauan	126	7 5S	118 15E
Pateros	78	48 4N	119 58W
Paterson, Austral.	136	32 37S	151 39E
Paterson, U.S.A.	71	40 55N	74 10W
Pathankot	124	32 18N	75 45E
Pathfinder Res.	78	42 30N	107 0W
Páti	127	6 45S	111 3E
Patiala	124	30 23N	76 26E
Patjitan	127	8 12S	111 8E
Patkai Bum	125	27 0N	95 30E
Pátmos, I.	109	37 21N	26 36E
Patna	125	25 35N	85 18E
Patos de Minas	87	18 35S	46 32W
Patos, Lag. dos	89	31 20S	51 0E
Patquía	88	30 0S	66 55W
Pátrai	109	38 14N	21 47E
Pátraikos, Kólpos	109	38 17N	21 30E
Patrick's Cove	37	47 3N	54 7W
Patrie, La	41	45 24N	71 15W
Patrocínio	87	18 57S	47 0W
Pattani	128	6 48N	101 15E
Patten	35	45 59N	68 28W
Patterson, Can.	50	43 54N	79 28W
Patterson, Calif., U.S.A.	80	37 30N	121 9W
Patterson, La., U.S.A.	75	29 44N	91 20W
Patterson, Mt.	80	38 29N	119 20W
Patti	108	38 8N	14 57E
Patton	70	40 38N	78 40W
Pattonsburg	76	40 3N	94 8W
Patuakhali	125	22 20N	90 25E
Patuca, Punta	84	15 49N	84 14W
Patuca, R.	84	15 20N	84 40W
Patung	131	31 0N	110 30E
Pátzcuaro	82	19 30N	101 40W
Pau	102	43 19N	0 25W
Pauillac	102	45 11N	0 46W
Pauini, R.	86	1 42S	62 50W
Pauk	125	21 55N	94 30E
Paul I.	36	56 30N	61 20W
Paul-Sauvé, L.	40	50 15N	78 20W
Paulatuk	67	69 25N	124 0W
Paulding	77	41 8N	84 35W
Paulhan	102	43 33N	3 28E
Paulistana	87	8 9S	41 9W
Paullina	74	42 55N	95 40W
Paulo Afonso	87	9 21S	38 15W
Paul's Valley	75	34 40N	97 17W
Pauma Valley	81	33 16N	116 58W
Pavia	108	45 10N	9 10E
Pavlodar	120	52 33N	77 0E
Pavlof Is.	67	55 30N	161 30W
Pavlovo	121	63 5N	115 25E
Paw-Paw	76	41 41N	88 59W
Paw Paw	77	42 13N	85 53W
Pawhuska	75	36 40N	96 25W
Pawling	71	41 35N	73 37W
Pawnee, U.S.A.	76	39 35N	89 35W
Pawnee, Okla., U.S.A.	75	36 24N	96 50W
Pawnee City	74	40 8N	96 10W
Pawtucket	71	41 51N	71 22W
Paxton, Ill., U.S.A.	77	40 25N	88 0W
Paxton, Nebr., U.S.A.	74	41 12N	101 27W
Paya Bakri	128	2 3N	102 44E
Payakumbah	126	0 20S	100 35E
Payen	129	45 57N	127 58E
Payette	78	44 0N	117 0W
Payne	77	41 5N	84 44W
Payne = Bellin	36	60 1N	70 1W
Paynesville	74	45 21N	94 44W
Paysandú	88	32 19S	58 8W
Payson, Ariz., U.S.A.	79	34 17N	111 15W
Payson, Utah, U.S.A.	78	40 8N	111 41W
Paz, Bahía de la	82	24 15N	110 25W
Paz Centro, La	84	12 20N	86 41W
Paz, La, Entre Ríos, Argent.	88	30 50S	59 45W
Paz, La, San Luis, Argent.	88	33 30S	67 20W
Paz, La, Boliv.	86	16 20S	68 10W
Paz, La, Hond.	84	14 20N	87 47W
Paz, La, Mexico	82	24 10N	110 20W
Paz, La, Bahía de	82	24 20N	110 40W
Paz, R.	84	13 44N	90 10W
Pazar	122	41 10N	40 50E
Pazardzhik	109	42 12N	24 20E
Pe Ell	80	46 30N	123 18W
Peabody	71	42 31N	70 56W
Peace Point	54	59 7N	112 27W
Peace, R.	54	59 0N	111 25W
Peace River	60	56 15N	117 18W
Peace River Res.	54	55 40N	123 40W
Peach Springs	79	35 36N	113 30W
Peachland	63	49 47N	119 45W
Peak Hill	134	32 39S	148 11E
Peak Range	135	22 50S	148 20E
Peak, The	94	53 24N	1 53W
Peale Mt.	79	38 25N	109 12W
Pearblossom	81	34 30N	117 55W
Pearce	79	31 57N	109 56W
Pearl, Can.	52	48 40N	88 40W
Pearl, U.S.A.	76	39 28N	90 38W
Pearl City, U.S.A.	76	42 16N	89 50W
Pearl City, Hawaii, U.S.A.	67	21 24N	158 0W
Pearl Harbor	67	21 20N	158 0W
Pearl, R.	75	31 50N	90 0W
Pearsall	75	28 55N	99 8W
Pearse I.	54	54 52N	130 14W
Peary Land	17	82 40N	33 0W
Pease, R.	75	34 18N	100 15W
Pebane	117	17 10S	38 8E
Pebas	86	3 10S	71 55W
Pebble Beach	80	36 34N	121 57W
Pec	109	42 40N	20 17E
Pecatonica	76	42 19N	89 22W
Pecatonica, R.	76	42 26N	89 17W
Pechenga	120	69 30N	31 25E
Pechora, R.	120	62 30N	56 30E
Pechorskaya Guba	120	68 40N	54 0E
Peck	46	43 16N	82 49W
Pecos	75	31 25N	103 35W
Pecos, R.	75	31 22N	102 30W
Pécs	107	46 5N	18 15E
Pedasí	84	7 32N	80 3W
Pedernales	85	18 2N	71 44W
Pedjantan, I.	126	0 5S	106 15E
Pedra Azul	87	16 2S	41 17W
Pedreiras	87	4 32S	44 40W
Pedrera, La	86	1 18S	69 43W
Pedro Afonso	87	9 0S	48 10W
Pedro Antonio Santos	83	18 54N	88 15W
Pedro Cays	84	17 5N	77 48W
Pedro Chico	86	1 4N	70 25W
Pedro de Valdivia	88	22 33S	69 38W
Pedro Juan Caballero	89	22 30S	55 40W
Pedro Miguel Locks	84	9 1N	79 36W
Peebles, U.K.	96	55 40N	3 12W
Peebles, U.S.A.	77	38 57N	83 23W
Peekshill	71	41 18N	73 57W
Peel	94	54 14N	4 40W
Peel □	50	43 45N	79 47W
Peel, R.	64	67 0N	135 0W
Peerless L.	60	56 37N	114 40W
Peerless Lake	60	56 30N	114 35W
Peers	60	53 40N	116 0W
Pegasus Bay	133	43 20S	173 10E
Peggy's Cove	39	44 30N	63 55W
Pegu	125	17 20N	96 29E
Pegu Yoma, mts.	125	19 0N	96 0E
Peh K.	131	24 20N	113 20E
Pehan	129	48 17N	120 31E
Pehpei	131	29 44N	106 29E
Pehtaiho	130	39 50N	119 30E
Pehuajó	88	36 0S	62 0W
Peine	88	23 45S	68 8W
Peiping	130	39 50N	116 20E
Peixe	87	12 0S	48 40W
Pekalongan	127	6 53S	109 40E
Pekan	128	3 30N	103 25E
Pékans, R.	38	52 12N	66 49W
Pekin	76	40 35N	89 40W
Peking = Peiping	130	39 50N	116 20E
Pelabuhan Ratu, Teluk	127	7 5S	106 30E
Pelabuhanratu	127	7 0S	106 32E
Pelaihari	126	3 55S	114 45E
Peleaga, mt.	107	45 22N	22 55E
Pelee I.	46	41 47N	82 40W
Pelée, Mt.	85	14 40N	61 0W
Pelee, Pt.	46	41 54N	82 31W
Peleng, I.	127	1 20S	123 30E
Pelham, Can.	49	43 3N	79 21W
Pelham, U.S.A.	73	31 5N	84 6W
Pelham Union	49	43 5N	79 23W
Pelican	67	58 12N	136 28W
Pelican L.	57	52 28N	100 20W
Pélican, L.	36	59 47N	73 35W
Pelican L., U.S.A.	52	48 4N	92 58W
Pelican L., U.S.A.	52	46 36N	94 5W
Pelican Narrows	55	55 10N	102 56W
Pelican Portage	54	55 51N	113 0W
Pelican Rapids	57	52 45N	100 42W

Peligre, L. de **Pine Flat Res**

Peligre, L. de **85** 19 1N 71 58W
Pelkosenniemi **110** 67 6N 27 28 E
Pella **76** 41 30N 93 0W
Pelletier Sta. **41** 47 33N 69 26W
Pellston **46** 45 33N 84 47W
Pelly **57** 51 52N 101 56W
Pelly Bay **65** 68 0N 89 50W
Pelly Crossing **64** 62 49N 136 34W
Pelly L. **64** 66 0N 102 0W
Pelly Pt. **66** 49 7N 123 12W
Pelly, R. **64** 62 15N 133 30W
Peloponnese = Pelóponnisos **109** 37 10N 22 0 E
Pelopónnisos Kai Dhitiktí Iprotikí Ellas □ **109** 37 10N 22 0 E
Peloro, C. **108** 38 15N 15 40 E
Pelorus Sound **133** 40 59 S 173 59 E
Pelotas **89** 31 42 S 52 23W
Pelvoux, Massif de **103** 44 52N 6 20 E
Pemalang **127** 6 53 S 109 23 E
Pematang Siantar **126** 2 57N 99 5 E
Pemba **117** 16 30 S 27 28 E
Pemba, I. **117** 5 0 S 39 45 E
Pemberton, Austral. **134** 34 30 S 116 0 E
Pemberton, Can. **63** 50 25N 122 50W
Pembina **57** 48 58N 97 15W
Pembina, R., Alta., Can. **60** 54 45N 114 17W
Pembina, R., Man., Can. **57** 49 0N 98 12W
Pembine **72** 45 38N 87 59W
Pembroke, Can. **47** 45 50N 77 7W
Pembroke, N.Z. **133** 44 33 S 169 9 E
Pembroke, U.K. **95** 51 41N 4 57W
Pembroke, U.S.A. **73** 32 5N 81 32W
Pen-y-Ghent **94** 54 10N 2 15W
Peña de Francia, Sierra de **104** 40 32N 6 10W
Peñalara, Pico **104** 40 51N 3 57W
Penang = Pinang **128** 5 25N 100 15 E
Penápolis **89** 21 30 S 50 0W
Peñas, C. de **104** 43 42N 5 52W
Peñas, G. de **90** 47 0 S 75 0W
Peñas, Pta. **86** 11 17N 70 28W
Pend Oreille, L. **63** 48 0N 116 30W
Pend Oreille, R. **78** 49 4N 117 37W
Pendembu **114** 9 7N 12 14W
Pendleton, U.S.A. **77** 40 0N 85 45W
Pendleton, Calif., U.S.A. **81** 33 16N 117 23W
Pendleton, Oreg., U.S.A. **78** 45 35N 118 50W
Penedo **87** 10 15 S 36 36W
Penetanguishene, Newf., Can. **37** 47 36N 52 45W
Penetanguishene, Ont., Can. **46** 44 50N 79 55W
Pengalengan **127** 7 9 S 107 30 E
Pengan **131** 31 0N 106 18 E
Pengchia Yu (Agincourt) Is. **131** 25 4N 122 2 E
Penghu (Pescadores) **131** 23 34N 119 30 E
Penglai (Tengchowfu) **130** 37 50N 120 50 E
Pengpu **131** 33 0N 117 25 E
Pengshui **131** 29 20N 108 15 E
Penhold **61** 52 8N 113 52W
Peniche **104** 39 19N 9 22W
Penida, I. **126** 8 45 S 115 30 E
Penki **130** 41 20N 132 50 E
Penmarch **100** 47 49N 4 21W
Penmarch, Pte. de **100** 47 48N 4 22W
Pennant **56** 50 32N 108 14W
Penner, R. **124** 14 50N 78 20 E
Penniac **39** 46 2N 66 34W
Pennines **94** 54 50N 2 20W
Pennington **80** 39 15N 121 47W
Pennsylvania □ **72** 40 50N 78 0W
Pennville **77** 40 30N 85 9W
Penny **63** 53 51N 121 20W
Penny Highland **65** 67 19N 66 20W
Penny Str. **65** 76 30N 97 0W
Pennyan **70** 42 39N 77 7W
Penola **136** 37 25 S 140 47 E
Penong **134** 31 59 S 133 5 E
Penonomé **84** 8 31N 80 21W
Penrhyn Is. **15** 9 0 S 150 30W
Penrith, Austral. **136** 33 43 S 150 38 E
Penrith, U.K. **94** 54 40N 2 45W
Pensacola **73** 30 30N 87 10W
Pensacola Mts. **91** 84 0 S 40 0W
Pense **56** 50 25N 104 59W
Pentecôte, L. **38** 49 53N 67 20W
Pentecôte, R. **38** 49 46N 67 10W
Penticton **63** 49 30N 119 30W
Pentland **135** 20 32 S 145 25 E
Pentland Corners **49** 43 40N 80 30W
Pentland Firth **96** 58 43N 3 10W
Pentland Hills **96** 55 48N 3 25W
Penylan L. **55** 61 50N 106 20W
Penza **120** 53 15N 45 5 E
Penzance **95** 50 7N 5 32W
Penzhinskaya Guba **121** 61 30N 163 0 E
Peoria, Ariz., U.S.A. **79** 33 40N 112 15W
Peoria, Ill., U.S.A. **76** 40 40N 89 40W
Peoria Heights **76** 40 45N 89 35W
Peotone **77** 41 20N 87 48W
Pepperwood **78** 40 23N 124 0W
Perabumilih **126** 3 27 S 104 15 E
Peraki, R. **128** 5 10N 101 4 E
Percé **38** 48 31N 64 13W
Perche **100** 48 31N 1 1 E
Perche, Collines de la **100** 42 30N 2 5 E
Percy, France **100** 48 55N 1 11W
Percy, U.S.A. **76** 38 5N 89 41W
Perdido, Mte. **104** 42 40N 0 50 E
Perdue **56** 52 4N 107 33W
Pereira **86** 4 49N 75 43W
Perez, I. **83** 22 24N 89 42W
Pergamino **88** 33 52 S 60 30W
Perham **74** 46 36N 95 36W
Perhentian, Kepulauan **128** 5 54N 102 42 E
Péribonca, L. **41** 50 1N 71 10W
Péribonca, R. **36** 48 45N 72 5W
Peribonka **41** 48 46N 72 3W
Perico **88** 24 20 S 65 5W
Pericos **82** 25 3N 107 42W
Périers **100** 49 11N 1 25W
Périgord **102** 45 0N 0 40 E
Périgueux **102** 45 10N 0 42 E
Perija, Sierra de **86** 9 30N 73 3W
Perkam, Tg. **127** 1 35 S 137 50 E
Perlas, Arch. de las **84** 8 41N 79 7W
Perlas, Punta de **84** 11 30N 83 30W
Perlis □ **128** 6 30N 100 15 E
Perm (Molotov) **120** 58 0N 57 10 E
Pernambuco = Recife **87** 8 0 S 35 0W
Pernambuco □ **87** 8 0 S 37 0W
Péronne **101** 49 55N 2 57 E
Perouse Str., La **118** 45 40N 142 0 E
Perow **54** 54 35N 126 10W
Perpignan **102** 42 42N 2 53 E
Perrington **77** 43 12N 84 42W
Perris **81** 33 47N 117 14W
Perros-Guirec **100** 48 49N 3 28W
Perrot, Île **44** 45 22N 73 57W
Perry, U.S.A. **77** 42 50N 84 13W
Perry, Fla., U.S.A. **73** 30 9N 83 40W
Perry, Ga., U.S.A. **73** 32 25N 83 41W
Perry, Iowa, U.S.A. **76** 41 48N 94 5W
Perry, Maine, U.S.A. **73** 44 59N 67 20W
Perry, Mo., U.S.A. **76** 39 26N 91 40W
Perry, N.Y., U.S.A. **70** 42 44N 77 59W
Perry, Okla., U.S.A. **75** 36 20N 97 20W
Perry River **65** 67 43N 102 14W
Perrysburg **77** 41 34N 83 38W
Perryton **75** 36 28N 100 48W
Perryville, Alas., U.S.A. **67** 55 54N 159 10W
Perryville, Mo., U.S.A. **76** 37 42N 89 50W
Persepolis **123** 29 55N 52 50 E
Persia = Iran **123** 35 0N 50 0 E
Persian Gulf **123** 27 0N 50 0 E
Perth, Austral. **134** 31 57 S 115 52 E
Perth, N.B., Can. **34** 46 43N 67 42W
Perth, N.B., Can. **39** 46 44N 67 42W
Perth, Ont., Can. **47** 44 55N 76 15W
Perth, U.K. **96** 56 24N 3 27W
Perth, U.S.A. **71** 40 33N 74 36W
Perth Amboy **72** 40 30N 74 25W
Perthus, Le **102** 42 30N 2 53 E
Pertuis **103** 43 42N 5 30 E
Peru, Ill., U.S.A. **76** 41 18N 89 12W
Peru, Ind., U.S.A. **77** 40 42N 86 0W
Peru ■ **86** 8 0 S 75 0W
Perúgia **108** 43 6N 12 24 E
Péruwelz **105** 50 31N 3 36 E
Pervouralsk **120** 56 55N 60 0 E
Pésaro **108** 43 55N 12 53 E
Pesca, La **83** 23 46N 97 47W
Pescadores = Penghu **131** 23 34N 119 30 E
Pescara **108** 42 28N 14 13 E
Peshawar **124** 34 2N 71 37 E
Peshawar □ **124** 35 0N 72 50 E
Peshtigo **72** 45 4N 87 46W
Pesqueira **87** 8 20 S 36 42W
Pesquiería **82** 29 23N 110 54W
Pesquieria, R. **82** 25 54N 99 11W
Pessac **102** 44 48N 0 37W
Petaling Jaya **128** 3 4N 101 42 E
Petaluma **80** 38 13N 122 39W
Petange **105** 49 33N 5 55 E
Petatlán **82** 17 31N 101 16W
Petauke **117** 14 14 S 31 12 E
Petawawa **47** 45 54N 77 17W
Petén Itza, Lago **84** 16 58N 89 50W
Peter 1st, I. **91** 69 0 S 91 0W
Peter Pond L. **55** 55 55N 108 44W
Peterbell **53** 48 36N 83 21W
Peterboro **71** 42 55N 71 59W
Peterborough, S. Australia, Austral. **135** 32 58 S 138 51 E
Peterborough, Victoria, Austral. **135** 38 37 S 142 50 E
Peterborough, Can. **47** 44 20N 78 20W
Peterborough, U.K. **95** 52 35N 0 14W
Peterhead **96** 57 30N 1 49W
Peters, L. **36** 59 41N 70 53W
Petersburg, U.S.A. **76** 40 1N 89 51W
Petersburg, Alas., U.S.A. **54** 56 50N 133 0W
Petersburg, Ind., U.S.A. **77** 38 30N 87 15W
Petersburg, Va., U.S.A. **72** 37 17N 77 26W
Petersburg, W. Va., U.S.A. **72** 38 59N 79 10W
Petersfield **57** 50 18N 96 58W
Petit Bois I. **73** 30 16N 88 25W
Petit-Brûlé **44** 45 35N 74 2W
Petit-Cap **38** 48 3N 64 30W
Petit-de-Grat **39** 45 30N 60 58W
Petit Étang **39** 46 39N 60 58W
Petit Goâve **85** 18 27N 72 51W
Petit-Mécatina, I. du **36** 50 30N 59 25W
Petit-Quevilly, Le **100** 49 26N 1 0 E
Petit-Rocher **39** 47 46N 65 43W
Petitcodiac **39** 45 57N 65 11W
Petite Baleine, R. **36** 56 0N 76 45W
Petite-Cascapédia, Parc Prov. de la **38** 48 30N 65 45W
Petite-Rivière **41** 47 20N 70 33W
Petite Rivière Bridge **39** 44 14N 64 27W
Petite Saguenay **41** 48 15N 70 4W
Petitsikapau, L. **36** 54 37N 66 25W
Petlad **124** 22 30N 72 45 E
Peto **83** 20 10N 89 0W
Petone **133** 41 13 S 174 53 E
Petoskey **46** 45 22N 84 57W
Petra, Ostrova **17** 76 15N 118 30 E
Petrich **109** 41 24N 23 13 E
Petrolândia **87** 9 5 S 38 20W
Petrolia **46** 42 54N 82 9W
Petrolina **87** 9 24 S 40 30W
Petropavlovsk **120** 55 0N 69 0 E
Petropavlovsk-Kamchatskiy **121** 53 16N 159 0 E
Petrópolis **89** 22 33 S 43 9W
Petroşeni **107** 45 28N 23 20 E
Petrovaradin **109** 45 16N 19 55 E
Petrovsk-Zabaykalskiy **121** 51 26N 108 30 E
Petrozavodsk **120** 61 41N 34 20 E
Petty Harbour Long Pond **37** 47 31N 52 58W
Peumo **88** 34 21 S 71 19W
Peureulak **126** 4 48N 97 45 E
Pevek **121** 69 15N 171 0 E
Peyrehorade **102** 43 34N 1 7W
Peyruis **103** 44 1N 5 56 E
Pézenas **102** 43 28N 3 24 E
Pforzheim **106** 48 53N 8 43 E
Phagwara **124** 31 10N 75 40 E
Phala **117** 23 45 S 26 50 E
Phalodi **124** 27 12N 72 24 E
Phalsbourg **101** 48 46N 7 15 E
Phan Rang **128** 11 40N 109 9 E
Phan Thiet **128** 11 1N 108 9 E
Phangnga **128** 8 28N 98 30 E
Phanh Bho Ho Chi Minh **128** 10 58N 106 40 E
Phanom Dang Raek, mts. **128** 14 45N 104 0 E
Pharo Dzong **129** 27 45N 89 14 E
Phatthalung **128** 7 39N 100 6 E
Phelps, N.Y., U.S.A. **70** 42 57N 77 5W
Phelps, Wis., U.S.A. **74** 46 2N 89 2W
Phelps L. **55** 59 15N 103 15W
Phenix City **73** 32 30N 85 0W
Phetchabun **128** 16 25N 101 8 E
Phetchaburi **128** 13 1N 99 55 E
Phichai **128** 17 22N 100 10 E
Philadelphia, Miss., U.S.A. **75** 32 47N 89 5W
Philadelphia, N.Y., U.S.A. **71** 44 9N 75 40W
Philadelphia, Pa., U.S.A. **72** 40 0N 75 10W
Philip **74** 44 4N 101 42W
Philip Smith Mts. **67** 68 0N 146 0W
Philippeville **105** 50 12N 4 33 E
Philippines ■ **127** 12 0N 123 0 E
Philipsburg, Can. **43** 45 2N 73 5W
Philipsburg, Mont., U.S.A. **78** 46 20N 113 21W
Philipsburg, Pa., U.S.A. **70** 40 53N 78 10W
Phillip, I. **136** 38 30 S 145 12 E
Phillips, Texas, U.S.A. **75** 35 48N 101 17W
Phillips, Wis., U.S.A. **74** 45 41N 90 22W
Phillipsburg, Kans., U.S.A. **74** 39 48N 99 20W
Phillipsburg, Penn., U.S.A. **71** 40 43N 75 12W
Philmont **71** 42 14N 73 37W
Philomath **78** 44 28N 123 21W
Phitsanulok **128** 16 50N 100 12 E
Phnom Penh **128** 11 33N 104 55 E
Phnom Thbeng **128** 13 50N 104 56 E
Phoenix, Ariz., U.S.A. **79** 33 30N 112 10W
Phoenix, N.Y., U.S.A. **71** 43 13N 76 18W
Phoenix Is. **14** 3 30 S 172 0W
Phoenixville **71** 40 12N 75 29W
Phong Saly **128** 21 42N 102 9 E
Phra Chedi Sam Ong **128** 15 16N 98 23 E
Phra Nakhon Si Ayutthaya **128** 14 25N 100 30 E
Phrae **128** 18 7N 100 9 E
Phrao **128** 19 23N 99 15 E
Phu Doan **128** 21 40N 105 10 E
Phu Loi **128** 20 14N 103 14 E
Phu Ly (Ha Nam) **128** 20 35N 105 50 E
Phu Qui **128** 19 20N 105 20 E
Phuket **128** 8 0N 98 28 E
Phuoc Le (Baria) **128** 10 39N 107 19 E
Pi Ho **131** 32 0N 116 20 E
Piacenza **108** 45 2N 9 42 E
Pialba **135** 25 20 S 152 45 E
Piana **103** 42 15N 8 34 E
Piapot **56** 49 59N 109 8W
Piashti, L. **38** 50 29N 62 52W
Piatra Neamţ **107** 46 56N 26 21 E
Piauí □ **87** 7 0 S 43 0W
Piave, R. **108** 45 50N 13 9 E
Piazza Armerina **108** 37 21N 14 20 E
Pic I. **53** 48 43N 86 37W
Pic, R. **53** 48 36N 86 18W
Pica **86** 20 35 S 69 25W
Picardie **101** 50 0N 2 15 E
Picardie, Plaine de **101** 50 0N 2 0 E
Picardy = Picardie **101** 50 0N 2 15 E
Picayune **75** 30 40N 89 40W
Piccadilly **37** 48 34N 58 55W
Pichieh **131** 27 20N 105 20 E
Pichilemu **88** 34 22 S 72 9W
Pickerel L. **52** 48 40N 91 25W
Pickering **51** 43 52N 79 2W
Pickering Beach **51** 43 50N 78 59W
Pickford **46** 46 10N 84 22W
Pickle Lake **52** 51 30N 90 12W
Pico **93** 38 28N 28 18W
Pico Truncado **90** 46 40 S 68 10W
Picquigny **101** 49 56N 2 10 E
Picton, Austral. **136** 34 12 S 150 34 E
Picton, Can. **47** 44 1N 77 9W
Picton, N.Z. **133** 41 18 S 174 3 E
Pictou **39** 45 41N 62 42W
Pictou I. **39** 45 49N 62 33W
Picture Butte **61** 49 55N 112 45W
Picún-Leufú **90** 39 30 S 69 5W
Pidurutalagala, mt. **124** 7 10N 80 50 E
Pie I. **52** 48 15N 89 6W
Piedad, La **82** 20 20N 102 1W
Piedecuesta **86** 6 59N 73 3W
Piedmont, Can. **43** 45 54N 74 8W
Piedmont, U.S.A. **73** 33 55N 85 39W
Piedmont = Piemonte **108** 45 0N 7 30 E
Piedmont Plat. **73** 34 0N 81 30W
Piedras Blancas Pt. **79** 35 45N 121 18W
Piedras Negras **82** 28 35N 100 35W
Piedras, R. de las **86** 11 40 S 70 50W
Piemonte □ **108** 45 0N 7 30 E
Pierce **78** 46 46N 115 53W
Piercefield **71** 44 13N 74 35W
Pierceland **56** 54 20N 109 46W
Pierre, France **101** 46 54N 5 13 E
Pierre, U.S.A. **74** 44 23N 100 20W
Pierrefeu **103** 43 8N 6 9 E
Pierrefonds, Can. **44** 45 29N 73 52W
Pierrefonds, France **101** 49 20N 3 0 E
Pierrefontaine **101** 47 14N 6 32 E
Pierrefort **102** 44 55N 2 50 E
Pierrelatte **103** 44 23N 4 43 E
Pierreville **41** 46 4N 72 49W
Pierson **57** 49 11N 101 15W
Piestany **69** 48 35N 17 50 E
Piet Retief **117** 27 1 S 30 50 E
Pietarsaari **110** 63 41N 22 40 E
Pietermaritzburg **117** 29 35 S 30 25 E
Pietersburg **117** 23 54 S 29 25 E
Pietrosul **107** 47 35N 24 43 E
Pigeon **46** 43 50N 83 17W
Pigeon Hill **43** 45 3N 72 56W
Pigeon L., Alta., Can. **61** 53 1N 114 2W
Pigeon L., Ont., Can. **47** 44 27N 78 30W
Pigeon, R. **34** 48 1N 89 42W
Piggott **75** 36 20N 90 10W
Pigü **88** 37 36 S 62 25W
Pike River **43** 45 4N 73 6W
Pikes Peak **74** 38 50N 105 10W
Piketberg **117** 32 55 S 18 40 E
Pikeville **72** 37 30N 82 30W
Pikwitonei **55** 55 35N 97 9W
Pilar, Brazil **87** 9 36 S 35 56W
Pilar, Parag. **88** 26 50 S 58 10W
Pilas, I. **127** 6 39N 121 37 E
Pilbara Cr. **134** 21 15 S 118 22 E
Pilcomayo, R. **88** 25 21 S 57 42W
Pilibhit **124** 28 40N 79 50 E
Pilica, R. **107** 51 25N 20 45 E
Pilos **109** 36 55N 21 42 E
Pilot Butte **56** 50 28N 104 25W
Pilot Grove **76** 38 53N 92 55W
Pilot Mound **57** 49 15N 98 54W
Pilot Point **75** 33 26N 97 0W
Pilot Rock **78** 45 30N 118 58W
Pilsen = Plzen **106** 49 45N 13 22 E
Pimba **135** 31 18 S 136 46 E
Pimenta Bueno **86** 11 35 S 61 10W
Pimentel **86** 6 45 S 79 55W
Pin-Blanc, L. **40** 46 45N 78 8W
Pinacle, Le, mt. **43** 45 2N 72 45W
Pinang, I. **128** 5 25N 100 15 E
Pinar del Río **84** 22 26N 83 40W
Pinawa **57** 50 9N 95 50W
Pincher Creek **61** 49 30N 113 57W
Pinchi L. **54** 54 38N 124 30W
Pinckneyville **76** 38 5N 89 20W
Pinconning **46** 43 52N 83 57W
Pincourt **44** 45 23N 74 0W
Pinczów **107** 50 30N 20 35 E
Pindos Óros **109** 40 0N 21 0 E
Pindus Mts. = Pindos Óros **109** 40 0N 21 0 E
Pine **79** 34 27N 111 30W
Pine Bluff **75** 34 10N 92 0W
Pine, C. **37** 46 37N 53 32W
Pine City **74** 45 46N 93 0W
Pine Creek **134** 13 50 S 131 49 E
Pine Dock **57** 51 38N 96 48W
Pine Falls **57** 50 34N 96 11W
Pine Flat Res. **80** 36 50N 119 20W

Pine Grove **Pontian Kechil**

Pine Grove	50	43 48N	79 35W
Pine Hill	43	45 44N	74 29W
Pine, La	78	40 53N	80 45W
Pine Pass	54	55 25N	122 42W
Pine Point	54	60 50N	114 28W
Pine Portage	52	49 20N	88 26W
Pine, R.	55	58 50N	105 38W
Pine Ridge, Can.	58	50 0N	96 50W
Pine Ridge, U.S.A.	74	43 0N	102 35W
Pine River, Can.	57	51 45N	100 30W
Pine River, U.S.A.	52	46 43N	94 24W
Pine Valley	81	32 50N	116 32W
Pinecrest	80	38 12N	120 1W
Pinedale, Ariz., U.S.A.	79	34 23N	110 16W
Pinedale, Calif., U.S.A.	80	36 50N	119 48W
Pinega, R.	120	64 20N	43 0E
Pinerolo	108	44 47N	7 21E
Pinetop	79	34 10N	109 57W
Pinetown	117	29 48S	30 54E
Pinetree	74	43 42N	105 52W
Pineview	63	53 50N	122 38W
Pineville, Ky., U.S.A.	73	36 42N	83 42W
Pineville, La., U.S.A.	75	31 22N	92 30W
Pinewood	55	48 45N	94 10W
Piney, Can.	55	49 5N	96 10W
Piney, France	101	48 22N	4 21E
Ping, R.	128	15 42N	100 9E
Pinghua	131	24 14N	117 2E
Pingkiang	131	28 45N	113 30E
Pingliang	130	35 20N	106 40E
Pinglo, Kwangsi-Chuang, China	131	24 30N	110 45E
Pinglo, Ningsia Hui, China	130	38 58N	106 30E
Pingnam	131	23 30N	110 15E
Pingsiang, Kiangsi, China	131	27 43N	113 50E
Pingsiang, Kwangsi-Chuang, China	131	22 2N	106 55E
Pingtung	131	22 36N	120 30E
Pingyang	131	27 45N	120 25E
Pingyao	130	37 12N	112 0E
Pingyuan	130	37 5N	106 40E
Pinhal	89	22 10S	46 46W
Pinhel	104	40 18N	7 0W
Pini, I.	126	0 10N	98 40E
Piniós, R.	109	39 55N	22 10E
Pinjarra	134	32 37S	115 52E
Pink, R.	55	56 50N	103 50W
Pinnacles	80	36 33N	121 8W
Pinnaroo	136	35 13S	140 56E
Pinon Hills	81	34 26N	117 39W
Pinos	82	22 20N	101 40W
Pinos, I. de	84	21 40N	82 40W
Pinos, Mt	81	34 49N	119 8W
Pinos Pt.	79	36 50N	121 57W
Pinotepa Nacional	83	16 25N	97 55W
Pinrang	127	3 46S	119 34E
Pins, Pte. aux	46	42 15N	81 51W
Pinsk	120	52 10N	26 8E
Pintados	86	20 35S	69 40W
Pintendre	42	46 45N	71 8W
Pinting	130	37 45N	113 34E
Pinto Butte Mt.	55	49 22N	107 27W
Pinware	37	51 37N	56 42W
Pinware R.	37	51 39N	56 42W
Pinyang	131	23 17N	108 47E
Pinyug	120	60 5N	48 0E
Pioche	79	38 0N	114 35W
Piombino	108	42 54N	10 30E
Pioner, I.	121	79 50N	92 0E
Piorini, L.	86	3 15S	62 35W
Piotrków Trybunalski	107	51 23N	19 43E
Pip	123	26 45N	60 10E
Pipestone	74	44 0N	96 20W
Pipestone Cr., Man., Can.	57	49 38N	100 15W
Pipestone Cr., Sask., Can.	55	53 37N	109 46W
Pipestone, R.	34	52 53N	89 23W
Pipinas	88	35 30S	57 19W
Pipmuacan, Rés.	41	49 45N	70 30W
Pipriac	100	47 49N	1 58W
Piqua	77	40 10N	84 10W
Piquiri, R.	89	24 3S	54 14W
Piracicaba	89	22 45S	47 30W
Piracuruca	87	3 50S	41 50W
Piræus = Piraiévs	109	37 57N	23 42E
Piraiévs	109	37 57N	23 42E
Pirajui	89	21 59S	49 29W
Pirane	88	25 25S	59 30W
Pirapora	87	17 20S	44 56W
Pirgos	109	37 40N	21 27E
Piriac-sur-Mer	100	47 22N	2 33W
Piribebuy	88	25 26S	57 2W
Pirin Planina	109	41 40N	23 30E
Pirineos, mts.	104	42 40N	1 0E
Piripiri	87	4 15S	41 46W
Piritu	86	9 23N	69 12W
Pirmasens	105	49 12N	7 30E
Pirot	109	43 9N	22 39E
Pirtleville	79	31 25N	109 35W
Piru	81	34 25N	118 48W
Pisa	108	43 43N	10 23E
Pisagua	86	19 40S	70 15W
Pisco	86	13 50S	76 5W
Pisek	106	49 19N	14 10E
Pising	127	5 8S	121 53E
Pismo Beach	81	35 9N	120 38W
Pissos	102	44 19N	0 49W
Pistoia	108	43 57N	10 53E
Pistol B.	55	62 25N	92 37W
Pistolet B.	37	51 35N	55 45W
Pisuerga, R.	104	42 10N	4 15W
Pitalito	86	1 51N	76 2W
Pitcairn I.	15	25 5S	130 5W
Pite älv	110	65 44N	20 50E
Piteå	110	65 20N	21 25E
Piteşti	107	44 52N	24 54E
Pithapuram	125	17 10N	82 15E
Pithiviers	101	48 10N	2 13E
Pitiquito	82	30 42N	112 2W
Pitlochry	96	56 43N	3 43W
Pitt I.	62	53 30N	129 50W
Pitt L.	63	49 25N	122 32W
Pitt Meadows	66	49 13N	122 42W
Pitt, R.	66	49 13N	122 46W
Pittsburg, Calif., U.S.A.	80	38 1N	121 50W
Pittsburg, Kans., U.S.A.	75	37 21N	94 43W
Pittsburg, Tex., U.S.A.	75	32 59N	94 58W
Pittsburgh	70	40 25N	79 55W
Pittsfield, Ill., U.S.A.	76	39 35N	90 46W
Pittsfield, Mass., U.S.A.	71	42 28N	73 17W
Pittsfield, N.H., U.S.A.	71	43 17N	71 18W
Pittston	71	41 19N	75 50W
Piura	86	5 5S	80 45W
Pivabiska, R.	53	50 13N	82 52W
Pivijay	86	10 28N	74 37W
Pixley	80	35 58N	119 18W
Pizarro	86	4 58N	77 22W
Pizzo	108	38 44N	16 10E
Placentia	37	47 20N	54 0W
Placentia B.	37	47 0N	54 40W
Placerville	80	38 47N	120 51W
Placetas	84	22 15N	79 44W
Plage-St-Blaise	43	45 12N	73 16W
Plain	76	43 17N	90 3W
Plain Dealing	75	32 56N	93 41W
Plaine, La	44	45 47N	73 46W
Plainfield, U.S.A.	77	41 37N	88 12W
Plainfield, N.J., U.S.A.	71	40 37N	74 28W
Plains, Kans., U.S.A.	75	37 20N	100 35W
Plains, Mont., U.S.A.	78	47 27N	114 57W
Plains, Tex., U.S.A.	75	33 11N	102 50W
Plainview, Nebr., U.S.A.	74	42 25N	97 48W
Plainview, Tex., U.S.A.	75	34 10N	101 40W
Plainville	74	39 18N	99 19W
Plainwell	72	42 28N	85 40W
Plaisance	102	43 36N	0 3E
Pláka	109	36 45N	24 26E
Plakhino	120	67 45N	86 5E
Plamondon	60	54 51N	112 32W
Plana Cays	85	22 38N	73 30W
Planada	80	37 18N	120 19W
Planaltina	87	15 30S	47 45W
Plancoët	100	48 32N	2 13W
Planeta Rica	86	8 25N	75 36W
Plankinton	74	43 45N	98 27W
Plano	75	33 0N	96 45W
Plant City	73	28 0N	82 15W
Plant, La	74	45 11N	100 40W
Plaquemine	75	30 20N	91 15W
Plasencia	104	40 3N	6 8W
Plaster City	81	32 47N	115 51W
Plaster Rock	39	46 53N	67 22W
Plata, La, Argent.	88	35 0S	57 55W
Plata, La, U.S.A.	76	40 2N	92 29W
Plata, La, Río de	88	35 0S	56 40W
Platani, R.	108	37 28N	13 23E
Plateau	91	70 55S	40 0E
Plateau du Coteau du Missouri	74	47 9N	101 5W
Platí, Ákra	109	40 27N	24 0E
Platinum	67	59 2N	161 50W
Plato	86	9 47N	74 47W
Platte	74	43 28N	98 50W
Platte City	76	39 22N	94 47W
Platte, R., Minn., U.S.A.	52	45 47N	94 17W
Platte, R., Nebr., U.S.A.	76	41 04N	95 53W
Platteville, U.S.A.	76	42 44N	90 29W
Platteville, Colo., U.S.A.	74	40 18N	104 47W
Plattsburg	76	39 34N	94 27W
Plattsburgh	71	44 41N	73 30W
Plattsmouth	74	41 0N	95 50W
Plauen	106	50 29N	12 9E
Playa Azul	82	17 59N	102 24W
Playgreen L.	57	54 0N	98 15W
Pleasant Bay	35	46 51N	60 48W
Pleasant Hill, Ill., U.S.A.	76	39 27N	90 52W
Pleasant Hill, Mo., U.S.A.	76	38 48N	94 14W
Pleasant Ridge Park	77	38 9N	85 50W
Pleasantdale	56	52 35N	104 30W
Pleasanton	75	29 0N	98 30W
Pleasantville, U.S.A.	76	41 23N	93 18W
Pleasantville, N.J., U.S.A.	72	39 25N	74 30W
Pléaux	102	45 8N	2 13E
Pledger L.	53	50 53N	83 42W
Pleiku (Gia Lai)	128	14 3N	108 0E
Plélan-le-Grand	100	48 0N	2 7W
Plémet	100	48 11N	2 36W
Pléneuf-Val-André	100	48 35N	2 32W
Plenty	56	51 47N	108 38W
Plenty, Bay of	133	37 45S	177 0E
Plentywood	74	48 45N	104 35W
Plessisville	41	46 14N	71 47W
Plestin-les-Grèves	100	48 40N	3 39W
Pletipi L.	36	51 44N	70 6W
Pleven	109	43 26N	24 37E
Plevlja	109	43 21N	19 21E
Plevna	47	44 58N	76 59W
Ploëmeur	100	47 44N	3 26W
Ploërmel	100	47 55N	2 26W
Ploieşti	107	44 57N	26 5E
Plomb du Cantal	102	45 2N	2 48E
Plombières	101	47 59N	6 27E
Plonge, Lac La	55	55 8N	107 20W
Plouay	100	47 55N	3 21W
Ploudalmézeau	100	48 34N	4 41W
Plougasnou	100	48 42N	3 49W
Plouha	100	48 41N	2 57W
Plouhinec	100	48 0N	4 29W
Plovdiv	109	42 8N	24 44E
Plum Coulee	57	49 11N	97 45W
Plum I.	71	41 10N	72 12W
Plumas, Can.	57	50 23N	99 5W
Plumas, U.S.A.	80	39 45N	119 4W
Plummer	78	47 21N	116 59W
Plumtree	117	20 27S	27 55E
Plunkett	56	51 55N	105 27W
Pluvigner	100	47 46N	3 1W
Plymouth, U.K.	95	50 23N	4 9W
Plymouth, U.S.A.	76	40 29N	90 58W
Plymouth, Calif., U.S.A.	80	38 29N	120 51W
Plymouth, Ind., U.S.A.	77	41 20N	86 19W
Plymouth, Mass., U.S.A.	71	41 58N	70 40W
Plymouth, Mich., U.S.A.	46	42 22N	83 28W
Plymouth, N.C., U.S.A.	73	35 54N	76 55W
Plymouth, N.H., U.S.A.	71	43 44N	71 41W
Plymouth, Pa., U.S.A.	71	41 17N	76 0W
Plymouth, Wis., U.S.A.	72	43 42N	87 58W
Plymouth Sd.	95	50 20N	4 10W
Plympton	39	44 30N	65 55W
Plynlimon = Pumlumon Fawr	95	52 29N	3 47W
Plzen	106	49 45N	13 22E
Po Hai	130	38 30N	119 0E
Po, R.	108	45 0N	10 45E
Pobedino	120	49 51N	142 49E
Pobedy Pik	120	40 45N	79 58E
Pocahontas, Arkansas, U.S.A.	75	36 18N	91 0W
Pocahontas, Ill., U.S.A.	76	38 50N	89 33W
Pocahontas, Iowa, U.S.A.	76	42 41N	94 42W
Pocatello	78	42 50N	112 25W
Pocatière, La	41	47 22N	70 2W
Pochontas	54	53 10N	117 51W
Pochutla	83	15 50N	96 31W
Pocita Casas	82	28 32N	111 6W
Pocomoke City	72	38 4N	75 32W
Poços de Caldas	89	21 50S	46 45W
Podensac	102	44 40N	0 22W
Podgorica = Titograd	109	42 30N	19 19E
Podkamennaya Tunguska	121	61 50N	90 26E
Pofadder	117	29 10S	19 22E
Pogamasing	53	46 55N	81 50W
Pogranichnyy	130	44 21N	131 23E
Poh	127	0 46S	122 51E
Pohang	130	36 1N	129 23E
Pohsien	131	33 53N	115 48E
Poile, La	37	47 41N	58 24W
Point Baker	67	56 20N	133 35W
Point-du-Jour	45	45 41N	72 59W
Point Edward	46	43 0N	82 30W
Point Fortin	85	10 9N	61 46W
Point Gatineau	40	45 28N	75 42W
Point Hope	67	68 20N	166 50W
Point L.	64	65 15N	113 4W
Point Lay	67	69 45N	163 10W
Point Leamington	37	49 20N	55 24W
Point Pedro	124	9 50N	80 15E
Point Pelee Nat. Park	46	41 57N	82 31W
Point Pleasant, Can.	39	44 37N	63 34W
Point Pleasant, U.S.A.	72	38 50N	82 7W
Point Roberts	66	48 59N	123 13W
Point Sapin	39	46 58N	64 50W
Pointe-à-la-Frégate	38	49 12N	64 55W
Pointe-à-la Hache	75	29 35N	89 55W
Pointe-à-Maurier	38	50 20N	59 48W
Pointe-à-Pitre	85	16 10N	61 30W
Pointe au Baril Sta.	46	45 35N	80 23W
Pointe-au-Pic	41	47 38N	70 9W
Pointe-aux-Anglais	38	49 41N	67 10W
Pointe-aux-Outardes	41	49 3N	68 26W
Pointe-Aux-Trembles	43	45 39N	73 30W
Pointe-aux-Trembles	45	45 40N	73 30W
Pointe-Calumet	43	45 30N	73 58W
Pointe-Cavagnal	44	45 27N	74 4W
Pointe-Claire	44	45 26N	73 50W
Pointe-des-Cascades	44	45 20N	73 58W
Pointe du Bois	57	50 18N	95 33W
Pointe-Fortune	43	45 34N	74 23W
Pointe-Gatineau	48	45 28N	75 42W
Pointe-Lebel	41	49 10N	68 12W
Pointe-Noire	116	4 48S	12 0E
Pointe-Parent	38	50 8N	61 47W
Pointe Verte	39	47 51N	65 46W
Poisson-Blanc, L. du	40	46 0N	75 45W
Poissy	101	48 55N	2 0E
Poitiers	100	46 35N	0 20E
Poitou, Plaines du	102	46 30N	0 1W
Poix	101	49 47N	2 0E
Poix-Terron	101	49 38N	4 38E
Pojoaque	79	35 55N	106 0W
Pokaran	124	27 0N	71 50E
Pokegama Res.	52	47 12N	93 39W
Poko	116	5 41N	31 55E
Pokotu	129	48 47N	122 7E
Pokpak	131	22 20N	109 45E
Pokrovsk	121	61 29N	129 6E
Pola	129	57 30N	32 0E
Polacca	79	35 52N	110 25W
Polan	123	25 30N	61 10E
Poland ■	107	52 0N	20 0E
Polar Bear Prov. Park	34	54 30N	83 20W
Polcura	88	37 10S	71 50W
Polden Hills	95	51 7N	2 50W
Polewali, Sulawesi, Indon.	127	4 8S	119 43E
Polewali, Sulawesi, Indon.	127	3 21S	119 31E
Poli	129	45 43N	130 28E
Poligny	101	46 50N	5 42E
Polillo I.	127	14 56N	122 0E
Polis	122	35 3N	32 30E
Políyiros	109	40 23N	23 25E
Polk	70	41 22N	79 57W
Pollachi	124	10 35N	77 0E
Pollock	74	45 58N	100 18W
Polnovat	120	63 50N	66 5E
Polo, Ill., U.S.A.	76	42 0N	89 38W
Polo, Mo., U.S.A.	76	39 33N	94 3W
Polotsk	120	55 30N	28 50E
Polson	78	47 45N	114 12W
Poltava	120	49 35N	34 35E
Poltimore	40	45 47N	75 43W
Polynesia	15	10 0S	162 0W
Pomaro	82	18 20N	103 18W
Pombal, Brazil	87	6 55S	37 50W
Pombal, Port.	104	39 55N	8 40W
Pomeroy, Ohio, U.S.A.	72	39 0N	82 0W
Pomeroy, Wash., U.S.A.	78	46 30N	117 33W
Pomme de Terre, Res.	76	37 54N	93 19W
Pomona	81	34 2N	117 49W
Pompano Beach	73	26 12N	80 6W
Pompey	101	48 50N	6 2E
Pompeys Pillar	78	46 0N	108 0W
Ponape I.	14	6 55N	158 10E
Ponask, L.	34	54 0N	92 41W
Ponass L.	56	52 16N	103 58W
Ponca	74	42 38N	96 41W
Ponca City	75	36 40N	97 5W
Ponce	85	18 1N	66 37W
Ponchatoula	75	30 27N	90 25W
Poncheville, L.	40	50 10N	76 55W
Poncin	103	46 6N	5 25E
Pond	81	35 43N	119 20W
Pond Inlet	65	72 30N	77 0W
Pondicherry	124	11 59N	79 50E
Ponds, I. of	36	53 27N	55 52W
Ponferrada	104	42 32N	6 35W
Ponnani	124	10 45N	75 59E
Ponnyadaung	125	22 0N	94 10E
Ponoi, R.	120	67 10N	39 0E
Ponoka	61	52 42N	113 40W
Ponorogo	127	7 52S	111 29E
Pons	102	45 35N	0 34W
Ponsonby	49	43 38N	80 22W
Pont-à-Mousson	101	45 54N	6 1E
Pont Audemer	100	49 21N	0 30E
Pont Aven	100	47 51N	3 47W
Pont-Château	44	45 20N	74 12W
Pont-de-Roide	101	47 23N	6 45E
Pont-de-Salars	102	44 18N	2 44E
Pont-de-Vaux	101	46 26N	4 56E
Pont-de-Veyle	103	46 17N	4 53E
Pont-l'Abbé	100	47 52N	4 15W
Pont Lafrance	35	47 40N	64 58W
Pont-l'Evêque	100	49 18N	0 11E
Pont-Mousseau	43	45 52N	73 39W
Pont-Rouge	41	46 45N	71 42W
Pont-St.-Esprit	103	44 16N	4 40E
Pont-sur-Yonne	101	48 18N	3 10E
Pont-Viau	44	45 34N	73 41W
Ponta Grossa	89	25 0S	50 10W
Ponta Pora	89	22 20S	55 35W
Pontacq	102	43 11N	0 8W
Pontailler	101	47 18N	5 24E
Pontarlier	101	46 54N	6 20E
Pontaubault	100	48 40N	1 20W
Pontaumur	102	45 52N	2 40E
Pontcharra	103	45 26N	6 1E
Pontchartrain, L.	75	30 12N	90 0W
Pontchâteau	100	47 25N	2 5W
Ponte Leccia	103	42 28N	9 13E
Ponte Nova	89	20 25S	42 54W
Pontedera	108	43 40N	10 37E
Pontefract	94	53 42N	1 19W
Ponteix	56	49 46N	107 29W
Pontemacassar Naikliu	127	9 30S	123 58E
Pontevedra	104	42 26N	8 40W
Pontiac, Ill., U.S.A.	77	40 50N	88 40W
Pontiac, Mich., U.S.A.	77	42 40N	83 20W
Pontiac, Parc	40	46 30N	76 30W
Pontian Kechil	128	1 29N	103 23E

Pontianak **Presidio**

Pontianak	**126**	0 3S	109 15E
Pontine Mts. = Karadeniz D.	**122**	41 30N	35 0E
Pontivy	**100**	48 5N	3 0W
Pontoise	**101**	49 3N	2 5E
Ponton, R.	**54**	58 27N	116 11W
Pontorson	**100**	48 34N	1 30W
Ponts-de Cé, Les	**100**	47 25N	0 30W
Pontypool, Can.	**47**	44 6N	78 38W
Pontypool, U.K.	**95**	51 42N	3 1W
Pontypridd	**95**	51 36N	3 21W
Ponziane, Isole	**108**	40 55N	13 0E
Poole	**95**	50 42N	2 2W
Pooley I.	**62**	52 45N	128 15W
Poona = Pune	**124**	18 29N	73 57E
Pooncarie	**136**	33 22S	142 31E
Poopelloe, L.	**136**	31 40S	144 0E
Poopó, Lago de	**86**	18 30S	67 35W
Poorman	**67**	64 5N	155 48W
Popak	**128**	22 15N	109 56E
Popakai, Austral.	**87**	32 12S	141 46E
Popakai, Surinam	**87**	3 20N	55 30W
Popayán	**86**	2 27N	76 36W
Poperinge	**105**	50 51N	2 42E
Popigay	**121**	71 55N	110 47E
Poplar, Mont., U.S.A.	**74**	48 3N	105 9W
Poplar, Wis., U.S.A.	**52**	46 35N	91 48W
Poplar Bluff	**75**	36 45N	90 22W
Poplar Point	**57**	50 4N	97 59W
Poplar, R., Man., Can.	**57**	53 0N	97 19W
Poplar, R., N.W.T., Can.	**54**	61 22N	121 52W
Poplarfield	**57**	50 53N	97 36W
Poplarville	**75**	30 55N	89 30W
Popocatepetl, vol.	**83**	19 10N	98 40W
Popokabaka	**116**	5 49S	16 40E
Porbandar	**124**	21 44N	69 43E
Porcher I.	**62**	53 50N	130 30W
Porcupine	**53**	48 30N	81 11W
Porcupine Plain	**56**	52 36N	103 15W
Porcupine, R., Can.	**55**	59 11N	104 46W
Porcupine, R., U.S.A.	**67**	67 0N	143 0W
Pore	**86**	5 43N	72 0W
Pori	**111**	61 29N	21 48E
Porjus	**110**	66 57N	19 50E
Porkkala	**111**	59 59N	24 26E
Porlamar	**86**	10 57N	63 51W
Pornic	**100**	47 7N	2 5W
Poronaysk	**121**	49 20N	143 0E
Porreta Pass	**108**	44 0N	11 10E
Porsangen	**110**	70 40N	25 40E
Port	**101**	47 43N	6 4E
Port Alberni	**62**	49 40N	124 50W
Port Albert	**136**	38 42S	146 42E
Port Albert Victor	**124**	21 0N	71 30E
Port Alexander	**67**	56 13N	134 40W
Port Alfred, Can.	**41**	48 18N	70 53W
Port Alfred, S. Afr.	**117**	33 36S	26 55E
Port Alice	**62**	50 20N	127 25W
Port Allegany	**70**	41 49N	78 17W
Port Allen	**75**	30 30N	91 15W
Port Angeles	**80**	48 7N	123 30W
Port Antonio	**84**	18 10N	76 30W
Port Aransas	**75**	27 49N	97 4W
Port Arthur, Austral.	**135**	43 7S	147 50E
Port Arthur, U.S.A.	**75**	30 0N	94 0W
Port Arthur = Lüshun	**130**	38 51N	121 20E
Port Arthur = Thunder Bay	**52**	48 25N	89 10W
Port au Choix	**37**	50 43N	57 22W
Port au Port	**37**	48 33N	58 43W
Port au Port B.	**37**	48 40N	58 50W
Port-au-Prince	**85**	18 40N	72 20W
Port Augusta	**135**	32 30S	137 50E
Port Augusta West	**135**	32 29S	137 47E
Port Austin	**46**	44 3N	82 59W
Port Bergé Vaovao	**117**	15 33S	47 40E
Port Blair	**128**	11 40N	92 30E
Port Blandford	**37**	48 20N	54 10W
Port Bolivar	**75**	29 20N	94 40W
Port Burwell	**46**	42 40N	80 48W
Port Canning	**125**	22 17N	88 48E
Port Carling	**46**	45 7N	79 35W
Port-Cartier	**38**	50 2N	66 50W
Port-Cartier-Ouest	**38**	50 1N	66 52W
Port Chalmers	**133**	45 49S	170 30E
Port Chester	**71**	41 0N	73 41W
Port Clements	**62**	53 40N	132 10W
Port Clinton	**77**	41 30N	83 0W
Port Colborne	**46**	42 50N	79 10W
Port Coquitlam	**66**	49 15N	122 45W
Port Credit	**50**	43 33N	79 35W
Port Dalhousie	**49**	43 13N	79 16W
Port-Daniel, Parc Prov. de	**38**	48 11N	64 58W
Port Darwin	**90**	51 50S	59 0W
Port-de-Bouc	**103**	43 24N	4 59E
Port de Paix	**85**	19 50N	72 50W
Port Dickson	**128**	2 30N	101 49E
Port Dover	**46**	42 47N	80 12W
Port Dufferin	**39**	44 55N	62 23W
Port Edward	**62**	54 12N	130 10W
Port Elgin, N.B., Can.	**39**	46 3N	64 5W
Port Elgin, Ont., Can.	**34**	44 25N	81 25W
Port Elizabeth	**117**	33 58S	25 40E
Port Erin	**94**	54 5N	4 45W
Port Fairy	**136**	38 22S	142 12E
Port Gamble	**80**	47 51N	122 35W
Port-Gentil	**116**	0 47S	8 40E
Port Gibson	**75**	31 57N	91 0W
Port Glasgow	**96**	55 57N	4 40W
Port Greville	**39**	45 24N	64 33W
Port Guichon	**66**	49 5N	123 7W
Port Hammond	**66**	49 12N	122 39W
Port Harcourt	**114**	4 40N	7 10E
Port Hardy	**62**	50 41N	127 30W
Port Hastings	**39**	45 39N	61 24W
Port Hawkesbury	**39**	45 36N	61 22W
Port Hedland	**134**	20 25S	118 35E
Port Heiden	**67**	57 0N	158 40W
Port Henry	**71**	44 0N	73 30W
Port Hood	**39**	46 0N	61 32W
Port Hope, Can.	**47**	43 56N	78 20W
Port Hope, U.S.A.	**46**	43 57N	82 43W
Port Howe	**39**	45 51N	63 45W
Port Hueneme	**81**	34 7N	119 12W
Port Huron	**46**	43 0N	82 28W
Port Isabel	**75**	26 12N	97 9W
Port Jackson	**135**	33 50S	151 18E
Port Jefferson	**71**	40 58N	73 5W
Port Jervis	**71**	41 22N	74 42W
Port-Joinville	**100**	46 45N	2 23W
Port Kaituma	**86**	8 3N	59 58W
Port Kelang	**128**	3 0N	101 23E
Port Kells	**66**	49 10N	122 42W
Port Kembla	**136**	34 29S	150 56E
Port-la-Nouvelle	**102**	43 1N	3 3E
Port Laoise	**97**	53 2N	7 20W
Port Lavaca	**75**	28 38N	96 38W
Port Lewis	**43**	45 10N	74 17W
Port Lincoln	**134**	34 42S	135 52E
Port Loring	**46**	45 55N	80 0W
Port Lorne	**39**	44 57N	65 16W
Port Louis, France	**100**	47 42N	3 22W
Port Louis, Maur.	**16**	20 10S	57 30E
Port McNeill	**62**	50 35N	127 5W
Port Macquarie	**135**	31 25S	152 54E
Port Maitland	**70**	42 53N	79 35W
Port Mann	**66**	49 12N	122 49W
Port Maria	**84**	18 25N	76 55W
Port Medway	**39**	44 8N	64 35W
Port Mellon	**63**	49 32N	123 31W
Port-Menier	**38**	49 51N	64 15W
Port Moody	**66**	49 17N	122 51W
Port Morant	**84**	17 54N	76 19W
Port Moresby	**14**	9 24S	147 8E
Port Mouton	**39**	43 58N	64 50W
Port-Navalo	**100**	47 34N	2 54W
Port Nelson, Man., Can.	**55**	57 3N	92 36W
Port Nelson, Ont., Can.	**48**	43 20N	79 46W
Port Nolloth	**117**	29 17S	16 52E
Port Nouveau-Quebec (George R.)	**36**	58 30N	65 50W
Port O'Connor	**75**	28 26N	96 24W
Port of Spain	**85**	10 40N	61 20W
Port Orchard	**80**	47 31N	122 38W
Port Oxford	**78**	42 45N	124 28W
Port Pegasus	**133**	47 12S	167 41E
Port Perry	**47**	44 6N	78 56W
Port Phillip B.	**136**	38 10S	144 50E
Port Pirie	**135**	33 10S	137 58E
Port Pleasant	**71**	40 5N	74 4W
Port Renfrew	**62**	48 30N	124 20W
Port Robinson	**49**	43 2N	79 13W
Port Rowan	**46**	42 40N	80 30W
Port Royal	**39**	44 43N	65 36W
Port Ryerse	**70**	42 47N	80 15W
Port Said = Bûr Sa'îd	**115**	31 16N	32 18E
Port St. Joe	**73**	29 49N	85 20W
Port-St.-Louis-du-Rhône	**103**	43 23N	4 49E
Port St. Servain	**35**	51 21N	58 0W
Port Sanilac	**46**	43 26N	82 33W
Port Saunders	**37**	50 40N	57 18W
Port Severn	**46**	44 48N	79 43W
Port Shepstone	**117**	30 44S	30 28E
Port Simpson	**54**	54 30N	130 20W
Port Stanley	**46**	42 40N	81 10W
Port Stephens	**136**	32 38S	152 12E
Port Talbot	**95**	51 35N	3 48W
Port Townsend	**80**	48 7N	122 50W
Port-Vendres	**102**	42 32N	3 8E
Port Wallace	**39**	44 42N	63 33W
Port Washington	**72**	43 25N	87 52W
Port Weld	**128**	4 50N	100 38E
Port Weller East	**49**	43 14N	79 13W
Port Whitby	**51**	43 51N	78 56W
Port Wing	**52**	46 47N	91 23W
Portachuelo	**86**	17 10S	63 20W
Portadown (Craigavon)	**97**	54 27N	6 26W
Portage, Can.	**35**	46 40N	64 5W
Portage, U.S.A.	**74**	43 31N	89 25W
Portage B.	**57**	51 33N	98 50W
Portage L.	**52**	47 3N	88 30W
Portage La Prairie	**57**	49 58N	98 18W
Portage Mt. Dam	**54**	56 0N	122 0W
Portage, R.	**77**	41 32N	82 58W
Portageville	**75**	36 25N	89 40W
Portalegre	**104**	39 19N	7 25W
Portalegre □	**104**	39 20N	7 40W
Portales	**75**	34 12N	103 25W
Portarlington	**97**	53 10N	7 10W
Porte City, La	**76**	42 19N	92 12W
Porte, La	**77**	41 36N	86 43W
Porter	**77**	41 36N	87 4W
Porter L., N.W.T., Can.	**55**	61 41N	108 5W
Porter L., Sask., Can.	**55**	56 20N	107 20W
Porterville	**80**	36 5N	119 0W
Portet	**102**	43 34N	0 11W
Porthill	**61**	49 0N	116 30W
Portile de Fier	**107**	44 42N	22 30E
Portimão	**104**	37 8N	8 32W
Portland, N.S.W., Austral.	**136**	33 20S	150 0E
Portland, Victoria, Austral.	**136**	38 20S	141 35E
Portland, Can.	**47**	44 42N	76 12W
Portland, Conn., U.S.A.	**71**	41 34N	72 39W
Portland, Ind., U.S.A.	**77**	40 26N	84 59W
Portland, Me., U.S.A.	**35**	43 40N	70 15W
Portland, Mich., U.S.A.	**77**	42 52N	84 58W
Portland, Oreg., U.S.A.	**80**	45 35N	122 40W
Portland B.	**136**	38 15S	141 45E
Portland Bill	**95**	50 31N	2 27W
Portland, C.	**135**	40 46S	148 0E
Portland Creek Pond	**37**	50 11N	57 32W
Portland, I. of	**95**	50 32N	2 25W
Portland Prom.	**36**	58 40N	78 33W
Portneuf	**42**	46 43N	71 55W
Portneuf, Parc Prov. de	**41**	47 10N	72 25W
Portneuf, R.	**41**	48 38N	69 5W
Pôrto	**104**	41 8N	8 40W
Pôrto Alegre, Mato Grosso, Brazil	**87**	21 40S	53 30W
Pôrto Alegre, Rio Grande do Sul, Brazil	**89**	30 5S	51 3W
Porto Alexandre	**117**	15 55S	11 55E
Pôrto de Moz	**87**	1 41S	52 22W
Porto Empédocle	**108**	37 18N	13 30E
Pôrto Esperança	**86**	19 37S	57 29W
Pôrto Franco	**87**	6 20S	47 24W
Porto, G. de	**103**	42 17N	8 34E
Porto Mendes	**89**	24 30S	54 15W
Porto Murtinho	**86**	21 45S	57 55W
Pôrto Nacional	**87**	10 40S	48 30W
Porto Novo	**114**	6 23N	2 42E
Pôrto São José	**89**	22 43S	53 10W
Pôrto Seguro	**87**	16 26S	39 5W
Porto Tórres	**108**	40 50N	8 23E
Pôrto União	**89**	26 10S	51 10W
Pôrto Válter	**86**	8 5S	72 40W
Porto-Vecchio	**103**	41 35N	9 16E
Pôrto Velho	**86**	8 46S	63 54W
Portobelo	**84**	9 35N	79 42W
Portoferráio	**108**	42 50N	10 20E
Portola	**80**	39 49N	120 28W
Portoscuso	**108**	39 12N	8 22E
Portoviejo	**86**	1 0S	80 20W
Portpatrick	**96**	54 50N	5 7W
Portree	**96**	57 25N	6 11W
Portrush	**97**	55 13N	6 40W
Portsall	**100**	48 37N	4 45W
Portsmouth, Can.	**71**	44 14N	76 34W
Portsmouth, Domin.	**85**	15 34N	61 27W
Portsmouth, U.K.	**95**	50 48N	1 6W
Portsmouth, N.H., U.S.A.	**71**	43 5N	70 45W
Portsmouth, Ohio, U.S.A.	**72**	38 45N	83 0W
Portsmouth, R.I., U.S.A.	**71**	41 35N	71 44W
Portsmouth, Va., U.S.A.	**72**	36 50N	76 20W
Porttipahta	**110**	68 5N	26 30E
Portugal ■	**104**	40 0N	7 0W
Portuguesa □	**86**	9 10N	69 15W
Portuguese Timor ■ = Timor	**127**	8 0S	126 30E
Portumna	**97**	53 5N	8 12W
Portville	**70**	42 3N	78 21W
Porvenir	**90**	53 10S	70 30W
Porvoo	**111**	60 24N	25 40E
Posadas	**89**	27 30S	56 0W
Poseh	**131**	23 50N	106 0E
Posen	**46**	45 16N	83 42W
Poseyville	**77**	38 10N	87 47W
Poso	**127**	1 20S	120 55E
Poso Colorado	**88**	23 30S	58 45W
Poso, D.	**127**	1 20S	120 55E
Posse	**87**	14 4S	46 18W
Possel	**116**	5 5N	19 10E
Possession I.	**91**	72 4S	172 0E
Post	**75**	33 13N	101 21W
Post Falls	**78**	47 50N	116 59W
Poste de la Baleine	**36**	55 17N	77 45W
Postiljon, Kepulauan	**127**	6 30S	118 50E
Postojna	**107**	45 46N	14 12E
Poston	**81**	34 0N	114 24W
Postville	**76**	43 5N	91 34W
Potchefstroom	**117**	26 41S	27 7E
Poteau	**75**	35 5N	94 37W
Poteet	**75**	29 4N	98 35W
Potenza	**108**	40 40N	15 50E
Poteriteri, L.	**133**	46 5S	167 10E
Potgietersrus	**117**	24 10S	29 3E
Potomac, R.	**72**	38 0N	76 23W
Potosi	**86**	19 38S	65 50W
Potosi	**76**	37 56N	90 47W
Potosí □	**86**	20 31S	67 0W
Potosi Mt.	**81**	35 57N	115 29W
Potow	**130**	38 8N	116 31E
Potrerillos	**88**	26 20S	69 30W
Potros, Cerro del	**88**	28 32S	69 0W
Potsdam, Ger.	**106**	52 23N	13 4E
Potsdam, U.S.A.	**71**	44 40N	74 59W
Pottageville	**50**	43 59N	79 37W
Potter	**74**	41 15N	103 20W
Pottstown	**71**	40 17N	75 40W
Pottsville	**71**	40 39N	76 12W
Pottuvil	**124**	6 55N	81 50E
Pouancé	**100**	47 44N	1 10W
Pouce Coupé	**54**	55 40N	120 10W
Pouch Cove	**37**	47 46N	52 46W
Poughkeepsie	**71**	41 40N	73 57W
Pouilly	**101**	47 18N	2 57E
Poulaphouca Res.	**97**	53 8N	6 30W
Pouldu, Le	**100**	47 41N	3 36W
Poulin-de-Courval, L.	**41**	48 52N	70 27W
Poulsbo	**80**	47 45N	122 39W
Pouso Alegre, Mato Grosso, Brazil	**87**	11 55S	57 0W
Pouso Alegre, Minas Gerais, Brazil	**89**	22 14S	45 57W
Poutrincourt, L.	**41**	49 11N	74 7W
Pouzages	**102**	46 40N	0 50W
Povenets	**120**	62 50N	34 50E
Poverty Bay	**133**	38 43S	178 2E
Póvoa de Varzim	**104**	41 25N	8 46W
Povungnituk	**36**	60 2N	77 10W
Povungnituk, B.	**36**	60 0N	77 30W
Povungnituk, Mts. de	**36**	61 22N	75 5W
Povungnituk, R.	**36**	60 3N	77 15W
Powassan	**46**	46 5N	79 25W
Poway	**81**	32 58N	117 2W
Powder, R.	**74**	46 47N	105 12W
Powell	**78**	44 45N	108 45W
Powell Creek	**134**	18 6S	133 46E
Powell L.	**62**	50 2N	124 25W
Powell River	**62**	49 50N	124 35W
Powers, Mich., U.S.A.	**72**	45 40N	87 32W
Powers, Oreg., U.S.A.	**78**	42 53N	124 2W
Powers Lake	**74**	48 37N	102 38W
Powis, Vale of	**98**	52 40N	3 10W
Powys □	**95**	52 20N	3 20W
Poyang	**131**	28 59N	116 40E
Poyang Hu	**131**	29 10N	116 10E
Poyarkovo	**121**	49 36N	128 41E
Poza Rica	**83**	20 33N	97 27W
Požarevac	**109**	44 35N	21 18E
Poznan	**106**	52 25N	17 0E
Pozo	**81**	35 20N	120 24W
Pozo Almonte	**86**	20 10S	69 50W
Pozoblanco	**104**	38 23N	4 51W
Prachin Buri	**128**	14 0N	101 25E
Prachuap Khiri Khan	**128**	11 49N	99 48E
Pradelles	**102**	44 46N	3 52E
Pradera	**86**	3 25N	76 15W
Prades	**102**	42 38N	2 23E
Prado	**87**	17 20S	39 13W
Prague = Praha	**106**	50 5N	14 22E
Praha	**106**	50 5N	14 22E
Prahecq	**102**	46 19N	0 26W
Praid	**107**	46 32N	25 10E
Prainha, Amazonas, Brazil	**86**	7 10S	60 30W
Prainha, Pará, Brazil	**87**	1 45S	53 30W
Prairie City	**78**	44 27N	118 44W
Prairie du Chien	**76**	43 1N	91 9W
Prairie du Rocher	**76**	38 5N	90 6W
Prairie, La	**45**	45 25N	73 30W
Prairie, R.	**75**	34 45N	101 15W
Prairies, R. des	**44**	45 42N	73 29W
Praja	**126**	8 39S	116 27E
Prapat	**126**	2 41N	98 58E
Prata, Minas Gerais, Brazil	**87**	19 25S	49 0W
Prata, Pará, Brazil	**87**	1 10S	47 35W
Prato	**108**	43 53N	11 5E
Prats-de-Mollo	**102**	42 25N	2 27E
Pratt	**75**	37 40N	98 45W
Prattville	**73**	32 30N	86 28W
Pravia	**104**	43 30N	6 12W
Pré-en-Pail	**100**	48 28N	0 12W
Precordillera	**88**	30 0S	69 1W
Preeceville	**56**	51 57N	102 40W
Préfailles	**100**	47 9N	2 11W
Pregonero	**86**	8 1N	71 46W
Preissac, L.	**40**	48 20N	78 20W
Prelate	**56**	50 51N	109 24W
Premier	**54**	56 4N	129 56W
Premier Downs	**134**	30 30S	126 30E
Premont	**75**	27 19N	98 8W
Prentice	**74**	45 31N	90 19W
Prenzlau	**106**	53 19N	13 51E
Prepansko Jezero	**109**	40 45N	21 0E
Preparis North Channel	**128**	15 12N	93 40E
Preparis South Channel	**128**	14 36N	93 40E
Prerov	**107**	49 28N	17 27E
Prescott, Can.	**47**	44 45N	75 30W
Prescott, Ariz., U.S.A.	**79**	34 35N	112 30W
Prescott, Ark., U.S.A.	**75**	33 49N	93 22W
Prescott □	**43**	45 32N	74 30W
Prescott I.	**62**	54 6N	130 37W
Présentation, La	**45**	45 39N	73 3W
Preservation Inlet	**133**	46 8S	166 35E
Presho	**74**	43 56N	100 4W
Presidencia de la Plaza	**88**	27 0S	60 0W
Presidencia Roque Sáenz Peña	**88**	26 45S	60 30W
Presidente Dutra	**82**	5 15S	44 30W
Presidente Hayes □	**88**	24 0S	59 0W
Presidente Hermes	**86**	11 0S	61 55W
Presidente Prudente	**89**	22 5S	51 25W
Presidente Rogue Saena Peña	**88**	34 33S	58 30W
Presidio, Mexico	**82**	29 29N	104 23W
Presidio, U.S.A.	**75**	29 30N	104 20W

Presque Isle Quilán, C

Presque Isle 35 46 40N 68 0W
Presteigne 95 52 17N 3 0W
Preston, Can. 49 43 23N 80 21W
Preston, U.K. 94 53 46N 2 42W
Preston, U.S.A. 76 42 6N 90 24W
Preston, Idaho, U.S.A. 78 42 10N 111 55W
Preston, Minn., U.S.A. 74 43 39N 92 3W
Preston, Nev., U.S.A. 78 38 59N 115 2W
Preston, C. 134 20 51S 116 12E
Prestonpans 96 55 58N 3 0W
Prestwick 96 55 30N 4 38W
Pretoria 117 25 44S 28 12E
Preuilly-sur-Claise 100 46 51N 0 56E
Préveza 109 38 57N 20 47E
Préville 45 45 29N 73 30W
Prevost 43 45 52N 74 5W
Prey-Veng 128 11 35N 105 29E
Pribilov Is. 17 56 0N 170 0W
Pribram 106 49 41N 14 2E
Price, Can. 38 48 36N 68 7W
Price, U.S.A. 78 39 40N 110 48W
Price I. 62 52 23N 128 41W
Prieska 117 29 40S 22 42E
Priest L. 63 48 30N 116 55W
Priest River 78 48 11N 116 55W
Priest Valley 80 36 10N 120 39W
Priestly 54 54 8N 125 20W
Prilep 109 41 21N 21 37E
Primrose L. 55 54 55N 109 45W
Prince 56 52 58N 108 23W
Prince Albert 56 53 15N 105 50W
Prince Albert Nat. Park 56 54 0N 106 25W
Prince Albert Pen. 64 72 30N 116 0W
Prince Albert Sd. 64 70 25N 115 0W
Prince Alfred C. 64 74 20N 124 40W
Prince Charles I. 64 67 47N 76 12W
Prince Edward I. □. 39 46 30N 63 30W
Prince Edward Is. 16 45 15S 39 0E
Prince Edward Island Nat. Pk. 39 46 26N 63 12W
Prince Edward Pt. 47 43 56N 76 52W
Prince George 63 53 55N 122 50W
Prince Gustav Adolf Sea 64 78 30N 107 0W
Prince of Wales, C. 67 65 50N 168 0W
Prince of Wales I. 67 73 0N 99 0W
Prince of Wales, I. 67 53 30N 131 30W
Prince of Wales Is. 135 10 40S 142 10E
Prince of Wales Str. 64 73 0N 117 0W
Prince Patrick I. 64 77 0N 120 0W
Prince Regent Inlet 65 73 0N 90 0W
Prince Rupert 62 54 20N 130 20W
Prince William Sd. 67 60 20N 146 30W
Princess Charlotte B. 135 14 25S 144 0E
Princess Margaret Range 65 80 30N 92 0W
Princess Royal Chan. 62 53 0N 128 31W
Princess Royal I. 62 53 0N 128 40W
Princeton, B.C., Can. 63 49 27N 120 30W
Princeton, Ont., Can. 49 43 10N 80 32W
Princeton, Calif., U.S.A. 80 39 24N 122 1W
Princeton, Ill., U.S.A. 76 41 23N 89 28W
Princeton, Ill., U.S.A. 76 41 25N 89 25W
Princeton, Ind., U.S.A. 77 38 20N 87 35W
Princeton, Ky., U.S.A. 72 37 6N 87 55W
Princeton, Mo., U.S.A. 76 40 23N 93 35W
Princeton, N.J., U.S.A. 71 40 18N 74 40W
Princeton, W. Va., U.S.A. 72 37 21N 81 8W
Princeville, Can. 41 46 10N 71 53W
Princeville, U.S.A. 76 40 56N 89 46W
Principe Chan. 62 53 28N 130 0W
Principe da Beira 86 12 20S 64 30W
Principe, I. de 112 1 37N 7 27E
Prineville 78 44 17N 120 57W
Prins Harald Kyst 91 70 0S 35 1E
Prinzapolca 84 13 20N 83 35W
Pripet, R. = Pripyat, R. 120 51 30N 30 0E
Pripyat, R. 120 51 30N 30 0E
Priština 109 42 40N 21 13E
Pritchard 73 30 47N 88 5W
Privas 103 44 45N 4 37E
Prizren 109 42 13N 20 45E
Probolinggo 127 7 46S 113 13E
Procter 63 49 37N 116 57W
Proddatur 124 14 45N 78 30E
Progreso 83 21 20N 89 40W
Prokopyevsk 120 54 0N 87 3E
Prome = Pyè 125 18 45N 95 30E
Prophet, R. 54 58 48N 122 40W
Prophetstown 76 41 40N 89 56W
Propriá 87 10 13S 36 51W
Propriano 103 41 41N 8 52E
Proserpine 135 20 21S 148 36E
Prosser 78 46 11N 119 52W
Prostějov 106 49 30N 17 9E
Protection 75 37 16N 99 30W
Prøven 65 72 10N 55 8W
Provence 103 43 40N 5 46E
Providence, Ky., U.S.A. 72 37 25N 87 46W
Providence, R.I., U.S.A. 71 41 41N 71 15W
Providence Bay 46 45 41N 82 15W
Providence, La 45 45 37N 72 57W
Providence Mts. 79 35 0N 115 30W
Providencia 86 0 28S 76 28W
Providencia, I. de 84 13 25N 81 26W
Provideniya 121 64 23N 173 18E
Province Wellesley 128 5 15N 100 20E
Provincetown 72 42 5N 70 11W
Provins 101 48 33N 3 15E
Provo 78 40 16N 111 37W
Provost 61 52 25N 110 20W
Prudhoe Bay 67 70 20N 148 20W
Prudhoe Land 17 78 1N 65 0W
Prud'homme 56 52 20N 105 54W
Pruszków 107 52 9N 20 49E
Prut, R. 107 46 3N 28 10E
Prydz B. 91 69 0S 74 0E
Pryor 75 36 17N 95 20W
Przemyśl 107 49 50N 22 45E
Przeworsk 107 50 6N 22 32E
Przhevalsk 120 42 30N 78 20E
Pskov 120 57 50N 28 25E
Puán 88 37 30S 63 0W
Pubnico 35 43 47N 65 50W
Pucallpa 86 8 25S 74 30W
Pucheng 131 28 0N 118 30E
Puchi 131 29 42N 113 54E
Pudukkottai 124 10 28N 78 47E
Puebla 83 19 0N 98 10W
Puebla □ 83 18 30N 98 0W
Pueblo 74 38 20N 104 40W
Pueblo Bonito 79 36 4N 107 57W
Pueblo Hundido 88 26 20S 69 30W
Pueblo Nuevo 86 8 26N 71 26W
Pueblonuevo 104 38 16N 5 16W
Puelches 88 38 5S 66 0W
Puelén 88 37 32S 67 38W
Puente Alto 88 33 32S 70 35W
Puente Genil 104 37 22N 4 47W
Puerco, R. 79 35 10N 109 45W
Puerh 129 23 11N 100 56E
Puerto Aisén 90 45 10S 73 0W
Puerto Angel 83 15 40N 96 29W
Puerto Arista 83 15 56N 93 48W
Puerto Armuelles 84 8 20N 83 10W
Puerto Ayacucho 86 5 40N 67 35W
Puerto Barrios 84 15 40N 88 40W
Puerto Belgrano 131 38 50S 62 0W
Puerto Bermejo 88 26 55S 58 34W
Puerto Bermúdez 86 10 20S 75 0W
Puerto Bolívar 86 3 10S 79 55W
Puerto Cabello 86 10 28N 68 1W
Puerto Cabezas 84 14 0N 83 30W
Puerto Cabo Gracias a Dios 84 15 0N 83 10W
Puerto Carreño 86 6 12N 67 22W
Puerto Casado 88 22 19S 57 56W
Puerto Castilla 84 16 0N 86 0W
Puerto Chicama 86 7 45S 79 20W
Puerto Coig 90 50 54S 69 15W
Puerto Columbia 86 10 59N 74 58W
Puerto Cortés, C. Rica 84 8 20N 82 20W
Puerto Cortés, Hond. 84 15 51N 88 0W
Puerto Cuemani 86 0 5N 73 21W
Puerto Cumarebo 86 11 29N 69 21W
Puerto de Morelos 83 20 49N 86 52W
Puerto de Santa María 104 36 36N 6 13W
Puerto Deseado 90 47 45S 66 0W
Puerto Heath 86 12 25S 68 45W
Puerto Huitoto 86 0 18N 74 3W
Puerto Juárez 83 21 11N 86 49W
Puerto La Cruz 86 10 13N 64 38W
Puerto Leguízamo 86 0 12S 74 46W
Puerto Libertad 82 29 55N 112 41W
Puerto Limón, Meta, Colomb. 86 3 23N 73 30W
Puerto Limón, Putumayo, Colomb. 86 1 3N 76 30W
Puerto Lobos 90 42 0S 65 3W
Puerto López 86 4 5N 72 58W
Puerto Madryn 90 42 48S 65 4W
Puerto Maldonado 86 12 30S 69 10W
Puerto Manotí 84 21 22N 76 50W
Puerto Mercedes 86 1 11N 72 53W
Puerto Montt 90 41 22S 72 40W
Puerto Natales 90 51 45S 72 25W
Puerto Nuevo 86 5 53N 69 56W
Puerto Ordaz 86 8 16N 62 44W
Puerto Padre 84 21 13N 76 35W
Puerto Páez 86 6 13N 67 28W
Puerto Peñasco 82 31 20N 113 33W
Puerto Pinasco 88 22 43S 57 50W
Puerto Pirámides 90 42 35S 64 20W
Puerto Plata 85 19 40N 70 45W
Puerto Quellón 90 43 7S 73 37W
Puerto Quepos 84 9 29N 84 6W
Puerto Rico 86 1 54N 75 10W
Puerto Rico ■ 85 18 15N 66 45W
Puerto Rico Trough 12 20 0N 63 0W
Puerto Sastre 88 22 25S 57 55W
Puerto Suárez 86 18 58S 57 52W
Puerto Tejada 86 3 14N 76 24W
Puerto Umbria 86 0 52N 76 33W
Puerto Vallarta 82 20 26N 105 15W
Puerto Villamizar 86 8 25N 72 30W
Puerto Wilches 86 7 21N 73 54W
Puertollano 104 38 43N 4 7W
Pueyrredón, L. 90 47 20S 72 0W
Pugachev 120 52 0N 48 55E
Puget Sd. 78 47 15N 122 30W
Puget-Théniers 103 43 58N 6 53E
Púglia □ 108 41 0N 16 30E
Pugwash 39 45 51N 63 40W
Puhute Mesa 80 37 25N 116 50W
Puigcerdá 104 42 24N 1 50E
Puisaye, Collines de 101 47 34N 3 28E
Puiseaux 101 48 11N 2 30E
Pukaki L. 133 44 4S 170 1E
Pukaskwa Nat. Park 53 48 20N 86 0W
Pukatawagan 55 55 45N 101 20W
Pukekohe 133 37 12S 174 55E
Pukoo 67 21 4N 156 48W
Pukow 131 32 15N 118 45E
Pula 108 39 0N 9 0E
Pulantien 130 39 25N 122 0E
Pulaski, N.Y., U.S.A. 71 43 32N 76 9W
Pulaski, Tenn., U.S.A. 73 35 10N 87 0W
Pulaski, Va., U.S.A. 72 37 4N 80 49W
Pulga 80 39 48N 121 29W
Pulicat, L. 124 13 40N 80 15E
Pullman 78 46 49N 117 10W
Pulog, Mt. 127 16 40N 120 50E
Puloraja 126 4 55N 95 24E
Pumlumon Fawr 95 52 29N 3 47W
Puna 86 19 45S 65 28W
Puna de Atacama 88 25 0S 67 0W
Puná, I. 86 2 55S 80 5W
Punakha 125 27 42N 89 52E
Punata 86 17 25S 65 50W
Punch 124 33 48N 74 4E
Pune 124 18 29N 73 57E
Punjab □ 124 31 0N 76 0E
Punnichy 56 51 23N 104 18W
Puno 86 15 55S 70 3W
Punta Alta 90 38 53S 62 4W
Punta Arenas 90 53 0S 71 0W
Punta de Diaz 88 28 0S 70 45W
Punta de Piedras 86 10 54N 64 6W
Punta del Lago Viedma 90 49 45S 72 0W
Punta Gorda, Belize 83 16 10N 88 45W
Punta Gorda, U.S.A. 73 26 55N 82 0W
Punta Prieta 82 28 58N 114 17W
Puntarenas 84 10 0N 84 50W
Punto Fijo 86 11 42N 70 13W
Puntzi L. 62 52 12N 124 2W
Punxsutawney 70 40 56N 79 0W
Punyu 131 22 58N 113 16E
Puquio 86 14 45S 74 10W
Pur, R. 120 65 30N 77 40E
Purace, vol. 86 2 21N 76 23W
Purbeck, Isle of 95 50 40N 2 5W
Purcell 75 35 0N 97 25W
Puri 125 19 50N 85 58E
Purificación 86 3 51N 74 55W
Purísima, La 82 26 10N 112 4W
Purmerend 105 52 30N 4 58E
Purnea 125 25 45N 87 31E
Pursat 128 12 34N 103 50E
Puruey 86 7 35N 64 48W
Purukcahu 126 0 35S 114 35E
Purulia 125 23 17N 86 33E
Purus, R. 86 5 25S 64 0W
Purwakarta 127 6 35S 107 29E
Purwodadi, Jawa, Indon. 127 7 51S 110 0E
Purwodadi, Jawa, Indon. 127 7 7S 110 55E
Purworejo 127 7 43S 110 2E
Pusan 130 35 5N 129 0E
Pushchino 121 54 20N 158 10E
Puskitamika L. 34 49 20N 76 30W
Puslinch 49 43 26N 80 5W
Puslinch, L. 49 43 25N 80 16W
Putahow L. 55 59 54N 100 40W
Putao 125 27 28N 97 30E
Putaruru 133 38 2S 175 50E
Putehachi (Chalantun) 129 48 4N 122 45E
Puthein Myit, R. 125 15 56N 94 18E
Putien 131 25 28N 119 0E
Putignano 108 40 50N 17 5E
Putnam 71 41 55N 71 55W
Putorana, Gory 121 69 0N 95 0E
Puttalam 124 8 1N 79 55E
Putten 105 52 16N 5 36E
Puttgarden 106 54 28N 11 15E
Putumayo □ 86 1 30S 70 0W
Putumayo, R. 86 1 30S 70 0W
Putussibau, G. 126 0 45N 113 50E
Puy-de-Dôme 102 45 46N 2 57E
Puy-de-Dôme □ 102 45 47N 3 0E
Puy-de-Sancy 102 45 32N 2 41E
Puy Guillaume 102 45 57N 3 28E
Puy, Le 102 45 3N 3 52E
Puy l'Êvêque 102 44 31N 1 9E
Puyallup 80 47 10N 122 22W
Puyang 130 35 45N 115 22E
Puyjalon, L. 38 50 30N 63 25W
Puylaurens 102 43 35N 2 0E
Puyôo 102 43 33N 0 56W
Pweto 116 8 25S 28 51E
Pwllheli 94 52 54N 4 26W
Pyapon 125 16 5N 95 50E
Pyasina, R. 121 72 30N 90 30E
Pyatigorsk 120 44 2N 43 0E
Pyinmana 125 19 45N 96 20E
Pyŏngyang 130 39 0N 125 30E
Pyote 75 31 34N 103 5W
Pyramid L. 78 40 0N 119 30W
Pyramid Pk. 81 36 25N 116 37W
Pyrénées 102 42 45N 0 18E
Pyrenees = Pyrénées 102 42 45N 0 18E
Pyrénées-Atlantiques □ 102 43 15N 1 0W
Pyrénées-Orientales □ 102 42 35N 2 26E
Pyu 125 18 30N 96 35E

Q

Qadam 123 32 55N 66 45E
Qadhimah 122 22 20N 39 13E
Qala-i-Kirta 123 32 15N 63 0E
Qala Nau 123 35 0N 63 5E
Qala Punja 123 37 0N 72 40E
Qal'at al Akhdar 122 28 0N 37 10E
Qal'eh Shaharak 124 34 10N 64 20E
Qamruddin Karez 124 31 45N 68 20E
Qarachuk 122 37 0N 42 2E
Qarah 122 29 55N 40 3E
Qasr-e-Qand 123 26 15N 60 45E
Qatar ■ 123 25 30N 51 15E
Qattara Depression = Q. Munkhafed el 115 29 30N 27 30E
Qattâra, Munkhafed el 115 29 30N 27 30E
Qâyen 123 33 40N 59 10E
Qazvin 122 36 15N 50 0E
Qeisari, (Caesarea) 115 32 30N 34 53E
Qena 115 26 10N 32 43E
Qesari 115 32 30N 34 53E
Qeshm 123 26 55N 56 10E
Qeshm, I. 123 26 50N 56 0E
Qila Saifulla 124 30 45N 68 17E
Qom 123 34 40N 51 0E
Quadra I. 62 50 10N 125 15W
Quakerstown 71 40 27N 75 20W
Qualicum Beach 62 49 22N 124 26W
Quan Long 128 9 7N 105 8E
Quanan 75 34 20N 99 45W
Quang Nam 128 15 55N 108 15E
Quang Ngai 128 15 13N 108 58E
Quang Yen 128 21 3N 106 52E
Quantock Hills, The 95 51 8N 3 10W
Qu'Appelle 56 50 33N 103 53W
Qu'Appelle, R. 56 50 26N 101 19W
Quaraî 88 30 15S 56 20W
Quarré les Tombes 101 47 21N 4 0E
Quarryville 39 46 50N 65 47W
Quartzsite 81 33 44N 114 16W
Quathiaski Cove 62 50 3N 125 12W
Quatsino 62 50 30N 127 40W
Quatsino Sd. 62 50 25N 127 58W
Qūchān 123 37 10N 58 27E
Que Que 117 18 58S 29 48E
Queanbeyan 136 35 17S 149 14E
Québec 42 46 52N 71 13W
Québec □ 35 50 0N 70 0W
Queen Alexandra Ra. 91 85 0S 170 0E
Queen Bess Mt. 54 51 13N 124 35W
Queen Charlotte 62 53 15N 132 2W
Queen Charlotte Is. 62 53 20N 132 10W
Queen Charlotte Mts. 62 53 5N 132 15W
Queen Charlotte Sd. 62 51 30N 130 0W
Queen Charlotte Str. 62 51 0N 128 0W
Queen City 76 40 25N 92 34W
Queen Elizabeth Is. 10 76 0N 95 0W
Queen Mary Coast 91 70 0S 95 0E
Queen Maud G. 64 68 15N 102 30W
Queen's Chan. 134 15 0S 129 30E
Queens Sd. 62 51 57N 128 20W
Queensborough 66 49 12N 122 56W
Queenscliff 136 38 16S 144 39E
Queensland □ 135 15 0S 142 0E
Queenston 49 43 10N 79 3W
Queenstown, Austral. 135 42 4S 145 35E
Queenstown, Can. 39 45 41N 66 7W
Queenstown, N.Z. 133 45 1S 168 40E
Queenstown, S. Afr. 117 31 52S 26 52E
Queets 80 47 32N 124 20W
Queguay Grande, R. 88 32 9S 58 9W
Queimadas 87 11 0S 39 38W
Quela 116 9 10S 16 56E
Quelimane 117 17 53S 36 58E
Quelpart = Cheju Do 131 33 29N 126 34E
Quemado, N. Mex., U.S.A. 79 34 17N 108 28W
Quemado, Tex., U.S.A. 75 28 58N 100 35W
Quemoy = Kinmen 131 24 25N 118 24E
Quemú-Quemú 88 36 3S 63 36W
Quequén 88 38 30S 58 30W
Querétaro 82 20 40N 100 23W
Querétaro □ 82 20 30N 100 30W
Quesnel 63 53 0N 122 30W
Quesnel L. 63 52 30N 121 20W
Quesnel, R. 63 52 58N 122 29W
Questa 79 36 45N 105 35W
Questembert 100 47 40N 2 28W
Quetico 34 48 45N 90 55W
Quetico Prov. Park 52 48 30N 91 45W
Quetta 124 30 15N 66 55E
Quetta □ 124 30 15N 66 55E
Quévillon, L. 40 49 4N 76 57W
Quezaltenango 84 14 40N 91 30W
Quezon City 127 14 38N 121 0E
Qui Nhon 128 13 40N 109 13E
Quiaca, La 88 22 5S 65 35W
Quibaxi 116 8 24S 14 27E
Quibdó 86 5 42N 76 40W
Quiberon 100 47 29N 3 9W
Quíbor 86 9 56N 69 37W
Quick 54 54 36N 126 54W
Quidi Vidi 37 47 35N 52 41W
Quiet L. 54 61 5N 133 5W
Quiindy 88 25 58S 57 14W
Quila 82 24 23N 107 13W
Quilán, C. 90 43 15S 74 30W

Quilcene Reefton

Quilcene 80 47 49N 122 53W
Quilchena 63 50 10N 120 30W
Quilengues 117 14 12S 14 12E
Quilimarí 88 32 5S 70 30W
Quilino 88 30 14S 64 29W
Quill Lake 56 52 4N 104 15W
Quillabamba 86 12 50S 72 50W
Quillagua 88 21 40S 69 40W
Quillaicillo 88 31 17S 71 40W
Quillan 102 42 53N 2 10E
Quillebeuf 100 49 28N 0 30E
Quillota 88 32 54S 71 16W
Quilmes 88 34 43S 58 15W
Quilon 124 8 50N 76 38E
Quilpie 135 26 35S 144 11E
Quilpué 88 33 5S 71 33W
Quimilí 88 27 40S 62 30W
Quimper 100 48 0N 4 9W
Quimperlé 100 47 53N 3 33W
Quinault, R. 80 47 23N 124 18W
Quincy, Calif., U.S.A. 80 39 56N 121 0W
Quincy, Fla., U.S.A. 73 30 34N 84 34W
Quincy, Ill., U.S.A. 74 39 55N 91 20W
Quincy, Mass., U.S.A. 72 42 14N 71 0W
Quincy, Wash., U.S.A. 78 47 22N 119 56W
Quines 88 32 13S 65 48W
Quinga 117 15 49S 40 15E
Quingey 101 47 7N 5 52E
Quinhagak 67 59 45N 162 0W
Quintana Roo □ 83 19 0N 88 0W
Quintanar de la Orden 104 39 36N 3 5W
Quintanar de la Sierra 104 41 57N 2 55W
Quintero 88 32 45S 71 30W
Quintin 100 48 26N 2 56W
Quinton 56 51 23N 104 24W
Quinze, L. des 40 47 35N 79 5W
Quirihue 88 36 15S 72 35W
Quiriquire 86 9 59N 63 13W
Quisiro 86 10 53N 71 17W
Quissac 103 43 55N 4 0E
Quissanga 117 12 24S 40 28E
Quitilipi 88 26 50S 60 13W
Quitman, Ga., U.S.A. 73 30 49N 83 35W
Quitman, Miss., U.S.A. 73 32 2N 88 42W
Quitman, Tex., U.S.A. 75 32 48N 95 25W
Quito 86 0 15S 78 35W
Quixadá 87 4 55S 39 0W
Quneitra 115 33 7N 35 48E
Quorn, Austral. 135 32 25S 138 0E
Quorn, Can. 34 49 25N 90 55W
Quruq Tagh, mts. 129 41 30N 90 0E
Quseir 115 26 7N 34 16E
Quyon 40 45 31N 76 14W

R

Raahe 110 64 40N 24 28E
Raanes Pen. 65 78 30N 85 45W
Raasay I. 96 57 25N 6 4W
Raasay, Sd. of 96 57 30N 6 8W
Raba 127 8 36S 118 55E
Rabastens, Hautes Pyrénées, France 102 43 25N 0 10E
Rabastens, Tarn, France 102 43 50N 1 43E
Rabat, Malta 108 35 53N 14 25E
Rabat, Moroc. 114 34 2N 6 48W
Rabaul 14 4 24S 152 18E
Rabbit L. 55 47 0N 79 38W
Rabbit Lake 56 53 8N 107 46W
Rabbit, R. 54 59 41N 127 12W
Rabbitskin, R. 54 61 47N 120 42W
Rabigh 122 22 50N 39 5E
Raccoon Cr. 77 39 47N 87 23W
Raccoon, R. 76 41 35N 93 37W
Race, C. 37 46 40N 53 5W
Rach Gia 128 10 5N 105 5E
Rachaya 115 33 30N 35 50E
Racine 77 42 41N 87 51W
Racine L. 53 48 2N 83 20W
Rackerby 80 39 26N 121 22W
Radauti 107 47 53N 25 48E
Radcliff 77 37 51N 85 57W
Radford 72 37 8N 80 32W
Radisson 56 52 30N 107 20W
Radium Hill 135 32 30S 140 42E
Radium Hot Springs 61 50 35N 116 2W
Radnor Forest 95 52 17N 3 10W
Radom 107 51 23N 21 12E
Radomir 109 42 37N 23 4E
Radomsko 107 51 5N 19 28E
Radstock 95 51 17N 2 25W
Radstock, C. 134 33 12S 134 20E
Radville 56 49 30N 104 15W
Radway 60 54 4N 112 57W
Rae 54 62 50N 116 3W
Rae Bareli 125 26 18N 81 20E
Rae Isthmus 65 66 40N 87 30W
Raeside, L. 134 29 20S 122 0E
Raetihi 133 39 25S 175 17E
Rafaela 88 31 10S 61 30W
Rafai 116 4 59N 23 58E
Rafhā 122 29 35N 43 35E
Rafsanjān 123 30 30N 56 5E
Ragama 124 7 0N 79 50E
Raglan 133 37 55S 174 55E
Ragueneau 35 49 11N 68 18W
Ragusa 108 36 56N 14 42E
Raha 127 8 20S 118 40E
Raichur 124 16 10N 77 20E
Raigarh 125 21 56N 83 25E
Raiis 122 23 33N 38 43E
Raijua 127 10 37S 121 36E
Rainbow Lake 54 58 30N 119 23W
Rainier 80 46 4N 123 0W
Rainier, Mt. 80 46 50N 121 50W
Rainy L. 52 48 42N 93 10W
Rainy, R. 52 48 43N 94 29W
Rainy River 52 48 43N 94 29W
Raipur 125 21 17N 81 45E
Raith 34 48 50N 90 0W
Raj Nandgaon 125 21 0N 81 0E
Raja Empat, Kepulauan 127 0 30S 129 40E
Raja, Ujung 126 3 40N 96 25E
Rajahmundry 125 17 1N 81 48E
Rajang, R. 126 2 30N 113 30E
Rajapalaiyarm 124 9 25N 77 35E
Rajasthan □ 124 26 45N 73 30E
Rajasthan Canal 124 30 31N 71 0E
Rajgarh 124 24 2N 76 45E
Rajkot 124 22 15N 70 56E
Rajojooseppi 110 68 25N 28 30E
Rajpipla 124 21 50N 73 30E
Rajshahi 125 24 22N 88 39E
Rajshahi □ 125 25 0N 89 0E
Rakaia 133 43 45S 172 1E
Rakaia, R. 133 43 26S 171 47E
Rakan, Ras 123 26 10N 51 20E
Rakaposhi, mt. 124 36 20N 74 30E
Raleigh, Can. 37 51 34N 55 44W
Raleigh, U.S.A. 34 35 46N 78 38W
Raleigh B. 73 34 50N 76 15W
Ralls 75 33 40N 101 20W
Ralston 61 50 15N 111 10W
Rām Allāh 115 31 55N 35 10E
Ram Hd. 136 37 47S 149 30E
Ram, R., Alta., Can. 61 52 23N 115 25W
Ram, R., N.W.T., Can. 54 62 1N 123 41W
Rama, Can. 56 51 46N 103 0W
Rama, Nic. 84 12 9N 84 15W
Ramadi 122 33 28N 43 15E
Ramah 36 58 52N 63 15W
Ramah B. 36 58 52N 63 13W
Ramanathapuram 124 9 25N 78 55E
Rambervillers 101 48 20N 6 38E
Rambipudji 127 8 12S 113 37E
Rambouillet 101 48 40N 1 48E
Rambre Kyun 125 19 0N 94 0E
Ramea, Can. 35 47 28N 57 4W
Ramea, Newf., Can. 37 47 31N 57 23W
Ramea Is. 37 47 31N 57 22W
Ramechhap 125 27 25N 86 10E
Ramelau, Mte. 127 8 55S 126 22E
Ramgarh, Bihar, India 125 23 40N 85 35E
Ramgarh, Rajasthan, India 124 27 30N 70 36E
Rāmhormoz 122 31 15N 49 35E
Ramla 115 31 55N 34 52E
Ramnad = Ramanathapuram 124 9 25N 78 55E
Ramona 81 33 1N 116 56W
Ramore 34 48 30N 80 25W
Ramos Arizpe 82 23 35N 100 59W
Ramos, R. 82 25 35N 105 3W
Rampart 67 65 0N 150 15W
Rampur 124 28 50N 79 5E
Rampurhat 125 24 10N 87 50E
Ramsay L. 62 52 33N 131 23W
Ramsayville 48 45 23N 75 34W
Ramsey, Can. 53 47 25N 82 20W
Ramsey, U.K. 94 54 20N 4 21W
Ramsey, U.S.A. 76 39 8N 89 7W
Ramsey L. 53 47 13N 82 15W
Ramsgate 95 51 20N 1 25E
Ramtek 124 21 20N 79 15E
Ranaghat 125 23 15N 88 35E
Ranau 126 6 2N 116 40E
Rancagua 88 34 10S 70 50W
Rance, R. 100 48 34N 1 59W
Rancheria, R. 54 60 13N 129 7W
Ranchester 78 44 57N 107 12W
Ranchi 125 23 19N 85 27E
Rand 136 35 33S 146 32E
Randall 52 46 9N 94 28W
Randan 102 46 2N 3 21E
Randers 111 56 29N 10 1E
Randle 80 46 32N 121 57W
Randolph, N.Y., U.S.A. 70 42 10N 78 59W
Randolph, Utah, U.S.A. 78 41 43N 111 10W
Randolph, Vt., U.S.A. 71 43 55N 72 39W
Random I. 37 48 8N 53 44W
Randsburg 81 35 26N 117 44W
Råne älv 110 66 26N 21 10E
Råneå 110 65 53N 22 18E
Ranfurly 60 53 25N 111 41W
Rang-des-Dusseau 43 45 11N 73 9W
Rangaunu B. 133 34 51S 173 15E
Rangeley 71 44 58N 70 33W
Rangely 78 40 3N 108 53W
Ranger 75 32 30N 98 42W
Ranger L. 53 46 52N 83 35W
Rangia 125 26 15N 91 20E
Rangiora 133 43 19S 172 36E
Rangitaiki 14 38 52S 176 23E
Rangitaiki, R. 133 37 54S 176 49E
Rangitata, R. 133 43 45S 171 15E
Rangkasbitung 127 6 22S 106 16E
Rangon, R. 125 16 28N 96 40E
Rangoon 125 16 45N 96 20E
Rangpur 125 25 42N 89 22E
Ranibennur 124 14 35N 75 30E
Raniganj 125 23 40N 87 15E
Raniwara 124 24 50N 72 10E
Rankin, U.S.A. 77 40 28N 87 54W
Rankin, Tex., U.S.A. 75 31 16N 101 56W
Rankin Inlet 65 62 30N 93 0W
Rankin's Springs 136 33 49S 146 14E
Rannoch 96 56 41N 4 20W
Rannoch L. 96 56 41N 4 20W
Ranohira 117 22 29S 45 24E
Ranoke 53 50 26N 81 35W
Ranong 128 9 56N 98 40E
Ransom 77 41 9N 88 39W
Ransomville 49 43 15N 78 55W
Rantau 126 4 15N 98 5E
Rantauprapat 126 2 15N 99 50E
Rantemario 127 3 15S 119 57E
Rantoul 77 40 18N 88 10W
Raon-l'Étape 101 48 24N 6 50E
Rapa Iti, I. 15 27 35S 144 20W
Rapang 127 3 45S 119 55E
Rāpch 123 25 40N 59 15E
Raper, C. 65 69 44N 67 6W
Rapid City, Can. 57 50 7N 100 2W
Rapid City, Mich., U.S.A. 46 44 50N 85 17W
Rapid City, S.D., U.S.A. 74 44 0N 103 0W
Rapid, R., Can. 54 59 15N 129 5W
Rapid, R., U.S.A. 52 48 42N 94 26W
Rapid River 72 45 55N 87 0W
Rapide-Blanc 41 47 48N 73 2W
Rapide-Mascouche 44 45 46N 73 40W
Rapide-Sept 40 47 46N 78 19W
Rapides des Joachims 40 46 13N 77 43W
Rarotonga, I. 15 21 30S 160 0W
Ras al Khaima 123 25 50N 56 5E
Ra's at Tannūrah 122 26 40N 50 10E
Ras Dashan, mt. 116 13 8N 37 45E
Rasa, Punta 90 40 50S 62 15W
Rasht 122 37 20N 49 40E
Raso, C. 87 1 50N 50 0W
Rason, L. 134 28 45S 124 25E
Rat Buri 128 13 30N 99 54E
Rat, Is. 67 51 50N 178 15E
Rat, R., Man., Can. 54 56 0N 99 30W
Rat, R., Man., Can. 57 49 35N 97 10W
Rat River 54 61 7N 112 36W
Ratangarh 124 28 5N 74 35E
Rath Luirc (Charleville) 97 52 21N 8 40W
Rathbun Res. 76 40 49N 93 53W
Rathdrum, Ireland 97 52 57N 6 13W
Rathdrum, U.S.A. 78 47 50N 116 58W
Rathenow 106 52 38N 12 23E
Rathkeale 97 52 32N 8 57W
Rathlin I. 97 55 18N 6 14W
Rathlin O'Birne I. 97 54 40N 8 50W
Ratlam 124 23 20N 75 0E
Ratnagiri 124 16 57N 73 18E
Raton 75 37 0N 104 30W
Rats, R. aux 41 48 53N 72 14W
Rattray Hd. 96 57 38N 1 50W
Ratz, Mt. 54 57 23N 132 12W
Raub 128 3 47N 101 52E
Rauch 88 36 45S 59 5W
Raufarhöfn 110 66 27N 15 57W
Raukumara Ra. 133 38 5S 177 55E
Rauma 111 61 10N 21 30E
Raung, Mt. 127 8 8S 114 4E
Rāvar 123 31 20N 56 51E
Ravena 71 42 28N 73 49W
Ravenna, Italy 108 44 28N 12 15E
Ravenna, U.S.A. 77 43 11N 85 56W
Ravenna, U.S.A. 77 37 42N 83 55W
Ravenna, Nebr., U.S.A. 74 41 3N 98 58W
Ravenna, Ohio, U.S.A. 70 41 11N 81 15W
Ravensburg 106 47 48N 9 38E
Ravenshoe 135 17 37S 145 29E
Ravensthorpe 134 33 35S 120 2E
Ravenswood 72 38 58N 81 47W
Raventasón 86 6 10S 81 0W
Ravenwood 76 40 23N 94 41W
Ravi, R. 124 31 0N 73 0E
Rawalpindi 124 33 38N 73 8E
Rawalpindi □ 124 33 10N 72 50E
Rawāndūz 122 36 40N 44 30E
Rawang 128 3 20N 101 35E
Rawdon 41 46 3N 73 40W
Rawene 133 35 25S 173 32E
Rawlinna 134 30 58S 125 28E
Rawlins 78 41 50N 107 20W
Rawlinson Range 134 24 40S 128 30E
Rawson 90 43 15S 65 0W
Ray 74 48 21N 103 6W
Ray, C. 37 47 33N 59 15W
Ray Mts. 67 66 0N 152 10W
Rayadrug 124 14 40N 76 50E
Rayagada 125 19 15N 83 20E
Raychikhinsk 121 49 46N 129 25E
Rayin 123 29 40N 57 22E
Rayleigh 63 50 49N 120 17W
Raymond, Can. 61 49 30N 112 35W
Raymond, U.S.A. 76 39 19N 89 34W
Raymond, Calif., U.S.A. 80 37 13N 119 54W
Raymond, Wash., U.S.A. 80 46 45N 123 48W
Raymondville 75 26 30N 97 50W
Raymore 56 51 25N 104 31W
Rayne 75 30 16N 92 16W
Rayón 82 29 43N 110 35W
Rayong 128 12 40N 101 20E
Raytown 76 39 1N 94 28W
Rayville 75 32 30N 91 45W
Raz, Pte. du 100 48 2N 4 47W
Razgrad 109 43 33N 26 34E
Razor Back Mt. 54 51 32N 125 0W
Ré, Île de 102 46 12N 1 30W
Read Island 64 69 12N 114 31W
Reading, Can. 49 43 50N 80 13W
Reading, U.K. 95 51 27N 0 57W
Reading, Mich., U.S.A. 77 41 50N 84 45W
Reading, Ohio, U.S.A. 77 39 13N 84 26W
Reading, Pa., U.S.A. 71 40 20N 75 53W
Realicó 88 35 0S 64 15W
Réalmont 102 43 48N 2 10E
Ream 128 10 34N 103 39E
Reata 82 26 8N 101 5W
Reay 96 58 33N 3 48W
Rebais 101 48 50N 3 10E
Rebi 127 5 30S 134 7E
Rebun-jima 132 45 20N 142 45E
Recherche, Arch. of the 134 34 15S 122 50E
Recife 87 8 0S 35 0W
Recklinghausen 105 51 36N 7 10E
Reconquista 88 29 10S 59 45W
Recreo 88 29 25S 65 10W
Red Bank 71 40 21N 74 4W
Red Bay, Newf., Can. 36 51 44N 56 25W
Red Bay, Newf., Can. 37 51 44N 56 25W
Red Bluff 78 40 11N 122 11W
Red Bluff L. 75 31 59N 103 58W
Red Bud 76 38 13N 90 0W
Red Cloud 74 40 8N 98 33W
Red Deer 61 52 20N 113 50W
Red Deer L., Alta., Can. 61 52 43N 113 2W
Red Deer L., Man., Can. 57 52 55N 101 20W
Red Deer, R. 61 50 58N 110 0W
Red Deer R. 57 52 53N 101 1W
Red Hill South 136 38 25S 145 2E
Red I. 37 47 23N 54 10W
Red Indian L. 37 48 35N 57 0W
Red L. 52 51 3N 93 49W
Red Lake 52 51 3N 93 49W
Red Lake Falls 74 47 54N 96 15W
Red Lake Road 52 49 59N 93 25W
Red Lodge 78 45 10N 109 10W
Red Mountain 81 35 37N 117 38W
Red Oak 74 41 0N 95 10W
Red Pass 63 53 0N 119 0W
Red, R., Can. 58 50 24N 96 48W
Red, R., Minn., U.S.A. 74 48 10N 97 0W
Red, R., Tex., U.S.A. 75 33 57N 95 30W
Red River Floodway 58 49 50N 96 57W
Red Rock, B.C., Can. 63 53 42N 122 40W
Red Rock, Ont., Can. 52 48 55N 88 15W
Red Rock, L. 76 41 30N 93 15W
Red Sea 115 25 0N 36 0E
Red Slate Mtn. 80 37 31N 118 52W
Red Sucker L 55 54 9N 93 40W
Red Tower Pass = Turnu Rosu P. 107 45 33N 24 17E
Red Wing 74 44 32N 92 35W
Redberry L. 56 52 45N 107 14W
Redbridge 95 51 35N 0 7E
Redcar 94 54 37N 1 4W
Redcliff 61 50 10N 110 50W
Redding 78 40 30N 122 25W
Redditch 95 52 18N 1 57W
Redditt 52 49 59N 94 24W
Redfield 74 45 0N 98 30W
Redkey 77 40 21N 85 9W
Redknife, R. 54 61 14N 119 22W
Redlands 81 34 0N 117 11W
Redmond, Oreg., U.S.A. 78 44 19N 121 11W
Redmond, Wash., U.S.A. 80 47 40N 122 7W
Redon 100 47 40N 2 6W
Redonda, I. 85 16 58N 62 19W
Redonda Is. 62 50 15N 124 50W
Redondela 104 42 15N 8 38W
Redondo 104 38 39N 7 37W
Redondo Beach 81 33 52N 118 26W
Redondz Bay 62 50 17N 124 57W
Redrock Pt. 54 62 11N 115 2W
Redruth 95 50 14N 5 14W
Redvers 57 49 35N 101 40W
Redwater 60 53 55N 113 6W
Redwillow, R. 60 55 2N 119 18W
Redwood 71 44 18N 75 48W
Redwood City 80 37 30N 122 15W
Redwood Falls 74 44 30N 95 2W
Ree, L. 97 53 35N 8 0W
Reed City 72 43 52N 85 30W
Reed, L 55 54 38N 100 30W
Reed, Mt. 35 52 5N 68 5W
Reeder 74 46 7N 102 52W
Reedley 80 36 36N 119 27W
Reedsburg 74 43 34N 90 5W
Reedsport 78 43 45N 124 4W
Reef Pt. 133 35 10S 173 5E
Reefton 133 42 6S 171 51E

Reese Robe-Noire

Reese 46 43 27N 83 42W
Refugio 75 28 18N 97 17W
Regensburg 106 49 1N 12 7E
Regent Park 58 50 28N 104 39W
Réggio di Calábria 108 38 7N 15 38E
Réggio nell' Emilia 108 44 42N 10 38E
Regina 58 50 27N 104 35W
Regina Beach 56 50 47N 105 0W
Registan □ 124 30 15N 65 0E
Registro 89 24 29S 47 49W
Rehoboth 117 23 15S 17 4E
Reichenbach 106 50 36N 12 19E
Reid L. 56 50 0N 108 9W
Reid Lake 62 53 58N 123 6W
Reidsville 73 36 21N 79 40W
Reigate 95 51 14N 0 11W
Reims 101 49 15N 4 0E
Reina Adelaida, Arch. 90 52 20S 74 0W
Reinbeck 76 42 18N 92 0W
Reindeer I. 57 52 30N 98 0W
Reindeer L. 55 57 15N 102 15W
Reindeer, R. 55 55 36N 103 11W
Reine, La 40 48 50N 79 30W
Reinga, C. 133 34 25S 172 43E
Reinland 57 49 2N 97 52W
Reliance 55 63 0N 109 20W
Remanso 87 9 41S 42 4W
Rembang 127 6 42S 111 21E
Remedios, Colomb. 86 7 2N 74 41W
Remedios, Panama 84 8 15N 81 50W
Remer 52 47 3N 93 55W
Remeshk 123 26 55N 58 50E
Remi Lake Prov. Park 53 49 30N 82 15W
Rémigny 40 47 46N 79 12W
Remington 77 40 45N 87 8W
Remiremont 101 48 0N 6 36E
Remoulins 103 43 55N 4 35E
Remscheid 105 51 11N 7 12E
Remus 46 43 36N 85 9W
Renata 63 49 27N 118 7W
Rencontre East 37 47 38N 55 12W
Rend L. 76 38 2N 88 58W
Rendsburg 106 54 18N 9 41E
Rene 121 66 2N 179 25W
Renews 37 46 56N 52 56W
Renfrew, Can. 47 45 30N 76 40W
Renfrew, U.K. 96 55 52N 4 24W
Rengat 126 0 30S 102 45E
Rengo 88 34 24S 70 50W
Renison 53 50 58N 81 7W
Renkum 105 51 58N 5 43E
Renmark 135 34 11S 140 43E
Rennell Sd. 62 53 23N 132 35W
Renner Springs Teleg. Off. 134 18 20S 133 47E
Rennes 100 48 7N 1 41W
Rennie 57 49 51N 95 33W
Rennison I. 62 52 50N 129 20W
Reno 80 39 30N 119 50W
Reno, R. 108 44 45N 11 40E
Renovo 70 41 20N 77 47W
Rens 104 54 54N 9 5E
Rensselaer, Ind., U.S.A. 77 41 0N 87 10W
Rensselaer, N.Y., U.S.A. 71 42 38N 73 41W
Renton 80 47 30N 122 9W
Réole, La 102 44 35N 0 1W
Repentigny 45 45 44N 73 28W
Republic, Mich., U.S.A. 53 46 25N 87 59W
Republic, Wash., U.S.A. 63 48 38N 118 42W
Republican City 74 40 9N 99 20W
Republican, R. 74 40 0N 98 30W
Repulse B., Antarct. 91 64 30S 99 30E
Repulse B., Austral. 135 20 31S 148 45E
Repulse Bay 65 66 30N 86 30W
Requena, Peru 86 5 5S 73 52W
Requena, Spain 104 39 30N 1 4W
Reserve, Can. 56 52 28N 102 39W
Reserve, U.S.A. 79 33 50N 108 54W
Resht = Rasht 122 37 20N 49 40E
Resistencia 88 27 30S 59 0W
Reşiţa 107 45 18N 21 53E
Resolute 65 74 42N 94 54W
Resolution I., Can. 23 61 30N 65 0W
Resolution I., N.Z. 133 45 40S 166 40E
Restigouche, R. 39 47 50N 67 0W
Reston 57 49 33N 101 6W
Restrepo 86 4 15N 73 33W
Retalhuleu 84 14 33N 91 46W
Rethel 101 49 30N 4 20E
Réthímnon 109 35 15N 24 40E
Rétiers 100 47 55N 1 25W
Retiro 88 35 59S 71 47W
Réunion, Î. 16 22 0S 56 0E
Reutlingen 106 48 28N 9 13E
Revel 102 43 28N 2 0E
Revelstoke 63 51 0N 118 10W
Revigny 101 48 50N 5 0E
Revilla Gigedo, Is. de 15 18 40N 112 0W
Revillagigedo I. 54 55 50N 131 20W
Revin 101 49 55N 4 39E
Rewa 125 24 33N 81 25E
Rewari 124 28 15N 76 40E
Rex 67 64 10N 149 20W
Rexburg 78 43 55N 111 50W
Rexdale 50 43 43N 79 33W
Rexton, Can. 39 46 39N 64 52W
Rexton, U.S.A. 46 46 10N 85 14W
Rey Malabo 116 3 45N 8 50E
Reyes, Pt. 80 37 59N 123 2W
Reykjahlið 110 65 40N 16 55W
Reykjanes 110 63 48N 22 40W
Reykjavík 110 64 10N 21 57E
Reynolds, Can. 57 49 40N 95 55W
Reynolds, U.S.A. 76 41 20N 90 40W
Reynolds Ra. 134 22 30S 133 0E
Reynoldsville 70 41 5N 78 58W
Reynosa 83 26 5N 98 18W
Rezā'iyeh, Daryāchech-ye 122 37 30N 45 30E
Rhayader 95 52 19N 3 30W
Rhein 57 51 25N 102 15W
Rhein, R. 106 51 42N 6 20E
Rheine 105 52 17N 7 25E
Rheinland-Pfalz □ 105 50 50N 7 0E
Rheydt 105 51 10N 6 24E
Rhinau 101 48 19N 7 43E
Rhine, R. = Rhein 106 51 42N 6 20E
Rhinelander 74 45 38N 89 29W
Rhode Island □ 71 41 38N 71 37W
Rhodes = Ródhos 109 36 15N 28 10E
Rhodesia ■ 117 20 0S 30 0E
Rhodope Mts. = Rhodopi Planina 109 41 40N 24 20E
Rhodopi Planina 109 41 40N 24 20E
Rhön, mts. 106 50 24N 9 58E
Rhondda 95 51 39N 3 30W
Rhône □ 103 45 54N 4 35E
Rhône, R. 103 43 28N 4 42E
Rhum, I. 96 57 0N 6 20W
Rhyl 94 53 19N 3 29W
Riachão 87 7 20S 46 37W
Rialto 81 34 6N 117 22W
Rians 103 43 37N 5 44E
Riasi 124 33 10N 74 50E
Riau □ 126 0 0 102 35E
Riau, Kepulauan 126 0 30N 104 20E
Ribadeo 104 43 35N 7 5W
Ribat 117 29 50N 60 55E
Ribatejo □ 104 39 15N 8 30W
Ribble, R. 94 54 13N 2 20W
Ribe 111 55 19N 8 44E
Ribeauvillé 101 48 10N 7 20E
Ribécourt 101 49 30N 2 55E
Ribeirão Prêto 89 21 10S 47 50W
Ribémont 101 49 47N 3 27E
Ribérac 102 45 15N 0 20E
Riberalta 86 11 0S 66 0W
Ribstone Cr. 61 52 52N 110 5W
Riccarton 133 43 32S 172 37E
Rice 81 34 5N 114 51W
Rice L., Can. 47 44 12N 78 10W
Rice L., U.S.A. 52 46 30N 93 22W
Rice Lake 74 45 30N 91 42W
Riceburg 43 45 8N 72 56W
Riceton 56 50 7N 104 19W
Rich, C. 46 44 43N 80 38W
Rich Hill 75 38 5N 94 22W
Rich Valley 60 53 51N 114 21W
Richan 52 49 59N 92 49W
Richards Deep 13 25 0S 73 0W
Richards I. 64 68 0N 135 0W
Richards L. 55 59 10N 107 10W
Richardson 58 50 23N 104 27W
Richardson Mts. 64 68 20N 135 45W
Richardson Pt. 51 43 50N 78 59W
Richardson, R. 55 58 25N 111 14W
Richardson Springs 80 39 51N 121 46W
Richardton 74 46 56N 102 22W
Riche, Pte. 37 50 42N 57 25W
Richelieu, Can. 45 45 27N 73 15W
Richelieu, France 100 47 0N 0 20E
Richelieu □ 43 45 55N 73 0W
Richelieu, R. 45 45 28N 73 18W
Richey 74 47 42N 105 5W
Richfield, Idaho, U.S.A. 78 43 2N 114 5W
Richfield, Utah, U.S.A. 79 38 50N 112 0W
Richford 71 45 0N 72 40W
Richibucto 39 46 42N 64 54W
Richland, Ga., U.S.A. 73 32 7N 84 40W
Richland, Iowa, U.S.A. 76 41 13N 91 58W
Richland, Mo., U.S.A. 76 37 51N 92 26W
Richland, Oreg., U.S.A. 78 44 49N 117 9W
Richland, Wash., U.S.A. 78 46 15N 119 15W
Richland Center 74 43 21N 90 22W
Richlands 72 37 7N 81 49W
Richmond, N.S.W., Austral. 136 33 35S 150 42E
Richmond, Queens., Austral. 135 20 43S 143 8E
Richmond, N.S., Can. 39 44 40N 63 36W
Richmond, Ont., Can. 47 45 11N 75 50W
Richmond, Qué., Can. 41 45 40N 72 9W
Richmond, N.Z. 133 41 4S 173 12E
Richmond, S. Afr. 117 29 51S 30 18E
Richmond, N. Yorks., U.K. 94 54 24N 1 43W
Richmond, Surrey, U.K. 95 51 28N 0 18W
Richmond, Calif., U.S.A. 80 38 0N 122 21W
Richmond, Ind., U.S.A. 77 39 50N 84 50W
Richmond, Ky., U.S.A. 77 37 40N 84 20W
Richmond, Mich., U.S.A. 46 42 47N 82 45W
Richmond, Mo., U.S.A. 74 39 15N 93 58W
Richmond, N.Y., U.S.A. 71 40 35N 74 6W
Richmond, Tex., U.S.A. 75 29 32N 95 42W
Richmond, Va., U.S.A. 72 37 33N 77 27W
Richmond □ 66 49 9N 123 7W
Richmond Gulf 34 56 20N 75 50W
Richmond Hill 50 43 52N 79 27W
Richmound 56 50 27N 109 45W
Richton 73 31 23N 88 58W
Richvale 50 43 51N 79 26W
Richwood, U.S.A. 77 40 26N 83 18W
Richwood, W. Va., U.S.A. 72 38 17N 80 32W
Rideau Canal 48 44 53N 76 0W
Rideau, R. 48 45 27N 75 42W
Ridge Farm 77 39 54N 87 39W
Ridge, R. 53 50 25N 84 20W
Ridgecrest 81 35 38N 117 40W
Ridgedale 56 53 0N 104 10W
Ridgefield 80 45 49N 122 45W
Ridgeland 73 32 30N 80 58W
Ridgetown 46 42 26N 81 52W
Ridgeville 77 40 18N 85 2W
Ridgway, Ill., U.S.A. 77 37 48N 88 16W
Ridgway, Pa., U.S.A. 70 41 25N 78 43W
Riding Mt. Nat. Park 57 50 50N 100 0W
Ried 106 48 14N 13 30E
Rietfontein 117 26 44S 20 1E
Rieti 108 42 23N 12 50E
Rieupeyroux 102 44 19N 2 12E
Riez 103 43 49N 6 6E
Rifle 78 39 40N 107 50W
Rifstangi 110 66 32N 16 12W
Riga 120 56 53N 24 8E
Rigaud 43 45 29N 74 18W
Rigby 78 43 41N 111 58W
Riggins 78 45 29N 116 26W
Rignac 102 44 25N 2 16E
Rigolet 36 54 10N 58 23W
Riihimäki 111 60 45N 24 48E
Riiser-Larsen halvøya 91 68 0S 35 0E
Riishiri-Tō 132 45 11N 141 15E
Rijeka (Fiume) 108 45 20N 14 21E
Rijkevorsel 105 51 21N 4 46E
Rijssen 105 52 19N 6 30E
Rijswijk 105 52 4N 4 22E
Rilly 101 49 11N 4 3E
Rimbey 61 52 35N 114 15W
Rímini 108 44 3N 12 33E
Rîmnicu Sărat 107 45 26N 27 3E
Rîmnicu Vîlcea 107 45 9N 24 21E
Rimouski 41 48 27N 68 30W
Rimouski-Est 41 48 28N 68 31W
Rimouski, Parc Prov. de 41 48 0N 68 15W
Rimouski, R. 41 48 27N 68 32W
Rimrock 80 46 38N 121 10W
Rinca 127 8 45S 119 35E
Rincón de Romos 82 22 14N 102 18W
Rinconada 88 22 26S 66 10W
Rineanna 97 52 42N 85 7W
Ringkøbing 111 56 5N 8 15E
Ringling 78 46 16N 110 56W
Ringvassøy 110 69 36N 19 15E
Ringwood 50 43 58N 79 17W
Rinia, I. 109 37 23N 25 13E
Rio Arica 86 1 35S 75 30W
Rio Branco 86 9 58S 67 49W
Rio Branco 89 32 40S 53 40W
Rio Brilhante 89 21 48S 54 33W
Rio Chico 86 10 19N 65 59W
Rio Claro, Brazil 89 22 19S 47 35W
Rio Claro, Trin 85 10 20N 61 25W
Rio Colorado 90 39 0S 64 0W
Rio Cuarto 88 33 10S 64 25W
Rio de Janeiro 89 23 0S 43 12W
Rio de Janeiro □ 89 22 50S 43 0W
Rio do Sul 89 27 95S 49 37W
Rio Gallegos 90 51 35S 69 15W
Rio Grande 90 53 50S 67 45W
Rio Grande 89 32 0S 52 20W
Rio Grande, Mexico 82 23 50N 103 2W
Rio Grande, Nic. 84 12 54N 83 33W
Rio Grande City 75 26 30N 98 55W
Rio Grande del Norte, R. 68 26 0N 97 0W
Rio Grande do Norte □ 87 5 40S 36 0W
Rio Grande do Sul □ 89 30 0S 53 0W
Rio Grande, R. 79 37 47N 106 15W
Rio Hato 84 8 22N 80 10W
Rio Lagartos 83 21 36N 88 10W
Rio Largo 87 9 28S 35 50W
Rio Mulatos 86 19 40S 66 50W
Rio Muni □ = Mbini □ 114 1 30N 10 0E
Rio Negro 89 26 0S 50 0W
Rio Oriente 84 22 17N 81 13W
Rio Pardo, Minas Gerais, Brazil 87 15 55S 42 30W
Rio Pardo, Rio Grande do Sul, Brazil 89 30 0S 52 30W
Río Segundo 88 31 40S 63 59W
Río Tercero 88 32 15S 64 8W
Rio Verde 83 21 56N 99 59W
Rio Vista 80 38 11N 121 44W
Riobamba 86 1 50S 78 45W
Riohacha 86 11 33N 72 55W
Rioja, La, Argent. 88 29 20S 67 0W
Rioja, La, Spain 104 42 20N 2 20W
Rioja, La □ 88 29 30S 67 0W
Riom 102 45 54N 3 7E
Riom-ès-Montagnes 102 45 17N 2 39E
Rion-des-Landes 102 43 55N 0 56W
Riondel 63 49 46N 116 51W
Rionegro 86 6 9N 75 22W
Riosucio, Caldas, Colomb. 86 5 30N 75 40W
Riosucio, Choco, Colomb. 86 7 27N 77 7W
Riou L. 55 59 7N 106 25W
Ripley, Can. 46 44 4N 81 35W
Ripley, U.S.A. 77 38 45N 83 51W
Ripley, Calif., U.S.A. 81 33 32N 114 39W
Ripley, N.Y., U.S.A. 70 42 16N 79 44W
Ripley, Tenn., U.S.A. 75 35 43N 89 34W
Ripon, Can. 40 45 45N 75 10W
Ripon, U.K. 94 54 8N 1 31W
Ripon, Calif., U.S.A. 80 37 44N 121 7W
Ripon, Wis., U.S.A. 72 43 51N 88 50W
Riscle 102 43 39N 0 5W
Rising Sun 77 38 57N 84 51W
Risle, R. 100 48 55N 0 41E
Rison 75 33 57N 92 11W
Risør 111 58 43N 9 13E
Ritchie L. 38 52 58N 66 1W
Ritchie's Archipelago 128 12 5N 94 0E
Rittman 70 40 57N 81 48W
Ritzville 78 47 10N 118 21W
Riva Bella 100 49 17N 0 18W
Rivadavia, Buenos Aires, Argent. 88 35 29S 62 59W
Rivadavia, Mendoza, Argent. 88 33 13S 68 30W
Rivadavia, Salta, Argent. 88 24 5S 63 0W
Rivadavia, Chile 88 29 50S 70 35W
Rivas 84 11 30N 85 50W
Rive-de-Gier 103 45 32N 4 37E
River Hébert 39 45 42N 64 23W
River John 39 45 45N 63 3W
River Jordan 62 48 26N 124 3W
River of Ponds 37 50 32N 57 24W
River of Ponds L. 37 50 30N 57 20W
River Rouge 77 42 16N 83 9W
River Valley 46 46 35N 80 11W
Rivera 89 31 0S 55 50W
Rivercrest 58 50 0N 97 3W
Riverdale 80 36 26N 119 52W
Riverfield 43 45 9N 73 49W
Riverhead, Can. 37 46 58N 53 31W
Riverhead, U.S.A. 71 40 53N 72 40W
Riverhurst 56 50 55N 106 50W
Riverina 135 35 30S 145 20E
Riverport 39 44 18N 64 20W
Rivers 57 50 2N 100 14W
Rivers Inl. 62 51 40N 127 20W
Rivers Inlet 62 51 42N 127 15W
Rivers, L. of the 56 49 49N 105 44W
Riversdal 117 34 7S 21 15E
Riverside, Can. 70 42 17N 82 59W
Riverside, Calif., U.S.A. 81 34 0N 117 22W
Riverside, Wash., U.S.A. 63 48 29N 119 30W
Riverside, Wyo., U.S.A. 78 41 12N 106 57W
Riverside-Albert 39 45 42N 64 45W
Riverton, Can. 57 51 1N 97 0W
Riverton, N.Z. 133 46 21S 168 0E
Riverton, U.S.A. 76 39 51N 89 33W
Riverton, Wyo., U.S.A. 78 43 1N 108 27W
Riverview Heights 39 46 4N 64 48W
Rives 103 45 21N 5 31E
Rivesaltes 102 42 47N 2 50E
Rivière -Ste.-Marguerite 38 50 8N 66 37W
Rivière-à-la-Chaloupe 38 50 17N 65 6W
Rivière-à-Pierre 41 46 59N 72 11W
Rivière-au-Renard 38 48 59N 64 23W
Rivière-aux-Rats 41 47 13N 72 53W
Rivière-Beaudette 43 45 14N 74 20W
Rivière-Bersimis 41 48 56N 68 42W
Rivière-Bleue 35 47 26N 69 2W
Rivière-de-la-Chaloupe 38 49 8N 62 32W
Rivière-des-Hurons 45 45 30N 73 9W
Rivière-des-Prairies 44 45 39N 73 33W
Rivière-du-Loup 41 47 50N 69 30W
Rivière-Ouelle 41 47 26N 70 1W
Rivière-Pigou 38 50 16N 65 35W
Rivière-Pontecôte 38 49 57N 67 1W
Rivière-Portneuf 41 48 38N 69 6W
Rivière-St-Jean 38 50 17N 64 19W
Rivière Verte 39 47 19N 68 9W
Rivierre-au-Tonnère 38 50 16N 64 47W
Riyadh = Ar Riyād 122 24 41N 46 42E
Rize 122 41 0N 40 30E
Rizzuto, C. 108 38 54N 17 5E
Rjukan 111 59 54N 8 33E
Roachdale 77 39 51N 86 48W
Road Town 85 18 27N 64 37W
Roag, L. 96 58 10N 6 55W
Roanne 103 46 3N 4 4E
Roanoke, U.S.A. 77 40 58N 85 22W
Roanoke, Ala., U.S.A. 73 33 9N 85 23W
Roanoke, Va., U.S.A. 72 37 19N 79 55W
Roanoke I. 73 35 55N 75 40W
Roanoke, R. 73 36 15N 77 20W
Roanoke Rapids 73 36 36N 77 42W
Roatán 84 16 18N 86 35W
Robb 60 53 13N 116 58W
Robe, Mt. 136 31 40S 141 20E
Robe-Noire, L. de la 38 50 42N 62 42W

Robe, R **Ruel**

Robe, R.	**97**	53 38N	9 10W
Robert Lee	**75**	31 55N	100 26W
Roberts, U.S.A.	**77**	40 37N	88 11W
Roberts, Idaho, U.S.A.	**78**	43 44N	112 8W
Robert's Arm	**37**	49 29N	55 49W
Roberts Bank Superport	**66**	49 1N	123 9W
Roberts Creek	**63**	49 26N	123 38W
Roberts, Pt.	**63**	49 0N	123 6W
Robertson, Austral.	**134**	34 37S	150 36E
Robertson, S. Afr.	**117**	33 46S	19 50E
Robertson I.	**91**	68 0S	75 0W
Robertsonville	**41**	46 9N	71 13W
Robertville	**39**	47 42N	65 46W
Roberval	**41**	48 32N	72 15W
Robeson Kanal	**17**	82 0N	61 30W
Robinson	**77**	39 0N	87 44W
Robinson Ranges	**134**	25 40S	118 0E
Robinvale	**136**	34 40S	142 45E
Robla, La	**104**	42 50N	5 41W
Roblin	**57**	51 14N	101 21W
Roblin Park	**58**	49 52N	97 17W
Roboré	**86**	18 10S	59 45W
Robsart	**56**	49 23N	109 17W
Robson, Mt.	**63**	53 10N	119 10W
Robstown	**75**	27 47N	97 40W
Roca, C. da	**104**	38 40N	9 31W
Roca Partida, I.	**82**	19 1N	112 2W
Roçadas	**117**	16 45S	15 0E
Rocanville	**57**	50 23N	101 42W
Rocas, I.	**87**	4 0S	34 1W
Rocha	**89**	34 30S	54 25W
Rochdale	**94**	53 36N	2 10W
Roche-Bernard, La	**100**	47 31N	2 19W
Roche-Canillac, La	**102**	45 12N	1 57E
Roche, La	**103**	46 4N	6 19E
Roche Percée	**56**	49 4N	102 48W
Roche-sur-Yon, La	**100**	46 40N	1 25W
Rochebaucourt	**40**	48 41N	77 30W
Rochechouart	**102**	45 50N	0 49E
Rochefort, Belg.	**105**	50 9N	5 12E
Rochefort, France	**102**	45 56N	0 57W
Rochefort-en-Terre	**100**	47 42N	2 22W
Rochefoucauld, La	**102**	45 44N	0 24E
Rochelle	**76**	41 55N	89 5W
Rochelle, La	**102**	46 10N	1 9W
Rocher River	**54**	61 23N	112 44W
Roches, R.	**38**	50 2N	66 55W
Rocheservière	**100**	46 57N	1 30W
Rochester, Austral.	**136**	36 22S	144 41E
Rochester, Can.	**60**	54 22N	113 27W
Rochester, U.K.	**95**	51 22N	0 30E
Rochester, Ind., U.S.A.	**77**	41 5N	86 15W
Rochester, Mich., U.S.A.	**77**	42 41N	83 8W
Rochester, Minn., U.S.A.	**74**	44 1N	92 28W
Rochester, N.H., U.S.A.	**71**	43 19N	70 57W
Rochester, N.Y., U.S.A.	**70**	43 10N	77 40W
Rochester, Pa., U.S.A.	**70**	40 41N	80 17W
Rock Creek	**63**	49 4N	119 0W
Rock Falls	**76**	41 47N	89 41W
Rock Hill	**73**	34 55N	81 2W
Rock Island, Can.	**41**	45 26N	73 34W
Rock Island, U.S.A.	**76**	41 30N	90 35W
Rock Lake	**74**	48 50N	99 13W
Rock Port	**74**	40 26N	95 30W
Rock, R.	**54**	60 7N	127 7W
Rock Rapids	**74**	43 25N	96 10W
Rock River	**78**	41 49N	106 0W
Rock Sound	**84**	24 54N	76 12W
Rock Sprs., Ariz., U.S.A.	**79**	34 2N	112 11W
Rock Sprs., Mont., U.S.A.	**78**	46 55N	106 11W
Rock Sprs., Tex., U.S.A.	**75**	30 2N	100 11W
Rock Sprs., Wyo., U.S.A.	**78**	41 40N	109 10W
Rock Valley	**74**	43 10N	96 17W
Rockall I.	**93**	57 37N	13 42W
Rockburn	**43**	45 1N	74 1W
Rockcliffe Park	**48**	45 27N	75 41W
Rockdale, Tex., U.S.A.	**75**	30 40N	97 0W
Rockdale, Wash., U.S.A.	**80**	47 22N	121 28W
Rockefeller Plat.	**91**	84 0S	130 0W
Rockford, Ill., U.S.A.	**76**	42 20N	89 0W
Rockford, Iowa, U.S.A.	**76**	43 3N	92 57W
Rockford, Mich., U.S.A.	**77**	43 7N	85 34W
Rockford, Ohio, U.S.A.	**77**	40 41N	84 39W
Rockglen	**56**	49 11N	105 57W
Rockhampton	**135**	23 22S	150 32E
Rockingham	**39**	44 41N	63 39W
Rockingham For.	**95**	52 28N	0 42W
Rocklake	**57**	48 47N	99 15W
Rockland, Can.	**47**	45 33N	75 17W
Rockland, Idaho, U.S.A.	**78**	42 37N	112 57W
Rockland, Me., U.S.A.	**35**	44 0N	69 0W
Rockland, Mich., U.S.A.	**52**	46 40N	89 10W
Rocklands Reservoir	**136**	37 15S	142 5E
Rocklin	**80**	38 48N	121 14W
Rockmart	**73**	34 1N	85 2W
Rockport, U.S.A.	**77**	37 53N	87 3W
Rockport, Tex., U.S.A.	**75**	28 2N	97 3W
Rockport, Wash., U.S.A.	**63**	48 30N	121 38W
Rockton	**49**	43 17N	80 7W
Rockville, U.S.A.	**77**	39 46N	87 14W
Rockville, Conn., U.S.A.	**71**	41 51N	72 27W
Rockville, Md., U.S.A.	**72**	39 7N	77 10W
Rockwall	**75**	32 55N	96 30W
Rockway	**49**	43 6N	79 20W
Rockwell	**136**	32 3S	141 32E
Rockwell City	**76**	42 20N	94 35W
Rockwood, Can.	**49**	43 37N	80 8W
Rockwood, U.S.A.	**77**	42 4N	83 15W
Rockwood, Tenn., U.S.A.	**73**	35 52N	84 40W
Rocky Ford	**74**	38 7N	103 45W
Rocky Fork Lake	**77**	39 12N	83 23W
Rocky Harbour	**37**	49 36N	57 55W
Rocky Island L.	**53**	46 55N	83 0W
Rocky Lane	**54**	58 31N	116 22W
Rocky Mount	**73**	35 55N	77 48W
Rocky Mountain House	**61**	52 22N	114 55W
Rocky Mts.	**54**	55 0N	121 0W
Rocky Pt.	**134**	33 30S	123 57E
Rocky, R.	**61**	53 8N	117 59W
Rockyford	**61**	51 14N	113 10W
Rocroi	**101**	49 55N	4 30E
Rod	**124**	28 10N	63 5E
Roda, La	**104**	39 13N	2 15W
Rødby Havn	**111**	54 39N	11 22E
Roddickton	**37**	50 51N	56 8W
Roden	**105**	53 8N	6 26E
Roderick I.	**62**	52 38N	128 22W
Rodez	**102**	44 21N	2 33E
Ródhos	**109**	36 15N	28 10E
Ródhos, I.	**109**	36 15N	28 10E
Rodney	**46**	42 34N	81 41W
Rodney, C.	**133**	36 17S	174 50E
Rodoni, C.	**109**	41 32N	19 30E
Rodriguez, I.	**16**	20 0S	65 0E
Roe, R.	**97**	55 0N	6 56W
Roebling	**71**	40 7N	74 45W
Roebourne	**134**	20 44S	117 9E
Roebuck B.	**134**	18 5S	122 20E
Roermond	**105**	51 12N	6 0E
Roes Welcome Sd.	**65**	65 0N	87 0W
Roeselare	**105**	50 57N	3 7E
Rogagua, L.	**86**	14 0S	66 50W
Rogaland fylke □	**111**	59 12N	6 20E
Roger, L.	**40**	47 50N	78 59W
Rogers	**75**	36 20N	94 0W
Rogers City	**46**	45 25N	83 49W
Rogerson	**78**	42 10N	114 40W
Rogersville, Can.	**39**	46 44N	65 26W
Rogersville, U.S.A.	**73**	36 27N	83 1W
Roggan	**36**	54 25N	79 32W
Roggan L.	**36**	54 8N	77 50W
Rogliano	**103**	42 57N	9 30E
Rogoaguado, L.	**86**	13 0S	65 30W
Rogue, R.	**78**	42 30N	124 0W
Rohan	**100**	48 4N	2 45W
Rohault, L.	**41**	49 23N	74 20W
Rohnert Park	**80**	38 16N	122 40W
Rohrbach	**101**	49 3N	7 15E
Rohri	**124**	27 45N	68 51E
Rohtak	**124**	28 55N	76 43E
Roi Et	**128**	15 56N	103 40E
Roisel	**101**	49 58N	3 6E
Rojas	**88**	34 10S	60 45W
Rojo, C., Mexico	**83**	21 33N	97 20W
Rojo, C., W. Indies	**67**	17 56N	67 11W
Rokan, R.	**126**	1 30N	100 50E
Roland	**57**	49 22N	97 56W
Rolândia	**89**	23 5S	52 0W
Rolette	**74**	48 42N	99 50W
Rolfe	**76**	42 49N	94 31W
Rolla, Kansas, U.S.A.	**75**	37 10N	101 40W
Rolla, Missouri, U.S.A.	**76**	37 56N	91 42W
Rolla, N. Dak., U.S.A.	**57**	48 50N	99 36W
Rollet	**40**	47 55N	79 15W
Rolling Hills	**61**	50 13N	111 46W
Rolling, R.	**77**	38 0N	85 56W
Roma, Austral.	**135**	26 32S	148 49E
Roma, Italy	**108**	41 54N	12 30E
Roma, Sweden	**111**	57 32N	18 26E
Romaine, R.	**36**	50 18N	63 47W
Roman	**107**	43 8N	23 54E
Romana, La	**85**	18 27N	68 57W
Romang, I.	**127**	7 30S	127 20E
Romano, Cayo	**84**	22 0N	77 30W
Romanzof, C.	**67**	62 0N	165 50W
Rome, Ga., U.S.A.	**73**	34 20N	85 0W
Rome, N.Y., U.S.A.	**71**	43 14N	75 29W
Rome = Roma	**108**	41 54N	12 30E
Romenay	**103**	46 30N	5 1E
Romilly	**101**	48 31N	3 44E
Romney, Can.	**70**	42 9N	82 23W
Romney, U.S.A.	**72**	39 21N	78 45W
Romney Marsh	**95**	51 0N	1 0E
Romorantin-Lanthenay	**101**	47 21N	1 45E
Romsdalen	**110**	62 25N	7 50E
Ronan	**78**	47 30N	114 11W
Roncador Cay	**84**	13 40N	80 4W
Roncador, Serra do	**87**	12 30S	52 30W
Ronceverte	**72**	37 45N	80 28W
Ronda	**104**	36 46N	5 12W
Rondane	**111**	61 57N	9 50E
Rondeau Prov. Park	**46**	42 19N	81 51W
Rondón	**86**	6 17N	71 6W
Rondônia □	**86**	11 0S	63 0W
Rong, Koh	**128**	10 45N	103 15E
Ronge, La	**55**	55 5N	105 20W
Ronge, Lac La	**55**	55 6N	105 17W
Rønne	**111**	55 6N	14 44E
Ronne Land	**91**	83 0S	70 0W
Ronse	**105**	50 45N	3 35E
Roodepoort-Maraisburg	**117**	26 8S	27 52E
Roodhouse	**76**	39 29N	90 24W
Roof Butte	**79**	36 29N	109 5W
Roorkee	**124**	29 52N	77 59E
Roosendaal	**105**	51 32N	4 29E
Roosevelt, Minn., U.S.A.	**74**	48 51N	95 2W
Roosevelt, Utah, U.S.A.	**78**	40 19N	110 1W
Roosevelt I.	**91**	79 0S	161 0W
Roosevelt, Mt.	**54**	58 20N	125 20W
Roosevelt Res.	**79**	33 46N	111 0W
Roosville	**61**	49 0N	115 3W
Roper, R.	**134**	14 43S	135 27E
Ropesville	**75**	33 25N	102 10W
Roque Pérez	**88**	35 25S	59 24W
Roquefort	**102**	44 2N	0 20W
Roquefort-sur-Soulzon	**102**	43 58N	2 59E
Roquemaure	**103**	44 3N	4 48E
Roquevaire	**103**	43 20N	5 36E
Roraima □	**86**	2 0N	61 30W
Roraima, Mt.	**86**	5 10N	60 40W
Rorketon	**57**	51 24N	99 35W
Røros	**110**	62 35N	11 23E
Rosa, U.S.A.	**78**	38 15N	122 16W
Rosa, Zambia	**116**	9 33S	31 15E
Rosa, Monte	**106**	45 57N	7 53E
Rosalia	**78**	47 26N	117 25W
Rosalind	**61**	52 47N	112 27W
Rosamund	**81**	34 52N	118 10W
Rosans	**103**	44 24N	5 29E
Rosario	**88**	33 0S	60 50W
Rosário, Maran., Brazil	**87**	3 0S	44 15W
Rosário, Rio Grande do Sul, Brazil	**90**	30 15S	55 0W
Rosario, Baja California, Mexico	**82**	30 0N	116 0W
Rosario, Durango, Mexico	**82**	26 30N	105 35W
Rosario, Sinaloa, Mexico	**82**	23 0N	106 0W
Rosario, Venez.	**86**	10 19N	72 19W
Rosario de la Frontera	**88**	25 50S	65 0W
Rosario de Lerma	**88**	24 59S	65 35W
Rosario del Tala	**88**	32 20S	59 10W
Rosário do Sul	**89**	30 15S	54 55W
Rosarito, Mexico	**82**	28 38N	114 4W
Rosarito, U.S.A.	**81**	32 18N	117 4W
Rosas	**104**	42 19N	3 10E
Rosas, G. de,	**104**	42 10N	3 15E
Roscoe	**76**	37 58N	93 48W
Roscoff	**100**	48 44N	4 0W
Roscommon, Ireland	**97**	53 38N	8 11W
Roscommon, U.S.A.	**46**	44 27N	84 35W
Roscommon □	**97**	53 40N	8 15W
Roscrea	**97**	52 58N	7 50W
Rose Blanche	**37**	47 38N	58 45W
Rose City	**46**	44 25N	84 7W
Rose Harbour	**62**	52 15N	131 10W
Rose Pt.	**62**	54 11N	131 39W
Rose Valley	**56**	52 19N	103 49W
Roseau, Domin.	**85**	15 20N	61 30W
Roseau, U.S.A.	**57**	48 51N	95 46W
Rosebud, Austral.	**136**	38 21S	144 54E
Rosebud, U.S.A.	**75**	31 5N	97 0W
Rosebud, R.	**61**	51 25N	112 38W
Roseburg	**78**	43 10N	123 10W
Rosedale, Can.	**63**	49 10N	121 48W
Rosedale, U.S.A.	**77**	39 38N	87 17W
Rosedale, Miss., U.S.A.	**75**	33 51N	91 0W
Roseisle	**57**	49 30N	98 20W
Roseland	**80**	38 25N	122 43W
Rosemary	**61**	50 46N	112 5W
Rosemère	**44**	45 38N	73 48W
Rosemont	**58**	50 27N	104 39W
Rosenberg	**75**	29 30N	95 48W
Rosendaël	**101**	51 3N	2 24E
Rosendale	**76**	40 4N	94 51W
Rosenheim	**106**	47 51N	12 9E
Rosetown	**56**	51 35N	107 59W
Roseville, U.S.A.	**76**	40 44N	90 40W
Roseville, Calif., U.S.A.	**80**	38 46N	121 17W
Roseville, Mich., U.S.A.	**46**	42 30N	82 56W
Rosières	**101**	48 36N	6 20E
Rosignol	**86**	6 15N	57 30W
Roskilde	**111**	55 38N	12 3E
Roslavl	**120**	53 57N	32 55E
Rosporden	**100**	47 57N	3 50W
Ross, N.Z.	**133**	42 53S	170 49E
Ross, U.K.	**95**	51 55N	2 34W
Ross Dependency	**91**	70 0S	170 5W
Ross I.	**91**	77 30S	168 0E
Ross Ice Shelf	**91**	80 0S	180 0W
Ross L.	**63**	48 50N	121 5W
Ross on Wye	**95**	51 55N	2 34W
Ross Pt.	**51**	43 51N	78 54W
Ross River	**67**	62 30N	131 30W
Ross Sea	**91**	74 0S	178 0E
Rossan Pt.	**97**	54 42N	8 47W
Rossburn	**57**	50 40N	100 49W
Rosseau, Can.	**70**	45 26N	79 39W
Rosseau, Ont., Can.	**46**	45 16N	79 39W
Rosseau L.	**46**	45 10N	79 35W
Rosser	**58**	49 59N	97 27W
Rossford	**77**	41 36N	83 34W
Rossignol, L., N.S., Can.	**39**	44 12N	65 0W
Rossignol, L., Qué., Can.	**36**	52 43N	73 40W
Rossland	**63**	49 6N	117 50W
Rosslare	**97**	52 17N	6 23W
Rossmore	**47**	44 8N	77 23W
Rossosh	**120**	50 15N	39 20E
Rossport	**53**	48 50N	87 30W
Røssvatnet	**110**	65 45N	14 5E
Rossville	**77**	40 25N	86 35W
Rosthern	**56**	52 40N	106 20W
Rostock	**106**	54 4N	12 9E
Rostov	**120**	47 15N	39 45E
Rostrenen	**100**	48 14N	3 21W
Roswell	**75**	33 26N	104 32W
Rosyth	**96**	56 2N	3 26W
Rotan	**75**	32 52N	100 30W
Rothaargebirge	**106**	51 0N	8 20E
Rother, R.	**95**	50 59N	0 40W
Rotherham	**94**	53 26N	1 21W
Rothes	**96**	57 31N	3 12W
Rothesay, Can.	**39**	45 23N	66 0W
Rothesay, U.K.	**96**	55 50N	5 3W
Roti, I.	**127**	10 50S	123 0E
Roto	**136**	33 0S	145 30E
Rotoroa Lake	**133**	41 55S	172 39E
Rotorua	**133**	38 9S	176 16E
Rotorua, L.	**133**	38 5S	176 18E
Rotterdam	**105**	51 55N	4 30E
Rottweil	**106**	48 9N	8 38E
Rotuma, I.	**14**	12 25S	177 5E
Roubaix	**101**	50 40N	3 10E
Rouen	**100**	49 27N	1 4E
Rouergue	**103**	44 20N	2 20E
Rouge Hill	**51**	43 48N	79 8W
Rouge, R., Ont., Can.	**51**	43 48N	79 7W
Rouge, R., Qué., Can.	**40**	45 17N	74 10W
Rougemont	**45**	45 26N	73 3W
Rouillac	**102**	45 47N	0 4W
Rouleau	**56**	50 10N	104 56W
Round Hill, Alta., Can.	**61**	53 10N	112 38W
Round Hill, N.S., Can.	**39**	44 46N	65 24W
Round L., Newf., Can.	**37**	51 15N	56 32W
Round L., Ont., Can.	**47**	45 38N	77 30W
Round Mt.	**135**	30 26S	152 16E
Round Mountain	**78**	38 46N	117 3W
Round Pond	**37**	48 11N	56 0W
Round Valley	**60**	53 21N	114 57W
Roundup	**78**	46 25N	108 35W
Rousay, I.	**96**	59 10N	3 2W
Rouses Point	**43**	44 58N	73 22W
Rousse, L'Île	**103**	42 27N	8 57E
Roussillon, Can.	**43**	45 41N	74 26W
Roussillon, France	**103**	45 24N	4 49E
Routhierville	**38**	48 11N	67 9W
Rouville □	**45**	45 33N	73 10W
Rouvray, L.	**41**	49 18N	70 49W
Rouyn	**40**	48 20N	79 0W
Rovaniemi	**110**	66 29N	25 41E
Rovereto	**108**	45 53N	11 3E
Rovigo	**108**	45 4N	11 48E
Rovinj	**108**	45 5N	13 40E
Rovira	**86**	4 15N	75 20W
Rovno	**120**	50 40N	26 10E
Rowan L.	**52**	49 18N	93 32W
Rowatt	**58**	50 20N	104 37W
Rowley I.	**65**	69 6N	77 52W
Rowley Shoals	**134**	17 40S	119 20E
Rowood	**79**	32 18N	112 54W
Roxas	**127**	11 36N	122 49E
Roxboro, Can.	**44**	45 31N	73 48W
Roxboro, U.S.A.	**73**	36 24N	78 59W
Roxburgh, N.Z.	**133**	45 33S	169 19E
Roxburgh, U.K.	**96**	55 34N	2 30W
Roxton Falls	**41**	45 34N	72 31W
Roy, U.S.A.	**78**	47 17N	109 0W
Roy, N. Mex., U.S.A.	**75**	35 57N	104 8W
Roy, Le, U.S.A.	**77**	40 21N	88 46W
Roy, Le, Kans., U.S.A.	**75**	38 8N	95 35W
Royal Center	**77**	40 52N	86 30W
Royal Oak, Can.	**63**	48 29N	123 23W
Royal Oak, U.S.A.	**77**	42 30N	83 5W
Royan	**102**	45 37N	1 2W
Roye	**101**	47 40N	6 31E
Rozay	**101**	48 40N	2 56E
Rozier, Le	**102**	44 13N	3 12E
Rozoy-sur-Serre	**101**	49 40N	4 8E
Rtishchevo	**120**	52 35N	43 50E
Ruahine Ra.	**133**	39 55S	176 2E
Ruapehu	**133**	39 17S	175 35E
Ruapuke I.	**133**	46 46S	168 31E
Rub 'al Khali	**115**	21 0N	51 0E
Rubicon, R.	**80**	38 53N	121 4W
Rubicone, R.	**108**	44 0N	12 20E
Rubio	**86**	7 43N	72 22W
Rubtsovsk	**120**	51 30N	80 50E
Ruby	**67**	64 40N	155 35W
Ruby L.	**78**	40 10N	115 28W
Ruby Mts.	**78**	40 30N	115 30W
Rudbar	**123**	30 0N	62 30E
Rudh a'Mhail, C.	**96**	55 55N	6 25W
Rudnogorsk	**121**	57 15N	103 42E
Rudnyy	**120**	52 57N	63 7E
Rudok	**129**	33 30N	79 40E
Rudyard	**46**	46 14N	84 35W
Rue	**101**	50 15N	1 40E
Rue, La	**77**	40 35N	83 23W
Ruel	**53**	47 15N	81 28W

Ruelle **St-Eustacht**

Ruelle	**102**	45 41N	0 14E
Ruffec Charente	**102**	46 2N	0 12E
Rufiji, R.	**116**	7 50S	38 15E
Rufino	**88**	34 20S	62 50W
Rugby, U.K.	**95**	52 23N	1 16W
Rugby, U.S.A.	**74**	48 21N	100 0W
Rügen, I.	**106**	54 22N	13 25E
Rugles	**100**	48 50N	0 40E
Ruhr, R.	**105**	51 25N	7 15E
Ruidosa	**75**	29 59N	104 39W
Ruidoso	**79**	33 19N	105 39W
Ruisseau-des-Anges	**43**	45 48N	73 40W
Ruisseau-Vert	**41**	49 4N	68 28W
Rukwa L.	**116**	7 50S	32 10E
Rully	**85**	46 52N	4 44E
Rum Jungle	**134**	13 0S	130 59E
Rumâh	**122**	25 35N	47 10E
Rumania ■	**107**	46 0N	25 0E
Rumford	**71**	44 30N	70 30W
Rumilly	**103**	45 53N	5 56E
Rummelhardt	**49**	43 27N	80 34W
Rumoi	**132**	43 56N	141 39W
Rumorosa, La	**81**	32 33N	116 4W
Rumsey	**61**	51 51N	112 48W
Runanga	**133**	42 25S	171 15E
Runaway, C.	**133**	37 32S	178 2E
Runcorn	**94**	53 20N	2 44W
Rungwa	**116**	6 55S	33 32E
Runton Ra.	**136**	23 35S	123 15E
Rupa	**125**	27 15N	92 30E
Rupat, I.	**126**	1 45N	101 40E
Rupert B.	**36**	51 35N	79 0W
Rupert House = Fort Rupert	**36**	51 30N	78 40W
Rupert, R.	**36**	51 29N	78 45W
Rupununi, R.	**87**	3 30N	59 30W
Rurrenabaque	**86**	14 30S	67 32W
Rusagonis	**39**	45 48N	66 37W
Rusape	**117**	18 35S	32 8E
Ruschuk = Ruse	**109**	43 48N	25 59E
Ruse	**109**	43 48N	25 59E
Rush L.	**53**	47 47N	82 11W
Rush Lake	**56**	50 24N	107 24W
Rushden	**95**	52 17N	0 37W
Rushford	**74**	43 48N	91 46W
Rushoon	**37**	47 21N	54 55W
Rushville, Ill., U.S.A.	**76**	40 6N	90 35W
Rushville, Ind., U.S.A.	**77**	39 38N	85 22W
Rushville, Nebr., U.S.A.	**74**	42 43N	102 20W
Rushworth	**136**	36 32S	145 1E
Russell, Man., Can.	**55**	50 50N	101 20W
Russell, Que., Can.	**71**	45 16N	75 21W
Russell, N.Z.	**133**	35 16S	174 10E
Russell, U.S.A.	**74**	38 56N	98 55W
Russell I.	**65**	74 0N	98 25W
Russell L., Man., Can.	**55**	56 15N	101 30W
Russell L., N.W.T., Can.	**54**	63 5N	115 44W
Russellkonda	**125**	19 57N	84 42E
Russelltown	**43**	45 4N	73 45W
Russellville, Ala., U.S.A.	**73**	34 30N	87 44W
Russellville, Ark., U.S.A.	**75**	35 15N	93 0W
Russellville, Ky., U.S.A.	**73**	36 50N	86 50W
Russian Mission	**67**	61 45N	161 25W
Russian, R.	**80**	38 27N	123 8W
Russian S.F.S.R. □	**121**	62 0N	105 0E
Russiaville	**77**	40 25N	86 16W
Russkoye Ustie	**17**	71 0N	149 0E
Rustenburg	**117**	25 41S	27 14E
Ruston	**75**	32 30N	92 58W
Rutba	**122**	33 4N	40 15E
Ruteng	**127**	8 26S	120 30E
Ruth, Mich., U.S.A.	**46**	43 42N	82 45W
Ruth, Nev., U.S.A.	**78**	39 15N	115 1W
Rutherford	**80**	38 26N	122 24W
Rutherglen, Austral.	**136**	36 5S	146 29E
Rutherglen, U.K.	**96**	55 50N	4 11W
Rutland	**71**	43 38N	73 0W
Rutland I.	**128**	11 25N	92 40E
Rutledge L.	**55**	61 33N	110 47W
Rutledge, R.	**55**	61 4N	112 0W
Rutshuru	**116**	1 13S	29 25E
Rutter	**46**	46 6N	80 40W
Ruvuma, R.	**116**	11 30S	36 10E
Ruwaidha	**122**	23 40N	44 40E
Ruwandiz	**122**	36 40N	44 32E
Ruwenzori Mts.	**116**	0 30N	29 55E
Ruwenzori, mt.	**116**	0 30N	29 55E
Ruzomberok	**107**	49 3N	19 17E
Rwanda ■	**116**	2 0S	30 0E
Ryan, L.	**96**	55 0N	5 2W
Ryans B.	**36**	59 35N	64 3W
Ryazan	**120**	54 50N	39 40E
Rybache	**120**	46 40N	81 20E
Rybinsk (Shcherbakov)	**120**	58 5N	38 50E
Ryckman	**48**	43 15N	79 54W
Rycroft	**60**	55 45N	118 40W
Ryde	**95**	50 44N	1 9W
Ryderwood	**80**	46 23N	123 3W
Rye	**95**	50 57N	0 46E
Rye Patch Res.	**78**	40 45N	118 20W
Rye, R.	**94**	54 12N	0 53W
Ryegate	**78**	46 21N	109 27W
Ryley	**60**	53 17N	112 26W
Rypin	**107**	53 3N	19 32E
Ryūkyū Is. = Nansei-Shotō	**132**	26 0N	128 0E
Ryūkyū-rettō	**131**	26 0N	127 0E
Rzeszów	**107**	50 5N	21 58E
Rzhev	**120**	56 20N	34 20E

S

Sa Dec	**128**	10 20N	105 46E
Sa'ādatābād	**123**	30 10N	53 5E
Saale, R.	**106**	51 25N	11 56E
Saanich	**63**	48 28N	123 22W
Saar, R.	**106**	49 25N	6 35E
Saar (Sarre), □	**101**	49 20N	6 45E
Saarbrücken	**105**	49 15N	6 58E
Saaremaa	**120**	58 30N	22 30E
Saariselkä	**110**	68 16N	28 15E
Saarland □	**15**	49 20N	6 45E
Saarlouis	**105**	49 19N	6 45E
Saba I.	**85**	17 30N	63 10W
Sabadell	**104**	41 28N	2 7E
Sabagalel	**126**	1 36S	98 40E
Sabah □	**126**	6 0N	117 0E
Sabak	**128**	3 46N	100 58E
Sábana de la Mar	**85**	19 7N	69 40W
Sábanalarga	**86**	10 38N	74 55W
Sabang	**126**	5 50N	95 15E
Sabará	**87**	19 55S	43 55W
Sabarania	**127**	2 5S	138 18E
Sabattis	**71**	44 6N	74 40W
Sabaudia	**108**	41 17N	13 2E
Sabhah	**114**	27 9N	14 29E
Sabina	**77**	39 29N	83 38W
Sabinal, Mexico	**82**	30 50N	107 25W
Sabinal, U.S.A.	**75**	29 20N	99 27W
Sabinas	**82**	27 50N	101 10W
Sabinas Hidalgo	**82**	26 40N	100 10W
Sabinas, R.	**82**	27 37N	100 42W
Sabine	**75**	29 42N	93 54W
Sabine, R.	**75**	31 30N	93 35W
Sablayan	**127**	12 5N	120 50E
Sable	**100**	47 50N	0 21W
Sable, C., Can.	**39**	43 29N	65 38W
Sable, C., U.S.A.	**84**	25 5N	81 0W
Sable I.	**35**	44 0N	60 0W
Sable River	**39**	43 51N	65 3W
Sablé-sur-Sarthe	**100**	47 50N	0 20W
Sables-D'Olonne, Les	**102**	46 30N	1 45W
Sables, R. aux	**46**	46 13N	82 3W
Sabourin, L.	**40**	47 58N	77 41W
Sabrevois	**43**	45 12N	73 14W
Sabrina Coast	**91**	67 0S	120 0E
Sabtang I.	**131**	20 15N	121 30E
Sabula	**76**	42 5N	90 23W
Sabzevār	**123**	36 15N	57 40E
Sabzvāran	**123**	28 45N	57 50E
Sac City	**76**	42 26N	95 0W
Sachigo, L.	**34**	53 50N	92 12W
Sachigo, R.	**34**	55 6N	88 58W
Sachs Harbour	**64**	71 59N	125 15W
Sackett's Harbor	**71**	43 56N	72 38W
Sackville	**39**	45 54N	64 22W
Saco, Me., U.S.A.	**73**	43 30N	70 27W
Saco, Mont., U.S.A.	**78**	48 28N	107 19W
Sacramento	**80**	38 39N	121 30E
Sacramento Mts.	**79**	32 30N	105 30W
Sacramento, R.	**80**	38 3N	121 56W
Sacramento Valley	**80**	39 0N	122 0W
Sacré-Coeur-de-Jésus	**41**	48 14N	69 48W
Sadaba	**104**	42 19N	1 12W
Sa'dani	**116**	5 58S	38 35E
Sadao	**128**	6 38N	100 26E
Saddle Mt.	**80**	45 58N	123 41W
Sadieville	**77**	38 23N	84 32W
Sado	**132**	38 0N	138 25E
Sado, Shima	**132**	38 15N	138 30E
Saegerstown	**70**	80 10N	41 42W
Safaniya	**122**	28 5N	48 42E
Saffron Walden	**95**	52 2N	0 15E
Safi	**114**	32 18N	9 14W
Safiah	**100**	31 27N	34 46E
Sag Harbor	**71**	40 59N	72 17W
Saga	**127**	2 40S	132 55E
Saga-ken □	**132**	33 15N	130 20E
Sagaing	**125**	23 30N	95 30E
Saganaga L.	**52**	48 14N	90 52W
Saganash L.	**53**	49 4N	82 35W
Sagar	**124**	23 50N	78 50E
Sagil	**129**	50 15N	91 15E
Saginaw	**46**	43 26N	83 55W
Saginaw B.	**46**	43 50N	83 40W
Sagleipie	**103**	45 25N	7 0E
Saglek B.	**36**	58 30N	63 0W
Saglek Fd.	**36**	58 29N	63 15W
Saglouc	**36**	62 14N	75 38W
Sagone	**103**	42 7N	8 42E
Sagone, G. de	**103**	42 4N	8 40E
Sagra, La, Mt.	**104**	38 0N	2 35W
Sagres	**104**	37 0N	8 58W
Sagua la Grande	**84**	22 50N	80 10W
Saguache	**79**	38 10N	106 4W
Saguenay, R.	**41**	48 22N	71 0W
Sagunto	**104**	39 42N	0 18W
Sahagún, Colomb.	**86**	8 57N	75 27W
Sahagún, Spain	**104**	42 18N	5 2W
Sahara	**114**	23 0N	5 0W
Saharanpur	**124**	29 58N	77 33E
Sahiwal	**124**	30 45N	73 8E
Sahtaneh, R.	**54**	59 2N	122 28W
Sahuaripa	**82**	29 30N	109 0W
Sahuarita	**79**	31 58N	110 59W
Sahuayo	**82**	20 4N	102 43W
Sa'idabad	**123**	29 30N	55 45E
Saidapet	**124**	13 0N	80 15E
Saidu	**124**	34 50N	72 15E
Säe	**111**	59 8N	12 55E
Saighan	**123**	35 10N	67 55E
Saignes	**102**	45 20N	2 31E
Saigon = Phanh Bho Ho Chi Minh	**128**	10 58N	106 40E
Saih-al-Malih	**123**	23 37N	58 31E
Saijō	**132**	34 0N	133 5E
Saikhoa Ghat	**125**	27 50N	95 40E
Saiki	**132**	32 58N	131 57E
Saillans	**103**	44 42N	5 12E
Sailolof	**127**	1 7S	130 46E
St-Hyacinthe	**45**	45 40N	72 58W
St-Jean-Port-Joli	**41**	47 15N	70 13W
St Jovite	**40**	46 8N	74 38W
St.-Julien-du-Sault	**101**	48 1N	3 17E
St. Abb's Head	**96**	55 55N	2 10W
St-Adalbert	**41**	46 51N	69 53W
St-Adolphe-d'Howard	**43**	45 58N	74 20W
St-Affrique	**102**	43 57N	2 53E
St-Agapitville	**41**	46 34N	71 26W
St-Agrève	**103**	45 0N	4 23E
St.-Aignan	**100**	47 16N	1 22E
St. Alban's	**37**	47 51N	55 50W
St. Albans, U.K.	**95**	51 44N	0 19W
St. Albans, Vt., U.S.A.	**71**	44 49N	73 7W
St. Albans, W. Va., U.S.A.	**72**	38 21N	81 50W
St. Alban's Head	**95**	50 34N	2 3W
St. Albert	**60**	53 37N	113 40W
St-Alexandre, Qué., Can.	**41**	47 41N	69 38W
St-Alexandre, Qué., Can.	**45**	45 14N	73 7W
St-Alexis	**43**	45 56N	73 37W
St-Alexis-des-Monts	**41**	46 28N	73 8W
St-Amable	**45**	45 39N	73 18W
St-Amand	**101**	50 25N	3 6E
St-Amand-en-Puisaye	**101**	47 32N	3 5E
St-Amand-Mont-Rond	**102**	46 43N	2 30E
St-Amarin	**101**	47 54N	7 0E
St-Ambroise	**41**	48 33N	71 20W
St-Amour	**103**	46 26N	5 21E
St-Anaclet	**41**	48 29N	68 26W
St-André	**39**	47 8N	67 45W
St-André-Avellin	**40**	45 43N	75 3W
St-André-de-Cubzac	**102**	44 59N	0 26W
St-André de l'Eure	**100**	48 54N	1 16E
St-André-Est	**43**	45 34N	74 20W
St-André-les-Alpes	**103**	43 58N	6 30E
St. Andrews	**39**	45 7N	67 5W
St. Andrew's	**37**	47 45N	59 15W
St. Andrews	**96**	56 20N	2 48W
St-Angèle-de-Monnoir	**45**	45 23N	73 6W
St-Anicet	**43**	45 8N	74 22W
St. Ann B.	**39**	46 22N	60 25W
St. Anne	**100**	49 43N	2 11W
St Anne	**77**	41 1N	87 43W
St. Annes	**57**	49 40N	96 39W
St. Anns	**49**	43 5N	79 30W
St. Ann's Bay	**84**	18 26N	77 15W
St-Anselme, N.B., Can.	**39**	46 4N	64 43W
St-Anselme, Qué., Can.	**41**	46 37N	70 58W
St. Anthony, N.B., Can.	**39**	46 22N	64 45W
St. Anthony, Newf., Can.	**37**	51 22N	55 35W
St. Anthony, U.S.A.	**78**	44 0N	111 49W
St-Antoine	**44**	45 46N	73 59W
St-Antoine-des-Laurentides	**44**	45 46N	73 59W
St-Antoine-sur-Richelieu	**45**	45 46N	73 11W
St-Antonin	**41**	47 46N	69 29W
St-Antonin-Noble-Val	**102**	44 10N	1 45E
St-Apolline	**41**	46 48N	70 12W
St. Arnaud	**136**	36 32S	143 16E
St. Arthur	**39**	47 33N	67 46W
St. Asaph	**94**	53 15N	3 27W
St-Astier	**102**	45 8N	0 31E
St-Aubert	**41**	47 11N	70 13W
St-Aubin-du-Cormier	**100**	48 15N	1 26W
St-Augustin	**44**	45 38N	73 59W
St-Augustin-de-Desmaures	**42**	46 45N	71 30W
St-Augustin, L.	**42**	46 45N	71 23W
St-Augustin, R.	**36**	51 16N	58 40W
St-Augustin-Saguenay	**37**	51 13N	58 38W
St. Augustine	**73**	29 52N	81 20W
St. Austell	**95**	50 20N	4 48W
St-Avc•l	**101**	49 6N	6 43E
St-Barnabé-Sud	**45**	45 44N	72 55W
St-Barthélémy	**41**	46 11N	73 8W
St. Barthélemy, I.	**85**	17 50N	62 50W
St-Basile	**39**	47 21N	68 14W
St-Basile-le-Grand	**45**	45 32N	73 17W
St-Basile-Sud	**41**	46 45N	71 49W
St. Bee's Hd.	**94**	54 30N	3 38E
St. Benedict	**56**	52 34N	105 23W
St-Benoît	**44**	45 34N	74 6W
St-Benoît-du-Sault	**102**	46 26N	1 24E
St-Bernard-de-Lacolle	**43**	45 5N	73 25W
St-Blaise	**43**	45 13N	73 17W
St. Boniface	**58**	49 53N	97 5W
St-Bonnet	**103**	44 40N	6 5E
St. Brendan's	**37**	48 52N	53 40W
St-Brévin-les-Pins	**100**	47 14N	2 10W
St-Brice-en-Coglès	**100**	48 25N	1 22W
St. Bride's	**37**	46 56N	54 10W
St. Bride's B.	**95**	51 48N	5 15W
St-Brieuc	**100**	48 30N	2 46W
St. Brieux	**56**	52 38N	104 54W
St-Bruno	**41**	48 28N	71 39W
St-Bruno-de-Montarville	**45**	45 32N	73 21W
St-Calais	**100**	47 55N	0 45E
St-Calixte-de-Kilkenny	**43**	45 57N	73 51W
St-Calixte-Nord	**43**	45 59N	73 55W
St-Canut	**44**	45 43N	74 5W
St-Casimir	**41**	46 40N	72 8W
St-Cast	**100**	48 37N	2 18W
St. Catharines	**49**	43 10N	79 15W
St. Catherines I.	**73**	31 35N	81 10W
St. Catherine's Pt.	**95**	50 34N	1 18W
St-Céré	**102**	44 51N	1 54E
St-Cernin	**102**	45 5N	2 25E
St-Césaire	**45**	45 25N	73 0W
St-Chamond	**103**	45 28N	4 31E
St. Charles	**58**	49 53N	97 19W
St-Charles	**42**	46 46N	70 57W
St. Charles, Ill., U.S.A.	**77**	41 55N	88 21W
St. Charles, Mich., U.S.A.	**46**	43 18N	84 9W
St. Charles, Mo., U.S.A.	**76**	38 46N	90 30W
St-Charles, L.	**42**	46 55N	71 23W
St-Charles, R.	**42**	46 49N	71 13W
St-Charles-sur-Richelieu	**45**	45 41N	73 11W
St-Chély-d'Apcher	**102**	44 48N	3 17E
St-Chinian	**102**	43 25N	2 56E
St. Christopher (St. Kitts)	**85**	17 20N	62 40W
St-Chrysostôme	**43**	45 6N	73 46W
St-Ciers-sur-Gironde	**102**	45 17N	0 37W
Saint Clair	**76**	38 21N	90 59W
St. Clair, Mich, U.S.A.	**46**	42 47N	82 27W
St. Clair, Pa., U.S.A.	**71**	40 42N	76 12W
St. Clair, L.	**46**	42 30N	82 45W
St. Clair, R.	**70**	42 40N	82 20W
St. Clairsville	**70**	40 5N	80 53W
St-Claud	**102**	45 54N	0 28E
St. Claude	**57**	49 40N	98 20W
St-Claude	**103**	46 22N	5 52E
St-Clet	**43**	45 21N	74 13W
St-Cloud	**100**	48 51N	2 12E
St. Cloud, Fla., U.S.A.	**73**	28 15N	81 15W
St. Cloud, Minn., U.S.A.	**74**	45 30N	94 11W
St-Coeur de Marie	**41**	48 39N	71 43W
St-Colomban	**44**	45 44N	74 8W
St-Côme	**41**	46 16N	73 47W
St-Constant	**44**	45 22N	73 37W
St-Croix	**39**	45 34N	67 26W
St. Croix Falls	**74**	45 18N	92 22W
St. Croix, I.	**85**	17 45N	64 45W
St.	**39**	45 5N	67 6W
St. Croix, R., U.S.A.	**52**	46 16N	91 35W
St. Croix, R., U.S.A.	**74**	45 20N	92 50W
St-Cyprien	**102**	42 37N	3 0E
St-Cyr	**103**	43 11N	5 43E
St-Cyrille-de-L'Islet	**41**	47 2N	70 17W
St. Cyrus	**96**	56 47N	2 25W
St-Damase	**45**	45 31N	73 1W
St. David	**76**	40 30N	90 3W
St-David-de-l'Auberivière	**42**	46 47N	71 12W
St-David-d'Yamaska	**43**	45 57N	72 51W
St. David's	**37**	48 12N	58 52W
St. Davids	**49**	43 10N	79 6W
St. David's	**95**	51 54N	5 16W
St. David's Head	**95**	51 54N	5 16W
St-Denis, Can.	**45**	45 47N	73 9W
St-Denis, France	**101**	48 56N	2 22E
St.-Denis	**16**	20 52S	55 27E
St-Denis-d'Orques	**100**	48 2N	0 17W
St-Dié	**101**	48 17N	6 56E
St-Dizier	**101**	48 40N	5 0E
St-Dominique	**44**	45 20N	74 8W
St-Donat-de-Montcalm	**41**	46 19N	74 13W
St-Edouard-de-Napierville	**43**	45 14N	73 31W
St-Egrève	**103**	45 14N	5 41E
St-Eleanors	**39**	46 25N	63 49W
St. Elias, Mt.	**67**	60 20N	141 59W
St Elias Mts.	**54**	60 33N	139 28W
Saint Elmo	**77**	39 2N	88 51W
St-Éloi	**41**	48 2N	69 14W
St-Élouthère	**41**	47 30N	69 15W
St.-Eloy-les-Mines	**102**	46 10N	2 51E
St-Émile	**42**	46 52N	71 20W
St-Émilion	**102**	44 53N	0 9W
St-Éphrem-de-Tring	**41**	46 2N	70 59W
St-Esprit	**43**	45 54N	73 40W
St-Étienne	**103**	45 27N	4 22E
St-Étienne-de-Tinée	**103**	44 16N	6 56E
St-Étienne-de-Beauharnois	**44**	45 15N	73 55W
St. Eugène	**47**	45 30N	74 28W
St-Eugène	**43**	45 30N	74 29W
St-Eusèbe	**41**	47 33N	68 55W
St. Eustache	**57**	49 59N	97 47W
St-Eustache	**44**	45 33N	73 54W

St-Sulpice San Gabriel

St-Sulpice 43 45 50N 73 21W
St-Sulpice-Laurière 102 46 3N 1 29E
St-Sulpice-la-Pointe 102 43 46N 1 41E
St-Télesphore 43 45 17N 74 23W
St-Thégonnec 100 48 31N 3 57W
St. Thomas 46 42 45N 81 10W
St-Thomas-d'Aquin 45 45 39N 72 59W
St. Thomas, I. 85 18 21N 64 55W
St-Timothée 44 45 18N 74 2W
St-Tite 41 46 45N 72 40W
St-Tite-des-Caps 41 47 8N 70 47W
St-Tropez 103 43 17N 6 38E
St-Ulric 38 48 47N 67 42W
St-Urbain 41 47 33N 70 32W
St-Urbain-de-Châteauguay 43 45 13N 73 44W
St-Vaast-la-Hougue 100 49 35N 1 17W
St-Valérien 43 45 34N 72 48W
St-Valéry 101 50 10N 1 38E
St-Valéry-en-Caux 100 49 52N 0 43E
St.-Vallier 103 45 11N 4 50E
St-Vallier-de-Thiey 103 43 42N 6 51E
St.-Varent 100 46 53N 0 13W
St-Vianney 38 48 37N 67 25W
St. Victor 56 49 26N 105 52W
St. Vincent 12 18 0N 26 1W
St. Vincent C. 117 21 58S 43 20E
St-Vincent-de-Tyrosse 102 43 39N 1 18W
St-Vincent-de-Paul 44 45 37N 73 39W
St. Vincent, G. 135 35 0S 138 0E
St. Vincent, I. 85 13 10N 61 10W
St. Vincent Passage 85 13 30N 61 0W
St. Vincent's 37 46 48N 53 38W
St. Vital 58 49 51N 97 7W
St-Vith 105 50 17N 6 9E
St. Walburg 56 53 39N 109 12W
St-Yrieux-la-Perche 102 45 31N 1 12E
St-Yvon 38 49 10N 64 48W
St-Zotique 43 45 15N 74 15W
Ste-Adèle 43 45 57N 74 7W
Ste-Adresse 100 49 31N 0 5E
Ste. Agathe 57 49 34N 97 11W
Ste-Agathe 41 46 23N 71 25W
Ste-Agathe-des-Monts 41 46 3N 74 17W
Ste-Agnès-de-Dundee 43 45 1N 74 25W
Ste-Angèle-de-Mérici 38 48 32N 68 5W
Ste-Angèle-de-Monnoir 43 45 23N 73 6W
Ste. Anne 85 14 26N 60 53W
Ste Anne de Beaupré 41 47 2N 70 58W
Ste-Anne-de-Bellevue 44 45 24N 73 57W
Ste-Anne-de-Madawaska 39 47 15N 68 2W
Ste. Anne de Portneuf 35 48 38N 69 8W
Ste-Anne-de-Prescott 43 45 26N 74 29W
Ste-Anne-des-Monts 38 49 8N 66 30W
Ste-Anne-des-Plaines 44 45 47N 73 49W
Ste-Anne-du-Lac 40 46 48N 75 25W
Ste-Anne, L. 38 50 0N 67 42W
Ste. Anne, Lac 60 53 42N 114 25W
Ste-Blandine 41 48 22N 68 28W
Ste-Brigide-d'Iberville 45 45 19N 73 4W
Ste. Cecile 35 47 56N 64 34W
Ste-Cécile-de-Milton 43 45 29N 72 44W
Ste-Claire 41 46 36N 70 51W
Ste-Clothilde-de-Châteauguay 43 45 10N 73 41W
Ste-Croix, Can. 41 46 38N 71 44W
Ste-Croix, Switz. 101 46 49N 6 34W
Ste-Dorothée 44 45 32N 73 49W
Ste-Enimie 102 44 22N 3 26E
Ste-Famille 41 46 58N 70 58W
Ste-Félicité 38 48 54N 67 20W
Ste-Florence 38 48 16N 67 14W
Ste-Foy 42 46 47N 71 17W
Ste-Foy-la-Grande 102 44 50N 0 13E
Ste-Françoise 41 48 6N 69 4W
Ste-Geneviève 44 45 29N 73 52W
Ste. Genevieve 76 37 59N 90 2W
Ste. Germaine 35 46 24N 70 24W
Ste-Hélène-de-Bagot 43 45 44N 72 44W
Ste-Hermine 102 46 32N 1 4W
Ste-Julie 45 45 35N 73 19W
Ste-Julienne 43 45 58N 73 43W
Ste-Justine-de-Newton 43 45 22N 74 25W
Ste-Livrade-sur-Lot 102 44 24N 0 36E
Ste-Madeleine 45 45 36N 73 6W
Ste-Marguerite, R. 36 50 9N 66 36W
Ste. Marie 85 14 48N 61 1W
Ste-Marie-aux-Mines 101 48 10N 7 12E
Ste-Marie de la Madeleine 41 46 26N 71 0W
Ste. Marie, I. 117 16 50S 49 55E
Ste-Marie-Salomé 43 45 56N 73 30W
Ste-Marthe 43 45 24N 74 18W
Ste-Marthe-de-Gaspé 38 49 12N 66 10W
Ste-Marthe-sur-le-Lac 44 45 32N 73 57W
Ste-Martine 44 45 15N 73 48W
Ste-Maure-de-Touraine 100 47 7N 0 37E
Ste-Maxime 103 43 19N 6 39E
Ste-Menehould 101 49 5N 4 54E
Ste-Mère-Église 100 49 24N 1 19W
Ste-Monique 41 48 44N 71 51W
Ste-Monique-des-Deux-Montagnes 44 45 40N 74 0W
Ste-Pudentienne 44 45 28N 72 40W
Ste-Rosalie 43 45 38N 72 54W
Ste-Rose 43 45 37N 73 48W
Ste. Rose 85 16 20N 61 45W
Ste.-Rose du lac 57 51 4N 99 30W
Ste-Sabine 43 45 15N 73 2W
Ste-Scholastique 44 45 39N 74 5W
Ste. Teresa 88 33 33S 60 54W
Ste-Thècle 41 46 49N 72 31W
Ste-Thérèse 44 45 38N 73 51W
Ste-Thérèse-de-Lisieux 42 46 56N 71 12W
Ste-Thérèse, Île, Qué., Can. 45 45 40N 73 29W
Ste Thérèse, Île, Qué., Can. 45 45 41N 73 28W
Ste-Thérèse-Ouest 44 45 37N 73 50W
Ste-Victoire 43 45 57N 73 5W
Saintes 102 45 45N 0 37W
Saintes, I. des 85 15 50N 61 35W
Saintes-Maries-de-la-Mer 103 43 26N 4 26E
Saintonge 102 45 40N 0 50W
Sairang 125 23 50N 92 45E
Sairecábur, Cerro 88 22 43S 67 54W
Sairs, L. 40 46 49N 78 26W
Saitama-ken □ 132 36 25N 137 0E
Sajama, Nevada 86 18 0S 68 55W
Såkahka 122 30 0N 40 8E
Sakai 132 34 30N 135 30E
Sakai Shimane 132 35 30N 133 25E
Sakaimachi 132 35 30N 133 15E
Sakami, L. 36 53 15N 76 45W
Sakania 117 12 43S 28 30E
Sakata 132 36 38N 138 19E
Sakhalin, Ostrov 121 51 0N 143 0E
Sakishima-guntō 131 24 30N 124 0E
Sakon Nakhon 128 17 10N 104 9E
Sala 111 59 58N 16 35E
Sala-y-Gomez, I. 15 26 28S 105 28W
Salaberry-de-Valleyfield 44 45 15N 74 8W
Salaberry, Île de 44 45 17N 74 7W
Salada, La 82 24 30N 111 30W
Saladas 88 28 15S 58 40W
Saladillo 88 35 40S 59 55W
Salado, R., Buenos Aires, Argent. 88 35 40S 58 10W
Salado, R., Santa Fe, Argent. 88 27 0S 63 40W
Salado, R., Mexico 82 26 52N 99 19W
Salamanca, Chile 88 32 0S 71 25W
Salamanca, Spain 104 40 58N 5 39W
Salamanca, U.S.A. 70 42 10N 78 42W
Salamina 86 5 25N 75 29W
Salamis 109 37 56N 23 30E
Salamonie, R. 77 40 47N 85 40W
Salamonie, Resvr. 77 40 45N 85 35W
Salar de Atacama 90 23 30S 68 25W
Salar de Uyuni 86 20 30S 67 45W
Salatu 130 44 25N 107 58E
Salaverry 86 8 15S 79 0W
Salayar, I. 127 6 15S 120 30E
Salbris 101 47 25N 2 3E
Saldaña 104 42 32N 4 48W
Saldanha 117 33 0S 17 58E
Sale, Austral. 136 38 6S 147 6E
Sale, U.K. 94 53 26N 2 19W
Salebabu 127 3 45N 125 55E
Sālehābād 123 35 40N 61 2E
Salekhard 120 66 30N 66 25E
Salem, Can. 49 43 42N 80 27W
Salem, India 124 11 40N 78 11E
Salem, U.S.A. 76 38 38N 88 57W
Salem, Ind., U.S.A. 77 38 38N 86 0W
Salem, Mass., U.S.A. 71 42 29N 70 53W
Salem, Mo., U.S.A. 75 37 40N 91 30W
Salem, N.J., U.S.A. 72 39 34N 75 29W
Salem, Ohio, U.S.A. 70 40 52N 80 50W
Salem, Oreg., U.S.A. 78 45 0N 123 0W
Salem, Va., U.S.A. 72 37 19N 80 8W
Salembu, Kepulauan 126 5 35S 114 30E
Salen 111 64 41N 11 27E
Salernes 103 43 34N 6 15E
Salerno 108 40 40N 14 44E
Salford 94 53 30N 2 17W
Salies-de-Béarn 102 43 28N 0 56W
Salima 117 13 47S 34 28E
Salina 74 38 50N 97 40W
Salina Cruz 83 16 10N 95 10W
Salina, I. 108 38 35N 14 50E
Salina, La 86 10 22N 71 27W
Salinas, Brazil 87 16 20S 42 10W
Salinas, Chile 88 23 31S 69 29W
Salinas, Ecuador 86 2 10S 80 50W
Salinas, Mexico 82 23 37N 106 8W
Salinas, U.S.A. 80 36 40N 121 31W
Salinas Ambargasta 88 29 0S 65 30W
Salinas, B. de 84 11 4N 85 45W
Salinas (de Hidalgo) 82 22 30N 101 40W
Salinas Grandes 88 30 0S 65 0W
Salinas, Pampa de las 88 31 58S 66 42W
Salinas, R., Mexico 83 16 28N 90 31W
Salinas, R., U.S.A. 80 36 45N 121 48W
Saline 46 42 12N 83 49W
Saline, R. 74 39 10N 99 5W
Salinópolis 87 0 40S 47 20W
Salins-les-Bains 101 46 58N 5 52E
Salisbury, Can. 39 46 2N 65 3W
Salisbury, Rhod. 117 17 50S 31 2E
Salisbury, U.K. 95 51 4N 1 48W
Salisbury, U.S.A. 76 39 25N 92 48W
Salisbury, Md., U.S.A. 72 38 20N 75 38W
Salisbury, N.C., U.S.A. 73 35 42N 80 29W
Salisbury I. 65 63 30N 77 0W
Salisbury Plain 95 51 13N 1 50W
Salle, La 76 41 20N 89 6W
Salles-Curan 102 44 11N 2 48E
Sallisaw 75 35 26N 94 45W
Sally's Cove 37 49 44N 57 56W
Salmo 63 49 10N 117 20W
Salmon 78 45 12N 113 56W
Salmon Arm 63 50 40N 119 15W
Salmon Falls 78 42 55N 114 59W
Salmon, R., B.C., Can. 54 54 3N 122 40W
Salmon, R., N.B., Can. 39 46 6N 65 56W
Salmon, R., Qué., Can. 38 49 25N 62 15W
Salmon, R., U.S.A. 78 46 0N 116 30W
Salmon Res. 37 48 05N 56 00W
Salmon River 39 44 3N 66 10W
Salmon River Mts. 78 45 0N 114 30W
Salo 111 60 22N 23 3E
Salome 81 33 51N 113 37W
Salon-de-Provence 103 43 39N 5 6E
Salonta 107 46 49N 21 42E
Salop □ 95 52 36N 2 45W
Salsacate 88 31 20S 65 5W
Salses 102 42 50N 2 55E
Salso, R. 108 37 6N 13 55E
Salt Fork R. 75 37 25N 98 40W
Salt Lake City 78 40 45N 111 58W
Salt, R., Can. 54 60 0N 112 25W
Salt, R., U.S.A. 76 39 29N 91 5W
Salt, R., U.S.A. 77 37 54N 85 51W
Salt, R., Ariz., U.S.A. 79 33 50N 110 25W
Salta 88 24 47S 65 25W
Salta □ 88 24 48S 65 30W
Saltair 62 48 57N 123 46W
Saltcoats, Can. 57 51 5N 102 15W
Saltcoats, U.K. 96 55 38N 4 47W
Saltee Is. 97 52 7N 6 37W
Saltery Bay 62 49 47N 124 10W
Saltfjorden 110 67 15N 14 20E
Salthólmavík 110 65 24N 21 57W
Saltillo 82 25 30N 100 57W
Salto, Argent. 88 34 20S 60 15W
Salto, Uruguay 88 31 20S 57 59W
Salto □ 88 31 20S 57 59W
Salto Augusto, falls 88 8 30S 58 0W
Salton City 81 33 21N 115 59W
Salton Sea 81 33 20N 115 50W
Saltspring 54 48 54N 123 37W
Salula, R. 73 34 12N 81 45W
Salûm 115 31 31N 25 7E
Salur 125 18 27N 83 18E
Saluzzo 108 44 39N 7 29E
Salvador, Brazil 87 13 0S 38 30W
Salvador, Can. 56 52 10N 109 25W
Salvador ■ 82 13 50N 89 0W
Salvador, L. 75 29 46N 90 16W
Salvail 45 45 40N 73 4W
Salvail, R. 45 45 49N 73 58W
Salvisa 77 37 54N 84 51W
Salwa 123 24 45N 50 55E
Salween, R. 125 16 31N 97 37E
Salzburg 106 47 48N 13 2E
Salzburg □ 106 47 15N 13 0E
Salzgitter 106 52 2N 10 22E
Sam Neua 128 20 29N 104 0E
Sam Ngao 128 17 18N 99 0E
Sam Rayburn Res. 75 31 15N 94 20W
Sama 120 60 12N 60 22E
Sama de Langreo 104 43 18N 5 40W
Samales Group 127 6 0N 122 0E
Samana Cay 85 23 3N 73 45W
Samanco 86 9 10S 78 30W
Samangan □ 123 36 15N 67 40E
Samar, I. 127 12 0N 125 0E
Samarkand 120 39 40N 67 0E
Samarra 122 34 16N 43 55E
Samatan 102 43 29N 0 55E
Sambalpur 125 21 28N 83 58E
Sambas, S. 126 1 20N 109 20E
Sambava 117 14 16S 50 10E
Sambhal 124 28 35N 78 37E
Sambhar 124 26 52N 75 10E
Sambiase 108 38 58N 16 16E
Sambor 128 12 46N 106 0E
Sambre, R. 105 50 27N 4 52E
Sambro 39 44 28N 63 36W
Samchŏk 130 37 30N 129 10E
Same 116 4 2S 37 38E
Samer 101 50 38N 1 44E
Samo Alto 88 30 22S 71 0W
Samoan Is. 10 14 0S 171 0W
Samoëns 103 46 5N 6 45E
Samoorombón, Bahía 88 36 5S 57 20W
Sámos, I. 109 37 45N 26 50E
Samosir, P. 126 2 35N 98 50E
Samothráki, I. 109 40 25N 25 40E
Sampacho 88 33 20S 64 50W
Sampang 127 7 11S 113 13E
Sampit 126 2 20S 113 0E
Samra 122 25 35N 41 0E
Samshui 131 23 7N 112 58E
Samsun 122 41 15N 36 15E
Samut Prakan 128 13 32N 100 40E
Samut Sakhon 128 13 31N 100 20E
Samut Songkhram (Mekong) 128 13 24N 100 1E
San Agustín 86 1 53N 76 16W
San Agustin, C. 127 6 20N 126 13E
San Agustín de Valle Fértil 88 30 35S 67 30W
San Ambrosio, I. 15 26 35S 79 30W
San Andreas 80 38 17N 120 39W
San Andrés, I. de 84 12 42N 81 46W
San Andres Mts. 79 33 0N 106 45W
San Andrés Tuxtla 83 18 30N 95 20W
San Angelo 75 31 30N 100 30W
San Anselmo 80 37 49N 122 34W
San Antonio, Belize 83 16 15N 89 2W
San Antonio, Chile 88 33 40S 71 40W
San Antonio, N. Mex., U.S.A. 79 33 58N 106 57W
San Antonio, Tex., U.S.A. 75 29 30N 98 30W
San Antonio, Venez. 86 3 30N 66 44W
San Antonio, C., Argent. 88 36 15S 56 40W
San Antonio, C., Cuba 84 21 50N 84 57W
San Antonio de Caparo 86 7 35N 71 27W
San Antonio de los Baños 84 22 54N 82 31W
San Antonio de los Cobres 88 24 16S 66 2W
San Antonio do Zaire 116 6 8S 12 11E
San Antonio, Mt. (Old Baldy Pk.) 81 34 17N 117 38W
San Antonio Oeste 90 40 40S 65 0W
San Antonio, R. 75 28 30N 97 14W
San Ardo 80 36 1N 120 54W
San Augustine 75 31 30N 94 7W
San Benedetto 108 45 2N 10 57E
San Benedicto, I. 82 19 18N 110 49W
San Benito 75 26 5N 97 32W
San Benito Mt. 80 36 22N 120 37W
San Benito, R. 80 36 53N 121 50W
San Bernardino 81 34 7N 117 18W
San Bernardo 88 33 40S 70 50W
San Bernardo, I. de 86 9 45N 75 50W
San Blas 82 26 10N 108 40W
San Blas, C. 73 29 40N 85 25W
San Blas, Cord. de 84 9 15N 78 30W
San Borja 86 15 0S 67 12W
San Buenaventura 82 27 5N 101 32W
San Buenaventura = Ventura 81 34 17N 119 18W
San Carlos, Argent. 88 33 50S 69 0W
San Carlos, Chile 130 36 25S 72 0W
San Carlos, Mexico 82 29 0N 101 10W
San Carlos, Nic. 84 11 12N 84 50W
San Carlos, Phil. 127 10 29N 123 25E
San Carlos, Uruguay 89 34 46S 54 58W
San Carlos, U.S.A. 79 33 24N 110 27W
San Carlos, Amazonas, Venez. 86 1 55N 67 4W
San Carlos, Cojedes, Venez. 86 9 40N 68 36W
San Carlos de Bariloche 90 41 10S 71 25W
San Carlos del Zulia 86 9 1N 71 55W
San Carlos L. 79 33 20N 110 10W
San Clara 57 51 29N 101 26W
San Clemente, Chile 88 35 30S 71 39W
San Clemente, U.S.A. 81 33 29N 117 45W
San Clemente I. 81 32 53N 118 30W
San Cristóbal, Argent. 88 30 20S 61 10W
San Cristóbal, Dom. Rep. 85 18 25N 70 6W
San Cristóbal, Venez. 86 7 46N 72 14W
San Cristóbal de las Casas 83 16 50N 92 33W
San Diego, Calif., U.S.A. 81 32 43N 117 10W
San Diego, Tex., U.S.A. 75 27 47N 98 15W
San Diego, C. 90 54 40S 65 10W
San Diego de la Unión 82 21 28N 100 52W
San Estanislao 88 24 39S 56 26W
San Felipe, Chile 88 32 43S 70 42W
San Felipe, Mexico 82 31 0N 114 52W
San Felipe, Venez. 86 10 20N 68 44W
San Felipe, R. 81 33 12N 115 49W
San Feliu de Guixols 104 41 45N 3 1E
San Félix 86 8 20N 62 35W
San Felix, I. 15 26 30S 80 0W
San Fernando, Chile 88 34 30S 71 0W
San Fernando, Mexico 82 30 0N 115 10W
San Fernando, Luzon, Phil. 127 16 40N 120 23E
San Fernando, Luzon, Phil. 127 15 5N 120 37E
San Fernando, Spain 104 36 22N 6 17W
San Fernando, Trin 85 10 20N 61 30W
San Fernando, U.S.A. 81 34 15N 118 29W
San Fernando de Apure 86 7 54N 67 28W
San Fernando de Atabapo 86 4 3N 67 42W
San Fernando, R. 82 25 0N 99 0W
San Francisco, Córdoba, Argent. 88 31 30S 62 5W
San Francisco, San Luis, Argent. 88 32 45S 66 10W
San Francisco, U.S.A. 80 37 47N 122 30W
San Francisco de Macorîs 85 19 19N 70 15W
San Francisco del Monte de Oro 88 32 36S 66 8W
San Francisco del Oro 82 26 52N 105 50W
San Francisco, Paso de 88 35 40S 70 24W
San Francisco, R. 79 33 30N 109 0W
San Francisco Solano, Pta. 86 6 18N 77 29W
San Francisville 75 30 48N 91 22W
San Gabriel 86 0 36N 77 49W

San German	**67**	18 5N	67 3W
San Gil	**86**	6 33N	73 8W
San Gorgonio Mt.	**81**	34 7N	116 51W
San Gottardo, Paso del	**106**	46 33N	8 33 E
San Gregorio, Uruguay	**89**	32 37 S	55 40W
San Gregorio, U.S.A.	**80**	37 20N	122 23W
San Ignacio, Boliv.	**86**	16 20 S	60 55W
San Ignacio, Mexico	**82**	27 27N	112 51W
San Ignacio, Parag.	**88**	26 52 S	57 3W
San Ignacio, Laguna	**82**	26 50N	113 11W
San Ildefonso, C.	**127**	16 0N	122 10 E
San Isidro	**88**	34 29 S	58 31W
San Jacinto, Colomb.	**86**	9 50N	75 8W
San Jacinto, U.S.A.	**81**	33 47N	116 57W
San Javier, Misiones, Argent.	**89**	27 55 S	55 5W
San Javier, Santa Fe, Argent.	**88**	30 40 S	59 55W
San Javier, Boliv.	**86**	16 18 S	62 30W
San Javier, Chile	**88**	35 40 S	71 45W
San Jerónimo, Sa. de	**86**	8 0N	75 50W
San Joaquin	**80**	36 36N	120 11W
San Joaquín	**86**	10 16N	67 47W
San Joaquin R.	**80**	37 4N	121 51W
San Joaquin Valley	**80**	37 0N	120 30W
San Jorge	**88**	31 54 S	61 50W
San Jorge, Bahía de	**82**	31 20N	113 20W
San Jorge, Golfo de	**90**	46 0 S	66 0W
San Jorge, G. de	**104**	40 50N	0 55W
San José, Boliv.	**86**	17 45 S	60 50W
San José, C. Rica	**84**	10 0N	84 2W
San José, Guat.	**82**	14 0N	90 50W
San José, Luzon, Phil.	**127**	15 45N	120 55 E
San José, Mindoro, Phil.	**127**	10 50N	122 5 E
San Jose, U.S.A.	**76**	40 18N	89 36W
San Jose, Calif., U.S.A.	**80**	37 20N	121 53W
San Jose, N. Mex., U.S.A.	**75**	35 26N	105 30W
San José Carpizo	**83**	19 26N	90 32W
San José de Feliciano	**88**	30 26 S	58 46W
San José de Jáchal	**88**	30 5 S	69 0W
San José de Mayo	**88**	34 27 S	56 27W
San José de Ocuné	**86**	4 15N	70 20W
San José del Cabo	**82**	23 0N	109 50W
San José del Guaviare	**86**	2 35N	72 38W
San José, I.	**82**	25 0N	110 50W
San Juan, Argent.	**88**	31 30 S	68 30W
San Juan, Antioquía, Colomb.	**86**	8 46N	76 32W
San Juan, Meta, Colomb.	**86**	3 26N	73 50W
San Juan, Dom. Rep.	**67**	18 49N	71 12W
San Juan, Coahuila, Mexico	**82**	29 34N	101 53W
San Juan, Jalisco, Mexico	**82**	21 20N	102 50W
San Juan, Querétaro, Mexico	**82**	20 25N	100 0W
San Juan, Phil.	**127**	8 35N	126 20 E
San Juan, Pto Rico	**85**	18 28N	66 37W
San Juan □	**88**	31 9 S	69 0W
San Juan Bautista, Parag.	**88**	26 37 S	57 6W
San Juan Bautista, U.S.A.	**80**	36 51N	121 32W
San Juan, C.	**67**	18 23N	65 37W
San Juan Capistrano	**81**	33 29N	117 40W
San Juan de Guadalupe	**82**	24 38N	102 44W
San Juan de los Cayos	**86**	11 10N	68 25W
San Juan de los Morros	**86**	9 55N	67 21W
San Juan de Norte, B. de	**84**	11 30N	83 40W
San Juan del Norte	**84**	10 58N	83 40W
San Juan del Río	**83**	24 47N	104 27W
San Juan del Sur	**84**	11 20N	86 0W
San Juan I.	**80**	48 32N	123 5W
San Juan Mts.	**79**	38 30N	108 30W
San Juan, Presa de	**82**	17 45N	95 15W
San Juan, R., Argent.	**88**	32 20 S	67 25W
San Juan, R., Colomb.	**86**	4 0N	77 20W
San Juan, R., Nic.	**84**	11 0N	84 30W
San Juan, R., Calif., U.S.A.	**80**	36 14N	121 9W
San Juan, R., Utah, U.S.A.	**79**	37 20N	110 20W
San Julián	**90**	49 15 S	68 0W
San Justo	**88**	30 55 S	60 30W
San Lázaro, C.	**82**	24 50N	112 18W
San Lázaro, Sa. de	**82**	23 25N	110 0W
San Leandro	**80**	37 40N	122 6W
San Lorenzo, Argent.	**88**	32 45 S	60 45W
San Lorenzo, Ecuador	**86**	1 15N	78 50W
San Lorenzo, Parag.	**88**	25 20 S	57 32W
San Lorenzo, Venez.	**86**	9 47N	71 4W
San Lorenzo, I., Mexico	**82**	28 35N	112 50W
San Lorenzo, I., Peru	**86**	12 20 S	77 35W
San Lorenzo, Mt.	**90**	47 40 S	72 20W
San Lorenzo, R.	**82**	24 15N	107 24W
San Lucas, Boliv.	**86**	20 5 S	65 0W
San Lucas, Baja California S., Mexico	**82**	22 53N	109 54W
San Lucas, Baja California S., Mexico	**82**	27 10N	112 14W
San Lucas, U.S.A.	**80**	36 8N	121 1W
San Lucas, C. de	**82**	22 50N	110 0W
San Luis, Argent.	**88**	33 20 S	66 20W
San Luis, Cuba	**84**	22 17N	83 46W
San Luis, Guat.	**84**	16 14N	89 27W
San Luis, U.S.A.	**79**	37 14N	105 26W
San Luis, Venez.	**86**	11 7N	69 42W
San Luis □	**88**	34 0 S	66 0W
San Luis de la Loma	**82**	17 18N	100 55W
San Luís de la Paz	**82**	21 19N	100 32W
San Luís de Potosí	**82**	22 9N	100 59W
San Luís de Potosí □	**82**	22 10N	101 0W
San Luis, I.	**82**	29 58N	114 26W
San Luis Obispo	**79**	35 21N	120 38W
San Luis Res.	**80**	37 4N	121 5W
San Luis Río Colorado	**82**	32 29N	114 48W
San Luis, Sierra de	**88**	37 25N	66 10W
San Marcos, Guat.	**84**	14 59N	91 52W
San Marcos, U.S.A.	**75**	29 53N	98 0W
San Marcos, I.	**82**	27 13N	112 6W
San Marino	**108**	43 56N	12 25 E
San Marino ■	**108**	43 56N	12 25 E
San Martín, Argent.	**88**	33 5 S	68 28W
San Martín, Colomb.	**86**	3 42N	73 42W
San Martín, L.	**90**	48 50 S	72 50W
San Mateo	**80**	37 32N	122 19W
San Matías	**86**	16 25 S	58 20W
San Matías, Golfo de	**90**	41 30 S	64 0W
San Miguel, El Sal.	**84**	13 30N	88 12W
San Miguel, Panama	**84**	8 27N	78 55W
San Miguel, U.S.A.	**80**	35 45N	120 42W
San Miguel, Venez.	**86**	9 40N	65 11W
San Miguel de Tucumán	**88**	26 50 S	65 20W
San Miguel del Monte	**88**	35 23 S	58 50W
San Miguel I.	**81**	34 2N	120 23W
San Miguel, R., Boliv.	**86**	16 0 S	62 45W
San Miguel, R., Ecuador/Ecuador	**86**	0 25N	76 30W
San Narcisco	**127**	15 2N	120 3 E
San Nicolás de los Arroyas	**88**	33 17 S	60 10W
San Nicolas I.	**68**	33 16N	119 30W
San Onafre	**81**	33 22N	117 34W
San Onofre	**86**	9 44N	75 32W
San Pablo, Boliv.	**88**	21 43 S	66 38W
San Pablo, Colomb.	**86**	5 27N	70 56W
San Pedro, Buenos Aires, Argent.	**89**	33 43 S	59 45W
San Pedro, Jujuy, Argent.	**88**	24 12 S	64 55W
San Pedro, Chile	**88**	21 58 S	68 30W
San Pedro, Colomb.	**86**	4 56N	71 53W
San Pedro, Dom. Rep.	**85**	18 30N	69 18W
San Pedro, Mexico	**82**	23 55N	110 17W
San Pedro □	**88**	24 0 S	57 0W
San Pedro Channel	**81**	33 35N	118 25W
San Pedro de Arimena	**86**	4 37N	71 42W
San Pedro de Atacama	**88**	22 55 S	68 15W
San Pedro de Jujuy	**88**	24 12 S	64 55W
San Pedro de las Colonias	**82**	25 50N	102 59W
San Pedro de Lloc	**86**	7 15 S	79 28W
San Pedro del Norte	**84**	13 4N	84 33W
San Pedro del Paraná	**88**	26 43 S	56 13W
San Pedro Mártir, Sierra	**82**	31 0N	115 30W
San Pedro Mixtepec	**83**	16 2N	97 0W
San Pedro Ocampo = Melchor Ocampo	**82**	24 52N	101 40W
San Pedro, Pta.	**88**	25 30 S	70 38W
San Pedro, R., Chihuahua, Mexico	**82**	28 20N	106 10W
San Pedro, R., Michoacan, Mexico	**82**	19 23N	103 51W
San Pedro, R., Nayarit, Mexico	**82**	21 45N	105 30W
San Pedro, R., U.S.A.	**79**	32 45N	110 35W
San Pedro Sula	**84**	15 30N	88 0W
San Pedro Tututepec	**83**	16 9N	97 38W
San Pedro,Pta.	**88**	25 30 S	70 38W
San Quintín, Mexico	**82**	30 29N	115 57W
San Quintín, Phil.	**127**	16 1N	120 56 E
San, R.	**107**	50 25N	22 20 E
San Rafael, Argent.	**88**	34 40 S	68 30W
San Rafael, Colomb.	**86**	6 2N	69 45W
San Rafael, Calif., U.S.A.	**80**	38 0N	122 32W
San Rafael, N. Mex., U.S.A.	**79**	35 6N	107 58W
San Rafael, Venez.	**86**	10 42N	71 46W
San Rafael Mt.	**81**	34 41N	119 52W
San Ramón de la Nueva Orán	**88**	23 10 S	64 20W
San Remo	**108**	43 48N	7 47 E
San Román, C.	**86**	12 12N	70 0W
San Roque	**88**	28 15 S	58 45W
San Rosendo	**88**	37 10 S	72 50W
San Saba	**75**	31 12N	98 45W
San Salvador	**84**	13 40N	89 20W
San Salvador de Jujuy	**88**	23 30 S	65 40W
San Salvador (Watlings) I.	**85**	24 0N	74 40W
San Sebastián, Argent.	**90**	53 10 S	68 30W
San Sebastián, Spain	**104**	43 17N	1 58W
San Sebastián, Venez.	**86**	9 57N	67 11W
San Severo	**108**	41 41N	15 23 E
San Simeon	**80**	35 39N	121 11W
San Simon	**79**	32 14N	109 16W
San Telmo	**82**	30 58N	116 6W
San Tiburcio	**82**	24 8N	101 32W
San Valentin, Mte.	**90**	46 30 S	73 30W
San Vicente de la Barquera	**104**	43 30N	4 29W
San Vicente del Caguán	**86**	2 7N	74 46W
San Vicenzo	**123**	43 9N	10 32 E
San Yanaro	**86**	2 47N	69 42W
San Ygnacio	**75**	27 6N	99 24W
San Ysidro	**79**	32 33N	117 5W
San'a	**115**	15 27N	44 12 E
Sana, R.	**108**	44 40N	16 43 E
Sanaga, R.	**116**	3 35N	9 38 E
Sanak I	**67**	53 30N	162 30W
Sanaloa, Presa	**82**	24 50N	107 20W
Sanana	**127**	2 5 S	125 50 E
Sanandaj	**122**	35 25N	47 7 E
Sanandita	**88**	21 40 S	63 35W
Sanary	**103**	43 7N	5 48 E
Sancergues	**101**	47 10N	2 54 E
Sancerre	**101**	47 20N	2 50 E
Sancha Ho	**131**	26 20N	105 30 E
Sánchez	**85**	19 15N	69 36W
Sanco, Pt.	**127**	8 15N	126 24 E
Sancoins	**101**	46 47N	2 55 E
Sancti-Spíritus	**84**	21 52N	79 33W
Sand Creek, R.	**77**	39 5N	85 52W
Sand I.	**52**	46 59N	91 0W
Sand L.	**52**	50 10N	94 35W
Sand Lake	**34**	47 46N	84 31W
Sand Pt.	**46**	43 54N	83 27W
Sand Point	**67**	55 20N	160 32W
Sand, R.	**60**	54 23N	111 2W
Sand Springs	**75**	36 12N	96 5W
Sandakan	**126**	5 53N	118 10 E
Sandan	**128**	12 46N	106 0 E
Sanday, I.	**96**	59 15N	2 30W
Sandbank L.	**53**	51 8N	82 41W
Sanders, U.S.A.	**77**	38 40N	84 56W
Sanders, Ariz., U.S.A.	**79**	35 12N	109 25W
Sanderson	**75**	30 5N	102 30W
Sandfell	**110**	63 57N	16 48W
Sandfly L.	**55**	55 43N	106 6W
Sandhill	**49**	43 50N	79 52W
Sandia	**86**	14 10 S	69 30W
Sandikli	**122**	38 30N	30 20 E
Sandnes	**111**	58 50N	5 45 E
Sandoa	**116**	9 48 S	23 0 E
Sandomierz	**107**	50 40N	21 43 E
Sandona	**86**	1 17N	77 28W
Sandoval	**76**	38 37N	89 7W
Sandover, R.	**135**	21 43 S	136 32 E
Sandoway	**125**	18 20N	94 30 E
Sandpoint	**78**	48 20N	116 40W
Sandringham	**94**	52 50N	0 30 E
Sandspit	**62**	53 14N	131 49W
Sandstone	**134**	27 59 S	119 16 E
Sandusky, Mich., U.S.A.	**46**	43 26N	82 50W
Sandusky, Ohio, U.S.A.	**70**	41 25N	82 40W
Sandusky, R.	**77**	41 27N	83 0W
Sandviken	**111**	60 38N	16 46 E
Sandwich	**77**	41 39N	88 37W
Sandwich B.	**36**	53 40N	57 15W
Sandwich Group	**91**	57 0 S	27 0W
Sandwip Chan.	**125**	22 35N	91 35 E
Sandy, Nev., U.S.A.	**81**	35 49N	115 36W
Sandy, Oreg., U.S.A.	**80**	45 24N	122 16W
Sandy Beach	**49**	43 4N	78 59W
Sandy C., Queens., Austral.	**135**	24 42 S	153 15 E
Sandy C., Tas., Austral.	**135**	41 25 S	144 45 E
Sandy Cay	**85**	23 13N	75 18W
Sandy Cove	**37**	51 21N	56 40W
Sandy Cr.	**78**	42 20N	109 30W
Sandy Hook	**76**	38 5N	83 8W
Sandy L., Alta., Can.	**60**	53 47N	114 2W
Sandy L., Newf., Can.	**37**	49 15N	57 0W
Sandy L., Ont., Can.	**34**	53 2N	93 0W
Sandy Lake	**34**	53 0N	93 15W
Sandy Narrows	**55**	55 5N	103 4W
Sandy Point	**39**	43 42N	65 19W
Sandy, R.	**36**	55 30N	68 21W
Sandybeach L.	**52**	49 49N	92 21W
Sanford, Fla., U.S.A.	**73**	28 45N	81 20W
Sanford, Me., U.S.A.	**71**	43 28N	70 47W
Sanford, N.C., U.S.A.	**73**	35 30N	79 10W
Sanford, R.	**134**	27 22 S	115 53 E
Sanga Tolon	**121**	61 50N	149 40 E
Sangamner	**124**	19 30N	74 15 E
Sangamon R.	**76**	40 2N	90 21W
Sangar	**121**	63 55N	127 31 E
Sangasanga	**126**	0 29 S	117 13 E
Sangchih	**131**	29 25N	109 30 E
Sangeang, I.	**127**	8 12 S	119 6 E
Sanger	**80**	36 47N	119 35W
Sanggau	**126**	0 5N	110 30 E
Sangihe, Kep.	**127**	3 0N	126 0 E
Sangihe, P.	**127**	3 45N	125 30 E
Sangkan Ho	**130**	40 24N	115 19 E
Sangkapura	**126**	5 52 S	112 40 E
Sangli	**124**	16 55N	74 33 E
Sangmélina	**116**	2 57N	12 1 E
Sangonera, R.	**104**	37 39N	2 0W
Sangre de Cristo Mts.	**75**	37 0N	105 0W
Sangsang	**129**	29 30N	86 0 E
Sangudo	**60**	53 50N	114 54W
Sanguinaires, Is.	**103**	41 51N	8 36 E
Sanish	**74**	48 0N	102 30W
Sankiang	**131**	25 39N	109 30 E
Sankt Moritz	**106**	46 30N	9 50 E
Sankuru, R.	**116**	4 17 S	20 25 E
Sanlúcar de Barrameda	**104**	37 26N	6 18W
Sanmaur	**41**	47 54N	73 47W
Sanmen Hu	**131**	34 40N	111 0 E
Sanmen Wan	**131**	29 10N	121 45 E
Sanmenhsia	**131**	34 46N	111 30 E
Sannicandro Gargánico	**108**	41 50N	15 34 E
Sanok	**107**	49 35N	22 10 E
Sanquhar	**96**	55 21N	3 56W
Santa Ana, Ecuador	**86**	1 10 S	80 20W
Santa Ana, El Sal.	**84**	14 0N	89 40W
Santa Ana, Mexico	**82**	30 31N	111 8W
Santa Ana, U.S.A.	**81**	33 48N	117 55W
Santa Ana, El Beni	**86**	13 50 S	65 40W
Santa Bárbara, Brazil	**87**	16 0 S	59 0W
Santa Bárbara, Colomb.	**86**	5 53N	75 35W
Santa Barbara	**84**	14 53N	88 14W
Santa Bárbara	**82**	26 48N	105 50W
Santa Barbara	**81**	34 25N	119 40W
Santa Bárbara	**86**	7 47N	71 10W
Santa Barbara Channel	**81**	34 20N	120 0W
Santa Barbara I.	**81**	33 29N	119 2W
Santa Barbara Is.	**79**	33 31N	119 0W
Santa Catalina	**86**	10 36N	75 17W
Santa Catalina, G. of	**81**	33 0N	118 0W
Santa Catalina, I., Mexico	**82**	25 40N	110 50W
Santa Catalina, I., U.S.A.	**81**	33 20N	118 30W
Santa Catarina □	**89**	27 25 S	48 30W
Santa Catarina, I. de	**89**	27 30 S	48 40W
Santa Cecília	**89**	26 56 S	50 27W
Santa Clara, Cuba	**84**	22 20N	80 0W
Santa Clara, Calif., U.S.A.	**80**	37 21N	122 0W
Santa Clara, Utah, U.S.A.	**79**	37 10N	113 38W
Santa Clara de Olimar	**89**	32 50 S	54 54W
Santa Clotilde	**86**	2 25 S	73 45W
Santa Cruz, Argent.	**90**	50 0 S	68 50W
Santa Cruz, Boliv.	**86**	17 43 S	63 10W
Santa Cruz, Canary Is.	**114**	28 29N	16 26W
Santa Cruz, Chile	**88**	34 38 S	71 27W
Santa Cruz, C. Rica	**84**	10 15N	85 41W
Santa Cruz, Phil.	**127**	14 20N	121 30 E
Santa Cruz, Calif., U.S.A.	**80**	36 55N	122 1W
Santa Cruz, N. Mexico, U.S.A.	**79**	35 59N	106 1W
Santa Cruz □	**86**	17 43 S	63 10W
Santa Cruz de Barahona	**85**	18 12N	71 6W
Santa Cruz del Norte	**84**	23 9N	81 55W
Santa Cruz del Sur	**84**	20 50N	78 0W
Santa Cruz do Rio Pardo	**89**	22 54 S	49 37W
Santa Cruz do Sul	**89**	29 42 S	52 25W
Santa Cruz I.	**68**	34 0N	119 45W
Santa Cruz, Is.	**14**	10 30 S	166 0 E
Santa Cruz, R.	**90**	50 10 S	70 0W
Santa Elena, Argent.	**88**	30 58 S	59 47W
Santa Elena, Ecuador	**86**	2 16 S	80 52W
Santa Elena C.	**85**	10 54N	85 56W
Santa Fe, Argent.	**88**	31 35 S	60 41W
Santa Fe, U.S.A.	**75**	35 40N	106 0W
Santa Fé □	**88**	31 50 S	60 55W
Santa Filomena	**87**	9 0 S	45 50W
Santa Genoveva, Mt.	**82**	23 18N	109 52W
Santa Inés, I.	**90**	54 0 S	73 0W
Santa Isabel, Argent.	**88**	36 10 S	67 0W
Santa Isabel, Brazil	**87**	13 45 S	56 30W
Santa Lucía, Corrientes, Argent.	**88**	28 58 S	59 5W
Santa Lucía, San Juan, Argent.	**88**	31 30 S	68 45W
Santa Lucia	**88**	34 27 S	56 24W
Santa Lucia Range	**80**	36 0N	121 20W
Santa Magdalena, I.	**82**	24 50N	112 15W
Santa Margarita, Argent.	**88**	38 18 S	61 35W
Santa Margarita, U.S.A.	**80**	35 23N	120 37W
Santa Margarita, I.	**82**	24 30N	112 0W
Santa Margarita, R.	**81**	33 13N	117 23W
Santa María, Argent.	**88**	26 40 S	66 0W
Santa Maria, Brazil	**89**	29 40 S	53 40W
Santa María, Mexico	**82**	27 40N	114 40W
Santa Maria	**81**	34 58N	120 29W
Santa María, Bahía de	**82**	25 10N	108 40W
Santa Maria da Vitória	**87**	13 24 S	44 12W
Santa María del Oro	**82**	25 30N	105 20W
Santa Maria di Leuca, C.	**109**	39 48N	18 20 E
Santa María, R.	**82**	31 0N	107 14W
Santa Marta	**86**	11 15N	74 13W
Santa Marta Grande, C.	**89**	28 43 S	48 50W
Santa Marta, Sierra Nevada de	**67**	10 55N	73 50W
Santa Monica	**81**	34 0N	118 30W
Santa Napa	**78**	38 28N	122 45W
Santa Paula	**81**	34 20N	119 2W
Santa Rita, U.S.A.	**79**	32 50N	108 0W
Santa Rita, Guarico, Venez.	**86**	8 8N	66 16W
Santa Rita, Zulia, Venez.	**86**	10 32N	71 32W
Santa Rosa, La Pampa, Argent.	**88**	36 40 S	64 30W
Santa Rosa, San Luis, Argent.	**88**	32 30 S	65 10W
Santa Rosa, Boliv.	**86**	10 25 S	67 20W
Santa Rosa, Brazil	**89**	27 52 S	54 29W
Santa Rosa, Colomb.	**86**	3 32N	69 48W
Santa Rosa, Hond.	**82**	14 40N	89 0W

Sebewaing **Sheldon**

Sebewaing 46 43 45N 83 27W
Sebinkarahisar 122 40 22N 38 28E
Sebring, Fla., U.S.A. 73 27 36N 81 20W
Sebring, Ohio, U.S.A. 70 40 55N 81 2W
Sebringville 46 43 24N 81 4W
Sebuku, I. 126 3 30S 116 25E
Sebuku, Teluk 126 4 0N 118 10E
Sechelt 62 49 25N 123 42W
Sechura, Desierto de 86 6 0S 80 30W
Seclin 101 50 33N 3 2E
Second Narrows 66 49 18N 123 2W
Secondigny 100 46 37N 0 26W
Secretary I. 133 45 15S 166 56E
Secunderabad 124 17 28N 78 30E
Sedalia 76 38 40N 93 18W
Sedan, France 101 49 43N 4 57E
Sedan, U.S.A. 75 37 10N 96 11W
Seddon 133 41 40S 174 7E
Seddonville 133 41 33S 172 1E
Sedgewick 61 52 48N 111 41W
Sedley 56 50 10N 104 0W
Sedova, Pik 120 73 20N 55 10E
Sedro Woolley 80 48 30N 122 15W
Seeheim 117 26 32S 17 52E
Seeley's Bay 47 44 29N 76 14W
Sées 100 48 38N 0 10E
Seg-ozero 120 63 0N 33 10E
Segamat 128 2 30N 102 50E
Seget 127 1 24S 130 58E
Segonzac 102 45 36N 0 14W
Ségou 114 13 30N 6 10W
Segovia 104 40 57N 4 10W
Segré 100 47 40N 0 52W
Segre, R. 104 41 40N 0 43E
Seguam 67 52 0N 172 30W
Seguam Pass. 67 53 0N 175 30W
Séguéla 114 7 55N 6 40W
Segula I. 67 52 0N 178 5W
Segundo 75 37 12N 104 50W
Segundo, R. 88 30 53S 62 44W
Segura, R. 104 38 9N 0 40W
Sehithwa 117 20 30S 22 30E
Sehore 124 23 10N 77 5E
Seilandsjøkelen 110 70 25N 23 16E
Seiling 75 36 10N 99 5W
Seille, R. 103 46 31N 4 57E
Sein, I. de 100 48 2N 4 52W
Sein, R. 58 49 54N 97 7W
Seinäjoki 110 62 48N 22 43E
Seine-Maritime □ 100 49 40N 1 0E
Seine □ 101 49 0N 3 0E
Seine-et-Marne □ 101 48 45N 3 0E
Seine, R. 100 49 28N 0 15E
Seine-Saint-Denis □ 101 48 58N 2 24E
Seistan 123 30 50N 61 0E
Sejal 86 2 45N 68 0W
Sekaju 126 2 58S 103 58E
Sekibi-shō 131 25 45N 124 35E
Sekiu 78 48 30N 124 29W
Sekondi-Takoradi 114 5 0N 1 48W
Selah 78 46 44N 120 30W
Selama 128 5 12N 100 42E
Selangor □ 128 3 20N 101 30E
Selaru, I. 127 8 18S 131 0E
Selawik 67 66 55N 160 10W
Selby, U.K. 94 53 47N 1 5W
Selby, U.S.A. 74 45 34N 99 55W
Selby Lake 43 45 6N 72 48W
Selden 74 39 24N 100 39W
Seldovia 67 59 30N 151 45W
Sele, R. 108 40 27N 15 0E
Selenga, R. = Selenge Mörön 130 49 25N 103 45E
Selenge 129 49 25N 103 59E
Selenge Mörön 130 52 16N 106 16E
Selenge Mörön, R. 129 52 16N 106 16E
Sélestat 101 48 10N 7 26E
Seletan, Tg. 126 4 10S 114 40E
Selfridge 74 46 3N 100 57W
Sélibaby 114 15 20N 12 15W
Seligman 79 35 17N 112 56W
Selkirk, Man., Can. 57 50 10N 96 55W
Selkirk, Ont., Can. 46 42 49N 79 56W
Selkirk, U.K. 96 55 33N 2 50W
Selkirk I. 57 53 20N 99 6W
Selkirk Mts. 54 51 15N 117 40W
Selles-sur-Cher 101 47 16N 1 33E
Sellières 101 46 50N 5 32E
Sells 79 31 57N 111 57W
Selma, Ala., U.S.A. 73 32 30N 87 0W
Selma, Calif., U.S.A. 80 36 39N 119 39W
Selma, N.C., U.S.A. 73 35 32N 78 15W
Selmer 73 35 9N 88 36W
Selongey 101 47 36N 5 10E
Selpele 127 0 1S 130 5E
Selsey Bill 95 50 44N 0 47W
Seltz 101 48 48N 8 4E
Selu, I. 127 7 26S 130 55E
Selukwe 117 19 40S 30 0E
Sélune, R. 100 48 38N 1 22W
Selva 88 29 50S 62 0W
Selva Beach, La 80 36 56N 121 51W
Selvas 86 6 30S 67 0W
Selwyn 135 21 30S 140 29E
Selwyn L. 55 60 0N 104 30W
Selwyn Mts. 67 63 0N 130 0W
Selwyn Ra. 135 21 10S 140 0E
Semani, R. 109 40 45N 19 50E
Semans 56 51 25N 104 44W
Semarang 127 7 0S 110 26E
Semeru, Mt. 127 8 4S 113 3E
Semiahmoo B. 66 49 1N 122 50W
Seminoe Res. 78 42 0N 107 0W
Seminole, Okla., U.S.A. 75 35 15N 96 45W
Seminole, Tex., U.S.A. 75 32 41N 102 38W
Semiozernoye 120 52 22N 64 8E
Semipalatinsk 120 50 30N 80 10E
Semirara Is. 127 12 0N 121 20E
Semisopochnoi I. 67 52 0N 179 40W
Semitau 126 0 29N 111 57E
Semiyarskoye 120 50 55N 78 30E
Semmering Pass. 106 47 41N 15 45E
Semnān 123 35 55N 53 25E
Semnan □ 123 36 0N 54 0E
Semois, R. 105 49 53N 4 44E
Semporna 127 4 30N 118 33E
Semuda 126 2 51S 112 58E
Semur-en-Auxois 101 47 30N 4 20E
Sen, R. 128 13 45N 105 12E
Sena Madureira 86 9 5S 68 45W
Senai 128 1 38N 103 38E
Senaja 126 6 49S 117 2E
Senanga 117 16 2S 23 14E
Senatobia 75 34 38N 89 57W
Sendai, Kagoshima, Japan 132 31 50N 130 20E
Sendai, Miyagi, Japan 132 38 15N 141 0E
Seneca, Oreg., U.S.A. 78 44 10N 119 2W
Seneca, S.C., U.S.A. 73 34 43N 82 59W
Seneca Falls 70 42 55N 76 50W
Seneca L. 70 42 40N 76 58W
Sénécal, L. 38 52 5N 63 20W
Senegal ■ 114 14 30N 14 30W
Senegal, R. 114 16 30N 15 30W
Seney 53 46 25N 86 0W
Senge Khambab (Indus), R. 125 28 40N 70 10E
Senhor-do-Bonfim 87 10 30S 40 10W
Senigállia 108 43 42N 13 12E
Senj 108 45 0N 14 58E
Senja 110 69 25N 17 20E
Senkaku-guntō 131 25 50N 123 30E
Senlis 101 49 13N 2 35E
Senmonorom 128 12 27N 107 12E
Sennâr 115 13 30N 33 35E
Senneterre 40 48 25N 77 15W
Senneville 44 45 27N 73 57W
Senonches 100 48 34N 1 2E
Sens 101 48 11N 3 15E
Senta 109 45 55N 20 3E
Sentein 102 42 53N 0 58E
Sentinel 79 32 56N 113 13W
Sentolo 127 7 55S 110 13E
Seo de Urgel 104 42 22N 1 23E
Seoul = Sŏul 130 37 31N 127 6E
Separation Point 36 53 37N 57 25W
Sepone 128 16 45N 106 13E
Sept-Îles 36 50 13N 66 22W
Sequart L. 38 52 26N 63 47W
Sequim 80 48 3N 123 9W
Sequoia Nat. Park 80 36 30N 118 30W
Seraing 105 50 35N 5 32E
Seram, I. 127 3 10S 129 0E
Seram Sea 127 2 30S 128 30E
Serampore 125 22 44N 88 30E
Serang 127 6 8S 106 10E
Serasan, I. 126 2 29N 109 4E
Serbia = Srbija 109 43 30N 21 0E
Seremban 128 2 43N 101 53E
Serena, La 88 29 55S 71 10W
Serenje 117 13 14S 30 15E
Sergipe □ 87 10 30S 37 30W
Seria 126 4 37N 114 30E
Serian 126 1 10N 110 40E
Sérifontaine 101 49 20N 1 45E
Sérignan 102 43 17N 3 17E
Sérigny, R. 36 56 47N 66 0W
Serik 122 36 55N 31 10E
Sermaize-les-Bains 101 48 47N 4 54E
Sermata, I. 127 8 15S 128 50E
Sernovdsk 120 61 20N 73 28E
Serov 120 59 36N 60 35E
Serowe 117 22 25S 26 43E
Serpentine, R. 66 49 5N 122 51W
Serpent's Mouth 86 10 0N 61 30W
Serpukhov 120 54 55N 37 28E
Serrai 109 41 0N 23 30E
Serres 103 44 26N 5 43E
Serrezuela 88 30 40S 65 20W
Sertânia 87 8 5S 37 20W
Sertanópolis 89 23 4S 51 2W
Sertão 87 10 0S 40 20W
Serua, P. 127 6 18S 130 1E
Serui 127 1 45S 136 10E
Serule 117 21 57S 27 11E
Serviceton 136 36 25S 141 55E
Sesajap Lama 126 3 32N 117 11E
Sesepe 127 1 30S 127 59E
Sesfontein 117 19 7S 13 39E
Sesheke 117 17 29S 24 13E
Sesser 76 38 7N 89 3W
Sessy 130 42 40N 110 30E
Sestao 104 43 18N 3 0W
Sète 102 43 25N 3 42E
Sete Lagoas 87 19 27S 44 16W
Seto Naikai 132 34 20N 133 30E
Seton L. 63 50 42N 122 8W
Seton Portage 63 50 42N 122 17W
Setté Cama 116 2 32S 9 57E
Setting L. 55 55 0N 98 38W
Settle 94 54 5N 2 18W
Settlement Pt. 73 26 40N 79 0W
Setúbal 104 38 30N 8 58W
Setúbal, B. de 104 38 40N 8 56W
Seul L. 34 50 25N 92 30W
Seul Réservoir, Lac 52 50 25N 92 30W
Seulimeum 126 5 27N 95 15E
Sevastopol 120 44 35N 33 30E
Seven Islands B. 36 59 25N 63 45W
Seven Sisters Falls 57 50 7N 96 2W
Seven Sisters, mt 54 54 56N 128 10W
Seventy Mile House 63 51 18N 121 23W
Sévérac-le-Château 102 44 20N 3 5E
Severn L. 34 53 54N 90 48W
Severn, R., Can. 34 56 2N 87 36W
Severn, R., U.K. 95 51 35N 2 38W
Severnaya Zemlya 121 79 0N 100 0E
Severo-Kurilsk 121 50 40N 156 8E
Severodvinsk 120 64 27N 39 58E
Sevier 79 38 39N 112 11W
Sevier L. 78 39 0N 113 20W
Sevier, R. 79 39 10N 112 50W
Sevilla, Colomb. 86 4 16N 75 57W
Sevilla, Spain 104 37 23N 6 0W
Seville = Sevilla 104 37 23N 6 0W
Seward 67 60 0N 149 40W
Seward Pen. 67 65 0N 164 0W
Sewell, Can. 62 53 47N 132 16W
Sewell, Chile 88 34 10S 70 45W
Sewer 127 5 46S 134 40E
Sewickley 70 40 33N 80 12W
Sexsmith 60 55 21N 118 47W
Seychelles, Is. 16 5 0S 56 0E
Seyðisfjörður 110 65 16N 14 0W
Seymchan 121 62 40N 152 30E
Seymour, Austral. 136 37 0S 145 10E
Seymour, U.S.A. 76 40 45N 93 7W
Seymour, Conn., U.S.A. 71 41 23N 73 5W
Seymour, Ind., U.S.A. 77 39 0N 85 50W
Seymour, Tex., U.S.A. 75 33 35N 99 18W
Seymour, Wis., U.S.A. 72 44 30N 88 20W
Seymour Arm 63 51 15N 118 57W
Seymour Heights 66 49 19N 123 0W
Seymour Inlet 62 51 3N 127 0W
Seymour L. 66 49 27N 122 57W
Seymour, Mt. 66 49 24N 122 57W
Seymour, R. 66 49 18N 123 1W
Seyne 103 44 21N 6 22E
Seyne-sur-Mer, La 103 43 7N 5 52E
Sézanne 101 48 40N 3 40E
Sfax 114 34 49N 10 48E
Sfîntu Gheorghe 107 45 52N 25 48E
Shaba 116 8 0S 25 0E
Shabani 117 20 17S 30 2E
Shabogamo L., Can. 35 48 40N 77 0W
Shabogamo L., Newf., Can. 36 53 15N 66 30W
Shabunda 116 2 40S 27 16E
Shabuskwia L. 52 51 15N 89 0W
Shackleton 91 78 30S 36 1W
Shackleton Inlet 91 83 0S 160 0E
Shadrinsk 120 56 5N 63 58E
Shafer, L. 77 40 46N 86 46W
Shafter 81 35 32N 119 14W
Shaftesbury 95 51 0N 2 12W
Shāhābād 123 37 40N 56 50E
Shāhbād 122 34 10N 46 30E
Shahcheng 130 40 18N 115 27E
Shahdād 123 30 30N 57 40E
Shahdadkot 124 27 50N 67 55E
Shahgarh 124 27 15N 69 50E
Shāhī 123 36 30N 52 55E
Shaho 131 28 29N 113 2E
Shahpūr 122 38 12N 44 45E
Shahr Kord 123 32 15N 50 55E
Shahraban 122 34 0N 45 0E
Shahrezâ 123 32 0N 51 55E
Shahrig 124 30 15N 67 40E
Shahriza 123 32 0N 51 50E
Shāhrūd 123 36 30N 55 0E
Shahrukh 123 33 50N 60 10E
Shahsavār 123 36 45N 51 12E
Shahsien 131 26 25N 117 50E
Shajapur 124 23 20N 76 15E
Shakespeare I. 52 49 38N 88 25W
Shakhty 120 47 40N 40 10E
Shakhunya 120 57 40N 47 0E
Shaki 114 8 41N 3 21E
Shakopee 74 44 45N 93 30W
Shaktolik 67 64 30N 161 15W
Shalalth 63 50 43N 122 13W
Shallow Lake 46 44 36N 81 5W
Shalu 131 24 24N 120 26E
Sham, J. ash 123 23 10N 57 5E
Shamattawa 55 55 51N 92 5W
Shamattawa, R. 34 55 1N 85 23W
Shamil 123 27 30N 56 55E
Shammar, Jabal 122 27 40N 41 0E
Shamo (Gobi) 129 44 0N 111 0E
Shamokin 71 40 47N 76 33W
Shamrock, Can. 56 50 10N 106 37W
Shamrock, U.S.A. 75 35 15N 100 15W
Shamva 117 17 20S 31 32E
Shan □ 125 21 30N 98 30E
Shanchengtze 130 42 29N 125 30E
Shandon 80 35 39N 120 23W
Shangani, R. 117 18 35S 27 45E
Shangch'eng 131 31 44N 115 22E
Shangchih, (Chuho) 130 45 10N 127 59E
Shangchwan Shan 131 21 35N 112 45E
Shanghai 131 31 10N 121 25E
Shanghsien 131 33 30N 109 58E
Shangjao 131 28 25N 117 57E
Shangkao 131 28 16N 114 50E
Shangkiu 131 34 28N 115 42E
Shangpancheng 130 40 52N 118 4E
Shangshui 131 33 42N 114 34E
Shangsze 131 22 0N 107 45E
Shangtu 130 41 31N 113 35E
Shangyu 131 25 59N 114 29E
Shanh 129 47 5N 103 5E
Shaniko 78 45 0N 120 50W
Shannon, Greenl. 17 75 10N 18 30W
Shannon, N.Z. 133 40 33S 175 25E
Shannon I. 17 75 0N 18 0W
Shannon L., Can. 53 49 48N 83 24W
Shannon L., U.S.A. 63 48 37N 121 42W
Shannon, R. 97 53 10N 8 10W
Shansi □ 130 37 30N 112 15E
Shantar, Ostrov Bolshoi 121 55 9N 137 40E
Shantou (Chan-t'eou) 131 23 23N 116 41E
Shantow (Swatow) 131 23 25N 116 40E
Shantung □ 130 36 0N 117 30E
Shanyang 131 33 39N 110 2E
Shaohing 131 30 0N 120 32E
Shaowu 131 27 25N 117 30E
Shaoyang 131 27 10N 111 30E
Shapinsay, I. 96 59 2N 2 50W
Shaqra 122 25 15N 45 16E
Sharbot Lake 47 44 46N 76 41W
Sharhjui 123 32 30N 67 22E
Shari 122 27 20N 43 45E
Sharin Gol 129 49 12N 106 27E
Sharjah 123 25 23N 55 26E
Shark B. 134 11 20S 130 35E
Sharon, U.S.A. 77 42 30N 88 44W
Sharon, Mass., U.S.A. 71 42 5N 71 11W
Sharon, Pa., U.S.A. 70 41 18N 80 30W
Sharpe, L. 34 54 10N 93 21W
Sharpe L. 55 54 5N 93 40W
Sharpsburg 70 40 30N 79 56W
Sharpsville 70 41 16N 80 28W
Shashi 117 21 15S 27 27E
Shasi 131 30 16N 112 20E
Shasta, Mt. 78 41 30N 122 0W
Shasta Res. 78 40 50N 122 15W
Shattuck 75 36 17N 99 55W
Shaunavon 56 49 35N 108 25W
Shaver Lake 80 37 9N 119 18W
Shaw, R. 134 20 21S 119 17E
Shawan 129 44 21N 85 37E
Shawanaga 46 45 31N 80 17W
Shawano 72 44 45N 88 38W
Shawbridge 43 45 52N 74 5W
Shawinigan 41 46 35N 72 50W
Shawinigan Sud 41 46 31N 72 45W
Shawnee, U.S.A. 76 39 1N 94 43W
Shawnee, N.Y., U.S.A. 49 43 9N 78 53W
Shawnee, Okla., U.S.A. 75 35 15N 97 0W
Shawville 40 45 36N 76 30W
Shcherbakov = Rybinsk 120 58 5N 38 50E
Shchuchinsk 120 52 56N 70 12E
Shebandowan 52 48 38N 90 4W
Sheboygan 72 43 46N 87 45W
Shediac 39 46 14N 64 32W
Sheelin, Lough 97 53 48N 7 20W
Sheep Haven 97 55 12N 7 55W
Sheerness 95 51 26N 0 47E
Sheet Harbour 39 44 56N 62 31W
Sheffield, Can. 49 43 19N 80 12W
Sheffield, N.Z. 94 43 23S 172 2E
Sheffield, U.K. 94 53 23N 1 28W
Sheffield, Ala., U.S.A. 73 34 45N 87 42W
Sheffield, Ill., U.S.A. 76 41 21N 89 44W
Sheffield, Iowa, U.S.A. 76 42 54N 93 13W
Sheffield, Mass., U.S.A. 71 42 6N 73 23W
Sheffield, Pa., U.S.A. 70 41 42N 79 3W
Sheffield, Tex., U.S.A. 75 30 42N 101 49W
Sheffield L. 37 49 20N 56 34W
Sheguiandah 46 45 54N 81 55W
Sheho 56 51 35N 103 13W
Sheila 39 47 29N 64 55W
Shekhupura 124 31 42N 73 58E
Shekichen 131 33 10N 113 0E
Shekki 131 22 30N 113 15E
Sheklung 131 23 5N 113 55E
Shelbina 76 39 47N 92 2W
Shelburn 77 39 10N 87 24W
Shelburne, N.S., Can. 39 43 47N 65 20W
Shelburne, Ont., Can. 46 44 4N 80 15W
Shelburne, U.S.A. 71 44 23N 73 15W
Shelburne B. 135 11 50S 143 0E
Shelburne Falls 71 42 36N 72 45W
Shelby, Mich., U.S.A. 72 43 34N 86 27W
Shelby, Mont., U.S.A. 78 48 30N 111 59W
Shelby, N.C., U.S.A. 73 35 18N 81 34W
Shelby, Ohio, U.S.A. 70 40 52N 82 40W
Shelbyville, U.S.A. 76 39 48N 92 2W
Shelbyville, Ill., U.S.A. 77 39 25N 88 45W
Shelbyville, Ind., U.S.A. 77 39 30N 85 42W
Shelbyville, Ky., U.S.A. 77 38 13N 85 14W
Shelbyville, Tenn., U.S.A. 73 35 30N 86 25W
Shelbyville, Res. 77 39 26N 88 46W
Sheldon, U.S.A. 76 37 40N 94 18W
Sheldon, Iowa, U.S.A. 74 43 6N 95 51W

Sheldon Point **Sinkiang-Uighur**

Sheldon Point 67 62 30N 165 0W
Sheldrake 36 50 20N 64 51W
Shelikef, Str. 67 58 0N 154 0W
Shelikhova, Zaliv 121 59 30N 157 0 E
Shell Lake 56 53 19N 107 2W
Shellbrook 56 53 13N 106 24W
Shelley 63 54 0N 122 37W
Shellharbour 136 34 31 S 150 51 E
Shellmouth 57 50 56N 101 29W
Shellsburg 76 42 6N 91 52W
Shelter Bay 35 50 30N 67 20W
Shelton, Conn., U.S.A. 71 41 18N 73 7W
Shelton, Wash., U.S.A. 80 47 15N 123 6W
Shenandoah, Iowa, U.S.A. 74 40 50N 95 25W
Shenandoah, Pa., U.S.A. 71 40 49N 76 13W
Shenandoah, Va., U.S.A. 72 38 30N 78 38W
Shenandoah, R. 72 38 30N 78 38W
Shenchih 130 39 12N 112 2 E
Shenmu 130 38 56N 110 19 E
Shensi □ 131 34 50N 109 25 E
Shentsa 129 30 56N 88 25 E
Shenyang (Mukden) 130 41 35N 123 30 E
Sheopur Kalan 124 25 40N 76 40 E
Shepard 59 50 57N 113 55W
Shepherd 46 43 32N 84 41W
Shepherdsville 77 37 59N 85 43W
Shepparton 136 36 23 S 145 26 E
Sheppton 71 40 52N 76 10W
Sher Khan Qala 124 29 55N 66 10 E
Sherborne 95 50 56N 2 31W
Sherbro I. 114 7 30N 12 40W
Sherbrooke 39 45 28N 71 57W
Sheridan, Can. 50 43 31N 79 40W
Sheridan, U.S.A. 76 40 31N 94 37W
Sheridan, Ark., U.S.A. 75 34 20N 92 25W
Sheridan, Col., U.S.A. 74 39 44N 105 3W
Sheridan, Ill., U.S.A. 77 41 32N 88 41W
Sheridan, Ind., U.S.A. 77 40 8N 86 13W
Sheridan, Wyo., U.S.A. 78 44 50N 107 0W
Sheridan L. 63 51 31N 120 54W
Sherman, Can. 66 49 21N 123 14W
Sherman, U.S.A. 75 33 40N 96 35W
Sherridon 55 55 8N 101 5W
Sherrington 43 45 10N 73 31W
Sherwood, U.S.A. 77 41 17N 84 33W
Sherwood, N.D., U.S.A. 57 48 59N 101 36W
Sherwood, Tex., U.S.A. 75 31 18N 100 45W
Sherwood For. 94 53 5N 1 5W
Sherwood Park 59 53 31N 113 19W
Sheshеke 117 17 14 S 24 22 E
Sheslay 54 58 17N 131 45W
Sheslay, R. 54 58 48N 132 5W
Shethanei L. 55 58 48N 97 50W
Shetland □ 96 60 30N 1 30W
Shetland Is. 96 60 30N 1 30W
Shevchenko 120 44 25N 51 20 E
Sheyenne 75 47 52N 99 8W
Sheyenne, R. 74 47 40N 98 15W
Shiawassea, R. 46 43 38N 83 50W
Shibeli, R. 115 2 0N 44 0 E
Shiberghan □ 123 35 45N 66 0 E
Shibogama L. 34 53 35N 88 15W
Shibushi 132 31 25N 131 0 E
Shiel, L. 96 56 48N 5 32W
Shifnal 96 52 40N 2 23W
Shiga-ken □ 132 35 20N 136 0 E
Shigatse 129 29 10N 89 0 E
Shih Ho 131 31 45N 115 50 E
Shihchwan 131 33 5N 108 30 E
Shihkiachwang 130 38 0N 114 32 E
Shihkwaikow 130 40 59N 110 4 E
Shihlu 131 19 15N 109 0 E
Shihpu 131 29 12N 121 58 E
Shihtao 130 36 55N 122 25 E
Shihtsien 131 27 28N 108 3 E
Shihwei 129 51 28N 119 59 E
Shikarpur 124 27 57N 68 39 E
Shikohabad 123 27 6N 78 38 E
Shikoku 132 33 30N 133 30 E
Shikoku □ 132 33 30N 133 30 E
Shikoku-Sanchi 132 33 30N 133 30 E
Shilka 121 52 0N 115 55 E
Shilka, R. 121 57 30N 93 18 E
Shillelagh 97 52 46N 6 32W
Shillong 125 25 35N 91 53 E
Shilo 57 49 49N 99 38W
Shimabara 132 32 48N 130 20 E
Shimada 132 34 49N 138 19 E
Shimane-ken □ 132 35 0N 132 30 E
Shimano-gawa 132 36 50N 138 30 E
Shimenovsk 121 52 15N 127 30 E
Shimizu 132 35 0N 138 30 E
Shimodate 132 36 20N 139 55 E
Shimoga 124 13 57N 75 32 E
Shimonoseki 132 33 58N 131 0 E
Shin Dand 124 33 12N 62 8 E
Shin, L. 96 58 7N 4 30W
Shinankow 129 48 40N 121 32 E
Shingleton 53 46 25N 86 33W
Shingu 132 33 40N 135 55 E
Shinkiachwang 130 38 0N 114 31 E
Shinyanga 116 3 45 S 33 27 E
Shio-no-Misaki 132 33 25N 135 45 E
Ship I. 75 30 16N 88 55W
Shipka 109 42 46N 25 33 E
Shipki La 124 31 45N 78 40 E
Shippegan 39 47 45N 64 45W
Shippegan I. 39 47 50N 64 38W
Shippensburg 70 40 4N 77 32W
Shiprock 79 36 51N 108 45W
Shir Kūh 123 31 45N 53 30 E
Shirāz 123 29 42N 52 30 E
Shire, R. 117 16 30 S 35 0 E
Shiriya-Zaki 132 41 25N 141 30 E
Shirley 77 39 53N 85 35W
Shirvan 123 37 30N 57 50 E
Shirwa L. = Chilwa L. 117 15 15 S 35 40 E
Shishmaref 67 66 15N 166 10W
Shiukwan 131 24 58N 113 3 E
Shively 77 38 12N 85 49W
Shivpuri 124 25 18N 77 42 E
Shizuoka 132 35 0N 138 30 E
Shizuoka-ken □ 132 35 15N 138 40 E
Shkoder = Shkodra 109 42 6N 19 20 E
Shkodra 109 42 6N 19 20 E
Shkumbini, R. 109 41 5N 19 50 E
Shmidt, O. 121 81 0N 91 0 E
Shoal Cr. 76 39 39N 93 35W
Shoal L. 52 49 33N 95 1W
Shoal Lake 57 50 30N 100 35W
Shoalhaven, R. 136 34 54 S 150 42 E
Shoals 77 38 40N 86 47W
Shoals Prov. Park 47 50 50N 83 50W
Shoeburyness 95 51 31N 0 49 E
Shohsien 130 39 30N 112 25 E
Sholapur 124 17 43N 75 56 E
Shologontsy 121 66 13N 114 14 E
Shongopovi 79 35 49N 110 37W
Shoshone, Calif., U.S.A. 81 35 58N 116 16W
Shoshone, Idaho, U.S.A. 78 43 0N 114 27W
Shoshone L. 78 44 30N 110 40W
Shoshone Mts. 78 39 30N 117 30W
Shoshong 117 22 56 S 26 31 E
Shoshoni 78 43 13N 108 5W
Show Low 79 34 16N 110 0W
Showyang 130 38 0 S 113 4 E
Shreveport 75 32 30N 93 50W
Shrewsbury 94 52 42N 2 45W
Shropshire (□) = Salop 95 52 36N 2 45W
Shubenacadie 39 45 5N 63 24W
Shucheng 131 31 25N 117 2 E
Shuikiahu 131 32 14N 117 4 E
Shulan 130 44 27N 126 57 E
Shullsburg 76 42 35N 90 15W
Shumagin Is. 67 55 0N 159 0W
Shumikha 120 55 10N 63 15 E
Shunan 131 29 37N 119 0 E
Shunchang 131 26 52N 117 48 E
Shungnak 67 66 55N 157 10W
Shuntak 131 22 54N 113 8 E
Shur, R. 123 28 30N 55 0 E
Shūsf 123 31 50N 60 5 E
Shūshtar 122 32 0N 48 50 E
Shuswap L. 63 50 55N 119 3W
Shuyak I. 67 58 35N 152 30W
Shuyang 131 34 9N 118 51 E
Shwangcheng 130 45 30N 126 20 E
Shwangliao 130 43 39N 123 40 E
Shwebo 125 22 30N 95 45 E
Shwegu 125 18 49N 95 26 E
Shweli, R. 125 23 45N 96 45 E
Shyok 124 34 15N 78 5 E
Shyok, R. 124 34 30N 78 15 E
Si Racha 128 13 10N 100 56 E
Siah 122 22 0N 47 0 E
Siahan Range 124 27 30N 64 40 E
Siahoyen 130 42 30N 120 30 E
Siaksriinderapura 126 0 51N 102 0 E
Siakwan 129 25 45N 100 10 E
Sialkot 124 32 32N 74 30 E
Siam, G. of 128 11 30N 101 0 E
Sian 131 34 2N 109 0 E
Siang K., Hunan, China 131 27 10N 112 45 E
Siang K., Kwangsi-chuang, China 131 23 20N 107 40 E
Siangcheng 131 33 16N 115 2 E
Siangfan 131 32 15N 112 2 E
Siangning 130 36 0N 110 50 E
Siangsiang 131 27 50N 112 30 E
Siangtan 131 28 0N 112 55 E
Siangyang 131 32 18N 111 0 E
Siangyin 131 28 45N 113 0 E
Siantan, P. 126 3 10N 106 15 E
Siao Hingan Ling 129 49 0N 127 0 E
Siaohaotze 129 46 52N 124 22 E
Siapu 131 26 53N 120 0 E
Siāreh 123 28 5N 60 20 E
Siargao, I. 127 9 52N 126 3 E
Siasi 127 5 34N 120 50 E
Siau, I. 127 2 50N 125 25 E
Sibbald 55 51 24N 110 10W
Sibenik 108 43 48N 15 54 E
Siberia 121 60 0N 100 0 E
Siberut, I. 126 1 30 S 99 0 E
Sibi 124 29 30N 67 48 E
Sibil 127 4 59 S 140 35 E
Sibiti 116 3 38 S 13 19 E
Sibiu 107 45 45N 24 9 E
Sibley, U.S.A. 77 40 35N 88 23W
Sibley, Iowa, U.S.A. 74 43 21N 95 43W
Sibley, La., U.S.A. 75 32 34N 93 16W
Sibley Prov. Park 52 48 30N 88 45W
Sibolga 126 1 50N 98 45 E
Sibsagar 125 27 0N 94 36 E
Sibuco 127 7 20N 122 10 E
Sibuguey B. 127 7 50N 122 45 E
Sibuko 127 7 20N 122 10 E
Sibut 116 5 52N 19 10 E
Sibutu, I. 127 4 45N 119 30 E
Sibutu Passage 127 4 50N 120 0 E
Sibuyan, I. 127 12 25N 122 40 E
Sicamous 63 50 49N 119 0W
Sicapoo 127 18 9N 121 34 E
Sicasica 68 17 20 S 67 45W
Sichang 129 28 0N 102 10 E
Sichwan 131 33 6N 111 30 E
Sicilia □ 108 37 30N 14 30 E
Sicilia, I. 108 37 30N 14 30 E
Sicily = Sicilia 108 37 30N 14 30 E
Sicuani 86 14 10 S 71 10W
Siddipet 124 18 0N 79 0 E
Sideburned L. 53 47 45N 83 15W
Sidell 77 39 55N 87 49W
Sidi-Bel-Abbès 114 35 13N 0 10W
Sidlaw Hills 96 56 32N 3 10W
Sidmouth 95 50 40N 3 13W
Sidnaw 52 46 30N 88 43W
Sidney, B.C., Can. 63 48 39N 123 24W
Sidney, Man., Can. 57 49 54N 99 4W
Sidney, Mont., U.S.A. 74 47 51N 104 7W
Sidney, N.Y., U.S.A. 71 42 18N 75 20W
Sidney, Ohio, U.S.A. 77 40 18N 84 6W
Sidoardjo 127 7 30 S 112 46 E
Sidon = Saydā 115 33 35N 35 25 E
Sidon, (Saida) 122 33 38N 35 28 E
Siedlce 107 52 10N 22 20 E
Siegburg 105 50 48N 7 12 E
Siegen 105 50 52N 8 2 E
Siem Reap 128 13 20N 103 52 E
Siena 108 43 20N 11 20 E
Sienfeng 131 29 45N 109 10 E
Sienyang 131 34 20N 108 48 E
Sierck-les-Bains 101 49 26N 6 20 E
Sierpe, Bocas de la 86 10 0N 61 30W
Sierra Blanca 79 31 11N 105 17W
Sierra Blanca, mt. 79 33 20N 105 54W
Sierra City 80 39 34N 120 42W
Sierra Colorado 90 40 35 S 67 50W
Sierra Gorda 88 23 0 S 69 15W
Sierra Leone ■ 114 9 0N 12 0W
Sierra Majada 82 27 19N 103 42W
Sierraville 80 39 36N 120 22W
Sífnos 109 37 0N 24 45 E
Sifton 57 51 21N 100 8W
Sifton Pass 54 57 52N 126 15W
Sigaboy 127 6 39N 126 10 E
Sigean 102 43 2N 2 58 E
Sighetul Marmatiei 107 47 57N 23 52 E
Sighişoara 107 46 12N 24 50 E
Sigli 126 5 25N 96 0 E
Siglufjörður 110 66 12N 18 55W
Sigma 127 11 29N 122 40 E
Signal 81 34 30N 113 38W
Signal Hill 37 47 35N 52 41W
Signal Pk. 81 33 25N 114 4W
Signy I. 91 60 45 S 46 30W
Signy-l'Abbaye 101 49 40N 4 25 E
Sigourney 76 41 20N 92 12W
Sigsig 86 3 0 S 78 50W
Sigtuna 111 59 36N 17 44 E
Sigüenza 104 41 3N 2 40W
Siguiri 114 11 31N 9 10W
Sigurd 79 38 57N 112 0W
Sigutlat L. 62 52 57N 126 12W
Sihanoukville = Kompong Som 128 10 40N 103 30 E
Siho 131 34 0N 105 0 E
Sihsien, Anwhei, China 130 29 55N 118 23 E
Sihsien, Shansi, China 131 36 54N 111 0 E
Siirt 122 37 57N 41 55 E
Sijsele 91 51 12N 3 20 E
Sikandra Rao 123 27 43N 78 24 E
Sikar 124 27 39N 75 10 E
Sikeston 75 36 52N 89 35W
Sikhote Alin, Khrebet 121 46 0N 136 0 E
Síkinos, I. 109 36 40N 25 8 E
Sikkani Chief, R. 54 57 47N 122 15W
Sikkim ■ 125 27 50N 88 50 E
Siku 131 33 48N 104 18 E
Sil, R. 104 42 23N 7 30W
Silacayoapán 83 17 30N 98 9W
Silamulun Ho 130 43 30N 123 35 E
Silchar 125 24 49N 92 48 E
Silcox 55 57 12N 94 10W
Siler City 73 35 44N 79 30W
Silesia 106 51 0N 16 30 E
Silesia = Slask 106 51 0N 16 30 E
Silgarhi Doti 125 29 15N 82 0 E
Silghat 125 26 35N 93 0 E
Silifke 122 36 22N 33 58 E
Siliguri 125 26 45N 88 25 E
Silin 131 24 10N 105 36 E
Silinhot 130 43 16N 116 0 E
Silistra 109 44 6N 27 19 E
Siljan, L. 111 60 55N 14 45 E
Silkeborg 111 56 10N 9 32 E
Sillajhuay, Cordillera 86 19 40 S 68 40W
Sillé-le Guillaume 100 48 10N 0 8W
Sillery 42 46 46N 71 15W
Siloam Springs 75 36 15N 94 31W
Silogui 126 1 10 S 98 46 E
Silsbee 75 30 20N 94 8W
Silver Bay 52 47 17N 91 16W
Silver City, Pan. C. Z. 84 9 21N 79 53W
Silver City, Calif., U.S.A. 78 36 19N 119 44W
Silver City, N. Mex., U.S.A. 79 32 50N 108 18W
Silver Cr., R. 78 43 30N 119 30W
Silver Creek 70 42 33N 79 9W
Silver Grove 77 39 2N 84 24W
Silver Islet 52 48 20N 88 45W
Silver L. 80 38 39N 120 6W
Silver Lake, Calif., U.S.A. 81 35 21N 116 7W
Silver Lake, Ind., U.S.A. 77 41 4N 85 53W
Silver Lake, Oreg., U.S.A. 78 43 9N 121 4W
Silver Lake, Wis., U.S.A. 77 42 33N 88 13W
Silver Ridge 57 50 48N 98 52W
Silver Star Prov. Park 63 50 23N 119 5W
Silver Water 46 45 52N 82 52W
Silverlake 80 38 38N 120 7W
Silvertip Mt. 63 49 10N 121 13W
Silverton, Austral. 136 31 52 S 141 10 E
Silverton, Can. 63 49 57N 117 21W
Silverton, Colo., U.S.A. 79 37 51N 107 45W
Silverton, Tex., U.S.A. 75 34 30N 101 16W
Silverton, Wash., U.S.A. 63 48 5N 121 34W
Silvia 86 2 37N 76 21W
Silvies, R. 78 43 57N 119 5W
Silvis 76 41 33N 90 28W
Silwani 123 23 18N 78 27 E
Simanggang 126 1 15N 111 25 E
Simard, L. 40 47 40N 78 40W
Simarun 123 31 16N 51 40 E
Simcoe 46 42 50N 80 20W
Simcoe Co. 50 43 59N 79 49W
Simcoe, L. 46 44 25N 79 20W
Simenga 121 62 50N 107 55 E
Simeulue, I. 126 2 45N 95 45 E
Simferopol 120 44 55N 34 3 E
Simi Valley 81 34 16N 118 47W
Simikot 125 30 0N 81 50 E
Simiti 86 7 58N 73 57W
Simla 124 31 2N 77 15 E
Simmie 56 49 56N 108 6W
Simmler 81 35 21N 119 59W
Simmons 48 45 26N 75 49W
Simmons Pen. 65 76 40N 89 7W
Simojärvi 110 66 5N 27 10 E
Simojoki 110 65 46N 25 15 E
Simojovel 83 17 12N 92 38W
Simonette, R. 60 55 9N 118 15W
Simonhouse 57 54 26N 101 23W
Simpang 128 4 50N 100 40 E
Simplon Pass 106 46 15N 8 0 E
Simpson 56 51 27N 105 27W
Simpson Des. 135 25 0 S 137 0 E
Simpson I. 53 48 46N 87 41W
Simpson Pen. 65 68 34N 88 45W
Simpsons Corners 49 43 46N 80 18W
Simunjan 126 1 25N 110 45 E
Simushir, Ostrov 121 46 50N 152 30 E
Sinabang 126 2 30N 46 30 E
Sinaloa 82 25 50N 108 20W
Sinaloa □ 82 25 0N 107 30W
Sinamaica 86 11 5N 71 51W
Sincé 86 9 15N 75 9W
Sincelejo 86 9 18N 75 24W
Sincheng, Honan, China 131 34 25N 113 56 E
Sincheng, Kwangsi, China 131 24 1N 108 35 E
Sinchengtu 131 23 55N 108 30 E
Sinclair 78 41 47N 107 35W
Sinclair Mills 54 54 5N 121 40W
Sinclair Pass 61 50 40N 115 58W
Sincorá, Serra do 87 13 30 S 41 0W
Sind Sagar Doab 124 32 0N 71 30 E
Sindangan 127 8 10N 123 5 E
Sindangbarang 127 7 27 S 107 9 E
Sindjai 127 5 0 S 120 20 E
Sines 104 37 56N 8 51W
Sinfeng, Kiangsi, China 131 25 28N 114 40 E
Sinfeng, Kweichow, China 131 26 59N 106 55 E
Singa 115 13 10N 33 57 E
Singaparna 127 7 23 S 108 4 E
Singapore ■ 128 1 17N 103 51 E
Singapore, Straits of 128 1 15N 104 0 E
Singaraja 126 8 15 S 115 10 E
Singida 116 4 49 S 34 48 E
Singitikós, Kólpos 109 40 6N 24 0 E
Singkang 127 4 8 S 120 1 E
Singkawang 126 1 0N 109 5 E
Singkep, I. 126 0 30 S 104 20 E
Singleton 136 32 33 S 151 10 E
Singleton, Mt. 134 29 27 S 117 15 E
Singtai 130 37 2N 114 30 E
Singtze 131 29 30N 116 4 E
Singyang 131 32 10N 114 0 E
Sinhailien 131 34 31N 119 0 E
Sinhsien 130 38 25N 112 45 E
Sinhwa 131 27 36N 111 6 E
Sining 129 36 35N 101 50 E
Sinkan 131 27 45N 115 30 E
Sinkiang 130 35 35N 111 25 E
Sinkiang-Uighur □ 129 42 0N 86 0 E

Sinkin **South Bend**

Sinkin	**130**	39 30N	122 29 E
Sinlo	**130**	38 25N	114 50 E
Sinmak	**130**	38 25N	126 15 E
Sinmin	**130**	42 0N	122 50 E
Sinni, R.	**108**	40 6N	16 15 E
Sinoia	**117**	17 20S	30 8 E
Sinop	**122**	42 1N	35 11 E
Sinpin	**130**	41 50N	125 0 E
Sinsiang	**131**	35 15N	113 55 E
Sinskoye	**121**	61 8N	126 48 E
Sint Eustatius, I.	**85**	17 30N	62 59W
Sint Maarten, I.	**85**	18 4N	63 4W
Sintai	**131**	30 59N	105 0 E
Sintaluta	**56**	50 29N	103 27W
Sintang	**126**	0 5N	111 35 E
Sinti, (Hunghu)	**131**	29 49N	113 30 E
Sinton	**75**	28 1N	97 30W
Sintra	**104**	38 47N	9 25W
Sinŭiju	**130**	40 5N	124 24 E
Sinuk	**67**	64 42N	166 22W
Sinyang	**131**	32 6N	114 2 E
Sióma	**117**	16 25S	23 28 E
Sion	**106**	46 14N	7 20 E
Sioux City	**74**	42 32N	96 25W
Sioux Falls	**74**	43 35N	96 40W
Sioux Lookout	**52**	50 10N	91 50W
Sioux Narrows	**52**	49 25N	94 10W
Sipa	**131**	33 34N	118 59 E
Sipera, I.	**126**	2 18S	99 40 E
Siping	**131**	33 25N	114 10 E
Sipiwesk L.	**55**	55 5N	97 35W
Siquia, R.	**84**	12 30N	84 30W
Siquijor, I.	**127**	9 12N	123 45 E
Siquirres	**84**	10 6N	83 30W
Siquisique	**86**	10 34N	69 42W
Sir Edward Pellew Group	**135**	15 40S	137 10 E
Sir Francis Drake, Mt.	**62**	50 49N	124 48W
Sir Sandford, Mt.	**63**	51 40N	117 52W
Siracusa	**108**	37 4N	15 17 E
Sirajganj	**125**	24 25N	89 47 E
Siret, R.	**107**	47 58N	26 5 E
Sirohi	**124**	24 52N	72 53 E
Sironj	**124**	24 5N	77 45 E
Siros, I.	**109**	37 28N	24 57 E
Sirretta Pk.	**81**	35 56N	118 19W
Sirsa	**124**	29 33N	75 4 E
Sisak	**108**	45 30N	16 21 E
Sisaket	**128**	15 8N	104 23 E
Sisiang	**131**	33 2N	107 48 E
Sisipuk I.	**55**	55 40N	102 0W
Sisipuk L.	**55**	55 45N	101 50W
Sisophon	**128**	13 31N	102 59 E
Sisseton	**74**	45 43N	97 3W
Sissonne	**101**	49 34N	3 51 E
Sistan-Baluchistan □	**123**	27 0N	62 0 E
Sisteron	**103**	44 12N	5 57 E
Sisters	**78**	44 21N	121 32W
Sitapur	**125**	27 38N	80 45 E
Sitges	**104**	41 17N	1 47 E
Sitka	**67**	57 9N	134 58W
Sittang Myit, R.	**125**	18 20N	96 45 E
Sittard	**105**	51 0N	5 52 E
Situbondo	**127**	7 45S	114 0 E
Siuna	**84**	13 37N	84 45W
Siuwu	**131**	35 10N	113 30 E
Siuyen	**130**	40 20N	123 15 E
Sivand	**123**	30 5N	52 55 E
Sivas	**122**	39 43N	36 58 E
Siverek	**122**	37 50N	39 25 E
Sivrihisar	**122**	39 30N	31 35 E
Sivry	**105**	50 10N	4 12 E
Siwalik Range	**125**	28 0N	83 0 E
Siwan	**125**	26 13N	84 27 E
Sixteen Island Lake	**43**	45 56N	74 28W
Sizewell	**95**	52 13N	1 38 E
Sjaelland	**111**	55 30N	11 30 E
Sjiptjenski P.	**109**	42 46N	25 33 E
Sjumen = Kolarovgrad	**109**	43 27N	26 42 E
Skagafjörður	**110**	65 54N	19 35W
Skagastölstindane, mt.	**111**	61 25N	8 10 E
Skagen	**111**	68 37N	14 27 E
Skagerrak	**111**	57 30N	9 0 E
Skagit, R.	**80**	48 20N	122 25W
Skagway	**67**	59 30N	135 20W
Skaidi	**110**	70 26N	24 30 E
Skandia	**53**	46 25N	87 16W
Skance	**52**	46 53N	88 20W
Skara	**111**	58 25N	13 30 E
Skaraborgs län □	**111**	58 20N	13 30 E
Skardu	**124**	35 20N	75 35 E
Skeena Mts.	**54**	56 40N	128 30W
Skeena, R.	**62**	54 9N	130 5W
Skeggjastadir	**110**	66 3N	14 50W
Skegness	**94**	53 9N	0 20 E
Skeldon	**86**	6 0N	57 20W
Skellefte älv	**110**	65 30N	18 30 E
Skellefteå	**110**	64 45N	20 58 E
Skelleftehamn	**110**	64 41N	21 14 E
Skellig Rocks	**97**	51 47N	10 32W
Skerries, The	**94**	53 27N	4 40W
Skibbereen	**97**	51 33N	9 16W
Skiddaw, Mt.	**94**	54 39N	3 9W
Skidegate	**62**	53 15N	132 1W
Skien	**111**	59 12N	9 35 E
Skierniewice	**107**	51 58N	20 19 E
Skihist, Mt.	**63**	50 12N	121 54W
Skikda	**114**	36 50N	6 58 E
Skillett Fork, Little Wabash, R.	**77**	38 6N	88 9W
Skipton	**94**	53 57N	2 1W
Skiros, I.	**109**	38 55N	24 34 E
Skive	**111**	56 33N	9 2 E
Skjálfandafljót	**110**	65 15N	17 25W
Skjálfandi	**110**	66 5N	17 30W
Skoghall	**111**	59 20N	13 30 E
Skopje	**109**	42 1N	21 32 E
Skövde	**111**	58 15N	13 59 E
Skovorodino	**121**	54 0N	125 0 E
Skowhegan	**35**	44 49N	69 40W
Skownan	**57**	51 58N	99 35W
Skudeneshavn	**111**	59 10N	5 10 E
Skull	**97**	51 32N	9 40W
Skunk, R.	**76**	40 42N	91 7W
Skwaner, Pegunungan	**126**	1 0S	112 30 E
Skwierzyna	**106**	52 46N	15 30 E
Skye, I.	**96**	57 15N	6 10W
Skykomish	**78**	47 43N	121 16W
Slamet, G.	**126**	7 16S	109 8 E
Slaney, R.	**97**	52 52N	6 45W
Slaokan	**131**	30 57N	114 2 E
Slask	**106**	51 25N	16 0 E
Slate Is.	**34**	48 40N	87 0W
Slater	**76**	39 13N	93 4W
Slatina	**107**	44 28N	24 22 E
Slaton	**75**	33 27N	101 38W
Slave Lake	**60**	55 17N	114 50W
Slave Pt.	**54**	61 11N	115 56W
Slave, R.	**54**	61 18N	113 39W
Slavgorod	**120**	53 10N	78 50 E
Slavkov (Austerlitz)	**106**	49 10N	16 52 E
Sleaford	**94**	53 0N	0 22W
Sleat, Sd. of	**96**	57 5N	5 47W
Sleepy Eye	**74**	44 15N	94 45W
Sleman	**127**	7 40S	110 20 E
Slemon L.	**54**	63 13N	116 4W
Slidell	**75**	30 20N	89 48W
Sliedrecht	**105**	51 50N	4 45 E
Slieve Aughty	**97**	53 4N	8 30W
Slieve Bloom	**97**	53 4N	7 40W
Slieve Donard	**97**	54 10N	5 57W
Slieve Gullion	**97**	54 8N	6 26W
Slieve Mish	**97**	52 12N	9 50W
Slievenamon Mt.	**97**	52 25N	7 37W
Sligo	**97**	54 17N	8 28W
Sligo □	**97**	54 10N	8 35W
Sligo B.	**97**	54 20N	8 40W
Slite	**111**	57 42N	18 48 E
Sliven	**109**	42 42N	26 19 E
Sloan	**81**	35 57N	115 13W
Sloansville	**71**	42 45N	74 22W
Slocan	**63**	49 48N	117 28W
Slocan L.	**63**	49 50N	117 23W
Slochteren	**105**	53 12N	6 48 E
Slough	**95**	51 30N	0 35W
Sloughhouse	**80**	38 26N	121 12W
Slovakia □	**107**	48 30N	19 0 E
Slovenia = Slovenija	**108**	45 58N	14 30 E
Slovenija □	**108**	45 58N	14 30 E
Slovenské Rhudhorie	**107**	48 45N	19 0 E
Slyne Hd.	**97**	53 25N	10 10W
Slyudyanka	**121**	51 40N	103 30 E
Smalltree L.	**55**	61 0N	105 0W
Smallwood Reservoir	**35**	54 20N	63 10W
Smartville	**80**	39 13N	121 18W
Smeaton	**56**	53 30N	104 49W
Smederevo	**109**	44 40N	20 57 E
Smethport	**70**	41 50N	78 28W
Smidovich	**121**	48 36N	133 49 E
Smilde	**105**	52 58N	6 28 E
Smiley	**56**	51 38N	109 29W
Smith	**60**	55 10N	114 0W
Smith Arm	**54**	66 15N	123 0W
Smith Center	**74**	39 50N	98 50W
Smith I.	**36**	54 13N	58 18W
Smith Pen.	**65**	77 12N	78 50W
Smith, R.	**54**	59 34N	126 30W
Smith Sund	**65**	78 30N	74 0W
Smithers	**54**	54 45N	127 10W
Smithfield	**73**	35 31N	78 16W
Smiths Cove	**39**	44 37N	65 42W
Smiths Falls	**47**	44 55N	76 0W
Smithville, Can.	**49**	43 6N	79 33W
Smithville, U.S.A.	**76**	39 23N	94 35W
Smithville, Tex., U.S.A.	**75**	30 2N	97 12W
Smjörfjöll	**110**	65 30N	15 42W
Smoky Falls	**53**	50 4N	82 10W
Smoky Hill, R.	**74**	38 45N	98 0W
Smoky Lake	**60**	54 10N	112 30W
Smoky, R.	**60**	56 10N	117 21W
Smola	**110**	63 23N	8 3 E
Smolensk	**120**	54 45N	32 0 E
Smolikas, Óros	**109**	40 9N	20 58 E
Smolyan	**109**	41 36N	24 38 E
Smooth Rock Falls	**53**	49 17N	81 37W
Smoothrock L.	**52**	50 30N	89 30W
Smoothstone L.	**55**	54 40N	106 50W
Smyrna = İzmir	**122**	38 25N	27 8 E
Snaefell	**94**	54 18N	4 26W
Snaefells Jökull	**110**	64 45N	23 25W
Snake I.	**136**	38 47S	146 33 E
Snake L.	**55**	55 32N	106 35W
Snake, R.	**78**	46 31N	118 50W
Snake Ra., Mts.	**78**	39 0N	114 30W
Snake River Plain	**78**	43 13N	113 0W
Snaring	**61**	53 5N	118 4W
Sneek	**105**	53 2N	5 40 E
Snelgrove	**49**	43 44N	79 49W
Snelling	**80**	37 31N	120 26W
Sněžka	**106**	50 14N	15 50 E
Snipe L.	**60**	55 7N	116 47W
Snizort, L.	**96**	57 33N	6 28W
Snohetta	**110**	62 19N	9 16 E
Snohomish	**80**	47 53N	122 6W
Snow Hill	**72**	38 10N	75 21W
Snow L.	**55**	54 52N	100 3W
Snow Mt.	**80**	39 22N	122 44W
Snowbird L.	**55**	60 45N	103 0W
Snowdon, Mt.	**94**	53 4N	4 8W
Snowdrift	**55**	62 24N	110 44W
Snowdrift, R.	**55**	62 24N	110 44W
Snowflake, Can.	**57**	49 3N	98 39W
Snowflake, U.S.A.	**79**	34 30N	110 4W
Snowshoe	**54**	53 43N	121 0W
Snowville	**78**	41 59N	112 47W
Snowy Mts.	**136**	36 30S	148 20 E
Snowy, R.	**136**	37 46S	148 30 E
Snug Corner	**85**	22 33N	73 52W
Snyder, Can.	**49**	42 57N	79 3W
Snyder, Okla., U.S.A.	**75**	34 40N	99 0W
Snyder, Tex., U.S.A.	**75**	32 45N	100 57W
Soacha	**86**	4 35N	74 13W
Soalala	**117**	16 6S	45 20 E
Soap Lake	**78**	47 29N	119 31W
Sobat, R.	**115**	8 32N	32 40 E
Sobral	**87**	3 50S	40 30W
Soc Trang = Khonh Hung	**128**	9 37N	105 50 E
Socha	**86**	6 0N	72 41W
Soche (Yarkand)	**129**	38 24N	77 20 E
Sochi	**120**	43 35N	39 40 E
Société, Is. de la	**15**	17 0S	151 0W
Society Is. = Société, Is. de la	**15**	17 0S	151 0W
Socompa, Portezuelo de	**88**	24 27S	68 18W
Socorro, Colomb.	**86**	6 29N	73 16W
Socorro, U.S.A.	**71**	34 3N	106 58W
Socorro, I.	**82**	18 45N	110 58W
Socotra, I.	**115**	12 30N	54 0 E
Soda Creek	**54**	52 25N	122 10W
Soda L.	**79**	35 7N	116 2W
Soda Springs	**78**	42 40N	111 40W
Söderhamn	**111**	61 18N	17 10 E
Söderköping	**111**	58 31N	16 35 E
Södermanlands län □	**111**	59 10N	16 30 E
Södertälje	**111**	59 12N	17 50 E
Sodo	**115**	7 0N	37 57 E
Sodus	**70**	43 13N	77 5W
Sodus Pt.	**70**	43 15N	77 0W
Soest	**105**	51 34N	8 7 E
Soeurs, Île des	**45**	45 28N	73 33W
Sofia = Sofiya	**109**	42 45N	23 20 E
Sofia, R.	**117**	15 25S	48 40 E
Sofiya	**109**	42 45N	23 20 E
Sogad	**127**	10 30N	125 0 E
Sogamoso	**86**	5 43N	72 56W
Sogn og Fjordane fylke □	**111**	61 40N	6 0 E
Sogndalsfjøra	**111**	61 14N	7 5 E
Sognefjorden	**111**	61 10N	5 50 E
Sohâg	**115**	26 27N	31 43 E
Soignies	**105**	50 35N	4 5 E
Sointula	**62**	50 38N	127 0W
Soissons	**101**	49 25N	3 19 E
Söke	**122**	37 48N	27 28 E
Sokhta Chinar	**123**	35 5N	67 35 E
Sokó'ka	**107**	53 25N	23 30 E
Sokoto	**114**	13 2N	5 16 E
Sol Iletsk	**120**	51 10N	55 0 E
Solano	**127**	16 25N	121 15 E
Soledad, Colomb.	**86**	10 55N	74 46W
Soledad, U.S.A.	**80**	36 27N	121 16W
Soledad, Venez.	**86**	8 10N	63 34W
Solemint	**81**	34 25N	118 27W
Solent, The	**95**	50 45N	1 25W
Solenzara	**103**	41 53N	9 23 E
Solesmes	**101**	50 10N	3 30 E
Solfonn, Mt.	**111**	60 2N	6 57 E
Solikamsk	**120**	59 38N	56 50 E
Solimões, R.	**86**	2 15S	66 30W
Solina	**49**	43 58N	78 47W
Solingen	**105**	51 10N	7 4 E
Sollefteå	**110**	63 12N	17 20 E
Soller	**104**	39 43N	2 45 E
Solok	**126**	0 55S	100 40 E
Sololá	**84**	14 49N	91 10 E
Solomon Is.	**14**	6 0S	155 0 E
Solomon, N. Fork, R.	**74**	39 45N	99 0W
Solomon, S. Fork, R.	**74**	39 25N	99 12W
Solon Springs	**52**	46 19N	91 47W
Solor, I.	**127**	8 27S	123 0 E
Solothurn	**106**	47 13N	7 32 E
Soltanābād	**123**	36 29N	58 5 E
Soltāniyeh	**122**	36 20N	48 55 E
Solun	**129**	46 40N	120 40 E
Solunska Glava	**109**	41 44N	21 31 E
Solvang	**81**	34 36N	120 8W
Solvay	**71**	43 5N	76 17W
Solvesborg	**111**	56 5N	14 35 E
Solway Firth	**96**	54 45N	3 38W
Solwezi	**117**	12 20S	26 21 E
Somali Rep. ■	**115**	7 0N	47 0 E
Sombernon	**101**	47 20N	4 40 E
Sombor	**109**	45 46N	19 17 E
Sombra	**46**	42 43N	82 29W
Sombrerete	**82**	23 40N	103 40W
Sombrero I.	**85**	18 30N	63 30W
Somers	**78**	48 4N	114 18W
Somerset, Can.	**57**	49 25N	98 39W
Somerset, Colo., U.S.A.	**79**	38 55N	107 30W
Somerset, Ky., U.S.A.	**72**	37 5N	84 40W
Somerset, Mass., U.S.A.	**71**	41 45N	71 10W
Somerset, Pa., U.S.A.	**70**	40 1N	79 4 E
Somerset □	**95**	51 9N	3 0W
Somerset East	**117**	32 42S	25 35 E
Somerset, I.	**65**	73 30N	93 0W
Somersworth	**71**	43 15N	70 51W
Somerton	**79**	32 41N	114 47W
Somerville	**71**	40 34N	74 36W
Someş, R.	**107**	47 15N	23 45 E
Somme □	**101**	50 0N	2 20 E
Somme, B. de la	**100**	5 22N	1 30 E
Sommepy-Tahure	**101**	49 15N	4 31 E
Sommesous	**101**	48 44N	4 12 E
Sommières	**103**	43 47N	4 6 E
Somoto	**84**	13 28N	86 37W
Somovit	**109**	43 40N	24 45 E
Somport, Puerto de	**104**	42 48N	0 31W
Son La	**128**	21 20N	103 50 E
Soná	**84**	8 0N	81 10W
Sønderborg	**111**	54 55N	9 49 E
Söndre Stromfjord	**17**	66 30N	50 52W
Sonepat	**124**	29 0N	77 5 E
Sonepur	**125**	20 55N	83 50 E
Song Cau	**128**	13 20N	109 18 E
Songea	**116**	10 40S	35 40 E
Songeons	**101**	49 20N	1 50 E
Songkhla	**128**	7 13N	100 37 E
Sonmiani	**124**	25 25N	66 40 E
Sonningdale	**56**	52 23N	107 44W
Sono, R.	**87**	8 58S	48 11W
Sonora, Can.	**39**	45 4N	61 54W
Sonora, Calif., U.S.A.	**80**	37 59N	120 27W
Sonora, Texas, U.S.A.	**75**	30 33N	100 37W
Sonora □	**82**	28 0N	111 0W
Sonora I.	**62**	50 22N	125 15W
Sonora P.	**78**	38 17N	119 35W
Sonora, R.	**82**	28 30N	111 33W
Sonoyta	**82**	31 51N	112 50W
Sonsonate	**84**	13 43N	89 44W
Soo Junction	**72**	46 20N	85 14W
Soochow	**131**	31 18N	120 41 E
Sooke	**63**	48 13N	123 43W
Sopi	**127**	2 40N	128 28 E
Sopot	**107**	54 27N	18 31 E
Sopron	**106**	47 41N	16 37 E
Sop's Arm	**37**	49 46N	56 56W
Sør-Rondane	**91**	72 0S	25 0 E
Sør Trøndelag fylke □	**110**	63 0N	11 0 E
Sorata	**86**	15 50S	68 50W
Sorel	**41**	46 0N	73 10W
Sorento	**76**	39 0N	89 34W
Sorgono	**108**	40 0N	9 0 E
Sorgues	**103**	44 1N	4 53 E
Soria	**104**	41 43N	2 32W
Soriano	**88**	33 24S	58 19W
Soriano □	**90**	33 30S	58 0W
Sorocaba	**89**	23 31S	47 35W
Sorong	**127**	0 55S	131 15 E
Sororoca	**86**	0 43N	61 31W
Soroti	**116**	1 43N	33 35 E
Soröy Sundet	**110**	70 25N	23 0 E
Soröya	**110**	70 35N	22 45 E
Sorrento	**108**	40 38N	14 23 E
Sorsele	**110**	65 31N	17 30 E
Sorsogon	**127**	13 0N	124 0 E
Soscumica, L.	**40**	50 15N	77 27W
Sosnowiec	**107**	50 20N	19 10 E
Sospel	**103**	43 52N	7 27 E
Soto la Marina, R.	**83**	23 40N	97 40W
Sotteville-lès-Rouen	**100**	49 24N	1 5 E
Souanké	**116**	2 10N	14 10 E
Soucy	**40**	48 10N	75 30W
Soúdhas, Kólpos	**109**	35 31N	24 10 E
Soufrière	**85**	13 51N	61 4W
Soufrière, vol.	**85**	13 10N	61 10W
Souillac	**102**	44 53N	1 29 E
Sŏul	**130**	37 31N	127 6 E
Soulac-sur-Mer	**102**	45 30N	1 7W
Soulanges □	**44**	45 18N	74 3W
Soulanges, Canal de	**44**	45 20N	73 58W
Soultz	**101**	48 57N	7 52 E
Sound, The	**111**	56 7N	12 30 E
Sounding Cr.	**61**	52 6N	110 28W
Sounding L.	**61**	52 8N	110 29W
Sources, Mt. aux	**117**	28 45S	28 50 E
Sourdeval	**100**	48 43N	0 55W
Soure	**87**	0 35S	48 30W
Souris, Man., Can.	**55**	49 40N	100 20W
Souris, P.E.I., Can.	**39**	46 21N	62 15W
Souris, R.	**57**	49 40N	99 34W
Sousa	**87**	6 45S	38 10W
Sousel	**87**	2 38S	52 29W
Soustons	**102**	43 45N	1 19W
Souterraine, La	**102**	46 15N	1 30 E
South Africa, Rep. of, ■	**117**	30 0S	25 0 E
South Aulatsivik I.	**36**	56 45N	61 30W
South Australia □	**134**	32 0S	139 0 E
South Baldy, Mt.	**79**	34 6N	107 27W
South Baymouth	**46**	45 33N	82 1W
South Beloit	**76**	42 29N	89 2W
South Bend, Indiana, U.S.A.	**77**	41 38N	86 20W
South Bend, Wash., U.S.A.	**80**	46 44N	123 52W

Stigler **Sussex, W. □**

Stigler	**75**	35 19N	95 6W
Stikine, R.	**67**	58 0N	131 12W
Stillwater, Minn., U.S.A.	**74**	45 3N	92 47W
Stillwater, N.Y., U.S.A.	**71**	42 55N	73 41W
Stillwater, Okla., U.S.A.	**75**	36 5N	97 3W
Stillwater Mts.	**78**	39 45N	118 6W
Stilwell	**75**	35 52N	94 36W
Stimson	**34**	48 58N	80 30W
Štip	**109**	41 42N	22 10E
Stiring Wendel	**101**	49 12N	6 57E
Stirling, Alta., Can.	**61**	49 30N	112 30W
Stirling, Ont., Can.	**47**	44 18N	77 33W
Stirling, U.K.	**96**	56 17N	3 57W
Stirling Ra.	**134**	34 0S	118 0E
Stittsville	**47**	45 15N	75 55W
Stockbridge	**46**	42 27N	84 11W
Stockerau	**106**	48 24N	16 12E
Stockett	**78**	47 23N	111 7W
Stockholm, Can.	**57**	50 39N	102 18W
Stockholm, Sweden	**111**	59 20N	18 3E
Stockinbingal	**136**	34 30S	147 53E
Stockport	**94**	53 25N	2 11W
Stockton, Austral.	**136**	32 56S	151 47E
Stockton, Calif., U.S.A.	**80**	38 0N	121 20W
Stockton, Ill., U.S.A.	**76**	42 21N	90 1W
Stockton, Kans., U.S.A.	**74**	39 30N	99 20W
Stockton, Mo., U.S.A.	**76**	37 40N	93 48W
Stockton I.	**52**	46 57N	90 35W
Stockton-on-Tees	**94**	54 34N	1 20W
Stockton, Reservoir	**76**	37 42N	93 46W
Stoke-on-Trent	**94**	53 1N	2 11W
Stokes Bay, Can.	**34**	45 0N	81 22W
Stokes Bay, Can.	**46**	45 0N	81 28W
Stokkseyri	**110**	63 50N	20 58W
Stokksnes	**110**	64 14N	14 58W
Stolac	**109**	43 8N	17 59E
Stolberg	**105**	50 48N	6 13E
Stolbovaya	**121**	64 50N	153 50E
Stonecliffe	**34**	46 13N	77 56W
Stoneham	**41**	47 0N	71 22W
Stonehaven	**96**	56 58N	2 11W
Stonehenge	**95**	51 9N	1 45W
Stoner	**63**	53 38N	122 40W
Stonewall	**57**	50 10N	97 19W
Stoney Creek	**48**	43 14N	79 45W
Stonington	**76**	39 44N	89 12W
Stony L., Man., Can.	**55**	58 51N	98 40W
Stony L., Ont., Can.	**47**	44 30N	78 0W
Stony Mountain	**57**	50 5N	97 13W
Stony Plain	**60**	53 32N	114 0W
Stony Rapids	**55**	59 16N	105 50W
Stony River	**67**	61 48N	156 48W
Stony Tunguska = Tunguska, Nizhmaya	**121**	64 0N	95 0E
Stonyford	**80**	39 23N	122 33W
Stora Lulevatten	**110**	67 10N	19 30E
Stora Sjøfallet	**110**	67 29N	18 40E
Storavan	**110**	65 45N	18 10E
Store Bælt	**111**	55 20N	11 0E
Storen	**110**	63 3N	10 18E
Storkerson B.	**64**	72 56N	124 50W
Storm B.	**135**	43 10S	147 30E
Storm Lake	**74**	42 35N	95 5W
Stormberg	**117**	31 16S	26 17E
Stormy L.	**52**	49 23N	92 18W
Stornoway	**96**	58 12N	6 23W
Storsjön	**110**	62 50N	13 8E
Storuman, L.	**110**	65 5N	17 10E
Story City	**76**	42 11N	93 36W
Stouffville	**50**	43 58N	79 15W
Stoughton, Can.	**56**	49 40N	103 0W
Stoughton, U.S.A.	**76**	42 55N	89 13W
Stour, R., Dorset, U.K.	**95**	50 48N	2 7W
Stour, R., Heref. & Worcs., U.K.	**94**	52 25N	2 13W
Stour, R., Kent, U.K.	**95**	51 15N	0 57E
Stour, R., Suffolk, U.K.	**95**	51 55N	1 5E
Stourbridge	**95**	52 28N	2 8W
Stout, L.	**55**	52 0N	94 40W
Stove Pipe Wells Village	**81**	36 35N	117 11W
Stowmarket	**95**	52 11N	1 0E
Strabane	**97**	54 50N	7 28W
Strabane □	**97**	54 45N	7 25W
Strachan, Mt.	**66**	49 25N	123 12W
Strahan	**135**	42 9S	145 20E
Stralsund	**106**	54 17N	13 5E
Strand	**117**	34 9S	18 48E
Strangford	**97**	54 23N	5 34W
Strangford, L.	**97**	54 30N	5 37W
Stranraer, Can.	**56**	51 43N	108 29W
Stranraer, U.K.	**96**	54 54N	5 0W
Strasbourg, Can.	**56**	51 4N	104 55W
Strasbourg, France	**101**	48 35N	7 42E
Strasburg	**74**	46 12N	100 9W
Stratford, Austral.	**136**	37 59S	147 7E
Stratford, Can.	**46**	43 23N	81 0W
Stratford, N.Z.	**133**	39 20S	174 19E
Stratford, Calif., U.S.A.	**80**	36 10N	119 49W
Stratford, Conn., U.S.A.	**71**	41 13N	73 8W
Stratford, Tex., U.S.A.	**75**	36 20N	102 3W
Stratford-on-Avon	**95**	52 12N	1 42W
Strath Spey	**96**	57 15N	3 40W
Strathclyde □	**96**	56 0N	4 50W
Strathcona Prov. Park	**62**	49 38N	125 40W
Strathmore, Can.	**61**	51 5N	113 25W
Strathmore, U.K.	**96**	56 40N	3 4W
Strathmore, U.S.A.	**80**	36 9N	119 4W
Strathnaver	**63**	53 20N	122 33W
Strathroy	**46**	42 58N	81 38W
Strathy Pt.	**96**	58 35N	4 0W
Stratton, Can.	**52**	48 41N	94 10W
Stratton, U.S.A.	**74**	39 20N	102 36W
Straumnes	**110**	66 26N	23 8W
Strawberry Hill	**66**	49 8N	122 53W
Strawberry Point	**76**	42 41N	91 32W
Strawberry Res.	**78**	40 0N	111 0W
Strawn	**75**	32 36N	98 30W
Streaky Bay	**134**	32 48S	134 13E
Streator	**77**	41 9N	88 52W
Streetsville	**50**	43 35N	79 42W
Strelka	**121**	58 5N	93 10E
Strezhevoy	**120**	60 42N	77 34E
Strezhnoye	**120**	57 45N	84 2E
Strezlecki	**136**	38 16S	145 50E
Strómboli, I.	**108**	38 48N	15 12E
Strome	**61**	52 48N	112 4W
Stromeferry	**96**	57 20N	5 33W
Ströms Vattudal L.	**110**	64 0N	15 30E
Strömstad	**111**	58 55N	11 15E
Stromsund	**110**	63 51N	15 35E
Strongfield	**56**	51 20N	106 35W
Stronghurst	**76**	40 45N	91 55W
Strongs Corners	**46**	46 18N	84 55W
Stronsay, I.	**96**	59 8N	2 38W
Stroud, Can.	**46**	44 19N	79 37W
Stroud, U.K.	**95**	51 44N	2 12W
Stroud Road	**136**	32 18S	151 57E
Stroudsberg	**71**	40 59N	75 15W
Struer	**111**	56 30N	8 35E
Struma, R.	**109**	41 50N	23 18E
Strumica	**109**	41 28N	22 41E
Struthers, Can.	**53**	48 41N	85 51W
Struthers, U.S.A.	**70**	41 6N	80 38W
Stryker	**61**	48 40N	114 44W
Strzelecki Creek	**135**	29 37S	139 59E
Stuart, U.S.A.	**76**	41 30N	94 19W
Stuart, Fla., U.S.A.	**73**	27 11N	80 12W
Stuart, Nebr., U.S.A.	**74**	42 39N	99 8W
Stuart I.	**67**	63 55N	164 50W
Stuart L.	**54**	54 30N	124 30W
Stuart, R.	**54**	54 0N	123 35W
Stuart Range	**134**	29 10S	134 56E
Stuart Town	**136**	32 44S	149 4E
Stull, L.	**55**	54 24N	92 34W
Stung-Treng	**128**	13 31N	105 58E
Stupart, R.	**55**	56 0N	93 25W
Sturgeon B.	**57**	52 0N	97 50W
Sturgeon Bay	**72**	44 52N	87 20W
Sturgeon Cr.	**58**	49 52N	97 16W
Sturgeon Falls	**46**	46 25N	79 57W
Sturgeon L., Alta., Can.	**60**	55 6N	117 32W
Sturgeon L., Ont., Can.	**47**	44 28N	78 43W
Sturgeon L., Ont., Can.	**52**	50 0N	90 45W
Sturgeon L., Ont., Can.	**52**	48 29N	91 38W
Sturgeon, R., Alta., Can.	**59**	53 46N	113 10W
Sturgeon, R., Ont., Can.	**46**	46 35N	80 11W
Sturgeon, R., Sask., Can.	**56**	53 12N	105 52W
Sturgis, Can.	**56**	51 56N	102 36W
Sturgis, Mich., U.S.A.	**77**	41 50N	85 25W
Sturgis, S.D., U.S.A.	**74**	44 25N	103 30W
Sturt, R.	**134**	34 58S	138 31E
Stutterheim	**117**	32 33S	27 28E
Stuttgart, Ger.	**106**	48 46N	9 10E
Stuttgart, U.S.A.	**75**	34 30N	91 33W
Stuyvesant	**71**	42 23N	73 45W
Stykkishólmur	**110**	65 2N	22 40W
Suakin	**115**	19 0N	37 20E
Suancheng	**131**	30 58N	118 57E
Süanen	**131**	30 0N	109 30E
Suanhan	**131**	31 17N	107 46E
Suanhwa	**130**	40 35N	115 0E
Suao	**131**	24 32N	121 42E
Suaqui	**82**	29 12N	109 41W
Suay Rieng	**128**	11 9N	105 45E
Subang	**127**	7 30S	107 45E
Subansiri, R.	**125**	26 48N	93 50E
Subi, I.	**126**	2 58N	108 50E
Subotica	**109**	46 6N	19 29E
Success	**56**	50 28N	108 6W
Suceava	**107**	47 38N	26 16E
Suchil	**82**	23 38N	103 55W
Suchitoto	**84**	13 56N	89 0W
Süchow	**131**	34 10N	117 20E
Sucio, R.	**86**	6 40N	77 0W
Suck, R.	**97**	53 17N	8 10W
Sucre, Boliv.	**86**	19 0S	65 15W
Sucre, Venez.	**86**	10 25N	64 5W
Sucre □, Colomb.	**86**	8 50N	75 40W
Sucre □, Venez.	**86**	10 25N	63 30W
Sucunduri, R.	**86**	6 20N	58 35W
Sud-Ouest, Pte. du	**38**	49 23N	63 36W
Sud, Pte.	**38**	49 3N	62 14W
Sudan ■	**115**	15 0N	30 0E
Sudan, The	**112**	11 0N	9 0E
Sudbury	**46**	46 30N	81 0W
Sudetan Mts. = Sudety	**106**	50 20N	16 45E
Sudety	**106**	50 20N	16 45E
Sudirman, Pengunungan	**127**	4 30N	137 0E
Sueca	**104**	39 12N	0 21W
Sueur, Le	**74**	44 25N	93 52W
Suez = El Suweis	**115**	29 58N	32 31E
Suez Canal	**115**	31 0N	32 20E
Sufaina	**122**	23 6N	40 44E
Suffield	**61**	50 12N	111 10W
Suffolk	**72**	36 47N	76 33W
Suffolk □	**95**	52 16N	1 0E
Suffolk, East, □	**95**	52 16N	1 10E
Suffolk, West, □	**95**	52 16N	0 45E
Sufu	**129**	39 44N	75 53E
Sufuk	**123**	23 50N	51 50E
Sugar City	**74**	38 18N	103 38W
Sugar Cr.	**76**	40 12N	89 41W
Sugar L.	**63**	50 24N	118 30W
Sugar, R., Ill., U.S.A.	**76**	42 25N	89 15W
Sugar, R., Ind., U.S.A.	**77**	39 50N	87 23W
Sugarloaf Head	**37**	47 37N	52 39W
Sugarloaf Pt.	**136**	32 22S	152 30E
Suggi L.	**56**	54 22N	102 47W
Suhār	**123**	24 20N	56 40E
Suhbaatar	**130**	50 17N	106 10E
Suhsien	**131**	33 40N	117 0E
Suichung	**130**	40 20N	120 20E
Suichwan	**131**	26 26N	114 32E
Suifenho	**130**	44 30N	131 2E
Suihsien	**131**	31 58N	113 20E
Suihwa	**130**	46 40N	126 57E
Suiknai	**131**	21 17N	110 19E
Suining	**131**	26 11N	109 5E
Suiping	**131**	33 15N	114 6E
Suippes	**101**	49 8N	4 30E
Suir, R.	**97**	52 31N	7 59W
Suiteh	**130**	37 35N	110 5E
Sukabumi	**127**	6 56S	106 57E
Sukadana	**126**	1 10S	110 0E
Sukandja	**126**	2 28S	110 25E
Sukarnapura = Jajapura	**127**	2 28N	140 38E
Sukarno, G. = Jaja, Puncak	**127**	3 57S	137 17E
Sukhona, R.	**120**	60 30N	45 0E
Sukhumi	**120**	43 0N	41 0E
Sukkur	**124**	27 50N	68 46E
Sukkur Barrage	**124**	27 50N	68 45E
Sukunka, R.	**54**	55 45N	121 15W
Sula, Kepulauan	**127**	1 45S	125 0E
Sulaco, R.	**84**	15 2N	87 44W
Sulaiman Range	**124**	30 30N	69 50E
Sulawesi □	**127**	2 0S	120 0E
Sulawesi, I.	**127**	2 0S	120 0E
Sulina	**107**	45 10N	29 40E
Sulitälma	**110**	67 17N	17 28E
Sulitjelma	**110**	61 7N	16 8E
Sullana	**86**	5 0S	80 45W
Sullivan, B.C., Can.	**66**	49 7N	122 48W
Sullivan, Qué., Can.	**40**	48 7N	77 50W
Sullivan, Ill., U.S.A.	**77**	39 40N	88 40W
Sullivan, Ind., U.S.A.	**77**	39 5N	87 26W
Sullivan, Mo., U.S.A.	**76**	38 10N	91 10W
Sullivan Bay	**62**	50 55N	126 50W
Sullivan L.	**61**	52 0N	112 0W
Sully	**76**	41 34N	92 50W
Sully-sur-Loire	**101**	47 45N	2 20E
Sulphur, La., U.S.A.	**75**	30 20N	93 22W
Sulphur, Okla., U.S.A.	**75**	34 35N	97 0W
Sulphur Pt.	**54**	60 56N	114 48W
Sulphur Springs	**75**	33 5N	95 30W
Sulphur Springs, Cr.	**75**	32 50N	102 8W
Sultan, Can.	**53**	47 36N	82 47W
Sultan, U.S.A.	**80**	47 51N	121 49W
Sultanpur	**125**	26 18N	82 10E
Sulu Arch.	**127**	6 0N	121 0E
Sulu Sea	**127**	8 0N	120 0E
Suluq	**115**	31 44N	20 14E
Sulzbach-Rosenburg	**105**	49 30N	11 46E
Sumalata	**127**	1 0N	122 37E
Sumampa	**88**	29 25S	63 29W
Sumatera, I.	**126**	0 40N	100 20E
Sumatera Selatan □	**126**	3 30S	104 0E
Sumatera Tengah □	**126**	1 0S	100 0E
Sumatera Utara □	**126**	2 0N	99 0E
Sumatra	**78**	46 45N	107 37W
Sumatra = Sumatera	**126**	0 40N	100 20E
Sumba, I.	**127**	9 45S	119 35E
Sumba, Selat	**127**	9 0S	118 40E
Sumbawa	**126**	8 26S	117 30E
Sumbawa, I.	**127**	8 34S	117 17E
Sümber	**129**	46 21N	108 25E
Sumbing, mt.	**127**	7 19S	110 3E
Sumburgh Hd.	**96**	59 52N	1 17W
Sumedang	**127**	6 49S	107 56E
Sumenep	**127**	7 3S	113 51E
Summer L.	**78**	42 50N	120 50W
Summerford	**37**	49 29N	54 47W
Summerland	**63**	49 32N	119 41W
Summerside, Newf., Can.	**37**	48 59N	57 59W
Summerside, P.E.I., Can.	**39**	46 24N	63 47W
Summerstown	**43**	45 4N	74 32W
Summerville, Newf., Can.	**37**	48 27N	53 33W
Summerville, Ont., Can.	**50**	43 37N	79 34W
Summerville, Ga., U.S.A.	**73**	34 30N	85 20W
Summerville, S.C., U.S.A.	**73**	33 2N	80 11W
Summit, Can.	**34**	47 50N	72 20W
Summit, U.S.A.	**67**	63 20N	149 20W
Summit Lake	**54**	54 20N	122 40W
Summit Pk.	**79**	37 20N	106 48W
Summitt	**77**	41 48N	87 48W
Sumner, U.S.A.	**77**	38 42N	87 53W
Sumner, Iowa, U.S.A.	**76**	42 49N	92 7W
Sumner, Wash., U.S.A.	**80**	47 12N	122 14W
Sumperk	**106**	49 59N	17 0E
Sumter	**73**	33 55N	80 10W
Sumy	**120**	50 57N	34 50E
Sun City	**81**	33 41N	117 11W
Sun Prairie	**76**	43 11N	89 13W
Sunart, L.	**96**	56 42N	5 43W
Sunburst	**61**	48 56N	111 59W
Sunbury, Can.	**66**	49 9N	122 59W
Sunbury, U.S.A.	**71**	40 50N	76 46W
Sunchales	**88**	30 58S	61 35W
Suncho Corral	**88**	27 55S	63 14W
Sunchŏn	**131**	34 52N	127 31E
Suncook	**71**	43 8N	71 27W
Sunda Ketjil, Kepulauan	**126**	7 30S	117 0E
Sunda, Selat	**126**	6 20S	105 30E
Sundance	**74**	44 27N	104 27W
Sundarbans, The	**125**	22 0N	89 0E
Sundargarh	**125**	22 10N	84 5E
Sunderland, Can.	**47**	44 16N	79 4W
Sunderland, U.K.	**94**	54 54N	1 22W
Sunderland, U.S.A.	**71**	42 27N	72 36W
Sundown	**57**	49 6N	96 16W
Sundre	**61**	51 49N	114 38W
Sundridge	**46**	45 45N	79 25W
Sundsvall	**110**	62 23N	17 17E
Sung-hua Hu	**130**	43 0N	127 0E
Sung-hua Kiang (Sungari)	**130**	47 0N	130 50E
Sungaipakning	**126**	1 19N	102 0E
Sungaipenuh	**126**	2 1S	101 20E
Sungaitiram	**126**	0 45S	117 8E
Sungari = Sung-hua Kiang	**130**	47 0N	130 50E
Sungei Lembing	**128**	2 53N	103 4E
Sungei Patani	**128**	5 38N	100 29E
Sungei Siput	**128**	4 51N	101 6E
Sungguminasa	**127**	5 17S	119 30E
Sunghsien	**131**	34 10N	112 10E
Sungkiang	**131**	31 0N	121 20E
Sungpan	**129**	32 50N	103 20E
Sungtao	**131**	28 12N	109 12E
Sungtzu	**131**	30 25N	111 46E
Sungtzu Hu	**131**	30 10N	111 45E
Sungurlu	**122**	40 12N	34 21E
Sungyang	**131**	28 16N	119 29E
Sunny Corner	**39**	46 57N	65 49W
Sunnybrae	**39**	45 24N	62 30W
Sunnyside, Can.	**37**	47 51N	53 55W
Sunnyside, Utah, U.S.A.	**78**	39 40N	110 24W
Sunnyside, Wash., U.S.A.	**78**	46 24N	120 2W
Sunnyvale	**80**	37 23N	122 2W
Sunray	**75**	36 1N	101 47W
Sunshine	**136**	37 48S	144 52E
Suntar	**121**	62 15N	117 30E
Sunwapta Pass	**61**	52 13N	117 10W
Supai	**79**	36 14N	112 44W
Supaul	**125**	26 10N	86 40E
Superior, Ariz., U.S.A.	**79**	33 19N	111 9W
Superior, Mont., U.S.A.	**78**	47 15N	114 57W
Superior, Nebr., U.S.A.	**74**	40 3N	98 2W
Superior, Wis., U.S.A.	**52**	46 45N	92 5W
Superior, L.	**69**	47 40N	87 0W
Suphan Buri	**128**	14 30N	100 10E
Supu	**131**	27 57N	110 15E
Supung Hu	**130**	40 40N	125 0E
Sūr, Leb.	**115**	33 19N	35 16E
Sūr, Oman	**123**	22 34N	59 32E
Sur, Pt.	**80**	36 18N	121 54W
Sura, R.	**120**	55 30N	46 20E
Surabaja = Surabaya	**127**	7 17S	112 45E
Surabaya	**127**	7 17S	112 45E
Surakarta	**127**	7 35S	110 48E
Surat	**124**	21 12N	72 55E
Surat Thani	**128**	9 6N	99 14E
Suratgarh	**124**	29 18N	73 55E
Sûre, R.	**105**	49 51N	6 6E
Surf	**81**	34 41N	120 36W
Surf Inlet	**54**	53 8N	128 50W
Surgères	**102**	46 7N	0 47W
Suri	**125**	23 50N	87 34E
Suriapet	**124**	17 10N	79 40E
Surin	**128**	14 50N	103 34E
Surinam ■	**87**	4 0N	56 15W
Suriname, R.	**87**	4 30N	55 30W
Surprise L.	**54**	59 40N	133 15W
Surprise, L.	**40**	49 20N	74 55W
Surrey	**66**	49 12N	122 51W
Surrey □, Can.	**66**	49 9N	122 46W
Surrey □, U.K.	**95**	51 16N	0 30W
Surrey Centre	**66**	49 7N	122 45W
Surtsey	**110**	63 20N	20 30W
Suruga-Wan	**132**	34 45N	138 30E
Surup	**127**	6 27N	126 17E
Surur	**123**	23 20N	58 10E
Susa	**108**	45 8N	7 3E
Süsangerd	**122**	31 35N	48 20E
Susanino	**121**	52 50N	140 14E
Susanville	**78**	40 28N	120 40W
Susquehanna Depot	**71**	41 55N	75 36W
Susquehanna, R.	**71**	41 50N	76 20W
Susques	**88**	23 35S	66 25W
Sussex, Can.	**39**	45 45N	65 37W
Sussex, U.S.A.	**71**	41 12N	74 38W
Sussex, E. □	**95**	51 0N	0 0E
Sussex, W. □	**95**	51 0N	0 30W

Sustut, R Taohsien

Sustut, R. 54 56 20N 127 30W
Susuman 121 62 47N 148 10 E
Susuna 127 3 20 S 133 25 E
Sutherland, Can. 55 52 15N 106 40W
Sutherland, S. Afr. 117 32 33 S 20 40 E
Sutherland, U.S.A. 74 41 12N 101 11W
Sutherland Falls 133 44 48 S 167 46 E
Sutherland Pt. 135 28 15 S 153 35 E
Sutherlin 78 43 28N 123 16W
Sutlej, R. 124 30 0N 73 0 E
Sutter 80 39 10N 121 45W
Sutter Creek 80 38 24N 120 48W
Sutton, Can. 71 45 8N 72 36W
Sutton, Ont., Can. 46 44 18N 79 22W
Sutton, Qué., Can. 41 45 6N 72 37W
Sutton, U.S.A. 74 40 40N 97 50W
Sutton-in-Ashfield 94 52 8N 1 16W
Sutton, R. 34 55 15N 83 45W
Sutwik I. 67 56 35N 157 10W
Suva 133 17 40 S 178 8 E
Suva Planina 109 43 10N 22 5 E
Suvorov Is. 15 13 15 S 163 30W
Suwałki 107 54 8N 22 59 E
Suwannee, R. 73 30 0N 83 0W
Suwanose Jima 132 29 26N 129 30 E
Suwen 131 20 27N 110 2 E
Suwŏn 130 37 17N 127 1 E
Suyung 131 28 12N 105 10 E
Suze, La 100 47 54N 0 2 E
Suzuka 132 34 55N 136 36 E
Svalbard, Arctica 17 78 0N 17 0 E
Svalbard, Iceland 110 66 12N 15 43W
Svanvik 110 69 38N 30 3 E
Svappavaari 110 67 40N 21 03 E
Svartenhuk Pen. 65 71 50N 54 30W
Svartisen 110 66 40N 14 16 E
Svealand □ 111 59 55N 15 0 E
Sveg 111 62 2N 14 21 E
Svendborg 111 55 4N 10 35 E
Sverdlovsk 120 56 50N 60 30 E
Sverdrup Chan. 65 79 56N 96 25W
Sverdrup Is. 65 79 0N 97 0W
Svishov 109 43 36N 25 23 E
Svobodnyy 121 51 20N 128 0 E
Svolvær 110 68 15N 14 34 E
Swain Reefs 135 21 45 S 152 20 E
Swainsboro 73 32 38N 82 22W
Swakopmund 117 22 37 S 14 30 E
Swale, R. 94 54 18N 1 20W
Swan Hill 136 35 20 S 143 33 E
Swan Hills 60 54 42N 115 24W
Swan Islands 84 17 22N 83 57W
Swan L. 57 52 30N 100 40W
Swan, R., Austral. 134 32 3 S 115 35 E
Swan, R., Alta., Can. 60 55 30N 115 18W
Swan, R., Man., Can. 57 52 30N 100 45W
Swan River 57 52 10N 101 16W
Swanage 95 50 36N 1 59W
Swansea, Austral. 136 33 3 S 151 35 E
Swansea, Can. 50 43 38N 79 28W
Swansea, U.K. 95 51 37N 3 57W
Swartz Creek 46 42 58N 83 50W
Swastika 34 48 7N 80 6W
Swatow = Shantow 131 23 25N 116 40 E
Swaziland ■ 117 26 30 S 31 30 E
Sweden ■ 111 67 0N 15 0 E
Sweet Home 78 44 26N 122 38W
Sweet Springs 76 38 58N 93 25W
Sweetwater, Nev., U.S.A. 80 38 27N 119 9W
Sweetwater, Tex., U.S.A. 75 32 30N 100 28W
Sweetwater, R. 78 42 31N 107 30W
Swellendam 117 34 1 S 20 26 E
Swidnica 106 50 50N 16 30 E
Swiebodzin 106 52 15N 15 37 E
Swift Current, Newf., Can. 37 47 53N 54 12W
Swift Current, Sask., Can. 56 50 20N 107 45W
Swiftcurrent Cr. 56 50 38N 107 44W
Swilly L. 97 55 12N 7 35W
Swindle, I. 62 52 30N 128 35W
Swindon 95 51 33N 1 47W
Swinemünde = Świnoujście 106 53 54N 14 16 E
Świnoujście 106 53 54N 14 16 E
Switzerland ■ 106 46 30N 8 0 E
Swords 97 53 27N 6 15W
Sydenham, R. 46 42 33N 82 25W
Sydney, Austral. 136 33 53 S 151 10 E
Sydney, Can. 39 46 7N 60 7W
Sydney, U.S.A. 74 41 12N 103 0W
Sydney L. 52 50 41N 94 25W
Sydney Mines 39 46 18N 60 15W
Sydney River 39 46 7N 60 13W
Sydproven 17 60 30N 45 35W
Syktyvkar 120 61 45N 50 40 E
Sylacauga 73 33 10N 86 15W
Sylarna, Mt. 110 63 2N 12 11 E
Sylhet 125 24 54N 91 52 E
Sylvan L. 61 52 21N 114 10W
Sylvan Lake 61 52 20N 114 10W
Sylvania, Can. 56 52 42N 104 0W
Sylvania, U.S.A. 77 41 43N 83 42W
Sylvania, Ga., U.S.A. 73 32 45N 81 37W
Sylvester, Can. 60 55 0N 119 41W
Sylvester, U.S.A. 73 31 31N 83 50W
Sym 120 60 20N 87 50 E
Symón 82 24 42N 102 35W
Syr Darya 120 45 0N 65 0 E
Syracuse, U.S.A. 77 41 28N 85 47W
Syracuse, Kans., U.S.A. 75 38 0N 101 40W
Syracuse, N.Y., U.S.A. 71 43 4N 76 11W
Syria ■ 122 35 0N 38 0 E
Syrian Des. 122 31 30N 40 0 E
Syuldzhyukyor 121 63 25N 113 40 E
Syzran 120 53 12N 48 30 E
Szczecin 106 53 27N 14 27 E
Szczecinek 106 53 43N 16 41 E
Szechwan □ 129 30 15N 103 15 E
Szeged 107 46 16N 20 10 E
Székesfehérvár 107 47 15N 18 25 E
Szekszárd 107 46 22N 18 42 E
Szemao 129 22 50N 101 0 E
Szenan 131 27 50N 108 25 E
Szengen, Kwangsi-Chuang, China 131 23 20N 108 5 E
Szengen, Kwangsi-Chuang, China 131 24 50N 108 0 E
Szentes 107 46 39N 20 21 E
Szeping 130 43 10N 124 18 E
Szeshui 94 34 50N 113 20 E
Szewui 131 23 30N 112 35 E
Szolnok 107 47 10N 20 15 E
Szombathely 106 47 14N 16 38 E

T

Ta Fengman 130 43 45N 126 35 E
Ta Hinghan Ling 129 48 0N 121 0 E
Ta Liang Shan 129 28 0N 103 0 E
Tabacal 88 23 15 S 64 15W
Tabaco 127 13 22N 123 44 E
Tābah 122 26 55N 42 30 E
Tabas, Khorasan, Iran 123 32 48N 60 12 E
Tabas, Khorasan, Iran 123 33 35N 56 55 E
Tabasará, Serranía de 84 8 35N 81 40W
Tabasco □ 83 17 45N 93 30W
Tabatière, La 37 50 50N 58 58W
Tabatinga 86 4 11 S 69 58W
Tabatinga, Serra da 87 10 30 S 44 0W
Taber 61 49 47N 112 8W
Tablas, I. 127 12 25N 122 2 E
Table B. 36 53 40N 56 25W
Table Grove 76 40 20N 90 27W
Table Mt. 117 34 0 S 18 22 E
Tábor 106 49 25N 14 39 E
Tabora 116 5 2 S 32 57 E
Tabrīz 122 38 7N 46 20 E
Tabūk 122 28 30N 36 25 E
Tacámbaro 82 19 14N 101 28W
Tacarigua, L. de 86 11 3N 68 25W
Tachick L. 62 53 57N 124 12W
Tachintala 130 45 13N 121 37 E
Tachira 86 8 7N 72 21W
Tachira □ 86 8 7N 72 15W
Tachu 131 30 45N 107 13 E
Tacloban 127 11 15N 124 58 E
Tacna 86 18 0 S 70 20W
Tacoma 80 47 15N 122 30W
Tacuarembó 89 31 45 S 56 0W
Tademaït, Plateau du 114 28 30N 2 30 E
Tadmor, N.Z. 133 41 27 S 172 45 E
Tadmor, Syria 122 34 30N 37 55 E
Tado 86 5 16N 76 32W
Tadoule, L. 55 58 36N 98 20W
Tadoussac 41 48 11N 69 42W
Tadzhik S.S.R. □ 120 35 30N 70 0 E
Taegu 130 35 50N 128 37 E
Taejŏn 130 36 20N 127 28 E
Taerh Hu 130 43 25N 116 40 E
Taf, R. 95 51 55N 4 36W
Tafalla 104 42 30N 1 41W
Tafermaar 127 6 47 S 134 10 E
Tafí Viejo 88 26 43 S 65 17W
Taft, Phil. 127 11 57N 125 30 E
Taft, Calif.., U.S.A. 81 35 10N 119 28W
Taft, Tex., U.S.A. 75 27 58N 97 23W
Taga Dzong 125 27 5N 90 0 E
Taganrog 120 47 12N 38 50 E
Tagbilaran 127 9 39N 123 51 E
Tagish 54 60 19N 134 16W
Tagish L. 67 60 10N 134 20W
Tagliamento, R. 108 45 38N 13 5 E
Tagua, La 86 0 3N 74 40W
Taguatinga 87 12 26 S 46 26W
Tagum (Hijo) 127 7 33N 125 53 E
Tagus = Tajo, R. 104 39 44N 5 50W
Tahahbala, I. 126 0 30 S 98 30 E
Tahakopa 133 46 30 S 169 23 E
Tahan, Gunong 128 4 45N 102 25 E
Tahcheng 129 46 50N 83 1 E
Taheiho 130 50 10N 127 20 E
Tāherī 123 27 43N 52 20 E
Tahiti, I. 15 17 37 S 149 27W
Tahoe 80 39 12N 120 9W
Tahoe, L. 80 39 0N 120 9W
Taholah 80 47 21N 124 17W
Tahoua 114 14 57N 5 16 E
Tahsien 131 31 17N 107 30 E
Tahsis 62 49 55N 126 40W
Tahulandang, I. 127 2 27N 125 23 E
Tahuna 127 3 45N 125 30 E
Tai Hu 131 31 10N 120 0 E
Taian 130 36 20N 117 0 E
Taichow 131 32 30N 119 50 E
Taichow Wan. 131 28 55N 121 10 E
Taichung 131 24 10N 120 35 E
Taieri, R. 133 46 3 S 170 12 E
Taihan Shan 130 36 0N 114 0 E
Taihape 133 39 41 S 175 48 E
Taiho 131 26 50N 114 54 E
Taihsien 130 39 9N 112 58 E
Taihu 131 30 30N 116 25 E
Taikang 131 34 3N 115 0 E
Taikiang 131 26 45N 108 44 E
Taiku 130 37 46N 112 28 E
Taikung 131 26 50N 108 40 E
Tailagein Shara 130 44 10N 106 0 E
Tailai 129 46 28N 123 18 E
Taīma 122 27 35N 38 45 E
Taimyr = Taymyr 121 75 0N 100 0 E
Taimyr, Oz. 121 74 20N 102 0 E
Tain 96 57 49N 4 4W
Tainan 131 23 0N 120 15 E
Taínaron, Ákra 109 36 22N 22 27 E
Taining 131 27 0N 117 15 E
Taipei 131 25 2N 121 30 E
Taiping 128 4 51N 100 44 E
Taishan 131 27 29N 119 34 E
Taitao, Pen. de 90 46 30 S 75 0W
Taitung 131 22 43N 121 4 E
Taivalkoski 110 65 33N 28 12 E
Taiwan (Formosa) ■ 131 23 30N 121 0 E
Taiwara 123 33 30N 64 24 E
Taïyetos Óros 109 37 0N 22 23 E
Taiyüan 130 38 0N 112 30 E
Tajicaringa 82 23 15N 104 44W
Tajitos 82 30 58N 112 18W
Tajo, R. 104 40 35N 1 52W
Tajumulco, Volcán de 83 15 20N 91 50W
Tak 128 16 52N 99 8 E
Takada 132 37 7N 138 15 E
Takaka 133 40 51N 172 50 E
Takamatsu 132 34 20N 134 5 E
Takanabe 132 32 8N 131 30 E
Takaoka 132 36 40N 137 0 E
Takapuna 133 36 47 S 174 47 E
Takasaki 132 36 20N 139 0 E
Takatsuki 132 34 51N 135 37 E
Takaungu 116 3 38 S 39 52 E
Takayama 132 36 18N 137 11 E
Takefu 132 35 50N 136 10 E
Takeo 128 10 59N 104 47 E
Tākestān 122 36 0N 49 50 E
Takhing 131 23 10N 111 45 E
Takingeun 126 4 45N 96 50 E
Takiyuak L. 64 65 30N 113 5W
Takla L. 54 55 15N 125 45W
Takla Landing 54 55 30N 125 50W
Takla Makan 129 39 0N 83 0 E
Taku, R. 54 58 30N 133 50W
Takushan 130 39 55N 123 30 E
Takysie Lake 62 53 53N 125 53W
Tala, Uruguay 89 34 21 S 55 46W
Tala, U.S.S.R. 121 72 40N 113 30 E
Talachih 130 36 45N 105 0 E
Talagante 88 33 40 S 70 50W
Talai 130 45 30N 124 20W
Talamanca, Cordillera de 84 9 20N 83 20W
Talara 86 4 30 S 81 10 E
Talas 120 42 45N 72 0 E
Talaud, Kepulauan 127 4 30N 127 10 E
Talavera de la Reina 104 39 55N 4 46W
Talayan 127 6 52N 124 24 E
Talbot, C. 134 13 48 S 126 43 E
Talbot L. 57 54 0N 99 55W
Talbragar, R. 136 32 5 S 149 15 E
Talca 88 35 20 S 71 46W
Talca □ 88 35 20 S 71 46W
Talcahuano 88 36 40 S 73 10W
Talcher 125 20 55N 85 3 E
Taldy Kurgan 120 45 10N 78 45 E
Talesh, Kūhā-Ye 122 39 0N 48 30 E
Talguppa 124 14 10N 74 45 E
Tali, Shensi, China 131 34 48N 109 48 E
Tali, Yunnan, China 129 25 45N 100 5 E
Taliabu, I. 127 1 45 S 125 0 E
Taliang Shan 129 28 0N 103 0 E
Talien, (Dairen) 130 38 53N 121 37 E
Talihina 75 34 45N 95 1W
Taling Sung 128 15 5N 99 11 E
Taliwang 126 8 50 S 116 55 E
Talkeetna 67 62 20N 150 0W
Talkeetna Mts. 67 62 20N 149 0W
Talladega 73 33 28N 86 2W
Tallahassee 73 30 25N 84 15W
Tallangatta 136 36 15 S 147 10 E
Tallering Pk 134 28 6 S 115 37 E
Tallinn (Reval) 120 59 29N 24 58 E
Tallulah 75 32 25N 91 12W
Talmage 55 49 46N 103 40W
Talmont 102 46 27N 1 37W
Talpa de Allende 82 20 23N 104 51W
Taltal 88 25 23 S 70 40W
Taltson L. 55 61 30N 110 15W
Taltson R. 54 61 24N 112 46W
Talunkwan I. 62 52 50N 131 45W
Talyawalka Cr. 136 32 28 S 142 22 E
Tama 76 41 56N 92 37W
Tama Abu, Pegunungan 126 3 10N 115 0 E
Tamalameque 86 8 52N 73 49W
Tamale 114 9 22N 0 50W
Tamano 132 34 35N 133 59 E
Tamanrasset 114 22 56N 5 30 E
Tamaqua 71 40 46N 75 58W
Tamar, R. 95 50 33N 4 15W
Támara 86 5 50N 72 10W
Tamaroa 76 38 8N 89 14W
Tamatave 117 18 10 S 49 25 E
Tamaulipas □ 83 24 0N 99 0W
Tamaulipas, Sierra de 83 23 30N 98 20W
Tamazula 82 24 55N 106 58W
Tamazunchale 83 21 16N 98 47W
Tambelan, Kepulauan 126 1 0N 107 30 E
Tambo de Mora 86 13 30 S 76 20W
Tambora, G. 126 8 12 S 118 5 E
Tambov 120 52 45N 41 20 E
Tambuku, G. 127 7 8 S 113 40 E
Tame 86 6 28N 71 44W
Tamega, R. 104 41 12N 8 5W
Tamenglong 125 25 0N 93 35 E
Tamerfors 111 61 30N 23 50 E
Tamgak, Mts. 114 19 12N 8 35 E
Tamiahua, Laguna de 83 21 30N 97 30W
Tamil Nadu □ 124 11 0N 77 0 E
Taming 130 36 20N 115 10 E
Tammisaari (Ekenäs) 111 60 0N 23 26 E
Tampa 73 27 57N 82 30W
Tampa B. 73 27 40N 82 40W
Tampere 111 61 30N 23 50 E
Tampico, Mexico 83 22 20N 97 50W
Tampico, U.S.A. 76 41 38N 89 47W
Tampin 128 2 28N 102 13 E
Tamsagbulag 130 47 15N 117 5 E
Tamu 125 24 13N 94 12 E
Tamworth, Austral. 135 31 0 S 150 58 E
Tamworth, Can. 47 44 29N 77 0W
Tamworth, U.K. 95 52 38N 1 41W
Tan Kiang 131 33 25N 111 0 E
Tana 110 70 7N 28 5 E
Tana, L. 115 13 5N 37 30 E
Tana, R. 116 0 50 S 39 45 E
Tanacross 67 63 40N 143 30W
Tanafjorden 110 70 45N 28 25 E
Tanahdjampea, I. 127 7 10 S 120 35 E
Tanahgrogot 126 1 55 S 116 15 E
Tanahmasa, I. 126 0 5 S 98 29 E
Tanahmerah 127 6 0 S 140 7 E
Tanami Des. 134 18 50 S 132 0 E
Tanana 67 65 10N 152 15W
Tanana, R. 67 64 25N 145 30W
Tananarive = Antananarivo 117 18 55 S 47 31 E
Tánaro, R. 108 44 9N 7 50 E
Tancarville 100 49 29N 0 28 E
Tanchai 131 25 58N 107 49 E
Tanchŏn 130 40 27N 128 54 E
Tanchow 131 19 33N 109 22 E
Tandag 127 9 4N 126 9 E
Tandil 88 37 15 S 59 6W
Tandjungpandan 126 2 43 S 107 38 E
Tando Adam 124 25 45N 68 40 E
Tandou L. 136 32 40 S 142 5 E
Tane-ga-Shima 132 30 30N 131 0 E
Taneatua 133 38 4 S 177 1 E
Tanen Range 128 19 40N 99 0 E
Tanen Tong Dan 125 16 30N 98 30 E
Tanezrouft 114 23 9N 0 11 E
Tanga 116 5 5 S 39 2 E
Tanganyika, L. 116 6 40 S 30 0 E
Tanger 114 35 50N 5 49W
Tangerang 127 6 12 S 106 39 E
Tanghing 131 21 30N 108 2 E
Tangho 131 32 47N 113 2 E
Tanghsien 130 38 48N 114 54 E
Tangier 39 44 48N 62 42W
Tangkak 128 2 18N 102 34 E
Tangku 130 39 0N 117 40 E
Tanglha Shan 129 33 0N 90 0 E
Tangshan, Anhwei, China 131 34 17N 116 25 E
Tangshan, Hopei, China 130 39 40N 118 10 E
Tangtu 131 31 37N 118 39 E
Tangyang 131 30 50N 111 45 E
Tanhsien (Nata) 131 19 30N 109 17 E
Tanimbar, Kepulauan 127 7 30 S 131 30 E
Taning = Wuki 131 31 27N 109 46 E
Tanjay 127 9 30N 123 5 E
Tanjore = Thanjavur 124 10 48N 79 12 E
Tanjung 126 2 10 S 115 25 E
Tanjungbalai 126 2 55N 99 44 E
Tanjungbatu 126 2 23N 118 3 E
Tanjungkarang 126 5 20 S 105 10 E
Tanjungpinang 126 1 5N 104 30 E
Tanjungpriok 127 6 8 S 106 55 E
Tanjungredeb 126 2 9N 117 29 E
Tanjungselor 126 2 55N 117 25 E
Tannin 34 49 40N 91 0W
Tannu Ola 129 51 0N 94 0 E
Tanout 114 14 50N 8 55 E
Tanshui 131 25 10N 121 28 E
Tansley 49 43 25N 79 48W
Tanta 115 30 45N 30 57 E
Tantallon 57 50 32N 101 50W
Tantoyuca 83 21 21N 98 10W
Tanu I. 62 52 46N 131 40W
Tanus 102 44 8N 2 19 E
Tanzania ■ 116 6 40 S 34 0 E
Tanzilla, R. 54 58 8N 130 43W
Taohsien 131 25 37N 111 24 E

Taokow Teulon

Taokow 130 35 30N 114 30E
Taolaihao 130 44 51N 125 57E
Taonan 130 45 30N 122 20E
Taos 79 36 28N 105 35W
Taoyuan, Hunan, China 131 29 8N 111 15E
Taoyuan, Taiwan, China 131 25 0N 121 4E
Tapa Shan 131 31 45N 109 30E
Tapachula 83 14 54N 92 17W
Tapah 128 4 12N 101 15E
Tapajós, R. 87 4 30S 56 10W
Tapaktuan 126 3 30N 97 10E
Tapanshang = Palinyuchi 130 43 40N 118 20E
Tapanui 133 45 56S 169 18E
Tapauá 86 5 40S 64 20W
Tapauá, R. 86 6 0S 65 40W
Tapirapecó, Serra 86 1 10N 65 0W
Tapleytown 48 43 11N 79 44W
Tappahannock 72 37 56N 76 50W
Tapti, R. 124 21 25N 75 0E
Tapuaenuku, Mt. 133 41 55S 173 50E
Tapul Group, Is. 127 5 35N 120 50E
Taquara 89 29 36N 50 46W
Taquari, R. 89 18 10S 56 0W
Tar Island 54 57 03N 111 40W
Tara, Can. 46 44 28N 81 9W
Tara, U.S.S.R. 120 56 55N 74 30E
Tara, R. 109 43 5N 19 20E
Tarabagatay, Khrebet 121 48 0N 83 0E
Tarābulus, Leb. 122 34 31N 33 52E
Tarābulus, Libya 114 32 49N 13 7E
Tarakan 126 3 20N 117 35E
Taranaki □ 133 39 5S 174 51E
Taranga Hill 124 24 0N 72 40E
Táranto 108 40 30N 17 11E
Táranto, G. di 108 40 0N 17 15E
Tarapacá 86 2 56S 69 46W
Tarapacá □ 88 20 45S 69 30W
Tarare 103 45 54N 4 26E
Tararua Range 133 40 45S 175 25E
Tarascon, Ariège, France 102 42 50N 1 37E
Tarascon, Bouches-du-Rhône, France 103 43 48N 4 39E
Tarauacá 86 8 6S 70 48W
Tarauacá, R. 86 7 30S 70 30W
Taravo, R. 103 41 48N 8 52E
Tarawera 133 39 2S 176 36E
Tarawera L. 133 38 13S 176 27E
Tarbagatai 129 48 30N 99 0E
Tarbat Ness 96 57 52N 3 48W
Tarbela Dam 124 34 0N 72 52E
Tarbert, Can. 49 43 56N 80 20W
Tarbert, U.K. 96 57 54N 6 49W
Tarbes 102 43 15N 0 3E
Tarboro 73 35 55N 77 30W
Tarcoola 134 30 44S 134 36E
Tardets-Sorholus 102 43 8N 0 52W
Tardin 129 37 16N 92 30E
Taree 136 31 50S 152 30E
Tarentaise 103 45 30N 6 35E
Tarfaya 114 27 55N 12 55W
Targon 102 44 44N 0 16W
Tari Nur 130 43 25N 116 40E
Táriba 86 7 49N 72 13W
Tarifa 104 36 1N 5 36W
Tarija 88 21 30S 64 40W
Tarija □ 88 21 30S 63 30W
Tarim, R. 129 41 5N 86 40E
Taritoe, R. 127 3 0S 138 5E
Tarko Sale 120 64 55N 77 50E
Tarlac 127 15 29N 120 35E
Tarma 86 11 25S 75 45W
Tarn □ 102 43 49N 2 8E
Tarn-et-Garonne □ 102 44 8N 1 20E
Tarn, R. 102 44 5N 1 2E
Tarnów 107 50 3N 21 0E
Tarnowskie Góry 107 50 27N 18 54E
Taroom 135 25 36S 149 48E
Tarpon Springs 73 28 8N 82 42W
Tarragona 104 41 5N 1 17E
Tarrasa 104 41 26N 2 1E
Tarrytown 71 41 5N 73 52W
Tarsus 122 36 58N 34 55E
Tartagal 88 22 30S 63 50W
Tartas 102 43 50N 0 49W
Tartūs 122 34 55N 35 55E
Tarutao, Ko 128 6 33N 99 40E
Tarutung 126 2 0N 99 0E
Taschereau 40 48 40N 78 40W
Taseko L. 62 51 15N 123 35W
Taseko, R. 62 52 4N 123 9W
Tashauz 120 42 0N 59 20E
Tashi Chho Dzong 125 27 31N 89 45E
Tashigong 129 33 0N 79 30E
Tashihkao 130 40 47N 122 29E
Tashkent 120 41 20N 69 10E
Tashkumyr 120 41 40N 72 10E
Tashkurgan 129 37 51N 74 57E
Tashkurghan 123 36 45N 67 40E
Tashtagol 120 52 47N 87 53E
Tasi Ho 131 28 20N 119 40E
Tasikmalaya 127 7 18S 108 12E
Tasin (Yangli) 131 22 57N 107 15E
Tasjön 110 64 15N 15 45E
Tasman Bay 133 40 59S 173 25E
Tasman Glacier 133 43 45S 170 20E
Tasman Mts. 133 41 3S 172 25E
Tasman Pen. 135 43 10S 148 0E
Tasman Sea 135 36 0S 160 0E
Tasmania, I., □ 135 49 0S 146 30E
Tassialuk, L. 36 59 3N 74 0W
Tasu 62 52 45N 132 5W
Tasu Sd. 62 52 47N 132 2W
Tatamagouche 39 45 43N 63 18W
Tatar A.S.S.R. □ 120 55 30N 51 30E
Tatarsk 120 55 20N 75 50E
Tatarskiy Proliv 121 54 0N 141 0E
Tateyama 132 35 0N 139 50E
Tathlina L. 54 60 33N 117 39W
Tatien 131 25 45N 118 0E
Tating 131 27 0N 105 35E
Tatinnai L. 55 60 55N 97 40W
Tatla L. 62 52 0N 124 20W
Tatlayoko L. 62 51 35N 124 24W
Tatnam, C. 55 57 16N 91 0W
Tatsaitan 129 37 55N 95 0E
Tatsu 131 29 40N 105 45E
Tatta 124 24 42N 67 55E
Tatton 63 51 43N 121 22W
Tatuī 89 23 25S 48 0W
Tatuk, L. 62 53 32N 124 14W
Tatum 75 33 16N 103 16W
Tatung 130 30 50N 117 45E
Tatungkow 130 39 55N 124 10E
Tatura 136 36 29S 145 16E
Tatvan 122 37 28N 42 27E
Taubaté 89 23 5S 45 30W
Tauern, mts. 106 47 15N 12 40E
Taumarunui 133 38 53S 175 15E
Taumaturgo 86 9 0S 73 50W
Taungdwingyi 125 20 1N 95 40E
Taunggyi 125 20 50N 97 0E
Taungup Taunggya 125 18 20N 93 40E
Taunton, Can. 49 43 56N 78 49W
Taunton, U.K. 95 51 1N 3 7W
Taunus 106 50 15N 8 20E
Taupo 133 38 41S 176 7E
Taupo, L. 133 38 46S 175 55E
Tauq 122 35 12N 44 29E
Tauramena 86 5 1N 72 45W
Tauranga 133 37 35S 176 11E
Tauranga Harb. 133 37 30S 176 5E
Taureau, Lac 34 46 50N 73 40W
Taurianova 108 38 22N 16 1E
Taurus Mts. = Toros Dağlari 122 37 0N 35 0E
Tava Wan 131 22 35N 114 35E
Tavani 55 62 10N 93 30W
Tavas 122 37 35N 29 8E
Tavda 120 58 7N 65 8E
Tavda, R. 120 59 30N 63 0E
Taverny 101 49 2N 2 13E
Taveta 116 3 31N 37 37E
Taviche 83 16 38N 96 32W
Tavignano, R. 103 42 7N 9 33E
Tavira 104 37 8N 7 40W
Tavistock, Can. 46 43 19N 80 50W
Tavistock, U.K. 95 50 33N 4 9W
Tavoy 128 14 7N 98 18E
Tavoy, I. = Mali Kyun 125 13 0N 98 20E
Taw, R. 95 50 58N 3 58W
Tawas City 46 44 16N 83 31W
Tawau 126 4 20N 117 55E
Tawu 131 22 30N 120 50E
Tay, Firth of 96 56 25N 3 8W
Tay, L. 96 56 30N 4 10W
Tay Ninh 128 11 20N 106 5E
Tay, R. 96 56 37N 3 38W
Tayabamba 86 8 15S 77 10W
Tayen 131 30 4N 115 0E
Taylor, Can. 54 56 13N 120 40W
Taylor, Alaska, U.S.A. 67 65 40N 164 50W
Taylor, Pa., U.S.A. 71 41 23N 75 43W
Taylor, Tex., U.S.A. 75 30 30N 97 30W
Taylor Mt. 79 35 16N 107 50W
Taylorsville 77 38 2N 85 21W
Taylorville 76 39 32N 89 20W
Taymyr, Oz. 121 74 50N 102 0E
Taymyr, P-ov. 121 75 0N 100 0E
Tayport 96 56 27N 2 52W
Tayshet 121 55 58N 97 25E
Tayside □ 96 56 25N 3 30W
Taytay 127 10 45N 119 30E
Tayu 131 25 38N 114 9E
Tayulehsze 129 29 15N 98 1E
Tayung 131 29 8N 110 30E
Taz, R. 120 65 40N 82 0E
Tazin L. 55 59 44N 108 42W
Tazin, R. 55 60 26N 110 45W
Tazovskiy 120 67 30N 78 30E
Tbilisi (Tiflis) 120 41 50N 44 50E
Tchad, Lac 114 13 30N 14 30E
Tchentlo L. 54 55 15N 125 0W
Tchibanga 116 2 45S 11 12E
Tchpao (Tienpao) 131 23 25N 106 47E
Te Anau L. 133 45 15S 167 45E
Te Aroha 133 37 32S 175 44E
Te Awamutu 133 38 1S 175 20E
Te Horo 133 40 48S 175 6E
Te Kuiti 133 38 20S 175 11E
Te Puke 133 37 46S 176 22E
Te Waewae B. 133 46 13S 167 33E
Teague 75 31 40N 96 20W
Teapa 83 17 35N 92 56W
Tebicuary, R. 88 26 36S 58 16W
Tebing Tinggi 126 3 38S 102 1E
Tecapa 81 35 51N 116 14W
Tecate 82 32 34N 116 38W
Tecomán 82 18 55N 103 53W
Tecoripa 82 28 37N 109 57W
Tecuci 107 45 51N 27 27E
Tecumseh, Can. 46 42 19N 82 54W
Tecumseh, U.S.A. 77 42 1N 83 59W
Tedzhen 120 37 23N 60 31E
Tee Lake 40 46 40N 79 0W
Teepee Creek 60 55 22N 118 24W
Tees B. 94 54 37N 1 10W
Tees, R. 94 54 36N 1 25W
Teesside 94 54 37N 1 13W
Teeswater 46 43 59N 81 17W
Tefé 86 3 25S 64 50W
Tegal 127 6 52S 109 8E
Tegid, L. 94 52 53N 3 38W
Tegucigalpa 84 14 10N 87 0W
Tehachapi 81 35 11N 118 29W
Tehachapi Mts. 81 35 0N 118 40W
Tehchow 130 37 29N 116 11E
Tehping 130 37 26N 117 0E
Tehrān 123 35 44N 51 30E
Tehrān □ 123 35 0N 49 30E
Tehtsin (Atuntze) 129 28 45N 98 58E
Tehuacán 83 18 20N 97 30W
Tehuantepec 83 16 10N 95 19W
Tehuantepec, Golfo de 83 15 50N 95 0W
Tehuantepec, Istmo de 83 17 0N 94 30W
Teich, Le 102 44 38N 0 59W
Teifi, R. 95 52 4N 4 14W
Teign, R. 95 50 41N 3 42W
Teignmouth 95 50 33N 3 30W
Teil, Le 103 44 33N 4 40E
Teilleul, Le 100 48 32N 0 53W
Tejo, R. 104 39 15N 8 35W
Tejon Pass 81 34 49N 118 53W
Tekamah 74 41 48N 96 14W
Tekapo, L. 133 43 53S 170 33E
Tekax 83 20 20N 89 30W
Tekeli 120 44 50N 79 0E
Tekirdağ 122 40 58N 27 30E
Tekkali 125 18 43N 84 24E
Tekoa 78 47 19N 117 4W
Tel Aviv-Jaffa 115 32 4N 34 48E
Tel Aviv-Yafo 115 32 4N 34 48E
Tela 84 15 40N 87 28W
Telanaipura = Jambi 126 1 38S 103 30E
Telegraph Cove 62 50 32N 126 50W
Telegraph Cr. 54 58 0N 131 10W
Telemark fylke □ 111 59 25N 8 30E
Telén 88 36 15S 65 31W
Teles Pires (São Manuel), R. 86 8 40S 57 0W
Telescope Peak, Mt. 81 36 6N 117 7W
Telford 94 52 42N 2 31W
Telisze 130 39 50N 112 0E
Telkwa 54 54 41N 126 56W
Tell City 77 38 0N 86 44W
Teller 67 65 12N 166 24W
Tellicherry 124 11 45N 75 30E
Telluride 79 37 58N 107 54W
Telok Anson 128 4 3N 101 0E
Teloloapán 83 18 21N 99 51W
Telom, R. 128 4 20N 101 46E
Telsen 90 42 30S 66 50W
Telukbetung 126 5 29S 105 17E
Telukdalem 126 0 45N 97 50E
Tema 114 5 41N 0 0E
Temagami L. 34 47 0N 80 10W
Temanggung 127 7 18S 110 10E
Temapache 83 21 4N 97 38W
Temax 83 21 10N 88 50W
Tembeling, R. 128 4 20N 102 23E
Temblor Ra, mts. 81 35 30N 120 0W
Teme, R. 95 52 23N 2 15W
Temecula 81 33 26N 117 6W
Temerloh 128 3 27N 102 25E
Temir Tau 120 53 10N 87 20E
Temirtau 120 50 5N 72 56E
Témiscamie, R. 36 50 59N 73 5W
Témiscaming 40 46 44N 79 5W
Témiscamingue, L. 40 47 10N 79 25W
Temora 136 34 30S 147 30E
Temosachic 82 28 58N 107 50W
Tempe, S. Afr. 79 29 1S 26 13E
Tempe, U.S.A. 79 33 26N 111 59W
Temperance Vale 39 46 4N 67 15W
Temperanceville 50 43 56N 79 28W
Tempestad 86 1 20S 74 56W
Tempino 126 1 55S 103 23E
Tempiute 80 37 39N 115 38W
Temple 75 31 5N 97 28W
Temple B. 135 12 15S 143 3E
Temple Sowerby 95 54 38N 2 33W
Templeman, Mt. 63 50 42N 117 12W
Templemore 97 52 48N 7 50W
Templeton, Can. 48 45 29N 75 35W
Templeton, U.S.A. 80 35 33N 120 42W
Tempoal 83 21 31N 98 23W
Temuco 90 38 50S 72 50W
Temuka 133 44 14S 171 17E
Ten Mile L. 37 51 6N 56 42W
Tena 86 0 59S 77 49W
Tenabo 83 20 2N 90 12W
Tenaha 75 31 57N 94 15W
Tenali 124 16 15N 80 35E
Tenancingo 83 19 0N 99 33W
Tenango 83 19 0N 99 40W
Tenasserim 128 12 6N 99 3E
Tenasserim □ 128 14 0N 98 30E
Tenay 103 45 55N 5 30E
Tenby 95 51 40N 4 42W
Tende 103 44 5N 7 35E
Tende, Col de 103 44 9N 7 32E
Tenerife, I. 114 28 20N 16 40W
Teng, R. 128 20 30N 98 10E
Tengah □ 127 2 0S 122 0E
Tengah Kepulauan 126 7 5S 118 15E
Tengchowfu = Penglai 130 37 50N 120 50E
Tenggara □ 127 3 0S 122 0E
Tenghsien, Kwangsi-Chuang, China 131 23 20N 111 0E
Tenghsien, Shantung, China 131 35 10N 117 10E
Tengiz, Ozero 120 50 30N 69 0E
Tengkow 130 39 45N 106 40E
Tenille 73 32 58N 82 50W
Tenino 80 46 51N 122 51W
Tenkasi 124 8 55N 77 20E
Tenke 116 10 32S 26 7E
Tennant Creek 134 19 30S 134 0E
Tennessee □ 69 36 0N 86 30W
Tennyson 77 38 5N 87 7W
Tenom 126 5 4N 115 38E
Tenosique 83 17 30N 91 24W
Tenryū-gawa, R. 132 35 39N 137 48E
Tent L. 55 62 25N 107 54W
Tenterfield 135 29 0S 152 0E
Teófilo Otôni 87 17 50S 41 30W
Tepalcatepec, R. 82 18 35N 101 59W
Tepehuanes 82 25 21N 105 44W
Tepetongo 82 22 28N 103 9W
Tepic 82 21 30N 104 54W
Teplice 106 50 39N 13 50E
Tepoca, C. 82 29 20N 112 25W
Tequila 82 20 54N 103 47W
Ter Apel 105 52 53N 7 5E
Ter, R. 104 42 0N 2 30E
Téramo 108 42 40N 13 40E
Terang 136 38 15S 142 55E
Tercan 122 39 50N 40 30E
Terceira 93 38 43N 27 13W
Tercero, R. 88 32 58S 61 47W
Terence Bay 39 44 28N 63 43W
Terengganu □ 128 4 55N 103 0E
Teresina 87 5 2S 42 45W
Terezinha 86 0 44N 69 27W
Tergnier 101 49 40N 3 17E
Termas de Chillan 88 36 50S 71 31W
Termez 120 37 0N 67 15E
Términi Imerese 101 37 59N 13 51E
Términos, Laguna de 83 18 35N 91 30W
Térmoli 108 42 0N 15 0E
Ternate 127 0 45N 127 25E
Terneuzen 105 51 20N 3 50E
Terney 121 45 3N 136 37E
Terni 108 42 34N 12 38E
Terra Bella 81 35 58N 119 3W
Terra Cotta 49 43 43N 79 56W
Terra Nova 37 48 30N 54 13W
Terra Nova B. 91 74 50S 164 40E
Terra Nova Nat. Park 37 48 33N 53 58W
Terra Nova, R. 37 48 40N 54 0W
Terrace 54 54 30N 128 35W
Terrace Bay 53 48 47N 87 5W
Terracina 108 41 17N 13 12E
Terralba 108 39 42N 8 38E
Terranova = Ólbia 108 40 55N 9 30E
Terrasse-Vaudreuil 44 45 24N 73 59W
Terrasson 102 45 7N 1 19E
Terre Haute 77 39 28N 87 25W
Terrebonne 44 45 42N 73 38W
Terrebonne □ 44 45 50N 74 0W
Terrebonne B. 75 29 15N 90 28W
Terrebonne Heights 44 45 44N 73 38W
Terrell 75 32 44N 96 19W
Terrenceville 37 47 40N 54 44W
Terry 74 46 47N 105 20W
Terschelling, I. 105 53 25N 5 20E
Teruel 104 40 22N 1 8W
Tervola 110 66 6N 24 49E
Tešanj 109 44 38N 17 59E
Teshio-Gawa, R. 132 44 53N 141 45E
Tesiyn Gol 129 50 40N 93 20E
Teslin 67 60 10N 132 43W
Teslin L. 54 60 15N 132 57W
Teslin, R. 54 61 34N 134 35W
Tessenderlo 105 51 4N 5 5E
Tessier 55 51 48N 107 26W
Test, R. 95 51 7N 1 30W
Teste, La 102 44 37N 1 8W
Tetachuck L. 62 53 18N 125 55W
Tetas, Pta. 88 23 31S 70 38W
Tete 117 16 13S 33 33E
Tête-à-la-Baleine 37 50 41N 59 20W
Teteven 109 42 58N 24 17E
Tethull, R. 54 60 35N 112 12W
Tetlin 67 63 14N 142 50W
Tetlin Junction 67 63 29N 142 55W
Teton, R. 78 47 58N 111 0W
Tétouan 114 35 35N 5 21W
Tetovo 109 42 1N 21 2E
Tetu L. 52 50 11N 95 2W
Tetuán = Tétouan 114 35 30N 5 25W
Tetyukhe 121 44 45N 135 40E
Teuco, R. 88 25 30S 60 25W
Teulon 57 50 23N 97 16W

Teutoburger Wald Togo

Teutoburger Wald	**106**	52 5N	8 20 E
Tevere, R.	**108**	42 30N	12 20 E
Teviot, R.	**96**	55 21N	2 51W
Tewkesbury	**95**	51 59N	2 8W
Texada I.	**62**	49 40N	124 25W
Texarkana, Ark., U.S.A.	**75**	33 25N	94 0W
Texarkana, Tex., U.S.A.	**75**	33 25N	94 3W
Texas □	**75**	31 40N	98 30W
Texas City	**75**	29 20N	95 20W
Texel, I.	**105**	53 5N	4 50 E
Texhoma	**75**	36 32N	101 47W
Texline	**75**	36 26N	103 0W
Texoma L.	**75**	34 0N	96 38W
Teziutlán	**83**	19 50N	97 30W
Tezpur	**125**	26 40N	92 45 E
Tezzeron L.	**54**	54 43N	124 30W
Tha-anne, R.	**55**	60 31N	94 37W
Tha Nun	**128**	8 12N	98 17 E
Thabana Ntlenyana, Mt.	**117**	29 30 S	29 9 E
Thabazimbi	**117**	24 40 S	26 4 E
Thai Nguyen	**128**	21 35N	105 46 E
Thailand (Siam) ■	**128**	16 0N	102 0 E
Thakhek	**128**	17 25N	104 45 E
Thal	**124**	33 28N	70 33 E
Thal Desert	**124**	31 0N	71 30 E
Thala La	**125**	28 25N	97 23 E
Thame	**95**	51 44N	0 58W
Thame, R.	**95**	51 52N	0 47W
Thames	**70**	42 35N	82 1W
Thames, R., Can.	**46**	42 20N	82 25W
Thames, R., N.Z.	**133**	37 32 S	175 45 E
Thames, R., U.K.	**95**	51 30N	0 35 E
Thames, R., U.S.A.	**71**	41 18N	72 9W
Thamesford	**46**	43 4N	81 0W
Thamesville	**46**	42 33N	81 59W
Thana	**124**	19 12N	72 59 E
Thanet, I. of	**95**	51 21N	1 20 E
Thang Binh	**128**	15 50N	108 20 E
Thanh Hoa	**128**	19 48N	105 46 E
Thanjavur (Tanjore)	**124**	10 48N	79 12 E
Thann	**101**	47 48N	7 5 E
Thaon	**101**	48 15N	6 25 E
Thar (Great Indian) Desert	**124**	28 25N	72 0 E
Tharad	**124**	24 30N	71 30 E
Thargomindah	**135**	27 58 S	143 46 E
Tharrawaddy	**125**	17 38N	95 48 E
Tharthār, Bahr ath	**122**	34 0N	43 0 E
Thásos, I.	**109**	40 40N	24 40 E
Thatcher, Ariz., U.S.A.	**79**	32 54N	109 46W
Thatcher, Colo., U.S.A.	**79**	37 38N	104 6W
Thaton	**125**	16 55N	97 22 E
Thau, Étang de	**102**	43 23N	3 36 E
Thaungdut	**125**	24 30N	94 40 E
Thayer	**75**	36 34N	91 34W
Thayetmyo	**125**	19 20N	95 18 E
Thazi	**125**	21 0N	96 5 E
The Bight	**85**	24 19N	75 24W
The Dalles	**78**	45 40N	121 11W
The Grampians, Mts.	**136**	37 0 S	142 30 E
The Great Divide	**136**	35 0 S	149 17 E
The Grenadines, Is.	**85**	12 30N	61 30W
The Hague = 's-Gravenhage	**106**	52 7N	7 14 E
The Lake	**85**	21 5N	73 34W
The Pas	**57**	53 45N	101 15W
The Rock	**136**	35 15 S	147 2 E
The Vale	**136**	33 34 S	143 49 E
Thedford, Can.	**46**	43 9N	81 51W
Thedford, U.S.A.	**74**	41 59N	100 31W
Thekulthili L.	**55**	61 3N	110 0W
Thelon, R.	**55**	62 35N	104 3W
Thénezay	**100**	46 44N	0 2W
Thenon	**102**	45 9N	1 4 E
Theodore, Austral.	**135**	24 55 S	150 3 E
Theodore, Can.	**56**	51 26N	102 55W
Thérain, R.	**101**	49 15N	2 27 E
Theresa	**71**	44 13N	75 50W
Thermaïkos Kólpos	**109**	40 15N	22 45 E
Thermopílai P.	**109**	38 48N	22 45 E
Thermopolis	**78**	43 35N	108 10W
Thesiger B.	**64**	71 30N	124 5W
Thessalía □	**109**	39 30N	22 0 E
Thessalon	**46**	46 20N	83 30W
Thessaloníki	**109**	40 38N	23 0 E
Thessaly = Thessalía	**109**	39 30N	22 0 E
Thetford	**95**	52 25N	0 44 E
Thetford Mines	**41**	46 8N	71 18W
Theux	**105**	50 32N	5 49 E
Thévet, L.	**38**	51 50N	64 12W
Thiberville	**100**	49 8N	0 27 E
Thicket Portage	**55**	55 19N	97 42W
Thief River Falls	**75**	48 15N	96 10W
Thiérache	**101**	49 51N	3 45 E
Thiers	**102**	45 52N	3 33 E
Thies	**114**	14 50N	16 51W
Thika	**116**	1 1 S	37 5 E
Thikombia, I.	**133**	15 44 S	179 55W
Thillot, Le	**101**	47 53N	6 46 E
Thimphu (Tashi Chho Dzong)	**125**	27 31N	89 45 E
þingvallavatn	**110**	64 11N	21 9W
Thionville	**101**	49 20N	6 10 E
Thírá	**109**	36 23N	25 27 E
Thirsk	**94**	54 15N	1 20W
Thisted	**111**	56 58N	8 40 E
Thistle I.	**134**	35 0 S	136 8 E
Thistletown	**50**	43 44N	79 33W
Thiu Khao Phetchabun	**128**	16 20N	100 55 E
Thívai	**109**	38 19N	23 19 E
Thiviers	**102**	45 25N	0 54 E
Thizy	**103**	46 2N	4 18 E
þjorsa	**110**	63 47N	20 48W
Thlewiaza, R., Man., Can.	**55**	59 43N	100 5W
Thlewiaza, R., N.W.T., Can.	**55**	60 29N	94 40W
Thoa, R.	**55**	60 31N	109 47W
Thoissey	**103**	46 12N	4 48 E
Thom Bay	**65**	70 9N	92 25W
Thomas, Okla., U.S.A.	**75**	35 48N	98 48W
Thomas, W. Va., U.S.A.	**72**	39 10N	79 30W
Thomas Hubbard, C.	**65**	82 0N	94 25W
Thomas Resr.	**76**	39 34N	92 39W
Thomastown	**97**	52 32N	7 10W
Thomasville, Ala., U.S.A.	**73**	31 55N	87 42W
Thomasville, Ga.., U.S.A.	**73**	30 50N	84 0W
Thomasville, N.C., U.S.A.	**73**	35 55N	80 4W
Thompson, B.C., Can.	**63**	50 15N	121 24W
Thompson, Man., Can.	**55**	55 45N	97 52W
Thompson Falls	**78**	47 37N	115 26W
Thompson Landing	**55**	62 56N	110 40W
Thompson, R., Can.	**63**	50 15N	121 24W
Thompson, R., U.S.A.	**74**	39 46N	93 37W
Thompsons	**79**	39 0N	109 50W
Thompsonville, U.S.A.	**77**	37 55N	88 46W
Thompsonville, Vt., U.S.A.	**71**	42 0N	72 37W
Thomson	**76**	41 58N	90 6W
Thomson, R.	**135**	25 11 S	142 53 E
Thonburi	**128**	13 50N	100 36 E
Thônes	**103**	45 54N	6 18 E
Thonon-les-Bains	**103**	46 22N	6 29 E
Thorburn	**39**	45 34N	62 33W
Thorhild	**60**	54 10N	113 7W
þorlákshöfn	**110**	63 51N	21 22W
Thornaby on Tees	**94**	54 36N	1 19W
Thornburn Road	**37**	47 35N	52 51W
Thornbury	**46**	44 34N	80 26W
Thorne Glacier	**91**	87 30N	150 0 E
Thornhill, Man., Can.	**57**	49 12N	98 14W
Thornhill, Ont., Can.	**50**	43 48N	79 25W
Thornton	**76**	42 57N	93 23W
Thorntown	**77**	40 8N	86 36W
Thorold	**49**	43 7N	79 12W
Thorold South	**49**	43 6N	79 12W
Thorsby	**60**	53 14N	114 3W
Thouarcé	**101**	47 17N	0 30W
Thousand Oakes	**81**	34 10N	118 50W
Thrace = Thráki	**109**	41 10N	25 30 E
Thráki	**109**	41 9N	25 30 E
Three Forks	**78**	45 55N	111 40W
Three Hills	**61**	51 43N	113 15W
Three Kings Is.	**133**	34 10 S	172 10 E
Three Lakes	**74**	45 41N	89 10W
Three Mile Plains	**39**	44 58N	64 7W
Three Oaks	**77**	41 48N	86 36W
Three Rivers, U.S.A.	**77**	41 57N	85 38W
Three Rivers, Calif., U.S.A.	**80**	36 26N	118 54W
Three Rivers, Tex., U.S.A.	**75**	28 30N	98 10W
Three Sisters, Mt.	**78**	44 10N	121 52W
þ risvatn	**110**	64 50N	19 26W
Throop	**71**	41 24N	75 39W
Throssell Ra.	**134**	17 24 S	126 4 E
þ rshöfn	**110**	66 12N	15 20W
Thrumster	**96**	58 24N	3 8W
Thubun Lakes	**55**	61 30N	112 0W
Thuddungra	**136**	34 8 S	148 8 E
Thueyts	**103**	44 41N	4 9 E
Thuin	**105**	50 20N	4 17 E
Thuir	**102**	42 38N	2 45 E
Thule	**65**	77 30N	69 0W
Thun	**106**	46 45N	7 38 E
Thunder B., Can.	**52**	48 20N	89 0W
Thunder B., U.S.A.	**70**	45 0N	83 20W
Thunder Bay	**52**	48 25N	89 15W
Thunder Cr.	**56**	50 23N	105 32W
Thunder River	**54**	52 13N	119 20W
Thung Song	**128**	8 10N	99 40 E
Thunkar	**125**	27 55N	91 0 E
Thüringer Wald	**106**	50 35N	11 0 E
Thurles	**97**	52 40N	7 53W
Thursday I.	**135**	10 30 S	142 3 E
Thurso, Can.	**40**	45 36N	75 15W
Thurso, U.K.	**96**	58 34N	3 31W
Thurso, R.	**96**	58 36N	3 30W
Thurston	**70**	39 50N	82 33W
Thurston I.	**91**	72 0 S	100 0W
Thury-Harcourt	**100**	49 0N	0 30W
Thutade L.	**54**	57 0N	126 55W
Tiahualilo	**82**	26 20N	103 30W
Tiaret	**114**	30 52N	10 10 E
Tibagi	**89**	24 30 S	50 24W
Tibagi, R.	**89**	22 47 S	51 1W
Tibati	**114**	6 22N	12 30 E
Tiber = Tevere, R.	**108**	42 30N	12 20 E
Tiber Res.	**78**	48 20N	111 15W
Tiberias	**115**	32 47N	35 32 E
Tibesti	**114**	21 0N	17 30 E
Tibet □	**129**	32 30N	86 0 E
Tibooburra	**135**	29 26 S	142 1 E
Tibugá, Golfo de	**86**	5 45N	77 20W
Tiburón, I.	**82**	29 0N	112 30W
Ticino □	**106**	46 20N	8 45 E
Ticino, R.	**108**	45 23N	8 47 E
Ticonderoga	**71**	43 50N	73 28W
Ticul	**83**	20 20N	89 50W
Tiddim	**125**	23 20N	93 45 E
Tide Head	**39**	47 59N	66 47W
Tidore	**127**	0 40N	127 25 E
Tiehling	**130**	42 25N	123 51 E
Tiel	**105**	51 53N	5 26 E
Tielt	**105**	51 0N	3 20 E
Tien Shan	**129**	42 0N	80 0 E
Tienchen	**130**	40 32N	114 0 E
Tienen	**105**	50 48N	4 57 E
Tienho	**131**	24 58N	108 35 E
Tieno	**131**	25 3N	107 3 E
Tienpao	**131**	23 25N	106 47 E
Tienshui	**131**	34 30N	105 34 E
Tientsin	**130**	39 10N	117 0 E
Tientu	**131**	18 12N	109 33 E
Tientung	**131**	23 47N	107 2 E
Tierra Alta	**86**	8 11N	76 4W
Tierra Amarilla	**88**	27 28 S	70 18W
Tierra Colorada	**83**	17 10N	99 35W
Tierra de Campos	**104**	42 10N	4 50W
Tierra del Fuego, I. Gr. de	**90**	54 0 S	69 0W
Tiétar, R.	**104**	39 55N	5 50W
Tieté, R.	**87**	20 40 S	51 35W
Tiffin	**77**	41 8N	83 10W
Tiffin, R.	**77**	41 20N	84 24W
Tiflis = Tbilisi	**120**	41 50N	44 50 E
Tifton	**73**	31 28N	83 32W
Tifu	**127**	3 39 S	126 18 E
Tigalda I.	**67**	54 9N	165 0W
Tigil	**121**	58 0N	158 10 E
Tignish	**39**	46 58N	64 2W
Tigre, R.	**86**	3 30 S	74 58W
Tigyaing	**125**	23 45N	96 10 E
Tihua	**129**	43 40N	87 50 E
Tijiamis	**127**	7 16 S	108 29 E
Tijibadok	**127**	6 53 S	106 47 E
Tijuana	**82**	32 30N	117 3W
Tikal	**84**	17 2N	89 35W
Tikamgarh	**124**	24 44N	78 57 E
Tikang	**131**	31 7N	118 2 E
Tikhoretsk	**120**	45 56N	40 5 E
Tikrit	**122**	34 35N	43 37 E
Tiksi	**121**	71 50N	129 0 E
Tilamuta	**127**	0 40N	122 15 E
Tilburg	**105**	51 31N	5 6 E
Tilbury, Can.	**46**	42 17N	82 23W
Tilbury, U.K.	**95**	51 27N	0 24 E
Tilcara	**88**	23 30 S	65 23W
Tilden	**74**	42 3N	97 45W
Tilichiki	**121**	61 0N	166 5 E
Till, R.	**94**	55 35N	2 3W
Tillamook	**78**	45 29N	123 55W
Tilley	**54**	50 28N	111 38W
Tillsonburg	**46**	42 53N	80 44W
Tilos, I.	**109**	36 27N	27 27 E
Tilston	**57**	49 23N	101 19W
Tilt, R.	**96**	56 50N	3 50W
Tilton	**71**	43 25N	71 36W
Timaru	**133**	44 23 S	171 14 E
Timber Lake	**74**	45 29N	101 0W
Timber Mtn.	**80**	37 6N	116 28W
Timberlea	**39**	44 40N	63 45W
Timbilica	**136**	37 22 S	149 42 E
Timbío	**86**	2 20N	76 40W
Timbiqui	**86**	2 46N	77 42W
Timboon	**136**	38 30 S	142 58 E
Timbuktu = Tombouctou	**114**	16 50N	3 0W
Timişoara	**107**	45 43N	21 15 E
Timmins	**53**	48 28N	81 25W
Timok, R.	**109**	44 10N	22 40 E
Timon	**87**	5 8 S	42 52W
Timor, I.	**127**	9 0 S	125 0 E
Timor Sea	**135**	10 0 S	127 0 E
Timur □	**127**	9 0 S	125 0 E
Tin Mtn.	**80**	36 54N	117 28W
Tinaca Pt.	**127**	5 30N	125 25 E
Tinaco	**86**	9 42N	68 26W
Tinambacan	**127**	12 5N	124 32 E
Tinaquillo	**86**	9 55N	68 18W
Tinchebray	**100**	48 47N	0 45W
Tindouf	**114**	27 50N	8 4W
Tingan	**131**	19 42N	110 18 E
Tinghai	**131**	30 0N	122 10 E
Tingnan	**131**	24 45N	114 50 E
Tingo María	**86**	9 10 S	76 0W
Tingpien	**130**	37 30N	107 50 E
Tingsi	**130**	35 50N	104 17 E
Tinnia	**88**	27 0 S	62 45W
Tinnoset	**111**	59 45N	9 3 E
Tinogasta	**88**	28 0 S	67 40W
Tínos	**109**	37 33N	25 8 E
Tinpak	**131**	21 40N	111 15 E
Tintagel	**62**	54 12N	125 35W
Tintina	**88**	27 2 S	62 45W
Tioga	**70**	41 54N	77 9W
Tioman, I.	**128**	2 50N	104 10 E
Tioman, Pulau, Is.	**128**	2 50N	104 10 E
Tionaga	**34**	48 0N	82 0W
Tionesta	**70**	41 29N	79 28W
Tipongpani	**125**	27 20N	95 55 E
Tipp City	**77**	39 58N	84 11W
Tippecanoe, R.	**77**	40 31N	86 47W
Tipperary	**97**	52 28N	8 10W
Tipperary □	**97**	52 37N	7 55W
Tipton, U.K.	**95**	52 32N	2 4W
Tipton, Calif., U.S.A.	**80**	36 3N	119 19W
Tipton, Ind., U.S.A.	**77**	40 17N	86 0W
Tipton, Iowa, U.S.A.	**76**	41 45N	91 12W
Tipton, Mo., U.S.A.	**76**	38 41N	92 48W
Tipton, Mt.	**81**	35 32N	114 16W
Tiptonville	**75**	36 22N	89 30W
Tīrān	**123**	32 45N	51 0 E
Tirana	**109**	41 18N	19 49 E
Tiraspol	**120**	46 55N	29 35 E
Tire	**122**	38 5N	27 50 E
Tirebolu	**122**	40 58N	38 45 E
Tiree, I.	**96**	56 31N	6 55W
Tîrgovişte	**107**	44 55N	25 27 E
Tîrgu-Jiu	**107**	45 5N	23 19 E
Tîrgu Mureş	**107**	46 31N	24 38 E
Tirich Mir Mt.	**124**	36 15N	71 35 E
Tirodi	**124**	21 35N	79 35 E
Tirol □	**106**	47 3N	10 43 E
Tirso, R.	**108**	40 33N	9 12 E
Tiruchchirappalli	**124**	10 45N	78 45 E
Tirunelveli (Tinnevelly)	**124**	8 45N	77 45 E
Tirupati	**124**	13 45N	79 30 E
Tiruvannamalai	**124**	12 10N	79 12 E
Tisa, R.	**107**	45 30N	20 20 E
Tisdale	**56**	52 50N	104 0W
Tishomingo	**75**	34 14N	96 38W
Tit-Ary	**121**	71 50N	126 30 E
Titicaca, L.	**86**	15 30 S	69 30W
Titograd	**109**	42 30N	19 19 E
Titov Veles	**109**	41 46N	21 47 E
Titovo Užice	**109**	43 55N	19 50 E
Tittabawassee, R.	**46**	43 23N	83 59W
Titule	**116**	3 15N	25 31 E
Titumate	**86**	8 19N	77 5W
Titusville	**70**	41 35N	79 39W
Tiverton, N.S., Can.	**39**	44 23N	66 13W
Tiverton, Ont., Can.	**46**	44 16N	81 32W
Tiverton, U.K.	**95**	50 54N	3 30W
Tívoli	**108**	41 58N	12 45 E
Tiwī	**123**	22 45N	59 12 E
Tizmín	**83**	21 0N	88 1W
Tiznados, R.	**86**	8 50N	67 50W
Tiznit	**114**	29 48N	9 45W
Tjalang	**127**	4 30N	95 43 E
Tjangkuang, Tg.	**126**	7 0 S	105 0 E
Tjareme, G.	**127**	6 55 S	108 27 E
Tjeggelvas	**110**	66 37N	17 45 E
Tjepu	**127**	7 12 S	111 31 E
Tjiandjur	**127**	6 51 S	107 7 E
Tjibatu	**127**	7 8 S	107 59 E
Tjikadjang	**127**	7 25 S	107 48 E
Tjimahi	**127**	6 53 S	107 33 E
Tjirebon = Cirebon	**127**	6 45 S	108 32 E
Tjörnes	**110**	66 12N	17 9W
Tjurup	**126**	4 26 S	102 13 E
Tlacolula	**83**	16 57N	96 29W
Tlacotalpán	**83**	18 37N	95 40W
Tlaquepaque	**82**	20 39N	103 19W
Tlaxcala	**83**	19 20N	98 14W
Tlaxcala □	**83**	19 30N	98 20W
Tlaxiaco	**83**	17 10N	97 40W
Tlell	**62**	53 34N	131 56W
Tlemcen	**114**	34 52N	1 15W
Toad, R.	**54**	59 25N	124 57W
Toay	**88**	36 50 S	64 30W
Toba	**132**	34 30N	136 45 E
Toba Inlet	**62**	50 25N	124 35W
Toba Kakar	**124**	31 30N	69 0 E
Toba, L.	**126**	2 40N	98 50 E
Tobago, I.	**85**	11 10N	60 30W
Tobelo	**127**	1 25N	127 56 E
Tobermory, Can.	**46**	45 12N	81 40W
Tobermory, U.K.	**96**	56 37N	6 4W
Tobin	**80**	39 55N	121 19W
Tobin L.	**56**	53 35N	103 30W
Tobique, R.	**39**	46 46N	67 42W
Toboali	**126**	3 0 S	106 25 E
Tobol	**120**	52 40N	62 39 E
Toboli	**127**	0 38 S	120 12 E
Tobolsk	**120**	58 0N	68 10 E
Tobruk = Tubruq	**115**	32 7N	23 55 E
Toby Creek	**63**	50 20N	116 25W
Tobyhanna	**71**	41 10N	75 15W
Tocantinópolis	**87**	6 20 S	47 25W
Tocantins, R.	**87**	14 30 S	49 0W
Tocca	**73**	34 32N	83 17W
Tochigi	**132**	36 25N	139 45 E
Tochigi-ken □	**132**	36 45N	139 45 E
Toconao	**88**	34 35N	83 19W
Tocópero	**86**	11 30N	69 16W
Tocopilla	**88**	22 5 S	70 10W
Tocumwal	**136**	35 45 S	145 31 E
Tocuyo, R.	**86**	10 50N	69 0W
Todeli	**127**	1 38 S	124 34 E
Todenyang	**116**	4 35N	35 56 E
Todjo	**127**	1 20 S	121 15 E
Todos os Santos, Baía de	**87**	12 48 S	38 38W
Todos Santos	**82**	23 27N	110 13W
Todos Santos, Bahia de	**82**	31 48N	116 42W
Tofield	**60**	53 25N	112 40W
Tofua I.	**133**	19 45 S	175 05W
Toghral Ombo	**129**	35 10N	81 40 E
Togian, Kepulauan	**127**	0 20 S	121 50 E
Togliatti	**120**	53 37N	49 18 E
Togo	**57**	51 24N	101 35W

Troyes — Udmurt, A.S.S.R. □

Troyes **101** 48 19N 4 3E
Trucial States = Utd. Arab Emirates **123** 24 0N 54 30E
Truckee **80** 39 20N 120 11W
Truite, L. à la **40** 47 20N 78 20W
Trujillo, Colomb. **86** 4 10N 76 19W
Trujillo, Hond. **84** 16 0N 86 0W
Trujillo, Peru **86** 8 0S 79 0W
Trujillo, Spain **104** 39 28N 5 55W
Trujillo, U.S.A. **75** 35 34N 104 44W
Trujillo, Venez. **86** 9 22N 70 26W
Truk Is. **15** 7 25N 151 46E
Trumann **75** 35 42N 90 32W
Trumbull, Mt. **79** 36 25N 113 32W
Trun **100** 48 50N 0 2E
Trundle **136** 32 53S 147 42E
Truro, Can. **39** 45 21N 63 14W
Truro, U.K. **95** 50 17N 5 2W
Truth or Consequences **79** 33 9N 107 16W
Trutnov **106** 50 37N 15 54E
Truyère, R. **102** 44 38N 2 34E
Tryon **73** 35 15N 82 16W
Tryonville **70** 41 42N 79 48W
Tsacha L. **62** 53 3N 124 50W
Tsagaan-Ükr **129** 50 20N 105 3E
Tsaidam **129** 37 0N 95 0E
Tsamkong = Chan Kiang **131** 21 15N 110 20E
Tsanghsien **130** 38 24N 116 57E
Tsangpo **129** 29 40N 89 0E
Tsaochwang **86** 35 11N 115 28E
Tsaohsien **131** 34 50N 115 45E
Tsaratanana **117** 16 47S 47 39E
Tsaring Nor **129** 34 40N 97 20E
Tsau **117** 20 8S 22 29E
Tsawassen **66** 49 1N 123 6W
Tselinograd **120** 51 10N 71 30E
Tsenkung **131** 27 3N 108 40E
Tsetserleg **129** 47 36N 101 32E
Tsetserling **130** 47 29N 101 10E
Tshabong **117** 26 2S 22 29E
Tshane **117** 24 5S 21 54E
Tshela **116** 5 4S 13 0E
Tshikapa **116** 6 17S 21 0E
Tshofa **116** 5 8S 25 8E
Tshwane **117** 22 24S 22 1E
Tsian **130** 41 12N 126 5E
Tsiaotso **131** 35 11N 113 37E
Tsihombe **117** 25 10S 45 41E
Tsimlyanskoye Vdkhr. **120** 48 0N 43 0E
Tsimo **130** 36 25N 120 29E
Tsin Ling Shan **131** 34 0N 107 30E
Tsinan **130** 34 50N 105 40E
Tsincheng **130** 35 30N 113 0E
Tsinghai **129** 35 10N 96 0E
Tsinghsien **131** 26 30N 109 30E
Tsingkiang **131** 27 50N 114 38E
Tsingliu **131** 26 0N 116 50E
Tsinglo **130** 38 40N 112 0E
Tsingning **130** 35 25N 105 50E
Tsingshih **131** 29 43N 112 13E
Tsingshuiho **130** 39 56N 111 55E
Tsingsi **130** 38 1N 114 4E
Tsingsi (Kweishun) **131** 23 6N 106 25E
Tsingtao **130** 36 0N 120 25E
Tsingtung Hu **130** 37 34N 105 40E
Tsingyuan **130** 37 43N 104 35E
Tsingyun **131** 23 45N 112 55E
Tsining **131** 35 30N 116 35E
Tsitsihar **129** 47 20N 124 0E
Tsitsutl Pk. **62** 52 43N 125 47W
Tsivory **117** 24 4S 46 5E
Tsowhsien **131** 35 29N 117 0E
Tsu **132** 34 45N 136 25E
Tsu L. **54** 60 40N 111 52W
Tsuchiura **132** 36 12N 140 15E
Tsugaru-Kaikyō **132** 41 35N 141 0E
Tsuiluan **130** 47 58N 28 27E
Tsumeb **117** 19 9S 17 44E
Tsumis **117** 23 39S 17 29E
Tsungfa **131** 23 35N 113 35E
Tsungming Tao **131** 31 40N 121 40E
Tsungsin **130** 35 2N 107 0E
Tsungtso **131** 22 26N 107 34E
Tsunhwa **130** 40 10N 117 57E
Tsuniah L. **62** 51 33N 124 4W
Tsuruga **132** 35 45N 136 2E
Tsushima, I. **132** 34 20N 129 20E
Tsushima-kaikyō **132** 34 20N 130 0E
Tsuyama **132** 35 0N 134 0E
Tual **127** 5 30S 132 50E
Tuam **97** 53 30N 8 50W
Tuamotu Arch = Touamotou **15** 17 0S 144 0W
Tuan **131** 23 59N 108 3E
Tuao **127** 17 47S 121 30E
Tuatapere **133** 46 8S 167 41E
Tuba City **79** 36 8N 111 12W
Tubac **79** 31 45N 111 2W
Tubai Is. = Toubouai, Îles **15** 25 0S 150 0W
Tuban **126** 6 57S 112 4E
Tubarão **89** 28 30S 49 0W
Tubau **126** 3 10N 113 40E
Tubbergen **105** 52 24N 6 48E
Tübingen **106** 48 31N 9 4E
Tubruq, (Tobruk) **115** 32 7N 23 55E
Tucacas **86** 10 48N 68 19W
Tuchang **131** 29 15N 116 15E
Tuchodi, R. **54** 58 17N 123 42W
Tucson **79** 32 14N 110 59W
Tucumán **88** 26 50S 65 20W
Tucumán □ **88** 26 48S 66 2W
Tucumcari **75** 35 12N 103 45W
Tucupido **86** 9 17N 65 47W
Tucupita **86** 9 14N 62 3W
Tucuracas **86** 11 45N 72 22W
Tucuruí **87** 3 42S 49 27W
Tudela **104** 42 4N 1 39W
Tudor, Lac **36** 55 50N 65 25W
Tugaske **56** 50 52N 106 17W
Tugidak I. **67** 56 30N 154 40W
Tuguegarao **127** 17 35N 121 42E
Tugur **121** 53 50N 136 45E
Tuhshan **131** 25 40N 107 30E
Tukangbesi, Kepulauan **127** 6 0S 124 0E
Tukarak I. **36** 56 15N 78 45W
Tuktoyaktuk **64** 69 27N 133 2W
Tukuyu **116** 9 17S 33 35E
Tukzar **124** 35 55N 66 25E
Tula, Hidalgo, Mexico **83** 20 0N 99 20W
Tula, Tamaulipas, Mexico **83** 23 0N 99 40W
Tula, U.S.S.R. **120** 54 13N 37 32E
Tulak **123** 33 55N 63 40E
Tulan **129** 37 24N 98 1E
Tulancingo **83** 20 5N 98 22W
Tulare **80** 36 15N 119 26W
Tulare Basin **80** 36 0N 119 48W
Tulare Lake **79** 36 0N 119 53W
Tularosa **79** 33 4N 106 1W
Tulbagh **117** 33 16S 19 6E
Tulcán **86** 0 48N 77 43W
Tulcea **107** 45 13N 28 46E
Tuléar **117** 23 21S 43 40E
Tulemalu L. **55** 62 58N 99 25W
Tuli, Indon. **127** 1 24S 122 26E
Tuli, Rhod. **117** 21 58S 29 13E
Tulkarm **115** 32 19N 35 10E
Tulla **75** 34 35N 101 44W
Tullahoma **73** 35 23N 86 12W
Tullamore, Can. **50** 43 47N 79 46W
Tullamore, Ireland **97** 53 17N 7 30W
Tulle **102** 45 16N 1 47E
Tullins **103** 45 18N 5 29E
Tullow **97** 52 48N 6 45W
Tulsa **75** 36 10N 96 0W
Tulsequah **54** 58 39N 133 35W
Tulua **86** 4 6N 76 11W
Tulun **121** 54 40N 100 10E
Tulungagung **127** 8 5S 111 54E
Tum **127** 3 28S 130 21E
Tuma, R. **84** 13 18N 84 50W
Tumaco **86** 1 50N 78 45W
Tumatumari **86** 5 20N 58 55W
Tumba, L. **116** 0 50S 18 0E
Tumbarumba **136** 35 44S 148 0E
Tumbaya **88** 23 50S 65 20W
Tumbes **86** 3 30S 80 20W
Tumen **130** 42 58N 129 49E
Tumen K. **130** 42 30N 130 0E
Tumeremo **86** 7 18N 61 30W
Tumkur **124** 13 18N 77 12E
Tummel, L. **96** 56 43N 3 55W
Tummo **114** 22 45N 14 8E
Tump **124** 26 7N 62 16E
Tumpat **128** 6 11N 102 10E
Tumucumaque, Serra de **87** 2 0N 55 0W
Tumut **136** 35 16S 148 13E
Tumwater **78** 47 0N 122 58W
Tuna, Pta. **67** 17 59N 65 53W
Tunas de Zaza **84** 21 39N 79 34W
Tunbridge Wells **95** 51 7N 0 16E
Tunduru **116** 11 0S 37 25E
Tundzha, R. **109** 42 0N 26 35E
Tung-Pei **121** 44 0N 126 0E
Tung-Shan **131** 23 40N 117 25E
Tungabhadra, R. **124** 15 30N 77 0E
Tungcheng **131** 31 0N 117 3E
Tungchow **130** 39 58N 116 50E
Tungchuan **131** 35 4N 109 2E
Tungfanghsien, (Paso) **131** 18 50N 108 33E
Tunghwa **130** 41 46N 126 0E
Tungien **131** 27 45N 109 3E
Tungjen **131** 27 40N 109 10E
Tungkang **131** 22 18N 120 29E
Tungkiang, Heilungkiang, China **130** 47 40N 132 30E
Tungkiang, Szechwan, China **131** 31 55N 107 30E
Tungkingcheng **130** 44 5N 129 15E
Tungkun **131** 23 0N 113 45E
Tungkwan **131** 34 40N 110 10E
Tungla **84** 13 24N 84 15W
Tunglan **131** 24 30N 107 23E
Tungliao **130** 43 42N 122 11E
Tungliu **131** 31 0N 117 54E
Tunglu **131** 29 50N 119 35E
Tungnafellsjökull **110** 64 45N 17 55W
Tungping **130** 35 50N 116 20E
Tungshan, Fukien, China **131** 23 40N 117 31E
Tungshan, Hupeh, China **131** 29 36N 114 28E
Tungsheng **130** 39 57N 110 0E
Tungsten, Can. **54** 61 57N 128 16W
Tungsten, U.S.A. **78** 40 50N 118 10W
Tungtai **131** 32 55N 120 15E
Tungtao **131** 26 15N 109 25E
Tungting Hu **131** 29 15N 112 30E
Tungtze **131** 27 59N 106 56E
Tunguska, Nizhmaya, R. **121** 64 0N 95 0E
Tunguska, Podkammenaya, R. **121** 61 0N 98 0E
Tungyang **131** 29 12N 120 12E
Tunhwa **130** 43 27N 128 16E
Tunhwang **129** 40 5N 94 46E
Tunia **86** 2 41N 76 31W
Tunica **75** 34 43N 90 23W
Tunis **114** 36 50N 10 11E
Tunisia ■ **114** 33 30N 9 10E
Tunja **86** 5 40N 73 25W
Tunkhannock **71** 41 32N 75 56W
Tunki **131** 29 44N 118 4E
Tunliu **130** 36 15N 112 54E
Tunnsjøen **110** 64 45N 13 25E
Tuntatuliag **67** 60 20N 162 45W
Tunulic, R. **36** 58 57N 66 50W
Tunungayualok I. **36** 56 0N 61 0W
Tunuyán **88** 33 55S 69 0W
Tunuyán, R. **88** 33 33S 67 30W
Tuolumne **80** 37 59N 120 16W
Tuolumne, R. **80** 37 36N 121 13W
Tuoy-Khaya **121** 62 32N 111 18E
Tupã **89** 21 57S 50 28W
Tuparro, R. **86** 5 0N 68 40W
Tupelo **73** 34 15N 88 42W
Tupik **121** 54 26N 119 57E
Tupinambaranas, I. **86** 3 0S 58 0W
Tupiza **88** 21 30S 65 40W
Tupman **81** 35 18N 119 21W
Tupper **54** 55 32N 120 1W
Tupper L. **71** 44 18N 74 30W
Tupungato, Cerro **88** 33 15S 69 50W
Tuque, La **41** 47 30N 72 50W
Túquerres **86** 1 5N 77 37W
Tura **121** 64 20N 99 30E
Turagua, Serranía **86** 7 20N 64 35W
Tūrān **123** 35 45N 56 50E
Turan **121** 51 38N 101 40E
Turek **107** 52 3N 18 30E
Turen **86** 9 17N 69 6W
Turfan **129** 43 6N 89 24E
Turfan Depression **129** 42 45N 89 0E
Turgeon, L. **40** 49 2N 79 4W
Turgeon, R. **40** 50 0N 78 56W
Turgutlu **122** 38 30N 27 48E
Turhal **122** 40 24N 36 19E
Turia, R. **104** 39 43N 1 0W
Turiaçl **87** 1 40S 45 28W
Turiaçl, R. **87** 3 0S 46 0W
Turin, Can. **54** 49 47N 112 24W
Turin, Alta., Can. **61** 49 58N 112 31W
Turin = Torino **108** 45 3N 7 40E
Turiy Rog **130** 45 5N 131 45E
Turkana, L. **116** 4 10N 32 10E
Turkestan **120** 43 10N 68 10E
Turkey ■ **122** 39 0N 36 0E
Turkey, R. **76** 42 43N 91 2W
Turkmen S.S.R. □ **120** 39 0N 59 0E
Turks Is. **85** 21 20N 71 20W
Turks Island Passage **85** 21 30N 71 20W
Turku (Åbo) **111** 60 30N 22 19E
Turlock **80** 37 30N 120 55W
Turnagain, C. **133** 40 28S 176 38E
Turnagain, R. **54** 59 12N 127 35W
Turnberry **55** 53 25N 101 45W
Turneffe Is. **83** 17 20N 87 50W
Turner **78** 48 52N 108 25W
Turner Valley **61** 50 40N 114 17W
Turners Falls **71** 42 36N 72 34W
Turnhout **105** 51 19N 4 57E
Turnor L. **55** 56 35N 108 35W
Turnour I. **62** 50 36N 126 27W
Turnovo **109** 43 5N 25 41E
Turnu Măgurele **107** 43 46N 24 56E
Turnu Rosu Pasul **107** 45 33N 24 17E
Turnu-Severin **107** 44 39N 22 41E
Turon **75** 37 48N 98 27W
Turriff **96** 57 32N 2 28W
Turtle L., Can. **56** 53 36N 108 38W
Turtle L., U.S.A. **74** 45 22N 92 10W
Turtle Lake **74** 47 30N 100 55W
Turtle Mt. Prov. Park **57** 49 3N 100 15W
Turtle, R. **52** 48 51N 92 45W
Turtleford **56** 53 23N 108 57W
Turūbah **122** 28 20N 43 15E
Turukhansk **121** 65 50N 87 50E
Turun ja Porin lä?ni □ **111** 60 27N 22 15E
Tuscaloosa **73** 33 13N 87 31W
Tuscar Rock **97** 52 10N 6 15W
Tuscola, Ill., U.S.A. **77** 39 48N 88 15W
Tuscola, Tex., U.S.A. **75** 32 15N 99 48W
Tuscumbia, U.S.A. **76** 38 14N 92 28W
Tuscumbia, Ala., U.S.A. **73** 34 42N 87 42W
Tushikow **130** 41 25N 115 55E
Tuskar Rock **97** 52 12N 6 10W
Tuskegee **73** 32 24N 85 39W
Tusket **39** 43 52N 65 58W
Tusket, R. **39** 43 41N 65 57W
Tutóia **87** 2 45S 42 20W
Tutong **126** 4 47N 114 34E
Tutrakan **109** 44 2N 26 40E
Tutshi L. **54** 59 56N 134 30W
Tuttlingen **106** 47 59N 8 50E
Tutuaia **127** 8 25S 127 15E
Tutuila, I. **133** 14 19S 170 50W
Tuul Gol, R. **130** 48 30N 104 25E
Tuva, A.S.S.R. □ **121** 51 30N 95 0E
Tuxedo **58** 49 52N 97 13W
Tuxford **56** 50 34N 105 35W
Tuxpan **83** 20 50N 97 30W
Tuxtla Gutiérrez **83** 16 50N 93 10W
Tuy **104** 42 3N 8 39W
Tuy Hoa **128** 13 5N 109 17E
Tuya L. **54** 59 7N 130 35W
Tuyen Hoa **128** 17 50N 106 10E
Tuyun **131** 26 15N 107 32E
Tuz Gölü **122** 38 45N 33 30E
Tuz Khurmatli **122** 34 52N 44 41E
Tūz Khurmātu **122** 34 50N 44 45E
Tuzla **109** 44 34N 18 41E
Twain **80** 40 1N 121 3W
Twain Harte **80** 38 2N 120 14W
Tweed **47** 44 29N 77 19W
Tweed, R. **94** 55 42N 2 10W
Tweedmuir **56** 53 34N 105 57W
Tweedside, N.B., Can. **39** 45 38N 67 1W
Tweedside, Ont., Can. **49** 43 10N 79 41W
Tweedsmuir Prov. Park **62** 53 0N 126 20W
Twelve Mile L. **56** 49 29N 106 14W
Twelve Pins **97** 53 32N 9 50W
Twenty Mile Creek, R. **49** 43 10N 79 22W
Twentynine Palms **81** 34 10N 116 4W
Twillingate **37** 49 42N 54 45W
Twin Bridges **78** 45 33N 112 23W
Twin City **52** 48 22N 89 25W
Twin Falls **78** 42 30N 114 30W
Twin Valley **74** 47 18N 96 15W
Twisp **63** 48 21N 120 5W
Two Creeks **60** 54 18N 116 21W
Two Harbors **52** 47 1N 91 40W
Two Hills **60** 53 43N 111 45W
Two Rivers **72** 44 10N 87 31W
Twofold B. **136** 37 8S 149 59E
Tyler, Minn., U.S.A. **74** 44 18N 96 15W
Tyler, Tex., U.S.A. **75** 32 18N 94 58W
Tyndall **57** 50 5N 96 40W
Tyndinskiy **121** 55 10N 124 43E
Tyne & Wear □ **94** 54 55N 1 35W
Tyne, R. **94** 54 58N 1 28W
Tyne Valley **39** 46 35N 63 56W
Tynemouth **94** 55 1N 1 27W
Tyre = Sūr **115** 33 19N 35 16E
Tyrell Creek **136** 35 22S 143 0E
Tyrell L. **136** 35 22S 143 0E
Tyrifjorden **111** 60 2N 10 8E
Tyrma **130** 50 0N 132 2E
Tyrol = Tirol **106** 46 50N 11 20E
Tyrone **70** 40 39N 78 10W
Tyrone □ **97** 54 40N 7 15W
Tyrone, Co. **97** 54 40N 7 15W
Tyrrell Arm **55** 62 27N 97 30W
Tyrrell, L. **136** 35 20S 142 50E
Tyrrell L. **55** 63 7N 105 27W
Tyrrell, R. **136** 35 26S 142 51E
Tyrrhenian Sea **108** 40 0N 12 30E
Tysfjörden **110** 68 10N 16 10E
Tyumen **120** 57 0N 65 18E
Tywi, R. **95** 51 48N 4 20W
Tzaneen **117** 23 47S 30 9E
Tzechung **131** 29 47N 104 50E
Tzehsien **130** 36 25N 114 24E
Tzeki **131** 27 40N 117 5E
Tzekwei **131** 31 0N 110 46E
Tzepo **130** 36 28N 117 58E
Tzetung **131** 31 31N 105 1E
Tzuyang **131** 35 44N 116 51E

U

Uainambi **86** 1 43N 69 51W
Uasadi-jidi, Sierra **86** 4 54N 65 18W
Uato-Udo **127** 4 3S 126 6E
Uatumã, R. **86** 1 30S 59 25W
Uaupés **86** 0 8S 67 5W
Uaxactún **84** 17 25N 89 29W
Ubá **89** 21 0S 43 0W
Ubaitaba **87** 14 18S 39 20W
Ubangi, R. = Oubangi **116** 1 0N 17 50E
Ubaté **86** 5 19N 73 49W
Ubauro **124** 28 15N 69 45E
Ube **132** 33 56N 131 15E
Ubeda **104** 38 3N 3 23W
Uberaba **87** 19 50S 47 55W
Uberlândia **87** 19 0S 48 20W
Ubon Ratchathani **128** 15 15N 104 50E
Ubundi **116** 0 22S 25 30E
Ucayali, R. **86** 6 0S 75 0W
Uchi Lake **52** 51 5N 92 35W
Uchiura-Wan **132** 42 25N 140 40E
Ucluelet **62** 48 57N 125 32W
Uda, R. **121** 54 42N 135 14E
Udaipur **124** 24 36N 73 44E
Udaipur Garhi **125** 27 0N 86 35E
Uddevalla **111** 58 21N 11 55E
Uden **105** 51 40N 5 37E
Udgir **124** 18 25N 77 5E
Udhampur **124** 33 0N 75 5E
Udine **108** 46 5N 13 10E
Udipi **124** 13 25N 74 42E
Udmurt, A.S.S.R. □ **120** 57 30N 52 30E

Udon Thani **Valrita**

Udon Thani 128 17 29N 102 46 E
Ueda 132 36 24N 138 16 E
Uedineniya, Os. 17 78 0N 85 0 E
Uelen 121 66 10N 170 0W
Uelzen 106 53 0N 10 33 E
Uere, R. 116 3 45N 24 45 E
Ufa 120 54 45N 55 55 E
Ugad R. 117 20 55S 14 30 E
Ugalla, R. 116 6 0S 32 0 E
Uganda ■ 116 2 0N 32 0 E
Ugine 103 45 45N 6 25 E
Uhrichsville 70 40 23N 81 22W
Uiju 130 40 15N 124 35 E
Uinta Mts. 78 40 45N 110 30W
Uitenhage 117 33 40S 25 28 E
Uithuizen 105 53 24N 6 41 E
Uivuk, C. 36 58 29N 62 34W
Uji-guntō 131 31 15N 129 25 E
Ujjain 124 23 9N 75 43 E
Ujpest 107 47 22N 19 6 E
Ujung Pandang 127 5 10S 119 20 E
Uka 121 57 50N 162 0 E
Ukerewe Is. 116 2 0S 33 0 E
Ukhrul 125 25 10N 94 25 E
Ukhta 120 63 55N 54 0 E
Ukiah 80 39 10N 123 9W
Ukraine S.S.R. □ 120 48 0N 35 0 E
Ulaan Nuur 130 44 30N 103 40 E
Ulaanbaatar 130 47 54N 106 52 E
Ulaangom 129 50 0N 92 10 E
Ulak I. 67 51 24N 178 58W
Ulan-Bator = Ulaanbaatar 130 47 54N 106 52 E
Ulan Ude 121 52 0N 107 30 E
Ulanhot 130 46 5N 122 1 E
Ulcinj 109 41 58N 19 10 E
Uldz Gol 130 49 30N 114 0 E
Ulhasnagar 124 19 15N 73 10 E
Ulladulla 136 35 21S 150 29 E
Ullapool 96 57 54N 5 10W
Ullswater, L. 94 54 35N 2 52W
Ullŭng Do 130 37 30N 130 30 E
Ulm 106 48 23N 10 0 E
Ulricehamn 111 57 46N 13 26 E
Ulster □ 97 54 45N 6 30W
Ulverston 94 54 13N 3 7W
Ulverstone 135 41 11S 146 11 E
Ulya 121 59 10N 142 0 E
Ulyanovsk 120 54 25N 48 25 E
Ulyasutay, (Javhlant) 129 47 56N 97 28 E
Ulysses 75 37 39N 101 25W
Umala 86 17 25S 68 5W
Umánaé 17 70 40N 52 10W
Umánaé Fjord 10 70 40N 52 0W
Umanak 65 70 58N 52 0W
Umaria 125 23 35N 80 50 E
Umarkot 70 25 15N 69 40 E
Umatilla 78 45 58N 119 17W
Umba 120 66 50N 34 20 E
Umbrella Mts. 133 45 35S 169 5 E
Umbria □ 108 42 53N 12 30 E
Ume, R. 110 64 45N 18 30 E
Umeå 110 63 45N 20 20 E
Umera 127 0 12S 129 30 E
Umfreville L. 52 50 18N 94 45W
Umiat 67 69 25N 152 20W
Umm al Qaiwain 123 25 30N 55 35 E
Umm az Zamul 123 22 35N 55 18 E
Umm Lajj 122 25 0N 37 23 E
Umm Said 123 25 0N 51 40 E
Umnak. 67 53 20N 168 20W
Umnak I. 67 53 0N 168 0W
Umniati, R. 117 18 0S 29 0 E
Umpang 128 16 3N 98 54 E
Umpqua, R. 78 43 30N 123 30W
Umtali 117 18 58S 32 38 E
Umtata 117 31 36S 28 49 E
Umvuma 117 19 16S 30 30 E
Umzimvubu, R. 117 31 38S 29 33 E
Unac, R. 108 44 42N 16 15 E
Unadilla 71 42 20N 75 17W
Unalanaska I. 67 54 0N 164 30W
Uncia 86 18 25S 66 40W
Uncompahgce Pk., Mt. 79 38 5N 107 32W
Underbool 136 35 10S 141 51 E
Ungarie 136 33 38S 146 56 E
Ungava B. 36 59 30N 67 30W
Ungava Pen. 36 60 0N 75 0W
Unggi 130 42 16N 130 28 E
União 87 4 50S 37 50W
União da Vitória 89 26 5S 51 0W
Unimak I. 67 54 30N 164 30W
Unimak Pass. 67 53 30N 165 15W
Union, Mo., U.S.A. 76 38 25N 91 0W
Union, N.J., U.S.A. 71 40 47N 74 3W
Union, S.C., U.S.A. 73 34 49N 81 39W
Union Bay 62 49 35N 124 53W
Union City, N.J., U.S.A. 71 40 47N 74 5W
Union City, Ohio, U.S.A. 77 40 11N 84 49W
Union City, Pa., U.S.A. 70 41 53N 79 50W
Union City, Tenn., U.S.A. 71 36 25N 89 0W
Union Gap 73 46 38N 120 29W
Union Grove 77 42 41N 88 3W
Union I. 62 50 0N 127 16W
Unión, La, Chile 90 40 10S 73 0W
Unión, La, Colomb. 86 1 35N 77 5W
Unión, La, El Sal. 83 13 20N 87 50W
Union, La 82 17 58N 101 49W
Unión, La 86 7 28N 67 53W
Union, Mt. 79 34 34N 112 21W
Union of Soviet Soc. Rep. ■ 121 47 0N 100 0 E
Union Springs 73 32 9N 85 44W
Union Star 76 39 59N 94 36W
Uniontown, U.S.A. 77 37 47N 87 56W
Uniontown, Pa., U.S.A. 72 39 54N 79 45W
Unionville, Can. 50 43 52N 79 18W
Unionville, U.S.A. 76 40 29N 93 1W
Unionville, Mich., U.S.A. 46 43 39N 83 28W
United Arab Emirates ■ 123 23 50N 54 0 E
United Arab Republic ■ 113 27 5N 30 0 E
United States of America ■ 69 37 0N 96 0W
United States Range 65 82 25N 68 0W
Unity 56 52 30N 109 5W
University City 76 38 40N 90 20W
University, R. 53 47 55N 85 12W
Unnao 125 26 35N 80 30 E
Unst, I. 96 60 50N 0 55W
Unturán, Sierra de 86 1 35N 64 40W
Unuk, R. 54 56 5N 131 3W
Ünye 122 41 5N 37 15 E
Upata 86 8 1N 62 24W
Upemba, L. 116 8 30S 26 20 E
Upernavik 65 72 49N 56 20W
Upington 117 28 25S 21 15 E
Uplands, B.C., Can. 63 48 27N 123 17W
Uplands, Sask., Can. 58 50 29N 104 36W
Upolu, I. 133 13 58S 172 0W
Upolu Pt. 67 20 16N 155 52W
Upper Alkali Lake 78 41 47N 120 0W
Upper Arlington 77 40 0N 83 4W
Upper Arrow L. 63 50 30N 117 50W
Upper Blackville 39 46 39N 65 52W
Upper Campbell L. 62 49 55N 125 39W
Upper Foster L. 55 56 47N 105 20W
Upper Goose L. 52 51 43N 92 43W
Upper Humber R. 37 49 11N 57 28W
Upper Hutt 133 41 8S 175 5 E
Upper Klamath L. 78 42 16N 121 55W
Upper L. Erne 97 54 14N 7 22W
Upper Lachute 43 45 40N 74 14W
Upper Lake 80 39 10N 122 55W
Upper Manitou L. 52 49 24N 92 48W
Upper Musquodoboit 39 45 10N 62 58W
Upper Red L., U.S.A. 52 48 10N 94 40W
Upper Red L., U.S.A. 74 48 0N 95 0W
Upper Sandusky 77 40 50N 83 17W
Upper Stewiacke 39 45 13N 63 0W
Upper Volta ■ 114 12 0N 0 30W
Uppsala 111 59 53N 17 38 E
Uppsala län □ 111 60 0N 17 30 E
Upsala 52 49 3N 90 28W
Upton, Can. 41 45 39N 72 41W
Upton, U.S.A. 74 44 8N 104 35W
Ur 122 30 55N 46 25 E
Urabá, Golfo de 86 8 25N 76 53W
Uracará 86 2 20S 57 50W
Ural Mts. = Uralskie Gory 120 60 0N 59 0 E
Ural, R. 120 49 0N 52 0W
Uralsk 120 51 20N 51 20 E
Uralskie Gory 120 60 0N 59 0 E
Urana 136 35 15S 146 21 E
Urandangi 135 21 32S 138 14 E
Uranium City 55 59 34N 108 37W
Uraricaá, R. 86 3 20N 61 56W
Urawa 132 35 50N 139 40 E
Uray 120 60 5N 65 15 E
Urbana, U.S.A. 76 37 51N 93 10W
Urbana, Ill., U.S.A. 77 40 7N 88 12W
Urbana, Ohio, U.S.A. 77 40 9N 83 44W
Urbana, La 86 7 8N 66 56W
Urbandale 76 41 38N 93 43W
Urbino 108 43 43N 12 38 E
Urbión, Picos de 104 42 1N 2 52W
Urcos 86 13 30S 71 30W
Urdinarrain 88 32 37S 58 52W
Urdos 102 42 51N 0 35W
Urdzhar 120 47 5N 81 38 E
Ure, R. 94 54 20N 1 25W
Ures 82 29 30N 110 30W
Urfa 122 37 12N 38 50 E
Urfahr 106 48 19N 14 17 E
Urgench 120 41 40N 60 30 E
Urgun 123 32 55N 69 12 E
Uribante, R. 86 7 25N 71 50W
Uribe 86 3 13N 74 24W
Uribia 86 11 43N 72 16W
Uriondo 88 21 41S 64 41W
Urique 82 27 13N 107 55W
Urique, R. 82 26 29N 107 58W
Urk 105 52 39N 5 36 E
Urla 122 38 20N 26 55 E
Urmia, L. 122 37 30N 45 30 E
Urmia (Rezā'iyeh) 122 37 40N 45 0 E
Urrao 86 6 20N 76 11W
Ursula Chan. 62 53 25N 128 55W
Uruaca 87 15 30S 49 41W
Uruapán 82 19 30N 102 0W
Urubamba 86 13 5S 72 10W
Urubamba, R. 86 11 0S 73 0W
Uruçuí 87 7 20S 44 28W
Uruguai, R. 89 24 0S 53 30W
Uruguaiana 88 29 50S 57 0W
Uruguay ■ 88 32 30S 55 30W
Uruguay, R. 88 28 0S 56 0W
Urumchi = Wulumuchi 129 43 40N 87 50 E
Urungu 129 46 30N 88 50 E
Urup, I. 121 43 0N 151 0 E
Uruyén 86 5 41N 62 25W
Uruzgan □ 124 33 30N 66 0 E
Usa 120 2 23S 36 52 E
Uşak 122 38 43N 29 28 E
Usakos 117 22 0S 15 31 E
Usedom 106 53 50N 13 55 E
Useko 116 5 8S 32 24 E
Ush-Tobe 120 45 16N 78 0 E
Ushakova, O. 17 82 0N 80 0 E
Ushant = Ouessant, Île d' 100 48 25N 5 5W
Ushuaia 90 54 50S 68 23W
Ushumun 121 52 47N 126 32 E
Usk, R. 95 51 37N 2 56W
Üsküdar 122 41 0N 29 5 E
Usolye Sibirskoye 121 52 40N 103 40 E
Uspallata, P. de 88 32 30S 69 28W
Uspenskiy 120 48 50N 72 55 E
Ussel 102 45 32N 2 18 E
Ussuriysk 130 43 40N 131 50 E
Ust Aldan = Batamay 121 63 30N 129 15 E
Ust Amginskoye = Khandyga 121 62 30N 134 50 E
Ust-Bolsheretsk 121 52 40N 156 30 E
Ust Ilga 121 55 5N 104 55 E
Ust Ilimpeya = Yukti 121 63 20N 105 0 E
Ust-Ilimsk 121 58 3N 102 39 E
Ust Ishim 120 57 45N 71 10 E
Ust Kamchatsk 121 56 10N 162 0 E
Ust Kamenogorsk 120 50 0N 82 20 E
Ust Karenga 121 54 40N 116 45 E
Ust Khayryuzova 121 57 15N 156 55 E
Ust Kut 121 56 50N 105 10 E
Ust Kuyga 121 70 1N 135 36 E
Ust Maya 121 60 30N 134 20 E
Ust Mil 121 59 50N 133 0 E
Ust Nera 121 64 35N 143 15 E
Ust Olenek 121 73 0N 120 10 E
Ust-Omchug 121 61 9N 149 38 E
Ust Port 120 70 0N 84 10 E
Ust Tsilma 120 65 25N 52 0 E
Ust-Tungir 121 55 25N 120 15 E
Ust Urt = Ustyurt 120 44 0N 55 0 E
Ust Vorkuta 120 67 7N 63 35 E
Ustaritz 102 43 24N 1 27W
Ustí nad Labem 106 50 41N 14 3 E
Ustica, I. 108 38 42N 13 10 E
Ustye 121 55 30N 97 30 E
Ustyurt, Plato 120 44 0N 55 0 E
Usuki 132 33 8N 131 49 E
Usulután 84 13 25N 88 28W
Usumacinta, R. 83 17 0N 91 0W
Utah □ 78 39 30N 111 30W
Utah, L. 78 40 10N 111 58W
Ute Cr. 75 36 5N 103 45W
Utete 116 8 0S 38 45 E
Uthai Thani 128 15 22N 100 3 E
Uthmaniyah 122 25 5N 49 6 E
Utiariti 86 13 0S 58 10W
Utica, Mich., U.S.A. 46 42 38N 83 2W
Utica, N.Y., U.S.A. 71 43 5N 75 18W
Utica, Ohio, U.S.A. 70 40 13N 82 26W
Utik L. 55 55 15N 96 0W
Utikuma L. 60 55 50N 115 30W
Utrecht, Neth. 105 52 3N 5 8 E
Utrecht, S. Afr. 117 27 38S 30 20 E
Utrecht □ 105 52 6N 5 7 E
Utrera 104 37 12N 5 48W
Utsjoki 110 69 51N 26 59 E
Utsunomiya 132 36 30N 139 50 E
Uttar Pradesh □ 124 27 0N 80 0 E
Uttaradit 128 17 36N 100 5 E
Utterson 70 45 13N 79 20W
Uttoxeter 94 52 53N 1 50W
Uudenmaan lä ni □ 111 60 25N 25 0 E
Uuldza 130 49 8N 112 10 E
Uusikaarlepyy 110 63 32N 22 31 E
Uusikaupunki 111 60 47N 21 25 E
Uvalde 75 29 15N 99 48W
Uvat 120 59 5N 68 50 E
Uvinza 116 5 5S 30 24 E
Uvira 116 3 22S 29 3 E
Uvs Nuur 129 50 20N 92 30 E
Uwainid 122 24 50N 46 0 E
Uwajima 132 33 10N 132 35 E
Uxbridge 46 44 6N 79 7W
Uxmal 83 20 22N 89 46W
Uyuni 88 20 35S 66 55W
Uyuni, Salar de 88 20 10S 68 0W
Uzbekistan S.S.R. □ 120 40 5N 65 0 E
Uzerche 102 45 25N 1 35 E
Uzès 103 44 1N 4 26 E

V

Vaal, R. 117 27 40S 25 30 E
Vaasan lääni □ 110 63 2N 22 50 E
Vabre 102 43 42N 2 24 E
Vác 107 47 49N 19 10 E
Vacaria 89 28 31S 50 52W
Vacaville 80 38 21N 122 0W
Vach, R. 120 60 56N 76 38 E
Vache, I.-à 85 18 2N 73 35W
Vadodara 124 22 20N 73 10 E
Vadsø 110 70 3N 29 50 E
Vaerøy 110 67 40N 12 40 E
Vagney 101 48 1N 6 43 E
Váh, R. 107 49 10N 18 20 E
Vaigach 120 70 10N 59 0 E
Vaiges 100 48 2N 0 30W
Vaihsel B. 91 75 0S 35 0W
Vailly Aisne 101 49 25N 3 30 E
Vaison 103 44 14N 5 4 E
Val-Alain 41 46 24N 71 45W
Val-Barrette 40 46 30N 75 21W
Val Brillant 38 48 32N 67 33W
Val Caron 46 46 37N 81 1W
Val d' Ajol, Le 101 47 55N 6 30 E
Val-de-Marne □ 101 48 45N 2 28 E
Val-des-Bois 40 45 54N 75 35W
Val-d'Espoir 38 48 31N 64 24W
Val-d'Oise □ 101 49 5N 2 0 E
Val d'Or 40 48 7N 77 47W
Val Marie 56 49 15N 107 45W
Val-St-Michael 42 46 52N 71 27W
Valahia 107 44 35N 25 0 E
Valcheta 90 40 40S 66 20W
Valcourt 41 45 29N 72 18W
Valdahon, Le 101 47 8N 6 20 E
Valdepeñas 104 38 43N 3 25W
Valdes I. 63 49 4N 123 39W
Valdes Pen. 90 42 30S 63 45W
Valdez 67 61 14N 146 10W
Valdezia 97 23 5S 30 14 E
Valdivia 90 39 50S 73 14W
Valdivia □ 90 40 0S 73 0W
Valdivia, La 88 34 43S 72 5W
Valdosta 73 30 50N 83 20W
Vale 78 44 0N 117 15W
Valemount 63 52 50N 119 15W
Valença 87 13 20S 39 5W
Valença do Piauí 87 6 20S 41 45W
Valence 103 44 57N 4 54 E
Valence-d'Agen 102 44 8N 0 54 E
Valencia, Spain 104 39 27N 0 23W
Valencia, Venez. 86 10 11N 68 0W
Valencia □ 104 39 20N 0 40W
Valencia, Albufera de 104 39 20N 0 27W
Valencia de Alcántara 104 39 25N 7 14W
Valencia, G. de 104 39 30N 0 20 E
Valencia, L. de 85 10 13N 67 40W
Valenciennes 101 50 20N 3 34 E
Valensole 103 43 50N 5 59 E
Valentia Hr. 97 51 56N 10 17W
Valentia I. 97 51 54N 10 22W
Valentine, Nebr., U.S.A. 74 42 50N 100 35W
Valentine, Tex., U.S.A. 75 30 36N 104 28W
Valenton 78 48 45N 2 28 E
Valera 86 9 19N 70 37W
Valier 78 48 25N 112 9W
Valinco, G. de 103 41 40N 8 52 E
Valjevo 109 44 18N 19 53 E
Valkeakoski 111 61 16N 24 2 E
Valkenswaard 105 51 21N 5 29 E
Valladolid, Mexico 83 20 30N 88 20W
Valladolid, Spain 104 41 38N 4 43W
Valle d'Aosta □ 108 45 45N 7 22 E
Valle de la Pascua 86 9 13N 66 0W
Valle de las Palmas 81 32 20N 116 43W
Valle de Santiago 82 20 25N 101 15W
Valle de Zaragoza 82 27 28N 105 49W
Valle del Cauca □ 86 3 45N 76 30W
Valle Fértil, Sierra del 88 30 20S 68 0W
Valle Hermosa 83 25 35N 102 25 E
Valle Nacional 83 17 47N 96 19W
Vallecas 104 40 23N 3 41W
Valledupar 86 10 29N 73 15W
Vallée-Jonction 41 46 22N 70 55W
Vallejo 80 38 12N 122 15W
Vallenar 88 28 30S 70 50W
Valleraugue 102 44 6N 3 39 E
Vallet 100 47 10N 1 15W
Valletta 108 35 54N 14 30 E
Valley Center 81 33 13N 117 2W
Valley City 74 46 57N 98 0W
Valley Falls 78 42 33N 120 8W
Valley Park 76 38 33N 90 29W
Valley Springs 80 38 11N 120 50W
Valley Station 77 38 10N 85 50W
Valley Wells 81 35 27N 115 46W
Valleyfield 34 45 15N 74 8W
Valleyview, Alta., Can. 60 55 5N 117 17W
Valleyview, B.C., Can. 63 50 10N 120 13W
Vallimanca, Arroyo 88 35 40S 59 10W
Vallon 103 44 25N 4 23 E
Valls 104 41 18N 1 15 E
Valmeyer 76 38 18N 90 19W
Valmont 100 49 45N 0 30 E
Valmy 101 49 5N 4 45 E
Valognes 100 49 30N 1 28W
Valora 52 49 46N 91 13W
Valparaíso, Chile 88 33 2S 71 40W
Valparaíso, Mexico 82 22 50N 103 32W
Valparaiso 77 41 27N 87 2W
Valparaiso □ 88 33 2S 71 40W
Valréas 103 44 24N 5 0 E
Valrita 53 49 27N 82 33W

Vals-les-Bains Villa Guillermina

Vals-les-Bains 103 44 42N 4 24E
Vals, Tanjung 127 8 32S 137 32E
Valsbaai 117 34 15S 18 40E
Valverde del Camino 104 37 35N 6 47W
Van 122 38 30N 43 20E
Van Alstyne 75 33 25N 96 36W
Van Bruyssel 41 47 56N 72 9W
Van Buren, Can. 39 47 10N 67 55W
Van Buren, Ark., U.S.A. 75 35 28N 94 18W
Van Buren, Me., U.S.A. 73 47 10N 68 1W
Van Buren, Mo., U.S.A. 75 37 0N 91 0W
Van Diemen, C. 135 11 9S 130 24E
Van Diemen G. 134 11 45S 131 50E
Van Gölü 122 38 30N 43 0E
Van Horn 79 31 3N 104 55W
Van Horne 76 42 1N 92 4W
Van Tassell 74 42 40N 104 3W
Van Wert 77 40 52N 84 31W
Vananda 62 49 46N 124 33W
Vanavara 121 60 22N 102 16E
Vanceburg 77 38 36N 83 19W
Vancouver, Can. 66 49 15N 123 10W
Vancouver, U.S.A. 80 45 44N 122 41W
Vancouver Harb. 66 49 18N 123 5W
Vancouver I. 62 49 50N 126 0W
Vancouver I. Ranges 62 49 30N 125 40W
Vancouver International Airport 66 48 12N 123 11W
Vandalia, Ill., U.S.A. 76 38 57N 89 4W
Vandalia, Mo., U.S.A. 76 39 19N 91 29W
Vandalia, Mo., U.S.A. 76 39 18N 91 30W
Vandalia, Ohio, U.S.A. 77 39 54N 84 12W
Vandenburg 81 34 35N 120 44W
Vanderbijlpark 118 26 42S 27 54E
Vanderbilt 46 45 9N 84 40W
Vandergrift 70 40 36N 79 33W
Vanderhoof 62 54 0N 124 0W
Vanderlin I. 135 15 44S 137 2E
Vandry 41 47 52N 73 34W
Vänern 111 58 47N 13 30E
Vänersborg 111 58 26N 12 27E
Vanessa 49 42 58N 80 24W
Vang Vieng 128 18 58N 102 32E
Vanga 116 4 35S 39 12E
Vangaindrano 117 23 21S 47 36E
Vanguard 56 49 55N 107 20W
Vanier, Ont., Can. 48 45 27N 75 40W
Vanier, Qué., Can. 42 46 49N 71 15W
Vankleek Hill 47 45 32N 74 40W
Vanna 110 70 6N 19 50E
Vannas 110 63 58N 19 48E
Vannes 100 47 40N 2 47W
Vanoise, Massif de la 103 45 25N 6 40E
Vanrhynsdorp 117 31 36S 18 44E
Vans, Les 103 44 25N 4 7E
Vansbro 111 60 32N 14 15E
Vanscoy 56 52 0N 106 59W
Vansittart B. 134 14 3S 126 17E
Vansittart I. 65 65 50N 84 0W
Vanua Levu, I. 133 16 33S 178 8E
Vanua Mbalavu, I. 133 17 40S 178 57W
Var □ 103 43 27N 6 18E
Varades 100 47 25N 1 1W
Varanasi (Benares) 125 25 22N 83 8E
Varangerfjorden 110 70 3N 29 25E
Varazdin 108 46 20N 16 20E
Varberg 111 57 17N 12 20E
Vardar, R. 109 41 25N 22 20E
Varennes 43 45 39N 73 28W
Varennes-sur-Allier 102 46 19N 3 24E
Varese 108 45 49N 8 50E
Varginha 89 21 33S 45 25W
Varillas 88 24 0S 70 10W
Värmlands län □ 111 59 45N 13 20E
Varna, Bulg. 109 43 13N 27 56E
Varna, U.S.A. 76 41 2N 89 14W
Varnamo 111 57 10N 14 3E
Vars 47 45 21N 75 21W
Varto 122 39 10N 41 28E
Varzaneh 123 32 25N 52 40E
Varzy 101 47 22N 3 20E
Vasa 110 63 6N 21 38E
Vasa Barris, R. 87 11 10S 37 10W
Vascongadas 104 42 50N 2 45W
Vasht = Khāsh 123 28 20N 61 6E
Vaslui 107 46 38N 27 42E
Vassa 110 63 6N 21 38E
Vassar, Can. 57 49 10N 95 55W
Vassar, U.S.A. 46 43 23N 83 33W
Västerås 111 59 37N 16 38E
Västerbottens län □ 110 64 58N 18 0E
Västerdalälven 111 60 30N 13 25E
Västernorrlands län □ 110 63 30N 17 40E
Västervik 111 57 43N 16 43E
Västmanland □ 111 59 55N 16 30E
Vasto 108 42 8N 14 40E
Vatan 101 47 4N 1 50E
Vatnajökull 110 64 30N 16 48W
Vatneyri 110 65 35N 24 0W
Vatoa, I. 133 19 50S 178 13W
Vatomandry 117 19 20S 48 59E
Vatra-Dornei 107 47 22N 25 22E
Vättern, L. 111 58 25N 14 30E
Vaucluse 43 45 54N 73 26W
Vaucluse □ 103 44 3N 5 10E
Vaucouleurs 101 48 37N 5 40E
Vaudreuil 44 45 24N 74 1W
Vaudreuil □ 44 45 25N 74 15W
Vaudreul-sur-le-Lac 44 45 25N 74 3W
Vaughan 79 34 37N 105 12W
Vaughn 78 47 37N 111 36W
Vaupés □ 86 1 0N 71 0W
Vaupés, R. 86 1 0N 71 0W
Vauvert 103 43 42N 4 17E
Vauxhall 61 50 5N 112 9W
Vavàu, I. 133 18 36S 174 0W
Vavenby 63 51 36N 119 43W
Vavincourt 101 48 49N 5 12E
Växjö 111 56 52N 14 50E
Vaygach, Ostrov 120 70 0N 60 0E
Vaza Barris, R. 87 10 0S 37 30W
Vedea, R. 107 44 0N 25 20E
Vedia 88 34 30S 61 31W
Vedrin 105 50 30N 4 52E
Veendam 105 53 5N 6 52E
Vefsna 110 65 48N 13 10E
Vega 75 35 18N 102 26W
Vega Baja 67 18 27N 66 23W
Vega Fd. 110 65 37N 12 0E
Vega, I. 110 65 42N 11 50E
Vega, La 85 19 20N 70 30W
Veghel 105 51 37N 5 32E
Vegreville 60 53 30N 112 5W
Veinticino de Mayo 88 38 0S 67 40W
Vejer de la Frontera 104 36 15N 5 59W
Vejle 111 55 43N 9 30E
Velarde 79 36 11N 106 1W
Velas, C. 84 10 21N 85 52W
Velasco 75 29 0N 95 20W
Velasco, Sierra de. 88 29 20S 67 10W
Velay, Mts. du 102 45 0N 3 40E
Velebit Planina 108 44 50N 15 20E
Vélez 86 6 1N 73 41W
Vélez Málaga 104 36 48N 4 5W
Vélez Rubio 104 37 41N 2 5W
Velhas, R. 87 17 13S 44 49W
Velikiye Luki 120 56 25N 30 32E
Velikonda Range 124 14 45N 79 10E
Velletri 108 41 43N 12 43E
Vellir 110 65 55N 18 28W
Vellore 124 12 57N 79 10E
Velsen-Noord 105 52 27N 4 40E
Velva 74 48 6N 100 56W
Venado 82 22 50N 101 10W
Venado Tuerto 88 33 50S 62 0W
Venarey-les-Laumes 101 47 32N 4 26E
Vence 103 43 43N 7 6E
Vendée □, France 100 46 50N 1 35W
Vendée □, France 102 46 40N 1 20W
Vendée, Collines de 100 46 35N 0 45W
Vendée, R. 100 46 30N 0 45W
Vendeuvre-sur-Barse 101 48 14N 4 28E
Vendôme 100 47 47N 1 3E
Venetie 67 67 0N 146 30W
Véneto □ 108 45 40N 12 0E
Venézia 108 45 27N 12 20E
Venézia, Golfo di 108 45 20N 13 0E
Venezuela ■ 86 8 0N 65 0W
Venezuela, Golfo de 86 11 30N 71 0W
Vengurla 124 15 53N 73 45E
Venice = Venézia 108 45 27N 12 20E
Venise 43 45 5N 73 8W
Vénissieux 103 45 43N 4 53E
Venkatapuram 125 18 20N 80 30E
Venlo 105 51 22N 6 11E
Venosta 40 45 52N 76 1W
Venraij 105 51 31N 6 0E
Venta, La 83 18 8N 94 3W
Ventana, Punta de la 82 24 4N 109 48W
Ventnor 95 50 35N 1 12W
Ventspils 111 57 25N 21 32E
Ventuari, R. 86 5 20N 66 0W
Ventucopa 81 34 50N 119 29W
Ventura 81 34 16N 119 18W
Ventura, La 82 24 38N 100 54W
Venturosa, La 86 6 8N 68 48W
Vera, Argent. 88 29 30S 60 20W
Vera, Spain 104 37 15N 1 15W
Veracruz 83 19 10N 96 10W
Veracruz □ 83 19 0N 96 15W
Veraval 124 20 53N 70 27E
Vercelli 108 45 19N 8 25E
Verchères 45 45 47N 73 21W
Verchères □ 43 45 45N 73 15W
Verdalsøra 110 63 48N 11 30E
Verde, R., Argent. 90 41 55S 66 0W
Verde, R., Chihuahua, Mexico 82 26 59N 107 58W
Verde, R., Oaxaca, Mexico 82 15 59N 97 50W
Verde, R., Veracruz, Mexico 83 21 10N 102 50W
Verde, R., Parag. 88 23 9S 57 37W
Verden 107 52 58N 9 18E
Verdi 80 39 31N 119 59W
Verdigre 74 42 38N 98 0W
Verdon-sur-Mer, Le 102 45 33N 1 4W
Verdun, Can. 44 45 27N 73 34W
Verdun, France 101 49 12N 5 24E
Verdun-sur-le Doubs 101 46 54N 5 0E
Vereeniging 117 26 38S 27 57E
Veregin 57 51 35N 102 5W
Vérendrye, Parc Prov. de la 40 47 20N 76 40W
Vergennes 71 44 9N 73 15W
Vergt 102 45 2N 0 43E
Verkhoyansk 121 67 50N 133 50E
Verkhoyanskiy Khrebet 121 66 0N 129 0E
Verlo 56 50 19N 108 35W
Vermenton 101 47 40N 3 42E
Vermeulle, L. 36 54 43N 69 24W
Vermilion 60 53 20N 110 50W
Vermilion, B. 75 29 45N 91 55W
Vermilion Bay 52 49 51N 93 34W
Vermilion Chutes 54 58 22N 114 51W
Vermilion L. 52 50 3N 92 13W
Vermilion Pass 63 51 15N 116 2W
Vermilion, R., Alta., Can. 60 53 22N 110 51W
Vermilion, R., Qué., Can. 41 47 38N 72 56W
Vermilion, R., Ill., U.S.A. 77 41 19N 89 5W
Vermilion, R., Ind., U.S.A. 77 39 57N 87 27W
Vermillion 74 42 50N 96 56W
Vermillion L. 52 47 53N 92 25W
Vermont 76 40 18N 90 26W
Vermont □ 71 43 40N 72 50W
Vernal 78 40 28N 109 35W
Vernalis 80 37 36N 121 17W
Verner 46 46 25N 80 8W
Verneuil-sur-Avre 100 48 45N 0 55E
Vernon, Can. 63 50 20N 119 15W
Vernon, France 100 49 5N 1 30E
Vernon, U.S.A. 75 34 10N 99 20W
Vernon, U.S.A. 76 38 48N 89 5W
Vernon, U.S.A. 77 38 59N 85 36W
Vernonia 80 45 52N 123 11W
Vero Beach 73 27 39N 80 23W
Véroia 109 40 34N 22 18E
Véron, L. 38 51 48N 65 7W
Verona, Can. 47 44 29N 76 42W
Verona, Italy 108 45 27N 11 0E
Verona, U.S.A. 76 42 59N 89 32W
Veropol 121 66 0N 168 0E
Versailles, France 101 48 48N 2 8E
Versailles, Ill., U.S.A. 76 39 53N 90 39W
Versailles, Ind., U.S.A. 77 39 4N 85 15W
Versailles, Ky., U.S.A. 77 38 3N 84 44W
Versailles, Mo., U.S.A. 76 38 26N 92 51W
Versailles, Ohio, U.S.A. 77 40 13N 84 29W
Vert I. 52 48 55N 88 3W
Verte, I. 41 48 2N 69 26W
Vertou 100 47 10N 1 28W
Vertus 101 48 54N 4 0E
Verviers 105 50 37N 5 52E
Vervins 101 49 50N 3 53E
Verwood 55 49 30N 105 40W
Vesle, R. 101 49 17N 3 50E
Vesoul 101 60 40N 6 11E
Vest-Agder fylke □ 111 58 30N 7 15E
Vesta 84 9 43N 83 3W
Vesterålen 110 68 45N 14 30E
Vestfjorden 110 67 55N 14 0E
Vestfold fylke □ 111 59 15N 10 0E
Vestmannaeyjar 110 63 27N 20 15W
Vestspitsbergen 17 78 40N 17 0E
Vestvågøy 110 68 18N 13 50E
Vesuvio 108 40 50N 14 22E
Vesuvius, Mt. = Vesuvio 108 40 50N 14 22E
Veszprém 107 47 8N 17 57E
Veteran 61 52 0N 111 7W
Vetlanda 111 57 24N 15 3E
Vetlugu, R. 120 57 0N 45 25E
Vettore, Mte. 108 44 38N 7 5E
Vevay 77 38 45N 85 4W
Veys 122 31 30N 49 0E
Vézelise 101 48 30N 6 5E
Vezhen, mt. 109 42 50N 24 20E
Viacha 86 16 30S 68 5W
Viana, Brazil 87 3 0S 44 40W
Viana, Port. 104 38 20N 8 0W
Viana do Castelo 104 41 42N 8 50W
Vianópolis 87 16 40S 48 35W
Vibank 56 50 20N 103 56W
Viborg 111 56 27N 9 23E
Vic-en-Bigorre 102 43 24N 0 3E
Vic-Fézensac 102 43 47N 0 19E
Vic-sur-Cère 102 44 59N 2 38E
Vic-sur-Seille 101 48 45N 6 33E
Vicenza 108 45 32N 11 31E
Viceroy 56 49 28N 105 22W
Vich 104 41 58N 2 19E
Vichada □ 86 5 0N 69 30W
Vichy 102 46 9N 3 26E
Vicksburg, Ariz., U.S.A. 81 33 45N 113 45W
Vicksburg, Mich., U.S.A. 77 42 10N 85 30W
Vicksburg, Miss., U.S.A. 75 32 22N 90 56W
Viçosa, Min. Ger., Brazil 87 20 45S 42 53W
Viçosa, Pernambuco, Brazil 87 9 28S 36 14W
Victor, Colo., U.S.A. 74 38 43N 105 7W
Victor, N.Y., U.S.A. 70 42 58N 77 24W
Victor Harbour 135 35 30S 138 37E
Victor, L. 38 50 35N 61 50W
Victoria, Argent. 88 32 40S 60 10W
Victoria, Camer. 116 4 1N 9 10E
Victoria, B.C., Can. 63 48 30N 123 25W
Victoria, Newf., Can. 37 47 46N 53 14W
Victoria, Ont., Can. 49 43 46N 79 53W
Victoria, Chile 90 38 13S 72 20W
Victoria, H. K. 131 22 25N 114 15E
Victoria, Malay. 126 5 20N 115 20E
Victoria, Seychelles 16 5 0S 55 40E
Victoria, U.S.A. 76 41 2N 90 6W
Victoria, Kans., U.S.A. 74 38 52N 99 8W
Victoria, Tex., U.S.A. 75 28 50N 97 0W
Victoria & Albert Mts. 65 80 45N 72 0W
Victoria □ 136 37 0S 144 0E
Victoria Beach 57 50 40N 96 35W
Victoria de las Tunas 84 20 58N 76 59W
Victoria Falls 117 17 58S 25 45E
Victoria, Grand L. 40 47 31N 77 30W
Victoria Harbour 46 44 45N 79 45W
Victoria I. 64 71 0N 111 0W
Victoria, L., Austral. 136 38 2S 147 34E
Victoria, L., E. Afr. 116 1 0S 33 0E
Victoria, La 86 10 14N 67 20W
Victoria Ld. 91 75 0S 160 0E
Victoria Pk. 61 49 18N 114 8W
Victoria Pk 62 50 3N 126 5W
Victoria, R. 134 15 10S 129 40E
Victoria Res. 37 48 20N 57 27W
Victoria Square 50 43 54N 79 22W
Victoria Taungdeik 125 21 15N 93 55E
Victoria West 117 31 25S 23 4E
Victoriaville 41 46 4N 71 56W
Victorica 88 36 20S 65 30W
Victorino 86 2 48N 67 50W
Victorville 81 34 32N 117 18W
Vicuña 88 30 0S 70 50W
Vicuña Mackenna 88 33 53S 64 25W
Vidal 81 34 7N 114 31W
Vidalia 73 32 13N 82 25W
Vidauban 103 43 25N 6 27E
Vidin 109 43 59N 22 28E
Vidisha (Bhilsa) 124 23 28N 77 53E
Viedma 90 40 50S 63 0W
Viedma, L. 90 49 30S 72 30W
Viejo Canal de Bahama 84 22 10N 77 30W
Vien Pou Kha 128 20 45N 101 5E
Vienna, Can. 46 42 41N 80 48W
Vienna, U.S.A. 76 38 11N 91 57W
Vienna, Illinois, U.S.A. 75 37 29N 88 54W
Vienna = Wien 106 48 12N 16 22E
Vienne 103 45 31N 4 53E
Vienne □ 102 46 30N 0 42E
Vienne, R. 100 47 5N 0 30E
Vientiane 128 17 58N 102 36E
Vieques, I. 67 18 8N 65 25W
Viersen 105 51 15N 6 23E
Vierzon 101 47 13N 2 5E
Vietnam ■ 128 19 0N 106 0E
Vieux-Boucau-les-Bains 102 43 48N 1 23W
Vif 103 45 5N 5 41E
Vigan 127 17 35N 120 28E
Vigan, Le 102 44 0N 3 36E
Vigia 87 0 50S 48 5W
Vigia Chico 83 19 46N 87 35W
Vignacourt 101 50 1N 2 15E
Vignemale, Pic du 102 42 47N 0 10W
Vigneulles 101 48 59N 5 40E
Vigo 104 42 12N 8 41W
Vihiers 100 47 10N 0 30W
Vijayawada (Bezwada) 125 16 31N 80 39E
Viking 61 53 7N 111 50W
Vikna 111 64 52N 10 57E
Vikulovo 120 56 50N 70 40E
Vila Arriaga 117 14 35S 13 30E
Vila Bittencourt 86 1 20S 69 20W
Vila Coutinho 117 14 37S 34 19E
Vila da Maganja 117 17 18S 37 30E
Vila de Aljustrel 117 13 30S 19 45E
Vila de Liquica 127 8 40S 125 20E
Vila de Manica 117 18 58S 32 59E
Vila Fontes 117 17 51S 35 24E
Vila Franca de Xira 104 38 57N 8 59W
Vila Machado 117 19 15S 34 14E
Vila Marechal Carmona = Uige 116 7 30S 14 40E
Vila Murtinho 86 10 20S 65 20W
Vila Nova do Seles 117 11 35S 14 22E
Vila Real 104 41 17N 7 48W
Vila Real de Santo Antonio 104 37 10N 7 28W
Vila Salazar 127 5 25S 123 50E
Vila Velha 89 20 20S 40 17W
Vila Verissimo Sarmento 116 8 15S 20 50E
Vilaine, R. 100 47 35N 2 10W
Vilanculos 117 22 1S 35 17E
Vilhelmina 110 64 35N 16 39E
Vilhena 86 12 30S 60 0W
Viliga 121 60 2N 156 56E
Villa Abecia 88 21 0S 68 18W
Villa Ahumada 82 30 30N 106 40W
Villa Ana 88 28 28S 59 40W
Villa Ángela 88 27 34S 60 45W
Villa Bella 86 10 25S 65 30W
Villa Cañ!s 88 34 0S 61 35W
Villa Cisneros = Dakhla 114 23 50N 15 53W
Villa Colón 88 31 38S 68 20W
Villa Constitución 88 33 15S 60 20W
Villa de Cura 86 10 2N 67 29W
Villa de María 88 30 0S 63 43W
Villa de Rosario 88 24 30S 57 35W
Villa Dolores 88 31 58S 65 15W
Villa Franca 88 26 14S 58 20W
Villa Frontera 82 26 56N 101 27W
Villa Grove 77 39 52N 88 10W
Villa Guillermina 88 28 15S 59 29W

Villa Hayes Walton

Villa Hayes 88 25 0S 57 20W
Villa Iris 88 38 12S 63 12W
Villa Julia Molina 85 19 5N 69 45W
Villa Madero 82 24 28N 104 10W
Villa María 88 32 20S 63 10W
Villa Mazán 88 28 40S 66 30W
Villa Mentes 88 21 10S 63 30W
Villa Montes 88 21 10S 63 30W
Villa Ocampo, Argent. 88 28 30S 59 20W
Villa Ocampo, Mexico 82 26 29N 105 30W
Villa Ojo de Agua 88 29 30S 63 44W
Villa San Agustín 88 30 35S 67 30W
Villa San José 88 32 12S 58 15W
Villa San Martín 88 28 9S 64 9W
Villa Unión 82 23 12N 106 14W
Villach 106 46 37N 13 51E
Villagarcía de Arosa 104 42 34N 8 46W
Villagrán 83 24 29N 99 29W
Villaguay 88 32 0S 58 45W
Villahermosa 83 17 45N 92 50W
Villaines-la-Juhel 100 48 21N 0 20W
Villalba 104 40 36N 3 59W
Villamblard 102 45 2N 0 32E
Villanueva, Colomb. 86 10 37N 72 59W
Villanueva, U.S.A. 79 35 16N 105 31W
Villanueva de la Serena 104 38 59N 5 50W
Villard 103 45 4N 5 33E
Villard-Bonnet 103 45 14N 5 53E
Villard-de-Lans 103 45 3N 5 33E
Villarreal 104 39 55N 0 3W
Villarrica, Chile 90 39 15S 72 30W
Villarrica, Parag. 88 25 40S 56 30W
Villarrobledo 104 39 18N 2 36W
Villars 103 46 0N 5 2E
Villavicencio, Argent. 88 32 28S 69 0W
Villavicencio, Colomb. 86 4 9N 73 37W
Villaviciosa 104 43 32N 5 27W
Villazón 88 22 0S 65 35W
Ville de Paris □ 101 48 50N 2 20E
Ville-Guay 42 46 50N 71 5W
Ville-Marie 40 47 20N 79 30W
Ville Platte 75 30 45N 92 17W
Villebon, L. 40 47 58N 77 17W
Villedieu 100 48 50N 1 12W
Villefort 102 44 28N 3 56E
Villefranche 101 47 19N 1 46E
Villefranche-de-Lauragais 102 43 25N 1 44E
Villefranche-de-Rouergue 102 44 21N 2 2E
Villefranche-du-Périgord 102 44 38N 1 5E
Villefranche-sur-Saône 103 45 59N 4 43E
Villemaur 101 48 14N 3 40E
Villemontel 40 48 38N 78 22W
Villemur-sur-Tarn 102 43 51N 1 31E
Villena 104 38 39N 0 52W
Villenauxe 101 48 36N 3 30E
Villenave 102 44 46N 0 33W
Villeneuve 101 48 42N 2 25E
Villeneuve-l'Archevêque 101 48 14N 3 32E
Villeneuve-lès-Avignon 103 43 57N 4 49E
Villeneuve-sur-Allier 102 46 40N 3 13E
Villeneuve-sur-Lot 102 44 24N 0 42E
Villeréal 102 44 38N 0 45E
Villers Bocage 100 49 3N 0 40W
Villers Bretonneux 101 49 50N 2 30E
Villers-Cotterêts 101 49 15N 3 4E
Villers-sur-Mer 100 49 21N 0 2W
Villersexel 101 47 33N 6 26E
Villerupt 101 49 28N 5 55E
Villerville 100 49 26N 0 5E
Villieu 42 46 44N 71 17W
Villisca 76 40 55N 94 59W
Vilna 60 54 7N 111 55W
Vilnius 120 54 38N 25 25E
Vilvoorde 105 50 56N 4 26E
Vilyuy, R. 121 63 58N 125 0E
Vilyuysk 121 63 40N 121 20E
Vimont 44 45 36N 73 43W
Vimoutiers 100 48 57N 0 10E
Viña del Mar 88 33 0S 71 30W
Vinaroz 104 40 30N 0 27E
Vincennes 77 38 42N 87 29W
Vincent 81 34 33N 118 11W
Vinchina 88 28 45S 68 15W
Vindel älv 110 64 20N 19 20E
Vindeln 110 64 12N 19 43E
Vindhya Ra. 124 22 50N 77 0E
Vine Grove 77 37 49N 85 59W
Vineland, Can. 49 43 9N 79 24W
Vineland, U.S.A. 72 39 30N 75 0W
Vinh 128 18 45N 105 38E
Vinita 75 36 40N 95 12W
Vinkovci 109 45 19N 18 48E
Vinnitsa 120 49 15N 28 30E
Vinton, Calif., U.S.A. 80 39 48N 120 10W
Vinton, Iowa, U.S.A. 76 42 8N 92 1W
Vinton, La., U.S.A. 75 30 13N 93 35W
Viola 76 41 12N 90 35W
Viqueque 127 8 42S 126 30E
Virac 127 13 30N 124 20E
Virago Sd. 62 54 0N 132 30W
Viramgam 124 23 5N 72 0E
Virden, Can. 57 49 50N 100 56W
Virden, U.S.A. 76 39 30N 89 46W
Vire 100 48 50N 0 53W
Vírgenes, C. 90 52 19S 68 21W
Virgil 49 43 13N 79 8W
Virgin Gorda, I. 85 18 45N 64 26W
Virgin Is. 85 18 40N 64 30W
Virgin, R., Can. 55 57 2N 108 17W
Virgin, R., U.S.A. 79 36 50N 114 10W
Virginia, U.S.A. 76 39 57N 90 13W
Virginia, Minn., U.S.A. 52 47 30N 92 32W
Virginia □ 72 37 45N 78 0W
Virginia Beach 72 36 54N 75 58W
Virginia City, Mont., U.S.A. 78 45 25N 111 58W
Virginia City, Nev., U.S.A. 80 39 19N 119 39W
Virginia Falls 54 61 38N 125 42W
Virginiatown 34 48 9N 79 36W
Virgins, C. 90 52 10S 68 30W
Virieu-le-Grand 103 45 51N 5 39E
Viroqua 74 43 33N 90 57W
Virton 105 49 35N 5 32E
Virudhunagar 124 9 30N 78 0E
Vis, I. 108 43 0N 16 10E
Visalia 80 36 25N 119 18W
Visayan Sea 127 11 30N 123 30E
Visby 111 57 37N 18 18E
Viscount 56 51 57N 105 39W
Viscount Melville Sd. 64 74 10N 108 0W
Visé 105 50 44N 5 41E
Višegrad 109 43 47N 19 17E
Viseu, Brazil 87 1 10S 46 20W
Viseu, Port. 104 40 40N 7 55W
Vishakhapatnam 125 17 45N 83 20E
Visikoi I. 91 56 30S 26 40E
Viso, Mte. 108 44 38N 7 5E
Vista 81 33 12N 117 14W
Vistula, R. = Wisła, R. 107 53 38N 18 47E
Vitebsk 120 55 10N 30 15E
Viterbo 108 42 25N 12 8E
Viti Levu, I. 133 17 30S 177 30E
Vitim 121 59 45N 112 25E
Vitim, R. 121 58 40N 112 50E
Vitlal Junction 81 34 11N 114 34W
Vitória 87 20 20S 40 22W
Vitoria 104 42 50N 2 41W
Vitória da Conquista 87 14 51S 40 51W
Vitória de São Antão 87 8 10S 37 20W
Vitré 100 48 8N 1 12W
Vitry-le-François 101 48 43N 4 33E
Vitteaux 101 47 24N 4 30E
Vittel 101 48 12N 5 57E
Vittoria 70 42 48N 81 21W
Vittória 108 36 58N 14 30E
Vittório Véneto 108 45 59N 12 18E
Vivero 104 43 39N 7 38W
Viviers 103 44 30N 4 40E
Vivonne 102 46 36N 0 15E
Vizcaíno, Desierto de 82 27 40N 113 50W
Vizcaíno, Sierra 82 27 30N 114 0W
Vizianagaram 125 18 6N 83 10E
Vizille 103 45 5N 5 46E
Vlaardingen 105 51 55N 4 21E
Vladimir 120 56 0N 40 30E
Vladivostok 130 43 10N 131 53E
Vlieland, I. 105 53 30N 4 55E
Vlissingen 105 51 26N 3 34E
Vlonë = Vlórë 109 40 32N 19 28E
Vlórë 109 40 32N 19 28E
Vltava, R. 106 49 35N 14 10E
Vogar 57 50 57N 98 39W
Vogelkop = Doberai, Jazirah 127 1 25S 133 0E
Vogelsberg 106 50 37N 9 30E
Vohémar 117 13 25S 50 0E
Vohipeno 117 22 22S 47 51E
Voi 116 3 25S 38 32E
Void 101 48 40N 5 36E
Voiron 103 45 22N 5 35E
Voisey B. 36 56 15N 61 50W
Vojmsjön 110 64 55N 16 40E
Volborg 74 45 50N 105 44W
Volda 110 62 9N 6 5E
Volendam 105 52 30N 5 4E
Volga, R. 120 52 20N 48 0E
Volgograd 120 48 40N 44 25E
Völklingen 105 49 15N 6 50E
Vollenhove 105 52 40N 5 58E
Volochayevka 121 48 40N 134 30E
Vologda 120 59 25N 40 0E
Vólos 109 39 24N 22 59E
Volsk 120 52 5N 47 28E
Volta, L. 114 7 30N 0 15E
Volta, R. 114 8 0N 0 10W
Volta Redonda 89 22 31S 44 5W
Volterra 108 43 24N 10 50E
Volturno, R. 108 41 18N 14 20E
Vonda 56 52 19N 106 6W
Voorburg 105 52 5N 4 24E
Vopnafjörður 110 65 45N 14 40W
Vorarlberg □ 106 47 20N 10 0E
Voreppe 103 45 18N 5 39E
Voriai Sporádhes 109 39 15N 23 30E
Vorkuta 120 67 48N 64 20E
Voronezh 120 51 40N 39 10E
Voroshilovgrad 120 48 38N 39 15E
Vorovskoye 121 54 30N 155 50E
Vosges 101 48 20N 7 10E
Vosges □ 101 48 12N 6 20E
Voss 111 60 38N 6 26E
Vostok I. 15 10 5S 152 23W
Vostotnyy Sayan 121 54 0N 96 0E
Votkinsk 120 57 0N 53 55E
Vouga, R. 104 40 46N 8 10W
Voulte-sur-Rhône, La 103 44 48N 4 46E
Vouziers 101 49 22N 4 40E
Voves 101 48 15N 1 38E
Voyageurs Nat. Park 52 48 30N 92 55W
Voznesenye 120 61 0N 35 45E
Vrangelja, Ostrov 121 71 0N 180 0E
Vranje 109 42 34N 21 54E
Vratsa 109 43 13N 23 30E
Vrbas, R. 109 44 30N 17 10E
Vrede 117 27 24S 29 6E
Vredenburg 117 32 51S 18 0E
Vršac 109 45 8N 21 18E
Vryburg 117 26 55S 24 45E
Vryheid 117 27 54S 30 47E
Vught 105 51 38N 5 20E
Vulcan, Can. 61 50 25N 113 15W
Vulcan, U.S.A. 72 45 46N 87 51W
Vulcano, I. 108 38 25N 14 58E
Vung Tau 128 10 21N 107 4E
Vyazemskiy 121 47 32N 134 45E
Vyazma 120 55 10N 34 15E
Vychegda R. 120 61 50N 52 30E
Vychodné Beskydy 107 49 30N 22 0E
Vyrnwy, L. 94 52 48N 3 30W
Vyshniy Volochek 120 57 30N 34 30E
Vyssi Brod 122 48 36N 14 20E
Vytegra 120 61 15N 36 40E

W

Wa 114 10 7N 2 25W
Waal, R. 105 51 59N 4 8E
Waalwijk 105 51 42N 5 4E
Wabakimi L. 52 50 38N 89 45W
Wabamun 60 53 33N 114 28W
Wabana 35 47 40N 53 0W
Wabano, R. 41 48 20N 74 3W
Wabasca 54 55 57N 113 45W
Wabasca, R. 60 58 22N 115 20W
Wabash 77 40 48N 85 46W
Wabash, R. 72 39 10N 87 30W
Wabaskang L. 52 50 26N 93 13W
Wabassi, R. 53 51 45N 86 20W
Wabatongushi L. 53 48 26N 84 13W
Wabeno 72 45 25N 88 40W
Wabigoon 52 49 43N 92 35W
Wabigoon L. 52 49 44N 92 44W
Wabimeig L. 53 51 28N 85 36W
Wabinosh L. 52 50 5N 89 0W
Wabowden 55 54 55N 98 38W
Wabrzezno 107 53 16N 18 57E
Wabuk Pt. 34 55 20N 85 5W
Wabush 38 52 55N 66 52W
Wabuska 78 39 16N 119 13W
W.A.C. Bennett Dam 54 56 2N 122 6W
Waco, Can. 36 51 27N 65 37W
Waco, U.S.A. 75 31 33N 97 5W
Waconichi, L. 41 50 8N 74 0W
Wacouno, R. 38 50 54N 65 57W
Wad ar Rima 122 26 5N 41 30E
Wâd Medanî 115 14 28N 33 30E
Waddenzee 105 53 6N 5 10E
Waddington 71 44 51N 75 12W
Waddington, Mt. 62 51 23N 125 15W
Waddinxveen 105 52 2N 4 40E
Wadena, Can. 56 51 57N 103 38W
Wadena, U.S.A. 74 46 25N 95 2W
Wadesboro 73 35 2N 80 2W
Wadhams 62 51 30N 127 30W
Wadi Halfa 115 21 53N 31 19E
Wadi Sabha 122 23 50N 48 30E
Wadlin L. 60 57 44N 115 35W
Wadsley 66 49 21N 123 13W
Wadsworth 78 39 44N 119 22W
Wafra 122 28 33N 48 3E
Wageningen 105 51 58N 5 40E
Wager B. 65 65 26N 88 40W
Wager Bay 65 65 56N 90 49W
Wagga Wagga 136 35 7S 147 24E
Waghete 127 4 10S 135 50E
Wagin 134 33 17S 117 25E
Wagon Mound 75 36 10N 104 50W
Wagoner 75 36 0N 95 20W
Wahai 127 2 48S 129 35E
Wahiawa 67 21 30N 158 2W
Wahoo 74 41 15N 96 35W
Wahpeton 74 46 20N 96 35W
Waianae 67 21 25N 158 8W
Waiau, R. 133 42 47S 173 22E
Waibeem 127 0 30S 132 50E
Waigeo, I. 127 0 20S 130 40E
Waihi 133 37 23S 175 52E
Waihou, R. 133 37 15S 175 40E
Waikabubak 127 9 45S 119 25E
Waikaoti 15 45 36S 170 41E
Waikaremoana 133 38 42S 177 12E
Waikari 133 42 58S 172 41E
Waikato, R. 133 37 23S 174 43E
Waikawa Harbour 133 46 39S 169 9E
Waikokopu 133 39 3S 177 52E
Waikouaiti 133 45 36S 170 41E
Wailuku 67 20 53N 156 26W
Waimakariri, R. 133 42 23S 172 42E
Waimanola 67 21 19N 157 43W
Waimarino 133 40 40S 175 20E
Waimate 133 44 53S 171 3E
Waimea 67 21 57N 159 39W
Wainganga, R. 124 21 0N 79 45E
Waingapu 127 9 35S 120 11E
Wainiha 67 22 9N 159 34W
Wainwright, Can. 61 52 50N 110 50W
Wainwright, U.S.A. 67 70 39N 160 10W
Waiouru 133 39 28S 175 41E
Waipahu 67 21 23N 158 1W
Waipara 133 43 3S 172 46E
Waipawa 133 39 56S 176 38E
Waipiro 133 38 2S 176 22E
Waipori 15 45 50S 169 52E
Waipu 133 35 59S 174 29E
Waipukurau 133 40 1S 176 33E
Wairakei 133 38 37S 176 6E
Wairarapa I. 133 41 14S 175 15E
Wairoa 133 39 3S 177 25E
Waitaki, R. 133 44 23S 169 55E
Waitara 133 38 59S 174 15E
Waitsburg 78 46 15N 118 0W
Waiuku 133 37 15S 174 45E
Waiyeung 131 23 12N 114 32E
Wajima 132 37 30N 137 0E
Wajir 116 1 42N 40 20E
Wakamatsu 132 33 50N 130 45E
Wakasa-Wan 132 34 45N 135 30E
Wakatipu, L. 133 45 5S 168 33E
Wakaw 56 52 39N 105 44W
Wakayama 132 34 15N 135 15E
Wakayama-ken □ 132 33 50N 135 30E
Wake Forest 73 35 58N 78 30W
Wake I. 14 19 18N 166 36E
Wakefield, Can. 40 45 38N 75 56W
Wakefield, N.Z. 133 41 24S 173 5E
Wakefield, U.K. 94 53 41N 1 31W
Wakefield, Mass., U.S.A. 71 42 30N 71 3W
Wakefield, Mich., U.S.A. 52 46 28N 89 53W
Wakeham 38 48 50N 64 34W
Wakeham Bay = Maricourt 36 61 36N 71 58W
Wakerusa 77 41 32N 86 1W
Wakhan □ 123 37 0N 73 0E
Wakkanai 132 45 28N 141 35E
Wako 34 49 50N 91 22W
Wakomata L. 46 46 34N 83 22W
Wakre 127 0 30S 131 5E
Wakuach L. 36 55 34N 67 32W
Wałbrzych 106 50 45N 16 18E
Walcheren, I. 105 51 30N 3 35E
Walcott 78 41 50N 106 55W
Waldeck 56 50 22N 107 36W
Walden, Colo., U.S.A. 78 40 47N 106 20W
Walden, N.Y., U.S.A. 71 41 32N 74 13W
Waldheim 56 52 39N 106 37W
Waldo 77 40 28N 83 5W
Waldport 78 44 30N 124 2W
Waldron, Can. 55 50 53N 102 35W
Waldron, U.S.A. 75 34 52N 94 4W
Wales, Alas., U.S.A. 67 65 38N 168 10W
Wales, N.Dak., U.S.A. 57 48 55N 98 35W
Wales □ 95 52 30N 3 30W
Wales I. 36 62 0N 72 30W
Walgett 135 30 0S 148 5E
Walhachin 63 50 45N 120 59W
Walhalla 57 48 55N 97 55W
Walker, U.S.A. 76 37 54N 94 14W
Walker, Minn., U.S.A. 52 47 4N 94 35W
Walker L., Man., Can. 55 54 42N 95 57W
Walker L., Qué., Can. 36 50 20N 67 11W
Walker L., U.S.A. 78 38 56N 118 46W
Walkerton, Can. 46 44 10N 81 10W
Walkerton, U.S.A. 77 41 28N 86 29W
Wall 74 44 0N 102 14W
Wall Lake 76 42 16N 95 5W
Walla Walla 78 46 3N 118 25W
Wallace, N.S., Can. 39 45 48N 63 29W
Wallace, Ont., Can. 70 45 12N 78 9W
Wallace, Idaho, U.S.A. 78 47 30N 116 0W
Wallace, N.C., U.S.A. 73 34 50N 77 59W
Wallace, Nebr., U.S.A. 74 40 51N 101 12W
Wallaceburg 46 42 40N 82 23W
Wallachia = Valahia 107 44 35N 25 0E
Wallaroo 135 33 56S 137 39E
Wallasey 94 53 26N 3 2W
Wallowa 78 45 40N 117 35W
Wallowa, Mts. 78 45 20N 117 30W
Wallsend, Austral. 136 32 55S 151 40E
Wallsend, U.K. 94 54 59N 1 30W
Wallula 78 46 3N 118 59W
Walmore 49 43 7N 78 55W
Walmsley, L. 55 63 25N 108 36W
Walney, Isle of 94 54 5N 3 15W
Walnut 76 41 33N 89 36W
Walnut Ridge 75 36 7N 90 58W
Walsall 95 52 36N 1 59W
Walsenburg 75 37 42N 104 45W
Walsh, Can. 61 49 57N 110 3W
Walsh, U.S.A. 75 37 28N 102 15W
Walterboro 73 32 53N 80 40W
Walters 75 34 25N 98 20W
Waltham 71 42 22N 71 12W
Waltham Sta. 40 45 57N 76 57W
Waltman 78 43 8N 107 15W
Walton, Can. 39 45 14N 64 0W
Walton, U.S.A. 77 38 52N 84 37W
Walton, Mich., U.S.A. 46 44 30N 85 14W

Walton Wendesi

Walton, N.Y., U.S.A. 71 42 12N 75 9W
Waltonville 76 38 13N 89 2W
Walvis Ridge 13 30 0S 3 0E
Walvisbaai 117 23 0S 14 28E
Wamba 116 2 10N 27 57E
Wamego 74 39 14N 96 22W
Wamena 127 3 58S 138 50E
Wampsville 71 43 4N 75 42W
Wamsasi 127 3 27S 126 7E
Wan Ta Shan 130 46 20N 132 20E
Wana 124 32 20N 69 32E
Wanaka L. 133 44 33S 169 7E
Wanan 131 26 25N 114 50E
Wanapiri 127 4 30S 135 50E
Wanapitei 34 46 30N 80 45W
Wanapitei L. 46 46 45N 80 40W
Wanapitei, R. 46 46 2N 80 51W
Wanchuan 130 40 53N 114 32E
Wang Saphung 128 17 18N 101 46E
Wangal 127 6 8S 134 9E
Wanganui 133 39 35S 175 3E
Wangaratta 136 36 21S 146 19E
Wangching 130 43 15N 129 37E
Wangerooge I. 106 53 47N 7 52E
Wangiwangi, I. 127 5 22S 123 37E
Wangkiang 131 30 6N 116 45E
Wanham 60 55 44N 118 24W
Wanhsien, Kansu, China 130 36 45N 107 24E
Wanhsien, Szechwan, China 131 30 50N 108 30E
Wankie 117 18 18S 26 30E
Wanless 57 54 11N 101 21W
Wanning 131 18 45N 110 28E
Wannon, R. 136 37 38S 141 25E
Wantsai 131 28 5N 114 22E
Wanyang Shan, mts. 131 26 30N 113 45E
Wanyüan 131 32 4N 108 5E
Wapakoneta 77 40 35N 84 10W
Wapato 78 46 30N 120 25W
Wapawekka L. 55 54 55N 104 40W
Wapella 57 50 16N 101 58W
Wapello 76 41 11N 91 11W
Wapikopa L. 34 42 50N 88 10W
Wapiti, R. 34 55 5N 118 18W
Wappingers Fs. 71 41 35N 73 56W
Wapsipinicon, R. 76 41 44N 90 19W
Waranga Res. 136 36 32S 145 5E
Warangal 124 17 58N 79 45E
Waratah B. 136 38 54S 146 5E
Warba 52 47 9N 93 16W
Warburg 61 53 11N 114 19W
Warburton 136 37 47S 145 42E
Warburton, R. 133 27 30S 138 30E
Ward 133 41 49S 174 11E
Ward Cove 54 55 25N 132 10W
Ward Mt. 80 37 12N 118 54W
Wardha 124 20 45N 78 39E
Wardha, R. 124 19 57N 79 11E
Wardlow 61 50 56N 111 31W
Wardner 61 49 25N 115 26W
Wardoan 135 25 59S 149 59E
Ware, Can. 54 57 26N 125 41W
Ware, U.S.A. 71 42 16N 72 15W
Wareham 71 41 45N 70 44W
Warendorf 105 51 57N 8 0E
Warfield 63 49 6N 117 46W
Warialda 135 29 29S 150 33E
Wariap 127 1 30S 134 5E
Warkopi 127 1 12S 134 9E
Warley 95 52 30N 2 0W
Warm Springs, Mont., U.S.A. 78 46 11N 112 56W
Warm Springs, Nev., U.S.A. 79 38 16N 116 32W
Warman 56 52 19N 106 30W
Warmbad, Namibia 117 19 14S 13 51E
Warmbad, S. Afr. 117 24 51S 28 19E
Warmeriville 101 49 20N 4 13E
Warncoort 136 38 30S 143 45E
Warnemünde 106 54 9N 12 5E
Warner 61 49 17N 112 12W
Warner Range, Mts. 78 41 30S 120 20W
Warner Robins 73 32 41N 83 36W
Warracknabeal 136 36 9S 142 26E
Warragul 136 38 10S 145 58E
Warrego, R. 135 30 24S 145 21E
Warrego Ra. 135 25 15S 146 0E
Warren, Austral. 136 31 42S 147 51E
Warren, Can. 46 46 27N 80 18W
Warren, U.S.A. 77 42 31N 83 2W
Warren, Ark., U.S.A. 75 33 35N 92 3W
Warren, Ill., U.S.A. 76 42 30N 89 59W
Warren, Ohio, U.S.A. 70 41 18N 80 52W
Warren, Pa., U.S.A. 70 41 52N 79 10W
Warren, R.I., U.S.A. 71 41 43N 71 19W
Warrender, C. 65 74 28N 81 46W
Warrenpoint 97 54 7N 6 15W
Warrens Corners 49 43 13N 78 45W
Warren's Landing 55 53 40N 98 0W
Warrensburg, Ill., U.S.A. 76 39 56N 89 4W
Warrensburg, Mo., U.S.A. 74 38 45N 93 45W
Warrenton, S. Afr. 117 28 9S 24 47E
Warrenton, U.S.A. 76 38 49N 91 9W
Warrenton, Oreg., U.S.A. 80 46 11N 123 59W
Warrina 134 28 12S 135 50E
Warrington, U.K. 94 53 25N 2 38W
Warrington, U.S.A. 73 30 22N 87 16W
Warrnambool 136 38 25S 142 30E
Warroad 52 48 54N 95 19W
Warsaw, Ill., U.S.A. 76 40 22N 91 26W
Warsaw, Ind., U.S.A. 77 41 14N 85 50W
Warsaw, Ky., U.S.A. 77 38 47N 84 54W
Warsaw, Mo., U.S.A. 76 38 15N 93 23W
Warsaw, N.Y., U.S.A. 70 42 46N 78 10W
Warsaw, Ohio, U.S.A. 70 40 20N 82 0W
Warsaw = Warszawa 107 52 13N 21 0E
Warszawa 107 52 13N 21 0E
Warta, R. 106 52 40N 16 10E
Warthe, R. = Warta, R. 106 52 40N 16 10E
Waru 127 3 30S 130 36E
Warwick, Austral. 135 28 10S 152 1E
Warwick, U.K. 95 52 17N 1 36W
Warwick, U.S.A. 71 41 43N 71 25W
Warwick □ 95 52 20N 1 30W
Wasa 54 49 45N 115 50W
Wasaga Beach 46 44 31N 80 1W
Wasatch, Mt., Ra. 78 40 30N 111 15W
Wascana Cr. 58 50 39N 104 55W
Wascana L. 58 50 26N 104 36W
Wasco, Calif., U.S.A. 81 35 37N 119 16W
Wasco, Oreg., U.S.A. 78 45 45N 120 46W
Waseca, Can. 56 53 6N 109 28W
Waseca, U.S.A. 74 44 3N 93 31W
Wasekamio L. 55 56 45N 108 45W
Wash, The 94 52 58N 0 20W
Washago 46 44 45N 79 20W
Washburn, U.S.A. 76 40 55N 89 17W
Washburn, N.D., U.S.A. 74 47 23N 101 0W
Washburn, Wis., U.S.A. 52 46 38N 90 55W
Washi L. 53 51 24N 87 2W
Washington, Can. 49 43 18N 80 35W
Washington, Calif., U.S.A. 80 39 22N 120 48W
Washington, D.C., U.S.A. 72 38 52N 77 0W
Washington, Ga., U.S.A. 73 33 45N 82 45W
Washington, Ind., U.S.A. 77 38 40N 87 8W
Washington, Iowa, U.S.A. 76 41 20N 91 45W
Washington, Mo, U.S.A. 76 38 35N 91 20W
Washington, N.C., U.S.A. 73 35 35N 77 1W
Washington, N.J., U.S.A. 71 40 45N 74 59W
Washington, Pa., U.S.A. 70 40 10N 80 20W
Washington, Utah, U.S.A. 79 37 10N 113 30W
Washington □ 78 47 45N 120 30W
Washington Court House 77 39 34N 83 26W
Washington I., Pac. Oc. 15 4 43N 160 25W
Washington I., U.S.A. 72 45 24N 86 54W
Washington Mt. 71 44 15N 71 18W
Washir 124 32 15N 63 50E
Washougal 80 45 35N 122 21W
Wasian 127 1 47S 133 19E
Wasior 127 2 43S 134 30E
Waskada 57 49 6N 100 48W
Waskaiowaka, L. 55 56 33N 96 23W
Waskateena Beach 56 53 45N 105 15W
Waskatenau 60 54 7N 112 47W
Waskesiu L. 56 53 58N 106 12W
Waskesiu Lake 56 53 55N 106 5W
Waskish 52 48 11N 94 28W
Wassenaar 105 52 8N 4 24E
Wassy 101 48 30N 4 58E
Waswanipi 40 49 40N 75 59W
Waswanipi, L. 40 49 35N 76 40W
Waswanipi, R. 40 49 40N 76 25W
Watangpone 127 4 29S 120 25E
Watawaha, P. 127 6 30S 122 20E
Water Valley 75 34 9N 89 38W
Waterberg 117 20 30S 17 18E
Waterbury, Conn., U.S.A. 71 41 32N 73 0W
Waterbury, Vt., U.S.A. 71 44 22N 72 44W
Waterbury L. 55 58 10N 104 22W
Waterdown 48 43 20N 79 53W
Waterford, Can. 46 42 56N 80 17W
Waterford, Ireland 97 52 16N 7 8W
Waterford, U.S.A. 77 42 46N 88 13W
Waterford, Calif., U.S.A. 80 37 38N 120 46W
Waterford □ 97 51 10N 7 40W
Waterford Harb. 97 52 10N 6 58W
Waterford, R. 37 47 33N 52 43W
Waterhen L., Man., Can. 57 52 10N 99 40W
Waterhen L., Sask., Can. 55 54 28N 108 25W
Waterloo, Belg. 105 50 43N 4 25E
Waterloo, Ont., Can. 49 43 30N 80 32W
Waterloo, Ont., Can. 52 43 25N 80 30W
Waterloo, Qué., Can. 41 45 21N 72 31W
Waterloo, Que., Can. 71 45 22N 72 32W
Waterloo, U.S.A. 77 41 24N 85 2W
Waterloo, Ill., U.S.A. 76 38 22N 90 6W
Waterloo, Iowa, U.S.A. 76 42 27N 92 20W
Waterloo, N.Y., U.S.A. 70 42 54N 76 53W
Waterloo, Wis., U.S.A. 76 43 11N 88 59W
Waterman 77 41 46N 88 47W
Watermeet 74 46 15N 89 12W
Waterpoint 70 43 19N 78 15W
Waterton Lakes Nat. Park 61 49 5N 114 15W
Waterton Park 61 49 3N 113 55W
Watertown, Conn., U.S.A. 71 41 36N 73 7W
Watertown, N.Y., U.S.A. 71 43 58N 75 57W
Watertown, S.D., U.S.A. 74 44 57N 97 5W
Watertown, Wis., U.S.A. 77 43 15N 88 45W
Waterville, N.S., Can. 39 45 3N 64 41W
Waterville, Qué., Can. 41 45 16N 71 54W
Waterville, Me., U.S.A. 35 44 35N 69 40W
Waterville, N.Y., U.S.A. 71 42 56N 75 23W
Waterville, Pa., U.S.A. 70 41 19N 77 21W
Waterville, Wash., U.S.A. 78 47 45N 120 1W
Watervliet, U.S.A. 77 42 11N 86 18W
Watervliet, N.Y., U.S.A. 71 42 46N 73 43W
Wates 127 7 53S 110 6E
Watford, Can. 46 42 57N 81 53W
Watford, U.K. 95 51 38N 0 23W
Watford City 74 47 50N 103 23W
Wathaman, R. 55 57 16N 102 59W
Watkins Glen 70 42 25N 76 55W
Watlings I. 85 24 0N 74 35W
Watonga 75 35 51N 98 24W
Watrous, Can. 56 51 40N 105 25W
Watrous, U.S.A. 75 35 50N 104 55W
Watsa 116 3 4N 29 30E
Watseka 77 40 45N 87 45W
Watshishou, L. 38 50 20N 60 50W
Watson 56 52 10N 104 30W
Watson Lake 67 60 6N 128 49W
Watsonville 80 36 55N 121 49W
Wattle Hill 136 38 42S 143 17E
Watubela, Kepulauan 127 4 28S 131 54E
Waubamik 46 45 27N 80 1W
Waubaushene 46 44 45N 79 42W
Waubay 74 45 42N 97 17W
Waubra 136 37 21S 143 39E
Wauchope 136 31 28S 152 45E
Wauchula 73 27 35N 81 50W
Waugh 57 49 40N 95 2W
Waukegan 77 42 22N 87 54W
Waukesha 77 43 0N 88 15W
Waukon 74 43 14N 91 33W
Wauneta 74 40 27N 101 25W
Waupaca 74 44 22N 89 8W
Waupun 74 43 38N 88 44W
Waurika 75 34 12N 98 0W
Wausau 74 44 57N 89 40W
Wauseon 77 41 33N 84 8W
Wautoma 74 44 3N 89 20W
Wauwatosa 77 43 6N 87 59W
Wave Hill 134 17 32S 131 0E
Waveland 77 39 53N 87 3W
Waveney, R. 95 52 24N 1 20E
Waverley, Can. 39 44 47N 63 36W
Waverley, N.Z. 133 39 46S 174 37E
Waverly, Ill., U.S.A. 76 39 36N 89 57W
Waverly, Iowa, U.S.A. 76 42 40N 92 30W
Waverly, Mo., U.S.A. 76 39 13N 93 31W
Waverly, N.Y., U.S.A. 71 42 0N 76 33W
Wavre 105 50 43N 4 38E
Wâw 115 7 45N 28 1E
Wawa 53 47 59N 84 47W
Wawagosic, R. 40 49 58N 79 6W
Wawanesa 57 49 36N 99 40W
Wawang L. 52 49 25N 90 34W
Wawasee, L. 77 41 24N 85 42W
Wawona 80 37 32N 119 39W
Waxahachie 75 32 22N 96 53W
Way Way 136 33 30S 151 18E
Wayabula Rau 127 2 29N 128 17E
Wayagamac, L. 41 47 21N 72 39W
Waycross 73 31 12N 82 25W
Wayland 77 42 40N 85 39W
Wayne, Mich., U.S.A. 46 42 17N 83 23W
Wayne, Nebr., U.S.A. 76 42 16N 97 0W
Wayne, W. Va., U.S.A. 72 38 15N 82 27W
Wayne City 77 38 21N 88 35W
Waynesboro, Miss., U.S.A. 73 31 40N 88 39W
Waynesboro, Pa., U.S.A. 72 39 46N 77 32W
Waynesboro, Va., U.S.A. 72 38 4N 78 57W
Waynesburg 72 39 54N 80 12W
Waynesville, U.S.A. 76 37 50N 92 12W
Waynesville, U.S.A. 77 39 32N 84 5W
Waynesville, N.C., U.S.A. 73 35 31N 83 0W
Waynoka 75 36 38N 98 53W
Waza 124 33 22N 69 22E
Wazirabad, Afghan. 123 36 44N 66 47E
Wazirabad, Pak. 124 32 30N 74 8E
We 126 6 3N 95 56E
Weald, The 95 51 7N 0 9E
Wear, R. 94 54 55N 1 22W
Weatherford, Okla., U.S.A. 75 35 30N 98 45W
Weatherford, Tex., U.S.A. 75 32 45N 97 48W
Weaubleau 76 37 54N 93 32W
Webb 56 50 11N 108 12W
Webb City 75 37 9N 94 30W
Webbwood 46 46 16N 81 52W
Webster, Mass., U.S.A. 71 42 4N 71 54W
Webster, N.Y., U.S.A. 70 43 11N 77 27W
Webster, S.D., U.S.A. 74 45 24N 97 33W
Webster, Wis., U.S.A. 74 45 53N 92 25W
Webster City 76 42 30N 93 50W
Webster Green 74 38 38N 90 20W
Webster Springs 72 38 30N 80 25W
Weda 127 0 30N 127 50E
Weda, Teluk 127 0 30N 127 50E
Weddell I. 90 51 50S 61 0W
Weddell Sea 91 72 30S 40 0W
Wedge I. 134 30 50S 115 11E
Wedgeport 39 43 44N 65 59W
Weed 78 41 29N 122 22W
Weed Heights 80 38 59N 119 13W
Weedon-Centre 41 45 42N 71 27W
Weedsport 71 43 3N 76 35W
Weedville 70 41 17N 78 28W
Weekes 56 52 34N 102 52W
Weert 105 51 15N 5 43E
Weesp 105 52 18N 5 2E
Wei Ho, R. 131 34 38N 110 20E
Weichow Tao 131 21 0N 109 1E
Weifang 130 36 47N 119 10E
Weihai 130 37 30N 122 10E
Weimar 106 51 0N 11 20E
Weinan 131 34 30N 109 35E
Weipa 135 12 24S 141 50E
Weir, R. 55 56 54N 93 21W
Weir River 55 56 49N 94 6W
Weirdale 56 53 27N 105 15W
Weirton 70 40 22N 80 35W
Weiser 78 44 10N 117 0W
Weiyüan 130 35 10N 104 10E
Wejherowo 107 54 35N 18 12E
Wekusko 55 54 30N 99 45W
Wekusko L. 55 54 40N 99 50W
Welby 55 50 33N 101 29W
Welch 72 37 29N 81 36W
Weldon 56 53 1N 105 8W
Welkom 117 28 0S 26 50E
Welland 49 43 0N 79 15W
Welland Canal 49 43 3N 79 13W
Welland, R., Can. 49 43 4N 79 3W
Welland, R., U.K. 94 52 43N 0 10W
Wellandport 49 43 0N 79 29W
Weller Park 49 43 14N 79 13W
Wellesley Is. 135 17 20S 139 30E
Wellin 105 50 5N 5 6E
Wellingborough 95 52 18N 0 41W
Wellington, Austral. 136 32 35S 148 59E
Wellington, B.C., Can. 62 49 13N 123 58W
Wellington, Newf., Can. 37 48 53N 53 58W
Wellington, Ont., Can. 47 43 57N 77 20W
Wellington, P.E.I., Can. 39 46 27N 64 0W
Wellington, N.Z. 133 41 19S 174 46E
Wellington, U.K. 94 50 58N 3 13W
Wellington, U.S.A. 76 39 8N 93 59W
Wellington, Col., U.S.A. 74 40 43N 105 0W
Wellington, Kans., U.S.A. 75 37 15N 97 25W
Wellington, Nev., U.S.A. 80 38 47N 119 28W
Wellington, Ohio, U.S.A. 70 41 9N 82 12W
Wellington, Tex., U.S.A. 75 34 55N 100 13W
Wellington □, Can. 49 43 50N 80 30W
Wellington □, N.Z. 133 40 8S 175 36E
Wellington Chan. 65 75 0N 93 0W
Wellington, I. 90 49 30S 75 0W
Wellington, L. 136 38 6S 147 20E
Wellington (Telford) 94 52 42N 2 31W
Wells, Can. 63 53 6N 121 36W
Wells, Norfolk, U.K. 95 52 57N 0 51E
Wells, Somerset, U.K. 95 51 12N 2 39W
Wells, Me., U.S.A. 71 43 18N 70 35W
Wells, Minn., U.S.A. 74 43 44N 93 45W
Wells, Nev., U.S.A. 78 41 8N 115 0W
Wells Gray Prov. Park 63 52 30N 120 15W
Wells L. 134 26 44S 123 15E
Wells River 71 44 9N 72 4W
Wellsboro 70 41 46N 77 20W
Wellsburg 70 40 15N 80 36W
Wellsville, Mo., U.S.A. 76 39 4N 91 30W
Wellsville, N.Y., U.S.A. 70 42 9N 77 53W
Wellsville, Ohio, U.S.A. 70 40 36N 80 40W
Wellsville, Utah, U.S.A. 78 41 35N 111 59W
Wellton 79 32 46N 114 6W
Wels 106 48 9N 14 1E
Welsford 39 45 27N 66 20W
Welshpool 95 52 40N 3 9W
Welwyn 55 50 20N 101 30W
Wem 94 52 52N 2 45W
Wembley 60 55 9N 119 8W
Wenasaga, R. 52 50 38N 93 10W
Wenatchee 78 47 30N 120 17W
Wenchang 131 19 45N 110 50E
Wenchow 131 28 0N 120 35E
Wendell 78 42 50N 114 51W
Wenden 81 33 49N 113 33W
Wendesi 127 2 30S 134 10E

Wendover Williamston

Wendover 78 40 49N 114 1W
Wenebegon L. 53 47 23N 83 6W
Wenebegon, R. 53 46 53N 83 12W
Wengniu 130 43 2N 118 54E
Wengteng 130 37 15N 122 10E
Wenlock Edge 98 52 30N 2 43W
Wenlock, R. 135 12 2S 141 55E
Wenona 76 41 3N 89 3W
Wensi 131 35 25N 111 7E
Wensiang 131 34 35N 110 40E
Wensu 129 41 15N 80 14E
Wenteng 130 37 10N 122 0E
Wentworth, Austral. 136 34 2S 141 54E
Wentworth, Can. 39 45 38N 63 33W
Wentzville 76 38 49N 90 51W
Wenut 127 3 11S 133 19E
Weott 78 40 19N 123 56W
Wepener 117 29 42S 27 3E
Werda 117 25 24S 23 15E
Weri 127 3 10S 132 30E
Werne 105 51 38N 7 38E
Werra, R. 105 51 0N 10 0E
Werribee 136 37 54S 144 40E
Werris Creek 136 31 18S 150 38E
Wersar 127 1 30S 131 55E
Wesel 105 51 39N 6 34E
Weser, R. 106 53 33N 8 30E
Wesiri 127 7 30S 126 30E
Weslemkoon L. 47 45 2N 77 25W
Wesleyville, Can. 37 49 8N 53 36W
Wesleyville, U.S.A. 70 42 9N 80 1W
Wessel Is. 135 11 10S 136 45E
Wessington 74 44 30N 98 40W
Wessington Springs 74 44 10N 98 35W
West 75 31 50N 97 5W
West Allis 77 43 1N 87 0W
West, B. 75 29 5N 89 27W
West Bend 72 43 25N 88 10W
West Bengal □ 125 25 0N 90 0E
West Branch 46 44 16N 84 13W
West Bromwich 95 52 32N 2 1W
West Carrollton 77 39 33N 84 17W
West Chazy 71 44 49N 73 28W
West Chester 72 39 58N 75 36W
West Chicago 77 41 53N 88 12W
West Columbia 75 29 10N 95 38W
West Covina 81 34 4N 117 54W
West Des Moines 76 41 30N 93 45W
West Don, R. 50 43 42N 79 20W
West Duffin, R. 51 43 51N 79 4W
West End 84 26 41N 78 58W
West Falkland Island 90 51 30S 60 0W
West Fork, Cuivre, R. 76 39 2N 90 58W
West Frankfort 76 37 56N 89 0W
West Glamorgan □ 95 51 40N 3 55W
West Harbour 15 45 51S 170 33E
West Hartford 71 41 45N 72 45W
West Haven 71 41 18N 72 57W
West Helena 75 34 30N 90 40W
West Hill 50 43 47N 79 12W
West Humber, R. 50 43 44N 79 33W
West Indies 74 15 0N 70 0W
West Kildonan 58 49 56N 97 8W
West Lafayette 77 40 27N 86 55W
West Liberty, Iowa, U.S.A. 76 41 34N 91 16W
West Liberty, Ky., U.S.A. 77 37 55N 83 16W
West Liberty, Ohio, U.S.A. 77 40 15N 83 45W
West Lorne 46 42 36N 81 36W
West Louisville 77 37 42N 87 17W
West Magpie, R., Can. 38 51 2N 64 42W
West Magpie, R., Qué., Can. 36 52 0N 65 0W
West Manchester 77 39 55N 84 38W
West Memphis 75 35 5N 90 3W
West Midlands □ 95 52 30N 1 55W
West Milton 77 39 58N 84 20W
West Monroe 75 32 32N 92 7W
West Montrose 49 43 35N 80 29W
West Newton 70 40 14N 79 46W
West Nicholson 117 21 2S 29 20E
West Palm Beach 73 26 44N 80 3W
West Paris 128 44 18N 70 30W
West Pittston 71 41 19N 75 49W
West Plains 75 36 45N 91 50W
West Point, Jamaica 84 18 14N 78 30W
West Point, Ga., U.S.A. 73 32 54N 85 10W
West Point, Ill., U.S.A. 76 40 15N 91 11W
West Point, Iowa, U.S.A. 76 40 43N 91 27W
West Point, Ky., U.S.A. 77 37 59N 85 57W
West Point, Miss., U.S.A. 73 33 36N 88 38W
West Point, Nebr., U.S.A. 74 41 50N 96 43W
West Point, Va., U.S.A. 72 37 35N 76 47W
West Poplar 56 49 0N 106 22W
West Road R. 63 53 18N 122 53W
West Salem 77 38 31N 88 1W
West Spitsbergen 17 78 40N 17 0E
West Sussex □ 95 50 55N 0 30W
West Terre Haute 77 39 27N 87 27W
West Thurlow I. 62 50 25N 125 35W
West Union, Iowa, U.S.A. 76 42 57N 91 49W
West Union, Ohio, U.S.A. 77 38 48N 83 33W
West Unity 77 41 35N 84 26W
West Vancouver 66 49 21N 123 8W
West Virginia □ 72 39 0N 81 0W
West Walker, R. 80 38 54N 119 9W
West Wyalong 136 33 56S 147 10E
West Yellowstone 78 44 47N 111 4W
West Yorkshire □ 94 53 45N 1 40W
Westbank 54 49 50N 119 40W
Westbourne 57 50 8N 98 35W
Westbrook, Maine, U.S.A. 72 43 40N 70 22W
Westbrook, Tex., U.S.A. 75 32 25N 101 0W
Westby, Austral. 136 35 30S 147 24E
Westby, U.S.A. 74 48 52N 104 3W
Westdale 48 43 17N 79 53W
Westend 81 35 42N 117 24W
Western Australia □ 134 25 0S 118 0E
Western Duck I. 46 45 45N 83 0W
Western Ghats 124 15 30N 74 30E
Western Isles □ 96 57 30N 7 10W
Western Pen. 52 49 30N 94 50W
Western Samoa ■ 133 14 0S 172 0W
Western Shore 39 44 32N 64 19W
Westernport 72 39 30N 79 5W
Westerschelde, R. 105 51 25N 4 0E
Westerwald, mts. 105 50 39N 8 0E
Westfield, Can. 39 45 22N 66 14W
Westfield, Ill., U.S.A. 77 39 27N 88 0W
Westfield, Ind., U.S.A. 77 40 2N 86 8W
Westfield, Mass., U.S.A. 71 42 9N 72 49W
Westfield, N.Y., U.S.A. 70 42 20N 79 38W
Westfield, Pa., U.S.A. 70 41 54N 77 32W
Westfriesche Eilanden 105 53 20N 5 10E
Westham I. 66 49 5N 123 10W
Westhope 57 48 55N 101 0W
Westland □ 133 43 33S 169 59E
Westland Bight 133 42 55S 170 5E
Westlock 60 54 9N 113 55W
Westmeath □ 97 53 30N 7 30W
Westminster 72 39 34N 77 1W
Westmorland 79 33 2N 115 42W
Westmount 44 45 29N 73 36W
Weston, Can. 50 43 43N 79 31W
Weston, Malay. 126 5 10N 115 35E
Weston, Ohio, U.S.A. 77 41 21N 83 47W
Weston, Oreg., U.S.A. 78 45 50N 118 30W
Weston, W. Va., U.S.A. 72 39 3N 80 29W
Weston I. 36 52 33N 79 36W
Weston-super-Mare 95 51 20N 2 59W
Westover 49 43 19N 80 5W
Westphalia 76 38 26N 92 0W
Westport, Newf., Can. 37 49 47N 56 38W
Westport, N.S., Can. 39 44 15N 66 22W
Westport, Ont., Can. 47 44 40N 76 25W
Westport, Ireland 97 53 44N 9 31W
Westport, N.Z. 133 41 46S 171 37E
Westport, U.S.A. 77 39 11N 85 34W
Westport, Ore., U.S.A. 80 46 10N 123 23W
Westport, Wash., U.S.A. 78 46 48N 124 4W
Westray 57 53 36N 101 24W
Westray, I. 96 59 18N 3 0W
Westree 53 47 26N 81 34W
Westsyde 63 50 47N 120 21W
Westview 54 49 50N 124 31W
Westville, Can. 39 45 34N 62 43W
Westville, Calif., U.S.A. 80 39 8N 120 42W
Westville, Ill., U.S.A. 77 40 3N 87 36W
Westville, Ind., U.S.A. 77 41 35N 86 55W
Westville, N.Y., U.S.A. 43 44 58N 74 20W
Westville, Okla., U.S.A. 75 36 0N 94 33W
Westwood 78 40 26N 121 0W
Wetar, I. 127 7 30S 126 30E
Wetaskiwin 61 52 55N 113 24W
Wetteren 105 51 0N 3 53E
Wetupoa 136 35 16S 143 46E
Wetzlar 106 50 33N 8 30E
Wewaka 75 35 10N 96 35W
Wexford, Can. 50 43 45N 79 18W
Wexford, Ireland 97 52 20N 6 28W
Wexford □ 97 52 20N 6 25W
Wexford Harb. 97 52 20N 6 25W
Weyburn 56 49 40N 103 50W
Weyburn L. 54 63 0N 117 59W
Weymouth, Can. 39 44 30N 66 1W
Weymouth, U.K. 95 50 36N 2 28W
Weymouth, U.S.A. 71 42 13N 70 53W
Weymouth, C. 135 12 37S 143 27E
Wezep 105 52 28N 6 0E
Whakatane 133 37 57S 177 1E
Whale Cove 55 62 11N 92 36W
Whale, R. 36 58 15N 67 40W
Whales 91 78 0S 165 0W
Whaletown 62 50 7N 125 2W
Whalsay, I. 96 60 22N 1 0W
Whampoa 131 23 5N 113 20E
Whangamomona 133 39 8S 174 44E
Whangarei 133 35 43S 174 21E
Whangarei Harbour 133 35 45S 174 28E
Wharfe, R. 94 53 55N 1 30W
Wharton, N.J., U.S.A. 71 40 53N 74 36W
Wharton, Pa., U.S.A. 70 41 31N 78 1W
Wharton, Tex., U.S.A. 75 29 20N 96 6W
Whatcom, L. 63 48 43N 122 20W
Wheatfield 77 41 13N 87 4W
Wheatland, Calif., U.S.A. 80 39 1N 121 25W
Wheatland, Ind., U.S.A. 77 38 40N 87 19W
Wheatland, Wyo., U.S.A. 74 42 4N 105 58W
Wheatley 46 42 6N 82 27W
Wheaton, U.S.A. 77 41 52N 88 6W
Wheaton, Minn., U.S.A. 74 45 50N 96 29W
Wheelbarrow Pk. 80 37 26N 116 5W
Wheeler, Oreg., U.S.A. 78 45 45N 123 57W
Wheeler, Tex., U.S.A. 75 35 29N 100 15W
Wheeler Peak, Mt. 78 38 57N 114 15W
Wheeler, R., Qué., Can. 36 57 2N 67 13W
Wheeler, R., Sask., Can. 55 57 34N 104 15W
Wheeler Ridge 81 35 0N 118 57W
Wheeling 70 40 2N 80 41W
Whernside, Mt. 94 54 14N 2 24W
Whidbey I. 63 48 15N 122 40W
Whidbey Is. 134 34 30S 135 3E
Whiskey Gap 61 49 0N 113 3W
Whiskey Jack L. 55 58 23N 101 55W
Whistler 73 30 50N 88 10W
Whitbourne 37 47 25N 53 32W
Whitby, Can. 51 43 52N 78 56W
Whitby, U.K. 94 54 29N 0 37W
Whitcombe, Mt. 15 43 12S 171 0E
Whitcombe, P. 15 43 12S 171 0E
White B. 37 50 0N 56 35W
White Bear 56 50 53N 108 13W
White Bear Res. 37 48 10N 57 5W
White Bird 78 45 46N 116 21W
White Butte 72 46 23N 103 25W
White City 74 38 50N 96 45W
White Cliffs 133 43 26S 171 55E
White Deer 75 35 30N 101 8W
White Fox 56 53 27N 104 5W
White Hall 76 39 25N 90 27W
White Haven 71 41 3N 75 47W
White I. 133 37 30S 177 13E
White L., Ont., Can. 47 45 18N 76 31W
White L., Ont., Can. 53 48 47N 85 37W
White L., U.S.A. 75 29 45N 92 30W
White Mts. 80 37 30N 118 15W
White, Mts. 71 44 15N 71 15W
White Nile = Nîl el Abyad, Bahr 115 9 30N 31 40E
White Otter L. 52 49 5N 91 55W
White Owl L. 53 47 10N 82 35W
White Pass, Can. 67 59 40N 135 3W
White Pass, U.S.A. 80 46 38N 121 24W
White Pigeon 77 41 48N 85 39W
White Pine 52 46 44N 89 35W
White Plains 71 41 2N 73 44W
White, R., Can. 53 48 33N 86 16W
White, R., U.S.A. 77 38 25N 87 45W
White, R., Ark., U.S.A. 75 36 28N 93 55W
White, R., Colo., U.S.A. 78 40 8N 108 52W
White, R., Ind., U.S.A. 72 39 25N 86 30W
White, R., S.D., U.S.A. 74 43 10N 102 52W
White, R., Wash., U.S.A. 80 47 12N 122 15W
White River, Can. 53 48 35N 85 20W
White River, U.S.A. 74 43 48N 100 45W
White River Junc. 71 43 38N 72 20W
White Rock 66 49 2N 122 48W
White Sulphur Springs, Mont., U.S.A. 78 46 35N 111 0W
White Sulphur Springs, W. Va., U.S.A. 78 37 50N 80 16W
White Swan 80 46 23N 120 44W
Whiteclay L. 52 50 53N 88 45W
Whitecourt 60 54 10N 115 45W
Whiteface 75 33 35N 102 40W
Whiteface R. 52 46 58N 92 48W
Whitefield 71 44 23N 71 37W
Whitefish, Can. 46 46 23N 81 19W
Whitefish, U.S.A. 78 48 25N 114 22W
Whitefish Bay 77 43 23N 87 54W
Whitefish Falls 46 46 7N 81 44W
Whitefish L., Can. 55 62 41N 106 48W
Whitefish L., U.S.A. 52 46 40N 94 10W
Whitefish Pt. 53 46 45N 85 0W
Whitegull, L. 36 55 27N 64 17W
Whitehall, Mich., U.S.A. 72 43 21N 86 20W
Whitehall, Mont., U.S.A. 78 45 52N 112 4W
Whitehall, N.Y., U.S.A. 71 43 32N 73 28W
Whitehall, Wis., U.S.A. 74 44 20N 91 19W
Whitehaven 94 54 33N 3 35W
Whitehorse 67 60 43N 135 3W
Whitehorse, Vale of 95 51 37N 1 30W
Whiteman 76 38 45N 93 40W
Whitemouth 57 49 57N 95 58W
Whitemouth L. 57 49 15N 95 40W
Whitemouth, R. 57 50 7N 96 2W
Whitemud Cr. 59 53 31N 113 34W
Whitesail, L. 54 53 35N 127 45W
Whitesand, R. 56 51 34N 102 56W
Whitesboro, N.Y., U.S.A. 71 43 8N 75 20W
Whitesboro, Tex., U.S.A. 75 33 40N 96 58W
Whiteshell Prov. Park 57 50 0N 95 40W
Whiteside 76 39 12N 91 2W
Whiteswan Ls. 56 54 5N 105 10W
Whitetail 56 48 54N 105 15W
Whitevale 50 43 53N 79 9W
Whiteville 73 34 20N 78 40W
Whitewater 77 42 50N 88 45W
Whitewater Baldy, Mt. 79 33 20N 108 44W
Whitewater, Cr. 56 49 0N 108 0W
Whitewater L. 52 50 50N 89 10W
Whitewood 57 50 20N 102 20W
Whithorn 96 54 55N 4 25W
Whitianga 133 36 47S 175 41E
Whiting 77 41 41N 87 29W
Whitman 71 42 4N 70 55W
Whitmire 73 34 33N 81 40W
Whitney 47 45 31N 78 14W
Whitney, Mt. 80 36 35N 118 14W
Whitney Pt. 71 42 19N 75 59W
Whitstable 95 51 21N 1 2E
Whitsunday I. 135 20 15S 149 4E
Whittemore 76 43 4N 94 26W
Whittier 67 60 46N 148 48W
Whittington 49 43 59N 80 10W
Whitwell 73 35 15N 85 30W
Wholdaia L. 55 60 43N 104 20W
Whyalla 135 33 2S 137 30E
Whycocomagh 39 45 59N 61 7W
Wiarton 46 44 40N 81 10W
Wibaux 74 47 0N 104 13W
Wichita 75 37 40N 97 29W
Wichita Falls 75 33 57N 98 30W
Wick 96 58 26N 3 5W
Wicked Pt. 47 43 52N 77 15W
Wickenburg 79 33 58N 112 45W
Wickett 75 31 37N 102 58W
Wickham 41 45 45N 72 30W
Wickliffe 70 41 36N 81 29W
Wicklow 97 53 0N 6 2W
Wicklow □ 97 52 59N 6 25W
Wicklow Hd. 97 52 59N 6 3W
Wicklow Mts. 97 53 0N 6 30W
Widnes 94 53 22N 2 44W
Wieliczka 107 50 0N 20 5E
Wielun 107 51 15N 18 40E
Wien 106 48 12N 16 22E
Wiener Neustadt 106 47 49N 16 16E
Wiesbaden 105 50 7N 8 17E
Wigan 94 53 33N 2 38W
Wiggins, Colo., U.S.A. 74 40 16N 104 3W
Wiggins, Miss., U.S.A. 75 30 53N 89 9W
Wight, I. of 95 50 40N 1 20W
Wigtown 96 54 52N 4 27W
Wigtown B. 96 54 46N 4 15W
Wikwemikong 46 45 48N 81 43W
Wilber 74 40 34N 96 59W
Wilberforce, Can. 47 45 2N 78 13W
Wilberforce, U.S.A. 77 39 43N 83 52W
Wilburton 75 34 55N 95 15W
Wilcannia 136 31 30S 143 26E
Wilcock Lake 50 43 56N 79 25W
Wilcocks L. 50 43 57N 79 26W
Wilcox, Can. 56 50 6N 104 44W
Wilcox, U.S.A. 70 41 34N 78 43W
Wildcat Creek, R. 77 40 28N 86 48W
Wildfield 50 43 49N 79 44W
Wildgoose L. 53 49 44N 87 11W
Wildhay, R. 60 53 59N 117 20W
Wildrose, Calif., U.S.A. 81 36 14N 117 11W
Wildrose, N. Dak., U.S.A. 74 48 36N 103 17W
Wildwood, Can. 60 53 37N 115 14W
Wildwood, U.S.A. 72 38 59N 74 46W
Wilhelm II Coast 91 67 0S 90 0E
Wilhelmina, Mt. 87 3 50N 56 30W
Wilhelmshaven 106 53 30N 8 9E
Wilkes-Barre 71 41 15N 75 52W
Wilkes Land 91 69 0S 120 0E
Wilkesboro 73 36 10N 81 9W
Wilkie 56 52 27N 108 42W
Wilkinsburg 70 40 26N 79 50W
Willamina 78 45 9N 123 32W
Willandra Billabong Creek 136 33 22S 145 52E
Willapa, B. 78 46 44N 124 0W
Willapa Hills 80 46 35N 123 25W
Willard, N. Mex., U.S.A. 79 34 35N 106 1W
Willard, Utah, U.S.A. 78 41 28N 112 1W
Willcox 79 32 13N 109 53W
Willebroek 105 51 4N 4 22E
Willemstad 85 12 5N 69 0W
William A. Switzer Prov. Park 60 53 30N 117 48W
William L. 57 53 54N 99 21W
William, R. 55 59 8N 109 19W
Williams, Ariz., U.S.A. 79 35 16N 112 11W
Williams, Calif., U.S.A. 80 39 9N 122 9W
Williams, Minn., U.S.A. 52 48 45N 94 54W
Williams L. 52 51 48N 90 45W
Williams Lake 63 52 10N 122 10W
Williamsburg, Can. 49 43 24N 80 30W
Williamsburg, Ky., U.S.A. 73 36 45N 84 10W
Williamsburg, Pa., U.S.A. 70 40 27N 78 14W
Williamsburg, Va., U.S.A. 72 37 17N 76 44W
Williamsfield 76 40 55N 90 1W
Williamson, N.Y., U.S.A. 70 43 14N 77 15W
Williamson, W. Va., U.S.A. 72 37 46N 82 17W
Williamsport, Ind., U.S.A. 77 40 17N 87 17W
Williamsport, Pa., U.S.A. 70 41 18N 77 1W
Williamston, U.S.A. 77 42 41N 84 17W

Williamston **Xique-Xique**

Williamston, S.C., U.S.A. 73 35 50N 77 5W
Williamstown, Austral. 136 37 51S 144 52E
Williamstown, Can. 43 45 9N 74 34W
Williamstown, U.S.A. 77 38 38N 84 34W
Williamstown, Mass., U.S.A. 71 42 41N 73 12W
Williamstown, N.Y., U.S.A. 71 43 25N 75 54W
Williamsville, U.S.A. 76 39 57N 89 33W
Williamsville, Mo., U.S.A. 75 37 0N 90 33W
Willimantic 71 41 45N 72 12W
Willingdon 60 53 50N 112 8W
Willisburg 77 37 49N 85 8W
Williston, Fla, U.S.A. 73 29 25N 82 28W
Williston, N.D., U.S.A. 74 48 10N 103 35W
Williston L. 54 56 0N 124 0W
Willits 78 39 28N 123 17W
Willmar 74 45 5N 95 0W
Willmore Wilderness Park 60 53 45N 119 30W
Willoughby 70 41 38N 81 26W
Willow Bunch 56 49 20N 105 35W
Willow Bunch L. 56 49 27N 105 27W
Willow L. 54 62 10N 119 8W
Willow Lake 74 44 40N 97 40W
Willow River 54 54 6N 122 28W
Willow Springs 75 37 0N 92 0W
Willowbrook 56 51 12N 102 48W
Willowdale 50 43 47N 79 26W
Willowlake, R. 54 62 42N 123 8W
Willowmore 117 33 15S 23 30E
Willows 80 39 30N 122 10W
Wills Pt. 75 32 42N 95 57W
Wilmette 72 42 6N 87 44W
Wilmington, U.S.A. 77 39 27N 83 50W
Wilmington, Del., U.S.A. 72 39 45N 75 32W
Wilmington, Ill., U.S.A. 77 41 19N 88 10W
Wilmington, N.C., U.S.A. 73 34 14N 77 54W
Wilmot 39 46 2N 62 30W
Wilsall 78 45 59N 110 40W
Wilson, N.C., U.S.A. 73 35 44N 77 54W
Wilson, N.Y., U.S.A. 49 43 19N 78 50W
Wilson Creek 62 49 27N 123 43W
Wilson Landing 63 50 0N 119 30W
Wilson, Mt. 79 37 55N 108 3W
Wilsons Beach 39 44 56N 66 56W
Wilson's Promontory 136 38 55S 146 25E
Wilsonvale 44 45 18N 74 11W
Wilsonville 49 42 58N 80 19W
Wilton, U.K. 95 51 5N 1 52W
Wilton, U.S.A. 74 47 12N 100 53W
Wiltshire □ 95 51 20N 2 0W
Wiltz 105 49 57N 5 55E
Wiluna 134 26 36S 120 14E
Wimereux 101 50 45N 1 37E
Wimmera 135 36 30S 142 0E
Wimmera, R. 136 36 8S 141 56E
Winagami L. 60 55 37N 116 44W
Winagami Lake Prov. Park 60 55 37N 116 39W
Winamac 77 41 3N 86 36W
Winch 71 42 26N 71 9W
Winchendon 71 42 40N 72 3W
Winchester, Can. 47 45 6N 75 21W
Winchester, U.K. 95 51 4N 1 19W
Winchester, U.S.A. 76 39 38N 90 27W
Winchester, U.S.A. 77 38 57N 83 40W
Winchester, Conn., U.S.A. 71 41 53N 73 9W
Winchester, Idaho, U.S.A. 78 46 11N 116 32W
Winchester, Ind., U.S.A. 77 40 10N 84 56W
Winchester, Ky., U.S.A. 77 38 0N 84 8W
Winchester, Nev., U.S.A. 81 36 6N 115 10W
Winchester, N.H., U.S.A. 71 42 47N 72 22W
Winchester, Tenn., U.S.A. 73 35 11N 86 8W
Winchester, Va., U.S.A. 72 39 14N 78 8W
Wind Pt. 77 42 47N 87 46W
Wind, R. 78 43 30N 109 30W
Wind River Range, Mts. 78 43 0N 109 30W
Windber 70 40 14N 78 50W
Windemere L. 53 47 58N 83 47W
Winder 73 34 0N 83 40W
Windermere, Can. 61 50 28N 115 59W
Windermere, U.K. 94 54 24N 2 56W
Windermere, L. 94 54 20N 2 57W
Windfall, Can. 60 54 12N 116 13W
Windfall, U.S.A. 77 40 22N 85 57W
Windflower L. 54 62 52N 118 30W
Windhoek 117 22 35S 17 4E
Windigo, R. 41 47 46N 73 19W
Windom 74 43 48N 95 3W
Windorah 135 25 24S 142 36E
Window Rock 79 35 47N 109 4W
Windrush, R. 95 51 48N 1 35W
Windsor, Austral. 136 33 37S 150 50E
Windsor, Newf., Can. 37 48 57N 55 40W
Windsor, N.S., Can. 39 44 59N 64 5W
Windsor, Ont., Can. 46 42 18N 83 0W
Windsor, Qué., Can. 41 45 34N 72 0W
Windsor, U.K. 95 51 28N 0 36W
Windsor, U.S.A. 77 39 26N 88 36W
Windsor, Col., U.S.A. 74 40 33N 104 45W
Windsor, Conn., U.S.A. 71 41 50N 72 40W
Windsor, Mo., U.S.A. 76 38 32N 93 31W
Windsor, N.Y., U.S.A. 71 42 5N 75 37W
Windsor, Vt., U.S.A. 71 43 30N 72 25W
Windsor Heights 37 47 36N 52 49W
Windsor L. 37 47 36N 52 48W
Windthorst 56 50 6N 102 50W
Windward Is. 85 13 0N 63 0W
Windward Passage 85 20 0N 74 0W
Windy L., N.W.T., Can. 55 60 20N 100 2W
Windy L., Sask., Can. 56 54 22N 102 35W
Winefred L. 60 55 30N 110 30W
Winfield, Can. 61 52 58N 114 26W
Winfield, Ill., U.S.A. 76 41 5N 91 30W
Winfield, Kans., U.S.A. 75 37 15N 97 0W
Winfield, Mo., U.S.A. 76 39 0N 90 44W
Wingen Mt. 136 31 50S 150 58E
Wingham, Austral. 136 31 48S 152 22E
Wingham, Can. 46 43 55N 81 20W
Winifred 78 47 30N 109 28W
Winisk 34 55 20N 85 15W
Winisk L. 34 52 55N 87 22W
Winisk, R. 34 55 17N 85 5W
Wink 75 31 49N 103 9W
Winkler 57 49 10N 97 56W
Winlock 80 46 29N 122 56W
Winnebago, Ill., U.S.A. 76 42 15N 89 18W
Winnebago, Minn., U.S.A. 74 43 43N 94 8W
Winnebago L. 72 44 0N 88 20W
Winnemucca 78 41 0N 117 45W
Winnemucca, L. 78 40 25N 19 21W
Winner 74 43 23N 99 52W
Winnetka 72 42 8N 87 46W
Winnett 78 47 2N 108 28W
Winnfield 75 31 57N 92 38W
Winnibigoshish L. 52 47 25N 94 12W
Winnipeg 58 49 54N 97 9W
Winnipeg Beach 57 50 30N 96 58W
Winnipeg International Airport 58 49 55N 97 15W
Winnipeg, L. 57 52 0N 97 0W
Winnipeg, R. 57 50 38N 96 19W
Winnipegosis 57 51 39N 99 55W
Winnipegosis L. 57 52 30N 100 0W
Winnsboro, La., U.S.A. 75 32 10N 91 41W
Winnsboro, S.C., U.S.A. 73 34 23N 81 5W
Winnsboro, Tex., U.S.A. 74 32 56N 95 15W
Winokapau, L. 36 53 15N 62 50W
Winona, Can. 49 43 12N 79 39W
Winona, Miss., U.S.A. 75 33 30N 89 42W
Winona, Wis., U.S.A. 52 46 53N 88 55W
Winona, Wis., U.S.A. 74 44 2N 91 45W
Winooski 71 44 31N 73 11W
Winschoten 105 53 9N 7 3E
Winslow, U.S.A. 77 38 23N 87 13W
Winslow, Ariz., U.S.A. 79 35 2N 110 41W
Winslow, Wash., U.S.A. 80 47 37N 122 31W
Winstead 71 41 55N 73 5W
Winston-Salem 73 36 7N 80 15W
Winter Garden 73 28 33N 81 35W
Winter Harbour 62 50 31N 128 2W
Winter Haven 73 28 0N 81 42W
Winter Park 73 28 34N 81 19W
Winterbourne 49 43 33N 80 28W
Winterhaven 81 32 47N 114 39W
Wintering L. 53 49 26N 87 16W
Winters, Calif., U.S.A. 80 38 32N 121 58W
Winters, Tex., U.S.A. 75 31 58N 99 58W
Winterset 76 41 18N 94 0W
Wintersville 70 40 23N 80 38W
Winterswijk 105 51 58N 6 43E
Winterthur 106 47 30N 8 44E
Winterton 37 47 58N 53 20W
Winthrop, Minn., U.S.A. 74 44 31N 94 25W
Winthrop, Wash., U.S.A. 63 48 27N 120 6W
Winton, Austral. 135 22 24S 143 3E
Winton, N.Z. 133 46 8S 168 20E
Winton, N.C., U.S.A. 73 36 25N 76 58W
Winton, Pa., U.S.A. 71 41 27N 75 33W
Wirral 94 53 25N 3 0W
Wisbech 94 52 39N 0 10E
Wisconsin □ 74 44 30N 90 0W
Wisconsin Dells 74 43 38N 89 45W
Wisconsin, R. 74 45 25N 89 45W
Wisconsin Rapids 74 44 25N 89 50W
Wisdom 67 45 36N 113 1W
Wiserman 67 67 25N 150 15W
Wiseton 56 51 19N 107 39W
Wishart 56 51 33N 103 59W
Wishaw 96 55 46N 3 55W
Wishek 74 46 20N 99 35W
Wisła, R. 107 53 38N 18 47E
Wismar 106 53 53N 11 23E
Wisner 74 42 0N 96 46W
Wissant 101 50 52N 1 40E
Wissembourg 101 48 57N 7 57E
Wistaria 62 53 52N 126 22W
Witbank 117 25 51S 29 14E
Witham, R. 94 53 3N 0 8W
Withernsea 94 53 43N 0 2W
Withrow 61 52 23N 114 30W
Witney 95 51 47N 1 29W
Witten 105 51 26N 7 19E
Wittenberg 106 51 51N 12 39E
Wittenberge 106 53 0N 11 44E
Wittenoom 134 22 15S 118 20E
Wkra, R. 107 52 45N 20 30E
Wlen 78 51 0N 15 39E
Wlingi 127 8 5S 112 25E
Woburn, Can. 50 43 46N 79 13W
Woburn, U.S.A. 71 42 31N 71 7W
Wodonga 136 36 5S 146 50E
Woerth 101 48 57N 7 45E
Woëvre 101 49 15N 5 45E
Wokam, I. 127 5 45S 134 28E
Woking 54 55 35N 118 50W
Wolcottville 77 41 32N 85 22W
Wolf Bay 38 50 16N 60 8W
Wolf Creek 78 47 1N 112 2W
Wolf L. 54 60 24N 131 40W
Wolf Point 74 48 6N 105 40W
Wolf, R. 54 60 17N 132 33W
Wolfe I. 47 44 7N 76 20W
Wolfenden 54 52 0N 119 25W
Wolfville 39 45 5N 64 22W
Wolin 106 53 40N 14 37E
Wollaston, Islas 90 55 40S 67 30W
Wollaston L. 55 58 7N 103 10W
Wollaston Pen. 64 69 30N 115 0W
Wollondilly, R. 136 34 12S 150 18E
Wollongong 136 34 25S 150 54E
Wolseley 56 50 25N 103 15W
Wolstenholme, C. 36 62 35N 77 30W
Wolstenholme Fjord 65 76 0N 70 0W
Wolvega 105 52 52N 6 0E
Wolverhampton 95 52 35N 2 6W
Wolverine 46 45 16N 84 36W
Won Wron 136 38 23S 146 45E
Wondai 135 26 20S 151 49E
Wŏnju 130 37 22N 127 58E
Wonosari 127 7 38S 110 36E
Wŏnsan 130 39 11N 127 27E
Wonthaggi 136 38 37S 145 37E
Wood Buffalo Nat. Park 54 59 0N 113 41W
Wood L. 55 55 17N 103 17W
Wood Lake 74 42 38N 100 14W
Wood Mt. 55 49 14N 106 30W
Wood, R. 56 50 8N 106 13W
Wood River 76 38 52N 90 5W
Woodbridge 50 43 47N 79 36W
Woodburn 49 43 8N 79 45W
Woodchopper 67 65 25N 143 30W
Woodend 136 37 20N 144 33E
Woodfibre 63 49 41N 123 15W
Woodfords 80 38 47N 119 50W
Woodhill 50 43 45N 79 41W
Woodlake 80 36 25N 119 6W
Woodland 80 38 40N 121 50W
Woodlands 57 50 12N 97 40W
Woodpecker 63 53 30N 122 40W
Woodridge 57 49 20N 96 9W
Woodroffe, Mt. 134 26 20S 131 45E
Woodruff, Ariz., U.S.A. 79 34 51N 110 1W
Woodruff, Utah, U.S.A. 78 41 30N 111 4W
Woods, L., Austral. 134 17 50S 133 30E
Woods, L., Can. 36 54 30N 65 13W
Woods, L. of the 52 49 15N 94 45W
Woodside, Austral. 136 38 31S 146 52E
Woodside, Can. 39 44 39N 63 33W
Woodstock, N.B., Can. 39 46 11N 67 37W
Woodstock, Ont., Can. 46 43 10N 80 45W
Woodstock, U.K. 95 51 51N 1 20W
Woodstock, Ill., U.S.A. 77 42 17N 88 30W
Woodstock, Vt., U.S.A. 71 43 37N 72 31W
Woodsville 71 44 10N 72 0W
Woodville, N.Z. 133 40 20S 175 53E
Woodville, U.S.A. 77 41 27N 83 22W
Woodville, Tex., U.S.A. 75 30 45N 94 25W
Woodward 75 36 24N 99 28W
Woody 81 35 42N 118 50W
Woody Point 37 49 30N 57 55W
Woombye 136 26 40S 152 55E
Woomera 135 31 11S 136 47E
Woonona 136 34 21S 150 54E
Woonsocket 71 42 0N 71 30W
Woonsockett 74 44 5N 98 15W
Wooramel, R. 134 25 30S 114 30E
Wooster 70 40 38N 81 55W
Worcester, S. Afr. 117 33 39S 19 27E
Worcester, U.K. 95 52 12N 2 12W
Worcester, Mass., U.S.A. 71 42 14N 71 49W
Worcester, N.Y., U.S.A. 71 42 35N 74 45W
Worden 76 38 56N 89 50W
Workington 94 54 39N 3 34W
Worksop 94 53 19N 1 9W
Workum 105 52 59N 5 26E
Worland 78 44 0N 107 59W
Wormerveer 105 52 30N 4 46E
Wormhoudt 101 50 52N 2 28E
Worms 106 49 37N 8 21E
Worsley 60 56 31N 119 8W
Wortham 75 31 48N 96 27W
Worthing 95 50 49N 0 21W
Worthington, Ind., U.S.A. 77 39 7N 86 59W
Worthington, Minn., U.S.A. 74 43 35N 95 30W
Worthington, Ohio, U.S.A. 77 40 5N 83 1W
Wosi 127 0 15S 128 0E
Woss Camp 62 50 13N 126 35W
Woss L. 62 50 7N 126 36W
Wota (Shoa Ghimirra) 115 7 4N 35 51E
Wottonville 41 45 44N 71 48W
Wowoni, I. 127 4 5S 123 5E
Wrangell 67 56 30N 132 25W
Wrangell, I. 54 56 20N 132 10W
Wrangell Mts. 67 61 40N 143 30W
Wrath, C. 96 58 38N 5 0W
Wray 74 40 8N 102 18W
Wrekin, The, Mt. 94 52 41N 2 35W
Wrens 73 33 13N 82 23W
Wrexham 94 53 5N 3 0W
Wright, Can. 63 51 52N 121 40W
Wright, Phil. 127 11 42N 125 2E
Wright, Mt. 35 52 40N 67 25W
Wrightson, Mt. 79 31 49N 110 56W
Wrightwood 81 34 21N 117 38W
Wrigley 64 63 16N 123 27W
Wrigley Corners 49 43 17N 80 22W
Wrocław 106 51 5N 17 5E
Wrottesley, C. 64 74 32N 121 33W
Wroxton 57 51 14N 101 53W
Września 107 52 21N 17 36E
Wu K. 131 27 30N 107 45E
Wuchai 130 39 10N 111 36E
Wuchan 131 28 30N 108 10E
Wuchang 130 44 51N 127 10E
Wuchen 130 41 10N 108 32E
Wuchow 131 23 26N 111 19E
Wuchung 130 38 4N 106 12E
Wuhan 131 30 35N 114 15E
Wuhu 131 31 18N 118 20E
Wukang, Chekiang, China 131 30 35N 119 50E
Wukang, Hunan, China 131 26 50N 110 15E
Wuki (Taning) 131 31 27N 109 46E
Wukung Shan, mts. 131 27 20N 114 0E
Wuliaru, I. 127 7 10S 131 0E
Wulumuchi 129 43 40N 87 50E
Wuning 131 29 16N 115 0E
Wunnummin L. 34 52 55N 89 10W
Wuntho 125 23 55N 95 45E
Wuping 131 25 5N 116 20E
Wuppertal 105 51 15N 7 8E
Würzburg 106 49 46N 9 55E
Wushan 131 31 3N 109 57E
Wusih 131 31 30N 120 30E
Wusu 129 44 27N 84 37E
Wutai 130 41 16N 113 59E
Wuting Ho 130 37 8N 110 31E
Wutu 131 33 27N 104 37E
Wutunghliao 129 29 25N 104 0E
Wuwei 129 37 55N 102 48E
Wuyi, China 130 37 54N 116 0E
Wuyi, China 131 28 45N 119 56E
Wuyi Shan 131 26 40N 116 30E
Wuying 130 48 10N 129 20E
Wuyuan 130 41 15N 108 30E
Wuyun 129 46 16N 129 37E
Wyalong 136 33 54S 147 16E
Wyalusing 71 41 40N 76 16W
Wyandotte 77 42 14N 83 13W
Wyandra 135 27 12S 145 56E
Wyangala Res. 136 33 54S 149 0E
Wycheproof 136 36 0N 143 17E
Wye, R. 95 52 0N 2 36W
Wymark 56 50 7N 107 44W
Wymlet 136 34 52S 142 10E
Wymondham, Leicester, U.K. 95 52 45N 0 42W
Wymondham, Norfolk, U.K. 95 52 34N 1 7E
Wymore 74 40 10N 96 40W
Wynadotte 46 42 11N 83 14W
Wyndham, Austral. 134 15 33S 128 3E
Wyndham, N.Z. 133 46 20S 168 51E
Wyndham Hills 49 43 10N 80 17W
Wyniatt B. 64 72 45N 110 30W
Wynndel 61 49 11N 116 33W
Wynne 75 35 15N 90 50W
Wynyard 56 51 45N 104 10W
Wyoming, Can. 46 42 57N 82 7W
Wyoming, U.S.A. 77 42 53N 85 42W
Wyoming, Ill., U.S.A. 76 41 4N 89 47W
Wyoming, Iowa, U.S.A. 76 42 4N 91 3W
Wyoming, N.Y., U.S.A. 70 42 46N 78 4W
Wyoming □ 68 42 48N 109 0W
Wyong 136 33 14S 151 24E
Wytheville 72 37 0N 81 3W

X

Xanthi 109 41 10N 24 58E
Xapuri 86 10 35S 68 35W
Xavantina 89 21 15S 52 48W
Xenia, Ill., U.S.A. 77 38 38N 88 38W
Xenia, Ohio, U.S.A. 77 39 42N 83 57W
Xieng Khouang 128 19 17N 103 25E
Xinavane 117 25 2S 32 47E
Xingu, R. 87 2 25S 52 35W
Xique-Xique 87 10 50S 42 40W

Yaan Zeeland □

Y

Yaan 129 30 0N 102 59 E
Yaapeet 136 35 45 S 142 3 E
Yablonovyy Khrebet 121 53 0N 114 0 E
Yabrīn 122 23 7N 48 52 E
Yacuiba 88 22 0 S 63 25W
Yadgir 124 16 45N 77 5 E
Yadkin, R. 73 36 15N 81 0W
Yahatahama 132 33 25N 132 40 E
Yahk 61 49 6N 116 10W
Yahuma 116 1 0N 22 5 E
Yaicheng 131 18 14N 109 7 E
Yakataga 67 60 5N 142 32W
Yakima 78 46 42N 120 30W
Yakima, R. 78 47 0N 120 30W
Yakoshih 129 49 13N 120 35 E
Yakut A.S.S.R. □ 121 62 0N 130 0 E
Yakutat 67 59 50N 139 44W
Yakutsk 121 62 5N 129 40 E
Yala 128 6 33N 101 18 E
Yalabusha, R. 75 33 53N 89 50W
Yale, Can. 80 49 34N 121 25W
Yale, U.S.A. 46 43 9N 82 47W
Yalgoo 134 28 16 S 116 39 E
Yalinga 116 6 20N 23 10 E
Yalkubul, Punta 83 21 32N 88 37W
Yallourn 136 38 10 S 146 18 E
Yalu K. 130 41 30N 126 30 E
Yalung K. 129 32 0N 100 0 E
Yalutorovsk 120 56 30N 65 40 E
Yam Kinneret (L. Tiberias) 115 32 49N 35 36 E
Yamagata 132 38 15N 140 15 E
Yamagata-ken □ 132 38 30N 140 0 E
Yamaguchi 132 34 10N 131 32 E
Yamaguchi-ken □ 132 34 20N 131 40 E
Yamal, Poluostrov 120 71 0N 70 0 E
Yamana 122 24 5N 47 30 E
Yamanashi-ken □ 132 35 40N 138 40 E
Yamantau 120 54 20N 57 40 E
Yamantau, Gora 120 54 15N 58 6 E
Yamaska 41 46 0N 72 55W
Yamaska □ 43 46 50N 72 50W
Yamaska, Mt. 43 45 27N 72 52W
Yamaska, R. 45 45 17N 72 55W
Yambol 109 42 30N 26 36 E
Yamdena 127 7 45 S 131 20 E
Yamdrok Tso 129 29 0N 90 40 E
Yamethin 125 20 29N 96 18 E
Yamhsien 131 21 45N 108 31 E
Yamma-Yamma L. 135 26 16 S 141 20 E
Yampa, R. 78 40 37N 108 0W
Yampi Sd. 134 16 8 S 123 38 E
Yamuna (Jumna), R. 125 27 0N 78 30 E
Yana, R. 121 69 0N 134 0 E
Yanac 136 36 8 S 141 25 E
Yanaul 120 56 25N 55 0 E
Yanbu 'al Bahr 122 24 0N 38 5 E
Yanco 136 34 38 S 146 27 E
Yandoon 125 17 0N 95 40 E
Yangambi 116 0 47N 24 20 E
Yangchow 131 32 25N 119 25 E
Yangchuan 130 38 0N 113 29 E
Yangi-Yer 120 40 17N 68 48 E
Yangkao 130 40 20N 113 40 E
Yangshui (Hinghwa) 131 29 53N 115 3 E
Yangso 131 24 36N 110 32 E
Yangtsun 130 39 29N 117 4 E
Yangtze Kiang 131 31 40N 122 0 E
Yanhee Res. 128 17 30N 98 45 E
Yankton 74 42 55N 97 25W
Yanping 131 22 25N 112 0 E
Yao Shan 131 24 0N 110 0 E
Yaomen 130 44 31N 125 8 E
Yaoundé 116 3 50N 11 35 E
Yap Is. 127 9 30N 138 10 E
Yapen 127 1 50 S 136 0 E
Yapen, Selat 127 1 20 S 136 10 E
Yapero 127 4 59 S 137 11 E
Yapo, R. 86 0 30 S 77 0W
Yaqui, R. 82 28 28N 109 30W
Yar-Sale 120 66 50N 70 50 E
Yaracuy □ 86 10 20N 68 45W
Yaraka 135 24 53 S 144 3 E
Yare, R. 95 52 36N 1 28 E
Yarensk 120 61 10N 49 8 E
Yari, R. 86 1 0N 73 40W
Yarkand (Soche) 129 38 24N 77 20 E
Yarker 47 44 23N 76 46W
Yarkhun, R. 124 36 30N 72 45 E
Yarmouth 39 43 50N 66 7W
Yaroslavl 120 57 35N 39 55 E
Yarra, R. 136 37 50 S 144 53 E
Yarrawonga 136 36 0 S 146 0 E
Yarrow 63 49 5N 122 2W
Yartsevo 121 60 20N 90 0 E
Yarumal 86 6 58N 75 24W
Yasawa Group 133 17 00 S 177 23 E
Yasinski, L. 36 53 16N 77 35W
Yasothon 128 15 50N 104 10 E
Yass 136 34 49 S 148 54 E
Yass, Res. 136 34 50 S 149 0 E
Yates Center 75 37 53N 95 45W
Yathkyed L. 55 62 40N 98 0W
Yatsushiro 132 32 30N 130 40 E
Yauyos 86 12 10 S 75 50W
Yavari R. 86 4 50 S 72 0W
Yayama-rettō 131 24 30N 123 40 E
Yazd (Yezd) 123 31 55N 54 27 E
Yazdan 123 33 30N 60 50 E
Yazoo City 75 32 48N 90 28W
Yazoo, R. 75 32 35N 90 50W
Yding Skovhøj 111 55 59N 9 46 E
Yebyu 125 14 15N 98 13 E
Yecla 104 38 35N 1 5W
Yécora 82 28 20N 108 58W
Yegros 88 26 20 S 56 25W
Yehsien 130 37 12N 119 58 E
Yehuda, Midbar 115 31 35N 34 57 E
Yelanskoye 121 61 25N 128 0 E
Yelets 120 52 40N 38 30 E
Yell, I. 96 60 35N 1 5W
Yell Sd. 96 60 33N 1 15W
Yellow Creek 56 52 45N 105 15W
Yellow Grass 56 49 48N 104 10W
Yellow Mt. 136 32 31 S 146 52 E
Yellow River = Hwang Ho 131 38 0N 117 20 E
Yellow Sea 130 35 0N 123 0 E
Yellowhead P. 63 52 53N 118 25W
Yellowknife 54 62 27N 114 21W
Yellowknife, R. 54 62 31N 114 19W
Yellowstone L. 78 44 30N 110 20W
Yellowstone National Park 78 44 35N 110 0W
Yellowstone, R. 74 46 35N 105 45W
Yemen ■ 115 15 0N 44 0 E
Yemen, South ■ 115 15 0N 48 0 E
Yenangyaung 125 20 30N 95 0 E
Yenchang 130 36 44N 110 2 E
Yencheng, Honan, China 131 33 43N 114 10 E
Yencheng, Kiangsu, China 131 33 22N 120 12 E
Yenchwan 130 37 0N 110 5 E
Yenda 136 34 13 S 146 14 E
Yengchun 131 22 10N 111 27 E
Yenisey, R. 120 68 0N 86 30 E
Yeniseysk 121 58 39N 92 4 E
Yeniseyskiy Zaliv 120 72 20N 81 0 E
Yenki, Kirin, China 130 43 12N 129 30 E
Yenki, Sinkiang, China 129 42 12N 86 30 E
Yenking 130 40 30N 116 0 E
Yenne 103 45 43N 5 44 E
Yenshih 131 34 42N 112 50 E
Yentai 130 37 30N 121 22 E
Yenyuka 121 58 20N 121 30 E
Yeo, L. 134 28 0 S 124 30 E
Yeo, R. 95 51 1N 2 46W
Yeola 124 20 0N 74 30 E
Yeotmal 124 20 20N 78 15 E
Yeovil 95 50 57N 2 38W
Yeppoon 135 23 5 S 150 47 E
Yerbent 120 39 30N 58 50 E
Yerbogachen 121 61 16N 108 0 E
Yerevan 120 40 10N 44 20 E
Yerington 80 38 59N 119 10W
Yermakovo 121 52 35N 126 20 E
Yermo 81 34 58N 116 50W
Yerofey Pavlovich 121 54 0N 122 0 E
Yershov 120 51 15N 48 27 E
Yerville 100 49 40N 0 53 E
Yes Tor, Mt. 95 50 41N 3 59W
Yeso 75 34 29N 104 37W
Yeu, I. d' 100 46 42N 2 20W
Yeungchun 131 22 15N 111 40 E
Yeungkong 131 21 55N 112 0 E
Yeungshan 131 24 27N 112 15 E
Yeysk Staro 120 46 40N 38 12 E
Yhati 88 25 45 S 56 35W
Yhú 89 25 0 S 56 0W
Yi, R. 88 33 7 S 57 8W
Yiannitsa 109 40 46N 22 24 E
Yihsien 131 34 50N 117 50 E
Yilan 131 24 47N 121 44 E
Yin Shan, mts. 130 41 0N 112 0 E
Yincheng 131 31 0N 113 40 E
Yinchwan 130 38 30N 106 20 E
Yingcheng 131 31 0N 113 44 E
Yingchow 130 39 45N 113 30 E
Yingkiang 131 28 10N 108 40 E
Yingkow 130 40 43N 122 9 E
Yingshan 131 30 50N 115 45 E
Yingtak 131 24 10N 113 5 E
Yingtan 131 28 12N 117 0 E
Yinmabin 125 22 10N 94 55 E
Yipang 128 22 15N 101 26 E
Yithion 109 36 46N 22 34 E
Yitu 130 36 40N 118 25 E
Yixian 131 41 32N 121 15 E
Yiyang 131 28 45N 112 16 E
Ylitornio 110 66 19N 23 39 E
Ylivieska 110 64 4N 24 28 E
Ynykchanskiy 121 60 15N 137 43 E
Yoakum 75 29 20N 97 10W
Yog Pt. 127 13 55N 124 20 E
Yogyakarta 127 7 49 S 110 22 E
Yoho Nat. Park 63 51 25N 116 30W
Yojoa, L. de 84 14 53N 88 0W
Yokadouma 116 3 35N 14 50 E
Yōkaichi 132 35 6N 136 12 E
Yokkaichi 132 35 0N 136 30 E
Yokohama 132 35 27N 139 39 E
Yokosuka 132 35 20N 139 40 E
Yola 114 9 10N 12 29 E
Yolaina, Cordillera de 84 11 30N 84 0W
Yolgali 136 34 20 S 146 7 E
Yom Mae Nam 128 15 15N 100 20 E
Yonago 132 35 25N 133 19 E
Yonaguni 131 24 28N 122 59 E
Yong Peng 128 2 0N 103 3 E
Yŏngchŏn 130 35 55N 128 55 E
Yŏngwŏl 130 37 18N 128 20 E
Yonker 55 52 40N 109 40W
Yonkers 71 40 57N 73 51W
Yonne □ 101 47 50N 3 40 E
Yonne, R. 101 48 23N 2 58 E
York, Austral. 134 31 52 S 116 47 E
York, Ont., Can. 50 43 1N 79 53W
York, Ont., Can. 50 43 42N 79 27W
York, U.K. 94 53 58N 1 7W
York, Ala., U.S.A. 73 32 30N 88 18W
York, Nebr., U.S.A. 74 40 55N 97 35W
York, Pa., U.S.A. 72 39 57N 76 43W
York □ 49 43 55N 79 30W
York, C., Austral. 135 10 42 S 142 31 E
York, C., Can. 65 76 30N 68 0W
York Factory 55 57 0N 92 18W
York, Kap 17 75 55N 66 25W
York Mills 50 43 45N 79 25W
York, R. 38 48 49N 64 34W
York Sd. 134 14 50 S 125 5 E
York, Vale of 98 54 15N 1 25W
Yorke Pen. 135 34 50 S 137 40 E
Yorkshire, reg. 94 54 54N 1 0W
Yorkshire Wolds 94 54 0N 0 30W
Yorkton 57 51 11N 102 28W
Yorktown 75 29 0N 97 29W
Yorkville, U.S.A. 77 41 38N 88 27W
Yorkville, Calif., U.S.A. 80 38 52N 123 13W
Yoro 84 15 9N 87 7W
Yosemite National Park 80 38 0N 119 30W
Yosemite Village 80 37 45N 119 35W
Yŏsu 131 34 47N 127 45 E
Yotsing 131 28 10N 120 55 E
Youbou 62 48 53N 124 13W
Youghal 97 51 58N 7 51W
Youghal B. 97 51 55N 7 50W
Youghal Har. 97 51 55N 7 50W
Young, Austral. 136 34 19 S 148 18 E
Young, Can. 56 51 47N 105 45W
Young, Uruguay 88 32 44 S 57 36W
Young, U.S.A. 79 34 9N 110 56W
Youngstown, Can. 61 51 35N 111 10W
Youngstown, N.Y., U.S.A. 49 43 16N 79 2W
Youngstown, Ohio, U.S.A. 70 41 7N 80 41W
Youngsville 70 41 51N 79 21W
Yoyang 131 29 27N 113 10 E
Yozgat 122 39 51N 34 47 E
Ypané, R. 88 23 29 S 57 19W
Yport 100 49 45N 0 15 E
Ypsilanti 77 42 18N 83 40W
Yreka 78 41 44N 122 40W
Ysleta 79 31 45N 106 24W
Yssingeaux 103 45 9N 4 8 E
Ystad 111 55 26N 13 50 E
Ythan, R. 96 57 26N 2 12W
Ytyk-Kel 121 62 20N 133 28 E
Yu Shan, Mt. 131 23 30N 121 0 E
Yuan Kiang 131 28 40N 110 30 E
Yuanling 131 28 30N 110 5 E
Yuanyang 129 23 10N 102 58 E
Yuba City 80 39 12N 121 37W
Yuba, R. 80 39 8N 121 36W
Yūbetsu 132 43 13N 144 5 E
Yucatán □ 83 21 30N 86 30W
Yucatán Basin 12 20 0N 84 0W
Yucatán Channel 84 22 0N 86 30W
Yucca 81 34 56N 114 6W
Yucca Valley 81 34 8N 116 30W
Yucheng 130 36 55N 116 40 E
Yudino 120 55 10N 67 55 E
Yugoslavia ■ 109 44 0N 20 0 E
Yühsien 130 34 10N 113 30 E
Yuhsien 131 39 45N 114 33 E
Yuhwan 131 28 1N 121 12 E
Yukan 131 28 43N 116 35 E
Yukikow 131 31 29N 118 17 E
Yukon, R. 67 65 30N 150 0W
Yukon Territory □ 64 63 0N 135 0W
Yukti 121 63 20N 105 0 E
Yule, R. 134 20 24 S 118 12 E
Yülin 130 18 10N 109 31 E
Yülin (Watlam) 131 22 30N 110 50 E
Yuma, Ariz., U.S.A. 81 32 45N 114 37W
Yuma, Colo., U.S.A. 74 40 10N 102 43W
Yuma, B. de 85 18 20N 68 35W
Yumbo 86 3 35N 76 28W
Yumen 129 41 13N 96 55 E
Yun Ho 129 35 0N 117 0 E
Yün Ho, R. 131 33 15N 119 45 E
Yunaska I. 67 52 40N 170 40W
Yundamindra 136 29 4 S 122 3 E
Yungan 131 25 50N 117 25 E
Yungas 86 17 0 S 66 0W
Yungay 88 37 10 S 72 5W
Yungchun 131 25 20N 118 15 E
Yungfu 131 24 59N 109 59 E
Yunghing 131 26 12N 113 3 E
Yunghwo 130 36 58N 110 56 E
Yungshun 131 29 3N 109 50 E
Yungsin 131 26 55N 114 10 E
Yungtsi 131 34 50N 110 25 E
Yungyun 131 24 31N 113 28 E
Yunhsien 131 32 30N 111 0 E
Yunhwo 131 28 0N 119 32 E
Yunlin 131 23 45N 120 30 E
Yunnan □ 129 25 0N 102 30 E
Yunsiao 131 24 0N 117 20 E
Yur 121 59 52N 137 49 E
Yurga 120 55 42N 84 51 E
Yuribei 120 71 20N 76 30 E
Yurimaguas 86 5 55 S 76 0W
Yuscarán 84 13 58N 86 51W
Yushu = Fyekundo 129 33 6N 96 48 E
Yūtu 131 26 0N 115 24 E
Yutze 130 37 45N 112 45 E
Yuyang 131 28 44N 108 46 E
Yuyao 131 30 0N 121 20 E
Yuyu 130 40 20N 112 30 E
Yuzhno-Sakhalinsk 121 47 5N 142 5 E
Yvelines □ 101 48 40N 1 45 E
Yvetot 100 49 37N 0 44 E

Z

Zaandam 105 52 26N 4 49 E
Zabaykalskiy 121 49 40N 117 10 E
Zābol 123 31 0N 61 25 E
Zābolī 123 27 10N 61 35 E
Zabrze 107 50 18N 18 46 E
Zacapa 84 14 59N 89 31W
Zacapu 82 19 50N 101 43W
Zacatecas 82 22 49N 102 34W
Zacatecas □ 82 23 30N 103 0W
Zacatecolua 84 13 29N 88 51W
Zacaultipán 83 20 39N 98 36W
Zacoalco 82 20 10N 103 40W
Zadar 108 44 8N 15 8 E
Zadetkyi Kyun 128 10 0N 98 25 E
Zafra 104 38 26N 6 30W
Zagan 106 51 39N 15 22 E
Zagreb 108 45 50N 16 0 E
Zāgros, Kudhā-ye 123 33 45N 47 0 E
Zāhedān 123 29 30N 60 50 E
Zahlah 115 33 52N 35 50 E
Zaïre, R. 116 1 30N 28 0 E
Zaïre, Rep. of ■ 116 3 0 S 23 0 E
Zaječar 109 43 53N 22 18 E
Zakamensk 121 50 23N 103 17 E
ZāKhū 122 37 10N 42 50 E
Zákinthos 109 37 47N 20 54 E
Zákinthos, I. 109 37 45N 27 45 E
Zambèze, R. 117 18 46 S 36 16 E
Zambezi, R. 117 18 46 S 36 16 E
Zambia ■ 117 15 0 S 28 0 E
Zamboanga 127 6 59N 122 3 E
Zambrano 86 9 45N 74 49W
Zamora, Mexico 82 20 0N 102 21W
Zamora, Spain 104 41 30N 5 45W
Zamość 107 50 50N 23 22 E
Zamuro, Sierra del 86 4 0N 62 30W
Zanaga 116 2 48 S 13 48 E
Zandvoort 105 52 22N 4 32 E
Zanesville 70 39 56N 82 2W
Zanjan 122 36 40N 48 35 E
Zanthus 134 31 2 S 123 34 E
Zanzibar 116 6 12 S 39 12 E
Zanzibar I. 116 6 12 S 39 12 E
Zaouiet El Kahla 114 27 10N 6 40 E
Zaouiet Reggane 114 26 32N 0 3 E
Zapadnaya Dvina 120 56 15N 32 3 E
Západné Beskydy 107 49 30N 19 0 E
Zapala 90 39 0 S 70 5W
Zapaleri, Cerro 88 22 49 S 67 11W
Zapata 75 26 56N 99 17W
Zaporozhye 120 47 50N 35 10 E
Zara 122 39 58N 37 43 E
Zaragoza, Colomb. 86 7 30N 74 52W
Zaragoza, Coahuila, Mexico 82 28 30N 101 0W
Zaragoza, Nuevo León, Mexico 83 24 0N 99 36W
Zaragoza □ 104 41 35N 1 0W
Zarand 123 30 46N 56 34 E
Zarate 88 34 7 S 59 0W
Zaraza 86 9 21N 65 19W
Zarembo I. 54 56 20N 132 50W
Zaria 114 11 0N 7 40 E
Zaruma 86 3 40 S 79 30W
Zary 106 51 37N 15 10 E
Zarzal 86 4 24N 76 4W
Zashiversk 121 67 25N 142 40 E
Zaskar Mountains 124 33 15N 77 30 E
Zavareh 123 33 35N 52 28 E
Zavitinsk 121 50 10N 129 20 E
Zavodoski, I. 91 56 0 S 27 45W
Zawiercie 107 50 30N 19 13 E
Zāyandeh, R. 123 32 35N 32 0 E
Zayarsk 121 56 20N 102 55 E
Zaysan 120 47 28N 84 52 E
Zaysan, Oz. 120 48 0N 83 0 E
Zdunska Wola 107 51 37N 18 59 E
Zealand Station 39 46 3N 66 56W
Zealandia 56 51 37N 107 45W
Zearing 76 42 10N 93 20W
Zeballos 62 49 59N 126 50W
Zeebrugge 105 51 19N 3 12 E
Zeeland 77 42 49N 86 1W
Zeeland □ 105 51 30N 3 50 E

Zeerust	117	25 31 s	26 4 E	Zheleznogorsk-Ilimskiy	121	56 34N	104 8 E	Zionz L.	52	51 25N	91 52W	Zumbo	117	15 35 s	30 26 E
Zefat	115	32 58N	35 29 E	Zhigansk	121	66 35N	124 10 E	Zipaquirá	86	5 0N	74 0W	Zumpango	83	19 48N	99 6W
Zehner	58	50 34N	104 28W	Zhitomir	120	50 20N	28 40 E	Zitácuaro	82	19 20N	100 30W	Zungeru	114	9 48N	6 8 E
Zeigler	76	37 55N	89 5W	Zhupanovo	121	51 59N	15 9 E	Zlatograd	109	41 22N	25 7 E	Zuni	79	35 7N	108 57W
Zeila	115	11 15N	43 30 E	Ziel, Mt.	134	23 20 s	132 30 E	Zlatoust	120	55 10N	59 40 E	Zurich	46	43 26N	81 37W
Zeist	105	52 5N	5 15 E	Zielona Góra	106	51 57N	15 31 E	Zmeinogorsk	120	51 10N	82 13 E	Zürich	106	47 22N	8 32 E
Zeitz	106	51 3N	12 9 E	Zierikzee	105	51 40N	3 55 E	Znojmo	106	48 50N	16 2 E	Zutphen	105	52 9N	6 12 E
Zelouane	118	35 1N	2 58W	Zihuatanejo	82	17 38N	101 33W	Zomba	117	15 30 s	35 19 E	Zuwárrah	114	32 58N	12 1 E
Zelzate	105	51 13N	3 47 E	Zile	122	40 15N	36 0 E	Zongo	116	4 12N	18 0 E	Zverinogolovskoye	120	55 0N	62 30 E
Zémio	116	5 2N	25 5 E	Zilfi	122	26 12N	44 52 E	Zonguldak	122	41 28N	31 50 E	Zvolen	107	48 33N	19 10 E
Zemun	109	44 51N	20 25 E	Zilina	107	49 12N	18 42 E	Zorra Island	84	9 18N	79 52W	Zweibrücken	105	49 15N	7 20 E
Zenon Park	56	53 4N	103 45W	Zilling Tso	129	31 40N	89 0 E	Zorritos	86	3 50 s	80 40W	Zwetti	106	48 35N	15 9 E
Zerbst	106	51 59N	12 8 E	Zilwaukee	46	43 28N	83 55W	Zottegam	105	50 52N	3 48 E	Zwickau	106	50 43N	12 30 E
Zeya	121	54 2N	127 20 E	Zima	121	54 0N	102 5 E	Zoutkamp	105	53 20N	6 18 E	Zwolle	105	52 31N	6 6 E
Zeya, R.	121	53 30N	127 0 E	Zimapán	83	20 40N	99 20W	Zrenjanin	109	45 22N	20 23 E	Zymoelz, R.	54	54 33N	128 31W
Zeytin	122	37 53N	36 53 E	Zinder	114	13 48N	9 0 E	Zug	106	47 10N	8 31 E	Zyrardów	107	52 3N	20 35 E
Zhailma	120	51 30N	61 50 E	Zion	77	42 27N	87 50W	Zuid-Holland □	105	52 0N	4 35 E				
Zhanatas	120	43 11N	81 18 E	Zion Nat. Park	79	37 25N	112 50W	Zuid-horn	105	53 15N	6 23 E				
Zhdanov	120	47 5N	37 31 E	Zionsville	77	39 57N	86 16W	Zulia □	86	10 0N	72 10W				

Acknowledgment is made to the following for providing the photographs used in the atlas

Agent-Général for Québec; Air India; Brazilian Embassy, London; British Aircraft Corporation; British Airways; British Leyland; British Petroleum; British Rail; British Steel Corporation; British Tourist Authority; Calgary City Hall; Canadian National Railways; Central Electricity Generating Board; D. Chanter; Danish Embassy, London; Edmonton City Hall; Egypt Air; R. Estall; Fiat (England) Ltd.; Finnish Tourist Bureau; Freightliners Ltd.; H. Fullard; M. H. Fullard; Gas Council Exploration Ltd.; Commander H. R. Hatfield/Astro Books; H. Hawes; Israeli Govt. Tourist Office; Japan Air Lines; Lufthansa; M.A.T. Transport Ltd.; Meteorological Office, London; Moroccan Tourist Office; N.A.S.A. (Space Frontiers); National Coal Board, London; National Maritime Museum, London; Offshore Co.; Pan American World Airways; M. Rentsch; Royal Astronomical Society, London; Shell International Petroleum Co. Ltd.; Swan Hunter Group, Ltd.; Swiss National Tourist Office; Toronto City Hall; Vancouver City Engineers Dept.; B. M. Willett; Woodmansterne Ltd.

Geographical Terms

This is a list of some of the geographical words from foreign languages which are found in the place names on the maps and in the index. Each is followed by the language and the English meaning.

Afr. afrikaans
Alb. albanian
Amh. amharic
Ar. arabic
Ber. berber
Bulg. bulgarian
Bur. burmese

Chin. chinese
Cz. czechoslovakian
Dan. danish
Dut. dutch
Fin. finnish
Flem. flemish
Fr. french

Gae. gaelic
Ger. german
Gr. greek
Heb. hebrew
Hin. hindi
I.-C. indo-chinese
Ice. icelandic

It. italian
Jap. japanese
Kor. korean
Lapp. lappish
Lith. lithuanian
Mal. malay
Mong. mongolian

Nor. norwegian
Pash. pashto
Pers. persian
Pol. polish
Port. portuguese
Rum. rumanian
Russ. russian

Ser.-Cr. serbo-croat
Siam. siamese
Sin. sinhalese
Som. somali
Span. spanish
Swed. swedish
Tib. tibetan
Turk. turkish

A. (Ain) *Ar.* spring
–á *Ice.* river
a *Dan., Nor., Swed.* stream
–abad *Pers., Russ.* town
Abyad *Ar.* white
Ad. (Adrar) *Ar., Ber.* mountain
Ada, Adasi *Tur.* island
Addis *Amh.* new
Adrar *Ar., Ber.* mountain
Aïn *Ar.* spring
Ăkra *Gr.* cape
Akrotíri *Gr.* cape
Alb *Ger.* mountains
Albufera *Span.* lagoon
–ålen *Nor.* islands
Alpen *Ger.* mountain pastures
Alpes *Fr.* mountains
Alpi *It.* mountains
Alto *Port.* high
–älv, –älven *Swed.* stream, river
Amt *Dan.* first-order administrative division
Appennino *It.* mountain range
Arch. (Archipiélago) *Span.* archipelago
Arcipélago *It.* archipelago
Arq. (Arquipélago) *Port.* archipelago
Arr. (Arroyo) *Span.* stream
–Ås, –åsen *Nor., Swed.* hill
Autonomna Oblast *Ser.-Cr.* autonomous region
Ayios *Gr.* island
Ayn *Ar.* well, waterhole

B(a). (Baía) *Port.* bay
B. (Baie) *Fr.* bay
B. (Bahía) *Span.* bay
B. (Ben) *Gae.* mountain
B. (Bir) *Ar.* well
B. (Bucht) *Ger.* bay
B. (Bugt.) *Dan.* bay
Baai, –baai *Afr.* bay
Bâb *Ar.* gate
Bäck, –bäcken *Swed.* stream
Back, backen, *Swed.* hill
Bad, –baden *Ger.* spa
Bädiya, -t *Ar.* desert
Baek *Dan.* stream
Baelt *Dan.* strait
Bahía *Span.* bay
Bahr *Ar.* sea, river
Bahra *Ar.* lake
Baía *Port.* bay
Baie *Fr.* bay
Bajo, –a, *Span.* lower
Bakke *Nor.* hill
Bala *Pers.* upper
Baltă *Rum.* marsh, lake
Banc *Fr.* bank
Bander *Ar., Mal.* port
Bandar *Pers.* bay
Banja *Ser. Cr.* spa. resort
Barat *Mal.* western
Barr. (Barrage) *Fr.* dam
Barracão *Port.* dam, waterfall
Bassin *Fr.* bay
Bayt *Heb.* house, village
Bazar *Hin.* market, bazaar
Be'er *Heb.* well
Beit *Heb.* village
Belo-, Belyy, Belaya,

Beloye, *Russ.* white
Ben *Gae.* mountain
Bender *Somal.* harbour
Berg,(e) –berg(e) *Afr.* mountain(s)
Berg, –berg *Ger.* mountain
–berg, –et *Nor., Swed.* hill, mountain, rock
Bet *Heb.* house, village
Bir, Bîr *Ar.* well
Birket *Ar.* lake, bay, marsh
Bj. (Bordj) *Ar.* port
–bjerg *Dan.* hill, point
Boca *Span.* river mouth
Bodden *Ger.* bay, inlet
Bogaz, Boğaz, –ı *Tur.* strait
Boka *Ser.-Cr.* gulf, inlet
Bol. (Bolshoi) *Russ.* great, large
Bordj *Ar.* fort
–borg *Dan., Nor., Swed.* castle, fort
–botn *Nor.* valley floor
bouche(s) *Fr.* mouth
Br. (Burnu) *Tur.* cape
Braţul *Rum.* distributary stream
–breen *Nor.* glacier
–bruck *Ger.* bridge
–brunn *Swed.* well, spring
Bucht *Ger.* bay
Bugt, –bugt *Dan.* bay
Buheirat *Ar.* lake
Bukit *Mal.* hill
Bukten *Swed.* bay
–bulag *Mong.* spring
Bûr *Ar.* port
Burg. *Ar.* fort
Burg, –burg *Ger.* castle
Burnu *Tur.* cape
Burun *Tur.* cape
Butt *Gae.* promontory
–by *Dan., Nor., Swed.* town
–byen *Nor., Swed.* town

C. (Cabo) *Port., Span.* headland, cape
C. (Cap) *Fr.* cape
C. (Capo) *It.* cape
Cabeza *Span.* peak, hill
Camp *Port., Span.* land, field
Campo *Span.* plain
Campos *Span.* upland
Can. (Canal) *Fr., Span.* canal
Canale *It.* canal
Canalul *Ser.-Cr.* canal
Cao Nguyên *Thai.* plateau, tableland
Cap *Fr.* cape
Capo *It.* cape
Cataracta *Sp.* cataract
Cauce *Span.* intermittent stream
Causse *Fr.* upland (limestone)
Cayi *Tur.* river
Cayo(s) *Span.* rock(s), islet(s)
Cerro *Span.* hill, peak
Ch. (Chaîne(s)) *Fr.* mountain range(s)
Ch. (Chott) *Ar.* salt lake
Chaco *Span.* jungle
Chaîne(s) *Fr.* mountain range(s)
Chap. (Chapada) *Port.* hills, upland

Chapa *Span.* hills, upland
Chapada *Port.* hills, upland
Chaung *Bur.* stream, river
Chen *Chin.* market town
Ch'eng *Chin.* town
Chiang *Chin.* river
Ch'ih *Chin.* pool
Ch'ön *Kor.* river
–chôsuji *Kor.* reservoir
Chott *Ar.* salt lake, swamp
Chou *Chin.* district
Chu *Tib.* river
Chung *Chin.* middle
Chute *Fr.* waterfall
Co. (Cerro) *Span.* hill, peak
Coch. (Cochilla) *Port.* hills
Col *Fr., It.* Pass
Colline(s) *Fr.* hill(s)
Conca *It.* plain, basin
Cord. (Cordillera) *Span.* mountain chain
Costa *It., Span.* coast
Côte *Fr.* coast, slope, hill
Cuchillas *Spain* hills
Cu-Lao *I.-C.* island

D. (Dolok) *Mal.* mountain
Dágh *Pers.* mountain
Dağ(ı) *Tur.* mountain(s)
Dağları *Tur.* mountain range
Dake *Jap.* mountain
–dal *Nor.* valley
–dal, –e *Dan., Nor.* valley
–dal, –en *Swed.* valley, stream
Dalay *Mong.* sea, large lake
–dalir *Ice.* valley
–dalur *Ice.* valley
–damm, –en *Swed.* lake
Danau *Mal.* lake
Dao *I.-O.* island
Dar *Ar.* region
Darya *Russ.* river
Daryācheh *Pers.* marshy lake, lake
Dasht *Pers.* desert, steppe
Daung *Bur.* mountain, hill
Dayr *Ar.* depression, hill
Debre *Amh.* hill
Deli *Ser.-Cr.* mountain(s)
Denizi *Tur.* sea
Dépt. (Département) *Fr.* first-order administrative division
Desierto *Span.* desert
Dhar *Ar.* region, mountain chain
Dj. (Djebel) *Ar.* mountain
Dō *Jap., Kor.* island
Dong *Kor.* village, town
Dong *Thai.* jungle region
–dorf *Ger.* village
–dorp *Afr.* village
–drif *Afr.* ford
–dybet *Dan.* marine channel
Dzong *Tib.* town, settlement

Eil. -eiland(en) *Afr., Dut.* island(s)
–elv *Nor.* river
'emeq *Heb.* plain, valley
'erg *Ar.* desert with dunes
Estrecho *Span.* strait
Estuario *Span.* estuary

Étang *Fr.* lagoon
–ey(jar) *Ice.* island(s)

F. (Fiume) *It.* river
F. Folyô *Hung.* river
Fd. (Fjord) *Nor.* Inlet of sea
–feld *Ger.* field
–fell *Ice.* mountain, hill
–feng *Chin.* mountain
Fiume *It.* river
Fj. (–fjell) *Nor.* mountain
–fjall *Ice.* mountain(s), hill(s)
–fjäll(et) *Swed.* hill(s), mountain(s), ridge
–fjällen *Swed.* mountains
–fjard(en) *Swed.* fjord, bay, lake
Fjeld *Dan.* mountain
–fjell *Nor.* mountain, rock
–fjord(en) *Nor.* inlet of sea
–fjorden *Dan.* bay, marine channel
–fjörður *Ice.* fjord
Fl. (Fleuve) *Fr.* river
Fl. (Fluss) *Ger.* river
–flói *Ice.* bay, marshy country
Fluss *Ger.* river
foce, –i *It.* mouth(s)
Folyó *Hung.* river
–fontein *Afr.* fountain, spring
–fors, –en, *Swed.* rapids, waterfall
Foss *Ice., Nor.* waterfall
–furt *Ger.* ford
Fylke *Nor.* first-order administrative division

G. (Gebel) *Ar.* mountain
G. (Gebirge) *Ger.* hills, mountains
G. (Golfe) *Fr.* gulf
G. (Golfo) *It.* gulf
G. (Gora) *Bulg., Russ., Ser.-Cr.* mountain
G. (Gunong) *Mal.* mountain
–gang *Kor.* river
Ganga *Hin., Sin.* river
–gat *Dan.* sound
–gau *Ger.* district
Gave *Fr.* stream
–gawa *Jap.* river
Geb. (Gebirge) *Ger.* hills, mountains
Gebel *Ar.* mountain
Geziret *Ar.* island
Ghat *Hin.* range of hills
Ghiol *Rum.* lake
Ghubbat *Ar.* bay, inlet
Gji *Alb.* bay
Gjol *Alb.* lagoon, lake
Gl. (Glava) *Ser.-Cr.* mountain, peak
Glen. *Gae.* valley
Gletscher *Ger.* glacier
Gobi *Mong.* desert
Gol *Mong.* river
Golfe *Fr.* gulf
Golfo *It., Span.* gulf
Gomba *Tib.* settlement
Gora *Bulg., Russ., Ser.-Cr.* mountain(s)
Góry *Pol., Russ.* mountain
Gölü *Tur.* lake
–gorod *Russ.* small town
Grad *Bulg., Russ., Ser.-Cr.* town, city

Grada *Russ.* mountain range
Guba *Russ.* bay
–Guntō *Jap.* island group
Gunong *Mal.* mountain
Gură *Rum.* passage

H. Hadabat *Ar.* plateau
–hafen *Ger.* harbour, port
Haff *Ger.* bay
Hai *Chin.* sea
Haihsia *Chin.* strait
–hale *Dan.* spit, peninsula
Hals *Dan., Nor.* peninsula, isthmus
Halvø *Dan.* peninsula
Halvøya *Nor.* peninsula
Hāmad, Hamada, *Ar.* stony desert, plain
–hamn *Swed., Nor.* harbour, anchorage
Hāmūn *Ar.* plain
Hāmūn *Pers.* low-lying marshy area
–Hantō *Jap.* peninsula
Harju *Fin.* hill
Hassi *Ar.* well
–haug *Nor.* hill
Hav *Swed.* gulf
Havet *Nor.* sea
–havn *Dan., Nor.* harbour
Hegyseg *Hung.* forest
Heide *Ger.* heath
Hi. (hassi) *Ar.* well
Ho *Chin.* river
–hø *Nor.* peak
Hochland *Afr.* highland
Hoek, –hoek *Afr., Dut.* cape
Höfn *Ice.* harbour, port
–hög, –en, –högar, *Swed.* hill(s)
–högarna *Swed.* hill(s), peak, mountain
Höhe *Ger.* hills
Holm *Dan.* island
–holm, –holme, –holzen, *Swed.* island
Hon *I.-C.* island
Hora *Cz.* mountain
–horn *Nor.* peak
Hory *Cz.* mountain range, forest
–hoved *Dan.* point, headland, peninsula
Hráun *Ice.* lava
–hsi *Chin.* mountain, stream
–hsiang *Chin.* village
–hsien *Chin.* district
Hu *Chin.* lake
Huk *Dan., Ger.* point
Huken *Nor.* head

I. (Île) *Fr.* island
I. (Ilha) *Port.* island
I. (Insel) *Ger.* island
I. (Isla) *Span.* island
I. (Isola) *It.* island
Idehan *Ar., Ber.* sandy plain
Île(s) *Fr.* island(s)
Ilha *Port.* island
Insel(n) *Ger.* island(s)
Irmak *Tur.* river
Is. (Inseln) *Ger.* islands
Is. (Islas) *Span.* islands
Is. (Isola) *It.* island
Isola, –e *It.* island(s)
Istmo *Span.* isthmus

J. (Jabal) *Ar.* mountain
J. (Jazira) *Ar.* island
J. (Jebel) *Ar.* mountain
J. (Jezioro) *Pol.* lake
Jabal *Ar.* mountain, range
–jaur *Swed.* lake
–järvi *Fin.* lake, bay, pond
Jasovir *Bulg.* reservoir
Jazā'ir *Ar.* islands
Jazira *Ar.* island
Jazireh *Pers.* island
Jebel *Ar.* mountain
Jezero *Ser.-Cr.* lake
Jezioro *Pol.* lake
–Jima *Jap.* island
Jøkelen *Nor.* glacier
–joki *Fin.* stream
–jökull *Ice.* glacier
Jūras Līcis *Lat.* bay, gulf

K. (Kap) *Dan.* cape
K (Khalig) *Ar.* gulf
K. (Kiang) *Chin.* river
K. (Kuala) *Mal.* confluence, estuary
Kaap *Afr.* cape
Kai *Jap.* sea
Kaikyō *Jap.* strait
Kamennyy *Russ.* stony
Kampong *Mal.* village
Kan. (Kanal) *Ser.-Cr.* channel, canal
Kanaal *Dut., Flem.* canal
Kanal *Dan.* channel, gulf
Kanal *Ger., Swed.* canal, stream
kanal *Ser.-Cr.* channel, canal
Kang *Kor.* river, bay
Kangri *Tib.* mountain glacier
Kap *Dan., Ger.* cape
Kapp *Nor.* cape
Kas *I.-C.* island
–kaupstaður *Ice.* market town
–kaupunki *Fin.* town
Kavir *Pers.* salt desert
Kébir *Ar.* great
Kéfar *Heb.* village, hamlet
–ken *Jap.* first-order administrative division
Kep *Alb.* cape
Kepulauan *Mal.* archipelago
Ketjil *Mal.* lesser, little
Khalig, Khalij *Ar.* gulf
khamba, –idg *Tib.* source, spring
Khawr *Ar.* wadi
Khirbat *Ar.* ruins
Kho Khot *Thai.* isthmus
Khōr *Pers.* creek, estuary
Khrebet *Russ.* mountain range
Kiang *Chin.* river
–klint *Dan.* cliff
–Klintar *Swed.* hills
Kloof *Afr.* gorge
Knude *Dan.* point
Ko *Jap.* lake
Ko *Thai.* island
Kohi *Pash.* mountains
Kol *Russ.* lake
Kolymskoye *Russ.* mountain range
Kólpos *Gr., Tur.* gulf, bay
Kompong *Mal.* landing place
–kop *Afr.* hill

–köping *Swed.* market town
Körfezi *Tur.* gulf
Kosa *Russ.* spit
–koski *Fin.* cataract, rapids
–kraal *Afr.* native village
Krasnyy *Russ.* red
Kryash *Russ.* ridge, hills
Kuala *Mal.* confluence, estuary
kuan *Chin.* pass
Kuh –hha *Pers.* mountains
Kul *Russ.* lake
Kulle *Swed.* hill, shoal
Kum *Russ.* sandy desert
Kumpu *Fin.* hill
Kurgan *Russ.* mound
Kwe *Bur.* bay, gulf
Kyst *Dan.* coast
Kyun, –zu, –umya *Bur.* island(s)

L. (Lac) *Fr.* lake
L. (Lacul) *Rum.* lake
L. (Lago) *It., Span.* lake, lagoon
L. (Lagoa) *Port.* lagoon
L. (Límni) *Gr.* lake
L. (Loch) *Gae.* (lake, inlet)
L. (Lough) *Gae.* (lake, inlet)
La *Tib.* pass
La (Lagoa) *Port.* lagoon
–laagte *Afr.* watercourse
Läani *Fin.* first-order administrative division
Län *Swed.* first-order administrative division
Lac *Fr.* lake
Lacul *Rum.* lake, lagoon
Lago *It., Span.* lake, lagoon
Lagoa *Port.* lagoon
Laguna *It., Span.* lagoon, intermittent lake
Lagune *Fr.* lake
Lahti *Fin.* bay, gulf, cove
Lakhti *Russ.* bay, gulf
Lampi *Fin.* lake
Land *Ger.* first-order administrative division
–land *Dan.* region
–land *Afr., Nor.* land, province
Lido *It.* beach, shore
Liehtao *Chin.* islands
Lilla *Swed.* small
Límni *Gr.* lake
Ling *Chin.* mountain range, ice
Linna *Fin.* historical fort
Llano *Span.* prairie, plain
Loch *Gae.* (lake)
Lough *Gae.* (lake)
Lum *Alb.* river
Lund *Dan.* forest
–lund, –en *Swed.* wood(s)

M. (Maj, Mai) *Alb.* mountain, peak
M. (Mont) *Fr.* mountain peak
M. (Mys) *Russ.* cape
Madina(h) *Ar.* town, city
Madiq *Ar.* strait
Maj *Alb.* peak
Mäki *Fin.* hill, hillside
Mal *Alb.* mountain
Mal *Russ.* little, small
Mal/a, –i, –o *Ser.-Cr.* small, little
Man *Kor.* bay
Mar *Span.* lagoon, sea
Mare *Rum.* great
Marisma *Span.* marsh
–mark *Dan., Nor.* land
Marsá *Ar.* anchorage, bay, inlet
Masabb *Ar.* river mouth
Massif *Fr.* upland, plateau
Mato *Port.* forest
Mazar *Pers.* shrine, tomb
Meer *Afr., Dut., Ger.* lake sea

Mi., Mti. (Monti) *It.* mountains
Miao *Chin.* temple, shrine
Midbar *Heb.* wilderness
Mif. (Massif) *Fr.* upland, plateau
Misaki *Jap.* cape, point
–mo *Nor., Swed.* heath, island
–mon *Swed.* heath
Mong *Bur.* town
Mont *Fr.* hill, mountain
Montagna *It.* mountain
Montagne *Fr.* hill, mountain
Montaña *Span.* mountain
Monte *It., Port., Span.* mountain
Monti *It.* mountains
More *Russ.* sea
Mörön *Hung.* river
Mt. (Mont) *It.* mountain
Mt. (Monti) *It.* mountain
Mt. (Montaña) *Span.* mountain range
Mte. (Monte) *It., Port., Span.* mountain
Mţi. (Munţi) *Rum.* mountain
Mts. (Monts) *Fr.* mountains
Muang *Mal.* town
Mui *Ar., I.-C.* cape
Mull *Gae.* (promontory)
Mund, –mund *Afr.* mouth
Munkhafed *Ar.* depression
Munte *Rum.* mount
Munţi(i) *Rum.* mountain(s)
Muong *Mal.* village
Myit *Bur.* river
Myitwanya *Bur.* mouths of river
–mýri *Ice.* bog
Mys *Russ.* cape

N. (Nahal) *Heb.* river
Naes *Dan.* point, cape
Nafüd *Ar.* sandy desert
Nahal *Heb.* river
Nahr *Ar.* river, stream
Najd *Ar.* plateau, pass
Nakhon *Thai.* town
Nam *I.-C.* river
–nam *Kor.* south
–näs *Swed.* cape
–nes *Ice., Nor.* cape
Ness, –ness *Gae.* promontory, cape
Nez *Fr.* cape
–niemi *Fin.* cape, point, peninsula, island
Nizhne, –iy *Russ.* lower
Nizmennost *Russ.* plain, lowland
Nísos, Nísoi *Gr.* island(s)
Nor *Chin.* lake
Nor *Tib.* peak
Nos *Bulg., Russ.* cape, point
Nudo *Span.* mountain
Nuruu *Mong.* mountain range
Nuur *Mong.* lake

O. (Ostrov) *Russ.* island
O (Ouâdi, Oued) *Ar.* wadi
–ö *Swed.* island, peninsula, point
–öar, (–na) *Swed.* islands
Oblast *Russ.* administrative division
Öbor *Mong.* inner
Occidental *Fr., Span.* western
Odde *Dan., Nor.* point, peninsula, cape
Oji *Alb.* bay
Ojo *Span.* spring
Oki *Jap.* bay
–ön *Swed.* island peninsula
Ondör *Mong.* high, tall

–ör *Swed.* island, peninsula, point
Oraşul *Rum.* city
Ord *Gae.* point
Óri *Gr.* mountains
Oriental *Span.* eastern
Órmos *Gr.* bay
Óros *Gr.* mountain
Ort *Ger.* point, cape
Ostrov(a) *Russ.* island(s)
Otok(–i) *Ser.-Cr.* island(s)
Ouadi, –edi *Ar.* dry watercourse, wadi
Ouzan *Pers.* river
Ova (–si) *Tur.* plains, lowlands
–øy, (–a) *Nor.* island(s)
Oya *Hin.* point
Oya *Sin.* river
Oz. (Ozero, a) *Russ.* lake(s)

P. (Passo) *It.* pass
P. (Pasul) *Rum.* pass
P. (Pico) *Span.* peak
P. (Prokhod) *Bulg.* pass
–pää *Fin.* hill(s), mountain
Pahta *Lapp.* hill
Pampa, –s *Span.* plain(s) salt flat(s)
Pan. (Pantano) *Span.* Reservoir
Pantao *Chin.* peninsula
Parbat *Urdu* mountain
Pas *Fr.* gap
Paso *Span.* pass, marine channel
Pass *Ger.* pass
Passo *It.* pass
Pasul *Rum.* pass
Patam *Hin.* small village
Patna, –patnam *Hin.* small village
Pegunungan *Mal.* mountain, range
Pei, –pei *Chin.* north
Pélagos *Gr.* sea
Pen. (Península) *Span.* peninsula
Peña *Span.* rock, peak
Península *Span.* peninsula
Per. (Pereval) *Russ.* pass
Pertuis *Fr.* channel
Peski *Russ.* desert, sands
Phanom *I.-C., Thai.* mountain
Phnom *I.-C.* mountain
Phu *I.-C.* mountain
Pic *Fr.* peak
Pico(s) *Span.* peak(s)
Pik *Russ.* peak
Piz., pizzo *It.* peak
Pl. (Planina) *Ser.-Cr.* mountain, range
Plage *Fr.* beach
Plaine *Fr.* plain
Planalto *Span.* plateau
Planina *Bulg., Ser.-Cr.* mountain, range
Plat. (Plateau) *Fr.* level upland
Plato *Russ.* plateau
Playa *Span.* beach
P-ov. (Poluostrov) *Russ.* peninsula
Pointe *Fr.* point, cape
Pojezierze *Pol.* lakes plateau
Polder *Dut.* reclaimed farmland
–pólis *Gr.* city, town
Poluostrov *Russ.* peninsula
Połwysep *Pol.* peninsula
Pont *Fr.* bridge
Ponta *Port.* point, cape
Ponte *It.* bridge
Poort *Afr.* passage, gate
–poort *Dut.* port
Porta *Port.* pass
Porţil, –e *Rum.* gate
Portillo *Span.* pass
Porto *It.* port
Porto *Port., Span.* port

Pot. (Potámi, Potamós) *Gr.* river
Poulo *I.-C.* island
Pr. (Průsmyk) *Cz.* pass
Pradesh *Hin.* state
Presa *Span.* reservoir
Presqu'île *Fr.* peninsula
Prokhod *Bulg.* pass
Proliv *Russ.* strait
Prusmyk *Cz.* pass
Pso. (Passo) *It.* pass
Pta. (Ponta) *Port.* point, cape
Pta. (Punta) *It., Span.* point, cape, peak
Pte. (Pointe) *Fr.* point cape
Puerto *Span.* port, pass
Puig *Cat.* peak
Pulau *Mal.* island
Puna *Span.* desert plateau
Punta *It., Span.* point, peak
Puy *Fr.* hill

Qal'at *Ar.* fort
Qanal *Ar.* canal
Qasr *Ar.* fort
Qiryat *Heb.* town
Qolleh *Pers.* mountain

Ramla *Ar.* sand
Rann *Hin.* swampy region
Rao *I.-C.* river
Ras *Amh.* cape, headland
Rãs *Ar.* cape, headland
Recife(s) *Port.* reef(s)
Reka *Bulg., Cz., Russ.* river
Repede *Rum.* rapids
Represa *Port.* dam
Reshteh *Pers.* mountain range
–Rettō *Jap.* group of islands
Ría *Span.* estuary, bay
Ribeirão *Port.* river
Rijeka *Ser.-Cr.* river
Rio *Port.* river
Río *Span.* river
Riv. (Riviera) *It.* coastal plain, coast, river
Rivier *Afr.* river
Riviera *It.* coast
Rivière *Fr.* river
Roche *Fr.* rock
Rog *Russ.* horn
–rück *Ger.* ridge
Rüd *Pers.* stream, river
Rudohorie *Cz.* ore mountains
Rzeka *Pol.* river

S. (Sungei) *Mal.* river
Sa. (Serra) *It., Port.* range of hills
Sa. (Sierra) *Span.* range of hills
–saari *Fin.* island
Sadd *Ar.* dam
Sagar, –ara *Hin., Urdu* lake
Saharã *Ar.* desert
Sahrã *Ar.* desert
Sa'id *Ar.* highland
Sakar *Fin.* mountain
–Saki *Jap.* point
Sal. (Salar) *Span.* salt pan
Salina(s) *Span.* salt flat(s)
–salmi *Fin.* strait, sound, lake, channel
Saltsjöbad *Swed.* resort
Sammyaku *Jap.* mountain, range
Samut *Thai.* gulf
–San *Jap.* hill, mountain
Sap. (Sapadno) *Russ.* west
Sasso *It.* mountain
Se, Sé *I.-C.* river
Sebkha, –kra *Ar.* salt flats
See *Ger.* lake
–see *Ger.* sea
–şehir *Turk.* town
Selat *Mal.* strait
–selkä *Fin.* bay, lake, sound, ridge, hills

Selva *Span.* forest, wood
Seno *Span.* bay, sound
Serír *Ar.* desert of small stones
Serra *It., Port.* range of hills
Serranía *Span.* mountains
Sev. (Severo) *Russ.* north
–shahr *Pers.* city, town
Shan *Chin.* hills, mountains, pass
Shan-mo *Chin.* mountain range
Shatt *Ar.* river
–Shima *Jap.* island
Shimãli *Ar.* northern
–Shotõ *Jap.* group of islands
Shuik'u *Chin.* reservoir
Sierra *Span.* hill, range
Sjö, sjön *Swed.* lake, bay, sea
Sjøen *Dan.* sea
Skär *Swed.* island, rock, cape
Skog *Nor.* forest
–skog, –skogen *Swed.* wood(s)
–skov *Dan.* forest
Slieve *Gae.* range of hills
–sø *Dan., Nor.* lake
Sør *Nor.* south, southern
Solonchak *Russ.* salt lake, marsh
Souk *Ar.* market
Spitze *Ger.* peak, mountain
–spruit *Afr.* stream
–stad *Afr., Nor., Swed.* town
–stadt *Ger.* town
Staður *Ice.* town
Stausee *Ger.* reservoir
Stenón *Gr.* strait, pass
Step *Russ.* plain
Str. (Stretto) *It.* strait
–strand *Dan., Nor.* beach
–strede *Nor.* straits
Strelka *Russ.* spit
–strete *Nor.* straits
Stretto *It.* strait
Stroedet *Dan.* strait
–ström, –strömmen *Swed.* stream(s)
–stroom *Afr.* large river
Suidõ *Jap.* strait, channel
Sûn *Bur.* cape
Sund *Dan.* sound
–sund, –sundet *Swed.* sound, estuary, inlet
–sund(et) *Nor.* sound
Sungai, –ei *Mal.* river
Sungei *Mal.* river
Sur *Span.* south, southern
Sveti *Bulg.* pass
Syd *Dan., Swed.* south

Tai –tai *Chin.* tower
Tal *Mong.* plain, steppe
–tal *Ger.* valley
Tall *Ar.* hills, hummocks
Tandjung *Mal.* cape, headland
Tao *Chin.* island
Tassili *Ar.* rocky plateau
Tau *Russ.* mountain, range
Taung *Bur.* mountain, south
Taunggya *Bur.* pass
Tělok *I.-C., Mal.* bay bight
Teluk *Mal.* bay, gulf
Tg. (Tandjung) *Mal.* cape, headland
–thal *Ger.* valley
Thok *Tib.* town
Tierra *Span.* land, country
–tind *Nor.* peak
Tjärn, –en, –et *Swed.* lake
Tong *Nor.* village, town
Tong *Bur., Thai.* mountain range
Tonle *I.-C.* large river, lake
–träsk *Swed.* bog, swamp
Tsangpo *Tib.* large river
Tso *Tib.* lake

Tsu *Jap.* entrance, bay
Tulur *Ar.* hill
T'un *Chin.* village
Tung *Chin.* east
Tunnel *Fr.* tunnel
Tunturi *Fin.* hill(s), mountain(s), ridge

Uad *Ar.* dry watercourse, wadi
Udjung *Mal.* cape
Udd, udde, udden *Swed.* point, peninsula
Uebi *Somal.* river
Us *Mong.* water
Ust *Russ.* river mouth
Uul *Mong., Russ.* mountain, range

V. (Volcán) *Span.* volcano
–vaara *Fin.* hill, mountain, ridge, peak
–våg *Nor.* bay
Val *Fr., It.* valley
Valea *Rum.* valley
–vall, –vallen *Swed.* mountain
Valle *Span.* valley
Vallée *Fr.* valley
Valli *It.* lake, lagoon
Väst *Swed.* west
–vatn *Ice., Nor.* lake
Vatten *Swed.* lake
Vdkhr. (Vodokhranilishche) *Russ.* reservoir
–ved, –veden *Swed.* range, hills
Veld, –veld *Afr.* field
Velik/a, –e, –i, –o *Ser.Cr.* large
–vesi *Fin.* water, lake, bay sound, strait
Vest *Dan., Nor.* west
Vf. (Vîrful) *Rum.* peak, mountain
–vidda *Nor.* plateau
Vig *Dan.* bay, inlet, cove, lagoon, lake, bight
–vik, –vika, –viken *Nor., Swed.* bay, cove, gulf, inlet, lake
Vila *Port.* small town
Villa *Span.* town
Ville *Fr.* town
Vinh *I.-C.* bay
Vîrful *Rum.* peak, mountain
–vlei *Afr.* pond, pool
Vodokhranilishche *Russ.* reservoir
Vol. (Volcán) *Span.* volcano, mountain
Vorota *Russ.* gate
Vostochnyy *Russ.* eastern
Vozyshennost *Russ.* heights, uplands
Vrata *Bulg.* gate, pass
Vrchovina *Cz.* mountainous country
Vrchy *Cz.* mountain range
Vung *I.-C.* gulf
–vuori *Fin.* mountain, hill

W. (Wädï) *Ar.* dry watercourse
Wâhât *Ar.* oasis
Wald *Ger.* wood, forest
Wan *Chin., Jap.* bay
Webi *Amh.* river
Woestyn *Afr.* desert

Yam *Heb.* sea
Yang *Chin.* ocean
Yazovir *Bulg.* reservoir
Yoma *Bur.* mountain range
–yüan *Chin.* spring

–**Z**aki *Jap.* peninsula
Zalew *Pol.* lagoon, swamp
Zaliv *Russ.* bay
Zan *Jap.* mountain
Zatoka *Pol.* bay
Zee *Dut.* sea
Zemlya *Russ.* land, island(s)

Principal Cities of the World

The population figures used are from censuses or more recent estimates and are given in thousands for towns and cities over 200 000 (over 500 000 in China and over 250 000 in Japan and U.S.S.R.). Where possible the population of the metropolitan areas is given e.g. Greater London, Greater New York, etc.

AFRICA

ALGERIA (1974)
Algiers 1 504
Oran 485
Constantine 350
Annaba 313
Tizi-Ouzou 224
ANGOLA (1970)
Luanda 475
CAMEROON (1975)
Douala 486
Yaoundé 274
CANARY ISLANDS (1970)
Las Palmas 287
CONGO (1974)
Brazzaville 290
EGYPT (1974)
Cairo 5 715
Alexandria 2 259
El Giza 854
Suez 368
Subra el Khelma 346
Port Said 342
El Mahalla el Kubra 288
Tanta 278
Aswan 246
El Mansura 232
ETHIOPIA (1975)
Addis Abeba 1 161
Asmera 318
GABON (1974)
Libreville 251
GHANA (1970)
Accra 738
Kumasi 345
GUINEA (1972)
Conakry 526
IVORY COAST (1976)
Abidjan 850
Bouake 318
KENYA (1973)
Nairobi 630
Mombasa 301
LIBYA (1973)
Tripoli 551
Benghazi 282
MADAGASCAR (1971)
Tananarive 378
MOROCCO (1973)
Casablanca 1 753
Rabat-Salé 596
Marrakesh 436
Fès 426
Meknès 403
Oujda 349
Kénitra 341
Tétouan 308
Safi 215
Tanger 208
MOZAMBIQUE (1970)
Maputo 384
NIGERIA (1975)
Lagos 1 477
Ibadan 847
Ogbomosho 432
Kano 399
Oshogbo 282
Ilorin 282
Abeokuta 253
Port Harcourt 242
Zaria 224
Ilesha 224
Onitsha 220
Iwo 214
Ado-Ekiti 213
Kaduna 202
RHODESIA (1973)
Salisbury 502
Bulawayo 307
SENEGAL (1973)
Dakar 726
SIERRA LEONE (1974)
Freetown 214
SOMALI REP. (1972)
Mogadishu 230
SOUTH AFRICA (1970)
Johannesburg 1 434
Cape Town 1 096
Durban 843
Pretoria 562
Port Elizabeth 489
Germiston 281
SUDAN (1973)
Khartoum 784
TANZANIA (1975)
Dar-es-Salaam 517
TOGO (1974)
Lomé 214
TUNISIA (1966)
Tunis 648
UGANDA (1969)
Kampala 331
ZAÏRE (1972-4)
Kinshasa 2 008
Kananga 601
Lubumbashi 404
Mbuji Mayi 337
Kisangani 311
ZAMBIA (1972)
Lusaka 448
Kitwe 331
Ndola 235

ASIA

AFGHANISTAN (1976)
Kabul 588
BANGLADESH (1974)
Dacca 1 730
Chittagong 889
Narayanganj 443
Khulna 437
BURMA (1973)
Rangoon 3 189
Mandalay 401
CAMBODIA (1973)
Phnom Penh 2 000
CHINA (1970)
Shanghai 10 820
Peking 7 570
Tientsin 4 280
Shenyang 2 800
Wuhan 2 560
Canton 2 500
Chungking 2 400
Nanking 1 750
Harbin 1 670
Luta 1 650
Sian 1 600
Lanchow 1 450
Taiyuan 1 350
Tsingtao 1 300
Chengtu 1 250
Changchun 1 200
Kunming 1 100
Tsinan 1 100
Fushun 1 080
Anshan 1 050
Chengchow 1 050
Hangchow 960
Tangshan 950
Paotow 920
Tzepo 850
Changsha 825
Shihkiachwang 800
Tsitsihar 760
Soochow 730
Kirin 720
Suchow 700
Foochow 680
Nanchang 675
Kweiyang 660
Wusih 650
Hofei 630
Hwainan 600
Penki 600
Loyang 580
Nanning 550
Huhehot 530
Sining 500
Wulumchi 500
HONG KONG (1967)
Kowloon 2 195
Victoria 849
INDIA (1971)
Calcutta 7 005
Bombay 5 969
Delhi 3 630
Madras 2 470
Hyderabad 1 799
Bangalore 1 648
Ahmedabad 1 588
Kanpur 1 273
Nagpur 866
Pune 853
Lucknow 826
Agra 638
Jaipur 613
Varanasi 583
Indore 573
Madurai 548
Jabalpur 534
Allahabad 514
Patna 490
Surat 472
Vadodara 467
Jamshedpur 465
Cochin 438
Dhanbad 433
Amritsar 433
Trivandrum 410
Gwalior 407
Srinagar 404
Ludhiana 401
Sholapur 398
Bhopal 392
Hubli-Dharwar 380
Meerut 268
Visakhapatnam 362
Mysore 356
Coimbatore 353
Vijaywada 344
Calicut 334
Bareilly 326
Jodhpur 319
Salem 308
Tiruchurapalli 306
Rajkot 300
Jullundur 296
Moradabad 272
Guntur 270
Ajmer 262
Kolhapur 259
Ranchi 256
Aligarh 254
Durg-Bhilainagar 245
Chandigarh 233
Gorakhpur 231
Bhavnagar 226
Saharanpur 226
Jamnagar 215
Mangalore 214
Belgaum 214
Kota 213
Ujjain 209
Durgapur 207
Warangul 207
Raipur 206
INDONESIA (1971)
Jakarta 4 576
Surabaya 1 556
Bandung 1 202
Semarang 647
Medan 636
Palembang 583
Ujung Pandang 435
Malang 422
Surakarta 414
Yogyakarta 342
Banjarmasin 282
Pontianak 218
IRAN (1973)
Tehran 4 002
Esfahan 605
Mashhad 592
Tabriz 510
Shiraz 373
Abadan 312
Ahvaz 302
Kermanshah 249
IRAQ (1970)
Baghdad 2 969
Basra 371
Mosul 293
Kirkuk 208
ISRAEL (1974)
Tel Aviv-Jaffa 1 157
Haifa 354
Jerusalem 344
JAPAN (1973)
Tokyo 11 623
Osaka 2 780
Yokohama 2 620
Nagoya 2 080
Kyoto 1 460
Kobe 1 360
Sapporo 1 240
Kitakyushu 1 060
Kawasaki 1 020
Fukuoka 1 000
Hiroshima 761
Chiba 613
Sendai 576
Amagasaki 538
Higashiosaka 501
Okayama 501
Hamamatsu 467
Kumamoto 467
Nagasaki 446
Kagoshima 444
Shizuoka 444
Himeji 432
Niigata 413
Gifu 407
Kurishiki 405
Funabashi 391
Wakayama 387
Nishinomiya 384
Kanazawa 383
Yokosuka 382
Toyonaka 381
Matsuyama 366
Sagamihara 359
Iwaki 335
Utsunomiya 335
Kawaguchi 334
Matsudo 324
Urawa 322
Omiya 321
Takatsuki 318
Asahikawa 316
Naha 306
Oita 305
Hakodate 303
Nagano 303
Hachioji 299
Takamatsu 296
Ichikawa 294
Fukuyama 293
Suita 289
Toyama 287
Hirakata 285
Toyohashi 279
Kochi 275
Shimonoseki 266
Aomori 263
Sasebo 261
Fujisawa 261
Koriyama 258
Akita 254
JORDAN (1974)
Amman 598
Az Zarqa 226
KOREA, NORTH (1967-70)
Pyongyang 1 500
Chongjin 265
KOREA, SOUTH (1975)
Seoul 6 889
Pusan 2 454
Taegu 1 311
Inchon 800
Kwangju 607
Taejon 506
Masan 372
Chonju 311
Seongnam 272
Ulsan 253
Suweon 224
KUWAIT (1975)
Kuwait 295
LEBANON (1971)
Beirut 939
MACAU (1971)
Macau 248
MALAYSIA (1970)
Kuala Lumpur 452
Georgetown 270
Ipoh 248
MONGOLIA (1971)
Ulan Bator 282
PAKISTAN (1972)
Karachi 3 469
Lahore 2 148
Lyallpur 820
Hyderabad 624
Rawalpindi 615
Multan 544
Gujranwala 366
Peshawar 273
Sialkot 212
Sargodha 203
PHILIPPINES (1975)
Manila 1 438
Quezon City 995
Davao 591
Cebu 419
Caloocan 364
Zamboanga 250
Iloilo 248
Pasay 241
SAUDI ARABIA (1974)
Riyadh 667
Jedda 561
Mecca 367
Taif 205
SINGAPORE (1975)
Singapore 2 250
SRI LANKA (1973)
Colombo 618
SYRIA (1970)
Damascus 923
Aleppo 639
Homs 215
TAIWAN (1970-73)
Taipei 1 922
Kaohsiung 915
Tainan 495
Taichung 490
Chilung 334
Chiai 237
Shanchung 229
Hsinchu 205
THAILAND (1973)
Bangkok 3 967
TURKEY (1973)
Istanbul 3 135
Ankara 1 554
Izmir 819
Abana 454
Bursa 427
Gaziantep 353
Konya 324
Eskisehir 303
Kayseri 297
Diyarbakir 251
Samsun 242
Maras 237
Malatya 234
Izmit 233
Erzurum 226
Sivas 213
Siirt 211
UNITED ARAB EMIRATES (1976)
Abu Dhabi 236
Dubai 207
VIETNAM (1973)
Ho Chi Minh City 1 825
Hanoi 920
Da-Nang 492
Haiphong 390
Nha-trang 216
Qui-Nhon 214
Hue 209

AUSTRALASIA

AUSTRALIA (1973)
Sydney 2 874
Melbourne 2 584
Brisbane 911
Adelaide 868
Perth 739
Newcastle 358
Canberra 211
Wollongong 206
NEW ZEALAND (1976)
Auckland 743
Wellington 327
Christchurch 295

EUROPE

AUSTRIA (1971)
Vienna 1 859
Linz 357
Graz 314
BELGIUM (1971)
Brussels 1 075
Antwerp 673
Liège 440
Gent 225
Charleroi 214
BULGARIA (1974)
Sofia 962
Plovdiv 305
Varna 270
CZECHOSLOVAKIA (1974)
Prague 1 096
Brno 354
Bratislava 325
Ostrava 291
DENMARK (1974)
Copenhagen 1 378
Århus 245
FINLAND (1976)
Helsinki 868
Tampere 237
Turku 235
FRANCE (1975)
Paris 9 863
Lyon 1 167
Marseille 1 004
Lille 922
Bordeaux 589
Toulouse 495
Nantes 433
Nice 433
Rouen 389
Grenoble 389
Toulon 378
Strasbourg 356
St-Etienne 335
Lens 313
Nancy 278
Le Havre 265
Grasse-Cannes 254
Tours 246
Clermont-Ferrand 225
Valenciennes 224
Montpellier 223
Mulhouse 219
Rennes 213
Orléans 209
Dijon 208
Douai 203
GERMANY, EAST (1975)
East Berlin 1 094
Leipzig 569
Dresden 508
Karl-Marx-Stadt 304
Magdeburg 277
Halle 239
Rostock 212
Erfurt 203
GERMANY, WEST (1974)
West Berlin 2 048
Hamburg 1 752
München 1 337
Cologne 832
Essen 674
Frankfurt am Main 663
Dortmund 632
Düsseldorf 628
Stuttgart 625
Bremen 584
Nürnberg 515
Hannover 505
Duisburg 435
Wuppertal 410
Bochum 338